Stock Valuation and Returns

Value of a share of common stock:

$$P_0 = \frac{D_1}{(1 + r_e)^1} + \frac{D_2}{(1 + r_e)^2} + \frac{D_3}{(1 + r_e)^3} + \cdots + \frac{D_\infty}{(1 + r_e)^\infty}$$

Value of a share of common stock with constant growth in dividends:

$$P_0 = \frac{D_1}{r_e - g}$$

Required rate of return on equity, dividend valuation model:

$$r_e = \frac{D_1}{P_0} + g$$

Required rate of return on equity, capital asset pricing model:

$$r_e = r_f + (r_m - r_f)\beta$$

Notation:

β = security beta
D_t = dividends per share of stock at the end of period t
g = expected growth rate in dividends per share
P_0 = present value of a share of stock

r_e = required rate of return on equity
r_f = expected risk-free rate of interest
r_m = expected return on the market
t = number of discounting periods

Bond Valuation and Yields

Value of zero-coupon bond:

$$V = \frac{M}{(1 + r_d)^T}$$

Value of a bond with annual coupons:

$$V = \sum_{t=1}^{T} \frac{C}{(1 + r_d)^t} + \frac{M}{(1 + r_d)^T}$$

Value of a bond with semiannual coupons:

$$V = \sum_{t=1}^{T} \frac{C}{(1 + r_{d,\text{six months}})^t} + \frac{M}{(1 + r_{d,\text{six months}})^T}$$

Yield to maturity on a bond:

Annualized yield to maturity = $r_{d,\text{six months}} \times 2$
Effective yield to maturity = $(1 + r_{d,\text{six months}})^2 - 1$

Notation:

C = cash flow (interest) per compounding period
M = maturity value (face value) of a bond
r_d = annual yield
$r_{d,\text{six months}}$ = yield to maturity, six months

T = number of periods until maturity
t = number of discounting periods
V = present value of a bond

Financial Management and Analysis

McGraw-Hill Series in Finance

Consulting Editor
Charles A. D'Ambrosio, University of Washington

ARCHER AND KERR: Readings and Cases in Corporate Finance

BLAKE: Financial Market Analysis

BREALEY AND MYERS: Principles of Corporate Finance

DOHERTY: Corporate Risk Management: A Financial Exposition

DUBOFSKY: Options and Financial Futures: Valuation and Uses

EDMISTER: Financial Institutions: Markets and Management

EDWARDS AND MA: Futures and Options

FRANCIS: Investments: Analysis and Management

FRANCIS: Management of Investments

FULLER AND FARRELL: Modern Investments and Security Analysis

GARBADE: Securities Markets

GIBSON: Option Valuation: Analyzing and Pricing Standardized Option Contracts

JOHNSON: Financial Institutions and Markets: A Global Perspective

JOHNSON AND SLOTTJE: Case Studies in Finance Using Lotus 1-2-3

JOHNSON AND SLOTTJE: Case Studies in Finance Using Microsoft Excel

KESTER AND LUEHRMAN: Case Problems in International Finance

KOHN: Financial Institutions and Markets

LANG: Strategy for Personal Finance

LEVI: International Finance: The Market and Financial Management of Multinational Business

MARTIN, PETTY, AND KLOCK: Personal Financial Management

PETERSON: Financial Management and Analysis

SCHALL AND HALEY: Introduction to Financial Management

SHARPE: Portfolio Theory and Capital Markets

SMITH: Case Problems and Readings: A Supplement for Investments and Portfolio Management

Financial Management and Analysis

PAMELA P. PETERSON

Florida State University

McGraw-Hill, Inc.

New York • St. Louis • San Francisco • Auckland • Bogotá • Caracas •
Lisbon • London • Madrid • Mexico City • Milan • Montreal •
New Delhi • San Juan • Singapore • Sydney • Tokyo • Toronto

FINANCIAL MANAGEMENT AND ANALYSIS

This book is printed on acid-free paper.

2 3 4 5 6 7 8 9 0   VNH   VNH   9 0 9 8 7 6 5 4

ISBN 0-07-049667-6

This book was set in New Aster by York Graphic Services, Inc.
The editors were Michael R. Elia, Kenneth A. MacLeod, and Ira C. Roberts;
the designer was Gayle Jaeger; the cover artist was Jane Sterrett;
the production supervisor was Paula Keller.
Von Hoffmann Press, Inc., was printer and binder.

Library of Congress Cataloging-in-Publication Data

Peterson, Pamela P. (Pamela Parrish)
    Financial management and analysis / Pamela P. Peterson.
        p.   cm.—(McGraw-Hill series in finance)
    Includes bibliographical references and index.
    ISBN 0-07-049667-6
    1. Corporations—Finance.   I. Title.   II. Series.
HG4026.P465   1994
658.15—dc20   93-33419

INTERNATIONAL EDITION

About the Author

Pamela P. Peterson did her undergraduate work at Miami University in Oxford, Ohio, completing her degree in accounting in 1975. Following this, she was employed by Arthur Andersen & Co. in Chicago. She earned her Ph.D. in Business Administration at the University of North Carolina in Chapel Hill in 1981. She successfully completed the Chartered Financial Analyst (CFA) program in 1992.

At Florida State University since 1981, she has taught undergraduate and graduate courses: Introduction to Financial Management, Problems in Financial Management, Quantitative Methods in Business, and Empirical Research in Finance. Professor Peterson has been the advisor for the Florida State University student chapter of the Financial Management Association. She has also helped candidates prepare for the CFA examinations.

Professor Peterson has published over twenty-five articles in the *Financial Analysts Journal,* the *Journal of Banking and Finance,* the *Journal of Finance,* the *Journal of Financial Economics,* the *Journal of Financial and Quantitative Analysis,* and other journals. Her primary research interests are capital structure issues, dividend policy, and analysts' forecasts. She has been active in national and regional professional associations, serving as a member of the board of directors of the Financial Management Association, the Financial Management Association Student Chapters, and the Eastern Finance Association.

This book is dedicated to my kids, Erica and Ken, who let mom work on her book, and to my husband and colleague, David, who picked up the slack.

Contents in Brief

Preface xxii

PART I
Introduction 1

1 Introduction to Financial Management and Analysis 1

PART II
Fundamentals of Financial Analysis 31

2 Securities and Markets 32
3 Financial Statements, Taxation, and Cash Flows 58
4 Financial Analysis 96

PART III
Fundamentals of Valuation 165

5 Mathematics of Finance 166
6 Asset Valuation and Returns 228
7 Risk and Expected Return 287

PART IV
Management of Investments 343

8 Capital Investment Decisions 344
9 Evaluating Capital Projects 387
10 Capital Budgeting and Risk 461

PART V
Management of Financing 497

11 Common and Preferred Stock 498
12 Long-Term Debt 550
13 Capital Structure 589
14 The Cost of Capital 630

PART VI
Management of Working Capital 684

15 Management of Short-Term Assets 685
16 Management of Short-Term Financing 736

PART VII
Financial Management and Planning 779

17 Strategy and Financial Planning 780

APPENDIXES 818

A Keeping Up with Security Prices 818
B Financial Mathematics Tables 830
C Financial Math with Calculators 839
D Statistics Primer 852

Glossary 881
Brief Solutions to End-of-Chapter Problems 901
Index 921

Contents

Preface xxii

PART I
Introduction 1

1 Introduction to Financial Management and Analysis 1

Introduction 4
Overview of Financial Management and Analysis 4
    Financial decisions within the firm 4
    Financial management and financial analysis 6
Forms of Business Enterprise 8
    Sole proprietorships 8
    Partnerships 8
    Corporations 9
    Other forms of business enterprise 12
    Prevalence 13
The Objective of Financial Management 15
    The measure of owners' economic well-being 16
    Economic profit vs. accounting profit: share price vs. earnings per share 17
    Share prices and efficient markets 19
Managers Representing Owners: The Agency Relationship 20
    Problems with the agency relationship 20
    Costs of the agency relationship 21
    Shareholder wealth maximization and social responsibility 22
Summary 24
Questions 24
Problems 27
Further Readings 29

PART II
Fundamentals of Financial Analysis 31

2 Securities and Markets 32

Introduction 34
Securities 34
    Money market securities 34
    Capital market securities 35
    Derivative securities 38

Securities Markets 39
    Classification of markets 40
    Markets in the United States 43
    International markets 48
    Market indicators 50
    Efficient markets 51
Summary 53
Questions 54
Problems 55
Further Readings 57

3 Financial Statements, Taxation, and Cash Flows 58

Introduction 60
Financial Statements 60
    The balance sheet 61
    The income statement 65
    The statement of cash flows 67
    Footnotes 69
    Depreciation 69
The Role of Taxes in Financial Decisions 72
    Types of taxes 73
    Income taxation in the United States 73
    Taxation in other countries 86
Cash Flows 88
    Cash inflows and outflows 88
    Predicting cash flows 88
Summary 90
Questions 91
Problems 92
Further Readings 95

4 Financial Analysis 96

Additional Disclosures 99
Information Inputs to the Financial Analysis of a Firm 100
Financial Ratios 100
    Classification of ratios 100
    Liquidity ratios 102
    Profitability ratios 109

Activity ratios 111
Financial leverage ratios 113
Before- vs. After-Tax Dollars 117
Return-on-investment ratios 119
Shareholder ratios 123
Earnings per Share 126
Common-Size Analysis 128
An Application of Financial Analysis to Wal-Mart Stores, Inc. 128
The business 130
The industry 131
The economy 132
Financial ratios of the firm and the industry 133
Common-size analysis 138
Using Financial Analysis 140
Evaluating credit-worthiness and debt quality 140
Predicting bankruptcy 142
Problems and Dilemmas in Financial Analysis 143
Using accounting data 143
Using a benchmark 145
Selecting and interpreting ratios 145
Forecasting 146
Summary 148
Questions 149
Problems 150
Further Readings 155
Appendix 4A   Financial Ratios Recap 156
Appendix 4B   Sources of Financial Data and Analyses 163

**PART III
Fundamentals
of Valuation
165**

5 Mathematics of Finance 166
Introduction 168
The Time Value of Money 168
Translating a present value into its future value 168
The Code of Hammurabi 171
The Average Annual Return 174
Translating a value backward in time 174
Cutting Down on Steps 177
Short-cuts: Compound and discount factor tables 178
The Time Value of a Series of Cash Flows 181
Translating a series of values forward in time 181

Time Travel with Time Lines 186
Summation Notation 187
   Translating a series of values back from the future 188
   Short-cuts: Annuities 189
   Short-cuts: Tables of annuity factors 196
Complexities in the Time Value of Money 198
   Valuing a perpetual stream of cash flows 198
   Valuing an annuity due 199
   Valuing a deferred annuity 204
   Determining the unknown interest rate 207
   Determining the number of compounding periods 210
Cutting Logs Down to Size 212
The Calculation of Interest Rates 213
   The annual percentage rate 213
   Effective versus annualized rates of interest 214
Taking It to the Limit 216
Does It Pay to Discover? 217
Summary 218
Questions 219
Problems 221
Further Readings 227

6 Asset Valuation and Returns 228
Introduction 230
Asset Valuation 230
   The role of the marketplace in the valuation of assets 233
   Valuation of securities 234
The DVM and the P/E Ratio 241
Returns on Investments 255
   Return on investments with no intermediate cash flows 255
   Return on investments with even cash flows 256
   Average annual return: what kind of average? 257
   Return on investments with uneven cash flows 258
   The reinvestment assumption 258
   Return on stocks 260
Annual Returns from Quarterly Returns 264
   Return on bonds 265
   Transactions costs 278
Summary 279

Questions 280
Problems 282
Further Readings 286

7 Risk and Expected Return 287
Introduction 290
Risk 290
    Cash flow risk 291
    Reinvestment rate risk 298
    Interest rate risk 301
    Purchasing power risk 304
    Currency risk 307
Return and Risk 307
    Expected return 307
    Standard deviation of the possible outcomes 309
    Return and the tolerance for bearing risk 315
Expected Return, Risk, and Diversification 315
    Diversification and risk 317
    Portfolio size and risk 323
    Modern portfolio theory and asset pricing 325
    Financial decision-making and asset pricing 333
Summary 333
Questions 334
Problems 336
Further Readings 342

PART IV Management of Investments 343

8 Capital Investment Decisions 344
Introduction 346
The Investment Problem 346
    Capital investments 346
    Investment decisions and owners' wealth maximization 347
    Capital budgeting 349
    Classifying investment projects 350
Cash Flow from Investments 353
    Incremental cash flows 353
    Simplifications 368
    Example 1: The expansion of the Williams 5 & 10 368
    Example 2: The replacement of facilities at the Hirshleifer Company 374

Cash Flow Estimation in Practice 378
Summary 381
Questions 381
Problems 383
Further Readings 386

9 Evaluating Capital Projects 387

Introduction 389
Evaluation Techniques 389
  Payback period 391
  Discounted payback period 394
  Net present value 399
  Profitability index 406
  Internal rate of return 411
  Modified internal rate of return 420
Comparing Techniques 428
Capital Budgeting Techniques in Practice 432
Summary 434
Questions 435
Problems 437
Further Readings 443
Appendix 9A   Investments with Unequal Lives 444
Appendix 9B   The Leasing Decision 451

10 Capital Budgeting and Risk 461

Introduction 463
Risk and Cash Flows 464
  Relevant cash flow risk 464
  Different types of project risk 465
Measurement of Project Risk 466
  Measuring a project's stand-alone risk 467
  Measuring a project's market risk 481
Incorporating Risk in the Capital Budgeting Decision 484
  Risk-adjusted rate 484
  Certainty equivalents 486
Assessment of Project Risk in Practice 487
Summary 488
Questions 489
Problems 490
Further Readings 494

PART V
Management of Financing 497

11 Common and Preferred Stock 498

Introduction 501
General Characteristics of Stock 502
  Limited liability 502
  The corporate charter 503
  The number of shares 503
  Stock ownership 504
  Dividends 505
Common Stock 510
  Classified stock 510
  Voting rights 511
  The right to buy more stock 514
  Other rights 517
  Corporate democracy 517
  Common stock dividends 520
Preferred Stock 533
  Par and liquidation values 533
  Preferred stock dividends 534
  Convertibility 536
  Callability 537
  Voting rights 539
  Sinking funds 539
  Packaging features 539
Equity as a Source of Funds 541
Summary 542
Questions 543
Problems 545
Further Readings 547
Appendix 11A   How a Dutch Auction Rate is Determined 548

12 Long-Term Debt 550

Introduction 553
Term Loans 553
Notes and Bonds 554
  Denomination 555
  Maturity 556
  Interest 556
  Security 560
  Seniority 562

    Option like features 562
    Packaging debt features 567
Indentures 569
    Covenants 569
    The trustee 569
Risk 570
    Default risk 570
    Interest rate risk 573
    Reinvestment rate risk 576
    Purchasing power risk 579
    Marketability risk 579
Debt Retirement 579
Long-Term Debt as a Source of Capital 581
Summary 583
Questions 584
Problems 585
Further Readings 588

13 Capital Structure 589

Introduction 592
Capital Structure and Financial Leverage 595
Financial Leverage and Risk 598
    The leverage effect 598
    Quantifying the leverage effect 599
Capital Structure and Taxes 600
    What Modigliani and Miller told us 600
A Refresher on Uncertainty Statistics 601
    Interest deductibility and capital structure 605
Average vs. Marginal Tax Rates 608
    Personal taxes and capital structure 609
    Unused tax shields 610
Capital Structure and Financial Distress 612
    Costs of financial distress 612
    The role of limited liability 612
    Bankruptcy and bankruptcy costs 615
    Financial distress and capital structure 616
Putting Together Financial Leverage, Taxes, and the Costs of
        Financial Distress 617
Reconciling Theory with Practice 620

Topics such as mergers and acquisitions, bankruptcy, and international finance, which are extensions of the basic concepts, are interwoven within fundamentals. For example, bankruptcy appears with the capital structure decision (in Chapter 13, *Capital Structure*) because the possibility of financial distress and bankruptcy affects the choice of sources of funds.

DISTINGUISHING FEATURES OF THE TEXT

- *Logical structure.* The text begins with core principles and tools, followed by long-term investment and financing decisions. The first three parts lay out the basics, the fourth part is the "left side" of the balance sheet (assets), and the fifth part is the "right side" of the balance sheet (liabilities and equity). Working capital decisions, which are made to support day-to-day operations of the firm, are discussed in the sixth part. The last is a reprise of the objective of financial management: the maximization of owners' wealth.

- *Numerous illustrations.* Graphs and illustrations have been developed to clarify and visually reinforce mathematical concepts. For example, the growth of a bank balance is shown in several ways: mathematically, in a displayed time line, and with a bar graph.

- *Research questions and problems.* Each chapter contains questions or problems that require research on actual companies. These problems can be answered using library resources or computer databases, such as Standard & Poor's *Compustat PC Plus* (CD-ROM). Computer resources are not required to complete any end-of-chapter question or problem, but students are encouraged to gain experience in the use of these resources. A data disk from Standard & Poor's *Compustat* database is available for use by instructors and students.

- *Applications.* As much as possible, I develop concepts and mathematics using examples from actual practice. For example, first I present the basic ideas of financial analysis using a simplified set of financial statements for a fictitious company. Then I demonstrate the tools of financial analysis using real data from Wal-Mart Stores, Inc. To help students better grasp and retain major concepts and tools, I make use of over 200 actual company examples.

- *International and ethical issues.* As in the real world, international and ethical issues are integrated, not artificially separated from financial decision making. For example, international securities markets are discussed in Chapter 2, *Securities and Markets*, following the discussion of U.S. securities markets. In Chapter 16, *Management of Short-Term Financing*, the ethics related to late payments owed creditors is discussed with the techniques for managing accounts payable, making clear the ethics are an integral part of financial management.

- *Stand-alone nature of the chapters.* Chapters are written so that they may easily be rearranged to fit different course structures. An instructor can tailor this book to fit his or her course and its time frame, as well as the students' level of preparation (for example, if students enter the course with sufficient background in accounting and taxation, Chapter 3 could be skipped).

- *End-of-text material.* I've included student-friendly end-of-text material. Aside from the time-value-of-money tables, you will find appendixes illustrating how to use financial calculators, demonstrating how to read securities quotes in the financial press, and summarizing key statistical techniques. In addition to the appendixes, I have also included a thorough glossary. Along with brief solutions to each end-of-chapter problem in the text, you will find a set of hints for guiding students in problem solving without revealing the key elements in the solution.

SUPPLEMENTAL MATERIAL

Standard & Poor's *Compustat* Data Disk

Each adopting instructor can be provided with a data disk containing financial data on over thirty U.S. corporations. This data can be used to complete the research questions and problems requiring individual company data. These questions and problems are coded with a **PC+** "logo."

This disk contains a small portion of Standard & Poor's *Compustat* data, which is available on either magnetic tape or CD-ROM. Standard & Poor's *Compustat* data is a valuable research resource, consisting of twenty years of financial statement data on over 10,000 corporations.

Study Guide

Professor Marianne Westerman of the University of Colorado at Denver and I have prepared the *Study Guide* to accompany the text. It provides for each chapter:

- An outline.
- Fill-in questions.
- True-False questions.
- Multiple choice questions and problems.
- Short-answer questions and problems.

Instructor's Manual

I've prepared the *Instructor's Manual*, which contains material to assist in preparation of class lectures. It includes:

- A detailed chapter outline, suitable for use as a lecture outline.
- Additional real world examples to illustrate key concepts and applications.
- Additional questions and problems (with solutions).
- Additional problems and overhead masters to illustrate calculations.
- Sample solutions to end-of-chapter **Research** questions and problems.
- Overhead transparency acetates for key figures, tables, and equations developed in the text.
- References to resource material to assist in preparing and presenting class lectures and exams.
- Alternative chapter sequences and outlines for one-semester, one-quarter, two-semester, and two-quarter courses.

Solutions Manual

In addition to the hints and brief solutions at the end of the text, I have prepared detailed solutions to all end-of-chapter questions and problems.[1] Step-by-step solutions are provided with extra help for more challenging problems.

---

[1] Solutions to **Research** questions and problems are not provided in the manual since these require research on individual firms assigned by the instructor or chosen by the student. Sample solutions to **Research** questions and problems are provided in the *Instructor's Manual*.

Test Bank

Prepared by Professor Westerman, the *Test Bank* has over 1,000 questions. They are chosen to test students' understanding of both concepts and tools. A computerized *Test Bank* is also available.

Transparencies

Transparency masters in the *Instructor's Manual:*

- Describe or illustrate key concepts and tools.
- Demonstrate problems that are similar, but not identical, to examples shown in the text.
- Guide the students through lecture material.

In addition, color acetates for many illustrations in the text will be provided to adopters.

Spreadsheet Templates

Spreadsheet programs are available to assist the students solving end-of-chapter problems. Though these programs are not necessary to complete any problems in the text, they will help students understand how computer software can be used in financial analysis. Programs are provided for such uses as the calculation of the yield to maturity, the calculation of basic financial ratios, and the generation of pro forma financial statements.

Videos

A program of videos will be available to adopters of *Financial Management and Analysis*. These videos are useful in supplementing lecture material, bringing the real world of finance closer to the student.

PROBLEM CHECKING

All in text, end-of-chapter, *Test Bank*, and *Study Guide* problems and questions have been independently checked for accuracy. The efforts by Stuart Michelson, at Eastern Illinois University, and Stephen P. Huffman, at the University of Wisconsin—Oshkosh, to verify the accuracy of the text examples and solutions to the end-of-chapter problems are greatly appreciated.

ACKNOWLEDG-MENTS

I hope the following reviewers will see in this text how much I valued their time, effort, and suggestions: Bala G. Arshanapalli, Indiana University, NW; Paul Bolster, Northeastern University; John Byrd, Fort Lewis College; Jaeho Cho, Bernard M. Baruch College; Frank L. Clark, Eastern Illinois University; Stan Eakins, East Carolina University; M. E. Ellis, St. John's University; Atul Gupta, Bentley College; Simon Hakim, Temple University; Glenn V. Henderson, Jr., University of Cincinnati; Ronald Hoffmeister, Arizona State University; Robert Kleiman, Oakland University; David R. Lange, Auburn University at Montgomery; Christopher K. Ma, Texas Tech University; John A. MacDonald, SUNY at Albany; Abbas Mamoozadeh, Slippery Rock University; William Nelson, Indiana University, NW; William B. Riley, West Virginia University; John Settle, Portland State University; A. Charlene Sullivan, Purdue University; Michael Sullivan, University of Nevada at Las Vegas; Joseph Sulock, University of North Carolina at Asheville; George S. Swales, Jr., Southwest Missouri State University; Bruce Swenson, Adelphi College; John Thatcher, University of Wisconsin at Whitewater; Clifford F. Thies, Shenandoah College; Joe Walker, University of Alabama at Birmingham; Allen Webster, Bradley University; Marianne Westerman, University of Colorado at Denver; and Mark A. White, University of Virginia.

I would like to thank the people associated with McGraw-Hill who have devoted a great deal of time (and patience) toward this book: the editors, Mike Elia, Ken MacLeod, and Ira Roberts; the designer, Gayle Jaeger; and the proof-reader, Kalista Johnston.

I would also like to thank my students in FIN 3403 at Florida State University who have taught me how to teach. I would especially like to acknowledge two of them: John Hooker, who provided honest feedback on my work, and Tonja Mobley, whose diligence in working problems helped minimize any errors in the solutions to end-of-chapter problems.

Pamela P. Peterson

Financial Management and Analysis

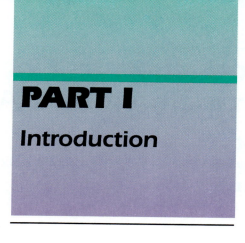

PART I

Introduction

1 Introduction to Financial Management and Analysis 2

Introduction to Financial Management and Analysis

INTRODUCTION 4

OVERVIEW OF FINANCIAL MANAGEMENT AND ANALYSIS 4

Financial Decisions within the Firm 4
    Investment Decisions 4
    Financing Decisions 5
    Investment and Financing Decisions 6
Financial Management and Financial Analysis 6
    Financial Management 6
    Financial Analysis 7

FORMS OF BUSINESS ENTERPRISE 8

Sole Proprietorships 8
Partnerships 8
Corporations 9
    Income and Taxation 10
    Ownership 11
    Financing 12
Other Forms of Business Enterprise 12
Prevalence 13

THE OBJECTIVE OF FINANCIAL MANAGEMENT 15

The Measure of Owners' Economic Well-Being 16
Economic Profit vs. Accounting Profit: Share Price vs. Earnings
  per Share 17
Share Prices and Efficient Markets 19

MANAGERS REPRESENTING OWNERS: THE AGENCY RELATIONSHIP 20

Problems with the Agency Relationship 20
Costs of the Agency Relationship 21
    Motivating Managers: Executive Compensation 21
Shareholder Wealth Maximization and Social Responsibility 22

Summary 24

Big Blue's Got the Blues

International Business Machines Corporation (IBM) had long been the leading company in the computer industry. Its primary products included mainframe computers, along with some software and communications services. But when IBM entered the personal computer business in 1981, it met stiffer competition than it was used to *(see top left graph)*. Earnings per share (earnings to owners for each share of ownership) varied *(see top right graph)*, while the company's dividends per share (the payments made to its owners, the shareholders) increased steadily *(see bottom left graph)*.

In 1992, IBM experienced a record loss requiring it to cut its dividend and make major changes in the top management of the firm. Was there much advance warning? Not through earnings. Not through dividends. But the market value of a share, which reflects investors' expectations about the future of the firm, declined steadily from 1985 through 1991 *(see bottom right graph)*.

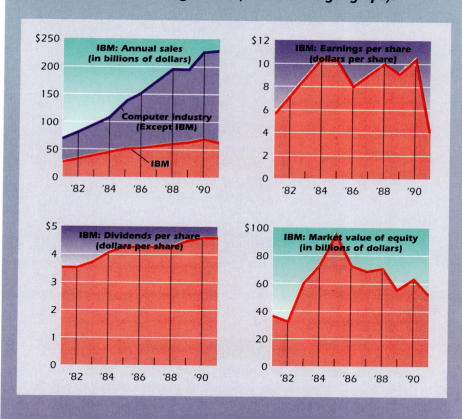

INTRODUCTION

Finance is the application of economic principles and concepts to business decision making and problem solving. Business situations that call for the theories and tools of finance generally involve either investing (using funds) or financing (raising funds). As a result, the field of finance can be considered to comprise three broad categories: financial management, investments, and financial institutions (see Figure 1–1).

FIGURE 1-1
The Three Primary Areas of Finance and Typical Decision Activities in Each Area

FINANCIAL MANAGEMENT (within the firm)	INVESTMENTS (for investors and investment managers)	FINANCIAL INSTITUTIONS (for banks and other finance firms)
Maintaining cash balances Extending credit Investing in new assets Replacing old assets Acquiring other firms Borrowing from banks Issuing stocks or bonds	Valuing common stocks Selecting securities Analyzing bonds Using options and futures Measuring portfolio performance	Making loans Managing cash balances Determining adequacy of capital Dealing with governmental regulation Setting interest rates on loans Setting interest rates on deposits

- *Financial management.* Sometimes called corporate finance. Primarily concerned with financial decision making within a business entity.
- *Investments.* Focuses on the behavior of financial markets and the pricing of securities.
- *Financial institutions.* Deals with banks and other firms that specialize in bringing the suppliers of funds together with the users of funds.

Managers who work in all three areas rely on the same basic knowledge of finance. This text introduces you to this common body of knowledge and shows how it is used in financial decision making.

OVERVIEW OF FINANCIAL MANAGEMENT AND ANALYSIS

Financial Decisions within the Firm

Let's look briefly at some examples of the types of decisions in financial management.

Investment Decisions

Investment decisions are concerned with the use of funds—the buying, holding, or selling of all types of assets: Should we buy a new stamping machine? Should we introduce a new product line? Sell the old production facility? Buy an existing company? Build a warehouse? Keep our cash in the bank?

Suppose you have invented a method of transcribing lecture notes directly onto a disk readable by any computer word processing program. If you want to produce and sell your new product, you must address questions such as:

- How much will it cost to purchase the equipment needed to manufacture this product and then to market it?
- Once you begin manufacturing, how much money will be tied up in inventories of raw materials, work-in-process, and finished goods?

- How much cash is expected to come in because of sales of the product, and how much cash is expected to flow out because of expenses? In other words, what cash flows do you expect from this product?
- By how much are actual future cash flows likely to vary from expected cash flows?
- Will you extend credit to purchasers of your product? If so, for how long? What else can you do with your money if you don't need to use all of it to produce and market this product?

Or, as another example, suppose we are considering how much of a firm's assets to keep available as cash. This is an investment decision because we will be investing in cash referred to as cash balances—tying up funds in cash that could be used elsewhere. It requires us to address at least the following questions:

- How large a cash balance do we need? Can a cash balance be too large?
- How certain are we about the amount of cash we will need in the future?
- Where should our cash balance be held? In the bank? Under a mattress? Invested in U.S. Treasury bills?
- Should the cash balance be kept constant throughout the year, or should it change as needs change?
- What else could we do with the money if we don't have it tied up in cash?

Here is an example that is personal. Your decision to spend your time and your money (or maybe your parents' money) on a college education is an investment decision. You are investing in your **human capital,** an intangible asset that may be defined as your future earning power. You can't really see this asset: You would look pretty much the same whether you went to college or you bagged groceries at the supermarket. But your future earning power— you hope—will be greater with a college education.

What are you investing? Your time and tuition dollars. Is it a good investment? To figure this out you would have to calculate the cost of your time (that is, what you could have earned if you went to work instead of going to class and studying) and your tuition; compare them with the expected future benefits from increased earnings; and somehow take into account uncertainty about your future earnings, since you don't know today exactly how much more you will make with a college degree. If the benefits exceed the costs, this is a good investment.

Financing Decisions

Financing decisions are concerned with the acquisition of funds with which to make investments and finance day-to-day operations. Should we use the money raised through the firm's revenues? Should we seek money from outside the business?

A company's operations and investments can be financed from outside the business by incurring debts, such as through bank loans and the sale of bonds, or by selling ownership interests. Since each method of financing obligates the business in different ways, financing decisions can be very important. The major differences are:

- Debts must be repaid, with interest, within a specified amount of time. Creditors (those lending the money) generally do not share in the control or profits of the borrowing firm.
- Proceeds from the sale of ownership interests do not need to be repaid. However, such sale dilutes the control of (and profits accruing to) the current owners.

The choice of financing method involves considering, at the least:

- The length of time the funds will be needed.
- The ability of the firm to make payments to a creditor on a fixed schedule.
- The willingness of current owners to have their ownership interest (and hence control) of the firm diluted.

Investment and Financing Decisions

Many business decisions simultaneously involve both investment and financing. For example, a company may wish to acquire another firm—an investment decision. However, the success of the acquisition may depend on how it is financed: by borrowing cash and using it to buy the firm or simply by selling additional shares in the original company and using the proceeds to buy other firms.

Whether a financial decision involves investment, financing, or both, it also will be concerned with two specific factors: expected return and risk. And throughout your study of finance, you will be concerned with these factors. *Expected return* is the difference between potential benefits and potential costs. *Risk* is the degree of uncertainty associated with these expected returns.

Financial Management and Financial Analysis

Financial Management

Financial management is the management of the cash flow of a firm to make a profit for its owners. The firm may be a business enterprise, such as a manufacturing company, an accounting firm, an oil producer, or a credit union, or it may be a charitable organization. The day-to-day purpose of a firm's financial management is to meet current and future operating needs. The financial managers' tasks include the development, application, and monitoring of policies and decisions regarding such business activities as:

- Collection of customer receipts.
- Investment in marketable securities.
- Investment in long-term assets, such as a factory building.
- Payment of obligations.
- Raising long-term funds.

Departments that perform financial management tasks include accounts payable (payments to suppliers), capital budgeting (investment in long-term assets), accounts receivable (collection of customer credit accounts), and financial planning (planning for cash inflows and outflows). In many organizations, some of the functions of financial management are integrated with accounting and economics functions.

These finance-oriented departments usually work in concert with other departments within the firm. For example, developing a new product takes the joint efforts of production management, marketing, and finance personnel to identify the new product, plan its production and distribution, and assess what future benefits it may provide for the firm.

Higher-level positions that focus primarily on financial management typically include controller, treasurer, and vice president for finance. The controller is typically charged with maintaining the company's financial health through accounting and auditing functions and the responsibility for planning cash inflows and outflows. The treasurer is charged with obtaining capital for investments and investing cash in other assets of the business. The vice president for finance is usually charged with policy-making duties and acts as a liaison between financial managers and other management personnel. Often the vice president for finance oversees the activities of the controller and the treasurer.

Financial Analysis

Financial analysis is a tool of financial management. It consists of the evaluation of the financial condition and operating performance of a business firm, an industry, or even the economy, and the forecasting of its future condition and performance. It is, in other words, a means for examining risk and expected return. Data for financial analysis may come from areas within the firm, such as marketing and production departments, from the firm's own accounting data, or from financial information vendors such as Dow Jones, Moody's, Standard & Poor's, and Value Line, as well as from government publications, such as the *Federal Reserve Bulletin*. Financial publications such as *Business Week, Forbes, Fortune,* and *The Wall Street Journal* also publish financial data (concerning individual firms) and economic data (concerning industries, markets, and economies).

Within the firm, financial analysis may be used not only to evaluate the performance of the firm, but also of its divisions or departments and its product lines. Analyses may be performed both periodically and as needed, not only to ensure informed investment and financing decisions, but also as an aid in implementing personnel policies and rewards systems.

Outside the firm, financial analysis may be used to determine the creditworthiness of a new customer, to evaluate the ability of a supplier to hold to the conditions of a long-term contract, and to evaluate the market performance of competitors.

Firms and investors that do not have the expertise, the time, or the resources to perform financial analysis on their own may purchase analyses from companies that specialize in providing this service. Such companies can provide reports ranging from detailed written analyses to simple creditworthiness ratings for businesses. As an example, Dun & Bradstreet, a financial services firm, evaluates the creditworthiness of many firms, from small local businesses to major corporations. Standard & Poor's publishes a *Bond Guide* that rates the bonds issued of perhaps 2,000 corporations.

FORMS OF BUSINESS ENTERPRISE

Financial management is not restricted to large corporations; it is necessary in all forms and sizes of businesses. The three major forms of business organization are the sole proprietorship, the partnership, and the corporation. These three forms differ in a number of factors, of which those most important to financial decision making are:

- The way the firm is taxed.
- The degree of control owners may exert on decisions.
- The liability of the owners.
- The ease of transferring ownership interests.
- The ability to raise additional funds.
- The longevity of the business.

Sole Proprietorships

The simplest and most common form of business enterprise is the ***sole proprietorship,*** a business owned and controlled by one person—the ***proprietor.*** The proprietor receives all income from the business and alone decides whether to reinvest the profits in the business or use them for personal expenses.

If more funds are needed to operate or expand the business than are generated by business operations, the owner either contributes his or her personal assets to the business or borrows. For most sole proprietorships, banks are the primary source of borrowed funds. However, there is a limit to how much banks will lend proprietorships, most of which are relatively very small businesses.

A proprietor is liable for all the debts of the business; in fact, it is the proprietor who *incurs* the debts of the business. If there are insufficient business assets to pay a business debt, the proprietor must pay the debt out of his or her personal assets.[1]

For tax purposes, the sole proprietor reports income from the business on his or her personal income tax return. Business income is treated as the proprietor's personal income.

The assets of a sole proprietorship may also be sold to some other firm, at which time the sole proprietorship ceases to exist. Or the life of a sole proprietorship ends with the life of the proprietor, although the assets of the business may pass to the proprietor's heirs.

Partnerships

A ***partnership*** is an agreement between two or more persons to operate a business. The partnership agreement describes how profits and losses are to be shared among the partners, and it details their responsibilities in the management of the business.

Most partnerships are ***general partnerships,*** consisting only of ***general partners*** who participate fully in the management of the business, share in its profits and losses, and are responsible for its liabilities. General partners are, in fact, "jointly and severally" responsible for the debts of their partnership; that is, each partner is personally and individually liable for the debts of the business, even if those debts were contracted by other partners.

[1] Some protections are provided in some states regarding the personal assets that can be seized to satisfy a claim on the business. For example, in Florida, the proprietor's residence is protected from creditors.

Whoa, Partner!

Let's see how this "joint and several" liability works. Suppose there are two general partners, Bert and Ernie, who have agreed to share profits and losses equally. Suppose the business is terminated and there are $10,000 of assets and $30,000 of partnership debts. Then $10,000 of the liability are recovered from the sale of the assets, leaving a $20,000 liability.

The creditors have the right to recover the remaining $20,000 of debts from *either* partner. If Ernie doesn't have any personal assets, the creditors can recover all of the $20,000 from Bert! Of course, Bert then has the right to try to recover half of the $20,000 from Ernie.

A *limited partnership* consists of at least one general partner and one limited partner, who does not participate in the management of the business and whose share in the profits and losses of the business is limited by the partnership agreement. In addition, a limited partner is not liable for the debts incurred by the business beyond his or her initial investment in the business.

A partnership is not taxed as a separate entity. Instead, each partner reports his or her share of the business profit or loss on his or her personal income tax return. Each partner's share is taxed as if it were from a sole proprietorship.

The life of a partnership may be limited by the partnership agreement. For example, the partners may agree that the partnership is to exist only for a specified number of years or only for the duration of a specific business transaction. The partnership must be terminated when any one of the partners dies, no matter what is specified in the partnership agreement. Partnership interests cannot be passed to heirs; at the death of any partner, the partnership is dissolved and perhaps renegotiated.

One of the drawbacks of partnerships is that a partner's interest in the business cannot be sold without the consent of the other partners. So a partner who needs to sell his or her interest because of, say, personal financial needs may not be able to do so.[2]

Another drawback is the partnership's limited access to new funds. Short of selling part of their own ownership interest, the partners can raise money only by borrowing from banks—and here, too, there is a limit to what a bank will lend a (usually small) partnership.

In certain businesses—including accounting, law, architecture, and physicians' services—firms are commonly organized as partnerships. The use of this business form may be attributed primarily to state laws, regulations of the industry, and certifying organizations meant to keep practitioners in those fields from limiting their liability.[3]

Corporations

A *corporation* is a legal entity created under state laws through the process referred to as *incorporation.* The corporation is an organization capable of entering into contracts and carrying out business under its own name, separate from its owners. State laws generally require that to become a corporation a firm must:

- File articles of incorporation.
- Adopt a set of bylaws.
- Form a board of directors.

The *articles of incorporation* is a document that specifies the legal name of the corporation, its place of business, and the nature of its business. This certificate gives "life" to a corporation in the sense that it represents a con-

---

[2] Still another problem involves ending a partnership and settling up, mainly because it is difficult to determine the value of the partnership and of each partner's share.

[3] As an example, Rule 505 of the American Institute of Certified Public Accountants restricts its members to sole proprietorships, partnerships, and professional corporations (essentially corporations with unlimited liability for their owners).

FIGURE 1-2

**Relationships among
Shareholders, the
Board of Directors,
and Management**

tract between the corporation and its owners. This contract authorizes the corporation to issue units of ownership, called **shares,** and specifies the rights of the owners, the **shareholders.**

The **bylaws** are the rules of governance for the corporation, specifically for its directors. In most large corporations, it is not possible for each owner to participate in or monitor the management of the business. For example, as of the end of 1992 there were 772,045 owners of IBM.[4] It would not be practical for each owner to watch over IBM's management directly. Therefore, the owners of a corporation elect a **board of directors** to represent them in the major business decisions and to monitor the activities of the corporation's management. The board of directors, in turn, appoints and oversees the officers of the corporation. Directors who are also officers are called **inside directors;** those who have no other position within the firm are **outside directors** (see Figure 1-2).

The state recognizes the existence of the corporation in the **corporate charter,** a contract between the state and the corporation, between the shareholders and the corporation, and between the shareholders and the state. The corporate charter has two parts:

- The articles of incorporation which, by reference, include the corporate bylaws.
- The corporate laws of the state in which the firm is incorporated. (The articles of incorporation cannot conflict with state laws.[5])

In effect, the state corporate laws serve as the boundary for the articles of incorporation. However, being incorporated in a certain state does not mean that the firm must do business—or even locate its headquarters—there.

Once created, the corporation is considered to be a business entity that can enter into contracts, adopt a legal name, sue or be sued, and continue in existence forever. Though owners may die, the corporation continues to live. The liability of owners is limited to the amounts they have invested in the corporation through the shares of ownership they purchased.

Income and Taxation

Unlike the sole proprietorship and partnership, the corporation is a taxable entity. It files its own income tax return and pays taxes on its income. That income is determined according to special provisions of the federal and state tax codes and is subject to corporate tax rates different from personal income tax rates.

If the board of directors decides to distribute cash to the owners, that money is paid out of income left over after the corporate income tax has been paid. The amount of that cash payment, or **dividend,** must also be included in the taxable income of the owners (shareholders). Therefore, a portion of the corporation's income (the portion paid out to owners) is subject to dou-

---

[4] *Value Line Investment Survey,* "Part 3: Ratings and Reports," vol. 48, no. 20, Jan. 29, 1993, p. 1097.

[5] Corporate laws in many states follow a uniform set of laws referred to as the Model Business Corporation Act.

Double Taxation

To see how income can be taxed twice, suppose that the Duplus Corporation has taxable income of $100,000 and is taxed at a flat rate of 40 percent of taxable income. Suppose further that Duplus pays all of its after-tax income to its shareholders whose income is taxed at an average rate of 30 percent.

Duplus pays $100,000 × 0.40 = $40,000 in taxes and pays the remainder, $100,000 − 40,000 = $60,000, to shareholders. The shareholders then must pay taxes of $60,000 × 0.30 = $18,000. Out of the $100,000 of income, shareholders are left with only $60,000 − 18,000 = $42,000. In effect, the shareholders' income has been taxed at the rate of

$$\text{Tax rate} = \frac{\text{taxes}}{\text{taxable income}} = \frac{\$58,000}{\$100,000} = 58\%$$

For each dollar of income for Duplus, 58 cents is paid in taxes. If Duplus were not a corporation, but was instead a sole proprietorship or a partnership with owners taxed at the rate of 30 percent, the total tax bill would be $100,000 × 30 percent = $30,000, instead of $58,000.

ble taxation: once as corporate income and once as the individual owner's income.

The dividend declared by the directors of a corporation is distributed to owners in proportion to the numbers of shares of ownership they hold. If Owner A has twice as many shares as Owner B, he or she will receive twice as much money.

Ownership

The ownership (sometimes called ownership interest) of a corporation, also referred to as **stock** or **equity,** is represented as shares of stock. A corporation that has just a few owners who exert complete control over the decisions of the corporation is referred to as a **closely held corporation.** A corporation whose ownership shares are sold outside of a closed group of owners is referred to as a **public corporation** or a **publicly held corporation.** Mars, producer of M&M candies and other confectionery products, is a closely held corporation; Hershey Foods, also a producer of candy products, is a publicly held corporation.

The shares of public corporations are freely traded in securities markets, such as the New York Stock Exchange. Hence, the ownership of a publicly held corporation is more easily transferred than the ownership of a proprietorship, a partnership, or a closely held corporation.

The Securities and Exchange Act of 1934 requires corporations in interstate commerce (1) whose stock is listed on national exchanges or (2) that have over 500 shareholders and over $3 million in assets to file an initial registration statement with the *Securities and Exchange Commission* (SEC), a federal agency created to oversee the enforcement of U.S. securities laws. The statement provides information regarding the nature of the business, the debt and stock of the corporation, the officers and directors, any individuals who own more than 10 percent of the stock, financial statements, articles of incorporation, and bylaws, among other items.

Each corporation required to file a registration statement must also make periodic reports to the SEC, updating the information in the registration statement, and must provide annual and quarterly financial statements. Both the registration statement and the updated information are made available to the public—and particularly the shareholders (and potential shareholders)—following review by the SEC.

Financing

A corporation can raise additional funds not only by borrowing, but also by issuing (selling) additional shares of stock. However, by selling more shares, the corporation dilutes the ownership of current shareholders. Each share then represents a smaller portion of the corporation because the ownership is divided among more shares. For that reason, current shareholders may balk at the use of new stock issues for financing. In many corporations, they have the right to vote on new stock issues, mergers, acquisitions, and other important matters.

Other Forms of Business Enterprise

In addition to the proprietorship, partnership, and corporate forms of business, an enterprise may be conducted using other forms of business, such as the master limited partnership, the professional corporation, and the joint venture.

The Virtual Entity

Joint ventures are becoming increasingly popular as a way of doing business. Participants—whether individuals, partnerships, or corporations—get together to exploit a specific business opportunity. Afterward, the venture can be dissolved. Recent alliances have sparked thought about what the future form of doing business will be. Some believe that what lies ahead is a virtual enterprise—a temporary alliance, without all the bureaucracy of the typical corporation, that can move quickly and decisively to take advantage of profitable business opportunities.

A *master limited partnership* is a partnership with limited partner ownership interests that are traded on an organized exchange. The ownership interests, which represent a specified ownership percentage, are traded in much the same way as the shares of a corporation. One difference, however, is that a corporation can raise new capital by issuing new ownership interests, increasing the number of shares of stock (but diluting existing shares), whereas a master limited partnership cannot. It is not possible to sell more than a 100 percent interest in the partnership, yet it is possible to sell additional shares of stock in a corporation.

Another variant of the corporate form of business is the professional corporation. A *professional corporation* is an organization formed under state law and is treated as a corporation for federal tax law purposes, yet has unlimited liability for its owners—the owners are personally liable for the debts of the corporation. The businesses that are likely to form such corporations are those that provide services and require state licensing. These service providers include public accountants, physicians, surgeons, architects, and attorneys, since it is generally felt that it is in the public interest to hold such professionals responsible for the liabilities of their business.

A business enterprise may be formed with a specific, limited purpose in mind. In this case, a more appropriate form of business operation is the joint venture. A *joint venture,* which may be structured as either a partnership or a corporation, is a business undertaken by a group of persons or entities (such as a partnership or corporation) for a specific business activity and, therefore, does not constitute a continuing relationship among the parties. A joint venture partnership is treated as a partnership for tax purposes, and a joint venture corporation is treated as a corporation for tax purposes.

Many major U.S. corporations currently participate in joint ventures. For example, IBM, CBS Inc., and Sears, Roebuck & Co. began a joint venture in 1984 to develop and market a videotext service, which eventually became the Prodigy® system. Though CBS withdrew in 1986, IBM and Sears are still participating in this videotext joint venture.

U.S. corporations have entered into joint ventures with foreign corporations, enhancing participation and competition in the global marketplace. For example, General Motors and Volvo of Sweden entered into a joint venture in 1986 to produce and market trucks in North America. Joint ventures are an easy way of entering a foreign market and of gaining an advantage (say, technological) in a domestic market.

Prevalence

The advantages and disadvantages of the three major forms of business from the point of view of finance are summarized in Table 1-1. They tend to produce an evolution from proprietorship to partnership to corporation as a firm grows and its need for financing increases. Sole proprietorship is the choice for starting a business, whereas the corporation is the choice to accommodate growth. As a result, the great majority of business firms are sole proprietorships—Figure 1-3(*a*)—but most business income is generated by corporations—Figure 1-3(*b*).

FIGURE 1-3(*a*)

Distribution of the Number of Business Enterprises in the United States, by Form of Business, 1989

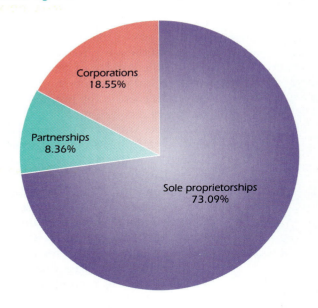

Corporations
18.55%

Partnerships
8.36%

Sole proprietorships
73.09%

FIGURE 1-3(*b*)

Distribution of Business Income in the United States, by Form of Business, 1989

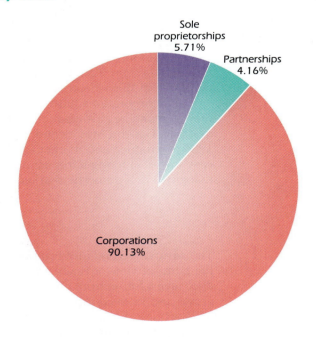

Sole
proprietorships
5.71%

Partnerships
4.16%

Corporations
90.13%

SOURCE: *Statistics of Income, SOI Bulletin*, U.S. Treasury Department, Internal Revenue Service, vol. 11, no. 1, Summer 1991, p. 123, and vol. 12, no. 1, Summer 1992, p. 154.

14

TABLE 1-1

Characteristics of the Three Forms of Business

SOLE PROPRIETORSHIP

Advantages
1. Proprietor is sole business decision maker.
2. Proprietor receives all income from business.
3. Income from business is taxed once, at the individual-taxpayer level.

Disadvantages
1. Proprietor is liable for all debts of the business (unlimited liability).
2. Proprietorship has a limited life.
3. Business has limited access to additional funds.

GENERAL PARTNERSHIP

Advantages
1. Partners receive income according to terms of partnership agreement.
2. Income from business is taxed once as partners' personal income.
3. Decision making rests with the general partners only.

Disadvantages
1. Each partner is liable for all the debts of the partnership.
2. Partnership life is determined by agreement or upon the death of any partner, whichever occurs first.
3. Business has limited access to additional funds.

CORPORATION

Advantages
1. Firm has perpetual life.
2. Owners are not liable for the debts of the firm; the most that owners can lose is their initial investment.
3. Firm can raise funds by selling additional ownership interest.
4. Income is distributed in proportion to ownership interest.

Disadvantages
1. Income paid to owners is subjected to double taxation.
2. Ownership and management (decision making) are separated in larger organization.

THE OBJECTIVE OF FINANCIAL MANAGEMENT

So far we have seen that financial managers are primarily concerned with investment decisions and financing decisions within business organizations. The great majority of these decisions are made within the corporate business structure, which better accommodates growth and is responsible for 90 percent of U.S. business income. Hence, most of our discussion in the remainder of this text will focus on financial decision making in corporations, but many of the issues apply generally to all forms of business.

One such issue concerns the objective of financial decision making. What goal (or goals) do managers have in mind when they choose between financial alternatives—say, between distributing current income among share-holders and investing it to increase future income? There is actually one financial objective: the maximization of the economic well-being, or wealth, of the owners. Whenever a decision is to be made, management should choose the alternative that most increases the wealth of the owners of the business.

The Measure of Owners' Economic Well-Being

The economic well-being of a corporation's shareholders is enhanced in two ways: (1) through dividends and (2) through increases in the price of a share of stock.

The price of a share of stock at any time—what buyers and sellers in a free market are willing to pay for it—is called its ***market value.*** The ***market value of shareholders' equity*** is the value of all owners' interest in the corporation and is calculated as the product of the market value of a share of stock and the number of shares of stock outstanding:

$$\text{Market value of shareholders' equity} = \text{Market value of a share of stock} \times \text{Number of shares of stock outstanding}$$

The "number of shares of stock outstanding" is the total number of shares that are owned by shareholders.

Investors buy shares of stock in anticipation of future dividends and increases in the market value of the stock. How much are they willing to pay today for this future—and hence uncertain—stream of dividends? They are willing to pay exactly what they believe it is worth *today*, an amount that is called its ***present value*** and that reflects:

- The uncertainty associated with receiving the future payments.
- The timing of these future payments.
- Compensation for tying up funds in this investment.

In other words, the market price of a share of stock at any time already includes investors' evaluation of both future dividends and the future market value of the stock. Consider a five-year investment horizon, that is, the situation in which an investor has expectations regarding the course of dividends and the price of the stock over the next five years. Then,

$$\text{Share price today} = \begin{array}{c}\text{present value of dividends expected during the next five years}\end{array} + \begin{array}{c}\text{present value of future share price at the end of five years}\end{array}$$

But since the share price after five years is *itself* a present value of future dividends (those after five years, *ad infinitum*):

$$\text{Share price today} = \begin{array}{c}\text{present value of dividends expected each period forever}\end{array}$$

Hence, to maximize the economic well-being of the corporation's owners, managers must maximize price of the stock. Market price is a measure of owners' economic well-being. Does this mean that if the share price goes up, management is doing a good job? Not necessarily. And if the share price goes down, is management doing a poor job? Not necessarily. Share prices can of-

A Split Decision

Suppose that there are 100,000 shares of stock outstanding that represent ownership interests in The Great Divide Company. Suppose further that the market price of a share is $20. The value of owners' equity in the company is:

$$\text{Market value of shareholders' equity} = \$20 \times 100,000 \text{ shares} = \mathbf{\$2,000,000}$$

Now let's suppose that the board of directors of The Great Divide Company declares a 2:1 stock split to lower the stock price. In a 2:1 stock split each share of old stock is exchanged for two new shares. Shareholders receive nothing of value in this split, which is simply a means of cutting the ownership "pie" into more pieces. Since this is merely a cosmetic change, the value of the shareholders' equity after the split should be the same as the value before the split, assuming all other things (such as economic and market conditions) are the same.

After the stock split, there are 200,000 shares of stock outstanding (100,000 × 2). But the market value of each share of stock drops from $20 to $10, in order to hold the value of shareholders' equity at $2 million:

$$\text{Market value of shareholders' equity} = \$10 \times 200,000 = \mathbf{\$2,000,000}$$

The price of the stock has gone down. Does this mean that the management of The Great Divide Company has done something wrong? No, because the total wealth of all shareholders and the wealth of each individual shareholder remains the same, even though the price of a share of stock is halved.

ten be influenced by factors beyond the control of management. These factors include expectations regarding the economy, returns available on investments, such as bonds (rather than shares of the firm), and even how investors view the firm and the idea of investing.

These factors influence the price of shares through their effects on expectations regarding future cash flows and investors' evaluation of those cash flows. Nonetheless, managers can still maximize the value of owners' equity, *given* current economic conditions and expectations. They do so by carefully considering the expected benefits, risk, and timing of the returns on proposed investments.

Economic Profit vs. Accounting Profit: Share Price vs. Earnings per Share

When you studied economics, you saw that the objective of the firm is to maximize profit. In finance, however, into which you have now stepped, the objective is to maximize owners' wealth. Is this a contradiction? No. We have simply used different terminology to express the same goal. The difference arises from the distinction between accounting profit and economic profit.

Accounting Profit vs. Economic Profit

Suppose you have $20,000 cash when you graduate from college and you own a building suitable for a retail business. Suppose further that you decide to open your own business in this building, using your $20,000 to buy inventory.

If after one year you have generated sales of $100,000 and made expenditures of $75,000, have you made a profit? Yes and no. Your accounting statement for your business would show a profit of $25,000. But is this truly a profit? Let's consider the other, less obvious costs.

The $20,000 that you used to buy inventory could have been invested elsewhere. If your next best alternative was to place it in a bank account and earn 5 percent, your opportunity cost is $20,000 × 0.05 = $1,000. If your building could have been rented to another business, say for $5,000 for the year, the forgone rental income is an opportunity cost. The use of the $20,000 elsewhere and the forgone rent are opportunity costs of your venture.

But what about you? You, the entrepreneur, have supplied your time and managerial talents to the business. What are your contributions worth? How much profit is necessary to compensate you for your time and talent and the risk of starting your new business? Suppose that your next best opportunity was as a manager of a local department store with an income of $30,000 for the year.

In summary, your venture has an accounting profit of $25,000, but an economic loss of at least $11,000.

Revenues	$ 100,000
Less: Expenditures	−75,000
Accounting profit	$ 25,000
Less: Interest forgone	$ −1,000
Rent forgone	−5,000
Salary forgone	−30,000
Economic loss	$−11,000

Economic profit is the difference between revenues and costs, where "costs" includes actual business costs plus the opportunity cost of invested funds and normal profits. An *opportunity cost* is the cost of not having the next best alternative; so, the opportunity cost of invested funds is the profit that could have been made by investing those funds elsewhere. A *normal profit* is the minimum return that investors will accept, given the risks of investment and the possibility of moving their funds elsewhere. This is different from the opportunity cost, which is what the business *could* have earned on alternative investments. In a sense, normal profit is the minimal return that will keep investors investing in the business. By maximizing stock price, we are also maximizing this economic profit and so are maximizing shareholder wealth. There is no contradiction between economics and finance.

18

Accounting profit, however, is the difference between revenues and costs, recorded according to accounting principles, where costs are primarily the actual costs of doing business. The implicit costs—opportunity cost and normal profit—which reflect the uncertainty and timing of future cash flows, are not taken into consideration in accounting profit. Moreover, accounting procedures, and hence the computation of accounting profit, can vary from firm to firm. For both these reasons, accounting profit is not a reasonable gauge of shareholders' return on their investment, and the maximization of accounting profit is not equivalent to the maximization of shareholder wealth.[6] This is also true of *earnings per share,* which is just accounting profit computed on a per-share basis; the maximization of earnings per share is not equivalent to the maximization of shareholder wealth.

Share Prices and Efficient Markets

Blue Big Blue

In late 1992, financial analysts expected IBM's dividend would be cut. Throughout the fall of 1992, IBM's share price continued to drop until, in late January 1993, the price had reached approximately half its previous year's value.

On January 26, 1993, IBM announced that its March 1993 quarterly dividend would be cut in half (from $1.21 per share to $0.54 per share) and that it had made other changes that suggested it was acting to restructure the firm's management and business to perform more competitively. The price of IBM's stock rose that day by $0.125 to $49 per share. What were investors thinking? We'll never really know, but most likely they thought the worst was over and IBM was on the mend.

We have seen that the price of a share of stock today is the present value of the dividends and share price the investor expects to receive in the future. What if these expectations change?

Suppose you buy a share of stock of IBM. The price you are willing to pay is the present value of future cash flows you expect from dividends paid on one share of IBM stock and from the eventual sale of that share. This price reflects the amount, the timing, and the uncertainty of these future cash flows. Now what happens if some news—good or bad—is announced that changes the expected IBM dividends? If the market in which these shares are traded is efficient, the new price will very quickly reflect that news.

In an *efficient market,* the price of assets—in this case shares of stock—reflects all publicly available information. As information is received by investors, share prices change rapidly to reflect the new information. How rapidly? In U.S. stock markets, which are efficient markets, information affecting a firm is reflected in share prices of its stock within minutes.

What are the implications for financing decisions? In efficient markets, the current price of a firm's shares reflect all publicly available information. Hence, there is no good time or bad time to issue a security. When a firm issues stock, it will receive what that stock is worth—no more and no less. Also, the price of the shares will change as information about the firm's activities is revealed. If the firm announces a new product, investors will use whatever information they have to figure out how this new product will change the firm's future cash flows and, hence, the value of the firm—and the share price will change accordingly. Moreover, in time, the price will be such that investors' economic profit approaches zero.

[6] When economic profit is zero, as an example, investors are getting a return that just compensates them for bearing the risk of the investment. When accounting profit is zero, investors would be much better off investing elsewhere and just as well off by keeping their money under their mattresses.

MANAGERS REPRESENTING OWNERS: THE AGENCY RELATIONSHIP

If you are the sole owner of a business, then you make the decisions that affect your own well-being. But what if you are a financial manager of a business and you are *not* the sole owner? In this case, you are making decisions for the owners, not for yourself; you, the financial manager, are an agent. An *agent* is a person who acts for—and exerts powers of—another person or group of persons. The person (or group of persons) the agent represents is referred to as the *principal.* The relationship between the agent and his or her principal is referred to as an *agency relationship.* There is an agency relationship between the managers and the shareholders of corporations.

Problems with the Agency Relationship

In an agency relationship, the agent is given the responsibility of acting for the principal. Is it possible the agent may not act in the best interest of the principal, but instead act in his or her own self-interest? Yes—because the agent has his or her own objective of maximizing personal wealth.

In a large corporation, for example, the managers may enjoy many fringe benefits, such as golf club memberships, access to private jets, and company cars. These benefits, also called *perquisites,* or "perks," may be useful in conducting business and may help attract or retain management personnel, but they contain room for abuse. What if the managers start spending more time at the golf course than at their desks? What if they use the company jets for personal travel? What if they buy company cars for their teenagers to drive? The abuse of perquisites imposes costs on the firm—and ultimately on the owners of the firm. There is also a possibility that managers who feel secure in their positions may not expend their best efforts toward the business. This is referred to as *shirking,* and it too imposes a cost to the firm.

Finally, there is the possibility that managers will act in their own self-interest, rather than in the interest of the shareholders when both interests clash. For example, the managers may fight the acquisition of their firm by some other firm even if the acquisition would benefit shareholders. Why? Put yourself in the position of a manager of a corporation. You have seen that in most takeovers of one firm by another, many managers of the *acquired* firm generally lose their jobs. Suppose some company makes an offer to acquire the firm you manage. Are you happy that the acquiring firm is offering the shareholders of your firm more for their stock than its current market value? If you are looking out for their best interests, you should be. Are you happy about the prospect of losing your job? Most likely not.

Many managers faced this dilemma in the "merger mania" of the 1980s. What did they do? Among the many tactics:

- Some fought acquisition of their firms—which they labeled *hostile takeovers*—by proposing changes in the corporate charter or even lobbying for changes in state laws to discourage takeovers.
- Some adopted lucrative executive compensation packages—called *golden parachutes*—that were to go into effect if they lost their jobs.

Such defensiveness by corporate managers in the case of takeovers, whether it is warranted or not, emphasizes the potential for conflict between the interests of the owners and the interests of management.

Costs of the Agency Relationship

There are costs involved with any effort to minimize the potential for conflict between the principal's interest and the agent's interest. Such costs are called *agency costs.* There are three types: monitoring costs, bonding costs, and residual loss.

Monitoring costs are costs that are incurred by the principal to monitor or limit the actions of the agent. In a corporation, shareholders may require managers to periodically report on their activities via audited accounting statements, which are sent to shareholders. The accountants' fees and the management time lost in preparing such statements are monitoring costs. Another example is the implicit cost incurred when shareholders limit the decision-making power of managers. By doing so, the owners miss profitable investment opportunities; the forgone profit is a monitoring cost.

The board of directors of a corporation has a *fiduciary duty* to shareholders—a legal responsibility to make decisions (or to see that decisions are made) that are in the best interests of shareholders. Part of that responsibility is to ensure that managerial decisions are also in the best interests of the shareholders. Therefore, at least part of the cost of having directors is a monitoring cost.

Bonding costs are incurred by agents to ensure that they will act in their principal's best interests. The name comes from the agent's *promise,* or *bond,* to take certain actions. A manager may enter into a contract that requires him or her to stay on with the firm even though another company acquires it; an implicit cost is then incurred by the manager, who forgoes other employment opportunities.

Even when monitoring and bonding devices are used, there may be some divergence between the interests of principals and those of agents. The resulting cost, called the *residual loss,* is the implicit cost that results because the principal's and the agent's interests cannot be perfectly aligned *even when* monitoring and bonding costs are incurred.

Motivating Managers: Executive Compensation

One way to encourage management to act in shareholders' best interests, and so minimize agency problems and costs, is through executive compensation—how top management is paid. There are several ways to compensate executives, including:

- *Salary.* The direct payment of cash of a fixed amount per period.
- *Bonus.* A cash reward based on some performance measure, say earnings of a division or the company.
- *Stock appreciation right.* A cash payment is based on the amount by which the value of a specified number of shares has increased over a specified period of time (supposedly due to the efforts of management).
- *Performance shares.* Shares of stock given the employees in an amount based on some measure of operating performance, such as earnings per share.
- *Stock options.* The right to buy a specified number of shares of stock in the company at a stated price—referred to as an *exercise price*—at

some time in the future. The exercise price may be above, at, or below the current market price of the stock.

- **_Restricted stock grant._** The grant of shares of stock to the employee at low or no cost, conditional on the shares not being sold for a specified time.

The salary portion of the compensation—the minimum cash payment an executive receives—must be enough to attract talented executives. But a bonus should be based on some measure of performance that is in the best interests of shareholders, not just on the past year's accounting earnings. For example, a bonus could be based on gains in market share.

The basic idea behind stock options and grants is to make managers into owners, since the incentive to consume excessive perks and to shirk are reduced if managers are also owners. As owners, managers not only share the costs of perks and shirks, but they also benefit financially, when their decisions maximize the wealth of owners. Hence, the key to motivation through stock is not really the _value_ of the stock, but the _ownership_ of the stock. For that reason, stock appreciation rights and performance shares, which do not involve an investment on the part of recipients, are not effective motivators.

Stock options do work to motivate performance if they require owning the shares over a long time period; are exercisable at a price _above_ the current market price of the shares, to encourage managers to get the share price up; and require managers to tie up their own wealth in the shares.

Currently, there is a great deal of concern in some corporations because executive compensation is not linked to performance. One problem is that compensation packages for top management are designed by the board of directors, which often includes top management. Moreover, reports disclosing these compensation packages to shareholders (the proxy statements) are often confusing. Both problems can be avoided by adequate and comprehensible disclosure of executive compensation to shareholders and with compensation packages determined by members of the board of directors who are not executives of the firm. Starting in 1993, SEC disclosure requirements will offer shareholders a clearer picture of executive salaries and stock options.

Owners have one more tool with which to motivate management—the threat of firing. As long as owners can fire managers, managers will be encouraged to act in owners' interest. However, if the owners are apathetic—as they often are in large corporations—or if they fail to monitor management's performance and the reaction of directors to that performance, the threat may not be credible. The removal of a few poor managers can, however, make this threat very believable.

Shareholder Wealth Maximization and Social Responsibility

When financial managers assess a potential investment in a new product, they examine the risks and the potential benefits and costs. If the risk-adjusted benefits do not outweigh the costs, they will not invest. Similarly, managers assess current investments for the same purpose; if benefits do not continue to outweigh costs, they will not continue to invest in the product but will shift their investment elsewhere. This is consistent with shareholder wealth maximization and with the allocative efficiency of the market economy.

Discontinuing investment in an unprofitable business may mean closing down plants, laying off workers, and perhaps, destroying the economy of an entire town that depends on the business for income. Thus decisions to invest or disinvest may affect great numbers of people.

All but the smallest business firms are linked in some way to groups of persons who are dependent to a degree on the business. These groups may include suppliers, customers, the community itself, and nearby businesses, as well as employees and shareholders. The various groups that depend on a firm are referred to as its ***stakeholders:*** They all have some *stake*, or interest, in the outcomes of the firm.

Can a firm maximize the wealth of shareholders and stakeholders at the same time? Probably. If a firm invests in the production of goods and services that meet the demand of consumers in such a way that benefits exceed costs, the firm will be allocating the resources of the community efficiently, employing assets in their most productive use. If later the firm must disinvest— perhaps close a plant—it has a responsibility to assist affected employees and other stakeholders. Failure to do so could tarnish its reputation, erode its ability to attract new stakeholder groups to new investments, and ultimately be detrimental to the interests of the shareholders.

The effects of a firm's actions on others are referred to as ***externalities*** and pollution is a very current example that keeps increasing in importance. Suppose the manufacture of a product creates air pollution. If the polluting firm takes action to reduce the pollution, it incurs a cost that either increases the price of its product or decreases profit and the market value of its stock. If competitors do not likewise incur costs to reduce their pollution, the firm is at a disadvantage and may be driven out of business through competitive pressure.

The firm may try to use its efforts at pollution control to enhance its reputation, in the hope that this will lead to a sales increase large enough to make up for the cost of reducing pollution. This is what is called a ***market solution.*** The market places a value on the pollution control and rewards the firm (or an industry) for it. If society really believes that pollution is bad and that pollution control is good, the interests of owners and society can be aligned.

It is more likely, however, that pollution control costs will be viewed as reducing owners' wealth. Then firms must be forced to reduce pollution through government laws or regulations. But such laws and regulations also come with a cost—the cost of enforcement. Again, if the benefits of mandatory pollution control outweigh the cost of government action, society is better off, and if the government requires all firms to reduce pollution, then pollution control costs simply become one of the conditions under which owner wealth-maximizing decisions are to be made.

SUMMARY

- Financial managers assess the potential risk and rewards associated with investment and financing decisions.

- Economic principles serve as the foundation of finance.

- The information necessary for financial decisions and analysis includes the accounting information that describes the company and its industry as well as economic information relating to the company, the industry, and the economy in general.

- A business enterprise may be formed as a sole proprietorship, a partnership, or a corporation. The choice of the form of business is influenced by concerns about the life of the enterprise, the liability of its owners, the taxation of income, and access to funds. In turn, the form influences financial decision making through its effect on taxes, governance, and the liability of owners.

- Most business income in the United States is generated by corporations. Corporations are entities created by law that limit the liability of owners and subject income to an additional layer of taxation. The corporation's owners—the shareholders—are represented by the board of directors, which oversees the management of the firm.

- The objective of financial decision making in a business is the maximization of the wealth of the owners. For a corporation, this is equivalent to the maximization of the market value of the stock.

- If markets for securities are efficient, share prices will reflect all available information. When information is revealed to investors, it is rapidly figured into share prices.

- Since managers' self-interest may not be consistent with owners' best interests, owners must devise ways to align managers' and owners' interests. One means of doing this is through executive compensation. By designing managers' compensation packages to encourage long-term investment in the stock of a corporation, the interests of managers and shareholders can be aligned.

- Shareholder wealth maximization is consistent with the best interests of stakeholders and society if either market forces reward firms for taking actions that are in society's interest or the government steps in to force actions that are in society's interest.

QUESTIONS

1-1   Which of the following actions are the result of a financing decision and which are the result of an investment decision?

    a.   A firm introduces a new product.
    b.   A firm issues new bonds.
    c.   A corporation issues new shares of stock.

d. A firm expands its existing manufacturing facilities.
e. A firm leases a new building to be used in its manufacturing.

1-2 Suppose you are the financial manager of a large, national food processing firm and in your travels, you run across a small regional processor that you believe will provide your firm with annual returns of over 30 percent, which are pretty good compared to the 20 percent on your firm's typical investments. Should you propose that your firm acquire this regional food processor? What factors do you need to consider in making this decision?

1-3 McDonald's Corporation, licenser and operator of a chain of fast-food restaurants, was founded in 1953 as a partnership and, within six months was incorporated. Why would this operator of fast-food restaurants incorporate so soon after being established? What factors influence the decision to incorporate?

1-4 Briefly describe each of the following forms of business:
a. Master limited partnership
b. Professional corporation
c. Joint venture

1-5 Corporations contribute the greatest share of business income in the United States, yet there are fewer corporations than sole proprietorships. Explain why these facts seem reasonable, considering the evolution of a firm.

1-6 If the share price of a corporation's stock declines, does this mean that the management of the company is not maximizing shareholder wealth? If the share price of a corporation's stock increases, does this mean that the management of the company is maximizing shareholder wealth? Explain.

1-7 Why is the maximizing of shareholder wealth not necessarily equivalent to the maximizing of earnings per share?

1-8 Through 1992, the Burlington Coat Factory Warehouse Corporation had not paid any dividends. Why were investors willing to pay over $20 for a share of Burlington stock in 1992?

1-9 The Rising Corporation has had twenty consecutive quarters of increasing earnings per share, but its share price has remained at about the same price over this same time period. Is this consistent? Explain.

1-10 The Lotus Development Corporation, one of the largest makers of personal computer software, had variable earnings per share, yet a falling stock price during the 1991–1992 period:

Year	Earnings per share	High	Low	Closing
		Price per share during year		
1989	$1.50	$33.50	$18.00	$31.000
1990	1.77	39.25	12.50	20.000
1991	1.40	40.75	14.75	26.250
1992	1.40	38.75	14.75	19.675

At the end of 1992, analysts expected Lotus's future earnings per share to increase, possibly to $1.65 per share in 1993. In spite of this prediction, the stock price remained at about $20 per share at the beginning of 1993. Are Lotus's earnings per share and share price consistent? Explain.

1-11   L. A. Gear Inc., markets athletic and leisure footwear. During 1991 and 1992, L. A. Gear lost money (negative earnings per share of $2.40 and $3.69 per share, respectively), but its share price has remained relatively constant, about $10 per share during this same period. Is the relationship between L. A. Gear's share price and its earnings inconsistent? Explain.

1-12   The Clockwork Corporation would like to issue $2 million in new shares of stock. The president of Clockwork believes that if the company waits two weeks, it could get a better price for its shares. The chairperson of the board of directors disputes this. She says that because markets are efficient, there is no "timing" possible on the stock issue and Clockwork should, therefore, issue the shares when it needs the funds, without worrying about "timing." Who is right?

1-13   What is an agency cost? Give three examples of agency costs.

1-14   The Sununu Corporation is having a bit of a problem: The executives are using the corporation's jets for personal reasons, such as to travel on vacation and to visit doctors in other cities. The board of directors wants management to cut down on this type of activity.
   a.   In terms of the different types of agency costs, how would we classify the misuse of corporate jets?
   b.   What measures can the board take to reduce or eliminate the misuse of the corporate jets?

1-15   Suppose that you start your own retail business. As business increases, you expand the hours of operation and hire someone to manage the business during the evening hours.
   a.   Describe the agency relationship involved in your business.
   b.   What possible problems can arise in this relationship?
   c.   How could you reduce the costs associated with this agency relationship?

1-16   List four kinds of compensation for a firm's management. Identify the arrangements that would be most effective in aligning the interests of shareholders and management.

1-17   Can shareholder wealth maximization be consistent with a firm's social responsibility? Explain. Consider IBM, whose headquarters are located in Armonk, New York, but whose manufacturing and sales operations span the globe. Who are IBM's stakeholders? If IBM trims its work force, what obligations does it have to its stakeholders?

1-18   On Tuesday, February 16, 1992, The Limited announced that its fourth quarter 1992 earnings per share rose to 67 cents, up from 55 cents for the fourth quarter of 1991. On the same day, Liz Claiborne Inc. announced fourth quarter earnings of 63 cents per share, compared to the year earlier's fourth quarter earnings of 66 cents. That same day, too, The Limited's share price fell from $27.375 to $25.375 and Liz Claiborne's share price fell from $40.125 to $37.375 (*The Wall Street Journal*, Feb. 17, 1993, pp. A5 and C4). Why did the share prices of both The Limited and Liz Claiborne fall after those earnings figures were announced?

1-19   **Research:**   Choose a major corporation and describe its history in terms of the forms of business that it has taken on since its inception as a business enterprise, noting the year the business was begun, when it was first incorporated, and any changes in its state of incorporation or other relevant factors.

Recommended sources of information:

- *Industrial Manual,* Moody's
- *Corporation Records,* Standard & Poor's

1-20   **Research:**   Choose a major corporation and describe the composition of its board of directors.

   a.   Identify the members of the board of directors as either inside directors or outside directors.

   b.   Determine the amount of stock of the corporation that is owned by each member of the board.

   c.   Determine whether the chairperson of the board of directors is also a member of the corporation's management.

   d.   Identify members of the compensation committee of the board of directors.

   e.   Discuss how the composition of the board may affect the role of the board as representatives of the shareholders.

Recommended sources of information:

- Proxy statements
- Annual reports
- *Industrial Manual,* Moody's

1-21   **Research:**   Select a major corporation and determine the compensation—in salary, bonuses, stock options, and other forms—of its chief executive officer for the past three years.

   a.   How has the company performed over the last five years in terms of the market value of equity?

   b.   How has the compensation of the chief executive officer changed over the past five years? Is there any relationship between the officer's compensation and the change in the market value of equity?

Recommended sources of information:

- Proxy statements
- "Executive Compensation Scoreboard," a special issue of *Business Week* published annually.

PROBLEMS

Forms of business

1-1   Mary, Martin, and Michael invested $20,000, $30,000 and $50,000, respectively, in a business enterprise. After operating the business unsuccessfully for five years, they decided to terminate it. At the time they ceased business operations, the assets of the business were worth only $40,000 and the debts of the business were $10,000.

    a. If this business was formed as a partnership, with the sharing of profits and losses based on the proportion of each partner's original investment, what will be the financial consequences of the dissolution of the business to Mary, Martin, and Michael?

    b. If this business was formed as a corporation, with the proportion of ownership based on the proportion of each shareholder's original investment, what will be the financial consequences of the dissolution of the business to Mary, Martin, and Michael?

1-2   Ivan and Dennis invested $100,000 and $300,000, respectively, in a business enterprise. They decided to terminate the business at a time when the assets of the business were worth only $200,000 and the debts of the business were $300,000.

    a. If this business was formed as a partnership, with the sharing of profits and losses based on the proportion of each partner's original investment, what will be the financial consequences of the dissolution of the business to Ivan and Dennis?

    b. If this business was formed as a corporation, with the proportion of ownership based on the proportion of each shareholder's original investment, what will be the financial consequences of the dissolution of the business to Ivan and Dennis?

1-3   Suppose the Flow Through Corporation pays all of its earnings in dividends to its shareholders. If the earnings of Flow Through are taxed at a rate of 40 percent and the earnings of its shareholders are taxed at 30 percent, what is the effective tax on each dollar of Flow Through Corporation income, considering both corporate and individual incomes taxes?

1-4   The Halfling Corporation pays half its earnings to its shareholders, retaining the other half to reinvest in new projects. Suppose Halfling's earnings are taxed at a rate of 30 percent and Halfling's shareholders are taxed at 40 percent. What is the effective tax on each dollar of Halfling earnings that are paid to shareholders?

Shareholders' wealth

1-5   Calculate the market value of equity for the corporations listed below, given the market price per share and the number of shares outstanding as of the

Corporation name	Market price per share	Number of shares outstanding (in thousands)
Corning Inc.	37\frac{1}{2}$	194,617
Fisher Price Inc.	25$\frac{1}{8}$	31,225
Lockheed Corporation	56$\frac{1}{2}$	61,030
Mattel Inc.	25$\frac{3}{8}$	97,937
Monsanto Company	57$\frac{5}{8}$	121,817
Wal-Mart Stores	64	1,149,028
Walt Disney Company	43	524,204

SOURCE: *Daily Stock Price Record, New York Stock Exchange, October November December 1992,* Standard & Poor's.

close of trading on December 31, 1992. Is that what these corporations are worth? Explain.

Potpourri

PC+   1-6   Research: What are the five largest U.S. corporations in terms of dollar sales for the most recent two years? What are the five largest U.S. corporations in terms of total assets for the most recent two years? Have the rankings changed? If so, is there any explanation for any of the firms' rank changes from year to year?

Recommended sources of information:

*   *Compustat PC Plus* (CD-ROM), Standard & Poor's
*   "The Business Week 1000," published annually by *Business Week,* McGraw-Hill.

PC+   1-7   Research: Choose a major corporation and calculate the market value of owners' equity at the end of the past five years. What has been the trend in owners' equity during this five years? Propose reasons why the market value of owners' equity has changed over this period.

Recommended sources of information:

*   *Daily Stock Price Record,* Standard & Poor's.
*   *Compustat PC Plus* (CD-ROM), Standard & Poor's.

PC+   1-8   Research: Choose a major corporation and find its earnings per share for each of the last sixteen quarters. Also, find the price of a share of its stock at the end of each of these quarters. Graph both the earnings per share and the share price over this four-year period.

a.   What has been the trend in earnings per share for your corporation?
b.   What has been the trend in the share price for your corporation?
c.   Is there any relationship between the two trends (earnings per share and share price)?

Recommended sources of information:

*   *Daily Stock Price Records,* Standard & Poor's.
*   *Compustat PC Plus* (CD-ROM), Standard & Poor's.
*   *Value Line Investment Survey,* Value Line.

FURTHER READINGS

The objective of financial management and its relation to the goal of profit maximization is discussed in a number of works, including:

RICHARD B. COFFMAN, "Is Profit Maximization vs. Value Maximization Also Economics vs. Finance," *Journal of Financial Education,* vol. 12, Fall 1983, pp. 37–40.

GORDON DONALDSON, "Financial Goals: Management vs. Stockholders," *Harvard Business Review,* vol. 41, May/June 1963, pp. 116–129.

———"Reflections on the Corporation as a Social Invention," *Midland Corporate Finance Journal,* Fall 1983, pp. 6–15.

G. BENNETT STEWART III, "Market Myths," *The Quest for Value: A Guide for Senior Management,* Harper & Row, New York, 1990, chap. 2.

JACK L. TREYNOR, "The Financial Objective in the Widely Held Corporation," *Financial Analysts Journal,* vol. 37, no. 1, March/April, 1981, pp. 68–71.

A more thorough (and theoretical) treatment of the objective of financial management and the role of agency costs is provided in:

WILLIAM H. MECKLING and MICHAEL C. JENSEN, "Theory of the Firm: Managerial Behavior, Agency Costs, and Ownership Structure," *Journal of Financial Economics,* vol. 3, no. 4, Oct. 1976, pp. 305–360.

The idea of stakeholders and the goal of financial management are elaborated in:

BRADFORD CORNELL and ALAN C. SHAPIRO, "Corporate Stakeholders and Corporate Finance," *Financial Management,* vol. 16, no. 1, Spring 1987, pp. 5–14.

The issue of relating the level of executive compensation to performance is discussed in:

KEVIN J. MURPHY, "Top Executives Are Worth Every Nickel They Get," *Harvard Business Review,* March/April 1986, pp. 125–132.

ALFRED RAPPAPORT, "Executive Incentives vs. Corporate Growth," *Harvard Business Review,* July/August 1978, pp. 81–88.

What executives actually earn, from salary, bonuses, and options, can be found in the corporation's proxy statement, which you can obtain by writing directly to the corporation. For a summary of executive compensation for hundreds of U.S. corporations, see:

"Executive Compensation Scoreboard," published each March in *Business Week,* which lists executives' compensation and corporate performance, and the annual survey of executive compensation (which includes highlights of key executives and their pay and performance) published each May in *Business Week.*

PART II

Fundamentals of Financial Analysis

2 Securities and Markets 32
3 Financial Statements, Taxation, and Cash Flows 58
4 Financial Analysis 96

CHAPTER 2

Securities and Markets

INTRODUCTION 34

SECURITIES 34

Money Market Securities 34

Capital Market Securities 35

    Equity 36

    Indebtedness 37

Derivative Securities 38

    Options 38

    Futures 39

    Asset-Backed Securities 39

SECURITIES MARKETS 39

Classification of Markets 40

    Primary and Secondary Markets 40

    Exchanges and Over-the-Counter Markets 43

Markets in the United States 43

    Money Markets 44

    Equity Markets 44

    Bond Markets 46

    Options and Futures Markets 46

International Markets 48

    Foreign Securities Exchanges 48

    The Global Market for Securities 50

Market Indicators 50

Efficient Markets 51

Summary 53

Changing the Blue-Light Special

K Mart Corporation is the second largest retailer in the world, with retail operations including K Mart discount stores, Pay Less Drug Stores, Builders Square home improvement centers, and Sports Authority stores. During the mid-1980s, K Mart began to lose its share of the discount retail market:

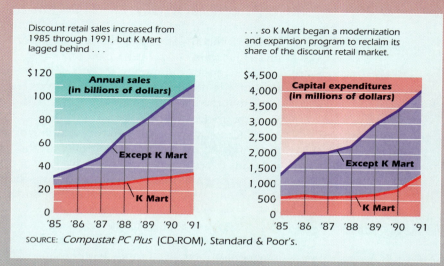

Discount retail sales increased from 1985 through 1991, but K Mart lagged behind . . .

. . . so K Mart began a modernization and expansion program to reclaim its share of the discount retail market.

SOURCE: *Compustat PC Plus* (CD-ROM), Standard & Poor's.

In 1989, K Mart embarked on a program to enlarge and modernize all its K Mart stores over a six-year period. In 1992 alone, the cost of modernization was over $1.3 billion, which exceeded 8 percent of its total assets in that year.

Where should K Mart get the funds it needs to pay for this program? One source is the cash it raises in day-to-day operations over and above its expenses. But K Mart needs more than that. The firm must also raise money by some other means, such as selling stock or borrowing.

Because of the different costs of raising funds it is cheaper for K Mart to raise funds infrequently in large amounts, instead of in the smaller, more frequently needed amounts that are required throughout its modernization program. But this presents a dilemma for the company's financial managers: What should K Mart do with money that has been raised but is not yet needed? K Mart wants the funds available for use as it incurs costs. But it doesn't want idle funds—money not being put to a productive use.

K Mart's modernization program thus presents its management with both financing and investment decisions. The financing decisions include what type of new capital to raise and when to raise it. The investment decisions include the rate at which the modernization should take place and where to invest extra funds temporarily so that they are available when needed but not idle in the meantime.

INTRODUCTION

The objective of any financial decision, whether concerned with financing or investment, is to maximize owners' wealth. For a corporation this translates into maximizing the market value of the ownership interest—the value of the stock. So a financial manager's decisions must be made with regard to the value of the firm's stock and the markets in which it is traded.

What about K Mart? Should the firm issue stock or borrow? If it issues new stock, will present investors lose? If it borrows, what interest rate will its lenders—the investors in its bonds—require? How soon could the loan be paid off? How soon *should* it be paid off?

How about the money K Mart raises? Should financial managers invest it until it is needed? In what kind of financial instrument? What characteristics must the investment vehicle have? What types of risk must they take on with their investment?

The answers require an understanding of the wide range of securities available and the markets in which they are bought and sold. This chapter provides an overview of both. First, we give you an idea how markets for securities function so that you will know how security prices are determined. Then we acquaint you with the terms and definitions we use in this book.

SECURITIES

A *security* is a document that gives its owner a claim on future cash flows. A security may represent an ownership claim on an asset or a claim on the repayment of borrowed funds with interest. The document may be in the form of a piece of paper (such as a stock certificate or a bond) or an entry in a register (which may, in turn, be a computer record). A *securities market* is an arrangement for buying and selling (that is, trading) securities; it may be a physical location or simply a computer or telephone network.

Securities are classified into three groups—money market securities, capital market securities, and derivative securities—based on their maturity and the source of their value.

The word "maturity" is often used loosely to refer to the repayment of a debt. Other terms involving "maturity" are more specific. The *maturity date* of a security is the specified future date on which the amount borrowed (called the *face value,* the *par value,* the *principal,* or the *maturity value*) is to be repaid. The security is said to mature on its maturity date. The *original maturity* is the time between the date a security is issued and its maturity date.

Money Market Securities

Money market securities are short-term claims. By "short term" we usually imply an original maturity of one year or less.[1] The most commonly used money market securities are Treasury bills, commercial paper, negotiable certificates of deposit, and banker's acceptances.

Treasury bills (T-bills) are short-term securities issued by the U.S. government; they have original maturities of either 91 days, 182 days, or 52 weeks. Unlike other money market securities, T-bills carry no stated interest rate. Instead, they are sold on a *discounted basis:* Purchasers obtain a return on their investment by buying these securities for less than their face value and

---

[1] Therefore, a bond issued in 1970 that matures in 1995 is *not* classified as a money market security in 1994.

then receiving the face value at maturity. T-bills are sold in $10,000 denominations, that is, the T-bill has a face value of $10,000.

Commercial paper is a promissory note—a written promise to pay—issued by a large, creditworthy corporation. These securities have original maturities ranging from 1 day to 270 days and usually trade in units of $100,000. Most commercial paper is backed by bank lines of credit, which means that a bank is standing by ready to pay the obligation if the issuer is unable to. Commercial paper may be either interest bearing or sold on a discounted basis.

Certificates of deposit (CDs) are written promises by a bank to pay a depositor. Nowadays they have original maturities ranging from six months to three years. *Negotiable certificates of deposit* are CDs issued by large commercial banks that can be bought and sold among investors. Negotiable CDs typically have original maturities of one month to one year and are sold in denominations of $100,000 or more. Negotiable certificates of deposit are sold to investors at their face value and carry a fixed interest rate. On the maturity date, the investor is repaid the amount borrowed, with interest.

Eurodollar certificates of deposit are CDs issued by foreign branches of U.S. banks, and *Yankee certificates of deposit* are CDs issued by foreign banks located in the United States. Both Eurodollar CDs and Yankee CDs are denominated in U.S. dollars, that is, interest payments and the repayment of principal are both in U.S. dollars.

Banker's acceptances are short-term loans, usually to importers and exporters, made by banks to finance specific transactions. An acceptance is created when a draft (a promise to pay) is written by a bank's customer and the bank "accepts" it, promising to pay. The bank's acceptance of the draft is a promise to pay the face amount of the draft to whoever presents it for payment. The bank's customer then uses the draft to finance a transaction, giving this draft to her supplier in exchange for goods. Since acceptances arise from specific transactions, they are available in a wide variety of principal amounts. Typically, banker's acceptances have maturities of less than 180 days. Banker's acceptances are sold at a discount from their face value, and the face value is paid at maturity. Since acceptances are backed by both the issuing bank *and* the purchaser of the goods, the likelihood of default is very small.

Money market securities are backed solely by the issuer's ability to pay. With money market securities, there is no *collateral;* that is, no item of value (such as real estate) is designated by the issuer to ensure repayment. The investor relies primarily on the reputation and repayment history of the issuer in expecting that he or she will be repaid. The features of these money market securities are summarized in Table 2-1.

Capital Market Securities

Capital market securities are long-term securities issued by corporations and governments. Here "long-term securities" refers to securities with original maturities greater than one year and perpetual securities (those with no maturity). There are two types of capital market securities: those that represent shares of ownership interest, also called *equity,* issued by corporations, and those that represent indebtedness, issued by corporations and by the U.S. and state and local governments.

TABLE 2-1
Summary of Features of Money Market Securities

Instrument	Borrower	Term to maturity	Interest payment	Denomination
U.S. Treasury bills	U.S. Government	91 days, 182 days, and 52 weeks	Discount from face value	$10,000
Commercial paper	Large corporations	Up to 270 days	Discount from face value or interest bearing	$100,000
Negotiable certificates of deposit	Commercial banks	Up to 1 year	Interest bearing	$100,000 or more
Banker's acceptances	Commercial banks	Up to 180 days	Discount from face value	Any denomination

Equity

The equity of a corporation is referred to as "stock"; ownership of stock is represented by shares. Investors who own stock are referred to as **shareholders.** Every corporation has common stock and some corporations may also have another type of stock, preferred stock.

Common stock is the most basic ownership interest in a corporation. Common shareholders are the residual owners of the firm. If the business is liquidated, the common shareholders can claim its assets, but only those assets that remain after all other claimants have been satisfied.

Since common stock represents ownership of the corporation and since the corporation has a perpetual life, common stock is a perpetual security; it has no maturity date. Common shareholders may receive cash payments—*dividends*—from the corporation. They may also receive a return on their investment in the form of increased value of their stock as the corporation prospers and grows.

Preferred stock, also, represents ownership interest in a corporation and, like common stock, is a perpetual security. However, preferred stock differs from common in several ways. First, preferred shareholders are usually promised a fixed annual dividend, whereas common shareholders receive the amount of dividends the board of directors decides to distribute to them. And although the corporation is not legally bound to pay the preferred stock's dividend, preferred shareholders must be paid their dividends before any common dividends are paid. Second, preferred shareholders are not residual owners; their claim on a liquidated corporation takes precedence over the claims of common shareholders. Finally, preferred shareholders generally do not have a say in corporate matters, whereas common stockholders have the right to vote for members of the board of directors and on major issues.

36

Indebtedness

A capital market debt security is a promise to repay the face amount of the security on the maturity date and to make periodic interest payments to the investor. Debt securities with original maturities of less than ten years are often referred to as *notes,* and those with original maturities greater than ten years are often referred to as *bonds.*[2]

We refer to the investor of debt as the *debtholder, bondholder,* or *noteholder.* The investor purchases the security on or after the issue date and either sells it to another investor at any time prior to the maturity date or presents it to the issuer for repayment on the maturity date.

Corporate notes and bonds may be backed by specific assets (as collateral), in which case they are referred to as *secured notes* or *secured bonds.* If they are not backed by specific assets, they are referred to as *debentures.* If a debt obligation is secured and the borrower is unable to make interest or principal payments when promised, the creditors may be able to force the sale of the collateral for the purpose of collecting what is due them. Collateral therefore reduces the security's riskiness; and if a security is less risky, investors are willing to accept a lower annual rate of return, or *yield,* when investing in it. The claims of debtholders take precedence over the claims of shareholders, although debtholders are unlikely to be paid the full face value for their securities if a corporation must be liquidated.

U.S. Government notes and bonds are interest-bearing securities backed by the "full faith and credit" of the United States; there is little uncertainty regarding whether the interest and principal will be paid as promised. The bonds and notes of U.S. government agencies, such as the Small Business Administration and the Tennessee Valley Authority, are also backed by the government.[3]

Bonds issued by state and local governments are called *municipal bonds.* They are either *general obligation bonds,* which are backed by the general taxing power of the issuing government, or *revenue bonds,* which are issued to finance a specific project and are repaid with the revenues from that project.

A curious feature of government bonds is the method of taxation of interest paid to the investors. Interest paid investors on federal government bonds is taxed as income by the federal government, but in most cases not by the states. The interest paid investors on municipal bonds is generally taxed as investor's income by the states, but not by the federal government.[4] The ex-

---

Wielding Yields

The yield on a security is, in general, composed of three parts:

- The opportunity cost of money, since investors do not have use of the funds while tied up in an investment.
- Compensation for anticipated inflation, since future cash flows may be worth less due to an erosion in the purchasing power of the currency.
- Compensation for bearing risk, since we generally assume that investors do not like risk; in fact, investors expect a greater yield for taking on a greater risk.

---

[2] This distinction between notes and bonds is not precisely true, but is consistent with common usage of the terms "note" and "bond." In fact, notes and bonds are distinguished by whether or not there is an indenture agreement, a legal contract specifying the terms of the borrowing and any restrictions, and identifying a trustee to watch out for the debtholders' interests. A bond has an indenture agreement, whereas a note does not. In this chapter, we use the terms "notes" and "bonds" in their common usage, that is, distinguished by the term to maturity.

[3] The securities of government-sponsored enterprises, such as the U.S. Postal Service and the Federal Home Loan Bank, are not explicitly backed by the federal government. However, there is little uncertainty about whether the interest and principal will be paid as promised.

[4] Many states do not tax interest on municipal bonds issued in their own state. In addition, a few states do not tax interest on municipal bonds issued by any state.

clusion of interest on municipal bonds from federal income tax makes these bonds attractive to investors. It also allows local governments to pay lower-than-average interest on their bonds.

Derivative Securities

A *derivative security* is any security that gets its value directly from another security or asset. The several types of derivative securities include options, futures, and asset-backed securities.

Options

An *option* is the right to buy or sell an asset at a specified price within a specified period of time. The specified price is referred to as the *exercise price* or *strike price.* The specified time period ends on the *expiration date* or maturity date.

We can classify options into two types: the right to buy, referred to as a *call option,* and the right to sell, referred to as a *put option.* The owner of an option has the right—but not the obligation—to exercise it. He or she can simply let it expire without taking any action.

There are many types of options that the financial manager will consider in making investment and financing decisions. These include:

- A *warrant,* which gives the holder the right to buy a given number of shares of common stock at a specified price within a specified time period. Warrants are often used to enhance the salability of debt securities; hence they are often referred to as "sweeteners."
- A *convertible feature* of a preferred stock or debt security, which gives the preferred stock or debt *owner* the right to exchange the security for shares of common stock.
- A *call feature* of a preferred stock or debt security, which gives the preferred stock or debt security *issuer* the right to buy back the security at a specified price.
- A *right* which gives the holder the privilege of buying stock at a specified price within a specified time period. Rights may be distributed to current shareholders to allow them to maintain their proportionate share of ownership.
- A *put feature,* in a debt security, which gives the debtholder the right to sell the security back to the issuer at a specified price.

In addition to these options, there are some less obvious—but still very important—options inherent in investment and financing decisions. Consider the following options:

- Suppose a firm decides to invest in a project. There may be an option to delay the investment in the project.
- Once a firm invests in a project, there is usually an option to abandon the project.
- Suppose a firm decides to issue a stock or debt security. The firm has an option to delay issuing the security.
- The shareholders of a firm have the option of not paying debtholders the interest or principal that is promised, but instead halt operations

Executive Compensation and Options

Options are one device used to motivate management to make decisions in the best interest of shareholders. *Executive stock options* granted to top managers of a firm give them the right to buy the stock of the firm at a specified price. If the exercise price is below the current market price per share, managers have an incentive to increase the share's price.

and liquidate the firm—selling off the assets and distributing the proceeds to the creditors and the owners.

Futures

Another type of derivative security is a futures contract. A ***futures contract*** is an arrangement to buy or sell a specific quantity of a commodity or other asset at a fixed price and at a fixed time in the future.

Originally, futures contracts were designed to reduce the effects of fluctuations in the prices of agricultural products (such as cattle, pork bellies, and orange juice) and mineral commodities (such as heating oil, copper, and gold). A recent innovation is futures contracts for foreign currencies, interest rates, stock indexes, and options.

Two types of investors use futures contracts. One is the ***hedger,*** an investor who buys futures contracts to ensure the future price of a commodity for supply or market purposes. For example, a cereal manufacturer may wish to lock in the price of grain at some future time via futures contracts. Or an importer may wish to buy currency futures to lock in a rate of exchange three months from now, when he will have to pay a supplier in Japanese yen. The second type of futures investor is the ***speculator,*** who buys futures contracts to bet on future changes in the prices of commodities or other assets. In general, hedgers use futures contracts to reduce their exposure to risk by unloading this risk onto the speculator.

Futures contracts are different from options because they involve the legal obligation (and not just the option) to buy the underlying asset. An investor who does not intend to buy the underlying asset must sell the futures contract prior to its stated expiration date. This is referred to as "closing out a position."

Asset-Backed Securities

A fairly new derivative security is the ***asset-backed security*** (ABS), a security created from the pooling of certain monetary assets. Typically, individual home mortgages, credit card debts, boat loans, or other types of debt are grouped together ("pooled"); then securities are issued that represent ownership in the principal and any interest received from this pool of debts.

This process of repackaging is referred to as ***securitization,*** and it entails creating a tradable security from loans that could not otherwise be readily traded. Practitioners of securitization are usually investment banks, commercial banks, and stock brokerage firms. The process itself permits lenders to concentrate on lending while investors finance the loans.

SECURITIES MARKETS

The primary function of a securities market—whether or not it has a physical location—is to permit buyers and sellers of securities to buy and sell them.

The earliest documented securities markets were operated by the Babylonians in 2000 B.C., where investors pooled funds to finance trade. The first formal securities markets were formed in the sixteenth century in western Europe, and the first stock exchange was formed in 1773 in London. Today, securities markets are firmly established in the United States, major European cities, and the Far East.

Classification of Markets

Securities markets can be classified by whether they are involved in original sales or resales of securities and by whether or not they involve a physical trading location.

Primary and Secondary Markets

When a security is first issued, it is sold in the ***primary market.*** This is the market in which new issues are sold and new capital is raised. So it is the market whose sales directly benefit the issuer of the securities.

There are three ways to raise capital in the primary market (see Figure 2-1). The first is the direct sale, in which the investor purchases stock, for example, directly from the issuer. Many venture capital firms invest in small, growing businesses in this way. Also, many corporations sell securities directly to large investors, such as pension funds. By doing so, the issuer can tailor the features of the security (such as maturity) to suit the desires of the investor. This type of selling is referred to as ***private placement.***

A second method is to raise capital in the primary market through ***financial institutions,*** which are firms that obtain money from investors in return for the institution's securities and then invest the money obtained. For example, a bank issues bank accounts in return for depositors' money and then loans that money to a firm. Besides banks, firms such as mutual funds and pension funds operate as financial institutions.

FIGURE 2-1

The Three Methods of Raising Capital in the Primary Market

Commercial Bankers vs. Investment Bankers

It may not be efficient for a firm that is raising money to negotiate with individual investors one at a time. Instead, the firm may seek the services of a financial *intermediary*, a firm that facilitates the flow of funds from providers to the ultimate users. There are two major financial intermediaries: investment bankers and commercial bankers.

Investment bankers specialize in marketing securities, buying securities from issuers and reselling them to investors. *Commercial bankers* borrow money from depositors and then lend it to others, usually on a short-term basis.

The Banking Act of 1933 (also known as the Glass-Steagall Act), which was one of the measures taken to reform the securities industry following the market crash of 1929, required separation of commercial banking and investment banking institutions. This act effectively separates those intermediaries that deal with relatively short-term financing (commercial banks) from those that deal with long-term financing (investment banks).

The third method is through investment bankers, who buy the securities issued by corporations and then sell those securities to investors for a higher price. This process of buying shares from the issuer and reselling them to investors is called *underwriting*.

Let's look at how a firm raises funds using an underwriter. Consider K Mart's issue of 23 million shares of preferred stock in August 1991. Morgan Stanley & Company, an investment banking firm, was the underwriter. K Mart sold the shares to Morgan Stanley at $42.90 per share, who then resold the shares to investors at $44.00 per share. K Mart raised almost a billion dollars through this one offering, while its underwriter earned $25 million.

A *secondary market* is one in which securities are resold among investors. No new capital is raised, and the issuer of the security does not benefit directly from the sale. Trading takes place among investors. Investors who buy and sell securities on the secondary market may obtain the services of *stock brokers*, individuals who buy or sell securities for their clients.

We can use the market for college textbooks to illustrate the difference between primary and secondary markets. Suppose one of your instructors decides to use McConnell and Brue's *Economics* as the class text. He notifies the school bookstore, which buys copies of the text from the publisher, McGraw-Hill, and then puts them up for sale at a somewhat higher price than was paid. You then buy your new copy of *Economics* from the bookstore. The market for new books, in which you, the publisher, and the bookstore have operated as buyer, seller, and intermediary, respectively, is a *primary market*. The bookstore has acted as a sort of textbook "investment banker," but most of the money invested in the book has gone to the issuer (the publisher). The bookstore received a profit for performing as an intermediary, a facilitator of the transaction between you and the publisher. The publisher would have been hard put to sell to each member of the class individually.

Federal Regulation of Securities Markets in the United States

Securities Act of 1933

Regulates new offerings of securities to the public. It requires the filing of a registration statement containing specific information about the issuing corporation and prohibits fraudulent and deceptive practices related to security offers.

Securities and Exchange Act of 1934

Establishes the Securities and Exchange Commission (SEC) to enforce securities regulations and extends regulation to the secondary markets.

Investment Company Act of 1940

Gives the SEC regulatory authority over publicly held companies that are in the business of investing and trading in securities.

Investment Advisers Act of 1940

Requires registration of investment advisers and regulates their activities.

Federal Securities Act of 1964

Extends the regulatory authority of the SEC to include the over-the-counter securities markets.

Securities Investor Protection Act of 1970

Creates the Securities Investor Protection Corporation, which is charged with the liquidation of securities firms that are in financial trouble and which insures investors' accounts with brokerage firms.

Insider Trading Sanctions Act of 1984

Provides for triple damages to be assessed against violators of securities laws.

Insider Trading and Securities Fraud Enforcement Act of 1988

Provides preventative measures against insider trading and establishes enforcement procedures and penalties for the violation of securities laws.

At the end of the term you may wish to sell your used copy of *Economics.* You can sell it directly to a friend who is about to take the course, or you can sell it back to the bookstore for resale to another student. Both these transactions take place in the secondary textbook market, because the publisher (the issuer) is not a party to them.

If a firm can raise new funds only through the primary market, why should financial managers be concerned about the secondary market on which the firm's securities trade? The reason is that investors are not interested in buying securities that are not liquid—that they could not sell at a fair price at any time—and the secondary markets provide the liquidity. For example, suppose K Mart wants to issue new common shares to pay for its expansion program; investors would not be willing to buy such shares if they could not expect to sell them on the secondary market should the need arise. K Mart counts on the existence of a healthy secondary market to entice investors to buy its *new* stock issue.

Exchanges and Over-the-Counter Markets

There are two types of secondary securities markets: exchanges and over-the-counter markets. ***Exchanges*** are actual places where buyers and sellers (or their representatives) meet to trade securities. ***Over-the-counter*** (OTC) ***markets*** are arrangements in which investors or their representatives trade securities without sharing a physical location. For the most part, computer and telephone networks are used for this purpose. These networks are owned and managed by the market's members.

Exchanges may be privately owned, as they are in the United States and the United Kingdom. Privately owned exchanges are managed by their owners, or members, who may pay hundreds of thousands of dollars for the privilege of owning a seat (a membership) on the exchange. Private exchanges are self-regulated, that is, they determine the rules and regulations that must be followed by their members, by traders, and by companies whose securities are ***listed,*** or accepted for trading, on the exchange.

Exchanges may be owned and operated by banks or banking organizations, as are many European exchanges—those in Luxembourg and Germany, for example. If the exchanges are owned by the banking institutions, these institutions then control both the primary and secondary markets for securities. Both bank-owned and privately owned exchanges are, of course, subject to regulation by the countries in which they are located.

Finally, there are state-controlled exchanges, such as those in France, Belgium, and several Latin American countries. These are generally the most restrictive exchanges and are characterized by stringent listing standards, especially for foreign companies.

Markets in the United States

[T]ake all your savings and buy some good stock and hold it till it goes up, then sell it. If it don't go up, don't buy it.

Will Rogers, 1924

Governments provide no guarantees regarding securities. However, through legislation and regulation of markets, transactions, and transactors, the U.S. government has attempted to guard against fraudulent practices and manipulative behavior on the part of market participants. The federal organization charged with the regulation of U.S. financial markets is the Securities and Exchange Commission (SEC). Major federal legislation is listed in the accompanying box. In addition, the states have all passed laws that reinforce or extend federal legislation.

Money Markets

Money market securities are not traded in a physical location; rather these securities are traded "over the counter" through banks and dealers that are joined in a network of telephone and computer lines. These intermediaries bring together buyers and sellers from around the world. In the United States, most of the trading is centered around large banks (called "money center banks") located in the major financial centers of the country. Many banks and dealers specialize in specific instruments, such as commercial paper or bankers' acceptances.

Government securities, such as T-bills, are traded through thirty-nine firms known as *primary dealers,* which serve as the intermediaries between the U.S. Treasury and investors. Primary dealers, such as Merrill Lynch & Co., and First Boston Corporation, facilitate trading in the world's biggest securities market, whose trading can exceed over $100 billion in a single day.[5]

Equity Markets

Exchanges

There are nine organized securities exchanges in the United States. Two are national (the New York Stock Exchange and the American Stock Exchange), and seven are regional.[6] The *New York Stock Exchange* (NYSE) was founded in 1792 and has grown to become the largest exchange in the United States. More than 1,800 different securities are listed on the NYSE, and the vast majority of exchange trading in the United States takes place there.

The other national exchange, the *American Stock Exchange* (AMEX), is somewhat smaller than the NYSE, in terms of both the number of securities listed and trading activity. By the terms of a 1910 agreement between the two, the NYSE handles the securities of large, more established firms and the AMEX handles the securities of smaller and usually newer firms. Approximately 860 securities are listed on the AMEX.

The seven regional U.S. stock exchanges are:

Boston Stock Exchange	Pacific Stock Exchange
Cincinnati Stock Exchange	Philadelphia Stock Exchange
Intermountain Stock Exchange	Spokane Stock Exchange
Chicago Stock Exchange	

Over-the-Counter Markets

The largest over-the-counter market for common stock in the United States is the *National Association of Securities Dealers Automated Quotation* (NASDAQ) *system* operated by the National Association of Securities Dealers

---

[5] A 1991 scandal involving a primary dealer, Salomon Brothers Inc., and its cornering of the U.S. Treasury security market has created interest in revising the system of relying on primary dealers.

[6] The words "national" and "regional" in the descriptions of U.S. exchanges refer mainly to investors' interest in the stocks listed (traded) on the exchange. The national exchanges list stocks that are of interest to investors across the nation; regional exchanges list stocks that are of primarily regional interest, along with a handful of NYSE-listed stocks.

(NASD). The NASDAQ system is a computerized quotation system initiated in 1971. More than 4,000 securities are listed in this system today. Most of them are small companies, many just starting to become known in their fields.

The more actively traded securities of the NASDAQ system are included in the ***National Market System*** (NMS). The NMS, begun in 1982, provides more information on transactions than the NASDAQ system. Over half of the NASDAQ-listed securities are included in the NMS, and these securities account for over 70 percent of the value of trading on the NASDAQ system.

The equity markets differ not only in the type of corporations they list, but also in trading activity. Total trading activity for 1991 is compared in Figure 2-2 for the NYSE, AMEX, the NASDAQ system, and the regional exchanges

FIGURE 2-2(*a*)

Trading Volume in U.S. Stock Markets, 1991

SOURCE: *Securities Industry Yearbook, 1992/1993,* Securities Industry Association, pp. 878 and 879.

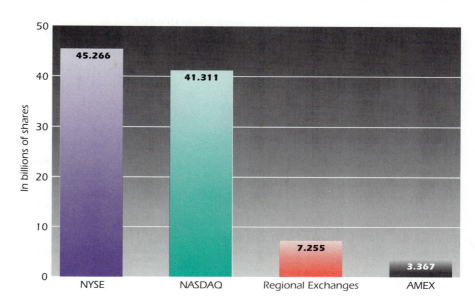

FIGURE 2-2(*b*)

The Market Value of Shares Traded in U.S. Stock Markets, 1991

SOURCE: *Securities Industry Yearbook, 1992/1993,* Securities Industry Association, pp. 878 and 879.

NOTE: NYSE = New York Stock Exchange; NASDAQ = National Association of Securities Dealers Automated Quotation System; and AMEX = American Stock Exchange.

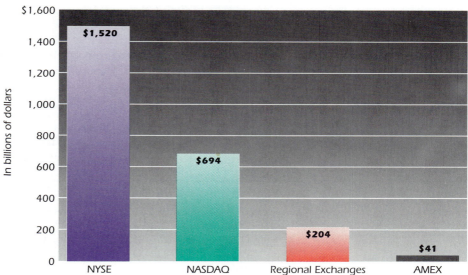

in terms of number of shares, panel *a*, and market value of shares, panel *b*.

The NYSE dominates the other markets in both the number and value of shares traded. The AMEX, though a national exchange, plays a relatively small role in securities trading in the United States. The NASDAQ system has become the second largest market for securities in the United States, but trading in the NASDAQ system is predominantly in lower-priced securities.[7]

Does it matter in which market a corporation's securities are traded? Yes and no. It is desirable to have your securities traded in a market where there is sufficient activity so that an investor who wants to buy or sell the security can do so readily. Therefore, the liquidity that the market provides to the security is important. The more easily a security can be bought and sold, the less its **marketability risk,** which is the risk that an owner will not be able to sell the security when he or she wishes to do so. Investors are willing to take a lower return when the marketability risk is lower, allowing the corporation to raise additional funds at a lower cost.

Bond Markets

Almost all bond trading takes place in over-the-counter markets, with the remainder (about 1 percent) occurring mainly on the New York Stock Exchange Fixed Income Market and the American Stock Exchange. The bond trading that does take place on exchanges consists primarily of small orders, whereas bond trading in the over-the-counter market is for larger—sometimes huge—blocks of bonds, purchased by pension funds and other institutional investors.

Within the over-the-counter market, large banks and firms, such as First Boston Corporation, "make a market" in bonds, that is, they connect buyers with sellers. They negotiate directly with large bond investors, such as pension funds, insurance companies, and corporations, and are connected among themselves through a computerized network.

Options and Futures Markets

The first formal options market was the ***Chicago Board Options Exchange*** (CBOE), begun in 1973. Soon after, several exchanges introduced options contracts in their "product line." Now options are traded on such exchanges as the CBOE, the Chicago Board of Trade (CBOT), the Pacific Stock Exchange, the Philadelphia Stock Exchange, and the American Stock Exchange. As an indicator of the growing interest in options, we note that the dollar value of options traded annually on the CBOE now exceeds the value of the stocks traded annually on the AMEX. Options are traded on both exchanges and in the over-the-counter market, with most of the recent growth in the over-the-counter market.

Futures markets have been around for a long time, with the first formal exchange appearing in the United States in 1848. Nowadays, futures contracts are traded on (among others) the CBOT, the Chicago Mercantile Exchange, the Mid-America Commodity Exchange, and the New York Futures Exchange.

---

[7] To see this, compare NASDAQ securities in Figure 2-2*(a)* and 2-2*(b)*.

The Crash of 1987

On Monday, October 19, 1987 the value of all U.S. stocks fell by $500 billion, a drop of approximately 25 percent. Since markets are interconnected both globally—securities trade on more than one country's exchange—and internally across different types of markets—stock, futures, and options—within countries, the effects of a drop in stock prices was felt in many places.

We cannot say precisely what caused this drop in prices, but most people believe the crash was precipitated by many factors, including the following:

- Interest rates had just risen sharply, with long-term interest rates over 10 percent. Since the value of stocks falls when discount rates increase—that is, a dollar of future cash flow from a share of stock is worth less today—the increase in interest rates exerted downward pressure on stock prices.
- A bill was proposed in Congress to deter merger activity, which had gone unabated for over a decade. Deterring merger activity, which had bolstered stock prices, was expected to reduce the potential gains from merging.
- The prior Friday, October 16, was a *triple-witching day*—with stock index futures, index options, and individual stock options expiring on the same day, bringing with it a great deal of trading activity.
- Recently, there was bad economic news, such as a large U.S. trade deficit, a weakening U.S. dollar, and falling markets in other parts of the world.

On Friday, October 16, and Monday, October 19, there was a great influx of sell orders, preventing many stocks from opening trading in the markets on Monday. Since some securities did not open, the values of securities and the options on these securities were not aligned, causing havoc in the markets. In addition, the influx of sell orders overwhelmed the computerized order-handling system (the Designated Order System) of the New York Stock Exchange.

There were two major outcomes of the crash. First, exchanges have instituted "circuit breakers" to take effect when there is a great deal of pressure on security prices that may overwhelm the system. Second, a dispute arose over who has regulatory authority over futures and options markets. Since the futures, options, and stock markets are interconnected, no one can agree on who should regulate the activity that spans the several markets.

Some futures markets specialize in certain contracts, either by preference or by state law. For example, the International Petroleum Exchange specializes in petroleum products, such as crude oil and gas oil. However, most commodity exchanges deal with a variety of futures contracts.

Like the equity markets, options and futures markets are subject to state and federal regulations (to different degrees), as well as to self-regulation by the markets themselves.[8]

International Markets

Foreign Securities Exchanges

Securities markets outside the United States have become increasingly more liberal in the 1980s and 1990s, with several countries deregulating their markets and moving them toward a U.S. style of governance. As part of this trend, some countries have relaxed constraints on foreign investment in domestic securities, as well as constraints on the listing of foreign securities on domestic exchanges.

Here's how various foreign markets stood in the mid-1990s:

United Kingdom	The London Stock Exchange is the largest exchange in the United Kingdom and the oldest in Europe. Its listings include primarily large multinational corporations. In October 1986, new guidelines were implemented to change the governance of the exchange to look more like the U.S. exchanges.
Germany	The foundation for today's markets in Germany occurred in 1585, when foreign currency and notes were first traded. Today there are eight exchanges (referred to as *bourses*) in Germany, of which the Frankfurt Stock Exchange is the largest. The exchanges are controlled by the large banking institutions and are in the main unregulated by the government. The banks also control the primary market.
France	The Paris Stock Exchange is the largest exchange in France, but it is small relative to other European exchanges. Its limited trading is dominated by fixed income securities, such as bonds. Restrictive listing standards and discriminatory taxation make this exchange unattractive to foreign investors and foreign companies. There is currently a move toward modernization and deregulation, but it is proceeding very slowly.
Canada	There are four exchanges in Canada, of which the Toronto Stock Exchange is the largest. The Canadian exchanges are regulated similarly to the U.S. exchanges, mainly by the Investment Dealers Association and the Canadian Securities Commission. In 1985, the Toronto and AMEX exchanges were linked electronically, introducing international communications among exchanges.

---

[8] For example, the **Commodity Futures Trading Commission** (CFTC) is a regulatory body established by Congress to approve new types of futures contracts and establish trading rules for futures exchanges.

Japan	Of the several exchanges in Japan, the Tokyo Stock Exchange is the largest and oldest. Japan has historically been isolationist in its markets, with its government restricting both foreign investment in Japanese securities and the listing of foreign companies on Japanese exchanges. In the 1980s, the markets were liberalized to allow some indirect trading in foreign securities.
Emerging markets	Many nations' securities markets are catching the attention of investors. Those nations include Venezuela, Greece, Taiwan, Turkey, and Zimbabwe, which are growing rapidly and deregulating their financial systems. However, since their financial infrastructures are immature, these markets are more volatile than the longer established markets of, say, the United States and the United Kingdom.

How much trading takes place in foreign securities markets relative to the U.S. markets? Figure 2-3 shows the market value of stocks traded on several markets during 1988. As you can see, the Tokyo Stock Exchange leads the world stock, or equity, markets. And although the U.S. markets are quite important in the global stock market, we cannot ignore markets outside of the United States.

FIGURE 2-3

Market Value of Shares in U.S. Dollars Traded in Major Markets Worldwide, 1988

SOURCE: *NASDAQ Fact Book*, National Association of Securities Dealers, 1989.

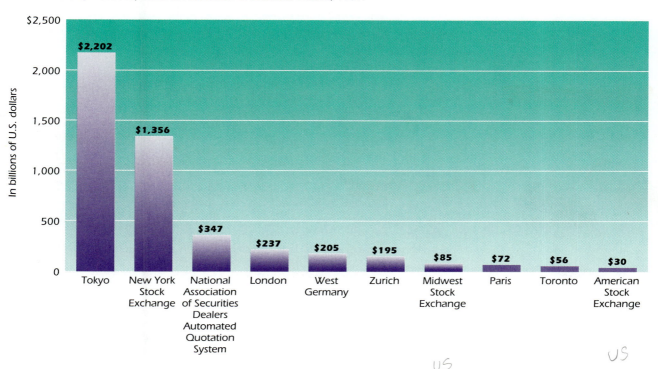

The Global Market for Securities

An enhanced ability to communicate around the world, the desire of investors to seek out investments with characteristics not available in their own countries, and the increasing sophistication and uniformity of financial markets in different countries all contribute to an accelerating globalization of securities markets.

One important ingredient of globalization is the ability of investors in one country to buy and sell securities issued in other countries. In that regard, there is a commitment on the part of the European Community (EC) to move toward a unified European securities market, which will provide uniformity among exchanges within the community. Likewise, in the United States the **Intermarket Trading System** (ITS) now connects seven U.S. exchanges and certain over-the-counter dealers for trading purposes. And recent linkages between exchanges in the United States, Canada, and the United Kingdom seem to be moving markets directly toward globalization.

Foreign stocks are typically not traded directly on U.S. exchanges but rather are traded indirectly through securities that represent ownership of shares of stock. The shares of foreign stock are deposited in a trust, either in the United States or abroad, and the trust issues securities that represent ownership of the trust's assets (the deposited stock). These securities are traded on U.S. exchanges and are called **American Depository Receipts** (ADRs).

A foreign investor may invest in a U.S. corporation by (1) buying shares of the U.S. corporation through a U.S. broker, or (2) buying shares in a **unit trust** for the U.S. corporation (similar to ADRs) on his or her country's domestic exchange. Many U.S. companies have their shares listed on foreign exchanges in the form of unit trusts. As an example, International Paper common stock is traded on the New York Stock Exchange as well as exchanges in Montreal, Basel, Geneva, Lausanne, Zurich, and Amsterdam. The laws of the particular investor's country regarding the purchase of foreign securities will, of course, influence the choice of method.

Market Indicators

Individual security prices are quoted each day in local newspapers and in the financial press.[9] However, individual prices are not indicative of how the security markets as a whole may be faring. Why would you care how the market is doing? There are at least two reasons. First, the prices of securities tend to move together in the same general direction—though not in perfect tandem. Second, such general movements of the market tend to precede economic developments. For example, a sustained upward movement in the market during a recession usually tells us that the end of the recession is nearing. Both of these factors have consequences for investors and for corporations contemplating new equity issues.

Market indicators provide a means of gauging the movement of market prices over time. Such an indicator may be calculated as an average of the prices of representative stocks, perhaps weighted in some way, or as an index.

---

[9] For information on how to read security prices in the financial press, take a look at Appendix A at the back of this book.

As an example, the oldest and most watched indicator is the Dow Jones Industrial Average (DJIA), composed of the stocks of thirty strong, well-established, and profitable firms (sometimes called "blue chip" firms) and weighted to reflect various events that have occurred during the histories of those firms. A more representative indicator is the Standard & Poor's 500 Stock Index (S&P 500), which includes 500 common stocks. The S&P 500 is reported relative to the base years 1941–1943, which are arbitrarily given an index value 10. So, for example, when that index reached 100 in 1977, we knew that stock prices were generally about ten times as high as in 1943.

In addition to general stock market indicators, like the DJIA and the S&P 500, a number of industry-specific stock indicators are computed and published. These include the Dow Jones Transportation Average and the S&P 400 Utilities Stock Index. There are also bond market indicators, such as the Shearson Lehman Long-Term Treasury Index.

Efficient Markets

Investors do not like risk, and they must be compensated for taking on risk—the more risk, the higher the compensation. But can investors earn a return on securities *beyond* that necessary to compensate them for the risk? In other words, can investors earn an **abnormal profit** on the secondary markets? Can they beat the market? The answer is maybe.

Recall from Chapter 1 that an efficient market is one in which asset prices rapidly reflect all available information and that the securities markets in the United States are typically thought of as being highly efficient. This means that all available information is already reflected in a security's price; so investors should expect to earn a return sufficient to compensate them for their opportunity cost and the effects of anticipated inflation and risk. That would seem to preclude abnormal profits. But according to at least one theory, there are several levels of efficiency: weak-form efficient, semistrong-form efficient, and strong-form efficient.[10]

In the **weak form of market efficiency,** current securities prices reflect all past prices and price movements. In other words, all worthwhile information about previous prices of the stock has been used to determine today's price; the investor cannot use that same information to predict tomorrow's price and earn abnormal profits.[11]

Empirical evidence shows that the securities markets are at least weak-form efficient. In other words, you cannot beat the market by using information on past securities prices.

In the **semistrong form of market efficiency** the current market prices of securities reflect all publicly available information. So if you trade on the basis of publicly available information, you cannot earn abnormal profits. This

---

[10] Eugene F. Fama, "Efficient Capital Markets: A Review of Theory and Empirical Work," *Journal of Finance*, vol. 25, no. 2, May 1970, pp. 383–417.

[11] This doesn't mean that trying it once may not prove fruitful. What it does mean is that, over the long run, you cannot earn abnormal profits by using information about past prices to predict future prices. Do investors actually try this? Well, there are financial services in business today that perform analyses of stock prices (called technical analysis). There is no evidence that investors can consistently earn abnormal profits using technical analysis.

does not mean that prices change instantaneously to reflect new information, but rather that new information is reflected in securities prices rapidly.

Empirical evidence supports the idea that U.S. securities markets are semi-strong-form efficient. This, in turn, implies that careful analysis of securities and issuing firms cannot produce abnormal profits.[12]

In the **_strong form of market efficiency_** stock prices reflect all public _and_ private information. In other words, the market (which includes all investors) knows everything about all securities, including information that has not been "formally" released to the public.

The strong form implies that you cannot make abnormal profits by trading on inside information, where inside information is information that is not yet public.[13] This form of market efficiency is not supported by the evidence. In fact, we know from recent events that the opposite is true; gains are available for someone with inside information.

As pointed out above, U.S. securities markets are essentially semistrong efficient. This means that investors can, for the most part, expect securities to be fairly priced. Therefore, when a firm issues new securities, it should expect investors to pay a price for those shares that reflects their value. This also means that if new information about the firm is revealed to the public (for example, concerning a new product), the price of the stock should change to reflect that new information.

But in a semistrong-efficient market an investor can make abnormal profits through trading by using information not known to the public. Such trading tends to distort the prices of affected securities and thus to harm at least some investors. For that reason and because investigators found evidence of such trading during the corporate merger mania of the 1980s, existing anti-insider trading legislation has recently been strengthened and reinforced. Strengthening such legislation tends to ensure the fairness of securities prices.

In essence, it is illegal for any person with an agency relationship to a firm to benefit financially through nonpublic information obtained as a result of that relationship. This does _not_ mean that executives of a corporation cannot buy and sell shares of the firm. Trading by insiders (members of the board of directors and the employees of the firm) is legal _if_ it is not motivated by the use of nonpublic information. What it _does_ mean is that insiders cannot use inside information to make their personal investment decisions; doing so would be **_illegal insider trading._** As another example, an investment banker who is negotiating the merger of two corporations cannot legally purchase the stock of those corporations knowing that the market prices will rise when news of the merger is made public.

---

[12] Does this mean that financial analysis is worthless? No. We still need financial analysis to help us sort out risk and expected return, so that we can properly manage our investments.

[13] There is no exact definition of "inside information" in law. Laws pertaining to insider trading remain a grey area, subject to clarification mainly through judicial interpretation.

SUMMARY

- A security represents ownership in an asset or debt obligation. Securities are classified as either money market securities, capital market securities, or derivative securities.

- Money market securities are marketable securities with original maturities of less than one year and include U.S. Treasury bills, commercial paper, certificates of deposit, and banker's acceptances. Capital market securities include common stocks, corporate bonds, and government bonds. Derivative securities are those that derive their value from some other security or asset; they include options, futures contracts, and asset-backed securities.

- A securities market is any arrangement in which securities can be bought and sold and can be a formalized market, such as a stock exchange, or an informal market, such as banks acting as dealers in the over-the-counter market for bonds. Securities are bought and sold in primary markets, which provide the issuer with new capital, or in secondary markets, which involves trading among investors and which does not generate new capital for the issuer.

- Stocks, bonds, options, and futures are traded in securities markets. These financial markets may be specialized for one type of security or may trade in more than one type of security. For example, bonds, futures, and options are all traded on markets organized under the New York Stock Exchange.

- More and more, securities are being bought and sold in countries other than their country of origin. The actual security may not trade outside its domestic market, yet there are means of trading securities that represent ownership of a foreign security, such as ADRs and unit trusts.

- Market indicators provide us with a gauge of the securities markets, giving us an idea of the general movements of securities prices.

- An efficient market is one in which information is quickly reflected in the prices of securities. We can classify efficient markets according to the kind of information that is reflected in the prices of securities traded: In weak-form markets all past price information is contained in securities prices; in semistrong-form markets all publicly available information is reflected in securities prices; and in strong-form markets, all public and private information is reflected in securities prices. Evidence supports the idea that U.S. securities markets are semistrong-form efficient markets. Trading on inside information, which disrupts market operations and efficiency, is illegal in the United States.

QUESTIONS

2-1   Ahsin Inc. is a publicly traded company, but it does not intend to raise any new capital in the next few years. Why should Ahsin's financial managers concern themselves with securities markets?

2-2   What is the primary distinction between a money market security and a capital market security? From an investor perspective, which security would tend to be riskier? Why?

2-3   How risky is buying the commercial paper of a corporation relative to, say, buying its common stock? What factors affect the riskiness of a corporation's commercial paper? What factors affect the riskiness of a corporation's common stock?

2-4   How does collateral affect a security's riskiness? How does collateral affect the return required by investors?

2-5   Suppose individual income tax rates increase. Ignoring any other changes that may be made in the tax law, how should this affect the demand for municipal bonds?

2-6   Consider a convertible security that gives the owner the right to exchange it for another security within a specified period of time. Is this right to exchange a call or a put option? Explain.

2-7   What is a derivative security? Consider a futures contract in U.S. Treasury bills. Who would be interested in buying such a contract? What economic factors might affect this contract's value?

2-8   Describe the maturity and cash flow characteristics of common stock, preferred stock, and corporate debt securities. Rank order these securities in terms of the uncertainty of their future cash flow.

2-9   What are the main differences between common and preferred stock? From the perspective of an investor, which security is riskier? Why?

2-10   Suppose you are asked by the university to help construct an option to sell to students. This option gives students the right to drop a class during a specified period of time.
   a.   What features of this option must be specified?
   b.   What factors determine how much a student would be willing to pay for such an option?

2-11   A toy manufacturer is considering a new product line based on a character in an upcoming movie. What options (that is, choices) does a financial manager face in this new product-line decision?

2-12   Suppose International Business Machines (IBM) needs to raise new capital. List and briefly describe the three methods of raising capital.

2-13   Blockbuster Entertainment initially listed its stock on the NASDAQ system in 1983 and then changed its listing to the NYSE in 1989. Why would Blockbuster initially list on the NASDAQ system? Why would the company want to change its listing to the NYSE?

2-14 Determine whether each statement is consistent with the semistrong-form of market efficiency.

> **Statement X** A local brokerage firm claims that following its strategy of investing in securities whose company name begins with the letter *M*, investors can earn a return that more than makes up for the risk associated with these securities.
>
> **Statement Y** Company Big invested in stocks during 1992 and earned a return of 10 percent. Company Little earned 15 percent during the same year.
>
> **Statement Z** Larry's investment strategy requires him to buy stocks of those companies that announced earnings higher than last year's. He claims that he can earn returns that are more than necessary to compensate him for the securities' risks.

2-15 What is insider trading? What is illegal insider trading?

> **a.** Suppose an executive exercises her stock options just prior to the end of the year, buying the shares and then selling them immediately, in order to avoid an anticipated increase in tax rates. Is this illegal inside trading?
>
> **b.** Suppose a member of the board of directors is involved in negotiating a merger of the firm with another firm. But suppose the negotiations will not be completed for several months. If the board member buys stock of the other company while the negotiations are going on, is this illegal insider trading?
>
> **c.** Suppose you are manager of a corporation, and you feel that it will do better in the future than most analysts believe. Can you buy stock of this firm? Is this illegal insider trading?

PROBLEMS

Money market securities

2-1 Match each of the following yields from January 1993 with a security listed below:

Yield	Security
3.15%	Commercial paper (six-month)
3.39	High-quality (low default risk), long-term corporate bond
6.95	U.S. T-bills (182-day)
12.18	Low-quality (high default risk), long-term corporate bond

Explain the reasoning behind your matching.

2-2 **Research:** Suppose a firm has funds that it desires to invest for a very short time (say, six months), and it wants to invest these funds in a liquid, safe security.

a. What securities are most appropriate for this investment?
b. What are the current yields on these securities?

Recommended sources of information:

- *Bond Market Roundup,* Salomon Brothers
- *Bond Record,* Moody's
- *The Wall Street Journal,* Dow Jones

Markets

PC+ **2-3** **Research:** On what market are the following common stocks traded? Do you see a pattern?

a. Cascade Natural Gas Co.
b. Apple Computer
c. A & W Brands
d. Showboat Inc.
e. Reebok International
f. International Business Machines
g. Microsoft Inc.

Recommended sources of information:

- *Industrial Manual,* Moody's
- *The Wall Street Journal,* Dow Jones
- *Value Line Investment Survey,* Value Line
- *Compustat PC Plus* (CD-ROM), Standard & Poor's

Raising capital

2-4 **Research:** Select a major corporation that has raised new capital within the past two years by issuing a security. You can find a corporation by looking at the securities described for that corporation in Moody's *Industrial Manual* or Standard & Poor's *Corporate Records.* For each new security the corporation has issued in the two-year period, determine:

a. The total amount of funds paid by investors for the security.
b. The amount paid to the underwriters (if underwritten).
c. The name of the underwriters.
d. The proceeds to the corporation.

Recommended sources of information:

- *Industrial Manual,* Moody's
- *Corporation Records,* Standard & Poor's
- *The Wall Street Journal,* Dow Jones

FURTHER READINGS

Listings of standards and statistics on U.S. markets are available in many forms, including the publications published by the markets themselves:

Fact Book, American Stock Exchange.

Fact Book, National Association of Securities Dealers.

New York Stock Exchange Fact Book, New York Stock Exchange.

In addition to Appendix A at the back of this book, there are several sources that help you make sense out of security quotations found in your local paper or in financial publications, such as *The Wall Street Journal:*

GERALD WARFIELD, *The Investor's Guide to Stock Quotations and Other Financial Listings,* 3d ed., Harper & Row, New York, 1990.

RICHARD SAUL WURMAN, ALAN SIEGEL, and KENNETH M. MORRIS, *The Wall Street Journal Guide to Understanding Money & Markets,* Access Press, New York, 1990.

Examining the two major market crashes of this century provides interesting insight into the function of markets. For a comparison of the two twentieth century market crashes see:

G. J. SANTONI, "The Great Bull Markets, 1924–29 and 1982–1987: Speculative Bubbles or Economic Fundamentals," *Review,* Federal Reserve Bank of St. Louis, Nov. 1987, pp. 16–29.

There are many studies that look at market efficiency and the efficiency of U.S. stock markets. For a recent perspective on market efficiency, see:

KEITH C. BROWN, W. VAN HARLOW and SEHA M. TINIC, "How Rational Investors Deal with Uncertainty (or Reports of the Death of Efficient Markets Theory Are Greatly Exaggerated)," in *The New Corporate Finance,* ed. Donald H. Chew, Jr., McGraw-Hill, New York, 1993, pp. 21–34.

GARY G. SCHLARBAUM, "Market Efficiency," in *Equity Markets and Valuation Methods,* Institute of Chartered Financial Analysts, Charlottesville, Va., 1988.

For a look at market efficiency theory, as set forth more than twenty years ago, and the evidence over the past twenty years, see:

EUGENE F. FAMA, "Efficient Capital Markets: A Review of Theory and Empirical Work," *Journal of Finance,* vol. 25, no. 2, May 1970, pp. 383–417.

———,"Efficient Capital Markets: II," *Journal of Finance,* vol. 46, no. 5, Dec. 1991, pp. 1575–1617.

The issues and legality of insider trading are discussed in:

JOHN G. GILLIS, "Insider Trading," in the *Financial Analysts' Handbook,* 2d ed., Sumner N. Levine, Dow Jones-Irwin, Homewood, Ill., 1988.

The recent insider trading scandal involving Ivan Boesky, Michael Milken, and others, is detailed in:

JAMES B. STEWART, *Den of Thieves,* Simon & Schuster, New York, 1992.

CHAPTER 3

Financial Statements, Taxation, and Cash Flows

INTRODUCTION 60

FINANCIAL STATEMENTS 60

The Balance Sheet 61
 Assets 61
 Liabilities 63
 Equity 64
The Income Statement 65
The Statement of Cash Flows 67
 Cash Flows from Operating Activities 67
 Cash Flows from Investing and Financing Activities 67
Footnotes 69
Depreciation 69
 Straight-Line Depreciation 70
 Accelerated Depreciation 70
 Comparison of Straight-Line and Accelerated Methods 71

THE ROLE OF TAXES IN FINANCIAL DECISIONS 72

Types of Taxes 73
Income Taxation in the United States 73
 Tax Rates 74
 Depreciation for Tax Purposes 77
 Investment Tax Credit 79
 Capital Gains 80
 Corporate Taxable Income 83
 Individual Taxable Income 84
 Net Operating Loss Carrybacks and Carryovers 84
 Subchapter S Corporations 85
 State and Local Taxes 86
Taxation in Other Countries 86

CASH FLOWS 88

Cash Inflows and Outflows 88
Predicting Cash Flows 88
 Cash Flow from Operating Activities 89
 Depreciation Tax Shields 89

Summary 90

Accounting and Reality

During the 1960s and 1970s, many U.S. companies began programs to provide their retired employees medical benefits in order to supplement Medicare, the government-sponsored medical program. Some of these programs were very explicit about the commitment of the firm; others were simply loose promises.

Nevertheless, many U.S. firms have some form of commitment to provide postretirement medical benefits. Escalating medical costs escalate the price of this commitment, which is really a liability because it is a promise to pay in the future. But this liability never showed up in any firm's financial statements; instead, payments made as medical benefits fulfilling the commitments showed up as expenses when they were actually made.

The Financial Accounting Standards Board (FASB), the body governing accounting standards, adopted a rule in 1990 [Statement of Financial Accounting Standards No. 106 or SFAS No. 106] that requires U.S. firms to recognize their postretirement obligations as a liability. Firms were not required to apply SFAS No. 106 until the 1993 calendar year, although they were permitted to adopt it earlier if they wanted to. In addition to recognizing the liability, SFAS No. 106 requires the company to recognize any expenses related to this liability. Furthermore, the FASB gives companies a choice: either amortize the cost over twenty years, or take a one-time hit on earnings.

The reaction of U.S. companies to this requirement has been mixed:

- Some firms, like International Business Machines, went ahead and took the one-shot hit on earnings during 1991, a period when earnings were depressed anyway from the recession.
- Some firms, such as Hewlett Packard, McGraw-Hill, and Borden, took the one-time hit in 1992 or 1993. For example, Inland Steel lost $5.83 per share in 1992 before considering the effect of SFAS No. 106, which lowered earnings per share by $25.82.
- And some firms, like Navistar International, chose to recognize the cost over twenty years.

In a reaction to SFAS No. 106, many firms, including Navistar, are cutting back or phasing out postretirement medical benefits to reduce their liability. But this raises an interesting issue: If companies have had the liability all along (but it just wasn't recorded as such), why should recognizing it on their financial statements encourage them to curtail these benefits? And even though companies' earnings will be lower because of the recognition of the expense, this expense does not reflect a cash flow out of the firm. So why did some companies react by cutting benefits to retirees?

Most likely they did so because SFAS No. 106 required firms to take a hard look at their obligations, which would eventually mean paying out cash. So while recognizing the liability and recording an expense do not relate directly to a firm's current cash flows, they tell us something about the firm's *future* cash flows.

INTRODUCTION

Cash flows are the inflows and outflows of spendable dollars to and from a firm, and investing and financing decisions depend strongly on such flows. This is true of individuals as well as firms. When a retail firm, such as K Mart, expands and modernizes its stores, it is spending money today, expecting to increase its cash flows in the future. If K Mart borrows money to finance its expansion and modernization, its management needs to know whether it will have sufficient money on hand to meet the interest and repayment obligations on its indebtedness.

Why then discuss financial statements in the same chapter as cash flows? Simply because these accounting statements contain information that we can use to determine and, ultimately, forecast cash flows.

Why discuss taxes in the same chapter as cash flows? Because taxes represent a significant cash flow and can affect investment or financing decisions. And since a firm's taxes are determined from its accounting information, we need to discuss financial statements, taxes, and cash flows all in the same chapter.

We use financial statements to estimate our cash flows from our operating and financing decisions. Financial statements contain the basic information we need to make these decisions. But our estimate of cash flows is not complete until we estimate the cash flow going to the government: taxes! Since taxes can represent a significant cash outflow—or even an inflow in some cases—we need to understand how taxation works so that we can estimate the cash flows associated with taxes.

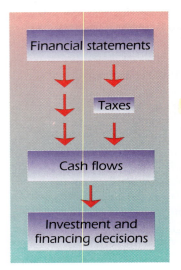

Financial statements

Taxes

Cash flows

Investment and financing decisions

FINANCIAL STATEMENTS

Financial statements are summaries of the operating, financing, and investment activities of a business. The *Financial Accounting Standards Board* (FASB), the governing body that develops the standards all firms follow in their financial accounting, maintains that financial statements should provide information useful to both investors and creditors in making their credit, investment, and other business decisions. By usefulness the FASB means that investors and creditors will be able to employ these statements to predict, compare, and evaluate the amount, timing, and uncertainty of potential cash flows.[1] In other words, financial statements provide the information a business needs to assess its future earnings and therefore the cash flows expected to result from those earnings.

The accounting data in financial statements are prepared by the firm's management according to a set of standards, referred to as *generally accepted accounting principles* (GAAP). The financial statements of firms whose stock is publicly traded must, by law, be audited at least annually by independent public accountants (that is, in this case, accountants who are not employees of the firm). In such an audit, the accountants examine the financial statements and the data from which these statements are prepared and attest that these statements have been prepared according to GAAP.

The financial statements and the auditors' findings are published in the firm's annual report. Also included in the annual report is a discussion by management, providing an overview of company events.

---

[1] The purpose, focus, and objectives of financial statements are detailed in Statement of Financial Accounting Concepts No. 1, "Objectives of Financial Reporting by Business Enterprises," FASB, Stamford, Conn., 1978, and Statement of Financial Accounting Concepts No. 2, "Qualitative Characteristics of Accounting Information," FASB, Stamford, Conn., 1980.

We look briefly at three financial statements: the balance sheet, the income statement, and the statement of cash flows.

The Balance Sheet

The **balance sheet** is a summary of the assets, liabilities, and equity of a business at a particular point in time—usually the end of the firm's fiscal year.

Assets are the resources of the business enterprise. They are used to generate future benefits. If a firm owns plant and equipment that will be used to produce goods for sale in the future, the firm can expect these assets (the plant and equipment) to generate cash inflows in the future.

Liabilities are obligations of the business. They represent commitments to creditors in the form of cash outflows. When a firm borrows, say, by issuing a long-term bond, it becomes obligated to pay interest and principal on this bond as promised.

Equity, also called **shareholders' equity** or **stockholders' equity,** reflects ownership. The equity of a firm represents the part of its value that is not owed to creditors and therefore is left over for the owners. In the most basic accounting terms, equity of an organization is the difference between what the firm owns—its assets—and what it owes its creditors—its liabilities.

The balance sheets for Fictitious Corporation, shown in Table 3-1, provide an example. At the end of the 1995 accounting year, the firm has $11 million in assets, financed by $5 million in liabilities and $6 million in equity.

Assets

There are four categories of assets: current assets, plant assets, investments, and intangible assets. Assets that do not fit neatly into any of these four categories may be recorded as either "other assets," "deferred charges," or "other noncurrent assets."

Current assets are assets that could be reasonably converted into cash within one operating cycle or one year, whichever takes longer. An **operating cycle** begins when the firm invests cash in the raw materials used to produce its goods or services and ends with the collection of cash for the sale of those same goods or services. Since the operating cycle of most businesses is less

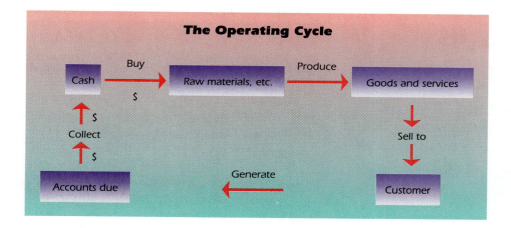

TABLE 3-1

Fictitious Corporation
Balance Sheets
For Years Ending December 31

	1995	1994
	In thousands	
ASSETS		
Cash	400	200
Marketable securities	200	–0–
Accounts receivable	600	800
Inventories	1,800	1,000
Total current assets	$ 3,000	$ 2,000
Gross plant and equipment	11,000	10,000
Less: Accumulated depreciation	4,000	3,000
Net plant and equipment	7,000	7,000
Intangible assets	1,000	1,000
Total assets	$11,000	$10,000
LIABILITIES AND SHAREHOLDERS' EQUITY		
Accounts payable	$ 500	$ 400
Other current liabilities	500	200
Long-term debt	4,000	5,000
Total liabilities	5,000	5,600
Preferred stock (12.5%; $100 par value)	800	800
Common stock: ($1 par value authorized 2 mil. shares; issued: 1.5 mil. and 1.2 mil. shares)	1,500	1,200
Additional paid-in capital	1,500	800
Retained earnings	2,200	1,600
Total shareholders' equity	6,000	4,400
Total liabilities and shareholders' equity	$11,000	$10,000

than one year, we tend to think of current assets as those assets that can be converted into cash in one year.

Current assets consist of cash, marketable securities, accounts receivable, and inventories.

- **Cash** comprises both currency—bills and coins—and assets that are immediately transformable into cash, such as deposits in bank accounts.
- **Marketable securities** are securities that can be readily sold when cash is needed. Every firm needs to have a certain amount of cash to fulfill

immediate needs, and any cash in excess of immediate needs is usually invested temporarily in marketable securities.

- *Accounts receivable* are amounts due from customers who have purchased the firm's goods or services but haven't yet paid for them. To encourage sales, many firms allow their customers to "buy now and pay later," perhaps at the end of the month or within thirty days of the sale. Accounts receivable therefore represents money that the firm expects to collect soon.
- *Inventories* represent the total value of the firm's raw materials, work-in-process, and finished (but as yet unsold) goods. A manufacturer of toy trucks would likely have plastic and steel on hand as raw materials, work-in-process consisting of truck parts and partly completed trucks, and finished goods consisting of trucks packaged and ready for shipping.

Plant assets are the physical assets, such as the equipment, machinery, and buildings, that are used in the operation of the business. We describe a firm's current investment in plant assets by using three values: gross plant assets, accumulated depreciation, and net plant assets. *Gross plant and equipment,* or *gross plant assets,* is the sum of the original costs of all equipment, buildings, and machinery the firm uses to produce its goods and services. *Depreciation,* as you will see later in this chapter, is a charge that accounts for the using up of an asset over the length of an accounting period; it is a means for allocating the asset's cost over its useful life. *Accumulated depreciation* is the sum of all the depreciation charges taken so far for all the firm's assets. *Net plant and equipment,* or *net plant assets,* is the difference between gross plant assets and accumulated depreciation.

Intangible assets are defined by the current value of nonphysical assets that represent long-term investments of the company. Such intangible assets include patents, copyrights, and goodwill. The cost of intangible assets is amortized ("spread out") over the life of the asset. *Amortization* is akin to depreciation: The asset's cost is allocated over the life of the asset; the reported value is the original cost of the asset, less whatever has been amortized.

Liabilities

Liabilities, a firm's obligations to its creditors, are made up of current liabilities, long-term liabilities, and deferred taxes.

Current liabilities are obligations that must be paid within one operating cycle or one year, whichever is longer. Current liabilities include:

- *Accounts payable,* which are obligations to pay suppliers. They arise from goods and services that have been purchased but not yet paid.
- *Wages and salaries payable,* which are obligations to the employees of the business. They represent wages that have been earned but not yet paid.
- Any portion of long-term indebtedness—obligations extending beyond one year—due within the year.
- Short-term loans from a bank.

Long-term liabilities are obligations that must be paid over a period beyond one year. They include notes, bonds, and capital lease obligations. *Notes* and *bonds* both represent loans on which the borrower promises to pay interest periodically and to repay the principal amount of the loan.

A *capital lease* obligates the lessee—the one leasing and using the leased asset—to pay specified rental payments for a period of time. Most capital leases are long-term, noncancellable commitments by the lessee and are therefore liabilities.[2]

Along with long-term liabilities, you may sometimes see another category, *deferred taxes,* which are taxes that will have to be paid to the federal and state governments based on accounting income, but are not due yet. Deferred taxes may arise when different methods of accounting are used for financial statements and for tax purposes.[3]

Equity

Equity is the owners' interest in the company. For a corporation, ownership is represented by common stock and preferred stock (if the firm has issued any preferred stock). Shareholders' equity is also referred to as the *book value of equity,* since this is the value of equity according to the records in the accounting books.

The value of the ownership interest of preferred stock is represented in financial statements as its *par value,* which is also the dollar value on which dividends are figured. For example, if you own a share of preferred stock that has a $100 par value and a 9 percent dividend rate, you receive $9 in dividends each year. Further, your ownership share of the company is $100. Preferred shareholders' equity is the product of the number of preferred shares outstanding and the par value of the stock; it is shown that way on the balance sheet.

The remainder of the equity belongs to the common shareholders. It consists of three parts: common stock outstanding (listed at par or at stated value), additional paid-in capital, and retained earnings. The par value of common stock is an arbitrary figure; it has no relation to market value or to dividends paid on common stock. Some stock has no par value, but may have an arbitrary value, or *stated value,* per share. Nonetheless, the total par value or stated value of all outstanding common shares is usually reported in an account entitled Capital Stock or Common Stock. Then, to inject reality into the equity part of the balance sheet, an entry called *additional paid-in capital* is added; this is the amount received by the corporation for its common stock

---

[2] The distinction between a capital lease and a noncapital lease—called an operating lease—is spelled out in Statement of Financial Accounting Standards No. 13, "Accounting for Leases," FASB, Stamford, Conn., Nov. 1976.

[3] There is some disagreement as to whether deferred taxes are truly liabilities or are equity. Some of the differences between the way we do our accounting and our taxes are permanent. For example, if a company purchases new depreciable assets each period, some portion of the deferred taxes is essentially permanent. If the deferral of taxes is permanent, these deferred taxes are not obligations but rather are part of owners' equity.

in excess of the par or stated value. If a firm sold 10,000 shares of $1 par value common stock at $40 a share, its equity accounts would show:

Common stock, $1 par value $ 10,000
Additional paid-in capital   390,000

Some corporations eliminate this arbitrary division of accounts and instead report the entire amount paid for the common stock as capital stock or common stock.

If some of the stock is bought back by the firm, the amount it pays for its own stock is recorded as **treasury stock.** Since these shares are not owned by shareholders, common shareholders' equity is reduced by subtracting this treasury stock.

We cannot really discuss shares of common stock without some sort of modifier, because there are actually four different labels that can be applied to shares of the same corporation:

- The number of shares *authorized* by the shareholders.
- The number of shares *issued* and sold by the corporation, which can be less than the number of shares authorized.
- The number of shares currently *outstanding*, which can be less than the number of shares issued if the corporation has bought back (repurchased) some of its issued stock.
- The number of shares of *treasury stock,* which is stock that the company has repurchased.

The outstanding stock is reported in the stock accounts, and adjustments must be made for any treasury stock. In the case of Fictitious Corporation, shown in Table 3-1, in 1995 there were 2 million authorized shares, 1.5 million issued shares, and (since there was no treasury stock) 1.5 million shares outstanding.

Retained earnings is the accumulated net income of the company, less any dividends that have been paid, over the life of the corporation. Retained earnings are *not* strictly cash. Any cash generated by the firm that has not been paid out in dividends has been reinvested in the firm's assets—to finance accounts receivable, inventories, equipment, etc.

The Income Statement

An **income statement** is a summary of the revenues and expenses of a business over a period of time, usually either one month, three months, or one year. It shows the results of the firm's operating and financing decisions during that time. Income statements for Fictitious Corporation are presented in Table 3-2.

The operating decisions of the company—those that apply to production and marketing—generate **sales** or **revenues** and incur the **cost of goods sold** (also referred to as the **cost of sales**). The difference between sales and cost of goods sold is **gross profit.** Operating decisions also result in administrative and general expenses, such as advertising fees and office salaries. Deducting these expenses from gross profit leaves **operating profit,** which is also referred to as **earnings before interest and taxes** (EBIT), **operating income,** or **operating earnings**.

TABLE 3-2

Retained Earnings vs. Retained Earnings

The entry "Retained earnings" in the balance sheet is the record of accumulated earnings, less any dividends paid, since the inception of the corporation. The entry "Retained earnings" in the income statement is the amount of earnings retained (that is, not paid out) during that period. As you can see, Fictitious retained $600,000 of its 1995 earnings (Table 3-2), increasing its retained earnings from $1.6 million in 1994 to $2.2 million in 1995 (Table 3-1).

Fictitious Corporation
Income Statements
For Years Ending December 31

	1995	1994
	In thousands	
Sales	$10,000	$9,000
Less: Cost of goods sold	6,500	6,000
Gross profit	3,500	3,000
Less: Lease expense	1,000	500
Administrative expenses	500	500
Earnings before interest and taxes (EBIT)	2,000	2,000
Less: Interest	400	500
Earnings before taxes	1,600	1,500
Less: Taxes	400	500
Net income	1,200	1,000
Less: Preferred dividends	100	100
Earnings available to common shareholders	1,100	900
Less: Common dividends	500	400
Retained earnings	$ 600	$ 500

So operating decisions take the firm from sales to EBIT on the income statement. Table 3-2 shows that Fictitious Corporation generated sales of $10 million in 1995, which produced an operating profit of $2 million.

The results of financing decisions are reflected in the remainder of the income statement. When interest expenses and taxes, which are both influenced by financing decisions, are subtracted from EBIT, the result is **net income.** Net income is, in a sense, the amount available to owners of the firm. First, preferred stock dividends must be paid before any common dividends can be paid, leaving **earnings available to common shareholders.** The board of directors may then distribute all or part of this as common stock dividends, retaining the remainder to help finance the firm. As shown in Table 3-2, Fictitious Corporation had net income for 1995 of $1.2 million. Of this, $100,000 was paid as dividends to preferred shareholders and $500,000 to common shareholders. The remaining $600,000 went into retained earnings.

It is important to note that net income does not represent the actual cash flow from operations and financing. Rather, it is a summary of operating performance measured over a given time period, using specific accounting procedures. Depending on these accounting procedures, net income may or may not correspond to cash flow.

The Statement of Cash Flows

The **statement of cash flows is** a relatively new requirement among financial statements; it is a summary, over a period of time, of a firm's cash flows from operating, investment, and financing activities.

Cash Flows from Operating Activities

The cash flow from operating activities is the most complex of the three. Ideally, we could obtain it directly, by summing all cash receipts (inflows) and disbursements (outflows) for the periods covered by the statement. However, in spite of its usefulness, this sum is, in practice, burdensome to prepare. Instead, the cash flow from operations is obtained indirectly. We begin with net income as reported on the income statement and adjust it for each change in current assets and current liabilities and each noncash operating item; what remains is the cash flow from operations.

The adjustments for changes in current assets and current liabilities are shown in Table 3-3. We adjust for noncash activities, such as depreciation, by adding them because they have been deducted in the computation for net income but do not require cash to be paid out.

We adjust for changes in current assets and liabilities because those changes represent cash flows and investment or financing activities related to current operating activities. For example, an increase in the inventories account is the result of an investment of cash to generate sales in the near future. Table 3-1 shows that Fictitious Corporation invested $800,000 in inventories during 1995 ($1 million in 1994 versus $1.8 million in 1995). Since that investment was an operating cash flow, we must *subtract* it from net income. As another example, Table 3-1 shows that accounts receivable decreased by $200,000. That decrease in a current asset represents a flow of cash to the firm—the return of cash invested in accounts receivable. So the $200,000 must be *added* to net income to obtain cash flow. These adjustments are shown in the "Cash flow from operating activities" section of Table 3-4, along with the other adjustments required to obtain Fictitious Corporation's operating activities.

Cash Flows from Investing and Financing Activities

The computation of the cash flows from investing and financing activities is straightforward. The **cash flow from investing activities** includes cash flow due to investments in plant assets, the disposal of plant assets, acquisitions

TABLE 3-3

Adjustment of Net Income for Changes in Working Capital Accounts to Arrive at Cash Flow from Operations

Change in Working Capital Account	Adjustment to Net Income
An increase in a *current asset* account	Deduct the change
A decrease in a *current asset* account	Add the change
An increase in a *current liability* account	Add the change
A decrease in a *current liability* account	Deduct the change

TABLE 3-4

Fictitious Corporation
Statement of Cash Flows
Years Ending December 31

	1995		1994	
	In thousands			
CASH FLOW FROM OPERATING ACTIVITIES				
Net income	$1,200		$1,000	
Add or deduct adjustments to cash basis				
Change in accounts receivables	$ 200		$ (200)	
Change in accounts payable	100		400	
Change in marketable securities	(200)		200	
Change in inventories	(800)		(600)	
Change in other current liabilities	300		–0–	
Depreciation	1,000		1,000	
		600		800
Net cash flow from operations		1,800		1,800
CASH FLOW FROM INVESTING ACTIVITIES				
Purchase of plant and equipment	(1,000)		–0–	
Net cash flow from investing activities		(1,000)		–0–
CASH FLOW FROM FINANCING ACTIVITIES				
Sale of common stock	1,000		–0–	
Repayment of long-term debt	(1,000)		(1,500)	
Payment of preferred dividends	(100)		(100)	
Payment of common dividends	(500)		(400)	
Net cash flow from financing activities		(600)		(1,900)
Net change in cash		200		(100)
Cash at the beginning of the year		200		300
Cash at the end of the year		$ 400		$ 200

of other companies, and divestitures of subsidiaries. For Fictitious Corporation, the $1 million invested in plant and equipment (see Table 3-1) shows up as a net cash outflow on the statement of cash flows.

The ***cash flow from financing activities*** includes cash flows due to the sale or repurchase of common or preferred stock, the issuing or retirement of long-term debt securities, and the payment of common and preferred dividends.

The flows due to these activities are shown in Table 3-4 for Fictitious Corporation. By design, the statement of cash flows is a reconciliation of the cash flows from the firm's three cash sources: operations, investment, and financing. It takes us from net income to the change in the cash account over the accounting period. For example, for Fictitious Corporation, the net change in the cash balance during 1995 is an increase of $200,000 as shown in the first line of Table 3-1. Table 3-4 shows us that this increase is the result of net cash flows during 1995 of $1.8 million from operations, *less* $1 million from investing activities, *less* $600,000 from financing activities.

Footnotes

The financial statements of a corporation contain information beyond that presented in the balance sheet, the income statement, and the statement of cash flows. This additional information is in the ***footnotes*** to these financial statements. A typical financial statement will have footnotes regarding:

- Significant accounting policies, such as inventory accounting and methods of depreciation.
- Detail on shares repurchased or issued during the report periods.
- Information on any stock options granted, options exercised, and shares granted to employees.
- A reconciliation of taxes paid, with the tax liability reported in the financial statements.
- A description of commitments and contingent liabilities that are not reported in the balance sheet.
- A description of long-term debt obligations, in terms of interest and principal payments.
- Obligations and funding under pension plans and postretirement benefit programs.

Depending on the circumstances of the company and the nature of its business, there may be additional footnotes providing, for example, supplemental balance sheet data, information on mergers or acquisitions in which the company is involved, or information on joint ventures.

Depreciation

We need to take a deeper look at depreciation, an expense that can have an important effect on the firm's financial statements. Depreciation arises directly from the firm's investing activities and directly affects the firm's reported new income and the reported asset values.

Depreciation allocates the cost of the asset, less residual value, over the expected economic life of the asset. The ***economic life,*** also referred to as the ***useful life,*** is the number of years the asset is expected to be of use to the company. The ***residual value,*** also referred to as the ***salvage value,*** is the expected value of the asset at the end of its useful life. Residual value may be an estimate of its scrap value or of its value as used equipment. Depreciation thus provides a means for expensing the portion of the asset's cost that is expected to be used up during its life.

Two types of depreciation methods are currently in use. The first consists of only a single method: ***straight-line depreciation.*** The second, called ***accelerated depreciation,*** primarily because it results in faster depreciation than straight-line in the earlier years of an asset's life, comprises several methods.

Straight-Line Depreciation

Straight-line depreciation is the simplest form of depreciation. The same depreciation expense is charged in each year of the asset's useful life:

$$\text{Depreciation} = \frac{\text{cost} - \text{salvage value}}{\text{useful life, in years}} \qquad [3\text{-}1]$$

Suppose you acquired a depreciable asset having a cost of $100,000, an expected useful life of five years, and an expected salvage value of $20,000. The depreciation expense each year is:

$$\text{Depreciation expense} = \frac{\$100,000 - \$20,000}{5} = \textbf{\$16,000}$$

Another way of looking at straight-line depreciation is to note that in this method, a constant annual depreciation rate is applied to the ***depreciable cost*** (cost *less* salvage value) of the asset. In our example, that rate is 20 percent which is applied to a depreciable cost of $80,000.

Accelerated Depreciation

The accelerated depreciation methods all give greater depreciation expense than the straight-line method in the asset's earlier years of use and less in its later years. Accelerated depreciation thus results in lower reported income and lower reported asset values during the earlier years of an asset's life, relative to straight-line. Over the life of the asset, of course, all must yield the same total depreciation, equal to the asset's depreciable cost.

Two accelerated depreciation methods, declining balance and sum-of-the-years' digits, are often used by firms for purposes of accounting (and financial statement reporting).

Declining balance method

In the ***declining balance method of depreciation,*** a constant annual rate of depreciation is applied each year to the declining, undepreciated cost of the asset. The constant rate is calculated as:

$$\text{Declining balance rate} = 1 - \sqrt[\text{useful life}]{\frac{\text{salvage value}}{\text{original cost}}} \qquad [3\text{-}2]$$

For the asset we depreciated in the straight-line example, with a five-year life:

$$\text{Declining rate balance} = 1 - \sqrt[5]{\frac{\$20,000}{\$100,000}} = 1 - \sqrt[5]{0.20} = \textbf{0.27522} \text{ or } \textbf{27.522\%} \text{ per year}$$

This rate is applied to the total cost, not the depreciable cost. So the first-year depreciation expense would be 27.522 percent of $100,000, or $27,522. The second-year depreciation expense would be 27.522 percent of what hasn't been depreciated, $100,000 − $27,522 = $72,478, resulting in a depreciation expense of 27.522 percent of $72,478, or $19,947. You might want to continue these computations to verify that the five-year total depreciation comes to $80,000, the depreciable cost.

Sum-of-the-years'-digits method

In the **sum-of-the-years'-digits method of depreciation** a declining annual rate is applied to the depreciable cost of the asset. The rate is calculated annually as:

$$\text{Sum-of-the-years'-digits rate} = \frac{\text{number of years' life remaining}}{\text{sum-of-the-years' digits}} \quad [3\text{-}3]$$

For our example where the asset has a five-year life, the denominator is $5 + 4 + 3 + 2 + 1 = 15$ and the rates for the five years are: 5/15, 4/15, 3/15, 2/15, and 1/15. The depreciation expense in the first year would be 5/15 of $80,000 or $26,667, and the depreciation expense in the second year would be 4/15 of $80,000, or $21,333.

Comparison of Straight-Line and Accelerated Methods

Figure 3-1 depicts the accumulation of depreciation over the life of the asset in the preceding example under each of the three methods. In particular, it shows that the accelerated methods do result in substantially faster depreciation than the straight-line method. All three methods, by design, accumulate the same amount of depreciation, in this case $80,000, over the five-year life of the asset. A related effect is a faster decrease in the Net Plant Assets account on the balance sheet, because of the faster depreciation of the accelerated methods.

Faster depreciation also has an effect on the earnings of a company. Earnings are lower in early years with accelerated depreciation, and higher in later years. Suppose the company buying the $100,000 asset has earnings before

FIGURE 3-1

Accumulated Depreciation Using Straight-Line, Declining Balance, and Sum-of-Years'-Digits Methods on a $100,000 Asset with a Useful Life of Five Years and a Salvage Value of $20,000

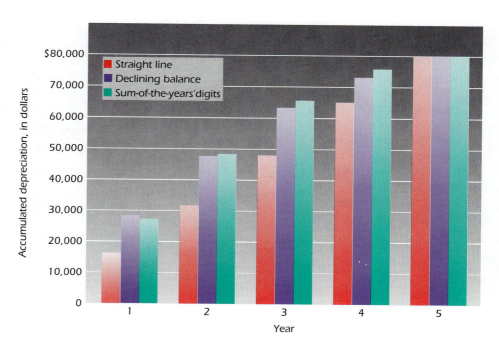

interest, taxes, and depreciation of $30,000 for each of the five years of the asset's life. Then the three depreciation methods would give first-year depreciation and earnings before interest and taxes (EBIT) as follows:

Method	First year depreciation expense	EBIT
Straight-line	$16,000	$14,000
Declining balance	27,522	2,478
Sum-of-the-years' digits	26,667	3,333

The first-year EBIT is more than four times greater with the straight-line method than with either accelerated method. Figure 3-2 shows what happens in the next four years if earnings before depreciation, interest, and taxes are $30,000 each year: With accelerated depreciation, earnings in the later years catch up and then surpass earnings under straight-line depreciation.

THE ROLE OF TAXES IN FINANCIAL DECISIONS

Our objective now is to acquaint you with the ways in which taxes affect financial decision making and analysis. The tax laws are changed almost constantly and are likely being changed as you read this chapter. Hence, no purpose would be served by covering all the details of present tax laws; they might be outdated as soon as you learn them. Instead, we discuss some of the principles behind the tax laws and in doing so provide an opportunity for you to learn some terminology and do some basic taxation calculations. We use the rates in the 1991 tax laws for demonstration purposes.

FIGURE 3-2

Earnings before Interest and Taxes When Earnings before Interest, Taxes, and Depreciation Are $30,000 and Alternative Methods of Depreciation Are Used on a $100,000 Asset with a Salvage Value of $20,000 and a Five-Year Useful Life

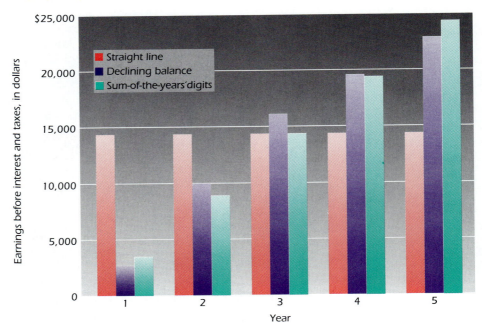

Types of Taxes

A *tax* is a transfer of financial resources from the private sector (meaning both individuals and businesses) to the public sector (meaning the government). Details such as the amount of the transfer, on whom it is levied, and how, are determined by law. A government may impose taxes to meet any number of objectives, including raising revenues, promoting economic stability, growth, and full employment, and redistributing wealth so as to achieve specific social goals. These objectives are achieved mainly through combinations of income taxes, employment taxes, excise taxes, and import-export taxes.

- *Income taxes* are taxes specifically levied on the basis of income.
- *Employment taxes* are also based on income, but specifically on wage and salary income. In the United States, employment taxes are paid by the employee and the employer, and they are designated specifically for retirement and unemployment insurance programs.
- *Excise taxes* are taxes on certain commodities, such as alcoholic beverages, tobacco products, telephone service, and gasoline. Excise taxes provide an easy way of raising revenue, and they can be imposed to discourage the use of specific products, such as tobacco.
- *Import and export taxes* (or tariffs) are taxes based on trade with other countries and are imposed to achieve specific economic goals in world trade.

We focus on income taxes and, specifically, federal income taxes. However, any of the other types of taxes may have a strong influence on decisions in specific industries or firms.

Income Taxation in the United States

In the United States, federal tax laws are the product of all three branches of federal government. Congress passes the tax legislation that comprises the *Internal Revenue Code* (IRC). The *Internal Revenue Service* (IRS), a part of the Treasury Department, interprets these laws, adds the details, and implements them. The IRS does this by providing and processing tax forms, collecting tax payments, explaining the law in its regulations, and even providing decisions regarding the law (called rulings) in some situations. The courts are also called on to interpret the law through specific court cases, and there

Are These Other Taxes Taxing?

We generally focus on federal income taxes in our analysis of financing and investment decisions. However, we cannot ignore other taxes that may arise from our decisions. These taxes can become significant.

The gas-guzzler tax is an excise tax on automobiles, based on how many miles you can drive them on one gallon of gas (mpg). The tax on an automobile that gets between 14.5 and 15.5 mpg was $2,250 in 1992. Depending on the cost of the automobile, this tax may affect its pricing and the revenues and profits obtained from selling it. Similarly, the excise tax on diesel fuel, at a rate of 15.1 cents per gallon in 1992, is likely to affect the pricing, sales, and profits in distributing diesel fuel.

is now a well-developed case law related to the IRC. Together the Internal Revenue Code, IRS regulations, IRS rulings, and the case law make up federal tax law.

The U.S. income tax originated in 1909 with a simple 1 percent tax on corporate income above $5,000 but has since become very complex. To indicate its complexity and the effects of the continual changes in the tax laws, Figure 3-3 shows the top tax rates for individuals and corporations from the beginning of the federal tax system to 1991. You should note that:

- Tax rates change often for both individuals and corporations, but seem to change more for the former than for the latter.
- Tax rates are higher during the years the country has been involved with wars: World War I (1917–1919), World War II (1941–1945), the Korean war (1950–1953), and the Vietnam war (1964–1975).
- Tax rates of individuals and corporations have recently tended to come together.

So what do changing tax rates mean to the financial manager? In forecasting future cash flows, the financial manager needs to be aware that tax rates change frequently. The financial manager cannot simply assume that the tax rate in existence today will be the same in five or ten years. Instead, the financial manager must understand the degree of uncertainty associated with tax rates, which affects the uncertainty of future cash flows.

Tax Rates

Table 3-5 shows the 1991 federal income tax rate schedules for single individuals and corporations. We can look at the schedule for a single person in panel *a* to see how the income tax is computed. Each line of the schedule rep-

FIGURE 3-3

Top Tax Rates for Federal Income Taxes for Individuals and Corporations, 1909–1991

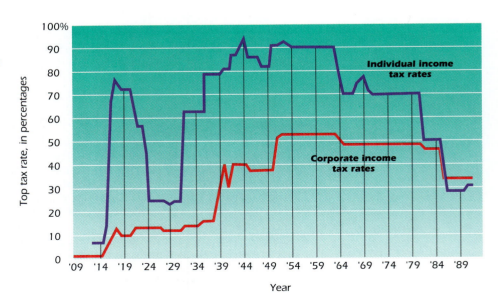

TABLE 3-5
1991 Tax Rate Schedules

(a) SINGLE TAXPAYER

Taxable income

Greater than this base amount . . .	But less than or equal to this amount	The tax on the base is . . .	Plus: Rate applied to the income over the base
$ –0–	$20,350	$ –0–	15%
20,350	49,300	3,052.50	28
49,300		11,158.50	31

(b) CORPORATION

Taxable income

Greater than this base amount . . .	But less than or equal to this amount	The tax on the base is . . .	Plus: Rate applied to the income over the base
$ –0–	$ 50,000	$ –0–	15%
50,000	75,000	7,500	25
75,000	100,000	13,750	34
100,000	335,000	22,250	39
335,000		113,900	34

resents a layer of taxable income, sometimes called a "tax bracket"; the lower limit of each bracket is called its base. So the first line, for example, represents the taxable income layer with base $0 and maximum taxable income of $20,350.

Each line of the schedule also tells us the dollar amount of the tax on the base and the rate at which income above the base is taxed in that bracket. A single taxpayer with a taxable income of, say, $100,000, would be in the "$49,300-and-over" bracket, also referred to by its tax rate as the "31 percent bracket." He or she would pay a federal income tax computed as:[4]

$$\text{Tax on \$100,000 (single individual, 1991)} = \frac{\text{tax on}}{\text{base income}} + \text{tax on amount } over \text{ the base}$$

$$= \$11,158.50 + 0.31(\$100,000 - \$49,300)$$
$$= \$11,158.50 + \$15,717.00$$
$$= \mathbf{\$26,875.50}$$

Suppose a corporation has taxable income of $500,000. Using the rate schedule in Table 3-5, panel *b*, we see that the tax is 15 percent of the first

[4] The tax on the base income is computed as the sum of taxes on all preceding brackets. For example, the tax on the $49,300 base is:

15% of $20,350	$ 3,052.50
plus: 28% of $28,950(= $49,300 − $20,350)	8,106.00
Tax on $49,300 base	**$11,158.50**

$50,000, 25 percent of the next $25,000, 34 percent of the next $25,000, 39 percent for the next $235,000, and 34 percent for income over $335,000:

$$\begin{aligned}\text{Tax on \$500,000}\atop\text{(corporation, 1991)} \quad &= \$113,900 + 0.34(\$500,000 - \$335,000)\\ &= \$113,900 + \$56,100\\ &= \mathbf{\$170,000}\end{aligned}$$

The ***marginal tax rate*** is the rate at which the *next* dollar of income would be taxed. It is the rate that defines the tax bracket. For a corporation with income falling between $100,000 and $335,000, the schedule shows that in 1991 the marginal tax rate was 39 percent. For our individual with $100,000 income, the marginal tax rate was 31 percent.

The ***average tax rate*** is the ratio of the tax paid on the taxable income. So, for example, our individual with $100,000 taxable income paid an average tax rate of:

$$\begin{aligned}\text{Average tax rate on \$100,000}\atop\text{(individual 1991)} \quad &= \frac{\text{tax}}{\text{taxable income}}\\[2mm] &= \frac{\$26,875.50}{\$100,000.00} = \mathbf{26.88\%}\end{aligned}$$

Note that this average tax rate is lower than the marginal tax rate, 31 percent. This is true for all progressive taxes, such as the federal income tax. A ***progressive tax*** is one that levies a higher average tax rate on higher incomes, and vice versa.

The marginal and average tax rates for a large range of 1991 taxable corporate incomes are graphed in Figure 3-4. It is apparent from this diagram that as corporate incomes increase, the average rate approaches the marginal

FIGURE 3-4

Marginal and Average Tax Rates, Corporate Tax Rate Schedule, 1991

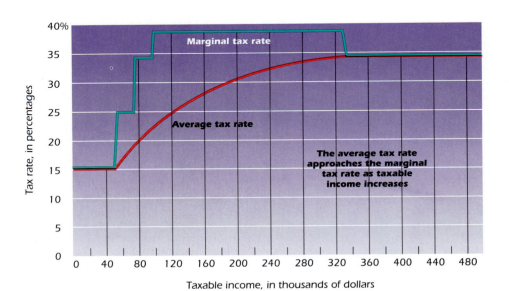

Taxable income, in thousands of dollars

rate of tax. It is also apparent that the corporate income tax is progressive. Note, however, that the corporate tax rate schedule in 1991 (shown in Table 3-5) has a "bubble" of 39 percent in the $100,000 to $335,000 bracket, where the rate is lower in the higher tax bracket. These bubbles appear occasionally in the corporate and individual income tax rate schedules mainly to increase revenues, and many times they disappear from the schedules after a year or two. They usually do not change the progressive nature of the tax.

It is important to realize that taxable income is taxed at the appropriate *marginal* rate for each bracket, and not at the average rate. Therefore, when a financing or investment decision is likely to affect taxable income—and hence cash flow—it will do so through the *marginal* income tax rate.

Depreciation for Tax Purposes

For accounting purposes, a firm can select a method of depreciation based on a number of factors, including the expected rate of physical depreciation of its asset and the effect on reported income. For federal income tax laws purposes, however, businesses are limited by law with regard to both the depreciation method and the period of time over which an asset can be depreciated.

The current depreciation tax laws are the result of an ongoing trend to create more uniformity in depreciation methods among business taxpayers while at the same time simplifying the calculations and allowing accelerated depreciation and shorter asset lives.

In 1991, the two methods of depreciation available to business taxpayers were straight-line method and an accelerated method. The accelerated method, referred to as the ***modified accelerated cost recovery system*** (MACRS), has four features:

1. The depreciation rate used each year is either 150 percent or 200 percent of the straight-line rate, depending on the type of property, applied against the undepreciated cost of the asset. Since the rate is applied against a declining amount, this method is a declining balance method, but not the same declining balance method as that used for financial statement reporting purposes.
2. The salvage value of the asset is ignored; so the depreciable cost is the original cost.
3. The ***half-year convention*** is used on most property, that is, a half year of depreciation is taken in the year the asset is acquired, no matter whether it is owned for one day or 365 days.[5]
4. The depreciation method is switched to the straight-line method when straight-line depreciation produces a higher depreciation expense than the accelerated method.

---

[5] Under 1991 law, there are three acceptable conventions for dealing with the first year's depreciation: half-year, midmonth, and midquarter. The half-year convention is used for most property.

TABLE 3-6

Modified Accelerated Cost Recovery System (MACRS)

(a) CLASSIFIED LIVES

Depreciable life, in years	Asset class
3-year	Tractor units, racehorses over two years old, special tools
5-year	Cars, light and heavy trucks, computer and peripheral equipment, semi-conductor manufacturing equipment
7-year	Office furniture and fixtures, railroad property
10-year	Means of water transportation, fruit trees, nut trees
15-year	Municipal wastewater plants, depreciable land improvements, pipelines, service station buildings
20-year	Farm buildings, municipal sewers
27.5-year	Residential rental property
31.5-year	Nonresidential real property, such as elevators and escalators
50-year	Railroad grading and tunnel bores

(b) DEPRECIATION RATES FOR 3-YEAR, 5-YEAR, 7-YEAR, 10-YEAR, 15-YEAR, AND 20-YEAR CLASSIFIED ASSETS

Year	Depreciation rate					
	3-year	5-year	7-year	10-year	15-year	20-year
1	33.33%	20.00%	14.29%	10.00%	5.00%	3.750%
2	44.45	32.00	24.49	18.00	9.50	7.219
3	14.81	19.20	17.49	14.40	8.55	6.677
4	7.41	11.52	12.49	11.52	7.70	6.177
5		11.52	8.93	9.22	6.93	5.713
6		5.76	8.92	7.37	6.23	5.285
7			8.93	6.55	5.90	4.888
8			4.46	6.55	5.90	4.522
9				6.56	5.91	4.462
10				6.55	5.90	4.461
11				3.28	5.91	4.462
12					5.90	4.461
13					5.91	4.462
14					5.90	4.461
15					5.91	4.462
16					2.95	4.461
17						4.462
18						4.461
19						4.462
20						4.461
21						2.231

NOTE: These rates reflect depreciation calculated using the 200 percent (for 3-year, 5-year, 7-year, and 10-year property) or 150 percent (for 15-year and 20-year property) declining balance method, with a switch to straight-line method, using the half-year convention.

Because the MACRS is an accelerated method, it yields greater depreciation expenses in earlier years and thus reduces taxable income and taxes relative to straight-line depreciation. However, the law allows some firms to use straight-line depreciation if they don't have the income necessary to take advantage of faster depreciation of the MACRS.

Congress (and the IRS) have taken much of the work out of calculating depreciation expenses for tax purposes. First, depreciable lives were assigned to the various classes of assets that might be used by businesses; these lives range from three to 50 years (see Table 3-6, panel *a*). Second, tables were provided showing the depreciation rates to be applied to the asset's cost for each year in the life of each class of asset; one such table is reproduced in Table 3-6, panel *b*.

Notice in panel *b* that each asset type is depreciated over its life plus one year: There are four years of depreciation for a three-year asset, six years of depreciation for a five-year asset, and so on. This is because of the half-year convention: only half of a year's depreciation is used up at the start, leaving half a year's depreciation to be taken after the asset's "life" is over for tax purposes.

Let's see how depreciation expense is calculated using the 1991 data in Table 3-6. Suppose a firm buys a truck for $50,000. According to panel *a* of the table, the truck has a five-year class life. According to panel *b*, the first year's depreciation rate is 20 percent; the next year's is 32 percent, and so on. The results of applying these rates to the cost of the truck over six years are shown in Table 3-7. The total cost is recouped over the six years, with most of the depreciation expense taken in the earlier years.

Investment Tax Credit

From time to time Congress allows businesses an ***investment tax credit*** (ITC), intended to stimulate investment spending; it is calculated as a specified percentage of the cost of the asset.

The ITC may or may not exist at the time you read this chapter. Even if it is not in existence right now, you need to understand about this credit for two reasons. First, the ITC affected the taxes companies paid in the past and

TABLE 3-7

MACRS Depreciation of a $50,000 Truck, Using 1991 MACRS Rates

Year	Depreciation rate	Depreciation expense = rate times $50,000
1991	20.00%	$ 10,000
1992	32.00	16,000
1993	19.20	9,600
1994	11.52	5,760
1995	11.52	5,760
1996	5.76	2,880
Total over six years		**$50,000**

**Give Congress
Credit**

The checkered history of
the investment tax credit
provides us with an ap-
preciation of how the
winds of change affect
Congress and our laws:

Introduced	1962
Liberalized	1964
Suspended	1966
Reinstated	1967
Deleted	1969
Reintroduced	1971
Liberalized	1975
Deleted	1986

Is it any wonder that it
is sometimes difficult to
consider taxes in mak-
ing future investment
plans?

influenced the payers' investment decisions. Second, it may be reinstated at
any time that Congress feels investment spending needs to be stimulated.

A tax credit is a direct reduction of the computed income tax. Suppose,
for example, that the tax code allows an ITC of 10 percent. If your firm invests $100,000 in, say, new machinery, it is entitled to a direct reduction of
$10,000 from its income tax bill. In effect, the government pays 10 percent of
the cost of the machinery.[6] Sometimes, such an ITC may be the deciding factor in a potential investment situation.

The ITC is not the only tax credit that Congress has offered business and
individuals. At one time or another there have been energy tax credits, targeted jobs credits, alcohol fuels credits, disabled access credits, and more. In
each case, the credit was designed to help meet some social, economic, or environmental goal.

Capital Gains

We tend to use the term "capital gain" loosely to mean an increase in the value
of an asset. However, in tax law a *capital gain* is specifically a realized gain
that results when an asset is sold for more than was paid for it.[7] Since tax
rates are progressive, taxing capital gains in one lump in one year at higher
rates seems unfair, so Congress has traditionally granted special treatment—
via lower effective tax rates—to capital gains.

Special treatment for capital gains has come in either of two ways: (1) an
exclusion or (2) a cap on the tax rate applied to capital gains. A cap is a "ceiling" on the tax rate applied to capital gains and is lower than the tax rate applied to other income. In 1991, for example, the tax rate cap on capital gains
was 28 percent for individuals and 34 percent for corporations.

Suppose that in 1991 the Taxit Corporation has ordinary taxable income
(that is, taxable income not including capital gains) of $50,000 and a capital
gain of $10,000. Taxit's tax bracket is 25 percent, which is below 1991's corpo-
rate capital gains rate of 34 percent. So Taxit's tax on its $60,000 of income is:

$$\text{Tax on } \$60,000 \text{ (corporation, 1991)} = \$7,500 + 0.25 \,(\$60,000 - \$50,000)$$
$$= \mathbf{\$10,000}$$

Now suppose you, an individual, have a 1991 ordinary taxable income of
$50,000 and a capital gain of $10,000. If you figured your taxes on the sum,
$60,000, it would put you in the 31 percent tax bracket, above the individual

---

[6] Of course, Congress did take some of the fun out of ITCs when it required taxpayers to reduce the depreciable cost of an asset by half of the ITC; so taxpayers got the ITC benefit immediately but obtained slightly less benefit from depreciation over the life of the asset.

[7] In the IRC, Sec. 1221, a *capital asset* is defined precisely as property, such as investment
property (stocks and bonds) or real estate and other property not used in trade or business. A
Section 1231 asset, as defined in that section of the code, is real or depreciable property used
in trade or business.

The Taxing Taxonomy of Taxation

Deductions and credits both reduce taxes payable. A *deduction* reduces taxable income and thus indirectly reduces the taxes paid. A tax *credit* is subtracted from the taxes paid, and thus directly reduces taxes.

Suppose you have $100,000 in taxable income, without considering a potential deduction or credit, and your tax rate is a flat 40 percent. Suppose also that you have a choice of taking a $10,000 deduction or a $10,000 credit. Which would you choose? Let's look at the consequences under three scenarios: (1) no deduction and no credit, (2) deduction, but no credit; and (3) credit, but no deduction.

	No deduction, no credit	Deduction, no credit	Credit, no deduction
Taxable income without deduction	$100,000	$100,000	$100,000
Deduction	–0–	10,000	–0–
Taxable income	$100,000	$ 90,000	$100,000
Tax rate	0.40	0.40	0.40
Tax before credit	$ 40,000	$ 36,000	$ 40,000
Credit	–0–	–0–	10,000
Tax	$ 40,000	$ 36,000	$ 30,000

The benefit from the deduction is $4,000, whereas the benefit from the credit is $10,000. Always, in the choice between equal dollar amounts of a credit and a deduction, the credit is more valuable.

capital gains rate of 28 percent. If the IRS laws allow, you would compute the taxes on the two types of income separately:

Tax on $50,000 ordinary income plus $10,000 capital gains (individual, 1991)

$$= \$11,375.50 + 0.28\,(\$10,000)$$

↑ Tax on ordinary income   ↑ Tax on capital gains income

$$= \mathbf{\$14,175.50}$$

The other way of giving special treatment to capital gains for tax purposes is the exclusion. A capital gains exclusion excludes a portion, say 60 percent, of the capital gain from taxation and taxes the remainder at the ordinary tax rate. Consider Taxit Corporation's income. If 60 percent of its capital gain is excluded, its income is $50,000 + 0.40 ($10,000), or $54,000. The tax on this income is computed using the rates in Table 3-5:

Tax on $54,000
(corporation, 1991) $= $7,500 + 0.25 ($54,000 − 50,000) = $8,500$
assuming 40%
capital gains exclusion

The exclusion of 40 percent of the gain reduces Taxit's tax from $10,000 to $8,500.

After a while, Congress caught on that for a depreciable asset, a part of the gain was really the result of "overdepreciating" it (for tax purposes) during its life; that is, depreciation expenses taken over the life of the asset (which reduced taxable income and taxes) do not represent the actual amount the asset depreciated in value. So, Congress inserted provisions in the tax laws that require breaking the gain into two parts:

> If the firm sells an asset for less than its book value (the original cost less accumulated depreciation), there is a **capital loss.** A capital loss is first combined with any existing capital gains; if that results in a net capital loss, the loss is used to reduce ordinary income.

1. The *recapture of depreciation,* the difference between (*a*) the lower of the original cost or the sales price and (*b*) the undepreciated portion of the asset's cost for tax purposes.
2. The capital gain, which is the sales price less the original cost.

The recapture portion of the gain is taxed at ordinary rates, and the capital gain portion is given special treatment (so, effectively it is taxed at less than ordinary rates).

Recapture of depreciation

Suppose Reclaim Inc. bought a depreciable asset ten years ago for $100,000, and its book value (cost less accumulated depreciation) for tax purposes is now $30,000. This means that the firm has taken $70,000 of depreciation expense over the ten years and has reduced its taxable income by that amount. If it now sells this asset for $125,000, it has a capital gain of $25,000.

Sales price	$125,000
Cost	100,000
Capital Gain	**$ 25,000**

But Reclaim has also recaptured its entire depreciation expense by selling the asset. The tax code requires that recaptured depreciation be added to ordinary income and, thus, taxed at the ordinary income tax rate. Reclaim would have to pay ordinary income tax on the recaptured $70,000 of depreciation and capital gains tax on $25,000.

Original cost	$100,000
Less: Book value	30,000
Yields recapture (taxed as ordinary income)	**$ 70,000**

If only part of the asset's depreciation is recaptured when it is sold, only the recaptured part is taxed, and there would be no capital gain. The recaptured portion is the difference between sales price and book value. For example, if Reclaim sold the asset for $75,000, instead of $125,000, it would have:

Sales price	$ 75,000
Less: book value	30,000
Yields recapture (taxed as ordinary income)	**$45,000**

As you can see, taxes, depreciation, and capital gains are all mutually related. Furthermore, they all become considerations in investment decisions, which almost always deal in some way with the purchase and sale of assets, and in cash flow, which is directly affected by tax law.

Corporate Taxable Income

The federal tax code defines gross income as all income not specifically excluded from gross income. In most cases, a corporation's gross income is different from the net income reported on its financial statements. The tax to be paid by the corporation is determined in two steps:

Step 1 Gross income less deductions yields taxable income.
Step 2 Tax on taxable income less tax credits yields tax payable.

However, the deductions for tax purposes differ from those for purposes of financial statement reporting. For example, for tax purposes corporations are permitted to deduct a part or all of any dividends they receive from another corporation.

The dividends-received deduction

We have seen that corporate income distributed to shareholders (in the form of dividends) is taxed twice—first as corporate income and then as shareholders' income—and then if the shareholder is another corporation, that income could be taxed a third time. To minimize the chance of triple (or even quadruple) taxation of the same income, the tax laws permit a ***dividends-received deduction:*** A corporate recipient of dividends may deduct a portion of its dividend income from its taxable income.

With respect to dividend income received by corporations, the 1991 tax law, for example, specifies deductions of either 100 percent, 80 percent, or 70 percent, as follows:

- Deduction of 100 percent of dividends received may be deducted if the corporation is (1) a small business investment company operated under the Small Business Investment Act or (2) a member of an affiliated group of corporations, as in the case of a parent corporation and its wholly owned subsidiaries.
- Deduction of 80 percent if the dividends are received from a 20 percent or more owned corporation.
- Deduction of 70 percent if none of the conditions above applies.

The dividends-received deduction either eliminates the tax on dividend income or reduces the effective tax rate considerably. Suppose a corporation has a marginal tax rate of 34 percent and the dividends it receives qualify for the 80 percent deduction. Then the effective tax rate is 20 percent of 34 percent, or 6.8 percent.

The dividends-received deduction increases the after-tax return of a corporation *investing* in another corporation's stock. Since corporate investors get a tax break on dividend income, they require a lower return on these securities, thus lowering the cost of capital for the corporation that *issues* these securities. The recent trend in tax law is to reduce the dividends-received deduction, increasing the multiple taxation effect and increasing the cost of capital to issuers of these securities.

Individual Taxable Income

Determining the tax to be paid by an individual is a three-step process:

Step 1   Gross income less adjustments to income, such as for IRA (individual retirement account) payments, yields adjusted gross income.

Step 2   Adjusted gross income less personal deductions, such as for charitable contributions or home mortgage payments, yields taxable income.

Step 3   Tax on taxable income less tax credits yields tax payable.

Gross income for an individual includes wages and salaries as well as income for proprietorships, partnerships, and investments. **Adjusted gross income** (AGI) is an intermediate figure that is used as a base for calculations, such as a limit on some types of deductions. The deductions from gross income are expenses directly related to producing income. For individuals, unlike corporations, there is no deduction for dividends received.

The deductions *from* the AGI include personal exemptions (a per-person reduction in taxable income) and *either* itemized deductions (for such payments as medical expenses, state and local taxes, and interest paid) *or* a standard deduction (lump sum) for those expenses. The standard deduction serves to simplify the tax-paying process for many taxpayers. Itemizing certain expenses (specifically identifying each expense and subtracting it from taxable income) permits a reduction of the taxes in cases of hardship (for example, for individuals with very large medical expenses). The general trend, however, appears to be toward a greater emphasis on the standard deductions and a phasing out of itemizing.

Net Operating Loss Carrybacks and Carryovers

A **net operating loss** is an excess of business deductions over business gross income in a tax year. The Internal Revenue Code allows businesses to carry back a net operating loss to preceding years and to carry forward the loss to future years to reduce the taxes payable for those years.[8] The 1991 tax law,

---

[8] Occasionally, individuals and corporations may not have taxable income for a tax year—in fact, they may have a loss. Congress recognized that with progressive taxation and because of the possibility that the income of some taxpayers may vary greatly from year to year, there should be a way for them to "even out" their tax burden. Section 172 of the Internal Revenue Code was created to allow carrybacks and carryovers or carryforwards of net operating losses.

for example, permits net operating losses of corporations to be carried back three years from the year of the loss and carried over (forward through time) fifteen years.

Here's how carrybacks and carryovers work. Suppose that for 1996, your firm has a $100,000 net operating loss. To simplify the calculations, let's also assume that the corporate tax rate is a flat 40 percent of income. Suppose further that you paid taxes on income as follows in the three years prior to 1996:

Year	Taxable income	Taxes paid
1993	$10,000	$ 4,000
1994	50,000	20,000
1995	50,000	20,000

To use the 1996 loss, you begin by carrying it back to the latest year (1993, in this example), applying it to reduce that year's taxable income and then re-computing the tax. Any loss that is left over is carried to the next year, and so on. If the 1996 tax law allows a three-year carryback, then your computation would look like this:

Year	Taxable income	Amount of loss applied	Refigured taxable income	Refigured taxes	Refund
1993	$10,000	$ 10,000	$ –0–	$ –0–	$ 4,000
1994	50,000	50,000	–0–	–0–	20,000
1995	50,000	40,000	10,000	4,000	16,000
		$100,000			**$40,000**

Your firm would then apply for a $40,000 refund of 1993-to-1995 taxes on the basis of its 1996 loss.

What if your loss was larger than the sum of your previous three years' taxable incomes? Then you could carryover any unused portion of the loss to future tax years, applying it to taxable income in the tax returns for those years. As an example, suppose your loss was $200,000, instead of $100,000. You would be able to apply $110,000 of that to taxable income and then could carryover the remaining loss of $90,000. You would apply as much as possible to your 1997 taxable income, carryover any remainder to 1998, and so on, until either the loss was exhausted or you reached the time limit prescribed in the IRC.

Subchapter S Corporations

Recall that income from a sole proprietorship or a partnership flows through directly to the owners—the individual who is the sole proprietor or the individuals who make up the partnership—and is taxed once on their individual tax returns; each owner's share of income and losses from these businesses is combined with the owner's other income and losses. However, corporate income is taxed once at the corporate level and then again if this income is distributed to the corporation's owners in the form of dividends. Moreover, losses stay at the corporate level; owners do not have the right to carry losses back or forward on their individual taxes.

The differences in taxation between proprietorships and partnerships, on the one hand, and corporations, on the other, presents a dilemma for fledgling businesses. The corporate form is attractive since it provides for limited liability; yet it will be taxed doubly if there is an operating profit, but cannot carry through any losses it incurs. Since losses are likely for smaller, younger businesses, this becomes an important consideration.

Subchapter S of the IRC allows small corporations to elect to file taxes as an S corporation and thus obtain the best of both types of business—limited liability and a flowthrough of income (and losses) to the owners, eliminating double taxation. We refer to a corporation electing this status as a **_Subchapter S corporation_** or a **_Sub S corporation._** The primary requirement (though not the only requirement) is that the number of shareholders not exceed a specified maximum, which has ranged from ten to the current thirty-five shareholders.[9] Keep in mind that the Subchapter S corporation is not a different form of business, but rather represents a tax break that certain small corporations may choose.

State and Local Taxes

In addition to the federal income tax, individuals and corporations may also be assessed state and local income taxes. State and local tax structures are, for the most part, dependent upon the federal tax system. With some exceptions and an occasional adjustment to taxable income, state and local taxes are levied as a percentage of the federal income.

State and local taxes can be significant. For example, in fiscal year 1992, the Walt Disney Company paid federal taxes—with a top rate of 34 percent—and state taxes—with an effective rate of 2.8 percent—together an effective marginal tax rate of 36.8 percent.[10]

Taxation in Other Countries

The countries of the world derive their revenues from the several types of taxes—income, employment, and import and export—in different combinations that reflect their individual goals and circumstances. The combinations of taxes used by some of the major industrial powers are shown in Figure 3-5. Japan relies more on income taxes than any of the other countries considered in this figure. France, the United Kingdom, and Canada rely greatly on taxes on goods and services, and France is heavily dependent on its social security (employment) taxes. An interesting feature of this graphical analysis is that income tax revenue from individuals exceeds income tax revenue from corporations in every one of these countries.

[9] The definition of a small business corporation has changed over the years since Subchapter S was created in 1958. For more complete details on qualifications under Subchapter S, see the IRC, Sec. 1361 (definition of a small business corporation) and Sec. 1362 (election of Subchapter S status).

[10] _The Walt Disney Company 1992 Annual Report,_ p. 57. Since state taxes are deductible for federal income tax purposes, the state tax rate of 2.8 percent reflects this benefit and, hence, is lower than the statutory state corporate tax rate.

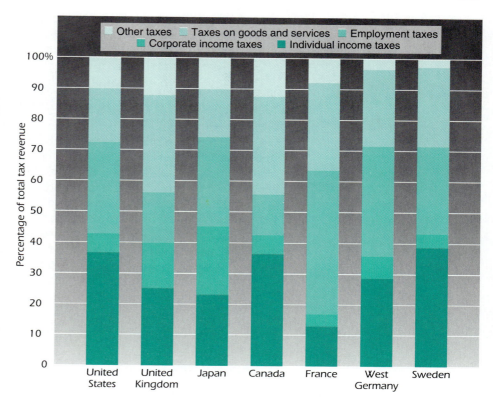

FIGURE 3-5

Tax Revenues of Major Countries, by Type of Tax

SOURCE: Organization for Economic Cooperation and Development, *Revenue Statistics of OECD Member Countries*, 1965–1985.

As an example of the differences that can exist among national tax systems, let us briefly compare Japan's system with that of the United States.

- Individual income tax rates in Japan are much higher than in the United States.
- In Japan, interest and dividend income of individuals are taxed at reduced rates; in the United States, this income is taxed at the same rate as other income.

The combined effect of the preferential treatment for interest and dividends has been a greater saving and investment rate for individuals in Japan, relative to other countries.

The Japanese corporate income tax is also different from the U.S. tax in several ways:

- Dividends received by a corporation are fully excluded from income; in the United States they are partially excluded (unless the paying and receiving corporations are part of an affiliated group).
- The capital gains of corporations are fully taxed in Japan; they are given special treatment in the United States.
- In Japan, different tax rates are applied to distributed profits (those paid as dividends) and undistributed profits (those retained by the corporation), with distributed profits taxed at the lower rate; in the United States, no distinction is made between distributed and undistributed profits.

The first and third of these differences take the Japanese corporate tax system a bit further than the U.S. system in reducing the effects of double taxation.

CASH FLOWS

Cash Inflows and Outflows

We have noted several times that cash flows and the ability to generate them considerably influence a firm's financial decision making. Since we've now covered financial statements (which summarize the operating results and condition of the firm) and taxes (which affect a firm's cash flow), we're ready to look at cash flows.

The firm's statement of cash flows lists separately its cash flows from operations, from investing activities, and from financing activities. By analyzing these individual flows, current and potential owners, managers, and creditors can examine such aspects of the business as:

- The sources of financing for the business operations, whether through internally generated funds or external sources of funds.
- The ability of the company to meet debt obligations (interest and principal payments).
- The ability of the company to finance expansion through operating cash flow.
- The ability of the company to pay dividends to shareholders.
- The flexibility the business has in financing its operations.

A firm that generates cash flows only by selling off its assets (obtaining cash flows from investments) or by issuing more securities (obtaining cash flows from financing) cannot keep that up for very long. For future prosperity the firm must be able to generate cash flows from its operations.

Predicting Cash Flows

A firm invests current cash flows in the hope of generating future cash flows. A part of financial analysis and decision making, then, is to forecast future cash flows to be expected from today's investments. Because predictions of future cash flows are based on idealized data, itself a prediction, future cash flow statements are easier to construct than past years' statements.

Suppose your firm is deciding whether to invest in a new product—a Gizmo—today by buying manufacturing equipment for $100,000. To predict future cash flows from Gizmo sales, we need at least the following:

- The number of Gizmos to be sold each year and the expected selling price.
- The cost of producing a Gizmo.
- The expected depreciation rate for the equipment for tax purposes.
- The firm's marginal tax rate.

According to your marketing department, the first year's forecasted sales are 100,000 Gizmos, at $5 each. The production department estimates that it will cost $3 to produce each Gizmo. Checking with your tax accountant, you find that the IRC classifies Gizmo's production equipment as a five-year-life asset, with depreciation of 20 percent of its cost in the first year, and that the firm's marginal tax rate is 34 percent. To simplify the problem, we can assume that all sales and production expenses will be paid in cash; this eliminates the need to include changes in current assets or current liabilities in our computations.

The firm's net income from this project in the first year will be:

Revenues	$ 500,000	←	$5 times 100,000 units
Less: expenses	300,000	←	$3 times 100,000 units
Gross profit	$ 200,000		
Less: depreciation	20,000	←	20% of $100,000 *cost of machine*
Income before taxes	$ 180,000		
Less: taxes	61,200	←	34% of $180,000
Net income	**$118,800**		

Cash Flow from Operating Activities

We can calculate a predicted first-year operating cash flow from this investment using either of two methods. The first is the indirect approach, similar to what is used in the statement of cash flows: Start with net income and adjust for noncash items and changes in current assets and liabilities. Here, we should have:

$$\text{Operating cash flow} = \text{net income} + \text{depreciation}$$
$$= \$118,800 \quad + \$20,000$$
$$= \textbf{\$138,800}$$

Because we are working with a project situation with simple assumptions, we can also predict the first year's cash flow using the direct approach: Start with cash revenues (sales) and deduct cash payments. Here, we would have:

$$\text{Operating cash flow} = \text{revenues} - \text{expenses} - \text{taxes}$$
$$= \$500,000 - \$300,000 - \$61,200$$
$$= \textbf{\$138,800}$$

Both approaches produce the same result, as they should. If we had projected changes in the firm's working capital accounts—that is, current assets and current liabilities—we would probably have used the direct approach. But we could also adjust the cash flow determined in each approach by the amount of the change in working capital. For example, if Gizmo's projection required an increase in inventories of $10,000 in the first year, we could deduct that $10,000 from the $138,800 to arrive at an operating cash flow of $128,800.

The calculated cash flow from operations must then be combined with projected first-year cash flows from financing and investment activities to produce the estimated cash flow for the period. The cash flows for succeeding years can then be predicted similarly from predicted operating, financing, and investment data.

Depreciation Tax Shields

A ***depreciation tax shield*** is an amount saved from a firm's taxes because it is allowed to deduct depreciation, a noncash expense. It is the product of the marginal tax rate and the depreciation expense. In the Gizmo example, the first-year depreciation tax shield is:

Depreciation tax shield = marginal tax rate × depreciation expense
= 0.34   × $20,000
= **$6,800**

The depreciation tax shield isolates the effect of depreciation on cash flow. Suppose in the Gizmo example that your accountants speculate that Congress may change the first-year depreciation rate from 20 percent to 10 percent. We can easily determine the sensitivity of cash flow to this change by computing the tax shield at 20 percent and 10 percent. The tax shield at 10 percent is:

Depreciation tax shield = 0.34 × [0.10 ($100,000)] = **$3,400**

Clearly, the greater the allowable depreciation, the greater the income it shields from taxes.

You must be sure to understand that the depreciation expense is not itself a cash flow, but it creates a cash flow by reducing the amount of taxes.

SUMMARY

- Financial statements, taxes, and cash flows provide information needed to make the financing and investment decisions of a business.
- The three financial statements (the balance sheet, income statement, and statement of cash flows), along with the accompanying footnotes, provide information necessary to assess the operating performance and financial condition of the firm. Using this information, in conjunction with our understanding of accounting, we can see where a business has been, which very likely will tell us where it is going.
- Taxes affect cash flows. Key elements of the tax system that affect financial decisions are the tax rate structure, the dividends-received deduction, capital gains taxation, net operating loss carryovers, and Subchapter S corporate status.
- The value of any decision we make today depends on expected future cash flows. We can estimate future cash flows from projections of sales and expenses, adjusting for taxes we expect to pay. We can arrive at our estimate of cash flow either directly (by looking at inflows and outflows), or indirectly (by adjusting net income).

QUESTIONS

3-1 Describe the type of information provided in each of the three financial statements:
  a. The balance sheet.
  b. The income statement.
  c. The statement of cash flows.

3-2 How does the choice of depreciation method between straight-line and an accelerated method affect the firm's:
  a. Reported net income.
  b. Reported value of assets.

3-3 Consider the following statement:

  Over the life of an asset, the total cost of the asset will be expensed, no matter which method of depreciation we choose. Therefore, the choice of depreciation method does not matter.

  Do you agree or disagree? Explain.

3-4 In calculating cash flows from operations indirectly, we adjust for changes in the current asset and current liabilities accounts. Why is this adjustment necessary?

3-5 In fiscal year 1991, Sears, Roebuck & Co. paid $688.90 million in U.S. income taxes and reported a marginal tax rate of 36.5 percent. Its U.S. income before taxes according to its income statement was $1,369.70 million. How could Sears pay more than 50 percent of its reported income in taxes if its marginal tax rate was 36.5 percent? Explain.

3-6 What is the basis for this statement?

  The ceiling on taxation of capital gains reflects the natural belief that speculation is a more worthwhile way to make a living than work.

3-7 XYZ Corporation has just purchased an asset that cost $1 million. Suppose you are the financial manager of XYZ and are responsible for selecting the method of depreciation for this asset for financial reporting purposes and for tax purposes. To reduce administration costs, it is recommended that you select the same method for both purposes. Suppose you have a choice between straight-line and MACRS methods.
  a. Which method provides the greatest reported earnings in the first year?
  b. Which method provides the lowest tax bill in the first year?
  c. Which method is in the best interests of shareholders? Why?

3-8 What is the role of the dividends-received deduction?

3-9 What is a Subchapter S corporation? How does a business become a Subchapter S corporation?

3-10 Suppose you have a full-time job and are also starting a part-time business on the side. You expect your business to generate losses for the first couple of years. What form of business is most appropriate for your new enterprise? Explain.

3-11 Distinguish between an average tax rate and a marginal tax rate. Under what circumstance are the two the same?

3-12 How can the choice of depreciation method affect the attractiveness of investments?

PROBLEMS

Tax computation

3-1 Using the tax rate schedule provided in Table 3-5, determine the amount of tax, the marginal tax rate, and the average tax rate for a corporation with the following taxable income:
  a. $35,000
  b. $120,000
  c. $300,000
  d. $1,000,000
  e. $2,000,000

3-2 Using the tax rate schedule provided in Table 3-5, determine the amount of tax, the marginal tax rate, and the average tax rate for an individual with the following taxable income:
  a. $35,000
  b. $120,000
  c. $300,000
  d. $1,000,000
  e. $2,000,000

Depreciation

3-3 The SL Company has purchased an asset for $1 million that has a useful life of five years and a salvage value of $200,000. What is the depreciation for accounting purposes each year using the straight-line method?

3-4 The EAC Company is debating whether to depreciate their new asset using the straight-line or the declining balance method. The asset cost $2 million and has a salvage value of $200,000 and a useful life of five years. EAC has no other assets. EAC's expected income before taxes and depreciation is $1 million each year for the next five years.
  a. What is EAC's depreciation expense each year under the two methods?
  b. What is EAC's net income before taxes each year for the two methods?

Dividends-received deduction

3-5 The PARENT Corporation received $3 million in dividends from the SUB Corporation. PARENT's income is taxed at a flat rate of 40 percent. How much tax must PARENT Corporation pay on these dividends in 1991 if the relationship between the two companies for purposes of the dividends-received deduction is:
  a. SUB and PARENT have no affiliation.
  b. SUB is 10-percent-owned by PARENT.
  c. SUB is wholly owned by PARENT.

3-6 DIV Corporation received $5 million in dividends and had $10 million in other taxable income. DIV's income is taxed at a flat rate of 30 percent.

    a. What is DIV's tax bill if there is no dividends-received deduction?

    b. What is DIV's tax bill if a 60 percent dividends-received deduction is allowed?

    c. What is DIV's tax bill if a 70 percent dividends-received deduction is allowed?

Net operating losses

3-7 The NOL Company had a loss of $1 million for 1995. The firm had income and paid taxes in the four prior years of:

Year	Taxable income	Taxes paid (30% of taxable income)
1991	$2,000,000	$600,000
1992	500,000	150,000
1993	300,000	90,000
1994	100,000	30,000

Suppose the tax law allows losses to be carried back three years and forward fifteen.

    a. How much of a refund of prior taxes can NOL receive?

    b. How much of the loss can be carried forward to future years?

3-8 The Loser Corporation had a loss of $200,000 in 1994. The firm had income and paid taxes in the three prior years of:

Year	Taxable income	Taxes paid (40% of taxable income)
1991	$100,000	$40,000
1992	200,000	80,000
1993	100,000	40,000

Suppose the tax law allows losses to be carried back three years and forward fifteen.

    a. How much of a refund of prior taxes can Loser receive?

    b. How much of the loss can be carried forward to future years?

Cash flows

3-9 The Mayberry Company purchased equipment for $100,000. Assume that this equipment qualifies as a five-year asset under the MACRS.

    a. What is the depreciation expense for tax purposes for each year the equipment is depreciated?

    b. If the marginal tax rate is 34 percent, what is the depreciation tax shield for each year?

3-10   The USA Company purchased equipment for $1 million in 1991. Assume this equipment qualifies as a seven-year asset under the MACRS.

    a. What is the depreciation expense for tax purposes for each year the equipment is depreciated?

    b. If the marginal tax rate is 34 percent, what is the depreciation tax shield for each year?

3-11   In 1993, NI Corporation had sales of $1 million, cost of goods sold of $600,000, and depreciation of $100,000. The corporation received $200,000 in dividends, paid $100,000 in dividends, and bought equipment for $300,000. Its tax rate was 30 percent, and the 1993 dividends-received deduction was 80 percent.

    a. What was the net income of NI Corporation?

    b. What was the cash flow from operations?

    c. What was the cash flow from financing activities?

    d. What was the cash flow from investment activities?

3-12   In 1994, TI Corporation had sales of $2 million, cost of goods sold of $1 million, and depreciation of $500,000. The firm received $300,000 in dividends and $100,000 in interest income, and paid $150,000 in dividends and $200,000 in interest. It bought equipment for $300,000. The firm's tax rate was 30 percent, and the dividends-received deduction was 70 percent.

    a. What was the net income of TI Corporation?

    b. What was the cash flow from operations?

    c. What was the cash flow from financing activities?

    d. What was the cash flow from investment activities?

Potpourri

3-13   **Research:** Select a corporation and find the following information from the footnotes in its most recent financial statements:

    a. Depreciation method for financial statement purposes.

    b. Average federal tax rate.

    c. Average state and local tax rate.

3-14   **Research:** Select a major corporation and examine the footnotes in its most recent financial statements for the liability related to its pension plans and its postretirement benefits programs, if any.

    a. What is the amount of the firm's liability for its pension plan? Is this liability shown in the firm's balance sheet?

    b. What is the amount of the firm's liability for its postretirement benefit programs? Is this liability shown in the firm's balance sheet?

PC+   **3-15**   **Research:** Select a major corporation and determine its cash flow from the three sources (operating activities, financing activities, and investment activities) for each of the past four fiscal years. Describe the trend in the firm's sources of cash flow over these four years.

Recommended sources of information:

- Annual reports
- *Industrial Manual,* Moody's
- *Compustat PC Plus* (CD-ROM), Standard & Poor's

FURTHER READINGS

Interpretation of financial statements of firms outside the United States requires an understanding of the International Accounting Standards adopted by many non-U.S. firms. For an overview of these standards and their comparison with GAAP, see:

"Dealing with International Accounting Diversity: International Accounting Standards," prepared by David F. Hawkins, Merrill Lynch Capital Markets, Accounting Bulletin 1, May 1990, Merrill, Lynch, Pierce, Fenner & Smith Incorporated.

You can get an overview of individual income taxes from the following free publication, which is updated each year:

Your Federal Income Tax, U.S. Treasury Department, Internal Revenue Service, Publication 17, catalog no. 10311G.

The tax system of Japan is summarized in:

HIROMITSU ISHI, *The Japanese Tax System*, Oxford University Press, New York, 1989.

Financial Analysis

INTRODUCTION 98

FINANCIAL RATIOS 100

Classification of Ratios 100
    Ratio Construction 101
    Ratios and Financial Characteristics 102
Liquidity Ratios 102
    The Operating Cycle 103
    Measures of Liquidity 106
Profitability Ratios 109
Activity Ratios 111
    Inventory Management 111
    Accounts Receivable Management 111
    Overall Asset Management 112
Financial Leverage Ratios 113
Return-on-Investment Ratios 119
    The Du Pont System 121
Shareholder Ratios 123

COMMON-SIZE ANALYSIS 128

**AN APPLICATION OF FINANCIAL ANALYSIS TO
    WAL-MART STORES INC. 128**

The Business 130
The Industry 131
The Economy 132
Financial Ratios of the Firm and the Industry 133
    Liquidity Ratios 133
    Profitability Ratios 134
    Activity Ratios 135
    Financial Leverage Ratios 136
    Return Ratios 137
    Shareholder Ratios 137
Common-Size Analysis 138

USING FINANCIAL ANALYSIS 140

Evaluating Creditworthiness and Debt Quality 140
Predicting Bankruptcy 142

**PROBLEMS AND DILEMMAS IN FINANCIAL
    RATIO ANALYSIS 143**

Using Accounting Data 143
    Historical Costs and Inflation 143
    Methods of Accounting 144
    Extraordinary Items 144
    Classification of "Fuzzy" Items 144
Using a Benchmark 145
Selecting and Interpreting Ratios 145
Forecasting 146
    Methods of Forecasting 146
    Analysts' Forecasts 147

Summary 148

Warning Signs

Wang Laboratories is a leader in the information processing industry, and its products include software and desktop systems that improve office productivity. In August 1992, Wang Laboratories filed for bankruptcy because its debt obligations became too much for it to handle.

Were there any warning signs of financial difficulty? Yes.

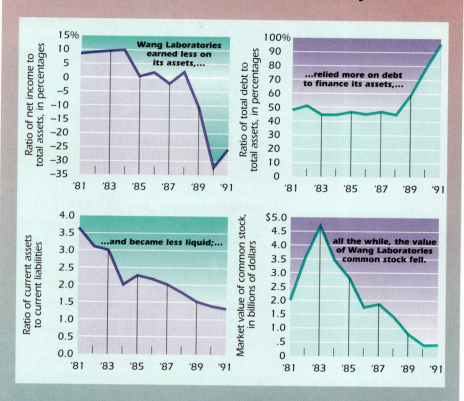

As you can see, by looking at financial data and relationships among this data we can get an idea of Wang's deteriorating financial position through time. In fact, we could see Wang Laboratories' financial difficulties well in advance of 1992.

INTRODUCTION

Many decisions made by a firm's managers, its investors, and its creditors are based on an evaluation of the firm's operating performance—how well it uses its assets to generate a return—and its firm's financial condition—its ability to meet its financial obligations, such as paying the interest it owes on its debts when promised.

As a manager, you may want to reward employees on the basis of their performance. How do you know how well they have done? How can you determine what departments or divisions have performed well? As a lender, how do you decide whether or not the borrower will be able to pay back as promised? As a manager of a corporation, how do you know when existing capacity will be exceeded and enlarged capacity will be needed? As an investor, how do you predict how well the securities of one firm will perform relative to those of another? How can you tell whether one security is riskier than another? All of these questions can be addressed through financial analysis.

Financial analysis is the selection, evaluation, and interpretation of financial data, along with other pertinent information, to assist in investment and financial decision making. Financial analysis may be used internally to evaluate issues such as employee performance, the efficiency of operations, and credit policies, and externally to evaluate potential investments and the creditworthiness of borrowers, among other things.

The financial data needed in financial analysis come from many sources. The primary source is the data provided by the firm itself in its annual report and required disclosures. The annual report comprises the income statement, the balance sheet, and the statement of cash flows, as well as footnotes to these statements. Certain businesses are required by securities laws to disclose additional information.

Besides information that companies are required to disclose through financial statements, other information is readily available for financial analysis. For example, information such as the market prices of securities of publicly traded corporations can be found in the financial press and the electronic media daily. The financial press also provides information on stock price indexes for industries and for the market as a whole.

Another source of information is economic data, such as the gross domestic product and consumer price index, which may be useful in assessing the recent performance or future prospects of a firm or industry. Suppose you are evaluating a firm that owns a chain of retail outlets. What information do you need to judge the firm's performance and financial condition? You need financial data, but they do not tell the whole story. You also need information on consumer spending, producer prices, consumer prices, and the competition. These are economic data that are readily available from government and private sources.

Besides financial statement data, market data, and economic data, in financial analysis you also need to examine events that may help explain the firm's present condition and may have a bearing on its future prospects. For example, did the firm recently incur some extraordinary losses? Is the firm developing a new product? Or acquiring another firm? Current events can provide information that may be incorporated in financial analysis.

Additional Disclosures

A publicly traded firm must provide additional disclosures in documents, including the following:

- **Registration statement.** Contains financial statement information as well as information that describes the business and management of the firm.
- **8-K statement.** Describes significant events that are of interest to investors and are filed as these events occur.
- **10-K statement.** Contains the financial statement data found in the firm's annual report as well as additional financial disclosures.
- **10-Q statement.** Contains financial statement data that are not as comprehensive as those in the 10-K statement. Issued quarterly.

The financial analyst must select the pertinent information, analyze it, and interpret the analysis, enabling judgments on the current and future financial condition and operating performance of the firm.

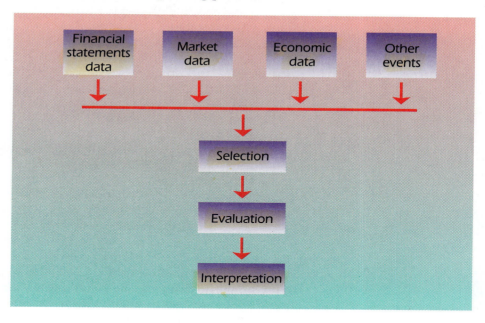

In this chapter, we introduce you to financial ratios—a tool of financial analysis. In financial ratio analysis we select the relevant information—primarily the financial statement data—and evaluate it. We show how to incorporate market data and economic data in the analysis and interpretation of financial ratios. And we show how to interpret financial ratio analysis, warning you of the pitfalls that occur when it's not used properly.

Information Inputs to the Financial Analysis of a Firm

The assessment of the current and future financial condition and operating performance of a firm requires information concerning the economy, the industry in which the firm operates, and the firm itself. Examples of the type of information that may be used in the financial analysis of a firm include current information and projections on:

The Economy

Production and income
Employment
Consumption
Investment activity
Interest rates
Stock prices
Inflation

The Industry

Nature of competition (highly competitive? monopoly? oligopoly?)
Market share for each firm in the industry
Labor conditions (unionized? contract renewals? benefits?)
Regulatory conditions
Price elasticity of demand and supply
Sensitivity of demand to economic conditions

The Firm

Financial statement data (annual report, 10-K statement)
Position in industry
International investment
Rate of growth
Breakdowns by product, divisions, or subsidiaries
Research and development efforts
Major litigation

We begin the analysis with a fictitious firm as our example, allowing us to use simplified financial statements and allowing you to become more comfortable with the tools of financial analysis. After we cover the basics, we use these same tools with data from an actual firm.

FINANCIAL RATIOS

Classification of Ratios

A *ratio* is a mathematical relation between one quantity and another. Suppose you have 200 apples and 100 oranges. The ratio of apples to oranges is 200/100, which we can more conveniently express as 2:1 or 2.

A financial ratio is a comparison between one bit of financial information and another. Consider the ratio of current assets to current liabilities, which we refer to as the current ratio. This ratio is a comparison between assets that can be readily turned into cash—current assets—and the obligations that are due in the near future—current liabilities. A current ratio of 2 or 2:1 means that we have twice as much in current assets as we need to satisfy obligations due in the near future.

Ratios can be classified according to the way they are constructed and their general characteristics.

Ratio Construction

Ratios can be constructed in four ways:

1. Coverage ratio
2. Return ratio
3. Turnover ratio
4. Component percentage

A ***coverage ratio*** is a measure of a firm's ability to "cover," or meet, a particular financial obligation:

$$\text{Coverage} = \frac{\text{funds available to meet an obligation}}{\text{amount of that obligation}} \qquad [4\text{-}1]$$

The denominator may be any obligation, such as interest or rent. The numerator is the amount of the funds available to satisfy that obligation. For example, you may want to know a firm's ability to meet current liabilities. What funds are available to meet current liabilities? For many firms those funds would be represented in its current assets, which are assets that can be liquidated quite readily (usually within one year). So, the ratio of current assets to current liabilities indicates the ability of the firm to cover its current liabilities. A coverage ratio equal to 1 indicates that the firm can *just meet* its obligations; a coverage ratio above 1 indicates the firm has some funds to spare.

A ***return ratio*** indicates a net benefit received from a particular investment of resources. The net benefit is what is left over after expenses, such as operating earnings or net income. The resources may be total assets, fixed assets, inventory, or any other investment.

$$\text{Return} = \frac{\text{net benefit}}{\text{resources employed to generate that benefit}} \qquad [4\text{-}2]$$

The net benefit is a measure of how much better off the firm will be from the investment in the resource, considering any relevant expenses. For example, the investment in total assets generates net income; so the return on assets is the ratio of net income to total assets. A return on investment in total assets of, say, 10 percent would mean that for every dollar invested in total assets, there is a net income of 10 cents.

A ***turnover ratio*** is a measure of how much a firm gets out of its assets. This ratio compares the gross benefit from an activity or investment with the resources employed in it. For example, by investing in inventory, a firm generates sales. The gross benefit is the dollar amount of sales, and the investment is the balance in inventory. This inventory turnover tells us how fast inventories are moving through the firm, from raw materials to sold goods.

$$\text{Turnover} = \frac{\text{gross benefit}}{\text{resource employed to generate that benefit}} \qquad [4\text{-}3]$$

A turnover ratio tells us how often resources are used, which can provide information on the efficiency of operations.

A **component percentage** is the ratio of one amount in a financial statement to the total of amounts in that financial statement. For example, the ratio of cash to total assets is a component percentage that measures the amount invested in cash relative to all assets.

$$\text{Component percentage} = \frac{\text{item amount}}{\text{total amount of all items}} \qquad [4\text{-}4]$$

In addition to these four ways to construct ratios, we can also express data in terms of time—say, how many days' worth of inventory we have on hand—or on a per share basis—say, how much a firm has earned for each share of stock. Both are measures we can use to evaluate operating performance or financial condition.

Ratios and Financial Characteristics

When we assess a firm's operating performance, we want to know if it is applying its assets in an efficient and profitable manner. When we assess a firm's financial condition, we want to know if it is able to meet its financial obligations.

There are six aspects of operating performance and financial condition we can evaluate from financial ratios:

1. Liquidity
2. Profitability
3. Activity
4. Return on investment
5. Financial leverage
6. Shareholder ratios

Many different financial ratios can be formed from items appearing in financial statements. But not all possible ratios are meaningful or useful. Learning which data you need to form which ratios to evaluate operating performance or financial condition is a fundamental part of financial analysis.

There are several ratios reflecting each of the six aspects of a firm's operating performance and financial condition. We apply these ratios to the Fictitious Corporation, whose balance sheets, income statements, and statement of cash flows were discussed in Chapter 3 and were presented in Tables 3-1, 3-2, and 3-4. The ratios we introduce now are by no means the only ones that can be formed using financial data, though they are some of the more commonly used. After becoming comfortable with the tools of financial analysis, you will be able to create ratios that serve your particular evaluation objective.

Liquidity Ratios

Liquidity reflects the ability of a firm to meet its short-term obligations using those assets that are most readily converted into cash. Assets that may be converted into cash in a short period of time are referred to as *liquid assets;*

they are listed in financial statements as current assets. Current assets are often referred to as **working capital,** since they represent the resources needed for the day-to-day operations of the firm's long-term capital investments. Current assets are used to satisfy short-term obligations, or current liabilities. The amount by which current assets exceed current liabilities is referred to as the **net working capital.**

The Operating Cycle

How much liquidity a firm needs depends on its operating cycle. The **operating cycle** is the duration from the time cash is invested in goods and services to the time that investment produces cash. For example, a firm that produces and sells goods has an operating cycle comprising four phases:

1. Purchase raw material and produce goods, investing in inventory.
2. Sell goods, generating sales, which may or may not be for cash.
3. Extend credit, creating accounts receivable.
4. Collect accounts receivable, generating cash.

These four phases make up the cycle of cash use and generation. The operating cycle would be somewhat different for companies that produce services rather than goods, but the idea is the same—the operating cycle is the length of time it takes to *generate* cash through the *investment* of cash.

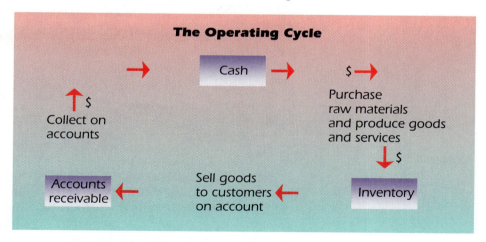

To measure an operating cycle we need to know:

1. The time it takes to convert the investment in inventory into sales (that is, cash → inventory → sales → accounts receivable).
2. The time it takes to collect sales on credit (that is, accounts receivable → cash).

We can estimate the operating cycle for Fictitious Corporation for 1995, using the balance sheet and income statement data in Tables 3-1 and 3-2.

The number of days Fictitious ties up funds in inventory is determined by:

1. The total amount of money represented in inventory.
2. The average day's cost of goods sold.

The current investment in inventory—that is, the money "tied up" in inventory—is the ending balance of inventory on the balance sheet.

The **average day's cost of goods sold** is the cost of goods sold on an average day in the year, which can be estimated by dividing the cost of goods sold, which is found on the income statement, by the number of days in the year. The average day's cost of goods sold for 1995 is:

$$\text{Average day's cost of goods sold} = \frac{\text{cost of goods sold}}{365 \text{ days}} \qquad \text{[4-5]}$$

$$= \frac{\$6,500,000}{365 \text{ days}}$$

$$= \textbf{\$17,808 per day}$$

In other words, Fictitious incurs, on average, a cost of producing goods sold of $17,808 per day.

Fictitious has $1.8 million of inventory on hand at the end of the year. How many days' worth of goods sold is this? One way to look at this is to imagine that Fictitious stopped buying more raw materials and just finished producing whatever was on hand in inventory, using available raw materials and work in process. How long would it take Fictitious to run out of inventory?

We compute the **number of days of inventory** by calculating the ratio of the amount of inventory on hand (in dollars) to the average day's cost of goods sold (in dollars per day):

$$\frac{\text{Number of days}}{\text{of inventory}} = \frac{\text{amount of inventory on hand}}{\text{average day's cost of goods sold}} \qquad \text{[4-6]}$$

$$= \frac{\$1,800,000}{\$17,808 \text{ per day}}$$

$$= \textbf{101 days}$$

In other words, Fictitious has approximately 101 days of goods on hand at the end of 1995. If sales continued at the same pace, it would take Fictitious 101 days to run out of inventory.

If the ending inventory is representative of the inventory throughout the year, then it takes about 101 days to convert the investment in inventory into sold goods. Why worry about whether the year-end inventory is representative of inventory at any day throughout the year? Well, if inventory at the end of the fiscal year-end is lower than on any other day of the year, we have understated the number of days of inventory. Indeed, in practice most companies try to choose fiscal year-ends that coincide with the slow period of their business. That means the ending balance of inventory would be *lower* than the typical daily inventory of the year. To get a better picture of the firm, we could, for example, look at quarterly financial statements and take averages of quarterly inventory balances. However, here for simplicity we make a note of the problem of representativeness and deal with it later in the discussion of financial ratios.

We can extend the same logic for calculating the number of days between a sale—when an account receivable is created—to the time it is collected in cash. If we assume that Fictitious sells all goods on credit, we can first calculate the average credit sales per day and then figure out how many days' worth of credit sales are represented by the ending balance of receivables. The average credit sales per day are:

$$\text{Credit sales per day} = \frac{\text{credit sales}}{365 \text{ days}} \qquad [4\text{-}7]$$

$$= \frac{\$10,000,000}{365 \text{ days}}$$

$$= \mathbf{\$27{,}397 \text{ per day}}$$

Therefore, Fictitious generates $27,397 of credit sales per day. With an ending balance of accounts receivable of $600,000, the **number of days of credit** in this ending balance is calculated by taking the ratio of the balance in the accounts receivable account to the credit sales per day:

$$\frac{\text{Number of}}{\text{days of credit}} = \frac{\text{accounts receivable}}{\text{credit sales per day}} \qquad [4\text{-}8]$$

$$= \frac{\$600,000}{\$27,397 \text{ per day}}$$

$$= \mathbf{22 \text{ days}}$$

If the ending balance of receivables at the end of the year is representative of the receivables on any day throughout the year, then it takes, on average, approximately 22 days to collect the accounts receivable. In other words, it takes 22 days for a sale to become cash.

Using what we have determined for the inventory cycle and cash cycle, we see that for Fictitious:

$$\text{Operating cycle (total)} = \frac{\text{number of days}}{\text{of inventory}} + \frac{\text{number of}}{\text{days of credit}} \qquad [4\text{-}9]$$

$$= 101 \text{ days} + 22 \text{ days}$$

$$= \mathbf{123 \text{ days}}$$

What does the operating cycle have to do with liquidity? The longer the operating cycle, the more current assets are needed (relative to current liabilities) since it takes longer to convert inventories and receivables into cash. In other words, the longer the operating cycle, the greater is the amount of net working capital required.

We also need to look at the liabilities on the balance sheet to see how long it takes a firm to pay its short-term obligations. We can apply the same logic to accounts payable as we did to accounts receivable and inventories. How long does it take a firm, on average, to go from creating a payable (buying on credit) to paying for it in cash?

First, we need to determine the amount of an **average day's purchases** on credit. If we assume all the Fictitious purchases are made on credit, then the total purchases for the year would be the cost of goods sold less any amounts included in cost of goods sold that are not purchases. For example, depreciation is included in the cost of goods sold yet is not a purchase. Since we do not have a breakdown on the company's cost of goods sold showing how much was paid for in cash and how much was on credit, let's assume for simplicity that purchases are equal to cost of goods sold less depreciation. The average day's purchases then become:

$$\text{Average day's purchases} = \frac{\text{cost of goods sold} - \text{depreciation}}{365 \text{ days}} \qquad [4\text{-}10]$$

$$= \frac{\$6,500,000 - \$1,000,000}{365 \text{ days}}$$

$$= \mathbf{\$15,068 \text{ per day}}$$

The **number of days of purchases** represented in the ending balance in accounts payable is calculated as the ratio of the balance in the accounts payable account to the average day's purchases:

$$\frac{\text{Number of days}}{\text{of purchases}} = \frac{\text{accounts payable}}{\text{average day's purchases}} \qquad [4\text{-}11]$$

For Fictitious in 1995:

$$\frac{\text{Number of days}}{\text{of purchases}} = \frac{\$500,000}{\$15,068 \text{ per day}} = \mathbf{33 \text{ days}}$$

This means that on average Fictitious takes 33 days to pay out cash for a purchase.

The operating cycle tells us how long it takes to convert an investment in cash *back into* cash (by way of inventory and accounts receivable). The number of days of purchases tells us how long it takes to pay on purchases made to create the inventory. If we put these two pieces of information together, we can see how long, on net, we tie up cash. The difference between the operating cycle and the number of days of purchases is the **net operating cycle:**

$$\frac{\text{Net operating}}{\text{cycle}} = \frac{\text{operating}}{\text{cycle}} - \frac{\text{number of days}}{\text{of purchases}} \qquad [4\text{-}12]$$

or, substituting for the operating cycle,

$$\frac{\text{Net operating}}{\text{cycle}} = \frac{\text{number of days}}{\text{of inventory}} + \frac{\text{number of}}{\text{days of credit}} - \frac{\text{number of days}}{\text{of purchases}}$$

Using Equation 4-12, the net operating cycle for Fictitious in 1995 is:

$$\frac{\text{Net operating}}{\text{cycle}} = 101 + 22 - 33 = \mathbf{90 \text{ days}}$$

The net operating cycle therefore tells us how long it takes for the firm to get cash back from its investment in inventory and accounts receivable, considering that purchases may be made on credit. By not paying for purchases immediately (that is, using trade credit), the firm reduces its liquidity needs. Therefore, the longer the net operating cycle, the greater the required liquidity.

Measures of Liquidity

We can describe a firm's ability to meet its current obligations in several ways. One, the **current ratio,** indicates the firm's ability to meet or cover its current liabilities using its current assets:

$$\text{Current ratio} = \frac{\text{current assets}}{\text{current liabilities}} \qquad [4\text{-}13]$$

A current ratio of 1.0 indicates that the firm can just meet its current obligations during the year. For the Fictitious Corporation, the current ratio for 1995 is the ratio of current assets, $3 million, to current liabilities, the sum of accounts payable and other current liabilities, or $1 million.

$$\text{Current ratio} = \frac{\$3,000,000}{\$1,000,000} = \mathbf{3.0}$$

The current ratio of 3.0 indicates that Fictitious has three times as much as it needs to cover its current obligations during the year. However, the current ratio groups all current asset accounts together, assuming they are all as easily converted to cash. Even though, by definition, current assets can be transformed into cash within a year, not all current assets can be transformed into cash in a short period of time.

An alternative to the current ratio is the **quick ratio,** also called the **acid-test ratio,** which uses a slightly different set of current accounts to cover the same current liabilities as in the current ratio. In the quick ratio, the least liquid of the current asset accounts, inventory, is excluded. Hence:

$$\text{Quick ratio} = \frac{\text{current assets} - \text{inventories}}{\text{current liabilities}} \qquad [4\text{-}14]$$

We leave out inventories in the quick ratio because receivables can be converted into cash sooner than inventories, as we saw when we looked at the operating cycle. By leaving out the least liquid asset, the quick ratio provides a more conservative view of liquidity. For Fictitious, for 1995:

$$\text{Quick ratio} = \frac{\$3,000,000 - \$1,800,000}{\$1,000,000}$$

$$= \frac{\$1,200,000}{\$1,000,000}$$

$$= \mathbf{1.2}$$

Still another way to measure the firm's ability to satisfy short-term obligations is the **net working capital-to-sales ratio,** which compares net working capital (current assets less current liabilities) with sales:

$$\text{Net working capital-to-sales ratio} = \frac{\text{net working capital}}{\text{sales}} \qquad [4\text{-}15]$$

or

$$\text{Net working capital-to-sales ratio} = \frac{\text{current assets} - \text{current liabilities}}{\text{sales}}$$

This ratio tells us the "cushion" available to meet short-term obligations relative to sales. Consider two firms with identical working capital of $100,000, but one has sales of $500,000 and the other sales of $1,000,000. If they have identical operating cycles, this means that the firm with the greater sales has more funds flowing in and out of its current asset investments (inventories and receivables). The firm with more funds flowing in and out needs a larger cushion to protect itself in the case of a disruption in the cycle, such as a labor strike or unexpected delays in customer payments.

The longer the operating cycle, the more of a cushion (net working capital) we need for a given level of sales. For Fictitious Corporation:

$$\text{Net working capital-to-sales ratio} = \frac{\$3,000,000 - \$1,000,000}{\$10,000,000}$$

$$= \mathbf{0.2000} \text{ or } \mathbf{20\%}$$

The ratio of 0.20 tells us that for every dollar of sales, Fictitious has 20 cents of net working capital to support it.

Recap: Liquidity Ratios

Operating cycle and liquidity ratio information for Fictitious, using data from 1995, in summary, is:

Number of days of inventory	= 101 days
Number of days of credit	= 22 days
Operating cycle	= 123 days
Number of days of purchases	= 33 days
Net operating cycle	= 90 days
Current ratio	= 3.0
Quick ratio	= 1.2
Net working capital-to-sales ratio	= 20%

Given the measures of time related to the current accounts—the operating cycle and the net operating cycle—and the three measures of liquidity—current ratio, quick ratio, and net working capital-to-sales ratio—we know the following about Fictitious Corporation's ability to meet its short-term obligations:

- Inventory is less liquid than accounts receivable (comparing days of inventory with days of credit).
- Current assets are greater than needed to satisfy current liabilities in a year (from the current ratio).
- Even when inventory is not considered, Fictitious can meet its short-term obligations (from the quick ratio).
- Net working capital "cushion" is 20 cents for every dollar of sales (from the net working capital-to-sales ratio).

What don't ratios tell us about liquidity? They don't tell us:

- How liquid are the accounts receivable? How much of the accounts receivable will be collectible? While we know it takes, on average, 22 days to collect, we do not know how much will never be collected.
- What is the nature of the current liabilities? How much of current liabilities consists of items that reoccur (such as accounts payable and wages payable) each period and how much of occasional items (such as income taxes payable)?
- Are there any unrecorded liabilities (such as leases) that are not included in current liabilities?

Profitability Ratios

Profit margin ratios compare components of income with sales. They give us an idea of what makes up a firm's income and are usually expressed as a portion of each dollar of sales. The profit margin ratios we discuss here differ only in the numerator. It's in the numerator that we reflect and thus can evaluate performance for different aspects of the business.

Let's say we want to evaluate how well production facilities are managed. We simply focus on gross profit (sales less cost of goods sold), a measure of income—the direct result of production management. Comparing gross profit with sales produces the ***gross profit margin:***

$$\text{Gross profit margin} = \frac{\text{sales} - \text{cost of goods sold}}{\text{sales}} \qquad [4\text{-}16]$$

This ratio tells us the portion of each dollar of sales that remains after deducting production expenses. For Fictitious Corporation for 1995:

$$\text{Gross profit margin} = \frac{\$10,000,000 - \$6,500,000}{\$10,000,000} = \frac{\$3,500,000}{\$10,000,000}$$

$$= \textbf{0.3500 or 35\%}$$

For each dollar of sales, the firm's gross profit is 35 cents. Looking at sales and cost of goods sold, we can see that the gross profit margin is affected by:

- Changes in sales volume (affects cost of goods sold *and* sales).
- Changes in sales price (affects sales).
- Changes in the cost of production (affects cost of goods sold).

Any change in this margin from one period to the next is caused by one or more of those three factors. Similarly, differences in gross margin ratios among firms are the result of differences in those factors.

To evaluate operating performance, we need to consider operating expenses in addition to the cost of goods sold. To do this, we remove operating expenses from gross profit, leaving us with operating profit, also referred to as earnings before interest and taxes (EBIT). The ***operating profit margin*** is therefore:

$$\text{Operating profit margin} = \frac{\text{sales} - \text{cost of goods sold} - \text{operating expenses}}{\text{sales}}$$

$$= \frac{\text{earnings before interest and taxes}}{\text{sales}} \qquad [4\text{-}17]$$

For Fictitious for 1995:

$$\text{Operating profit margin} = \frac{\$2,000,000}{\$10,000,000} = \textbf{0.20 or 20\%}$$

Therefore, for each dollar of sales, Fictitious has 20 cents of operating income. The operating profit margin is affected by the same factors as gross profit margin, plus factors that affect other costs as well. The difference between gross profit and operating profit is any income or expense related to operations, such as:

- Office rent and lease expenses.
- Miscellaneous income (for example, income from investments).

- Advertising expenditures.
- Bad debt expense.

Most of these expenses are related in some way to sales, though they are not included directly in the cost of goods sold. Therefore, the difference between the gross profit margin and the operating profit margin is due to these indirect items that are included in computing the operating profit margin.

Both gross profit margin and operating profit margin reflect operations. But they do not consider how these operations have been financed. To evaluate both operating *and* financing decisions, we need to compare net income (that is, earnings after deducting interest and taxes) with sales. Doing so, we obtain the **net profit margin:**

$$\text{Net profit margin} = \frac{\text{sales} - \frac{\text{cost of}}{\text{goods sold}} - \frac{\text{operating}}{\text{expenses}} - \text{interest} - \text{taxes}}{\text{sales}}$$

$$= \frac{\text{net income}}{\text{sales}} \qquad\qquad [4\text{-}18]$$

Net profit margin tells us the net income generated from each dollar of sales; it considers financing costs that the operating profit margin doesn't consider. For Fictitious, for 1995:

$$\text{Net profit margin} = \frac{\$1,200,000}{\$10,000,000} = \textbf{0.12 or 12\%}$$

For every dollar of sales, Fictitious generates 12 cents.

Recap: Profitability Ratios

The profitability ratios for Fictitious in 1995 are:

Gross profit margin   = 35%
Operating profit margin = 20%
Net profit margin   = 12%

They tell us the following about the operating performance of Fictitious:

- Each dollar of sales contributes 35 cents to gross profit and 20 cents to operating profit.
- Every dollar of sales contributes 12 cents to owners' earnings.
- By comparing the 20-cent operating profit margin with the 12-cent net profit margin, we see that Fictitious has 8 cents of financing costs for every dollar of sales.

What these ratios do not tell us about profitability is the sensitivity of gross, operating, and net profit margins to:

- Changes in the sales price.
- Changes in the volume of sales.

Looking at the profitability ratios for one firm for one period gives us very little information that can be used to make judgments regarding future profitability. Nor do these ratios give us any information about why the profitability is the way it is. We need more information to make these kinds of judgments, particularly regarding the future profitability of the firm.

Activity Ratios

Activity ratios are measures of how well assets are used. Activity ratios—for the most part, turnover ratios—can be used to evaluate the benefits produced by specific assets, such as inventory or accounts receivable to evaluate the benefits produced by the totality of the firm's assets.

Inventory Management

The ***inventory turnover ratio*** indicates how well a firm has used inventory to generate the goods and services that are sold. The inventory turnover is the ratio of the cost of goods sold to inventory:[1]

$$\text{Inventory turnover ratio} = \frac{\text{cost of goods sold}}{\text{inventory}} \qquad [4\text{-}19]$$

For Fictitious, for 1995:

$$\text{Inventory turnover ratio} = \frac{\$6,500,000}{\$1,800,000} = \textbf{3.61}$$

This ratio tells us that Fictitious turns over its inventory 3.61 times per year: On average, cash is invested in inventory, goods and services are produced, and these goods and services are sold 3.6 times a year. Looking back to the number of days of inventory, we see that this turnover measure is consistent with the results of that calculation: We have 101 calendar days of inventory on hand at the end of the year; dividing 365 days by 101 days, or 365/101 days, we find that inventory cycles through (from cash to sales) 3.61 times a year.

Accounts Receivable Management

In much the same way we evaluated inventory turnover, we can evaluate a firm's management of its accounts receivable and its credit policy. The ***accounts receivable turnover ratio*** is a measure of how effectively a firm is using credit extended to customers. The benefit from extending credit is a sale that would not have been generated without it. The downside to extending credit is the possibility of default—customers not paying when promised. The benefit from extending credit is referred to as net credit sales—sales on credit less returns and refunds.

$$\text{Accounts receivable turnover ratio} = \frac{\text{net credit sales}}{\text{accounts receivable}} \qquad [4\text{-}20]$$

Looking at the Fictitious Corporation income statement we see an entry for sales, but we do not know how much of these amounts stated is on credit. This is often the case when we analyze companies from the outside looking in. Let's assume that the entire sales amount represents net credit sales. For Fictitious, for 1995:

$$\text{Accounts receivable turnover ratio} = \frac{\$10,000,000}{\$600,000} = \textbf{16.67}$$

---

[1] A common alternative to this is the ratio of sales to inventory. But there is a problem with this alternative: The numerator is in terms of sales (based on selling prices) whereas the denominator is in terms of costs. By including the sales price in the numerator, the result of this measure is not easily interpreted.

Therefore, almost seventeen times in the year there is, on average, a cycle that begins with a sale on credit and finishes with the receipt of cash for that sale. In other words, there are seventeen cycles of sales to credit to cash during the year.

The number of times accounts receivable cycle through the year is consistent with the number of days of credit of 22 that we calculated earlier—accounts receivable turn over seventeen times during the year and the average number of days of sales in the accounts receivable balance is 365 days/16.67 times = 22 days.

Overall Asset Management

The inventory and accounts receivable turnover ratios reflect the benefits obtained from the use of specific assets (inventory and accounts receivable). For a more general picture of the productivity of the firm, we can compare the sales during the period with the total assets that generated these sales.

One way is with the **total asset turnover,** which tells us how many times during the year the value of a firm's total assets is generated in sales:

$$\text{Total asset turnover ratio} = \frac{\text{sales}}{\text{total assets}} \qquad [4\text{-}21]$$

For Fictitious Corporation in 1995:

$$\text{Total asset turnover ratio} = \frac{\$10,000,000}{\$11,000,000} = \textbf{0.91}$$

The turnover ratio of 0.91 indicates that during 1995 every dollar invested in total assets generates 91 cents of sales. Or, stated differently, the total assets of Fictitious "turn over" almost once during the year. Since total assets include both tangible and intangible assets, this turnover tells us about how well all assets were used.

An alternative is to focus only on fixed assets, the long-term, tangible assets of the firm. The **fixed asset turnover** is the ratio of sales to fixed assets:

$$\text{Fixed asset turnover ratio} = \frac{\text{sales}}{\text{fixed assets}} \qquad [4\text{-}22]$$

For Fictitious Corporation for 1995:

$$\text{Fixed asset turnover ratio} = \frac{\$10,000,000}{\$7,000,000} = \textbf{1.43}$$

Therefore, for every dollar of fixed assets, Fictitious is able to generate $1.43 of sales.

Recap: Activity Ratios

The activity ratios for Fictitious Corporation are:

Inventory turnover ratio   =   3.61
Accounts receivable turnover ratio = 16.67
Total asset turnover ratio   =   0.91
Fixed asset turnover ratio   =   1.43

From these ratios we can determine that:

- Inventory flows in and out almost four times a year (from the inventory turnover ratio).
- Accounts receivable are collected in cash, on average, 22 days after a sale (from the number of days of credit). In other words, accounts receivable flow in and out almost seventeen times during the year (from the accounts receivable turnover ratio).

What these ratios do not tell us about the firm's use of its assets:

- The number of sales not made because credit policies are too stringent.
- How much of credit sales is not collectible.
- Which assets contribute most to the turnover.

Financial Leverage Ratios

A firm can finance its assets either with equity or debt. Financing through debt involves risk because debt legally obligates the firm to pay interest and to repay the principal as promised. Equity financing does not obligate the firm to pay anything, because dividends are paid at the discretion of the board of directors. There is always some risk, which we refer to as business risk, inherent in any operating segment of a business. But how a firm chooses to finance its operations—the particular mix of debt and equity—may add financial risk on top of business risk. *Financial risk* is the extent to which debt financing is used relative to equity.

Financial leverage ratios are used to assess how much financial risk the firm has taken on. There are two types of financial leverage ratios: component percentages and coverage ratios. Component percentages compare a firm's debt with either its total capital (debt plus equity) or its equity capital. Coverage ratios reflect a firm's ability to satisfy fixed obligations, such as interest, principal repayment, or lease payments.

A ratio that indicates the proportion of assets financed with debt is the *total debt-to-assets ratio*, which compares total liabilities (short-term + long-term debt) with total assets:

$$\text{Total debt-to-assets ratio} = \frac{\text{total debt}}{\text{total assets}} \qquad [4\text{-}23]$$

For Fictitious in 1995:

$$\text{Total debt-to-assets ratio} = \frac{\$5,000,000}{\$11,000,000} = \textbf{0.4546 or 45.46\%}$$

This ratio tells us that 45 percent of the firm's assets are financed with debt.

We could focus on long-term debts using the *long-term debt-to-assets ratio* to see the proportion of assets financed with long-term obligations:

$$\text{Long-term debt-to-assets ratio} = \frac{\text{long-term debt}}{\text{total assets}} \qquad [4\text{-}24]$$

For Fictitious, for 1995:

$$\text{Long-term debt-to-assets ratio} = \frac{\$4,000,000}{\$11,000,000} = \textbf{0.3636 or 36.36\%}$$

Fictitious finances 36.36 percent of its assets using long-term debt.

We may also look at the financial risk in terms of the use of debt relative to the use of equity. One definition of the *long-term debt-to-equity ratio* tells us how the firm finances its operations with debt relative to the *book value* of its shareholders' equity:

$$\text{Long-term debt-to-equity ratio (definition 1)} = \frac{\text{long-term debt}}{\text{book value of shareholders' equity}} \qquad [4\text{-}25]$$

For Fictitious, for 1995, using the book-value definition:

$$\text{Long-term debt-to-equity ratio (definition 1)} = \frac{\$4,000,000}{\$6,000,000} = \mathbf{0.6667} \text{ or } \mathbf{66.67\%}$$

For every one dollar of book value of shareholders' equity, Fictitious uses 67 cents of debt.

One problem (as we shall see) with using a financial ratio based on the book value of equity (the stock) to look at risk is that most often there is little relation between the book value of stock and its market value. The book value of equity consists of:

1. The proceeds to the firm of all the stock issues since it was first incorporated, less any treasury stock (stock repurchased by the firm).
2. The accumulation of all the earnings of the firm, less any dividends, since it was first incorporated.

Let's look at an example of the book value versus the market value of equity. IBM was incorporated in 1911. So the book value of its equity represents the sum of all its stock issued and all its earnings, less all dividends paid since 1911. As of the end of 1991, IBM's book value of equity was $3,698,870,909 and the market value of its equity was $5,079,455,499. The book value understates market value by almost $1.4 billion!

The book value generally does not give a true picture of the investment of shareholders in the firm because:

1. Earnings are recorded according to accounting principles, which may not reflect the true economics of transactions.
2. Because of inflation, the dollars from earnings and proceeds from stock issued in the past do not reflect today's values.

The market value, on the other hand, is the value of equity as perceived by investors. It is what investors are willing to pay, its worth. So why bother with the book value of equity? For two reasons: First, it is easier to obtain the book value than the market value of a firm's securities, and second, many financial services report ratios using book value rather than market value.

We may use the market value of equity in the denominator, replacing the book value of equity. To do this, we need to know the current number of shares outstanding and the current market price per share of stock and multiply to get the market value of equity.

The long-term debt-to-equity ratio using market value is:

$$\text{Long-term debt-to-equity ratio (definition 2)} = \frac{\text{long-term debt}}{\text{market value of shareholders' equity}} \quad [4\text{-}26]$$

Since Fictitious has both preferred and common shares outstanding, we must determine the market value of each and add them. Suppose the market value of the firm's common stock is $17 per share and preferred stock is $100 per share. For Fictitious, in 1995, using the market-value definition of equity:

$$
\begin{aligned}
\text{Long-term debt-to-equity ratio (definition 2)} &= \frac{\$4,000,000}{(8,000 \times \$100.00) + (1,500,000 \times \$17.00)} \\
&= \frac{\$4,000,000}{\$800,000 + \$25,500,000} \\
&= \textbf{0.1521} \text{ or } \textbf{15.21\%}
\end{aligned}
$$

Therefore, the firm's use of debt financing relative to equity financing appears to reflect lower risk when we look at the market value of its stock rather than the book value.[2]

The ratios that compare debt to equity or debt to total assets tell us about the amount of financial leverage, information enabling us to assess the financial condition of a firm. Another way of looking at the financial condition and the amount of financial leverage used by the firm is to see how well it can handle the financial burdens associated with its debt or other fixed commitments.

One measure of a firm's ability to handle financial burdens is the ***interest coverage ratio,*** also referred to as the ***times interest-covered ratio.*** This ratio tells us how well the firm can cover or meet the interest payments associated with debt. The ratio compares the funds available to pay interest (that is, earnings before interest and taxes) with the interest expense:

$$\text{Interest coverage ratio} = \frac{\text{EBIT}}{\text{interest expense}} \quad [4\text{-}27]$$

The greater the interest coverage ratio, the better able the firm is to pay its interest expense. For Fictitious, for 1995:

$$\text{Interest coverage ratio} = \frac{\$2,000,000}{\$400,000} = \textbf{5}$$

---

[2] You may have noticed that we were silent on whether the long-term debt in the ratios was book value or market value. Since debt is traded by investors and its value changes with time and interest rate movements, the value of debt for accounting purposes—the amount that shows up on the balance sheet—may differ from its true value. Ideally, we would like to use the market value of debt in our financial leverage ratios, since we are most concerned about the burden of debt. But it is not always practical to do so because, unlike common and preferred shares, the market value of bonds is not readily available: (1) Many bonds are not traded and (2) the price quotes of most publicly traded bonds are not easy to obtain because they aren't traded often. The ratios in the examples in this chapter use the *book value* of debt.

An interest coverage ratio of 5 means that the firm's earnings before interest and taxes are five times greater than its interest payments.

The interest coverage ratio tells us about a firm's ability to cover the interest related to its debt financing. However, there are other costs, which do not arise from debt but which nevertheless must be considered in the same way we consider the cost of debt in a firm's financial obligations. For example, lease payments are fixed costs incurred in financing operations. They represent legal obligations and therefore expenses that must be paid, just like interest.

What funds are available to pay debt and debtlike expenses? We can start with EBIT and back into the available funds by *adding back* expenses that were deducted to arrive at EBIT. The ability of a firm to satisfy its fixed financial costs—its fixed charges—is referred to as the ***fixed charge coverage ratio.*** One definition of the fixed charge coverage considers only the lease payments:

$$\text{Fixed charge coverage ratio (definition 1)} = \frac{\text{EBIT} + \text{lease expense}}{\text{interest} + \text{lease expense}} \qquad [4\text{-}28]$$

For Fictitious Corporation, for 1995:

$$\begin{aligned}
\text{Fixed charge coverage ratio (definition 1)} &= \frac{\$2,000,000 + \$1,000,000}{\$400,000 + \$1,000,000} \\
&= \frac{\$3,000,000}{\$1,400,000} \\
&= \mathbf{2.14}
\end{aligned}$$

This ratio tells us that Fictitious can cover its fixed charges (interest and lease payments) more than two times.

What fixed charges to consider is not entirely clear-cut. For example, if the firm is required to set aside funds to eventually or periodically retire debt—referred to as a sinking fund—is the amount set aside a fixed charge? As another example, since preferred dividends represent a fixed financing charge, should they be included as a fixed charge? From the perspective of the common shareholder, the preferred dividends must be covered to enable either the payment of common dividends or to retain earnings for future growth. Since debt principal and preferred stock dividends are paid on an after-tax basis—paid out of dollars remaining after taxes are paid—we must translate this fixed charge into equivalent before-tax dollars.

The fixed charge coverage ratio can be expanded to accommodate the sinking funds and preferred stock dividends as fixed charges. In this second definition:

$$\text{Fixed charge coverage ratio (definition 2)} = \frac{\text{EBIT} + \text{lease expense}}{\text{interest expense} + \text{lease expense} + \dfrac{\text{sinking fund payment} + \text{preferred dividends}}{(1 - \text{tax rate})}} \qquad [4\text{-}29]$$

Before- vs. After-Tax Dollars

There are many instances when we need to figure out how many before-tax dollars are equivalent to a specified amount of after-tax dollars. Suppose you must pay $100 in debt principal. This must come out of after-tax dollars, since Congress does not allow deductions for the repayment of debt. How many before-tax dollars are needed to pay off $100 after-tax dollars? Say the tax rate is 30 percent.

After-tax earnings = taxable income − (tax rate × taxable income)
$100 = taxable income − (0.30 × taxable income)
$100 = taxable income (1 − 0.30)

Rearranging,

$$\text{Taxable income} = \frac{\$100}{(1 - 0.30)} = \mathbf{\$142.86}$$

As a check, let's now suppose you have $142.86 in before-tax earnings. How much will you have after paying 30 percent in taxes?

After-tax earnings = $142.86 − 0.30($142.86)
= $142.86 − $42.86
= **$100**

Therefore, dividing after-tax dollars by (1 − tax rate) translates after-tax dollars into before-tax dollars.

If we assume that Fictitious must set aside 10 percent of the debt principal in a sinking fund each year, then for 1995:

$$\text{Fixed charge coverage ratio (definition 2)} = \frac{2,000,000 + \$1,000,000}{\$400,000 + \$1,000,000 + \dfrac{\$400,000 + \$100,000}{(1 - 0.25)}}$$

$$= \frac{\$3,000,000}{\$1,400,000 + \$666,667}$$

$$= \frac{\$3,000,000}{\$2,066,667}$$

$$= \mathbf{1.45}$$

Fictitious Corporation is able to cover fixed obligations that include interest, lease payments, sinking fund payments, and preferred dividends.

Up to now we looked toward earnings before interest and taxes as funds available to meet fixed financial charges. The EBIT we have used thus far included noncash items such as depreciation and amortization. Since we are trying to compare funds available to meet obligations, a better measure of available funds is cash flow from operations, which we can find in the statement of cash flows. A ratio that considers cash flows from operations as funds available to cover interest payments is referred to as the ***cash flow interest coverage ratio.***

$$\text{Cash flow interest coverage ratio} = \frac{\text{cash flow from operations} + \text{interest} + \text{taxes}}{\text{interest}} \quad [4\text{-}30]$$

The amount of cash flow from operations that is in the statement of cash flows is net of interest and taxes. So we have to add back interest and taxes to cash flow from operations to arrive at the cash flow amount *before* interest and taxes in order to determine the cash flow available to cover interest payments.

For Fictitious Corporation in 1995:

$$\text{Cash flow interest coverage ratio} = \frac{\$1,800,000 + \$400,000 + \$400,000}{\$400,000}$$

$$= \frac{\$2,600,000}{\$400,000}$$

$$= \mathbf{6.5}$$

This coverage ratio tells us that, in terms of cash flows, Fictitious has six and one-half times more cash than is needed to pay its interest. This is a much better picture of interest coverage than the five times reflected by EBIT. Why the difference? Because cash flow considers not just the accounting income, but cash flows arising from operations. In the case of Fictitious, depreciation is a noncash charge that reduced EBIT but not cash flow from operations—it is added back to net income to arrive at cash flow from operations.

Recap: Financial Leverage Ratios

Summarizing, the financial leverage ratios for Fictitious Corporation for 1995 are:

Total debt-to-assets ratio = 45.45%
Long-term debt-to-assets ratio = 36.36%
Long-term debt-to-equity ratio (definition 1) = 66.67%
Long-term debt-to-equity ratio (definition 2) = 15.21%
Interest coverage ratio = 5.00
Fixed charge coverage ratio (definition 1) = 2.14
Fixed charge coverage ratio (definition 2) = 1.45
Cash flow interest coverage ratio = 6.50

These ratios tell us Fictitious uses its financial leverage as follows:

• Assets are 45 percent financed with debt, measured using book values.
• Long-term debt is approximately two-thirds of equity. When equity is measured in market value terms, long-term debt is approximately one-sixth of equity.

These ratios do not tell us:

• What other fixed, legal commitments the firm has that are not included on the balance sheet (for example, pension benefits and operating leases).

The weighted average number of shares outstanding, considering that 200,000 shares were outstanding during half the year and 250,000 shares were outstanding during the other half, is:

Weighted average
number of shares = 0.50 (200,000 shares) + 0.50 (250,000 shares)
outstanding

$$= 100,000 \text{ shares} + 125,000 \text{ shares}$$
$$= 225,000 \text{ shares}$$

What are the earnings per share for 1996?

$$\text{Earnings per share} = \frac{\$2,000,000}{225,000} = \$8.89 \text{ per share}$$

We can represent the earnings per share adjusted for the change in the shares outstanding as:

$$\text{Earnings per share} = \frac{\text{earnings available to owners}}{\text{weighted average number of shares outstanding}}$$

For a firm having securities that are potentially dilutive—meaning they could share in net income—we need to represent its primary earnings per share and its fully diluted earnings per share. *Primary earnings per share* reflect the dilutive effects of the potentially dilutive securities *likely* to be transformed into common stock. *Fully diluted earnings per share* reflect the dilutive effects of all potentially dilutive securities.

Recap: Shareholder Ratios

The shareholder ratios for Fictitious for 1995 are:

Earnings per share	= $0.73 per share
Book value of equity per share	= $3.47 per share
Price-earnings ratio	= 23.29
Dividends per share	= $0.33 per share
Dividend payout ratio	= 45.46%

These ratios tell us that:

- Fictitious pays almost half of its earnings to its shareholders in the form of cash dividends.
- Its equity's market value is higher than its book value.

These ratios don't tell us:

- What will be the ability of Fictitious to pay dividends in the future.
- How the market values of the firm's equity relates to cash flows.

COMMON-SIZE ANALYSIS

We have looked at a firm's operating performance and financial condition through ratios that relate various items of information contained in the financial statements. Another way to analyze a firm is to look at its financial data more comprehensively.

Common-size analysis is a method of analysis in which the components of a financial statement are compared with each other. The first step in common-size analysis is to break down a financial statement—either the balance sheet or the income statement—into its parts. The next step is to calculate the proportion that each item represents relative to some benchmark. In common-size analysis of the balance sheet, the benchmark is total assets. For the income statement, the benchmark is sales.

Let's see how it works by doing some common-size financial analysis for the Fictitious Corporation. Comparing Table 4-2 with Table 3-1, you see that the data in Table 4-2 are not precisely the same as the data in the Fictitious balance sheet shown in Table 3-1. Nevertheless, the data are the same but reorganized. Each item in the original balance sheet has been restated as a proportion of total assets for the purpose of common size analysis. Hence, we refer to this as the ***common-size balance sheet.***

In this balance sheet, we see, for example, that in 1995 cash is 3.6 percent of total assets $400,000/$11,000,000 = 0.036. We can also see that the largest investment is in plant and equipment, which comprises 63.6 percent of the total assets. On the liabilities side, we can see that current liabilities are a small portion (9.1 percent) of liabilities and equity.

The common-size balance sheet tells us in very general terms how Fictitious has raised capital and where this capital has been invested. Like financial ratios, however, the picture is not complete until we look at trends and compare these proportions with those of other firms in the same industry.

In the income statement, also, as in the balance sheet, we can restate items as a proportion of sales; this statement is referred to as the ***common-size income statement.*** The common-size income statement for Fictitious for 1995 and 1994 is shown in Table 4-3. For 1995 we see that the major costs are associated with goods sold (65 percent); lease expense, other expenses, interest, taxes, and dividends make up smaller portions of sales. Looking at gross profit, EBIT, and net income, you will notice that these proportions are the profit margins that we calculated earlier. The common-size income statement provides information on the profitability of different aspects of the firm's business. Again, the picture is not complete until we look at trends over time and comparisons with other companies in the same industry.

AN APPLICATION OF FINANCIAL ANALYSIS TO WAL-MART STORES INC.

The financial ratios that we have looked at up to this point are summarized in Appendix 4A, Table 4A-1, which also includes the calculated financial ratios for Fictitious for both 1994 and 1995.

Financial ratios that reflect just one point in time tell us very little about earnings performance or financial condition. For example, suppose your data result in a current ratio of 2.0. Is this good or bad? It does tell us that the firm could pay off twice its amount of current liabilities using its current assets, but: Does it tell us how well the firm is managing its assets? Does it tell us whether the firm can pay off its liabilities in the future? Does it tell us about the amount of coverage needed for the type of business? The current ratio you calculated answers none of these questions.

To analyze financial ratios we must look at them over time so that we can get an idea of trends. For example, by looking at the current ratio over time we can see whether it is improving or deteriorating, giving us an idea of where the firm is heading. If we look at the current ratio for Wang Laboratories, shown at the beginning of this chapter, we see the company becoming less liquid over time. Considering this trend, along with the downward trend in its return on assets and upward trend in its use of debt, we see that Wang Laboratories was heading for financial trouble.

TABLE 4-2

Fictitious Corporation
Common-Size Balance Sheets
For Years Ending December 31

	1995	1994
ASSET COMPONENTS		
Cash	0.036	0.020
Marketable securities	0.018	0.000
Accounts receivable	0.055	0.080
Inventory	0.164	0.100
Current assets	0.273	0.200
Net plant and equipment	0.636	0.700
Intangible assets	0.091	0.100
Total assets	1.000[a]	1.000[a]
LIABILITY AND SHAREHOLDERS' EQUITY COMPONENTS		
Accounts payable	0.046	0.040
Other current liabilities	0.046	0.010
Long-term debt	0.364	0.500
Total liabilities	0.454	0.560
Preferred stock	0.073	0.080
Common stock	0.473	0.360
Total shareholders' equity	0.546	0.440
Total liabilities and shareholders' equity	1.000[a]	1.000[a]

EXAMPLES:

$$\text{Cash as a proportion of total assets} = \frac{\$400}{\$11,000} = \mathbf{0.036}$$

$$\begin{array}{l}\text{Common stock as a proportion of total} \\ \text{liabilities and shareholders' equity}\end{array} = \frac{\$3,000 + 2,200}{\$11,000} = \mathbf{0.473}$$

[a]All proportions add to 1.000, or 100 percent.

TABLE 4-3

Fictitious Corporation
Common-Size Income Statements
For Years Ending December 31

	1995	1994
Sales	1.000[a]	1.000[a]
Less: Cost of goods sold	0.650	0.667
Gross profit	0.350	0.333
Less: Lease and administrative expenses	0.150	0.167
Earnings before interest and taxes	0.200	0.167
Less: Interest	0.040	0.056
Earnings before taxes	0.160	0.167
Less: Taxes	0.040	0.057
Net income	0.120	0.111
Less: Preferred dividends	0.010	0.011
Earnings available to common shareholders	0.110	0.100
Less: Common dividends	0.050	0.044
Retained earnings	0.060	0.056

EXAMPLES:

$$\text{Earnings before interest and taxes as a proportion of sales} = \frac{\$2,000}{\$10,000} = \mathbf{0.200}$$

$$\text{Common dividends as a proportion of sales} = \frac{\$500}{\$10,000} = \mathbf{0.050}$$

[a]All proportions add to 1.000, or 100 percent.

Another way to analyze financial ratios is to compare the ratios of one firm with corresponding benchmark ratios, typically those of other companies in the same industry. Since firms in the same industry have similar product lines and similar markets, they are all likely to have similar business risks. Firms in the same industry compete against one another. They face similar consumer demand, competitive pressures on price and quantity of goods or services sold, and sensitivity to change in the economy. They also face similar production cost structures (the mixture of fixed and variable production costs).

Now that you are familiar with the concepts behind the financial ratios, we can put aside the convenient but fabricated data of Fictitious Corporation. Instead, we will demonstrate how to look at ratios over time and across an industry using data for an actual firm that has a past (and a future). Let's look at and analyze the financial ratios of Wal-Mart Stores. But first we'll take a brief look at the business of Wal-Mart, the industry, and the economy, which we must always do to properly analyze any financial ratio.

The Business   Wal-Mart Stores Inc. was founded in 1945 and incorporated in 1969. Its main business is operating discount department stores and wholesale clubs. By the end of 1990, Wal-Mart had grown to 1,402 discount department stores, 123 wholesale club stores, and 3 hypermarkets—large stores that combine department and grocery stores under one roof to make possible one-stop shopping. However, Wal-Mart owns only 200 of the buildings in which its stores are located—the rest are leased from developers or local governments.

The Industry

Wal-Mart is a discount retailer. What other companies are in the same industry? The retail industry includes many types of business operations, from the discounter to the upscale retailer to the mom-and-pop local store. Wal-Mart, through both its Discount City Stores and its Wholesale Clubs, is best characterized as a discount retailer. Other discount retailers include K Mart (Wal-Mart's closest competitor), Dayton Hudson, and the Price Company. The share of discount retail industry sales of the major discount retailers in 1990 is shown in Figure 4-1.

There are seven major players and many minor ones in this industry, and it has undergone many changes in the past twenty years. There have been a number of bankruptcies (e.g., W. T. Grant and Ames Department Stores) and a number of acquired companies (e.g., Kuhn's Big-K was acquired by Wal-Mart).

In our time series analysis, we have included companies that later disappeared, through bankruptcy or merger, for those years in which they were still viable, independent entities. We did so to get a picture of the industry during its early years. If we left out firms that later disappeared, we would be biasing our picture of the performance and condition of the industry toward the larger, healthier companies and away from what it really was like as it developed.

There is a great deal of competition between the two major players—Wal-Mart and K Mart. In addition to competition among the discount retail stores,

FIGURE 4-1

Breakdown of Discount Retail Store Industry Sales, by Company, 1990

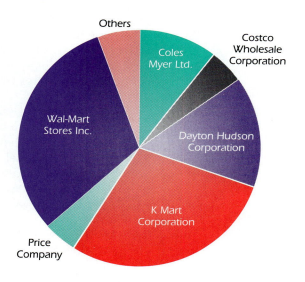

there is competition with stores not generally considered discounters, such as Sears, Roebuck and J. C. Penney. The prospects for the discount retail store industry in the future (from 1990 onward) include greater competition, which may mean that firms seeking to maintain their market share may be forced to accept lower profit margins.

The Economy

To evaluate Wal-Mart's financial condition and operating performance with an eye on the future, we need to look at how it has done under different economic conditions: Has the firm fared well during recessions? Has it fared well during periods of high inflation? How has it done during periods of economic prosperity?

To gain a perspective on the firm's management under different economic conditions, we have to evaluate the financial ratios within the economic climate over which they are measured. To do this we could look back at economic history, mapping out the indicators, such as ***gross domestic production*** (GDP), which is a measure of the goods and services produced in a nation, and the ***consumer price index*** (CPI), which measures the general level of

FIGURE 4-2

Percentage Change in Wal-Mart's Sales and Net Income, 1972–1990

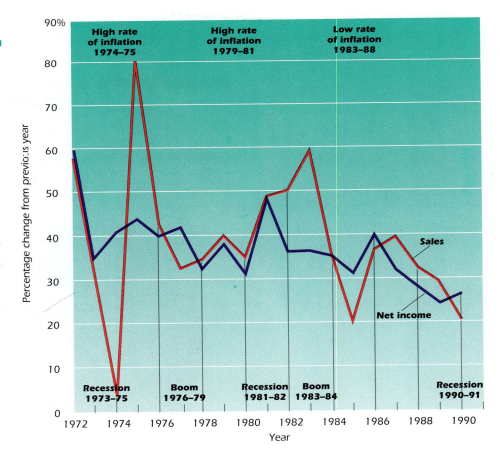

prices, to get an idea of economic conditions and how Wal-Mart fared under different conditions.

The changes in annual sales and net income for Wal-Mart over the period 1972–1990 are shown in Figure 4-2, with economic climates indicated. What we find is that Wal-Mart does well in poor economic climates: The growth in sales and net income is strongest during recessionary and inflationary periods.

Financial Ratios of the Firm and the Industry

Let's look at a few of the ratios from the six groups to make this analysis manageable. Each of the Wal-Mart ratios we look at will be graphed over the 1971–1990 period, along with the corresponding average ratio for the industry.

Liquidity Ratios

The current and quick ratios for Wal-Mart and the retail store industry for the years 1971–1990 are graphed in Figure 4-3. We can easily see that Wal-Mart is less liquid than the other companies in the industry, as indicated by

FIGURE 4-3

Liquidity Ratios for Wal-Mart and the Discount Retail Store Industry, 1971–1990

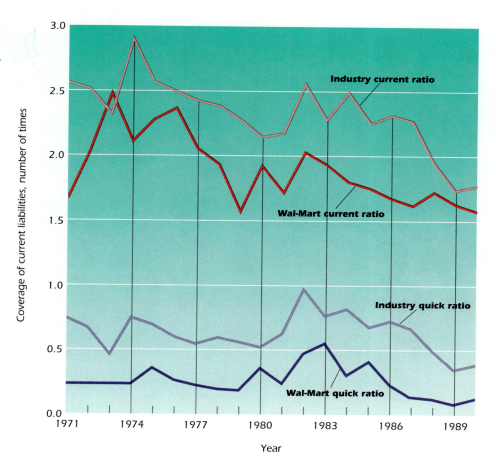

both lower current and lower quick ratios. Both the industry and Wal-Mart have experienced declining liquidity over time.

We can't tell whether this is good or bad because we are looking at only one piece in the puzzle. On the one hand, relatively lower liquidity could mean that Wal-Mart is having difficulty meeting its short-term obligations, perhaps forcing it to seek additional short-term financing. On the other hand, relatively lower liquidity could mean that Wal-Mart is managing its current assets efficiently. Since current assets provide low return—a firm earns less from its current asset investment than from its investment in plant and equipment—a smaller investment in current assets may mean that Wal-Mart is investing in noncurrent assets that provide a higher return. So, let's withhold judgment on a declining current ratio until we examine Wal-Mart's profitability.

Profitability Ratios

The operating and net profit margins for both Wal-Mart and the industry are graphed in Figure 4-4. Using either measure of profitability, we see that Wal-

FIGURE 4-4
Profitability Ratios for Wal-Mart and the Discount Retail Store Industry, 1971–1990

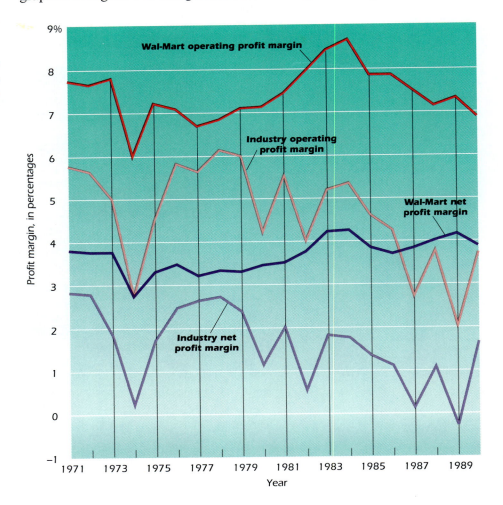

Mart is more profitable than the industry. In addition, it's quite clear that the profitability of Wal-Mart is much less volatile than that of the rest of the industry. The recession in 1974 is evident in the profitability of Wal-Mart and the industry. Wal-Mart did not seem to be affected seriously by the recession of 1982, though the rest of industry appears to have been. Wal-Mart also seemed to benefit from the boom periods of 1976–1977 and 1984, more so than the rest of the industry. During the periods of higher inflation, Wal-Mart seems to have been less affected than other members of the industry.

Activity Ratios

The inventory turnover for Wal-Mart and the industry is shown in Figure 4-5. Inventory turnover is slower for Wal-Mart than the rest of the industry. This indicates that there may be a difference between either the type of inventory or the inventory management systems of Wal-Mart and its competitors.

The total asset turnover for Wal-Mart and the industry is also shown in Figure 4-5. Wal-Mart turns over its assets much faster than the other firms in the industry.

These two measures of activity may indicate that Wal-Mart tends to invest less in plant assets than other companies. Therefore, though their in-

FIGURE 4-5

Activity Ratios for Wal-Mart and the Discount Retail Store Industry, 1971–1990

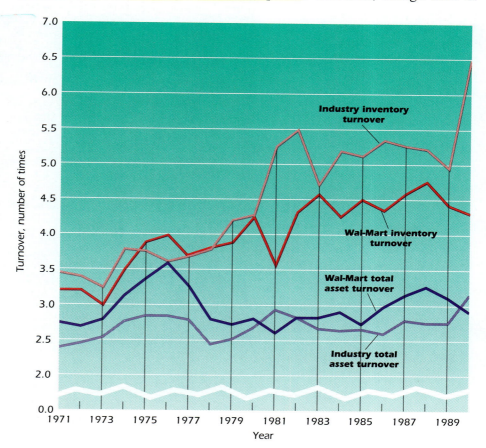

ventory turnover is slower, their total asset turnover is faster. Put together with the fact that Wal-Mart owns less than one-seventh of its store buildings, we see that Wal-Mart invests little in plant facilities.

Financial Leverage Ratios

The total debt-to-assets ratio for Wal-Mart and the industry is shown in Figure 4-6. We see that Wal-Mart took on debt greater than its typical debt load during the 1978–1980 period, but this additional debt was reduced over the subsequent years. The debt ratio of the industry declined in the last year, 1990.

Combining the information on Wal-Mart's acquisitions with what we see in the graph representing its financial leverage, we conclude that Wal-Mart did the right things at the right time:

- Increased its debt with the acquisitions in the 1977–1981 period.
- Sold and leased back stores in 1983, providing cash to pay down some debt.
- Pared down its debt burden after 1981.

FIGURE 4-6

Total Debt-to-Assets Ratios for Wal-Mart and the Discount Retail Store Industry, 1971–1990

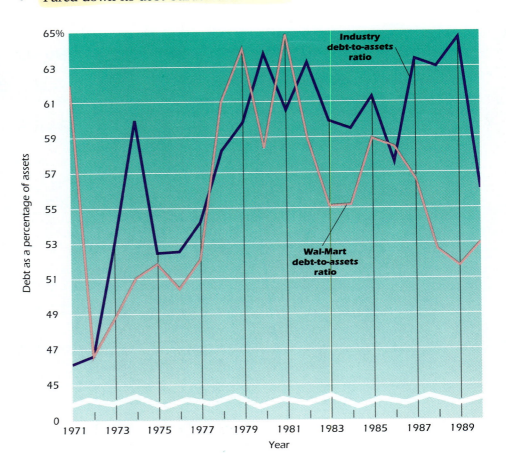

Return Ratios

Figure 4-7 shows that Wal-Mart's return on assets is better than the industry's. This greater return is due to the company's greater profitability and better asset turnover relative to the industry. The graph shows that the industry return on assets is more volatile over time, appearing to be more sensitive to changes in economic conditions.

Blending this information with the economic data, we see that Wal-Mart tends to weather economic storms better than other members of the industry. It even appears that Wal-Mart performs better in poor economic climates. Perhaps when times are tough, consumers tend to look for more bargains and discounted goods.

Shareholder Ratios

Wal-Mart's P/E ratios and the average P/Es for all firms in the industry are shown in Figure 4-8. We can easily see that the price-earnings ratios for Wal-Mart are above the industry averages. It's also clear that the trend for both is

FIGURE 4-7

Return on Assets for Wal-Mart and the Discount Retail Store Industry, 1971–1990

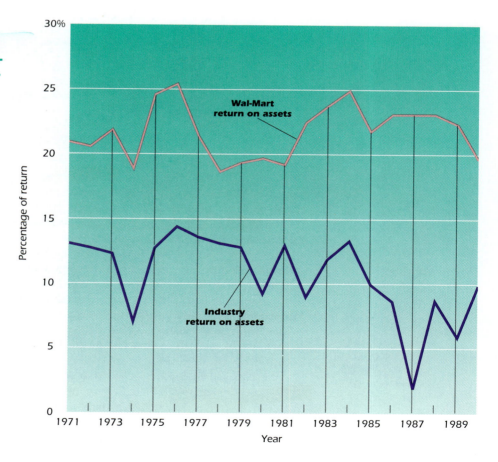

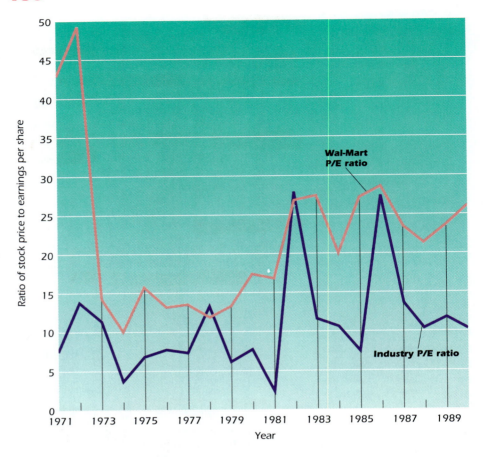

FIGURE 4-8
Price-Earnings (P/E) Ratio for Wal-Mart and the Retail Store Industry, 1971–1990

upward since 1974, though the industry average P/E ratios are more volatile than Wal-Mart's. Also, the industry was especially sensitive to economic downturns, such as those in 1974, 1981, and 1989.

The growth in Wal-Mart's P/E ratios coincides with expansion of its stores. As Wal-Mart grew, so did investors' expectations about future cash flows.

Common-Size Analysis

A thorough common-size analysis requires looking at financial statement components over time. Let's return to Wal-Mart to see how this works. Figure 4-9(a) uses a bar graph to represent each of the three major components of Wal-Mart's assets as a proportion of total assets. Hence, this is a graph of the proportions in the asset section of Wal-Mart's common-size balance sheet. Figure 4-9(b) uses the same bar graph format to represent the three major components of liabilities as proportions of total liabilities.

We can see in Figure 4-9(a) that Wal-Mart increased its percentage investment in plant assets, starting in 1978. This is the same period in which Wal-Mart took on more debt, which we can see by looking at the long-term debt component in Figure 4-9(b). Long-term debt increased in 1978, but has slowly declined over the years. This tells us the investment in plant assets was financed for the most part by debt and that this debt has slowly been reduced.

FIGURE 4-9(a)

Common-Size Balance Sheets for Wal-Mart, 1971–1990

Asset components

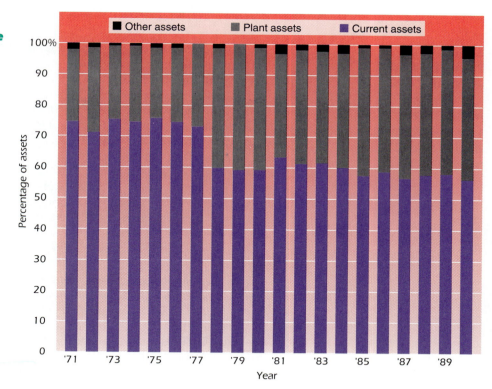

FIGURE 4-9(b)

Common-Size Balance Sheets for Wal-Mart, 1971–1990

Liability and equity components

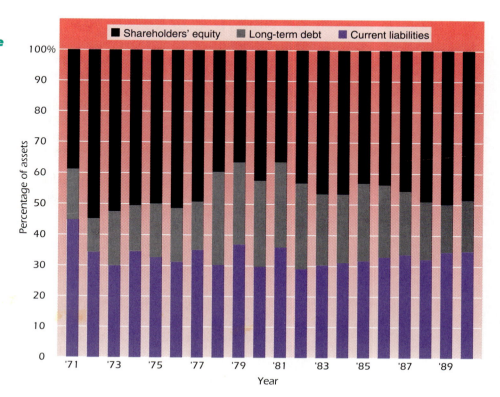

USING FINANCIAL ANALYSIS

Evaluating Creditworthiness and Debt Quality

If you are considering lending a firm some money, it is natural to be concerned about getting your money back (the principal) and receiving compensation for lending the money (the interest). As a creditor, you must evaluate the financial condition of the firm to determine whether or not its promises to pay you in the future will actually be met. The best you can do is evaluate the financial soundness of the business and make an assessment of whether cash flows in the future will be sufficient to pay you what is promised. We can calculate financial ratios and evaluate them in the context of other data (market and economic data) and other information about the firm and its industry. Putting all that together in some meaningful context should enable us to make a judgment about the firm's future cash flows.

We can perform the analysis ourselves or rely on financial services that provide assessments of the creditworthiness of companies. There are many financial services available, including Dun & Bradstreet, Moody's, and Standard & Poor's.

Dun & Bradstreet provides credit ratings for companies ranging from your local bookstore to those whose stock is traded on the major stock exchanges. Moody's and Standard & Poor's evaluate stock and bond quality, but specialize more in rating the latter. Each service has a rating scheme, described in Table 4-4, that classifies a debt in categories ranging from the highest credit grade to default. Debt classified in the top two categories—considered to have the least risk of default—is considered *high-grade debt.* Debt classified in the top four categories is considered *investment-grade debt.* Since many institutional investors (such as pension funds) are required to invest prudently, they tend to restrict their investments to investment-grade debt. Debt issues with a rating below investment grade are referred to as *speculative bonds,* or *junk bonds.*

Though not shown in Table 4-4, Standard & Poor's also delineates and rates debt *within* each class, assigning pluses and minuses to bonds within the classes AA to CCC to distinguish debt within those categories; for example, debt rated AA+ is considered to be higher in quality than debt rated AA−. Similarly, Moody's assigns numbers 1 through 3 alongside the ratings in the Aa through B categories to distinguish among debt in those classes; for example, debt rated Aa1 is considered to be of higher quality than debt rated Aa3.

Financial services assign ratings based on their analysis of both the features of a debt and the characteristics of the firm issuing it. Some debt (such as a mortgage bond) may contain provisions that protect the creditor. Which ratios do the financial services use, and how do they make the judgments that result in their rating of debt? Well, they are not about to tell us much beyond the general description of the ratings classes. If they told us, we wouldn't need them any more!

Each debt obligation is rated individually, so it is possible for a firm to have debt with different ratings. How can this be? Because debt issued by the same firm may have different features regarding seniority (priority in the case of liquidation), callability, and protections. For example, Illinois Bell Telephone has some bonds rated Aaa and others rated Aa1 by Moody's. The Aaa bonds are secured bonds (that is, they are backed by specific property), whereas the Aa1 bonds are debentures (and therefore backed only by the gen-

TABLE 4-4

Bond Rating Classifications: Standard & Poor's, Moody's

STANDARD & POOR'S

Investment grade

AAA	Highest quality. Ability to pay interest and principal very strong.
AA	High quality. Ability to pay interest and principal strong.
A	Medium to high quality. Ability to pay interest and principal, but more susceptible to changes in circumstances and the economy.
BBB	Medium quality. Adequate ability to pay, but highly susceptible to adverse circumstances.

Speculative grade

BB	Speculative. Less near-term likelihood of default relative to other speculative issues.
B	Current capacity to pay interest and principal, but highly susceptible to changes in circumstances.
CCC	Likely to default, where payment of interest and principal is dependent on favorable circumstances.
CC	Debt subordinate to senior debt rated CCC.
C	Debt subordinate to senior debt rated CCC−.
D	Currently in default, where interest or principal has not been paid as promised.

SOURCE: "Long-term Rating Definitions," *CREDITWEEK*, Standard & Poor's, Feb. 11, 1991, p. 128.

MOODY'S

Investment grade

Aaa	Best quality. Smallest investment risk.
Aa	High quality.
A	Upper to medium grade. Favorable investment attributes.
Baa	Medium grade. Adequate ability to pay interest and principal.

Speculative grade

Ba	Speculative. Ability to pay interest and principal uncertain in the future.
B	Lack of desirable investment characteristics. Likelihood of paying interest and principal in the future is small.
Caa	Poor standing. May be in default or other problems with respect to payment of interest and principal.
Ca	Very speculative. May be in default.
C	Poor prospects of becoming investment standing.

SOURCE: "Key to Moody's Corporate Bond Ratings," *Industrial Manual*, Moody's, 1991, pp. vi–vii.

eral creditworthiness of Illinois Bell). If Illinois Bell has difficulty paying interest or principal (which is doubtful, given their high ratings) the secured bonds are protected, but the debentures must wait in line for payment after the secured bonds have been paid.

Predicting Bankruptcy

Financial ratios have been used since the 1930s to predict whether a firm will go bankrupt. The idea behind a prediction of bankruptcy is that prior to bankruptcy, certain aspects of a firm's financial condition and operating performance deteriorate. By comparing the financial ratios of companies that go bankrupt with those that do not, we can get a profile of the aspects that mark a firm on the verge of bankruptcy. Since financial ratios are useful for summarizing the major financial aspects of a firm, they are utilized to help discriminate between healthy companies and those at risk of bankruptcy.

The earlier studies of bankruptcy prediction found that liquidity ratios—especially those that compare net working capital with total assets—and financial leverage ratios—those that compare long-term debt to equity—were most helpful in predicting bankruptcies.[4]

More recent studies suggest a number of ratios, in combination, are useful in predicting bankruptcy. One of the most often cited studies in this area is by Edward Altman.[5] He found five key ratios that help distinguish between bankruptcy-prone and healthy firms:

- The ratio of working capital to total assets (liquidity).
- The ratio of retained earnings to total assets (combines profitability over time and the age of the firm).
- The basic earning power ratio (profitability).
- The ratio of the market value of equity to the book value of debt (financial leverage).
- The total asset turnover.

Models of bankruptcy prediction use information on the past financial characteristics of bankrupt and healthy firms to predict the likelihood of bankruptcy in the future. These models are able to identify the basic financial characteristics that distinguish bankruptcy-prone firms from healthy ones; nevertheless they can only correctly predict the firms that will remain healthy versus those that will go bankrupt about 68 to 98 percent of the time, depending on the particular model and the period over which it is tested.[6]

---

[4] These early studies include analyses by Arthur Winakor and Raymond F. Smith, *Changes in Financial Structure of Unsuccessful Firms,* Bureau of Business Research, University of Illinois Press, Urbana, 1935; Paul J. Fitzpatrick, *Symptoms of Industrial Failures,* Catholic University of America Press, Washington, D.C., 1931; and Fitzpatrick, *A Comparison of the Ratios of Successful Industrial Enterprises with Those of Failed Companies,* The Accountants Publishing, Washington, D.C., 1932.

[5] Edward Altman, "Financial Ratios, Discriminant Analysis, and the Prediction of Corporate Bankruptcy," *Journal of Finance,* vol. 22, Sept. 1968, pp. 589–609.

[6] Comparisons of the predictive accuracy of the widely used bankruptcy models are made by Ismael G. Dambolena and Joel M. Shulman, "A Primary Rule for Detecting Bankruptcy: Watch the Cash," *Financial Analysts Journal,* vol. 44, Sept.–Oct. 1988, pp. 74–78. Dambolena and Shulman also demonstrate the importance of liquid assets in bankruptcy models.

PROBLEMS AND DILEMMAS IN FINANCIAL RATIO ANALYSIS

Financial analysis provides information concerning a firm's operating performance and financial condition. This information is useful to a financial manager in evaluating a firm's operations and to an investor in evaluating the risk and potential returns to investing in a firm's securities.

But financial ratio analysis cannot tell the whole story and must be interpreted and used with care. When we discussed each ratio, we noted what we needed to assume or what it might not tell us. For example, in calculating inventory turnover, we need to assume that the inventory shown on the balance sheet is representative of inventory throughout the year. Another example is in the calculation of accounts receivable turnover: We assumed that all sales were on credit. If we are on the outside looking in—that is, evaluating a firm based on its financial statements only—and therefore do not have data on credit sales, we have to start making assumptions, which may or may not be correct.

In addition, there are other areas of concern you should be aware of in using financial ratios:

- Limitations in the accounting data used to construct the ratios.
- Selection of an appropriate benchmark firm or firms for comparison purposes.
- Interpretation of the ratios.
- Pitfalls in forecasting future operating performance and financial condition based on past trends.

Let's take a closer look at these concerns.

Using Accounting Data

In using accounting data we need to beware of several problems, including:

- Lack of representativeness of the data because they may be historical cost data or inaccurate.
- Inability to compare data presented by different methods of accounting.
- Distortions because of the presence of extraordinary items, such as losses due to a plant closing.
- Inability to classify some items.

Historical Costs and Inflation

Accounting principles dictate that an asset be recorded at its cost or market value, whichever is lower. But this means that if an asset's value increases over time, it is recorded at its original cost, understating its current, true value. In periods of inflation, asset values are likely to increase. The longer an asset is on the books and the greater the rate of inflation, the more likely the value of the asset will be recorded at less than its true value. And because of the understatement of asset values on the balance sheet, income is overstated.

FIFO vs. LIFO

FIFO (first-in, first-out) inventory assumes that inventory items sold are the ones that have been in inventory the longest; so the cost of the *older* inventory items is recorded as the cost of goods sold. LIFO (last-in, first-out) inventory assumes that any items sold are the ones that have been acquired recently; so the cost of the *newer* inventory items is recorded as the cost of goods sold.

In a period of inflation, FIFO results in a value of inventory on the balance sheet that is close to its current value, whereas LIFO understates the value of inventory. However, since FIFO uses older costs in determining cost of goods sold, the cost of goods sold is understated and gross profit is overstated on the income statement in a period of inflation. Using LIFO, the cost of goods sold is closest to the current cost, so gross profit is more accurate than if the firm had used FIFO in a period of inflation.

The accounting profession has attempted to represent the effects of changing price levels. Nevertheless, there is currently no required disclosure in financial statements on the effects of price-level changes.

Methods of Accounting

A firm is allowed to choose among different methods of accounting for purposes of financial statement reporting, including method of inventory accounting, method of depreciation, and period of amortization.

Different companies use different accounting methods; so financial comparisons among them is more difficult. Suppose you want to compare the profitability of two companies, one of which uses LIFO and the other FIFO. How can you adjust for the differences? In the case of inventory accounting, companies using LIFO provide a footnote in their financial statements, disclosing the difference between the value of inventory using LIFO and using FIFO. For example, International Paper uses LIFO for raw materials and finished goods inventory. A footnote to their 1990 annual report discloses that total inventory was $971 million, but that if FIFO had been used for all categories of inventory, total inventory would have been $185 million more, or $1,156 million. By using this information to adjust the balance sheet and income statement appropriately, International Paper could be compared with a firm that uses FIFO accounting.

In cases other than inventory, footnotes may not be available to help you evaluate what you're looking at.

Do companies in the same industry really use different methods of accounting? Yes! In fact, some companies use different methods of accounting for different accounts. How can you tell what method of accounting they use? Check the footnotes: The first footnote in the financial statements describes significant accounting policies.

Extraordinary Items

When we analyze the performance of a firm, we focus on the bottom line: net income. Alas, there is not one bottom line, but two: net income *before* extraordinary items and net income *after* extraordinary items. ***Extraordinary items*** are nonrecurring, so we do not expect them again. But they did affect past cash flows. So which bottom line do we look at?

We really should look attentively at each extraordinary item. The extraordinary items tell us about past decisions by management, such as disposal of assets and settlements of large law suits.

This is important information in analyzing a firm. But it's not important when we are trying to use past information to make predictions about the future. The trend of profitability should be based on net income *before* extraordinary items. That is what represents the ability of a firm to generate earnings and, hence, future cash flows.

Classification of "Fuzzy" Items

Several items in the financial statements are difficult to classify. For example, a firm may have deferred taxes. Does this represent debt or equity? It depends. If there are permanent differences between taxes expensed in the financial statements and taxes payable to the government, then deferred taxes represent equity. If deferred taxes arise from temporary differences, then they represent a liability and should be included in our analysis of financial leverage as an obligation. For a given firm, deferred taxes may be composed of both permanent and temporary differences; so we should (if we had sufficient information) allocate a portion to liabilities and a portion to equity.

There are many other "fuzzy" items that challenge or defy classification, including operating leases, investment income, pension obligations, and foreign currency futures contracts. What to do with "fuzzy" items depends on the firm's particular situation and may require examining footnotes and digging deeper into the analysis of the firm.

Using a Benchmark

To interpret a firm's financial ratios we need to compare them with the ratios of other firms in the industry since these other firms are in a similar line of business and face some of the same market pressures—for example, competition in the input and output markets—as the firm we are evaluating.

But finding the appropriate comparable firms is difficult for many large firms that have operations spanning many different lines of business. For example, in 1991, the Walt Disney Company received 46 percent of its revenues from its theme parks and 42 percent from film entertainment. Looking at its asset investments, we can see that 46 percent of its assets are identified with its theme park and only 6 percent with its film entertainment. In what industry do we classify the Walt Disney Company? What are the comparable companies? It is not always clear. In the case of Disney, there are no companies with the same *mix* of lines of business, so we end up comparing it with similar companies, such as Time Warner, that are in the same lines of business—amusements and film entertainment—but with different revenue and asset mixes.

Suppose we find a comparable firm or set of firms. The average ratios of these comparable firms do not necessarily constitute a good benchmark. Finding that a firm is about average is not necessarily the same as saying that it is doing well. A better comparison is with those firms that are in similar lines of business and are also industry leaders.

Selecting and Interpreting Ratios

It is difficult to say whether a comparison is good or bad. Suppose we find a firm has a current ratio greater than the industry leaders. This could mean the firm is more liquid than the others; so there is less risk that it cannot meet its near-term obligations. But it may also mean that the company is tying up its assets in low- or no-earning assets, which reduces its profitability.

Since ratios cannot be viewed in isolation, we need to look at several different characteristics of a firm *at the same time* in order to make judgments regarding its operating performance and financial condition. Statistical models have been developed that incorporate several aspects of a firm's operating performance and financial conditions at the same time in order to make assessments of a firm's creditworthiness. With the help of computers, these models enable us to translate financial ratios into meaningful measures.

Another issue of interpretation is the appropriateness of particular ratios to the firm. Consider an electric utility whose sole line of business is generating electricity. The only inventory that such a utility has on hand will be nuts, bolts, and a few spare parts—which do not amount to much. Calculating an inventory turnover doesn't make sense for this type of firm—and any attempts to do so will result in an absurd inventory turnover, perhaps over 2,000 times! The selection of ratios must make sense for the firm being analyzed.[7]

Still another issue is trying to make sense out of ratios that are out of reasonable bounds. Suppose a firm has a loss, that is, net income is negative. If we calculate a P/E ratio for this firm, we arrive at a negative value. Does a negative P/E ratio make sense? No; we cannot interpret a negative P/E.

As another example, consider a firm that has a negative book value of equity—it can happen.[8] If we calculate its total debt-to-assets ratio, we get a value greater than 1.0, meaning that more than 100 percent of the firm's assets are financed with debt! In this case, some other ratio—say, total debt-to-market-value of equity—should be used instead.

Forecasting

Methods of Forecasting

One goal in financial analysis is to forecast future cash flows. Using past financial data in conjunction with other information about the economy, the industry, and the company itself, we can look at trends in operating performance and financial condition to forecast the future.

To see how we use these trends, let's look at Wal-Mart, specifically its sales over the period 1971–1990, shown in Figure 4-10. Sales have increased dramatically over this period of time. Where are they heading? If we look at sales over the period and continue their path into the future, we see that if Wal-Mart's sales continued to grow at a rate of 37.39 percent per year—the average growth rate over the twenty years, 1991 sales would be $44,792 million. Wal-Mart's actual sales for 1991 were $43,887 million—almost $1 billion less than expected if we had simply extrapolated from prior years' sales.

In addition to extrapolating a particular item or ratio through time, we can also apply statistical methods to predict future items. Again, we are using past information to predict the future.

Can Wal-Mart continue to grow at such a pace? Considering the burgeoning competition, especially from traditionally nondiscount retailers, it may not be appropriate to extrapolate from the past. Rather, we should make a judgment about the future course of Wal-Mart, the economy, and the industry to forecast future sales. We would need to consider several items to make reasonable estimates about future sales:

- Forecasts about the economy (Wal-Mart seems to do well in recessions).

---

[7] Other examples of inappropriate ratios include: (1) accounts receivable turnover for a firm that doesn't extend credit, (2) inventory turnover for a service firm, and (3) return on fixed assets for a bank.

[8] A negative book value of equity can occur and results from the use of historical costs. In the late 1980s, a number of firms recapitalized—that is, made a wholesale change in the way they financed their assets—producing negative book values of equity.

FIGURE 4-10
Wal-Mart Sales,
1971–1990

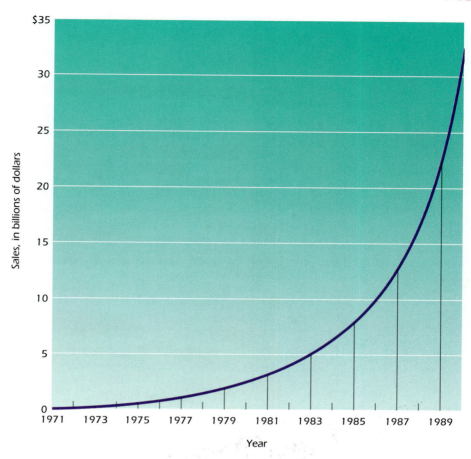

- Forecasts about competitiveness in the industry (no matter what the economy, consumers can only spend so much).
- Forecasts about Wal-Mart's intention to grow. (Do they intend to open more stores? Close any stores?)

Analysts' Forecasts

Many financial service firms offer projections on different aspects of a company's performance. The most commonly forecast financial ratio is future earnings per share, though projections of cash flows and stock prices are available. Examples of services that provide financial forecasting include:

- Standard & Poor's, *Earnings Forecaster.*
- Institutional Brokers Estimate System (I/B/E/S).
- Zacks Investment Research, Inc.
- Value Line's *Investment Survey.*

These financial service firms have access to a wealth of information on the economy, the industry, and individual firms.

SUMMARY

- Financial analysis is the basis for investment and financing decisions. The basic data for financial analysis are those in the financial statement. We use these data to analyze relationships between different elements of a firm's financial statements. Through this analysis, we develop a picture of the operating performance and financial condition of a firm.

- Looking at the calculated financial ratios, in conjunction with industry and economic data, we can make judgments about past and future financial performance and condition.

- We can classify ratios by type—coverage, return, turnover, or component percentage—or by the financial characteristic that we wish to measure—liquidity, profitability, activity, financial leverage, or return.

- Liquidity ratios tell us about a firm's ability to satisfy short-term obligations. These ratios are related closely to a firm's operating cycle, which tells us how long it takes a firm to turn its investment in current assets back into cash.

- Profitability ratios tell us how well a firm manages its assets, typically in terms of the proportion of revenues that are left over after expenses.

- Activity ratios tell us how efficiently a firm manages its assets, that is, how effectively a firm uses its assets to generate sales.

- Financial leverage ratios tell us (1) to what extent a firm uses debt to finance its operations and (2) its ability to satisfy debt and debtlike obligations.

- Return-on-investment ratios tell us how much of each dollar of an investment is generated in a period. The Du Pont System breaks down return ratios into their profit margin and activity ratios, allowing us to analyze changes in return on investments.

- Shareholder ratios represent financial data, such as earnings and dividends, on a per share basis.

- Common-size analysis expresses financial statement data relative to some benchmark item—usually total assets for the balance sheet and sales for the income statement. Representing financial data in this way allows us to spot trends in investments and profitability.

- Among the problems in using financial data are the composition of the accounting data, selection of benchmarks, interpretation of ratios, and forecasting of future performance or condition.

QUESTIONS

4-1 What is the relation between a firm's operating cycle and its need for liquidity?

4-2 Why is inventory removed from assets available to cover current liabilities in the calculation of the quick ratio?

4-3 Suppose you calculate the following ratios for two firms, A and B.

	Firm A	Firm B
Current ratio	2.0	2.0
Quick ratio	1.0	1.5

What can you say about their relative investment in inventory?

4-4 Suppose you are comparing two firms that are in the same line of business. Firm C has an operating cycle of 40 days, and D has an operating cycle of 60 days. Firm C has a current ratio of 3, and D has a current ratio of 2.5. Comment on the liquidity of the two firms. Which firm has more risk of not satisfying its near-term obligations? Why?

4-5 A rule of thumb in financial analysis is that a current ratio of 2 is adequate.
  a. If this is so, how much could a firm's current assets shrink and still be sufficient to satisfy current obligations?
  b. Explain how a current ratio of 2 may be inadequate to meet current obligations.
  c. Explain how a current ratio of 2 may be more than sufficient to meet current obligations.

4-6 Suppose you calculate an inventory turnover for the Rapid Corporation of three times.
  a. Explain why a high turnover may be seen as favorable information about the management of the firm.
  b. Explain why a low turnover may be seen as unfavorable information about the management of the firm.
  c. Explain how you would determine whether Rapid's inventory turnover indicates good operating performance.

4-7 Suppose you calculate a return on fixed assets of 20 percent for 1992 and 15 percent for 1993 for a company. Explain how you would use the Du Pont System to further investigate this change in the return on fixed assets.

4-8 Suppose you must select ratios to evaluate the returns on assets of a manufacturing firm. Which ratios would you select? Why?

4-9 Suppose you must select ratios to evaluate the returns on assets of an airline. Which ratios would you select? Why?

4-10 In examining the trend of returns on assets over a twenty-year period for a firm, you find that the returns have been declining gradually over this period. What information would you look at to further explain this trend?

4-11 In preparing your financial ratio analysis of a firm, your supervisor has suggested you add another ratio:

$$\text{Working capital-to-assets ratio} = \frac{\text{net working capital}}{\text{total assets}}$$

where net working capital is the difference between current assets and current liabilities.

  a. What type of ratio is this: coverage, return, turnover, or component percentage?
  b. What financial characteristic of a firm does this ratio capture?
  c. Suppose you calculated a value of 10 percent for this ratio. What does that mean?

PROBLEMS

Problems 4-1 and 4-2 use data provided for the Ray Shio Corporation.

4-1 Calculate the following ratios for the Ray Shio Corporation:
  a. Current ratio
  b. Quick ratio
  c. Inventory turnover ratio
  d. Total asset turnover ratio
  e. Gross profit margin
  f. Operating profit margin
  g. Net profit margin

Ray Shio Corporation
Balance Sheet
As of December 31, 1993
In millions

Cash	$ 100	Accounts payable	$ 300
Marketable securities	300	Other current liabilities	200
Accounts receivable	600	Long-term debt	500
Inventory	1,000	Common stock	2,000
Net plant and equipment	4,000	Retained earnings	3,000
Total assets	$6,000	Total liabilities and equity	$6,000

Fixed charge coverage ratio (definition 2)

$$= \frac{\text{earnings before interest and taxes} + \text{lease expense}}{\text{interest expense} + \text{lease expense} + \dfrac{\text{sinking fund payment} + \text{preferred dividends}}{(1 - \text{tax rate})}}$$

[4-29] Coverage ratio

Cash flow interest coverage ratio

$$= \frac{\text{cash flow from operations} + \text{interest} + \text{taxes}}{\text{interest}}$$

[4-30] Coverage ratio

FINANCIAL CHARACTERISTIC: RETURN ON INVESTMENT

Return on assets (definition 1)

$$= \frac{\text{earnings before interest and taxes}}{\text{total assets}}$$

[4-31] Return ratio

Return on assets (definition 2)

$$= \frac{\text{net income}}{\text{total assets}}$$

[4-32] Return ratio

Return on equity

$$= \frac{\text{net income}}{\text{book value of shareholders' equity}}$$

[4-33] Return ratio

Return on common equity

$$= \frac{\text{earnings available to common shareholders}}{\text{book value of common equity}}$$

[4-34] Return ratio

FINANCIAL CHARACTERISTIC: SHAREHOLDER RATIO

Earnings per share

$$= \frac{\text{earnings available to owners}}{\text{number of common shares outstanding}}$$

[4-37] Per share

Book value of equity per share

$$= \frac{\text{book value of common shareholders' equity}}{\text{number of common shares outstanding}}$$

[4-38] Per share

Price-earnings ratio

$$= \frac{\text{market price per share}}{\text{earnings per share}}$$

[4-39] Per share

Dividends per share

$$= \frac{\text{dividends}}{\text{number of common shares outstanding}}$$

[4-40] Per share

Dividend payout ratio

$$= \frac{\text{dividends}}{\text{earnings available to common shareholders}}$$

[4-41] Component percentage

TABLE 4A-2
Summary of Financial Ratios Applied to Fictitious Corporation, 1994 and 1995

	1995		1994	
LIQUIDITY RATIOS				
Average day's cost of goods sold	$\dfrac{\$6,500,000}{365 \text{ days}}$	$= \$17,808$	$\dfrac{\$6,000,000}{365}$	$= \$16,438$
Number of days of inventory	$\dfrac{\$1,800,000}{\$17,808}$	$= 101 \text{ days}$	$\dfrac{\$1,000,000}{\$16,438}$	$= 61 \text{ days}$
Credit sales per day	$\dfrac{\$10,000,000}{365 \text{ days}}$	$= \$27,397$	$\dfrac{\$9,000,000}{365}$	$= \$24,658$
Number of days of credit	$\dfrac{\$600,000}{\$27,397}$	$= 22 \text{ days}$	$\dfrac{\$800,000}{\$24,659}$	$= 32 \text{ days}$
Operating cycle	$101 \text{ days} + 22 \text{ days}$	$= 123 \text{ days}$	$61 \text{ days} + 32 \text{ days}$	$= 93 \text{ days}$
Average day's purchases	$\dfrac{\$6,500,000 - \$1,000,000}{365}$	$= \$15,068$	$\dfrac{\$5,000,000}{365}$	$= \$13,699$
Number of days of purchases	$\dfrac{\$500,000}{\$15,068}$	$= 33 \text{ days}$	$\dfrac{\$400,000}{\$13,699}$	$= 29 \text{ days}$
Net operating cycle	$101 \text{ days} + 22 \text{ days} - 33 \text{ days} = 90 \text{ days}$		$61 \text{ days} + 32 \text{ days} - 29 \text{ days} = 64 \text{ days}$	
Current ratio	$\dfrac{\$3,000,000}{\$1,000,000}$	$= 3 \text{ times}$	$\dfrac{\$2,000,000}{\$600,000}$	$= 3.33 \text{ times}$
Quick ratio	$\dfrac{\$1,200,000}{\$1,000,000}$	$= 1.2 \text{ times}$	$\dfrac{\$1,000,000}{\$600,000}$	$= 1.67 \text{ times}$
Net working capital-to-sales ratio	$\dfrac{\$2,000,000}{\$10,000,000}$	$= 20.00\%$	$\dfrac{\$1,400,000}{\$9,000,000}$	$= 15.56\%$
PROFITABILITY RATIOS				
Gross profit margin	$\dfrac{\$3,500,000}{\$10,000,000}$	$= 35\%$	$\dfrac{\$3,000,000}{\$9,000,000}$	$= 33\%$
Operating profit margin	$\dfrac{\$2,000,000}{\$10,000,000}$	$= 20\%$	$\dfrac{\$2,000,000}{\$9,000,000}$	$= 22\%$
Net profit margin	$\dfrac{\$1,200,000}{\$10,000,000}$	$= 12\%$	$\dfrac{\$1,000,000}{\$9,000,000}$	$= 11\%$

ACTIVITY RATIOS

Inventory turnover ratio	$\dfrac{\$6,500,000}{\$1,800,000}$ = 3.61 times	$\dfrac{\$6,000,000}{\$1,000,000}$ = 6 times
Accounts receivable turnover ratio	$\dfrac{\$10,000,000}{\$600,000}$ = 16.67 times	$\dfrac{\$9,000,000}{\$800,000}$ = 11.25 times
Total asset turnover ratio	$\dfrac{\$10,000,000}{\$11,000,000}$ = 0.91 times	$\dfrac{\$9,000,000}{\$10,000,000}$ = 0.90 times
Fixed asset turnover ratio	$\dfrac{\$10,000,000}{\$7,000,000}$ = 1.43 times	$\dfrac{\$9,000,000}{\$7,000,000}$ = 1.29 times

FINANCIAL LEVERAGE RATIOS

Total debt-to-assets ratio	$\dfrac{\$5,000,000}{\$11,000,000}$ = 45.46%	$\dfrac{\$5,600,000}{\$10,000,000}$ = 56.00%
Long-term debt-to-assets ratio	$\dfrac{\$4,000,000}{\$11,000,000}$ = 36.36%	$\dfrac{\$5,000,000}{\$10,000,000}$ = 50.00%
Long-term debt-to-equity ratio (definition 1)	$\dfrac{\$4,000,000}{\$6,000,000}$ = 66.67%	$\dfrac{\$5,000,000}{\$4,400,000}$ = 113.64%
Long-term debt-to-equity ratio[a] (definition 2)	$\dfrac{\$4,000,000}{\$26,300,000}$ = 15.21%	$\dfrac{\$5,000,000}{\$21,500,000}$ = 23.26%
Interest coverage ratio	$\dfrac{\$2,000,000}{\$400,000}$ = 5 times	$\dfrac{\$2,000,000}{\$500,000}$ = 4 times
Fixed charge coverage ratio (definition 1)	$\dfrac{\$3,000,000}{\$1,400,000}$ = 2.14 times	$\dfrac{\$2,500,000}{\$1,000,000}$ = 2.5 times
Fixed charge coverage ratio (definition 2)	$\dfrac{\$3,000,000}{\$2,066,667}$ = 1.45 times	$\dfrac{\$2,500,000}{\$1,900,000}$ = 1.32 times
Cash flow interest coverage ratio	$\dfrac{\$2,600,000}{\$400,000}$ = 6.5 times	$\dfrac{\$2,800,000}{\$500,000}$ = 5.6 times

(*Continued*)

TABLE 4A-2
Summary of Financial Ratios Applied to Fictitious Corporation, 1994 and 1995 *(Continued)*

	1995		1994	
RETURN RATIOS				
Return on assets (definition 1)	$\dfrac{\$2,000,000}{\$11,000,000}$	= 18.18%	$\dfrac{\$2,000,000}{\$10,000,000}$	= 20.00%
Return on assets (definition 2)	$\dfrac{\$1,200,000}{\$11,000,000}$	= 10.91%	$\dfrac{\$1,000,000}{\$10,000,000}$	= 10.00%
Return on equity	$\dfrac{\$1,200,000}{\$6,000,000}$	= 20.00%	$\dfrac{\$1,000,000}{\$4,400,000}$	= 22.73%
Return on common equity	$\dfrac{\$1,100,000}{\$5,200,000}$	= 21.15%	$\dfrac{\$900,000}{\$3,600,000}$	= 25.00%
SHAREHOLDER RATIOS				
Earnings per share	$\dfrac{\$1,100,000}{1,500,000 \text{ shares}}$	= $0.73 per share	$\dfrac{\$900,000}{1,200,000 \text{ shares}}$	= $0.75 per share
Book value of equity per share	$\dfrac{\$5,200,000}{1,500,000 \text{ shares}}$	= $3.47 per share	$\dfrac{\$3,600,000}{1,200,000 \text{ shares}}$	= $3.00 per share
Price-earnings ratio	$\dfrac{\$17.00}{\$0.73}$	= 23.29 times	$\dfrac{\$17.00}{\$3.00}$	= 5.67 times
Dividends per share	$\dfrac{\$500,000}{1,500,000 \text{ shares}}$	= $0.33 per share	$\dfrac{\$400,000}{1,200,000 \text{ shares}}$	= $0.33 per share
Dividend payout ratio	$\dfrac{\$500,000}{\$1,100,000}$	= 45.46%	$\dfrac{\$400,000}{\$900,000}$	= 44.44%

[a]Assuming a market price per share of common stock of $17 in 1995 and $17.25 in 1994, and a market price per share of preferred stock of $100 in both 1995 and 1994.

Sources of Financial Data and Analyses

Accounting data

Individual firm's annual reports and 10-K statements.

MOODY'S, *Handbook of Common Stocks.*

——— , *Industrial Manual.*

——— , *Banking and Finance Manual.*

——— , *OTC Manual.*

STANDARD & POOR'S, *Compustat PC Plus* (from S&P's Compustat Services Inc; available on CD-ROM).

——— , *Corporation Records.*

——— , *Stock Reports.*

——— , *Stock Market Encyclopedia of the S&P 500.*

VALUE LINE INC., *Value Line Investment Survey.*

Industry data

DUN & BRADSTREET, *Key Business Ratios.*

ROBERT MORRIS ASSOCIATES (Philadelphia, Pennsylvania), *RMA Annual Statement Studies.*

STANDARD & POOR'S, *Compustat PC Plus* (from S&P's Compustat Services, Inc.; available on CD-ROM).

——— , *Industry Survey.*

——— , *Statistical Service.*

LEO TROY, *Almanac of Business and Industrial Financial Ratios,* Prentice-Hall, N.J.

U.S. BUREAU OF THE CENSUS, *Quarterly Financial Report for Manufacturing, Mining, and Trade Corporations.*

VALUE LINE, INC., *Value Line Investment Survey.*

WEISS RESEARCH INC., *Thrift Safety Directory.*

Economic and market data

CONFERENCE BOARD, *Statistical Bulletin.*

DOW JONES & CO., *Wall Street Journal.*

FEDERAL RESERVE BANK OF NEW YORK, *Federal Reserve Bulletin.*

INVESTOR'S DAILY INC., *Investor's Daily.*

STANDARD & POOR'S, *Statistical Service.*

PART III

Fundamentals of Valuation

5 Mathematics of Finance 166

6 Asset Valuation and Returns 228

7 Risk and Expected Return 287

Mathematics of Finance

INTRODUCTION 168

THE TIME VALUE OF MONEY 168

Translating a Present Value into Its Future Value 168

Translating a Value Backward in Time 171

Shortcuts: Compound and Discount Factor Tables 178

THE TIME VALUE OF A SERIES OF CASH FLOWS 181

Translating a Series of Values Forward in Time 181

Translating a Series of Values Back from the Future 188

Shortcuts: Annuities 189

Shortcuts: Tables of Annuity Factors 196

COMPLEXITIES IN THE TIME VALUE OF MONEY 198

Valuing a Perpetual Stream of Cash Flows 198

Valuing an Annuity Due 199

Valuing a Deferred Annuity 204

Determining the Unknown Interest Rate 207

Determining the Number of Compounding Periods 210

THE CALCULATION OF INTEREST RATES 213

The Annual Percentage Rate 213

Effective vs. Annualized Rates of Interest 214

Summary 218

Speeding Up Your Refund

Many tax preparers offer to file your tax return electronically to speed up your refund of federal income taxes—for a small fee. Filing electronically speeds up your refund by about four weeks. Is speeding up your refund worthwhile? It depends.

Suppose you are due a refund of $500 and your tax preparer charges $30 to file electronically. Suppose also that when you get the money you invest it to earn 5 percent per year. By paying $30, you get the use of this $500 four weeks sooner.

We know the cost of filing electronically: $30. What is the benefit? Having the use of the $500 four weeks sooner. This benefit amounts to the earnings on the $500 for four weeks (one thirteenth of a year):

$$\text{Earnings for four weeks on } \$500 = \$500 \times 5\% \times \frac{1}{13} = \$1.92$$

Is it worth it? Not if your refund is only $500 and the best you can do with your money is 5 percent.

How large a refund would you need to justify the $30 charge if you earn 5 percent on your money? In other words, how large a refund must you have so that the earnings on the refund over the four-week period will be equal to the $30 cost?

$$\text{Earnings for four weeks on refund} = \$30 = \text{Refund} \times 5\% \times \frac{1}{13}$$

Using algebra to solve for the refund, the refund would have to be $7,800!

Let's look at this from another direction. What would you have to earn on your money to justify the $30 charge if your refund is $500?

$$\text{Earnings for four weeks on refund} = \$30$$
$$= \$500 \times \frac{\text{return on}}{\text{investment}} \times \frac{1}{13}$$

Using algebra to solve for the return on investment, your return would have to be 78 percent per year!

Knowing a little about financial mathematics can help you make financing and investment decisions—even if they are personal finance decisions.

INTRODUCTION

Financial managers are expected to make decisions about whether, for example, to invest in a new product, to purchase securities with idle cash, to sell bonds to raise cash, or to acquire another company. In decisions like these, there is a value—the value it represents to the firm.

It would be simple to determine the value of a decision that involves making or receiving funds today or in the immediate future. But most financial transactions involve a number of payments or receipts that occur over many years. We refer to a series of payments or receipts as cash flows. Figuring out today's value of future (or even past) cash flows requires familiarity with financial mathematics.

To determine the value of financial transactions that occur over long periods, we must understand two things:

- Cash flows occurring at different points in time have different values relative to any one point in time.

   One dollar one year from now is not as valuable as one dollar today. After all, you can invest a dollar today and earn interest so that the value it grows to next year is *greater* than the one dollar today. This means we have to take into account the ***time value of money*** to quantify the relation between cash flows at different points in time.

- Cash flows are uncertain.

   Expected cash flows may not materialize. Uncertainty stems from the nature of forecasts of the timing or the amount of cash flows. We do not know for sure the timing, certainty, or amount of cash flows in the future. This uncertainty regarding future cash flows must somehow be taken into account in assessing the value of a financial decision.

Translating a cash flow into its future value is referred to as ***compounding***. Translating a future cash flow into its value in a prior period is referred to as ***discounting***. This chapter outlines the basic mathematical techniques used to translate the value of one or more cash flows from one period to another. The implications of uncertain cash flows are discussed in a later chapter.

THE TIME VALUE OF MONEY

Translating a Present Value into Its Future Value

If someone wants to borrow $100 from you today and promises to pay you back in one month, would you lend it? Would you consider the repayment of only the $100 to be fair? Probably not. There are two things to consider.

First, if you didn't lend the $100, what could you do with it? Perhaps you could have put it into a savings account and earned interest or simply bought pizzas. By lending the money, don't you forgo the possibility of earning interest or enjoying the pizzas?

Second, is there a chance that the borrower may not pay you back? If you kept the money under a mattress instead of lending it out, at least you could be sure that the $100 would be there at the end of the month. Are you sure that by lending the money you will get all of it back? Will you get it back exactly when promised?

So, when you consider lending money, you must consider the opportunity cost (what you could have earned or enjoyed) as well as the uncertainty associated with getting the money back as promised.

Let's say that you are willing to lend the money, but that you require repayment of the $100 plus some compensation for the opportunity cost *and* any uncertainty the loan will be paid as promised. The amount of the loan, the $100, is the ***principal.*** The compensation that you require for allowing someone else to use your $100 is the ***interest.***

Looking at this same situation in terms of time and value, the amount that you are willing to lend today is the loan's ***present value*** and the amount that you require to be paid at the end of the loan period is the loan's ***future value.*** A future period's value comprises two parts:

Future value = present value + interest

Interest is the compensation for the use of funds for a specific period. It consists of (1) compensation for the length of time the money is borrowed and (2) compensation for the risk that it will not be repaid exactly as promised.

Compensation for the time the money is borrowed is called the ***price of time.*** It is an opportunity cost—the cost of not having the funds available for any other use during that time. Compensation for risk is called the ***price of risk*** and is the reward for bearing risk.

To focus on the mathematics of the time value of money, we are going to lump together the price of time and of risk as the interest rate. We will worry about how these components of the interest rate are calculated in another chapter.

Of Interest

The word "interest" is derived from the Latin word *intereo,* which means "to be lost." The word "interest" developed from the concept that lending goods or money resulted in a loss to the lender since he or she did not have the use of the goods or money loaned.

In the English language, the word "usury" is associated with lending at excessive or illegal interest rates. In earlier times, however, usury (from the Latin *usura,* meaning "use") was the price paid for the use of money or goods.

Though "interest" and "usury" appear to have similar meanings, it is curious that there were restrictions on usury, but not interest. For example, the Bible states: "Thou shalt not lend upon usury to thy brother; usury of money, usury of victuals, usury of anything that is lent upon usury: unto a stranger thou mayest lend upon usury, but unto thy brother thou shalt not lend upon usury" (Deut. 23:19–20; ca. 650 B.C.).

You could lend to a stranger and profit, but you could not profit in a loan to a friend. This doctrine caused problems in commerce, since lenders could require compensation for the loss from lending (interest), but could not profit from the transaction otherwise.

If you place $1,000 into a savings account that promises to pay 10 percent interest per period, you would have $1,100 at the end of one period. This $1,100 consists of your principal (the amount of the original investment) and the interest, or return, on your investment (the $100). Let's label these values:

- $1,000 is the value today, or present value, PV.
- $1,100 is the value at the end of one period, or future value, FV.
- 10 percent is the rate at which interest is earned in one period, or interest rate, r.

To get to the future value from the present value:

$$FV = \quad PV \quad + (PV \times r)$$

$$\uparrow \qquad\qquad \uparrow$$

(Principal   Interest)

This is equivalent to:

$$FV = PV(1 + r)$$

In terms of our example,

$$FV = \$1,000 + (\$1,000 \times 0.10)$$
$$= \$1,000(1 + 0.10)$$
$$= \mathbf{\$1,100}$$

If you withdraw the $100 interest at the end of the period, you have the principal left to earn interest at the 10 percent rate. Whenever you do this, you earn **simple interest.** It is simple because it repeats itself in exactly the same way from one period to the next as long as you take out the interest at the end of each period and the principal remains the same.

If you leave both the principal and the interest on deposit at your savings and loan institution, you will earn interest on your interest, referred to as **compound interest.** Earning interest on interest is called compounding, since the balance at any time is a combination of the principal, interest on principal, and *interest on accumulated interest*. With compounding, the initial investment grows from one period to the next.

If you compound interest for one more period in our example, the original $1,000 grows to $1,210.00:

$$FV = \text{principal} \quad + \text{first-period interest} + \text{second-period interest}$$
$$= \$1,000.00 \ + (\$1,000.00 \times 0.10) \ + (\$1,100.00 \times 0.10)$$
$$= \$1,000.00 \ + \$100.00 \qquad\qquad + \$110.00$$
$$= \$1,000.00 \ + \$210.00$$
$$= \mathbf{\$1,210.00}$$

The present value of the investment is $1,000, the interest earned over two years is $210, and the future value of the investment after two years is $1,210.

The relation between the present value and future value after two periods, breaking out the second-period interest into interest on the principal and interest on interest, is:

$$FV = \quad PV \quad + \ (PV \times r) \ + \ (PV \times r) \ + \ (PV \times r \times r)$$

$$\uparrow \qquad\qquad \uparrow \qquad\qquad \uparrow \qquad\qquad \uparrow$$

Principal	First-period	Second-	Second-period
	interest on	period	interest on
	principal	interest on	first-period
		principal	interest

or, collecting the PVs from each term:

$$FV = PV(1 + 2r + r^2)$$

The Code of Hammurabi

Before money was coined, around 1000 B.C., grain and silver were used as mediums of exchange. If a farmer borrowed seeds from his neighbor, he had to repay this loan at harvest by giving his neighbor a like amount of seeds plus some additional seeds to compensate his neighbor for doing without the borrowed seeds.

The Code of Hammurabi, which governed commerce in the Babylonian period (1900–732 B.C.), specified the terms of credit. A lender of seeds could not demand repayment until after the harvest. Further, a lender could not require that the additional seeds be more than one-third of the original amount loaned. Therefore, there was a maximum interest of 33.3 percent on loans of grain.

But what if you lived in the city and needed to borrow? Silver was the medium of exchange for city dwellers. The rate of interest on loans of silver was 20 percent. A city dweller who borrowed silver for a specified time period had to repay, according to weight, the amount borrowed (the principal) plus 20 percent (the interest).

Borrowers were protected from unscrupulous lenders. All contracts involving interest had to be witnessed; otherwise, repayment was not necessary. In addition, if a lender required more than the legal maximum interest, repayment of the loan was not necessary.

Lenders were also protected. A lender could require the borrower to pledge his wife, children, house, or land. If the loan and interest were not paid as promised, the lender could take the property or require the servitude of the wife or children of the borrower for up to three years.

Applying a bit of elementary algebra (it's called factoring, as you may remember), we see that:

$$(1 + 2r + r^2) = (1 + r)(1 + r)$$

Therefore, the future value after two periods is:

$$FV = PV(1 + r)(1 + r) = PV(1 + r)^2$$

Let's see if using this equation produces the identical future value in our savings problem:

$$FV = \$1,000(1 + 0.10)^2 = \$1,000(1.10)^2$$
$$= \$1,000(1.21)$$
$$= \mathbf{\$1,210.00}$$

The balance in the account two years from now, $1,210, comprises three parts:

1. The principal, $1,000.
2. Interest on principal, $100 in the first period plus $100 in the second period.
3. Interest on interest, 10 percent of the first period's interest, or $10.

To determine the future value with compound interest for *more* than two periods, we follow along the same lines:

Future value after one period $= PV(1 + r)$
Future value after two periods $= PV(1 + r)^2$
Future value after three periods $= PV(1 + r)^3$

$$\cdot$$
$$\cdot$$
$$\cdot$$

Future value after ten periods $= PV(1 + r)^{10}$

$$\cdot$$
$$\cdot$$
$$\cdot$$

Future value after t periods $= PV(1 + r)^t$ [5-1]

The value of t is the number of **compounding periods,** where a compounding period is the unit of time after which interest is paid at the rate r[1]. The term $(1 + r)^t$ is referred to as the **compound factor.** It is the rate of exchange between present dollars and dollars t compounding periods into the future. Equation 5-1 is the **basic valuation equation**—the foundation of financial mathematics. It relates a value at one point in time to a value at another point in time, considering the compounding of interest.

The relation between present and future values for principal = $1,000 and interest = 10 percent per period through ten compounding periods is shown graphically in Figure 5-1. For example, the value of $1,000, earning interest at 10 percent per period, is $2,593.70 ten periods into the future:

$$FV = \$1,000(1 + 0.10)^{10}$$
$$= \$1,000(2.5937)$$
$$= \mathbf{\$2,593.70}$$

As you can see in this figure, the $2,593.70 balance in the account at the end of ten periods comprises three parts:

1. The principal, $1,000.
2. Interest on the principal of $1,000: $100 per period for 10 periods, which equals $1,000.
3. Interest on interest, totaling $593.70.

We can express the change in the value of our savings balance (the difference between the ending value and the beginning value) as a growth rate. A **growth rate** is the rate at which a value appreciates (a positive growth) or depreciates (a negative growth) over time. Our $1,000 grew at a rate of 10 percent per year over the ten-year period to $2,593.70. The average annual growth rate of our investment of $1,000 is 10 percent—the value of the savings account balance increased 10 percent per year.

---

[1] A period may be any length of time: a minute, a day, a month, a year. The important thing is to make sure the same compounding period is reflected throughout the problem being analyzed.

FIGURE 5-1

Growth in the Savings Account Balance over Ten-Year Period for $1,000 Deposited in an Account Today (End-of-Year 0) That Earns 10 Percent Interest Compounded per Year

How a $1,000 deposit earning 10 percent compounded interest per year grows over a period of ten years. Growth is from both the interest on the principal and the interest on the accumulated interest. The principal, $1,000, grows to $1,210 after two years, and to $2,593.70 after ten years.

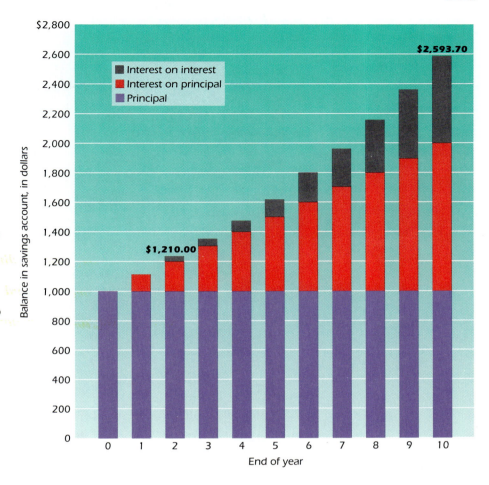

We could also express the appreciation in our savings balance in terms of a return. A ***return*** is the income on an investment, generally stated as a change in the value of the investment over each period divided by the amount of the investment at the beginning of the period. We could also say that our investment of $1,000 provides an average annual return of 10 percent per year.

As another example, suppose that Safety Savings and Loan promises to pay 2 percent interest compounded every six months. How much will a $100 deposit be worth after five years if there are no withdrawals during this five-year period? To determine this, we must recognize that:

- Present value is $100.
- Rate of interest is 2 percent per compounding period (six months).
- There are ten compounding periods in five years.

Therefore:

t = 10 periods
r = 2% or 0.02 per period
PV = $100

The Average Annual Return

The average annual return is *not* calculated by taking the change in value over the entire ten-year period ($2,593.70 − $1,000) and dividing it by $1,000. This would produce an **arithmetic average return** of 159.37 percent over the ten-year period, or 15.937 percent per year. The arithmetic average *ignores the process of compounding.*

The correct way of calculating the average annual return is to use a **geometric average return:**

$$\text{Return} = \sqrt[t]{\frac{FV}{PV}} - 1$$

which is a rearrangement of $FV = PV(1 + r)^t$. Using the values from the examples:

$$\text{Return} = \sqrt[10]{\frac{\$2,593.70}{\$1,000.00}} - 1.0000 = \left(\frac{\$2,593.70}{\$1,000.00}\right)^{1/10} - 1.0000$$

$$= 1.1000 - 1.0000 = \textbf{0.10 or 10\% per year}$$

Therefore, the annual return on the investment—sometimes referred to as the *compound average annual return* or the *true return* is 10 percent per year.

Using the basic valuation equation:

$$FV = \$100(1 + 0.02)^{10}$$
$$= \$100(1.2190)$$
$$= \textbf{\$121.90}$$

The compound factor in this example is 1.2190.

The growth of the savings account balance is shown in Figure 5-2. The value of the deposit at the end of five years (ten compounding periods) is $121.90: $100 of principal plus $21.90 of interest. The $21.90 of interest consists of $20.00 of interest on the principal ($2 for each of the ten compounding periods) and $1.90 of interest on interest.

Translating a Value Backward in Time

Suppose that for borrowing a specific amount of money today, the YENOM Company promises to pay lenders $5,000 in one year from today. How much are you willing to lend YENOM in exchange for this promise? This problem is different from that of figuring out a future value. Here we are given the future value and have to figure out the present value. But we can use the same basic ideas we applied in solving future value problems to solve present value ones.

If you can earn 10 percent on other investments that have the same amount of uncertainty as the $5,000 YENOM promises to pay, then:

- The future value, FV = $5,000.
- The number of compounding periods, t = 1.
- The interest rate, r = 10%.

174

FIGURE 5-2

Growth of Deposit in Safety Savings and Loan Account over Five–Year Period with 2 Percent Interest Compounded Every Six Months

How a deposit of $100 grows over a period of five years when interest is compounded at 2 percent every six months; the deposit grows to $121.90 after five years (that is, after ten six-month periods).

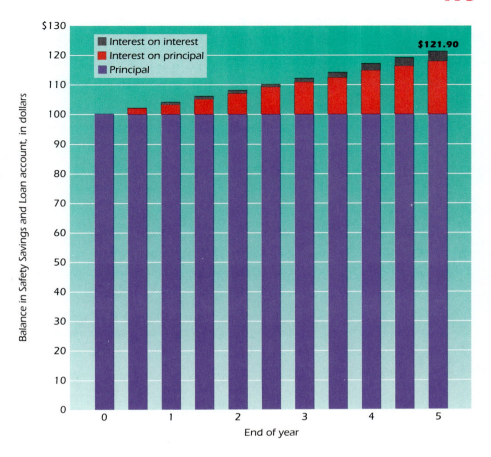

We also know the basic relation between the present and future values:

$$FV = PV(1 + r)^t$$

Substituting the known values into this equation:

$$\$5,000 = PV(1 + 0.10)^1$$

To determine how much you are willing to lend now, PV, to get $5,000 one year from now, FV, requires solving this equation for the unknown present value:

$$PV = \frac{\$5,000}{1 + 0.10} = \mathbf{\$4,545.45}$$

Therefore, you would be willing to lend $4,545.45 to receive $5,000 one year from today if your opportunity cost was 10 percent. We can check our calculations by reworking the problem from the reverse perspective. Suppose you invested $4,545.45, and it earned 10 percent over a year. What is the value of this investment at the end of the year?

We know:

PV = $4,545.45
r = 10% or 0.10
t = 1

Therefore the future value is:

$$FV = PV(1 + r)^t$$
$$= \$4{,}545.45(1 + 0.10)^1$$
$$= \mathbf{\$5{,}000.00}$$

Compounding translates a value at one point in time into a value at some future point in time. The opposite process, discounting, translates future values into present values. From the basic valuation equation:

$$FV = PV(1 + r)$$

we divide both sides by $1 + r$ and exchange sides to get the present value:

$$PV = \frac{FV}{1 + r} \quad \text{or} \quad PV = FV\left(\frac{1}{1 + r}\right)$$

The term $1/(1 + r)$ is referred to as the ***discount factor***, since it is used to translate a future (higher) value into its equivalent (lower) present value.

Suppose we wish to have $1,050 in a savings account at the end of one year. If the promised interest is 5 percent per year, to be paid at the end of the year, how much do we need to deposit at the beginning of the year?

$$PV = FV\left(\frac{1}{1 + r}\right)$$
$$= FV\left(\frac{1}{1 + 0.05}\right)$$
$$= \$1{,}050(0.9524)$$
$$= \mathbf{\$1{,}000}$$

To have $1,050 at the end of one year at a 5 percent annual interest rate, we need to deposit $1,000 today.

Discounting can be extended over more than one period in the same way we discounted a value over one period. What would you have to deposit today to have a balance of $1,050 two years from today if interest is compounded at 5 percent per year? We already know from the preceding calculation that we must have $1,000 *one* year from today to produce $1,050 *two* years from today. Backing up one more year:

$$PV = FV\left(\frac{1}{1 + 0.05}\right)$$
$$= \$1{,}000(0.9524)$$
$$= \mathbf{\$952.40}$$

Therefore, you would need to deposit $952.40 today at 5 percent per year to have $1,050.00 two years from today.

The discounting process for two years therefore consists of discounting a value from the end of the second period to the end of the first period, and then discounting that value from the end of the first period to the present:

Cutting Down on Steps

It is also possible to calculate the present value over two periods by multiplying the future value by the product of two one-period discount factors:

$$PV = \$1,050(0.9524)(0.9524)$$
$$= \$1,050(0.9071)$$
$$= \mathbf{\$952.42}$$

You will notice in this case, and as in other problems, that there are small numerical differences (in this case 2 cents) in answers when approaching the problem different ways. This is due to rounding differences. These small differences also pop up using different calculators or calculator settings. If these differences are small there is no need to worry.

What's small? It depends on the scale of the problem. One rule of thumb in time-value-of-money problems: If you are within 0.01 percent of the other answer, that's close enough.

$$PV = FV\left(\frac{1}{1+r}\right) \quad \times \quad \left(\frac{1}{1+r}\right)$$

Present value at the end of the first period

Discount factor to discount end-of-first-year value to today's value

or

$$PV = FV\left(\frac{1}{1+r}\right)^2$$

If we want to discount a value for three periods, we follow the same process:

$$PV = FV\left(\frac{1}{1+r}\right) \quad \times \quad \left(\frac{1}{1+r}\right) \quad \times \quad \left(\frac{1}{1+r}\right)$$

Present value at the end of the second period

Discount factor to discount end-of-second-period value to end-of-first-period value

Discount factor to discount end-of-first-period value to today's value

177

or

$$PV = FV\left(\frac{1}{1+r}\right)^3$$

Discounting further follows the same pattern:

Present value, discounting one period $= FV\left(\frac{1}{1+r}\right)$

Present value, discounting two periods $= FV\left(\frac{1}{1+r}\right)^2$

Present value, discounting three periods $= FV\left(\frac{1}{1+r}\right)^3$

$$\vdots$$

Present value, discounting ten periods $= FV\left(\frac{1}{1+r}\right)^{10}$

$$\vdots$$

Present value, discounting t periods $= FV\left(\frac{1}{1+r}\right)^t$

What If There Were No Interest?

Looking at Equation 5-2, we see that if the interest rate is zero, the discount factor is 1.0 and the present value is equal to the future value. From 5-2 we also see that present values are smaller than future values as long as there is an interest rate (that is, r > 0 percent). Further, the larger the number of compounding periods (that is, the larger is t), the smaller are the present values relative to the future values.

Note that the present value equation is a rearrangement of the basic valuation equation for future value:

$$PV = FV\left(\frac{1}{1+r}\right)^t = FV\frac{1}{(1+r)^t} = \frac{FV}{(1+r)^t} \qquad [5\text{-}2]$$

The relation between present values and future values for this example is shown in Figure 5-3. The present values of $1,050 for discounting periods from 1 to 10 are shown in this figure using an interest rate of 5 percent per period. For example, $1,050 discounted for *five* periods at 5 percent is $822.70:

$$PV = \$1,050\left(\frac{1}{1+0.05}\right)^5$$

$$= \$1,050(0.7835)$$

$$= \mathbf{\$822.70}$$

$1,050 received *ten* years from now is worth $644.61 today if interest is paid at a rate of 5 percent per period:

$$PV = \$1,050\left(\frac{1}{1+0.05}\right)^{10}$$

$$= \$1,050(0.6139)$$

$$= \mathbf{\$644.61}$$

Shortcuts: Compound and Discount Factor Tables

There are different ways to translate values forward and backward in time. The basic way is through Equations 5-1 or 5-2, using whichever values of PV, FV, t, or r are given and solving for the present or future value required by the problem.

FIGURE 5-3

Present Value of $1,050 Discounted up to Ten Periods of a 5 Percent Compound Interest Rate per Period

Discounting $1,050 five periods results in a present value of $822.70; discounting the $1,050 for ten periods results in a present value of $644.61.

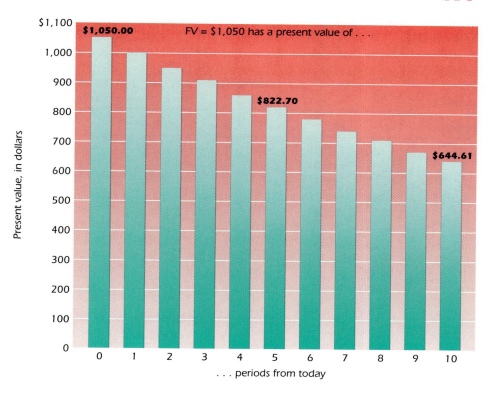

Another way is to use tables of discount and compound factors. A table of compound factors for periods ranging from 1 to 40 and for rates of interest from 1 percent to 40 percent is provided in Table B-1 in Appendix B, at the back of this book. Similarly, Table B-2 provides discount factors for the same range of periods and interest rates. The compound factor to use for a problem is determined by choosing the value in the table that corresponds to the row for the number of periods and the column for the interest rate per period given in the problem. A discount factor is determined in like manner.

In Table 5-1, a portion of Table B-1 is shown in panel *a* and a portion of Table B-2 is shown in panel *b*. To see how to use Table B-1, let's find the compound factors for several combinations of periods and interest rates. The compound factor for ten periods and an interest rate of 5 percent per period is 1.6289. The compound factor for five periods and an interest rate of 10 percent per period is 1.6105. The compound factor for three periods and an interest rate of 6 percent per period is 1.1910.

The table of compound factors can also be used for situations in which you need to determine the number of periods or the interest rate. For example, suppose that you are asked to find out how long it takes to double your money if the interest rate per period is 8 percent. Doubling your money would mean that the future value will be twice the present value. Using the equation:

$$FV = PV(1 + r)^t$$

TABLE 5-1

Portions of Compound and Discount Factor Tables, from Appendix B

(a) COMPOUND FACTORS (FROM TABLE B-1)

Number of periods, t	Interest rate per period, r									
	1%	2%	3%	4%	5%	6%	7%	8%	9%	10%
1	1.0100	1.0200	1.0300	1.0400	1.0500	1.0600	1.0700	1.0800	1.0900	1.1000
2	1.0201	1.0404	1.0609	1.0816	1.1025	1.1236	1.1449	1.1664	1.1881	1.2100
3	1.0303	1.0612	1.0927	1.1249	1.1576	1.1910	1.2250	1.2597	1.2950	1.3310
4	1.0406	1.0824	1.1255	1.1699	1.2155	1.2625	1.3108	1.3605	1.4116	1.4641
5	1.0510	1.1041	1.1593	1.2167	1.2763	1.3382	1.4026	1.4693	1.5386	1.6105
6	1.0615	1.1262	1.1941	1.2653	1.3401	1.4185	1.5007	1.5869	1.6771	1.7716
7	1.0721	1.1487	1.2299	1.3159	1.4071	1.5036	1.6058	1.7138	1.8280	1.9487
8	1.0829	1.1717	1.2668	1.3686	1.4775	1.5938	1.7182	1.8509	1.9926	2.1436
9	1.0937	1.1951	1.3048	1.4233	1.5513	1.6895	1.8385	1.9990	2.1719	2.3579
10	1.1046	1.2190	1.3439	1.4802	1.6289	1.7908	1.9672	2.1589	2.3674	2.5937

(b) DISCOUNT FACTORS (FROM TABLE B-2)

Number of periods, t	Interest rate per period, r									
	1%	2%	3%	4%	5%	6%	7%	8%	9%	10%
1	.9901	.9804	.9709	.9615	.9524	.9434	.9346	.9259	.9174	.9091
2	.9803	.9612	.9426	.9246	.9070	.8900	.8734	.8573	.8417	.8264
3	.9706	.9423	.9151	.8890	.8638	.8396	.8163	.7938	.7722	.7513
4	.9610	.9238	.8885	.8548	.8227	.7921	.7629	.7350	.7084	.6830
5	.9515	.9057	.8626	.8219	.7835	.7473	.7130	.6806	.6499	.6209
6	.9420	.8880	.8375	.7903	.7462	.7050	.6663	.6302	.5963	.5645
7	.9327	.8706	.8131	.7599	.7107	.6651	.6227	.5835	.5470	.5132
8	.9235	.8535	.7894	.7307	.6768	.6274	.5820	.5403	.5019	.4665
9	.9143	.8368	.7664	.7026	.6446	.5919	.5439	.5002	.4604	.4241
10	.9053	.8203	.7441	.6756	.6139	.5584	.5083	.4632	.4224	.3855

and inserting the known values:

$$\$2 = \$1(1 + 0.08)^t$$
$$2 = (1 + 0.08)^t$$

So, the compound factor for doubling your money at 8 percent per period over some unknown number of periods is 2. Looking down the 8 percent interest rate column in panel a, we see that the factor for nine periods is 1.9990. Therefore, it takes more than nine periods to double your money if interest is compounded at 8 percent per period. After nine periods, $1 is worth $1.999. After ten periods, $1 is worth $2.1589.

Consider another example. If you want to invest $1,000 for six periods, at what interest rate must the account pay compound interest in order for you to have $1,500 after six periods?

$$FV = PV(1 + r)^t$$
$$\$1,500 = \$1,000(1 + r)^6$$
$$1.5 = (1 + r)^6$$

Therefore, the compound factor is 1.5.

Using panel *a* of Table 5-1 and going across the row corresponding to six periods, we see that the compound factor is 1.5 at (approximately) a 7 percent interest rate. Therefore, if you save $1,000 in an account that provides compound interest at 7 percent per period, you will have a balance of approximately $1,500 after six periods.

To see how to use Table B-2, let's find the discount factors for several combinations of periods and interest rates in the panel *b* of Table 5-1. The discount factor for ten periods and an interest rate of 5 percent per period is 0.6139. The discount factor for five periods and an interest rate of 10 percent per period is 0.6209. The discount factor for three periods and an interest rate of 6 percent per period is 0.8396. Just as we did for the compound factors, we can use these discount factors to solve for t, given a value of the discount factor and an interest rate, or to solve for the interest rate, given the value for the discount factor and the number of discounting periods.

If we look at Equations 5-1 and 5-2 and think about them for a moment, it becomes apparent that inverting the values in one table produces the values in the other. For example, using the corresponding factors for t = 10 and r = 5 percent, we see this inverse relation:

$$\text{Compound factor} = \frac{1}{\text{discount factor}}$$

$$1.6289 = \frac{1}{0.6139}$$

Likewise,

$$\text{Discount factor} = \frac{1}{\text{compound factor}}$$

$$0.6139 = \frac{1}{1.6289}$$

The compound and discount factors are inversely related to one another for any pair of t and r values.

THE TIME VALUE OF A SERIES OF CASH FLOWS

Translating a Series of Values Forward in Time

Financial managers regularly need to determine the present or future value of a *series* of cash flows rather than simply a single cash flow. For example, we may want to determine the future value of a number of deposits made at different intervals of time or we may want to figure out the value of the lottery winnings we might hope to receive over the next twenty years. The principles for determining the future or present value of a series of cash flows are the same as for a single cash flow. The math becomes somewhat more cumbersome, however.

When the scenario includes multiple cash flows, we need to introduce additional notation to help us sort them out. Let CF_t represent the cash flow at the end of period t, where t is mathematical shorthand to mean any one of the periods. For example CF_1 is the cash flow at the end of the first period.

Is CF_t an inflow or an outflow? Well, that depends on the side of the deal that you are on. If you make deposits in an account in a savings and loan, CF_t represents cash outflows to you and cash inflows to the savings and loan.

The future value of a series of cash flows is the sum of the future values of each flow comprising the series. Suppose there are two deposits: $100 today, CF_0, and $100 one period from today, CF_1. If interest is earned at the rate of 4 percent per period, the future value of these deposits at the end of the second period is:

$$FV = [CF_0 + (CF_0 \times r) + (CF_0 \times r) + (CF_0 \times r \times r)] + [CF_1 + (CF_1 \times r)]$$

Value of first deposit at end of period 2   Value of second deposit at the end of period 2

$$= CF_0(1 + r)^2 + CF_1(1 + r)$$

Inserting the known values and solving for FV:

$$FV = \$100(1 + 0.04)^2 + \$100(1 + 0.04)$$
$$= \$100(1.0816) + \$100(1.0400)$$
$$= \$108.16 + \$104.00$$
$$= \mathbf{\$212.16}$$

The first deposit contributes $108.16 and the second contributes $104.00 to the future value of this series of two $100 cash flows.

As another example, suppose that the following deposits are made in a savings account paying 5 percent interest compounded annually:

Time at which deposit is made	Amount of deposit
Today	$1,000
At the end of the first year	2,000
At the end of the second year	1,500

What is the balance in the savings account at the end of the second year if no withdrawals are made and interest is paid annually?

Let's simplify any problems like this by referring to today as the end of period 0 and identifying the end of the first and each successive period as 1, 2, 3, and so on. Represent each end-of-period cash flow as CF with a subscript specifying the period to which it corresponds. Thus, CF_0 is a cash flow today, CF_{10} is a cash flow at the end of period 10, and CF_{25} is a cash flow at the end of period 25, and so on.

The Period 0

To describe a situation that involves values at different points in time, it is convenient to represent the points using some type of shorthand. To avoid becoming tangled in particular dates, we sometimes designate today as the end of period 0, and label the end of each period following as 1, 2, 3, and so on. So, the end of time period 0 could be March 3, 1979, or December 15, 1995, or any such date.

What we need to make sure of is that the periods are all of the same length of time; that is, the time from the end of period 0 to the end of period 1 must be the same length as the time from the end of period 1 to the end of period 2, and so on. This is important for the calculation of interest compounding, which is performed at the end of each period.

Representing the information in our example using cash flow and period notation:

Period	CF	End-of-period cash flow
0	CF_0	$1,000
1	CF_1	2,000
2	CF_2	1,500

The future value of the series of cash flows at the end of the second period is calculated as follows:

Period	End-of-period cash flow	Number of periods interest is earned	Compounding factor	Future value
0	$1,000	2	1.1025	$1,102.50
1	2,000	1	1.0500	2,100.00
2	1,500	0	1.0000	1,500.00
Future value of the series				**$4,702.50**

To see how we arrived at the future value of the series, let's look at the future value of today's cash flow of $1,000. At the end of two periods:

$$\text{Future value of today's cash flow} = \$1,000(1 + 0.05)^2$$
$$= \$1,000(1.1025)$$
$$= \mathbf{\$1,102.50}$$

The last cash flow, $1,500, was deposited at the very end of the second period, the point in time at which we wish to know the future value of the series. Therefore, this deposit earns no interest.[2] In more formal terms, its future value is precisely equal to its present value.

What we have just described can be illustrated in much the same way as in the diagram we used to portray future values and compounding earlier in this chapter. Series of cash flows and how they grow to their future value are illustrated graphically in Figure 5-4.

Today, the end of period 0, the balance in the account is $1,000, since the first deposit has been made but no interest has been earned. At the end of period 1, the balance in the account is $3,050, made up of three parts:

1. The first deposit, $1,000.
2. Interest of $50 on the first deposit.
3. The second deposit, $2,000.

---

[2] The compound factor is equal to 1 for this last cash flow. Using the basic valuation equation, if t is equal to zero, then $FV = PV(1 + r)^0$. Any value to the power of zero is equal to 1; therefore $FV = PV$ when the number of compounding periods is zero.

FIGURE 5-4

Illustration of the Growth in the Value of Three Deposits of $1,000, $2,000, and $1,500 (at End of Periods 0, 1, and 2, Respectively), That Earn 5 Percent Compound Interest Each Period

Deposits made at three different points in time contribute to the value of the account. The first deposit, $1,000, is made today (end of period 0); the second deposit, $2,000, is made at the end of period 1; and the third deposit, $1,500, is made at the end of period 2. The balance in the savings account grows from both the deposits and the interest on the balance in the account.

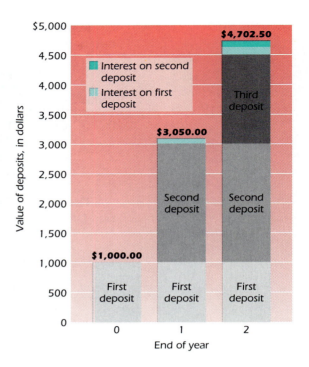

The balance in the account at the end of period 2 is $4,702.50, which is made up of five parts:

1. The first deposit, $1,000.
2. The second deposit, $2,000.
3. The third deposit, $1,500.
4. Interest of $102.50 on the first deposit, $50 earned at the end of the first period, and $52.50 more earned at the end of the second period.
5. Interest of $100 earned on the second deposit at the end of the second period.

These cash flows can also be represented in a time line. A **_time line_** is used to help graphically depict and sort out each cash flow in a series. The time line for this problem is shown in Figure 5-5. For example, you make a deposit of $1,000 today, at time 0. The initial deposit of $1,000 grows to $1,102.50 by the end of period 2, earning $50 interest on $1,000 in the first period and $52.50 interest on $1,050 in the second period. You also make deposits of $2,000 in period 1 and $1,500 in period 2. The period 1 deposit earns $100 in period 2. The balance in the account grows from $1,000.00 today to $3,050.00 at the end of the first period and to $4,702.50 at the end of the second period.

From this example, you can see that the future value of the entire series is the sum of each of the compounded cash flows comprising the series. In much the same way, we can determine the future value of a series comprising any number of cash flows. If we need to, we can also determine the future value of any number of cash flows before the end of the series (if there is any end).

FIGURE 5-5

Time Line for the Future Value of a Series of Uneven Cash Flows Deposited at 5 Percent Compound Interest per Period

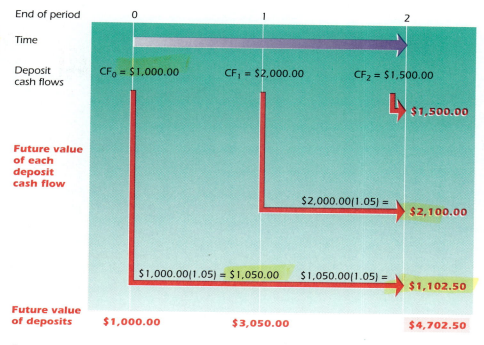

Breakdown of Future Value in Interest and Deposits

	Deposits and Interest	Future value at end of period 2
First deposit (CF$_0$) = deposit at time period 0	$1,000.00	
Interest in first period	50.00	
Interest in second period	52.50	
Future value of first deposit		$1,102.50
Second deposit (CF$_1$) = deposit at time period 1	2,000.00	
Interest in second period	100.00	
Future value of second deposit		2,100.00
Third deposit (CF$_2$) = future value of third deposit		1,500.00
Future value of all deposits		**$4,702.50**

For example, you're planning to deposit $1,000 today and at the end of each year for the next ten years on precisely the same date in a savings account paying 5 percent interest annually. If you want to know the future value of this series after four years, you compound each cash flow for the number of years it takes to reach four years. That is, you compound the first cash flow over four years, the second cash flow over three years, the third over two years, and the fourth over one year; you don't compound the fifth at all because you will have just deposited it in the bank at the end of the fourth year.

Suppose you want to know the future value of the series at the end of the sixth year. You compound the first cash flow over six years, the second over five years . . . Get the idea? But it need not be as tedious as it may seem. What helps alleviate the tedium is that the value of any series over any number of periods into the future may be represented in a form of mathematical shorthand. We simply have to be sure we know precisely what we mean by the notations used in the shorthand form.

Time Travel with Time Lines

A time line is a visual representation of cash flows and their values over time. In financial math, a time line is useful in depicting points in time at which there is a cash flow. Looking at the time line, we can see how each cash flow grows over time with compounding, or shrinks as it is brought back in time with discounting.

Consider the simple problem of calculating a future value at the end of three periods for a $1,000 deposit earning 10 percent interest compounded per period. Representing this on a time line:

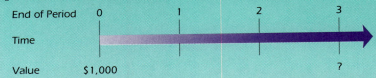

To depict the growth of the deposit, we can add the future values of the $1,000 deposit at the end of each of periods 1, 2, and 3 to the time line:

Or we can collapse the depiction of the value of the deposit at the end of each period as follows:

Keeping in mind the examples we just referred to, you should be able to see that the following equation can be used to find the future value of the cash flows after any period within any series of cash flows.

$$FV = CF_0(1 + r)^T + CF_1(1 + r)^{T-1} + CF_2(1 + r)^{T-2} + \cdots + CF_T(1 + r)^0$$

where T represents the number of periods into the series over which you want to determine the future value, and t = 1, 2, 3, ... , T. So if you want to know the future value of the series after four periods, then T = 4; if you want the value after eight periods, then T = 8.

Before proceeding, let's look at the last term in this general equation. Say a series comprises only three cash flows (three periods), each at the end of the period, and assume that you want to find the future value of the series at the end of the final period. Then the exponent in the last term of the general equation representing this series will be T − 3 or, substituting for T = 3, the exponent will be 3 − 3 = 0. In other words, a cash flow at the end of period

Summation Notation, Σ

When we are dealing with mathematical notation that tends to repeat itself somehow, we can represent it in shorthand form. If we have a series of items to add up, we can use notation to represent the summing of these items.

For example, let's say that we want to add together the following five present values: PV_1, PV_2, PV_3, PV_4, PV_5. We already know we can represent the sum of these values as:

$Sum = PV_1 + PV_2 + PV_3 + PV_4 + PV_5$

But there is a briefer way of representing the sum of any series like this one. This shorthand version uses the summation symbol Σ. All it means is "the sum of." So, we could actually write:

$Sum = \Sigma \ (PV_1, \ PV_2, \ PV_3, \ PV_4, \ and \ PV_5)$

A shorter version is $\Sigma \ PV_t$, where the subscript t is standard mathematical notation for $t = 1, 2, 3, 4, 5, 6, 7, \ldots$, up to infinity. But in this example, we are not looking for the sum of all PV terms up through infinity. So we need to indicate in this shorthand notation that we are adding up only the terms PV_1 through PV_5. We do this as follows:

$$Sum = \sum_{t=1}^{5} PV_t$$

where the "t=1" below the Σ symbol and the "5" above it means: Add up the PV terms from PV_1 through PV_5. Let's take a look at one more example.

Let's say that we want to represent the sum of only PV_2, PV_3, and PV_4. We can write this sum as:

$$Sum = \sum_{t=2}^{4} PV_t$$

Looking at the t=2, we know that the first term in the series to be summed is PV_2 and looking at the 4 above the Σ we know that we continue adding terms until we get to PV_4. The summation notation is the same as if we had written:

$$Sum = \sum_{t=2}^{4} PV_t = PV_2 + PV_3 + PV_4$$

Why bother with this shorthand notation? In complex situations, we can use summation notation to represent compactly the sum of a large number of items.

T is compounded zero periods or, more generally, is compounded $T - T = 0$ periods—meaning it is *not* compounded since interest is not yet earned on this final cash flow.

We can express the preceding equation even more succinctly using summation notation:

$$FV = \sum_{t=0}^{T} CF_t(1 + r)^{T-t} \tag{5-3}$$

Example: To represent the future value of a series of four cash flows that begin today and end after three years:

$$FV = \sum_{t=0}^{3} CF_t(1 + r)^{3-t} = CF_0(1 + r)^3 + CF_1(1 + r)^2 + CF_2(1 + r) + CF_3$$

Equation 5-3 tells us that the future value of a series of cash flows is the sum of the products of each cash flow and the corresponding compound factor for (T − t) periods.

If you still don't get the distinction between T and t, try to remember that in any cash flow series problem, t designates the number of periods a particular cash flow is compounded or discounted. When there is more than one cash flow in the discounting or compounding problem, we invoke T to indicate the entire length of time, which consists of a number of periods, t = 0, 1, 2, 3, … , T.

Translating a Series of Values Back from the Future

To determine the present value of a series of future cash flows, each cash flow is discounted back to the present, where the beginning of the first period, today, is designated as 0. As an example, in the series of cash flows of $1,000 today, $2,000 at the end of period 1, and $1,500 at the end of period 2, each cash flow is to be discounted to the present, the end of period 0, as follows:

Period	End-of-period cash flow	Number of periods of discounting	Discount factor at 5%	Present value of each cash flow
0	$1,000	0	1.0000	$1,000.00
1	2,000	1	0.9524	1,904.80
2	1,500	2	0.9070	1,360.50
	Total present value of series			$ 4,265.30

The present value of the series, $4,265.30, is the sum of the present value of the three cash flows. The time line representing this series and its present value is shown in Figure 5-6. For example, the $1,500 cash flow at the end of period 2 is worth $1,428.57 at the end of the first period and $1,360.50 today.[3]

The present value of a series of cash flows can be represented in notation form as:

$$PV = CF_0\left(\frac{1}{1 + r}\right)^0 + CF_1\left(\frac{1}{1 + r}\right)^1 + CF_2\left(\frac{1}{1 + r}\right)^2 + \cdots + CF_T\left(\frac{1}{1 + r}\right)^T$$

For example, if there are cash flows today and at the end of periods 1 and 2, today's cash flow is not discounted, the first-period cash flow is discounted one period, and the second-period cash flow is discounted two periods.

[3] Another way to look at this is to consider what the value of $1,360.50 at 5 percent per period would be after two periods. A deposit of $1,360.50 would grow to $1,500 after two periods by earning interest in the first period of $68.03 (= $1,360.50 × 0.05) and $71.43 [= ($1,360.50 + $68.03) × 0.05] in the second period.

FIGURE 5-6

Time Line for the Present Value of a Series of Uneven Cash Flows Deposited at 5 Percent Compound Interest per Period

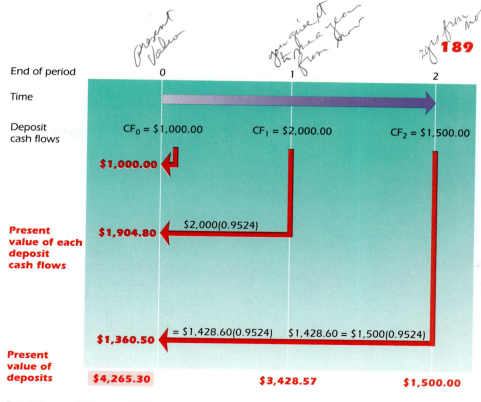

Breakdown of Present Value into Interest and Deposits

	Interest and deposits	Present value of deposits
CF_0 = Deposit at time period 0	$1,000.00	$1,000.00
CF_1 = Deposit at time period 1	2,000.00	
Interest in first period	−95.20	
Present value of period 1 deposit		1,904.80
CF_2 = Deposit at time period 2	1,500.00	
Interest in second period	−71.50	
Interest in first period	−68.00	
Present value of period 2 deposit		1,360.50
Present value of all deposits		**$4,265.30**

Representing the present value of a series using summation notation,

$$PV = \sum_{t=0}^{T} CF_t \left(\frac{1}{1+r} \right)^t \qquad \text{[5-4]}$$

Equation 5-4 tells us that the present value of a series of cash flows is the sum of the products of each cash flow and its corresponding discount factor.

Shortcuts: Annuities

Many finance problems require us to evaluate a series of level cash flows—each cash flow is the same amount as the others—received at regular intervals. Let's say you're saving money to buy a car. Suppose today is the last day of 1997. You don't have any money to deposit today, but you expect to deposit $2,000 at the end of each of the *next* four years (1998, 1999, 2000, and 2001) in an account earning 8 percent compound interest. How much will you have available to buy the car at the end of 2001, the fourth year?

As we just did for the future value of a series of uneven cash flows, we can calculate the future value (as of the end of 2001) of each $2,000 deposit, compounding interest at 8 percent:

$$
\begin{aligned}
FV &= \$2{,}000(1 + 0.08)^3 + \$2{,}000(1 + 0.08)^2 + \$2{,}000(1 + 0.08)^1 \\
&\quad + \$2{,}000(1 + 0.08)^0 \\
&= \$2{,}000(1.2597) + \$2{,}000(1.1664) + \$2{,}000(1.0800) + \$2{,}000(1.0000) \\
&= \$2{,}519.40 + \$2{,}332.80 + \$2{,}160.00 + \$2{,}000 \\
&= \mathbf{\$9{,}012.20}
\end{aligned}
$$

Figure 5-7 shows the contribution of each deposit and the accumulated interest at the end of each period.

- At the end of 1998, you would have $2,000.00 in the account since you have just made your first deposit.
- At the end of 1999, you would have $4,160.00 in the account: two deposits of $2,000 each plus $160 interest (8 percent of $2,000).
- At the end of 2000, you would have $6,492.80 in the account: three deposits of $2,000.00 each plus accumulated interest of $492.80, or [$160.00 + (0.08 × $4,000) + (0.08 × $160)].
- At the end of the fourth year, you would have $9,012.20 available to buy a car: four deposits of $2,000 each plus $1,012.20 accumulated interest, or [$160.00 + $492.80 + (0.08 × $6,000) + [0.08 × ($160.00 + 492.80)]].

Notice that in our calculations, each deposit of $2,000 is multiplied by a compound factor that corresponds to an interest rate of 8 percent and the

FIGURE 5-7

Growth in the Values of a Series of Deposits of $2,000 Each at the End of 1998, 1999, 2000, and 2001 at 8 Percent Compounded Interest per Period

Growth in the value of an account in which four deposits of $2,000 each are made at the end of 1998, 1999, 2000, and 2001. The balance in the account at the end of 2001 comprises the deposits (4 × $2,000 = $8,000) plus interest on the accumulated deposits ($1,012.20).

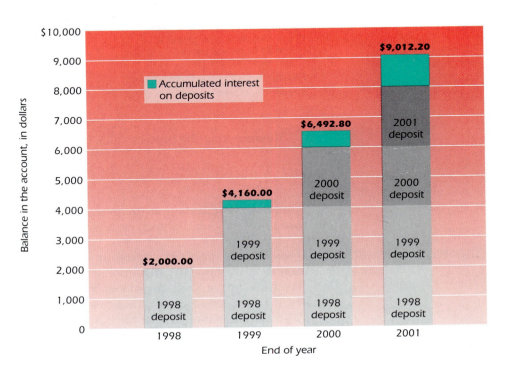

number of periods that the deposit has been in the savings account. Since the deposit of $2,000 is common to each multiplication, we can simplify the math somewhat by multiplying the $2,000 by the sum of the factors to get the same answer:

$$
\begin{aligned}
FV &= \$2{,}000(1.2597) + \$2{,}000(1.1664) + \$2{,}000(1.0800) + \$2{,}000(1.0000) \\
&= \$2{,}000(1.2597 + 1.1664 + 1.0800 + 1.0000) \\
&= \$2{,}000(4.5061) \\
&= \mathbf{\$9{,}012.20}
\end{aligned}
$$

A series of cash flows of equal amount, occurring at even intervals, is referred to as an ***annuity.*** Determining the value of an annuity, whether compounding it or discounting it, is not as cumbersome as valuing uneven cash flows. The arithmetic is simpler. If each CF_t is equal (that is, all the cash flows are the same in amount) *and* the first one occurs at the end of the first period ($t = 1$), we can express the future value of the series as:

$$
FV = \sum_{t=1}^{T} CF_t(1 + r)^{T-t}
$$

T is the last period—which in the case of an ordinary annuity is also the number of cash flows—and t indicates the time period corresponding to a particular cash flow, starting at 1 (not zero) for an ordinary annuity.

Since CF_t is shorthand for:

$$CF_1, CF_2, CF_3, \ldots , CF_T$$

and we know that $CF_1 = CF_2 = CF_3 \ldots = \ldots CF_T$, let's make things simple by using CF to indicate same-value periodic cash flows. Rearranging the future value equation:

$$
FV \quad = \quad CF \quad \times \quad \sum_{t=1}^{T} (1 + r)^{T-t} \tag{5-5}
$$

↑	↑	↑
Future value	Periodic cash flow	Sum of compound factors

This equation tells us that the future value of a level series of cash flows, occurring at regular intervals beginning one period from today (notice again that t starts at 1), is equal to the amount of cash flow multiplied by the sum of the compound factors.

In like manner, the equation for the present value of a series of level cash flows beginning after one period simplifies to:

$$
PV = \sum_{t=1}^{T} CF_t\left(\frac{1}{1 + r}\right)^{t}
$$

Using CF for level cash flows:

$$
PV = CF \sum_{t=1}^{T} \left(\frac{1}{1 + r}\right)^{t} = CF \sum_{t=1}^{T} \frac{1}{(1 + r)^{t}} \tag{5-6}
$$

This equation tells us that the present value of an annuity is equal to the amount of one cash flow multiplied by the sum of the discount factors.

Equations 5-5 and 5-6 are the valuation—future and present value—formulas for an **ordinary annuity.** An ordinary annuity is a special form of annuity, for which the first cash flow occurs *at the end of the first period*. Examples of ordinary annuities: If you take out a home mortgage, the first payment is not made immediately but at the end of the first month of the mortgage (that is, at the end of the first period). Many leasing arrangements are ordinary annuity contracts, for which the first lease payment is not due until the end of the first period.

To calculate the future value of an annuity we multiply the amount of the annuity (that is, the amount of one periodic cash flow) by the sum of compound factors. The sum of these factors for a given interest rate, r, and number of periods, T, is referred to as the **future value annuity factor.**

Likewise, to calculate the present value of an annuity we multiply one cash flow of the annuity by the sum of discount factors. The sum of the discounting factors for a given r and T is referred to as the **present value annuity factor.**

Let's demonstrate how using a sum of factors simplifies the calculations. Suppose you wish to determine the future value of a series of deposits of $1,000, to be made each year in the No Fault Vault Bank for five years, with the first deposit made at the end of the first year. If the NFV Bank pays 5 percent interest on the balance in the account at the end of each year and no withdrawals are made, what is the balance in the account at the end of the five years?

This problem is illustrated in Figure 5-8 with a time line indicating each of the five deposits. Each $1,000 is deposited at a different time; so it contributes a different amount to the future value. For example, the first deposit accumulates interest for four periods, contributing $1,215.50 to the future value (at the end of period 5), whereas the last deposit contributes only $1,000 to the future value since it is deposited at exactly the point in time at which we are determining the future value; hence, there is no interest on this deposit.

The future value of an annuity is the sum of the future value of each deposit:

Period	Amount of deposit	Number of periods interest is earned	Compound factor	Future value
1	$1,000	4	1.2155	$1,215.50
2	1,000	3	1.1576	1,157.60
3	1,000	2	1.1025	1,102.50
4	1,000	1	1.0500	1,050.00
5	1,000	0	1.0000	1,000.00
Total			**5.5256**	**$5,525.60**

The future value of the series of $1,000 deposits, with interest compounded at 5 percent, is $5,525.60. Since we know the amount of each level-period

FIGURE 5-8

Time Line for the Future Value of Five Periodic $1,000 Deposits, Earning 5 Percent Compound Interest in the No Fault Vault Bank

Each $1,000 deposit grows over time, earning 5 percent compound interest in each period in which the deposit is in the savings account. For example, the first deposit of $1,000 grows to $1,050.00 after one period (at the end of period 2), $1,102.50 after two periods (at the end of period 3), $1,157.60 after three periods (at the end of period 4), and $1,215.50 after four periods (at the end of period 5). The first deposit therefore contributes $1,215.50 of the $5,525.60 future value in the No Fault Vault Bank account at the end of period 5.

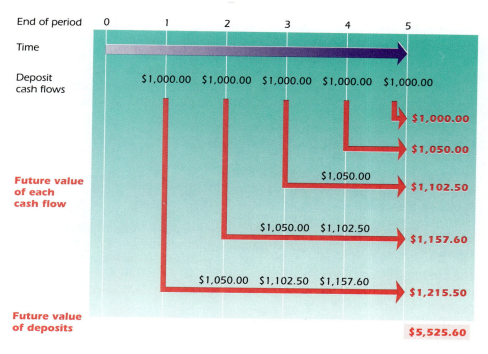

flow is $1,000, and the future value of the annuity is $5,525.60, and the sum of the individual compound factors is 5.5256, we should be getting the idea that maybe there is an easier way to calculate the future value of an annuity. If the sum of the individual compound factors for a specific interest rate and a specific number of periods were available, all we would have to do is multiply that sum by the value of one cash flow to get the future value of the entire annuity.

In this example, the shortcut is multiplying the amount of the annuity, $1,000, by the sum of the compound factors, 5.5256:

$$FV = \$1,000 \times 5.5256 = \mathbf{\$5,525.60}$$

For large numbers of periods, summing the individual factors can be a bit clumsy—with possibilities of errors along the way. An alternative formula for the sum of the compound factors—that is, the future value annuity factor—is:

$$\text{Future value annuity factor} = \frac{(1 + r)^T - 1}{r}$$

In the last example, T = 5 and r = 5 percent:

$$\text{Future value annuity factor} = \frac{(1 + 0.05)^5 - 1}{0.05}$$

$$= \frac{1.2763 - 1.0000}{0.05}$$

$$= 5.5256$$

Now let's use the long method to find the present value of the series of five deposits of $1,000 each, with the first deposit at the end of the first period. Then we'll do it using the shorter method. In Figure 5-9, we can see that the last deposit of $1,000 (end of period 5) is discounted five periods, contributing $783.50 to the present value. The calculations are similar to the fu-

FIGURE 5-9

Time Line for the Present Value of an Ordinary Annuity of $1,000 for Five Periods

The present value of each cash flow in a series of five deposits of $1,000 each, earning 5 percent compound interest per period. The last deposit (received at the end of period 5) is discounted over five periods, contributing $783.50 to the present value of the series today (end of period 0). This last deposit has a value of $952.40 at the end of period 4, $907.00 at the end of period 3, $863.80 at the end of period 2, $822.70 at the end of period 1, and finally $783.50 today.

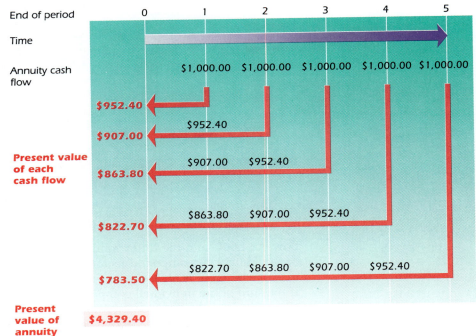

ture value of an ordinary annuity, except that we take each deposit back in time, instead of forward:

Period	Amount of deposit	Discounting periods	Discount factor	Present value
1	$1,000	1	0.9524	$ 952.40
2	1,000	2	0.9070	907.00
3	1,000	3	0.8638	863.80
4	1,000	4	0.8227	822.70
5	1,000	5	0.7835	783.50
Total			**4.3294**	**$4,329.40**

The present value of this series of five deposits is $4,329.40.

This same value is obtained by multiplying the annuity amount of $1,000 by the sum of the discount factors, 4.3294:

$$PV = \$1,000 \times 4.3294 = \textbf{\$4,329.40}$$

Another, more convenient way of solving for the present value of an annuity is to rewrite the factor as:

$$\text{Present value annuity factor} = \frac{1 - \dfrac{1}{(1 + r)^T}}{r}$$

This formula for the present value annuity factor is somewhat easier in terms of computations if there are many discount periods. In our last example,

$$\text{Present value annuity factor} = \frac{1 - \dfrac{1}{(1 + 0.05)^5}}{0.05} = \frac{1 - 0.7835}{0.05} = \textbf{4.3295}$$

which is different from the sum of the factors, 4.3294, due to rounding.

We can turn the problem of finding the present value of an annuity problem around to look at it from another angle. Suppose you borrow $4,329.40 at an interest rate of 5 percent per period and are required to pay back this loan in five installments ($T = 5$): one payment per period for five periods, starting one period from now. The payments are determined by equating the present value with the product of the cash flow and the sum of the discount factors:

$$PV = CF(\text{sum of discount factors})$$

$$= CF\left[\sum_{t=1}^{5}\left(\frac{1}{1 + 0.05}\right)^t\right]$$

$$= CF(0.9524 + 0.9070 + 0.8638 + 0.8227 + 0.7835)$$

$$= CF(4.3294)$$

substituting the known present value,

$$\$4,329.40 = CF(4.3294)$$

and rearranging to solve for the payment:

$$CF = \frac{\$4{,}329.40}{4.3294} = \mathbf{\$1{,}000.00}$$

We can convince ourselves that five installments of $1,000 each can pay off the loan of $4,329.40 by carefully stepping through the calculation of interest and the reduction of the principal:

Beginning-of-period loan balance	Payment	Interest (principal × 5%)	Reduction in loan balance (payment − interest)	End-of-period loan balance
$4,329.40	$1,000.00	$216.47	$783.53	$3,545.87
3,545.87	1,000.00	177.29	822.71	2,723.16
2,723.16	1,000.00	136.16	863.84	1,859.32
1,859.32	1,000.00	92.97	907.03	952.29
952.29	1,000.00	47.61	952.29[a]	0.00

[a]Small difference between calculated reduction ($952.38) and reported reduction, due to rounding differences.

For example, the first payment of $1,000 is used to (1) pay interest on the loan at 5%, that is, $4,329.40 × 0.05 = $216.47, and (2) pay down the principal or loan balance, that is, $1,000.00 − 216.47 = $783.53 paid off. Each successive payment pays off a greater amount of the loan—as the principal amount of the loan is reduced, less of each payment goes to paying off interest and more goes to reducing the loan principal. This analysis of the repayment of a loan is referred to as loan amortization. **Loan amortization** is the repayment of a loan with equal payments over a specified period of time. As we can see from the example of borrowing $4,329.40, each payment can be broken down into its interest and principal components.

Shortcuts: Tables of Annuity Factors

Annuity factor tables simplify the task of valuing annuities. Table B-3 in Appendix B shows future value of annuity factors for interest rates and periods from 1 percent to 40 percent and from 1 to 40 payments, respectively. Table B-4 is the corresponding table for present value of annuity factors.

For illustrative purposes here, representative portions of Tables B-3 and B-4 are provided in Table 5-2. For example, the future value annuity factor for five periodic payments and an interest rate of 10 percent is 6.1051; the factor for ten periodic payments and an interest rate of 5 percent is 12.5779. The present value annuity factor for five periodic payments and an interest rate of 10 percent is 3.7908; the factor for ten periodic payments and an interest rate of 5 percent is 7.7217.

Like the tables of compound and discount factors shown in Table 5-1, we can use the annuity factor tables to solve for T (given r and the appropriate factor) or for r (given T and the appropriate factor). Suppose that we deposit $1,000 at the end of each year in an account that pays 6 percent compounded annually. For how many years must we make deposits in the account to have a balance of $7,000? We can work this out using the future value annuity factor in panel *a* of Table 5-2. We know that the future value is $7,000, the interest rate is 6 percent, and the periodic payments are $1,000. We substitute this information into the formula for the future value of an annuity and solve for the future value annuity factor:

$$FV = CF \sum_{t=1}^{T} (1 + r)^{T-t}$$

where $\sum_{t=1}^{T} (1 + r)^{T-t}$ is the future value annuity factor. Rearranging terms slightly and substituting the known future value and the known value of CF:

$$\frac{\$7,000}{\$1,000} = \sum_{t=1}^{T} (1 + r)^{T-t} = 7 \qquad \text{(future value annuity factor)}$$

we find that the future value annuity factor is 7.

TABLE 5-2

Portions of Future Value and Present Value Annuity Factor Tables, from Appendix B

(a) FUTURE VALUE ANNUITY FACTORS (FROM TABLE B-3)

Number of cash flows, T	1%	2%	3%	4%	5%	6%	7%	8%	9%	10%
1	1.0000	1.0000	1.0000	1.0000	1.0000	1.0000	1.0000	1.0000	1.0000	1.0000
2	2.0100	2.0200	2.0300	2.0400	2.0500	2.0600	2.0700	2.0800	2.0900	2.1000
3	3.0301	3.0604	3.0909	3.1216	3.1525	3.1836	3.2149	3.2464	3.2781	3.3100
4	4.0604	4.1216	4.1836	4.2465	4.3101	4.3746	4.4399	4.5061	4.5731	4.6410
5	5.1010	5.2040	5.3091	5.4163	5.5256	5.6371	5.7507	5.8666	5.9847	6.1051
6	6.1520	6.3081	6.4684	6.6330	6.8019	6.9753	7.1533	7.3359	7.5233	7.7156
7	7.2135	7.4343	7.6625	7.8983	8.1420	8.3938	8.6540	8.9228	9.2004	9.4872
8	8.2857	8.5830	8.8923	9.2142	9.5491	9.8975	10.2598	10.6366	11.0285	11.4359
9	9.3685	9.7546	10.1591	10.5828	11.0266	11.4913	11.9780	12.4876	13.0210	13.5795
10	10.4622	10.9497	11.4639	12.0061	12.5779	13.1808	13.8164	14.4866	15.1929	15.9374

(b) PRESENT VALUE ANNUITY FACTORS (FROM TABLE B-4)

Number of cash flows, T	1%	2%	3%	4%	5%	6%	7%	8%	9%	10%
1	0.9901	0.9804	0.9709	0.9615	0.9524	0.9434	0.9346	0.9259	0.9174	0.9091
2	1.9704	1.9416	1.9135	1.8861	1.8594	1.8334	1.8080	1.7833	1.7591	1.7355
3	2.9410	2.8839	2.8286	2.7751	2.7232	2.6730	2.6243	2.5771	2.5313	2.4869
4	3.9020	3.8077	3.7171	3.6299	3.5460	3.4651	3.3872	3.3121	3.2397	3.1699
5	4.8534	4.7135	4.5797	4.4518	4.3295	4.2124	4.1002	3.9927	3.8897	3.7908
6	5.7955	5.6014	5.4172	5.2421	5.0757	4.9173	4.7665	4.6229	4.4859	4.3553
7	6.7282	6.4720	6.2303	6.0021	5.7864	5.5824	5.3893	5.2064	5.0330	4.8684
8	7.6517	7.3255	7.0197	6.7327	6.4632	6.2098	5.9713	5.7466	5.5348	5.3349
9	8.5660	8.1622	7.7861	7.4353	7.1078	6.8017	6.5152	6.2469	5.9952	5.7590
10	9.4713	8.9826	8.5302	8.1109	7.7217	7.3601	7.0236	6.7101	6.4177	6.1446

Examining the future value annuity table for the 6 percent interest rate, we don't find a factor of 7.0000, but we do see one that is very close, 6.9753, which corresponds to T = 6 payments. In this example, six payments of $1,000 each year produces very nearly $7,000 at the end of the sixth year.

COMPLEXITIES IN THE TIME VALUE OF MONEY

Valuing a Perpetual Stream of Cash Flows

Some cash flows are expected to continue forever. For example, a corporation may promise to pay dividends on preferred stock forever or a company may issue a bond that pays interest every six months forever. How do you value these cash flow streams? When we calculated the present value of an annuity, we took the amount of one cash flow and multiplied it by the sum of the discount factors that corresponded to the interest rate and number of payments. But what if the number of payments extends forever—into infinity?

A series of cash flows that occur at regular intervals forever is a **perpetuity.** Valuing a perpetual cash flow stream is just like valuing an ordinary annuity. It looks like this:

$$PV = CF_1\left(\frac{1}{1+r}\right)^1 + CF_2\left(\frac{1}{1+r}\right)^2 + CF_3\left(\frac{1}{1+r}\right)^3 + \cdots + CF_\infty\left(\frac{1}{1+r}\right)^{\text{infinity}}$$

Simplifying, recognizing that the cash flows, CF_t, are the same in each period, and using summation notation, we obtain:

$$PV = CF \sum_{t=1}^{\text{infinity}} \left(\frac{1}{1+r}\right)^{\text{infinity}}$$

As the number of discounting periods approaches infinity, the summation approaches 1/r. To see why, consider the present value annuity factor for an interest rate of 10 percent as the number of payments goes from 1 to 200:

Number of discounting periods, T	Present value of annuity factor for T cash flows $\sum_{t=1}^{T} \left(\frac{1}{1+r}\right)^t$
1	0.9091
10	6.1446
40	9.7791
100	9.9993
200	9.9999

For greater numbers of payments, the factor approaches 10, or 1/0.10. Therefore, the present value of a perpetual annuity is very close to:

$$PV = CF\left(\frac{1}{r}\right) = \frac{CF}{r} \qquad\qquad [5\text{-}7]$$

Suppose you are considering an investment that promises to pay $100 each period forever, and the interest rate you can earn on alternative invest-

Using this equation and factors in Table B-4, for T = 3 periods and r = 4 percent per period, we find the present value annuity factor is 2.7751; and in Table B-1, for T = 1 and r = 4 percent, we find the compound factor is 1.0400. Calculating the present value of the annuity due with these factors:

PV of annuity due of T cash flows = $500(2.7751)(1.0400)

= $500(2.8861)

= **$1,443.05**

The present value of the annuity due and ordinary annuity calculations with their cash flows are illustrated in the time lines in Figure 5-11. Since the cash flows in an annuity due situation are each discounted one less period than the corresponding cash flows in the ordinary annuity, the present value of the annuity due is greater than the present value of the ordinary annuity.

FIGURE 5-11

Time Line for the Present Value of an Annuity with Three Cash Flows

Discounted values of deposits for the ordinary annuity and annuity due cash flows. The value today of the ordinary annuity is $1,387.55, and the value of the annuity due is $1,443.05. The value of the ordinary annuity today is less than the annuity due since each ordinary annuity cash flow is discounted one more period.

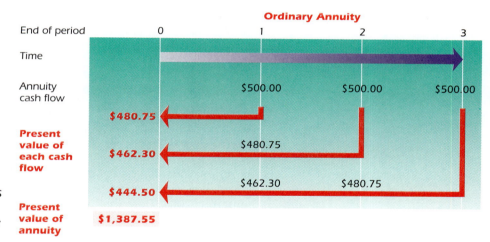

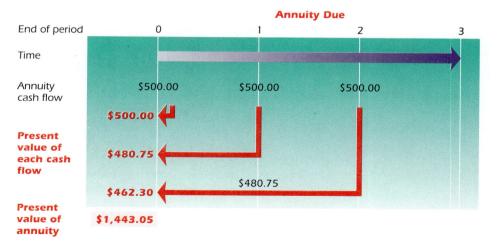

**Valuing a
Deferred Annuity**

A ***deferred annuity*** has a stream of cash flows of equal amounts at regular periods starting at some time after the end of the first period. Example: Say that today is January 1, 1995, and you are planning to enter graduate school January 1, 2001. Upon entering graduate school, you must pay tuition of $5,000 per year (on January 1 of each year) for three years. How much do you have to deposit in a savings account today to have enough money for graduate school if your savings earn 6 percent compound interest per year?

When we calculated the present value of an annuity, we brought a series of cash flows back to the beginning of the first period—or, equivalently the end of the period 0. For the sake of putting some meaning into our notation, the beginning of the first period coincides with the end of the period prior to period 1. That's why we refer to that point in time as $t = 0$. We can apply the same process to our problem, calculating the present value as of the beginning of the year before the first withdrawal is made:

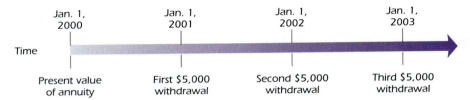

Therefore, we know how to calculate the present value of this annuity:

$$PV = \$5,000 \sum_{t=1}^{3} \left(\frac{1}{1 + 0.06} \right)^t = \$5,000(2.6730) = \mathbf{\$13,365.06}$$

Therefore, you must have a balance of $13,365.06 in your account on January 1, 2000 in order to be able to withdraw $5,000 per year each year beginning January 1, 2001. Does that mean that we must deposit $13,365.06 today? No, because today is January 1, 1995, *not* January 1, 2001. Whatever we deposit today will earn interest for five years (1995, 1996, 1997, 1998, and 1999):

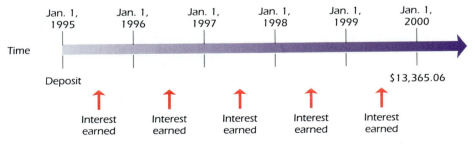

Therefore, we require a deposit today that will grow in five years compounded at 6 percent per year to a future value of $13,365.06:

$$\begin{aligned} FV &= PV(1 + r)^t \\ \$13,365.06 &= PV(1 + 0.06)^5 \end{aligned}$$

Rearranging,

$$PV = \$13{,}365.06\left(\frac{1}{1+0.06}\right)^5$$

$$= \$13{,}365.06(0.7473)$$

$$= \mathbf{\$9{,}987.15}$$

You can see in the time line in Figure 5-12 for this problem that the present value of a deferred annuity consists of two parts: the present value of an annuity and the present value of an amount.

Figures 5-13(*a*) and 5-13(*b*) show graphically how the balance in the account grows with interest during the five years after the initial deposit and then shrinks in the last three years because of withdrawals. In Figure 5-13(*a*), we see the deposit, interest on the deposit, and withdrawals. In Figure 5-13(*b*) we see the balance in the account—growing as deposits are made, declining as withdrawals are made.

As we can see from this savings problem, the value of a deferred annuity calculation requires two parts:

Part 1 The valuation of the annuity at some future point in time.
Part 2 The discounted value of this value of the annuity.

Let's look at a more complex deferred annuity. Consider making a series of deposits, beginning today, to provide for a steady cash flow beginning at some future time period. If interest is earned at a rate of 4 percent compounded per year, what amount must be deposited in a savings account each

FIGURE 5-12

Saving for Graduate School, Deferred Annuity Example Time Line

Two-step solution to the graduate school savings problem: (1) Determine the balance in the account on January 1, 2000, necessary to meet three tuition payments of $5,000 each beginning January 1, 2001; (2) Determine the deposit needed to grow to this amount by January 1, 2000, at 6 percent interest compounded per year.

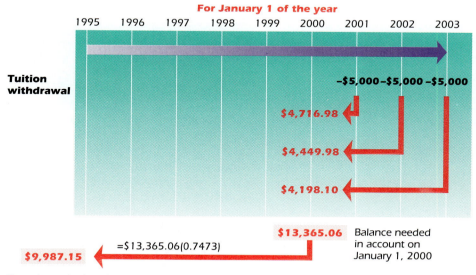

Deposit required on January 1, 1995, so that $13,365.06 will be available January 1, 2000, permitting annual withdrawals of $5,000 each, starting January 1, 2001

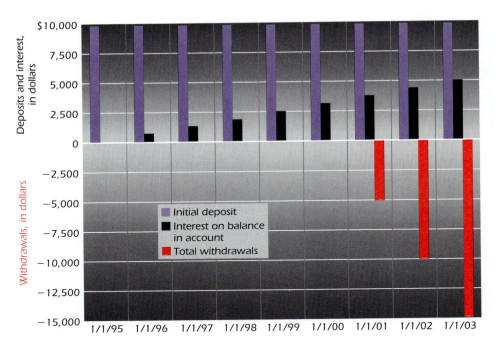

FIGURE 5-13(b)
Balance in the Account

The $9,987.15 will grow in five years to $13,365.06. Three annual withdrawals, of $5,000 each, will leave a zero balance in the account.

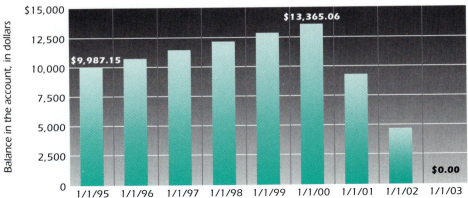

year for four years, starting today, so that $1,000 may be withdrawn each year for five years, beginning five years from today?

As with any deferred annuity, we need to:

Part 1 Calculate the present value of the $1,000 per year five-year ordinary annuity as of the end of the fourth year (or, equivalently, at the beginning of the fifth year).

Part 2 Calculate the cash flow needed to arrive at the future value of that annuity due, comprising four annual deposits earning 4 percent compound interest, starting today.[5]

---

[5] Why an annuity due? Because we are making our first deposit today.

Working out Part 1: The present value of the annuity deferred to the end of the fourth period is

$$PV = \sum_{t=1}^{5} \$1,000 \left(\frac{1}{1 + 0.04} \right)^t$$

$$= \$1,000 \left[\sum_{t=1}^{5} \left(\frac{1}{1 + 0.04} \right)^t \right]$$

$$= \$1,000(4.4518)$$

$$= \mathbf{\$4,451.80}$$

Therefore, there must be $4,451.80 in the account at the end of the fourth year to permit five $1,000 withdrawals at the end of each of the years 5, 6, 7, 8, and 9.

Working out Part 2: The present value of the annuity at the end of the fourth year, $4,451.80, is the future value of the annuity due of four payments. Using the formula for the future value of an annuity due,

$$\begin{array}{l} \text{FV of annuity due} \\ \text{at the end of 4 years} \end{array} = CF \sum_{t=0}^{T-1} (1 + r)^{T-t}(1 + r)$$

Substituting the known values for FV, r, and t:

$$\$4,451.80 = CF \sum_{t=0}^{3} (1 + 0.04)^{T-t}(1 + 0.04)$$

$$= CF(4.2465)(1.0400)$$

$$= CF(4.4164)$$

and rearranging,

$$CF = \frac{\$4,451.80}{4.4164} = \mathbf{\$1,008.02}$$

Therefore, by depositing $1008.02 today and the same amount on the same date in each of the next three years, we will have a balance in the account of $4,451.80 at the end of the fourth period. With this period-4 balance, we will be able to withdraw $1,000 at the end of the following five periods.

Figures 5-14(a) and 5-14(b) graphically show the increase in the account balance throughout the first four years as deposits are made and interest is earned and the reduction in the account balance, starting at the end of the fifth year, because of withdrawals. In Figure 5-14(a) we see the deposits, interest on the balance in the account, and the withdrawals. In Figure 5-14(b), we see the balance in the account—growing as deposits are made and declining as withdrawals are made. By the end of the ninth year, the balance in the account is exactly zero.

Determining the Unknown Interest Rate

Let's say that you have $1,000 to invest today and that in five years, you would like the investment to be worth $2,000. What interest rate would satisfy your investment objective? We know the present value (PV = $1,000), the future

FIGURE 5-14(a)

Total Deposits, Accumulated Interest, and Total Withdrawals in a Savings Account Earning 4 Percent Compound Interest per Year

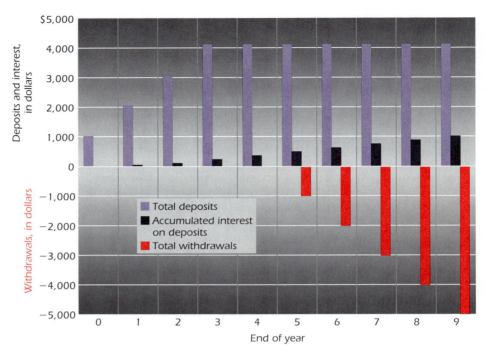

FIGURE 5-14(b)

Total Deposits, Accumulated Interest, and Total Withdrawals in a Savings Account Earning 4 Percent Compound Interest per Year

Growth as deposits of $1,008.02 are made each year for four years (starting at time 0) and decline of the balance with withdrawals of $1,000.00 each year for five years, starting at the end of period 5. The account balance after all deposits are made is $4,451.80 (at the end of period 4) and the account balance after all withdrawals are made is zero.

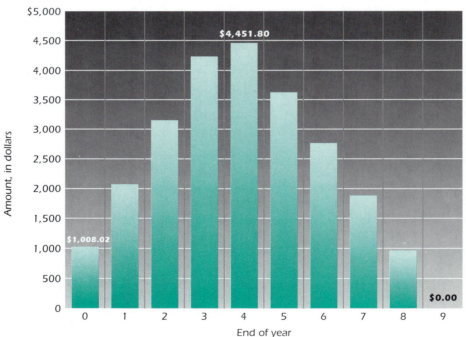

value (FV = \$2,000) and the number of compounding periods (t = 5). Using the basic valuation equation:

$$FV = PV(1 + r)^t$$

and substituting the known values of FV, PV, and t:

$$\$2,000 = \$1,000(1 + r)^5$$

Rearranging, we see that the ratio of the future value to the present value is equal to the compound factor for five periods:

$$\frac{\$2,000}{\$1,000} = (1 + r)^5 \quad \text{or} \quad 2 = (1 + r)^5$$

where 2 is the compound factor.

We therefore have one equation with one unknown, r. We can determine the unknown interest rate either mathematically or by using the table of compound factors in Table B-1. In that table, we see that for five compounding periods, the interest rate that produces a compound factor closest to 2 is 15 percent per year.

We can determine the interest rate more precisely, however, by solving for r mathematically:

$$2 = (1 + r)^5$$

Taking the fifth root of both sides, and representing this operation in several equivalent ways,

$$\sqrt[5]{2} = 2^{1/5} = 2^{0.20} = (1 + r)$$

You'll need a calculator to figure out the fifth root:

$$\sqrt[5]{2} = 1.1487 = (1 + r)$$
$$r = 1.1487 - 1 = \mathbf{0.1487} \text{ or } \mathbf{14.87\%}$$

Therefore, if you invested \$1,000 in an investment that pays 14.87 percent compound interest per year for five years, you would have \$2,000 at the end of the fifth year.

We can formalize an equation for finding the interest rate when we know PV, FV, and t by using the valuation equation and notation:

$$FV = PV (1 + r)^t$$

and dividing both sides by PV,

$$\frac{FV}{PV} = (1 + r)^t$$

Taking the tth root of both sides of the equation:

$$\sqrt[t]{\frac{FV}{PV}} = (1 + r) \quad \text{which is equivalent to} \quad \left(\frac{FV}{PV}\right)^{1/t} = (1 + r)$$

Subtracting 1 from each side and exchanging sides yields:

$$r = \sqrt[t]{\frac{FV}{PV}} - 1 = \left(\frac{FV}{PV}\right)^{1/t} - 1 \qquad \text{[5-10]}$$

As an example, suppose that the value of an investment today is $100 and the value of the investment in five years is expected to be $150. What is the annual rate of appreciation of this investment over the five-year period?

$$r = \sqrt[5]{\frac{\$150}{\$100}} - 1$$

$$= \sqrt[5]{1.5} - 1$$

$$= \mathbf{0.0845} \text{ or } \mathbf{8.45\% \text{ per year}}$$

As we saw earlier, we can approximate the interest rate using Table B-1 or B-2. From the formulas for the present value and future value, you can see that the compound factor is the ratio of the future value to the present value, whereas the discount factor is the ratio of the present value to the future value. That is,

$$\text{Compound factor} = (1 + r)^t = \frac{FV}{PV}$$

and

$$\text{Discount factor} = \left(\frac{1}{1 + r}\right)^t = \frac{PV}{FV}$$

In this example,

$$\frac{FV}{PV} = 1.5000 \quad \text{and} \quad \frac{PV}{FV} = 0.6667$$

In Table B-1, the factor closest to 1.5 in the row corresponding to five periods is in the column for a 9 percent interest rate. In Table B-2, the factor closest to 0.6667 in the row corresponding to five periods is in the 9 percent interest rate column. Therefore, investing $100 today will produce $150 five years from now if the investment appreciates approximately 9 percent per year, as before.

Determining the Number of Compounding Periods

Let's say that you place $1,000 in a savings account that pays 10 percent compound interest per year. How long would it take for that savings account balance to reach $5,000? In this case, we know the present value (PV = $1,000), the future value (FV = $5,000), and the interest rate (r = 10 percent per year). What we need to determine is the number of compounding periods.

Let's start with the basic valuation equation and insert the known values of PV, FV, and r:

$$FV = PV(1 + r)^t \quad \longrightarrow \quad \$5,000 = \$1,000(1 + 0.10)^t$$

Rearranging:

$$\frac{\$5,000}{\$1,000} = (1 + 0.10)^t = 5$$

Therefore, the compound factor is 5.

Like the determination of the unknown interest rate, we can determine the number of periods either mathematically or by using the table of compound factors. If we use the table of compound factors, Table B-1, we look down the column for the 10 percent interest rate to find the factor closest to 5. Then we look across the row containing this factor to find t. We see that the t that corresponds to a factor of 5 for a 10 percent interest rate is between 16 and 17, though closer to 17. Therefore, we approximate the number of periods as 17.

Solving the equation mathematically is a bit more complex. We know that:

$$5 = (1 + 0.10)^t$$

We must somehow rearrange this equation so that the unknown value, t, is on one side of the equation and all the known values are on the other. To do this, we must use logarithms and a bit of algebra. Taking the natural log of both sides:

$$\ln 5 = t \ln (1 + 0.10)$$

or

$$\ln 5 = t \ln 1.10$$

where ln indicates the natural log. Substituting the values of the natural logs of 5 and 1.10,

$$1.6094 = t(0.0953)$$

Rearranging:

$$t = \frac{1.6094}{0.0953} = \mathbf{16.8877}$$

Since the last interest payment is at the end of the last year, the number of annual periods is seventeen—it would take seventeen years for your $1,000 investment to grow to $5,000 if interest is compounded at 10 percent per year.

As you can see, given the present and future values, calculating the number of periods when we know the interest rate is somewhat more complex than calculating the interest rate when we know the number of periods. Nevertheless, we can develop an equation for determining the number of periods, beginning with the valuation formula:

$$FV = PV(1 + r)^t \qquad \text{and dividing both sides by PV,} \qquad \frac{FV}{PV} = (1 + r)^t$$

Taking logarithms of both sides:

$$\ln FV - \ln PV = t \ln (1 + r)$$

Dividing both sides by $\ln (1 + r)$ and exchanging sides:

$$t = \frac{\ln FV - \ln PV}{\ln (1 + r)} \qquad\qquad [5\text{-}11]$$

Suppose that the present value of an investment is $100 and you wish to determine how long it will take for the investment to double in value if the investment earns 6 percent per year compounded annually:

$$t = \frac{\ln 200 - \ln 100}{\ln 1.06} = \frac{5.2983 - 4.6052}{0.0583} = \mathbf{11.8885} \text{ or approximately 12 years}$$

Cutting Logs Down to Size

Logarithmic functions ("logs" for short) are mathematical transformations that can simplify some types of math problems. Let's say that we have the expression:

$$Y^z = X$$

The exponent of Y is Z. In the language of logs, Z is referred to as the *logarithm* of X to the *base* of Y. The base is the set of numbers used to represent values. The two most often used bases are 10 and e (where e is the value 2.71828). When 10 is used as a base, the logarithm is referred to as a *common logarithm*. To see how a logarithm works, let's look at a few examples. Representing a logarithm in base 10 as $\log_{10}$:

$\log_{10} 1,000 = 3$ since $10^3 = 1,000$
$\log_{10} 100 \ \ = 2$ since $10^2 = 100$
$\log_{10} 10 \ \ \ = 1$ since $10^1 = 10$
$\log_{10} 1 \ \ \ \ = 0$ since $10^0 = 1$

There are several rules of logarithms (applicable no matter which is the base) that make it easier for us to solve complex math problems:

Rule 1 $\log (ab) = \log a + \log b$

Rule 2 $\log \dfrac{a}{b} = \log a - \log b$

Rule 3 $\log a^b = b \log a$

Rule 4 $\log_a a^b = b$

A useful device is to use the logarithm to the base of e. When e is used as the base, the logarithm is referred to as a *natural logarithm* and $\log_e$ is represented by ln. For example,

$\log_e 1,000 = 6.9078$ $\log_e 10 = 2.3026$
$\log_e 100 \ \ = 4.6052$ $\log_e 1 \ \ = 0$

Logarithms can help us solve what otherwise looks unsolvable. For example, if we have to solve for t in the following equation,

$$5 = (1 + 0.10)^t$$

we take the natural log of each side, using Rule 3:

$$\ln 5 = t \ln (1 + 0.10)$$

We can then proceed to solve the equation by using our calculator for ln 5, 1.6094, and ln 1.10, 0.0953. We didn't have to use natural logs to solve this, but since many financial calculators have special keys for natural logs, we use the natural log in our examples.

You'll notice that we round off to the next whole period. To see why, consider this last example. After 11.8885 years, we have doubled our money if interest were paid 88.85 percent of the way through the twelfth year. But, we stated earlier, interest is paid *at the end of each period*—not part of the way through. At the end of the eleventh year, our investment is worth $189.93, and at the end of the twelfth year, our investment is worth $201.22. So, our investment's value doubles by the twelfth period—with a little extra, $1.22.

The tables in Appendix B can be used to approximate the number of periods. The approach is similar to the way we approximated the interest rate. The compound factor in this example is 2 and the discount factor is 0.5 (that is, FV/PV = 2.0000 and PV/FV = 0.5000). In Table B-1, following down in the column corresponding to the interest rate of 6%, we find that the compound factor closest to 2 is for twelve periods. Likewise, using Table B-2 and following down the column corresponding to the interest rate of 6 percent, we find that the discount factor closest to 0.5 is for twelve periods. We can use Tables B-3 and B-4 in a like manner to solve for the number of payments in the case of an annuity.

THE CALCULATION OF INTEREST RATES

A common problem in finance is comparing alternative financing or investment opportunities when the interest rates are specified in such a way as to make it difficult to compare terms. Interest rates are not always stated on the same basis. For example, one bank may advertise a savings account that pays 10 percent compounded semiannually, whereas another bank may advertise its savings account as paying 9 percent compounded daily. Which savings account pays more interest over a period, such as a year? We can't answer that without first figuring out how the stated rates translate into rates having the same basis—then we can compare them.

There are two ways to convert interest rates stated over different time intervals so that they have a common basis: the annual percentage rate and the effective annual interest rate.

The Annual Percentage Rate

One obvious way to represent rates stated in various time intervals on a common basis is to express them in the same unit of time—so we annualize them. The ***annualized rate*** is the product of the stated rate of interest per compounding period and the number of compounding periods in a year. Let r be the rate of interest per period and t be the number of compounding periods in a year. The annualized rate, also referred to as the ***nominal interest rate*** or the ***annual percentage rate*** (APR) is:

$$\text{APR} = r \times t \qquad [5\text{-}12]$$

Let's consider the Lucky Break Loan Company. Lucky's loan terms are simple: Pay back the amount borrowed, plus 50 percent, in six months. Suppose you borrow $10,000 from Lucky. After six months, you must pay back the $10,000 plus $5,000. The annual percentage rate on financing with Lucky is the interest rate per period (50 percent for six months) multiplied by the number of compounding periods in a year (two six-month periods in a year). For the Lucky Break financing arrangement:

$$\text{APR} = 0.50 \times 2 = 1.00 \text{ or } \textbf{100\% per year}$$

But what if you cannot pay Lucky back after six months? Lucky will let you off this time, but you must pay back the following at the end of the next six months:

- The $10,000 borrowed.
- The $5,000 interest from the first six months.
- The 50 percent of interest on both the unpaid $10,000 and the unpaid $5,000 interest ($15,000 × 0.50 = $7,500).

So, at the end of the year, knowing what is good for you, you pay off Lucky:

Amount of original loan	$ 10,000
Interest from first six months	5,000
Interest on second six months	7,500
Total payment at end of year	**$22,500**

Using the Lucky Break method of financing, you have to pay $12,500 interest to borrow $10,000 for one year's time.

Because you have to pay $12,500 interest to borrow $10,000 over one year's time, you pay not 100 percent interest, but rather 125 percent interest per year ($12,500/$10,000 = 1.25 = 125%). What's going on here? It looks like the APR in the Lucky Break example ignores the compounding (interest on interest) that takes place after the first six months.[6] And that's the way it is with all APRs. The APR ignores the effect of compounding. And therefore this rate understates the true annual rate of interest if interest is compounded at any time prior to the end of the year. Nevertheless, APR is an acceptable method of disclosing interest on many lending arrangements, since it is easy to understand and simple to compute. However, because it ignores compounding, it is not the best way to convert interest rates to a common basis.

Effective vs. Annualized Rates of Interest

Another way of converting stated interest rates to a common basis is the effective rate of interest. The ***effective annual rate*** (EAR), also referred to as the ***effective rate of interest,*** is the *true* economic return for a given time period because it takes into account the compounding of interest.

Using our Lucky Break example, we see that we must pay $12,500 interest on the loan of $10,000 for one year. Effectively, we are paying 125 percent annual interest. Thus, 125 percent is the effective annual rate of interest.

In this example, we can easily work through the calculation of interest and interest on interest. But for situations in which interest is compounded more frequently, we need a direct way to calculate the effective annual rate. We do that by resorting once again to our basic valuation equation:

$$FV = PV(1 + r)^t$$

Next, we consider that a return is the change in the value of an investment over a period and an annual return is the change in value over a year. Using

---

[6] It is unreasonable to assume that, after six months, Lucky would let you forget about paying interest on the $5,000 interest from the first six months. If Lucky *did* forget about the interest on interest, you would pay $20,000 at the end of the year—$10,000 in repayment of principal and $10,000 interest—which is a 100 percent interest rate.

our basic valuation equation, the relative change in value is the difference between the future value and the present value, divided by the present value:

$$EAR = \frac{FV - PV}{PV}$$

Substituting $PV(1 + r)^t$ for FV:

$$EAR = \frac{[PV(1 + r)^t] - PV}{PV}$$

Canceling PV in both the numerator and the denominator,

$$EAR = (1 + r)^t - 1 \qquad\qquad [5\text{-}13]$$

Let's look at how the EAR is affected by the compounding. Suppose that the Safe Savings and Loan Bank promises to pay 6 percent interest on accounts, compounded annually. Since interest is paid once, at the end of the year, the effective annual return, or EAR, is 6 percent.

If the 6 percent interest is paid on a semiannual basis—3 percent every six months—the effective annual return is larger than 6 percent, since interest is earned on the 3 percent interest earned at the end of the first six months. In this case, to calculate the EAR, the interest rate per compounding period—six months—is 0.03 (that is, 0.06/2), and the number of compounding periods in an annual period is 2:

$$
\begin{aligned}
EAR &= (1 + r)^t - 1 \\
&= (1 + 0.03)^2 - 1 = 1.0609 - 1 = \mathbf{0.0609} \text{ or } \mathbf{6.09\%}
\end{aligned}
$$

Extending this example to the case of quarterly compounding with a nominal interest rate of 6 percent, we first calculate the interest rate per period, r, and the number of compounding periods in a year, t:

$$r = \frac{0.06}{4} = 0.015 \text{ per quarter}$$

$$t = \frac{12 \text{ months}}{3 \text{ months}} = 4 \text{ quarters in a year}$$

Then:

$$EAR = (1 + 0.015)^4 - 1 = 1.0614 - 1 = \mathbf{0.0614} \text{ or } \mathbf{6.14\%}$$

As this example indicates the greater the frequency of compounding, the greater the EAR.

Effective Annual Rates of Interest Equivalent to an Annual Percentage Rate of 6%	Frequency of compounding per year	Calculation	EAR
	Annual	$(1 + 0.060)^1 - 1$	6.00%
	Semiannual	$(1 + 0.030)^2 - 1$	6.09
	Quarterly	$(1 + 0.015)^4 - 1$	6.14
	Continuous	$e^{0.06} - 1$	6.18

Figuring out the effective annual rate is useful when comparing interest rates for different investments. It doesn't make sense to compare the APRs

The extreme frequency of compounding is ***continuous compounding,*** in which interest is compounded at the *smallest* possible increment of time. In continuous compounding, the rate per period becomes extremely small:

$$r = \frac{\text{nominal interest rate}}{\text{infinity}}$$

And the number of compounding periods in a year, t, is infinite. As the rate of interest, r, gets smaller and the number of compounding periods approaches infinity, the EAR is:

$$EAR = 1 + \left(\frac{\text{nominal interest rate}}{\text{infinity}}\right)^{\text{infinity}}$$

What does all this mean? It means that r approaches 0 and t approaches infinity—at the same time! For a given nominal interest rate under continuous compounding, it can be shown that:

$$EAR = e^{APR} - 1$$

For the stated 6 percent annual interest rate compounded continuously, the EAR is:

$$
\begin{aligned}
EAR &= e^{0.06} - 1 \\
&= 1.0618 - 1 \\
&= \mathbf{0.0618 \text{ or } 6.18\%}
\end{aligned}
$$

among investments that differ in frequency of compounding within a year. But since the return on investments is often stated in terms of APRs, we need to understand how to work with them.

Looking again at the comparison of advertised rates for the two banks introduced at the beginning of this section, in which one bank offers 10 percent compounded semiannually and the other offers 9 percent compounded daily, we can compare these rates using the EARs. For the bank advertising a savings account that pays 10 percent compounded semiannually:

- The 10 percent is the nominal interest rate.
- The compounding period is six months.
- The rate of interest per six-month period is 5 percent.
- The effective annual rate is $(1 + 0.05)^2 - 1 = 0.1025$, or 10.25%.

For the bank advertising a savings account paying 9 percent compounded daily:

- The 9 percent is the nominal interest rate.
- The compounding period is one day.
- The rate of interest per day is 0.09/365, or 0.0247 percent.
- The effective annual rate is $(1 + 0.000247)^{365} - 1 = 0.0943$, or 9.43 percent.

Does It Pay to Discover?

The Discover credit card, like many credit cards, provides interest-free financing as long as you pay your balance in full each month. If you choose not to pay any of the balance due, Discover offers you the following financing terms (taken from the *Discover Cardmembers Agreement*, 1992):

". . . multiply each day's daily balance by a daily periodic rate of .05425%—an Annual Percentage Rate of 19.8%. . . . The daily balance for each day will include the previous day's finance charge."

As Discover tells you directly in the cardmember agreement, the APR is 0.0005425 × 365 = 19.8 percent. But is this the true cost of using Discover to finance your purchases? Since the agreement states that the daily balance on a given day includes any financing charges built up from previous days, you know that these financing charges, which are another name for interest, are compounding each day. So what is the effective annual rate?

We know that r = 0.05425 percent or 0.0005425 per day and that there are 365 days in the year (T = 365). Substituting these values into the EAR equation:

$$EAR = (1 + 0.0005424)^{365} - 1$$
$$= 1.2189 - 1 = \mathbf{0.2189} \text{ or } \mathbf{21.89\%}$$

Since the credit period does not begin until you fail to pay the monthly balance when due, the credit card allows interest-free financing for one month on your purchases. But when you use the Discover credit card to finance your purchases—by delaying payment beyond the monthly due date—you are paying an effective rate of almost 22% per year!

We see that the 10 percent APR with semiannual compounding provides a better effective annual return than the 9 percent APR with daily compounding. While the difference in APRs is 1 percent, the EAR difference is less than 1 percent. In this example, the investment with the higher APR provides the higher EAR. But this is not always the case.

Suppose there are two banks, Bank A, paying 12 percent interest compounded semiannually, and Bank B, paying 11.9 percent interest compounded monthly.

Which bank offers you the best return on your money? Comparing APRs, Bank A provides the higher return. But what about compound interest? The EARs for each account are calculated as:

Bank A:

$$EAR = \left(1 + \frac{0.12}{2}\right)^2 - 1$$

$$= (1 + 0.06)^2 - 1$$
$$= 1.1236 - 1$$
$$= \textbf{0.1236} \text{ or } \textbf{12.36\%}$$

Bank B:

$$EAR = \left(1 + \frac{0.119}{12}\right)^{12} - 1$$
$$= (1 + 0.0099)^{12} - 1$$
$$= 1.1255 - 1$$
$$= \textbf{0.1255} \text{ or } \textbf{12.55\%}$$

Bank B offers the better return on your money, even though it advertises a lower APR. If you deposit $1,000 in Bank A for one year, you will have $1,123.60 at the end of the year. If you deposit $1,000 in Bank B for one year, you will have $1,125.50 at the end of the year, providing the better return on your savings.

SUMMARY

- We can translate a present value into a value in the future through compounding. We can translate a future value into an equivalent value today through discounting. Financial mathematics consists of the mathematical tools we use to perform compounding and discounting.

- The basic valuation equation, $FV = PV(1 + r)^t$, is used to translate present values into future values and to translate future values into present values. This basic relationship includes interest compounding; that is, interest earnings on interest already earned.

- Using the basic valuation equation, we can translate any number of cash flows into a present or future value. When faced with a series of cash flows, we must value each cash flow individually and then sum these individual values to arrive at the present or future value of the series. Our work can be cut somewhat shorter if these cash flows are equal and occur at periodic intervals of time; this kind of flow is referred to as an annuity.

- Tables containing present value factors, future value factors, present value annuity factors, and future value annuity factors can be used to reduce the computations involved in financial math.

- We can use financial mathematics to value many different patterns of cash flows, including perpetuities, annuity dues, and deferred annuities. Applying the tools to these different patterns of cash flows requires us to take care in specifying the timing of the various cash flows.

- If the interest on alternative investments is stated in different terms, we can put these interest rates on a common basis so that we can determine the best alternative. Typically, we specify an interest rate on an annual basis, using either the annual percentage rate or the effective annual rate. The latter method is preferred since it takes into consideration the compounding of interest within a year.

QUESTIONS

5-1　What is the difference between compounding and discounting?

5-2　What is the relation between a future value of an amount and the present value of an amount?

5-3　If you offered two investments, one that pays 5 percent simple interest per year and one that pays 5 percent interest compounded per year, which would you choose? Why?

5-4　Suppose you make a deposit today in a bank account that pays compound interest annually. After one year, the balance in the account has grown. What has caused it to grow? After two years, the balance in the account has grown even more. What has caused the balance to increase during the second year?

5-5　Show how the basic valuation equation $[FV = PV(1 + r)^t]$ can be rearranged to solve for the present value, given a future value, an interest rate, and the number of compounding periods.

5-6　Show how the basic valuation equation $[FV = PV(1 + r)^t]$ can be rearranged to solve for the interest rate, given a future value, a present value, and the number of compounding periods.

5-7　Using the CF_t notation, draw two time lines, one showing the calculation of the present value of a four-payment ordinary annuity and one showing the calculation of the present value of an annuity due, when interest is compounded at the rate r.

5-8　Using the CF_t notation, draw two time lines, one showing the calculation of the future value of a four-payment ordinary annuity and one showing the calculation of the future value of an annuity due, when interest is compounded at the rate r.

5-9　The Florida lottery pays out winnings, after taxes, on the basis of twenty equal annual installments, providing the first installment at the time that the winning ticket is turned in. What type of cash flow pattern is the distribution of lottery winnings? How would you value such winnings?

5-10　Rent is typically paid on the first of each month. What pattern of cash flows, an ordinary annuity or an annuity due, does a rental agreement follow?

5-11　Under what conditions does the effective annual rate of interest (EAR) differ from the annual percentage rate (APR)? As the frequency of compounding increases within the annual period, what happens to the relation between the EAR and the APR?

5-12　Suppose you are planning for your retirement. Your goal is to set aside the same amount of money each year until you retire, so that you can withdraw an even amount each year during your retirement. You expect to retire in forty years and you also expect to live for twenty years following your retirement.

　　a.　What additional information do you need to figure out how much you need to save each year?

b. Diagram this problem on a time line, indicating savings and withdrawals.

c. Without actually performing any calculations, describe how you would approach solving this problem to determine the amount you need to save each year to retirement.

5-13 Using Table B-1, find the compound factor for each of the following combinations of interest rate per period and number of compounding periods:

Number of periods	Interest rate per period	Compound factor
2	2%	_____
4	3	_____
3	4	_____
6	8	_____
8	6	_____

5-14 Using Table B-2, find the discount factor for each of the following combinations of interest rate per period and number of discounting periods:

Number of periods	Interest rate per period	Discount factor
2	2%	_____
4	3	_____
3	4	_____
6	8	_____
8	6	_____

5-15 Using Table B-3, find the future value annuity factor for each of the following combinations of interest rate per period and number of payments:

Number of payments	Interest rate per period	Future value annuity factor
2	2%	_____
4	3	_____
3	4	_____
6	8	_____
8	6	_____

5-16 Using Table B-4, find the present value annuity factor for each of the following combinations of interest rate per period and number of payments:

Number of payments	Interest rate per period	Present value annuity factor
2	2%	_____
4	3	_____
3	4	_____
6	8	_____
8	6	_____

PROBLEMS

Translating a value into the future

5-1 Using an 8 percent compound interest rate per period, calculate the future value of a $100 investment:

a. One period into the future.
b. Two periods into the future.
c. Three periods into the future.
d. Four periods into the future.
e. Five periods into the future.
f. Forty periods into the future.

5-2 Suppose you deposit $1,000 into a savings account that earns interest at the rate of 4 percent compounded annually. What would be the balance in the account:

a. After two years?
b. After four years?
c. After six years?
d. After twenty years?

5-3 If you deposit $10,000 in an account that pays 6 percent compound interest per period, assuming no withdrawals:

a. What will be the balance in the account after two periods?
b. After the two periods, how much interest has been paid on the principal amount?
c. After the two periods, how much interest has been paid on the interest?

5-4 The No Problem Savings and Loan Association has begun promoting a new type of account that pays compound interest at a rate of 20 percent on account balances at the end of each calendar year (that is, December 31). If you deposit $1,000 in the account on January 1, 1995, what will be the balance in your account, assuming no withdrawals, on:

a. January 1, 1997?
b. January 1, 2000?
c. January 1, 2010?

Translating a value back from the future

5-5 Using an 8 percent compound interest rate, calculate the present value of $100 to be received:

   a. One period into the future.
   b. Two periods into the future.
   c. Three periods into the future.
   d. Four periods into the future.
   e. Five periods into the future.
   f. Forty periods into the future.

5-6 Ted wants to borrow from Fred. Ted is confident that he will have $1,000 available to pay off Fred in two years. How much will Fred be willing to lend to Ted in return for $1,000 two years from now if he uses a compound interest rate per year of:

   a. 5%?
   b. 10%?
   c. 15%?

5-7 How much would you have to deposit into a savings account that pays 2 percent interest compounded quarterly, in order to have a balance of $2,000 at the end of four years, if you make no withdrawals?

5-8 What is the present value of $5,000 to be received five years from now, if the nominal annual interest rate (APR) is 12 percent and interest is compounded:

   a. Annually?
   b. Semiannually?
   c. Quarterly?
   d. Monthly?

Translating a series of cash flows into the future

5-9 Calculate the future value at the end of the second period of this series of end-of-period cash flows, using an interest rate of 10 percent compounded per period:

Period	End-of-period cash flow
0	$100
1	200
2	400

5-10 An investor is considering the purchase of an investment at the end of 1995 that will yield the following cash flows:

Year	End-of-year cash flow
1996	$2,000
1997	3,000
1998	4,000
1999	5,000

If the appropriate return on this investment is 10 percent, what will this investment be worth at the end of 1999?

Translating a series of values back from the future

5-11 Calculate the present value (that is, the value at the end of period 0) of the following series of end-of-period cash flows if the discount rate is 6 percent:

Period	End-of-period cash flow
0	$100
1	200
2	400

5-12 Suppose that an investment promises to provide the following cash flows:

Year	End-of-year cash flow
2000	$ 0
2001	1,000
2002	0
2003	−1,000

If interest is compounded annually at 5 percent, what is the present value of these cash flows at the end of:

a. The year 2000?
b. The year 1999?

Annuities

5-13 Calculate the future value at the end of the third period of an ordinary annuity consisting of three cash flows of $2,000 each. Use a compound rate of 5 percent per period.

5-14 Calculate the present value of an ordinary annuity consisting of three cash flows of $1,000 each. Use a compound interest rate of 5 percent per period.

5-15 Suppose the Cookie Monster Cookie Company borrows $10,000 to finance the purchase of a new oven. If the loan specifies that the loan be paid off in four even end-of-year payments and if interest is compounded at the rate of 6 percent per year:

a. What is the amount of the annual payment that Cookie Monster must pay?
b. Provide a loan amortization schedule for the Cookie Monster loan, breaking down each of the annual payments into their interest and principal repayment pieces.

Perpetuities

What is the present value of $10 to be received each period, forever, if the interest rate is 6 percent.

5-17   Preferred stock is a security that promises to pay a fixed dividend amount at fixed intervals of time forever. If you have the opportunity to invest in a preferred stock that promises to pay $50 every three months forever, what would you be willing to pay for that stock if your opportunity cost of funds, expressed as an APR, is 7.5 percent per year?

5-18   If an investor is willing to pay $40 today to receive $2 every year forever, what opportunity cost should the investor use to value this investment?

Annuity due

5-19   Calculate the present value of an annuity due consisting of three cash flows of $1,000 each, each one year apart. Use a 6 percent compound interest rate per year.

5-20   Calculate the future value at the end of the third period of an annuity due consisting of three cash flows of $1,000 each, each one year apart. Use a 6 percent compound interest rate per year.

5-21   Suppose that you have won the Florida Lotto worth $18 million. Suppose further that the state of Florida will pay you the winnings in twenty annual installments, starting immediately, of $900,000 each. If your opportunity cost is 10 percent, what is the value today of these twenty installments?

Deferred annuity

5-22   Calculate the required deposit to be made today so that a series of ten withdrawals of $1,000 each can be made beginning five years from today. Assume an interest rate of 5 percent per period on end-of-period balances.

5-23   Suppose that you have just celebrated your twenty-fifth birthday. If you wish to make a deposit each year, starting on your twenty-sixth birthday, with the last deposit on your sixty-fourth birthday, so that you can begin making withdrawals of $10,000 each year for twenty years beginning on your sixty-fifth birthday, how much must each deposit be if interest is 5 percent compounded annually?

5-24   How much would you need to deposit today so that you can withdraw $4,000 per year for ten years starting three years from today, if the balance earns compound interest of 6 percent per year?

Determining the unknown interest rate

5-25   Suppose you wish to invest $2,000 today so that you will have $4,000 six years from now. What must the compound annual interest rate be in order to achieve your goal?

5-26   The Bert and Ernie Bathtub Company is planning to finance a new truck with a loan of $20,000. This loan requires them to pay five end-of-year-installments of $5,276 each. What is the effective annual interest rate that Bert and Ernie are paying for their new truck financing?

5-27   In 1980, a one-day adult pass to Disney World cost $15. In 1991, a one-day adult pass to Disney World cost $28. At what annual rate have ticket prices risen from 1980 to 1991?

Determining the number of compounding periods

5-28 If interest is earned at the rate of 5 percent compounded annually, how long will it take an investment of $10,000 to grow to:

a. $15,000?
b. $20,000?
c. $30,000?

5-29 If interest is earned at the rate of 5 percent compounded annually, how long would it take an investment to:

a. Double in value?
b. Triple in value?

5-30 Suppose you invest $2,500 today. How long will it take to grow to $5,000 if interest is compounded at the rate of 4 percent per quarter?

APR and EAR

5-31 If interest is paid at a rate of 5 percent per quarter, what is the:

a. Annual percentage rate?
b. Effective annual rate?

5-32 L. Shark is willing to lend you $10,000 for six months. At the end of six months, L. Shark requires you to repay the $10,000 plus 50%.

a. What is the length of the compounding period?
b. What is the rate of interest per compounding period?
c. What is the annual percentage rate associated with L. Shark's lending activities?
d. What is the effective annual rate of interest associated with L. Shark's lending activities?

5-33 The Consistent Savings and Loan is designing a new type of account that pays interest quarterly. The company wishes to pay, effectively, 16 percent per year on this account. Consistent desires to advertise the annual percentage rate on this new account, instead of the effective rate, since its competitors state their interest on an annualized basis. What is the APR that corresponds to an effective rate of 16 percent for this new account?

Potpourri

5-34 If you deposit $1,000 into a savings and loan account that earns 4 percent interest (APR) compounded quarterly, what will be the balance in the account at the end of four years if you make no withdrawals and the savings and loan is not insolvent prior to the end of the fourth year?

5-35 Which of the following financing arrangements offers the lowest cost of credit on an effective annual basis?

a. Simple interest loan of 15 percent per year.
b. Pawn shop credit, on terms 25 percent, payable after 50 days.
c. A bank loan with a nominal interest of 14 percent, with interest compounded monthly.

5-36 Suppose that you have an opportunity to invest at 12 percent interest compounded quarterly.

a. How much must you invest today so that you will have $2,000 four years from now?

b. How much must you invest today so that you can withdraw $2,000 at the end of each quarter for four years and have a zero balance at the end of that time?

c. If you invest $2,000 each quarter starting one quarter from today, how much will this be worth after four years?

d. If you invest $2,000 today, how much will this be worth after four years?

5-37 Ken invested $6,000 in a savings account that pays interest at the rate of 1 percent per quarter. At the end of five years, Ken withdraws only the interest. How much does he withdraw?

5-38 Erica deposited $2,000 in a savings account that pays 10 percent compound interest per year. At the end of five years, Erica withdraws only the interest on interest. How much does she withdraw?

5-39 The ABC Company wishes to invest a sum of money today in an investment that grows at a rate of 12 percent per year, so that ABC may withdraw $1,000 at the end of every year for the next ten years. How much must be invested?

5-40 If I deposit $25 per quarter, starting one quarter from now, in an account with a nominal annual interest rate of 12 percent, with interest compounded quarterly, what will be my balance in the account at the end of three years?

5-41 John Q. Public is planning to retire. John's goal is to set aside the same amount of money each year into a savings account until he retires so that he can withdraw $40,000 each year during his retirement. He expects to retire in forty years and expects to live for thirty years following his retirement. John expects to be able to earn 4 percent per year on his account balance. Calculate the amount of the deposit John must make for each of the following alternative deposit and withdrawal plans:

Plan 1 John's first deposit will be today and his last deposit will be forty years from today. He intends to make his first withdrawal forty-one years from today.

Plan 2 John's first deposit will be one year from today and his last deposit will be forty years from today. He intends to make his first withdrawal forty-one years from today.

Plan 3 John's first deposit will be one year from today and his last deposit will be thirty-nine years from today. He intends to make his first withdrawal forty years from today.

5-42 In 1987, Chirag Keith won the New York State lottery, which entitled him to receive twenty-one installments of $240,245 each. Unfortunately, Mr. Keith died after receiving only two installments. By the time his estate had been divided, his heirs had received three additional installments ("Pricey, but Perhaps the Only Way to Buy a Certain Lottery Winner," *The Wall Street Journal*, June 30, 1992, p. C1). To settle his estate, the right to receive the remaining sixteen installments was sold at auction, with the first of these sixteen installments to be received one year from the time this right was sold.

a. What would you be willing to pay for this right if your opportunity cost of funds was 4 percent?

b. What would you be willing to pay for this right if your opportunity cost of funds was 6 percent?

    c. If someone paid $2 million, what return would they receive on their investment?

5-43 In 1963, a McDonald's double hamburger cost 28 cents. In 1984, that same hamburger—well, not the *same* exact hamburger, but one just like it—cost $1.35. What was the annual rate of growth in a McDonald's hamburger's price from 1963 to 1984?

5-44 **Research:** Calculate the effective interest rate (the EAR) for a credit card other than the Discover card. Specify the APR and the method the credit card company uses to compute interest.

5-45 **Research:** Calculate the effective interest rate (the EAR) for a financing arrangement in your city or town for one of the following:

    a. The purchase of furniture, using the furniture store's credit arrangement.
    b. The purchase of an auto, using financing arranged by the auto dealer.
    c. The purchase of furniture from a "rent-to-own" dealer.
    d. Borrowing from a local pawn shop.
    e. A home mortgage financed by a local bank.

Identify clearly: (1) the lender, (2) the length of the loan, (3) the period of the loan, and (4) the method used by the lender to calculate the interest. Make sure to include any "financing charges" that are really interest and to include any up-front fees (such as points on a mortgage) in your calculations.

FURTHER READINGS

In addition to the instruction book that comes with your calculator, you can find calculator-specific instructions in Appendix C of this text as well as in:
MARK A. WHITE, "Financial Problem-Solving with an Electronic Calculator," *Financial Practice and Education*, vol. 1, no. 2, Fall/Winter 1991, pp. 73–88.

An alternative approach to determining present and future values, referred to as the wristwatch method, is demonstrated in:
BRUCE D. BAGAMERY, "Present and Future Values of Cash Flow Streams: The Wristwatch Method," *Financial Practice and Education*, vol. 1, no. 2, Fall/Winter 1991, pp. 89–91.

Several shortcuts that are commonly used to estimate the length of time necessary to multiply the value of an investment are discussed and compared in:
DANIEL T. WINKLER, "An Analysis of Shortcut Rules for Determining the Length of Time Required to Multiply an Investment," *Financial Practice and Education*, vol. 2 no. 1, Spring/Summer 1992, pp. 47–52.

Asset Valuation and Returns

CHAPTER 6

INTRODUCTION 230

ASSET VALUATION 230

The Role of the Marketplace in the Valuation of Assets 233

The Valuation of Securities 234

    Valuation of Common Stock 236

    Valuation of Preferred Stock 243

    Valuation of Long-Term Debt Securities 245

    Valuation of Options 251

RETURNS ON INVESTMENTS 255

Return on Investments with No Intermediate Cash Flows 255

Return on Investments with Even Cash Flows 256

Return on Investments with Uneven Cash Flows 258

The Reinvestment Assumption 258

Return on Stocks 260

    Return with No Dividends 260

    Return with Dividends at the End of the Period 260

Return on Bonds 265

    Effective Annual Return 266

    Yield to Maturity 268

    Yield to Call 276

Transaction Costs 278

Summary 279

Higgledy-Piggledy Apple Computer

Apple Computer Inc. is a leading developer, manufacturer, and marketer of personal computers. During the early 1980s, Apple's earnings showed phenomenal growth, growing from 12 cents to $1.20 a share from 1980 to 1986. That's a 47 percent annual growth in earnings per share.

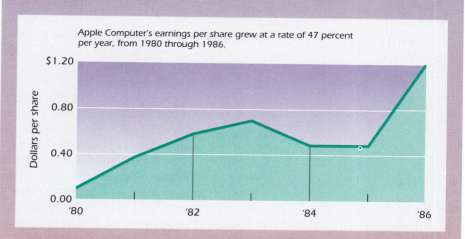

Apple Computer's earnings per share grew at a rate of 47 percent per year, from 1980 through 1986.

If Apple had kept up this growth in earnings, 1992 earnings per share would have been $12.11. But Apple's earnings per share in 1992 were $4.33. What happened?

Most firms experience high growth when their products are new, but as the market for the products matures, growth in sales and earnings wanes. Apple's experience was no different. The danger of using past growth rates of earnings, sales, or dividends to estimate growth rates in the *future* was pointed out by Little in ``Higgledy-Piggledy Growth.''[1]

Investors know that high rates of growth are not sustainable over the long run. Hence, while investors do not ignore what has taken place in the past, the value of a share of stock reflects investors' expectations regarding *future* prospects of the firm.

[1] I. Little, "Higgledy-Piggledy Growth," Institute of Statistics, vol. 24, no. 4, Nov. 1962.

INTRODUCTION

The financial manager regularly has to figure out whether a particular investment is good or bad. A good investment will enhance shareholder wealth. A bad one won't. To decide which, the manager must determine whether the benefits from the investment—often expected in future periods—will outweigh its costs. If its benefits exceed its cost, it has a positive value and is a good investment. If its benefits are less than its cost, it has a negative value and is not a good investment.

To make the best investment decisions, the financial manager must at the same time be aware of the consequences of whatever financing decisions are being considered to make these investments. If the firm takes on more debt, is this harmful to shareholders? If the firm issues more shares of equity, how does this affect the value of equity? Since we as financial managers are ultimately interested in maximizing owners' wealth, we must be aware of how investors value the equity of a firm. Furthermore, recognizing that the value of equity is the difference between the value of the firm's assets and its debt obligations, we must be aware of how debt securities are valued as well.

Valuation compares the benefits of a future investment decision with its cost. Another way of evaluating investments is to answer the question, Given its cost and its expected future benefits, what return will a particular investment provide? We will look at how to calculate the return on investments, focusing on the return on stocks and bonds.

ASSET VALUATION

Suppose I offer you the following investment opportunity: Give me $90 today, and I will pay you $100 one year from today. Whether or not this is a good investment depends on:

- What you could have done with your $90 instead of investing it with me.
- How uncertain you are that I will pay the $100 in one year.

If your other opportunities with the same amount of uncertainty provide a return of 10 percent, is this loan a good investment? There are two ways to evaluate this.

First, you can figure out what you could have wound up with after one year by investing your $90 at 10 percent:

$$\text{Value at end of one year} = \$90 + 10\% \text{ of } \$90$$
$$= \$90(1 + 0.10)$$
$$= \mathbf{\$99}$$

Since the $100 promised is more than $99, you are better off with the investment I am offering you.

Another way of looking at this is to figure out what the $100 promised in the future is worth today. To calculate its present value, we must discount the $100 at some rate. The rate we'll use is our opportunity cost of funds, which in this case is 10 percent:

$$\text{Value today of \$100 in one year} = \frac{\$100.00}{(1 + 0.10)^1} = \mathbf{\$90.91}$$

This means that you consider $90.91 today to be worth the same as $100.00 in one year. In other words, if you invested $90.91 today in an investment that yields 10 percent, you would end up with $100.00 in one year. Since today's value of the receipt of $100.00 in the future is $90.91 and it only costs $90.00 to get into this deal, the investment is attractive: It costs *less* than what you have determined it is worth.

Since there are two ways to look at this—through its future value or through its present value—which way should you go? While both approaches get you to the same decision, the approach in terms of the present value of the investment is usually easier.

Let's look at another example. Suppose you have an opportunity to buy an asset expected to give you $500 in one year and $600 in two years. If your other investment opportunities with the same amount of risk give you a return of 5 percent a year, how much are you willing to pay today to get those two future receipts?

We can figure this out by discounting the $500 for one period at 5 percent and the $600 for two periods at 5 percent:

$$\text{Present value of investment} = \frac{\$500.00}{(1 + 0.05)^1} + \frac{\$600.00}{(1 + 0.05)^2}$$

$$= \$476.19 + \$544.22$$

$$= \mathbf{\$1{,}020.41}$$

This investment is worth $1,020.41 today, so you would be willing to pay $1,020.41 *or less* for this investment:

- If you pay more than $1,020.41, you get a return of less than 5 percent.
- If you pay less than $1,020.41 you get a return of more than 5 percent.
- If you pay $1,020.41 you get a return of 5 percent.

Let's look at still another example. Suppose you are evaluating an investment that promises $10 every year forever. The value of this investment is the present value of the stream of $10s to be received each year to infinity, where each $10 is discounted the appropriate number of periods at some annual rate r:

$$\text{Present value of investment} = \frac{\$10}{(1 + r)^1} + \frac{\$10}{(1 + r)^2} + \frac{\$10}{(1 + r)^3} + \cdots + \frac{\$10}{(1 + r)^\infty}$$

which we can write in shorter form, using summation notation, as:

$$\text{Present value of investment} = \sum_{t=1}^{\infty} \frac{\$10}{(1 + r)^t} = \$10 \sum_{t=1}^{\infty} \frac{1}{(1 + r)^t}$$

Or, since $\sum_{t=1}^{\infty}[1/(1 + r)^t]$ is equal to 1/r, we can rewrite the present value of this perpetual stream as:

$$\text{Present value of investment} = \$10\left(\frac{1}{r}\right) = \frac{\$10}{r}$$

A Perpetuity Refresher

As the number of periods, T, becomes larger, the present value annuity factor:

$$\sum_{t=1}^{T} \frac{1}{(1 + r)^t}$$

approaches 1/r. This means that the present value of a perpetuity is equal to the amount of the level cash flow divided by the discount rate.

If the discount rate to translate this future stream into a present value is 10 percent, the value of the investment is $100:

$$\text{Present value of investment} = \frac{\$10}{0.10} = \$100$$

The 10 percent is the discount rate, also referred to as the ***capitalization rate,*** for the future cash flows comprising this stream. Let's look at this investment from another angle: If you consider the investment to be worth $100 today, you are capitalizing—translating future flows into a present value—the future cash flows at 10 percent per year.

As you see from these examples, the value of an investment depends on:

1. The amount and timing of the future cash flows.
2. The discount rate used to translate these future cash flows into a value today.

This discount rate represents the amount an investor is willing to pay today for the right to receive a future cash flow. Or, to put it another way, the discount rate is the rate of return the investor requires on an investment, given the price he or she is willing to pay for its expected future cash flow.

We can generalize this relationship a bit more. Let CF_t represent the cash flow from the investment in period t; so CF_1 is the cash flow at the end of period 1, CF_2 is the cash flow at the end of period 2, and so on, until we reach the last cash flow, CF_T, at the end of period T. If the investment produces cash flows for T periods and the discount rate is r, the value of the investment—the present value—is:

$$\text{Present value of investment} = \frac{CF_1}{(1 + r)^1} + \frac{CF_2}{(1 + r)^2} + \cdots + \frac{CF_T}{(1 + r)^T}$$

which we can write more compactly as:

$$\text{Present value of investment} = \sum_{t=1}^{T} \frac{CF_t}{(1 + r)^t} \qquad [6\text{-}1]$$

If the cash flows are all equal, we can simplify this by letting CF represent each cash flow and using CF in place of CF_1, CF_2, and so on. The valuation relation becomes:

$$\text{Present value of investment} = \sum_{t=1}^{T} \frac{CF}{(1 + r)^t}$$

or:

$$\text{Present value of investment} = CF \sum_{t=1}^{T} \frac{1}{(1 + r)^t} \qquad [6\text{-}2]$$

which we can write in terms of the annuity factor:

$$\text{Present value of investment} = CF\left(\begin{array}{c} \text{present value} \\ \text{annuity factor} \end{array}\right)$$

If the cash flow stream is level and is promised each period forever, T is infinite. As the number of future periods approaches infinity, for which the symbol is ∞, the present value annuity factor approaches 1/r. Therefore, the present value of a perpetual stream of cash flows is equal to:

$$\text{Present value of investment} = CF\left(\frac{1}{r}\right)$$

or:

$$\text{Present value of investment} = \frac{CF}{r} \qquad [6\text{-}3]$$

Whether we are talking about a single future cash flow, a series of level cash flows, a series of cash flows having different amounts, or a perpetual series of cash flows, to determine the present value we need to know:

- The amount and timing of the future cash flows.
- The discount rate that reflects the uncertainty of these cash flows.

The Role of the Marketplace in the Valuation of Assets

Both wise men and foolish will trade in the market, but no one group by itself will set the price. Nor will it matter what the majority, however overwhelming, may think; for the last owner, and he alone, will set the price. Thus marginal opinion will determine market price.

John Burr Williams, *The Theory of Investment Value*, North-Holland, Amsterdam, 1938, p. 12.

If you are faced with a decision whether to make a particular investment, you figure out what it is worth to you—its value—and compare its value with what it will cost you. If the investment costs less than you think it is worth, you will buy it; if it costs more than you think it is worth, you will not buy it.

Now suppose several different people are considering buying the same one-of-a-kind asset. Each potential investor determines whether the asset is priced at more or less than what he or she thinks it is worth by making the comparison between value and cost. By either buying or selling the asset based on whether the buyers and sellers (investors) think it is over- or underpriced, they determine its price.

Let's see how this works. Three investors, A, B, and C, have an opportunity to buy an asset expected to generate $100 each period forever. This is a perpetuity whose value is the ratio of the $100 to the discount rate.

If each investor thinks that this asset represents an investment that has a different amount of risk, then each will use a different discount rate to value it. If investors are **risk averse**—they do not like risk—they will value the asset using a higher discount rate the more uncertain they are about the future cash flows.

Suppose:

Investor	uses a discount rate of . . .	and values the asset as . . .
A	8.0%	$1,250
B	10.0	1,000
C	12.5	800

Now suppose the asset is owned by Investor C, who has been looking at alternative investment opportunities with similar risk that yield 12.5 percent and as a result figures that the asset is worth only $800. Both Investors A and B would be interested in buying it from C for more than $800, and C would be willing to sell it for more than $800. Since both A and B want this asset, they would bid for it.

So what is the market price of the asset? If its price is $1,000, Investor B would be indifferent between this asset and his other investments of similar risk. At $1,000, Investor A would still think the asset is underpriced and want to buy it. So the price is bid up to reflect the highest value investors are willing to pay: $1,250. If Investor A buys the asset for $1,250, he gets a return of 8 percent, which is what he thinks is appropriate, given his assessment of the asset's risk.

What makes this process work is the investors' desire to exploit profitable opportunities: C to sell it for more that she thinks it is worth and A and B to buy it for less than they think it is worth. If we assume that investors are interested in maximizing their wealth, those investors who think an asset is overpriced will want to sell it and those who think it is underpriced will want to buy it. Buyers and sellers will continue to buy and sell until they have exhausted what they believe are all the profitable opportunities. When that happens, the assets are neither over- nor underpriced. This point at which buying and selling are in balance is referred to as a **market equilibrium.** As John Burr Williams states, the price of an asset is determined by the investor with the highest valuation of the asset. If the price of an asset is above or below its market equilibrium price, investors will buy and sell it until its price is the market equilibrium price.

As long as an asset can be traded without any restrictions in a market, buying and selling the asset will determine its price. However, if there is a barrier to trading, such as a limit on the quantity that can be sold, this trading will be inhibited and the asset's price will not reflect the valuation of the highest valuer.

In addition, if there are costs to trading, such as a fee to be paid each time a trade is made, investors will figure the cost into their bidding. For example, if there is a $100 fee to buy the asset, the most Investor A would be willing to pay will be $1,150 and the most Investor B would be willing to pay will be $900, because they must pay a $100 fee to buy the asset.

The Valuation of Securities

When we value an investment, we need to know its expected future cash flows and the uncertainty of receiving them.

Let's look at three types of securities: common stock, preferred stock, and debt. These securities have different types of cash flows and the uncertainty of each is different also.

If you invest in common stock, you buy shares that represent an ownership interest in the firm. Shares of common stock are a perpetual security—there is no maturity. If you own shares of common stock, you have the right to receive a certain portion of any dividends—but dividends are *not* a sure thing. Whether a firm will pay dividends is up to its board of directors—the representatives of the common shareholders. Typically we see some pattern in the dividends companies pay: Dividends are either constant or grow at a constant rate. But there is no guarantee that dividends will be paid in the future.

Preferred shareholders are in a similar situation to that of the common shareholders, since both groups expect to receive cash dividends in the future, but the payment of these dividends is up to the board of directors. However, there are three major differences between dividends on preferred and common shares. First, the dividends on preferred stock usually are specified at a fixed rate or dollar amount, whereas the amount of dividends is not specified for common shares. Second, preferred shareholders are given preference: Their dividends must be paid before any dividends are paid on common stock. Third, if the preferred stock has a **cumulative feature,** dividends not paid in one period accumulate and are carried over to the next period. Therefore, the dividends on preferred stock are more certain than those on common shares.

Both notes and bonds are debt securities. Both are legal contracts to pay interest and principal. The primary difference between a note and a bond is that a bond has an indenture agreement, which is a document that specifies the conditions and restrictions the borrower must adhere to, such as maintaining a specified current ratio.

Most debt securities represent obligations of the borrower to pay interest at regular intervals and to repay the principal amount of the loan—referred to as the **maturity value** or the **face value**—at the end of the loan period, that is, at maturity. If you issue a debt security, you are entering into a contract with the purchaser of that debt security—the creditor—to repay the loan. Any interest and principal that you promise to pay are legal obligations—failure to pay as promised results in dire consequences.

Debt securities are senior to equity securities: The borrower must satisfy its obligations to the creditors before making payments to owners. Therefore, the cash flows from debt securities are more certain than the cash flows of either preferred or common stock.

The features of corporate debt, preferred stock, and common stock are summarized in Table 6-1.

TABLE 6-1
Summary of Features of Securities

Security	Cash flow	Certainty of cash flow	Maturity
Common stock	Dividend; no fixed rate or amount	No obligation to pay but rather paid at the discretion of the board of directors	None
Preferred stock	Dividend; generally a fixed rate or amount	No obligation to pay but preferential to common stock	None
Debt	Interest at regular intervals and face value at maturity	Legal obligation and given preference over common and preferred stock	Fixed

Valuation of Common Stock

"[A] stock is worth the present value of all the dividends ever to be paid upon it, no more, no less. The purchase of a stock represents the exchange of present goods for future goods. . . ."

Williams, *Theory of Investment Value*, p. 80.

When you buy a share of common stock, it is reasonable to figure that what you pay for it should reflect what you expect to receive from it—the return on your investment. What you receive are cash dividends in the future. How can we relate that return to what a share of common stock is worth? Well, the value of a share of stock should be equal to the present value of all the future cash flows you expect to receive from that share:

$$\text{Price of a share of common stock} = \frac{\text{dividends in first period}}{(1 + \text{discount rate})^1} + \frac{\text{dividends in second period}}{(1 + \text{discount rate})^2} + \cdots$$

Since common stock never matures, today's value is the present value of an infinite stream of cash flows. Also, common stock dividends are not fixed, as are those of preferred stock. Not knowing the amount of the dividends—or even if there will be future dividends—makes it difficult to determine the value of common stock.

So what are we to do? Well, we can grapple with the valuation of common stock by looking at its current dividend and making assumptions about any future dividends it may pay.

Dividend Valuation Model

If dividends are constant forever, the value of a share of stock is the present value of the dividends per share per period, in perpetuity. Let D represent the constant dividend per share of common stock expected next period and each period thereafter, forever; P_0 the price of a share of stock today; and r_e, the required rate of return on common stock. The **required rate of return** is the return shareholders demand to compensate them for the time value of money tied up in their investment and the uncertainty of the future cash flows from these investments.

The current price of a share of common stock, P_0, is:

$$P_0 = \frac{D}{(1 + r_e)^1} + \frac{D}{(1 + r_e)^2} + \cdots + \frac{D}{(1 + r_e)^\infty}$$

which we can write using summation notation:

$$P_0 = \sum_{t=1}^{\infty} \frac{D}{(1 + r_e)^t}$$

The summation of a constant amount discounted from perpetuity simplifies to:

$$P_0 = \frac{D}{r_e}$$

If the current dividend is $2 per share and the required rate of return is 10 percent, the value of a share of stock is:

$$P_0 = \frac{\$2}{0.10} = \$20$$

Therefore, if you pay $20 per share and dividends remain constant at $2 per share, you will earn a 10 percent return per year on your investment every year. But dividends on common stock often change over time.

If dividends grow at a constant rate, the value of a share of stock is the present value of a *growing* cash flow. Let D_0 indicate *this* period's dividend. If dividends grow at a constant rate, g, forever, the present value of the common stock is the present value of all *future* dividends:

$$P_0 = \frac{D_0(1 + g)^1}{(1 + r_e)^1} + \frac{D_0(1 + g)^2}{(1 + r_e)^2} + \cdots + \frac{D_0(1 + g)^\infty}{(1 + r_e)^\infty}$$

Pulling today's dividend D_0, from each term:

$$P_0 = D_0 \left[\frac{(1 + g)^1}{(1 + r_e)^1} + \frac{(1 + g)^2}{(1 + r_e)^2} + \cdots + \frac{(1 + g)^\infty}{(1 + r_e)^\infty} \right]$$

Using summation notation:

$$P_0 = D_0 \sum_{t=1}^{\infty} \frac{(1 + g)^t}{(1 + r_e)^t}$$

Because $\sum_{t=1}^{\infty} [(1 + g)^t/(1 + r_e)^t]$ is approximately equal to $(1 + g)/(r_e - g)$:[2]

$$P_0 = D_0 \frac{(1 + g)}{(r_e - g)}$$

If we represent the next period's dividend, D_1, in terms of this period's dividend, D_0, compounded one period at the rate g:

$$D_1 = D_0(1 + g) \qquad \text{or} \qquad D_0 = \frac{D_1}{1 + g}$$

and substitute the last expression for D_0 in the equation above for D_0 below:

$$P_0 = D_0 \frac{(1 + g)}{(r_e - g)} = \frac{D_1}{1 + g} \frac{1 + g}{r_e - g}$$

$$P_0 = \frac{D_1}{r_e - g} \qquad\qquad\qquad [6\text{-}4]$$

This equation is referred to as the ***dividend valuation model*** (DVM).[3]

---

[2] Our use of the term $(1 + g)/(r_e - g)$ to approximate for $\sum_{t=1}^{\infty} [(1 + g)^t/(1 + r_e)^t]$ is based on integration of the latter term (remember your calculus?). Since the approximation is well accepted, we will use it in our analysis.

[3] The dividend valuation model is attributed to Myron Gordon, who popularized the constant-growth model. A more formal presentation of this model can be found in published works by Gordon: "Dividends, Earnings and Stock Prices," *Review of Economics and Statistics,* May 1959, pp. 99–105, and *The Investment Financing and Valuation of the Corporation,* Irwin, Homewood, Ill., 1962. However, the foundation of common stock valuation is laid out—for both constant and growing dividends—by John Burr Williams, *The Theory of Investment Value,* North-Holland, Amsterdam, 1938, chaps. V, VI, and VII.

Consider a firm expected to pay a constant dividend of $2 per share forever. If this dividend is capitalized at 10 percent, the value of a share is $20:

$$P_0 = \frac{\$2}{0.10} = \mathbf{\$20}$$

If, however, the dividends are expected to be $2 in the *next* period and grow at a rate of 6 percent per year forever, the value of a share of stock is $50:

$$P_0 = \frac{\$2}{0.10 - 0.06} = \mathbf{\$50}$$

Does this make sense? Yes. If dividends are expected to grow in the future, the stock is worth more than if the dividends are expected to remain the same.

If today's value of a share is $50.00, what are we saying about the value of the stock next year? If we move everything up one period, D_1 is no longer $2.00, but $2.00 grown one period at 6 percent, or $2.12. Therefore, we expect the price of the stock at the end of one year, P_1, to be $53.00:

$$P_1 = \frac{\$2.12}{0.10 - 0.06} = \mathbf{\$53.00}$$

At the end of two years, the price will be even higher:

$$P_2 = \frac{\$2.2472}{0.10 - 0.06} = \mathbf{\$56.18}$$

Since we expect dividends to grow each period, we also expect the price of the stock to grow over time as well. In fact, the price is expected to grow at the same rate as the dividends: 6 percent per period.

The relation between the growth rate of dividends, g, and the price of the stock expected in the future is illustrated in Figure 6-1. For a given required rate of return and dividend—in this case r_e = 10 percent and D_1 = $2—we see that the price of a share of stock is expected to grow each period at the rate g.

What if the dividends are expected to decline each year? That is, what if g is negative? We can still use the dividend valuation model, but each dividend in the future is expected to be *less* than the one before it. For example,

FIGURE 6-1

Price One Year from Today of a Share of Stock with a Required Rate of Return of 10 Percent and a Dividend of $2, for Different Expected Rates of Growth in Dividends

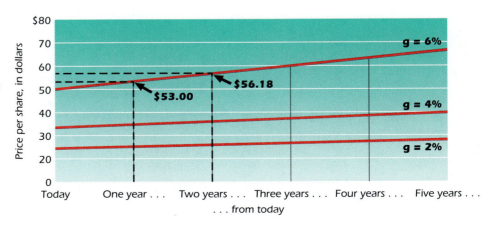

suppose a stock has a current dividend of $5 per share and the required rate of return is 10 percent. If dividends are expected to decline 3 percent each year, what is the value of a share of stock today? We know that $D_0 = \$5$, $r_e = 10$ percent, and $g = -3$ percent. Therefore,

$$P_0 = \frac{\$5.00(1 - 0.03)}{0.10 + 0.03} = \frac{\$4.85}{0.13} = \mathbf{\$37.31}$$

Next period's dividend, D_1, is expected to be $4.85. We capitalize this at 13 percent, that is, 10 percent $- (-3$ percent) or 10 percent $+ 3$ percent. What do we expect the price of the stock to be next period?

$$P_1 = \frac{\$5.00(1 - 0.03)^2}{0.13} = \frac{\$4.705}{0.13} = \mathbf{\$36.19}$$

The expected price goes the same way as the dividend: down 3 percent each year.

Let's look at another situation, one in which growth is expected to *change* but at different growth rates as time goes on. Consider a share of common stock whose dividend is currently $3.00 per share and is expected to grow at a rate of 4 percent per year for five years and afterward at a rate of 3 percent per year after five years. To tackle this problem, let's break it into two manageable parts: the first five years and the years after the first five, or:

$$P_0 = \underbrace{\frac{D_1}{(1 + 0.10)} + \frac{D_2}{(1 + 0.10)^2} + \frac{D_3}{(1 + 0.10)^3} + \frac{D_4}{(1 + 0.10)^4} + \frac{D_5}{(1 + 0.10)^5}}_{}$$

Dividends growing at a rate of 4 percent per year

$$+ \underbrace{\frac{D_6}{(1 + 0.10)^6} + \frac{D_7}{(1 + 0.10)^7} + \cdots + \frac{D_\infty}{(1 + 0.10)^\infty}}_{}$$

Dividends growing at a rate of 3 percent per year

or:

$$P_0 = \begin{matrix}\text{present value of dividends} \\ \text{received during first five years}\end{matrix} + \begin{matrix}\text{present value of dividends} \\ \text{received after the first five} \\ \text{years to infinity}\end{matrix}$$

The present value of the dividends in the first five years is:

$$\begin{matrix}\text{Present value of} \\ \text{dividends received} \\ \text{during first five years}\end{matrix} = \frac{D_1}{(1 + 0.10)^1} + \frac{D_2}{(1 + 0.10)^2} + \frac{D_3}{(1 + 0.10)^3}$$

$$+ \frac{D_4}{(1 + 0.10)^4} + \frac{D_5}{(1 + 0.10)^5}$$

$$= \frac{\$3.12}{1.1000} + \frac{\$3.24}{1.2100} + \frac{\$3.37}{1.3310} + \frac{\$3.51}{1.4641} + \frac{\$3.65}{1.6105}$$

$$= \$2.8364 + \$2.6777 + \$2.5319 + \$2.3974 + \$2.2664$$

$$= \mathbf{\$12.7098} \text{ or } \mathbf{\$12.71}$$

The present value of dividends received after the fifth year—evaluated five years from today—is the expected price of the stock in five years, P_5:

$$P_5 = \frac{D_6}{0.10 - 0.03} = \frac{D_5(1 + 0.03)}{0.10 - 0.03}$$

$$= \frac{\$3.00(1 + 0.04)^5(1 + 0.03)}{0.10 - 0.03} = \frac{\$3.65(1 + 0.03)}{0.10 - 0.03}$$

$$= \frac{\$3.76}{0.07} = \mathbf{\$53.71}$$

The price expected at the end of five years is $53.71, which we translate into a value today by discounting it five periods at 10 percent:

$$\text{Present value of dividends after the first five years to infinity} = \frac{P_5}{(1 + 0.10)^5}$$

$$= \frac{\$53.71}{(1 + 0.10)^5} = \mathbf{\$33.35}$$

Putting everything together:

$$P_0 = \text{present value of dividends received during first five years} + \text{present value of all dividends received after the fifth year}$$

$$= \$12.71 \qquad\qquad + \$33.35$$

$$= \mathbf{\$46.06}$$

The value of a share of this stock is $46.06. We can see the growth in the expected price of a share of stock in Figure 6-2, where the price grows at a rate of 4 percent the first five years and 3 percent after the fifth year.

FIGURE 6-2

Growth in Share Price If Dividends Grow at 4 Percent per Year for the First Five Years and 3 Percent Thereafter

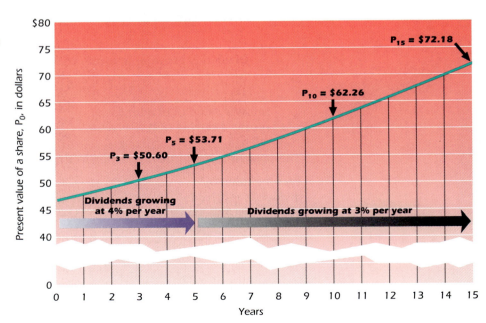

The DVM and the P/E Ratio

We can represent the dividend valuation model in terms of a share's P/E ratio. Let's start with a dividend valuation model with constant growth in dividends:

$$P_0 = \frac{D_1}{r_e - g}$$

If we divide both sides of this equation by earnings per share, we can represent the dividend valuation model in terms of the price-earnings (P/E) ratio:

$$\frac{P_0}{EPS_1} = \frac{D_1/EPS_1}{r_e - g}$$

$$\text{Price-earnings ratio} = \frac{\text{dividend payout ratio}}{r_e - g}$$

This tells us the P/E ratio is influenced by the dividend payout ratio, the required rate of return on equity, and the expected growth rate of dividends.

The dividend valuation model makes some sense regarding the relation between the value of a share of stock, the growth in dividends, and the discount rate:

- The greater the current dividend, the greater the value of a share of stock.
- The greater the expected growth in dividends, the greater the value of a share of stock.
- The more uncertainty regarding future dividends, the greater the discount rate and the lower the value of a share of stock.

However, the DVM has some drawbacks. How do you deal with dividends that do not grow at a constant rate? As you can see in our example, this model does not accommodate nonconstant growth easily.

What if the firm does not pay dividends now? In that case, D_0 would be zero and the expected price would be zero. But a zero price for a share of stock does not make any sense! Therefore, the DVM may be appropriate to use to value the stock of companies with stable dividend policies, but it is not applicable for all firms.

Required Rate of Return

Future cash flows—dividends in the case of common stock—are discounted to the present at some rate that reflects the shareowners' opportunity cost. This opportunity cost is what they could have earned on alternative investments having similar risks. Since investors could earn this return on alternative investments, they require at least the same return. This minimum return is the required rate of return—the discount rate that compensates the shareowners for the time value of money and risk:

$$\text{Required rate of return} = \text{time value of money} + \text{compensation for bearing risk} \qquad [6\text{-}5]$$

Since shareowners are risk averse, they require compensation in the form of a greater return for bearing risk. The greater the risk, the greater the required return.

If we start with the dividend valuation model with a constant growth rate:

$$P_0 = \frac{D_1}{r_e - g}$$

and solve for r_e:

$$r_e = \frac{D_1}{P_0} + g$$

we see that the required rate of return is made up of the ***dividend yield,*** D_1/P_0, plus the rate at which we expect the share price to grow, the ***capital yield,*** g:

$$r_e = \text{dividend yield} + \text{capital yield}$$

In other words, if we know next period's dividend, the current price, and the expected growth rate, we can determine the required rate of return. Suppose a share of ABC stock is currently selling for $40 per share. If next period's dividend is expected to be $2 and dividends are expected to grow at a rate of 4 percent per year, the required rate of return is:

$$r_e = \frac{\$2}{\$40} + 4\% = 5\% + 4\% = \mathbf{9\%}$$

In other words, a share of ABC stock will be valued at a price that yields the investor 9 percent.

Growth Rate of Future Dividends

If we assume that a constant proportion of earnings are paid in dividends—a constant dividend payout—we can tie the growth rate of dividends to the return on equity. Let's start with the dividend valuation model with constant growth:

$$P_0 = \frac{D_1}{r_e - g}$$

If we divide both sides by earnings per share for the next period, EPS_1, we get:

$$\frac{P_0}{EPS_1} = \frac{D_1/EPS_1}{r_e - g}$$

Inverting both sides:

$$\frac{EPS_1}{P_0} = \frac{r_e - g}{D_1/EPS_1}$$

Recognizing that the return on equity, r_e, is equal to EPS_1/P_0:

$$r_e = \frac{r_e - g}{D_1/EPS_1}$$

Simplifying and solving for the growth rate:

$$g = r_e\left(1 - \frac{D_1}{EPS_1}\right)$$

or:

$$\text{Expected growth rate of dividends} = \frac{\text{return}}{\text{on equity}}\,(1 - \text{dividend payout ratio})$$

From this we see that:

- The greater the return on equity, the greater the expected growth rate of dividends.
- The greater the dividend payout, the lower the growth rate of dividends.

Does this make sense? Yes. The more the firm can earn, the greater the expected future growth in dividends. Also, the more the firm pays out in dividends, the less it has to reinvest into the firm for the future and the lower will be the expected growth rate of dividends.

Valuation of Preferred Stock

The value of the preferred stock is the present value of all future dividends. If a share of preferred stock has a 5 percent dividend (based on a $100 par value), paid at the end of each year, today's price is the present value of the stream of $5s forever:

$$\text{Present value of preferred stock} = \frac{\$5}{(1+r)^1} + \frac{\$5}{(1+r)^2} + \cdots + \frac{\$5}{(1+r)^\infty}$$

which we can rewrite as:

$$\text{Present value of preferred stock} = \sum_{t=1}^{\infty} \frac{\$5}{(1+r)^t} = \frac{\$5}{r}$$

If the discount rate is 10 percent, then:

$$\text{Present value of preferred stock} = \frac{\$5}{0.10} = \mathbf{\$50}$$

That is, investors are willing to pay $50 today for the promised stream of $5 per period, since they consider 10 percent to be sufficient compensation for both the time value of money and the risk associated with the perpetual stream of $5s.

Let's rephrase this relation, letting P_p indicate today's price, D_p indicate the perpetual dividend per share per period, and r_p indicate the discount rate (the required rate of return on the preferred stock). Then:

$$P_p = \frac{D_p}{r_p} \qquad\qquad\qquad [6\text{-}6]$$

Consider a share of preferred stock with a par value of $100 and a dividend rate of 12 percent. If the required rate of return is 15 percent, the value of the preferred stock is less than $100:

$$P_p = \frac{\$12}{0.15} = \mathbf{\$80}$$

We can make some generalizations about the value of preferred stock:

- The greater the dividend stream, the greater the value of a share of stock.
- The greater the required rate of return—the discount rate—the lower the value of a share of stock.

Let's look at a feature of preferred stock that may affect its value: the call feature. If preferred stock has a **call feature,** the issuer has the right to call it—buy it back—at a specified price per share, referred to as the **call price.**

Suppose the dividend rate on preferred stock is $6 per share and the preferred stock is callable after three years at par value, $100. If the preferred stock has a required rate of return of 5 percent, the value of a share of preferred stock without the call is:

$$P_p = \frac{\$6}{0.05} = \mathbf{\$120}$$

To take account of the call feature, we need to alter our valuation equation so that we find the present value of the first three dividends and the present value of the call price:

$$P_p = \underbrace{\frac{\$6.00}{(1 + 0.05)^1} + \frac{\$6.00}{(1 + 0.05)^2} + \frac{\$6.00}{(1 + 0.05)^3}}_{\substack{\text{Present value of dividends} \\ \text{in next three years}}} + \underbrace{\frac{\$100.00}{(1 + 0.05)^3}}_{\substack{\text{Present value} \\ \text{of call price}}}$$

$$= \$5.71 \quad + \quad \$5.44 \quad + \quad \$5.18 \quad + \quad \$86.38$$

$$= \mathbf{\$102.71}$$

If the preferred shares did not have a call feature, they would be worth more; the call feature reduces the value of the shares. What is the likelihood that the firm will call in the preferred shares? If the required rate of return is 5 percent, that is, investors demand a 5 percent return, and the stock pays $6 on the par of $100, or 6 percent, the firm can call in the 6 percent preferred shares and issue 5 percent shares. Since calling in the preferred shares makes sense—the firm can lower its costs of raising capital—the firm will very likely call in the preferred shares if it can.

Valuation of Long-Term Debt Securities

Long-term debt securities, such as notes and bonds, are promises by the borrower to repay the principal amount. Notes and bonds may also require the borrower to pay interest periodically, typically semiannually or annually; the interest is generally stated as a percentage of the face value of the bond or note. We refer to the interest payments as coupon payments or *coupons* and the percentage rate as the *coupon rate.* If these coupons are a constant amount, paid at regular intervals, we refer to the security paying them as having a *straight coupon.* A debt security that does not have a promise to pay interest we refer to as a *zero-coupon* note or bond.

The value of a debt security today is the present value of the promised future cash flows—the interest and the maturity value. Therefore, the present value of a debt is the sum of the present value of the interest payments and the present value of the maturity value:

$$\text{Value of debt security} = \frac{\text{present value of future}}{\text{interest payments}} + \frac{\text{present value of}}{\text{maturity value}}$$

To figure out the value of a debt security, we have to discount the future cash flows—the interest and maturity value—at some rate that reflects both the time value of money and the uncertainty of receiving those future cash flows. We refer to this discount rate as the *yield.* The more uncertain the future cash flows, the greater the yield. It follows that the greater the yield, the lower the present value of the future cash flows—hence, the lower the value of the debt security. The present value of the maturity value is the present value of a future amount.

In the case of a straight-coupon security, the present value of the interest payments is the present value of an annuity. In the case of a zero-coupon security, the present value of the interest payments is zero; so the present value of the debt is the present value of the maturity value.

We can rewrite the formula for the present value of a debt security using some new notation and some familiar notation. Since there are two different cash flows—interest and maturity value—let C represent the coupon payment promised each period and M represent the maturity value. Also, let T be the number of periods until maturity; t, a specific period; and r_d, the yield. The present value of a debt security, V, is:

$$V = \sum_{t=1}^{T} \frac{C}{(1 + r_d)^t} + \frac{M}{(1 + r_d)^T} \qquad [6\text{-}7]$$

Present value of future interest payments   Present value of maturity value

To see how the valuation of future cash flows from debt securities works, let's look at the valuation of a straight-coupon bond and a zero-coupon bond.

Straight-Coupon Bond

Suppose you are considering investing in a straight-coupon bond that:

- Promises interest of $100, paid at the end of each year.
- Promises to pay the principal amount of $1,000 at the end of twelve years.
- Has a yield of 5 percent per year.

What is this bond worth today? We are given the following:

Interest, C $= \$100$ every year
Number of periods, T $= 12$ years
Maturity value, M $= \$1,000$
Yield, r_d $= 5\%$ per year

$$V = \sum_{t=1}^{12} \frac{\$100.00}{(1 + 0.05)^t} + \frac{\$1,000.00}{(1 + 0.05)^{12}}$$

$$= \$886.32 + \$556.84$$

$$= \mathbf{\$1,443.16}$$

This bond has a present value greater than its maturity value; so we say that the bond is selling at a ***premium*** from its maturity value. Does this make sense? Yes. The bond pays interest of 10 percent of its face value every year. But what investors require on their investment—the capitalization rate, which is based on the time value of money and the uncertainty of future cash flows—is 5 percent. So what happens? The bond paying 10 percent is attractive—*so* attractive that its price is bid upward to a price that gives investors the going rate, the 5 percent. In other words, an investor who buys the bond for $1,443.16 will get a 5 percent return on it if it is held until maturity. We say that at $1,443.16, the bond is priced to yield 5 percent per year.

Suppose, instead, that the interest on the bond is $50 every year—a 5 percent coupon rate—instead of $100 every year. Then:

Interest, C $= \$50$ every year
Number of periods, T $= 12$ years
Maturity value, M $= \$1,000$
Yield, r_d $= 5\%$ per year

$$V = \sum_{t=1}^{12} \frac{\$50.00}{(1 + 0.05)^t} + \frac{\$1,000.00}{(1 + 0.05)^{12}}$$

$$= \$443.16 + \$556.84$$

$$= \mathbf{\$1,000.00}$$

The bond's present value is equal to its face value, and we say that the bond is selling "at par." Investors will pay face value for a bond that pays the going rate for bonds of similar risk. In other words, if you buy the 5 percent bond for $1,000, you will earn a 5 percent annual return on your investment if you hold it until maturity.

Different Value, Different Coupon Rate, But Same Return?

How can a bond costing $1,443.16 and another costing $1,000.00 each give an investor a return of 5 percent per year if held to maturity? If the $1,443.16 bond has a higher coupon rate than the $1,000.00 bond (10 percent versus 5 percent), it is possible for the bonds to provide the same return. With the $1,443.16 bond you pay more now, but also get more each year ($100 versus $50). The extra $100 a year for twelve years makes up for the $443.16 extra you pay now to buy the bond.

Suppose, instead, the interest on the bond is $20 every year—a 2 percent coupon rate. Then,

Interest, C = $20 every year
Number of periods, T = 12 years
Maturity value, M = $1,000
Yield, r_d = 5% per year

$$V = \sum_{t=1}^{12} \frac{\$20.00}{(1 + 0.05)^t} + \frac{\$1,000.00}{(1 + 0.05)^{12}}$$

$$= \$177.26 + \$556.84$$

$$= \mathbf{\$734.10}$$

The bond sells at a ***discount*** from its face value. Why? Because investors are not going to pay face value for a bond that pays less than the going rate for bonds of similar risk. If an investor can buy other bonds that yield 5 percent, why pay the face value—$1,000.00 in this case—for a bond that pays only 2 percent? An investor wouldn't. Instead, the price of this bond would fall to a price that provides an investor a yield to maturity of 5 percent. In other words, if you buy the 2 percent bond for $734.10, you will earn a 5 percent annual return on your investment if you hold it until maturity.

So when we look at the value of a bond, we see that its present value is dependent on the relation between the coupon rate and the yield. We can see this relation in our example:

If a bond has a yield of 5% and a coupon rate of . . .	it will sell for . . .	so we say it is selling at . . .
10%	$1,443.16	a premium
5	1,000.00	par
2	734.10	a discount

Let's look at another example, this time keeping the coupon rate the same, but varying the yield. Suppose we have a bond with a $1,000 face value and a 10 percent coupon rate; the bond pays interest at the end of each year and matures in five years. If the yield is five percent, the value of the bond is:

$$V = \sum_{t=1}^{5} \frac{\$100.00}{(1 + 0.05)^t} + \frac{\$1,000.00}{(1 + 0.05)^5}$$

$$= \$432.95 + \$783.53$$

$$= \mathbf{\$1,216.48}$$

If the yield is 10 percent, the same as the coupon rate (10 percent), the bond sells at face value:

$$V = \sum_{t=1}^{5} \frac{\$100.00}{(1 + 0.10)^t} + \frac{\$1,000.00}{(1 + 0.10)^5}$$

$$= \$379.08 + \$620.92$$

$$= \mathbf{\$1,000.00}$$

If the yield is 15 percent, the bond's value is less than its face value:

$$V = \sum_{t=1}^{5} \frac{\$100.00}{(1 + 0.15)^t} + \frac{\$1,000.00}{(1 + 0.15)^5}$$

$$= \$335.21 + \$497.18$$

$$= \mathbf{\$832.39}$$

When we hold the coupon rate constant and vary the yield, we see that:

If a bond has a coupon rate of 10% and a yield of . . .	it will sell for . . .	so we say it is selling at . . .
5%	$1,216.48	a premium
10	1,000.00	par
15	832.39	a discount

We see a relation developing between the coupon rate, the yield, and the value of a debt security:

- If the coupon rate is more than the yield, the security is worth more than its face value—it sells at a premium.
- If the coupon rate is less than the yield, the security is worth less than its face value—it sells at a discount.
- If the coupon rate is equal to the yield, the security is worth its face value—it sells at par.

We can extend the valuation of debt to securities that pay interest every six months. But before we do this, we must grapple with a bit of semantics. In Wall Street parlance, the term **yield to maturity** is used to describe an *annualized* yield on a security if the security is held to maturity. For example, if a bond has a return of 5 percent over a six-month period, the annualized yield to maturity for a year is two times 5 percent, or 10 percent.

Annualized yield to maturity = yield over six months × 2   [6-8]

But is this the effective yield to maturity? Not quite. The **effective yield to maturity** is:

Effective yield to maturity = (1 + yield over six months)^2 − 1   [6-9]

That is, the effective yield to maturity considers the compounding of interest after the first six months. The yield to maturity, as commonly used on Wall Street, is the *annualized* yield to maturity.

Does it make a difference which you use? Let's look at an example. Suppose a bond has a six-month yield of 6 percent. Then:

Effective yield to maturity = (1 + 0.06)^2 − 1 = **12.36%**

and

Annualized yield to maturity = 6% × 2 = **12%**

Is this difference enough to worry about? Probably. If you invested $1 million, the difference between 12 percent and 12.36 percent is $3,600!

We didn't have to worry about whether the yield to maturity was "effective" or "annualized" in our previous example, since interest was paid once a year. In that case, the "effective" and "annualized" yields are the same. Considering the importance of the time value of money, let's focus on the *effective* yield to maturity from here on out: Whenever we mention *yield* or *yield to maturity*, assume we are referring to the rate that considers the time value of money unless we tell you otherwise.

If a debt security promises interest every six months, there are a couple of things to watch out for in calculating the security's value. First, the r_d we use to discount cash flows is the *six-month yield*, not an annual yield. Second, the number of periods is the number of *six-month periods* until maturity, not the number of years to maturity.

Suppose we are interested in valuing a $1,000-face-value bond that matures in five years and promises a coupon of 4 percent per year, with interest paid semiannually. This four percent coupon rate tells us that 2 percent, or $20, is paid every six months. What is the bond's value today if the *annualized* yield to maturity is six percent? From the bond's description we know that:

Interest, C $\quad\quad\quad\quad$ = $20 every six months
Number of periods, T = 5 times 2 = 10 six-month periods
Maturity value, M $\quad\;$ = $1,000
Yield, r_d $\quad\quad\quad\quad$ = 6%/2 = 3% for six-month period

The value of the bond is:

$$V = \sum_{t=1}^{10} \frac{\$20.00}{(1 + 0.03)^t} + \frac{\$1,000.00}{(1 + 0.03)^{10}}$$

$$= \$170.60 + \$744.09$$

$$= \mathbf{\$914.70}$$

If the annualized yield to maturity is 8 percent, then:

Interest, C $\quad\quad\quad\quad$ = $20 every six months
Number of periods, T = 5 times 2 = 10 six-month periods
Maturity value, M $\quad\;$ = $1,000
Yield, r_d $\quad\quad\quad\quad$ = 8%/2 = 4% for six-month period

and the value of the bond is:

$$V = \sum_{t=1}^{10} \frac{\$20.00}{(1 + 0.04)^t} + \frac{\$1,000.00}{(1 + 0.04)^{10}}$$

$$= \$162.22 + \$675.56$$

$$= \mathbf{\$837.78}$$

We can see the relation between the annualized yield to maturity and the value of the 4 percent coupon bond in Figure 6-3. The greater the yield, the lower the present value of the bond. This makes sense, since an increasing yield means that we are discounting the future cash flows at higher rates.

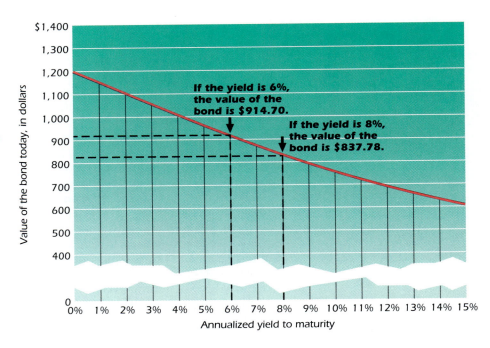

FIGURE 6-3

Relation between Annualized Yield to Maturity and Present Value of 4 Percent Coupon Bond, with Interest Paid Semiannually and Five Years Remaining until Maturity

If the yield is 6%, the value of the bond is $914.70.

If the yield is 8%, the value of the bond is $837.78.

Value of the bond today, in dollars

Annualized yield to maturity

Zero-Coupon Bond

The value of a zero-coupon bond is easier to figure out than the value of a straight-coupon bond. Let's see why.

Suppose we are considering investing in a zero-coupon bond that matures in five years and has a face value of $1,000. If this bond does not pay interest—explicitly at least—no one will buy it at its face value. Instead, investors pay some amount *less* than the face value, with the bond's return based on the difference between what they pay for it and—assuming they hold it to maturity—its maturity value.

If these bonds are priced to yield 10 percent, their present value is the present value of $1,000, discounted five years at 10 percent. We are given:

Maturity value, M   = $1,000
Number of periods, T = 5 years
Yield, r_d = 10% per year

The value of the debt security is:

$$V = \frac{\$1,000}{(1 + 0.10)^5} = \textbf{\$620.92}$$

If, instead, these bonds are priced to yield 5 percent:

Maturity value, M   = $1,000
Number of periods, T = 5 years
Yield, r_d = 5% per year

the value of a bond is:

$$V = \frac{\$1,000.00}{(1 + 0.05)^5} = \textbf{\$783.53}$$

250

FIGURE 6-4

Relation between Yield to Maturity and Present Value of Zero-Coupon Bond with Five Years Remaining until Maturity

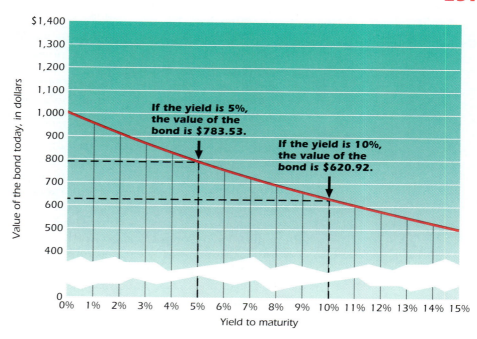

The price of the zero-coupon bond is sensitive to the yield: If the yield changes from 10 percent to 5 percent, the value of the bond increases from $620.92 to $783.53. We can see the sensitivity of the value of the bond's price over yields ranging from 1 percent to 15 percent in Figure 6-4.

Valuation of Options

The value of an option depends on:

1. The value of the underlying asset.
2. The exercise price.
3. The time value of money.
4. The volatility in the value of the underlying asset.
5. The time to maturity.

To see how these factors influence the value of an option, let's look at a simple one—a stock option. A **stock option** is the right to buy or sell a particular common stock at a specified price within a specified period. These options are not created by the company that issued the underlying stock; rather, they are created by the exchange on which the option is to be traded.

To illustrate the influence of these factors on an option's value, consider the following stock option: *the right to buy a share of ABC stock at $40 a share before December 15*. Since this is a right to buy an asset, we refer to this as a **call option.** It gives the investor the right to buy a share of ABC stock at the $40 price per share—the **strike price** (also called the **exercise price**)—before December 15, the **expiration date.**

If ABC stock is currently trading at $35 a share, this option is referred to as **out of the money,** that is, the current stock price is less than the strike price of $40. Is this option worthless? The answer is no. The option to buy ABC stock at $40 a share is valuable (that is, the option is worth more than $0) since there is *some* chance that the price of ABC stock will rise above $40 a share prior to December 15.[4]

If ABC stock is currently trading at $40 a share, this option is referred to as **at the money;** that is, the current stock price is equal to the strike price. Again, the option would be worth something, since ABC stock may rise above the strike price prior to December 15.

If the ABC stock is currently trading for $45 a share, this option is referred to as **in the money,** that is, the current stock price is greater than the strike price. The option will be worth more than $5. Why? Because an investor today can buy the stock at $40 (exercising the option) and then sell it for $45 in the market, making a $5 profit. Therefore, the option is worth at least $5. Again, since the stock price has a chance of rising further prior to December 15, the option will be worth more than $5.

From this analysis, we can see that the greater the price of the underlying asset (the stock, in this case), the greater the value of the call option. That is, there is a direct relation between the price of the underlying asset and the value of the call option.

The option value is also affected by the exercise price. For a given price of ABC stock, the lower the exercise price, the greater the value of the option. For example, assume that the price of ABC stock is $45. The option with the exercise price of $40 will have a value greater than $5. Compare this with an option on ABC with an exercise price of $35. In this latter case, the ABC option will trade for some value greater than $10. Therefore, there is an inverse relation between the exercise price and the value of the call option.

The value of the option is also affected by the time value of money. The call option is the right to buy an asset sometime in the future. Since the option represents a future purchase, the greater the opportunity cost of funds, the greater the value of the option. By delaying the purchase of the asset, you can invest your funds in other assets—the greater the return available, the greater is the value of deferring the purchase of the asset. In other words, the greater the opportunity cost, the more valuable it is to have the option, which allows you to purchase the asset in the future (instead of today).

The value of the option is also influenced by the volatility of the value of the underlying asset. If ABC stock is currently trading at $35 a share, the value of the option to buy ABC stock at $40 a share is influenced by the probability that ABC stock will rise above $40 prior to the expiration date. What affects this probability? The more volatile the value of the underlying asset, the greater the likelihood that it may increase in value prior to the expiration date. Therefore, there is a direct relation between the volatility of the underlying asset's value and the value of the call option.

The time remaining to expiration also affects the value of the option. For example, if today is October 15 and the ABC stock is trading for $35 a share, there are two months left before the option's expiration. If, instead, today is

---

[4] Of course, the price of the stock may fall below $40. If the price of the stock is below $40, the option owner will not choose to exercise the option (that is, the option owner will not purchase the stock). Since a call option is an option to buy and not an option to sell the stock, the option's value depends on the probability that the stock's price will be *above* the exercise price prior to expiration.

November 15 and the ABC stock is trading for $35 a share, one month is left before expiration. In which case is it more likely that the option will become in the money before expiration? October 15, because there is more time for the stock price to rise. Therefore, there is a direct relation between the time to maturity of an option and the option's value.

The factors that affect the value of a call option and their relation to the option's value are summarized in Table 6-2.

If we alter our example to make the option a **put option** in ABC stock—that is, an option to *sell* ABC stock—we would have a different set of relations between these factors and the value of the option. Consider the following put option on ABC stock: *The right to sell a share of ABC stock at $40 a share before December 15.*

The put becomes more valuable:

- The lower the value of the asset, since the investor in the put option gains when the exercise price (the sales price) is higher than the asset's actual value.
- The higher the exercise price, since this means the investor can sell the asset for a higher price.
- The lower the time value of money, since the investor is delaying selling the asset and getting the proceeds from that sale.
- The more volatile the underlying asset's value, since there is no profit if the price of the underlying asset does not move.
- The longer the time to maturity, since there is more time for the underlying asset's price to move below the exercise price.

TABLE 6-2

Relation between Call and Put Option Features and the Value of an Option

Feature	Relation to call option value	Relation to put option value
Value of underlying asset	**Direct relation.** The greater the value of the underlying asset, the greater the value of the option.	**Inverse relation.** The greater the value of the underlying asset, the lower the value of the option.
Exercise price	**Inverse relation.** The lower the exercise price, the greater the value of the option.	**Direct relation.** The greater the exercise price, the greater the value of the option.
Time value of money	**Direct relation.** The greater the time value of money, the greater the value of the option.	**Inverse relation.** The lower the time value of money, the greater the value of the option.
Volatility of underlying asset value	**Direct relation.** The greater the volatility of the value of the underlying asset, the greater the value of the option.	**Direct relation.** The greater the volatility of the value of the underlying asset, the greater the value of the option.
Time to maturity	**Direct relation.** The greater the time remaining to maturity, the greater the value of the option.	**Direct relation.** The greater the time remaining to maturity, the greater the value of the option.

The relation between the value of the put option and the factors that affect the value of the option are also summarized in Table 6-2. Incorporating these factors mathematically into the valuation of an option or optionlike security is quite complex. That's part of your advanced studies in finance.

In addition to options on stocks, as we discussed in our ABC example, there are other types of option securities.

- A *warrant* is the right to buy a specified stock at a specified price in a specified time period, generally attached to a corporate bond as a "sweetener" to make the bond more attractive. A warrant is therefore a call option.
- A ***detachable warrant*** is a warrant that can be sold separately from the bond and traded as a security.
- A *right* is a call option given to shareholders to buy additional stock in the issuing corporation (usually at a discount from the current market price) for a limited period of time. Rights can be sold by shareholders or exercised. If they are sold to another investor, they are traded as securities.

In addition to these option securities, there are also securities with optionlike features. A ***convertible bond*** is a bond that can be converted into common stock at the option of the investor. This bond is therefore a combination of a straight bond (a bond without such a conversion feature) and an option to convert the bond into shares of stock. Another example is the putable bond. A ***putable bond*** is a bond that gives the investor the right to put, or sell, the bonds back to the issuer at a specified price under certain specified conditions.

These optionlike features may affect the value of the security. A bond with a call feature gives the bond issuer the right to buy back the bond from the investor for a specified price during a specified period. This feature provides the issuer with flexibility—for example, if interest rates decline, the issuer can call, or buy back, the bonds and then sell new bonds with a lower interest rate. This feature therefore increases the risk of the bond, since it can be bought back by the issuer, leaving the investor with funds instead of an investment. Since the call feature adds risk to the security, investors—who, we assume, do not like risk—will demand a higher return on a callable security, thus increasing its cost to the issuer.

A bond with a convertible feature gives the investor the right to exchange the bond for common stock of the issuer at a specified rate of exchange. This feature gives the investor flexibility. For example, if the common stock's price increases sufficiently, the investor could exchange the bond for common stock. A convertible feature therefore increases the potential return on the bond since it could be turned into stock when it is attractive to do so.

We already know the value of a debt security is affected by its return (in the form of interest and principal payments) and the uncertainty associated with these interest and principal payments. Now we know features such as callability and convertibility also affect the value of debt securities.

In addition to the options found in securities, the financial manager faces investment decisions that have options. In deciding whether or not to invest in a new product, the financial manager has the option to postpone investment. This is a call option—the option to invest in the product at some future point in time.

Another example is the abandonment option. In evaluating an investment that was made in the past, the financial manager has the option to abandon the investment—stop production and sell off the assets. The option to abandon is a put option, since it is an option to *sell* the investment.

Looking at options in a broader perspective, we see that the owners of a firm have the option not to pay the creditors, halting operations, selling off assets, and distributing the proceeds. This is a put option held by the owners, since they determine whether or not to pay off creditors or to default.

Whether we are talking about securities that are options, securities with optionlike features, or financial decisions that contain options, the same five factors listed in Table 6-2 apply in valuing them. Though the precise calculation of the value of options is beyond the scope of this text, you should be able to recognize the factors affecting the value of an option and how they could influence the financial decisions you will have to make.

RETURNS ON INVESTMENTS

A *return,* the benefit an investor receives from an investment, can be in the form of:

- A change in the value of the asset, that is, its appreciation or depreciation.
- A cash flow from the investment, such as a dividend or an interest payment.
- Both a cash flow and a change in value.

The return on an investment is also referred to as the yield. We saw the role of the yield in determining the value of an asset. Now let's turn the tables and see how to calculate return on different investments.

Return on Investments with No Intermediate Cash Flows

Let's start by looking at an investment that involves no cash flows other than at its purchase and then its sale—no intermediate cash flows. Suppose you bought the *Official Handbook of the Marvel Universe (H–J)* comic book in 1983 for the cover price of $1. In 1989, this comic book, in mint condition, was worth $3.[5] If you sold at this time, your return on your investment would have been:

$$\text{Return on investment} = \frac{\text{sales price} - \text{cost}}{\text{cost}}$$

$$= \frac{\$3 - \$1}{\$1}$$

$$= \textbf{2 or 200\%}$$

Before any commission by the comic book dealer, you have made a return of 200 percent over the six years.

---

[5] Robert Overstreet, *The Official Overstreet Comic Book Price Guide 1989–1990,* 19th ed., The House of Collectibles, New York, 1989.

Since different investments have different lives or are valued at different points in their lives, we will need to put their yields on some common basis to compare them. The most common way of reporting a return or yield is on an annual basis, more precisely, the average annual return per year. Given the following, we can translate the six-year return on our comic book investment into a return per year:

Future value (sales price) = FV = $3.00
Present value (cost)   = PV = $1.00
Number of periods   = t   = 6 years

We can represent the return over the six years on a per-year basis. Let r be the annual return on the investment. Using the basic valuation equation, where FV is the future value, PV is the present value, t is the number of compounding periods, and r is the interest rate per period:

$$FV = PV(1 + r)^t$$
$$\$3.00 = \$1.00 \, (1 + r)^6$$

solving for r:

$$(1 + r)^6 = \frac{\$3}{\$1}$$

Taking the sixth root of both sides:

$$1 + r = \sqrt[6]{\frac{\$3}{\$1}} = \sqrt[6]{3}$$

which is equivalent to taking the value of 3 to the one-sixth power, or $3^{1/6}$:

$$1 + r = 3^{1/6} = 1.2009$$

Therefore, the annual return is:

$$r = 1.2009 - 1 = \mathbf{0.2009} \text{ or } \mathbf{20.09\%} \text{ per year}$$

Holding onto the comic book for six years provided a return of 20.09 percent per year. Another name for this return is the ***internal rate of return*** (IRR). Let's compare this annual return with the return on other investments.

Return on Investments with Even Cash Flows

For the comic book, we calculated a return that was solely from the appreciation of its value. Now let's look at an example in which the return is solely from a stream of cash inflows.

Suppose you buy an investment for $10,000 that promises to pay $4,000 per year for three years, beginning one year from the date you buy it. The return on this investment is the discount rate that equates its cost, $10,000, with the benefits it produces—the three cash inflows of $4,000 each—considering the time value of money. This is a present value problem. We use CF_t to indicate the cash flow at the end of period t:

Present value (cost of investment)   = PV = $10,000
Cash flow at the end of the first year   = CF_1 = $4,000
Cash flow at the end of the second year = CF_2 = $4,000
Cash flow at the end of the third year   = CF_3 = $4,000

Average Annual Return: What Kind of Average?

The average annual return on an investment is the geometric average, not the arithmetic average. What's the difference? Compounding.

Suppose you invest $100 today that will earn 5 percent per year for two years. After two years your investment is worth $100.00 $(1 + 0.05)^2 = \$110.25$. You have earned $10.25, or 10.25 percent, over two years.

But what have you earned per year? You have earned 5 percent, which happens to be, not coincidentally, the geometric average return:

$$\text{Geometric average annual return} = \sqrt{\frac{FV}{PV}} - 1 = \sqrt{\frac{\$110.25}{\$100.00}} - 1 = 1\sqrt{.1025} - 1$$

$$= 1.05 - 1 = 5\%$$

The arithmetic average annual return is:

$$\text{Arithmetic average annual return} = \frac{\$10.25/\$100.00}{2} = 5.13\%$$

But the arithmetic average ignores any compounding! It says that we earn 5.13 percent of $100 in both the first year and the second year and do not earn interest on interest during the second year.

If we want to compare investments that have different time horizons and different frequencies of compounding, we need to place returns on a common basis. Since the geometric average gives us a return that considers compounding, this is the average we can compare meaningfully. So, when we refer to the average annual return or average annual yield, we are talking about the average that considers compounding: the geometric average.

The return is the value of r that solves:

$$PV = \frac{CF_1}{(1 + r)^1} + \frac{CF_2}{(1 + r)^2} + \frac{CF_3}{(1 + r)^3}$$

Inserting the known values:

$$\$10,000 = \frac{\$4,000}{(1 + r)^1} + \frac{\$4,000}{(1 + r)^2} + \frac{\$4,000}{(1 + r)^3}$$

Because the cash flows are level, we can represent this equation in summation form:

$$\$10,000 = \sum_{t=1}^{3} \frac{\$4,000}{(1 + r)^t} = \$4,000 \sum_{t=1}^{3} \frac{1}{(1 + r)^t}$$

Recognizing that $\sum_{t=1}^{3} [1/(1 + r)^t]$ is the present value annuity factor for three periods and some unknown r, the equation becomes:

$\$10,000 = \$4,000$(present value annuity factor for t = 3 and r = ?)

We can calculate r either by:

1. Trial and error.
2. Using present value of annuity factors (Appendix B, Table B-4).
3. Using a financial calculator.

The value of r that solves this equation is r = 0.09701 = 9.701 percent per period. So, we say that this investment yields 9.701 percent per year compounded.

Return on Investments with Uneven Cash Flows

If we are calculating a return on an investment from a change in the value of an investment, we can use the basic valuation equation to back into the return on the investment. If we are calculating a return on an investment that produces even cash flows throughout the investment, we can use the annuity shortcut to figure out the return. But when the cash flows are neither in the same amount each period nor a single lump sum, it is more difficult to calculate the return. If an investment produces cash flows in different amounts, there are only two ways to solve for r:

1. By trial and error.
2. By using a financial calculator.

Suppose you are offered an investment costing $10,000 that promises cash flows of $1,000 after one year and $2,000 after two years and returns the original $10,000 at the end of the second year. The return on this investment is the rate r that solves:

$$\$10,000 = \frac{\$1,000}{(1 + r)^1} + \frac{\$2,000}{(1 + r)^2} + \frac{\$10,000}{(1 + r)^2}$$

Combining the cash flows that occur at the end of the second year,

$$\$10,000 = \frac{\$1,000}{(1 + r)^1} + \frac{\$12,000}{(1 + r)^2}$$

The discount rate that solves this problem is 14.66 percent per year, the annual return on this investment.

The Reinvestment Assumption

The discount rate that equates an investment's initial cost with value of the future cash flows it produces is the internal rate of return. The internal rate of return is aptly named since we are assuming that the cash inflows are reinvested at the same return as the rest of the investment—its internal return.

How does this reinvestment work? Let's look again at the preceding problem. Suppose that instead of reinvesting the $1,000 you received after the first year, you place it under your mattress where it earns nothing. The total value of the cash flows at the end of the second year is:

Year	Cash flow	Value at end of second year
1	$ 1,000	$ 1,000
2	12,000	12,000
Total		**$13,000**

This reinvestment strategy provides $13,000 at the end of the second year. The ***effective annual return*** on your investment—what you earn considering compounding—is calculated from the basic valuation equation:

$$FV = PV(1 + r)^t$$

Substituting the known values of FV, PV, and t:

$$\$13,000 = \$10,000(1 + r)^2$$

$$(1 + r)^2 = \frac{\$13,000}{\$10,000} = 1.3000$$

therefore:

$$r = \sqrt{1.3000} - 1 = \mathbf{0.1402} \text{ or } \mathbf{14.02\%} \text{ per year}$$

By stuffing your first year's end-of-period cash flow into a mattress, where it earns no interest during the second year, you reduce your return to 14.02 percent.

If, instead of padding the mattress, you invested the $1,000 for the one year at 10 percent, what would be the return on your total investment?

Year	Cash flow	Value at end of second year	
1	$ 1,000	$ 1,100	← $1,000 invested for one period at 10%
2	12,000	12,000	
Total		**$13,100**	

In this case, the return on your investment is:

$$r = \sqrt{\frac{\$13,100}{\$10,000}} - 1 = \mathbf{14.46\%} \textbf{ per year}$$

which is better than mattress stuffing because the $1,000 earns $100 of interest during the second period.

But suppose you reinvest this $1,000 at a return of 14.66 percent?

Year	Cash flow	Value at end of second year	
1	$ 1,000	$ 1,147	← $1,000 invested for one period at 14.66%
2	12,000	12,000	
Total		**$13,147**	

$$r = \sqrt{\frac{\$13,147}{\$10,000}} - 1 = \mathbf{0.1466} \text{ or } \mathbf{14.66\%}$$

In this case, the return on your investment is 14.66 percent, the IRR!

When we solve for the internal rate of return, whether by trial or error, or annuity tables, or by use of a financial calculator, we assume that the cash flows are reinvested at the same rate as the rate of the investment that generated those cash flows. This is true whether we are calculating yields on stocks, bonds, comic books, or any other investment.

If we assume the cash flows are reinvested at a different return, the return on the investment is referred to as the *modified internal rate of return* (MIRR). For example, if we reinvest the cash inflows at 10.00 percent, we receive a modified internal rate of return of 14.46 percent, which is less than the internal rate of return, 14.66 percent.

Return on Stocks

We can calculate the return on an investment in common stocks just as we did the internal rate of return in the preceding example. The return on stock comprises two components: (1) the appreciation (or depreciation) in the market price of the stock—the capital yield—and (2) the return in the form of dividends—the dividend yield:

Return on stock = capital yield + dividend yield

Return with No Dividends

Let's first ignore dividends. The return on common stock over a period of time during which there are no dividends is the change in the stock's price divided by the beginning share price:

$$\text{Return on a stock} = \frac{\text{end-of-period price} - \text{beginning-of-period price}}{\text{beginning-of-period price}}$$

Let's see how this works. At the beginning of 1991, Cyclops Industries stock was $11\frac{1}{4}$ per share, and at the end of 1991 Cyclops stock was $19\frac{1}{4}$ a share. The return on Cyclops during 1991 was:

$$\text{Return on Cyclops stock during 1991} = \frac{\$19.25 - \$11.25}{\$11.25}$$

$$= \frac{\$8.00}{\$11.25}$$

$$= \mathbf{0.7111} \text{ or } \mathbf{71.11\%} \text{ per year in 1991}$$

Cyclops stock appreciated $8.00 per share, providing a return of 71.11 percent for the year.

Return with Dividends at the End of the Period

If there are no dividends, we simply compare the change in the price of the shares with the original investment to arrive at the return. However, if there are dividends, we need to consider them as well as the change in the share's price, as cash inflows in determining the return. The simplest way to calculate the return is to assume that dividends are received at the end of the period:

$$\text{Return on a stock} = \frac{\text{end-of-period price} - \text{beginning-of-period price} + \text{dividends at end of period}}{\text{beginning-of-period price}}$$

Or if we let:

P_0 = beginning-of-period price
P_1 = end-of-period price
D_1 = dividends received at the end of period

we can write:

$$\text{Return on a stock} = \frac{P_1 - P_0 + D_1}{P_0}$$

We can break this return into two parts, one part representing the return due to the change in price and another part representing the return due to dividends:

$$\text{Return on a stock} = \underbrace{\frac{P_1 - P_0}{P_0}}_{\substack{\uparrow \\ \text{Capital} \\ \text{yield}}} + \underbrace{\frac{D_1}{P_0}}_{\substack{\uparrow \\ \text{Dividend} \\ \text{yield}}} \qquad [6\text{-}10]$$

The first part is the capital yield, and the second part is the dividend yield. If a company doesn't pay dividends, the dividend yield is zero and the return on the stock is its capital yield.

In using this equation, be careful to specify the timing of the prices at the beginning and end of the period and the timing of the dividends. Because we're dealing with the time value of money, we have to be very careful to be exact about the timing of all cash flows.

Example: To simplify our analysis, let's ignore our stock broker's commission, though we will discuss these costs later in this chapter. Suppose we bought 100 shares of Apple Computer common stock at the end of 1989 at $35\frac{1}{4}$. We have invested $100 \times \$35.25 = \$3,525.00$ in Apple stock. During 1990, Apple Computer paid $0.45 per share in dividends; so we earned $45.00 in dividends. If we sold the Apple shares at the end of 1990 at 43 ($43.00 per share, or $4,300.00 for all 100 shares), what was the return on our investment? It depends on when the dividends were received. If we assume that the dividends were all received at the end of 1990, our return was:

$$\begin{aligned}\frac{\text{Return on Apple Computer}}{\text{common stock in 1990}} &= \frac{\$4,300 - \$3,525 + \$45}{\$3,525} \\[2mm] &= \frac{\$820}{\$3,525} \\[2mm] &= \mathbf{0.2326} \text{ or } \mathbf{23.26\%} \text{ per year in 1990}\end{aligned}$$

We can break this return into its capital yield and dividend yield components:

$$\text{Return on Apple Computer common stock in 1990} = \underbrace{\frac{\$4,300 - \$3,525}{\$3,525}}_{\substack{\uparrow \\ \text{Capital yield}}} + \underbrace{\frac{\$45}{\$3,525}}_{\substack{\uparrow \\ \text{Dividend yield}}}$$

$$= 0.2198 + 0.0128$$
$$= 21.98\% + 1.28\%$$
$$= \mathbf{23.26\%}$$

Most of the return on Apple stock was from the capital yield—the appreciation in the stock's price.

But like most dividend-paying companies, Apple does not pay dividends in a lump sum at the end of the year, but rather pays dividends at the end of each quarter. Apple paid dividends per share at the end of each of the quarters of 11 cents, 11 cents, 11 cents, and 12 cents. The calculation of the return on the stock becomes a little more complicated now, since each quarter's dividend has a different time value of money. To solve for the yield on Apple stock during 1990, we:

1. Specify each of the cash flows, that is, the dividends, discounted at some unknown quarterly rate, for the appropriate number of periods.
2. Solve for the unknown quarterly return, r.
3. Translate this quarterly return into an effective annual return.

Why are we now working with a quarterly return and then figuring out the annual return? Since the dividends are received each quarter, we can take each dividend and reinvest it. Therefore, there is quarterly compounding in our investment: A period is defined in this case to be a quarter of a year. By translating the quarterly return into an equivalent annual return, we can more readily compare the return on this investment with other investments.

Let D_1 be the first quarter's dividend, D_2 be the second quarter's dividend, and so on. Also, since the end-of-year price is four quarters from the beginning-of-year-price, let's designate the ending price as P_4. We know the following:

$P_0 = \$3,525$
$P_4 = \$4,300$
$D_1 = \$11$
$D_2 = \$11$
$D_3 = \$11$
$D_4 = \$12$

We can diagram these cash flows as:

	End of 1989	End of first quarter, 1990	End of second quarter, 1990	End of third quarter, 1990	End of fourth quarter, 1990
Value of shares	$3,525				$4,300
Dividends		11	11	11	12
Total	**$3,525**	**$11**	**$11**	**$11**	**$4,312**

Viewing this as a present value problem, and using D_1, D_2, D_3, and D_4 to represent the four quarterly dividend payments:

$$P_0 = \frac{D_1}{(1+r)^1} + \frac{D_2}{(1+r)^2} + \frac{D_3}{(1+r)^3} + \frac{D_4}{(1+r)^4} + \frac{P_4}{(1+r)^4}$$

Substituting the known values:

$$\$3,525 = \frac{\$11}{(1+r)^1} + \frac{\$11}{(1+r)^2} + \frac{\$11}{(1+r)^3} + \frac{\$12}{(1+r)^4} + \frac{\$4,300}{(1+r)^4}$$

Where do we begin? When we assumed dividends were received at the end of the year, we hadn't figured in the return from reinvesting any dividends. In that situation, we calculated a 23 percent return on Apple stock. But since we now consider these dividends to be reinvested, the annual return on Apple stock is some value greater than 23 percent: If you receive dividends before the end of the year, you can put them to use by investing them. Because we know the lowest annual rate, we can figure out the lowest the quarterly rate must be. The 23 percent annual rate is equivalent to a quarterly rate of $\sqrt[4]{1.2300} - 1 = 0.0531$ or 5.31 percent per quarter. Therefore, the quarterly rate is some rate *greater than* 5.31 percent.

Since our problem is stated in the form of a present value setup we can use trial and error, starting with a quarterly rate of 6 percent:

$$\text{Present value} = \frac{\$11.00}{(1+0.06)^1} + \frac{\$11.00}{(1+0.06)^2} + \frac{\$11.00}{(1+0.06)^3}$$
$$+ \frac{\$12.00}{(1+0.06)^4} + \frac{\$4,300.00}{(1+0.06)^4}$$
$$= \$10.38 + \$9.79 + \$9.24 + \$9.51 + \$3,406.00$$
$$= \mathbf{\$3,444.93}$$

The present value of the quarterly cash flows discounted at 6 percent per quarter is $3,444.93. But the beginning price was $3,525.00. We are close! We have discounted a bit too much. That is, r is actually lower than 6 percent.

From financial mathematics, we learned that:

Effective annual return $= \left(1 + \dfrac{\text{rate per period}}{}\right)^{\text{number of compounding periods in a year}} - 1$ or $(1 + r)^t - 1$

Since there are four quarters in a year, the effective annual return or yield can be determined using the quarterly rate:

Effective annual return $= (1 + \text{quarterly rate})^4 - 1$

For example, a 2 percent quarterly rate is equivalent to an annual return of:

Effective annual return $= (1 + 0.02)^4 - 1 = \textbf{8.24\%}$

We get a more precise value of the quarterly yield by working with a financial calculator, which results in r = 5.39 percent.

The next step is to translate the quarterly yield into an annual yield, remembering our time-value-of-money principles:

Yield $= (1 + 0.0539)^4 - 1$
$= 1.2337 - 1 = \textbf{0.2337}$ or $\textbf{23.37\%}$ per year

Let's calculate the capital yield and dividend yield for this investment. First, we calculate the capital yield, then subtract it from the total yield to arrive at the dividend yield.

The capital yield is the annual rate that causes $3,525 to grow to $4,300 over four quarters. We are given:

PV = $3,525
FV = $4,300
t = 4 quarters

Substituting the known values into the basic valuation equation and solving for r, the capital yield is:

$\$4,300 = \$3,525(1 + r)^4$

$(1 + r)^4 = \dfrac{\$4,300}{\$3,525}$

$r = \sqrt[4]{1.2199} - 1 = (1.2199)^{0.25} - 1$

$= \textbf{0.0509}$ or $\textbf{5.09\%}$ per quarter

Since the 5.09 percent is a quarterly return, we can translate it into an annual return with compounding: $(1 + 0.0509)^4 - 1 = 21.97$ percent per year.

The dividend yield is therefore:

Dividend yield = total yield − capital yield
$$= 0.2337 - 0.2197$$
$$= \mathbf{0.0140\%} \text{ or } \mathbf{1.40\%} \text{ per year}$$

You can see that by taking into account the timing of the dividends, we can determine the return more precisely (even though in this example, the yield rates with and without taking account of timing are fairly close, 23.21 percent and 23.37 percent).

You will notice in many cases that the dividend yield is calculated by simply taking the ratio of the annual dividend to the beginning-of-period price. In *The Wall Street Journal,* the dividend yield is the ratio of next year's expected dividend to today's share price. While these shortcuts are convenient, remember that the true return should take into account the time value of money. This is especially important when you are considering large dividends relative to the stock price or when reinvestment rates are high.

In the preceding example, we assumed that you sold the investment at a specific point in time, realizing the capital appreciation or depreciation in the investment—that is, actually getting cash. But we can also think about a return without actually selling the investment. What if you didn't sell the Apple stock at the end of 1990? You would receive the dividends for 1990 whether or not you sold the stock at the end of the year; so you would have the dividend yield of 1.4 percent. Your investment would still have increased in value during the year, even if you didn't sell. If you don't sell the Apple stock, you still have a capital yield for the year; it's just not realized. A capital gain on a stock you haven't sold is what many refer to as a "paper gain."

You can see that we can compute returns on investments whether or not we have sold them. In the cases where we do not sell the asset represented in the investment, we compute the capital yield (gain or loss) based on the market value of the asset at the point in time at which we are evaluating the investment.

It becomes important to consider whether or not we actually realize the capital yield only when we are dealing with taxes. We must pay taxes on the capital gain only when we realize it. As long as we don't sell the asset, we are not taxed on its capital appreciation.

Return on Bonds

If you invest in a bond, you realize a return from the interest it pays (if it is a coupon bond) and from either the sale, the maturity, or call of the bond. We calculate the return on a bond in the same way we calculate the return on a stock, except that in the case of a stock the cash flow is dividend income rather than interest income.

There is another dimension to consider with bonds that we needn't consider with common stocks: Bonds have a finite life, since they either mature or are called. Therefore, we are not just interested in the effective annual yield, but also the yield if the bond is held to maturity or the yield to the point at which a bond is likely to be called.

Effective Annual Return

A bond's return comprises the return from the appreciation or depreciation in the value of the bond over the period—the capital yield and the return from the interest received during the period—the ***coupon yield:***

Effective annual return = capital yield + coupon yield

Let's look at an investment in 100 Georgia Power bonds that mature in the year 2000 with a coupon rate of $8\frac{7}{8}$ and a par value of 1000. At the beginning of 1990, these bonds were selling at $96\frac{1}{2}$ (that is, 96.5% of face value, or $965.00 per bond); at the end of 1990, they were selling for $97\frac{1}{2}$. The coupon rate of $8\frac{7}{8}$ means that they pay 8.875 percent on the par value of $1,000.00, or $88.75 for the year. If interest were paid at the end of the year, the return on 100 bonds for 1990 would be:

$$\text{Return on Georgia Power } 8\tfrac{7}{8} \text{ bonds maturing in 2000} = \frac{\$97,500 - \$96,500 + \$8,875}{\$96,500}$$

$$= \frac{\$9,875}{\$96,500}$$

$$= \mathbf{0.102332} \text{ or } \mathbf{10.2332\%} \text{ per year in 1990}$$

Breaking down this return into its capital yield and coupon yield:

$$\text{Return on Georgia Power } 8\tfrac{7}{8} \text{ bonds maturing in 2000} = \underbrace{\frac{\$97,500 - \$96,500}{\$96,500}}_{\substack{\text{Capital} \\ \text{yield}}} + \underbrace{\frac{\$8,875}{\$96,500}}_{\substack{\text{Coupon} \\ \text{yield}}}$$

$$= 1.0363\% + 9.1969\%$$

$$= \mathbf{10.2332\%} \text{ per year in 1990}$$

Since the interest is paid semiannually (each bond pays $44.375 on June 30 and December 31), what return could you have earned if you bought 100 of these bonds on January 1, 1990, and held them through December 31, 1990? The semiannual interest payments make our computations somewhat more complicated. But we can make our job easier if we lay out the cash flows in an orderly fashion:

	Beginning of January 1990	End of June 1990	End of December 1990
Bond values	$ 96,500.00		$ 97,500.00
Interest		$ 4,437.50	4,437.50
Total	**$96,500.00**	**$4,437.50**	**$101,937.50**

The yield on these bonds is such that an investment of $96,500.00 will produce cash flows of $4,437.50 after six months and $101,947.50 after twelve months. Stated in the form of a present value equation, with r_d representing the six-month yield,

$$\$96{,}500.00 = \frac{\$4{,}437.50}{(1 + r_d)^1} + \frac{\$101{,}937.50}{(1 + r_d)^2}$$

Where do we start to solve for r_d? We can begin at either of two places.

For one, we know these bonds are selling at a discount from their par value of $1,000. This tells us the yield is greater than the coupon rate because investors are not willing to pay full price, the $1,000, to get interest of 8.875 percent per year. Therefore, the market rate must be something greater than 8.875 percent. Therefore, we know the effective annual yield must be greater than 8.875 percent, which means that the six-month yield must be greater than 8.875 percent/2 = 4.4375 percent.

Alternatively, we can start with the 10.2332 percent annual yield we calculated when we assumed interest was received at the end of the year. Since the interest received after six months can be reinvested, the yield must be *greater than* 10.2332 percent. If the annual yield is greater than 10.2332 percent, the semiannual yield must be greater than the semiannual rate equivalent to 10.2332 percent per year, or $\sqrt{1 + 0.102332} - 1 = 0.04992$ or 4.992 percent.

What we know, then, is that the semiannual yield is above 4.992 percent. Using a financial calculator, we find that r_d is 5.1037 percent. If the yield over six months is 5.1037 percent, the effective annual yield for a year is 5.1087 percent compounded for two six-month periods:

$$\text{Effective annual yield} = (1 + 0.051037)^2 - 1$$
$$= \mathbf{0.1047} \text{ or } \mathbf{10.47\%}$$

We can determine how much of this return is due to interest—the coupon yield—and how much is due to capital appreciation—the capital yield—in the following way:

- First, calculate the capital yield.
- Then subtract the capital yield from the effective annual yield.

The effective capital yield is calculated from the r_d, the semiannual rate, that solves:

$$\$97{,}500 = \$96{,}500(1 + r_d)^2$$

Rearranging and solving for r:

$$(1 + r_d)^2 = \frac{\$97{,}500}{\$96{,}500} = 1.0104$$

$$1 + r_d \quad = 1.0104^{0.50} \text{ or } \sqrt{1.0104}$$

Therefore:

$$r_d = \mathbf{0.0052} = \mathbf{0.52\%} \text{ semiannually}$$

Putting this six-month yield on an annual basis gives us the annual capital yield:[6]

Capital yield $= (1 + 0.0052)^2 - 1$
$$= \mathbf{0.0104} \text{ or } \mathbf{1.04\%} \text{ per year}$$

Therefore:

Coupon yield $= 0.1047 - 0.0104$
$$= \mathbf{0.0943} \text{ or } \mathbf{9.43\%} \text{ per year}$$

Most of the return from these bonds is from the coupon rather than from capital appreciation. And the coupon yield isn't equal to 8.875 percent because:

1. The 8.875 percent interest is paid on a par value of $1,000, but we paid only $96,500, which is less than par value.
2. We have figured in the interest earned on reinvesting the interest received after six months.

Now let's look at an example of the return on a zero-coupon bond—a bond that does not pay interest. Suppose that on January 1, 1990, you bought 10 RJR Nabisco zero-coupon bonds maturing on December 31, 2001, for $47\frac{3}{4}$, or $477.50 per bond. On December 31, 1990, these bonds sold for $50\frac{1}{4}$ or $502.50 per bond. What is your effective annual return on these bonds during 1990?

$$\begin{aligned}\text{Return during 1990 on RJR Nabisco} \atop \text{zero-coupon bonds maturing in 2001} &= \frac{\$5{,}025 - \$4{,}775}{\$4{,}775} \\[6pt] &= \frac{\$250}{\$4{,}775} \\[6pt] &= \mathbf{0.0524} \text{ or } \mathbf{5.24\%} \text{ per year in 1990}\end{aligned}$$

Since we are looking at the beginning and ending prices over the year and there are no interest payments during the year, 5.24 percent is the effective annual return.

Yield to Maturity

Zero-Coupon Bonds

The effective annual return on a bond is a measure of the yield or benefit (realized or unrealized) over a year. But for some bonds, we may be interested in knowing what yield we would earn over the longer term, such as until ma-

---

[6] We can apply this compounding process to other period lengths. For example, the two-year rate equivalent to the semiannual rate of 0.52 percent is:

$$(1 + 0.0052)^4 - 1 = 2.10\%$$

since there are four six-month periods in two years.

Since there are two compounding periods in the year, we could have stopped at the step:

$$(1 + r)^2 = 1.0104$$

and had our annual return of 1.04 percent.

turity. Yield to maturity is the annual yield on an investment assuming you own it *until maturity*. Yield to maturity considers all an investment's expected cash flows—in the case of a bond, the interest and principal. When we look at yield to maturity, we once again see a relation between a bond's yield and its value today.

Looking again at the RJR Nabisco bonds, let's figure out the return if they are held to maturity. If you hold these bonds to maturity, you will receive the $1,000 par value on each of your bonds, or $10,000.[7] To make the calculations simpler, let's assume they mature on December 31, 2001. If you buy the bonds and hold them to maturity, you would have held them for twelve years.

The return on these bonds over the twelve-year period is:

$$\text{Return on RJR Nabisco zero-coupon bonds} \atop \text{maturing in 2001 and held until maturity} = \frac{\$10,000 - \$4,775}{\$4,775}$$

$$= \frac{\$5,225}{\$4,775}$$

$$= \mathbf{1.0942} \text{ or } \mathbf{109.42\%}$$

Looks impressive! But this return is over a period of twelve years. Let's see what this return is on an annual basis so that we can compare it with the annual return of other investments. For this example:

PV = $4,775
FV = $10,000
t = 12 years

Using the basic valuation equation and inserting the known values for FV, PV, and t, and solving for the annual return:

$$\text{FV} = \text{PV}(1 + r)^t$$

$$\$10,000.00 = \$4,775.00(1 + r_d)^{12}$$

$$(1 + r_d)^{12} = \frac{\$10,000.00}{\$4,775.00} = 2.0942$$

$$1 + r_d = \sqrt[12]{2.0942} = 1.0635$$

$$r_d = 1.0635 - 1 = \mathbf{0.0635} \text{ or } \mathbf{6.35\%} \text{ per year}$$

Buying these bonds at the beginning of 1990 and holding them to maturity provides an average annual return of 6.35 percent—the annual yield to maturity.

Straight-Coupon Bonds

The present value, V, of a bond is its current market price, which is the discounted value of all future cash flows of the bond—the interest and principal:

$$V = \frac{\text{Present value of}}{\text{future interest payments}} + \frac{\text{Present value of}}{\text{maturity value}}$$

[7] Of course we are assuming that the issuer of the bond, in this case RJR Nabisco, will be able to pay the principal at maturity.

or

$$V = \sum_{t=1}^{T} \frac{C}{(1 + r_d)^t} + \frac{M}{(1 + r_d)^T}$$

Since most bonds pay interest semiannually, C is the interest payment made every six months, M is the maturity value, T is the number of six-month periods remaining until maturity, t specifies which of the six-month periods we are evaluating, and r_d is the six-month yield.

The yield to maturity on a coupon bond is the discount rate, put on an annual basis, that equates the present value of the interest and principal payments to the present value of the bond. So, in the case of a bond that pays interest semiannually, we first solve for the six-month yield and then translate it to its equivalent annual yield to maturity.

Now let's look at the yield to maturity on a coupon bond. Going back to the Georgia Power $8\frac{7}{8}$ percent coupon bonds maturing in 2000 and with interest paid semiannually, what is the yield to maturity on these bonds if you bought them on January 1, 1990, for $96,500? Or, put another way, what annual yield equates the investment of $96,500 with the present value of the twenty-two interest cash flows and the maturity value?

In this example, we know the following:

$V = \$1,000.00 \times 96.5\% \times 100 = \$96,500.00$

$C = \dfrac{0.08875}{2} \times \$1,000.00 \times 100 \text{ bonds} = \$4,437.50$

$M = \$1,000.00 \times 100 \text{ bonds} = \$100,000.00$

$T = 11 \text{ years} \times 2 = 22 \text{ six-month periods}$

and t identifies the six-month period we're evaluating. Therefore:

$$\$96,500.00 = \sum_{t=1}^{22} \frac{\$4,437.50}{(1 + r_d)^t} + \frac{\$100,000.00}{(1 + r_d)^{22}}$$

Where do we start looking for a solution to r_d? Before we turn to our financial calculators, let's think about the value of r_d. If the bonds yielded $8\frac{7}{8}$ percent, they would be selling close to par ($100,000 for our 100 bonds). This would be equivalent to a six-month value of $r_d = \sqrt{1 + 0.08875}$ or $(1.08875)^{0.50}$ or 4.3432 percent for six months.

But these bonds are priced *below* par. That is, investors are not willing to pay full price for these bonds since they can get a better return on similar bonds elsewhere. As a result, the price of the bonds is driven downward until these bonds provide a return or yield to maturity equal to that of bonds with similar risk.

Given this reasoning, the yield on these bonds must be greater than the coupon rate; so the six-month yield must be greater than 4.34 percent. Using the trial-and-error approach, we start with 5 percent and look at the relation between the present value of the cash inflows (interest and principal) discounted at 5 percent and the price of the bonds (the $96,500.):

$$\text{Present value of bonds, using } r = 5\% = \sum_{t=1}^{22} \frac{\$4,437.50}{(1 + 0.05)^t} + \frac{\$100,000.00}{(1 + 0.05)^{22}}$$

$$= \$58,410.82 + \$34,184.99$$

$$= \mathbf{\$92,595.81}$$

We conclude:

Present value of bonds, using r = 5% ≠ present value of bonds

$92,595.81   ≠ $96,500.00

In fact, using 5 percent, we have discounted too much, since the present value of the bonds using 5 percent is less than their actual present value. Therefore, we know that r_d should be less than 5 percent. We now have an idea of where the yield lies: between 4.3432 percent and 5 percent. Using a financial calculator, we find the value of r_d = 4.70 percent, a six-month yield. Translating the six-month yield into an effective annual yield, we find that these bonds result in an effective yield to maturity of 9.61 percent:

Yield to maturity = $(1 + 0.0470)^2 - 1 = \mathbf{0.0961}$ or **9.61%** per year

Another way of saying this is that the bonds are priced to yield 9.61 percent per year.

Why is the effective yield to maturity different from the annual yield of 10.48 percent that we calculated earlier? The annual yield was calculated using the beginning- and end-of-year values of the bonds ($96,500 and $97,500) as well as the two interest payments. But the yield-to-maturity assumption is that we buy the bonds for $96,500 and *hold them until 2000*, getting twenty-two interest payments and the $100,000 principal. So we know that if we buy and hold these bonds for one year, we obtain a 10.48 percent annual return on our investment. But if we hold onto these bonds, we will get a 9.61 percent annual return. Remember: When we bought the bonds at the beginning of 1990, we didn't know if the price of the bonds was going to go up, down, or stay the same, since we didn't know what was going to happen to interest rates during the year, but we did know what we would get at maturity—assuming the bond issuer is able to pay the principal at that time.

The bond's price changes from January 1, 1990, to January 1, 1991, for two reasons:

1. As time progresses, the value of a bond tends toward its maturity value (we'll show why and how next).
2. The value of a bond changes as yields change.

We now take a brief look at both these considerations.

Value of Bonds as They Approach Maturity

Let's focus on maturity, holding the yield constant at the January 1, 1990, yield. What is the value of the bonds if the yield to maturity is 9.61 percent per year and there are now twenty interest payments left, instead of twenty-two? This is the same as asking: What is the value of the bonds as of December 1990—two six-month periods later—if the yield to maturity does not change?

$$\text{Present value of bonds on December 31, 1990} = \sum_{t=1}^{20} \frac{\$4,437.50}{(1 + 0.0470)^t} + \frac{\$100,000.00}{(1 + 0.0470)^{20}}$$

$$= \$56,735.24 + \$39,908.59$$

$$= \mathbf{\$96,643.83}$$

Moving ahead one more year, to December 1991:

$$\text{Present value of bonds on December 31, 1991} = \sum_{t=1}^{18} \frac{\$4,437.50}{(1 + 0.0470)^t} + \frac{\$100,000.00}{(1 + 0.0470)^{18}}$$

$$= \$53,110.12 + \$43,748.15$$

$$= \mathbf{\$96,858.27}$$

In Table 6-3, we continue this calculation for each year to maturity. We see that the value of the bonds increases until it approaches the maturity value. The interest payments contribute less to the bonds' present value as time goes on, since there are fewer interest payments left, yet the maturity value contributes more as the bonds near maturity.

To visualize this process, look at Figure 6-5. The value of the Georgia Power bonds is plotted against time, holding the effective yield to maturity constant at 9.61 percent per year—and therefore the six-month yield at 4.70

TABLE 6-3

Value of Georgia Power 8⅞ Percent Bonds, Interest Paid Semiannually, Maturing December 31, 2000, as Maturity Approaches

Date	Number of six-month periods remaining to maturity	Present value of interest payments	Present value of maturity value	Present value of bonds
December 31, 1990	20	$56,735.24	$ 39,908.59	$ 96,643.83
December 31, 1991	18	53,110.12	43,748.15	96,858.27
December 31, 1992	16	49,136.23	47,957.12	97,093.35
December 31, 1993	14	44,780.01	52,571.03	97,351.04
December 31, 1994	12	40,004.69	57,628.83	97,633.53
December 31, 1995	10	34,769.94	63,173.24	97,943.19
December 31, 1996	8	29,031.56	69,251.08	98,282.64
December 31, 1997	6	22,741.10	75,913.66	98,654.75
December 31, 1998	4	15,845.43	83,217.23	99,062.66
December 31, 1999	2	8,286.34	91,223.48	99,506.82
December 31, 2000	0	0.00	100,000.00	100,000.00

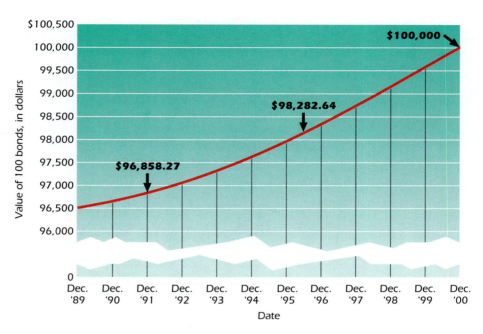

FIGURE 6-5

Value of 100 Georgia Power 8⅞ Percent Bonds Maturing in 2000, with Interest Paid Semiannually, and with a Constant Annual Yield to Maturity of 9.61 Percent

percent. For example, on December 31, 1996, the bonds would be worth $98,282.64. You can see how the value of bonds approaches their maturity value as they approach maturity in the year 2000. The change in the value of the bond as it approaches maturity is referred to as the ***time path*** of the bond.

Value of Bonds as Yields Change

If the yield to maturity had remained constant at 9.61 percent per year, what would these bonds be worth at the end of 1990? According to Table 6-3, $96,643.83. What is their value at the end of 1990? $97,500.00. Why has their value changed? Because yields have changed. At the beginning of 1990, the bonds were priced to yield 9.61 percent per year to maturity. At the end of 1990, however, the value of the bonds is greater than what we would expect, given simply the passage of time.

The effective yield to maturity as of December 31, 1990, given a value of $97,500, is calculated by solving for the six-month yield that equates the new market value to the present value of the interest and maturity value:

$$\$97,500.00 = \sum_{t=1}^{20} \frac{\$4,437.50}{(1 + r_d)^t} + \frac{\$100,000.00}{(1 + r_d)^{20}}$$

which gives us:

$r_d =$ **0.04632** or **4.632%** semiannually

We then find the yield to maturity:

Yield to maturity as of the end of 1990 for the Georgia Power bonds $= (1 + 0.04632)^2 - 1$

$= $ **0.0948** or **9.48%** per year

If yields did not change during the year and the bonds were valued to yield 9.61 percent per year to maturity, the value of the bonds would have crept up to $96,643.83 by the end of 1990. But instead, the value of the bonds increased from $96,500.00 to $97,500.00. Since the cash flows have not changed, the only thing that could cause the value of the bonds to deviate from $96,643.83 would be the discount rate—the yield.

As we saw from the calculations, the effective yield to maturity decreased from 9.61 percent to 9.48 percent per year. As the yield decreased, the value of the bond increased.

Let's look once again at the value of a bond:

$$V = \sum_{t=1}^{T} \frac{C}{(1 + r_d)^t} + \frac{M}{(1 + r_d)^T}$$

If we hold C, T, and M constant, we see that an increase in r_d—the six-month yield—decreases the present value of the bond. Likewise, a decrease in r_d increases the present value of the bond. The value of bonds is therefore sensitive to the yield.

How sensitive is the value to different yields? Let's look at an example, using the Georgia Power bonds as of the end of 1990. We saw that if the bonds are valued at $97,500.00, this is equivalent to saying their yield to maturity is 9.48 percent per year. We also saw that if the bonds are valued at $96,643.83, their yield to maturity is 9.61 percent per year.

Now let's turn the example around and ask: What is the value of the bonds if the yield to maturity is 10 percent per year? Our first step is to translate the annual yield of 10 percent into its equivalent six-month yield:

$0.10 = (1 + \text{six-month yield})^2 - 1$

Adding 1 to each side:

$1.10 = (1 + \text{six-month yield})^2$

and taking the square root of both sides:

$\sqrt{1.10} = (1 + \text{six-month yield}) \longrightarrow \text{six-month yield} = \textbf{0.0488}$ or **4.88%**

Therefore, a six-month yield of 4.88 percent is equivalent to a 10 percent annual yield. Using 4.88 percent in place of r_d:

$$\text{Present value of bonds with yield to maturity of 10\%} = \sum_{t=1}^{20} \frac{\$4,437.50}{(1 + 0.0488)^t} + \frac{\$100,000.00}{(1 + 0.0488)^{20}}$$

$$= \$55,868.09 + \$38,560.83$$

$$= \mathbf{\$94,428.92}$$

We can see the different values of the bonds as of December 1990 for different yields in Figure 6-6. If the bonds are priced to yield 1 percent, they would be worth $174,796. If the bonds are priced to yield 20 percent, they would be worth $55,134.

If the bonds are priced to return their coupon equivalent yield, they are priced at par. What is their coupon equivalent yield? Remember that a coupon rate is simply the six-month coupon rate multiplied by 2; so it ignores any

SUMMARY

- The value of any asset today depends on its expected future cash flows. The form of these future cash flows may be a level, perpetual stream (as in the case of a preferred stock), a growing stream of cash flows (as in the case of many common stocks), or a series of uneven cash flows (as in the case of a bond). No matter what the pattern of future cash flows, the basic valuation of these flows is the same: Each future cash flow is discounted to the present at a rate that reflects both the time value of money and the uncertainty of the flow.

- There is an inverse relation between the value of an asset and the discount rate applied to future cash flows: The higher this discount rate, the lower will be today's value, and the lower the discount rate, the higher will be today's value.

- The dividend valuation model is useful in assessing the value of a share of stock where dividends are either constant or growing at a constant rate.

- The value of a debt obligation changes as it approaches maturity, eventually converging upon its maturity value. The value of a debt obligation also changes as the yield to maturity changes.

- The value of an option—whether an actual security, a security with optionlike features, or a possible action embedded in an investment or financing decision—is influenced by the exercise price, the time remaining to maturity, the value of the underlying asset, the volatility of the value of the underlying asset, and time value of money.

- The valuation of an asset requires discounting the expected future cash flows at some rate—the yield. Turning the problem around, we can figure out, for a given asset value, the yield on the asset. It's the same math as we performed with valuation, but instead of solving for the present value of future cash flows, we solve for the discount rate—the yield.

- When we calculate the yield on a security, we are interested in translating that yield into some common basis—a year—so that we can compare alternative investments. Applying our understanding of time-value-of-money principles, we can translate a rate for some period less than a year—say, a six-month period—into the equivalent effective annual yield, and we can translate an annual yield into the equivalent yield for some period of time less than a year.

- When we consider transaction costs, we see that our return on an investment is reduced. If transaction costs are substantial, we need to figure them into our calculation of the return on our investments to obtain our actual return.

QUESTIONS

6-1   What is the relation between the discount rate applied to future cash flows from an investment and the value of the investment today?

6-2   What is meant by the required rate of return? What is the relation between the required rate of return and the discount rate used to value future cash flows?

6-3   Using the dividend valuation model with dividends growing at a constant rate, what is the relation between dividend growth, share price growth, and earnings growth?

6-4   Which of the following situations does *not* work with the dividend valuation model?

    a. No growth in dividends.
    b. Growth in dividends that is greater than the required rate of return.
    c. Negative growth in dividends.
    d. No current dividends.

6-5   What is the relation between the price-earnings ratio and the growth rate of dividends?

6-6   If the dividend rate on preferred stock is reset every year to the going market yield on preferred stocks of similar risk, at what price would a share of preferred stock trade?

6-7   Rank the following securities in order of the uncertainty of their producing a future cash flow:

    a. Common stock
    b. Preferred stock
    c. Callable preferred stock
    d. Long-term bond

What is the basis for your ranking?

6-8   What is the relation between the expected growth rate of common stock dividends and the dividend payout? What is the rationale behind this relation?

6-9   For each of the following pairs of coupon rates and yields, assuming interest is paid at the end of each year, determine whether the bond will sell for more than, at, or less than its par value:

Bond	Coupon rate	Yield to maturity
A	5%	7%
B	2	3
C	6	6
D	3	6
E	8	4
F	10	12
G	12	10
H	11	11

6-10   Consider two bonds, Bond X and Bond Y, each with a face value of $1,000 and maturing in five years. Bond X has a coupon rate of 5 percent, and Bond Y has no coupon. If Bond X and Bond Y are considered to be of equal risk, which bond will have a higher value today?

6-11   If companies tend to pay dividends on a quarterly basis and we calculate the return on a stock assuming these dividends are paid at the end of the year, what is the relation between our calculated return and the true return on the stock?

6-12   If a bond is priced to yield 10 percent and its coupon is 6 percent, is this bond selling for a premium or a discount from face value?

6-13   The ABC Company's bonds had a value of $900 per bond at the beginning of the year. By the end of the year, these bonds were valued at $950 per bond. What may have caused the price to change?

6-14   Suppose you buy a bond today for $1,000, its par value. If the yield on this bond changes from 10 percent to 12 percent tomorrow, what will happen to the value of your bond?

6-15   Consider this statement: If the coupon rate is the same as the yield to maturity, the bond's value will be equal to its par value. Is this true? Why or why not?

6-16   Consider the following three investments:

Investment 1   Invest $10,000 today, and get $15,000 three years from now.
Investment 2   Invest $10,000 today, and get $5,000 at the end of each of the next three years.
Investment 3   Invest $10,000 today, and get $2,500 at the end of every six months for three years.

If the cash flows from these investments have the same degree of uncertainty, which investment should you choose? Why?

6-17   Suppose you are offered an option on an asset. This option gives you the right to buy the asset for $1,000 any time before December 31 of this year. Currently, the asset is worth $800.

   a.   Is this a call option or a put option?
   b.   What determines the value of the option?
   c.   Currently, is the option at the money, in the money, or out of the money?
   d.   Since the exercise price is more than the asset's value today, does that mean the option is worthless? Explain.

6-18   Consider the option of dropping a course after the start of the semester. What determines the value of such an option? What is the relation between these determinants and the value of the option?

6-19   Under what circumstance(s) is the coupon rate of a bond equal to its effective yield to maturity?

6-20   If you determine that the yield to maturity on a bond with annual coupons is 10 percent, what rate of return are we assuming these coupons earn when they are reinvested?

PROBLEMS

General

6-1 Suppose you have an opportunity to invest $1,000 today and get back $1,200 one year from today. If your required rate of return on investments of similar risk is 10 percent, should you make the investment? Why?

6-2 Suppose you have the opportunity to invest in a project that provides you with $4,000 every year forever. If you require an 8 percent return on investments with similar risk, what is the most you would be willing to pay for this project?

Valuation of common stock

6-3 The Goofy Gadget Company currently pays a dividend of $2.50 per common share. If dividends are expected to grow at a rate of 5 percent per year and your required rate of return on Goofy common stock is 8 percent, what is the value to you of a share of Goofy stock?

6-4 The Common Company has paid dividends during the past four years as follows:

Year	Dividend per share
1990	$2.00
1991	2.10
1992	2.30
1993	2.52

If dividends are expected to grow at the same rate as during the period 1990–1993 and the required rate of return on Common common is 10 percent, what is the expected price of a share of Common common at the end of 1993?

6-5 The Grow-all Company has 1 million shares of common stock outstanding. The company paid dividends of $6 million on common stock this year. Dividends are expected to grow at a rate of 4 percent per year, and the required rate of return on common stock is 7 percent. Using the dividend valuation model, what is the value of a share of Grow-all common stock?

6-6 The Change-all Company currently pays dividends of $2 on each share of common stock. The required rate of return on Change-all stock is 10 percent.
  a. If the expected dividend growth rate is 5 percent each year forever, what is the value of a share of Change-all common stock?
  b. If the expected dividend growth rate is 2 percent each year forever, what is the value of a share of Change-all common stock?
  c. If the expected dividend growth is 5 percent for the next five years and 2 percent thereafter, what is the value of a share of Change-all common stock?

6-7 The AlterG Corporation currently pays $3 of dividends per share of common stock. The required rate of return on AlterG stock is 5 percent.

 a. If the expected dividend growth rate is 2 percent per year forever, what is the value of a share of AlterG common stock?

 b. If the expected dividend growth rate is 4 percent per year forever, what is the value of a share of AlterG common stock?

 c. If the dividend growth rate is expected to be 4 percent per year for the next four years and 2 percent thereafter, what is the value of a share of AlterG common stock?

Valuation of preferred stock

6-8 A share of Pampered Inc. preferred stock is currently selling to yield 10 percent. If dividends are $5 per share per period, what is the required rate of return on Pampered preferred?

6-9 Yodel Company preferred stock has a dividend of $6 per share and is priced to yield 10 percent.

 a. What is the value of a share of Yodel preferred stock?

 b. If the stock is callable at $100 in four years, what is the value of a share of Yodel callable preferred stock?

6-10 The Perpetual Corporation issued shares of preferred at a price of $90 per share. If the dividend is fixed at $9 per share, what is the yield on the preferred shares?

6-11 Suppose the Everlasting Company has shares of preferred stock outstanding that pay $5 per share and are priced to yield 10 percent. If the yield on this stock were to change to 8 percent, what would be the expected effect on the share price?

6-12 The PS Corporation currently has preferred stock outstanding that pays $5 per share and is valued at $80 per share. What is the yield on PS preferred stock?

Valuation of debt securities

6-13 Consider a bond with a face value of $1,000 and a coupon rate of 8 percent paid annually. The bond matures in three years. What is the value of the bond if it is priced to yield 6 percent?

6-14 The IO Company issued a bond that matures in five years. It has a face value of $1,000 and a coupon rate of 5 percent paid annually. What is the value of the IO bond today if the yield to maturity is 4 percent?

6-15 The OU Corporation issued a bond that has a 6 percent coupon rate paid semiannually, a face value of $1,000, and a maturity of five years. What is the value of the OU bond if the yield to maturity is 8 percent?

6-16 The Dettor Corporation issued a bond with a face value of $1,000 that matures in ten years. If the coupon rate is 10 percent and is paid semiannually, what is the value of the Dettor bond if the bond yields 8 percent?

6-17 Suppose you bought an ABC Company bond at its par value of $1,000 three years ago. The bond has a coupon rate of 6 percent per year paid semiannually and has three years to maturity.

 a. If you sell the bond when it is priced to yield 8 percent (annualized), what is your gain or loss on this investment?

    b. If you sell the bond when it is priced to yield 4 percent (annualized), what is your gain or loss on this investment?

    c. If you sell the bond when it is priced to yield 10 percent (annualized), what is your gain or loss on this investment?

6-18 Consider a bond with a par value of $1,000, maturing in five years. If the bond provides interest at a rate of 8 percent per year paid semiannually, but only starts paying interest two years from now, what is the value of the bond if it is priced to yield 6 percent (annualized) or 3 percent every six months?

6-19 Consider a bond with a par value of $1,000, maturing in ten years. Suppose the issuer promised to pay interest of 8 percent per year annually, but only for the first five years. What is the value of this bond if its yield to maturity is 6 percent?

Returns on investments

6-20 Rebecca purchased 100 shares of stock for $30 a share on January 1, 1994. On December 31, 1996, she sold these shares for $32 per share.

    a. What was the return on her investment?

    b. If transaction costs were 1 percent of the dollar value of the transaction both in purchasing and selling these shares, what was the return on her investment?

6-21 Ross purchased 100 shares of stock for $30 a share on January 1, 1990. On December 31, 1995, he sold these shares for $25 per share.

    a. What was the return on his investment?

    b. If transaction costs were 1 percent of the dollar value of the transaction both in purchasing and selling these shares, what was the return on his investment?

6-22 Jan purchased a zero-coupon bond on January 1, 1980, for $500. On December 31, 1991, she sold this bond for $750.

    a. What was the return on her investment?

    b. What was the return on her investment if she incurred a 2 percent transaction cost in both the purchase and sale of the bonds?

6-23 The Caitlin Company acquired a bond with a face value of $1,000 for $800 on January 1, 1992. The bond yields interest of 6 percent per year paid semiannually and matures on December 31, 1995.

    a. If the Caitlin Company sells the bond for $900 on December 31, 1992, what is the return on the investment?

    b. If the Caitlin Company sells the bond for $1,000 on December 31, 1993, what is the return on the investment?

    c. If the Caitlin Company holds the bond to maturity, what is the return on the investment?

6-24 Rose Company bonds were issued January 1, 1991, and will mature on December 31, 1995. These bonds have a face value of $1,000 and a coupon rate of 6 percent paid semiannually. Assume that these bonds have an annualized yield to maturity of 10 percent throughout their life. What is their value as of:

    a. January 1, 1992?

    b. January 1, 1993?

    c. January 1, 1994?

6-25 The Vashon Company issued bonds on January 1, 1992, that mature December 31, 1996. These bonds have a face value of $1,000 per bond and a coupon rate of 12 percent paid semiannually. What is the value of these bonds on January 1, 1994, if their annualized yield to maturity is:

   a. 8 percent?
   b. 10 percent?
   c. 12 percent?
   d. 14 percent?
   e. 16 percent?

6-26 Calculate the coupon-equivalent yield for the following coupon rates, where interest is paid semiannually:

   a. 6 percent
   b. 8 percent
   c. 10 percent
   d. 12 percent
   e. 14 percent

6-27 Consider a bond that has a current value of $1,081.11, a face value of $1,000.00, a coupon rate of 10 percent paid semiannually, and five years remaining to maturity.

   a. What is the bond's yield to maturity today?
   b. If the bond's yield does not change, what will be its value one year from today?
   c. If the bond's yield does not change, what will be its value two years from today?

6-28 Find the value today of a zero-coupon bond with a face value of $1,000 and five years remaining to maturity if it is priced to yield:

   a. 5 percent
   b. 8 percent
   c. 10 percent
   d. 12 percent
   e. 14 percent

6-29 Ferry Corporation has coupon bonds with a face value of $1,000 and five years remaining to maturity. If these bonds have a value of $900 and are priced to yield 10.25 percent to maturity, what is the coupon rate if interest is paid semiannually?

Potpourri

6-30 Island Corporation invested $1,000,000 in a new product on January 1, 1990. This product generated cash flows of $800,000 the first year, $400,000 the second year, and $200,000 the third year. At the end of the third year, Island abandoned the new product and at the same time disposed of the production equipment receiving $400,000. If these are the only cash flows from the new product, what was Island's return on its investment in the product?

6-31 Suppose you are considering investing in either the common or the preferred stock of the **CORP** Company. A share of **CORP** common stock is currently trading for $25 per share, and the current dividend is $5 per share.

The dividend is expected to decrease 5 percent per year. A share of CORP preferred stock is currently trading for $50 per share, and the current dividend is $5 per share.

a. If you require a return of 9 percent on the preferred shares and 15 percent on the common shares, should you buy the common, the preferred, or neither?

b. If you require a return on 11 percent on the preferred shares and 12 percent on the common shares, should you buy the common, the preferred, or neither?

PC+ 6-32 Research: Select a corporation that has paid dividends each quarter for the past ten years.

a. What is the effective annual growth rate of dividends for the first five years?

b. What is the effective annual growth rate of dividends for the most recent five years?

c. What is the effective annual growth rate of dividends over the entire ten years?

Recommended sources of information:

- *Industrial Manual,* Moody's
- *Compustat PC Plus* (CD-ROM), Standard & Poor's
- *Value Line Investment Survey*

FURTHER READINGS

The economic reasoning behind the value of assets is described clearly in:
JOHN BURR WILLIAMS, *The Theory of Investment Value,* North-Holland, Amsterdam, 1938.

There are many books devoted to the financial mathematics of bond valuation and yields. For a detailed look at bond valuation, the sensitivity of bond values to changes in yields, and the role of options embedded in bonds, see:
FRANK J. FABOZZI, *Fixed Income Mathematics,* Probus, Chicago, 1988.

Many textbooks provide in-depth coverage of options valuation. For example, see:
DAVID A. DUBOFSKY, *Options and Financial Futures,* McGraw-Hill, New York, 1992.

CHAPTER 7

Risk and Expected Return

INTRODUCTION 290

RISK 290

Cash Flow Risk 291

    Business Risk 291

    Financial Risk 294

    Operating and Financial Risk 296

    Default Risk 297

Reinvestment Rate Risk 298

Interest Rate Risk 301

Purchasing Power Risk 304

Currency Risk 307

RETURN AND RISK 307

Expected Return 307

Standard Deviation of the Possible Outcomes 309

Return and the Tolerance for Bearing Risk 315

EXPECTED RETURN, RISK, AND DIVERSIFICATION 315

Diversification and Risk 317

Portfolio Size and Risk 323

Modern Portfolio Theory and Asset Pricing 325

    The Capital Asset Pricing Model 326

    The Arbitrage Pricing Model 332

Financial Decision Making and Asset Pricing 333

Summary 333

No Guts, No Glory

We often look at past returns on securities to get an idea of the returns and risk we might expect in the future when we invest in these securities. Consider the returns on common stocks and long-term corporate bonds. The returns on stocks (as represented by the stocks that make up the Standard & Poor's 500 Stock Index) have been **more volatile** than those on corporate bonds, but the returns on stocks have also been **higher** than on bonds.

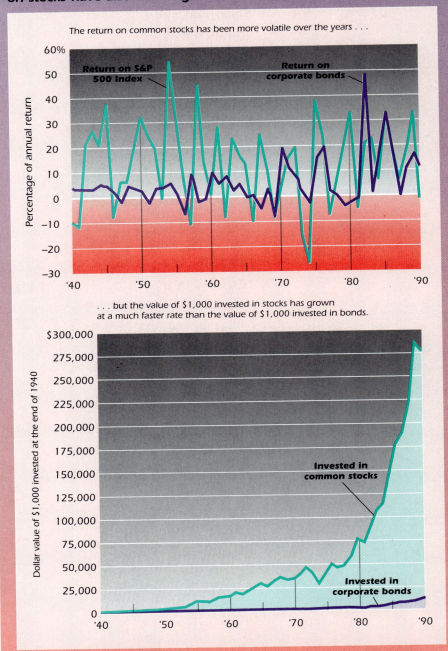

The return on common stocks has been more volatile over the years . . .

Return on S&P 500 Index

Return on corporate bonds

Percentage of annual return

. . . but the value of $1,000 invested in stocks has grown at a much faster rate than the value of $1,000 invested in bonds.

Dollar value of $1,000 invested at the end of 1940

Invested in common stocks

Invested in corporate bonds

How do the returns on common stocks and corporate bonds compare with investments in relatively "safe" securities, such as U.S. Treasury bills and bonds?

Consider $1,000 invested at the end of 1940, where any dividends or interest earned on the security are reinvested in that security:

	Value of $1,000 invested at the end of 1940 in . . .			
As of the end of . . .	U.S. Treasury bills	U.S. Treasury bonds	Corporate bonds	Common stocks
1940	$1,000	$1,000	$ 1,000	$ 1,000
1950	1,053	1,296	1,288	3,505
1960	1,286	1,464	1,520	15,703
1970	1,963	1,664	1,951	34,335
1980	3,778	2,564	2,936	76,785
1990	8,575	9,925	10,920	276,726

SOURCE: Returns on these securities are taken from *Johnson Charts*, Johnson's Charts, Inc., Williamsville, N.Y., 1991.

We can also put this in terms of the average annual return over the fifty years:[1]

	U.S. Treasury bills	U.S. Treasury bonds	Corporate bonds	Common stocks
Average annual return	4.39%	4.70%	4.90%	11.90%

If you are willing to take on more risk, you can earn more on your investment. In other words: no guts, no glory.

[1] This is the average annual return including compounding, which is also referred to as the geometric average annual return. If the present value is $1,000, the future value is $276,726, and the number of compounding periods is 50, the average annual return, r, is:

$$r = \sqrt[50]{\frac{\$276,726}{\$1,000}} - 1 = \mathbf{11.90\%}$$

INTRODUCTION

By now it should be clear that to make any investment or financing decision you have to make your best determination of the costs it will involve and the benefits, or return, that will result from it. What may not yet be clear is that there is risk that the returns may not turn out to be what you thought they would be. You will have to make your best determination of the returns and, at the same time, assess the uncertainty that the outcome will not meet your expectations. What we're getting at, of course, is the problem of risk. Specifying a return by itself doesn't mean very much unless you also specify its risk.

After we have explained the concept of risk, we will look at how to quantify the risk of an expected return and how to use risk in financial decision making. By becoming familiar with modern portfolio theory and the role of risk in valuing assets, we will see that a financial manager who understands risk and its relation to expected return can manage risk.

RISK

Risk is a most slippery and elusive concept. It's hard for investors—let alone economists—to agree on a precise definition.

　　　　　　　　　　Burton G. Malkiel, *A Random Walk Down Wall Street*, 1985, p. 187.

With any financing or investment decision, there is some uncertainty about its outcome. *Uncertainty* is not knowing exactly what will happen in the future. There is uncertainty in most everything we do as financial managers because no one knows precisely what changes will occur in such things as tax laws, consumer demand, the economy, or interest rates.

Though the terms "risk" and "uncertainty" are many times used to mean the same, there is a distinction between them. Uncertainty is not knowing what's going to happen. *Risk* is how we characterize *how much* uncertainty exists: the greater the uncertainty, the greater the risk. Risk is the degree of uncertainty. In financing and investment decisions there are many types of risk we must consider.[2]

The types of risk a financial manager faces include:

- Cash flow risk
- Reinvestment risk
- Interest rate risk
- Purchasing power risk
- Currency risk

Let's take a look at each of these types of risk.

---

[2] You should clearly understand two points regarding risk and uncertainty. First, in statistics, we generally refer to uncertainty as described in the text. Yet we refer to risk as a description of uncertainty only if there is some *objective* probability distribution associated with the possible outcomes reflecting that uncertainty. In financial decision making, we have only *subjective* distributions, since we cannot foresee the future. Therefore, in finance we use the term "risk" slightly differently than you may have used it in statistics.

Second, some refer to risk as the chance of a loss. While we are concerned with losses, we are also concerned about possible gains and how to figure them into our analysis. Therefore, in finance we adopt a broader definition of risk that includes the chance of incurring not only a loss but also a gain.

	Operating cash flow of $5,000	**Operating cash flow of $6,000**
Operating cash flow	$5,000	$6,000
Less: Interest	1,000	1,000
Cash flows to owners	$4,000	$5,000

A change in operating cash flow from $5,000 to $6,000—a 20 percent increase—increased cash flows to owners by $1,000—a 25 percent increase.

What if, instead, our fixed financial costs are $3,000? A 20 percent change in operating cash flows results in a 50 percent change in the cash flows available to owners:

	Operating cash flow of $5,000	**Operating cash flow of $6,000**
Operating cash flow	$5,000	$6,000
Less: Interest	3,000	3,000
Cash flows to owners	$2,000	$3,000

Using more debt financing increases the sensitivity of owners' cash flows.

We can describe the sensitivity of owners' cash flows to a change in operating cash flows as:

$$DFL = \frac{\left(\begin{array}{c}\text{number}\\\text{of units}\\\text{sold}\end{array}\right)\left(\begin{array}{ccc}\text{price}&&\text{variable}\\\text{per}&-&\text{cost}\\\text{unit}&&\text{per unit}\end{array}\right) - \left(\begin{array}{c}\text{fixed}\\\text{operating}\\\text{costs}\end{array}\right)}{\left(\begin{array}{c}\text{number}\\\text{of units}\\\text{sold}\end{array}\right)\left(\begin{array}{ccc}\text{price}&&\text{variable}\\\text{per}&-&\text{cost}\\\text{unit}&&\text{per unit}\end{array}\right) - \left(\begin{array}{c}\text{fixed}\\\text{operating}\\\text{costs}\end{array}\right) - \left(\begin{array}{c}\text{fixed}\\\text{financing}\\\text{costs}\end{array}\right)} \qquad [7\text{-}2]$$

where: Number of units sold = 1,000
Price per unit   = $30
Variable cost per unit = $20
Fixed operating costs = $5,000
Fixed financing costs = $1,000

$$DFL \text{ for 1,000 units} = \frac{1,000(\$30 - \$20) - \$5,000}{1,000(\$30 - \$20) - \$5,000 - \$1,000}$$

$$= \frac{\$5,000}{\$4,000}$$

$$= \mathbf{1.25}$$

Again, we need to qualify our degree of leverage by the level of production, since DFL is different for different levels of operating cash flows.[6]

---

[6] Like the DOL, the DFL approaches infinity as we approach the breakeven point. Breakeven in this case is at the point at which cash flows to owners—the denominator in the DFL formula—equals zero.

The greater the use of financing sources that require fixed obligations, such as interest, the greater the sensitivity of cash flows to owners to changes in operating cash flows.[7]

Operating and Financial Risk

The DOL gives us an idea of the sensitivity of operating cash flows to changes in sales, and the DFL gives us an idea of the sensitivity of owners' cash flows to changes in operating cash flows. But often we are concerned about the *combined* effect of operating leverage and financial leverage. Owners are concerned about the combined effect because both types of leverage contribute to the risk associated with their future cash flows. Financial managers are concerned about the combined effect because, in making decisions to maximize owners' wealth, managers need to consider how investment decisions (which affect the operating cost structure) and financing decisions (which affect the capital structure) affect owners' risk.

Let's look back on the example that uses fixed operating costs of $5,000 and fixed financial costs of $1,000. The sensitivity of owners' cash flow to a given change in units sold is affected by both operating and financial leverage.

Consider increasing the number of units sold by 50 percent. If there were no interest (and therefore no financial leverage), the owners' cash flow would equal operating cash flow. Then a 50 percent increase in units sold would result in a 100 percent increase in cash flows to owners. Now consider decreasing the number of units sold by 50 percent. This would result in a 100 percent decrease in cash flows to owners.

But if there is financial leverage, it will exaggerate the effect of operating leverage. Consider again the case in which there is $1,000 of interest payments:

	1,000 units sold	1,500 units sold	500 units sold
Sales	$30,000	$45,000	$ 15,000
Less: Variable costs	20,000	30,000	10,000
Fixed costs	5,000	5,000	5,000
Operating cash flow	$ 5,000	$10,000	$ 0
Less: Interest	1,000	1,000	1,000
Cash flows to owners	$ 4,000	$ 9,000	−$1,000

If the number of units sold increases by 50 percent, from 1,000 to 1,500 units:

- Operating cash flows increase by 100 percent.
- Cash flows to owners increase by 125 percent.

If units sold decrease by 50 percent, from 1,000 to 500 units:

- Operating cash flows decrease by 100 percent.
- Cash flows to owners decrease by 125 percent.

---

[7] If we had included taxes, we would have gotten the same result, since the effect of taxes is canceled from both the numerator and the denominator.

Combining a firm's degree of operating leverage with its degree of financial leverage results in the **degree of total leverage** (DTL), a measure of the sensitivity of owners' cash flows to changes in unit sales:

$$\text{DTL} = \frac{\text{percentage change in cash flows to owners}}{\text{percentage change in units sold}}$$

which is the same as:

$$\text{DTL} = \frac{\left(\begin{array}{c}\text{number}\\\text{of units}\\\text{sold}\end{array}\right)\left(\begin{array}{cc}\text{price}&\text{variable}\\\text{per}&-\text{cost}\\\text{unit}&\text{per unit}\end{array}\right)}{\left(\begin{array}{c}\text{number}\\\text{of units}\\\text{sold}\end{array}\right)\left(\begin{array}{cc}\text{price}&\text{variable}\\\text{per}&-\text{cost}\\\text{unit}&\text{per unit}\end{array}\right)-\left(\begin{array}{c}\text{fixed}\\\text{operating}\\\text{costs}\end{array}\right)-\left(\begin{array}{c}\text{fixed}\\\text{financing}\\\text{costs}\end{array}\right)} \quad [7\text{-}3]$$

and which simplifies to:

$$\text{DTL} = \text{DOL} \times \text{DFL}$$

Suppose: Number of units sold = 1,000
Price per unit = $30
Variable cost per unit = $20
Fixed operating costs = $5,000
Fixed financing costs = $1,000

Then,

$$\text{DTL for 1,000 units} = \frac{1{,}000(\$30-\$20)}{1{,}000(\$30-\$20)-\$5{,}000-\$1{,}000} = \frac{\$10{,}000}{\$4{,}000} = \textbf{2.5}$$

which we could also have gotten by multiplying the DOL, 2.00, by the DFL, 1.25. This means that a 1.0 percent increase in units sold results in a 2.5 percent increase in cash flows to owners, a 50.0 percent increase in units sold results in a 125.0 percent increase in cash flows to owners, a 5.0 percent decline in units sold results in a 12.5 percent decline in cash flows to owners, and so on.

In the case of operating leverage, the fixed operating costs act as a fulcrum: The greater is the proportion of operating costs that are fixed, the more sensitive are operating cash flows to changes in sales. In the case of financial leverage, the fixed financial costs, such as interest, act as a fulcrum: The greater is the proportion of financing with fixed cost sources, such as debt, the more sensitive are cash flows available to owners to changes in operating cash flows. Combining the effects of both types of leverage, we see that fixed operating and financial costs together act as a fulcrum that increases the sensitivity of cash flows available to owners.

Default Risk

When you invest in a bond, you expect interest to be paid as scheduled (usually semiannually) and the principal to be paid at the maturity date. But not all interest and principal payments may be made in the amount or on the date expected: Interest or principal may be late, or the principal may not be paid at all!

The more burdened a firm is with debt—required interest and principal payments—the more likely is the possibility that payments promised to bond-holders will not be made and that nothing may be left for the owners. We refer to the cash flow risk of a debt security as *default risk* or *credit risk*.

Technically, default risk on a debt security depends on the specific obligations the debt comprises. Default may result from:

- Failure to make an interest payment when promised (or within a specified period).
- Failure to make the principal payment as promised.
- Failure to make sinking fund payments (that is, amounts set aside to pay off the obligation), if these payments are required.
- Failure to meet any other condition of the loan.
- Bankruptcy.

Why do financial managers need to worry about default risk? Because they invest their firm's funds in the debt securities of other firms and they want to know what default risk lurks in those investments; because they are concerned about how investors perceive the risk of the debt securities their own firm issues; and because the greater the risk of a firm's securities, the greater the firm's cost of financing.

Default risk is affected by both business risk—which includes sales risk and operating risk—and financial risk. We need to consider the effects operating and financing decisions have on the default risk of the securities a firm issues since the risk accepted in the financing decisions affects the firm's cost of financing.

Reinvestment Rate Risk

Another type of risk is that associated with the reinvestment of cash flows, not surprisingly called *reinvestment rate risk.*

Suppose you buy a U.S. Treasury bond that matures in five years. There is no default risk, since the U.S. government could simply print more money to pay the interest and principal. Does this mean there is no risk when you own a Treasury bond? No. You need to do something with the interest payments as you receive them and with the principal amount when the bond matures. You could stuff the money under your mattress, reinvest in another Treasury bond, or invest in some asset. If yields have been falling, however, you cannot reinvest the interest payments from the bond and get the same return paid on the bond.

From the time that you bought the Treasury bond until its maturity five years later, yields on investments may have changed. While the yield on the mattress option hasn't changed (it's still zero), the yields on other investments may have changed. When your Treasury bond matures, you face reinvestment risk.

If we look at an investment that produces cash flows before maturity or sale, such as a stock (with dividends) or a bond (with interest), we face a more complicated reinvestment problem. In this case we're concerned not only with the reinvestment of the final proceeds (at maturity or sale), but also with the reinvestment of the intermediate dividend or interest cash flows (between purchase and maturity or sale).

Let's look at the case of a five-year bond issued by Company Y, which pays 10 percent interest at the end of each year (to keep things simple) and has a par value of $1,000. This bond is a *coupon bond;* that is, interest is paid at the coupon rate of 10 percent per year, or $100 per bond. If you buy the bond when it is issued at the beginning of 1990 and hold it to maturity, you will have the following cash flows:

COMPANY Y BOND

Date	Cash flow	
January 1, 1990	−$1,000	← Purchase of bond
December 31, 1990	100	
December 31, 1991	100	
December 31, 1992	100	
December 31, 1993	100	
December 31, 1994	1,100	← Proceeds of maturity and last interest payment

You face five reinvestment decisions during the life of this bond: the four intermediate flows at the end of each year and the final and largest cash flow, which consists of the final interest payment and the par value.

Suppose we wish to compare the investment in the Company Y bond with a five-year bond issued by Company Z, which has a different cash flow stream, but a yield that is nearly the same. Company Z's bond is a zero-coupon bond; that is, it has no interest payments, so the only cash flow to the investor is the face value at maturity:

COMPANY Z BOND

Date	Cash flow	
January 1, 1990	−1,000.00	← Purchase of bond
December 31, 1994	1,610.51	← Proceeds of maturity

Both bonds have the same annual yield to maturity of 10 percent. If the yield is the same for both bonds, does that mean they have the same reinvestment rate risk? No. Just by looking at the cash flows from these bonds we see there are intermediate cash flows to reinvest from Company Y's bond, but not from Company Z's bond.

Let's see just how sensitive the yield on the investment is to changes in the assumptions on the reinvestment of intermediate cash flows. Suppose we are not able to reinvest the interest payments at 10 percent, but only at 5 percent per year. We calculate the yield on the bonds assuming reinvestment at 5 percent—a modified internal rate of return—by calculating the future value of the reinvested cash flows and determining the discount rate that equates the original investment of $1,000 to this future value:

Date	Company Y bond		Company Z bond	
	Cash flow	Values as of December 31, 1994	Cash flow	Values as of December 31, 1994
December 31, 1990	$ 100.00	$ 121.55		
December 31, 1991	100.00	115.76		
December 31, 1992	100.00	110.25		
December 31, 1993	100.00	105.00		
December 31, 1994	1,100.00	1,100.00	$1,610.51	$ 1,610.51
Future value, with cash flows reinvested at 5%		**$1,552.00**		**$1,610.51**

Using the value of the cash flow as of December 31, 1994, as the future value and the $1,000 investment as the present value, the modified internal rates of return are 9.19 percent for Company Y's bond and 10 percent for Company Z's bond. You'll notice that the modified internal rate of return for Company Z's bond is the same as its yield to maturity because there are no intermediate cash flows.

If we compare two bonds with the same yield to maturity and the same coupon rate, the bond with the *longer* maturity has *more* reinvestment risk.[8] That's because it has more cash flows to reinvest throughout its life.

If we compare two bonds with the same yield to maturity and the same maturity date, the bond with the *greater* coupon rate has *more* reinvestment rate risk. That's because it has more of its value coming sooner in the form of cash flows.

Two types of risk closely related to the reinvestment risk of debt securities are prepayment risk and call risk. In the case of mortgage-backed securities—securities that represent a collection of home mortgages—a home owner may pay off her or his mortgage early. If the mortgage is paid off early, investors in the mortgage will have to scramble to reinvest earlier than expected. Therefore, investors in securities that can be paid off earlier than maturity face **prepayment risk**—the risk that the borrower may choose to prepay the loan—which causes the investor to have to reinvest the funds earlier than intended.

Call risk is the risk that the issuer may exercise the right in a callable security to buy it back. While you may receive a call premium (a specified amount above the par value), you will have to reinvest the funds you receive.

Modifying the Internal Rate

A bond's yield is the bond's internal rate of return. The internal rate of return assumes that any cash flows from the asset (interest, in the case of a bond) are reinvested at a rate equal to the bond's yield.

A *modified* internal rate of return is the return on an asset, assuming that intermediate cash flows are reinvested at a specific rate. The modified internal rate of return can provide a more realistic return on an investment, since it accounts for reinvestment at some rate *other* than the asset's internal rate.

---

[8] We can examine the reinvestment problem for different investments that have different cash flow patterns by looking at the investments' duration, which is a time-weighted measure of cash flow patterns. The concept and calculations of duration are, however, beyond the scope of this book.

There is reinvestment risk in assets other than stocks and bonds. If you invest in a new product, that is, in assets to manufacture and distribute it, you expect to have cash flows from the investment in future periods. You face a reinvestment problem with these cash flows: What can you earn by investing these cash flows? What are your future investment opportunities?[9]

If we assume that investors do not like risk—a safe assumption—then they will want to be compensated if they take on more reinvestment rate risk. The greater is the reinvestment rate risk, the greater will be the expected return demanded by investors.

Reinvestment rate risk is relevant in our investment decisions no matter the asset, and we must consider this risk in assessing the attractiveness of investments. The greater are the cash flows during the life of an investment, the greater will be the reinvestment rate risk of the investment, and that must be factored into our decision.

Interest Rate Risk

Interest rate risk is the sensitivity of the change in an asset's value to changes in market interest rates, and market interest rates determine the rate we must use to discount a future value to a present value. The value of any investment depends on the rate used to discount its cash flows to the present. If the discount rate changes, the investment's value changes.

Suppose we make an investment in a project that we expect to have in operation for ten years. Two years into the project, we look at our investment opportunities and see that the returns on alternative investments have increased. Does this affect the value to us of this two-year-old project? Sure. We now have a higher opportunity cost—the return on our best investment opportunity—and therefore the value of the two-year-old project is now less and we need to assess the situation in order to determine whether to continue or terminate the project. Reassessment is necessary, also, if the opportunity cost declines as well. If the return on our next best investment opportunity declines, the existing project will look even better.

Interest rate risk also is present in debt securities. If you buy a bond and intend to hold it until its maturity, you don't need to worry about its value changing as interest rates change: Your return is the bond's yield to maturity. But if you do not intend to hold the bond to maturity, you need to worry about how changes in interest rates affect the value of your investment. As interest rates go up, the value of your bond goes down. As interest rates go down, the value of your bond goes up. This may seem wrong to you. But it's not; it's correct. Here's why.

Let's compare the change in the value of the Company Y bond to the change in the value of the Company Z bond as the market interest rate changes. (We presented these bonds in the previous section.) Suppose that it

---

[9] Another reinvestment problem arises when we terminate a project before the end of its useful life. When a firm invests in a new product, buying buildings and equipment, there is always a possibility of abandoning the product before its projected useful life, requiring the firm to sell the buildings and equipment and reinvest the proceeds.

is now January 1, 1991. If yields remain at 10 percent, the values of the bonds are:

$$\text{Value of Company Y bond} = \frac{\$100.00}{(1 + 0.10)^1} + \frac{\$100.00}{(1 + 0.10)^2} + \frac{\$100.00}{(1 + 0.10)^3} + \frac{\$1,100.00}{(1 + 0.10)^4}$$

$$= \$90.91 + \$82.64 + \$75.13 + \$751.31$$

$$= \mathbf{\$1,000.00}$$

and

$$\text{Value of Company Z bond} = \frac{\$1,610.51}{(1 + 0.10)^4} = \mathbf{\$1,100.00}$$

If market interest rates rise to 12 percent, the market value of the Company Y and Company Z bonds will fall:

$$\text{Value of Company Y bond} = \frac{\$100.00}{(1 + 0.12)^1} + \frac{\$100.00}{(1 + 0.12)^2} + \frac{\$100.00}{(1 + 0.12)^3} + \frac{\$1,100.00}{(1 + 0.12)^4}$$

$$= \$89.29 + \$79.71 + \$71.18 + \$699.07$$

$$= \mathbf{\$939.25}$$

and

$$\text{Value of Company Z bond} = \frac{\$1,610.51}{(1 + 0.12)^4} = \mathbf{\$1,023.50}$$

If, instead, the market yield is 14 percent, the value of Company Y's and Company Z's bonds is even lower:

$$\text{Value of Company Y bond} = \frac{\$100.00}{(1 + 0.14)^1} + \frac{\$100.00}{(1 + 0.14)^2} + \frac{\$100.00}{(1 + 0.14)^3} + \frac{\$1,100.00}{(1 + 0.14)^4}$$

$$= \$87.72 + \$76.95 + \$67.50 + \$651.29$$

$$= \mathbf{\$883.46}$$

and

$$\text{Value of Company Z bond} = \frac{\$1,610.51}{(1 + 0.14)^4} = \mathbf{\$953.55}$$

If market interest rates fall to 8 percent, the market value of the Company Y and Company Z bonds is more than \$1,000:

$$\text{Value of Company Y bond} = \frac{\$100.00}{(1 + 0.08)^1} + \frac{\$100.00}{(1 + 0.08)^2} + \frac{\$100.00}{(1 + 0.08)^3} + \frac{\$1,100.00}{(1 + 0.08)^4}$$

$$= \$92.59 + \$85.73 + \$79.38 + \$808.53$$

$$= \mathbf{\$1,066.23}$$

and

$$\text{Value of Company Z bond} = \frac{\$1,610.51}{(1 + 0.08)^4} = \mathbf{\$1,183.77}$$

But how sensitive are the values of the bonds to changes in market interest rates? If the bonds' yield changed on January 1, 1991, from 10 percent to 12 percent, the value of the Company Y bond would drop from $1,000.00 to $939.25—a drop of $60.75, or 6.08 percent of the bond's value. The drop would be greater for Company Z's bond—a drop of $76.50, or 6.95 percent of its value. Looking at changes in the value of the bonds for different yield changes, we see that the value of Company Z's bond is more sensitive to changes in yields than Company Y's:

	Change in market value for change in market yield from 10% to:		
Bond	**12%**	**14%**	**8%**
Company Y	−$60.75, or −6.08%	−$116.54, or −11.65%	+$66.23, or +6.62%
Company Z	−$76.50, or −6.95%	−$146.45, or −13.31%	+$83.77, or +7.62%

The values of the two bonds for different yields, as of January 1, 1991, are shown in Figure 7-1. As you can see, the value of Company Z's bond is more sensitive to the yield changes than Company Y's.

We can make some generalizations about the sensitivity of a bond's value to changes in yields.

- For a given coupon rate, the *longer the maturity* of the bond, the *more sensitive* is the bond's value to changes in market interest rates. Why? Because more of the bond's value is further out into the future (the principal payments), its present value is influenced more by a change in the discount rate.

FIGURE 7-1

Value of Company Y Bond and Company Z Bond on January 1, 1991, for Different Yields to Maturity

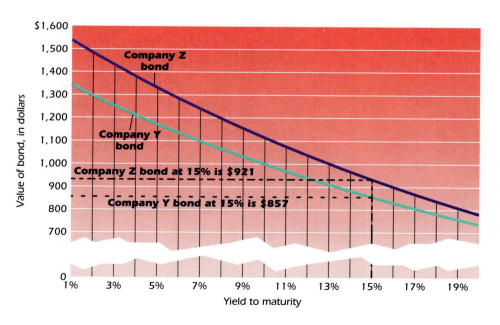

Example:
Compare the change in the value of two bonds that have the same coupon rate (10 percent) and the same face value ($1,000) and pay interest annually. If Bond SM has five years remaining to maturity and Bond LM has ten years remaining to maturity, a change in the yield on the bonds from 10 percent to 12 percent results in a greater change in Bond LM's value. When interest changes from 10 percent to 12 percent:

> Bond SM's value changes from $1,000 to $928, down 7.2 percent.
> Bond LM's value changes from $1,000 to $887, down 11.3 percent.

- For a given maturity, the *greater the coupon rate*, the *less sensitive* the bond's value to a change in the yield. Why? The greater the coupon rate, the more of the bond's present value is derived from cash flows that are affected less by discounting.

Example:
Compare two bonds that have the same time remaining to maturity (five years) and the same face value ($1,000); both are priced to yield 10 percent. If Bond HC has a 10 percent coupon and Bond LC has a 5 percent coupon, a change in the yield has a greater effect on the value of Bond LC than on Bond HC. When yields change from 10 percent to 12 percent:

> Bond HC's value changes from $1,000 to $928, down 7.20 percent.
> Bond LC's value changes from $810 to $748, down 7.65 percent.

Purchasing Power Risk

Purchasing power risk is the risk that the price level may increase unexpectedly. If a buyer locks in a price on your supply of raw materials through a long-term contract and the price level increases, the buyer benefits from the increase in the price level and you suffer a loss because the buyer pays you in cheaper currency. If a firm borrows funds by issuing a long-term bond with a fixed coupon rate, and the price level increases, the firm benefits from an increase in the price level and its creditor is harmed, since interest and the principal are repaid in a cheaper currency.

Consider the 11.0 percent and 9.1 percent inflation rates for the years 1974 and 1975, respectively. If you borrowed $1,000 at the beginning of 1974 and paid it back two years later, you would be paying it back in end-of-1975 dollars. But how much is an end-of-1975 dollar worth relative to a beginning-of-1974 dollar? We can use the compounding relation to work this out. We know that the future value is $1,000. We also know that the rate of inflation over the two-year period is determined by compounding the two inflation rates:

r = (1 + inflation rate for 1974)(1 + inflation rate for 1975) − 1
   = (1 + 0.110)(1 + 0.091) − 1 = 1.2110 − 1
   = **0.2110** or **21.10%** over 1974 and 1975

We can solve the basic valuation relation for today's value, PV, considering r to be a *two-year rate* (that is, a period is defined as the two-year stretch from the beginning of 1974 to the end of 1975):[10]

$$FV = PV(1 + r)$$
$$\$1,000 = PV(1 + 0.2110)$$

and rearranging to solve for PV,

$$PV = \frac{\$1,000.00}{(1 + 0.2110)} = \textbf{\$825.76}$$

Therefore, the $1,000 you paid back at the end of 1975 was really worth only $825.76 at the beginning of 1974. As a borrower, you have benefited from inflation and your lender has lost.

How much should your lender have demanded just to keep up with inflation? That is, how much should your lender have demanded without any compensation for the time value of money or for the uncertainty that you will pay it back?

$$FV = \$1,000(1 + 0.2110) = \textbf{\$1,211}$$

Demanding $1,211.00 in return at the end of 1975 would have *just* compensated your lender for the purchasing power lost since the beginning of 1974. We can check our work by calculating what $1,211 would be worth in terms of beginning-of-1975 dollars, $1,211.00/(1 + 0.091) = $1,109.99, and in terms of beginning-of-1974 dollars, $1,109.99/(1 + 0.11) = $1,000.00.

Since we know how to translate the purchasing power of dollars in one year into the purchasing power of dollars in another, let's see how inflation affects returns. Suppose you invest $100 today in an investment that pays a lump sum at the end of the year. You expect inflation to be 4 percent this year, and you want a return of 6 percent on your investment. What would the expected return on the investment have to be for you to get a 6 percent return after considering the expected loss in purchasing power?

If you lent $100.00 today and got $106.00 back at the end of the year, your return would be 6.00 percent before considering the effect of inflation. But the $106 is worth only $106.00/(1 + 0.04) = $101.92 in today's dollars; so effectively you have a return of 1.92 percent on your investment!

So, what must the investment's return be in order to provide you with a 6 percent return *after* inflation? We need to solve for the return, r, that equates the end-of-year cash flow after adjusting for inflation with the end-of-year cash flow if we had earned the 6 percent:

$$\frac{\text{Required loan repayment}}{\text{Adjustment for inflation}} = \frac{\text{desired loan repayment}}{\text{after considering inflation}}$$

---

[10] We could have solved for PV using the individual-year rates:

$$PV = \frac{\$1,000}{(1 + 0.110)(1 + 0.091)}$$

but we use the equivalent two-year rate instead to make the math somewhat simpler.

Inserting the rate of inflation and the initial loan balance:

$$\frac{\$100(1 + r)}{(1 + 0.04)} = \$100(1 + 0.06)$$

$$(1 + r) = (1 + 0.04)(1 + 0.06)$$

$$= 1.1024$$

Solving for r,

r = **0.1024** or **10.24%** per year

If you demand a return of 10.24%, which means the loan repayment should be $110.24, you have earned 6.00 percent after inflation.

Let's refer to the return after considering inflation as the ***real return*** and refer to the return before removing inflation as the ***nominal return.*** Therefore:

$$1 + \text{nominal return} = \left(1 + \frac{\text{inflation}}{\text{rate}}\right)\left(1 + \frac{\text{real}}{\text{return}}\right)$$

This relation between the nominal return, the inflation rate, and the real return is referred to as the ***Fisher effect.***[11]

If we solve for the nominal return,

$$\text{Nominal return} = \left(1 + \frac{\text{inflation}}{\text{rate}}\right)\left(1 + \frac{\text{real}}{\text{return}}\right) - 1$$

$$= \left[1 + \frac{\text{inflation}}{\text{rate}} + \frac{\text{real}}{\text{return}} + \left(\frac{\text{real}}{\text{return}}\right)\left(\frac{\text{inflation}}{\text{rate}}\right)\right] - 1$$

Hence:

$$\text{Nominal return} = \frac{\text{inflation}}{\text{rate}} + \frac{\text{real}}{\text{return}} + \left(\frac{\text{real}}{\text{return}}\right)\left(\frac{\text{inflation}}{\text{rate}}\right) \qquad [7\text{-}4]$$

As you can see, the nominal return comprises three parts: the inflation rate, the real return, and the cross-product of the inflation rate and the real return. Since the cross-product term is usually quite small—0.24 percent or 0.0024 in the last example—we often leave it out and consider the nominal return to be the sum of the inflation rate and the real return.

Nominal return = inflation rate + real return

The difference between the nominal return and the real return is often referred to as the ***inflation premium,*** since it is the additional return necessary to compensate for inflation.

Purchasing power risk is the risk that future cash flows may be worth less in the future because of inflation *and* that the return on the investment will not compensate for the unanticipated inflation. If there is risk that the purchasing power of a currency will change, investors—who do not like risk—will demand a higher return.

Inflation, 1941–1990

The average rate of inflation over the fifty-year period, 1941 through 1990, was 4.61 percent as measured by the Consumer Price Index. But this rate does differ over time. For example, looking at the average annual rate of inflation over different periods of time, we see quite a difference in inflation rates:

Decade	Average annual rate of inflation
1941–1950	5.91%
1951–1960	1.79
1961–1970	2.94
1971–1980	8.04
1981–1990	4.48

SOURCE: *Statistical Abstract of the United States*, U.S. Department of Commerce, Bureau of Census, 1992.

---

[11] This relation is so named because it is derived from the work of Irving Fisher, *The Theory of Interest*, Kelley, New York, 1965.

Financial managers need to assess purchasing power risk in terms of both their investment decisions, making sure to figure in the risk from a change in purchasing power of cash flows—and their financing decisions—in order to understand how purchasing power risk affects the costs of financing.

Currency Risk

In assessing the attractiveness of an investment, we estimated future cash flows from the investment to see whether their value today—the benefits—outweighs the cost of the investment. In an investment that generates cash flows in another currency (some other nation's currency), we face some risk that the value of the foreign currency will change relative to the value of our currency. We refer to the risk of the change in the value of the currency as *currency risk.*

Consider a U.S. firm making an investment that produces cash flows in British pounds. Suppose we invest 10,000 British pounds today and expect to get 12,000 pounds one year from today. Further suppose that a British pound is worth $1.48 today; so you are investing $1.48 times £10,000 = $14,800.00. If the British pound does not change in value relative to the U.S. dollar, you will have a return of 20 percent:

$$\text{Return} = \frac{£12,000 - £10,000}{£10,000} \quad \text{or} \quad \frac{\$17,760 - \$14,800}{\$14,800}$$

$$= \mathbf{20\%}$$

But what if one year from now the British pound is worth $1.30 instead of $1.48? Your return would be less than 20 percent because of the drop in the value of the pound vis-à-vis the U.S. dollar. You are making an investment of £10,000, or $14,800.00, and getting not $17,760.00, but rather $1.30 times £12,000 = $15,600.00 in one year.

If the dollar value of the pound falls from $1.48 to $1.30, your return on your investment is:

$$\text{Return} = \frac{\$15,600 - \$14,800}{\$14,800} = \frac{\$800}{\$14,800}$$

$$= \mathbf{5.41\%}$$

Currency risk is the risk that the *relative values* of the domestic and foreign currencies will change in the future, changing the value of the future cash flows. As financial managers, we need to consider currency risk in our investment decisions that involve other currencies and make sure that the returns on these investments are sufficient compensation for the risk of changing values of currencies.

RETURN AND RISK

Expected Return

We refer to both future benefits and future costs as expected returns. *Expected returns* are a measure of the tendency of returns on an investment. This doesn't mean that these are the only returns possible, just our best summary measure of what we expect.

Suppose we are evaluating the investment in a new product. We do not and cannot know precisely what the future cash flows will be. But from past experience, we can at least get an idea of possible flows and the likelihood—the probability—they will occur. After consulting with colleagues in market-

Financial Innovations Are Not without Their Risks

For more than two decades, Wall Street has been inventing new securities to satisfy investors' demands for a variety of securities in terms of risk and expected returns.

These security innovations are not without peril. Consider PERLS (short for Principal Exchange-Rate Linked Securities). PERLS are debt securities issued by U.S. government agencies and large, creditworthy corporations and pay above-market yields. What's the catch? The catch is that the principal amount of the debt is repaid not in U.S. dollars, but in another nation's currency.

The Student Loan Marketing Association (known as Sallie Mae), a government agency, issued $135 million of PERLS in 1990, with a maturity of five years and an interest rate of 11.75 percent (when the going yield on U.S. government five-year bonds was about 8.5 percent). But the principal amount was to be repaid in $270 million in British pounds *minus* $135 million in German marks, at exchange rates prevailing at the time the notes were issued. When these notes mature, the investor will get back what was originally paid only if the exchange rates among the mark, the pound, and the dollar remain the same as they were in 1990. If, for example, the pound falls and the mark rises, the investor gets back less than the debt's original amount.

Because of currency fluctuations following their issue, these notes were worth less than $135 million, even though they paid interest above the current market rates for other notes with similar maturity and risk (that is, notes that were default free or had low risk of default). In March 1993, these notes were worth only $88 million, despite the fact that interest rates in general had fallen since 1990.

Though there was little risk that the borrower would fail to repay the principal, there was uncertainty about just what that principal would be, since it depended on the relationships among three currencies. In addition to interest rate risk and reinvestment rate risk, these notes had currency risk.

ing and production management, we figure out that there are two possible cash flow outcomes, success or failure, and we estimate the probability of each outcome. Next, again consulting with colleagues in marketing and production to obtain sales prices, sales volume, and production costs, we develop the following possible schedule of cash flows in the first year:

Scenario	Cash flow	Probability of cash flow
Product success	$ 4,000,000	40%
Product flop	−2,000,000	60

But what is the expected cash flow in the first year? The expected cash flow is the average of the possible cash flows, weighted by their probabilities of occurrence:

$$\text{Expected cash flow} = 0.40(\$4{,}000{,}000) + 0.60(-\$2{,}000{,}000)$$
$$= \$1{,}600{,}000 + -\$1{,}200{,}000$$
$$= \mathbf{\$400{,}000}$$

The expected cash flow is $400,000.

The expected value is a guess about a future outcome. It is not necessarily the *most likely* outcome. The most likely outcome is the one with the highest probability. In the case of our example, the most likely outcome is $-\$2{,}000{,}000$.

A general formula for any expected value is:

$$\text{Expected value} = E(x) = p_1x_1 + p_2x_2 + p_3x_3 + \cdots + p_nx_n + \cdots + p_Nx_N$$

where $E(x)$ = the expected value
  n = possible outcome
  N = number of possible outcomes
  p_n = probability of the nth outcome
  x_n = value of the nth outcome

We can abbreviate this formula by using summation notation:

$$\text{Expected value} = E(x) = \sum_{n=1}^{N} p_nx_n \qquad\qquad [7\text{-}5]$$

Applying the general formula to our example:

$N = 2$ (there are two possible outcomes)
$p_1 = 0.40$
$p_2 = 0.60$
$x_1 = \$4{,}000{,}000$
$x_2 = -\$2{,}000{,}000$

$$E(\text{cash flow}) = \sum_{n=1}^{2} p_nx_n$$
$$= p_1x_1 + p_2x_2$$
$$= 0.40(\$4{,}000{,}000) + 0.60(-\$2{,}000{,}000)$$
$$= \mathbf{\$400{,}000}$$

Considering the possible outcomes and their likelihoods, we expect a $400,000 cash flow.

Standard Deviation of the Possible Outcomes

The expected return gives us an idea of the tendency of the future outcomes— what we expect to happen, considering all the possibilities. But the expected return is a single value and does not tell us anything about the diversity of the possible outcomes. Are the possible outcomes close to the expected value? Are the possible outcomes much different than the expected value? Just how much uncertainty *is* there about the future?

Since we are concerned about the degree of uncertainty (risk), as well as the expected return, we need some way of quantifying the risk associated with decisions.

Suppose we are considering two products, A and B, with estimated returns under different scenarios and their associated probabilities:

Scenario	Probability of possible outcome	Possible outcome
PRODUCT A		
Success	25%	24%
Moderate success	50	10
Failure	25	−4
PRODUCT B		
Success	10%	40%
Moderate success	30	30
Failure	60	−5

We refer to a product's set of the possible outcomes and their respective probabilities as the ***probability distribution*** of those outcomes.

We can calculate the expected cash flow for each product as follows:

Scenario	p_n	x_n	$p_n x_n$
PRODUCT A			
Success	0.25	0.24	0.0600
Moderate success	0.50	0.10	0.0500
Failure	0.25	−0.04	−0.0100
Expected return			**0.1000** or **10%**
PRODUCT B			
Success	0.10	0.40	0.0400
Moderate success	0.30	0.30	0.0900
Failure	0.60	−0.05	−0.0300
Expected return			**0.1000** or **10%**

Both Product A and Product B have the same expected return. Let's now see if there is any difference in the possible outcomes for the two products.

The possible returns for Product A range from −4 percent to 24 percent, and those for Product B range from −5 percent to 40 percent. The ***range*** is the span of possible outcomes. For Product A the span is 28 percent; for Product B it is 45 percent. A wider span indicates more risk; so Product B has more risk than Product A.

If we graph the possible cash flow outcomes for Products A and B, with their corresponding probabilities, as in Figure 7-2, we see there is more dis-

FIGURE 7-2

Probability Distribution for Products A and B

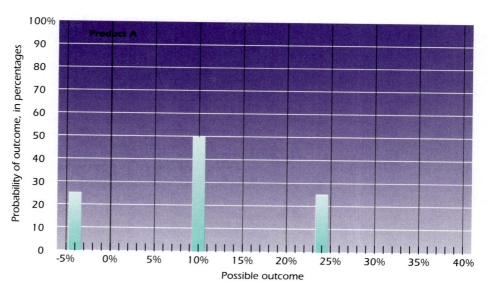

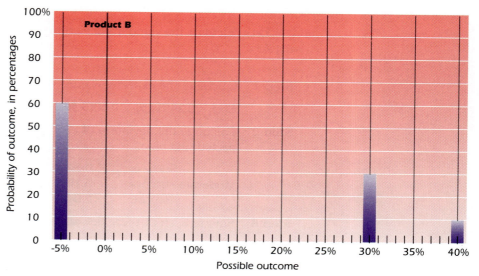

person of possible outcomes for Product B—they are more spread out—than for Product A. But the range by itself doesn't tell us much about either the possible cash flows or the probabilities at or within the extremes.

A measure of risk that does tell us something about how much cash flow to expect and the probability that it will happen is the standard deviation. The *standard deviation* is a measure of dispersion that considers the values and probabilities for each possible outcome. The larger the standard deviation, the greater the dispersion of possible outcomes from the expected value. The standard deviation considers the distance (deviation) of each possible outcome from the expected value and the probability associated with that distance.

The standard deviation of possible returns, represented by $\sigma(x)$, is calculated in six steps:

Step 1 *Calculate the expected value.* See the example in the previous section, where we calculated the expected value of the cash flow.

Step 2 *Calculate the deviation of each possible outcome from the expected value.* The deviation tells us how far each possible outcome is from the expected value.

Step 3 *Square each deviation.*

Step 4 *Weight each squared deviation, multiplying it by the probability of the outcome.*

Step 5 *Sum these weighted squared deviations.* This is the variance of the possible outcomes, $\sigma^2(x)$.

Step 6 *Take the square root of the sum of the squared deviations.* This is the standard deviation of the possible outcomes, $\sigma(x)$.

Let's calculate the standard deviation of the expected cash flows for Product A:

Step 1 Calculate the expected value.

$$E(x) = 0.24(0.25) + 0.10(0.50) + -0.04(0.25) = \mathbf{0.10} \text{ or } \mathbf{10\%}$$

Step 2 Calculate the deviation of each possible outcome from the expected outcome.

Success:	$0.2400 - 0.1000 =$	0.1400
Moderate success:	$0.1000 - 0.1000 =$	0.0000
Failure:	$-0.0400 - 0.1000 =$	-0.1400

Step 3 Square each of these deviations.

Success:	$0.1400^2 = 0.0196$
Moderate success:	$0.0000^2 = 0.0000$
Failure:	$-0.1400^2 = 0.0196$

Step 4 Weight each of the squared deviations by multiplying the probability of the outcome by the squared deviations.

Success:	$0.0196(0.25) = 0.0049$
Moderate success:	$0.0000(0.50) = 0.0000$
Failure:	$0.0196(0.25) = 0.0049$

Step 5 Sum these weighted squared deviations.

$$\text{Variance} = \sigma^2(x) = 0.0049 + 0.0000 + 0.0049 = \mathbf{0.0098}$$

The Variance and the Standard Deviation

The variance and standard deviation are both measures of dispersion. In fact, they are related: The standard deviation is the square root of the variance. So why do we go beyond the calculation of the variance to get the standard deviation? For two reasons.

First, the variance is in terms of squared units of measure (say, squared dollars or squared returns), whereas the standard deviation is in terms of the original unit of measure. It's hard to interpret squared dollars or squared returns.

Second, if the probability distribution is approximately normally distributed (that is, bell shaped, with certain other characteristics), we can use the standard deviation to compactly describe the probability distribution; not so with the variance. There are uses for the variance in statistical analysis, but for the purposes of describing and comparing probability distributions, we focus on the expected value and the standard deviation.

Step 6   Take the square root of the sum of the squared deviations.

$$\text{Standard deviation} = \sigma(x) = \sqrt{0.0098} = (0.0098)^{1/2}$$
$$= \mathbf{0.0990} \text{ or } \mathbf{9.90\%}$$

The standard deviation of Product A's returns is 9.90 percent.

We can represent these six steps in a single formula:

$$\text{Standard deviation of possible outcomes} = \sigma(x) = \sqrt{\sum_{n=1}^{N} p_n[x_n - E(x)]^2} \qquad [7\text{-}6]$$

The calculation of the standard deviation can be made manageable with a worksheet such as Table 7-1, used to calculate the standard deviations of possible outcomes for Products A and B.

Summarizing, we have calculated the following:

	Expected return	Standard deviation of possible outcomes
Product A	10%	9.90%
Product B	10	18.57

While both products have the same expected value, they differ in the distribution of their possible outcomes. When we calculate the standard deviation around the expected value, we see that Product B has a larger standard deviation. The larger standard deviation for Product B tells us that Product B has more risk than Product A, since its possible outcomes are more distant from its expected value.

TABLE 7-1

Calculation of Expected Values and Standard Deviations for Probability Distributions of Cash Flows for Product A and Product B

Scenario	Probability, p_n	Return, x_n	Probability times return, $p_n x_n$	Deviation from expected value, $x_n - E(x)$	Squared deviation from expected value, $[x_n - E(x)]^2$	Weighted squared deviation, $p_n[x_n - E(x)]^2$
			PRODUCT A			
Success	25%	24%	0.0600	−0.1400	0.0196	0.0049
Moderate success	50	10	0.0500	0.0000	0.0000	0.0000
Failure	25	−4	−0.0100	−0.1400	0.0196	0.0049
	100%		$E(x) = \mathbf{0.1000}$			$\sigma^2(x) = \mathbf{0.0098}$

$\sigma(x) = \sqrt{0.0098} = 0.0098^{1/2} = \mathbf{0.0990}$ or **9.90%**

Scenario	Probability, p_n	Return, x_n	Probability times return, $p_n x_n$	Deviation from expected value, $x_n - E(x)$	Squared deviation from expected value, $[x_n - E(x)]^2$	Weighted squared deviation, $p_n[x_n - E(x)]^2$
			PRODUCT B			
Success	10%	40%	0.0400	0.3000	0.0900	0.0090
Moderate success	30	30	0.0900	0.2000	0.0400	0.0120
Failure	60	−5	−0.0300	−0.1500	0.0255	0.0135
	100%		$E(x) = \mathbf{0.1000}$			$\sigma^2(x) = \mathbf{0.0345}$

$\sigma(x) = \sqrt{0.0345} = 0.345^{1/2} = \mathbf{0.1857}$ or **18.57%**

NOTE: p_n = probability of outcome n occurring; x_n = outcome n; $E(x)$ = expected value; $\sigma(x)$ = standard deviation; and $\sigma^2(x)$ = variance.

Return and the Tolerance for Bearing Risk

Which product investment do you prefer, A or B? Most people would choose A since it provides the same expected return, with less risk. Most people do not like risk—they are risk averse. **Risk aversion** is the dislike for risk. Does this mean a risk averse person will not take on risk? No. They will take on risk if they feel they are compensated for it.

A **risk neutral** person is indifferent toward risk. Risk neutral persons do not need compensation for bearing risk. A **risk preference** person likes risk—and may even be willing to pay to take on risk. Are there such people? Yes. Consider people who play the state lotteries, for which the expected value is always negative; that is, the expected value of the winnings is less than the cost of the lottery ticket.

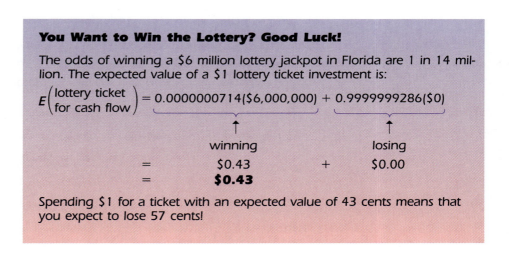

You Want to Win the Lottery? Good Luck!

The odds of winning a $6 million lottery jackpot in Florida are 1 in 14 million. The expected value of a $1 lottery ticket investment is:

$$E\left(\frac{\text{lottery ticket}}{\text{for cash flow}}\right) = \underbrace{0.0000000714(\$6,000,000)}_{\substack{\uparrow \\ \text{winning} \\ \$0.43}} + \underbrace{0.9999999286(\$0)}_{\substack{\uparrow \\ \text{losing} \\ \$0.00}}$$

$$= \$0.43$$

Spending $1 for a ticket with an expected value of 43 cents means that you expect to lose 57 cents!

When we consider financing and investment decisions, we assume that most people are risk averse. Managers, as agents for the owners, make decisions that treat risk as "bad." If risk must be borne, managers make sure there is sufficient compensation for bearing it. As agents for the owners, managers cannot have the "fun" of taking on risk for the pleasure of doing so.

Risk aversion is the link between return and risk. To evaluate a return you must consider its risk: Is there sufficient compensation (in the form of an expected return) for the investment's risk?

EXPECTED RETURN, RISK, AND DIVERSIFICATION

As managers, we rarely consider investing in only one project at one time. Small businesses and large corporations alike can be viewed as a collection of different investments, made at different points in time. We refer to a collection of investments as a **portfolio.**

While we usually think of a portfolio as a collection of securities (stocks and bonds), we can also think of a business in much the same way—a portfolio of assets such as buildings, inventories, trademarks, and patents. As managers, we are concerned about the overall risk of the firm's portfolio of assets.

Suppose you invested in two assets, Thing One and Thing Two, having the following expected returns over the next year:

Asset	Return on asset
Thing One	20%
Thing Two	8

Suppose we invest equal amounts, say $10,000, in each asset for one year. At the end of the year we expect to have $10,000(1 + 0.20) = $12,000 from Thing One and $10,000(1 + 0.08) = $10,800 from Thing Two, or a total value of $22,800 from our original $20,000 investment. The expected return on our portfolio is therefore:

$$\text{Return} = \frac{\$22,800 - \$20,000}{\$20,000} = \textbf{14\%}$$

If instead, we invested $5,000 in Thing One and $15,000 in Thing Two, the value of our investment at the end of the year would be:

$$
\begin{aligned}
\text{Value of investment} &= \$5,000(1 + 0.20) + \$15,000(1 + 0.08) \\
&= \$6,000 + \$16,200 \\
&= \textbf{\$22,200}
\end{aligned}
$$

and the return on our portfolio would be:

$$\text{Return} = \frac{[\$5,000(1 + 0.20) + \$15,000(1 + 0.08)] - \$20,000}{\$20,000} = \textbf{11\%}$$

which we can also write as:

$$\text{Return} = \frac{\$5,000}{\$20,000}(0.20) + \frac{\$15,000}{\$20,000}(0.08)$$

or:

$$\text{Return} = 0.25(0.20) + 0.75(0.08) = \textbf{11\%}$$

As you can see more readily in the second calculation, the return on our portfolio is the weighted average of the returns on the assets in the portfolio, where the weights are the proportions invested in each asset.

We can generalize the formula for a portfolio return, r_p, as the weighted average of the returns of *all* assets in the portfolio, letting:

i = a particular asset in the portfolio
w_i = proportion invested in asset i,
r_i = return on asset i,
S = number of assets in the portfolio

and

$$r_p = w_1 r_1 + w_2 r_2 + \cdots + w_S r_S$$

which we can write more compactly as:

$$r_p = \sum_{i=1}^{S} w_i r_i \qquad\qquad [7\text{-}7]$$

Diversification and Risk

My ventures are not in one bottom trusted,
Nor to one place; nor is my whole estate
Upon the fortune of this present year;
Therefore my merchandise makes me not sad.

William Shakespeare, *Merchant of Venice*, Act 1, Scene 1.

In any portfolio, one investment may do well while another does poorly. The cash flows in the projects may be "out of synch" with one another. Let's see how this might happen.

Suppose you own Asset P, which produces the returns over time shown in Figure 7-3(*a*). These returns vary up and down within a wide range. Suppose you also invested in Asset Q, whose returns over time are shown in Figure 7-3(*b*). These returns also vary over time within a wide band. But since the returns on Asset P and Asset Q are out of synch, each tends to provide positive returns when the other doesn't. The result is that your portfolio's returns vary within a narrower range, as shown in Figure 7-3(*c*).

Let's look at the idea of "out-of-synchness" in terms of expected returns, since this is what we face when we make financial decisions. Consider Investment C and Investment D and their probability distributions:

Scenario	Probability of scenario	Return on Investment C	Return on Investment D
Boom	30%	20%	−10%
Normal	50	0	0
Recession	20	−20	45

We see that when Investment C does well, in the boom scenario, Investment D does poorly. Also, when Investment C does poorly, as in the recession scenario, Investment D does well. In other words, these investments are out of synch with one another.

FIGURE 7-3

(*a*) Returns on Asset P over Time; (*b*) Returns on Asset Q over Time; (*c*) Returns on a Portfolio Composed of Asset P and Asset Q, over Time

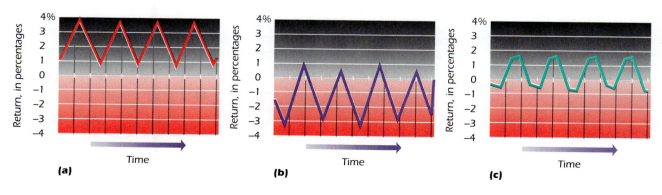

Now let's look at how their "out-of-synchness" affects the risk of the portfolio of C and D. If we invest an equal amount in C and D, the portfolio's return under each scenario is the weighted average of the returns on C and D, where each has a weight of 50 percent:

Scenario	Probability	Weighted average return
Boom	0.30	0.5(0.20) + 0.5(−0.10) = 0.0500 or 5.0%
Normal	0.50	0.5(0.00) + 0.5(0.00) = 0.0000 or 0.0%
Recession	0.20	0.5(−0.20) + 0.5(0.45) = 0.1250 or 12.5%

The calculation of the expected return and standard deviation for Investments C and D and the portfolio consisting of C and D is shown in Table 7-2. Summarizing the statistics:

Scenario	Probability of scenario	Return on Investment C	Return on Investment D	Return on portfolio comprising C and D
Boom	30%	20%	−10%	5.0%
Normal	50	0	0	0.0
Recession	20	−20	45	12.5
Expected return		2%	6%	4%
Standard deviation		14.00	19.97	4.77

The expected return on Investment C is 2 percent, and the expected return on Investment D is 6 percent. The return on a portfolio comprising equal investments of C and D is expected to be 4 percent. The standard deviation of the return on Investment C is 14 percent and that on Investment D is 19.97 percent, but the standard deviation of the *portfolio*, calculated using the weighted average of the returns on C and D in each scenario, is 4.77 percent. This is *less* than the standard deviations of each of the individual investments because the returns of the two investments do not move in the same direction at the same time, but rather tend to move in opposite directions.

The portfolio made up of Investments C and D has less risk than the individual investments because each moves in a direction opposite to the other. A statistical measure of how two variables—in this case, the returns on two different investments—move together is the **covariance,** which measures how one variable changes in relation to changes in another variable. Covariance is calculated in four steps:

Step 1 For each scenario and investment, subtract the expected value of the investment from its possible outcome.

Step 2 For each scenario, multiply the deviations for the two investments.

Step 3 Weight this product by the scenario's probability.

Step 4 Sum the weighted products to arrive at the covariance.

TABLE 7-2

Calculation of Expected Values and Standard Deviations for Investment C, Investment D, and the Portfolio Composed of Investment C and Investment D

Scenario	Probability, p_n	Return, x_n	Probability times return, $p_n x_n$	Deviation from expected value, $x_n - E(x)$	Squared deviation from expected value, $[x_n - E(x)]^2$	Weighted squared deviations $p_n[x_n - E(x)]^2$
INVESTMENT C						
Boom	30%	20.0%	0.0600	0.1800	0.0324	0.00972
Normal	50	0.0	0.0000	−0.0200	0.0004	0.00020
Recession	20	−20.0	−0.0400	−0.2200	0.0484	0.00968
	100%		$E(x) = \mathbf{0.0200}$			$\sigma^2(x) = \mathbf{0.01960}$
						$\sigma(x) = \mathbf{0.1400}$ or **14%**
INVESTMENT D						
Boom	30%	−10.0	−0.0300	−0.1600	0.0256	0.00768
Normal	50	0.0	0.0000	−0.0600	0.0036	0.00018
Recession	20	45.0	0.0900	0.3900	0.1521	0.03042
	100%		$E(x) = \mathbf{0.0600}$			$\sigma^2(x) = \mathbf{0.03828}$
						$\sigma(x) = \mathbf{0.1957}$ or **19.57%**
PORTFOLIO OF INVESTMENT C AND INVESTMENT D						
Boom	30%	5.0%	0.0150	0.0100	0.0001	0.00003
Normal	50	0.0	0.0000	−0.0400	0.0016	0.00080
Recession	20	12.5	0.0250	0.0850	0.0072	0.00145
	100%		$E(x) = \mathbf{0.0400}$			$\sigma^2(x) = \mathbf{0.00228}$
						$\sigma(x) = \mathbf{0.477}$ or **4.77%**

NOTE: p_n = probability of outcome n occurring; x_n = outcome n; $E(x)$ = expected value; $\sigma(x)$ = standard deviation; and $\sigma^2(x)$ = variance.

Scenario	Probability	**Step 1: Deviation of return on investment from its expected return**		**Step 2: Multiply deviations together**	**Step 3: Weight the product by the probability**
		Investment C	Investment D		
Boom	0.30	0.1800	−0.1600	−0.0288	−0.00864
Normal	0.50	−0.0200	−0.0600	0.0012	0.00060
Recession	0.20	−0.2200	0.3900	−0.0858	−0.01716
				Step 4: Covariance =	**−0.02520**

As you can see in these calculations, in a boom economic environment, when Investment C is above its expected return (deviation is positive), Investment D is below (deviation is negative). In a recession, Investment C's return is below its expected value and D's return is above. The tendency is for the returns on these portfolios to covary in *opposite* directions, producing a *negative* covariance of −0.0252.

Let's see the effect of this negative covariance on the risk of the portfolio. The portfolio's variance depends on:

- The weight of each asset in the portfolio.
- The standard deviation of each asset in the portfolio.
- The covariance of the returns on all assets.

Let $cov_{1,2}$ represent the covariance of the returns on two assets. We can write the portfolio variance as:

$$\text{Portfolio variance} = w_1^2\sigma_1^2 + w_2^2\sigma_2^2 + 2\,cov_{1,2}w_1w_2 \qquad [7\text{-}8]$$

The portfolio standard deviation is:

$$\text{Portfolio standard deviation} = \sqrt{\text{portfolio variance}} \qquad [7\text{-}9]$$

We can apply this general formula to our example, with Investment C's characteristics indicated with a 1 and D's with a 2:

w_1　　= 0.50 or 50%
w_2　　= 0.50 or 50%
σ_1　　= 0.1400 or 14.00%
σ_2　　= 0.1997 or 19.97%
$cov_{1,2}$ = −0.0252

Then:

$$\begin{aligned}\text{Portfolio variance} &= 0.50^2(0.1400^2) + 0.50^2(0.1997^2) + 2(-0.0252)(0.50)(0.50) \\ &= 0.25(0.01960) + 0.25(0.03988) + 2(-0.02520)0.2500 \\ &= 0.0049 + 0.0100 - 0.0126 \\ &= \mathbf{0.002275}\end{aligned}$$

and:

$$\text{Portfolio standard deviation} = \sqrt{0.002275} = \mathbf{0.0477 \text{ or } 4.77\%}$$

which, not coincidentally, is what we got when we calculated the standard deviation directly from the portfolio returns under the three scenarios.[12]

The standard deviation of the portfolio is lower than the standard deviations of each of the investments because the returns on Investments C and D are negatively related: When one is doing well the other may be doing poorly, and vice versa; that is, the covariance is negative.

Investment in assets whose returns are out of step with one another is the whole idea behind diversification. **Diversification** is the combination of assets whose returns do not vary with one another in the same direction at the same time.

If the returns on investments move together, we say that they are *correlated* with one another. **Correlation** is the tendency for two or more sets of data—in our case returns—to vary together. The returns on two investments are:

- Positively correlated if both investments tend to vary in the same direction at the same time.
- Negatively correlated if one investment tends to vary in the opposite direction with respect to the other.
- Uncorrelated if there is no relation between the changes in one investment with respect to changes in the other.

Statistically, we can measure correlation with a **correlation coefficient.** The correlation coefficient reflects the extent to which the returns of two securities vary together and is measured by the covariance of the two securities' returns, divided by the product of their standard deviations:

$$\text{Correlation coefficient} = \frac{\text{covariance of two assets' returns}}{\left(\begin{array}{c}\text{standard deviation of} \\ \text{returns on first asset}\end{array}\right)\left(\begin{array}{c}\text{standard deviation of} \\ \text{returns on second asset}\end{array}\right)} \qquad [7\text{-}10]$$

By construction, the correlation coefficient is bounded by -1 and $+1$.[13] We can interpret the correlation coefficient as follows, and we depict the interpretations in the accompanying figures:

- *A correlation coefficient of +1* indicates a perfect positive correlation between variables (the returns on the two assets).
- *A correlation coefficient of −1* indicates a perfect, negative correlation between the two variables.
- *A correlation coefficient of 0* indicates no correlation between the variables.

---

[12] If we can calculate the standard deviation directly from the portfolio's returns, why calculate it using the standard deviations of the individual assets and the covariance? We did it to illustrate the role of the covariance of the assets in assessing portfolio risk.

[13] Dividing the covariance by the product of the standard deviations ensures (mathematically) that this statistic is bounded by -1 and $+1$, allowing a cleaner interpretation of the relation between assets' returns.

- *A correlation coefficient falling between 0 and +1* indicates positive, but not perfect positive, correlation between the two variables.
- *A correlation coefficient falling between −1 and 0* indicates negative, but not perfect negative, correlation between the two variables.

Covariance and Correlation: The Basics

- If the returns on the two assets tend to move together, the covariance and the correlation are positive.
- If the returns tend to move in opposite directions, the covariance and correlation are negative.
- If the returns are unrelated—that is, there is no relation—the covariance and correlation are zero.

In the case of Investments C and D, the correlation of their returns is:

$$\text{Correlation of returns on Investments C and D} = \frac{\text{covariance of returns Investments C and D}}{\left(\begin{array}{c}\text{standard deviation}\\\text{of returns on}\\\text{Investment C}\end{array}\right)\left(\begin{array}{c}\text{standard deviation}\\\text{of returns on}\\\text{Investment D}\end{array}\right)}$$

$$= \frac{-0.0252}{(0.1400)(0.1997)}$$

$$= \mathbf{-0.9014}$$

Therefore, the returns on Investment C and Investment D are negatively correlated with one another.

By investing in assets with less than perfectly correlated cash flows, you are getting rid of—diversifying away—some risk. The less correlated the cash flows, the more risk you can diversify away—to a point.

Let's see how the correlation and portfolio standard deviation interact. Consider two investments, E and F, whose standard deviations are 5 percent and 3 percent, respectively. Suppose our portfolio consists of an equal investment in each; that is, $w_1 = w_2 = 50$ percent.

If the correlation between the assets' returns is . . .	this means that the covariance is . . .	and the portfolio's standard deviation is . . .
+1.0	+0.00150	4.00%
+0.5	+0.00075	3.50
0.0	0.00000	2.92
−0.5	−0.00075	2.18
−1.0	−0.00150	1.00

The less perfectly positively correlated are two assets' returns, the lower is the risk of the portfolio composed of these assets.

Let's think about what this means for a company. Consider Proctor & Gamble, whose products include Tide detergent, Prell shampoo, Pampers dia-

Correlation and Portfolio Risk

Let's look at the implications of different correlation coefficients for a portfolio's risk:

1. If the correlation is 1.0, the covariance is $\sigma_1\sigma_2$, and therefore:

    Portfolio variance = $w_1^2\sigma_1^2 + w_2^2\sigma_2^2 + 2\sigma_1\sigma_2 w_1 w_2$

    and

    Portfolio standard deviation $= \sqrt{w_1^2\sigma_1^2 + w_2^2\sigma_2^2 + 2\sigma_1\sigma_2 w_1 w_2} = w_1\sigma_1 + w_2\sigma_2$

    which is the same as saying the portfolio's standard deviation is the weighted average of the individual securities' standard deviations.

2. If the correlation is less than 1.0, the portfolio's standard deviation is *less than* the weighted average of the individual securities' standard deviations.

3. If the correlation is zero (and, therefore, $cov_{1,2} = 0$), the variance of the portfolio's expected return is equal to $w_1^2\sigma_1^2 + w_2^2\sigma_2^2$, which is the same as saying the portfolio's variance is the weighted average of the individual securities' variances.

4. If the correlation coefficient is -1.0, the covariance is equal to $-\sigma_1\sigma_2$, and the portfolio's variance and standard deviation are zero:

    Portfolio variance = $w_1^2\sigma_1^2 + w_2^2\sigma_2^2 - 2\sigma_1\sigma_2 w_1 w_2$

    which means that risk is *reduced substantially*.

pers, Jif peanut butter, and Old Spice cologne. Are the cash flows from these products positively correlated? To a degree, yes. The cash flows from these products depend on consumer spending for consumption goods. But are they *perfectly* correlated? No. For example, diaper sales are related to the size of the diaper-wearing population, whereas sales of men's cologne products are related to the size of the male cologne-wearing population. The cash flows of these different products are related also to the actions of competitors—the degree of competition may be different for the diaper market than the peanut butter market. Further, the cash flows of the products are affected by differences in input pricing—the cost of the inputs to make these products. If there is a bad year for the peanut crop, the price of peanuts may increase substantially, reducing cash flows from Jif—but this increase in peanut prices is not likely to affect the costs of, say, producing laundry detergent.

Portfolio Size and Risk

What we have seen for a portfolio with two assets can be extended to include any number of assets. Alas, the calculations get more complicated because we have to consider the covariance between *every possible pair of assets!* But the basic idea is the same. The risk of a portfolio declines as it is expanded with assets whose returns are not perfectly correlated with the returns of the assets already in the portfolio.

The idea of diversification is based on beliefs about what will happen in the future: expected returns, standard deviation of all possible returns, and expected covariances between returns. How valid are our beliefs about anything in the future? We can get an idea by looking at the past. So we look at historical returns on assets—returns over time—to get an idea of how some asset's returns increase while at the same time others do not or decline.

Let's look at the effects of diversification with common stocks. As we add common stocks to a portfolio, the standard deviation of returns on the portfolio declines—to a point. We can see this in Figure 7-4, in which the portfolio standard deviation is plotted against the number of different stocks in the portfolio. After the number reaches around twenty different stocks, the portfolio's standard deviation is about as low as it is going to get.

Why does the risk seem to reach some point and not decline any further? Because returns on common stocks, in general, are positively correlated with one another. There just aren't enough negatively correlated stock returns to reduce portfolio risk beyond a certain point.

We refer to the risk that declines as we add assets as ***diversifiable risk.*** We refer to the risk that *cannot* be reduced by adding more assets as ***nondiversifiable risk.*** The diversifiable and nondiversifiable components of a portfolio's risk are indicated in Figure 7-4.

Risk is not diversified with common stocks only. Consider a business that has many different product lines. While the returns on these product lines may not be perfectly correlated, they are influenced by similar forces—for example, the economy and industry competition; so that the returns are most likely positively correlated.

The idea that we can reduce the risk in a portfolio by introducing assets whose returns are not highly correlated with one another is the basis of ***modern portfolio theory*** (MPT). The MPT tells us that by combining assets whose returns are not correlated with one another, we can determine combinations of assets that provide the least risk for each possible expected portfolio return.

FIGURE 7-4
Role of Portfolio Size on the Risk of the Portfolio

FIGURE 7-5

(a) Expected Return and Risk for All Possible Portfolios of Assets; (b) Expected Return and Risk for All Possible Portfolios of Assets, Efficient Frontier Version

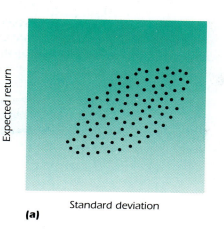

(a)

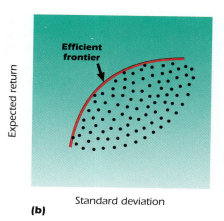

(b)

Though the mathematics involved in determining the optimal combinations of assets is beyond this text, the basic idea is provided in Figure 7-5(a) and Figure 7-5(b). In Figure 7-5(a), the expected return and standard deviation for all possible portfolios is shown. Each point in the graph represents a *possible* portfolio that can be put together comprising different assets and different weights. The points in this graph represent every possible portfolio. As you can see in this diagram:

- Some portfolios have a higher expected return than other portfolios with the same level of risk.
- Some portfolios have a lower standard deviation than other portfolios with the same expected return.

Since investors like more return rather than less and prefer less risk rather than more, some portfolios are better than others. The best portfolios—those that are unbeatable in terms of either the level of return for the amount of risk or the amount of risk for the level of return—make up what is called the *efficient frontier*. If investors are rational, they will choose portfolios that fall on this efficient frontier. All the possible portfolios and the efficient frontier are diagrammed in Figure 7-5(b).

So what is the relevance of the MPT to financial managers? The MPT tells us that:

- We can manage risk by judicious combinations of assets in our portfolios.
- There are some combinations of assets that are preferred over others.

Modern Portfolio Theory and Asset Pricing

The relation between portfolio returns and portfolio risk was recognized by two Nobel laureates in economics, Harry Markowitz and William Sharpe. Markowitz tuned us into the idea that investors hold portfolios of assets, and therefore their concern is focused upon the portfolio return and the portfolio risk, not on the return and risk of individual assets.[14] Is this reasonable?

---

[14] Harry M. Markowitz, "Portfolio Selection," *Journal of Finance,* March 1952, pp. 77–91.

Probably. Not many businesses consist of a single asset. Nor do investors invest in only one asset.

The **relevant risk** to an investor is the portfolio's risk, not the risk of an individual asset. If an investor holds assets in a portfolio and is considering buying an additional asset or selling an asset currently in the portfolio, what must be considered is how this change will affect the *risk* of the portfolio. This concept applies whether we are talking about an investor holding 30 different stocks or a business that has invested in 30 different projects. The important thing in valuing an asset is its contribution to the portfolio's return and risk.

The Capital Asset Pricing Model

Sharpe took the idea that portfolio return and risk are the only elements to consider and developed a model that deals with how assets are priced.[15] This model is referred to as the **capital asset pricing model** (CAPM).

We saw in Figure 7-5 that there is a set of portfolios that make up the efficient frontier—the best combinations of expected return and standard deviation. All the assets in each portfolio, even on the frontier, have some risk. Now let's see what happens when we add an asset with no risk—referred to as the risk-free asset. Suppose we have a portfolio along the efficient frontier that has a return of 4 percent and a standard deviation of 3 percent. Suppose we introduce into this portfolio the risk-free asset, which has an expected return of 2 percent and, by definition, a standard deviation of zero. If the risk-free asset's expected return is certain, there is *no* covariance between the risky portfolio's returns and the returns on the risk-free asset.

The new portfolio, of which 50 percent consists of the assets in the risky portfolio and 50 percent of the risk-free asset, has an expected return of $(0.50)4$ percent $+ (0.50)2$ percent $= 3$ percent and a portfolio standard deviation calculated as follows:

Portfolio variance
$$= 0.50^2(0.03) + 0.50^2(0.00) + 2(0.00)\,0.50(0.50)$$
$$= \mathbf{0.0075}$$

Portfolio standard deviation $= \sqrt{0.0075} = \mathbf{0.0866}$

If we look at all possible combinations of portfolios along the efficient frontier and the risk-free asset, we see that the best portfolios are no longer along the entire length of the efficient frontier, but rather are the combinations of the risk-free asset and one—and only one—portfolio of risky assets on the frontier. The combinations of the risk-free asset and this one portfolio are shown in Figure 7-6. These combinations differ from one another by the proportion invested in the risk-free asset: As less is invested in the risk-free asset, both the portfolio's expected return and standard deviation increase.

Sharpe demonstrates that one and only one portfolio of risky assets is the **market portfolio**—a portfolio that consists of all assets, with the weights of

---

[15] William F. Sharpe, "A Simplified Model of Portfolio Analysis," *Management Science*, vol. 9, Jan. 1963, pp. 277–293.

FIGURE 7-6

Expected Return and Risk for All Possible Portfolios of Assets, with Capital Market Line

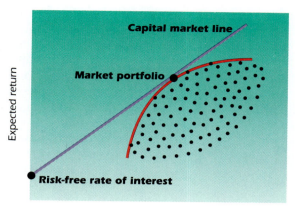

these assets being the ratio of their market value to the total market value of all assets.

If investors are all risk averse—they take on risk only if there is adequate compensation—and if they are free to invest in the risky assets as well as the risk-free asset, the best deals lie along the line that is tangent to the efficient frontier. This line is referred to as the ***capital market line*** (CML).

If the portfolios along the capital market line are the best deals and are available to all investors, it follows that the returns on these risky assets will be priced to compensate investors for the risk they bear *relative to that of the market portfolio*. Since the portfolios along the capital market line are the best deals, they are as diversified as they can get—no other combination of risky assets or risk-free asset provides a better expected return for the level of risk or provides a lower risk for the level of expected return.

The CML tells us about the returns an investor can expect for a given level of risk. The CAPM uses that relationship between expected return and risk to describe how assets are priced.

The CAPM specifies that the return on any asset is a function of the return on a risk-free asset plus a risk premium. The return on the risk-free asset is compensation for the time value of money. The ***risk premium*** is the compensation for bearing risk. Putting these components of return together, the CAPM says:

$$\text{Expected return on an asset} = \text{expected return on a risk-free asset} + \text{risk premium}$$

or,

$$\text{Expected return on an asset} = \text{compensation for the time value of money} + \text{compensation for bearing risk}$$

The market portfolio therefore represents the most well diversified portfolio—the only risk in a portfolio comprising all assets is the nondiversifiable risk. As far as diversification goes, the market portfolio is the best you can do, since you have included everything in it.

By the same token, if we assume that investors hold well diversified portfolios (approximating the market portfolio), the only risk they have is nondiversifiable risk. If assets are priced to compensate for the risk of assets *and* if the only risk in your portfolio is nondiversifiable risk, then it follows that the compensation for risk is only for nondiversifiable risk. Let's refer to this nondiversifiable risk as *market risk.*

Since the market portfolio is made up of all assets, each asset possesses some degree of market risk. Since market risk is systematic across assets, it is often referred to as *systematic risk* and diversifiable risk is referred to as *unsystematic risk.* Further, the risk that is not associated with the market as a whole is often referred to as *company-specific risk* when referring to stocks, since it is risk that is specific to the company's own situation, such as the risk of lawsuits and labor strikes, and is not part of the risk that pervades all securities.

The measure of an asset's return sensitivity to the market return, that is, the asset's market risk, is referred to as the asset's *beta.*

The expected return on an individual asset is the sum of the expected return on the risk-free asset and the premium for bearing market risk. Let r_i represent the expected return on asset i, r_f represent the expected return on the risk-free asset, r_m represent the expected return on the market, and β_i represent the degree of market risk for asset i. Then:

$$r_i = r_f + (r_m - r_f)\beta_i \qquad\qquad [7\text{-}11]$$

The term $(r_m - r_f)$ is the *market risk premium:* If you owned all the assets in the market portfolio, you would expect to be compensated $(r_m - r_f)$ for bearing the risk of those assets. β is a measure of market risk, which serves to finetune the risk premium for the individual asset. For example, if the market risk premium were 2 percent and the β for an individual asset were 1.5, you would expect to receive a risk premium of 3 percent, since you are taking on 50 percent more risk than the market.

For each asset there is a beta. If we represent the expected return on each asset and its beta as a point on a graph, and we do the same for every asset in the market, and connect all the points, the result is the *security market line* (SML), as shown in Figure 7-7.[16] As you can see in the figure:

1. The greater the β, the greater the expected return.
2. If there were no market risk (beta = 0.0) on an asset its expected return would be the expected return on the risk-free asset.
3. If the asset's risk is similar to the risk of the market as a whole (beta = 1.0), the asset's expected return is the return on the market portfolio.

For an individual asset, beta is a measure of sensitivity of its returns to changes in the return on the market portfolio. If beta is 1.0, we expect that for a given change of 1 percent in the market portfolio return, the asset's return will change by 1 percent. If beta is *less than* 1.0, then for a 1 percent

---

Sorting Out the Terminology

The risk that reflects the movement of an asset's returns with asset returns in general is referred to as:

   nondiversifiable risk or market risk or systematic risk.

The risk that reflects the returns on an asset that does not move along with asset returns in general is referred to as:

   diversifiable risk or company-specific risk or unsystematic risk.

---

[16] You'll notice that in the discussion of the asset-pricing models we refer to the risk and expected return for *assets,* which can be any asset, not exclusively stocks. The security market line describes a relation between expected return and market risk that is applicable to any asset, even though the name implies securities.

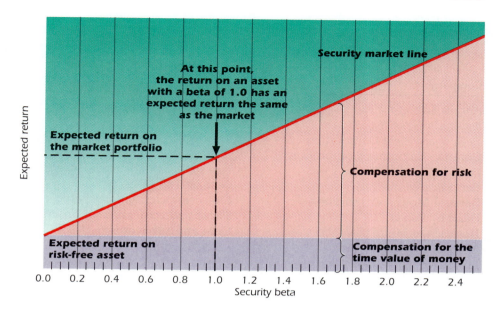

FIGURE 7-7

Security Market Line That Describes the Relation between Expected Asset Returns and Beta

change in the expected market return, the asset's return is expected to change by less than 1 percent. If beta is *greater than* 1.0, then for a 1 percent change in the expected market return, the asset's return is expected to change by more than 1 percent.

We typically estimate the beta for a common stock by looking at the historical relation between its return and the return in the market as a whole. The betas of the common stock of some U.S. companies are listed in Table 7-3.

The betas of some firms' stocks are close to 1.0, indicating that the returns on these stocks tend to move along with the market. There are some betas of about 0.3 (Homestake Mining and Southern Company, for example), indicating that the returns on these securities do not move along with the market: If the market were to go up 10 percent, we would expect the returns on these securities to go up only about 3 percent. Then there are some stocks whose betas are much higher than 1.0. For example, K Mart has a beta of 1.5. This means that if the market is expected to go up 1 percent, we expect K Mart's return to go up 1.5 percent; if the market is expected to go down 1 percent, we expect K Mart's return to go down 1.5 percent.

When we introduced the idea of risk, we discussed many different types of risk, many of which affect cash flows. For example, every firm has some type of business risk. And some of that business risk is common among all firms—all firms' sales are affected by the economy to some extent. But some of that business risk an investor can diversify away by buying stocks whose sensitivity to the economy is out of synch with one another. However, part of business risk cannot be diversified away—we are stuck with it. This is the risk that concerns investors, and they want to be compensated for it.

If we know part of the risk of a particular asset is common to all assets, and we have a large enough representation of all in the assets in our portfo-

TABLE 7-3

Security Betas of Common Stock, Selected U.S. Companies

Company	Industry	Security beta
Abbott Laboratories	Pharmaceutical preparations	0.9
Amerada Hess	Petroleum refining	0.8
Bethlehem Steel Corporation	Steel works and blast furnaces	1.5
Compaq Computer Corporation	Electronic computers	1.4
Dow Jones & Co. Inc.	Newspaper publishing	1.1
Echo Bay Mines Ltd	Gold and silver ores	0.1
General Motors Corporation	Motor vehicles and car bodies	1.0
Hershey Foods	Sugar and confectionery products	1.0
Homestake Mining	Gold and silver ores	0.3
Houston Industries	Electric services	0.3
International Business Machines	Computer and office equipment	0.7
K Mart Corporation	Variety stores	1.5
Marriott Corporations	Food service	1.5
Mattel Inc.	Dolls and stuffed toys	1.4
National Semiconductor Corporation	Semiconductor and related products	1.4
Procter & Gamble	Soap, detergent, and toilet preparations	0.8
Southern Co.	Electric services	0.3
Toys "R" Us	Hobby, toy, and game shops	1.2
Unisys	Computer and office equipment	1.5
Wal-Mart Stores	Variety stores	1.3

SOURCE: Standard & Poor's *Compustat PC PLUS* (CD-ROM).

lio, then we don't need to be concerned with the diversifiable risk. We are concerned about the market risk of each asset in the portfolio and how it contributes to the market risk of the entire portfolio.

We can get a good idea of the portfolio's market risk by using a beta that represents the composition of the assets in the portfolio. To determine the portfolio's beta, we need to calculate the weighted average of the betas of the assets that make up the portfolio, where each weight is the proportion invested in each asset. Let β_p indicate the beta of the portfolio, w_i indicate the proportion invested in the asset i, and β_i indicate the beta for asset i. If there are S assets in the portfolio, then:

$$\beta_p = w_1\beta_1 + w_2\beta_2 + w_3\beta_3 + \cdots + w_S\beta_S \qquad [7\text{-}12]$$

or more compactly:

$$\beta_p = \sum_{i=1}^{S} w_i\beta_i$$

Suppose we have three securities in our portfolio, with the amount invested in each and its security beta as follows:

Security	Security beta	Amount invested
AAA	1.00	$10,000
BBB	1.50	20,000
CCC	0.75	20,000

The portfolio's beta is:

$$\beta_p = \frac{\$10,000}{\$50,000} 1.00 + \frac{\$20,000}{\$50,000} 1.50 + \frac{\$20,000}{\$50,000} 0.75$$
$$= (0.20)1.00 + (0.40)1.50 + (0.40)0.75$$
$$= 0.20 + 0.60 + 0.30$$
$$= \mathbf{1.10}$$

If the expected risk-free rate of interest is 4 percent, and the expected return on the market is 7 percent, a $\beta_p = 1.1$ means:

Expected return on portfolio of AAA, BBB, and CCC $= 4\% + 1.10(7\% - 4\%) = \mathbf{7.3\%}$

The CAPM, with its description of the relation between expected return and risk and the importance of market risk in asset pricing, has some drawbacks:

1. A beta is an estimate. For stocks, the beta is typically estimated using historical returns. But the proxy for market risk depends on the method and period in which it is measured. For assets other than stocks, beta estimation is more difficult.
2. The CAPM includes some unrealistic assumptions.[17] For example, it assumes that all investors can borrow and lend at the same rate.
3. The CAPM is really not testable. The market portfolio is a theoretical construct and cannot be observed; so we cannot test the relation between the expected return on an asset and the expected return of the market to see if the relation specified in the CAPM holds.
4. In studies of the CAPM applied to common stocks, the CAPM does not explain the differences in returns for securities that differ over time, differ on the basis of dividend yield, and differ on the basis of the market value of equity (the so-called size effect).

Though it lacks realism and is difficult to apply, the CAPM makes some sense regarding the role of diversification and the type of risk we need to consider in investment decisions.

---

[17] There are a number of assumptions behind the CAPM. We will leave the discussion of these assumptions and the derivation of the CAPM for your advanced study of finance.

The Arbitrage Pricing Model

An alternative to the CAPM in relating risk and return is the arbitrage pricing model, which was developed by Stephen Ross. The ***arbitrage pricing model*** is an asset-pricing model that is based on the idea that identical assets in different markets should be priced identically.[18]

While the CAPM is based on a market portfolio of assets, the arbitrage pricing model doesn't mention a market portfolio at all. Instead, the model states that an asset's returns should compensate the investor for the risk of the asset, where the risk is due to a number of economic influences, or economic factors. Therefore, the expected return on the asset i, r_i, is:

$$r_i = r_f + \delta_1 \frac{\text{first}}{\text{factor}} + \delta_2 \frac{\text{second}}{\text{factor}} + \delta_3 \frac{\text{third}}{\text{factor}} + \cdots \qquad [7\text{-}13]$$

where each of the δ's reflects sensitivity of the asset's return to the corresponding economic factor. The arbitrage pricing model looks much like the CAPM, but the CAPM has only one factor—the market portfolio, whereas there are many factors in the arbitrage pricing model.

What if an asset's price is such that it is out of line with what is expected? That's where arbitrage comes in. Anytime an asset's price is out of line with how market participants feel it should be priced—based on the basic economic influences—investors will enter the market and buy or sell the asset until its price is in line with what investors think it should be.

What are these economic factors? They are not specified in the original arbitrage pricing model, though evidence suggests that these factors include:[19]

- Unanticipated changes in inflation.
- Unanticipated changes in industrial production.
- Unanticipated changes in risk premiums.
- Unanticipated changes in the difference between interest rates for short- and long-term securities.

Anticipated factors are already reflected in an asset's price. It is the *un*anticipated factors that cause an asset's price to change.

For example, consider a bond with a fixed coupon interest. The bond's current price is the present value of expected interest and principal payments, discounted at some rate that reflects the time value of money, the uncertainty of these future cash flows, and the expected rate of inflation. If there is an *un*anticipated increase in inflation, what will happen to the price of the bond? It will go down, since the discount rate increases as inflation increases. And if the price of the bond goes down, so too the return on the bond. Therefore, the sensitivity of a bond's price to changes in unanticipated inflation is negative.

[18] Stephen A. Ross, "The Arbitrage Theory of Capital Asset Pricing," *Journal of Economic Theory*, vol. 13, Dec. 1976, pp. 341–360.

[19] Some of the evidence on the identification of factors can be found in the study by Nai-fu Chen, Richard Roll, and Stephen Ross, "Economic Forces and the Stock Market: Testing the APT and Alternative Asset Pricing Theories," Working Paper No. 20-83. Graduate School of Management, University of California, Los Angeles, Dec. 1983.

The arbitrage pricing model is not without drawbacks. First, the factor sensitivities must be estimated. The model is based on the sensitivities of expected returns to unanticipated changes in the factors. Alas, the best we can do, much as we did for the CAPM, is look at historical relationships.

Second, some financial observers argue that a single factor, namely, the market portfolio, does just as good a job in explaining security returns as the more complex multiple-factor approach of the arbitrage pricing model.

Financial Decision Making and Asset Pricing

Portfolio theory and asset-pricing models lay the groundwork for financial decisions. While portfolio theory and asset-pricing theory are complex and rely on many assumptions, they do get us thinking about what is important:

- Return and risk must both be considered.
- Since investors must be compensated for risk, a greater return is expected for bearing greater risk.
- Investors hold portfolios of assets; therefore, the relevant risk in the valuation of assets is the portfolio's risk.

If a corporation is considering investing in a new product, there are two levels of thinking to work through in evaluating the product's risk and returns:

- If a firm takes on the product, it is adding the product to its portfolio of assets and needs to consider the effect of this product on the firm's overall risk.
- Since a firm is owned by investors who themselves may own portfolios of assets, the relevant risk to consider is how the change in the firm's risk affects the owners' portfolio risk.

Therefore, when we evaluate the new product's future cash flows, the discount rate that we apply to value these future cash flows must reflect how that product affects the owners' portfolio risk.

SUMMARY

- Financial decision makers must consider both expected return and risk from investments.
- To evaluate an investment, the financial manager needs to consider the different types of risk, including cash flow risk, reinvestment rate risk, interest rate risk, purchasing power risk, and currency risk.
- Cash flow risk comprises sales risk, operating risk, and financial risk. Sales risk is the degree of uncertainty regarding the number of units of a good or service the firm will be able to sell and the price of these units. Operating risk is the uncertainty arising from the mix of variable and fixed operating costs. Financial risk is the uncertainty arising from the firm's financing decisions.
- Interest rate risk is the uncertainty associated with the change in the value of an asset that is caused by changes in the discount rate used to translate future values into present ones. With a bond, for example,

interest rate risk is the sensitivity of the bond's price to changes in the yield on the bond.

■ Purchasing power risk is the uncertainty associated with the change in the value of the currency. The greater the unanticipated inflation, the greater the purchasing power risk.

■ Currency risk is the uncertainty arising from the change in exchange rates between different currencies. If future cash flows are denominated in a currency other than the domestic currency, the value of those cash flows is dependent, in part, on the exchange rate between the domestic and the foreign currency.

■ When a firm invests in assets whose cash flows are not perfectly correlated with the firm's other assets, the firm's risk may be reduced. This is diversification.

■ The risk that cannot be diversified away, the asset's market risk, is what investors demand compensation for in the form of higher expected returns.

■ The capital asset-pricing model and the arbitrage pricing model are descriptions of the relation between risk and expected return. The CAPM specifies the expected return on an asset in terms of the expected return on a risk-free asset plus a premium for market risk. The arbitrage pricing model specifies the expected return on an asset in terms of the expected return on the risk-free asset plus premiums for several risk factors.

QUESTIONS

7-1 The Global Company is considering investing in a project in another country. This project will generate cash flows—in the other country's currency—each year for ten years, at which time the project will be terminated. What types of risk does Global need to consider in its investment decision?

7-2 Consider the two firms Tweedle Dee and Tweedle Dum. Both firms operate in the same industry, but Tweedle Dum has a greater portion of fixed operating costs relative to variable costs than does Tweedle Dee. Which firm has greater operating risk? Which firm has a higher degree of operating leverage?

7-3 The airline industry is one that can be characterized as having a large portion of its operating costs in fixed, rather than variable, costs. What does this tell you about the sensitivity of the airline industry to changes in passenger traffic?

7-4 Abel, an astute investor, buys bonds and always holds them to maturity. He claims that because he holds these bonds to maturity, there is no risk. Is he correct? Explain.

7-5 U.S. government bonds are generally considered risk-free, since the government can always print the money necessary to cover any interest or principal payments. Are there risks associated with buying a long-term U.S. government bond? If so, what are these risks?

7-6 If you invest in corporate bonds, what types of risk do you assume?

7-7 Consider the following investments and their expected returns and the standard deviations:

Investment	Expected return	Standard deviation
1	10%	10%
2	11	10
3	9	9
4	11	9

If you are a risk averse investor, which investment would you prefer in each of the following pairs?

a. 1 and 2
b. 2 and 4
c. 3 and 4
d. 1 and 4

7-8 The covariance of returns on Asset A and Asset B are negative. What does this tell us about the correlation coefficient of their returns? If we form a portfolio comprising Asset A and Asset B, what is the relation between the portfolio's risk and that of Asset A and Asset B considered separately?

7-9 Consider the following common stocks and their return characteristics:

Stock	Expected return	Standard deviation	Security beta
1	10%	5%	1.00
2	8	5	1.20
3	10	6	0.80

Which stock would a risk averse investor prefer between:

a. 1 and 2?
b. 1 and 3?
c. 2 and 3?

7-10 What are the major features of the CAPM and the arbitrage pricing model that distinguish them from one another?

7-11 Consider the following securities and their security betas:

Security	Security beta
A	2.500
B	1.000
C	0.100
D	0.800
E	1.250

Rank these securities according to their market risk, from lowest to highest.

7-12   Describe the types of risk associated with each of the following security innovations:

   a.   *IOs (interest-only mortgage strips).* The interest portion of a collateralized mortgage obligation, on which the investor receives the interest a group of homeowners pay on their home mortgages.

   b.   *SURFs (step-up recovery floaters).* Securities whose interest is reset every six months according to some formula, but cannot fall below a predetermined rate (the floor) or above another predetermined rate (the cap).

   c.   *LYONS (liquid yield option notes).* Zero-coupon convertible bonds that are callable and putable. These securities are hybrids—part debt, part stock—and offer investors the opportunity to share in the common stock's appreciation, but with a more senior debt security.

   d.   *PERCS (preferred equity redemption cumulative stock).* Preferred stock that can be converted into common stock in a few years: convertible on a share-for-share basis if the common stock rises to the conversion price, but at less than share-for-share if the common stock rises above the conversion price.

PROBLEMS

Degrees of leverage

7-1   The Gearing Company has provided you with the following information regarding its operating and financing costs:

   Price per unit   = $50
   Variable cost per unit = $30
   Fixed operating cost   = $100,000
   Fixed financing cost   = $50,000

   a.   Calculate its degree of operating leverage at 10,000 units sold.
   b.   Calculate its degree of financial leverage at 10,000 units sold.
   c.   Calculate its degree of total leverage at 10,000 units sold.
   d.   If there is a 1 percent increase in units sold, what do you expect the change in operating cash flows will be?
   e.   If there is a 3 percent decrease in units sold, what do you expect the change in cash flows to owners will be?

7-2   The Hi-Gear Company and the Lo-Gear Company have provided you with the following information:

	Hi-Gear	Lo-Gear
Price per unit	$ 50	$ 50
Variable cost per unit	20	25
Fixed operating cost	400,000	300,000
Fixed financing cost	100,000	50,000

a. At 20,000 units sold, which firm has the highest DOL?
b. At 20,000 units sold, which firm has the highest DFL?
c. At 20,000 units sold, which firm has the highest DTL?
d. Which firm's cash flows are the most sensitive to changes in demand?

Purchasing power and interest rate risk

7-3 Consider two bonds, MM and NN:

- Bond MM has a face value of $1,000, matures in five years, and pays 6 percent interest semiannually.
- Bond NN has a face value of $1,000, matures in five years, and pays 2 percent interest semiannually.

a. If the annualized yield to maturity on these bonds changes from 4 percent to 6 percent, which bond's value changes the most?
b. Which bond has the greatest interest rate risk? Why?
c. Which bond has the greatest reinvestment rate risk? Why?

7-4 Consider two bonds, OO and PP:

- Bond OO is a zero-coupon bond that matures in ten years, and has a face value of $1,000.
- Bond PP is a straight-coupon bond that matures in ten years, and has a 10 percent coupon that is paid semiannually and a face value of $1,000.

a. If the annualized yield to maturity on these bonds changes from 5 percent to 15 percent, which bond's value changes the most?
b. Which bond has the greatest interest rate risk? Why?
c. Which bond has the greatest reinvestment rate risk? Why?

Purchasing power risk

7-5 Suppose you want to earn a rate of 8 percent after inflation. If you expect inflation to be 4 percent during the next year, what nominal rate of return would you require on your investment?

7-6 The XYZ Bank sets an interest rate on one-year loans at 10 percent. If the bank anticipates inflation of 4 percent, what real rate of return does it earn on its one-year loans?

Statistical measures of risk

7-7 Your firm is considering investing in a new product. Marketing researchers have determined that the sales of the new product depend, in large part, on whether or not competitors jump in to mimic the product. Their assessment of sales and the likelihood of mimicking are as follows:

Competitor's reaction	Probability	Sales
Mimic	80%	$ 1,000,000
Will not mimic	20	10,000,000

a. What are the expected sales from this new product?
b. What is the standard deviation of possible sales of this new product?

7-8 Suppose you are offered two investments with the following expected cash flows:

Economic scenario	Probability of economic scenario	Possible outcome for Investment 1	Possible outcome for Investment 2
Boom	20%	$1,000	$1,200
Normal	50	750	750
Recession	30	250	117

   a. Calculate the expected value of each investment.
   b. Calculate the standard deviation for each investment's possible outcomes.
   c. Which investment is riskier? Explain.

7-9 Consider two investments, A and B:

Economic scenario	Probability of economic scenario	Possible outcome for Investment A	Possible outcome for Investment B
Boom	10%	$10,000	$12,000
Normal	50	5,000	3,000
Recession	40	−2,000	−4,000

   a. Calculate the expected value of each investment.
   b. Calculate the standard deviation for each investment's possible outcomes.
   c. Which investment is riskier? Explain.

7-10 Consider two bonds, HI and LI. The HI bond has a 10 percent coupon rate, and the LI bond has a 5 percent coupon rate. Both bonds pay interest annually and are priced to yield 10 percent. Suppose the following interest scenarios are possible next year when both bonds have five years remaining to maturity:

Possible interest rate	Probability of interest rate
5%	10%
10	50
15	40

   a. Calculate the expected return of each bond.
   b. Calculate the standard deviation of possible returns for each bond.
   c. Which bond is riskier? Why?

Portfolio risk and return

7-11 Consider a portfolio that comprises Security A and Security B, with an equal investment in each. Security A has an expected return of 3 percent with a standard deviation of 4 percent. Security B has an expected return of 5 percent with a standard deviation of 6 percent. Complete the following table:

Correlation coefficient of returns on Securities A and B	Portfolio return	Covariance between returns on Securities A and B	Portfolio variance	Portfolio standard deviation
1.00	————	————	————	————
0.50	————	————	————	————
0.00	————	————	————	————
−0.50	————	————	————	————
−1.00	————	————	————	————

7-12 Consider a portfolio that comprises Security C and Security D, with an equal investment in each. Security C has an expected return of 5 percent with a standard deviation of 4 percent. Security D has an expected return of 2 percent with a standard deviation of 1 percent. Complete the following table:

Correlation coefficient of returns on Securities C and D	Portfolio return	Covariance between returns on Securities C and D	Portfolio variance	Portfolio standard deviation
1.00	————	————	————	————
0.50	————	————	————	————
0.00	————	————	————	————
−0.50	————	————	————	————
−1.00	————	————	————	————

7-13 Consider a portfolio that comprises Asset P and Asset Q. The expected return on Asset P is 10 percent, and the standard deviation is 6 percent. The expected return on Asset Q is 12 percent, and the standard deviation is 8 percent. The correlation between the returns on these two assets is 0.500. Complete the following table.

Proportion of portfolio invested in Asset P	Proportion of portfolio invested in Asset Q	Portfolio return	Covariance between returns on Assets P and Q	Portfolio variance	Portfolio standard deviation
100%	0%	————	————	————	————
0	100	————	————	————	————
50	50	————	————	————	————
25	75	————	————	————	————
75	25	————	————	————	————

7-14 Consider a portfolio that comprises Asset R and Asset S. The expected return on Asset R is 10 percent, and the standard deviation is 5 percent. The expected return on Asset S is 6 percent, and the standard deviation is 0%. The correlation between the returns on these two assets is 0.00. Complete the following table.

Proportion of portfolio invested in Asset R	Proportion of portfolio invested in Asset S	Portfolio return	Covariance between returns on Securities R and S	Portfolio variance	Portfolio standard deviation
100%	0%	_____	_____	_____	_____
0	100	_____	_____	_____	_____
50	50	_____	_____	_____	_____
25	75	_____	_____	_____	_____
75	25	_____	_____	_____	_____

Asset pricing

7-15 If the expected return on a risk-free asset is 5 percent and the market premium is 4 percent, what is the expected security return if the security's beta is:

  a. 0.00?
  b. 0.50?
  c. 1.00?
  d. 1.25?
  e. 2.00?

7-16 Suppose the expected risk-free rate is 5 percent and the expected market return is 8 percent. What is the expected return on a security whose security beta is:

  a. 1.00?
  b. 1.25?
  c. 1.50?
  d. 1.75?
  e. 2.00?

7-17 Suppose the expected risk-free rate is 5 percent, and the expected market return is 12 percent. Further suppose you have a portfolio that contains the four securities listed below, with equal investments in each:

Security	Security beta
AA	1.00
BB	1.25
CC	1.50
DD	1.00

  a. What is the expected return on each security in your portfolio?
  b. What is the portfolio's beta?
  c. What is the expected return on your portfolio?

7-18   Suppose the expected risk-free rate is 4 percent and the expected return on the market is 12 percent. Further suppose you have a portfolio that contains the four assets listed below, with an equal amount invested in each:

Asset	Asset beta
EE	0.50
FF	0.75
GG	1.00
HH	1.25

a.   What is the expected return on each security in your portfolio?
b.   What is the portfolio's beta?
c.   What is the expected return on your portfolio?

Potpourri

PC+   7-19   **Research:**   Select a corporate note or bond that has been outstanding for at least five years.

a.   Describe the security's features, noting its coupon rate and its remaining maturity.
b.   What has been the security's value at the end of each of the past five years?
c.   If the yield on the debt goes up 1 percent, what price do you expect for this security?
d.   What types of risk does the investor assume when she or he buys this security?

Recommended sources of information:

- *Bond Record,* Moody's
- *Bond Survey,* Moody's
- *Industrial Manual,* Moody's
- *Bond Guide,* Standard & Poor's
- *Corporation Records,* Standard & Poor's
- *The Wall Street Journal*

PC+   7-20   **Research:**   Select a major corporation that has at least ten years of financial statement data available.

a.   What is the trend in operating earnings over the past ten years? Are the firm's operating earnings sensitive to changes in the economy? If so, in what manner?
b.   Do earnings to owners change each year? Are these earnings sensitive to changes in the economy? If so, in what manner?
c.   Characterize this firm and its industry in terms of sales risk, operating risk, and financial risk. This characterization may include a discussion of (1) the degree of competitiveness in the market for the firm's products, (2) whether the firm can adjust its operating cost structure quickly to changes in demand, and (3) whether the firm has increased or decreased its financial risk over the past ten years.

Recommended sources of information:

- Annual reports and 10-K statements
- *Industrial Manual,* Moody's
- *Compustat PC Plus* (CD-ROM), Standard & Poor's
- *Value Line Investment Survey*

FURTHER READINGS

For an overview of asset pricing and market efficiency, see
CHARLES A. D'AMBROSIO, "Portfolio Management Basics," in *Managing Investment Portfolios: A Dynamic Process,* 2d ed., eds. John L. Maginn and Donald L. Tuttle, Warren Gorham & Lamont, New York, 1990.

A more detailed coverage of the arbitrage pricing theory can be found elsewhere, including:
DOROTHY H. BOWER and RICHARD S. BOWER, "A Primer on Arbitrage Pricing Theory," *Midland Corporate Finance Journal,* vol. 2, no. 3, Fall 1984.

Additional discussion on the statistics of expected return and risk can be found in Appendix D, "Statistical Primer," at the end of this text. For a more detailed coverage of the quantitative tools behind risk analysis, see:
STEPHEN J. BROWN and MARK P. KRITZMAN, *Quantitative Methods for Financial Analysis,* 2d ed., Dow Jones-Irwin, Homewood, Ill., 1990.

PART IV

Management of Investments

8 Capital Investment Decisions 344

9 Evaluating Capital Projects 387

10 Capital Budgeting and Risk 461

CHAPTER 8

Capital Investment Decisions

INTRODUCTION 346

THE INVESTMENT PROBLEM 346

Capital Investments 346

Investment Decisions and Owners' Wealth Maximization 347

Capital Budgeting 349

Classifying Investment Projects . . . 350

. . . According to Their Economic Life 350

. . . According to Their Risk 351

. . . According to Their Dependence on Other Projects 352

CASH FLOW FROM INVESTMENTS 353

Incremental Cash Flows 353

Investment Cash Flows 354

Operating Cash Flows 359

Net Cash Flows 367

Simplifications 368

Example 1: The Expansion of the Williams 5 & 10 368

The Problem 368

The Analysis 370

Example 2: The Replacement of Facilities at the Hirshleifer Company 374

The Problem 374

The Analysis 376

CASH FLOW ESTIMATION IN PRACTICE 378

Summary 381

To MBA or Not to MBA?

Determining whether to go to graduate school for a Master of Business Administration (MBA) degree is an investment decision. It's an investment in your human capital. Let's assume you are evaluating this decision after you've been working for a few years, since most MBA programs require you to have a few years of work experience. To make this decision you need to compare an MBA's costs (the opportunity cost and the direct tuition cost) with its benefits (the increased salary potential).

One side of that decision is not to pursue an MBA, to continue working, expecting pay raises each year (you hope) and an occasional promotion. The other side is to quit work, give up this income, and go to school. This forgone income is an opportunity cost. Is the opportunity cost the total forgone income? No, because a part of it would have been paid in taxes; only the part of your income left after paying taxes would be the opportunity cost.

To pursue an MBA, you most likely must pay tuition for two years. Tuition can be as high as $20,000 per year. And since tuition is not deductible on your tax return, the full amount of it is a direct cost of the MBA.

The objective of getting an MBA is to increase your future income. By how much depends on a number of factors. Recent surveys indicate that if you graduate from one of the top MBA programs, your starting salary will be approximately three times the annual tuition. So if you pay $20,000 in tuition, you would expect a starting salary of $60,000. The benefit from an MBA is the difference between the estimate of your salary **with** an MBA (after taxes, of course) and your after-tax salary **without** an MBA.

If we ignore the intangibles, such as your personal satisfaction in obtaining a degree and your delight in sitting through classes and taking exams, your decision whether or not to go for an MBA boils down to a process of comparing the costs and the benefits:

Benefits	Costs
• Present value of increased after-tax income after completion of degree for each year until retirement (or later if retirement benefits are enhanced by an MBA).	• Present value of forgone income during the two years you are working on your MBA • Present value of tuition payments for two years.

If the benefits outweigh the costs, obtaining an MBA is a good investment decision, since you will be better off with an MBA than without it.

INTRODUCTION

As long as a firm exists, it invests in assets. Indeed, a firm invests in assets to continue to exist and, moreover, to grow. By investing to grow, a firm is at the same time investing to maximize its owners' wealth. To maximize the wealth of a firm's owners, its managers must regularly evaluate investment opportunities and determine which ones provide a return commensurate with their risk.

Let's look at Firms A, B, and C, each having identical assets and investment opportunities, but with the following differences:

- Firm A's management does not take advantage of its investment opportunities and simply pays all of its earnings to its owners.
- Firm B's management makes only those investments necessary to replace any deteriorating plant and equipment, paying out any leftover earnings to its owners.
- Firm C's management invests in all those opportunities that provide a return better than that which the owners could have earned had they had the same amount of invested funds to invest themselves.

In the case of Firm A, the owners' investment in the firm will not be as good as it could be as long as the firm has investment opportunities that are better than those available to the owners but fails to take advantage of them. By not even making investments to replace deteriorating plant and equipment, Firm A will eventually shrink until it has no more assets.

In the case of Firm B, its management is not taking advantage of all profitable investments—investments that provide a higher return than the return required by its owners. This means that there are forgone opportunities, and owners' wealth is not maximized.

But in the case of Firm C, management is making all profitable investments, maximizing owners' wealth. Firm C will continue to grow as long as there are profitable investment opportunities and its management takes advantage of them.

THE INVESTMENT PROBLEM

Capital Investments

Firms continually invest funds in assets, and these assets produce income and cash flows that the firm can then either reinvest in more assets or pay to its owners. These assets represent the firm's capital. **Capital** is the firm's total assets and is composed of all tangible and intangible assets, including physical assets (such as land, buildings, equipment, and machinery) as well as assets that represent property rights (such as accounts receivable, notes, stocks, and bonds). When we refer to **capital investment**, we are referring to the firm's investment in its assets.

The term "capital" also has come to mean the funds used to finance the firm's assets. In this sense, capital consists of notes, bonds, stock, and short-term financing. We use the term "capital structure" to refer to the mix of these different sources of capital used to finance a firm's assets.

The term "capital" as used in financial management refers to a firm's resources and the funds committed to these resources. But in other fields the term has different meanings. In accounting, "capital" is the owners' equity: the difference between the amount of a firm's assets and its liabilities. In economics, "capital" is the physical (real) assets of the firm, and therefore excludes the assets that represent property rights. In law, "capital" is the amount of owners' equity required by statute for the protection of creditors. This amounts to the "stated capital," which often is the par value of the firm's stock.

The firm's capital investment decision may be composed of a number of distinct decisions, each referred to as a project. A *capital project* is a set of assets that are contingent on one another and are considered together. Suppose a firm is considering the production of a new product. The company must decide whether to produce this new product. This capital project requires the firm to acquire land, to build facilities, and to purchase production equipment. The firm may also need to increase its investment in its *working capital*—inventory, cash, or accounts receivable. Working capital is the collection of assets needed for the day-to-day operations that support a firm's long-term investments.

The investment decisions of the firm are decisions concerning a firm's capital investment. When we refer to a particular decision that financial managers must make, we are referring to a decision pertaining to a capital project.

Investment Decisions and Owners' Wealth Maximization

Let's see what we must evaluate in our investment decisions in order to maximize the wealth of owners of the firm we manage.

We already know that the value of the firm today is the present value of all its future cash flows. But we need to understand better where these future cash flows come from. They come from:

1. Assets that are already in place, which are the assets accumulated as a result of all past investment decisions.
2. Future investment opportunities.

$$\text{Value of firm} = \begin{matrix}\text{present value}\\\text{of all future}\\\text{cash flows}\end{matrix} = \begin{matrix}\text{present value}\\\text{of cash flows from}\\\text{all assets in place}\end{matrix} + \begin{matrix}\text{present value}\\\text{of cash flows from}\\\text{future investment}\\\text{opportunities}\end{matrix}$$

Future cash flows are discounted at a rate that represents investors' assessments of the uncertainty that these cash flows will flow in the amounts and at the time expected. To evaluate the value of the firm, we need to evaluate the risk of these future cash flows.

Cash flow risk comes from two basic sources:

- *Sales risk,* which is the degree of uncertainty related to the number of units that will be sold and the price of the good or service.
- *Operating risk,* which is the degree of uncertainty concerning operating cash flows that arises from the particular mix of fixed and variable operating costs.

Sales risk is related to the economy and the market in which the firm's goods and services are sold. Operating risk, for the most part, is determined by the product or service that the firm provides and is related to the sensitivity of operating cash flows to changes in sales. We refer to the combination of these two risks as *business risk*.

A project's business risk is reflected in the discount rate, which is the rate of return required to compensate the suppliers of capital (bondholders and owners) for the amount of risk they bear. From the investors' perspective, the discount rate is the ***required rate of return*** (RRR). From the firm's perspective, the discount rate is the ***cost of capital***—what it costs the firm to raise a dollar of new capital.

The Required Rate of Return and the Cost of Capital

What investors call the required rate of return and firms call the cost of capital are similar. The cost of capital includes the cost of raising capital from outside the firm. These costs are referred to as flotation costs. Flotation costs are paid to the intermediaries (such as underwriters) who assist a firm in raising new capital. Therefore:

$$\boxed{\text{Required rate of return}} + \boxed{\text{flotation costs}} = \boxed{\text{cost of capital}}$$

And, as we will see in Chapter 14, the cost of capital reflects the tax deductibility of interest.

Suppose a firm invests in a new project:

- If the project generates cash flows that *just* compensate the suppliers of capital for the risk they bear on this project (that is, it earns the cost of capital), the value of the firm does not change.
- If the project generates cash flows *greater* than needed to compensate the capital suppliers for the risk they take on, it earns more than the cost of capital, increasing the value of the firm.
- If the project generates cash flows *less* than needed, it earns less than the cost of capital, decreasing the value of the firm.

How do we know whether the cash flows are more than or less than needed to compensate for the risk that they will indeed flow? If we discount all the cash flows at the cost of capital, we can assess how this project affects the present value of the firm. If the expected change in the value of the firm from an investment is:

- Positive, the project returns more than the cost of capital.
- Negative, the project returns less than the cost of capital.
- Zero, the project returns the cost of capital.

Capital budgeting is the process of identifying and selecting investments in long-lived assets, where long-lived means assets expected to produce benefits over more than one year.

In this chapter, we first look at the capital budgeting process in general. After looking at the broad picture of how investment decisions are made, we look at how projects may be classified. This classification helps us identify the cash flows we need to consider in our decisions. We then look at the mechanics of estimating future cash flows, using estimates of future revenues, expenses, and depreciation. We summarize our analysis of cash flows with examples analyzing two different investment projects.

We discuss how to evaluate cash flows in investment decisions in Chapter 9. We cover how to determine cash flow risk and factor it into capital budgeting decisions in Chapter 10.

Capital Budgeting

A firm must continually evaluate possible investments. Investment decisions regarding long-lived assets are a part of the ongoing capital budgeting process. Ideas about what projects to invest in are generated through facts gathered at lower management levels, where they are evaluated and screened. The suggested investments that pass this first level filter up through successive management levels toward top management or the board of directors, who make the decisions about which projects to accept and how much capital to allot to each project.

Before a firm begins thinking about capital budgeting, it must first determine its **corporate strategy**—its broad set of objectives for future investment. For example, Anheuser-Busch Companies Inc's objective is ". . . to extend its position as the world's leading brewer of quality products; increase its share of the domestic beer market to 50% by the mid-1990s; and increase its presence in the international beer market."[1]

Consider the corporate strategy of Mattel Inc., manufacturer of toys such as Barbie and Disney toys. Mattel's strategy in the 1990s is to become a full-line toy company and grow through expansion into the international toy market. In 1990, 1991, and 1992, Mattel entered the activity-toy, games, and plush-toy markets, and, through acquisitions in Mexico, France, and Japan, increased its presence in the international toy market.[2]

How does a firm carry out its corporate strategy? By making investments in long-lived assets that will maximize owners' wealth. Selecting these projects is what capital budgeting is all about.

There are five stages in the capital budgeting process.

Stage 1 *Investment screening and selection.* Projects consistent with the corporate strategy are identified. But projects don't simply walk into corporate headquarters. The firm must have some system for seeking or generating investment opportunities. Identifying investment opportunities is not necessarily the task of the financial manager. This task typically lies with the production, marketing, and research and development management of the firm.

Once identified, projects are evaluated and screened by estimating how they affect the future cash flows of the firm and, hence, the value of the firm.

Stage 2 *Capital budget proposal.* A capital budget is proposed for the projects that survive the screening and selection process. The budget lists the recommended projects and the dollar amount of investment needed for each.

[1] *Annual Report, 1991,* p. 7.
[2] *Annual Report, 1991,* pp. 4–5, 15.

A proposal may start as an estimate of expected revenues and costs, but as the project analysis is refined, data from marketing, purchasing, engineering, accounting, and finance functions are collected and put together.

Stage 3   *Budgeting approval and authorization.* Projects included in the capital budget are authorized, allowing further fact gathering and analysis, and approved, allowing expenditures for the projects. In some firms, the projects are authorized and approved at the same time. In others, a project must first be authorized, requiring more research before it can be formally approved.

Formal authorization and approval procedures are typically used on larger expenditures; smaller expenditures are at the discretion of management. For example, Hershey Foods has three different approval processes, depending on the size of the investment. If the investment requires an outlay of less than $500,000, the project needs the approval of the division president. If the outlay is between $500,000 and $1 million, the project must be approved by both the chairman and chief executive officer or by both the president and chief operating officer, depending on whether the project is a new product or simply an expansion of existing facilities. If the investment outlay is above $1 million, the project must be approved by the board of directors.

Stage 4   *Project tracking.* After a project is approved, work on it begins. The manager reports periodically on its expenditures, as well as on any revenues associated with it. This is referred to as **project tracking**, the communication link between the decision makers and the operating management of the firm. For example, tracking can identify cost overruns; it can also uncover the need for more marketing research in order to better focus on the target market.

Stage 5   *Postcompletion audit.* Following a period of time, perhaps two or three years after approval, projects are reviewed to see whether they should be continued. This reevaluation is referred to as a **postcompletion audit**.

Thorough postcompletion audits are not usually performed on every project, since that would be too time consuming. Rather, they are performed on selected projects, usually the largest projects in a given year's budget for the firm or for each division. Postcompletion audits enable the firm's management to see how well the cash flows realized correspond with the cash flows forecasted several years earlier.

Classifying Investment Projects . . .

. . . According to Their Economic Life

An investment generally provides benefits over a limited period of time, referred to as its economic life. The *economic life,* or *useful life,* of an asset is determined by one or more of the following factors:

- Physical deterioration
- Obsolescence
- Degree of competition in the market for a product

The economic life is an estimate of the length of time that the asset will provide benefits to the firm. After its useful life ends, the revenues generated by the asset tend to decline rapidly and its expenses tend to increase.

Typically, an investment requires an expenditure up front—immediately—and provides benefits in the form of cash flows received in the future. If benefits are received only within the current period—within one year of making the investment—we refer to the investment as a ***short-term investment***. If these benefits are received beyond the current period, we refer to the investment as a ***long-term investment*** and refer to the expenditure as a ***capital expenditure***.

Any project representing an investment may comprise one or more assets. For example, a new product may require investment in production equipment, a building, and transportation equipment—all of them making up the bundle of assets that constitutes the project we are evaluating.

Short-term investment decisions involve, primarily, investments in current assets: cash, marketable securities, accounts receivable, and inventory. The objective of investing in short-term assets is the same as for long-term assets: maximizing owners' wealth. Nevertheless, we consider them separately for two practical reasons:

1. Decisions about long-term assets are based on projections of cash flows far into the future and require us to consider the time value of money.
2. Long-term assets do not figure into the daily operating needs of the firm.

Decisions regarding short-term investments, or current assets, are concerned with day-to-day operations. Furthermore, a firm needs some level of current assets to act as a cushion in case of unusually poor operating periods, when cash flows from operations are less than expected.

. . . According to Their Risk

Suppose you are faced with two investments, A and B, each promising a $100 cash inflow ten years from today. If A is riskier than B, what are they worth to you today? If you do not like risk, you would consider A less valuable than B because the chance of getting the $100 in ten years is less for A than for B. Therefore, valuing a project requires considering the risk associated with the project's future cash flows.

The project's risk can be classified according to the nature of the project represented by the investment:

- ***Replacement projects.*** Investments in the replacement of existing equipment or facilities.
- ***Expansion projects.*** Investments in projects that broaden existing product lines and existing markets.
- ***New products and markets.*** Projects that involve introducing a new product or entering into a new market.
- ***Mandated projects.*** Projects required by government laws or agency rules.

Replacement projects include the maintenance of existing assets to continue the current level of operating activity. Projects that reduce costs, such as replacing older technology with newer technology or improving the efficiency of equipment or personnel, are also considered replacement projects.

To evaluate replacement projects we need to compare the value of the firm *with* the replacement asset to the value of the firm *without* the same replacement asset. What we're really doing in this comparison is looking at **opportunity cost:** what cash flows would have been if the firm had stayed with the old asset.

There's little risk in the cash flows from replacement projects. The firm is simply replacing equipment or buildings already operating and producing cash flows. Furthermore, the firm typically has experience in managing similar new equipment.

Expansion projects are intended to enlarge a firm's established product or market. There is little risk associated with expansion projects. The reason: A firm with a history of experience in a product or market can estimate future cash flows with more certainty when considering expansion than when introducing a new product outside its existing product line.

Investment projects that involve introducing *new products* or *entering into new markets* are riskier than the replacement and expansion projects. That's because the firm has little or no management experience in the new product or market. Hence, there is more uncertainty about the future cash flows from investments in new-product or new-market projects.

A firm is forced or coerced into its *mandated projects*. These are government-mandated projects typically found in "heavy" industries, such as utilities, transportation, and chemicals, which have a large portion of their assets in production activities. Government agencies, such as the Occupational Health and Safety Agency (OSHA) or the Environmental Protection Agency (EPA), may impose requirements that firms install specific equipment or alter their activities (such as their method of disposal of waste).

We can further classify mandated projects into two types: contingent and retroactive. Suppose, as a steel manufacturer, we are required by law to include pollution control devices on all smoke stacks. If we are considering a new plant, this mandated equipment is really part of our new-plant investment decision—the investment in pollution control equipment is contingent on our decision to build the new plant.

On the other hand, if we are required by law to place pollution control devices on *existing* smoke stacks, the law is retroactive. We do not have a choice. We must invest in the equipment whether it increases the value of the firm or not. In this case either we select equipment that satisfies the mandate, or we decide whether to halt production in the offending plant.

. . . According to Their Dependence on Other Projects

In addition to considering the future cash flows generated by a project, a firm must consider how the project will affect the assets already in place—the results of previous project decisions—as well as other projects that may be undertaken. Projects can be classified according to the degree of their dependence on other projects as independent, mutually exclusive, contingent, or complementary.

A Capital Budget Can Be as Simple as This

"Some 53% of the capital budget for 1991 has been earmarked for cost efficiencies and replacement of plant and equipment, while 21% is slated for expansion of capacity and new products. The remaining 26% is budgeted for the purchase of additional rental assets, OSHA and environmental requirements and miscellaneous" (*Harsco Corporation Annual Report,* 1990, p. 31).

An ***independent project*** is one whose cash flows are not related to the cash flows of any other project. In other words, accepting or rejecting an independent project does not affect the acceptance or rejection of other projects. An independent project can be evaluated strictly on the effect it will have on the value of a firm without having to consider how it affects the firm's other investment opportunities.

Projects are ***mutually exclusive*** if the acceptance of one precludes the acceptance of other projects. There are some situations in which it is technically impossible to take on more than one project. For example, suppose a manufacturer is considering whether to replace its production facilities with more modern equipment. The firm may solicit bids among the different manufacturers of this equipment. Making the decision consists of comparing two choices:

1. Keeping its existing production facilities, or
2. Replacing the facilities with the modern equipment of one manufacturer.

Since the firm cannot use more than one production facility, it must evaluate each bid and determine the most attractive one. The alternative production facilities are mutually exclusive projects: the firm can accept only one bid.

The alternatives of keeping existing facilities or replacing them are also mutually exclusive projects. The firm cannot keep the existing facilities *and* replace them!

Contingent projects are dependent on the acceptance of another project. Suppose a greeting card company develops a new character, Pippy, and is considering starting a line of Pippy cards. If Pippy catches on, the firm will consider producing a line of Pippy T-shirts—but *only* if the Pippy character becomes popular. The T-shirt project is a contingent project. It is contingent on the company's taking on the Pippy project and on Pippy's success.

Another form of dependence is found in complementary projects. Projects are ***complementary projects*** if the investment in one enhances the cash flows of one or more other projects. Consider a manufacturer of personal computer equipment and software. If the firm develops new software that enhances the abilities of a computer pointing device, or "mouse," the introduction of the new software may enhance mouse sales as well.

Classification of Projects

By economic life:

- Short term
- Long term

By risk:

- Replacement
- Expansion
- New products or new markets
- Mandated

By dependence on other projects:

- Independent
- Mutually exclusive
- Contingent
- Complementary

CASH FLOW FROM INVESTMENTS

Incremental Cash Flows

A firm invests only to make its owners "better off," that is, to increase the value of their ownership interest. A firm will have cash flows in the future from its past investment decisions. When it invests in new assets, it expects the firm's future cash flows to be *greater than they would have been without this new investment*. Otherwise, it doesn't make sense to make this investment. The difference between the cash flows of the firm *with* the investment project and the cash flows of the firm *without* the investment project—both over the same period of time—is referred to as the project's ***incremental cash flow***.

To evaluate an investment, we have to find out how it will change the future cash flows of the firm. To do so, we need to determine how much the value of the firm changes as a result of the investment.

The change in a firm's value as a result of a new investment is the difference between its benefits and its costs:

$$\text{Change in the value of the firm due to the project} = \text{project's benefits} - \text{project's costs}$$

A more useful way of evaluating the change in the value is to break down the project's cash flows into two components:

1. The present value of the cash flows from the project's operating activities (revenues and operating expenses), referred to as the project's **operating cash flows** (OCF);
2. The present value of the **investment cash flows**, which are the expenditures needed to acquire the project's assets and any cash flows from disposing of the project's assets.

or,

$$\text{Change in the value of the firm} = \text{present value of the change in operating cash flows provided by the project} + \text{present value of investment cash flows}$$

The present value of a project's operating cash flows is typically positive (indicating predominantly cash inflows) and the present value of the investment cash flows is typically negative (indicating predominantly cash outflows).

Investment Cash Flows

When we consider the cash flows of an investment we must also consider all the cash flows associated with acquiring and disposing of assets in the investment.

An investment may comprise:

- One asset or many assets.
- One asset purchased and another sold.
- Cash outlays that occur at the beginning of the project or spread over several years.

Let's first become familiar with cash flows related to acquiring assets. Then we'll look at cash flows related to disposing assets.

Asset Acquisition

In acquiring any asset, there are three cash flows to consider:

1. Cost of the asset.
2. Setup expenditures, including shipping and installation.
3. Any tax credit.[3]

The tax credit may be an investment tax credit or a special credit—such as a credit for a pollution control device—depending on the tax law.

---

[3] Care must be taken in evaluating an asset's cash flows if there is a tax credit, since some tax credits require the firm to reduce amount of depreciation taken on the asset.

Cash flow associated with the acquisition of an asset is:

$$\text{Cash flow from the acquisition of assets} = \text{cost} + \text{setup expenditures} - \text{tax credit}$$

Suppose the firm buys equipment that costs $100,000 and pays $10,000 to install it. If the firm is eligible for a 10 percent tax credit on this equipment (that is, 10 percent of the total cost of buying and installing the equipment) the change in the firm's cash flow as a result of acquiring the asset is $99,000:

$$\text{Cash flow from the acquisition of assets} = \$100,000 + \$10,000 - 0.10(\$100,000 + \$10,000)$$

$$= \$100,000 + \$10,000 - \$11,000$$

$$= \mathbf{\$99,000}$$

The cash outflow is $99,000 when this asset is acquired: $110,000 *out* to buy and install the equipment and $11,000 *in* from the reduction in taxes.

What about expenditures made in the past for assets or research that would be used in the project we're evaluating? Suppose the firm spent $1 million over the past three years developing a new type of toothpaste. Should the firm consider this $1 million spent on research and development in deciding whether to engage in the proposed new project? No: These expenses have already been made and do not affect how the new product changes the future cash flows of the firm. We refer to this $1 million as a **sunk cost** and do not consider it in the analysis of our new project. Whether or not the firm goes ahead with the proposed new product, the $1 million has been spent. A sunk cost is any cost that has already been incurred and that does not affect future cash flows of the firm.

Let's consider another example. Suppose the firm owns a building that is currently empty. Let's say the firm suddenly has an opportunity to use it for the production of a new product. Is the cost of the building relevant to the new product decision? The cost of the building itself is a sunk cost, since it was an expenditure made as part of some *previous* investment decision. The cost of the building does not affect the decision to go ahead with the new product.

However, suppose the firm uses the building in some way to produce cash (say, by renting it) and the new project would take over the entire building. The cash flows given up represent opportunity costs that must be included in the analysis of the new project. However, these forgone cash flows are not asset acquisition cash flows. Because they represent operating cash flows that could have occurred but will not because of the new project, they must be considered part of the project's future operating cash flows. Furthermore, if we incur costs in renovating the building to manufacture the new product, the renovation costs are relevant and should be included in our asset acquisition cash flows.

Asset Disposition

Many new investments require getting rid of old assets. At the end of the useful life of an asset, the firm may be able to sell it or may have to pay someone to haul it away. If the firm is making a decision that involves replacing an existing asset, the cash flow from the disposal of the old asset must be figured in, since it is a cash flow relevant to the acquisition of the new asset.

If the firm disposes of an asset, whether at the end of its useful life or when it is replaced, two types of cash flows must be considered:

1. What the firm receives or pays out in disposing of the asset.
2. Any tax consequences resulting from the disposal.

$$\begin{array}{l}\text{Cash flow from} \\ \text{disposal of assets}\end{array} = \begin{array}{l}\text{proceeds or payment} \\ \text{from disposal of} \\ \text{assets}\end{array} - \begin{array}{l}\text{taxes from} \\ \text{disposal of assets}\end{array}$$

The proceeds are what you expect to sell the asset for if you can get someone to buy it. If the firm must pay for the disposal of the asset, this cost is a cash outflow.

Consider an investment in a gas station. The current owner may want to leave the business (retire, whatever), selling the station to another gas station proprietor. But if a buyer cannot be found, for whatever reason, and the station must be abandoned, the current owner may be required to remove the underground gasoline storage tanks to prevent environmental damage. Thus, a cost is incurred at the end of the asset's life.

The tax consequences are a bit more complicated. Taxes depend on (1) the expected sale price and (2) the book value of the asset for tax purposes at the time of disposition. If a firm sells the asset for more than its book value but less than its original cost, the difference between the sales price and the book value is a gain, taxable at ordinary tax rates. If a firm sells the asset for more than its original cost, then the gain is broken into two parts:

1. *Capital gain.* The difference between the sales price and the original cost.
2. *Recapture of depreciation.* The difference between the original cost and the book value.

The *capital gain* is the benefit from the appreciation in the value of the asset and may be taxed at special rates, depending on the tax law at the time of sale. The *recapture of depreciation* represents the amount by which the firm has *over*-depreciated the asset during its life; that is, more depreciation was deducted from income (reducing taxes) than was necessary to reflect the usage of the asset. The recapture portion is taxed at ordinary tax rates, since the excess depreciation taken in all those past years reduced taxable income.

If a firm sells an asset for less than its book value, the result is a *capital loss*. In this case, the asset's value has decreased by more than the amount taken for depreciation for tax purposes. A capital loss is given special tax treatment:

- If there are capital gains in the same tax year as the capital loss, they are combined, so that the capital loss reduces the taxes paid on capital gains.
- If there are no capital gains to offset against the capital loss, the capital loss is used to reduce ordinary taxable income.

The benefit from a loss on the sale of an asset is the amount by which taxes are reduced. The reduction in taxable income is referred to as a *tax shield,* since the loss *shields* some income from taxation. If the firm has a loss of $1,000 on the sale of an asset and is subject to a tax rate of 40 percent, then its taxable income will be $1,000 less and its taxes will be $400 less than they would have been without the sale of the asset.

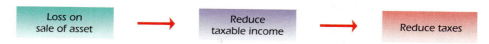

Suppose that you are evaluating an asset that costs $10,000 and that you expect to sell in five years. Suppose further that the book value of the asset for tax purposes will be $3,000 after five years and that the firm's tax rate is 40 percent. What are the expected cash flows from disposing of this asset?

If you expect the firm to sell the asset for $8,000 in five years, $10,000 − $3,000 = $7,000 of the asset's cost will be depreciated; yet the asset lost only $10,000 − $8,000 = $2,000 in value. Therefore, the firm has *over*depreciated the asset by $5,000. Since this overdepreciation represents deductions to be taken on the firm's tax returns over the five years and these deductions do not reflect the actual depreciation in value (the asset doesn't lose $7,000 in value, but only $2,000), the $5,000 is taxed at ordinary tax rates. If the firm's tax rate is 40 percent, the tax = 40% × $5,000 = $2,000.

The cash flow from disposition is the sum of the direct cash flow (someone pays the firm for the asset or the firm pays someone to dispose of it) and the tax consequences. In this example, the cash flow is the $8,000 we expect someone to pay the firm for the asset less the $2,000 in taxes we expect the firm to pay, leaving a cash inflow of $6,000.

Suppose, instead, that you expect the firm to sell the asset in five years for $12,000. Again, the asset is overdepreciated by $7,000. In fact, the asset is not expected to depreciate but rather to *appreciate* over the five years. The $7,000 in depreciation is recaptured after five years and taxed at ordinary rates: 40 percent of $7,000, or $2,800. The $2,000 capital gain is the appreciation in the value of the asset and may be taxed at special rates. If the tax rate on capital gain income is 30 percent, the firm can expect to pay 30 percent of $2,000, or $600, in taxes on this gain. Selling the asset in five years for $12,000 therefore results in an expected cash inflow of $12,000 − $2,800 − $600 = $8,600.

Suppose you expect the firm to sell the asset in five years for $1,000. If the firm can reduce its ordinary taxable income by the amount of the capital loss, $3,000 − $1,000 = $2,000, its tax bill will be 40 percent of $2,000, or $800, because of the loss. We refer to this reduction in the taxes as a tax shield, since the loss "shields" $2,000 of income from taxes. Combining the $800 tax reduction with the cash flow from selling the asset, the $1,000, gives the firm a cash inflow of $1,800.[4]

The calculations of the cash flow from disposition for the alternative sales prices of $8,000, $12,000, and $1,000 are shown in Table 8-1.

---

[4] However, if we expect other capital gains five years from now, the amount of tax shield would be less, since the loss would be used first to offset any capital gains taxed at 30 percent. In this case, the expected tax shield is only 30 percent of $2,000 or $600, since we must first use the capital loss to reduce any capital gains.

TABLE 8-1
Expected Cash Flows from the Disposition of an Asset

The firm pays $10,000 for an asset and expects to dispose of it in five years, when the asset will have a book value of $3,000. The firm's ordinary tax rate is 40 percent, and the tax rate on capital gains is 30 percent.

Original > Expected > Book
cost   sales price   value

Tax on disposition
Sales price	$ 8,000
Book value	3,000
Gain	$ 5,000
Ordinary tax rate	×0.40
Tax on recapture	$2,000

Cash flows
Proceeds from disposition	$ 8,000
Less tax on gain	2,000
Cash flow on disposition	$6,000

Expected > Original > Book
sales price   cost   value

Tax on disposition
Sales price	$12,000
Original cost	10,000
Capital gain	$ 2,000
Capital gains tax rate	×0.30
Tax on capital gain	$600

Original cost	$10,000
Book value	3,000
Gain (recapture)	$ 7,000
Ordinary tax rate	×0.40
Tax on recapture	$ 2,800

Cash flows
Proceeds from disposition	$12,000
Less tax on capital gain	600
Less tax on recapture	2,800
Cash flow on disposition	$ 8,600

Book > Expected
value   sales price

Tax shield on disposition
Book value	$ 3,000
Less sales price	1,000
Loss	$ 2,000
Ordinary tax rate	×0.40
Tax shield on loss	$800

Cash flows
Proceeds from disposition	$ 1,000
Plus tax shield on loss	800
Cash flow on disposition	$1,800

Let's also not forget about disposing of any existing assets. Suppose the firm bought equipment ten years ago and at that time expected to be able to sell it fifteen years later for $10,000. If the firm decides *today* to replace this equipment, it must consider what it is giving up by *not* disposing of an asset *as planned*. If the firm does not replace the equipment today, it would continue to depreciate the item for five more years and then sell it for $10,000; if the firm replaces the equipment today, it would not have five more years' depreciation on the replaced equipment and it would not have $10,000 in five years (but perhaps some other amount today). The expected $10,000 to be received in five years, less any taxes, is a forgone cash flow that we must figure into the investment cash flows. Also, the depreciation the firm would have had on the replaced asset must be considered in analyzing the replacement asset's operating cash flows.

Operating Cash Flows

In the simplest form of investment, there will be a cash outflow when the asset is acquired and there may be either a cash inflow or an outflow at the end of the investment's economic life. In most cases these are not the only cash flows: The investment may result in changes in revenues, expenditures, taxes, and working capital. These are operating cash flows, since they result directly from the operating activities—the day-to-day activities of the firm.

What we are after here are *estimates* of operating cash flows. We cannot know for certain what these cash flows will be in the future, but we must attempt to estimate them. What is the basis for these estimates? We base them on marketing research, engineering analyses, operations research, analysis of our competitors—and our managerial experience.

Change in Revenues

Suppose we are a food processor that produces a line of frozen dinner products, and we are now considering a new investment in a line of not-frozen dinner products. If we introduce a new ready-to-eat dinner product that is not frozen, our marketing research will indicate how much we should expect to sell. But where do these new-product sales come from? Some may come from consumers who do not already buy frozen dinner products. But some of the not-frozen dinner product sales may come from consumers who choose to buy the not-frozen dinner product *instead* of frozen dinners. We would be pleased if these consumers were to give up buying our *competitors'* frozen dinners. Yet some of them may give up buying *our* frozen dinners. So, when we introduce a new product, we are really interested in how it changes the sales of the entire firm (that is, the *incremental* sales), rather than the sales of the new product alone.

We also need to consider any forgone revenues—opportunity costs—related to our investment. Suppose our firm owns a building that is currently rented out to another firm. If we are considering terminating that rental agreement so that we can use the building for a new project, we need to consider the forgone rent—what we would have earned from the building. Therefore, the revenues from the new project are really only the additional revenues—

the revenues from the new project minus the revenue we could have earned by renting out the building.

So, when a firm undertakes a new project, the financial managers want to know how it changes the firm's total revenues, not merely the new product's revenues. In deciding whether to go to graduate school—the problem introduced at the beginning of this chapter—you needed to know how your income would change if you got an MBA—that's what matters, not just your total income after graduate school.

Change in Expenses

When a firm takes on a new project, all the costs associated with it will change the firm's expenses.

If the investment involves changing the sales of an existing product, we need an estimate of the change in unit sales. Once we have an estimate of how sales may change, we can consult with production management in order to develop an estimate of the additional costs of producing the additional number of units. And, we will want an estimate of how the product's inventory may change when production and sales of the product change.

If the investment involves changes in the costs of production, we compare the costs without this investment with the costs with this investment. For example, if the investment is the replacement of an assembly line machine with a more efficient version, we need to estimate the change in the firm's overall production costs, such as electricity, labor, materials, and management costs.

A new investment may change not only production costs but also operating costs, such as rental payments and administration costs. Changes in operating costs as a result of a new investment must be considered as a part of the changes in the firm's expenses.

Increases in cash expenses are cash outflows, and decreases in cash expense are cash inflows.

Change in Taxes

Taxes figure into the operating cash flows in two ways. First, if revenues and expenses change, taxable income and, therefore, taxes change. That means we need to estimate the change in taxable income resulting from the changes in revenues and expenses that arise from a new project in order to determine the effect of taxes on the firm.

Second, the deduction for depreciation reduces taxes. Depreciation itself is not a cash flow. But depreciation reduces the taxes that must be paid, shielding income from taxation. The tax shield from depreciation is like a cash inflow.

Suppose a firm is considering a new product that is expected to generate additional sales of $200,000 and increase expenses by $150,000. If the firm's tax rate is 40 percent and we consider only the changes in sales and expenses, taxes go up by $50,000 × 40 percent or $20,000. This means that the firm is expected to pay $20,000 more in taxes because of the increase in revenues and expenses.

Let's change this around and consider that the product will generate $200,000 in revenues and $250,000 in expenses. If we consider only the

Depreciation itself is not a cash flow. But in determining cash flows, we are concerned with the effect depreciation has on our taxes—and we all know that taxes are a cash outflow. Since depreciation reduces taxable income, depreciation reduces the tax outflow, which amounts to a cash inflow.

For tax purposes, firms are permitted to use either straight-line or accelerated depreciation [specifically, the rates specified under the modified accelerated cost recovery system (MACRS)]. An accelerated method is preferred in most situations, since it results in larger deductions sooner in the asset's life than straight-line depreciation. Therefore, accelerated depreciation, if otherwise appropriate, is preferable to straight line because of the time value of money.

Under the present tax code, assets are depreciated to a zero book value. *Salvage value*—what we expect the asset to be worth at the end of its life—is not considered in calculating depreciation.

So is salvage value totally irrelevant to the analysis? No. Salvage value is our best guess today of what the asset will be worth at the end of its useful life some time in the future. Salvage value is our estimate of how much we can get when we dispose of the asset. Just remember that you can't use it to figure depreciation for tax purposes.

changes in revenues and expenses and the tax rate is 40 percent, taxes go *down* by $50,000 × 40 percent, or $20,000.[5] This means that we reduce our taxes by $20,000, which is like having a cash inflow of $20,000 from taxes.

Now consider depreciation. When a firm buys an asset that produces income, the tax laws allow the asset to be depreciated, reducing taxable income by a specified percentage of the asset's cost each year. By reducing taxable income, the firm is reducing its taxes. The reduction in taxes is like a cash inflow, since it reduces the firm's cash outflow to the government.

Suppose a firm has taxable income of $50,000 before depreciation and a flat tax rate of 40 percent. If the firm is allowed to deduct depreciation of $10,000, how will this change the taxes it pays?

	Without depreciation	With depreciation
Taxable income	$ 50,000	$ 40,000
Tax rate	× 0.40	× 0.40
Taxes	**$20,000**	**$16,000**

[5] This loss creates an immediate cash inflow *if* (1) the firm has other income in the same tax year to apply the $50,000 loss against or (2) the firm has income in prior tax years so that it can carry back the loss and apply for a refund of the prior year's taxes. Otherwise, the loss is carried forward to reduce taxable income in future years. In this case, the loss is worth less because the benefit derived from the loss (the reduction in taxable income) is realized in the future, not today.

Depreciation *reduces* the firm's tax-related *cash outflow* by $20,000 − $16,000 = $4,000 or, equivalently by $10,000 × 40 percent = $4,000. A reduction in an outflow (taxes in this case) is an inflow.

We refer to the effect depreciation has on taxes as the ***depreciation tax shield.***

Let's look at another depreciation example, this time considering the effects that replacing an asset has on the depreciation tax-shield cash flow. Suppose you are replacing a machine that you bought five years ago for $75,000. You were depreciating the machine using straight-line depreciation over ten years, or $7,500 depreciation per year. If you replace it with a new machine that costs $50,000 and is depreciated over five years, or $10,000 each year, how does the change in depreciation affect the cash flows if the firm's tax rate is 30 percent?

We can calculate the effect two ways:

1. ***We can compare the depreciation and related tax shields of the old and new machines.*** The depreciation tax shield on the old machine is 30 percent of $7,500, or $2,250. The depreciation tax shield on the new machine is 30 percent of $10,000, or $3,000. Therefore, the change in the cash flow resulting from depreciation is $3,000 − $2,250 = $750.

2. ***We can calculate the change in depreciation and then calculate the tax shield related to the change in depreciation.*** The change in depreciation is $10,000 − $7,500 = $2,500. The change in the depreciation tax shield is 30 percent of $2,500, or $750.

Let's look at another example. Suppose a firm invests $50,000 in an asset and has a choice of depreciating the asset using either:

- An accelerated method over four years, with rates of 33.33, 44.45, 14.81, and 7.41 percent, respectively, where these depreciation rates are a percentage of the original cost of the asset, or
- The straight-line method over four years.

If the firm's tax rate is 40 percent and the cost of capital is 10 percent, what is the present value of the difference in the cash flows from the depreciation tax shield each year?

Year	Depreciation using the accelerated method	Depreciation using the straight-line method	Difference in depreciation	Difference in depreciation tax shield	Present value of difference
1	$ 16,665	$ 12,500	$ 4,165	$ 1,666	$ 1,515
2	22,225	12,500	9,725	3,890	3,215
3	7,405	12,500	−5,095	−2,038	−1,531
4	3,705	12,500	−8,795	−3,518	−2,403
	$50,000	**$50,000**	**$ 0**	**$ 0**	**$ 796**

With either the accelerated or straight-line method, the entire asset's cost is depreciated over the four years. But the accelerated method provides greater tax shields in the first and second years than the straight-line method. Since larger depreciation tax shields are generated under the accelerated method in the earlier years, the present value of the tax shields using the accelerated method is more valuable than the present value of the tax shields using the straight-line method. How much more? $796.

Change in Working Capital

Working capital consists of short-term assets, also referred to as current assets, that support the day-to-day operating activity of the business. **Net working capital** is the difference between current assets and current liabilities. Net working capital is what would be left over if the firm had to pay off its current obligations using its current assets.

The adjustment we make for changes in net working capital is attributable to two sources:

1. A change in current asset accounts for transactions or precautionary needs.
2. Use of the accrual method of accounting.

An investment may increase the firm's level of operations, resulting in an increase in its net working capital needs (also considered transaction needs). If the purpose of the investment is to produce a new product, the firm may have to invest more in inventory (raw materials, work in process, and finished goods). If the purpose is to increase sales by extending more credit, then the firm's accounts receivable will increase. If the investment will require the firm to maintain a higher cash balance in order to handle the increased level of transactions, the firm will need more cash. If the investment makes the firm's production facilities more efficient, the firm may be able to reduce the level of inventory.

Because of an increase in the level of transactions, the firm may want to keep more cash and inventory on hand for precautionary purposes. That is because as the level of operations increases, the effect of any fluctuations in demand for goods and services may increase, requiring the firm to keep additional cash and inventory "just in case." The firm may increase working capital as a precaution because if there is greater variability of cash and inventory, a greater safety cushion will be needed. However, if a project enables the firm to be more efficient or lowers costs, it may lower its investment in cash, marketable securities, or inventory, releasing funds for investment elsewhere in the firm.

We also use the change in working capital to adjust accounting income (revenues less expenses) to a cash basis because cash flow is ultimately what we are valuing, not accounting numbers. But since we generally have only the accounting numbers to work with, we use them, making adjustments to arrive at cash.

To see how this works, let's look at the cash flow from sales. Not every dollar of sales is collected in the year of sale. Customers may pay some time *after* the sale. Using information from the accounts receivable department about how payments are collected, we can determine the change in the cash flows from revenues. Suppose we expect sales in the first year to increase by $20,000 per month and customers typically take thirty days to pay. The change in cash flow from sales in the first year is $20,000 \times 11 = $220,000$, not $20,000 \times 12 = $240,000$. The way we adjust for this difference between what

---

MACRS Rates

A portion of the schedule of MACRS rates in Table 3-6 is shown below. As you can see, an asset classified under the MACRS as a three-year asset is depreciated over four years, a five-year asset is depreciated over six years, and so on. The reason is that the MACRS uses half a year's depreciation in the first year, leaving an extra half-year's depreciation beyond the classified life.

| | Depreciation rate | |
Year	Three years	Five years
1	33.33%	20.00%
2	44.45	32.00
3	14.81	19.20
4	7.41	11.52
5		11.52
6		5.76

is sold and what is collected in cash is to keep track of the change in working capital, which in this case is the change in accounts receivable. An increase in working capital is used to adjust revenues downward to calculate
cash flow:

Change in revenues	$240,000
Less: Increase in accounts receivable	20,000
Change in cash inflow from sales	$220,000

On the other side of the balance sheet, if the firm is increasing its purchases of raw materials and incurring more production costs, such as labor,
the firm may increase its level of short-term liabilities, such as accounts
payable and salary and wages payable. Suppose expenses for materials and
supplies are forecasted at $10,000 per month for the first year and the firm
takes thirty days to pay. Expenses for the first year are $10,000 \times 12 =
$120,000; yet cash outflow for these expenses is only $10,000 \times 11 = $110,000,
since the firm does not pay the last month's expenses until the following year.
Accounts payable increases by $10,000, representing one month's expenses.
The increase in net working capital (increase in accounts payable → increases
current liabilities → increases net working capital) reduces the cost of goods
sold to give us the cash outflow from expenses:

Cost of goods sold	$120,000
Less: Increase in accounts payable	10,000
Change in cash flow from expenses	$110,000

A new project may result in either:

1. An increase in net working capital;
2. A decrease in net working capital; or
3. No change in net working capital.

Furthermore, working capital may change at the beginning of the project and
at any point during the life of the project. For example, as a new product is
introduced, sales may be terrific in the first few years, requiring an increase
in cash, accounts receivable, and inventory to support the increased sales. But
all of this requires an increase in working capital—a cash outflow.

Later, however, sales may fall off as competitors enter the market. As sales
and production fall off, the need for the increased cash, accounts receivable,
and inventory falls off also. As cash, accounts receivable, and inventory are
reduced, there is a cash inflow that becomes available for other uses within
the firm.

A change in net working capital can be thought of specifically as part of
the initial investment—the amount necessary to get the project going. It can
also be considered generally as part of operating activity—the day-to-day business of the firm. Where do we classify the cash flow associated with net working capital? With the asset acquisition and disposition represented in the new
project or with the operating cash flows?

If a project requires a change in the firm's net working capital accounts that persists for the duration of the project—say, an increase in inventory levels starting at the time of the investment—we tend to classify the change as part of the acquisition costs at the beginning of the project and as part of disposition proceeds at the end of the project. If, however, the change in net working capital occurs because accrual accounting does not coincide with cash flows, we tend to classify the change as part of operating cash flows.

Putting It All Together

Here's what we need to put together in order to calculate the change in the firm's operating cash flows related to a new investment we are considering:

- Changes in revenues and expenses.
- Cash flow from changes in taxes arising from changes in revenues and expenses.
- Cash flow from changes in cash flows arising from depreciation tax shields.
- Changes in net working capital.

There are many ways of compiling the component cash flow changes to arrive at the change in operating cash flow. We start by first calculating taxable income, making adjustments for changes in taxes, noncash expenses, and net working capital to arrive at operating cash flow:

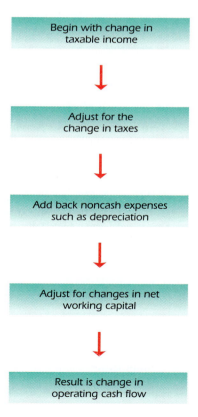

Classifying Working Capital Changes

In many applications, we can arbitrarily classify the change in working capital as either an investment cash flow or an operating cash flow. The classification doesn't really matter, since it's the bottom line, the net cash flow, that matters. How we classify the change in working capital doesn't affect a project's attractiveness.

However, we will take care in the examples in this text to classify the change in working capital as an operating or an investment cash flow so that you can see how to make the appropriate adjustments.

Suppose you are evaluating a project that is expected to increase sales by $200,000 and expenses by $150,000. Accounts receivable are expected to increase by $25,000, and accounts payable are expected to increase by $10,000, but no changes in cash or inventory are expected. Further suppose that the project's assets will have a $10,000 depreciation expense for tax purposes. If the tax rate is 40 percent, what is the operating cash flow from this project?

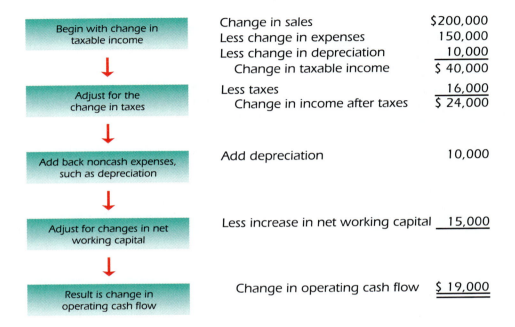

Change in sales	$200,000
Less change in expenses	150,000
Less change in depreciation	10,000
Change in taxable income	$ 40,000
Less taxes	16,000
Change in income after taxes	$ 24,000
Add depreciation	10,000
Less increase in net working capital	15,000
Change in operating cash flow	$ 19,000

Flowchart boxes (left column): Begin with change in taxable income → Adjust for the change in taxes → Add back noncash expenses, such as depreciation → Adjust for changes in net working capital → Result is change in operating cash flow

So that we can mathematically represent the way to calculate the change in operating cash flows for a project, we use the symbol Δ (the Greek capital letter delta) to indicate "change in":

ΔOCF = change in operating cash flow
ΔR   = change in revenues
ΔE   = change in expenses
ΔD   = change in depreciation
τ   = tax rate (the symbol is the Greek lower case letter tau)
ΔNWC = change in working capital

The change in the operating cash flow is:

$$\Delta OCF = (\Delta R - \Delta E - \Delta D)(1 - \tau) + \Delta D - \Delta NWC \qquad [8\text{-}1]$$

| Change in firm's operating cash flows | Change in after-tax income | Change in depreciation | Change in working capital |

We can also write this as:

$$\Delta OCF = \underbrace{(\Delta R - \Delta E)(1 - \tau)}_{} + \underbrace{\Delta D\tau}_{} - \underbrace{\Delta NWC}_{} \qquad [8\text{-}2]$$

$$\uparrow \qquad\qquad \uparrow \qquad\qquad \uparrow$$

Change in after-tax income without considering depreciation | Change in depreciation tax shield | Change in working capital

Applying Equation 8-1 to the previous example,

$$\begin{aligned}
\Delta OCF &= (\Delta R - \Delta E - \Delta D)(1 - \tau) + \Delta D - \Delta NWC \\
&= (\$200{,}000 - \$150{,}000 - \$10{,}000)(1 - 0.40) + \$10{,}000 - \$15{,}000 \\
&= \mathbf{\$19{,}000}
\end{aligned}$$

or, using the rearrangement as in Equation 8-2,

$$\begin{aligned}
\Delta OCF &= (\Delta R - \Delta E)(1 - \tau) + \Delta D\tau - \Delta NWC \\
&= (\$200{,}000 - \$150{,}000)(1 - 0.40) + \$10{,}000(0.40) - \$15{,}000 \\
&= \mathbf{\$19{,}000}
\end{aligned}$$

Let's look at one more example of the calculation of operating cash flows. Suppose you are evaluating modern equipment that you expect will reduce expenses by $100,000 during the first year. Since the new equipment is more efficient, you expect to be able to reduce the level of inventory by $20,000 during the first year. The old machine cost $200,000 and was depreciated on a ten-year basis, using the straight-line method; five years remain. The new machine cost $300,000 and will be depreciated using the straight-line method over ten years. If the firm's tax rate is 30 percent, what is the expected operating cash flow in the first year?

Let's identify the components:

$\Delta R \quad = \$0$ ← The new machine does not affect revenues.

$\Delta E \quad = -\$100{,}000$ ← The new machine reduces expenses, which will reduce taxes and increase cash flows.

$\Delta D \quad = +\$10{,}000$ ← The new machine increases the depreciation expense from $20,000 to $30,000.

$\Delta NWC = -\$20{,}000$ ← The firm can reduce its investment in inventory, releasing funds to be invested elsewhere.

$\tau \quad = 30\%$

The operating cash flow from the first year is therefore:

$$\begin{aligned}
\Delta OCF &= (\Delta R - \Delta E - \Delta D)(1 - \tau) + \Delta D - \Delta NWC \\
&= (+\$100{,}000 - \$10{,}000)(1 - 0.30) + \$10{,}000 - (-\$20{,}000) \\
&= \$63{,}000 + \$10{,}000 + \$20{,}000 \\
&= \mathbf{\$93{,}000}
\end{aligned}$$

Net Cash Flows

By now we should know that an investment's cash flows consist of (1) cash flows related to acquiring and disposing of the assets represented in the investment, and (2) cash flows from the investment's operations. To evaluate any investment project, we must consider both to determine whether or not the firm is better off with or without it.

The sum of the cash flows from asset acquisition and disposition and from operations is referred to as **net cash flows** (NCF). This sum is calculated for each period. In each period, we add the cash flow from asset acquisition and disposition and the cash flow from operations. For a given period:

$$\text{Net cash flow} = \frac{\text{investment}}{\text{cash flow}} + \frac{\text{change in operating}}{\text{cash flow } (\Delta\text{OCF})}$$

The analysis of the cash flows of investment projects can become quite complex. But by working through any problem systematically, line by line, you will be able to sort out the information and focus on those items that determine cash flows.

Simplifications

To actually analyze a project's cash flows, we need to make several simplifications:

- We assume that cash flows into or out of the firm at certain points in time, typically at the end of the year, although we realize a project's cash flows into and out of the firm at irregular intervals.
- We assume that the assets are purchased and put to work immediately.
- By combining inflows and outflows in each period, we are assuming that all inflows and outflows in a given period have the same risk.

Since there are so many flows to consider, we focus on flows within a period (say, a year), assuming they all occur at the end of the period. We assume this in order to reduce the number of things we have to keep track of. Whether or not this assumption matters depends on (1) the difference between the actual time of cash flow and the time at which we assume it flows at the end of the period (that is, a flow on January 2 is 364 days from December 31, but a flow on December 30 is only one day from December 31) and (2) the opportunity cost of funds. Also, assuming that cash flows occur at specific points in time simplifies the financial mathematics we use in valuing these flows.

Keeping track of the different cash flows of an investment project can be taxing. Developing a checklist of things to consider can help you wade through the analysis of a project's cash flows. Table 8-2 provides a checklist for the new investment and the replacement investment decisions. When you begin your analysis of an investment decision, take a look at the appropriate checklist to make sure you've covered everything.

Example 1: The Expansion of the Williams 5 & 10

The Problem

The Williams 5 & 10 Company is a discount retail chain that sells a variety of goods at low prices. Business has been very good lately, and the Williams 5 & 10 Company is considering opening one more retail outlet in a neighboring town at the end of 1999. Williams figures that it would be about five years before a large national chain of discount stores moves into that town to compete with its store. So Williams is looking at this expansion as a five-

TABLE 8-2

Capital Budgeting Checklists

Nonreplacement decision

- [ ] Asset cost
- [ ] Shipping and installation costs
- [ ] Asset disposition
- [ ] Tax effect of asset disposition
- [ ] Change in working capital (transactions or precautionary needs)

- [ ] Change in firm's revenues
- [ ] Change in firm's expenses
- [ ] Tax on change in firm's revenues and expenses
- [ ] Depreciation on asset
- [ ] Tax shield from depreciation
- [ ] Change in working capital to adjust accounting income to cash flows

Replacement decision

INVESTMENT CASH FLOWS

- [ ] New asset cost
- [ ] Shipping and installation costs on new asset
- [ ] Old asset disposition
- [ ] Tax effect of old asset disposition
- [ ] New asset disposition
- [ ] Tax effect of new asset disposition
- [ ] Change in working capital (transactions or precautionary needs)

CHANGE IN OPERATING CASH FLOWS

- [ ] Change in firm's revenues
- [ ] Change in firm's expenses
- [ ] Tax on change in firm's revenues and expenses
- [ ] Change in depreciation (new versus old)
- [ ] Tax shield from change in depreciation
- [ ] Change in working capital to adjust accounting income to cash flows

year project. After five years, the company would most likely retreat from the neighboring town.

Williams's managers have researched the expansion and determined that the building needed could be built for $400,000 and that $100,000 would have to be spent to buy the cash registers, shelves, and other equipment necessary to start up the new outlet. Under the MACRS, the building would be classified as a 31.5-year property and depreciated using the straight-line method, with no salvage value. This means that 1/31.5 of the $400,000 would be depreciated each year. Also under the MACRS, the equipment would be classified as five-year property. The Williams 5 & 10 expects to be able to sell the building for $350,000 and the equipment for $50,000 after five years.

The Williams 5 & 10 extends no credit on its sales and pays for all its purchases immediately. The projections for sales and expenses for the new store for the next five years are:

Year	Sales	Expenses
2000	$200,000	$100,000
2001	250,000	100,000
2002	300,000	100,000
2003	300,000	100,000
2004	50,000	20,000

The new store would require $50,000 of additional inventory. Since all sales are in cash, there is no expected increase in accounts receivable. However, the firm anticipates that more cash on hand will be needed to handle the increased level of sales. Projected cash on hand with and without this new store is as follows:

	Projected cash on hand	
End of year	Without new store	With new store
2000	$100,000	$120,000
2001	110,000	140,000
2002	130,000	160,000
2003	130,000	150,000
2004	120,000	120,000

The tax rate is a flat 30 percent, and there are no investment tax credits associated with this expansion. Also, capital gains are taxed at the ordinary tax rate of 30 percent.

The Analysis

To determine the relevant cash flows to evaluate this expansion, let's look at this problem bit by bit.

The Williams 5 & 10 Company is a discount retail chain that sells a variety of goods at low prices. Business has been very good lately, and the

Williams 5 & 10 Company is considering opening one more retail outlet in a neighboring town at the end of 1999.

This is an expansion of the business into a new market. Since Williams has other similar outlets, this is most likely a low-risk type of investment.

Williams figures that it would be about five years before a large national chain of discount stores moves into that town to compete with its store. So Williams is looking at this expansion as a five-year project. After five years, the company would most likely retreat from the neighboring town.

The economic life of this project is five years. Williams expects to expand into the prospective new market for only five years, leaving when a competitor enters.

Williams's managers have researched the expansion and determined that the building needed could be built for $400,000 and that $100,000 would have to be spent to buy the cash registers, shelves, and other equipment necessary to start up the new outlet.

The initial outlay for the building and equipment is $500,000. There are no setup charges, so we can assume that all other initial investment costs are included in these figures.

Under the MACRS, the building would be classified as a 31.5-year property and depreciated using the straight-line method, with no salvage value. This means that 1/31.5 of the $400,000 would be depreciated each year. Also under the MACRS, the equipment would be classified as five-year property.

The depreciation expense for each year is:

Year	Depreciation expense Building	Equipment	Total
1	$ 12,698	$ 20,000	$32,698
2	12,698	32,000	44,698
3	12,698	19,200	31,898
4	12,698	11,520	24,218
5	12,698	11,520	24,218
Total	**$63,490**	**$94,240**	

The book values of the building and equipment at the end of the fifth year are:

Book value of building = $400,000 − $63,490 = **$336,510**

and

Book value of equipment = $100,000 − $94,240 = **$5,760**

The Williams 5 & 10 expects to be able to sell the building for $350,000 and the equipment for $50,000 after five years.

The sale of the building is a cash inflow of $350,000 at the end of the fifth year. The building is expected to be sold for more than its book value, creating a taxable gain of $350,000 − $336,510 = $13,490. At the 30-percent rate, the tax on this gain is $4,047.

The sale of the equipment is a cash inflow of $50,000. The gain on the sale of the equipment is $50,000 − $5,760 = $44,240. The tax on this gain is 30 percent of 44,240, or $13,272.

The Williams 5 & 10 extends no credit on its sales and pays for all its purchases immediately. The projections for sales and expenses for the new store for the next five years are:

Year	Sales	Expenses
2000	$200,000	$100,000
2001	250,000	100,000
2002	300,000	100,000
2003	300,000	100,000
2004	50,000	20,000

The change in revenues, ΔR, and the change in cash expenses, ΔE, correspond to the sales and costs figures.

The new store would require $50,000 of additional inventory. Since all sales are in cash, there is no expected increase in accounts receivable. However, the firm anticipates that more cash on hand will be needed to handle the increased level of sales. Projected cash on hand with and without this new store is as follows:

End of year	Projected cash on hand	
	Without new store	With new store
2000	$100,000	$120,000
2001	110,000	140,000
2002	130,000	160,000
2003	130,000	150,000
2004	120,000	120,000

The increase in inventory is an investment of cash when the store is opened, that is, a $50,000 cash outflow. That's the amount Williams has to invest to maintain inventory while the store is in operation. Once the store is closed, five years later, there is no need to keep this increased level of inventory. If we assume that the inventory at the end of the fifth year can be sold for $50,000, that amount will be a cash inflow at that time. Since this is a change in working capital for the duration of the project, we include this cash flow in the calculation of asset acquisition (initially) and its disposition (at the end of the fifth year).

When additional cash is needed on hand, there is effectively a cash outflow, since Williams is tying up funds in the cash on hand. In 2000, Williams will need $120,000 on hand if it invests in the new store, but only $100,000 on hand if it does not. That means Williams is tying up $20,000 more of its cash during 2000.

If Williams invests in the new store, it will need a cash balance of $140,000 in the second year (instead of $110,000 without the new store). That means it has to tie up $30,000 more if it invests in the new store (as compared to not investing), and therefore, it needs to invest $10,000 more in cash above what was already tied up in 2000.

To determine the cash flow related to changes in cash on hand, we first calculate the change in the cash on hand each period. If cash on hand increases (in the first two years of operation), this is a cash outflow. If cash on hand decreases (in the later years of operation of the new store), that is a cash inflow, since the funds would be released for use elsewhere in the firm.

Year	Additional cash on hand	Change in cash on hand	Cash flow
2000	$20,000	+$20,000	−$20,000
2001	30,000	+10,000	−10,000
2002	30,000	0	0
2003	20,000	−10,000	+10,000
2004	0	−20,000	+20,000

In the first year, the firm is expected to invest $20,000 more in its cash on hand, which is, in effect, a negative cash flow. In the second year, an additional $10,000 will be required. In the fourth and fifth years, the cash balance is reduced, releasing cash that can be invested elsewhere in the firm.

Since the change in inventory and cash are both attributed to transactions and precautionary needs, we will classify them as part of the investment cash flows.

The tax rate is a flat 30 percent, and there are no investment tax credits associated with this expansion. Also, capital gains are taxed at the ordinary tax rate of 30 percent.

Once we know the tax rate we can calculate the cash flows related to acquiring and disposing of assets and the cash flow from operations. We can calculate the cash flows from operations by using Equation 8-1:[6]

Year	Change in revenues, ΔR	Change in expenses, ΔE	Change in depreciation, ΔD	Change in income after taxes, $(\Delta R - \Delta E - \Delta D)(1 - \tau)$	Change in operating cash flow, $(\Delta R - \Delta E - \Delta D)(1 - \tau) + \Delta D$
2001	$200,000	$100,000	$32,698	$ 47,111	$ 79,809
2002	250,000	100,000	44,698	73,711	118,409
2003	300,000	100,000	31,898	117,671	149,569
2004	300,000	100,000	24,218	123,047	147,265
2005	50,000	20,000	24,218	4,047	28,265

[6] Remember that the changes in working capital have been classified along with acquisition and disposition cash flows. Therefore, there is no ΔNWC to consider as part of the operating cash flows.

Or, we can calculate the incremental operating cash flows from the new store by using Equation 8-2:

Year	Change in revenues, ΔR	Change in expenses, ΔE	Change in revenues and expense after taxes, $(\Delta R - \Delta E)(1 - \tau)$	Change in depreciation tax shield, $\Delta D\tau$	Change in operating cash flow, $(\Delta R - \Delta E)(1 - \tau) + \Delta D\tau$
1	$200,000	$100,000	$ 70,000	$ 9,809	$ 79,809
2	250,000	100,000	105,000	13,409	118,409
3	300,000	100,000	140,000	9,569	149,569
4	300,000	100,000	140,000	7,265	147,265
5	50,000	20,000	21,000	7,265	28,265

The pieces of this cash flow puzzle are put together in Table 8-3, which identifies the cash inflows and outflows for each year, with acquisition and disposition cash flows at the top and operating cash flows below.

We can also summarize the project's net cash flows in a time line:

Investing $550,000 initially is expected to result in cash inflows during the following five years. Our next task, which we take up in the next chapter, will be to see whether investing in this project as represented by the cash flows in this time line will increase owners' wealth.

Example 2: The Replacement of Facilities at the Hirshleifer Company

The Problem

The management of the Hirshleifer Company is evaluating the replacement of its existing manufacturing equipment with new equipment. The old equipment cost $200,000 five years ago, currently has a book value of $100,000, and has been depreciated on a straight-line basis over a ten-year life with no salvage value. If the old equipment is kept, it is expected to last another five years, at which time the ten-year-old equipment could be sold for $10,000. The old equipment could be sold today for $120,000.

The new equipment costs $300,000 and is expected to have a useful life of five years. The new equipment will be depreciated for tax purposes using the MACRS and a five-year classified life.

At the end of its useful life, management expects be to able to sell the new equipment for $100,000. Meanwhile, the new equipment is expected to reduce production costs by $60,000 each year. In addition, since it is more efficient, Hirshleifer can reduce its raw material and work-in-process inventories. Hirshleifer expects to reduce its inventory by $10,000 as soon as the new equipment is placed in service.

TABLE 8-3

Estimated Incremental Cash Flows from the Williams 5 & 10 Expansion

				End of year		
	Initial	2001	2002	2003	2004	2005
Investment cash flows						
Purchase and sale of building	−$ 400,000					+$ 350,000
Tax on sale of building						−4,047
Purchase and sale of equipment	−100,000					+50,000
Tax on sale of equipment						−13,272
Change in working capital: Inventory	−50,000					+50,000
Cash		−$ 20,000	−$ 10,000	0	+$ 10,000	+20,000
Investment cash flows	−$ 550,000	−$ 20,000	−$ 10,000	0	+$ 10,000	+$ 452,681
Change in operating cash flows						
Change in revenues, ΔR		+$200,000	+$ 250,000	+$ 300,000	+$ 300,000	+$ 50,000
Change in expenses, ΔE		−100,000	−100,000	−100,000	−100,000	−20,000
Change in taxes resulting from:						
Change in revenues and expenses (ΔR − ΔE)τ		−30,000	−45,000	−60,000	−60,000	−9,000
Change in depreciation tax shield, ΔDτ		+9,809	+13,409	+9,569	+7,265	+7,265
Net change in taxes		−$ 20,191	−$ 31,591	−$ 50,431	−$ 52,735	−$ 1,735
Change in operating cash flows, ΔOCF		+$ 79,809	+$ 118,409	+$ 149,569	+$ 147,265	+$ 28,265
Net cash flows	−$550,000	+$ 59,809	+$108,409	+$149,569	+$157,265	+$480,946

Hirshleifer income is taxed at 35 percent. There are no tax credits available for this equipment.

What cash flows would the replacement equipment produce in each of the five years after purchase?

The Analysis

This is a replacement project. We need to decide whether to continue with the present equipment or replace it. To do this, we look at the effect on the cash flows if we replace the equipment relative to the effect if we keep the existing equipment. Instead of analyzing the problem line by line, as we did for the Williams 5 & 10, let's take a different approach, looking first at the cash flows related to the acquisition and disposal of the assets and then at the operating cash flows.

Investment Cash Flows

The new equipment requires an immediate cash outlay of $300,000. It will be depreciated using the specified rates, where $20.00\% + 32.00\% + 19.20\% + 11.52\% + 11.52\% = 94.24\%$ of its cost is depreciated by the end of the fifth year. That leaves a book value of 5.76% of $300,000, or $17,280. The expected selling price of the new equipment at the end of the fifth year is greater than the equipment's book value, so there is a gain on the sale of the equipment of $100,000 − $17,280 = $82,720.

Since the selling price is less than the original cost, the gain is taxed as a recapture of depreciation at ordinary tax rates. The sale of the new equipment in the fifth year creates a gain of $82,720. The cash outflow for taxes on this gain is $0.35 \times \$82,720 = \$28,952$.

The $200,000 cost of the old equipment is a sunk cost and is not directly relevant to our analysis. However, we need to consider the book value of the old equipment in computing a gain or loss on its sale. We also need to consider the cost of the old equipment to determine whether any gain on its sale would be a capital gain or a recapture of depreciation.

By selling the old equipment now for $120,000, which is greater than the book value, the firm incurs a gain of $20,000: $120,000 − $100,000 = $20,000. This is a recapture of depreciation—taxed at 35 percent—since the sales price is less than the original cost of $200,000.

Disposing of the old equipment produces two tax-related cash flows: the tax on the sale of the old equipment when the new equipment is purchased, which is an outflow of $0.35 \times \$20,000 = \$7,000$, and the tax the firm would have had to pay on the sale of the old equipment in the fifth year, which is an inflow of $0.35 \times \$10,000 = \$3,500$.

If the firm replaces the old equipment today, it forgoes the sale of the equipment in five years for $10,000. We need to consider both the forgone cash flow from this sale as well as any forgone taxes or tax benefit on this sale.

And let's not forget about the change in net working capital. The reduction in inventory is a cash inflow, since inventory can be reduced. If we assume it is reduced immediately, there is a $10,000 cash inflow initially. Assuming that inventory returns to its previous level at the end of the new equipment's life, there will be a $10,000 cash outflow at the end of the fifth year. Let's summarize the investment cash flows:

INITIALLY

Purchase of new equipment	−$ 300,000
Sale of old equipment	+120,000
Tax on sale of old equipment	−7,000
Decrease in inventory	+10,000
Total investment cash flow	**−$177,000**

FIFTH YEAR

Sale of new equipment	+$100,000
Tax on sale of new equipment	−28,952
Forgone sale of old equipment	−10,000
Forgone tax on sale of old equipment	+3,500
Increase in inventory	−10,000
Total investment cash flow	**+$ 54,548**

Operating Cash Flows

If the old equipment is kept, depreciation would continue to be $200,000/10 years = $20,000 per year for each of the next five years. If the equipment is replaced, the firm would no longer incur this depreciation expense.

The new equipment would be depreciated over five years. Comparing the depreciation expense for the old and the new equipment, we determine the change in taxes resulting from the change in the depreciation tax shield:

	New equipment			
Year	Rate of depreciation	Depreciation expense	Depreciation expense of old equipment	Change in depreciation expense[a]
1	20.00%	$ 60,000	$ 20,000	$40,000
2	32.00	96,000	20,000	76,000
3	19.20	57,600	20,000	37,600
4	11.52	34,560	20,000	14,560
5	11.52	34,560	20,000	14,560
		$282,720	$100,000	

[a]Depreciation expense of new equipment minus depreciation expense of old equipment.

The reduction in costs is a cash inflow: Less cash is paid out with the new equipment than with the old equipment. But there is also additional taxable income: The new machine will reduce expenses by $60,000 each year; so taxable income increases by $60,000 each year, increasing taxes each year.

Using equation 8-1:

Year	Change in revenues, ΔR	Change in expenses, ΔE	Change in depreciation, ΔD	Change in income after taxes, $(\Delta R - \Delta E - \Delta D)(1 - \tau)$	Change in operating cash flow, $(\Delta R - \Delta E - \Delta D)(1 - \tau) + \Delta D$
1	$0	−$60,000	$40,000	$13,000	$53,000
2	0	−60,000	76,000	−10,400	65,600
3	0	−60,000	37,600	14,560	52,160
4	0	−60,000	14,560	29,536	44,096
5	0	−60,000	14,560	29,536	44,096

Or, using equation 8-2:

Year	Change in revenues, ΔR	Change in expenses, ΔE	Change in revenues and expenses after taxes, $(\Delta R - \Delta E)(1 - \tau)$	Change in depreciation tax shield, $\Delta D\tau$	Change in operating cash flow, $(\Delta R - \Delta E)(1 - \tau) + \Delta D\tau$
1	$0	−$60,000	$39,000	$14,000	$53,000
2	0	−60,000	39,000	26,600	65,600
3	0	−60,000	39,000	13,160	52,160
4	0	−60,000	39,000	5,096	44,096
5	0	−60,000	39,000	5,096	44,096

The project's cash flows are shown in Table 8-4. We can summarize the net cash flows in a time line:

Investing $177,000 initially is expected to generate cash inflows shown in the time line in the next five years. Our task, which we will take up in the next chapter, is to evaluate these cash flows to see whether taking on this project will increase owners' wealth.

CASH FLOW ESTIMATION IN PRACTICE

So how do firms actually estimate cash flows for the projects they are considering investing in? We learn how cash flows are estimated for capital projects by looking at the results of surveys of U.S. corporations. This evidence indicates that:[7]

- The person estimating cash flows is an accountant, an analyst, treasurer, controller, vice president of finance, or a person reporting directly to the treasurer or vice president of finance.

[7] Randolph A. Pohlman, Emmanuel S. Santiago, and F. Lynn Markel, "Cash Flow Estimation Practices of Large Firms," *Financial Management*, vol. 17, Summer 1988, pp. 71–79.

TABLE 8-4

Estimated Incremental Cash Flows from the Replacement of Facilities at the Hirshleifer Company

	Initial	Year 1	Year 2	Year 3	Year 4	Year 5
Investment cash flows						
Purchase and sale of new equipment	−$ 300,000					+$100,000
Tax on sale of new equipment						−28,952
Sale of old equipment	+120,000					−10,000
Tax on sale of old equipment	−7,000					+3,500
Change in working capital	+10,000					−10,000
Investment cash flows	−$ 177,000					+$ 54,548
Change in operating cash flows						
Change in expenses, ΔE		+$ 60,000	+$ 60,000	+$ 60,000	+$ 60,000	+$ 60,000
Change in taxes resulting from:						
Change in expenses, $\Delta E\tau$		−21,000	−21,000	−21,000	−21,000	−21,000
Change in depreciation tax shield, $\Delta D\tau$		+14,000	+26,600	+13,160	+5,096	+5,096
Net change in taxes		−$ 7,000	+$ 5,600	−$ 7,840	−$ 15,904	−$ 15,904
Change in operating cash flows, ΔOCF		+$ 53,000	+$ 65,600	+$ 52,160	+$ 44,096	+$ 44,096
Net cash flows	−$177,000	+$53,000	+$65,500	+$52,160	+$44,096	+$ 98,644

- Most firms have standard procedures for estimating cash flows.
- Most firms arrive at cash flow estimates derived from a variety of sources, but rely mainly on the subjective judgment of management.
- Most firms consider working capital requirements in their analysis of cash flows.
- Most firms consider taxes in their analysis of cash flows.
- Sales and operating expense forecasts are a key ingredient in estimating cash flows.

Estimating cash flows for capital projects is perhaps the most difficult part of the investment screening and selection process.

We know that it is necessary to consider cash flows related to the acquisition and disposal of the assets, and to operations. In our analysis, we must not forget to consider working capital and the cash flows related to taxes, being aware, all the while, that we are working with estimates—forecasts of the future.

We are making our best guess as to:

- The cost of the assets.
- The benefits or costs of disposing of the assets at the end of the project.
- Sales in each future period.
- Expenses in each future period.
- Tax rates in each future period.
- Working capital needs in each future period.

Implicit in our forecasts are judgments pertaining to:

- Competitors' reactions to our investment.
- Changes in the tax code.
- The costs of materials and labor.
- The time it takes to get the project under way.

Looking at how cash flows are estimated, we see that corporations analyze all the key elements—sales, expenses, taxes, working capital—yet apply judgment in arriving at the estimates of these elements. Cash flow estimation is not a process that lends itself well to the application of mechanical formulas. Though we can apply formulas that help us put the key elements together, we should keep in mind that cash flow estimates are determined, in large part, by marketing analyses, engineering studies, and, most important, managerial experience.

SUMMARY

- The capital budgeting process requires identifying, screening, and selecting investment projects. These projects provide benefits in the future by increasing the firm's cash flows in future years.

- Estimating future cash flows requires estimating cash flows of the firm with and without the investment and observing how the cash flows change if the investment is made.

- Estimating changes in cash flows (that is, incremental cash flows) requires forecasting future sales, expenses, and taxes, as well as the effect of the project on net working capital.

- Calculation of cash flows from the acquisition and disposal of assets must take into account (1) the direct cash flows from purchases and sales of assets, (2) the tax consequences of sales, and (3) any forgone cash flows from the sale of assets.

- Changes in net working capital arise in an investment project from two sources: (1) an increased need for cash, accounts receivable, or inventory to meet a larger scale of operations or (2) a need to adjust accounting estimates that are on the accrual basis to a cash basis.

- Putting these estimates together with the estimated cash flows from the acquisition and disposal of the assets of the investment project, we calculate the net cash flows for each future period. We then determine whether this investment is consistent with the goal of owners' wealth maximization, applying evaluation techniques to be developed in the next chapter.

QUESTIONS

8-1 How does an investment in a new product five years ago affect the value of the firm today?

8-2 Why might the economic life of an asset be shorter than its actual, physical expected life?

8-3 While the objective of short-term and long-term investments is the same, the approaches we use to analyze these two types of investments are different. Why would the approaches to analyzing our investment in cash—the amount of cash we have on hand—be different from our investment in a new product?

8-4 Suppose a toy manufacturer is faced with the following collection of investment projects:
- **a.** Opening a retail outlet.
- **b.** Introducing a new line of dolls.
- **c.** Introducing a new action figure in an existing line of action figures.
- **d.** Adding another packaging line to the production process.

e. Adding pollution control equipment to avoid environmental fines.
f. Computerizing the doll-molding equipment.
g. Introducing a child's version of an existing adult board game.

Classify each project into one of the following four categories: expansion, replacement, new product or market, or mandated.

8-5 A shoe manufacturer is considering introducing a new line of boots. When evaluating the incremental revenues from this new line, what should be considered?

8-6 If you sell an asset for more than its book value, but less than its original cost, we refer to this gain as a recapture of depreciation, and it is taxed at ordinary income tax rates. Why?

8-7 How does a capital loss on the disposition of an asset generate a cash inflow?

8-8 If a project's projected revenues and expenses are on a cash basis, is there any need to adjust for a change in working capital? Explain.

8-9 If a firm replaces its production line with equipment with lower depreciation expenses, will the tax cash flow from depreciation be an inflow or an outflow? Explain.

8-10 Classify each of the following changes as an increase or decrease of the operating cash flow:

a. An increase in raw materials inventory.
b. An increase in salaries and wages payable.
c. An increase in accounts receivable.
d. A decrease in raw materials inventory.
e. A decrease in accounts receivable.
f. A decrease in accounts payable.
g. A decrease in finished goods inventory.
h. A decrease in accounts receivable.

8-11 Depreciation does not involve a cash flow; yet we consider cash flows from depreciation as a tax shield. What is the depreciation tax shield, and how does it produce a cash flow?

8-12 Suppose a firm buys an asset, depreciates it over its ten-year MACRS life, and then sells it for $100,000 fifteen years after it was bought. Without performing any calculations, describe the tax consequences related to the asset's purchase, depreciation, and sale.

PROBLEMS

Investment cash flows

8-1 Suppose you buy an asset for $1 million. If it costs $100,000 for shipping and installation, how much is your investment outlay?

8-2 Suppose you buy an asset for $100,000 that is depreciated for tax purposes over twenty years using the straight-line method. Break down the tax effects resulting from the sale of this asset five years later if the sales price is:

a. $125,000
b. $100,000
c. $75,000
d. $50,000

8-3 The Fester Electrical Equipment Company is considering the purchase of one of two different wire-soldering machines. Machine 1 has an initial cost of $100,000, costs $20,000 to set up, and is expected to be sold for $20,000 after ten years. Machine 2 has an initial cost of $80,000, costs $30,000 to set up, and is expected to be sold for $10,000 after ten years. Both machines would be depreciated over ten years using the straight-line method. Fester has a tax rate of 35 percent.

a. What are the cash flows related to the acquisition of each machine?
b. What are the cash flows related to the disposition of each machine?

8-4 The Morticia Casket Company is considering the purchase of a new polishing machine. The existing polishing machine cost $100,000 five years ago and is being depreciated on a straight-line basis over a ten-year life. Morticia's management estimates that it can sell the old machine for $60,000. The new machine costs $150,000 and would be depreciated over five years using the MACRS. At the end of the fifth year, Morticia's management expects to be able to sell the new polishing machine for $75,000. The marginal tax rate is 40 percent.

a. What are the cash flows related to the acquisition of the new machine?
b. What are the cash flows related to the disposition of the old machine?
c. What are the cash flows related to the disposition of the new machine?

8-5 Mama's Goulash Company is considering purchasing a dishwasher. The dishwasher costs $50,000 and would be depreciated over three years using the MACRS. After three years, Mama's plans to sell the dishwasher for $10,000. The marginal tax rate is 40 percent.

a. What are the cash flows related to the acquisition of the dishwasher?
b. What are the cash flows related to the disposition of the dishwasher?

Operating cash flows

8-6 If an investment is expected to increase revenues by $100,000 per year for five years, with no effect on expenses or working capital, what is the operating cash flow per year if depreciation is $20,000 each year and the tax rate is:

a. 20 percent?
b. 30 percent?
c. 40 percent?
d. 50 percent?

8-7 The Gomez Mustache Wax Company is evaluating the purchase of a new wax-molding machine. The machine costs $100,000 and has a useful life of five years. How do the cash flows differ when straight-line depreciation is used instead of MACRS depreciation for tax purposes, assuming a tax rate of 40 percent and no salvage value?

8-8 Calculate the operating cash flow for each year using the following information:

- The machine costs $1 million and is depreciated using the straight-line method over five years.
- The machine will increase sales by $150,000 per year for five years.
- The tax rate is 40 percent.
- Working capital needs will increase by $10,000 when the machine is placed in service and will be reduced at the end of the life of the machine.
- There is no salvage value at the end of the five years.

8-9 Calculate the operating cash flow for each year using the following information:

- The equipment costs $200,000, and is depreciated using the MACRS over five years.
- The equipment will reduce operating expenses by $25,000 per year for five years.
- The tax rate is 30 percent.
- Working capital needs will increase by $10,000 when the machine is placed in service and will be reduced at the end of the life of the machine.
- There is no salvage value at the end of the five years.

8-10 Calculate the operating cash flow for each year, using the following information:

- The asset costs $1 million and is depreciated using the MACRS for a three-year asset.
- The machine will reduce operating expenses by $120,000 per year for three years.
- The tax rate is 45 percent.
- Working capital needs will decrease by $10,000 when the machine is placed in service and will increase at the end of the life of the machine.
- The asset can be sold for $400,000 at the end of the three years.

Net cash flows

8-11 I. T. Company is a beauty products business that is considering the purchase of a new hair-growth product. The new product would encourage hair growth of persons with thinning hair. The new product is expected to generate sales of $500,000 per year and would cost $300,000 to produce each year. It is expected that the patent on the new product would prevent competition from entering the market for at least seven years.

I. T. Company spent $1 million to develop the new product over the past four years. The equipment to produce the new product would cost $1.5 million and would be depreciated for tax purposes as a five-year MACRS asset. I. T.'s management estimates that the equipment could be sold after seven years for $400,000. The company's marginal tax rate is 40 percent.

a. What are the initial cash flows related to the new product?
b. What are the cash flows related to the disposition of the equipment after the seven years?
c. What are the operating cash flows for each year?
d. What are the net cash flows for each year?

8-12 The Pugsly Dynamite Company is considering the purchase of a new packing machine. The existing packing machine cost $500,000 five years ago and is being depreciated on a straight-line basis over a ten-year life. Pugsly's management executives estimate they can sell the old machine for $100,000. The new machine costs $600,000 and would be depreciated over five years using the straight-line method. The new machine has no salvage value. The new machine is more efficient and would reduce packing expenses (damaged goods) by $120,000 per year for the next five years. The marginal tax rate is 30 percent.
a. What are the cash flows related to the acquisition of the new machine?
b. What are the cash flows related to the disposition of the old machine?
c. What are the cash flows related to the disposition of the new machine?
d. What are the operating cash flows for each year?
e. What are the net cash flows for each year?

8-13 The Wednesday Trench Company is considering the purchase of new digging equipment. The existing equipment cost $1 million five years ago and is being depreciated, using the MACRS, as a five-year asset. Wednesday's management estimates it can sell the old equipment for $200,000.

The new equipment costs $1.2 million and would be depreciated over five years using the MACRS. At the end of the fifth year, Wednesday's management intends to sell the new equipment for $400,000. The new equipment is more efficient and would reduce expenses by $200,000 per year for the next five years. The marginal tax rate is 35 percent.

a. What are the cash flows related to the acquisition of the new equipment?
b. What are the cash flows related to the disposition of the old equipment?
c. What are the cash flows related to the disposition of the new equipment?
d. What are the operating cash flows for each year?
e. What are the net cash flows for each year?

8-14 The Lurch Cleaning Service Company is considering replacing its cleaning equipment. The existing equipment cost $100,000 five years ago and was depreciated, using the MACRS, as a three-year asset. The management of Lurch estimates it can sell the old equipment for $10,000. The new equipment costs $120,000 and would be depreciated, using the MACRS, as a three-year asset. At the end of five years, Lurch's management expects to sell the new equipment for $200,000. The new equipment is more efficient and would reduce expenses by $20,000 per year for the next five years. The marginal tax rate is 30 percent.

a. What are the cash flows related to the acquisition of the new equipment?

b. What are the cash flows related to the disposition of the old equipment?

c. What are the cash flows related to the disposition of the new equipment?

d. What are the operating cash flows for each year?

e. What are the net cash flows for each year?

FURTHER READINGS

A discussion of how the capital budgeting of a business enterprise and its strategic plan are related can be found in:
STEWART C. MYERS, "Finance Theory and Financial Strategy," *Interfaces*, Jan.–Feb., 1984, pp. 126–137.

While capital budgeting tends to be a "bottoms-up" process and the development of a strategic plan tends to be a "top-down" process, consistency between the two is important.

American Can, like many large businesses, faces the dilemma of working with many business units, distinguishing between operating expenditures and capital investment expenditures, and linking its strategic plan to its capital budgeting decisions. The capital budgeting process of a U.S. corporation, American Can, is detailed in:
RICHARD MARSHUETZ, "How American Can Allocates Capital," *Harvard Business Review*, Jan.–Feb., 1985, pp. 82–91.

Project tracking and postcompletion analysis are important aspects of the investment project analysis. However, managers tend to resist terminating a losing project, as discussed in:
MEIR STATMAN and DAVID CALDWELL, "Applying Behavioral Finance to Capital Budgeting: Project Terminations," *Financial Management*, vol. 16, Winter 1987, pp. 7–15.

CHAPTER 9

Evaluating Capital Projects

INTRODUCTION 389

EVALUATION TECHNIQUES 389

Payback Period 391

    The Payback-Period Decision Rule 392

    Payback Period as an Evaluation Technique 393

Discounted Payback Period 394

    The Discounted-Payback Decision Rule 395

    Discounted Payback as an Evaluation Technique 396

Net Present Value 399

    The Net Present Value Decision Rule 401

    Net Present Value as an Evaluation Technique 402

    The Investment Profile 404

    The NPV and Further Considerations 405

Profitability Index 406

    The Profitability-Index Decision Rule 407

    Profitability Index as an Evaluation Technique 407

Internal Rate of Return 411

    The Internal-Rate-of-Return Decision Rule 414

    Internal Rate of Return as an Evaluation Technique 417

Modified Internal Rate of Return 420

    The Modified Internal-Rate-of-Return Decision Rule 425

    Modified Internal Rate of Return as an Evaluation Technique 426

COMPARING TECHNIQUES 428

CAPITAL BUDGETING TECHNIQUES IN PRACTICE 432

Summary 434

What's Next? The Brooklyn Bridge?

In 1991, Prudential Insurance Company of America sold the Empire State building in New York City for $40 million. If you were the buyer, what did you get when you bought this building? You got a building leased to a limited partnership for the next 84 years. In turn, the partnership leases space to tenants. The partnership receives about $40 million a year in lease income and pays a much smaller amount annually to the building's owner, as specified in the building's master lease. As the building's owner, you get a stream of future lease payments from the partnership, specifically:

- From 1992 through 2012: $1.9 million per year.
- From 2013 through 2075: $1.7 million per year.

Suppose you paid $40 million for the building and your tax rate is 34 percent. For simplicity, let's assume you pay no real estate taxes and no maintenance costs. What will you get on your investment?

Your only cost is that for the building itself, which is depreciated for tax purposes using the straight-line method over 31.5 years, or $1,269,841 per year. This, in effect, generates a positive cash flow, since it shields your income from taxes: 34 percent of $1,269,841, or $431,746 per year, for the first thirty-one years; half of that for the thirty-second year; and no depreciation tax shield after that.

Years	Lease income after taxes	Depreciation tax shield	Cash flow (lease income after taxes plus depreciation tax shield)
1992 through 2012	$1,900,000(1 − 0.34)	$431,746	$1,685,746
2013 through 2022	1,700,000(1 − 0.34)	431,746	1,553,746
2023	1,700,000(1 − 0.34)	215,873	1,337,873
2024 through 2075	1,700,000(1 − 0.34)		1,122,000

Let's ignore the cash flows beyond 2075, since they won't be worth much in 1991 (if the discount rate is 5 percent, $1 in 2075 is worth less than 2 cents in 1991).

What annual return do you get on your $40 million investment? Given the cash flows estimated above, the yield on this investment is 3.54 percent.[1] This yield is much lower than the yield on the default-free, long-term U.S. government bonds that were available in 1991 at about 8 percent.

[1] It is estimated that without the master lease to the limited partnership, the building would be worth $450 million (Neil Barsky, "Empire State Building to Be Sold to a Peter Grace Family Member," *The Wall Street Journal*, Oct. 31, 1991, p. B1). However, since the building is tied up in the lease for the next 84 years, the value of the building is substantially less.

INTRODUCTION

The value of a firm today is the present value of all its future cash flows. These future cash flows come from assets already in place and from future investment opportunities. The future cash flows are discounted at a rate that represents investors' assessments of the uncertainty that the sums will flow in the amounts and at the times expected:

$$\text{Value of a firm} = \begin{array}{c}\text{present value}\\\text{of all future}\\\text{cash flows}\end{array} = \begin{array}{c}\text{present value}\\\text{of cash flows from}\\\text{all assets in place}\end{array} + \begin{array}{c}\text{present value}\\\text{of cash flows from}\\\text{future investment}\\\text{opportunities}\end{array}$$

The objective of the financial manager is to maximize the value of the firm. In a corporation, the shareholders are the residual owners of the firm, so decisions that maximize the value of the firm also maximize shareholders' wealth.

The financial manager makes decisions regarding long-lived assets by carrying out a process referred to as **capital budgeting.** The capital budgeting decisions for a project require analysis of:

- Its future cash flows.
- The degree of uncertainty associated with these future cash flows.
- The value of these future cash flows after taking their uncertainty into consideration.

We looked at how to estimate cash flows in Chapter 8, in which we were concerned with a project's incremental cash flows, which comprise changes in operating cash flows (change in revenues, expenses, and taxes) and changes in investment cash flows (the firm's incremental cash flows from the acquisition and disposition of the project's assets).

We know the concept behind uncertainty: The more uncertain a future cash flow, the less it is worth today. The degree of uncertainty, or risk, is reflected in a project's cost of capital. The **cost of capital** is what the firm must pay for the funds to finance its investment. The cost of capital may be an explicit cost (for example, the interest paid on debt) or an implicit cost (for example, the expected price appreciation of its shares of common stock).

In this chapter, we focus on evaluating the future cash flows. *Given* estimates of incremental cash flows for a project and *given* a cost of capital that reflects the project's risk, we look at alternative techniques that are used to select projects.

For now all we need to understand about a project's risk is that we can incorporate risk in one of two ways: (1) We can discount future cash flows using a discount rate that reflects the risk of the flow (the greater the cash flow's risk, the higher the rate), or (2) we can require a level of annual return on the project that reflects the risk (the greater the risk of its cash flows, the higher the required annual return). We will look at specific ways of estimating risk and incorporating it into the discount rate in Chapter 10.

EVALUATION TECHNIQUES

Look at the incremental cash flows for Investments A and B shown in Table 9-1. Can you tell by looking at the cash flows for Investment A whether or not it enhances wealth? Or, can you tell by just looking at Investments A and B which one is better? Perhaps, with some projects, you may think you can

TABLE 9-1

Four Pairs of Projects for Evaluation Using Six Different Techniques

From these evaluations, we will learn what each technique can and cannot tell us about an investment under consideration.

INVESTMENTS A AND B

Each project requires an investment of $1 million at the end of the year 2000 and has a cost of capital of 10 percent per year.

	Cash flows	
End of year	Investment A	Investment B
2001	$400,000	$ 100,000
2002	400,000	100,000
2003	400,000	100,000
2004	400,000	1,000,000
2005	400,000	1,000,000

INVESTMENTS C AND D

Each project requires an investment of $1 million at the end of the year 2000 and has a cost of capital of 10 percent per year.

	Cash flows	
End of year	Investment C	Investment D
2001	$300,000	$ 300,000
2002	300,000	300,000
2003	300,000	300,000
2004	300,000	300,000
2005	300,000	10,000,000

INVESTMENTS E AND F

Each project requires an investment of $1 million at the end of the year 2000 and has a cost of capital of 5 percent per year.

	Cash flows	
End of year	Investment E	Investment F
2001	$300,000	0
2002	300,000	0
2003	300,000	0
2004	300,000	$1,200,000
2005	300,000	300,000

INVESTMENTS G AND H

Each project requires an investment of $1 million at the end of the year 2000. Investment G's cost of capital is 5 percent per year; Investment H's is 10 percent per year.

	Cash flows	
End of year	Investment G	Investment H
2001	$250,000	$250,000
2002	250,000	250,000
2003	250,000	250,000
2004	250,000	250,000
2005	250,000	250,000

pick out the better one simply by gut feeling or by eyeballing the cash flows. But why do it that way when there are precise methods to evaluate investments on the basis of their cash flows?

To screen investment projects and select the one that maximizes wealth, we must determine the cash flows from each investment and then assess their uncertainty.

We look at six techniques that are commonly used by firms to evaluate investments in long-term assets:

- Payback period
- Discounted-payback period
- Net present value

- Profitability index
- Internal rate of return
- Modified internal rate of return

We are interested in how well each technique discriminates among the different projects and steers us toward the projects that maximize owners' wealth.
An evaluation technique should:

- Consider all the future incremental cash flows from the project.
- Consider the time value of money.
- Consider the uncertainty associated with future cash flows.

Projects selected using a technique that satisfies all three criteria will, under most general conditions, maximize owners' wealth. It is also useful for there to be objective rules or criteria associated with a technique to determine which project or projects to select.

In addition to judging whether each technique satisfies the three criteria above, we will also look at which techniques can be used in special situations, such as when a dollar limit is placed on the capital budget.

We will demonstrate each technique and determine in what way and how well it evaluates each of the projects described in Table 9-1.

Payback Period

No gain is possible without attendant outlay, but there will be no profit if the outlay exceeds the receipts.

Plautus, c. 218 B.C.

The **payback period** for a project runs from the time when initial cash outflow takes place for investment in the project to the time when the project's cash inflows add up to the initial cash outflow—in other words, the length of time it takes to get your money back. The payback period is also referred to as the **payoff period** or the **capital recovery period**. If you invest $10,000 today and are promised $5,000 one year from today and $5,000 two years from today, the payback period is two years—it takes two years to get your $10,000 investment back.

Suppose you are considering Investments A and B, each requiring an investment of $1 million today (we're considering today to be the last day of the year 2000) and promising cash flows at the end of each of the following five years, as described in Table 9-1.

How long will it take to get your $1 million investment back? The payback period for Investment A is three years:

	Investment A		
End of year	Expected cash flow	Accumulated cash flow	
2001	$400,000	$ 400,000	
2002	400,000	800,000	
2003	400,000	1,200,000	← $1,000,000 investment is paid back
2004	400,000	1,600,000	
2005	400,000	2,000,000	

By the end of 2002, the full $1 million is not paid back, but by 2003, the accumulated cash flow hits (and exceeds) $1 million. Therefore, the payback period for Investment A is three years.

The payback period for Investment B is four years:

	Investment B			
End of year	Expected cash flow	Accumulated cash flow		
2001	$ 100,000	$ 100,000		
2002	100,000	200,000		
2003	100,000	300,000		
2004	1,000,000	1,300,000	←	$1,000,000 investment paid back
2005	1,000,000	2,300,000		

It is not until the end of 2004 that the original $1 million investment (and more) is paid back.

The Payback-Period-Decision Rule

Is Investment A or B more attractive? A shorter payback period is better than a longer payback period. Yet there is no clear-cut rule for how much shorter is better.

Investment A provides a quicker payback than B. But that doesn't mean it provides the better value for the firm. All we know is that A "pays for itself" more quickly than B. We do not know in this particular case whether quicker is better.

In addition to having no well-defined decision criteria, payback-period analysis favors investments with "front-loaded" cash flows: An investment looks better in terms of the payback period the sooner its cash flows are received, no matter what its later cash flows look like!

Payback-period analysis is a type of "break-even" measure. It tends to provide a measure of the economic life of the investment in terms of its payback period. The more likely it is that the life exceeds the payback period, the more attractive is the investment. The economic life beyond the payback period is referred to as the ***postpayback duration.*** If the postpayback duration is zero, the investment is worthless, *no matter how short the payback.* This is because the sum of the future cash flows is no greater than the initial investment outlay. And since these future cash flows are really worth less today than in the future, a zero postpayback duration means that the present value of the future cash flows is *less* than the project's initial investment.

Payback should be used only as a coarse initial screen of investment projects. But it can be a useful indicator of some things. Since a dollar of cash flow in the early years is worth more than a dollar of cash flow in later years, the payback-period method provides a simple, yet crude measure of the value of the investment.

The payback period also offers some indication on the risk of the investment. In industries in which equipment becomes obsolete rapidly or in which

Fractional Payback

We have assumed that the cash flows are received at the end of the year. So we always arrive at a payback period in terms of a whole number of years. If we assume that the cash flows are received, say, uniformly, such as monthly or weekly, throughout the year, we arrive at a payback period in terms of years and *fractions* of years.

For example, assuming we receive cash flows monthly throughout the year, the payback period for Investment A is 2.5 years (two years and six months), and the payback period for Investment B is 3.7 years (three years and eight and one-half months).

Our assumption of end-of-period cash flows may be unrealistic, but is helpful in demonstrating how to use the various evaluation techniques. We will continue to use this end-of-period assumption throughout the chapter.

conditions are very competitive, investments with earlier payback are more valuable. That's because cash flows further into the future are more uncertain and therefore have lower present value. In the personal computer industry, for example, the fierce competition and rapidly changing technology require investment in projects that have a payback of less than one year, since there is no expectation of project benefits beyond that.

Furthermore, the payback period gives us a rough measure of the liquidity of the investment—how soon we get cash flows from our investment.

However, because the payback method doesn't identify the particular payback period that maximizes wealth, we cannot use it as the primary screening device for investment in long-lived assets.

Payback Period as an Evaluation Technique

Does Payback Consider All Cash Flows?

Let's look at Investments C and D in Table 9-1. Let's assume that their cash flows have similar risk, require an initial outlay of $1 million each, and have cash flows at the end of each year.

Both investments have a payback period of four years. If we used only the payback period to evaluate them, it's likely we would conclude that both investments are identical. Yet, Investment D is more valuable because of the cash flow of $10 million in 2005. The payback method does not recognize the $10 million! We know C and D cannot be equal. Certainly Investment D's $10 million in the year 2005 is more valuable in 2000 than Investment C's $300,000.

The payback-period method ignores cash flows occurring after the payback period.

Does Payback Consider the Timing of Cash Flows?

Let's look at Investments E and F. They have similar risk, require an investment of $1 million each, and have the expected end-of-year cash flows described in Table 9-1. The payback period of both investments is four years. But the cash flows of Investment F are received later in the four-year period than those of Investment E. We know that there is a time value to money—receiving money sooner is better than later—that is not considered in a payback evaluation.

The payback-period method ignores the timing of cash flows.

Does Payback Consider the Riskiness of Cash Flows?

Let's look at Investments G and H. Each requires an investment of $1 million, and both have identical cash inflows. If we assume that the cash flows of Investment G are less risky than the cash flows of Investment H, can the payback period help us to decide which is preferable?

The payback period of both investments is four years. The payback period is *identical* for these two investments, even though the cash flows of Investment H are riskier and therefore less valuable today than those of Investment G. But we know that the more uncertain the future cash flow, the less valuable it is today.

The payback period ignores the risk associated with cash flows.

Is Payback Consistent with Owners' Wealth Maximization?

There is no connection between an investment's payback period and its profitability. The payback-period evaluation ignores the time value of money, the uncertainty of future cash flows, and the contribution of a project to the value of the firm.

Therefore, the payback-period method is not going to pick out projects that maximize owners' wealth.

Discounted-Payback Period

The *discounted-payback period* is the time needed to pay back the original investment in terms of *discounted* future cash flows.

Each cash flow is discounted back to the beginning of the investment at a rate that reflects both the time value of money and the uncertainty of the future cash flows. This rate is the cost of capital—the return required by the suppliers of capital (creditors and owners) to compensate them for the time value of money and the risk associated with the investment. The more uncertain are the future cash flows, the greater is the cost of capital.

Suppose that Investments A and B each have a cost of capital of 10 percent. The first step in determining the discounted-payback period is to discount each year's cash flow to the beginning of the investment (the end of the year 2000) at the cost of capital:

	Investment A		Investment B	
End of year	Cash flow	Value at end of 2000	Cash flow	Value at end of 2000
2001	$400,000	$363,636	$ 100,000	$ 90,909
2002	400,000	330,579	100,000	82,645
2003	400,000	300,526	100,000	75,131
2004	400,000	273,205	1,000,000	683,013
2005	400,000	248,369	1,000,000	620,921

How long does it take for each investment's discounted cash flows to pay back the $1 million investment? The discounted-payback period for A is four years:

End of year	Value at end of 2000	Accumulated discounted cash flows		
2001	$363,640	$ 363,640		
2002	330,580	694,220		
2003	300,530	994,750		
2004	273,205	1,267,955	←	$1,000,000 investment paid back
2005	248,369	1,516,324		

The Cost of
Capital, the
Required
Rate of
Return, and
the Discount
Rate

We discount an uncertain future cash flow to the present at some rate that reflects the degree of uncertainty associated with this future cash flow. The more uncertain is the cash flow, the less the cash flow is worth today—this means that a higher discount rate is used to translate it into a value today.

This discount rate is a rate that reflects the opportunity cost of funds. In the case of a corporation, we consider the opportunity cost of funds for the suppliers of capital (the creditors and owners). We refer to this opportunity cost as the cost of capital.

The cost of capital comprises the *required rate of return* (RRR) (the return suppliers of capital demand on their investment), adjusted for tax benefits from interest deductibility, and the cost of raising new capital if the firm cannot generate the needed capital internally (that is, from retaining earnings). Since the difference between the cost of capital and the required rate of return is usually quite small, and since the cost of capital and the required rate of return basically express the same concept, but from different perspectives, we sometimes use the terms interchangeably in our study of capital budgeting.

The discounted-payback period for B is five years:

| End of year | Investment B | |
	Value at end of 2000	Accumulated discounted cash flows
2001	$ 90,909	$ 90,909
2002	82,645	173,554
2003	75,131	248,685
2004	683,010	931,698
2005	620,921	1,552,619 ← $1,000,000 investment paid back

This example shows that it takes one more year to pay back each investment with discounted cash flows than with nondiscounted cash flows.

The Discounted-Payback-Decision Rule

It appears that the shorter the payback period, the better, whether using discounted or nondiscounted cash flows. But how much shorter is better? We don't know. All we know is that an investment breaks even in terms of discounted cash flows at the discounted-payback period—the point in time at which the accumulated discounted cash flows equal the amount of the investment.

The cash flow expected for Investment A at the end of 2001 is discounted one period—to the end of 2000—at 10 percent:

$$\text{Present value of cash flow at end of } 2000 = \frac{\text{end-of-2001 cash flow}}{(1 + 0.10)^1}$$

$$= \frac{\$400,000}{(1 + 0.10)^1} = \$363,636$$

Another example: The present value (at the end of 2000) of the cash flow expected at the end of 2004 is:

$$\text{Present value of cash flow at end of } 2000 = \frac{\$400,000}{(1 + 0.10)^4} = \$273,205$$

In terms of the basic valuation equation:

$$FV = PV (1 + r)^t$$

and

FV = future value = $400,000
t = number of compound periods = 4
r = rate per period = 10%

and the present value, PV, of the fourth period's cash flow is:

$$\$400,000 = PV (1 + 0.10)^4$$
$$PV = \$273,205$$

Using the length of the payback as a basis for selecting investments, A is preferred to B. But we've ignored some valuable cash flows for both investments.

Discounted Payback as an Evaluation Technique

Does Discounted Payback Consider All Cash Flows?

Let's look again at Investments C and D. The main difference between them is that D has a very large cash flow in 2005, relative to C. Discounting each cash flow at the 10 percent cost of capital:

	Investment C		Investment D	
End of year	Cash flow	Value at end of 2000	Cash flow	Value at end of 2000
2001	$300,000	$272,727	$ 300,000	$ 272,727
2002	300,000	247,934	300,000	247,934
2003	300,000	225,394	300,000	225,394
2004	300,000	204,904	300,000	204,904
2005	300,000	186,276	10,000,000	6,209,213

The discounted-payback period for C is five years:

End of year	Investment C	
	Value at end of 2000	Accumulated discounted cash flows
2001	$272,727	$ 272,727
2002	247,934	520,661
2003	225,394	746,055
2004	204,904	950,959
2005	186,276	1,137,235 ← $1,000,000 investment paid back

The discounted-payback period for D is also five years, with each year-end cash flow from 2001 through 2004 contributing the same amounts as that of Investment C. However, D's cash flow in 2005 contributes over $6 million more in terms of the present value of the project's cash flows:

End of year	Investment D	
	Value at end of 2000	Accumulated discounted cash flows
2001	$ 272,727	$ 272,727
2002	247,934	520,661
2003	225,394	746,055
2004	204,904	950,959
2005	6,209,213	7,160,172 ← $1,000,000 investment paid back

The discounted-payback-period method *ignores* the remaining discounted cash flows: $950,959 + $186,276 − $1,000,000 = $137,236 from Investment C in year 2005 and $950,959 + $6,209,213 − $1,000,000 = $6,160,172 from Investment D in year 2005.

Does Discounted Payback Consider the Timing of Cash Flows?

Let's look at Investments E and F. Using a cost of capital of 5 percent for both E and F, the discounted cash flows for each period are:

End of year	Investment E		Investment F	
	Cash flow	Value at end of 2000	Cash flow	Value at end of 2000
2001	$300,000	$285,714	0	0
2002	300,000	272,109	0	0
2003	300,000	259,151	0	0
2004	300,000	246,811	$1,200,000	$987,243
2005	300,000	235,058	300,000	235,058

The discounted-payback period for E is four years:

	Investment E		
End of year	**Value at end of 2000**	**Accumulated discounted cash flows**	
2001	$285,714	$ 285,714	
2002	272,109	557,823	
2003	259,151	816,974	
2004	246,811	1,063,785	← $1,000,000 investment paid back
2005	235,058	1,298,843	

The discounted-payback period for F is five years:

	Investment F		
End of year	**Value at end of 2000**	**Accumulated discounted cash flows**	
2001	0	0	
2002	0	0	
2003	0	0	
2004	$987,243	$ 987,243	
2005	235,058	1,222,301	← $1,000,000 investment paid back

The discounted-payback period is able to distinguish among investments that differ in the timing of their cash flows. E's cash flows are expected sooner than those of F. E's discounted-payback period is shorter than F's—four versus five years.

Does Discounted Payback Consider the Riskiness of Cash Flows?

Let's look at Investments G and H. Suppose the cost of capital for G is 5 percent and the cost of capital for H is 10 percent. We are assuming that H's cash flows are more uncertain than G's. The discounted cash flows for the two investments, using the appropriate discount rates, are:

	Investment G		Investment H	
End of year	**Cash flow**	**Value at end of 2000**	**Cash flow**	**Value at end of 2000**
2001	$250,000	$238,095	$250,000	$227,273
2002	250,000	226,757	250,000	206,612
2003	250,000	215,959	250,000	187,829
2004	250,000	205,676	250,000	170,753
2005	250,000	195,882	250,000	155,230

The discounted-payback period for G is five years:

	Investment G	
End of year	**Value at end of 2000**	**Accumulated discounted cash flows**
2001	$238,095	$ 238,095
2002	226,757	464,852
2003	215,959	680,811
2004	205,676	886,487
2005	195,882	1,082,369 ← $1,000,000 investment paid back

According to the discounted-payback-period method, H does not pay back its original $1 million investment—not in terms of discounted cash flows:

	Investment H	
End of year	**Value at end of 2000**	**Accumulated discounted cash flows**
2001	$227,273	$227,273
2002	206,612	433,885
2003	187,829	621,714
2004	170,753	792,467
2005	155,230	947,697 ← Less than $1,000,000 investment

Since risk is reflected through the discount rate, risk is explicitly incorporated into the discounted-payback-period analysis.

The discounted-payback-period method is able to distinguish between Investment G and the riskier Investment H.

Is Discounted Payback Consistent with Owners' Wealth Maximization?

Discounted payback cannot provide us with any information about how profitable an investment is because it ignores everything after the break-even point! The discounted-payback period can be used as an initial screening device—eliminating any projects that don't pay back over the expected term of the investment. But since the method ignores some of the cash flows that contribute to the present value of investment (those above and beyond what is necessary for the investment's payback), the discounted-payback-period technique is not consistent with owners' wealth maximization.

Net Present Value

If you are offered an investment that costs $5,000 today and that promises to pay you $7,000 two years from today and if your opportunity cost for projects of similar risk is 10 percent, would you make this investment? Whether or not this is a good investment, you need to compare your $5,000 investment with the $7,000 cash flow you expect in two years. Since you feel that a discount rate of 10 percent reflects the degree of uncertainty associated with the $7,000 expected in two years, today the investment is worth:

$$\text{Present value of \$7,000 to be received in two years} = \frac{\$7,000}{(1 + 0.10)^2} = \mathbf{\$5,785.12}$$

By investing $5,000, today you are getting in return a promise of a cash flow in the future that is worth $5,785.12 today. You increase your wealth by $785.12 when you make this investment.

Another way of stating this is that the present value of the $7,000 cash inflow is $5,785.12, which is more than the $5,000 current cash outflow necessary to make the investment. When we subtract today's cash outflow necessary to make the investment from the present value of the cash inflow from the investment, the difference is the increase or decrease in our wealth, which is referred to as the net present value.

The *net present value* (NPV) is the present value of *all* expected cash flows:

Net present value = present value of all expected cash flows

or, in terms of the incremental operating and investment cash flows,

$$\text{Net present value} = \frac{\text{present value of the change}}{\text{in operating cash flows}} + \frac{\text{present value of the}}{\text{investment cash flows}}$$

"Net" refers to the difference between the change in the operating cash flows and the investment cash flows causing the change in the firm's operating cash flows. Often the changes in operating cash flows are inflows and the investment cash flows are outflows. Therefore we tend to refer to the net present value as the difference between the present value of the cash inflows and the present value of the cash outflows.

We can represent the net present value using summation notation, where t indicates any particular period, CF_t represents the cash flow at the end of period t, r represents the cost of capital, and T the number of periods that make up the length of economic life of the investment:

$$NPV = \sum_{t=0}^{T} \frac{CF_t}{(1 + r)^t} \qquad\qquad [9\text{-}1]$$

Cash inflows are positive values of CF_t, and cash outflows are negative values of CF_t. For any given period t, we collect all the cash flows (positive and negative) and add them algebraically to obtain the net.

Example: In the Williams 5 & 10 expansion project detailed in Chapter 8, the investment cash flow in the second year was −$20,000 and the operating cash flow was +$79,809. Therefore, $CF_2 = -\$20,000 + 79,809 = \$59,809$. This cash flow would be discounted over two years. If the discount rate, r, is 10 percent, CF_2 would be worth $49,429 at the start of the project (end of 2000).

To make things a bit easier to track, let's just refer to cash flows as inflows or outflows and not specifically identify them as operating or investment cash flows.

Let's take another look at Investments A and B. Using a 10 percent cost of capital, the present values of the inflows are:

End of year	Investment A		Investment B	
	Cash flow	Value at end of 2000	Cash flow	Value at end of 2000
2001	$400,000	$ 363,636	$ 100,000	$ 90,909
2002	400,000	330,579	100,000	82,645
2003	400,000	300,526	100,000	75,131
2004	400,000	273,206	1,000,000	683,013
2005	400,000	248,369	1,000,000	620,921
Present value of the cash inflows		**$1,516,315**		**$1,552,619**

The present value of the cash outflows is the outlay of $1 million. The net present value of A is:

NPV of A = $1,516,315 − $1,000,000 = **$516,315**

Present value of the cash inflows   Present value of the cash outflows

and the net present value of B is:

NPV of B = $1,552,619 − $1,000,000 = **$552,619**

These NPVs tell us that if we invest in A, we expect to increase the value of the firm by $516,315. If we invest in B, we expect to increase the value of the firm by $552,619.

The Net Present Value Decision Rule

A positive net present value means that the investment increases the value of the firm—the return is more than sufficient to compensate for the required return on the investment. A negative net present value means that the investment decreases the value of the firm—the return is less than the cost of capital. A zero net present value means that the return just equals the return required by owners to compensate them for the degree of uncertainty of the investment's future cash flows and the time value of money. Therefore,

If . . .	This means that . . .	and you . . .
NPV > 0	the investment is expected to increase shareholder wealth . . .	should accept the project.
NPV < 0	the investment is expected to decrease shareholder wealth . . .	should reject the project.
NPV = 0	the investment is expected not to change shareholder wealth . . .	are indifferent between accepting or rejecting the project.

Investment A increases the value of the firm by $516,315 and B increases it by $552,620. If these are independent investments, both should be taken on because both increase the value of the firm. If A and B are **mutually exclusive,** that is, the choice is between A *or* B but not both, then B is preferred since it has the greater NPV. Projects are said to be mutually exclusive if accepting one precludes the acceptance of the other.

Net Present Value as an Evaluation Technique

Does Net Present Value Consider All Cash Flows?

Let's look at Investments C and D, which are similar except for the cash flows in 2005. The discounted value of each cash flow, using a cost of capital of 10 percent, is:

End of year	Investment C		Investment D	
	Cash flow	Value at end of 2000	Cash flow	Value at end of 2000
2001	$300,000	$ 272,727	$ 300,000	$ 272,727
2002	300,000	247,934	300,000	247,934
2003	300,000	225,394	300,000	225,394
2004	300,000	204,904	300,000	204,904
2005	300,000	186,276	10,000,000	6,209,213
Present value of the cash inflows		**$1,137,236**		**$7,160,172**

The net present value of each investment is:

NPV of C = $1,137,236 − $1,000,000 = **$137,236**
NPV of D = $7,160,172 − $1,000,000 = **$6,160,172**

Because C and D each have positive net present values, each is expected to increase the value of the firm. And because D has the higher NPV, it provides the greater increase in value. If we had to choose between them, D is the better choice, since it is expected to increase owners' wealth by over $6 million.

The net present value technique considers all future incremental cash flows. D's NPV with a large cash flow in year 2005 is much greater than C's NPV.

Does Net Present Value Consider the Timing of Cash Flows?

Let's look again at projects E and F, whose total cash flow is the same but whose yearly cash flows differ.

	Investment E		Investment F	
End of year	**Cash flow**	**Value at end of 2000**	**Cash flow**	**Value at end of 2000**
2001	$300,000	$ 285,714	0	0
2002	300,000	272,108	0	0
2003	300,000	259,151	0	0
2004	300,000	246,811	$1,200,000	$ 987,243
2005	300,000	235,058	300,000	235,058
Present value of the cash inflows		**$1,298,843**		**$1,222,301**

The net present values are:

NPV of E = $1,298,843 − 1,000,000 = **$298,843**
NPV of F = $1,222,301 − 1,000,000 = **$222,301**

Both E and F are expected to increase owners' wealth. But E, whose cash flows are received sooner, has a greater NPV.

Therefore, NPV does consider the timing of the cash flows.

Does Net Present Value Consider the Riskiness of Cash Flows?

For this we'll look again at Investments G and H. They have identical cash flows, although H's inflows are riskier than G's. The present value of each period's cash flows for these two investments are:

	Investment G		Investment H	
End of year	**Cash flow**	**Value at end of 2000**	**Cash flow**	**Value at end of 2000**
2001	$250,000	$ 238,095	$250,000	$ 227,273
2002	250,000	226,757	250,000	206,612
2003	250,000	215,959	250,000	187,829
2004	250,000	205,676	250,000	170,753
2005	250,000	195,882	250,000	155,230
Present value of the cash inflows		**$1,082,369**		**$947,697**

For G, the net present value is positive and for H it is negative.

NPV of G = $1,082,369 − $1,000,000 = **$82,369**
NPV of H = $947,697 − $1,000,000 = **−$52,303**

G is acceptable, since it is expected to *increase* owners' wealth. H is not acceptable, since it is expected to *decrease* owners' wealth.

The net present value method is able to distinguish among investments whose cash flows have different risks.

Is Net Present Value Consistent with Owners' Wealth Maximization?

Because the net present value is a measure of how much owners' wealth is expected to increase with an investment, NPV can help us identify projects that maximize owners' wealth.

The Investment Profile

We may want to see how sensitive our decision to accept a project is to changes in our cost of capital. We can see this sensitivity by looking at the way a project's net present value changes as the discount rate changes, that is, by looking at a project's **investment profile,** also referred to as the **net present value profile.** The investment profile is a graphical depiction of the relation between the net present value of a project and the discount rate: The profile shows the net present value of a project for each discount rate, within some range.

The net present value profile for Investment A is shown in Figure 9-1 for discount rates from 0 percent to 40 percent. To help you get the idea behind this graph, we've identified the NPVs of this project for discount rates of 10 percent and 20 percent. You should be able to see that the NPV is positive for discount rates from 0 percent to 28.65 percent and negative for discount rates higher than 28.65 percent. Therefore, Investment A increases owners' wealth if the cost of capital on this project is less than 28.65 percent and decreases owners' wealth if the cost of capital on this project is greater than 28.65 percent.

Let's impose A's NPV profile on the NPV profile of Investment B, as shown in the graph in Figure 9-2. If A and B are mutually exclusive projects—we invest in only one project or in neither—this graph clearly shows that the project we invest in depends on the discount rate. For higher discount rates, B's

FIGURE 9-1
Investment Profile of Investment A

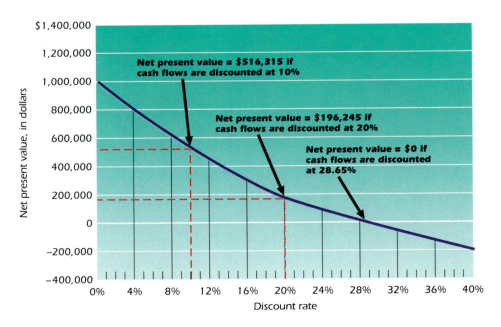

FIGURE 9-2

Investment Profile of
Investments A and B

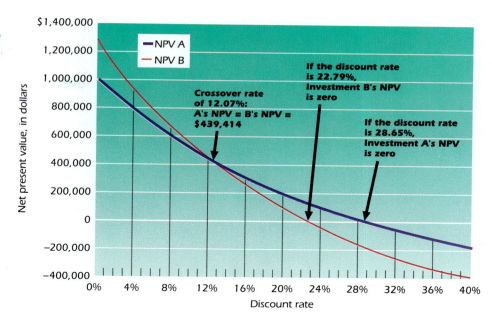

NPV falls faster than A's. This is because most of B's present value is attributed to the large cash flows four and five years into the future. The present value of the more distant cash flows is more sensitive to changes in the discount rate than is the present value of cash flows nearer the present.

If the discount rate is less than 12.07 percent, B increases wealth more than A. If the discount rate is more than 12.07 percent but less than 28.65 percent, A increases wealth more than B. If the discount rate is greater than 28.65 percent, we should invest in neither project, since both would decrease wealth.

The 12.07 percent is the *crossover discount rate,* which produces identical NPVs for the two projects. If the discount rate is 12.07 percent, the net present value of both investments is $1,439,414 − $1,000,000 = $439,414.

The NPV and Further Considerations

The net present value technique considers:

1. All expected future cash flows.
2. The time value of money.
3. The risk of the future cash flows.

Evaluating projects by using the NPV will lead us to select the ones that maximize owners' wealth. But there are a couple of things we need to take into consideration when we use net present value.

First, NPV calculations result in a dollar amount, say $500 or $23,413, which is the incremental value to owners' wealth. However, investors and managers tend to think in terms of percentage returns: Does this project return 10 percent? 15 percent?

Solving for the Crossover Discount Rate

For Investments A and B, the crossover rate is the rate, r, that solves:

$$-\$1,000,000 + \frac{\$400,000}{(1+r)^1} + \frac{\$400,000}{(1+r)^2} + \frac{\$400,000}{(1+r)^3} + \frac{\$400,000}{(1+r)^4} + \frac{\$400,000}{(1+r)^5}$$

↑

Net present value of Investment A

$$= -\$1,000,000 + \frac{\$100,000}{(1+r)^1} + \frac{\$100,000}{(1+r)^2} + \frac{\$100,000}{(1+r)^3} + \frac{\$1,000,000}{(1+r)^4} + \frac{\$1,000,000}{(1+r)^5}$$

↑

Net present value of Investment B

Combining like terms—those with the same denominators—as you would in simple algebra:

$$\frac{\$400,000 - \$100,000}{(1+r)^1} + \frac{\$400,000 - \$100,000}{(1+r)^2}$$

$$+ \frac{\$400,000 - \$100,000}{(1+r)^3} + \frac{\$400,000 - \$1,000,000}{(1+r)^4}$$

$$+ \frac{\$400,000 - \$1,000,000}{(1+r)^5} = \$0$$

Simplifying,

$$\frac{\$300,000}{(1+r)^1} + \frac{\$300,000}{(1+r)^2} + \frac{\$300,000}{(1+r)^3} + \frac{-\$600,000}{(1+r)^4} + \frac{-\$600,000}{(1+r)^5} = \$0$$

This last equation is in the form of a yield problem: the crossover rate is the rate of return of the *differences* in cash flows of the investments. The r that solves this equation is 12.07 percent, the crossover rate.

Second, to calculate the NPV we need to know the cost of capital. This is not so easy. The concept behind the cost of capital is simple. It is compensation to the suppliers of capital for (1) the time value of money and (2) the risk they accept that the cash flows they expect to receive may not materialize as promised. Getting an estimate of how much compensation is needed is not so simple. That's because to estimate a cost of capital we have to make a judgment about the risk of a project and how much return is needed to compensate for that risk—an issue we will address in the next chapter.

Profitability Index

The *profitability index* (PI) is the ratio of the present value of the change in operating cash inflows to the present value of investment cash outflows:

$$PI = \frac{\text{present value of the change in operating cash inflows}}{\text{present value of the investment cash outflows}} \qquad [9\text{-}2]$$

Instead of being the *difference* between the two present values, obtained as in Equation 9-1, the PI is the *ratio* of the two present values. Hence, the PI is a variation of the NPV. By construction, if the NPV is zero, the PI is one.

Suppose the present value of the change in cash inflows is $200,000 and the present value of the change in cash outflows is $200,000. The NPV (the difference between these present values) is zero, and the PI (the ratio of these present values) is 1.0.

Looking at Investments A and B:

$$PI \text{ of } A = \frac{\$1,516,315}{\$1,000,000} = \mathbf{1.5163}$$

$$PI \text{ of } B = \frac{\$1,552,619}{\$1,000,000} = \mathbf{1.5526}$$

The PI of 1.5163 means that for each $1.00 invested in A, we get approximately $1.52 in value; the PI of 1.5526 means that for each $1.00 invested in B, we get approximately $1.55 in value.

The PI is often referred to as the **benefit-cost ratio,** since it is the ratio of the benefit from an investment (the present value of cash inflows) to its cost (the present value of cash outflows).

The Profitability-Index Decision Rule

The profitability index tells us how much value we get for each dollar invested. If the PI is greater than one, we get more than $1 for each $1 invested—if the PI is less than one, we get less than $1 for each $1 invested. Therefore, a project that increases owners' wealth has a PI greater than one.

If . . .	This means that . . .	and you . . .
PI > 1	the investment returns more than $1 in present value for every $1 invested . . .	should accept the project.
PI < 1	the investment returns less than $1 in present value for every $1 invested . . .	should reject the project.
PI = 1	the investment returns $1 in present value for every $1 invested . . .	are indifferent between accepting or rejecting the project.

Profitability Index as an Evaluation Technique

Does the Profitability Index Consider All Cash Flows?

For Investment C:

$$PI \text{ of } C = \frac{\$1,137,236}{\$1,000,000} = \mathbf{1.1372}$$

which indicates that the present value of the change in operating cash flows exceeds the present value of the investment cash flows. For Investment D:

$$PI \text{ of } D = \frac{\$7,160,172}{\$1,000,000} = \textbf{7.1602}$$

which is much larger than the PI of C, indicating that D produces more value per dollar invested than C.

The PI includes all cash flows.

Does the Profitability Index Consider the Timing of Cash Flows?

From the data representing Investments E and F, which differ in the timing of their future cash flows:

$$PI \text{ of } E = \frac{\$1,298,843}{\$1,000,000} = \textbf{1.2988} \quad \text{and} \quad PI \text{ of } F = \frac{\$1,222,301}{\$1,000,000} = \textbf{1.2223}$$

The PI of Investment E, whose cash flows occur sooner, is higher than the PI of F.

The PI considers the time value of money.

Does the Profitability Index Consider the Riskiness of Cash Flows?

Back again to Investments G and H, which have different risk.

$$PI \text{ of } G = \frac{\$1,082,369}{\$1,000,000} = 1.0824 \quad \text{and} \quad PI \text{ of } H = \frac{\$947,697}{\$1,000,000} = 0.9477$$

The less risky project, G, has a higher PI and is therefore preferable to H, the riskier project.

The PI is able to distinguish between Investment G and the riskier investment, H. The PI of G is greater than the PI of H, even though the expected future cash flows of G and H are the same. The PI does consider the riskiness of the investment's cash flows.

Is the Profitability Index Consistent with Owners' Wealth Maximization?

Rejecting or accepting investments having PIs greater than 1.0 is consistent with rejecting or accepting investments whose NPV is greater than $0. However, in ranking projects, the PI might result in one ranking of the proposed investments while the NPV might result in a different ranking. This can happen when trying to rank projects that require different amounts to be invested. Consider the following:

Investment	Present value of cash inflows	Present value of cash outflows	PI	NPV
J	$110,000	$100,000	1.10	$10,000
K	315,000	300,000	1.05	15,000

Investment K has a larger net present value, so K is expected to increase the value of owners' wealth by more than J. But the profitability-index values are

The Profitability Index and Scale Differences

Consider two mutually exclusive projects, P and Q:

Project	Present value of inflows	Present value of outflows	PI	NPV
P	$110,000	$100,000	1.10	$10,000
Q	20,000	10,000	2.00	10,000

If we rank the projects according to the profitability index, Project Q is preferred, although they both contribute the same value, $10,000, to the firm.

Consider two mutually exclusive projects, P and R:

Project	Present value of inflows	Present value of outflows	PI	NPV
P	$110,000	$100,000	1.10	$10,000
R	11,000	10,000	1.10	1,000

According to the profitability index, P and R are the same, yet P contributes more value to the firm, $10,000 versus $1,000.

Consider two mutually exclusive projects, P and S:

Project	Present value of inflows	Present value of outflows	PI	NPV
P	$110,000	$100,000	1.10	$10,000
S	120,000	110,000	1.09	10,000

Ranking the projects on the basis of the profitability index, P is preferable to S, even though they contribute the same value to the firm, $10,000. Seen enough? If the projects are mutually exclusive and have different scales, selecting a project on the basis of the profitability index may not lead you to make the best decision in terms of owners' wealth.

different: J has a higher PI than K. According to the PI, J is preferred even though it contributes less to the value of the firm.

The source of this conflict is the different amounts of investments—scale differences. Because of the way the PI is calculated (as a ratio, instead of a difference), projects that produce the same present value may have different PIs.

As long as we can take on all profitable projects, using the PI will lead us to the same decision as the NPV. However, if the projects are *mutually exclusive* and are on *different scales,* the PI cannot be used.

If there is a limit on how much we can spend on capital projects, the PI is useful. Limiting the capital budget is referred to as **capital rationing.** Consider the following projects:

Project	Investment	NPV	PI
X	$10,000	$6,000	1.6
Y	10,000	5,000	1.5
Z	20,000	8,000	1.4

If there is a limit of $20,000 on what we can spend, which project or group of projects is best in terms of the goal of maximizing owners' wealth?

If we base our choice on the NPV, choosing the projects with the highest NPV, we would choose Z, whose NPV is $8,000. If we base our choice on the PI, we could choose Projects X and Y—those with the highest PI—providing an NPV of $6,000 + $5,000 = $11,000.

Our goal in selecting projects when the capital budget is limited is to select those that provide the highest *total NPV,* given our constrained budget. We could use the NPV to select projects, but we cannot *rank* projects on the basis of the NPV and always get the greatest value for our investment. As an alternative, we could calculate the total NPV for all possible combinations of investments or use a statistical technique, such as linear programming, to find the optimal set of projects. If we have many projects to choose from, we can also rank projects on the basis of their PIs and choose those projects with the highest PIs that fit into our capital budget.

When capital is limited, selecting projects on the basis of the PI provides us with the maximum total NPV for our total capital budget.

Capital Rationing and the Investment Decision

Capital rationing limits the amount that can be spent on capital investments during a particular period of time; that is, capital rationing sets a limit on the capital budget. These constraints may arise as a result of some policy of the board of directors or may arise externally, say, from creditor agreements that limit capital spending. If a firm has limited management personnel, the board's directors may not want to take on more projects than they feel they can effectively manage.

The overriding goal of the firm is to maximize owners' wealth. But if a limit is put on capital spending, the firm may have to forgo projects that are expected to increase owners' wealth and therefore owners' wealth will not be maximized. Capital rationing, whatever its cause, it is not in the best interest of owners.

Internal Rate of Return

Suppose you are offered an investment opportunity that requires you to put up $50,000 and has expected cash inflows of $28,809.52 at the end of each of the next two years. We can evaluate this opportunity using a time line:

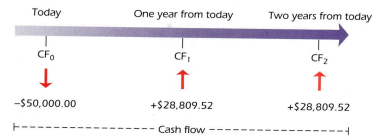

The return on this investment is the discount rate that causes the present value of the $28,809.52 cash inflows to equal the present value of the $50,000 cash outflow:

$$\$50,000 = \frac{\$28,809.52}{(1 + r)^1} + \frac{\$28,809.52}{(1 + r)^2}$$

Present value of the cash outflows

Present value of the cash inflows

Solving for the return, r:

$$\$50,000 = \$28,809.52 \left(\frac{1}{(1 + r)^1} + \frac{1}{(1 + r)^2} \right)$$

$$\frac{\$50,000}{\$28,809.52} = \frac{1}{(1 + r)^1} + \frac{1}{(1 + r)^2}$$

The right side we recognize as a present value annuity factor, and the expression equals 1.7355. Using Table B-4 or a calculator annuity function, we obtain r = **0.1000,** or **10.0 percent,** the yield on the investment.

Let's look at this problem from a different angle so that we can see the relation between the net present value and the internal rate of return. Calculate the net present value of this investment at 10 percent per year:

$$\text{Present value of all cash flows} = \frac{-\$50,000}{(1 + 0.10)^0} + \frac{\$28,809.52}{(1 + 0.10)^1} + \frac{\$28,809.52}{(1 + 0.10)^2}$$

$$= -\$50,000 + \$26,190.47 + \$23,809.52$$

$$= \mathbf{\$0.00}$$

Therefore, the net present value of the investment is zero when cash flows are discounted at the yield.

An investment's **_internal rate of return_** (IRR) is the discount rate that makes the present value of all expected future cash flows equal to zero:

0 = present value of the cash inflows + present value of the cash outflows

Or, in other words, the IRR is the discount rate that causes NPV = $0.

We can represent the IRR as the rate that solves the following equation:

$$\$0 = \sum_{t=0}^{T} \frac{CF_t}{(1 + IRR)^t} \qquad [9\text{-}3]$$

The Origins of the Concept of the Internal Rate of Return

The concept of the internal rate of return was developed by Kenneth Boulding: "We will now assume that there is some rate of return, i, which is characteristic of the investment as a whole. . . . That is to say, it is an internal rate, and while it may be equal to external rates of interest it must not be confused with them" ("The Theory of a Single Investment," *Quarterly Journal of Economics*, vol. 49, May 1935, p. 478). Boulding points out about the internal rate: ". . . the rate of return in an enterprise is that rate which will make the present value of the product of input which is now going into the enterprise equal to the value of that input" (p. 485).

In other words, the internal rate is the rate that equates the investment—the "value of that input"—with the present value of the benefits from the investment—the "product of input."

Let's return to Investments A and B. The IRR for Investment A is the discount rate that solves the relationship:

$$\$0 = -\$1,000,000 + \frac{\$400,000}{(1 + IRR)^1} + \frac{\$400,000}{(1 + IRR)^2} + \frac{\$400,000}{(1 + IRR)^3}$$
$$+ \frac{\$400,000}{(1 + IRR)^4} + \frac{\$400,000}{(1 + IRR)^5}$$

Since the cash inflows are the same in each period:

$$\$0 = -\$1,000,000 + \$400,000 \sum_{t=1}^{5} \frac{1}{(1 + IRR)^t}$$

where $\sum_{t=1}^{5}[1/(1 + IRR)^t]$ is the present value interest factor for an annuity. Rearranging the equation:

$$\$1,000,000 = \$400,000 \sum_{t=1}^{5} \frac{1}{(1 + IRR)^t}$$

Bringing the cash inflow $400,000 to the left-hand side, rearranging, and simplifying:

$$\sum_{t=1}^{5} \frac{1}{(1 + IRR)^t} = \frac{\$1,000,000}{\$400,000} = 1.2500$$

Using the present value annuity factor table (Table B-4), we see that the discount rate that solves this equation is approximately 30 percent per year. Using a calculator or a computer, we get the more precise answer of 28.65 percent per year. Let's calculate the IRR for B, then we'll see how we can use the IRR to value investments.

The IRR for Investment B is the discount rate that solves:

$$\$0 = \underbrace{-\$1,000,000}_{\substack{\uparrow \\ \text{Present value of} \\ \text{the cash outflows}}}$$

$$\underbrace{+\frac{\$100,000}{(1+\text{IRR})^1} + \frac{\$100,000}{(1+\text{IRR})^2} + \frac{\$100,000}{(1+\text{IRR})^3} + \frac{\$1,000,000}{(1+\text{IRR})^4} + \frac{\$1,000,000}{(1+\text{IRR})^5}}_{\substack{\uparrow \\ \text{Present value of the cash inflows}}}$$

Since the cash inflows are not the same amount each period, we cannot use the shortcut of solving for the present value annuity factor, as we did for Investment A. We can solve for the IRR of Investment B by (1) trial and error, (2) financial calculator, or (3) computer.

Trial and error requires a starting point. To make the trial and error a bit easier, let's rearrange the equation, putting the present value of the cash outflows on the left-hand side:

$$\$1,000,000 = \frac{\$100,000}{(1+\text{IRR})^1} + \frac{\$100,000}{(1+\text{IRR})^2} + \frac{\$100,000}{(1+\text{IRR})^3}$$
$$+ \frac{\$1,000,000}{(1+\text{IRR})^4} + \frac{\$1,000,000}{(1+\text{IRR})^5}$$

If we try IRR = 10 percent per year, the right-hand side is greater than the left-hand side:

$$\$1,000,000 \neq \$1,552,620$$

This tells us that we have not discounted enough. Increasing the discount rate to 20 percent per year:

$$\$1,000,000 \neq \$1,094,779$$

We *still* haven't discounted the cash flows enough. Increasing the discount rate still further, to 25 percent per year:

$$\$1,000,000 \neq \$932,480$$

We discounted *too* much—we drove the right-hand side below $1,000,000. But at least now we know the IRR is between 20 percent and 25 percent. Using a calculator or computer, we find that the precise value of IRR is 22.79 percent per year.[2]

The Internal Rate of Return by Any Other Name

The internal rate of return is known by other names, such as the:

- Marginal efficiency of capital
- True yield
- Interest rate of return
- Yield to maturity
- Expected rate of return

Solving for the internal rate of return is also referred to as the:

- Investors' method
- Scientific method

And, for those without financial calculators, the IRR is sometimes known as the *infernal* rate of return.

---

[2] Your calculator does not arrive at the solution directly. Your calculator's program uses trial and error also—and keeps you waiting as it tries different discount rates.

Looking back at Figure 9-2, which shows the investment profiles of Investments A and B, you'll notice that each profile crosses the horizontal axis (where NPV = $0) at the discount rate that corresponds to the investment's internal rate of return. This is no coincidence: By definition, the IRR is the discount rate that causes the project's NPV to equal zero.

The Internal-Rate-of-Return Decision Rule

The internal rate of return is a yield—what we earn, on average, per year. How do we use it to decide which investment, if any, to choose? Let's revisit Investments A and B and the IRRs we just calculated for each. If, for similar risk investments, owners earn 10 percent per year, then both A and B are attractive. They both yield *more* than the rate owners require for the level of risk of these two investments:

Investment	IRR, per year	Cost of capital, per year
A	28.65%	10%
B	22.79	10

The decision rule for the internal rate of return is to invest in a project if it provides a return *greater* than the cost of capital. The cost of capital, in the context of the IRR, is a **hurdle rate**—the minimum acceptable rate of return.

The IRR and Mutually Exclusive Projects

What if we were forced to choose *between* projects A and B because they are mutually exclusive? A has a higher IRR than B; so at first glance we might want to accept A. But wait! What about the NPV of A and B? What does the NPV tell us to do?

Investment	IRR, per year	NPV
A	28.65%	$516,315
B	22.79	552,619

If we use the higher IRR, we go with A. If we use the higher NPV, we go with B. Which is correct? If 10 percent is the cost of capital we used to determine both NPVs and we choose A, we will be forgoing value in the amount of $552,620 − $516,315 = $36,305. Therefore, we should choose B, the one with the higher NPV.

In this example, if for both A and B the cost of capital were different, say, 25 percent rather than 10 percent, we would calculate different NPVs and come to a different conclusion. In this case:

Investment	IRR, per year	NPV
A	28.65%	$75,712
B	22.79	−67,520

Investment A still has a positive NPV, since its IRR > 25 percent, but B has a negative NPV, since its IRR < 25 percent.

When evaluating mutually exclusive projects, the one with the highest IRR may not be the one with the best NPV. The IRR may point to a different decision than the NPV when mutually exclusive projects are evaluated, because of the reinvestment assumption:

- The NPV assumes cash flows are reinvested at the cost of capital.
- The IRR assumes cash flows are reinvested at the internal rate of return.

This reinvestment assumption may lead to different decisions in choosing among mutually exclusive projects when any of the following factors apply:

- The timing of the cash flows is different among the projects.
- There are scale differences (that is, very different cash flow amounts).
- The projects have different useful lives.

With respect to the role of the timing of cash flows in choosing between two projects: Investment A's cash flows are received sooner than B's. Part of the return on each is from the reinvestment of its cash inflows. And in the case of A, there is more return from the reinvestment of cash inflows. The question is, What do you do with the cash inflows when you get them? We generally assume that if you receive cash inflows, you'll reinvest them in other assets.

With respect to the reinvestment rate assumption in choosing between these projects: Suppose we can reasonably expect to earn only the cost of capital on our investments. Then for projects with an IRR above the cost of capital, we would be overstating the return on the investment using the IRR. Consider Investment A once again. If the best you can do is reinvest each of the $400,000 cash flows at 10 percent, these cash flows are worth $2,442,040:

Future value of Investment A's
cash flows with each invested = $400,000 × future value annuity factor
at 10%   for T = 5 and r = 10%

$$= \$400,000 \times 6.2051$$
$$= \mathbf{\$2,442,040}$$

Investing $1,000,000 at the end of 2000 produces a value of $2,442,040 at the end of 2005 (cash flows plus the earnings on these cash flows at 10 percent). This means that if the best you can do is reinvest cash flows at 10 percent, then you earn not the IRR of 28.65 percent, but rather 19.55 percent:

$$FV = PV(1 + r)^t$$
$$\$2,442,040 = \$1,000,000(1 + r)^5$$
$$r = \mathbf{19.55\%}$$

If we evaluate projects on the basis of their IRR, we may select one that does not maximize value.

With respect to the NPV method: The NPV assumes reinvestment at the cost of capital. If the best we can do is reinvest cash flows at the cost of capital, then the NPV has the more reasonable reinvestment rate assumption. If the reinvestment rate is assumed to be the project's cost of capital, we would evaluate projects on the basis of the NPV and select the one that maximizes owners' wealth.

The IRR and Capital Rationing

What if there is capital rationing? Suppose Investments A and B are ***independent projects,*** meaning that the acceptance of one does not prevent the acceptance of the other. Further suppose that the capital budget is limited to $1 million. We are therefore forced to choose between A or B. If we select the one with the highest IRR, we choose A. But A is expected to increase wealth *less* than B. Ranking investments on the basis of their IRRs may not maximize wealth.

We can see this dilemma in Figure 9-2. The discount rate at which A's NPV is $0.00 is A's IRR = 28.65 percent, where A's profile crosses the horizontal axis. Likewise, the discount rate at which B's NPV is $0.00 is B's IRR = 22.79 percent. The discount rate at which A and B's profiles cross is the crossover rate, 12.07 percent. For discount rates less than 12.07 percent, B has the higher NPV. For discount rates greater than 12.07 percent, A has the higher NPV. If A is chosen because it has a higher IRR and if A's cost of capital is more than 12.07 percent, we have not chosen the project that produces the greatest value.

Let's look at another situation. Suppose we evaluate four independent projects characterized by the following data:

Project	Investment outlay	NPV	IRR, per year
L	$ 2,000,000	$ 150,000	23%
M	3,000,000	250,000	22
N	5,000,000	500,000	21
O	10,000,000	1,000,000	20

If there is no capital rationing, we would spend $20 million, since all four have positive NPVs, and we would expect owners' wealth to increase by $1.9 million, the sum of the NPVs.

If the capital budget is limited to $10 million, we can select one or more of these four projects only up to the limit of the budget. If we select projects on the basis of their IRRs, we would choose projects L, M, and N. But is this optimal for maximizing owners' wealth? Let's look at the value added arising from different investment strategies:

	Investment selection	Amount of investment	Total NPV
Selection based on highest IRRs	L, M, and N	$10,000,000	$ 900,000
Selection based on highest NPVs	O	10,000,000	1,000,000

We can increase the owners' wealth more with Project O than with the combined investment in Projects L, M, and N. Therefore, when there is capital rationing, selecting investments on the basis of IRR rankings is not consistent with the goal of maximizing wealth.

The source of the problem in the case of capital rationing is that the IRR is a percentage, not a dollar amount. Because of this, we cannot determine how to distribute the capital budget to maximize wealth because the investment or group of investments producing the highest yield is not necessarily the one that produces the greatest wealth.

Internal Rate of Return as an Evaluation Technique

Does the IRR Consider All Cash Flows?

Looking at Investments C and D, the difference between them is D's cash flow in the last year.

The internal rate of return for C is the rate that solves the following equation:

$$\$0 = -\$1,000,000 + \frac{\$300,000}{(1 + IRR)^1} + \frac{\$300,000}{(1 + IRR)^2} + \frac{\$300,000}{(1 + IRR)^3}$$
$$+ \frac{\$300,000}{(1 + IRR)^4} + \frac{\$300,000}{(1 + IRR)^5}$$
$$= -\$1,000,000 + \$300,000 \sum_{t=1}^{5} \frac{1}{(1 + IRR)^t}$$

C's IRR = 15.24 percent per year.

For the IRR for D:

$$\$0 = -\$1,000,000 + \frac{\$300,000}{(1 + IRR)^1} + \frac{\$300,000}{(1 + IRR)^2} + \frac{\$300,000}{(1 + IRR)^3}$$
$$+ \frac{\$300,000}{(1 + IRR)^4} + \frac{\$10,000,000}{(1 + IRR)^5}$$

D's IRR = 73.46 percent per year.

The IRR considers all cash flows. As a result, D's IRR is much larger than C's because of the size of D's cash flow in the last period.

Does the IRR Consider the Timing of Cash Flows?

To see if the IRR can distinguish investments whose cash flows have different time values of money, let's look at Investments E and F. The IRR of E is the rate that solves the following equation:

$$\$0 = -\$1,000,000 + \frac{\$300,000}{(1 + IRR)^1} + \frac{\$300,000}{(1 + IRR)^2} + \frac{\$300,000}{(1 + IRR)^3}$$
$$+ \frac{\$300,000}{(1 + IRR)^4} + \frac{\$300,000}{(1 + IRR)^5}$$

E's IRR = 15.24 percent per year.

Similarly for F:

$$\$0 = -\$1,000,000 + \frac{\$1,200,000}{(1 + IRR)^4} + \frac{\$300,000}{(1 + IRR)^5}$$

and F's IRR = 10.15 percent per year.

Investment E, whose cash flows are received sooner, has a higher IRR than F. The IRR does consider the timing of cash flows.

The IRR and the Cost of Capital

Notice that Investments C and E have identical cash flows, but C's cost of capital is 10 percent per year and E's is 5 percent per year.

Do the different costs of capital affect the calculation of net present value? Yes, since cash flows for C and E are discounted at different rates.

Does this affect the calculation of the internal rate of return? No, since we are solving for the discount rate—we do not use the cost of capital. The cost of capital comes into play when we compare the IRR with the cost of capital in making a decision.

Does the IRR Consider the Riskiness of Cash Flows?

To examine whether the IRR considers the riskiness of cash flows, let's compare Investments G and H. The IRR for G is the rate that solves the following equation:

$$\$0 = -\$1,000,000 + \frac{\$250,000}{(1 + IRR)^1} + \frac{\$250,000}{(1 + IRR)^2} + \frac{\$250,000}{(1 + IRR)^3}$$

$$+ \frac{\$250,000}{(1 + IRR)^4} + \frac{\$250,000}{(1 + IRR)^5}$$

$$= -\$1,000,000 + \$250,000 \sum_{t=1}^{5} \frac{1}{(1 + IRR)^t}$$

The internal rate of return for G is close to 8 percent (7.93 percent to be precise). The cash flows of H are the same as those of G, so its IRR is the same: 7.93 percent per year.

The IRR of G exceeds the cost of capital (5 percent per year), so we would accept G. The IRR of H is less than its cost of capital (10 percent per year), so we would reject H. Then how does the IRR method consider risk? The calculation of the IRR doesn't consider risk, but when we compare a project's IRR with its cost of capital we do consider the risk of the cash flows.

Is the IRR Consistent with Owners' Wealth Maximization?

Evaluating projects with the IRR indicates the ones that maximize wealth so long as (1) the projects are independent and (2) they are not limited by capital rationing. If the projects are mutually exclusive or there is capital rationing, the IRR may sometimes lead to the selection of projects that do not maximize wealth.

Multiple Internal Rates of Return

The typical project usually involves only one large negative cash flow initially, followed by a series of future positive flows. But that's not always the case. Suppose you are involved in a project that uses environmentally sensitive chemicals. It may cost you a great deal to dispose of them and that will mean a negative cash flow at the end of the project.

Suppose you are considering a project that has cash flows as follows:

End of period	Cash flows
0	−$100
1	+474
2	−400

What is the internal rate of return on this project? Solving for the internal rate of return:

$$\$0 = -\$100 + \frac{\$474}{(1 + IRR)^1} + \frac{-\$400}{(1 + IRR)^2}$$

One possible solution is IRR = 10 percent:

$$\$0 = -\$100 + \frac{\$474}{(1 + 0.10)^1} + \frac{-\$400}{(1 + 0.10)^2}$$
$$= -\$100 + \$431 + -\$331$$

Yet *another* possible solution is IRR = 2.65 or 265 percent:

$$\$0 = -\$100 + \frac{\$474}{(1 + 2.65)^1} + \frac{-\$400}{(1 + 2.65)^2}$$
$$= -\$100 + \$130 + -\$30$$

Therefore, there are two possible solutions: IRR = 10 percent per year and IRR = 265 percent per year.

We can see this graphically in Figure 9-3, where the NPV of these cash flows is shown for discount rates from 0 percent to 300 percent. Remember that the IRR is the discount rate that causes the NPV to be zero. In terms of this graph, that means the IRR is the discount rate at which the NPV is $0, the point at which the present value changes sign from positive to negative or from negative to positive. In the case of this project, the present value changes from negative to positive at 10 percent and from positive to negative at 265 percent.

FIGURE 9-3

Investment Profile of a Project with an Initial Cash Outlay of $100, a First-Period Cash Inflow of $474, and a Second-Period Cash Outflow of $400, Resulting in Multiple Internal Rates of Return

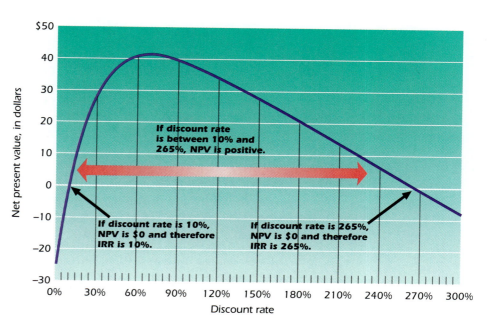

Multiple solutions to the yield on a series of cash flows occur whenever there is more than one change from plus to minus or from minus to plus in the sequence of cash flows. For example, the cash flows in the example above followed a pattern of $- + -$. There are two sign changes: from minus to plus and from plus to minus. There are also two possible solutions for IRR, one for each sign change.[3]

If you end up with multiple solutions, what do you do? Can you use any of these? None of these? If there are multiple solutions, there is no unique internal rate of return. If there is no unique solution, the solutions we get are worthless with respect to our making a decision based on the IRR. This is a strike against the IRR as an evaluation technique.

Modified Internal Rate of Return

There are situations in which it's not appropriate to use the IRR. Let's look again at A's IRR:

$$\$0 = -\$1,000,000 + \frac{\$400,000}{(1 + IRR)^1} + \frac{\$400,000}{(1 + IRR)^2} + \frac{\$400,000}{(1 + IRR)^3}$$
$$+ \frac{\$400,000}{(1 + IRR)^4} + \frac{\$400,000}{(1 + IRR)^5}$$

A's IRR is 28.65 percent per year. This means that when the first $400,000 comes into the firm, it is reinvested at 28.65 percent per year for four more periods; when the second $400,000 comes into the firm, it is reinvested at 28.65 percent per year for three more periods; and so on. If you reinvested all of A's cash inflows at the IRR of 28.65 percent—that is, you had other investments with the same 28.65 percent yield—you would have by the end of the project:

		Investment A
End of year	Cash inflow	Value at end of project
2001	$400,000	$400,000 $(1 + 0.2865)^4 = \$ 1,095,719$
2002	400,000	$400,000 $(1 + 0.2865)^3 =$ 851,705
2003	400,000	$400,000 $(1 + 0.2865)^2 =$ 662,033
2004	400,000	$400,000 $(1 + 0.2865)^1 =$ 514,600
2005	400,000	$400,000 $(1 + 0.2865)^0 =$ 400,000
		Total = **$3,524,057**

Investing $1,000,000 in A contributes $3,524,057 to the future value of the firm in the fifth year, providing a return on the investment of 28.65 percent per year. Let FV = $3,524,057, PV = $1,000,000, and t = 5.

---

[3] If there is only one sign change (positive to negative or negative to positive), there is a unique IRR that solves the equation. If there is more than one sign change, there is more than one discount rate that solves the equation. According to the Descartes rule of signs (which you can look up in an algebra textbook), there are at most as many solutions as there are sign changes.

Using the basic valuation equation,

$$FV = PV (1 + r)^t$$

Substituting the known values for FV, PV, and t, and solving for r (the IRR) we obtain:

$$\$3,524,057 = \$1,000,000 (1 + r)^5$$
$$r = 28.65\% \text{ per year}$$

Therefore, by using financial math to solve for the annual return, r, we have assumed that the cash inflows are reinvested at the IRR.

Assuming that cash inflows are reinvested at the IRR is strike two against the IRR as an evaluation technique if it is an unrealistic rate. One way to get around this problem is to modify the reinvestment rate built into the mathematics.

Suppose you have an investment with the following expected cash flows:

End of year	Cash flow
0	−$10,000
1	3,000
2	3,000
3	6,000

The IRR of this project is 8.55 percent per year. This IRR assumes you can reinvest each of the inflows at 8.55 percent per year. Let's see what happens when we change the reinvestment assumption.

If you invest in this project and each time you receive a cash inflow you stuff it under your mattress, you accumulate $12,000 by the end of the third year: $3,000 + $3,000 + $6,000 = $12,000. What return do you earn on your investment of $10,000?

You invest $10,000 and end up with $12,000 after three years. The $12,000 is the future value of the investment, which is also referred to as the investment's **terminal value.**

We solve for the return on the investment by inserting the known values (PV = $10,000, FV = $12,000, t = 3) into the basic valuation equation and solve for the discount rate, r:

$$\$12,000 = \$10,000(1 + r)^3$$

$$(1 + r)^3 = \frac{\$12,000}{\$10,000} = 1.2000$$

$$(1 + r) = \sqrt[3]{1.2000} = 1.0627$$

$$r = \textbf{0.0627} \text{ or } \textbf{6.27\%} \text{ per year}$$

The return from this investment, with no reinvestment of cash flows, is 6.27 percent. We refer to this return as a **modified internal rate of return** (MIRR) since we have *modified* the reinvestment assumption. In this case, we modified the reinvestment rate from the IRR of 8.55 percent to 0 percent. The calculations of the MIRR are represented in the time line in Figure 9-4.

FIGURE 9-4

Time-Line Representation of an Investment, Its Future Value, and Its Modified Internal Rate of Return, Where Cash Flows Generated from the Investment Are Reinvested at 0 Percent Per Period

STEP 1 Calculate the present value of the investment cash flows: PV = **$10,000**
STEP 2 Calculate the future value of cash inflows: FV = **$12,000**

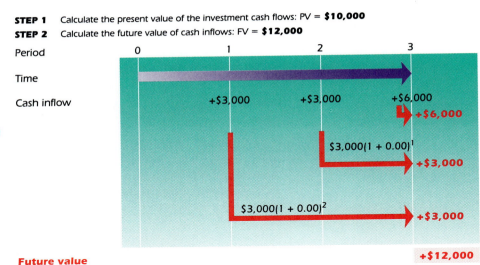

STEP 3 Solve for MIRR: $12,000 = $10,000(1 + MIRR)^3→ MIRR = **6.27%**

But what if, instead, you could invest the cash inflows in an investment that provides an annual return of 5 percent? Each cash flow earns 5 percent compound interest annually until the end of the third period. We can represent this problem in a time line, shown in Figure 9-5. The future value of the cash inflows, with reinvestment at 5 percent annually, is:

$$FV = \$3,000\ (1 + 0.05)^2 + \$3,000(1 + 0.05)^1 + \$6,000$$
$$= \$3,307.50 + \$3,150.00 + \$6,000$$
$$= \mathbf{\$12,457.50}$$

FIGURE 9-5

Time-Line Representation of an Investment, Its Future Value, and Its Modified Internal Rate of Return, Where Cash Flows Generated from the Investment Are Reinvested at 5 Percent Per Period

STEP 1 Calculate the present value of the investment cash flows: PV = **$10,000**
STEP 2 Calculate the future value of cash inflows: FV = **$12,457.50**

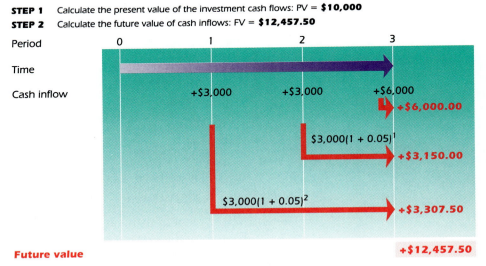

STEP 3 Solve for MIRR: $12,457.50 = $10,000(1 + MIRR)^3→ MIRR = **7.60%**

The MIRR is the return on the investment of $10,000 that produces $12,457.50 in three years:

$$\$12,457.50 = \$10,000(1 + MIRR)^3$$

$$(1 + MIRR)^3 = \frac{\$12,457.50}{\$10,000} = 1.2458$$

$$(1 + MIRR) = \sqrt[3]{1.2458} = 1.0759$$

$$MIRR = \mathbf{0.0760} \text{ or } \mathbf{7.60\%} \text{ per year}$$

A way to think about the modified return is to consider breaking down the return into its two components:

1. The return you get if there is no reinvestment (our mattress stuffing).
2. The return from reinvestment of the cash inflows.

We can also represent the MIRR in terms of a formula that combines terms we are already familiar with. Consider the three steps in the calculation of MIRR:

Step 1 Calculate the present value of all cash outflows, using the reinvestment rate as the discount rate.

Step 2 Calculate the future value of all cash inflows reinvested at some rate.

Step 3 Solve for the rate—the MIRR—that causes the future value of cash inflows to equal the present value of outflows:

Let COF_t represent the cash outflow in period t, and let CIF_t represent the cash inflow in period t. Let's also assume that cash inflows can be reinvested at some rate, RR. The MIRR is the rate that solves the following equation:

$$\begin{matrix}\text{Present value} \\ \text{of cash outflows}\end{matrix} = \begin{matrix}\text{future value of cash} \\ \text{inflows reinvested at RR}\end{matrix}\left[\frac{1}{(1 + MIRR)^T}\right]$$

Since the cash outflows may not occur all at the beginning, we can represent their present value as:

$$\begin{matrix}\text{Present value} \\ \text{of cash outflows}\end{matrix} = \sum_{t=0}^{T} \frac{COF_t}{(1 + RR)^t}$$

The future value of the cash inflows is

$$\sum_{t=0}^{T} CIF_t(1 + RR)^{T-t}$$

Putting all the pieces together, the MIRR is the rate that solves the following equation:

$$\begin{matrix}\text{Present value} \\ \text{of cash outflows}\end{matrix} = \frac{\sum_{t=0}^{T} CIF_t(1 + RR)^{T-t}}{(1 + MIRR)^T}$$

or

$$\underbrace{\sum_{t=0}^{T} \frac{COF_t}{(1 + RR)^t}}_{\substack{\text{Present value} \\ \text{of cash outflows}}} = \underbrace{\frac{\sum_{t=0}^{T} CIF_t(1 + RR)^{T-t}}{(1 + MIRR)^T}}_{\substack{\text{Present value} \\ \text{of cash inflows} \\ \text{reinvested at RR}}}$$

which we can rearrange to be:

$$(1 + MIRR)^T = \frac{\sum_{t=0}^{T} CIF_t(1 + RR)^{T-t}}{\sum_{t=0}^{T} \frac{COF_t}{(1 + RR)^t}} \qquad [9\text{-}4]$$

In the last example:

Reinvestment rate, RR	Modified internal rate of return, MIRR
0.00%	6.27%
5.00	7.60
8.55	8.55

If, instead of reinvesting each cash flow at 0 percent, we reinvest at 5 percent per year, then the reinvestment adds 7.60 percent − 6.27 percent = 1.33 percent to the investment's return. But wait—we reinvested at 5 percent. Why doesn't reinvestment add 5 percent? Because you only earn on reinvestment of intermediate cash flows—the first $3,000 for two periods at 5 percent and the second $3,000 for one period at 5 percent—not on all cash flows.

Let's calculate the MIRR for Investments A and B, assuming reinvestment at the 10 percent cost of capital.

Step 1   Calculate the present value of the cash outflows. In both A's and B's cases, this is $1 million.

Step 2   Calculate the future value by figuring the future value of each cash flow as of the end of 2005:[4]

---

[4] We have taken each cash flow and determined its value at the end of the year 2005. We could cut down our work by recognizing that these cash inflows are even amounts—simplifying the first step to the calculation of the future value of an ordinary annuity.

End of year	Investment A		Investment B	
	Cash flow	End-of-year 2005 cash flow	Cash flow	End-of-year 2005 cash flow
2001	$400,000	$ 585,640	$ 100,000	$ 146,410
2002	400,000	532,400	100,000	133,100
2003	400,000	484,000	100,000	121,000
2004	400,000	440,000	1,000,000	1,100,000
2005	400,000	400,000	1,000,000	1,100,000
Future value		**$2,442,040**		**$2,500,510**

Step 3 For A, solve for the rate that equates $2,442,040 in five years with $1,000,000 today:

$$\$2,442,040 = \$1,000,000(1 + \text{MIRR})^5$$

$$(1 + \text{MIRR})^5 = \frac{\$2,442,040}{\$1,000,000} = 2.4420$$

$$(1 + \text{MIRR}) = \sqrt[5]{2.4420}$$

$$\text{MIRR} = \textbf{0.1955 or 19.55\%} \text{ per year}$$

Following the same steps, we find the MIRR for Investment B to be 20.12 percent per year.

The Modified Internal-Rate-of-Return Decision Rule

The modified internal rate of return is a return on the investment, assuming a particular return on the reinvestment of cash flows. As long as the MIRR is greater than the cost of capital, that is, MIRR > cost of capital, the project should be accepted. If the MIRR is less than the cost of capital, the project does not provide a return commensurate with the amount of risk of the project.

If . . .	This means that . . .	and you . . .
MIRR > cost of capital	the investment is expected to return more than required . . .	should accept the project.
MIRR < cost of capital	the investment is expected to return less than required . . .	should reject the project.
MIRR = cost of capital	the investment is expected to return what is required . . .	are indifferent between accepting or rejecting the project.

Consider Investments A and B and their MIRRs with reinvestment at the cost of capital:

Investment	MIRR, per year	IRR, per year	NPV
A	19.55%	28.65%	$516,315
B	20.12	22.79	552,619

Assume for now that these are mutually exclusive investments. We saw the danger in trying to rank projects on their IRRs if the projects are mutually exclusive. But what if we ranked projects according to the MIRR? In this example, there seems to be a correspondence between the MIRR and the NPV. In the case of Investments A and B, the MIRR and the NPV provide identical rankings.

Modified Internal Rate of Return as an Evaluation Technique

Does the MIRR Consider All Cash Flows?

Assume the cash inflows from Investments C and D with reinvestment at the cost of capital of 10 percent per year:

End of year	Investment C		Investment D	
	Cash flow	End-of-year 2005 cash flow	Cash flow	End-of-year 2005 cash flow
2001	$300,000	$ 439,230	$ 300,000	$ 439,230
2002	300,000	399,300	300,000	399,300
2003	300,000	363,000	300,000	363,000
2004	300,000	330,000	300,000	330,000
2005	300,000	300,000	10,000,000	10,000,000
Future value		$1,831,530		$11,531,530

Solving for the rate that equates the terminal value with the $1 million present value of the outflows, we find that the modified internal rate of return for C is 12.87 percent per year and that for D is 63.07 percent per year. D's larger cash flow in 2005 is reflected in the larger MIRR.

The MIRR does consider all cash flows.

Does the MIRR Consider the Timing of Cash Flows?

To see whether the MIRR can distinguish investments whose cash flows occur at different points in time, let's calculate the MIRR for Investments E and F.

	Investment E		Investment F	
End of year	Cash flow	End-of-year 2005 cash flow	Cash flow	End-of-year 2005 cash flow
2001	$300,000	$ 439,230	0	0
2002	300,000	399,300	0	0
2003	300,000	363,000	0	0
2004	300,000	330,000	$1,200,000	$ 1,320,000
2005	300,000	300,000	300,000	300,000
Future value		**$1,831,530**		**$1,620,000**

Using these terminal values, we solve for the rate that equates the terminal value in five years with each investment's $1 million outlay. The MIRR of E is 12.87 percent per year and that of F is 10.13 percent per year. E's cash flows are expected sooner than F's. This is reflected in the higher MIRR.

Investment	MIRR, per year	Cost of capital per year	Decision
E	12.87%	5%	Accept
F	10.13	5	Accept

Both E and F are acceptable investments because they provide a return above the cost of capital. If we had to choose between E and F, we would choose E because it has the higher MIRR.

The MIRR does consider the timing of cash flows.

Does the MIRR Consider the Riskiness of Cash Flows?

Let's look at the modified internal rate of return for Investments G and H, which have identical expected cash flows, although H's inflows are riskier. Assuming that G's cash flows are reinvested at its 5 percent per year cost of capital and H's at 10 percent per year, the future values are:

	Investment G		Investment H	
End of year	Cash flow	End-of-year 2005 cash flow	Cash flow	End-of-year 2005 cash flow
2001	$250,000	$ 303,877	$250,000	$ 366,025
2002	250,000	289,406	250,000	332,750
2003	250,000	275,625	250,000	302,500
2004	250,000	262,500	250,000	275,000
2005	250,000	250,000	250,000	250,000
Future value		**$1,381,408**		**$1,526,275**

The MIRR for G is calculated using the investment of \$1,000,000 as the present value and \$1,381,408 as the terminal value.

$$\$1,381,408 = \$1,000,000(1 + \text{MIRR})^5$$

$$(1 + \text{MIRR})^5 = \frac{\$1,381,408}{\$1,000,000} = 1.3814$$

$$(1 + \text{MIRR}) = \sqrt[5]{1.3814} = 1.0668$$

$$\text{MIRR} = \textbf{0.0668} \text{ or } \textbf{6.68\%} \text{ per year}$$

Using the same procedure, the MIRR for H is 8.82 percent per year. Comparing the MIRR with the cost of capital:

Investment	MIRR, per year	Cost of capital, per year	Decision
G	6.68%	5%	Accept
H	8.82	10	Reject

If we reinvest cash flows at the cost of capital and if the costs of capital are different, we get different terminal values and hence different MIRRs for G and H. If we then compare each project's MIRR with the project's cost of capital, we can determine the projects that would increase owners' wealth.

The MIRR distinguishes between investments, but choosing the investment with the highest MIRR may not result in a value-maximizing decision. In the current example, H has the higher MIRR. But, when we compare each project's MIRR with its cost of capital, we see that Investment H should not be accepted. This points out the danger of using the MIRR when capital is rationed or when a choice must be made among mutually exclusive projects: Ranking and selecting projects on the basis of their MIRRs may lead to a decision that does not maximize owners' wealth.

If projects are not independent or if capital is rationed, we are faced with some of the same problems we encountered with the IRR in those situations: The MIRR may not produce the decision that maximizes owners' wealth.

Is the MIRR Consistent with Owners' Wealth Maximization?

The MIRR can be used to determine whether to invest in independent projects and to identify the ones that maximize owners' wealth. However, decisions made using the MIRR are not consistent with the goal of maximizing wealth when the selection must be made among mutually exclusive projects or when there is capital rationing.

COMPARING TECHNIQUES

The results of our calculations using the techniques ranging from the simple payback period to the more complex MIRR, are summarized in Table 9-2. If each of the eight projects is independent and is not limited by capital rationing, all projects except Investment H are expected to increase owners' wealth.

Suppose each project is independent, but we have a capital budget limit of \$5,000,000 on the total amount we can invest. Since each of the eight projects requires \$1,000,000, we can invest in only five of them. Which five proj-

TABLE 9-2
Summary of Techniques for Evaluation of Investment Projects

Investment	Cost of capital	Payback period	Discounted payback period	Net present value	Profitability index	Internal rate of return	Modified internal rate of return, assuming cash inflows reinvested at 5%
A	10%	3 years	4 years	$ 516,315	1.5163	28.65%	19.55%
B	10	4 years	5 years	552,619	1.5526	22.79	20.12
C	10	4 years	5 years	137,236	1.1372	15.24	12.87
D	10	4 years	5 years	6,160,172	7.1602	73.46	63.07
E	5	4 years	4 years	298,843	1.2988	15.24	12.87
F	5	4 years	5 years	222,301	1.2223	10.15	10.13
G	5	4 years	5 years	82,369	1.0823	7.93	6.68
H	10	4 years	Not paid back	−52,303	0.9477	7.93	8.82

ects do we invest in? In order of the NPV, we choose D, B, A, E, and F. We would expect the value of owners' wealth to increase by $6,160,172 + $552,620 + $516,315 + $298,843 + $222,301 = $7,750,251.

Now suppose that two projects in each pair of projects are mutually exclusive. Which project of each mutually exclusive pair is preferable? Investments B, D, E, and G are preferable if, in each pair, we choose the project with the higher NPV.

If we are dealing with mutually exclusive projects, the NPV method leads us to invest in projects that maximize wealth, that is, capital budgeting decisions consistent with the goal of owners' wealth maximization. If we are dealing with a limit on the capital budget, the NPV and PI methods lead us to invest in the set of projects that maximize wealth.

The advantages and disadvantages of each of the techniques for evaluating investments are summarized in Table 9-3. We see in this table that the discounted cash flow techniques are preferred to the nondiscounted cash flow techniques. The discounted cash flow techniques—the NPV, PI, IRR, MIRR—are preferable since they consider (1) all cash flows, (2) the time value of money, and (3) the risk of future cash flows. The discounted cash flow techniques are also useful because we can apply objective decision criteria that tell us when a project increases wealth and when it does not.

We also see in Table 9-3 that not all of the discounted cash flow techniques are right for every situation. There are questions we need to ask when evaluating an investment, and the answers will determine which technique is the one to use for that investment:

- Are the projects mutually exclusive or independent?
- Are the projects subject to capital rationing?
- Are the projects of the same risk?
- Are the projects of the same scale of investment?

The Scoop on Scale Differences

Scale differences—differences in the amounts of the cash flows—between projects can lead to conflicting investment decisions among the discounted cash flow techniques. Consider two projects, Project Big and Project Little, that each have a cost of capital of 5 percent per year with the following cash flows:

End of period	Project Big	Project Little
0	−$1,000,000	−$1.00
1	400,000	0.40
2	400,000	0.40
3	400,000	0.50

Applying the discounted cash flow techniques to each project:

Discounted cash flow technique	Project Big	Project Little
NPV	$89,299	$0.1757
PI	1.0893	1.1757
IRR	9.7010%	13.7789%
MIRR	8.0368%	10.8203%

Mutually Exclusive Projects

If Big and Little are mutually exclusive projects, which project should a firm prefer? If the firm goes strictly by the PI, IRR, or MIRR criteria, it would choose Project Little. But is this the better project? Project Big provides more value—$89,299 versus 18 cents. The techniques that ignore the scale of the investment—the PI, IRR, and MIRR—may lead to an incorrect decision.

Capital Rationing

If the firm is subject to capital rationing—say a limit of $1,000,000—and Big and Little are independent projects, which project should the firm choose? The firm can choose only one—can spend $1 or $1,000,000, but not $1,000,001. If you go strictly by the PI, IRR, or MIRR criteria, the firm would choose Project Little. But is this the better project? Again, the techniques that ignore the scale of the investment—the PI, IRR, and MIRR—lead to an incorrect decision.

TABLE 9-3

Summary of Characteristics of the Investment Evaluation Techniques

PAYBACK PERIOD

Advantages

1. Simple to compute.
2. Provides some information on the risk of the investment.
3. Provides a crude measure of liquidity.

Disadvantages

1. No concrete decision criteria to indicate whether an investment increases the firm's value.
2. Ignores cash flows beyond the payback period.
3. Ignores the time value of money.
4. Ignores the riskiness of future cash flows.

DISCOUNTED-PAYBACK PERIOD

Advantages

1. Considers the time value of money.
2. Considers the riskiness of the cash flows involved in the payback.

Disadvantages

1. No concrete decision criteria that indicate whether the investment increases the firm's value.
2. Requires estimate of cost of capital in order to calculate.
3. Ignores cash flows beyond the payback

NET PRESENT VALUE

Advantages

1. Tells whether the investment will increase the firm's value.
2. Considers all cash flows.
3. Considers the time value of money.
4. Considers the riskiness of future cash flows.

Disadvantages

1. Requires estimate of cost of capital in order to calculate.
2. Expressed in terms of dollars, not as a percentage.

PROFITABILITY INDEX

Advantages

1. Tells whether an investment increases the firm's value.
2. Considers all cash flows.
3. Considers the time value of money.
4. Considers the riskiness of future cash flows.
5. Useful in ranking and selecting projects when capital is rationed.

Disadvantages

1. Requires estimate of cost of capital in order to calculate.
2. May not give correct decision when used to compare mutually exclusive projects.

(Continued on p. 432)

INTERNAL RATE OF RETURN

Advantages	Disadvantages
1. Tells whether an investment increases the firm's value. 2. Considers the time value of money. 3. Considers all cash flows. 4. Considers riskiness of future cash flows.	1. Requires estimate of cost of capital in order to calculate. 2. May not give value-maximizing decision when used to compare mutually exclusive projects. 3. May not give value-maximizing decision when used to choose projects with capital rationing.

MODIFIED INTERNAL RATE OF RETURN

Advantages	Disadvantages
1. Tells whether the investment increases the firm's value. 2. Considers the time value of money. 3. Considers all cash flows. 4. Considers riskiness of future cash flows.	1. May not give value-maximizing decision when used to compare mutually exclusive projects with different investment scales or different risk. 2. May not give value-maximizing decision when used to choose projects with capital rationing.

If projects are independent and not subject to capital rationing, we can evaluate them and determine the ones that maximize wealth, basing our decision on any of the discounted cash flow techniques. If the projects are mutually exclusive, have the same investment outlay, and have the same risk, we must use only the NPV or the MIRR techniques to determine the projects that maximize wealth.

If projects are mutually exclusive and have different risks or are on different scales, the NPV is preferable to the MIRR.

If the capital budget is limited, we can use either the NPV or the PI. We must be careful, however, not to select projects on the basis of their NPVs (that is, we should not rank on NPV and select the highest NPV projects), but rather on how we can maximize the NPV of the *total* capital budget.

Which evaluation technique to use under different constraints is illustrated in Figure 9-6. By following the branches you can see that the evaluation technique to use depends on the project's constraints.

CAPITAL BUDGETING TECHNIQUES IN PRACTICE

Among the evaluation techniques in this chapter, the one we can be sure about is the net present value method. The NPV will steer us toward the project that maximizes wealth in the most general circumstances. But what evaluation technique do financial decision makers really use?

FIGURE 9-6
Determining the Appropriate Discounted Cash Flow Technique

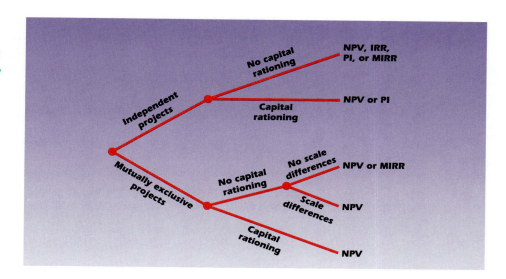

We learn about what goes on in practice by anecdotal evidence and through surveys.[5] We see that:

- There is an increased use of more sophisticated capital budgeting techniques.
- Most financial managers use more than one technique to evaluate the same projects, with a discounted cash flow technique (the NPV, IRR, or PI) used as a primary method and payback period as a secondary method.
- The most commonly used is the internal-rate-of-return method, though the net present value method is gaining acceptance.

The IRR is popular most likely because it is a measure of yield and therefore easy to understand. Moreover, since the NPV is expressed in dollars—the expected increment in the value of the firm—and financial managers are accustomed to dealing with yields, they may be more comfortable dealing with the IRR than the NPV.

The popularity of the IRR method is troubling, since it may lead to decisions about projects that are not in the best interest of owners in certain circumstances. However, the NPV method is becoming more widely accepted and, in time, may replace the IRR as the more popular method.

Is the use of payback period troubling? Not necessarily. The payback period is generally used as a screening device, eliminating those projects that cannot break even. Furthermore, the payback period can be viewed as a measure of a yield. If the amounts of the future cash flows are the same in each

[5] See Richard H. Pike, "An Empirical Study of the Adoption of Sophisticated Capital Budgeting Practices and Decision-Making Effectiveness," *Accounting and Business Research*, vol. 18, 1988, pp. 341–351; David F. Scott, Jr. and J. William Petty, "Capital Budgeting Practices in Large American Firms: A Retrospective Analysis and Synthesis," *Financial Review*, vol. 19, 1984, pp. 111–123; and Tarun K. Mukherjee, "Capital Budgeting Surveys: The Past and the Future," *Review of Business and Economic Research*, 1987, pp. 37–56.

period and if these future cash flows can be assumed to be received each period forever—essentially, a perpetuity—then 1/payback period is a rough guide to a yield on the investment. Suppose you invest $100 today and expect $20 each period forever. The payback period is five years. The inverse, 1/5 = 20 percent per year, is the yield on the investment.

Now let's turn this relation around and create a payback-period rule. Suppose we want a 10 percent per year return on our investment. This means that the payback period should be less than or equal to ten years. So while the payback period may seem to be a rough guide, there is some rationale behind it.

Use of the simpler techniques, such as payback period, does not mean that a firm's capital budgeting is unsophisticated. Remember that evaluating the cash flows is only one aspect of the process:

- Cash flows must first be estimated.
- Cash flows are evaluated using the NPV, PI, IRR, MIRR, or a payback method.
- Project risk must be assessed to determine the cost of capital.

SUMMARY

■ Techniques to evaluate the expected cash flows from investment projects include the payback period, the discounted-payback period, the net present value, the profitability index, the internal rate of return, and the modified internal rate of return.

■ Not all these six techniques consider all cash flows, the timing of the cash flows, and the risk of the cash flows, nor are they all consistent with the goal of the owners' wealth maximization.

■ The payback period and the discounted-payback period are measures of how long it takes the future cash flows to pay back the initial investment. The payback period looks only at the amount of the future cash flows, whereas the discounted-payback period looks at the present value of the future cash flows. Both methods give us some information on the attractiveness of an investment, though these methods provide little guidance in deciding whether a project will enhance owners' wealth.

■ The net present value is the dollar amount that the value of the firm is increased if the investment is made. It is the difference between the present value of the future operating cash flows and the present value of the investment cash flows.

■ The sensitivity of a project's worth can be represented as an investment profile, which is a graphical portrayal of a project's NPV for different discount rates.

■ The profitability index is the ratio of the present value of the future operating cash inflows to the present value of the investment cash flows. Similar to the net present value, the profitability index tells us whether the investment would increase owners' wealth. Since the profitability index does not give us a dollar measure of the increase in value, we cannot use it to choose among mutually exclusive projects, but the profitability index does help us rank projects when there is capital rationing.

■ The internal rate of return is the yield on the investment. It is the discount rate that causes the net present value to be equal to zero. The IRR is hazardous to use when selecting among mutually exclusive projects or when there is a limit on capital spending.

■ The modified internal rate of return is a yield on the investment, assuming that cash inflows are reinvested at some rate other than the internal rate of return. This method overcomes the problems associated with unrealistic reinvestment rate assumptions inherent in the internal-rate-of-return method. However, the MIRR is hazardous to use when selecting among mutually exclusive projects or when there is a limit on capital spending.

■ Each technique we look at offers some advantages and some disadvantages. The discounted flow techniques—the NPV, PI, IRR, and MIRR—are superior to the non-discounted cash flow technique—the payback period.

■ To evaluate mutually exclusive projects or projects subject to capital rationing, we have to be careful about the techniques we use. The net present value method is consistent with the objective of maximizing owners' wealth whether or not we have mutually exclusive projects or capital rationing.

■ Looking at capital budgeting in practice, we see that firms do use the discounted cash flow techniques, with the IRR the most widely used. Over time, however, we see a growing use of the NPV technique.

QUESTIONS

9-1 What is the objective of evaluating investments?

9-2 What criteria must be satisfied for an investment evaluation technique to be ideal?

9-3 Distinguish between the payback period and the discounted-payback period.

9-4 In our examples using the payback period and discounted-payback period, we end up with a payback period in terms of a whole number of periods, instead of a fractional number of periods. Why?

9-5 Why is it that when the postpayback duration is zero, the investment is not profitable and should be rejected without further analysis?

9-6 Can the payback-period method of evaluating projects identify the ones that will maximize wealth? Explain.

9-7 Can the discounted-payback-period method of evaluating projects identify the ones that will maximize wealth? Explain.

9-8 Consider two projects, AA and BB, that have identical positive net present values, but Project BB is riskier than AA. If these projects are mutually exclusive, what is your investment decision?

9-9 Can the net present value method of evaluating projects identify the ones that will maximize wealth? Explain.

9-10 The decision rules for the net present value and the profitability index methods are related. Explain the relationship between these two sets of decision rules.

9-11 What is the source of the conflict between net present value and the profitability index decision rules in evaluating mutually exclusive projects?

9-12 Suppose you calculate a project's net present value to be $3,000. What does that mean?

9-13 Suppose you calculate a project's profitability index to be 1.4. What does that mean?

9-14 The internal rate of return is often referred to as the yield on an investment. Explain the analogy between the internal rate of return on an investment and the yield to maturity on a bond.

9-15 The net present value method and the internal-rate-of-return method may produce different decisions when selecting among mutually exclusive projects. What is the source of this conflict?

9-16 The net present value method and the internal-rate-of-return method may produce different decisions when selecting projects under capital rationing. What is the source of this conflict?

9-17 The modified internal rate of return is designed to overcome a deficiency in the internal-rate-of-return method. Specifically, what problem is the MIRR designed to overcome?

9-18 Based upon our analysis of the alternative techniques to evaluate projects, which method or methods are preferable if our goal is to maximize owners' wealth?

9-19 According to the results of studies of capital project evaluation in practice, which method or methods are preferred by those actually using these techniques?

9-20 Why do we find a gap between what we prefer in terms of owners' wealth maximization and what is used in practice for capital project evaluation?

PROBLEMS

Calculations using evaluation techniques

9-1 You are evaluating Investment Project ZZ, with the following cash flows:

End of period	Cash flow
0	−$100,000
1	35,027
2	35,027
3	35,027
4	35,027

Calculate the following:

a. Payback period.
b. Discounted-payback period, assuming a 10 percent cost of capital.
c. Discounted-payback period, assuming a 16 percent cost of capital.
d. Net present value, assuming a 10 percent cost of capital.
e. Net present value, assuming a 16 percent cost of capital.
f. Profitability index, assuming a 10 percent cost of capital.
g. Profitability index, assuming a 16 percent cost of capital.
h. Internal rate of return.
i. Modified internal rate of return, assuming reinvestment at 0 percent.
j. Modified internal rate of return, assuming reinvestment at 10 percent.

9-2 You are evaluating Investment Project YY, with the following cash flows:

End of period	Cash flow
0	−$100,000
1	43,798
2	43,798
3	43,798

Calculate the following:

a. Payback period.
b. Discounted-payback period, assuming a 10 percent cost of capital.
c. Discounted-payback period, assuming a 14 percent cost of capital.
d. Net present value, assuming a 10 percent cost of capital.
e. Net present value, assuming a 14 percent cost of capital.
f. Profitability index, assuming a 10 percent cost of capital.
g. Profitability index, assuming a 14 percent cost of capital.
h. Internal rate of return.
i. Modified internal rate of return, assuming reinvestment at 10 percent.
j. Modified internal rate of return, assuming reinvestment at 14 percent.

9-3 You are evaluating Investment Project XX, with the following cash flows:

End of period	Cash flow
0	−$200,000
1	65,000
2	65,000
3	65,000
4	65,000
5	65,000

Calculate the following:

a. Payback period.
b. Discounted-payback period, assuming a 10 percent cost of capital.
c. Discounted-payback period, assuming a 15 percent cost of capital.
d. Net present value, assuming a 10 percent cost of capital.
e. Net present value, assuming a 15 percent cost of capital.
f. Profitability index, assuming a 10 percent cost of capital.
g. Profitability index, assuming a 15 percent cost of capital.
h. Internal rate of return.
i. Modified internal rate of return, assuming reinvestment at 10 percent.
j. Modified internal rate of return, assuming reinvestment at 15 percent.

9-4 You are evaluating Investment Project WW, with the following cash flows:

End of period	Cash flow
0	−$100,000
1	0
2	0
3	0
4	174,901

Calculate the following:

a. Payback period.
b. Discounted-payback period, assuming a 10 percent cost of capital.
c. Discounted-payback period, assuming a 12 percent cost of capital.
d. Net present value, assuming a 10 percent cost of capital.
e. Net present value, assuming a 12 percent cost of capital.
f. Profitability index, assuming a 10 percent cost of capital.
g. Profitability index, assuming a 12 percent cost of capital.
h. Internal rate of return.
i. Modified internal rate of return, assuming reinvestment at 10 percent.

9-5   You are evaluating Investment Project VV, with the following cash flows:

End of period	Cash flow
0	−$100,000
1	20,000
2	40,000
3	60,000

Calculate the following:

a. Payback period.
b. Discounted-payback period, assuming a 5 percent cost of capital.
c. Discounted-payback period, assuming a 10 percent cost of capital.
d. Net present value, assuming a 5 percent cost of capital.
e. Net present value, assuming a 10 percent cost of capital.
f. Profitability index, assuming a 5 percent cost of capital.
g. Profitability index, assuming a 10 percent cost of capital.
h. Internal rate of return.

Selecting among mutually exclusive projects

9-6   Suppose you are evaluating two mutually exclusive projects, Thing 1 and Thing 2, with the following cash flows:

	Cash flows	
End of year	Thing 1	Thing 2
2000	−$10,000	−$10,000
2001	3,293	0
2002	3,293	0
2003	3,293	0
2004	3,293	14,641

a. If the cost of capital on both projects is 5 percent, which project, if any, would you choose? Why?
b. If the cost of capital on both projects is 8 percent, which project, if any, would you choose? Why?
c. If the cost of capital on both projects is 11 percent, which project, if any, would you choose? Why?
d. If the cost of capital on both projects is 14 percent, which project, if any, would you choose? Why?
e. At what discount rate would you be indifferent between choosing Thing 1 and Thing 2?
f. On the same graph, draw the investment profiles of Thing 1 and Thing 2. Indicate the following items:

   • Crossover discount rate.
   • NPV of Thing 1 if the cost of capital is 5 percent.
   • NPV of Thing 2 if the cost of capital is 5 percent.
   • IRR of Thing 1.
   • IRR of Thing 2.

9-7 Suppose you are evaluating two mutually exclusive projects, Thing 3 and Thing 4, with the following cash flows:

| End of year | Cash flows | |
	Thing 3	Thing 4
2000	−$10,000	−$10,000
2001	3,503	0
2002	3,503	0
2003	3,503	0
2004	3,503	19,388

a. If the cost of capital on both projects is 5 percent, which project, if any, would you choose? Why?

b. If the cost of capital on both projects is 10 percent, which project, if any, would you choose? Why?

c. If the cost of capital on both projects is 15 percent, which project, if any, would you choose? Why?

d. If the cost of capital on both projects is 20 percent, which project, if any, would you choose? Why?

e. At what discount rate would you be indifferent between choosing Thing 3 and Thing 4?

f. On the same graph, draw the investment profiles of Thing 3 and Thing 4. Indicate the following items:

- Crossover discount rate.
- NPV of Thing 3 if the cost of capital is 10 percent.
- NPV of Thing 4 if the cost of capital is 10 percent.
- IRR of Thing 3.
- IRR of Thing 4.

9-8 Suppose you are evaluating two mutually exclusive projects, Thing 5 and Thing 6, with the following cash flows:

| End of year | Cash flows | |
	Thing 5	Thing 6
2000	−$10,000	−$10,000
2001	2,000	0
2002	5,000	0
2003	6,000	13,500

a. If the cost of capital on both projects is 0 percent, which project, if any, would you choose? Why?

b. If the cost of capital on both projects is 10 percent, which project, if any, would you choose? Why?

c. If the cost of capital on both projects is 15 percent, which project, if any, would you choose? Why?

d. If the cost of capital on both projects is 20 percent, which project, if any, would you choose? Why?

e. At what discount rate would you be indifferent between choosing Thing 5 and Thing 6?

f. On the same graph, draw the investment profiles of Thing 5 and Thing 6. Indicate the following items:

- Crossover discount rate.
- NPV of Thing 5 if the cost of capital is 15 percent.
- NPV of Thing 6 if the cost of capital is 15 percent.
- IRR of Thing 5.
- IRR of Thing 6.

Capital rationing

9-9 Consider the results obtained for the following five projects:

Project	Initial outlay	NPV
AA	$300,000	$10,000
BB	400,000	20,000
CC	200,000	10,000
DD	100,000	10,000
EE	200,000	−15,000

Suppose there is a limit on the capital budget of $600,000. Which projects should we invest in, given our capital budget?

9-10 Consider these three independent projects:

	Cash flows		
End of period	FF	GG	HH
0	−$100,000	−$200,000	−$300,000
1	30,000	40,000	40,000
2	30,000	40,000	40,000
3	30,000	40,000	40,000
4	40,000	120,000	240,000
Cost of capital	5%	6%	7%

a. If there is no limit on the capital budget, which projects would you choose? Why?

b. If there is a limit on the capital budget of $300,000, which projects would you choose? Why?

9-11   Consider the following four independent projects:

Project	Investment outlay	Net present value
JJ	$100,000	$ 50,000
KK	100,000	60,000
LL	200,000	100,000
MM	200,000	80,000

If there is a limit of $400,000 for capital projects, which projects should you select? Why?

Potpourri

9-12   The Mighty Mouse Computer Company is considering the purchase of a packaging robot. The robot costs $500,000, including shipping and installation. The robot can be depreciated as a five-year asset, using the MACRS. The robot is expected to last for five years, at which time Mighty Mouse expects to sell it for parts for $100,000. The robot is expected to replace five persons in the shipping department, saving the company $150,000 each year. Mighty Mouse's tax rate is 30 percent. The MACRS depreciation rates for a five-year asset are 20 percent, 32 percent, 19.2 percent, 11.52 percent, 11.52 percent, and 5.76 percent.

   a.   What are the net cash flows for each year of the robot's five-year life?
   b.   What is the net present value of the robot investment if the cost of capital is 10 percent?
   c.   What is the net present value of the robot investment if the cost of capital is 5 percent?
   d.   What is the profitability index of this investment if the cost of capital is 5 percent?
   e.   What is the payback period of the robot investment?
   f.   What is the discounted-payback period of the robot investment if the cost of capital is 5 percent?
   g.   What is the internal rate of return of the robot investment?
   h.   What is the modified internal rate of return of the robot investment if the cash flows are reinvested at 5 percent?
   i.   If the cost of capital is 5 percent, should Mighty Mouse invest in this robot?

9-13   The Sopchoppy Motorcycle Company is considering an investment of $600,000 in a new motorcycle. They expect to increase sales in each of the next three years by $400,000, while increasing expenses by $200,000 each year. They expect that they can carve out a niche in the marketplace for this new motorcycle for three years, after which they intend to cease production on this model and sell the manufacturing equipment for $200,000. Assume the equipment is depreciated at the rate of $200,000 each year. Sopchoppy's tax rate is 40 percent.

   a.   What are the net cash flows for each year of the motorcycle's three-year life?
   b.   What is the net present value of the investment if the cost of capital is 10 percent?
   c.   What is the net present value of the motorcycle investment if the cost of capital is 5 percent?

   d. What is the profitability index of this investment if the cost of capital is 5 percent?

   e. What is the payback period of the investment?

   f. What is the discounted payback of the investment if the cost of capital is 5 percent?

   g. What is the internal rate of return of the investment?

   h. What is the modified internal rate of return of the motorcycle investment if the cash flows are reinvested at 5 percent?

   i. If the cost of capital is 10 percent, should Sopchoppy invest in this motorcycle?

9-14 Using the cash flows provided in Chapter 8 for the Williams 5 & 10, calculate the net present value of opening the new retail store if the cost of capital is 10 percent.

9-15 Using the cash flows provided in Chapter 8 for the Hirshleifer Company, calculate the net present value of the investment to replace facilities if the cost of capital is 10 percent.

FURTHER READINGS

The development of our modern theories on investment decision making is reviewed in:

MICHAEL C. JENSEN and CLIFFORD W. SMITH, "The Theory of Corporate Finance: An Historical Overview," *Modern Theory of Corporate Finance,* McGraw-Hill, New York, 1983.

The rationale for the persistence of simpler techniques in capital budgeting is discussed in:

H. MARTIN WEINGARTNER, "Some New Views on the Payback Period and Capital Budgeting Decisions," *Management Science,* vol. 15, Aug. 1969, pp. 594–607.

H. LEVY, "A Note on the Payback Method," *Journal of Financial and Quantitative Analysis,* vol. 3, no. 4, Dec. 1968, pp. 433–443.

There are a number of surveys of capital budgeting practices by firms, including:

LAWRENCE J. GITMAN and JOHN R. FORRESTER, JR., "A Survey of Capital Budgeting Techniques Used by Major US Firms," *Financial Management,* vol. 6, no. 3, Fall 1977, pp. 66–71.

THOMAS KLAMMER and MICHAEL C. WALKER, "The Continuing Increase in the Use of Sophisticated Budgeting Techniques," *California Management Review,* vol. 27, no. 1, Fall 1984, pp. 137–148.

Investments with Unequal Lives

Suppose a bakery needs to replace its dough-kneading machine. This machine has a relatively short life, but the bakery will need a dough-kneader as far as we can see into the future. However, we can fit only one machine into the company's plant.

There are two machines that can satisfy the bakery's needs: Machine 1 and Machine 2, with expected economic lives of three and five years, respectively. To make things simpler, let's assume that the two machines have cash flows of identical risk, with a cost of capital of 5 percent per year. The expected cash flows for each kneading machine are:

	Cash flows	
End of year	Machine 1	Machine 2
0	−$10,000	−$10,000
1	4,500	3,000
2	4,500	3,000
3	4,500	3,000
4		3,000
5		3,000

Discounting each of the cash flows to the end of Year 0 at 5 percent,

	Machine 1		Machine 2	
End of year	Cash flow	Present value of cash flows at end of Year 0	Cash flow	Present value of cash flows at end of Year 0
1	$4,500	$ 4,285.72	$3,000	$ 2,857.14
2	4,500	4,081.63	3,000	2,721.09
3	4,500	3,887.27	3,000	2,591.51
4			3,000	2,468.11
5			3,000	2,350.58
Sum of present value of cash inflows		**$12,254.62**		**$12,988.43**

The NPV of Machine 1 is $2,254.62, and that of Machine 2 is $12,988.43.

But we have a problem in comparing these two investments on the basis of their NPVs. They have different economic lives. If the bakery invests in Machine 1, which lasts only three years, the bakery would have to invest in another kneader at the end of three years. The replacement in three years also creates value (that is, has an NPV > 0). This practical consideration is beginning to make it seem there is no point in trying to compare an NPV for a project whose economic life is three years with the NPV of a project whose economic life is five years.

So how do we compare projects with different economic lives? There are two techniques we can use: the replacement chain method and the equivalent annuity approach.

The Replacement Chain Method

To see what the ***replacement chain method*** is, let's assume that:

1. The bakery replaces the three-year machine, Machine 1, four times after the initial purchase, for a total of five sequential investments, amounting to an investment horizon of fifteen years.
2. The bakery replaces the five-year machine, Machine 2, twice after the initial purchase, for a total of three sequential investments in the machine, amounting to an investment horizon of fifteen years.

Because we have expanded our view of each machine from its economic life to a broader investment horizon, and both machines can now be regarded over identical investment horizons, referred to as the ***common life,*** we can now compare their NPVs meaningfully over this span.

Machine 1: One Investment Plus Four Replacements

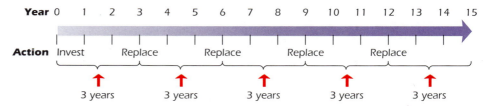

Machine 2: One Investment Plus Two Replacements

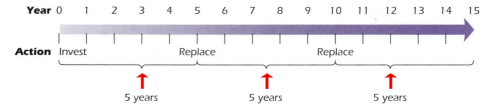

To compare projects having different economic lives using the replacement chain method, we assume that we replace each project enough times (a finite number of times) so that they have identical investment horizons.

Once we determine the number of investments and replacements for each project, we calculate the net present value of the project *considering the initial investments and all replacements.*

For Machine 1, the net present value is the sum of the *discounted* net present values of the investment and four replacements:

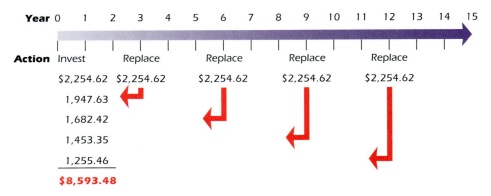

If the bakery invests in Machine 1 initially (at time 0), the bakery increases its value by $2,254.62. If the bakery invests in Machine 1 at the end of the third year, the bakery increases its value by $2,254.62 in terms of end-of-year-three dollars. But investing in Machine 1 at the end of the third year increases the value of the bakery today (the end of time 0) by only $2,254.62/$(1 + 0.05)^3$ = $1,947.63. Continuing this process for the other three replacements, we find that the value of investing in Machine 1 (initially and its four replacements) is $8,593.48.

For Machine 2, the net present value is the sum of the *discounted* net present values of the initial investment and two replacements:

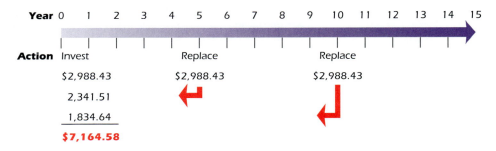

The value of investing in Machine 2 (initially and with two replacements) is $7,164.58.

Since we have now compared the net present values of the two machines on the basis of a common life (fifteen years), we can evaluate these two projects on the basis of their present values. Since Machine 1 provides the higher NPV with replacements, $8,593.48 versus $7,164.58, it is preferred.

Equivalent Annual Annuity Approach

Using the replacement chain to analyze dough-kneading Machines 1 and 2 with different economic lives, we assumed a finite number of replacements (four for Machine 1 and two for Machine 2) so that we could compare the two machines over a common life span (fifteen years).

We could have assumed that replacements are made forever—every three years for Machine 1 and every five years for Machine 2. How do we value a project that is reinvested forever? By using what we know about the value of a perpetuity.

Our objective is to determine the NPV of the perpetual investment in the project. Remember how we value a perpetuity: We divide the cash flow per period by the discount rate per period:

$$\text{Present value of a perpetuity} = \frac{\text{cash flow per period}}{\text{discount rate per period}}$$

If we apply this to Machine 1, we obtain a value of $2,254.62 every three years forever: $2,254.62 is the cash flow, and we need a *three-year discount rate*. If we apply this to Machine 2, we obtain a value of $2,988.43 every five years forever: $2,988.43 is the cash flow, and we need a *five-year discount rate*.

Since this involves figuring a three-year and a five-year discount rate, an alternative is to express the cash flow (the NPV) in terms of an equivalent annual annuity and find the value of the perpetuity by dividing this equivalent annual annuity by the discount rate.

$$\text{Present value of a perpetuity} = \frac{\text{equivalent annual annuity}}{\text{discount rate}}$$

The ***equivalent annual annuity approach*** assumes that the investment in each project is made forever—perpetually. Therefore, we find the annuity that is equivalent in value to the net present value calculated over the asset's original life and then value this annuity in perpetuity.

Finding the annuity equivalent to the net present value is straightforward: We can use the table of present value annuity factors or an annuity function in our calculators. Let's look at Machine 1. What three-period annuity is equivalent to a present value of $2,254.62, using a discount rate of 5 percent?

$$\$2,254.62 = \sum_{t=1}^{3} \frac{\text{equivalent annual annuity}}{(1 + 0.05)^t}$$

$$= \frac{\text{equivalent}}{\text{annual annuity}} \times \frac{\text{present value annuity factor}}{\text{for T = 3 and r = 5\%}}$$

Rearranging:

$$\frac{\text{Equivalent}}{\text{annual annuity}} = \frac{\$2,254.62}{\text{present value annuity factor}} = \frac{\$2,254.62}{2.7232} = \mathbf{\$827.93}$$
$$\text{for T = 3 and r = 5\%}$$

Receiving $827.93 per year for three years is equivalent to receiving $2,254.62 today if it can earn 5 percent interest per year compounded annually, and receiving $827.93 each year forever is worth $16,558.61 today:

$$\text{Net present value of Machine 1 in perpetuity} = \frac{\$827.93}{0.05} = \mathbf{\$16,558.61}$$

Replacement Chain Method Procedure

Step 1 Determine the common life—the length of time into which the economic life of each project divides equally.

Step 2 Calculate the net present value over the original economic life of each project.

Step 3 Calculate the sum of the discounted net present values for the initial investment and the replacements, using the cost of capital to discount NPVs in the future.

Step 4 Compare the sum of the discounted net present values, selecting the project with the greatest sum.

Equivalent Annual Annuity Approach Procedure

Step 1 Calculate the net present value of each project.

Step 2 For each project, solve for the annuity that is equivalent in value to the NPV.

Step 3 Calculate the present value of the annuity assuming the annuity to be a perpetuity, using the cost of capital as the discount rate.

Step 4 Compare the present value of the perpetuities, selecting the project with the greatest value. If the projects have identical discount rates, this step is not necessary, since the project with the greater equivalent annual annuity has the greater value in perpetuity.

The net present value produced by Machine 2 with perpetual investments is calculated in the same manner. We solve for the equivalent annuity by equating the net present value to the present value of a five-period annuity:

$$\$2,988.43 = \sum_{t=1}^{5} \frac{\text{equivalent annual annuity}}{(1 + 0.05)^t}$$

$$= \frac{\text{equivalent}}{\text{annual annuity}} \times \frac{\text{present value annuity factor}}{\text{for } T = 5 \text{ and } r = 5\%}$$

Rearranging:

$$\frac{\text{Equivalent}}{\text{annual annuity}} = \frac{\$2,988.43}{\frac{\text{present value annuity factor}}{\text{for } T = 5 \text{ and } r = 5\%}} = \frac{\$2,988.43}{4.3295} = \mathbf{\$690.25}$$

The net present value invested perpetually of Machine 2 is:

$$\text{Net present value of Machine 2 in perpetuity} = \frac{\$690.25}{0.05} = \mathbf{\$13,804.97}$$

The NPV of Machine 1 is greater than that of Machine 2, $16,558.51 versus $13,804.97, assuming perpetual investments in the assets. Therefore, Machine 1 is preferable.

SUMMARY

- In evaluating mutually exclusive projects that have different economic lives and that we plan to replace upon expiration of their lives, we need to look beyond net present value in order to make our comparisons.

- Some type of adjustment for the unequal lives is necessary. We can use either the replacement chain method or the equivalent annuity approach.

- The replacement chain method assumes a finite number of replacements of each project so that they can be compared over a common life. The annual equivalent annuity approach assumes a perpetual replacement of each project.

PROBLEMS

9A-1 Suppose there are two pieces of equipment that satisfy your production needs. The Felix equipment costs $10,000 and is expected to generate cash flows of $4,021 per year for three years. The Oscar equipment costs $5,000 and is expected to generate cash flows of $2,765 per year, but will last only two years. If your need for the equipment is continuous—that is, you will replace either piece of equipment at the end of its life with the same equipment as far as you can forecast into the future, which equipment should you choose? Assume a cost of capital of 5 percent for both.

9A-2 Consider the two mutually exclusive projects UX and UY:

	Cash flows	
End of year	**Project UX**	**Project UY**
2000	−$20,000	−$20,000
2001	15,000	7,600
2002	15,000	7,600
2003		7,600
2004		7,600

Both projects have a cost of capital of 10 percent, and a similar project will be needed for the foreseeable future. Which project should be selected? Why?

9A-3   Consider three mutually exclusive projects with the following cash flows:

	Cash flows		
End of year	**Project 1**	**Project 2**	**Project 3**
2000	−$100,000	−$100,000	−$100,000
2001	42,000	34,000	25,000
2002	42,000	34,000	25,000
2003	42,000	34,000	25,000
2004		34,000	25,000
2005			25,000
2006			25,000

Each project is capable of satisfying our requirements, and we will need this type of project for the foreseeable future. The cost of capital for each of the three projects is 10 percent. Which project should we select? Why?

APPENDIX 9B   The Leasing Decision

INTRODUCTION

A **lease** is an agreement giving to another party the right to use an asset for a specified period in exchange for a periodic payment referred to as the rent or lease payment. The party who owns the asset is the **lessor**; the party granted the right to use it is the **lessee**.

Leasing an asset is often an alternative to purchasing it. But there is a difference between leasing and buying: A firm buying an asset can finance it using debt, equity, or some mix of both; a firm leasing that same asset is essentially financing it with debt. This difference affects how we analyze a decision to buy or to lease.

TYPES OF LEASES

A lease contract specifies the conditions and terms of the leasing arrangement, including:

- The leasing period.
- The amount and timing of the rental payments.
- The parties responsible for the costs of maintaining and repairing the asset.
- Cancellation privileges.
- The option, if any, to purchase the asset at the end of the lease.

Since there are many different combinations of terms that can be negotiated in a lease, there are many different types of lease arrangements. The two main types are operating leases and capital leases.[1] An **operating lease** is usually for a term that is less than the asset's useful life and is cancelable. A **capital lease**, also referred to as a **financial lease**, usually has a lease term extending to the economic life of the asset and is not cancelable. To compare buying and leasing, we will focus on capital leases because they represent an alternative to buying an asset.

Within the broad class of capital leases, there are alternative forms of leasing, including:

- A **direct lease**, which grants the lessee the right to use an asset that it did not already own.
- The **sale-leaseback arrangement**, in which the owner of an asset sells it to another party and then leases it back from the new owner.
- A **leveraged lease**, in which the lessor borrows a substantial portion of the funds used to purchase the asset. A leveraged lease therefore involves a lessee, a lessor, and a lender.

From the perspective of the lessee, it doesn't matter what form the capital lease takes because the cost of the lease is the lease payment promised. However, the lease payments are fully deductible for tax purposes by the lessee if:

1. The leasing period is for less than 90 percent of the asset's economic life.
2. Any purchase option at the end of the lease is close to the asset's expected fair market value.

> ### Capital or Operating
>
> To be classified as a capital lease for financial statement purposes, the lease must satisfy one of the following conditions:
>
> - The leasing period is greater than or equal to 75 percent of the economic life of the asset.
> - The present value of the lease payments, determined at the beginning of the lease, exceeds 90 percent of the current market value of the leased property.
> - The lease transfers title to the asset to the lessee at the end of the lease period.
> - The lease contains an option to purchase the asset at a bargain price.

---

[1] The distinction between these two types of leases is clarified in Statement of Financial Accounting Standards No. 13, "Accounting for Leases," FASB, Stamford, Conn., Nov. 1976.

If these conditions are not met, the lease is viewed as a disguised installment sale, in which case the lessee deducts from taxable income the depreciation on the asset and the implied interest, but not the lease payment.

From the perspective of the lessor, it doesn't matter what form the capital lease takes unless the lease is construed as an installment sale. In that case, the lessor reports any gain or loss on the sale of the asset and any interest income on the loan, but does not deduct depreciation on the asset.

ANALYSIS OF THE LEASE VS. BUY DECISION

Evaluating an asset that can be leased or bought and deciding which to do is an investment decision that should be based on whether the asset increases the value of the firm, not on how the acquisition is financed. And the decision follows along the same lines as those for any other type of investment decision: Do the firm's future cash flows increase? If so, does the present value of these future cash flows exceed the cost of the asset? To analyze any investment, we estimate its future incremental cash flows and discount them at a rate that reflects the investment's uncertainty of producing those flows. And we don't include the financing arrangements for the project when we analyze the investment decision: We separate the investment and financing decisions.

But in analyzing a lease versus buy decision, the financing decision and investment decision are intertwined. And because we want to compare leasing and buying on the same terms, we have to compare the financing cash flows of each.

If we have already determined to acquire an asset, apart from how we choose to finance it, then we must decide whether to borrow to buy it or to lease it. If we're deciding between buying an asset, financing it with a mix of debt and equity, and leasing (which is effectively all debt financing) the analysis becomes complex. That's because the rate we use to discount future cash flows is different for different capital structures. Let's simplify the decision and compare leasing with borrowing to buy.

Cash Flows Related to Leasing

Suppose we have decided to acquire an asset that has a three-year useful life and costs $200,000 today if we buy it outright. How much must we pay in rent? Let us assume that:

1. The lessor wants a 9 percent return (before taxes).
2. There is no expected salvage value at the end of the lease.
3. The lease payments are to be made at the beginning of each period (the typical arrangement).

Then the rental payment must be:

$$\$200{,}000 = \text{rent} + \frac{\text{rent}}{(1 + 0.09)^1} + \frac{\text{rent}}{(1 + 0.09)^2}$$

$$= \text{rent}(1 + 0.9174 + 0.8417)$$

$$= 2.7591(\text{rent})$$

Rent = **$72,487**

The lessee's cash flows to finance the asset would be the $72,487 rent payment (cash outflow) at the beginning of each year (or the end of the prior year) less any tax shield from the deduction of the lease payment. If we designate the beginning of the lease as the end of the year 0, the cash outflows are at the end of year 0, year 1, and year 2.

But that's not the complete story. What is the tax shield from the lease payment deduction, and when is it realized? Not at the end of year 0, but some time later, because it reduces the taxes to be paid during year 1. Let's assume the lease payment tax shield reduces taxes paid at the end of the year *following* the payment. Like the depreciation tax shield, the lease payment tax shield is the product of the tax rate and the lease payment. If the tax rate is 40 percent, the tax shield in each year is:

Lease payment tax shield = 40% × $72,487 = **$28,995**

The cash flows related to leasing are therefore:

End of year	Lease payment	Lease payment tax shield	Net cash flow from lease
0	−$72,487	$ 0	−$72,487
1	−72,487	+28,995	−43,492
2	−72,487	+28,995	−43,492
3	0	+28,995	+28,995

Now that we have the cash flows related to leasing, we must translate them into the value they represent at the beginning of the lease, the end of year 0. To do this requires a discount rate that reflects the uncertainty of these cash flows. Since the lease payment is contractual, there is little uncertainty regarding these values from the perspective of the lessee who must pay the rent, since the rent is a fixed amount, specified in the lease agreement.[2] But the tax rate and the lessee firm's ability to use the lease payment deduction on its tax return are uncertain. The common approach is to use the lessee's after-tax cost of debt.[3] Suppose the lessee firm's cost of debt is 10 percent. The after-tax cost of debt is:

After-tax cost of debt = 0.10(1 − 0.40) = **0.06** or **6%**

Discounting the lease-related cash flows at 6 percent:

End of year	Net cash flow from lease	Present value
0	+$72,487	−$72,487
1	−43,492	−41,030
2	−43,492	−38,708
3	+28,995	+24,345

Net present value of leasing cash flows **−$127,880**

[2] If we were analyzing the lease from the lessor's perspective, the uncertainty of receiving these payments must be considered. There is evidence that suggests there is a high rate of default (19 percent) in lease contracts (Ronald C. Lease, John J. McConnell, and James S. Schallheim, "Realized Returns and the Default and Prepayment Experience of Financial Leasing Contracts," *Financial Management*, vol. 19, no. 2, Summer 1990, pp. 11–20).

[3] For a discussion of this controversy, see Richard S. Bower, "Issues in Lease Financing," *Financial Management*, vol. 2, no. 4, Winter 1973, pp. 25–34.

Cash Flows Related to Borrowing

Now let's look at the cash flows related to borrowing, including:

1. The cash outflow for the loan repayment.
2. The cash inflow for the interest tax shield.
3. The depreciation tax shield.
4. The salvage value (and any related taxes) at the end of the asset's useful life.

First, we know the firm can borrow at 10 percent. Next, let's assume that the first payment is made immediately, at the end of the year 0 (so that we can compare it on the same time basis as the lease payments). The three lease payments constitute a three-period cash flow annuity due:

$$\$200,000 = \text{loan payment} + \frac{\text{loan payment}}{(1 + 0.10)^1} + \frac{\text{loan payment}}{(1 + 0.10)^2}$$

$$= \text{loan payment}(1 + 0.9091 + 0.8264)$$

$$= 2.7355(\text{loan payment})$$

Loan payment = **$73,113**

This would mean that there are three payments of $73,113 each, paid at the end of year 0, year 1, and year 2.

To determine the interest deduction, we need to first amortize the loan, separating each payment into the interest paid on the principal balance at the start of the year and the amount by which that payment reduces the loan's principal:

Year	Loan balance, beginning of year	Loan payment	Interest, beginning loan balance × 10%	Reduction in loan principal	Loan balance, end of year
0	$200,000	$73,113	$ 0	$73,113	$126,887
1	126,887	73,113	12,689	60,424	66,463
2	66,463	73,113	6,646	66,463[a]	0[a]

[a]Small rounding difference.

Because the first payment is made immediately, the principal reduction at the end of the first year is $73,113. The payment is a cash outflow, but the interest component is deducted for tax purposes, effectively creating a cash inflow of 40 percent of the interest deduction: 40 percent × $12,689 = $5,076 in year 1 and 40 percent × $6,646 = $2,658 in year 2.

If the asset is a three-year MACRS asset, its depreciation and tax shield each year are:

Year	Depreciation	Depreciation tax shield
1	$66,000	$26,400
2	90,000	36,000
3	30,000	12,000

The cash flows related to borrowing, ignoring any salvage value, are therefore:

End of year	Loan payment	Interest tax shield	Depreciation tax shield	Net cash flow from borrowing	Present value
0	−$73,113	$ 0	$ 0	−$73,113	−$ 73,113
1	−73,113	+5,076	+26,400	−41,637	−39,280
2	−73,113	+2,658	+36,000	−34,455	−30,665
3	0	0	+12,000	+26,000	+21,830
Net present value of loan cash flows					**−$121,228**

Now let's include salvage value. The book value of the asset at the end of the third year is $200,000 − $66,000 − $90,000 − $30,000 = $14,000. Suppose the asset could be sold at the end of the third year for $14,000. The firm would have a cash inflow of $14,000 and no inflow or outflow for taxes. The present value of the $14,000 inflow, discounting it at 6 percent, is $11,755. This would increase the net present value of the loan cash flows to −$121,228 + $11,755 = − $109,473.

If, instead, the asset could be sold for, say $20,000, there would be a $20,000 cash inflow but a ($20,000 − $14,000) × 40 percent = $2,400 cash outflow for taxes, or a net inflow at the end of the third year of $20,000 − $2,400 = $17,600. If we discount this cash flow at 6 percent and add it to the present value of the other cash flows from the loan, the net borrowing-to-buy cash flows are −$106,451.

Since the salvage value has a different level of uncertainty than the lease, depreciation, or interest payments, any expected cash flows from the sale of the asset at the end of the lease term should be discounted at some other (most likely higher) rate. The $17,600 cash flow at the end of the third year should be discounted at a higher rate than the 6 percent we used to discount the other loan-related cash flows.

Leasing vs. Borrowing

In this example, the present value of the leasing cash flows is −$127,880 and the present value of the borrowing cash flows (ignoring the benefit from any salvage value) is −$121,228. Leasing the asset is more costly than borrowing to buy it.

There are several reasons for any difference between a lease and a borrow-to-purchase situation.

The difference in costs arises from several sources:

- The return required by the lessor may be different from the interest cost of borrowing. In our example, the cost of borrowing was 10 percent; yet the lessor required only a 9 percent (before-tax) return on the lease.
- Lease payments are even throughout the life of the lease. However, if the asset is purchased, the owner can depreciate the asset using an accelerated method, which provides earlier tax deductions.

- Another source of difference is the asset's salvage value. If the asset is leased, any salvage value reverts to the lessor; if the asset is purchased, the owner can sell it at the end of its useful life.

Analysis When Leasing Is the Only Option

There are many instances when leasing is the only option. For example, a retail chain that wants to open a store in a mall has to decide to lease the space or not do business in the mall at all—the space cannot be purchased.

When leasing is the only choice, the decision we need to make is whether to undertake the project. In this case, we need to evaluate the project as an investment decision. But we don't know the cost of the asset the project represents. What we do have is a stream of lease payments. One way to evaluate this situation is to calculate the present value of the lease payments, discounted at some rate that reflects the degree of uncertainty associated with the lease, which is typically less than other projects. Once the present value is calculated, we determine the project's other cash flows and discount them at the project's cost of capital—a discount rate that reflects the uncertainty of these future cash flows.[4]

Suppose the Sell All Company is considering opening another store in a mall where the only available space must be leased at a cost of $50,000 per year. And suppose Sell All expects to increase its sales by $200,000 and its expenses by $100,000 each year for the next five years if it takes the space for a new store. If Sell All's marginal tax rate is 40 percent, its cost of debt is 10 percent, and its estimate of the project's cost of capital is 12 percent, should it open the new store?

Because the lease payments are discounted at one rate and the incremental sales and expenses are discounted at another rate, there are two cash flows to be analyzed. The present value of the lease payments for the next five years is the $50,000 discounted at the after-tax cost of debt, 10 percent $\times$ $(1 - 0.40) = 6$ percent:

$$\text{Present value of lease payments} = \sum_{t=0}^{4} \frac{\$50,000}{(1 + 0.06)^t} = \mathbf{\$223,255}$$

The after-tax change in sales and expenses each year is ($200,000 - 100,000) \times (1 - 0.40) = $60,000$. If we assume that each cash flow is not realized until the end of each year, the present value of these cash flows, discounted at the project's cost of capital, 12 percent, is:

$$\text{Present value of future benefits} = \sum_{t=1}^{5} \frac{\$60,000}{(1 + 0.12)^t} = \mathbf{\$216,287}$$

Since the present value of the lease payments exceeds the present value of the benefits from the new store, the new store should not be opened.

---

[4] It may be tempting to analyze cash flows as we did for a nonleasing project and include the after-tax lease payments as a cash outflow. But this is not correct, since the uncertainty of the lease payments will most likely be much less than the uncertainty of the project's other cash flows.

LEASING AND PERFECT MARKETS

In a world with perfect markets, there would be no cost to bankruptcy and no taxes. And we would be indifferent between borrowing to acquire an asset or leasing it: The lease payment would reflect the uncertainty of the project's future cash flows, and the debt cost would reflect the same uncertainty. As a result, the return required by lessors would be the same return required by lenders. But bankruptcy costs and taxes create a demand for leasing.

In a bankruptcy, the lessor has the right to take possession of the leased asset. A lender does not. Even in the case of a secured loan, the lender's position is inferior to that of a lessor: (1) the secured lender incurs costs in bankruptcy proceedings; and (2) there is delay before a secured asset can be legally acquired in default, sold, and its proceeds taken in hand.

Taxes enter into the analysis from the deductions for lease payments (in the lease analysis) and from the deductions for depreciation and interest (in the borrowing analysis). Suppose Firm A is a taxable entity and Firm B is a nontaxable entity (such as a university). If Firm B buys an asset costing $1 million, the asset does not affect its taxes, since it doesn't pay any.

If Firm A buys the asset (depreciating it) and leases it to Firm B, there may be a net gain in terms of the reduction of taxes: Firm A can take deductions for depreciation (using an accelerated method, such as the MACRS), and generate depreciation tax shields. Firm B doesn't do any of this because it doesn't pay taxes.

Suppose the asset can be depreciated as a three-year MACRS asset. If Firm A's tax rate is 40 percent, the depreciation tax shields are:

Year	Depreciation	Depreciation tax shield
1	$330,000	$132,000
2	450,000	180,000
3	150,000	60,000
4	70,000	28,000

If Firm A charges Firm B rent for four years to get a 10 percent before-tax return and the rent is paid annually at the beginning of the year, the annual lease payments would be $286,792. Taxes on the lease income are $286,792 × 40 percent = $114,717 per year. If we assume that the lease payments are made at the beginning of the year, but that taxes are not paid on this income until the end of the year, Firm A's cash flows would be:

Year	Purchase	Depreciation tax shield	Lease income	Tax on lease income	Net cash flow
0	−$1,000,000		+$286,792		−$713,208
1		+$132,000	+286,792	−$114,717	+304,075
2		+180,000	+286,792	−114,717	+352,075
3		+60,000	+286,792	−114,717	+232,075
4		+28,000		−114,717	−86,717

Discounting the cash flows at 6 percent, the net present value is $13,167. Firm A has created value by the purchase and subsequent lease of the asset to Firm B.

And this extends as well to the case in which one of the firms in the transaction cannot use the depreciation and interest tax deductions because of insufficient taxable income. Suppose a firm generating operating losses wants to acquire an asset. Depreciation deductions do not mean much to this firm because they would only serve to reduce taxes in future years (through net operating loss carryovers). If another, profitable firm buys the asset, it can use the depreciation deductions.

If the lessor has a higher tax rate than the lessee, the depreciation tax shield is more valuable to the lessor than the lessee. So it may be beneficial for higher-taxed firms to buy and lease assets to lower-taxed firms.

In addition to bankruptcy cost and tax considerations, there may be other reasons for leases. For example, lessors may be able to take advantage of economies of scale in purchasing assets, enabling them to purchase assets at a lower cost than an individual customer considering buying the same asset. Also, the lessor may face lower borrowing costs than that same potential lessee.

Considering the advantages one firm may have over another in purchasing an asset and the many lessors and lessees negotiating lease arrangements, market forces may provide an opportunity for the leasing firm to share some of these advantages by offering lease payments lower than any debt obligation the lessee may have incurred by buying the asset.

SUMMARY

- A lease is an arrangement whereby the owner of an asset, the lessor, gives another party, the lessee, the right to use it. There are many types of leases. Two main types are operating leases and capital leases. A capital lease may be in the form of a direct lease, a sale-leaseback arrangement, or a leveraged lease.

- Leasing is, effectively, a means of acquiring an asset through a form of financing similar to debt. To determine whether to lease, you need to compare the costs of leasing with the costs of borrowing to buy the asset.

- In comparing the cash flows related to leasing versus the flows related to borrowing, future cash flows are discounted to the present using a discount rate that reflects the after-tax cost of borrowing.

- If leasing is the only way to acquire an asset, analyzing the lease is like analyzing the purchase of the asset, except that the cost of the asset is replaced by the present value of the lease payments (discounted at the after-tax cost of debt).

QUESTIONS

9B-1   Is renting an apartment for one year an operating lease or a capital lease? Explain.

9B-2   What distinguishes a sale-leaseback arrangement from a direct lease?

9B-3   In evaluating a lease versus borrow decision, why is the discount rate not the project's cost of capital?

9B-4   If there were no taxes and no costs to bankruptcy, would there still be a demand for leasing? Explain.

9B-5   If leasing is the only option available to acquire the use of an asset, why should we discount the project's cash flows at the project's cost of capital and not at the after-tax cost of debt?

PROBLEMS

9B-1   What would the lease payments have to be for an asset costing $200,000 (with no salvage value) in order for the lessor to get a return of 8 percent if lease payments are made at the beginning of each year for four years?

9B-2   What would the loan payments need to be on a three-year loan of $2 million if the interest rate is 5 percent per year and payments are made at the beginning of each year? Calculate the loan amortization, breaking out the interest payments from the principal repayment.

9B-3   The Barrow Company is considering acquiring a new machine. In the company's analysis, it found that acquiring the machine would increase the value of the firm. Now Barrow needs to decide whether to lease the machine or purchase it. The machine would cost $1 million and has a useful life of five years. It would be depreciated using a five-year life under the MACRS. The Barrow Company expects that the machine could be sold for $20,000 at the end of the fifth year. Assume a marginal tax rate of 30 percent. The discount rate appropriate for the salvage value, if the asset is purchased, is 10 percent.

   a. If the lessor requires a 10 percent before-tax return from the lease payments, ignoring any salvage value, what annual payment (paid at the beginning of each year) would the lessor require?
   b. If the cost of borrowing is 10 percent, what loan payment must be made each year for five years (beginning immediately)?
   c. If both the lessor and the lender require a 10 percent return, should Barrow lease the asset or buy it? Explain.

9B-4 Arice Company is considering acquiring a new machine. In Arice's analysis, it found that acquiring the machine would increase the value of the firm. Now Arice must decide whether to lease the machine or purchase it. The machine would cost $100,000, has a useful life of three years, and would be depreciated using a three-year life under the MACRS. Arice expects that the machine would have a $20,000 salvage value at the end of the third year. The discount rate appropriate for this salvage value is 10 percent. Assume a marginal tax rate of 40 percent.

    a. If the lessor requires a 10 percent before-tax return from the lease payments, what annual payment (paid at the beginning of each year) would the lessor require for the three-year lease?

    b. If the cost of borrowing is 12 percent, what loan payment must be made each year for three years (beginning immediately)?

    c. If both the lessor and the lender require a 10 percent return, should Arice lease the asset, or buy it? Explain.

9B-5 Suppose the Mall-O Store Company is considering opening a new store in the Llama Mall. They can lease the space for five years at $100,000 per year, payable at the beginning of each year. Over the five years, they expect to increase sales by $600,000 each year and incur additional expenses of $450,000 per year. Mall-O's marginal tax rate is 35 percent. If Mall-O's cost of debt is 10 percent and its cost of capital appropriate for the store's revenues and expenses is 10 percent, should it open the new store?

FURTHER READINGS

A debate on some of the thornier issues in lease analysis can be found in the following four articles:

H. MARTIN WEINGARTNER, "Leasing, Asset Lives and Uncertainty: Guides to Decision Making," *Financial Management*, vol. 16, no. 2, Summer 1987, pp. 5–12.

ROGER L. CASON, "Leasing, Asset Lives and Uncertainty: A Practitioner's Comments," ibid., pp. 13–16.

LAWRENCE D. SCHALL, "Analytic Issues in Lease vs. Purchase Decisions," ibid., pp.17–20.

H. MARTIN WEINGARTNER, "Rejoinder," ibid., pp. 21–23.

A survey of companies' approaches to the analysis of leasing decisions can be found in:

TARUN K. MUKHERJEE, "A Survey of Corporate Leasing Analysis," *Financial Management*, vol. 20, no. 3, Autumn 1991, pp. 96–107.

CHAPTER 10

Capital Budgeting and Risk

INTRODUCTION 463

RISK AND CASH FLOWS 464

Relevant Cash Flow Risk 464

Different Types of Project Risk 465

MEASUREMENT OF PROJECT RISK 466

Measuring a Project's Stand-Alone Risk 467

    Statistical Measures of Cash Flow Risk 467

    Sensitivity Analysis 475

    Simulation Analysis 477

Measuring a Project's Market Risk 481

    Market Risk and Financial Leverage 481

    Using a Pureplay 483

INCORPORATING RISK IN THE CAPITAL BUDGETING DECISION 484

Risk-Adjusted Rates 484

    Required Return for a Project's Market Risk 485

    Adjusting a Firm's Cost of Capital 486

Certainty Equivalents 486

ASSESSMENT OF PROJECT RISK IN PRACTICE 487

Summary 488

A Product That Became Too Hot

In 1992, Larami Corporation, a closely held corporation and a producer and distributor of toys, introduced what became the summer season's hottest toy: the Super Soaker toy gun, capable of shooting large spurts of water long distances. Despite imitations by rival toy makers, Larami's toy gun was the best-seller and was by far its most profitable toy in 1992. Alas, some users were filling their toy guns with harmful liquids, causing injuries.

So what do you do if your new product becomes popular but doused in controversy? Do you pull it from the shelves and discontinue selling it? If you do, you lose your most successful product. If you stop selling it, there's no guarantee your competitors will stop selling their imitations of your product. Do you continue selling it, even though parents and police departments protest against its continued sale? If you do, your company looks insensitive to its consumers.

Many products have been misused by consumers. But the response by the companies that make and sell these products has been varied: Some add warning labels (such as that printed on Liquid Paper correction fluid), fight governmental restrictions (such as with lawn darts), or voluntarily limit advertising (such as with alcoholic beverages).

Larami didn't expect controversy with its new toy. With any new product—or even established products—there can be many surprises that affect future sales or expenses. The point here is that financial managers need to understand that there is uncertainty regarding future cash flows.

INTRODUCTION *To understand uncertainty and risk is to understand the key business problem—and the key business opportunity.*

David B. Hertz, 1972

The capital budgeting decisions that a financial manager makes require analyzing for each project:

- Future cash flows.
- Degree of uncertainty of these future cash flows.
- Value of these future cash flows, considering their uncertainty.

We looked at how to estimate future cash flows in Chapter 8, in which we saw that a project's incremental cash flows comprise two types: (1) operating cash flows (the change in the revenues, expenses, and taxes) and (2) investment cash flows (the acquisition and disposition of the project's assets).

In Chapter 9, we focused on evaluating future cash flows. *Given* estimates of incremental cash flows for a project and *given* a discount rate that reflects the uncertainty that the project will produce those flows as expected, we looked at alternative techniques that are used to select projects to invest in.

When we look at the available investment opportunities, we want to determine which projects will maximize the value of the firm and, hence, maximize owners' wealth. That is, we analyze each project, evaluating how much its benefits exceed its costs. The projects that are expected to increase owners' wealth the most are the best ones.

In deciding whether a project increases shareholder wealth, we have to weigh its benefits and its costs. The costs are:

1. The cash flow we need to make the investment (the investment outlay).
2. The opportunity costs of using the cash we tie up in the investment.

The benefits are the future cash flows generated by the investment. But we know that anything in the future is uncertain; so we know those future cash flows are not certain. Therefore, for an evaluation of any investment to be meaningful, we must represent how much risk there is that the cash flows of an investment will differ from what is expected in terms of their amount and timing. **Risk** is the *degree* of uncertainty.

We can incorporate risk in one of two ways: (1) we can discount future cash flows using a discount rate that reflects the cash flow's risk (the greater the risk, the higher the rate) or (2) we can require an annual return on the project that reflects the cash flow's risk (the greater the cash flow's risk, the higher the required annual return). And, of course, we must incorporate risk into our investment decisions in order to maximize owners' wealth. In this chapter, we look at the sources of cash flow uncertainty and how to incorporate risk in the capital budgeting decision.

We begin by describing what we mean by risk in the context of long-lived projects. We then propose several commonly used statistical measures of risk, taking what we learned about risk in Chapter 7, expanding on what we learned, and applying it to capital projects. Then we look at the relation between risk and return, specifically for capital projects, and we conclude by showing how risk can be incorporated in the capital budgeting decision and how the process of incorporation is applied in practice.

RISK AND CASH FLOWS

When we estimate (which is the best we can do) what it costs to invest in a given project and what its benefits will be in the future, we are coping with uncertainty. The uncertainty arises from different sources, depending on the type of investment under consideration, as well as the circumstances and the industry in which the investment will take place. Uncertainty may be due to:

1. *Economic conditions.* Will consumers be spending or saving? Will the economy be in a recession? Will the government stimulate spending? Will there be inflation?
2. *Market conditions.* Is the market competitive? How long does it take for competitors to enter into the market? Are there any barriers, such as patents or trademarks, that will keep competitors away? Is there a sufficient supply of raw materials and labor? How much will raw materials and labor cost in the future?
3. *Taxes.* What will tax rates be? Will Congress alter the tax system?
4. *Interest rates.* What will be the cost of raising capital in future years?
5. *International conditions.* Will currency exchange rates change? Are the governments of the countries in which the firm does business stable?

These sources of uncertainty influence future cash flows. To evaluate and select among projects that will maximize owners' wealth, we need to assess the uncertainty associated with a project's cash flows. In evaluating a capital project, we are concerned with measuring its risk.

Relevant Cash Flow Risk

Financial managers worry about risk because the suppliers of capital—the creditors and owners—demand compensation for taking on risk. They can either provide their funds to your firm to make investments or they could invest their funds elsewhere. Therefore, there is an opportunity cost to consider: what the suppliers of capital could earn elsewhere for the same level of risk. We refer to the return required by the suppliers of capital as the *required rate of return,* which comprises the compensation to suppliers of capital for their opportunity cost of not having the funds available (the time value of money) and compensation for risk.

$$\text{Required rate of return} = \frac{\text{compensation for the}}{\text{time value of money}} + \frac{\text{compensation}}{\text{for risk}}$$

Using the net present value criterion, if the present value of the future cash flows is greater than the present value of the cost of the project, the investment is expected to increase the value of the firm, and therefore is acceptable. If the present value of the future cash flows is less than the present value of the costs of the project, the investment should be rejected. And under certain circumstances, using the internal rate of return criterion, if the project's return exceeds the project's cost of capital, the project increases owners' wealth.

From the perspective of the firm, this required rate of return is what it costs to raise capital; so we also refer to this rate as the *cost of capital.*

The Required Rate of Return and the Cost of Capital

You'll notice that we tend to use "required rate of return" and "cost of capital" as synonymous terms. They are very close concepts: The required rate of return is the return suppliers of capital demand in return for the use of their funds; the cost of capital is the cost, expressed in the form of a return.

However, there is a subtle distinction: The required rate of return ignores the cost of issuing additional capital (such as underwriter fees), whereas the cost of capital includes those costs. In most cases, however, the costs are so small we just ignore them; hence, the required rate of return and the cost of capital are very close figures.

We refer to the compensation for risk as a ***risk premium***—the additional return necessary to compensate investors for the risk they bear. How much compensation for risk is enough? 2 percent? 4 percent? 10 percent?

How do we assess the risk of a project? We begin by recognizing that the assets of a firm are the result of its prior investment decisions. What this means is that the firm is really a collection, or portfolio, of projects. So when the firm adds another project to its portfolio, should we be concerned only about the risk of that additional project? Or should we be concerned about the risk of the entire portfolio when the new project is included in it? To see which, let's look at the different dimensions of risk of a project.

Different Types of Project Risk

If we have some idea of the uncertainty associated with a project's future cash flows—its possible outcomes—and the probabilities associated with these outcomes, we will have a measure of the risk of the project. But this is the project's risk in isolation from the firm's other projects. This is the risk of ignoring the effects of diversification in assessing the project and is referred to as the project's total risk, or ***stand-alone risk.***

Since most firms have other assets, the stand-alone risk of the project under consideration may not be the relevant risk for analyzing the project. A firm is a portfolio of assets and the returns on these different assets do not necessarily move together, that is, they are not perfectly positively correlated with one another. We are therefore not concerned about the stand-alone risk of a project, but rather *how the addition of the project to the firm's portfolio of assets changes the risk of the portfolio.*

Now let's take it a step further. The shares of many firms may be owned by investors who *themselves* hold diversified portfolios. These investors are concerned about how the firm's investments affect the risk of their own personal portfolios. When owners demand compensation for risk, they are requiring compensation for market risk, the risk they can't get rid of by diversifying. Recognizing this, a firm considering taking on a new project should be concerned with how the project would change the market risk of a firm. Therefore, if the firm's owners hold diversified investments, it is the project's *market* risk that is relevant to the firm's decision making.

Even though we generally believe that it's the project's market risk that is important to analyze, stand-alone risk should not be ignored. If we are mak-

Diversifiable versus Nondiversifiable Risk: A Brief Review

Suppose we invest in only one asset and its future cash flows are uncertain. They may be one value or another, depending on how the economy, the market, and our competitors behave in the future. These things are the source of the risk associated with the asset's cash flows.

Now suppose we invest in a second asset. Its cash flows are uncertain also. But the cash flows of this second asset do not necessarily vary with economic and market conditions in the same way as the cash flows of the first asset. That is, the second asset's future cash flows may not be perfectly positively correlated with the future cash flows of the first asset. When the economy slumps, perhaps the cash flows of the first asset are up and cash flows of the second asset are down or, perhaps, the cash flows of the first asset are up and those of the second asset are up but not by as much.

So what does the risk of the two assets look like when considered together? The risk of our portfolio composed of these two assets is lower than the risk of the portfolio composed of only the first asset. Why? Because the total investment—the two assets—is not as risky. That's because as we add assets to our portfolio, we are most likely adding assets whose cash flows are not perfectly positively correlated. As assets are added whose cash flows are not perfectly correlated with the assets already in the portfolio, the portfolio's risk declines.

We refer to the portion of the risk that is reduced as assets are added as the ***diversifiable risk***. The remaining risk is the ***nondiversifiable risk*** and is the risk that we cannot get rid of through diversification. We also refer to the nondiversifiable risk as the ***market risk***.

ing decisions for a small, closely held firm whose owners do not hold well-diversified portfolios, the stand-alone risk gives us a good idea of the project's risk. And many small businesses fit into this category.

And even if we are making investment decisions for large corporations that have many products and whose owners are well diversified, the analysis of stand-alone risk is useful. Stand-alone risk is often closely related to market risk: In many cases, projects with higher stand-alone risk may also have higher market risk. Furthermore, a project's stand-alone risk is easier to measure than market risk. To get an idea of a project's stand-alone risk, we can evaluate the project's future cash flows by means of statistical measures, sensitivity analysis, and simulation analysis.

MEASUREMENT OF PROJECT RISK

Take calculated risks. That is quite different from being rash.

George S. Patton, 1944

The financial decision maker needs to measure risk in order to evaluate risk and incorporate it into the capital budgeting decision. We next look at sev-

A Review of Probability

A **probability** is the likelihood of the particular outcome's occurrence in the future—the higher the probability, the more likely the outcome. For example, there is a 25 percent probability of drawing a card from the heart suit from a standard deck of playing cards comprising four suits and fifty-two cards. This means that we would draw a heart 25 percent of the time—one out of every four draws—*if* we kept drawing cards forever and *if* we put the drawn card back into the deck after each draw.

A **probability distribution** is the mathematical description of all the possible outcomes and their associated probabilities. This description merely tells us the likelihood of each possible outcome. For example, in the standard card deck:

Suit	Probability of drawing a card from the suit
Heart	25%
Diamond	25
Spade	25
Club	25
All	100%

If we have considered all possible outcomes, for example, all possible economic conditions, the probabilities of all outcomes must sum to 1.00 or 100 percent.

eral methods of evaluating risk, focusing first on stand-alone risk and then on market risk.

Measuring a Project's Stand-Alone Risk

Statistical Measures of Cash Flow Risk

We will look at three statistical measures that are used to evaluate the risk associated with a project's possible outcomes: the range, the standard deviation, and the coefficient of variation. Let's demonstrate each using new products as examples. Based on experience with our firm's current product lines and the market research for our new product, A, we can estimate that it may generate one of three different cash flows in its first year, depending on economic conditions:

Economic condition	Cash flow	Probability
Boom	$10,000	20% or 0.20
Normal	5,000	50% or 0.50
Recession	−1,000	30% or 0.30

The table shows that there are three possible outcomes, each representing a possible cash flow, and the probability of occurrence of each. Product A's three possible cash flows are represented graphically in Figure 10-1. This is a graph of a probability distribution where the probability of an outcome is represented on the vertical axis and the value of the outcome is represented on the horizontal axis.

Looking at this graph, we see that there is some chance of getting a −$1,000 cash flow and some chance of getting a +$10,000 cash flow, though the most likely possibility (the one with the greatest probability) is a +$5,000 cash flow.

But to get an idea of Product A's risk, we need to know a bit more. The more spread out the possible outcomes, the greater the degree of uncertainty (the risk) of what is expected in the future. We refer to the degree to which future outcomes are "spread out" as **dispersion.** In general, the greater the dispersion, the greater the risk.

There are several measures we could use to describe the dispersion of future outcomes. We will focus on the range, the standard deviation, and the coefficient of variation.

The Range

The **range** is a statistical measure representing how far apart are the two extreme outcomes of the probability distribution. The range is calculated as the difference between the best and the worst possible outcomes:

Range = best possible outcome − worst possible outcome

FIGURE 10-1
Probability Distribution for Product A's Cash Flows

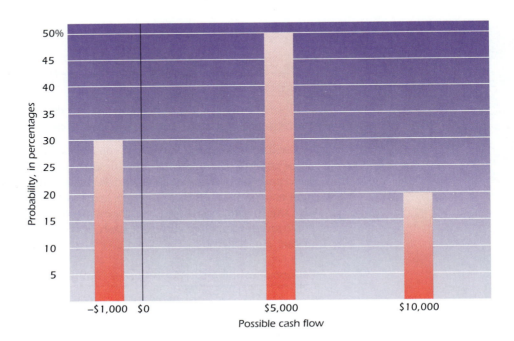

For Product A, the range of possible outcomes is $10,000 − (−$1,000) = $11,000. The greater the range, the farther apart are the two extreme possible outcomes and therefore the greater the risk of undertaking the project.

The Standard Deviation

Though easy to calculate, the range doesn't tell us anything about the likelihood of the possible cash flows at or between the extremes. In financial decision making, we are interested not just in the extreme outcomes, but in all the possible outcomes.

One way to characterize the dispersion of all possible future outcomes is to look at how the outcomes differ from one another. This would require looking at the differences between all possible outcomes and trying to summarize these differences in a usable measure.

An alternative to this is to look at how each possible future outcome differs from a single value, comparing each possible outcome with this one value. A common approach is to use a measure of central location of a probability distribution, the *expected value.*

Let's use N to designate the number of possible future outcomes, x_n to indicate the nth possible outcome, p_n to indicate the probability of the nth outcome's occurrence, and $E(x)$ to indicate the expected outcome. The expected cash flow is the weighted average of the cash flows, where the weights are the probabilities:

$$E(x) = p_1 x_1 + p_2 x_2 + p_3 x_3 + \cdots + p_n x_n + \cdots + p_N x_N$$

or, using summation notation,

$$E(x) = \sum_{n=1}^{N} p_n x_n \qquad \text{[10-1]}$$

The ***standard deviation*** (σ or "sigma") is a measure of how each possible outcome deviates—that is, differs—from the expected value. The standard deviation provides information about the dispersion of possible outcomes by providing information on the distance each outcome is from the expected value and the likelihood the outcome will occur. The standard deviation is:

$$\sigma(x) = \sqrt{\sum_{n=1}^{N} p_n [x_n - E(x)]^2} \qquad \text{[10-2]}$$

We begin our calculation of the standard deviation by first calculating the expected outcome, $E(x)$. In our example, there are three possible outcomes, so N = 3. Adding the probability-weighted outcome of each of these three outcomes results in the expected cash flow:

$$\begin{aligned} E(\text{cash flow for Product A}) &= (0.20)\$10,000 + (0.50)\$5,000 + (0.30)(-\$1,000) \\ &= \$2,000 + \$2,500 - \$300 \\ &= \mathbf{\$4,200} \end{aligned}$$

With this value for the expected cash flow from Product A, we can calculate A's standard deviation. If you follow the columns in Table 10-1, you

Properties of the Standard Deviation

- *A standard deviation of zero tells us there is no risk.* If the standard deviation is zero, there is no dispersion of possible outcomes around the expected value: All possible outcomes equal the expected value.

- *The greater the standard deviation, the more the possible outcomes differ from the expected value and therefore the greater is the risk.* The standard deviation is calculated using deviations of outcomes from the expected value; so the greater are these differences (that is, the more dispersed the possible outcomes) the greater is the risk.

- *We are more concerned about outcomes farthest from the expected value than those close to the expected value. The farthest outcomes have a greater influence on the standard deviation.* The standard deviation is calculated using *squared* deviations from the expected value, giving more weight to the more extreme outcomes.

- *The standard deviation is in the same unit of measurement as the expected value.* The standard deviation is the square root of another statistical measure of dispersion, the variance. The variance is in squared units (for example, squared dollars), but the standard deviation is in the same unit of measure as the expected value (for example, dollars).

TABLE 10-1

Calculation of Standard Deviation of Possible Cash Flows of Product A

Economic conditions	Cash flow, x_n	Probability, p_n	$p_n x_n$	$x_n - E(x)$	$[x_n - E(x)]^2$	$p_n[x_n - E(x)]^2$
Boom	$10,000	0.20	$2,000	$5,800	33,640,000	6,728,000
Normal	5,000	0.50	2,500	800	640,000	320,000
Recession	−1,000	0.30	−300	−5,200	27,040,000	8,112,000
			$E(x) = \$4,200$			$\sigma^2(x) = \mathbf{15{,}160{,}000}$

Standard deviation $= \sigma(x) = \sqrt{15{,}160{,}000} = \mathbf{\$3{,}894}$

NOTE: $E(x)$ = expected value, $\sigma^2(x)$ = variance of possible outcomes, $\sigma(x)$ = standard deviation of possible outcomes.

should be able to see that they represent the sequence of steps in solving Equation 10-2 and obtaining a standard deviation of $3,894.

The standard deviation is a statistical measure of dispersion of the possible outcomes about the expected outcome. The larger is the standard deviation, the greater is the dispersion and, hence, the greater is the risk.

Let's look at another example. Suppose the possible cash flows and their corresponding probabilities in the first year for Product B are:

PRODUCT B

Cash flow	Probability
$10,000	5%
9,000	10
8,000	20
7,000	30
6,000	20
5,000	10
4,000	5

The probability distribution of Product B's possible cash flows is graphed in Figure 10-2. Expected value and standard deviation calculations are in Table 10-2. We can describe the probability distribution with several measures:

FIGURE 10-2

Probability Distribution for Product B's Cash Flows

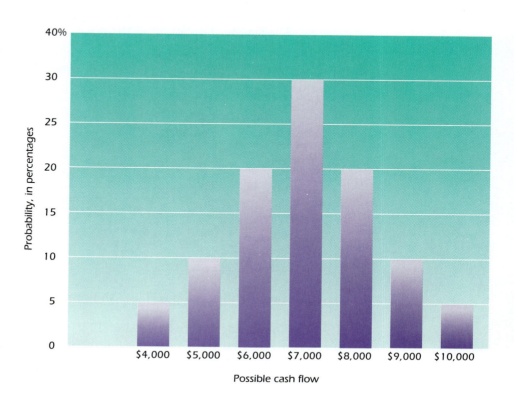

TABLE 10-2

Calculation of Standard Deviation of Possible Cash Flows of Product B

Cash flow, x_n	Probability, p_n	$p_n x_n$	$x_n - E(x)$	$[x_n - E(x)]^2$	$p_n[x_n - E(x)]^2$
$10,000	0.05	$ 500	$3,000	$9,000,000	$ 450,000
9,000	0.10	900	2,000	4,000,000	400,000
8,000	0.20	1,600	1,000	1,000,000	200,000
7,000	0.30	2,100	0	0	0
6,000	0.20	1,200	−1,000	1,000,000	200,000
5,000	0.10	500	−2,000	4,000,000	400,000
4,000	0.05	200	−3,000	9,000,000	450,000
		$E(x) = \$7,000$			$\sigma^2(x) = \$2,100,000$

Standard deviation $= \sigma(x) = \sqrt{2,100,000} = \$1,449$

NOTE: $E(x)$ = expected value, $\sigma^2(x)$ = variance of possible outcomes, $\sigma(x)$ = standard deviation of possible outcomes.

- The expected value is $7,000.
- The most likely outcome—the one that has the highest probability of occurring—is $7,000.
- The range of possible outcomes is $10,000 − $4,000 = $6,000.
- The standard deviation of the possible outcomes is $1,449.

Let's compare the risk associated with Product B's cash flows with the risk of still another project, Product C, which has the following possible cash flows:

PRODUCT C

Cash flow	Probability
$10,000	2%
9,000	8
8,000	20
7,000	40
6,000	20
5,000	8
4,000	2

The probabilities and possible cash flows of Product C are graphed in Figure 10-3.

Comparing Figures 10-3 and 10-2, we see that C's cash flows are less dispersed than B's. Describing the possible outcomes for Product C (which you can determine on your own, applying the process we used for Products A and B):

472

FIGURE 10-3
Probability Distribu-
tion for Product C's
Cash Flows

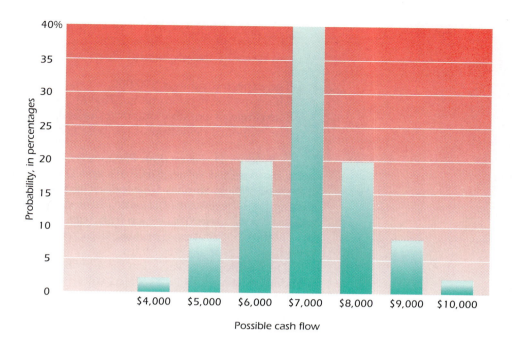

- The expected value is $7,000.
- The most likely outcome is $7,000.
- The range of possible outcomes is $6,000.
- The standard deviation of the possible outcomes is $1,183.

Both B and C have the same most likely outcome, the same expected value, and the same range of possible outcomes. But the standard deviation of the cash flows for C is less than it is for B. This confirms what we see when we compare Figures 10-2 and 10-3: The distribution of possible outcomes of Product C is less dispersed than that of Product B.

The Coefficient of Variation

The standard deviation provides a useful measure of dispersion. It is a measure of how widely dispersed the possible outcomes are from the expected value. However, we cannot compare standard deviations of different projects' cash flows if they have different expected values. To see this, consider the possible cash flows from Product D:

PRODUCT D

Cash flow	Probability
$100,000	5%
90,000	10
80,000	20
70,000	30
60,000	20
50,000	10
40,000	5

We can describe the probability distribution of D's possible cash flows:

- The expected value is $70,000.
- The most likely outcome is $70,000.
- The range of possible outcomes is $60,000.
- The standard deviation of the possible outcomes is $14,491.

Is Product D riskier than Product B? D's standard deviation is larger, but so is its expected value. Since B's and D's cash flows are of different sizes, comparing their standard deviations is meaningless without somehow adjusting for difference in the *scale* of the cash flows. We can do that with the **coefficient of variation,** which translates the standard deviations of different probability distributions (because their scales differ) so that they can be compared.

The coefficient of variation for a probability distribution is the ratio of its standard deviation to its expected value:

$$\text{Coefficient of variation} = \frac{\text{standard deviation}}{\text{expected value}}$$

or:

$$\text{Coefficient of variation} = \frac{\sigma(x)}{E(x)} \qquad \text{[10-3]}$$

Calculating the coefficient of variation of the probability distribution of each of the four products in our examples:

Product	Expected value	Range	Standard deviation	Coefficient of variation
A	$ 4,200	$11,000	$ 3,894	0.9271
B	7,000	6,000	1,449	0.2070
C	7,000	6,000	1,183	0.1690
D	70,000	6,000	14,491	0.2070

Comparing coefficients of variation among these products, we see that:

- Product A is the most risky.
- Product C is the least risky.
- Products B and D have identical risk.

Risk can be expressed statistically in terms of measures such as the range, the standard deviation, and the coefficient of variation. Now that we know how to calculate and apply these statistical measures, all we need are the probability distributions of a project's future cash flows so that we can apply these statistical tools to evaluate the project's risk.

Where do we get these probability distributions? From research, judgment, and experience. We can use sensitivity analysis or simulation analysis to get an idea of a project's possible future cash flows and their risk.

Sensitivity Analysis

Estimates of cash flows are based on assumptions about the economy, competitors, consumer tastes and preferences, construction costs, and taxes, among a host of other possible assumptions. One of the first things we have to consider about our estimates is how sensitive they are to these assumptions. For example, if we sell only 2 million units of a product in the first year instead of 3 million, is the project still profitable? Or, if Congress increases the tax rates, will the project still be attractive?

We can analyze the sensitivity of cash flows to changes in the assumptions by re-estimating the cash flows for different scenarios. **Sensitivity analysis,** also called **scenario analysis,** is a method of looking at the possible outcomes, given a change in one of the factors in the analysis. Sometimes we refer to this as "what if" analysis: What if this changes? What if that changes? and so on.

Sensitivity Analysis and Bond Value

In a bond valuation, we often look at what happens to the present value of the bond if market yields change. We see that the value of the bond increases when market yields go down and decreases when market yields go up. This is sensitivity analysis: the sensitivity of a bond's value to changes in market yields. We perform this sensitivity analysis to look at a bond's interest rate risk.

To see how sensitivity analysis works, let's look at the Williams 5 & 10 cash flows we determined in Chapter 8, where the detailed calculations were shown in Table 8-3. The net cash flow for each year is:

Year	Net cash flow
Initial	−$550,000
2001	59,809
2002	108,409
2003	149,569
2004	157,265
2005	480,946

Now let's play with the assumptions. Suppose that the tax rate is not known with certainty, but instead the tax rate may be 20 percent, 30 percent, or 40 percent. The tax rate that we assume affects:

- The expected tax on the sale of the building and equipment in the last year.
- The cash outflow for taxes and thus the change in revenues and expenses.
- The cash inflow from the depreciation tax shield.

Each different tax assumption changes the project's net cash flows:

| | Net cash flow | | |
Year	Tax rate = 20%	Tax rate = 30%	Tax rate = 40%
Initial	−$550,000	−$550,000	−$550,000
2001	66,540	59,809	53,079
2002	118,940	108,409	97,879
2003	166,380	149,569	132,759
2004	174,844	157,265	139,687
2005	437,298	480,946	459,987

We can see that the value of this project and, hence, any decision made that is based on this value, is sensitive to what we assume will be the tax rate.

We could take each of the "what if" tax rate assumptions and recalculate the value of the investment.

If the tax rate is . . .	. . . the net present value using a cost of capital of 5% is . . .
20%	$251,456
30	201,536
40	179,346

But when we do this, we have to be careful—the net present value requires discounting the cash flows at a rate that reflects risk—but *that* is what we are trying to figure out! So we shouldn't be using the net present value method in evaluating a project's risk in our sensitivity analysis.

An alternative is to recalculate the internal rate of return under each "what if" scenario.

If the tax rate is . . .	. . . the internal rate of return will be . . .
20%	16.42%
30	14.21
40	13.05

And this illustrates one of the attractions of using the internal rate of return to evaluate projects. Despite its drawbacks in the case of mutually exclusive projects and in capital rationing, as pointed out in Chapter 9, the internal rate of return is more suitable to use in assessing a project's attractiveness under different scenarios and, hence, that project's risk. Why? Because the net present value approach requires us to use a cost of capital to arrive at a project's value, but the cost of capital is what we set out to determine! We would be caught in a vicious circle if we used the net present value approach in sensitivity analysis. But the internal-rate-of-return method does not require a cost of capital; instead, we can look at the possible internal rates of return of a project and use this information to measure a project's risk.

If we can specify the probability distribution for tax rates, we can put sensitivity analysis together using the statistical measures of risk. Suppose that in the analysis of the Williams project it is most likely that tax rates will be 30 percent, though there is a slight probability that tax rates will be lowered and a chance that tax rates will be increased. More specifically, suppose the probability distribution of future tax rates and, hence, the project's internal rate of return, is as follows:

Probability . . .	that the tax rate will be . . .	and hence the internal rate of return will be . . .
10%	20%	16.42%
50	30	14.21
40	40	13.05

Applying the calculations for the statistical measures of risk to this distribution we obtain:

Expected internal rate of return	= 13.967%
Standard deviation of possible internal rates of return =	0.980%
Coefficient of variation	= 0.070

We can now judge whether the project's expected return is sufficient considering its risk (as measured by the standard deviation). We can also use the statistical results to compare this project with other projects under consideration.

Sensitivity analysis illustrates the effects of changes in assumptions. But because sensitivity analysis focuses only on one change at a time, it is not very realistic. We know that not one, but *many* factors can change throughout the life of the project. In the case of the Williams project, there are a number of assumptions built into the analysis that are based on uncertainty, including the sales prices of the building and equipment in five years and the entrance of competitors no sooner than five years. And you can use your imagination and envision any new product and the attendant uncertainties regarding many factors that could affect it, including the economy, the firm's competitors, and the price and supply of raw material and labor.

Simulation Analysis

Sensitivity analysis becomes unmanageable if we start changing two factors at the same time (change more than two and it's even worse). A manageable approach to changing two or more factors at the same time is computer simulation. *Simulation analysis* allows the financial manager to develop a probability distribution of possible outcomes, given a probability distribution for each variable that may change.

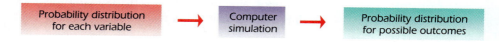

Suppose you have three possible outcomes, $100, $200, and $400, with probabilities of occurrence of:

Outcome	Probability
$100	1/6
200	3/6 = 1/2
400	2/6 = 1/3

We can use the outcome of the roll of a die (a single cube with the numbers 1 through 6 on each one of its faces) to simulate this uncertain situation, that is, the probabilities represented in the example above. If you think about the number on each face of the die, you should be able to see how the following table is similar to the table above:

Outcome	Dice role outcome	Probability
$100	1 (out of 6)	1/6
200	2, 3, or 4 (out of 6)	1/2
400	5 or 6 (out of 6)	1/3

If you roll a "3," the $200 outcome is selected. If you roll a "5," $400 is selected. And so on. By rolling the die a large number of times and selecting the outcome that corresponds to the assigned die roll, you can simulate the probability distribution of these outcomes.

Suppose you are analyzing a project having the following uncertain elements:

- Sales (number of units and price)
- Costs
- Tax rate

Suppose further that the initial outlay for the project is known with certainty and so is the rate of depreciation. Using results from the firm's marketing research, you estimate a probability distribution for dollar sales. And from the firm's engineers and production management and purchasing agents, you estimate the probability distribution for costs, which depends, in part, on the number of units sold. The firm's economists estimate the probability distribution of possible tax rates.

You have three probability distributions to work with. Now you need a computer simulation program to meet your needs, one that can:

* Randomly select a possible value of unit sales for each year, given the probability distribution.
* Randomly select a possible value of costs for each year, given the unit sales and the probability distribution of costs.
* Randomly select a tax rate for each year, given the probability distribution of tax rates.

While the computer cannot roll a die, spin a wheel as the emcees do in TV game shows, or select Ping-Pong balls with numbers as in lotteries, computers can be programmed to randomly select values based on whatever probability distribution you want. For example, Lotus Development Corporation has a program, called @Risk, that allows the financial manager to assume probability distributions for different variables in an analysis and perform a simulation.

Once the computer selects the number of units sold, the cost per unit, and the tax rate, the cash flows are calculated, as well as the project's internal rate of return. You now have one internal rate of return. Then you start all over, with the computer repeating this process, calculating an internal rate of return each time. After a large number of trials, you will have a frequency distribution of the return on investments. A *frequency distribution* is a description of the number of times you've arrived at each different return. Using the statistical measures of risk, you can evaluate the risk associated with the return on investments by applying those measures to this frequency distribution.[1]

Simulation analysis is more realistic than sensitivity analysis because it introduces uncertainty for many variables in the analysis. But if you use your imagination, this analysis may become complex since there are interdependencies among many variables in a given year and interdependencies among the variables in different time periods.

However, simulation analysis looks at a project in isolation, ignoring the diversification effects of projects, focusing instead on a single project's total risk. And simulation analysis also ignores the effects of diversification for the owners' personal portfolios. If owners hold diversified portfolios, then their

---

[1] Because the frequency distribution is a *sampling* distribution (that is, it is based on a sample of observations instead of a probability distribution), its standard deviation is calculated in a slightly different manner than the standard deviation of possible outcomes:

$$\text{Standard deviation of frequency distribution} = \sqrt{\frac{\sum(x_i - \bar{x})^2 \, f_i}{N - 1}}$$

where x_i is the value of a particular outcome, $\bar{x}$ is the average of the outcomes, f_i is the number of times the particular outcome is observed (its frequency), and N is the number of trials (e.g., number of times a coin is flipped). The interpretation of this standard deviation is similar to the interpretation of the sample standard deviation.

There are two differences between the standard deviation of the frequency distribution and that of the probability distribution: The weights in the former are the frequencies, and the sum of the weighted outcomes is divided by the number of trials (less one).

On a Roll

Consider two sources of uncertainty, the number of units sold and the cost of manufacturing a unit. Each source has its own probability distribution:

FIRST SOURCE			**SECOND SOURCE**	
Probability	Number of units sold		Probability	Cost per unit
1/6	1,000		1/2	$8
3/6	2,000		1/2	9
2/6	3,000			

To keep things simple, let's assume the sales price per unit is $10 and there are no taxes. So if we sell 1,000 units and the cost per unit is $8, sales are $10,000 and profits are $2,000. And let's use two dice instead of a computer, assigning the following:

Probability	Number of units sold	Roll of die 1	Probability	Cost per unit	Roll of die 2
1/6	1,000	1	1/2	$8	1, 2, 3
3/6	2,000	2, 3, 4	1/2	$9	4, 5, 6
2/6	3,000	5, 6			

Let the dice roll:

Roll number	Die 1	Die 2	Profit
1	2	3	$4,000
2	3	2	4,000
3	1	5	1,000
4	2	3	4,000
5	5	4	3,000
6	5	2	6,000

and so on. We keep the dice rolling for a large number of trials, say, 100. Once we finish, we will have a large number of operating profit outcomes, ranging from $1,000 (1,000 units at $9 per unit) to $6,000 (3,000 units at $8 per unit). We can then form a frequency distribution (how many $1,000 observations, how many $2,000 observations, and so on) and apply our statistical tools to measure the risk.

While we kept this example simple (we didn't, say, have the cost per unit vary according to the number of units we produced), the basic idea should be apparent to you: Let more than one probability distribution enter into the picture.

concern is how a project affects their portfolios' risk, not the project's total risk.

Measuring a Project's Market Risk

If we are considering an investment in a share of stock, we could look at the stock's returns and the returns of the entire market over the same period of time as a way of measuring its market risk. While this is not a perfect measurement, it at least provides an estimate of the sensitivity of that particular stock's returns as compared to the returns of the market as a whole. But what if we are evaluating the market risk of a new product? We can't look at how the new product has affected the firm's stock return! So what do we do?

Though we can't look at a project's returns and see how they relate to the returns on the market as a whole, we can do the next best thing: estimate the market risk of the stock of *another* firm whose only line of business is the same as the project's. If we could find such a company, we could look at its stock's market risk and use that as a first step in estimating the project's market risk.

Let's use a measure of market risk, referred to as beta and represented by the Greek letter β. β is a measure of the sensitivity of an asset's returns to changes in market returns. β is an elasticity measure: If the return on the market increases by 1 percent, we expect the return on an asset with a β of 2.0 to increase by 2 percent; if the return on the market decreases by 1 percent, we expect the returns on an asset with a β of 1.5 to decrease by 1.5 percent, and so on. The β of an asset, therefore, is a measure of the asset's market risk. To distinguish the beta of an asset from the beta we used for a firm's stock, we refer to an asset's beta as β_{asset} and the beta of a firm's stock as β_{equity}.

Market Risk and Financial Leverage

You were introduced to β in Chapter 7. So you see, we are refining this concept, looking at the β in a firm's assets as well as a firm's equity.

If a firm has no debt, the market risk of its common stock is the same as the market risk of its assets; that is, the beta of its equity, β_{equity}, is the same as its assets' beta, β_{asset}.

Financial leverage is the use of fixed payment obligations, such as notes or bonds, to finance a firm's assets. The greater is the use of debt obligations, the more financial leverage there is and the more risk there is associated with cash flows to owners. So, the effect of using debt is to increase the risk of the firm's equity.

If the firm has debt obligations, the market risk of its common stock is *greater* than its assets' risk (that is, $\beta_{equity} > \beta_{asset}$), due to financial leverage. Let's see why.

β_{asset} depends on an asset's risk, *not* on how a firm chooses to finance it. The firm can choose to finance it with equity only, in which case $\beta_{asset} = \beta_{equity}$. But what if, instead, the firm chooses to finance the asset partly with debt and partly with equity? When it does this, the creditors and the owners share the risk of the asset; so the asset's risk is split between them, but not equally because of the nature of the claims. Creditors have seniority and receive a fixed amount (interest and principal); so there is less risk associated with a dollar of debt financing than a dollar of equity financing of the same asset. Therefore, the market risk borne by the creditors is different from the market risk borne by owners.

Let's represent the market risk of creditors as β_{debt} and the market risk of owners as β_{equity}. Since the asset's risk is shared between creditors and owners, we can represent the asset's market risk as the weighted average of the firm's debt beta, β_{debt}, and equity beta, β_{equity}:[2]

$$\beta_{asset} = \beta_{debt}\left(\begin{array}{c}\text{proportion of assets}\\\text{financed with debt}\end{array}\right) + \beta_{equity}\left(\begin{array}{c}\text{proportion of assets}\\\text{financed with equity}\end{array}\right)$$

$$= \beta_{debt}\left(\frac{\text{debt}}{\text{debt + equity}}\right) + \beta_{equity}\left(\frac{\text{equity}}{\text{debt + equity}}\right)$$

But interest on debt is deducted to arrive at taxable income; so the claim that creditors have on the firm's assets does not cost the firm the full amount, but rather the after-tax claim. Therefore, the burden of debt financing is actually reduced to the extent that interest is tax deductible.[3]

$$\beta_{asset} = \beta_{debt}\left[\frac{(1 - \text{marginal tax rate})\text{debt}}{(1 - \text{marginal tax rate})\text{debt} + \text{equity}}\right]$$

$$+ \beta_{equity}\left[\frac{\text{equity}}{(1 - \text{marginal tax rate})\text{debt} + \text{equity}}\right]$$

If the firm's debt does not have market risk, $\beta_{debt} = 0$. This means that the returns on debt do not vary with returns on the market, a situation we generally assume to be true for most large firms. In that case, the first term after the equal sign in the equation above reduces to zero, but the market risk of the firm's equity is affected, as before, by both the market risk of the assets and the nondiversifiable portion of the firm's financial risk. That is, if $\beta_{debt} = 0$:

$$\beta_{asset} = \beta_{equity}\left[\frac{\text{equity}}{(1 - \text{marginal tax rate})\text{debt} + \text{equity}}\right]$$

or:

$$\beta_{asset} = \beta_{equity}\left[\frac{1}{1 + \dfrac{(1 - \text{marginal tax rate})\text{debt}}{\text{equity}}}\right] \qquad [10\text{-}4]$$

This means that an asset's beta is related to the firm's equity beta, with adjustments for financial leverage.[4] You'll notice that if the firm does not use debt, $\beta_{asset} = \beta_{equity}$, and if the firm does use debt, $\beta_{asset} < \beta_{equity}$.

---

[2] The process of breaking down the firm's beta into equity and debt components is attributed to Robert S. Hamada, "The Effect of the Firm's Capital Structure on the Systematic Risk of Common Stocks," *Journal of Finance*, vol. 27, no. 2, May 1972, pp. 435–452.

[3] The tax deductibility of interest reduces the cost of debt to the firm, which we will demonstrate in Chapters 13 and 14.

[4] This means that we can also specify the firm's equity beta in terms of its asset beta:

$$\beta_{equity} = \beta_{asset}\left[1 + \frac{(1 - \text{marginal tax rate})\text{ debt}}{\text{equity}}\right]$$

The greater is a firm's use of debt (relative to equity), the greater is its equity's beta and hence the greater is its equity's market risk.

Therefore, we can translate a β_{equity} into a β_{asset} by removing the firm's financial risk from its β_{equity}. As you can see in Equation 10-4, to do this we need to know:

- The firm's marginal tax rate.
- The amount of the firm's debt financing.
- The amount of the firm's equity financing.

The process of translating an equity beta into an asset beta is referred to as "unleveraging" since we are removing the effects of financial leverage from the equity beta, β_{equity}, to get a beta for the firm's assets, β_{asset}.[5]

Using a Pureplay

A firm with a single line of business is referred to as a ***pureplay.*** Selecting the firm, or firms, with a single line of business similar to that of the proposed project helps in estimating the project's market risk. We estimate a project's asset beta by starting with the pureplay's equity beta. We can estimate the pureplay's equity beta by looking at the relation between the returns on the pureplay's stock and the returns on the market. Once we have the pureplay's equity beta, we can then "unleverage" it by adjusting it for the financial leverage of the pureplay firm.

Examples of pureplay equity betas are shown in Table 10-3. The firms listed in this table have one primary line of business. Using the information in Table 10-3 for Alcan Aluminum and assuming a marginal tax rate of 34 percent, we see that the asset beta for aluminum products is 0.6970:

$$\beta_{asset} = 1.1 \left[\frac{1}{1 + \dfrac{(1 - 0.34)\$3,914 \text{ million}}{\$4,468 \text{ million}}} \right]$$

$$= 1.1(0.6336)$$

$$= \mathbf{0.6970}$$

As another example, using the data for J. M. Smucker Co., we see that the asset beta for food products, assuming a marginal tax rate of 34 percent, is 0.7909:

$$\beta_{asset} = 0.8 \left[\frac{1}{1 + \dfrac{(1 - 0.34)\$12 \text{ million}}{\$685 \text{ million}}} \right]$$

$$= 0.8(0.9885)$$

$$= \mathbf{0.7909}$$

Since Smucker's has very little debt, its asset beta is close to its equity beta.

---

[5] The effect of financial leverage on equity betas and the process of leveraging and unleveraging betas is attributed to Hamada, "The Effect of the Firm's Capital Structure on the Systematic Risk of Common Stocks."

TABLE 10-3

The Equity beta (β_{equity}), Book Value of Long-Term Debt, and Market Value of Equity for Selected Firms with a Single Line of Business ("Pureplays"), 1991

Company	Line of business	Equity beta (β_{equity})	Book value of long-term debt, in millions[a]	Market value of equity, in millions
Alcan Aluminum	Aluminum	1.1	$ 3,914	$ 4,468
Beverly Enterprises	Nursing facilities	1.3	746	653
Commonwealth Edison	Electric service	0.4	11,523	8,480
Digital Equipment	Computers	1.2	160	6,885
Gap	Casual and activewear apparel	1.7	139	7,625
Hannaford, Brothers	Retail foods	1.1	270	913
McDonald's	Food service	1.0	5,226	13,631
J. C. Penney	Retailing	1.2	5,923	6,416
Reebok International	Athletic shoes	1.7	183	3,014
Smucker	Food products	0.8	12	685

[a]The book value of debt is used in place of the market value of debt, since the latter is not readily available. The market value of equity is the product of the number of shares outstanding and the closing share price as of the end of the year.

SOURCE: *Compustat PC Plus* (CD-ROM), Standard and Poor's.

Since many U.S. corporations for which stock return data are readily available have more than one line of business, *finding* an appropriate pureplay firm may be difficult. Care must be taken to identify those that have lines of business similar to the project's.

INCORPORATING RISK IN THE CAPITAL BUDGETING DECISION

In using the net present value method to value future cash flows, we know we should apply a discount rate that reflects the project's risk. In using the internal-rate-of-return method, we know we should apply a hurdle rate—the minimum rate of return on the project—that reflects the project's risk. Both the net present value and the internal-rate-of-return methods, therefore, depend on using a cost of capital that reflects the project's risk.

Risk-Adjusted Rates

The cost of capital is the cost of funds (from creditors and owners). This cost is the return required by those suppliers of capital. The greater the risk of a project, the greater the return required and, hence, the greater the cost of capital.

The cost of capital can be viewed as the sum of the price suppliers of capital would demand for providing funds if the project were risk-free plus compensation for the risk the suppliers take on.

The compensation for the time value of money includes compensation for any anticipated inflation. We typically use a risk-free rate of interest, such as the yield on a long-term U.S. Treasury bond, to represent the time value of money.

The compensation for risk is the extra return required because the project's future cash flows are uncertain. If we assume that the relevant risk is the stand-alone risk (say, for a small, closely held business), investors would require a greater return, the greater the project's stand-alone risk. If we assume that the relevant risk is the project's market risk, investors would require a greater return, the greater the project's market risk.

Required Return for a Project's Market Risk

Now let's explain how to determine the premium for bearing market risk. We do this by first specifying the premium for bearing the average amount of risk for the market as a whole and then, using our measure of market risk, we fine-tune this to reflect the market risk of the asset.

The market risk premium for the market as a whole is the difference between the average expected market return, r_m, and the risk-free rate of interest, r_f. If you bought an asset whose market risk was the same as that of the market as a whole, you would expect a return of $r_m - r_f$ to compensate you for market risk.

Next, let's adjust this market risk premium for the market risk of the particular project by multiplying it by that project's asset beta, β_{asset}:

Compensation for market risk = $\beta_{asset} (r_m - r_f)$

This is the extra return necessary to compensate for the project's market risk. The β_{asset} fine-tunes the risk premium for the market as a whole to reflect the market risk of the particular project. If we then add the risk-free interest rate, we arrive at the cost of capital:

Cost of capital = $r_f + \beta_{asset} (r_m - r_f)$ [10-5]

Suppose the expected risk-free rate of interest is 4 percent and the expected return on the market as a whole is 10 percent. If the β_{asset} is 2.00, this means that if there is a 1 percent change in the market risk premium, we expect a 2 percent change in the return on the project. In this case, the cost of capital is 16 percent:

$$
\begin{aligned}
\text{Cost of capital} &= 0.04 + 2.00(0.10 - 0.04) \\
&= 0.04 + 2.00(0.06) \\
&= 0.04 + 0.12 \\
&= \mathbf{0.16} \text{ or } \mathbf{16\%}
\end{aligned}
$$

If β_{asset} is 0.75, instead, the cost of capital is 8.5 percent.

$$
\begin{aligned}
\text{Cost of capital} &= 0.04 + 0.75(0.06) \\
&= 0.04 + 0.045 \\
&= \mathbf{0.085} \text{ or } \mathbf{8.5\%}
\end{aligned}
$$

If we are able to gauge the market risk of a project, we estimate the risk-free rate and the premium for market risk and put them together. But often we are not able to measure the market risk or even the risk-free rate. So we need another way to approach the estimation of the project's cost of capital.

Adjusting a Firm's Cost of Capital

Another way to estimate the cost of capital for a project without estimating the risk premium directly is to use the firm's average cost of capital as a starting point. The average cost of capital is the firm's marginal cost of raising one more dollar of capital—the cost of raising one more dollar in the context of all the firm's projects considered altogether, not just the proposed new project. We can adjust the average cost of capital of the firm to suit the perceived risk of the project:

- If a proposed new project is *riskier* than the average project of the firm, the cost of capital of the new project is *greater* than the average cost of capital.
- If the new project is *less risky,* its cost of capital is *less* than the average cost of capital.
- If the project is *as risky* as the average project of the firm, the new project's cost of capital is *equal to* the average cost of capital.

As you can tell, altering the firm's cost of capital to reflect a project's cost of capital requires the exercise of judgment. By how much do we adjust the firm's cost of capital? If the project is riskier than the typical project, do we add 2 percent? 4 percent? 10 percent? There is no prescription here. It depends on the judgment and experience of the decision maker. But this is where we can use the measures of a project's stand-alone risk to help form that judgment.

Certainty Equivalents

An alternative to adjusting the discount rate to reflect risk is to adjust the cash flow to reflect risk. We do this by converting each cash flow and its risk into its ***certainty equivalent.*** A certainty equivalent is the certain cash flow that is considered to be equivalent to the risky cash flow.

The certainty-equivalent approach of incorporating risk into the net present value analysis is useful for several reasons:

- It separates the time value of money and risk. Risk is accounted for in the adjusted cash flows while the time value of money is accounted for in the discount rate.
- It allows each period's cash flows to be adjusted separately for risk. This is accomplished by converting each period's cash flows into a certainty equivalent for that time period. The certainty-equivalent factor may be different for each period.
- The decision maker can incorporate preferences for risk. This is done in determining the certainty-equivalent cash flows.

However, there are some disadvantages to using the certainty-equivalent approach that stymie its application in practice:

- The net present value of the certainty equivalent is not easily interpreted. We no longer have the clearer interpretation of the net present value as the increment in shareholder wealth.
- There is no reliable way of determining the certainty-equivalent value for each period's cash flow.

While it sounds great in principle, it is really hard to apply in practice. We will leave the calculation and use of certainty equivalents to your more advanced courses in finance.

ASSESSMENT OF PROJECT RISK IN PRACTICE

Most U.S. firms consider risk in some manner in evaluating investment projects.[6] But considering risk is usually a subjective analysis as opposed to the more objective results that can be obtained by simulation of sensitivity analysis.

Firms that use discounted cash flow techniques, such as internal-rate-of-return and net present value methods, tend to use a single cost of capital. But using a single cost of capital for all projects can be hazardous.

Suppose you use the same cost of capital for all your projects. If all of them have the same risk and the cost of capital you are using is appropriate for this level of risk, there is no problem. But what if you use the same cost of capital but each of your projects has a *different* level of risk?

Alternatively, suppose you use a cost of capital that is the cost of capital for the firm's average-risk project. What happens when you apply discounted cash flow techniques, such as the net present value or the internal rate of return, and use this one rate? You will end up:

- Rejecting profitable projects (which would have increased owners' wealth) that have risk *below* the risk of the average-risk project because you discounted their future cash flows too much.
- Accepting unprofitable projects whose risk is *above* the risk of the average project, because you did not discount their future cash flows enough.

Firms that use a risk-adjusted discount rate usually do so by classifying projects into risk classes by the type of project. For example, based on its experience, a firm with a cost of capital of 10 percent might develop the following classes and discount rates:

Type of project	Cost of capital
New product	14%
New market	12
Expansion	10
Replacement	8

Given this set of costs of capital, the financial manager need only figure out which class a project belongs to and then apply the rate assigned to that class.

Firms may also make adjustments in the cost of capital for factors other than the type of project. For example, firms investing in projects in foreign

[6] David F. Scott, Jr., and J. William Petty II, "Capital Budgeting Practices in Large American Firms: A Retrospective Analysis and Synthesis," *Financial Review,* vol. 19, 1984, pp. 111–123; David J. Oblak and Roy J. Helm, Jr., "Survey and Analysis of Capital Budgeting Methods Used by Multinationals," *Financial Management,* vol. 9, no. 4, Winter 1980, pp. 37–41; and L. R. Runyon, "Capital Expenditure Decision Making in Small Firms," *Journal of Business Research,* vol. 11, 1983, pp. 389–397.

countries will sometimes make an adjustment for the additional risk of the foreign project, such as exchange rate risk, inflation risk, and political risk.

The cost of capital is generally based on an assessment of the firm's overall cost of capital. First, the firm evaluates the cost of each source of capital—debt, preferred stock, and common equity. Then each cost is weighted by the proportion of each source to be raised. This average is referred to as the ***weighted average cost of capital*** (WACC). The estimation of a firm's cost of capital is discussed in more detail in Chapter 14.

There are tools available to assist the decision maker in measuring and evaluating project risk. But much of what is actually done in practice is subjective. Judgment, with a large dose of experience, is used more often than scientific means of incorporating risk. Is this bad? Well, the scientific approaches to measurement and evaluation of risk depend, in part, on subjective assessments of risk, the probability distribution of future cash flows, and judgments about market risk. So it is possible that bypassing the more technical analyses in favor of a completely subjective assessment of risk may result in cost-of-capital estimates that better reflect the project's risk. But then again it may not. The proof may be in the pudding, but it is difficult to assess the "proof," since we cannot tell how well firms could have done had they used more technical techniques!

SUMMARY

- To screen and select among investment projects, the financial manager must estimate future cash flows for each project, evaluate the riskiness of those cash flows, and evaluate each project's contribution to the firm's value and, hence, to owners' wealth.

- The financial manager has to evaluate future cash flows—cash flows that are estimates, which means they are uncertain.

- The financial manager has to incorporate risk into the analysis of projects to identify the ones that maximize owners' wealth.

- Statistical measures that can be used to evaluate the risk of a project's cash flows are the range, the standard deviation, and the coefficient of variation.

- Sensitivity analysis and simulation analysis are tools that can be used, in conjunction with the statistical measures, to evaluate a project's risk. Both techniques give us an idea of the relation between a project's return and its risk. However, since the firm is itself a portfolio of projects and it is typically assumed that owners hold diversified portfolios, the relevant risk of a project is not its stand-alone risk, but rather how the risk of the project affects the risk of owners' portfolios, that is, the project's market risk.

- Risk is typically figured into our decision making by using a cost of capital that reflects the project's risk.

- The relevant risk for the evaluation of a project is the project's market risk, which is also referred to as the asset beta. This risk can be estimated by looking at the market risk of pureplays (firms in a single line of business) in businesses similar to that of the project.

- An alternative to finding a pureplay is to classify projects according to the type of project (e.g., expansion) and assign costs of capital to each project type according to subjective judgments of risk.

- Most firms adjust for risk in their assessment of the attractiveness of projects. However, this adjustment is typically done by evaluating risk subjectively and making ad hoc adjustments to the firm's cost of capital to arrive at a cost of capital for a particular project.

QUESTIONS

10-1 Are the required rate of return and the cost of capital the same thing? Explain.

10-2 Suppose a discount retail chain is considering opening a new outlet in another city. What should the company consider in assessing the risk associated with the future cash flows of the new outlet?

10-3 Suppose a cereal manufacturer is considering producing a new cereal based on a new, yet to be released, feature film. What should the cereal manufacturer consider in assessing the risk associated with the future cash flows from this new cereal?

10-4 What distinguishes the standard deviation from the coefficient of variation.

10-5 Suppose you perform calculations for a proposed project and determine that the expected value of first-year cash flows is $1,200 and the standard deviation is $500. What does this mean?

10-6 Outline a procedure you would use to determine the risk of a project.

10-7 What distinguishes sensitivity analysis from simulation analysis?

10-8 Suppose you are responsible for determining the cost of capital of a project. Explain how your approach would differ if the firm is a small, one-owner business, as compared to a large, publicly held corporation.

10-9 Suppose the Shell Point Shell Company evaluates most projects using the net present value method and a single discount rate that reflects its marginal cost of raising new capital. Can you see any problem with their method?

10-10 Suppose the Destin Sand Company's management evaluates investment opportunities by grouping projects into three risk classes: low, average, and high risk. The management assigns a cost of capital to each group and uses this cost of capital to discount a project's future cash flows: 5 percent for low-risk, 10 percent for average-risk, and 15 percent for high-risk projects. Critique the company's method of adjusting for risk.

PROBLEMS

Measures of project risk

10-1 Consider the probability distribution of the first-year cash flows for the ABC Project:

Possible cash flow	Probability
$1,000	20%
2,000	60
3,000	20

    a. Calculate the range of possible cash flows.
    b. Calculate the expected cash flow.
    c. Calculate the standard deviation of the possible cash flows.
    d. Calculate the coefficient of variation of the possible cash flows.

10-2 Consider the probability distribution of the first-year cash flows for the DEF Project:

Possible cash flow	Probability
$1,000	10%
2,000	60
3,000	30

    a. Calculate the range of possible cash flows.
    b. Calculate the expected cash flow.
    c. Calculate the standard deviation of the possible cash flows.
    d. Calculate the coefficient of variation of the possible cash flows.

10-3 Consider the probability distributions of the first-year cash flows of two projects, GHI and JKL:

GHI		JKL	
Possible cash flow	Probability	Possible cash flow	Probability
−$5,000	30%	−$2,000	30%
0	30	+3,000	40
+7,000	40	+4,000	30

    a. Calculate the range of possible cash flows for each project.
    b. Calculate the expected cash flow for each project.
    c. Calculate the standard deviation of the possible cash flows for each project.

d. Calculate the coefficient of variation of the possible cash flows for each project.
e. Which project is the riskiest? Why?

10-4 Consider the probability distributions of the first-year cash flows of two projects, MNO and PQR:

MNO		PQR	
Possible cash flow	Probability	Possible cash flow	Probability
−$10,000	20%	−$20,000	25%
0	60	+30,000	50
+20,000	20	+40,000	25

a. Calculate the range of possible cash flows for each project.
b. Calculate the expected cash flow for each project.
c. Calculate the standard deviation of the possible cash flows for each project.
d. Calculate the coefficient of variation of the possible cash flows for each project.
e. Which project is the riskiest? Why?

Sensitivity analysis

10-5 The Avalanche Snow Company is evaluating the purchase of a new snow-making machine. The marketing and production managers have provided the following data on the increases in revenues and expenses associated with the new machine, and the accountant has calculated the depreciation on the machine for the next four years. Assume that there are no changes in working capital in each year.

Year	Sales	Expenses	Depreciation
2001	$100,000	$50,000	$25,000
2002	150,000	75,000	25,000
2003	125,000	75,000	25,000
2004	100,000	75,000	25,000

a. What is the operating cash flow for each year if the tax rate is 30 percent?
b. What is the operating cash flow for each year if the tax rate is 40 percent?
c. What is the operating cash flow for each year if the tax rate is 50 percent?
d. Suppose the probability of a 30 percent tax rate is 10 percent, the probability of a 40 percent tax rate is 30 percent and the probability of a 50 percent tax rate is 60 percent. What is the expected operating cash flow for Avalanche? What is the standard deviation of the operating cash flows?

10-6   The Sopchoppy Motorcycle Company is considering an investment of
$600,000 in a new model of motorcycle. They expect sales in each of the
next three years to increase by $400,000, and expenses to increase by
$200,000. They expect that they can carve out a niche in the marketplace
for the new motorcycle for three years, after which they intend to cease
producing it. Assume the equipment is depreciated at the rate of $200,000
each year. Sopchoppy's tax rate is 40 percent.

a.   What is the internal rate of return of this project if Sopchoppy sells the
manufacturing equipment for $200,000 at the end of the three years?

b.   What is the internal rate of return of this project if the company sells
the manufacturing equipment for $100,000 at the end of the three
years?

c.   What is the internal rate of return of this project if the company sells
the manufacturing equipment for $300,000 at the end of the three
years?

d.   Suppose the following distribution of possible sales prices on the equipment is developed:

Sales price	Probability
$100,000	25%
200,000	50
300,000	25

What is the expected internal rate of return for Sopchoppy? What is the
standard deviation of these possible internal rates of return?

Simulation analysis

10-7   Consider the probability of possible cash flow outcomes for Project XYZ:

Possible cash flow	Probability
$2,000	1/6
4,000	2/3
6,000	1/6

Construct a simulation of the future cash flows, using a six-sided die.

a.   If you roll the die thirty times, what will be the distribution of the possible cash flows?

b.   If you roll the die a total of sixty times, what will be the distribution of
the possible cash flows?

c.   Draw a frequency distribution of the results of rolling the die sixty
times, plotting the frequency of occurrence on the vertical axis and the
possible outcomes on the horizontal axis. How does this frequency distribution compare with the probability distribution?

Risk-adjusted discount rate

10-8   Calculate the cost of capital for each of the possible combinations of the compensation for the time value of money and the compensation for risk:

	Compensation for time value of money	Compensation for risk
a.	2%	5%
b.	4	6
c.	5	5
d.	4	6

10-9   Suppose that the compensation for risk is based on the market risk and that market risk is estimated as the product of the asset's beta and the market risk premium for the market as a whole (that is, $r_m - r_f$). Calculate the cost of capital for each of the possible combinations of compensation for the time value of money and compensation for risk:

	Risk-free rate of interest	Asset beta	Market risk premium
a.	3%	1.00	4%
b.	4	0.50	5
c.	5	1.50	6
d.	4	1.00	4
e.	5	1.25	4

10-10   Consider the following information on firms that are in a single line of business:

Company	Equity beta (β_{equity})	Debt, in millions of dollars	Equity, in millions of dollars
Airborne Freight Corporation	1.6	$ 320	$ 461
Albertson's Inc.	0.8	365	5,186
Arco Chemical Company	1.3	1,447	3,811
Arkla Inc.	0.7	2,332	1,456
Arrow Electronics Inc.	1.1	334	314

SOURCE: *Compustat PC Plus* (CD-ROM), Standard & Poor's; 1991 financial data.

Calculate the asset beta for each firm, assuming a marginal tax rate of 34 percent.

10-11 **Research:** Consider the following probability distribution of cash flows one year from today:

Cash flow	Probability
$1,000	10%
2,000	50
3,000	40

a. Survey at least thirty persons, showing each person this probability distribution and asking them what amount of money, to be received in one year with certainty, would be equivalent to the *uncertain* cash flow one year from today. In other words, what "sure thing" (certainty equivalent) would each person demand in exchange for the uncertain cash flow.

b. Tabulate your results. Is there agreement on the certainty-equivalent cash flow? How much disagreement is there? Why do you believe that there is disagreement?

PC+ **10-12** **Research:** Select a company that meets the following requirements:

- Its common stock is traded on the New York Stock Exchange.
- It is in a single, well-defined line of business.
- Its financial data are not already shown in Table 10-3.

Calculate the asset beta for your selected firm.
  Recommended sources of information:

- *Industrial Manual,* Moody's
- *Compustat PC Plus* (CD-ROM), Standard and Poor's
- *Value Line Investment Survey*

FURTHER READINGS

There are many surveys of the capital budgeting practices of firms and several that address the firms' use of risk in their analysis:
EUGENE F. BRIGHAM, "Hurdle Rates for Screening Capital Expenditure Proposals," *Financial Management,* vol. 5, no. 3, Autumn 1975, pp. 17–26.
EUGENE F. BRIGHAM and RICHARD H. PETTWAY, "Capital Budgeting by Utilities," *Financial Management,* vol. 3, no. 3, Autumn 1973, pp. 11–22.
SUK H. KIM, TREVOR CRICK, and SUNG H. KIM, "Do Executives Practice What Academics Preach?" *Management Accounting,* Nov. 1986, pp. 49–52.
THOMAS KLAMMER, "Empirical Evidence of the Adoption of Sophisticated Capital Budgeting Techniques," *Journal of Business,* vol. 45, no. 3, July 1972, pp. 387–397.
WILLIAM J. PETTY, DAVID F. SCOTT, JR., and MONROE M. BIRD, "The Capital Expenditure Decision-Making Process of Large Corporations," *The Engineering Economist,* Spring 1975, pp. 159–172.
RICHARD H. PIKE, "An Empirical Study of the Adoption of Sophisticated Capital Budgeting Practices and Decision-Making Effectiveness," *Accounting and Business Research,* vol. 18, no. 72, Autumn 1988, pp. 341–351.
MARC ROSS, "Capital Budgeting Practices of Twelve Large Manufacturers," *Financial Management,* vol. 15, no. 4, Winter 1986, pp. 15–22.

LAWRENCE D. SCHALL, GARY L. SUNDEM, and WILLIAM R. GEIJSBECK, JR., "Survey and Analysis of Capital Budgeting Methods," *Journal of Finance,* vol. 33, no. 1, March 1978, pp. 281–287.

For an overall view of survey evidence on risk adjustments in capital budgeting, see:

DAVID R. SCOTT and J. WILLIAM PETTY II, "Capital Budgeting Practices in Large American Firms: A Retrospective Analysis and Synthesis," *Financial Review,* vol. 19, no. 1, March 1984, pp. 111–123.

Examples of methods of determining asset betas and betas for divisions of firms can be found in:

RUSSELL J. FULLER and HALBERT S. KERR, "Estimating the Divisional Cost of Capital: An Analysis of the Pure-Play Technique," *Journal of Finance,* vol. 36, no. 4, Dec. 1981, pp. 997–1008.

BENTON E. GUP and SAMUEL W. NORWOOD III, "Divisional Cost of Capital: A Practical Approach," *Financial Management,* vol. 11, no. 1, Spring 1982, pp. 20–24.

ROBERT S. HARRIS, THOMAS J. O'BRIEN, and DOUG WAKEMAN, "Divisional Cost-of-Capital Estimation for Multi-Industry Firms," *Financial Management,* vol. 18, no. 2, Summer 1989, pp. 74–84.

PART V

Management of Financing

11 Common and Preferred Stock 498

12 Long-Term Debt 550

13 Capital Structure 589

14 The Cost of Capital 630

Common and Preferred Stock

INTRODUCTION 501

GENERAL CHARACTERISTICS OF STOCK 502

Limited Liability 502

The Corporate Charter 503

The Number of Shares 503

Stock Ownership 504

Dividends 505

    Types of Dividends 505

    The Mechanics of Paying a Dividend 508

COMMON STOCK 510

Classified Stock 510

Voting Rights 511

    Cumulative Voting 513

    Classified Boards of Directors 514

The Right to Buy More Stock 514

Other Rights 517

Corporate Democracy 517

Common Stock Dividends 520

    Dividends: To Pay or Not to Pay, That Is the Issue 524

    Dividend Reinvestment Plans 528

    Stock Repurchases 529

PREFERRED STOCK 533

Par and Liquidation Values 533

Preferred Stock Dividends 534

    Fixed vs. Variable Rate Dividends 535

    Cumulative vs. Noncumulative Dividends 535

    Participating vs. Nonparticipating Dividends 536

Convertibility 536

Callability 537

Voting Rights 539

Sinking Funds 539

Packaging Features 539

EQUITY AS A SOURCE OF FUNDS 541

Summary 542

It's Public. No, It's Private. No, It's Public.

The RJR Nabisco Holdings Corporation is one of the largest U.S. producers of tobacco products as well as the largest U.S. producer of cookies. Though RJR Nabisco went public in 1991, that is not when the company began.

June 1985
R. J. Reynolds Corporation acquired Nabisco Brands by buying Nabisco Brands stock in exchange for cash, preferred stock, and notes valued at $4.9 million. This was the fourth largest merger of 1985. The combined company was named RJR Nabisco Corporation, and its stock was traded on the New York Stock Exchange.

April 1989
Kohlberg Kravis Roberts & Co. acquired RJR Nabisco, taking the firm private in a leveraged buyout that was financed by almost $30 billion of debt. The new privately held company was renamed RJR Nabisco Holdings Corporation. [This transaction was the basis of Bryan Burrough and John Helyar's *Barbarians at the Gate: The Fall of RJR Nabisco* (Harper & Row, New York, 1990) and the HBO movie by the same title.]

March 1991
RJR Nabisco Holdings went public, listing its stock on the New York Stock Exchange, and following up, the next month, with a public offering of new common shares of $1.3 billion.

The $30 billion of debt used to take the company private in 1989 has been slowly pared down *(left)* and the company's net income has recovered somewhat *(right)*.

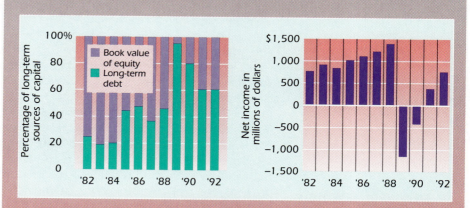

SOURCE: *Value Line Investment Survey;* end-of-year data.

But RJR Nabisco Holdings has struggled under the burden of the debt it took on and its newly issued shares have been dropping in price, despite an upward movement in stock prices in general, a recovering economy, and recovering company earnings.

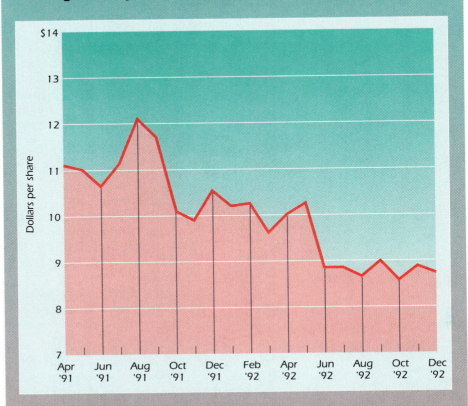

SOURCE: Standard & Poor's Daily Stock Price Index; end-of-month data.

The share price suffered for a number of reasons, most notably because (1) the firm continued to bear a great deal of debt and (2) concerns existed regarding liability claims related to the firm's tobacco products.

In 1993, RJR Nabisco Holdings devised a plan to raise additional money to reduce its debt: issue another class of common stock whose future cash flows would be specifically tied to the performance of the firm's food products. This would raise additional capital, allowing the firm to reduce its debt. In addition, the share price of this new class of stock would reflect the brighter prospects of the food products group rather than the gloomy prospects of the tobacco-related products.

INTRODUCTION

Different types of capital are nothing new. During the seventeenth century, the East India Company of England divided its ownership shares into two classes, one entitled to regular payments of 8 percent on their investment and the other entitled to the profits made in trading.

Suppose you buy a new car costing $12,000 and you pay cash for it. You will own it completely. The value of your investment in the car—your equity—is the value of the car, $12,000. If, instead, you pay 10 percent in cash and finance the rest with a car loan, your equity is 10 percent of the value of the car, or $1,200. Your equity in the car is the value of the car less any debt obligation. As you pay off your debt or as the car changes in value, your equity in the car changes also.

If you joined with your roommate to buy the car, each putting up $6,000 in cash, you own 50 percent of the equity in the car and your roommate owns 50 percent. By sharing ownership, you are sharing the equity.

Like the equity in your car, the equity of a corporation is the value of its ownership. We have come to refer to the equity of a corporation as *stock.* The word "stock" has evolved to mean a store of value or wealth, deriving from the word *stukko,* which meant trunk or log in Old Teutonic.

Just as a log can be split into pieces so, too, can the stock of a corporation be cut into pieces.[1] A corporation's stock may be divided into two major types—preferred stock and common stock. Both may be split into different, smaller classes of stock. And each of these classes is split into yet smaller pieces called *shares.* This smallest unit of ownership, one share, is represented by a stock certificate. When you buy a share of stock, you are buying a share of the ownership of a corporation, and it is represented by the stock certificate.

Owners of these shares are referred to as *shareholders* or *stockholders.* As a shareholder you are not buying something that is tangible (other than the stock certificate itself), but rather you are buying rights: rights to income, rights to have a say in the corporation's activities, and so on.

And the Image Is . . .

U.S. corporations have tried to project their images on stock certificates by providing a picture or sketch on the certificates. Until 1990, Playboy Enterprises Inc. had a nude picture of the February 1971 Playmate on their certificate. In 1990 Playboy changed the picture to one of a clothed woman. This was done in part to project a more modern image of women and in part to cut down on the number of people buying single shares of stock just to get the certificate. (For more examples, see Steven E. Levingston, "Stock Certificates Get a Makeover for the '90s," *The Wall Street Journal,* Feb. 19, 1993, p. C1.)

Preferred stock and common stock have different rights. Preferred shareholders are given *preference* over common shareholders: They have rights to receive income *ahead* of common shareholders. The reason is that shareholders receive part of the return on their investment from *dividends,* which

---

[1] Jason Zweig provides an interesting tracing of the origin of the word "stock" in his article, from which the quotation in the top sidebar on this page is taken.

are periodic cash payments from the corporation. Dividends promised to preferred shareholders must be paid *before* common shareholders can be paid.

If the firm is liquidated—that is, the business operations are ended—the assets are sold and the proceeds of the sale are distributed to creditors and owners. Preferred shareholders receive preference over common shareholders when liquidation proceeds are distributed among the owners. Preferred shareholders receive the liquidation value of their shares before common shareholders can receive anything.

Common stock represents the residual ownership of a corporation. The claims of creditors and preferred shareholders come before the claims of common shareholders to the income and assets of a corporation. Common shareholders get what is left over, that is, the residual income and assets.

In this chapter, we take a closer look at the specific features of common and preferred stock. In particular, we examine the rights of shareholders, how a corporation's funds are distributed to its shareholders, and how shareholders obtain a say in the firm they own.

> In England, the two types of equity interests are referred to as *ordinary shares* (equivalent to common stock) and *preference shares* (equivalent to preferred stock).

GENERAL CHARACTERISTICS OF STOCK

Both common stock and preferred stock have similar characteristics, such as limited liability. We'll begin with these characteristics and then see how rights are granted in the corporate charter and what distributions are made to shareholders.

Limited Liability

The corporate form of doing business is attractive to owners of a business because the corporate form limits their liability. The most owners can lose is the amount of their investment. But this is not quite true. The amount owners—the shareholders—can lose depends on whether there is a par value for their shares.

Each share of stock may have a *par value,* indicated on the stock certificate. Par value represents the maximum amount of each share stockholders can be responsible for if the firm becomes insolvent (that is, unable to pay its debts).

If shares are sold at or above par value, the most shareholders can lose in case of insolvency is what they paid for their shares. Suppose a share of stock has a $100 par value and is sold for $110. If the corporation is liquidated and the proceeds are not enough to pay all the creditors, the stock is worthless and shareholders have lost the $110 invested in each share.

If shares are sold for less than their par value, the laws of some states require that shareholders be held liable for the difference between what they paid for the shares and the par value. Suppose a share of stock has a $100 par value and is sold for $90. If the corporation is liquidated and the proceeds are not enough to pay all the creditors, the owner of each share is liable for $10 per share—the difference between what the owner paid for the stock and its par value.

This potential for liability has encouraged corporations to issue stock with very low par values—say $1 or even 1 cent—or no par at all. Shares of stock issued without a par value are referred to as *no-par stock.* This creates a problem for accountants—they like to record something in the balance sheet to represent the value of the stock. Firms that issue no-par stock assign an arbitrary value per share, referred to as the *stated value,* which implies no liability.

The Corporate Charter

A corporation comes into being through *incorporation*—the process in which a business files a document, referred to as the *articles of incorporation,* with the state. The articles of incorporation include:

- The name and address of the business.
- A statement of the purpose of the business.
- A description of the types and classes of stock, specifying the rights and privileges of the owners.
- A description of the responsibilities of officers and members of the board of directors who represent the interest of shareholders.
- The bylaws, which are the rules governing the internal affairs of the corporation, such as meetings of the board of directors and meetings of shareholders.

The state accepts this document and grants a corporate charter, giving life to the corporation. The *corporate charter* is simultaneously the contract between the state and the corporation, between the shareholders and the corporation, and between the shareholders and the state. The charter consists of both the articles of incorporation and state law. The corporation is obligated to follow the articles of incorporation and the laws of the state in which it is incorporated.

So You Want to Incorporate?

The procedures and fees differ from state to state, but the basic process is the same. In Florida, for example, you file your articles of incorporation with the Division of Corporations, a part of Florida's Department of State. All you need are (1) the articles of incorporation, (2) a corporate name that is not already in use, and (3) the $122.50 filing fee.

The Number of Shares

The equity pie can be split into any number of pieces. For example, there can be one share that represents 100 percent ownership or there can be 100,000 shares, each share representing a 0.001 percent ownership share.

How many shares of stock may a corporation issue? The number—referred to as the *authorized shares*—is specified in the corporate charter. If a firm wishes to issue more shares than specified, the charter must be amended to change the number of authorized shares. But a firm does not have to issue the entire number of shares authorized. The number of *issued shares*—the number of shares sold—is equal to or fewer than the number of authorized shares.

An Example of the Number of Shares

As of May 1990, the management of ConAgra Inc. was authorized to issue 600,000,000 of common stock. At that time, there were 122,729,283 shares outstanding. In addition to the shares outstanding, there were 6,569,843 shares issued but not outstanding: 123,167 shares held in treasury for unspecified reasons, 6,045,049 shares reserved in case management exercised its stock options, and 401,627 shares reserved in case the owners of preferred stock converted—exchanged—their stock into common stock (Moody's *Industrial Manual,* 1991, vol. 1, p. 1079).

If a firm buys back stock from investors, the number of shares left in the hands of investors—referred to as *outstanding shares*—will be fewer than the number of issued shares. Shares bought back from investors may be either retired (that is, eliminated from existence), reducing the number of issued shares, or held as treasury stock. Shares held as treasury stock are not considered outstanding shares and, for example, can be used by the firm to provide shares to employees when they exercise their stock options rights.

Stock Ownership

A Close Call

A private corporation whose stock is owned among a very few individuals is referred to as a **closely held corporation** or a **close corporation.** In a close corporation, the stock is owned by a single shareholder or a tightly knit group of shareholders who are active in the management of the firm.

We saw in Chapter 1 that the securities laws require registration with the Securities and Exchange Commission.

We can classify a corporation according to whether its shares of stock can be traded in financial markets. A corporation whose shares of stock are traded in financial markets is considered a **public corporation.** A corporation whose shares cannot be traded in financial markets is considered a **private corporation.**

Federal securities laws—specifically the Securities Exchange Act of 1934, as modified in 1982—require a corporation to *register* its securities if it has more than 500 shareholders and more than $3 million in assets. To register securities, a corporation must file a detailed description of the firm and the securities as well as the following:

- Quarterly financial reports, on Form 10-Q.
- Annual reports, on Form 10-K, providing financial statement information, along with other descriptive information about the firm.
- Form 8-K, detailing specific events, such as the acquisition or disposition of assets, as they occur.

If a corporation has either less than 500 shareholders or less than $3 million in assets, it can choose not to register and is referred to as a private corporation or a **privately held corporation,** in which case its shares cannot be traded on a securities exchange. If it does register with the Securities and Exchange Commission, it's considered a public corporation.

The shares of stock of a public corporation—also referred to as a **publicly held corporation**—can be owned by and traded among the general public. Anyone can buy and sell the shares of stock in a public corporation and these shares can be traded in the financial markets—on national or regional stock exchanges or in the over-the-counter market.

What difference does it make whether the corporation's stock is privately held or publicly held? There are many differences.

One difference is in the stock's marketability. If the shares are publicly traded, they are marketable. Investors can easily buy or sell the shares. If shares are privately held, there may be restrictions as to whom you can sell your shares to, possibly making it difficult to get cash when you need it.

Another difference is in the diversification of the owners' wealth. If the shares are closely held, the owners are usually also the managers. Owner-managers have a great deal of their wealth tied up with the corporation. Not only does the value of their stock depend on the fortunes of the company; so does their income. In a publicly held corporation, owner-managers can sell off parts of their ownership.

Still another difference is in the firm's access to capital. A publicly traded corporation can raise new capital by issuing more shares to the general public. A privately held corporation may not be able to do this, since ownership may be restricted to a few shareholders. In addition, the number of shareholders and the size of a privately held corporation may increase to the point at which registration of the firm's securities is required, changing its status from private to public.

A further difference is in confidentiality. A publicly held corporation is required to disclose information to shareholders and the investing public through financial statements, annual reports, and press releases. Securities laws and exchange rules require publicly traded corporations to disclose to investors important information, such as a merger, a new product or discovery, the sale of a significant asset, and labor disputes. Private corporations do not have to reveal any information to the public. They can keep it all secret! Therefore, a private corporation has an advantage because its publicly traded competitors will have difficulty trying to figure out what it is doing.

Another difference is in the cost of communication. A publicly traded corporation must file annual financial statements with the Securities and Exchange Commission, prepare and send annual reports to shareholders, and correspond with shareholders (Securities Exchange Act of 1934, Rule 13a). The costs of these communications can add up, in terms of both the direct expenses for accountants, lawyers, and other personnel, and the indirect expense of tying up management's time in handling shareholders' affairs instead of managing the firm.

All these differences must be weighed in deciding whether to be a private or a public corporation. There are over 3.5 million corporations in the United States. Only about 9,000 have publicly traded stock! The fact that there are some private and some public corporations tells us that the evaluation of the advantages and disadvantages can go either way.

Corporations do *change* their status, going from public to private or private to public. It is possible that as a corporation changes—in terms of its ownership, the types of investments it makes, and its need for capital—a change from public to private or private to public may be appropriate. RJR Nabisco went private in 1989, only to go public once again as RJR Nabisco Holdings two years later when it needed more capital.

Dividends

A dividend is the cash, stock, or any type of property a corporation distributes to its shareholders. The board of directors may declare a dividend at any time, but dividends are not a legal obligation of the corporation—it is the board's choice. Unlike interest on debt securities, if a corporation fails to pay a dividend there is no violation of a contract and no legal recourse for shareholders.

Types of Dividends

Most dividends are in the form of cash. Cash dividends are paid on all outstanding shares of stock. That means no dividends are paid on treasury stock.

In addition to cash dividends, corporations may provide shareholders with dividends in the form of additional shares of stock or, rarely, some type of property owned by the corporation.

Distributions of property as dividends to shareholders can be cumbersome. If a brewer decides to pay a dividend of one six-pack of beer per share of stock, there are a few problems: How to get the beer to the shareholders, what to do about dividends to be paid to institutions such as pension funds, and what is a shareholder of 100,000 shares to do with all that beer!

When dividends aren't in cash, they are usually additional shares of stock. Additional shares of stock can be distributed to shareholders two ways: by paying a stock dividend and by splitting the stock.

A **_stock dividend_** is the distribution of additional shares of stock to shareholders. Stock dividends are generally stated as a percentage of existing shareholdings. For example, if you own 1,000 shares of stock and the firm pays a 5 percent stock dividend, you receive 5 percent more shares, or 50 shares. Before the dividend, you owned 1,000 shares; after the dividend, you own 1,050 shares.

If a corporation pays a stock dividend, it is not transferring anything of value to the shareholders. The assets of the corporation remain the same, and each shareholder's proportionate share of ownership remains the same. All the firm is doing is cutting its equity pie into more slices and at the same time cutting each shareholder's portion of that equity into more slices. So why pay a stock dividend?

There are a couple of reasons for stock dividends. One is to provide information to the market. A firm may want to communicate good news to the shareholders without paying cash. For example, if the firm has an attractive investment opportunity and needs funds for it, paying a cash dividend doesn't make sense; so the firm pays a stock dividend instead. But is this an effective way of communicating good news to the shareholders? It costs very little to pay a stock dividend: just minor expenses for recordkeeping, printing, and distribution. But if it costs very little, do investors really believe in devices in which management is not putting "its money where its mouth is"?

Another reason for paying a stock dividend is to reduce the price of the stock. If the price of a stock is high, relative to most other stocks, there may be higher costs related to investors' transactions in the stock, that is, a higher broker's commission. By paying a stock dividend, which slices the equity pie into more pieces, the price of the stock should decline.

Let's see how this works. Suppose you own 1,000 shares, each worth $50 per share, for a total investment of $50,000. If the firm pays you a 5 percent stock dividend, you own 1,050 shares after the dividend. Is there any reason for your holdings to change in value? Nothing economic has gone on here—the firm has the same assets, the same liabilities, and the same equity—total equity has just been cut up into smaller pieces. There is no reason for the value of the portion of the equity you own to change. But the price _per share_ may decline: from $50 per share to $50,000/1,050 = $47.62 per share. The argument in favor of reducing share price works only if you can bring down the price substantially, from an unattractive trading range to a more attractive trading range in terms of reduced brokerage commissions and of enabling small investors to purchase even lots of 100 shares. Brokerage commissions are usually lower for shares trading in the range from $20 to $40, compared to shares trading above or below that price range, and for even lots of 100 shares.

A stock split is something like a stock dividend. A ***stock split*** splits the number of existing shares into more shares. For example, in a 2:1 split—referred to as "two for one"—each shareholder gets two shares for every one owned. If you own 1,000 shares and the stock is split 2:1, you own 2,000 shares after the split. Has the portion of your ownership in the firm changed? No. You simply own twice as many shares—and so does every other shareholder. If you owned 1 percent of the corporation's stock before the split, you still own 1 percent after the split.

So why split? Like a stock dividend, the split reduces the trading price of shares. If your 1,000 shares of stock were trading at $50 per share prior to the 2:1 split, your shares can be expected to trade for $50,000/2,000 = $25 per share after the split.

> A stock split that creates additional shares is sometimes referred to as a forward stock split.

Aside from a minor difference in accounting, stock splits and stock dividends are essentially the same.[2] A 2:1 split has the same effect on a stock's price as a 100 percent stock dividend, a 1.5:1 split has the same effect on a stock's price as a 50 percent stock dividend, and so on.[3]

A ***reverse stock split*** raises the price of a stock by reducing the number of shares of stock outstanding. It's the opposite of a stock split. Reducing the number of shares increases the stock's price because the equity is transformed into fewer but *larger* pieces. A 1:2 reverse split—one share given in exchange for two shares—doubles the price of the stock. If you own 1,000 shares of stock and the stock is trading for $5 per share, with a 1:2 reverse split you own 500 shares after the split, each worth around $10 per share.

There are several reasons to reverse-split.

First, you may want to steer the price of your firm's stock toward a more attractive trading range, reducing investors' transactions costs for trading in the stock. You may also want to raise the price of the stock so that it is not a *penny stock*, a stock trading under $1 per share, since there is a negative connotation to penny stocks.[4]

Another reason to reverse-split may be to take the company private. If your firm has fewer than 500 shareholders, you can avoid the disclosure requirements of the SEC—go private. While there are other ways to go private, a reverse split is an inexpensive way.

Let's see how a reverse split can be used to go private. Suppose there are 10,000 shares outstanding spread among 600 shareholders, each owning dif-

---

[2] The stock dividend requires a shift within the stockholders' equity accounts, from retained earnings to paid-in capital, for the amount of the distribution, whereas the stock split requires only a memorandum entry.

[3] The basis of the accounting rules is related to the reasons behind the distribution of additional shares. If firms want to bring down their share price, they tend to declare a stock split; if firms want to communicate news, they often declare a stock dividend.

[4] There have been a number of well-publicized fraud and market manipulation cases involving stocks that trade at very low prices. For example, the Stuart-James Co. brokerage firm was fined in 1990 by the National Association of Securities Dealers for overcharging customers on low-priced stocks (Anne Newman, "Stuart-James Is Fined $1.9 Million; Agrees to Drop Many Penny Stocks," *The Wall Street Journal,* May 11, 1990, p. C1).

ferent numbers of shares. The firm declares a 1:1,000 reverse split, and the firm will pay cash for each partial share of new stock. There will be 10 shares outstanding after the split and anyone who owned less than 1,000 shares before the split is paid off in cash. Since there are only 10 whole shares after the split, the number of shareholders is well below 500; therefore the firm can become privately held.

How can we tell what the motivation is behind stock dividends, stock splits, and reverse splits? We can't. But we can get a general idea of how investors interpret these actions by looking at what happens to the firm's share price when a corporation announces its decision to pay a stock dividend, split its stock, or reverse-split. If the share price tends to go up when the announcement is made, the decision is probably good news; if the price goes down, the decision is probably bad news. This is supported by evidence that indicates firms' earnings tend to increase following stock splits and payments of stock dividends.[5]

The share price of companies announcing stock distributions and stock splits generally increases at the time of the announcement.[6] The most likely explanation is that this distribution is interpreted as good news—that management believes that the future prospects of the firm are favorable or that the share price is more attractive to investors.

The stock price of companies announcing a reverse stock split usually decreases at the time of the announcement.[7] The most likely explanation for this decrease is that the firm is unable to increase the share price in any way *other* than through a reverse split. That is, the prospects of the firm are so bleak that this is the only way to increase the share price.

The Mechanics of Paying a Dividend

The board of directors decides whether or not to pay a dividend. The board announces a decision to pay a dividend, specifying:

- The amount of the dividend (dollars per share for a cash dividend, amount of stock for a stock dividend).
- Who is to receive the dividend, specified in terms of who owns the stock on a specified date, referred to as the **record date.**
- When the dividend is to be paid, the **payment date.**

The date the board of directors declares the dividend is referred to as the **declaration date.**

[5] See, for example, Maureen McNichols and Ajay Dravid, "Stock Dividends, Stock Splits, and Signaling," *Journal of Finance,* vol. 45, no. 3, July 1990, pp. 857–879.

[6] The stock price typically increases by 1 or 2 percent when the split or stock dividend is announced. When the stock dividend is distributed or the split is effected (on the "ex" date, which we'll discuss shortly), the share's price typically declines according to the amount of the distribution. Suppose a firm announces a 2:1 split. Its share price may increase by 1 or 2 percent when this is announced, but when the shares are split, the share price will go down to approximately half of its presplit value. See, for example, Mark Grinblatt, Ronald Masulis, and Sheridan Titman, "The Valuation Effects of Stock Splits and Stock Dividends," *Journal of Financial Economics,* vol. 13, no. 4, Dec. 1984, pp. 461–490.

[7] See, for example, David Peterson and Pamela Peterson, "A Further Evidence of Stock Distributions: The Case of Reverse Stock Splits," *Journal of Financial Research,* vol. 15, no. 3, Fall 1992, pp. 189–206.

Dividend Dates

Declaration date	The day the board of directors meets and decides on the dividend.
Record date	The date specified by the board on which any shareholders who are on record as owning shares on that date are eligible to receive the dividend.
Ex-dividend date	The date, established by the stock exchanges as four business days prior to the record date, that determines who receives the dividend (whoever purchased and held onto the shares prior to this date) and who does not (whoever buys the shares on or after this date).
Payment date	The date the dividend checks are mailed.

An Example of How Dividend Dates Work Out: International Paper Company

The board of directors of the International Paper Company met on July 10, 1992, and declared a 42 cent dividend per share payable on September 17, 1992, to all shareholders of record as of August 24, 1992. Since the date of record was a Friday, the International Paper Company stock was traded ex-dividend—that is, without the dividend—on Monday, August 20, 1992.

Declaration date	Ex-dividend date	Record date	Payment date
↑	↑	↑	↑
Tuesday	Monday	Friday	Monday
July 10, 1992	Aug. 20, 1992	Aug. 24, 1992	Sept. 17, 1992

If you bought International Paper Company common stock *before* August 20, 1992, and did not sell it before that same date, you were entitled to the dividend paid September 17, 1992. If you bought the stock on August 20, 1992 or after, you would *not* have received the dividend paid September 17.

Figuring out who are actually the owners of stock on the record date can be somewhat of a problem because it takes up to three or four days for the paperwork to be completed following a sale of shares. Recognizing this situation, the stock exchanges have adopted a system for figuring out who has the right to the dividend, called the ***five-day settlement plan.*** The stock exchanges identify the trading day four business days *prior* to the record date as the ***ex-dividend date.*** If you buy the shares on the day before the ex-dividend date, you are entitled to the forthcoming dividend. If you buy the shares *on* the ex-dividend date or after, you are not entitled to the forthcoming dividend.

As you might well imagine, the price of the stock on the ex-dividend date reflects the fact that you are not entitled to the next dividend. Suppose a stock is trading for $25 the day prior to the ex-dividend date. If the dividend is $1 per share, what would you be willing to pay for a share on the ***ex-dividend date?*** Remember: If you buy the share on this date, you are not entitled to the $1 dividend, *but* if you had bought it the day before, you would be getting the $1 in the near future. If nothing else happens to affect the share price, you would be willing to pay only $24 a share on the ex-dividend date. Therefore, we expect a share's price on the ex-dividend date to be less than it was the day before by approximately the amount of the dividend per share.

COMMON STOCK

Residual ownership in a firm is common stock ownership and is represented by shares. Since the corporation has a perpetual existence, granted by its charter, common stock ownership interest—also referred to as common equity—is perpetual too.

Common equity is created either by retaining and reinvesting earnings in the firm or by selling more shares. Whatever is left from earnings after paying what is due the creditors and preferred shareholders may be reinvested in the firm or paid as dividends to common shareholders. If these residual funds are reinvested by the firm in profitable investment opportunities, they increase the value of the firm, increasing the value of the common stock. If these residual funds are paid to shareholders, they can reinvest the dividends they receive as they wish.

Let's focus on how the following factors set common stock apart from preferred stock and on what affects the value of common stock:

- The classification of common stock.
- The rights given to common shareholders.
- The participation of common shareholders in the management of the firm.
- The issues related to the payment of dividends.

Classified Stock

Corporations may have more than one class of common stock, each with different rights. There is no limit on the number of different classes of common stock a corporation may issue. The different classes are usually designated Class A, Class B, etc. There is no rule as to how these classes must be designated.

We often find different classes of stock owned by the family that founded the corporation and stock in the same corporation owned by the public. Until 1956, Ford Motor Company was a privately held corporation: only Ford family members owned the stock. When the company went public, the Ford family members did not want to lose control of the management of the business, so they divided the shares into Class A and Class B. Class A shares are publicly owned, and Class B shares are owned only by Ford family members and their descendants.[8] Class B shares give their shareholders better voting rights than the Class A shares (as you will see in the next section).

Multiple classes of common stock may also arise from acquisitions. For example, General Motors (GM) acquired Hughes Aircraft Co. in 1985. As a

---

[8] In addition to family members and descendants, Class B stock may be owned by trusts or corporations controlled by Ford family members or descendants.

Classified Common Stock: Turner Broadcasting

Turner Broadcasting, owner of the Atlanta Hawks, TBS Productions, and Turner Network Television, among other holdings, has two classes of common stock, Class A and Class B. These two classes differ with respect to their voting rights and their rights to dividends.

Each share of Class A stock has one vote per share, whereas each share of Class B stock has one-fifth of a vote per share. Since there are 75 million Class A shares and 300 million Class B shares, this means that there are 75 million + 60 million = 135 million votes: Class A controls 55.6 percent of the votes and Class B controls 44.4 percent.

At the end of 1989, the founder, Ted Turner, owned 77.2 percent of Class A stock and 80.7 percent of Class B stock. This gave him 106.32 million out of 135 million votes, or 78.8 percent of the total votes:

Class A 77.2% of 75 million votes = 57.90 million votes
Class B 80.7% of 60 million votes = 48.42 million votes
Total = 106.32 million votes

The dividends differ between the two classes: The total dividends paid on Class A stock are 90 percent of the total paid on Class B stock. Shares of both classes are traded on the American Stock Exchange.

condition of the acquisition, Hughes Aircraft shareholders were given a special class of GM stock, designated Class H. When GM acquired Electronic Data Systems (EDS) in 1985 it created still another, Class E. General Motors common stock (which doesn't have a class designation), General Motors Class H common, and General Motors Class E common all have different rights to vote and different rights to dividends. For example, Class H shares have one-half of a vote per share, whereas Class E common shares have one-quarter of a vote per share.

Voting Rights

Common shareholders are generally granted rights to

- Elect members of the board of directors.
- Vote on the merger of the corporation with another corporation.
- Authorize additional shares of common stock.
- Vote on amendments to the articles of incorporation.

The number of votes granted per share of stock is determined by the articles of incorporation and the particular class of common stock. A share generally has one vote, though it is possible to have different classes of stock, each with a different number of votes per share, or different classes, each class with a specified percentage of the votes. For example, Ford Class B gets

Killer Bs

Powerful voting shares are sometimes referred to as Killer Bs because the class of stock with superior voting power is often referred to as Class B. With up to ten votes per share, holders of these shares are very powerful and can put together enough votes to scuttle a takeover attempt.

40 percent of the vote and Class A gets 60 percent, even though there are more than twelve times the number of Class A shares than Class B shares.

Special classes of common stock with better voting rights (that is, more votes per share than the common shares already outstanding) were created during the 1980s as a defense against takeovers. By issuing a class of common stock with superior voting rights—say, ten votes per share instead of one vote per share—to a friendly party, the management of a corporation could derail a takeover attempt.

The proliferation of multiple classes of common stock during the 1980s, along with the potential to take control of the firm from current shareholders, raised concern over whether there *should* be different classes of stock with different rights. Suppose a firm has one class of stock with 1,000 shares outstanding, and each share has one vote. If you own 100 shares, you have 10 percent of the stock with 10 percent of the votes. Now suppose the firm issues 1,000 shares of a new class of stock, with each share having ten votes per share. What happens to your control of the firm? After it issues these shares, you have 5 percent of the outstanding shares of stock, but only $100/[1,000 + (10 \times 1,000)] = 0.91$ percent of the votes. No federal securities law prohibits multiple classes of stock with different rights, though there may be state laws that prohibit them.

The markets on which the stock is traded may have prohibitions on listing multiple classes of stock. For example, the New York Stock Exchange (NYSE) and the National Association of Securities Dealers Automated Quotation (NASDAQ) system require each share to have one vote for common stocks traded in their markets. The only exceptions are for (1) classes already outstanding at the time the rule went into effect and (2) multiple classes of stock that are part of an initial public offering (when they go public). The American Stock Exchange (ASE), however, allows companies to list classes of stock with different voting rights.

Shareholders exercise their voting rights either by voting directly at annual meetings and special shareholder meetings or by giving their vote to another party through a proxy. A **proxy** is a written authorization for someone

The Revealing Proxy Statement

The proxy statement can be very revealing about a corporation. It summarizes the issues that are subject to shareholder vote, including the ratification of the selection of the independent public accountants, the election of members of the board of directors, and any proposals made by shareholders.

In addition to the issues subject to a vote, the proxy statement provides information on the officers of the corporation, describing their compensation: not just their annual salary, but their holdings of the company's stock and any stock options they may have. The proxy also reveals any severance agreements—which, when very lucrative are called **golden parachutes**—triggered if the company is taken over by another company.

else to vote in place of the shareholder in the manner the shareholder prescribes. Corporations whose stock is publicly traded are required by the Securities Exchange Act to send a *proxy statement,* detailing the issues subject to shareholder voting, along with the *proxy card,* the document in which the shareholder indicates her or his vote.

The use of proxies is governed by the Securities Exchange Act of 1934.[9] Though intended to encourage corporate democracy through greater disclosure of information, the regulation of the proxy system resulted in the creation of barriers among shareholders and limits on shareholder proposals.[10] For example, the Securities and Exchange Commission instituted rules (rules 14a-6 and 14a-7) intended to enhance the disclosure of information to shareholders, but which instead slowed down the process, inhibiting shareholder-to-shareholder communication and increasing the expense of communications among shareholders.

Cumulative Voting

Because shareholders elect the board of directors, the board should be the voice of the shareholders. But if every shareholder receives one vote per share to cast for each board seat, there is no way for minority shareholders to get representation on the board of directors. Those who own the majority of shares can elect every one of the directors!

Cumulative voting is designed to alleviate this problem, allowing a minority of shareholders to gain representation on the board. With cumulative voting, shareholders can accumulate their votes for members of the board of directors. Let's see how this works.

Suppose there are 1,000 shares outstanding and seven director positions up for election, and you own 400 shares. If there is *no* cumulative voting, you would have 400 votes that you can cast for each director position. If there *is* cumulative voting, you have 7 times 400, or 2,800 votes, that you can cast any way you want:

- Cast 400 for each position ($400 \times 7 = 2,800$).
- Cast 2,800 toward one position and none for the other six ($2,800 \times 1$ plus $0 \times 6 = 2,800$).
- Cast 1,400 toward each of two positions and none for the other five ($1,400 \times 2$ plus $0 \times 5 = 2,800$).
- Or any other possible allocation of your 2,800 votes.

Cumulative voting allows shareholders to pile up their votes for one or more seats, leading to more active participation in the corporation's governance, especially by shareholders with smaller holdings.

Most states permit cumulative voting rights to be included in the corporate charter. In some states, corporate law requires cumulative voting for common shareholders; a few states prohibit it.

> **Not Just for Stock**
>
> A cumulative voting system is used in Illinois to elect members of the legislature. The purpose is to allow for minority representation in the legislature.

---

[9] Regulation 14A, Solicitation of Proxies.

[10] John Pound provides a review of the history of the proxy system and an analysis of proposed changes in the proxy system in his "Proxy Voting and the SEC," *Journal of Financial Economics,* vol. 28, no. 2, Oct. 1991, pp. 241–286.

Classified Boards of Directors

In most corporations, shareholders elect the members of the board of directors annually, without cumulative voting. If a majority of shareholders desires to gain representation on the board, they simply wait until the next annual meeting or, in some cases, call a special shareholders' meeting.

Some corporations have divided their director positions into classes, and only one class of directors is voted on each year, instead of the entire board. This system is referred to as a **classified board of directors** or a **staggered board of directors.** Consider Flowers Industries, which has twelve members on its board of directors: four positions voted on each year, with each member serving a three-year term.

There is a good side and a bad side to classified boards.

The good side: By staggering terms so that each director serves a term of, say, three to four years, there is continuity in the board of directors. Having multiyear terms ensures that there are experienced members on the board and allows the board as a group to work on projects or issues that extend beyond one year.

The bad side: As a deterrent to a changeover in the board, some corporations have classified their board positions into several classes—typically three—so only a few positions are put to a vote each year. If a shareholder wanted to elect representatives to this board and eventually get control of the board, it would take two or more years. A classified board cannot prevent a majority of shareholders from gaining control of the board, but it can slow the process down.

The Right to Buy More Stock

If a corporation issues additional shares of stock, they will be available for purchase by anyone—existing shareholders and others. This opens up the possibility that a shareholder's interest in the corporation may be diluted. If you own 1,000 shares of stock in a corporation, representing 10 percent of the 10,000 common shares outstanding, you control 10 percent of that corporation. If the corporation issues 10,000 more shares and you do not buy any of these shares, your ownership drops to 1,000/20,000 = 5 percent.

Corporations can give current shareholders the right to buy additional shares of new common stock through a formal procedure called a **rights offering.** How does this work? First, the corporation issues **warrants** to each shareholder. The warrant is the physical document that gives each shareholder the right to buy a *specified number of shares* at a *specified price*, within a *specified period of time*, according to the number of shares the shareholder already owns. When a shareholder receives warrants, he or she can do one of the following:

- Throw the warrants away.
- Exercise the rights contained in the warrants by buying the shares.
- Sell the rights.

In some corporations, a current shareholder's right to buy shares of any new common stock offering is granted directly in the corporate charter. This is referred to as the **preemptive right** and is the current shareholder's right to buy additional shares of common stock to maintain her or his proportionate share of ownership in the corporation.

Keeping Jaws Away

The provision of classified boards is only one of a number of antitakeover strategies—sometimes referred to as **shark repellants**—that can be instituted to discourage or prevent the takeover of a corporation. Some shark repellants are innocuous, whereas others are powerful.

The real question is whether the management of a firm should attempt to repel a takeover. If a party is willing to pay shareholders more than the current market price for their shares, should management discourage this?

If defenses against takeovers provide a firm's managers with bargaining strength, enabling them to hold out for a better offer, then these defenses are in the best interest of shareholders. If defenses discourage attractive offers, they are not in the best interest of shareholders.

Considering that in many cases the managers of the firm taken over in a merger or acquisition lose their jobs, there is a conflict of interest: management's self-preservation versus its fiduciary duty to shareholders.

The evidence indicates that antitakeover defenses, in general, are not viewed favorably by shareholders.

NOTE: See the survey article by Gregg A. Jarrell, James A. Brickley, and Jeffry M. Netter, "The Market for Corporate Control: The Empirical Evidence Since 1980," *Journal of Economic Perspectives*, vol. 2, no. 1, Winter 1988, pp. 49–68.

Suppose you own 10 percent of the stock of a corporation. If the corporation has a rights offering, you have the right to buy 10 percent of any new stock before it is offered to the public. You don't have to exercise the right, but you have the right and will be given the opportunity to exercise it.

A corporation makes a rights offering for two reasons.

First, shareholders may view a preemptive right as attractive, since they are able to maintain their proportionate ownership interest and, hence, their control of a corporation. If shareholders view this as valuable, this right has the effect of increasing the value of the stock. If the price of shares is higher, a firm needn't issue as many new shares when it wants to raise new capital.

Second, it usually costs a corporation less to issue shares in a rights offering than to sell new shares to the public. And a savings for the corporation is valuable to the owners—the shareholders.

Let's look at an example of a rights offering. In 1991, Time Warner issued rights to its common shareholders.[11] For each share owned, shareholders received six-tenths of a right to buy Time Warner stock at $80 per share. If you

> A rights offering grants shareholders a call option: the option to buy additional shares of stock.

[11] Prior to this rights offering, Time Warner did attempt another offering whose terms were not in the best interests of the shareholders. Dennis E. Logue and James K. Seward discuss the Time Warner rights offerings in detail in "Time Warner Rights Offering: Strategy, Articulation and Destruction of Shareholder Value," *Financial Analysts Journal*, vol. 48, no. 2, March/April 1992, pp. 37–45.

owned 100 shares, you were entitled to buy 60 shares of stock at $80 per share. The rights were granted July 16 and expired three weeks later, on August 5. During that period, the higher the price of Time Warner stock rose, the more valuable the right became.

At the time the rights were granted, Time Warner common stock was trading at $86.75 per share, making the right to buy at $80 worth *at least* $6.75 per right. But early on in this three-week period the value of the right—the price of the rights traded on the stock exchange—was *greater* than the difference between the Time Warner stock price and $80. Why? Because the investors buying the rights at this price felt that before the three weeks were up, the price of the stock would increase even more, making the right *even more* valuable. But as time passed, investors began to lose confidence that the stock would increase in price. So the value of the right wound up equal to the difference between the stock price and the $80.

We can see the relation between the value of the right and the value of the share of Time Warner stock in Figure 11-1. The value of the right and the value of the stock move almost parallel. As the price of Time Warner stock increases, so does the value of the right to buy it at $80. Finally, just before expiration, the value of the right is equal to the difference between the Time Warner stock price and $80.

FIGURE 11-1

Market Value of a Time Warner Common Share and the Right to Buy a Time Warner Common Share at $80 per Share, July 16, 1991–August 5, 1991

SOURCE: Standard & Poor's Daily Stock Price Record.

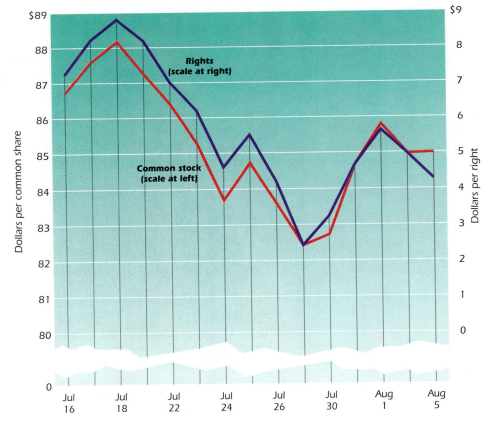

Other Rights

Corporate charters may also grant shareholders other rights besides voting and preemptive rights, such as:

- The right to inspect shareholder lists in order to obtain the names and addresses of shareholders.
- The right to receive dividends declared by the board of directors.
- The right to share assets in the event the corporation is liquidated.
- The right to inspect the books of the corporation.
- The right to call a special shareholders' meeting.
- The right to propose amendments to the corporate charter.

These rights of shareholders are spelled out in the corporate charter. Since the corporate charter is determined, in part, by the laws of the state in which it is incorporated, these rights may differ among corporations because of either differences in their articles of incorporation or differences in state law.

Corporate Democracy

In most large corporations, it is not practical for each shareholder to participate in or monitor the management of the business. Therefore, shareholders require a way to be represented in the major business decisions and to monitor the activities of management. That's why shareholders elect representatives—the members of the board of directors. The board then appoints and oversees the officers and managers of the corporation, making the major decisions and delegating other decisions to the officers and managers. The corporate charter may specify, however, specific decisions that must be voted upon by shareholders, such as the authorization of new shares.

Corporate democracy gives owners of the corporation a say in how to manage it. By law, shareholders are not allowed to interfere with the ordinary business—the day-to-day operations—of a corporation. But they elect representatives—the members of the board of directors—to oversee the management of the firm. The board of directors may be composed of officers of the corporation or may include persons not employed by the corporation—referred to as ***outside directors.***

It is not always clear just what constitutes the ordinary business of a corporation: Doing business in South Africa? Obtaining golden parachutes (attractive severance packages) for top management? Devising salary and stock options for management?

Any shareholder owning either $1,000 worth of the common stock or 1 percent of the outstanding shares is permitted to introduce a proposal to be voted on by shareholders.[12] To avoid having proposals that are inappropriate—in the sense that they are really about ordinary business or simply a nui-

---

[12] This requirement is set forth in the Securities Exchange Act of 1934, rule 14a-8.

sance—the management may petition the Securities and Exchange Commission (SEC) to remove a proposal from the proxy. In the past, the SEC has allowed corporate management to remove shareholder proposals that dealt with management compensation issues, but more recently has forced companies to include these proposals in the proxies.

Corporate democracy as practiced in the United States is imperfect. Many problems have been brought out during the mergers and acquisitions frenzy in the 1980s.

One of the problems that became quite noticeable during the 1980s merger mania is that most large institutional investors tended to vote as recommended by management and that individual investors were, in large part, apathetic toward corporate issues. This is changing as both institutional investors and individual investors form coalitions to encourage shareholder participation in corporation issues.

Second, for most corporations voting is not confidential. Management receives your votes and, if not pleased with how you voted, may contact you to try to persuade you to change your vote. In many cases, shareholders and managers of institutional investors have been pressured to vote in favor of the present management. When AT&T was trying to buy NCR in 1990, the chairman of NCR met with owners and managers of large holdings of NCR stock to persuade them not to sell their shares to AT&T (AT&T eventually bought NCR).[13]

Third, even if a shareholder proposal succeeds, it is nonbinding. Management can simply ignore it! Consider the case of USX. In 1990, a shareholder proposal calling for confidential proxy voting and third-party tabulation of votes received a majority of votes. Subsequent to this vote, the USX board adopted a weaker confidential voting policy that exempted proxy voting and did not guarantee third-party tabulation.[14]

Shareholder proposals represent a weak method of effecting change in a corporation. This is due to the apathetic nature of shareholders, the possibility of arm-twisting by management, and the nonbinding character of the proposals. An alternative method of getting a corporation to change is to wage a **proxy fight,** gaining a voice in the corporation by getting seats on the board of directors. Usually, the board members elected each year are nominated by the current board members and run unopposed. In a proxy fight, an alternative slate of board members is nominated by someone interested in gaining representation on the board. And the battle begins.

The proxy fight pits current board members against the alternative slate—each side vying for the votes, that is, the proxies, of the shareholders. Each side advertises its position in the financial press and through mailings to shareholders. The process is time-consuming, expensive and sometimes nasty.

Some interesting issues arise from the process. Let's say that the party opposing the current board's slate owns 10 percent of the stock. While the battle to unseat the present board may be beneficial to all or most shareholders, the one doing battle pays the expenses of the battle—the others are free-

---

[13] "NCR Sets Up Meetings with Big Holders to Lobby for Support to Fight AT&T Bid," *The Wall Street Journal*, Dec. 13, 1990, p. A6.

[14] "USX Offers Weak Response to Shareholder Votes," United Shareholders Association *Advocate*, vol. 15, no. 12, Dec. 1990, p. 5.

FIGURE 11-3(a)

Dividends per Share and Earnings per Share, General Electric, 1976–1991

SOURCE: Standard & Poor's, *Compustat PC Plus* (CD-ROM)

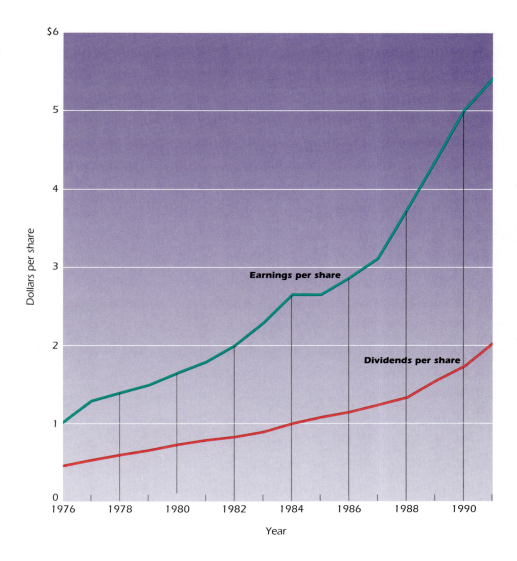

Many firms are reluctant to cut dividends because the firm's share price usually falls when a dividend reduction is announced.[15] They tend to raise their regular quarterly dividend only when they are sure they can keep it up in the future. By giving a special or extra dividend, the firm is able to provide more cash to the shareholders without committing itself to paying an increased dividend each period into the future. Let's look at an example. The

[15] A number of studies have documented the fall in share price that accompanies a cut in dividends. See, for example, Richardson Pettit, "Dividend Announcements, Security Performance, and Capital Market Efficiency," *Journal of Finance*, vol. 27, no. 5, Dec. 1972, pp. 86–96; and Joseph Aharony and Itzhak Swary, "Quarterly Dividend and Earnings Announcements and Stockholders' Returns: An Empirical Analysis," *Journal of Finance*, vol. 35, no. 1, March 1980, pp. 1–12. But just how much the share price falls depends on the reasons for the cut, as documented by J. Randall Woolridge and Chinmoy Gosh, "Dividend Cuts: Do They Always Signal Bad News?" *Midland Journal of Corporate Finance*, Summer 1985, pp. 20–32.

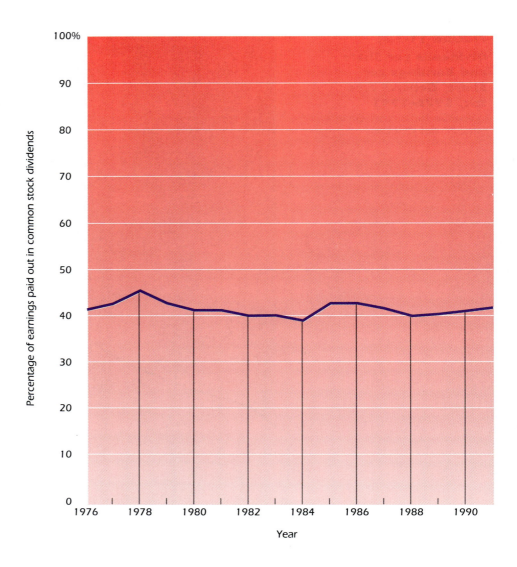

fortunes of Longview Fibre, a timber-growing and -harvesting firm, vary depending on construction demand and timber cutting availability on public land, both of which are quite uncertain. Longview Fibre pays a regular quarterly dividend of about 10 cents a share, but Longview also pays special dividends every October (for example, 3 cents in 1990 and 12 cents in 1991) that vary according to its earnings.

Dividends: To Pay or Not to Pay, That Is the Issue

There is no general agreement about whether dividends should or should not be paid. Here are several views:

- *The Dividend Irrelevance Explanation.* The payment of dividends does not affect the value of the firm, since the investment decision is independent of the financing decision.

- *The Bird-in-Hand Explanation.* Investors prefer a certain dividend stream to an uncertain price appreciation.
- *The Tax-Preference Explanation.* Because of the way in which dividends are taxed vis-à-vis capital gains, investors prefer the retention of funds over the payment of dividends.
- *The Signaling Explanation.* Dividends provide a way for the management of the firm to communicate information to investors regarding the future prospects of the firm.
- *The Agency Explanation.* The payment of dividends forces the firm to seek more external financing, which subjects the firm to the scrutiny of investors.

Let's take a further look at each view.

The Dividend Irrelevance Explanation

The dividend irrelevance argument was developed by Merton Miller and Franco Modigliani.[16] Basically, the argument is that if there is a **perfect market**—no taxes, no transaction costs, no costs related to the issuing of new securities, and no costs of sending or receiving information—the value of the firm is unaffected whether or not the firm pays a dividend.

How can this be? Suppose investment decisions are fixed, that is, the firm will invest in certain projects *regardless* of how they are financed. The value of the firm is the present value of all future cash flows of the firm, which are dependent on the investment decisions that it makes, *not* on how these investments are financed. If the investment decision is fixed, the value of the firm is unaffected whether or not the firm pays a dividend.

A firm raises additional funds either through earnings or by selling securities sufficient to meet its investment and dividend decisions. The dividend decision therefore affects only the financing decision: how much capital the firm needs to raise in order to carry out its investment decisions.

The implication of the Miller and Modigliani argument is that the dividend decision is a residual decision. If the firm has no profitable investments to undertake, it can pay out funds that would have gone to investments to shareholders. And whether or not the firm pays dividends is of no consequence to the value of the firm. In other words, dividends are irrelevant.

But we don't live in a perfect world with a perfect market. Are the imperfections (taxes, transactions costs, etc.) enough to alter the conclusions of Miller and Modigliani? It isn't clear.

The Bird-in-Hand Explanation

A popular view is that dividends represent a *sure thing* relative to share price appreciation. The return to shareholders is composed of two parts: the return from dividends—the **dividend yield**—and the return from the change in the share price—the **capital yield.** Firms generate earnings and can either pay them out in cash dividends or reinvest earnings in profitable investments, increasing the value of the stock and, hence, the share price. Once a dividend is paid, it is a certain cash flow. Shareholders can cash their quarterly divi-

---

[16] "Dividend Policy, Growth and the Valuation of Shares," *Journal of Business,* Oct. 1961, pp. 411–433.

dend checks and reinvest the funds. But an increase in share price is not a sure thing. It becomes a sure thing only when the share price rises higher than the price the shareholder paid and he or she sells the shares. Not before!

We can see that prices of dividend-paying stocks are less volatile than non-dividend-paying stocks. But are dividend-paying stocks less risky because they pay dividends? Or are less risky firms more likely to pay dividends? Most of the evidence supports the latter. Firms that have greater risk—business risk, financial risk, or both—tend to pay little or no dividends. Firms whose cash flows are more variable tend to avoid large dividend commitments that they might not be able to satisfy during periods of poorer financial performance.

The Tax-Preference Explanation

The dividend income shareholders receive is taxed like any other income, such as wages or salaries. If shareholders sell their stock, any gain they make (called capital gains) is given preferential tax treatment—taxed effectively at a lower rate than dividend income.

Capital gains are taxed at lower rates due to two aspects of the tax law.

First, capital gains are only taxed when realized—when you sell the stock. If you receive $20 of dividends in 1995, you pay taxes on that income in 1995. If you bought stock in 1980 and sell it in 2000, you do not pay tax on any gain until 2000! So, while the price of the stock may go up $20 in 1995, you don't pay any tax on that $20 until you sell the stock in 2000. And since the taxes you pay on this gain are in the future, you effectively pay lower taxes on the capital gain as compared to an equivalent amount of dividends.

Second, capital gains have often been taxed at lower rates. Whether through a special capital gain exclusion—that means part of the gain does not get figured into your taxable income—or through a special tax rate, capital gains have been taxed at lower rates than dividend income throughout most of U.S. tax history.

But the tax impact is different for different types of shareholders. An individual taxpayer includes dividend income along with other income, such as wages, to determine taxable income. But a corporation receiving a dividend from another corporation may take a **dividends-received deduction**—a deduction of a large portion of the dividend income.[17] Therefore, corporations pay taxes on only a small portion of their dividend income. Still other shareholders may not even be taxed on dividend income. For example, a pension fund does not pay taxes on the dividend income it gets from its investments (these earnings are eventually taxed when the pension is paid out to the employee after retirement).

Dividends are taxed at rates higher than capital gains, though there are two things that could affect this difference for some investors. First, investors who have high marginal tax rates may gravitate toward stocks that pay little or no dividends. This means the shareholders of dividend-paying stocks have lower marginal tax rates. This is referred to as a **tax clientele**—investors who choose stocks on the basis of the taxes they have to pay.

---

[17] The dividends-received deduction ranges from 70 to 100 percent, depending on the ownership relation between the two corporations.

Second, investors with high marginal tax rates can use legitimate investment strategies—such as borrowing to buy stock and using the deduction from the interest payments on the loan to offset the dividend income, in order to reduce the tax impact of dividends.[18]

The Signaling Explanation

Firms that pay dividends seem to maintain a relatively stable payout policy, either in terms of a constant or growing dividend payout or in terms of a constant or growing dividend per share. And when firms change their dividend—either increasing or reducing ("cutting") the dividend—the price of the firm's shares seems to be affected: When a dividend is increased, the price of its shares goes up; when a dividend is cut, the price goes down. This reaction is attributed to investors' perception of the meaning of the dividend change: Increases are good news, decreases are bad news.

Managers likely have some information that investors do not have. A change in dividend may be a way for managers to signal this private information. Since we observe that when dividends are lowered, the price of a share falls, we would expect managers not to increase a dividend unless they thought they could maintain it into the future. Realizing this, investors may view a dividend increase as a sign of management's increased confidence in the future operating performance of the firm.

The Agency Explanation

The relation between the owners and managers of a firm is an **agency relationship:** The owners are the **principals,** and the managers are the **agents.** The managers are charged with acting in the best interests of the owners. Nevertheless, there are possibilities for conflicts between the interests of the two. If the firm pays a dividend, managers may be forced to raise new capital outside of the firm—that is, issue new securities instead of using internally generated capital—thus subjecting themselves to the scrutiny of investment bankers, banks, and other investors. This extra scrutiny helps reduce the possibility that managers will not work in the best interests of the shareholders. But issuing new securities is not cost-free. There are costs in issuing new securities—*flotation costs.* In agency-theory jargon, these costs are part of *monitoring costs:* They are incurred to help monitor the managers' behavior and ensure that it is consistent with shareholder wealth maximization.

The payment of dividends also reduces the amount of free cash flow under control of management. *Free cash flow* is the cash in excess of the amount needed to finance profitable investment opportunities. A profitable investment opportunity is any investment that provides the firm with a return greater than what shareholders could get elsewhere on their money, that is, a return greater than the shareholders' opportunity cost.

---

[18] Several strategies that can be used to reduce the taxes on dividend income are discussed by Merton Miller and Myron Scholes in "Dividends and Taxes," *Journal of Financial Economics,* vol. 6, no. 4, 1978, pp. 333–364. However, Pamela Peterson, David Peterson, and James Ang, in "Direct Evidence on the Marginal Rate of Taxation on Dividend Income," *Journal of Financial Economics,* vol. 14, no. 2, 1985, pp. 267–282, document the apparent failure of investors to take advantage of these strategies, with the result that the taxpayers end up paying substantial taxes on their dividend income.

What's the Cost to Issue Stock?

The cost of issuing common stock is approximately 4 percent of the proceeds raised. If $100 million of common stock is sold, the underwriters—the investment banking firms that sell the stock to investors—receive $4 million and the issuing firm receives $96 million.

Free cash flow is the cash flow left over after all profitable projects are undertaken—the only projects left are the unprofitable ones. Should free cash be reinvested in the unprofitable investments or paid out to shareholders? Of course, if managers make decisions consistent with shareholder wealth maximization, any free cash flow should be paid out to shareholders, since—by the definition of a profitable investment opportunity—the shareholders could get a better return investing the funds they receive elsewhere.

If the firm pays a dividend, funds are paid out to shareholders. If the firm needs funds, they could be raised by issuing new securities. If the shareholders wish to reinvest the funds received as their dividends in the firm, they could buy these new securities. The payment of dividends therefore reduces the cash flow in the hands of management, reducing the possibility that managers will invest funds in unprofitable investment opportunities.

Summing Up: To Pay or Not to Pay Dividends

We can figure out reasons why a firm should or should not pay dividends, but not why they actually do or do not—that is the "dividend puzzle."[19] But what we do know from looking at dividends and the market's reaction to them is that:

- If a firm increases its dividends or pays a dividend for the first time, the action is viewed as good news—the firm's share price increases.
- If a firm decreases its dividend or even omits it completely, the action is viewed as bad news—the firm's share price declines.

That's why financial managers must be aware of the relation between dividends and the value of the common stock in establishing or changing dividend policy.

Dividend Reinvestment Plans

Many U.S. corporations allow shareholders automatically to reinvest their dividends in the shares of the corporation paying them. A ***dividend reinvestment plan*** (DRP) is a program that allows shareholders to reinvest their dividends, buying additional shares of stock of the company instead of receiving the cash dividend. Over 500 corporations whose stock is traded on the New York Stock Exchange or American Stock Exchange have dividend reinvestment plans.

These additional shares representing dividends reinvested may be currently outstanding (the firm buys them in the open market) or newly issued. The dividends are reinvested according to a prescribed formula. For example, you may be able to reinvest your dividend in new shares based on the average market price of a share five days prior to the dividend payment date. If you get $100 in dividends and the average price of the stock during the five preceding days was $20, you receive five more shares. The corporation keeps track of the shares you are "buying," much as in a savings account. You never see the cash dividend or the shares, but you receive a periodic accounting of

---

[19] The phrase "dividend puzzle" originates in Fischer Black's "The Dividend Puzzle," *Journal of Portfolio Management,* vol. 2, Winter 1976, pp. 5–8.

the shares you own. You can sell or keep the shares that accumulate in your account.

To encourage participation, especially in plans providing newly issued shares, some firms allow shareholders to reinvest their dividends at a discount from the current market price. These discounts range from 2 to 10 percent, typically 5 percent.

A DRP offers benefits to both shareholders and the firm. Shareholders buy shares without transaction costs—brokers' commissions—and at a discount from the current market price. The firm is able to retain cash without incurring the cost of a new stock issue.

Alas, the dividends are taxed as income before they are reinvested, even though the shareholders never see the dividend. The result is similar to a dividend cut—shareholders are getting less cash because they're paying more taxes! Many firms are finding high rates of participation in DRPs. If so many shareholders want to reinvest their dividends—even after considering the tax consequences—why is the firm paying dividends? This suggests that there is some rationale, such as signaling, that compels firms to pay dividends.

Stock Repurchases

Recently, many corporations have repurchased their common stock from their shareholders. A corporation repurchasing its own shares is effectively paying a cash dividend, with one important difference: taxes. Cash dividends are ordinary taxable income to the shareholder: The dividends are income, lumped with his or her other ordinary income. A firm's repurchase of shares, on the other hand, results in a capital gain or loss for the shareholder, depending on the price paid when they were originally purchased. If the shares are repurchased at a higher price, the difference may be treated as a capital gain, which may be taxed at a rate lower than ordinary income.

Methods of Repurchasing Stock

A corporation may repurchase its own stock by means of (1) a tender offer, (2) open market purchases, or (3) a targeted share repurchase.

A *tender offer* is an offer made to all shareholders, with a specified deadline and a specified number of shares the corporation is willing to buy back. The tender offer may be a fixed price offer, in which the corporation specifies the price it is willing to pay and solicits purchases of shares of stock at that price.

The tender offer may also be conducted as a ***Dutch auction,*** in which the corporation specifies a minimum and a maximum price, soliciting bids from shareholders for any price within this range at which they are willing to sell their shares. After the corporation receives these bids, they pay all tendering shareholders the maximum price sufficient to buy back the number of shares they want. A Dutch auction reduces the chance that the firm will pay a price higher than needed to acquire the shares.

A corporation may also buy back shares directly in the open market. This involves buying the shares through a broker. A corporation that wants to buy shares may have to spread its purchases over time so as not to drive the share's price up temporarily by buying large numbers of shares.

How a Dutch Auction Works

Suppose a corporation wants to buy back 1 million shares of common stock currently trading at $25 a share. If the firm makes a tender offer for the shares, it must specify the price it is willing to pay. The price has to be higher than $25, or else no one will be willing to sell back the shares.

Since it is sometimes difficult to figure out just how much more to offer, the firm can use a Dutch auction. A Dutch auction—a system used since the early 1900s by Holland bulb growers—sets the buying price for the item based on the basis of bids.

For example, the firm could make a Dutch auction tender offer, specifying that it wants to buy back 1 million shares and offering to pay a minimum price of $26 and a maximum price of $29. Shareholders who want to tender their shares—sell them back to the corporation—specify how many shares they are willing to sell and at what price. Suppose the shareholders respond as follows:

Number of shares willing to tender	Specified price
200,000	$26
600,000	27
200,000	28
400,000	29

The corporation will accept the first 1 million shares in order of price, paying only one price, and that not higher than necessary, to get that 1 million shares. In this example, the corporation will pay $28 per share for the 1 million shares. The shareholders who specified they would tender their shares at $29 per share are out of luck. The shareholders who bid $26 and $27 will be paid more than the price at which they were willing to tender.

We saw earlier in this chapter, greenmail is one of several tactics available to fend off an unwanted takeover.

The third method of repurchasing stock is to buy it from a specific shareholder. This involves direct negotiation between the corporation and the shareholder. This method is referred to as a ***targeted block repurchase,*** since there is a specific shareholder (the "target") and there are a large number of shares (a "block") to be purchased at one time. Targeted block repurchases, also referred to as greenmail, were used in the 1980s to fight takeovers.

Reasons for Repurchasing Stock

Corporations repurchase their stock for a number of reasons: First, a repurchase is a way to distribute cash to shareholders at a lower cost to both the firm and the shareholders than dividends. If capital gains are taxed at rates lower than ordinary income, which is often the case with our tax law, repurchasing is a lower-cost way of distributing cash. However, since shareholders have different tax rates—especially corporate shareholders compared with individual shareholders—the benefit is mixed. Why? Because some shareholders are tax-free (e.g., pension funds), some shareholders are only taxed on a portion of dividends (e.g., corporations that receive dividends from other corporations), and some shareholders are taxed on the full amount of dividends (e.g., individual taxpayers).

Another reason to repurchase stock is to increase earnings per share. A firm repurchasing its shares increases its earnings per share simply because there are fewer shares outstanding after the repurchase. But there are two problems with this motive:

1. Cash is paid to the shareholders; so less cash is available for the corporation to reinvest in profitable projects.
2. There are fewer shares; so, other things being held constant, the reduction in shares means that the earnings pie is sliced in fewer pieces—resulting in higher earnings per share—not that the pie is any bigger.

Looking at how share prices respond to gimmicks that manipulate earnings, we know that you cannot fool the market by playing an earnings-per-share game. The market can see through the earnings-per-share gimmick to what is really happening—the firm will have less cash to invest.

Still another reason for stock repurchase is that it could tilt the debt-equity ratio so as to increase the value of the firm. By buying back stock—thereby reducing equity—the firm's assets are financed to a greater degree by debt. Does this seem wrong? It's not. To see this, suppose a corporation has the following balance sheet:

Assets $100   Debt $50
                     Equity 50

The corporation has financed 50 percent of its assets with debt, 50 percent with equity. If this corporation uses $20 of its assets to buy back stock worth $20, its balance sheet will be:

Assets $80   Debt $50
                     Equity 30

It now finances $50/$80 = 62.5 percent of its assets with debt and 37.5 percent with equity.

If financing the firm with more debt is good—that is, the benefits from deducting interest on debt outweigh the cost of increasing the risk of bankruptcy—repurchasing stock may increase the value of the firm. But there is the flip side to this argument: Financing the firm with more debt may be bad if the risk of financial distress—difficulty paying legal obligations—outweighs the benefits from the tax deductibility of interest. Therefore, from this perspective a proposal to repurchase shares would have to be judged on a case-by-case basis to determine if it's beneficial or detrimental.

One more reason for a stock repurchase is that it reduces total dividend payments without seeming to. If you cut down on the number of shares out-

> ### Some Companies Miss the Mark
>
> Although you would think that companies would try to sell new shares when their share prices are high and would repurchase their shares when prices are low, that is not always the case. For example, Westinghouse Electric repurchased 5.3 million of its common stock from May 1990 through February 1991, paying an estimated $32.42 per share. Needing cash later in 1991, Westinghouse issued 21.5 million shares of common stock at $26.50 per share.
>
> SOURCE: Laurie P. Cohen, "Why Companies Buy Their Stock High, Then Sell Low," *The Wall Street Journal*, July 15, 1991, p. C1. Other companies cited in this article as buying high and selling low included Tenneco Inc. and the Marriott Corporation.

Is a Shrinking Firm Consistent with Shareholder Wealth Maximization?

Repurchasing shares of a firm tends to shrink the firm: Cash is paid out and the value of the firm declines. Can repurchasing shares be consistent with wealth maximization? Yes.

If the best use of funds is to pay them out to shareholders, repurchasing shares maximizes shareholders' wealth. If the firm hasn't any profitable investment opportunities, it is better for a firm to shrink by paying funds to the shareholders than to shrink by investing in poor investments.

standing, you can still pay the same amount of dividends *per share*, but your *total* dividend payments are reduced. Suppose you pay a regular quarterly dividend of $2.00 per share. If there are 1 million shares of stock outstanding, your quarterly dividend payment is $2 million. If you repurchase 10 percent of the outstanding shares and keep the dividends per share the same, your total quarterly dividend payment is $2.00 times 900,000 shares, or $1.8 million. You have reduced your payment by $200,000, but you have not changed the dividends per share.

If the shares are correctly valued in the market (there is no reason to believe otherwise), the payment for the repurchased shares equals the reduction in the value of the firm—and the remaining shares are worth the same as they were before. In our example, the repurchase reduces the equity pie by 10 percent, and the smaller pie comprises 10 percent fewer shares. Suppose the shares traded at $50 per share before the repurchase. Then total equity is $50 times 1 million, or $50 million. If the firm buys back 10 percent of the shares—100,000 shares at $50 each—the value of the firm should decline by $5 million. This leaves equity worth $45 million. Split among the remaining 900,000 shares, the value per share is $50—the same as before the repurchase.

Some argue that a repurchase is a signal about future prospects. That is, by buying back the shares, the management is communicating to investors that the firm is generating sufficient cash to be able to buy back shares. But does this make sense? Not really. If the firm has profitable investment opportunities, the cash could be used to finance these investments, instead of paying it out to the shareholders.

A stock repurchase may also reduce agency costs by reducing the amount of cash the management has on hand. Just as for dividend payments, as we explained earlier, repurchasing shares reduces the amount of free cash flow and, hence, reduces the possibility that management will invest it unprofitably.

So how does the market react to a firm's intention to repurchase shares? A number of studies have looked at how the market reacts to such announcements.[20] In general, the share price goes up when a firm announces it is going to repurchase its own shares.

It is difficult to identify the reason the market reacts favorably to such announcements, since so many other things are happening at the same time. By piecing bits of evidence together, however, we see that it is likely investors view the announcement of a repurchase as good news—a signal of good things to come.

PREFERRED STOCK

During the late 1800s, many U.S. railroads were having problems paying the interest and principal on their debt obligations. As part of the reorganization of these railroads, bondholders took an equity interest in exchange for their debt obligations: Lenders became owners. But these bondholders wanted some priority over the other equity owners, so they exchanged their debt for shares of stock with a *prior* claim over common shareholders—hence, preferred stock.

We've already covered the basics of common stock, which is the residual ownership of a firm. Some firms also have preferred stock: a form of ownership that has *preference* over common stock ownership. Like common stock, preferred stock also represents equity.

Preferred shareholders have a claim on income and assets ahead of that of common shareholders. Preferred shareholders are promised a dividend that must be paid before common shareholders receive any dividends. The consequences of not paying the preferred stock dividend are not so drastic as not paying, say, interest on a debt obligation: Preferred shareholders do not have a legal claim to receive the dividend—they cannot force the firm into bankruptcy for failure to pay. But creditors can!

If the business is liquidated—all the assets sold and the proceeds used to pay off all the creditors and owners—the preferred shareholders get all that's coming to them before common shareholders get anything. While few corporations are actually liquidated, this prior claim provides preferred shareholders with an advantage in the reorganization of firms in distress or bankruptcy.

Just as there may be different classes of common stock, there may also be different classes of preferred stock, each with a different dividend rate and rights. Some classes of preferred stock are junior to others, that is, they wait in line behind owners of more senior preferred issues in the case of dividend payments or liquidation. Nevertheless, all preferred shareholders have preference over the common shareholders.

Par and Liquidation Values

Preferred stocks may have a par value, though it is not legally required. Nevertheless, some specified value is convenient to have for accounting purposes. Some corporations specify a ***stated value,*** that is, an arbitrary value for the stock, say, $100.

---

[20] For a review of the pertinent evidence, see the article by Larry Dann, "Common Stock Repurchases: What Do They Really Accomplish?" *Chase Financial Quarterly.*

Depositary Preferred Shares

As a way of making their preferred stock more marketable, some corporations deposit some or all of the preferred stock in a trust, issuing shares in the trust for a fraction of the share's par value. These trust shares are referred to as ***depositary preferred shares.*** They receive a portion of the dividend on a preferred share. For example, if ten depositary preferred shares are created from each share of $100 par value preferred stock that has an 8 percent annual dividend, the dividend on the depositary shares is one-tenth of the dividend on the preferred stock, or $0.80.

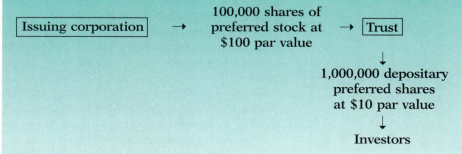

Depositary preferred shares are created to increase the marketability of the preferred shares: Each of the depositary shares trades at a fraction of the price of the preferred stock. This lower price may reduce investors' transactions costs and make purchases of even lots of 100 shares each more affordable for smaller investors.

Each preferred stock does have a ***liquidation value,*** the amount that preferred shareholders are paid if the firm is liquidated and there remain sufficient assets to pay off this value. Often, the liquidating value is equal to the stated or par value of the stock.

Preferred Stock Dividends

Although a firm announces it will pay a dividend on its preferred stock, payment is not a legal obligation. That is, if a firm does not pay the dividend, preferred shareholders cannot legally force payment. Nevertheless, almost all firms pay their specified preferred dividend. When dividends are paid, preferred dividends must be paid first; what remains may be paid as dividends to common shareholders. Most preferred share dividends are paid in cash, though a few preferred stock issues allow the issuing firm to pay preferred dividends in cash or shares of stock.

Preferred dividends are declared by the board of directors, and most are paid quarterly, though monthly, semiannual, and annual dividends are possible. Furthermore, preferred dividends may be paid at either a fixed or variable rate per period.

Fixed vs. Variable Rate Dividends

Fixed dividends are expressed as either a percentage of the par value or a fixed dollar amount per period. If you own a preferred stock with a $100 par value and an 8 percent annual dividend, you receive $8 in dividends per year. This dividend could have also been stated simply as $8 per share annually.

In the early 1980s, corporations began issuing preferred stock having a dividend rate that varied. This *adjustable rate preferred stock* (ARPS) has a dividend that changes or "floats" as a specified benchmark rate changes. Common benchmarks include the yield on long-term U.S. Treasury bonds and the *London interbank offered rate* (LIBOR). An adjustable preferred dividend rate may change each year or each quarter.

In addition, some adjustable rate preferred stocks specify a maximum and a minimum dividend rate. The maximum and minimum rates are referred to as a *collar.* From the perspective of the issuer, a collar's maximum ensures that the costs of financing with preferred stock are limited; from the perspective of the investors, a collar's minimum ensures that the return on the preferred stock has a lower limit.

Another twist on the variable preferred dividend rate is a rate determined by shareholders bidding in a Dutch auction (described earlier). This kind of preferred dividend is changed periodically—usually annually—according to the bidding. Investors buy and sell the preferred shares depending on how the dividend rate they bid differs from the dividend rate resulting from the auction. A Dutch auction to set the dividend rate ensures that the firm pays a dividend that is determined by the market.

For a demonstration of the determination of a dividend in a Dutch auction, see Appendix 11A.

Cumulative vs. Noncumulative Dividends

Since there is no legal requirement to pay dividends to preferred shareholders, these shareholders may want some assurance that their dividend payment is not skipped and the funds paid instead to common shareholders. Remember: The members of the board of directors are, for the most part, elected by the common shareholders.

But there is a way to ensure that common shareholders do not take advantage of the preferred shareholders' lack of legal claim on dividends. With *cumulative preferred stock,* any dividend not paid in one period must be paid the next period before any other dividend for that class of preferred stock is paid and before any common stock dividend is paid. With *noncumulative preferred stock,* any dividend not paid in a period is not paid in any other period—it is simply forgotten and does not affect the preferred or common dividend in any future period.

If a preferred stock dividend is cumulative, any dividend passed over in one period is carried over from year to year. The passed over dividend is referred to as the *arrearage,* and the preferred stock dividend is said to be in *arrears.* Most preferred stock issued in the United States is cumulative preferred stock.

Some companies can chalk up quite a bit of dividends in arrears. For example, Gulf States Utilities began to have cash problems in 1987 and stopped paying dividends on its twenty-three different preferred stock issues as well as on its common stock. Preferred dividend arrearages grew to over $282 million in the twenty-four quarters from 1987 until mid-1991, when Gulf States began to whittle down the arrearage.

Participating vs. Nonparticipating Dividends

Preferred shareholders may also participate in the earnings of the firm, along with the common shareholders. If the preferred stock is *participating,* preferred shareholders receive a portion of the earnings according to some prescribed formula. The portion is either in addition to a stated preferred dividend or varies according to the common stock dividend.

There are very few participating preferred stock issues. There are two reasons for this. First, preferred stock originated as a substitute for debt in cases in which firms were in poor financial condition. Since the prospects are viewed as dim for a firm issuing preferred stock, so is the value of participating in the firm's future earnings. Preferred shareholders prefer receiving their promised dividend rather than gambling on an uncertain share of earnings.

Second, participating preferred stock reduces the benefits to common shareholders. If the firm does poorly, common shareholders are protected on the downside by limited liability. If the firm does well, common shareholders do not have to share the good earnings with others. Management, acting on behalf of the common shareholders, simply pays the bondholders and preferred shareholders the promised interest or dividend and no more, keeping the rest for the holders of the common. The existence of participating preferred shares would limit this leveraging effect.

One example is the participating preferred issued by Intermark, Inc. in 1986. The dividend on this preferred stock is not fixed, but rather is 1 cent per share less than the common stock dividend each quarter. The preferred shareholders of Intermark therefore have the opportunity to share in the earnings along with the common shareholders and are not limited by a specified dividend rate or amount.

Convertibility

A preferred stock that is exchangeable for common shares is called a *convertible preferred stock.* The conversion feature gives the shareholder the right to convert the preferred shares into common shares at a predetermined rate of exchange.

Conversion Jargon

Conversion ratio. The number of shares of common stock that you get when you exchange a share of preferred stock for common stock.

Market conversion price. The market value of the common stock you would have if you exchange your preferred stock, that is, the conversion ratio multiplied by the market value of a share of common stock. Also referred to as the conversion value.

Conversion premium. The difference between the market price of the preferred stock and the conversion price.

To see how the conversion feature works, consider the convertible preferred stock issued in November 1991 by the Ford Motor Company. Ford sold 46 million shares of its convertible preferred stock at $50.00 each, for a total sale of $2.3 billion. The annual dividend yield is 8.4 percent of the $50.00 par, or $4.20 per share. Each preferred share is convertible into a share of Ford Motor Company Class A common stock.

To Convert or Not to Convert

The decision to convert preferred stock into common stock requires weighing (1) the more certain preferred dividend against the less certain common stock dividend and (2) the limited stock price appreciation of the preferred stock against the unlimited stock price appreciation of the common stock.

When is it best for a shareholder to convert preferred stock into common stock? You have to weigh several factors. If you keep the Ford preferred stock, you have a stream of dividends of $4.20 each year forever. While these dividends are not certain, you at least have preference over Ford's common shareholders, whose annual dividends were recently cut from around $3.00 to $1.60 per share. But sticking with the preferred stock, you are limited in your profit potential—if the value of Ford common increases, the only way to share in this appreciation is to convert to the common stock. At the time the preferred stock was issued, Ford common was trading at about $25.75 a share; so exchanging the preferred stock for the common was not attractive then, but may be in the future.

Recently, several firms have issued **mandatory convertible preferred stock.** This type of stock requires the investor to convert the preferred shares into common shares within a specified period of time, say, five years. From the perspective of the issuer, mandatory convertible preferred is attractive, since it releases the firm from the obligation to pay preferred dividends and is, in effect, a deferred issue of common shares. From the perspective of the investor, mandatory convertible preferred provides the opportunity to convert but only within a specific period and is much like a common stock with a set dividend rate for a limited period of time.

Callability

Since preferred stock has no maturity, the issuer usually has only two ways to retire it:

1. Buy the stock in the open market.
2. Exchange preferred shares for another security, such as common shares, with a conversion feature.

If the stock is callable, the firm has another alternative: exercise its right to call the stock—buy it—from the investor. **Callable preferred stock** gives the issuer the right to buy it from the shareholder at a predetermined price. If the issuing corporation wants to buy back the stock by using the call—referred to as **exercising** the call—the issuer pays the specified **call price.** The call price may be a set amount forever, or may change according to a preset schedule. The call price is generally greater than or equal to the stated or par value of the stock.

The Value of a Perpetuity

The dividend on a share of preferred stock is a perpetuity. Since the value of a perpetuity is the cash flow divided by the discount rate (the yield), the value of a preferred share is:

$$\text{Market value of a share} = \frac{\text{dividend per period}}{\text{yield per period}}$$

and the yield on the preferred share is:

$$\text{Yield per period} = \frac{\text{dividend per period}}{\text{market value of a share}}$$

Conversion and Call Features Are Options

The conversion feature gives the owner of the stock the right to exchange the stock for another type of stock, according to preset conditions. This is an option to buy the new stock (a conversion option).

The call feature gives the issuer of the stock the right to buy it back according to preset conditions. This is an option to buy from the perspective of the issuer (a call option).

Suppose a corporation issued preferred stock at $100 par that pays a 9 percent dividend. If the yield on the preferred stock falls to 5 percent, two things happen:

1. The price of the 9 percent preferred stock increases to $9/0.05 = $180, a premium of $80 above par value.
2. The corporation sees an opportunity to issue preferred stock at a lower dividend cost.

Buying the preferred stock in the open market means that the corporation pays $180 for each share. But if the preferred stock is callable at, say, $104, the corporation can buy it back at $104 a share, retire the 9 percent preferred stock, and issue 5 percent preferred stock.

The call feature provides the issuer with flexibility. But it increases the risk to the investor, since the stock may be called just when it is looking especially good. Since the call feature increases the risk to the investor, investors demand a greater return—and therefore the issuer faces a greater cost—on callable preferred stock relative to noncallable preferred stock.

Forcing the Issue

If a callable preferred stock is combined with a conversion feature, the firm can force conversion. When callable stock is called, shareholders are given notice—usually thirty or sixty days—before the stock is actually called away from them. If the stock is convertible, the shareholders are faced with the choice of either taking the cash, in the amount of the call price, or converting the shares. If the conversion price is greater than the call price, shareholders will convert rather than take the cash.

Voting Rights

The vast majority of preferred stock issues do not have the right to vote. Instead, preferred shareholders generally have ***contingent voting rights***—voting rights that become active only when the firm fails to pay the promised preferred stock dividend. Contingent voting rights may be designed in any manner. But the typical voting right is triggered once the dividends are in arrears and is limited to voting on representation on the board of directors and the issuance of other securities. For example, the New York Stock Exchange requires that all preferred stock issues listed on the exchange have contingent voting rights that allow preferred shareholders the right to vote for at least two members of the board of directors as long as dividends are in arrears.

Sinking Funds

Because there is no legal obligation to pay the preferred dividend and because bondholders and other creditors get the first crack at a firm's income and liquidation rights, preferred shareholders want some assurance they will receive preferred stock dividends. A corporation can provide this assurance in the form of a sinking fund.

A ***sinking fund*** is like a savings account. The corporation deposits funds with a trustee, who uses these funds to periodically retire preferred stock, buying it from shareholders at a specified price, the ***sinking fund call price.*** The trustee acquires these shares either by buying them in the open market—calling up a broker and buying the shares—or by calling in the preferred stock at a specified sinking fund call price. The amount of the periodic retirement, which is predetermined, may be specified in terms of the number of shares or the percentage of total shares to be retired each year. By retiring preferred stock periodically, the firm is better able to meet the dividend payments on the remaining preferred shares.

Packaging Features

A corporation may combine any of the features we just described into their preferred stock. If the company hopes to sell its preferred shares, it must package them in a way that is attractive to investors and at a reasonable cost.

When preferred stock was first introduced, the primary concern was dividends and who gets them. Bondholders who became shareholders wanted priority over other shareholders. And since preferred stock was issued to replace bond issues when a firm was having trouble paying interest, most early preferred stocks were noncumulative to prevent further financial difficulties. There were no features such as voting rights, conversion, and callability in early preferred stock issues because they weren't needed.

Preferred stock issues became popular in the 1920s, since they were more senior to common stock and therefore less risky, but provided a better return than bonds. As preferred stocks were issued by more financially sound firms, the cumulative dividend feature was added to many. In the late 1920s, preferred stock issues tended to have priority not just for dividends, but in liquidation as well. At about the same time, a call feature was added to many preferred stocks. When the stock market collapsed in 1929, preferred stocks fell out of favor because they did not offer investors protective features.

It was not until the 1940s, when protections were built into preferred stocks, that they regained investor confidence. Today's preferred stocks protect the investor with contingent voting rights, sinking funds, and restrictions on common stock dividends. All these protective features, and those to be developed, are in response to what investors want. Marketing preferred stock is like marketing anything else.

Features that give the issuer flexibility, such as a call feature, introduce uncertainty for investors. Investors do not know when (or if) the firm will call in the issue. Since investors do not like risk, they will demand a greater return on callable preferred shares to compensate them for the additional risk implicit in its uncertainty. Providing a greater return increases the issuer's cost.

Features that give the investor something of additional value, such as a conversion feature, lower the issuer's cost. Investors are willing to accept a lower return in exchange for convertibility. And if investors are willing to accept a lower return, the issuer's cost of capital is lower.

And as with common stock, dividends *received* by corporations are partially excluded from taxation. Since most of the investors in preferred stock are corporations, the dividend-received deduction lowers the return demanded by investors, lowering the issuing corporation's cost of financing.

Packaging a new issue of preferred stock requires considering investors' need for greater returns and lower risk and the issuer's need for greater flexibility and lower costs.

FIGURE 11-4

U.S. Corporate Profits after Taxes, Broken Down by Dividends and Retained Earnings, 1980–1990

SOURCE: *Survey of Current Business.*

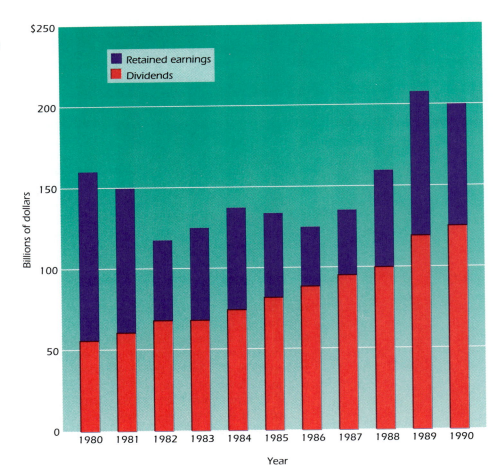

EQUITY AS A SOURCE OF FUNDS

In the heyday of preferred stock, 1927–1929, corporations raised approximately one-fifth of their new capital through preferred stock offerings.

SOURCE: *Survey of Current Business,* 1938 Supplement, p. 70.

Corporations generate common equity as they operate by generating more funds than they need for operating and financing expenses. Any earnings that the firm does not pay out to its owners in the form of dividends are reinvested in the business. We refer to these reinvested funds as ***retained earnings.***

How much U.S. corporations reinvest is shown in Figure 11-4, where we see that dividends grew at a steady pace from 1980 through 1990, but retained earnings varied each year.

If the firm doesn't get enough funds for profitable investment projects from the retained earnings, where does it get the funds it needs? By issuing more preferred stock, or more common stock, or more debt, or more of each.

We can see corporations' increasing reliance on capital from stock issues in Figure 11-5, where the amount raised in preferred stock and common stock is shown for 1950–1990. Beginning around 1980, the increase in new common stock grew dramatically. Even with the increased issuance of common and preferred stock, together they represent less than 40 percent of the new capital raised by U.S. corporations. Debt makes up the other 60 percent!

As you can see in Figure 11-5, preferred stock is not issued as often as common stock. That's because preferred stock is usually associated with firms

FIGURE 11-5

Common and Preferred Stock Issued by U.S. Corporations, 1950–1990

SOURCE: Moody's *Industrial Manual,* 1991, p. a39.

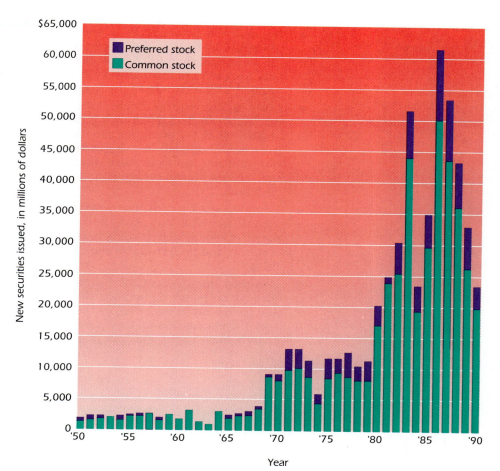

in financial difficulties.[21] Preferred stock does not have the legal protections of bonds and since the dividend on preferred is most often nonparticipating, it is a limited dividend. Considerations like these make preferred stock unattractive to many investors.

SUMMARY

- Stock represents ownership in a corporation in units called shares. There are two types of stock: preferred and common. Both are forms of equity but have different priorities with respect to their claim on the firm's income and assets.

- Part of shareholders' return is in the form of cash payments called dividends. Whether a corporation should pay dividends is debatable, given the higher tax rate on dividend income relative to capital gain income. Some believe that dividends serve a purpose: either providing information about the firm's future prospects or forcing the corporation to sell more securities in order to raise the money to pay the dividends.

- Besides cash dividends, firms may distribute additional shares of stock to shareholders through a stock dividend or a stock split. While distributing additional shares does not change the value of the stock, the announcement of the distribution may provide information about management's expectations of the firm's future prospects.

- Corporations may repurchase their own shares, resulting in lesser tax consequences than when cash is distributed to shareholders in the form of a dividend. Corporations can repurchase shares in the open market, use a tender offer, or buy shares in a targeted block repurchase. Corporations can repurchase shares either to change their capital structure, reduce dividend payments, signal future prospects, or reduce free cash flow.

- Common stock represents ownership that is the last to receive any income as well as any assets if the firm is liquidated. If the firm is liquidated, common shareholders have to wait until all claimants, such as creditors and preferred shareholders, are satisfied before receiving anything.

- Common shareholders are the ultimate owners of the corporation and through corporate democracy, elect members of the board of directors and have a say in major issues that affect the firm. While the existing system of corporate democracy is imperfect, the current movement in shareholders' rights may put this system back on track.

---

[21] R. Charles Moyer, M. Wayne Marr, and Robert E. Chatfield examined the financial condition of firms that issued preferred stock from 1970 through 1980 and found evidence that preferred stock was typically issued by firms in a poor financial condition ("Nonconvertible Preferred Stock Financing and Financial Distress: A Note," *Journal of Economics and Business,* Feb. 1987, pp. 81–89.

- Common shareholders get a return from their investment in the form of dividends and any increase (or decrease) in the market value of their shares. But dividends are not a sure thing. The corporation is not obligated to pay dividends to common shareholders.

- Preferred stock is also equity. Preferred stock has some of the features of common stock—a perpetual security with dividends. But there is more variety in the features of preferred stock, such as convertibility, callability, and sinking funds.

- Unlike common shareholders, preferred shareholders do not have a say in the corporation. Only in extreme circumstances do preferred shareholders vote for representation on the board of directors. Therefore, features such as cumulative dividends and contingent voting rights have developed to protect the preferred shareholders' rights.

- Preferred stock and common stock issues make up about 40 percent of the new capital raised by U.S. corporations. There has been an increase in firms' reliance on equity as a source of funds.

QUESTIONS

11-1 What are the primary differences between common and preferred stock?

11-2 What is the role of the par value of a stock? If a stock has no par value, does this mean that it is worthless? Explain.

11-3 Explain why the number of shares of a corporation's stock may differ among authorized, issued, and outstanding shares.

11-4 List the advantages of being a publicly held corporation. List the advantages of being a privately held corporation. Why would a large, publicly traded corporation such as RJR Nabisco go private? Why would it go public shortly thereafter?

11-5 What distinguishes a stock dividend from a stock split?

11-6 Why might a firm use a reverse stock split? How might a reverse stock split affect the market value of a firm's equity?

11-7 Describe the information provided in the board of director's declaration of a dividend. Who determines the ex-dividend date?

11-8 Explain how cumulative voting makes possible minority shareholder representation on the board of directors.

11-9 Describe how a classified board of directors could be used to thwart or discourage a takeover of control of a corporation's board.

11-10 In a rights offering, the corporation gives shareholders the right to buy shares of the stock at a discount from the current market price. Why would a corporation offer a discount?

11-11 Suppose you are a disgruntled shareholder of a major U.S. corporation. What can you do to change the policies of the corporation?

11-12 What are some of the problems with the current system of corporate democracy in the United States?

11-13 List the various rationales for paying dividends. For each rationale, determine whether the rationale favors or does not favor the payment of dividends.

11-14 If a firm has more cash than it needs for its profitable investment opportunities and wishes to pay this cash out to common shareholders, would you recommend that the firm do this with a special cash dividend or by repurchasing stock? Explain your choice.

11-15 What is a tax clientele? What role does a tax clientele play in explaining dividend policies?

11-16 Explain how an increase in dividends per share may be interpreted as good news from the perspective of the shareholders.

11-17 Explain how an increase in dividends per share may be interpreted as bad news from the perspective of the shareholders.

11-18 From the perspective of a shareholder, would you rather receive a 5 percent stock dividend or a $2 per share cash dividend? Explain.

11-19 If a firm pays a cash dividend and sells new shares of stock, both in the same year, does this make sense? Why?

11-20 What is a dividend reinvestment plan? From the perspective of shareholders, what are the advantages and disadvantages of participating in such a plan? From the perspective of the corporation, what are the advantages of offering such a plan?

11-21 If a firm makes a Dutch auction tender offer to repurchase shares and sets a range of prices of $20 to $25, with the current share price at $19, would you tender your shares? At what price would you tender your shares? Explain your decision.

11-22 Explain why a corporation would issue preferred stock rather than a debt security or common shares.

11-23 Why would an investor prefer to buy preferred shares rather than a bond or common shares?

11-24 Suppose the Multi-Facet Corporation issues a convertible, callable sinking fund preferred stock. From the perspective of the issuer, which of these features contributes to financing flexibility? From the perspective of the investor, which features contribute to the uncertainty of the share's value?

11-25 Suppose ABC Corporation is issuing convertible, callable, fixed-rate preferred stock. What option does ABC Corporation have after it issues this stock? What option does the investor buying this stock have?

11-26 Some preferred stock issues give the preferred shareholders rights to vote if dividends are in arrears. Why is this provision necessary? Explain what might happen if the preferred shareholders did not have this right.

PROBLEMS

Common stock

11-1 The GHI Corporation has paid dividends on common stock over the past ten years as follows:

Year	Dividends	Earnings
1981	$3,000	$5,000
1982	3,100	5,100
1983	3,200	4,500
1984	3,300	5,400
1985	3,500	5,500
1986	3,725	5,300
1987	3,975	5,200
1988	4,200	5,600
1989	4,500	5,800

During this ten-year period, there were 1,000 common shares outstanding.
a. What are the dividends per share in each year?
b. What is the dividend payout in each year?
c. How would you describe the dividend policy of GHI Corporation?

11-2 The JKL Corporation currently has a stock price of $100 per share. What would be the expected price of the JKL stock under each of the following types of distribution?

a. A 2:1 stock split
b. A 100 percent stock dividend
c. A 4:1 stock split
d. A 50 percent stock dividend

11-3 MNO Corporation currently has 10 million common shares outstanding, trading at $2 per share. If MNO does a reverse split of 1:4, how many shares will be outstanding after the split? What price would you expect MNO shares to be trading at after this split?

11-4 The Repo Corporation currently has 1 million common shares outstanding and has been paying a $1 dividend per share each quarter on its common shares. The Repo Corporation has decided to repurchase 10 percent of its common shares.

a. If Repo maintains its current dividend per share, how much will it be paying in dividends each quarter after the repurchase?
b. If Repo decides to keep the total dividend payments the same, what would be its new dividend per share?

11-5 The Fissure Corporation currently has 2 million common shares of stock outstanding that are trading at $80 per share. The board of directors has decided that the current price per share is too high, preventing many smaller investors from buying even lots of 100 shares. The board has decided that a more attractive stock price would be about $40 per share.

a. If Fissure decides to use a stock dividend to reduce the share price, what would be the size of the stock dividend that would reduce the share price to the desirable level?

b. If Fissure decides to use a stock split to reduce the share price, what would be the size of the stock split that would reduce the share price to the desirable level?

11-6 Lowly Worm Corporation's common share price is currently at about $5 per share. The board of directors has decided that a more respectable share price level would be about $20. The board also realizes that in the company's current circumstance, share price cannot be increased other than by a reverse stock split. What size of reverse split is necessary to increase the share price to the desirable level?

11-7 Calculate the stock dividend rate equivalent to each of the following stock splits:

a. 1.5:1
b. 2:1
c. 3:1
d. 7:5

Preferred stock

11-8 PQR has 1 million shares of 9 percent cumulative preferred stock outstanding with a stated value of $100 per share. If PQR does not pay dividends for two years, what will be the amount of arrearage?

11-9 Suppose you own 1,000 shares of STU Corporation 10 percent convertible preferred stock. If each preferred share is convertible into forty common shares, what is the conversion value of your 1,000 preferred shares if the common stock is trading at:

a. $20 per share?
b. $30 per share?
c. $40 per share?

11-10 The Top Down Corporation has 1 million callable convertible preferred shares outstanding with a par value of $100 and a dividend rate of 5 percent per year, paid quarterly. The shares are callable at $105 per share and are convertible into four common shares.

a. What is the dividend payment on preferred shares each quarter?
b. Suppose Top Down determines that it can issue preferred stock that pays 3 percent per year. What are Top Down's possible courses of action?
c. Suppose the common stock is currently trading at $30 per share and the preferred stock is trading at $150 per share. Is it attractive to convert to common stock? Explain.

Potpourri

11-11 **Research:** Select a corporation that has more than one class of common stock outstanding. Describe the differences between the two classes in terms of voting rights and dividends. What proportion of the firm's votes are controlled by each class of shares?

Recommended source of information: *Industrial Manual,* Moody's.

PC+ **11-12** **Research:** Select a corporation that has paid quarterly dividends in each quarter during the past five years.

a. Plot the quarterly dividends per share for the past twenty quarters.
b. Plot the quarterly dividend payout rate for the past twenty quarters.
c. Describe the dividend policy of this corporation.

Recommended sources of information:

- *Industrial Manual,* Moody's
- *Compustat PC Plus* (CD-ROM), Standard & Poor's
- *Value Line Investment Survey*

FURTHER READINGS

The debate over whether firms should pay dividends is summarized in a number of articles, including:
PATRICK HESS, "The Dividend Debate: 20 Years of Discussion," in *The Revolution in Corporate Finance,* eds. Joel M. Stern and Donald H. Chew, United Kingdom: Basil Blackwell, 1986, pp. 310–319.
RICHARD BREALEY, "Does Dividend Policy Matter?" *Midland Corporate Finance Journal,* vol. 1, no. 1, Spring 1983, pp. 17–25.

Management's views on dividend policy are surveyed in:
H. KENT BAKER, GAIL E. FARRELLY, and RICHARD B. EDELMAN, "A Survey of Management Views on Dividend Policy," *Financial Management,* vol. 14, no. 3, Autumn 1985, pp. 78–84.

Management's views of stock repurchases are surveyed in:
H. KENT BAKER, PATRICIA L. GALLAGHER, and KAREN E. MORGAN, "Management's View of Stock Repurchase Programs," *Journal of Financial Research,* vol. 4, no. 3, Fall 1981, pp. 233–247.
JAMES W. WANSLEY, WILLIAM R. LANE, and SALIL SARKAR, "Management View on Share Repurchase and Tender Offer Premiums," *Financial Management,* vol. 18, no. 3, Autumn 1989, pp. 97–110.

John and Lewis Gilbert reported their activities in defense of shareholders' rights annually. The last of these reports, which reflects their dedication to shareholders' rights, was issued in 1979:
LEWIS D. GILBERT and JOHN J. GILBERT, *Fortieth Annual Report of Stockholder Activities at Corporation Meetings during 1979,* Corporate Democracy, New York, 1979.

How a Dutch Auction Rate Is Determined

A Dutch auction rate on a preferred stock is determined by bidding among investors. Investors place bids for the dividend rate that they want, indicating:

Hold   The number of shares they wish to hold, regardless of the dividend rate.

Sell   The number of shares they wish to sell, regardless of the dividend rate.

Bid   The number of shares they will continue to hold if the dividend rate is not less than a rate they specify or the number of additional shares they want to buy at a specified rate.

In most cases, investors other than current shareholders are permitted to bid. Once all the bids are in, the issuer of the preferred stock compares the buy and sell bids and determines the dividend rate that will sell out the issue.

Suppose we hold a Dutch auction bid for an annual dividend rate for a preferred stock issue with 1,000 shares outstanding and the following orders placed by shareholders and other investors:

Investor	Bid by each shareholder or other investor
1	Hold 200 shares
2	Sell 100 shares
3	Bid to hold 400 shares at 6% by an existing shareholder
4	Bid to buy 300 shares at 7% by other investor
5	Bid to hold 100 shares and buy 200 shares at 7% by an existing shareholder
6	Bid to buy 200 shares at 8% by an existing shareholder

The minimum dividend rate so that all 1,000 shares will be purchased or held is 7 percent, so all shareholders receive an annual dividend of 7 percent. Since Investor 6 has a bid greater than the 7 percent necessary, he does not buy any preferred shares. Investor 1 wants to hang onto her 200 shares no matter the rate. That leaves 800 shares for other investors.

Since Investor 2 wants to sell 100 shares, these can be sold to existing shareholders or to other investors. Going along in order of their bids (lowest rate upward), Investor 3 keeps his 400 shares. This leaves 400 shares (1,000 − 200 − 400 = 400).

Since Investor 4 wants to buy 300 shares at 7 percent and 5 wants to buy 200 shares and hold 100 at 7 percent, we split the 400 shares between them pro rata—in proportion to the number they wish to buy or hold. Therefore, Investor 4 buys 200 shares, and Investor 5 keeps 100 shares and buys 100 shares.

Following the Dutch auction, the shares are distributed among the shareholders as follows:

Investor	Shares owned	Transaction
1	200	Keeps shares
2	0	Sells shares
3	400	Keeps shares
4	200	Buys shares
5	200	Keeps 100 shares and buys 100 shares
6	0	Sells 200 shares

What happens here is that shares are swapped. The issuer benefits from the swap, paying the lowest dividend rate necessary to keep all shares outstanding. Shareholders benefit from a dividend rate set by market demand.

Long-Term Debt

INTRODUCTION 553

TERM LOANS 553

NOTES AND BONDS 554

Denomination 555

Maturity 556

Interest 556

    Fixed Rate 556

    Zero-Coupon 557

    Floating Rate 558

    Deferred Interest 558

    Income 559

    Participating 560

Security 560

    Sinking Funds 561

    Defeasance 561

Seniority 562

Optionlike Features 562

    Call Feature 563

    Conversion Feature 563

    Put Feature 565

    Warrants 566

Packaging Debt Features 567

INDENTURES 569

Covenants 569

The Trustee 569

RISK 570

Default Risk 570

Interest Rate Risk 573

Reinvestment Rate Risk 576

Purchasing Power Risk 579

Marketability Risk 579

DEBT RETIREMENT 579

LONG-TERM DEBT AS A SOURCE OF CAPITAL 581

Summary 583

And It Comes Fully Loaded

USX Corporation's primary lines of business are integrated steel production (through its USX-U.S. Steel Group) and oil production and refining (through its USX-Marathon Group). In August 1990, just before it split its common stock into two classes (USX-U.S. Steel and USX-Marathon), USX Corporation issued a bond that had quite a few features:

Convertible Each bond is convertible into USX stock. Because USX split its stock into two classes, one tied to its steel business and the other to its oil business, the bonds are convertible into both classes of shares: 1.64 shares of USX-U.S. Steel *and* 8.21 shares of USX-Marathon stock. This means that the investor can exchange a bond into shares of both of USX's common stock.

Zero-coupon The bond pays no interest, but pays $1,000 at maturity in 2005.

Putable The investor can sell the bond back to USX for a specified price ($466.93) starting in August 1995. But USX can decide whether the payment will be in cash, stock, or notes.

Callable USX can buy the bonds from the investor ("call" them) at a specified price, starting in August 1995. The call price rises from $461.91 in August 1995 to $925.67 in August 2004.

So what type of yield can an investor earn on these bonds? Suppose an investor buys the bond in December 31, 1992 for $377.50. The investor can choose to hold the bonds to maturity at an annual yield of 8.05 percent. Or the investor can:

Convert An investor who immediately converted the bonds to stock on December 31, 1992, got stock worth:

1.64 shares USX-U.S. Steel at $34.00 per share	$ 55.76
8.21 shares USX Marathon at $17.25 per share	141.62
	$197.38

The only way the investor can benefit from the bond's convertibility is for the share price of one or both of these classes of stock to increase substantially above its current price.

Put Sell the bonds to USX Corporation for $466.93 at the earliest time possible and, assuming the investor receives cash, the yield will be 8.58 percent.

USX Corporation can, if it wishes, call the bonds. If the bonds are called away at the earliest possible date, the yield is 8.12 percent. If the bonds are called away at the latest possible date, they yield 8.05 percent.

The bonds provide the investor with flexibility, since she or he can hold the bonds, convert them, or sell them back to the issuer. The bonds also provide the issuer with flexibility, since the issuer can retire the bonds prior to the maturity date.

But these features also affect the bonds' risk, since investors do not know whether or not the issuer will call them and the issuer does not know whether the investor will convert them, hold them, or sell them back.

INTRODUCTION

Running into debt isn't so bad, it's running into creditors that hurts.

Jacob M. Braude, *Treasury of Wit and Humor*

A firm may raise new funds internally—through its operations—or externally—by selling ownership interest or borrowing. Borrowing can be short term, meaning repayment will be made within one year, or long term, meaning repayment will be made after one year.

The borrower receives money in exchange for her promise to repay it at some future time. The obligation to repay is referred to as the ***debt*** or ***indebtedness;*** the borrower is the ***debtor,*** and the lender is the ***creditor.***

The creditor is also an investor, because he is lending money at one point in time, expecting it back in the future along with compensation for lending his money. We refer to indebtedness between a borrower and a lender as a ***loan.*** If the borrower issues a security to represent the indebtedness, we usually refer to the borrower as the ***issuer*** and the lenders as ***noteholders*** or ***bondholders,*** depending on the type of security representing the indebtedness.

The amount borrowed is called the ***principal*** and is repaid either at the end of the period of indebtedness or at regular intervals during this period. The lender receives ***interest*** to compensate him for lending his funds. For some types of debt the interest is paid periodically, and for other types the interest is paid at the end of the debt period.

The lender cannot be absolutely sure that the borrower will repay the principal and pay the interest when promised. Realizing that, borrowers typically specify this assurance in the form of a promise to repay with property they own, if necessary. If the debtor fails to pay as promised, the creditors have the right to force the sale of this property and to be repaid from the proceeds of the sale.

We refer to debt backed by property as a ***secured*** debt and to the property as ***security.*** If there is no security, the creditor relies entirely on the ability of the borrower to make the promised payments. We refer to this type of debt as ***unsecured.***

There are three types of long-term indebtedness—term loans, notes, and bonds—and they are the focus of this chapter. We will look at the features of each and how a firm uses debt to finance its business.

TERM LOANS

Term loans are negotiated directly between borrower and creditor, where the creditor is typically a commercial bank or an insurance company. Term loans range in maturity from two to ten years, though any repayment term is possible. We refer to these debts as term loans because there is a fixed term (fixed maturity) for the loan, as opposed to a loan that is payable on demand.

Term loans are commonly unsecured; the creditor has no claim on specific assets of the borrower for failure to pay the interest or principal of the loan as promised. However, creditors could require that a loan be secured by specific property owned by the borrower.

The interest rate on term loans is usually variable, tied to some other security, such as the 91-day U.S. Treasury bill (T-bill) rate.

Term loans are usually repaid in installments: either monthly, quarterly, semiannually, or annually. These periodic payments include both interest and a repayment of principal; so the debt obligation is reduced steadily throughout the loan period.

NOTES AND BONDS

A firm may borrow money by issuing notes or bonds. Both are ***certificates of indebtedness,*** which are written obligations of the borrower to repay the amount borrowed under specified terms. The terms can vary, but most include provisions regarding interest payments, security, and priority of claims.

There is a technical difference between a note and a bond. A bond has an indenture agreement; a note does not. An ***indenture agreement*** spells out the rights and duties of the borrower and appoints a trustee to look out for the bondholders' interests. Though both a note and a bond are represented by legal contracts stipulating the rights and duties of the borrower, the contract representing a note is typically considered an agreement, less formal than a bond's contract, and is not referred to as an indenture.

In common usage, however, the terms "bond" and "note" have taken on slightly different meanings. Since bonds are often secured with collateral and notes are typically not secured, many people use "bond" to refer to secured indebtedness and "note" for indebtedness that is not secured. Further, since bonds have longer maturities than notes, many people refer to intermediate-term (three to ten years) indebtedness as notes and longer-term indebtedness as bonds. However, there are notes that are secured with property, and there are bonds with four-year maturities and notes with thirty-year maturities.

Bonds and notes may be either registered or bearer. For ***registered*** bonds or notes, the issuer maintains records of who owns them (the creditors) and sends any interest or principal to the registered owners. For ***bearer*** bonds or notes, whoever physically possesses the certificates representing them owns them. If interest is payable, the bearer simply clips a coupon attached to the certificate and sends it in or cashes it at a specified bank. Bearer debt is a bit riskier for investors because they will no longer own it if the debt certificate is lost or stolen—in which case the finder or thief would own it.

The bond or note issuer (the borrower) pays interest and repays the principal amount of the debt (the face value) at the end of the debt period (at maturity). The interest may be a fixed amount per period, it may vary throughout the debt period, or it may be paid in a lump sum at the end of the debt period. Bonds and notes may also have optionlike features that give the borrower, the creditor, or both, opportunities to retire or exchange the debt.

What used to be a simple indebtedness—a fixed interest rate, interest paid every six months, and a fixed maturity date—now has lots of "bells and whistles." In the 1970s and 1980s, ***financial engineering*** designed and created new types of debt securities, tailoring notes and bonds to the borrowers' and lenders' needs and desires. But it sure made them complex! Nevertheless, we can understand any note or bond if we understand its basic characteristics:

- Denomination
- Maturity
- Interest
- Security
- Seniority
- Optionlike features

Secret Identity

The government of Pakistan advertised bearer bonds in March 1992 with the selling feature of "No Questions Asked About Source of Funds! No Identity to Be Disclosed!" (*The Wall Street Journal,* March 17, 1992, p. C15).

Subsequently, however, the bond offer was withdrawn, since the Pakistan government had failed to register the securities with the Securities and Exchange Commission (*The Wall Street Journal,* March 24, 1992, p. C15).

Euro-what?

Eurobonds and **Euronotes** are terms for indebtedness issued and traded in markets other than the currency in which the debts are denominated. For example, American Brands issued $150 million $8\frac{7}{8}$ percent Eurodollar notes in 1987 that matured in 1992. These notes were issued outside the United States by a foreign subsidiary of a U.S. corporation. "Eurodollar" indicates that they are denominated in U.S. dollars, just as "Euroyen" indicates denomination in Japanese yen and "Eurosterling" indicates denomination in the British pound.

The advantage of issuing "Euro" notes and bonds is that the issuer need not register them with the Securities and Exchange Commission. Since securities laws in other countries may not be as stringent (for example, requiring semiannual financial statements instead of quarterly ones), it may be less costly for a U.S. firm to issue securities outside the United States.

Euronotes and Eurobonds have some unique characteristics:

- They are issued with the aid of multinational syndicates of underwriting banks and brokerages.
- They are issued only in bearer form.
- Many are listed on one or more exchanges, but most of the trading is over the counter by large international banks.
- Interest payments are not subject to withholding taxes, which makes the Eurodebt more attractive for U.S. investors.
- Interest payments are generally made on an annual basis.

We will look at each characteristic to see how it can be varied and packaged with others to meet the needs of borrowers and lenders. We will also look at debt ratings and how they reflect a debt's risk.

Denomination

Par value means very little for preferred and common stock, but is meaningful for debt since it is used for the calculation of any interest and is the amount that is repaid at maturity.

Bonds and notes are issued in denominations, referred to as *face value,* representing the amount of indebtedness. The face value is also referred to as the *par value* or *maturity value.* A face value of $1,000 means the issuer is borrowing $1,000 and will, it is hoped, repay the $1,000 at the end of the debt period. Though they are typically issued with face values of $1,000, we can find notes and bonds with face values of $500, $5,000, or $10,000. Bonds with small denominations—$100 or less—are referred to as *baby bonds.*

Most bonds sold in the United States are denominated in dollars—the interest and principal are paid in U.S. dollars. But it is possible to denominate bonds in any currency. You can borrow funds in the United States that are denominated in Japanese yen and promise to pay a specified interest and the principal in yen. There are even some bonds denominated in foreign currency that give the lender a choice between receiving interest and principal in U.S. dollars or some other currency.

Maturity

If you borrow by issuing a bond or a note, you generally must repay the loan at some specified point in time referred to as the ***maturity date***—the date the bond or note "matures."

Bonds and notes are often classified in terms of their maturity, though this is a loose classification. One rule of thumb for classifying notes and bonds is:

Maturity	Referred to as
5–15 years	Short term
16–40 years	Medium term
Over 40 years	Long term

There is no limit to the maturity. Bonds have been issued with a maturity of 999 years![1] We do see, from time to time, a bond or note *without* a maturity date, referred to as ***perpetual debt.*** For example, the Canadian Pacific Limited perpetual 4 percent bonds were issued in 1921 and never mature. Why would an investor be interested in such a security? Because it is less risky than buying the firm's preferred or common stock (this perpetual debt has a prior claim on the firm's earnings) and the cash flow (the interest) is fixed forever.

Firms also may issue ***serial debt,*** which is a group of notes or bonds designed to mature at different times. For example, you could issue a serial debt with some of the bonds maturing in five years, some maturing in ten years, and the rest maturing in twenty years.

Interest

Interest is the compensation paid to the lenders for the use of their funds. In the United States, most interest is paid twice a year at six-month intervals. For example, a bond may pay interest on January 1 and July 1 of each year of the bond's life.

But semiannual interest is not the only way to go. For example, most bonds issued in other countries pay interest in annual coupons. You can design a bond to pay interest monthly, daily, quarterly—any way you like. You want to design the interest payments to be attractive to investors but, at the same time, you want to minimize the costs of administering the bonds—writing and mailing interest payments.

Interest is also referred to as a ***coupon.*** The reference to coupons originates with bearer bonds. If you own a bearer bond, you receive the interest by clipping coupons off the side of the bond and redeeming them for cash. But over time, the interest received on both registered and bearer debt has come to be referred to as the coupon payment.

Interest is generally stated as a percentage of the face value of the bond or note and the rate or interest is referred to as the ***interest rate*** or ***coupon rate.***

Fixed Rate

Interest payments may be fixed, may vary according to the interest rate on some other security, or may vary according to the firm's earnings. Tradition-

---

[1] The Elmira and Williamsport Railroad Company issued bonds in 1863 that mature in 2862.

ally, notes and bonds have fixed coupons—the same amount paid at regular intervals. This type of debt is referred to as having a ***straight coupon.***

Let's look at an example of a straight coupon debt. International Business Machines (IBM) issued notes in April 1988 with a total face value of $500 million—0.5 million notes, each with a face value of $1,000—that pay 9 percent interest and mature on May 1, 1998. Interest is paid semiannually, on May 1 and November 1 of each year, for a total of twenty-one interest payments: The first interest was paid May 1, 1988, and the last interest will be paid May 1, 1998. IBM pays 4.5 percent interest on each bond on each interest payment date, or $45 per bond, for a total of $45 times 0.5 million, or $22 million every six months.

In the past twenty years, there have been many innovations in debt interest; so there is no longer any "typical" debt. These innovations include zero-coupon, deferred interest, floating rate, and dual-coupon debt.

Zero-Coupon

Zero-coupon debt does not have a coupon. Since there are no coupons, the only return an investor gets is the difference between what was paid for the debt and either what it was sold for or its face value at maturity. That is why zero-coupon notes and bonds are issued and traded at a discount from their face value. Effectively, you earn interest, but you do not receive it until the maturity date: The interest is part of the face value. Consider the Walt Disney Company zero-coupon subordinated notes, due 2005. The notes were issued in June 1990 at 41.199, that is, at 41.199 percent of their face value. An investor who bought a $1,000 face value note in June 1990 and held on to it until maturity would pay $411.99, would not receive interest during the life of the note, and would receive $1,000 in June 2005.

Zero-coupon securities were first issued by corporations in 1981 and rapidly became very popular.[2] As with interest paid on any kind of debt, the issuer may deduct the implicit interest to determine taxable income. The investors are taxed on the debt's interest income—the implicit interest—even though they receive no cash.

Consider the Disney notes. If you bought a note for $411.99 in June 1990 and hold it until maturity, you earn an annual return of 6.0899 percent:

J. C. Penney Company Inc. issued the first corporate zero-coupon note in April 1981. The notes were issued at 33.427 (that is, at 33.427 percent of par value), with a yield to investors of 14.25 percent.

Present value of the investment = $411.99
Future value of the investment = $1,000.00
Number of periods = 15

$$\text{Return} = \sqrt[15]{\frac{\$1,000.00}{\$411.99}} - 1 = \mathbf{6.0899\%}$$

[2] Initially, they provided an attractive tax advantage for the issuer. But this was eliminated with the Tax Equity and Fiscal Responsibility Act of 1982. Before this change in the tax code, the issuer deducted an even amount of implicit interest, which overstates the interest deduction in the early years of the bond. In the case of the Disney notes, this would mean $588.01/15 = $39.20 interest each year. But the actual implicit interest is only $25.09 in the first year. An even amount of interest results in greater interest deductions in the early years than is warranted.

Implied interest for the first year is $411.99 multiplied by 6.0899 percent, or $25.09. Implied interest for the second year is ($411.99 + $25.09) = $437.08 multiplied by 6.0899 percent, or $26.62. As time passes, the value of the note increases and the implicit interest on the note in any period is the increased value multiplied by the 6.0899 percent. Implicit interest on the Disney notes over its life is shown for each year in Table 12-1.

Floating Rate

Debt issuers were reluctant to be locked into paying the escalating interest rates that prevailed during the 1970s. As a result, the variable rate on debt was conceived. Borrowers began to issue debt instruments whose interest rates changed as interest rates in general changed, so the borrowers ended up paying the "going rate" instead of a fixed rate.

One form of variable rate is the *floating rate,* which changes, or "floats," according to the rate on some other debt. Different benchmarks for floating rates include:

- The *London interbank offered rate* (LIBOR)
- The U.S. 91-day Treasury bill (T-bill) rate
- A rate fixed by a Dutch auction[3]

A floating rate changes periodically, such as annually, as specified in the bond contract, and may be bounded by some minimum rate—the "floor"—and maximum rate—the "cap."

Floating rate debt may specify:

- The benchmark rate, such as the LIBOR or the T-bill rate.
- How often the floating rate is reset according to the benchmark rate.
- The spread between the floating rate and the benchmark.
- Any cap (maximum rate) or floor (minimum rate).

For example, Manufacturers Hanover Corporation issued floating rate notes in 1983 that matured in 1992. Interest was paid quarterly, although the interest rate was adjusted each week according to the interest rate on that week's auction of 91-day Treasury bills. The interest rate each week on the Manufacturers Hanover notes was set at 75 basis points, that is, the concurrent T-bill rate plus 0.0075.

Deferred Interest

Somewhere between a zero-coupon and a fixed coupon bond lies a deferred interest bond—a bond whose interest payments do not start until some time after it is issued. Most deferred interest debt has no interest for the first three to seven years and sells at a discount from its face value.

Deferred interest debt is usually used when cash flow problems are anticipated. For example, if a firm borrows heavily to restructure its operations,

---

[3] In a Dutch auction, the interest rate on the debt is determined by a process that assures that the rate paid on the debt is the going market rate, since it is determined by bidding among investors. For a more detailed description of this bidding process, see Appendix 11A.

TABLE 12-1

Implied Interest on Disney Zero-Coupon Subordinated Notes, Due 2005, That Were Issued June 1990 at 41.199 or $411.99 per Bond, for Years Ending June, 1991–2005

Year ending June	Beginning-of-year value	Implied interest = yield × beginning value	End-of-year value of bond = beginning value + implied interest
1991	$411.99	$ 25.09	$ 437.08
1992	437.08	26.62	463.70
1993	463.70	28.24	491.94
1994	491.94	29.96	521.90
1995	521.90	31.78	553.68
1996	553.68	33.72	587.40
1997	587.40	35.77	623.17
1998	623.17	37.95	661.12
1999	661.12	40.26	701.38
2000	701.38	42.71	744.10
2001	744.10	45.32	789.41
2002	789.41	48.07	837.49
2003	837.49	51.00	888.49
2004	888.49	54.11	942.60
2005	942.60	57.40	1,000.00
Total implied interest		**$588.01**	

NOTE: Yield calculation:

$$\text{Yield} = \sqrt[T]{\frac{\text{future value}}{\text{present value}}} - 1 = \sqrt[15]{\frac{\$1,000.00}{\$411.99}} - 1 = \mathbf{6.0899\%}$$

Check on the calculations:

Total implied interest + price when issued = face value

$588.01   + $411.99   = $1,000.00

deferred interest debt gives the firm some time for it to turn its operations around.

Income

An *income bond* pays interest only when there are sufficient earnings to pay it. If earnings are not sufficient, the firm need not pay the interest to its income bondholders. Unlike other types of debt, failure to pay interest on an income bond is *not* necessarily an act of default.

Income bonds and notes are seldom issued, for two reasons. First, since they do not carry a fixed interest obligation, they are issued by companies that foresee financial difficulties, so this stigma is attached to income bonds. Second, since paying interest depends on accounting earnings, which can be manipulated, there is a potential problem, a possible conflict of interests between management, which represents the shareholders, and the bondholders, who are the creditors.

Income bonds and notes look a lot like preferred stock—they provide for a fixed payment but nonpayment is not a cause for default. However, there are three important differences:

1. For the borrower, the interest paid on income bonds and notes is tax deductible, whereas the dividend paid on preferred stock is not.
2. Income debtholders have a prior claim to assets and income over preferred and common shareholders.
3. The interest income to the income debtholders is fully taxable, whereas the dividend income of corporate owners of preferred stock is partially deductible.

From an issuer's perspective, income bonds and notes are more attractive than, say, preferred stock. Income bonds may be more attractive to noncorporate investors than preferred stock, since bondholders have a prior claim on income and assets over preferred and common shareholders. But preferred stock may be more attractive than income bonds from the perspective of the *corporate* investor, since a portion of preferred dividends is not taxed.

Despite the tax deductibility of interest to the issuer and the seniority of debt over preferred stock, few income bonds have ever been issued. This suggests that the stigma of and concern over the potential accounting manipulation outweigh the tax benefits to issuers.

Participating

From the viewpoint of the owners (the shareholders) of the firm issuing debt, debt securities with fixed coupons provide financial leverage: When earnings are high, the owners (who are not only the shareholders, but simultaneously the debt issuers) need pay bondholders or noteholders only a fixed amount and no more.

However, bondholders and noteholders can share in the fortunes of the firm if they hold participating debt. A ***participating*** bond or note—also called a ***profit-sharing*** bond or note—is a debt security with a specified rate of interest plus a specified share of earnings. Like the income bond, participating debt suffers from the potential accounting earnings manipulation problem.

We do not see many participating debt securities issued today. The most likely reason is that it is possible to put together a "package deal" of bonds and equity that gives the investor the same result as a participating bond.

Security

In the case of a mortgage debt, the borrower is referred to as the **mortgagor** and the creditor or lender is referred to as the **mortgagee.**

A debt may be unsecured or secured with the pledge of specific property called ***collateral.*** A debt that is not secured by specific property is referred to as a ***debenture.*** In the case of secured debt, if the obligations of the loan are not satisfied, the creditor has the right to recoup the amount of the principal, any accrued interest, and penalties from the proceeds from the sale of the pledged property. Unsecured debt, as well as secured debt, is backed by the general credit of the firm—the ability of the firm to generate cash flows that are sufficient to meet its obligations.

There are different types of secured debt, classified by the type of property pledged:

- If the pledged property is real property—such as land or buildings—the debt is referred to as a ***mortgage.***

- If the pledged property is any type of financial asset, such as stocks or bonds of other corporations, the debt is referred to as **collateral trust** debt, since the stocks and bonds are held in a trust account until the debt is satisfied.
- If the pledged property is equipment, the secured debt is referred to as **equipment obligation** or **equipment trust debt.** Equipment trust debt, also referred to as **equipment trust certificates,** is often used by airlines to finance the purchase of aircraft.

Sinking Funds

A bond may be secured with a sinking fund instead of specific property. With a **sinking fund,** the bond issuer makes periodic payments to a trust for the purpose of retiring the bonds. The sinking fund trust can be established in either of two ways.

One way is to treat it as a savings account, with the bond issuer making payments in sufficient amounts so that just enough will accumulate in the trust to pay off the face value of the bonds when they mature.

Another way is to use the payments to retire bonds periodically at a price, referred to as the **sinking fund call price,** specified in the debt agreement. An example is the sinking fund debentures of Bristol-Myers (5.70 debentures due 1992). The bonds were issued in 1963. Starting in 1973, 5 percent of the $50 million issue was called in at par each year. Bristol-Myers had to make sure that each year starting in 1973 there were sufficient funds (considering its deposits and interest earned on the funds) to pay off 5 percent of $50 million, or $2.5 million.

A sinking fund adds extra comfort to the creditor—the fund reduces the risk associated with the bond. If the borrower fails to make a scheduled contribution to the sinking fund, the trustee may declare the debt security in default; this has the same consequences as not paying interest or principal.

> A sinking fund is so named since it is used to "sink"—get rid of—the debt.

Defeasance

Another way of making a bondholder or noteholder comfortable is to **defease** the debt by setting up a trust to pay it off.[4] To do this, the firm establishes an irrevocable trust (that is, the firm cannot get back any funds it puts into the trust) and deposits risk-free securities into the trust (such as U.S. government bonds) in amounts sufficient to generate enough cash flow (from interest and principal) to pay the obligations of the debt. The interest and principal of the defeased debt are then paid by the trust. For example, UAL Corporation defeased its 5 percent and $4\frac{1}{4}$ percent debentures in 1984 by placing U.S. government securities into a trust.

Defeasing debt requires three steps:

> The term "defease" comes from the French *defaire,* which means to void or undo.

Step 1 Create a trust dedicated to making payments due on the debt.

---

[4] Pamela Peterson, David Peterson, and James Ang, "The Extinguishment of Debt Through In-Substance Defeasance," *Financial Management,* vol. 14, no. 1, Spring 1985, pp. 59–67, present a discussion of defeasance transactions, with examples of how the trust is established.

Step 2 Place in the trust U.S. government bonds having cash inflows (interest and principal) that match the cash outflows on the firm's debt (interest and principal).

Step 3 Place the debt in the trust. The debt's interest and principal payments are made by the trust.

An issuer would do this for several reasons:

- If the debt cannot be bought back from the bondholders (which is referred to as a "call"), defeasance provides a way of retiring debt.
- If interest rates on the securities in the trust is high relative to the interest rate on the defeased debt, this difference ends up increasing the firm's reported earnings.
- If certain requirements are met, as set forth in the Financial Accounting Standards Board's Statement of Financial Accounting Standards No. 76, the debt obligation is removed from the borrower's financial statements, which should lead to an improved credit evaluation.

Owners of defeased debt securities are assured they will be paid interest and principal as promised, so their risk is reduced on the investment.

Seniority

A firm can issue different kinds of debt. But not all debt is created equal. There is a pecking order of sorts with respect to each debt's claim on the firm's assets and income. This pecking order is referred to as **seniority**. One debt is **senior** to another if it has a prior claim on assets and income; one debt is **junior** to another if the other debt has a prior claim on assets and income. A **subordinated debt** is a debt that is junior to another.

> **Subordinated to Whom?**
>
> Among Disney's several debt issues outstanding in 1992 were $9\frac{1}{8}$ percent Euronotes, due 1995, and $4\frac{3}{4}$ percent Swiss franc bonds, due 1996, both ranked equally with any unsecured, unsubordinated obligations of Disney. Its zero-coupon notes, due 2005, are subordinated to *all* senior obligations, which include the Euronotes and Swiss franc bonds.

Optionlike Features

Part of the value of a note or bond can be derived from the value of another security in much the same way as a stock option derives its value from the underlying stock. The optional features that can be included in a debt security include:

- A call feature, which allows the issuer to buy back the debt from the investor at a specified price.
- A conversion feature, which allows the investor to exchange the debt for shares of stock at a specified exchange rate.
- A put feature, which allows the investor to sell the debt back to the issuer at a specified price.

- A warrant, which allows the investor to buy shares of stock of the issuer at a specified price.

Let's take a closer look at each.

Call Feature

A *call feature* is the right of the bond issuer to buy back the bond from the investor at a predetermined price. Indebtedness that has a call feature is referred to as *callable.*

The call feature specifies the **call price** the issuer must pay to buy back the debt from the investor. This price is above the face value of the debt. In addition to the call price, the issuer must pay any accrued interest, that is, interest earned but not yet paid up to the date of the call. The difference between the call price and the face value is the **call premium.** Often, callable debt may specify that the debt is not callable within a specified period of time. This is referred to as a *deferred call.*

For example, Champion International Corporation convertible subordinated $4\frac{7}{8}$ debentures due 1997 were issued in 1972. In 1991, they were callable at 100.488—that is, at 100.488 percent of par value, or $1,004.88 per bond— and in 1992 they were callable at 100.244. Since 1992, they have been callable at 100 (par value). Champion International need give the bondholders only thirty days' notice to call these bonds.

Conversion Feature

While a callable debt allows the issuer to buy back the debt from the investor— exchanging the debt for cash—the investor can also be given an option to exchange the debt for another security. A *conversion feature* gives the investor the right to exchange the debt for some other security of the issuer, typically shares of common stock, at a predetermined rate of exchange. Indebtedness that has such a feature is *convertible debt.* Not all bonds are convertible when issued. Some conversion features kick in at some specified future date.

The conversion feature must specify the *conversion ratio,* the number of shares of stock that the debt may be exchanged for, or the *conversion price,* the price of a share of the other security to be acquired. For example, if you own $1,000 par value bonds of ABC Company convertible into 20 shares of common stock, you can exchange one of your bonds for 20 shares of common stock.

If the current market value of the bond is $1,000, this means that you are effectively paying $1,000/20 = $50 per share. This has the same effect as if the debt had a conversion price of $50 per share:

$$\text{Conversion price} = \frac{\$1,000}{20} = \mathbf{\$50}$$

which we can generalize as:

$$\text{Conversion price} = \frac{\text{face value of debt}}{\text{conversion ratio}} \qquad [12\text{-}1]$$

The conversion ratio, the ratio of the bond's face value to the market value of a share, is 20:

$$\text{Conversion ratio} = \frac{\$1{,}000}{\$50} = \mathbf{20}$$

Expressing the ratio generally:

$$\text{Conversion ratio} = \frac{\text{face value of debt}}{\text{conversion price}} \qquad [12\text{-}2]$$

Another way of describing a convertible security is in terms of the market value of the stock received upon exchange. For example, if the current price of the common share is $30 per share and a bond may be converted into 20 shares of common stock, the market conversion value is $30 × 20, or $600. We refer to this market value of the stock as the ***market conversion price:***

$$\text{Market conversion price} = \frac{\text{price per share}}{\text{of common stock}} \times \text{conversion ratio} \qquad [12\text{-}3]$$

The market conversion price is also referred to as the ***conversion value***—the value of what you get when you convert.

Still another way of describing the convertible security is in terms of the effective price to be paid for each share, considering the current market price of the bond, called the ***effective conversion price:***

$$\text{Effective conversion price} = \frac{\text{market value of bond}}{\text{conversion ratio}} \qquad [12\text{-}4]$$

If the current price of a convertible bond is $800 and the bond is convertible into 20 common shares, you are effectively paying $40 per share for the common stock; that is, you are giving up something worth $800 to get the 20 common shares.

At the time the convertible securities are issued, the effective conversion price is about 15 to 20 percent above the current market price of the common share.[5] You must hold the debt until converting it into shares of stock becomes attractive. It won't be worth converting unless the price of the shares of stock increases.

But the market price of the common shares is not the only factor that influences your decision to convert the debt. If you hold onto the debt, you continue to get interest. If you exchange the debt for stock, you do not get this interest but, instead, you may (or may not) receive dividends. So you have to weigh the benefits of holding the debt against the benefits of converting to stock.

Why does a firm needing funds issue a convertible security? Conversion is attractive to investors because they can switch their convertible debt to common stock if the shares do well. Therefore, investors are willing to accept

> In the case of the USX bonds described at the beginning of the chapter, the market conversion price as of December 31, 1992, was $197.38, substantially below the bond's value at that date of $377.50.

---

[5] If the effective conversion price weren't above the current market price, investors would buy the bonds and immediately convert them into stock. In that case, the issuer could have skipped this step and simply issued common stock!

a lower yield on convertible debt. This means a lower cost of financing for the issuer. Another reason a firm may issue convertible debt is weak demand for its common stock. But by issuing a convertible security, the firm is, in effect, issuing a stock at a later time if the stock price increases.

Put Feature

A **put** is the right of the investor to sell the debt back to the issuer. In other words, the issuer must buy it when the investor wants to sell it back. Debt with a put feature is referred to as **putable debt.** The right to sell the debt back is usually restricted, meaning it can be done only under special circumstances.

In the late 1980s, many firms took on a great deal of debt, increasing the risk of default on all their debt obligations. Many debtholders found themselves with debt whose default risk increased dramatically.

For example, when RJR Nabisco went private in a leveraged buyout in 1989, credit rating services lowered their rating of the debt from investment grade to speculative grade, which indicates an increase in the uncertainty that bondholders will receive interest and principal when promised.

Put features were added to debt instruments as a way of protecting new debtholders. If an event affecting the debt issue takes place, such as a leveraged buyout or a downgrade in the debt quality, and if the debt has a put feature, debtholders have the right to sell the bonds back to the issuer.[6]

A variation on the put is the **soft put,** which allows the debt owner to sell the debt back to the issuer in exchange for cash, notes, stock, or some combination of these instruments, all at the option of the issuer. The put feature in the USX bonds discussed in the chapter opening is an example of a soft put.

In the late 1980s, some firms issued puts designed specifically to make takeovers more expensive. Called **poison puts,** they take effect only under some specified change in control of the firm, such as if some one acquires more than 20 percent of the common stock. By designing putable debt, the management is able to make any takeover more expensive. Investors will want to sell the debt back to the firm for its face value, draining the company of cash. For example, ICN Pharmaceuticals Inc. $12\frac{7}{8}$ sinking fund debentures, due 1998, have a "change in control" put:

> *In the event of a change-in-control of Co., each holder, will have the one-time optional right to require Co. to repurchase each holder's debentures at the principal amount thereof, plus accrued interest (Moody's Industrial Manual, 1991, p. 3127).*

If there is a change in control, as defined in more detail in the indenture, the bondholder can "put" the bond back to the issuer at par value.

---

[6] Leland Crabbe reviews the history of putable bonds and examines the relation between put features and the cost of raising debt capital in "Event Risk: An Analysis of Losses to Bondholders and 'Super Poison Put' Bond Covenants," *Journal of Finance,* vol. 46, no. 2, June 1991, pp. 689–706.

Warrants

In addition to option features that cause the retirement of the debt, there are features that do not involve debt retirement. One such feature is a warrant. Warrants do not displace debt securities; they are appended to a debt security.

A *warrant* is the right to buy the common stock of a company at a specified price, the exercise price. So a warrant is like a call option. It represents the right to buy the stock. How then is a warrant different from a convertible debt? With convertible debt, the debt owner exchanges the debt for shares of stock. With a warrant, the debt owner exercises the warrant—buying the shares of stock at a specified price—but still has the debt!

Some firms add warrants as a "sweetener" or "equity kicker" to debt to entice investors to buy bonds. By buying the debt, investors not only get the debt security, with its promised interest and maturity value, but also a chance to participate in the good fortune of the firm if the price of its stock increases.

Warrants may have a fixed life—use it or lose it—or may have a perpetual life—and then are called *perpetual warrants.* The debt and its warrant together are referred to as a *unit.* Some warrants—called *detachable warrants*—can be separated from the debt and sold by the debt owner. These warrants can be traded in the market just like shares of stock.

A warrant is an option and, like other types of options, its value depends on many factors. Suppose you buy a warrant that gives you the right to buy stock for $5 per share within the next five years. The $5 is the exercise price. If the current share price is $1 per share, this right is not very valuable. But it is still worth something. However small, there is some chance that the price of the stock will get above $5 and make exercising this warrant valuable.

Factors that affect a warrant's value are:

- *The common stock's share price.* The greater the share's price, the more valuable the warrant. In the example above, if the share's price were $6 instead of $1, the warrant would be more valuable.
- *The exercise price.* The lower is the warrant's exercise price—$5 in our example—the more valuable is the warrant. If the exercise price were $2 instead of $5, there would be a greater chance that the warrant gives us the right to buy shares at a price below the prevailing market price.
- *The warrant's life.* The longer the life of the warrant, the more valuable it is, since there is more time for the share price to increase and the warrant to become attractive. If the warrant in our example expired in ten years instead of the five years, it would be more valuable, since there is a greater chance of the share's price rising above $5 in ten years than in five years.
- *The opportunity cost of funds.* The greater is the opportunity cost, the more valuable is the warrant because it allows us to postpone our stock purchase to a later time. Suppose the underlying stock price were $6 instead of $1. We could hold onto the warrant and buy the stock at a later time. The value of the warrant would increase along with the stock's price, so we could share in the stock's appreciation without laying out the cash.

The use of warrants in the United States began in the 1926–1929 market boom. Prior to this period, warrants were usually given to placate owners of worthless securities in reorganizations. During the market boom, the role of warrants changed from pacifier to sweetener.

- *The common stock's share price volatility.* The more volatile is the share's price, the more valuable is the warrant, since a more volatile price means that there is a greater chance the share's price will change before the warrant expires. If the share's price is very stable—relatively constant at around $1—there is little chance that the price of the stock will go above $5. But if the share's price is volatile—with the price taking on a much wider range of values—there is more chance that the share price will go above the exercise price of $5.

Packaging Debt Features

An issuer wants to issue a security with the lowest cost and the flexibility to retire the debt if interest rates fall. An investor wants a security that provides the highest yield, lowest risk, and the flexibility to sell it if other, more profitable investment opportunities arise. The best "package" of debt features will provide what investors are looking for (in terms of risk and return) and simultaneously what the firm is willing to offer (in terms of risk and cost).

Let's see how this works for the Disney zero-coupon notes. The Disney zero-coupon subordinated notes were issued in June 1990 and will mature in June 2005. The notes were initially sold at a price of 41.199, that is, $411.99 per note, which represents a yield to maturity of 6.0899 percent. These notes:[7]

- Have a face value of $1,000 per note.
- Have no coupon; so they are priced at less than maturity value.
- Can be exchanged for cash on the basis of the price of shares of Euro-Disney any time before maturity.
- Can be sold back to Disney on two dates: June 27, 1995, and June 27, 2000.
- Are callable on June 26 of each year through 2004, at call prices specified in a schedule; for example, the notes are callable at $744.10 in 2000 and callable at $837.29 in 2002.
- Have a change-in-control provision (the put), allowing the noteholder to sell the notes back to Disney at a price equal to the original issue price, plus accrued interest, if there is a change in control of Disney prior to June 27, 1995.

From Disney's perspective, there are several considerations:

- Interest is not paid during the life of the notes, even though Disney gets to deduct the accrued interest expense each year.
- If investors decide to exchange the notes for cash at any time, the amount of cash depends on the success of Euro-Disney: The more successful is the venture, the more cash will be paid.
- There are two times that investors can sell the notes back to Disney without regard to the price of the Euro-Disney shares; the firm must be prepared for this possibility.
- Disney can call the notes back each year, giving itself the opportunity to retire these notes if it wishes to issue lower cost debt.

---

[7]Characteristics of this security are described in Moody's *Industrial Manual*, 1991, p. 6458.

Forcing the Issue

Suppose you hold convertible bonds but are waiting for the common share price to move upward before converting into stock. If the bonds are callable and the issuer wants to stop paying interest and convince you to convert into stock, the issuer can call the bonds. Then you have to decide whether to accept the call price of the bonds or to convert into stock.

For example, in March 1992, View-Master Ideal Group Inc., a subsidiary of Tyco Toys Inc., called its $6\frac{7}{8}$ percent convertible subordinated debentures, due 2006. If you owned these debentures, you had the choice of:

1. Converting the debentures into shares of stock, with each debenture convertible into 23.07 shares of common stock, selling at $42\frac{1}{2}$ per share at the time, plus 13.92 warrants, exercisable at $16.50 per share until the end of the next year. The warrants were trading at $26\frac{1}{8}$ at the time. The total value of the conversion was:

Value of common stock: 23.07 shares at $42.500 per share	$ 980.475
Value of warrants: 13.92 warrants at $26.125 per warrant	363.660
Total value of conversion	**$1,344.135**

2. Having the debentures called away at 102.75 percent of face value, or $1,027.50 per bond.

Given the choice, wouldn't you convert?

From the perspective of the investor, there are also several considerations:

- Investors must pay taxes on any accrued interest income each year, even though they receive no cash interest payment.
- The callability of the notes limits the yield on these bonds to 6.09 percent.
- There is some protection in the event of an acquisition—the put option—that may reduce the creditworthiness of Disney, since the noteholder could sell the bond back to Disney, forcing cash to be paid out to noteholders.
- There is a possibility that Disney could call these notes, requiring investors to find another investment vehicle for their funds.

The many available features, in terms of interest, maturity, security, interest, and options, make it possible to design debt instruments to meet both the issuer's and investors' needs.

INDENTURES

"Creditors have better memories than debtors" (Benjamin Franklin, *Poor Richard's Almanac,* 1758).

Do not confuse a *series* of bonds with a *serial* debt issue. A bond *series* is a set of several bond issues offered at different times but under one blanket indenture; *serial* debt is debt issued at one time but composed of bonds or notes that have different maturities.

A debt security is a contract between issuer and debtholders that obligates the issuer to pay the interest and principal and to abide by other terms as well.

The rights of the creditors (the investors or the lenders) and the obligations of the issuer (the borrower) are spelled out in the indenture agreement. All debt sold to the public (with few exceptions) is governed by the Trust Indenture Act of 1939 (TIA). The TIA requires each issue of debt to have a trustee who watches out for the debtholders' interests. The duties and powers of the trustee—what the trustee can and cannot do to monitor the firm and enforce the provisions of the contract—are spelled out in the indenture agreement. In addition, the indenture contains:

- A description of the bonds, including the bonds' denominations and the amount of the interest payments and their payment dates.
- Remedies, such as the ability to dispose of equipment or other property, in case the borrower fails to live up to provisions of the bond agreement.
- The borrowers' responsibilities to keep the bondholders informed regarding its financial condition.
- Covenants, which are provisions that limit or restrict the borrower's activities to ensure that sufficient funds will be available to pay the debt's obligations.

Each firm's debt issue may have a separate indenture, or the firm may have a **blanket indenture** covering all its debt issues. Several debt issues covered under the same indenture are referred to as a series, and each issue within the series is usually labeled A, B, C, and so on.

Covenants

Covenants protect the bondholder and limit management actions that could damage the bondholder's position. A covenant's typical provisions require the borrower to:

- Pay interest and principal as specified.
- Pay any real estate taxes on any secured property.
- Provide adequate insurance coverage on any secured property.

In addition to these usual provisions, others may be added to further protect the bondholder. For example, a covenant may specify a minimum amount of working capital or restrictions on the payment of dividends.

The Trustee

The bond indenture specifies that the *trustee* must watch out for the bondholders' interests (meaning both the bondholders' welfare and the interest and principal payments due the bondholder). Specifically, the trustee is responsible for making sure that all provisions of the indenture are carried out, including:

- Authenticating bonds to prevent overissue or forgery (so that, for example, the firm doesn't issue $10 million in bonds for a $1 million issue).
- Collecting and disbursing interest and principal according to the terms of the indenture.
- If a sinking fund is required, collecting money for it and performing the tasks of sinking funds management.
- Making sure that any collateral is properly maintained.

RISK

Because investors are concerned about the risk of their investment, so must borrowers be concerned about the risk of the debt that they are issuing. That's because investors will demand a higher yield for debts with more risk. And a higher yield to investors means a higher cost to borrowers.

There are different types of risk associated with debt securities. The degree of each type of risk depends, in part, on the characteristics of the debt. The primary types of risk with debt securities include:

- Default risk
- Interest rate risk
- Reinvestment rate risk
- Purchasing power risk
- Marketability risk

We will look at each type of risk and describe how it is affected by characteristics of the debt obligations.

Default Risk

We say that a borrower who fails to live up to the debt agreement is in default. Since there is always some chance the borrower will not pay interest or principal when promised or will not abide by some other part of the debt agreement, there is always some chance of default. For some firms, this chance is extremely small; for others default is likely. The risk that the debtor will default is referred to as **default risk.**

Financial service firms evaluate the quality of debt securities, focusing on the likelihood of default. Firms such as Moody's, Standard & Poor's, Fitch Investors, and Duff and Phelps are called rating services because they classify, or rate, debt securities into broad categories based on the service's judgment of the borrower's ability to meet the interest and principal payments as promised.

The rating services rank debt issues on the basis of the ability of the borrower to generate the cash necessary to "service" its obligations, that is, to pay interest and repay principal when due. We can see the classification system of Moody's and Standard & Poor's in Table 12-2, which shows that the issues with the lowest probability of default are rated the highest: Aaa in Moody's, AAA in Standard & Poor's. The rating services further break down some of the classes into three subclasses. For example, Standard & Poor's breaks down the lower medium grade rating into three groups: BBB+, BBB, and BBB−.

Since rating services are rating the *issues*, not the *issuers*, it is possible for the same issuer to have several issues, each with a different rating. The ratings differ because the debt securities they reflect differ in seniority or security. For example, in 1992, Moody's rated Disney's $9\frac{1}{8}$ percent Euronotes, due 1995, Aa3, but rated the zero-coupon subordinated notes, due 2005, A1.

The top *four* classes—AAA through BBB for Standard & Poor's, Aaa through Baa for Moody's—are called **investment grade** debt and the top *two* classes—AAA and AA for Standard & Poor's, Aaa and Aa for Moody's—are referred to as **high-quality** debt. Any debt that is not investment grade (that is, any debt rated below the top four classes) is referred to as **junk bonds.** Junk bonds are considered speculative because they represent substantial risk that interest and principal may not be paid as promised.

General description	Standard & Poor's	Moody's
INVESTMENT GRADE		
Maximum safety	AAA	Aaa
High quality	AA+	Aa1
	AA	Aa2
	AA−	Aa3
Upper medium grade	A+	A1
	A	A2
	A−	A3
Lower medium grade	BBB+	Baa1
	BBB	Baa2
	BBB−	Baa3
NONINVESTMENT GRADE		
Low grade, speculative	BB+	Ba1
	BB	Ba2
	BB−	Ba3
Highly speculative	B+	B1
	B	B2
	B−	B3
Substantial risk	CCC+	
	CCC	Caa
	CCC−	
Extremely speculative	CC	Ca
Very extremely speculative	C	C
Default	D	

SOURCE: "Key to Moody's Corporate Bond Ratings," Moody's, *Industrial Manual*, 1991, pp. vi–vii.; and "Long-Term Rating Definitions," *CREDITWEEK*, Standard & Poor's, Feb. 11, 1991, p. 128.

Ratings on debt change as the issuer's ability to handle its debt obligations changes. If there is an economic downturn and firms that issued debt are perceived as adversely affected, their debt ratings may be revised downward. If there is a general decrease in interest rates, firms with variable rate debt may be better able to handle their obligations, so their debt ratings may be revised upward.

Debt ratings are important for the marketability and cost of debt. Many financial institutions and governmental bodies are restricted from investing in securities that are not investment-grade debt. Since institutions such as banks and pension funds make up a large portion of debt investors, packaging debt with sufficient seniority and security is important to ensure that it will be attractive to investors.

And, since investors want to be compensated for risk, the greater the default risk associated with debt—as represented by the debt ratings—the greater

Debt issues whose ratings are changed from investment grade to noninvestment grade are referred to as "fallen angels."

571

will be the yield on debt demanded by investors. We can see the relation between debt yields and debt ratings in Figure 12-1. Here we see that Baa debt has a higher yield than A debt, A debt has higher yields than Aa debt, and Aa debt has higher yields than Aaa debt.

Some limitations in relying upon debt ratings in an investment decision are these:

- Debt ratings reflect credit quality only; no evaluation is made of other risks associated with the debt.
- Since debt security prices are affected largely by changes in interest rates and debt ratings do not represent a forecast of future interest rates, debt ratings cannot be used to select investments that will necessarily increase in value.
- Debt ratings reflect the judgment of the rating service analysts, who look at the operating and financial performance of the borrowing firm, the economic environment, and the market in which the firm operates, along with the features and indenture of the particular debt issue.

Therefore, a rating is ultimately a subjective interpretation of the information it is based on.

FIGURE 12-1

Average Annualized Yields on Corporate Debt by Moody's Ratings Classes, 1980–1991

SOURCE: Moody's, *Industrial Manual*, 1991; annualized monthly data.

Interest Rate Risk

The value of a debt at any point in time is related to its yield—the return necessary to compensate the lender for the time value of money and the risk associated with the debt. We can see this by expressing the value of debt as:

$$\text{Value of debt} = \frac{\text{present value of}}{\text{interest payments}} + \frac{\text{present value of}}{\text{the maturity value}}$$

or, in general terms:

$$\text{Value of debt} = \sum_{t=1}^{T} \frac{C}{(1+r)^t} + \frac{M}{(1+r)^T}$$

where t = payment period
T = number of periods to maturity
C = coupon payment per period
M = maturity value
r = yield per period

The interest payments and the maturity value are discounted to the present—today's value—using the rate that we refer to as the yield. If the yield increases, the present value of the interest payments and maturity value decline; if the yield decreases, the present value of the interest and maturity value increases.

Consider a bond with five years to maturity, a face value of $1,000, and a coupon rate of 6 percent, paid semiannually. If the annualized yield to maturity is 10 percent (making the six-month discount rate 5 percent), the value of this bond is calculated as follows:

$$\text{Value of bond} = \sum_{t=1}^{10} \frac{\$30}{(1+0.05)^t} + \frac{\$1,000}{(1+0.05)^{10}}$$

$$= \$30\left[\sum_{t=1}^{10} \frac{1}{(1+0.05)^t}\right] + \$1,000\left[\frac{1}{(1+0.05)^{10}}\right]$$

$$= \$30(\text{present value annuity factor}) + \$1,000(\text{discount factor})$$

$$= \$231.65 + \$613.91$$

$$= \mathbf{\$845.56}$$

If the yield changes, so does the value of the debt. If the yield decreases to 8 percent (4 percent per sixth-month period), the value of the bond increases:

$$\text{Value of bond} = \sum_{t=1}^{10} \frac{\$30}{(1+0.04)^t} + \frac{\$1,000}{(1+0.04)^{10}}$$

$$= \mathbf{\$918.89}$$

Interest rate risk is the risk that yields will change, changing the value of the debt. Interest rate risk is the sensitivity of a debt's price to changes in interest rates. An investor who holds a debt security until its maturity need

Coupon Rates and Yields

The *coupon rate* is the rate at which interest is paid: 6 percent paid semiannually on a $1,000 bond means that $30 is paid every six months. The *yield to maturity* is the discount rate used to determine the value of the bond's future cash flows today, and the *discount rate* is a reflection of the expected going market interest rates.

The yield to maturity is usually quoted on an annualized basis; the discount rate for a six-month period is multiplied by two if interest is paid semiannually:

Annualized yield to maturity = six-month yield × 2

The effective yield to maturity in the case of semiannual compounding is the six-month yield compounded two periods:

Effective yield to maturity = $(1 + \text{six-month yield})^2 - 1$

If interest is paid annually, the annualized yield to maturity is equivalent to the effective yield to maturity.

The yield investors require on a security is influenced by changes in interest rates in the marketplace—the interest rates they could get from alternative securities. If yields in the marketplace change, the yield investors require on a given security changes. Therefore, the yield on a security (and hence the security's price) is sensitive to changes in market interest rates.

not worry that its value will change as interest rates change. But an investor who does not hold the debt to maturity needs to worry about how changes in interest rates affect its value. As market interest rates go up, the value of your bond goes down. As market interest rates go down, the value of your bond goes up.

Just how sensitive is a debt security's value to changes in yields? It depends on the security's time to maturity and its coupon rate.

Suppose we have a $1,000 bond with a 10 percent coupon, paid semiannually. If there are ten years remaining to maturity and market rates have changed so that the yield to maturity on the bond changes from 8 percent to 9 percent, then the value of the bond changes from $1,135.90 to $1,065.04—a drop in value of $70.86, or 6.24 percent. If, instead, there are twenty-five years to maturity and the yield changes from 8 percent to 9 percent, the value of the bond changes from $1,214.82 to $1,098.81—a drop of $116.01 or 9.55 percent.

In Table 12-3, we can see how this shift in yield to maturity changes the value of the bond as the number of years remaining to maturity changes. If there is one year to maturity, the effect of a change in the yield from 8 per-

TABLE 12-3

Sensitivity of a Bond's Value to Changes in the Yield to Maturity of a 10 Percent Coupon Bond and Changes in the Number of Years Remaining to Maturity

Breakdown of the value of a 10 percent coupon bond into the present value of interest and the present value of the maturity value with yields of 8 percent and 9 percent and different numbers of years remaining to maturity

Years to maturity	8% yield to maturity			9% yield to maturity		
	Present value of interest	Present value of maturity value	Present value of bond	Present value of interest	Present value of maturity value	Present value of bond
1	$ 94.30	$924.56	$1,018.86	$ 93.63	$915.73	$1,009.36
5	405.54	675.56	1,081.11	395.64	643.93	1,039.56
10	679.52	456.39	1,135.90	650.40	414.64	1,065.04
15	864.60	308.32	1,172.92	814.44	267.00	1,081.44
20	989.64	208.29	1,197.93	920.08	171.93	1,092.01
25	1,074.11	140.71	1,214.82	988.10	110.71	1,098.81
30	1,131.17	95.06	1,226.23	1,031.90	71.29	1,103.19

Change in a bond's value when the yield to maturity changes from 8 percent to 9 percent for different numbers of years remaining to maturity:

Years to maturity	Present value of bond with an 8% yield to maturity	Present value of bond with a 9% yield to maturity	Change in the value of the bond In dollars	Percentage change in the value of the bond In percentages
1	$1,018.86	$1,009.36	−$ 9.50	−0.93%
5	1,081.11	1,039.56	−41.55	−3.84
10	1,135.90	1,065.04	−70.86	−6.24
15	1,172.92	1,081.44	−91.48	−7.80
20	1,197.93	1,092.01	−105.08	−8.44
25	1,214.82	1,098.81	−116.01	−9.55
30	1,226.23	1,103.19	−123.04	−10.03

cent to 9 percent is very small, changing the present value of interest by less than $1 and the present value of the maturity value by less than $9. If there are thirty years to maturity, a change from 8 percent to 9 percent changes the present value of the interest by almost $100 and the present value of the maturity value by almost $24.

The change in the value of the 10 percent coupon bond for different years remaining to maturity is shown in Figure 12-2, where you can see how the value of the bond changes for different maturities. The longer the time to maturity, the more of the debt's value is further out into the future and the more

FIGURE 12-2

Value of a 10 Percent Coupon Bond for 8 Percent and 9 Percent Yields to Maturity and for Different Numbers of Years Remaining to Maturity

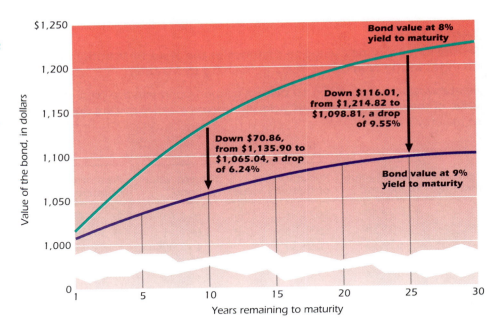

the present value is affected by a change in the going market interest rate. To sum up: *For a given coupon rate, the longer is the maturity of the debt, the more sensitive will be the debt's value to changes in market interest rates.*

The higher the coupon rate, the more of the debt's present value is derived from cash flows earlier on in the debt's life. The higher the coupon rate, the sooner these debt cash flows are received; therefore, the less sensitive will be the present value of the cash flows to changes in the yield, which is the discount rate used to translate future cash flows into present values.

Suppose we have a bond with ten years remaining to maturity. If the bond's yield changes from 8 percent to 9 percent, its price changes also. How much it changes depends on the bond's coupon rate. The higher the coupon rate, the less sensitive will be the bond's price to the change in the yield. We can see this at work in Table 12-4, where the calculation of the change in a bond's value is shown for different coupon rates from 0 percent (zero-coupon) to 20 percent. For a zero-coupon bond, a change in the yield from 8 percent to 9 percent changes the bond's value by almost $42, or 9.15 percent; for a 20 percent coupon bond, the change in the yield changes the bond's value by a larger dollar amount, almost $100, which is a smaller percentage, 5.51 percent. Zero-coupon debt has the greatest interest rate risk, since *all* of its value is derived from the maturity value. To sum up: *For a given maturity, the greater is the coupon rate, the less sensitive is the debt's value to a change in the yield.*

Reinvestment Rate Risk

As investors receive the interest and principal, they may reinvest these funds in other investments. **Reinvestment rate risk** is the risk that interest rates will change, affecting the return on the reinvestment of cash flows.

Consider a $1,000 bond with an 8 percent coupon rate paid annually and a maturity of five years. If you reinvest each of the $80 coupon receipts in an investment that yields 8 percent at the end of the five years you will have:

Coupon received at the end of year . . .	and reinvested at 8% for . . .	results in a future value of . . .
1	4 years	$ 108.84
2	3 years	100.78
3	2 years	93.31
4	1 years	86.40
5	0 years	80.00
Total value of reinvested coupons		**$469.33**

The return on the investment is determined by comparing the amount invested, $1,000, with what we get back, the principal repayment of $1,000 plus

TABLE 12-4

Sensitivity of a Bond's Value to Changes in the Yield to Maturity of a Bond with Ten Years Remaining to Maturity for Different Coupon Rates, Interest Paid Semiannually

Breakdown of a bond's value into the present value of interest and the present value of the maturity value, with ten years remaining to maturity, yields to maturity of 8 and 9 percent, and different coupon rates:

Coupon rate	8% yield to maturity			9% yield to maturity		
	Present value of interest	Present value of maturity value	Present value of bond	Present value of interest	Present value of maturity value	Present value of bond
0%	$ 0.00	$456.39	$ 456.39	$ 0.00	$414.64	$ 414.64
5	339.76	456.39	796.15	325.20	414.64	739.84
10	679.52	456.39	1,135.90	650.40	414.64	1,065.04
15	1,019.27	456.39	1,475.66	975.60	414.64	1,390.24
20	1,359.03	456.39	1,815.42	1,300.79	414.64	1,715.44

Changes in the value of the bond when the yield to maturity changes from 8 percent to 9 percent, for different coupon rates:

Coupon rate	Present value of bond with an 8% yield to maturity	Present value of bond with a 9% yield to maturity	Change in the value of the bond — In dollars	Percentage change in the value of the bond — In percentages
0%	$ 456.39	$ 414.64	−$41.74	−9.15%
5	796.15	739.84	−56.30	−7.07
10	1,135.90	1,065.04	−70.86	−6.24
15	1,475.66	1,390.24	−85.42	−5.79
20	1,815.42	1,715.44	−99.98	−5.51

interest (which includes interest on interest) of $469.33 in five years. In other words,

Present value, PV = $1,000.00

Future value, FV = $1,469.33

Number of periods, T = 5

$$\text{Return} = \sqrt[T]{\frac{FV}{PV}} - 1 = \sqrt[5]{\frac{\$1,469.33}{\$1,000.00}} - 1 = 8\% \text{ per year}$$

Therefore, if we can invest the interest to earn 8 percent, we get a return of 8 percent on our investment. If, instead, our best investment opportunity yields 6 percent annually:

Coupon received at the end of year . . .	and reinvested at 6% for . . .	results in a future value of . . .
1	4 years	$ 101.00
2	3 years	95.28
3	2 years	89.89
4	1 years	84.80
5	0 years	80.00
Total value of reinvested coupons		**$450.97**

we have a lower return on our investment:

$$\text{Return} = \sqrt[5]{\frac{\$1,450.97}{\$1,000.00}} - 1 = 7.73\% \text{ per year}$$

What you get out of your investing depends not just on an investment's cash flows, but on what you can do with the flows once you get them.

Investors in debt securities face reinvestment rate risk with respect to the reinvestment of interest payments and the reinvestment of maturity value:

> In evaluating capital projects, we also consider alternative reinvestment rates when we calculate the return. In that case, we refer to the future value as the *terminal value* and the return as the *modified internal rate of return*.

- *The larger are the coupon payments, relative to the entire present value of the bond, the greater is the reinvestment rate risk.* The higher the coupon, the more of a bond's cash flows are received sooner in its life and the more important reinvestment becomes.
- *The shorter is the maturity of the bond, the greater is the reinvestment rate risk.* The shorter is the maturity, the sooner a large cash flow—the maturity value—is received and the sooner you have to worry about reinvesting it.
- *Debt that is callable—either through a call feature or a sinking fund call—has a greater reinvestment risk than the equivalent noncallable debt; we refer to this risk as **call risk.*** If debt is called, you end up with a large cash flow (the call price) that you need to reinvest somewhere.
- *Zero-coupon debt has less reinvestment rate risk than a coupon bond with the same maturity because there are no cash flows to investors until maturity.* Without any interest payments, you don't have to worry about reinvesting what you didn't receive.

Purchasing Power Risk

Purchasing power risk is the risk that the price level may change. This type of risk has its winners and its losers. If a firm locks in a price on its supply of raw materials through a long-term contract and the price level increases, it is a winner and its supplier is the loser—the firm pays the supplier in cheaper currency. If a firm borrows funds by issuing a long-term bond with a fixed coupon rate and the price level increases, it is the winner and its creditor is the loser—the firm pays the interest and the principal in cheaper currency.

How large can the effect be? Consider the inflation rate for 1991: 4.2 percent. If you borrowed $1,000 at the beginning of 1991 and paid it back at the end of 1991, you paid back $1,000 in end-of-1991 dollars. Each dollar that you paid back was worth less than each dollar that you borrowed: You borrowed $1,000 but paid back an amount worth only $1,000/(1 + 0.042) = $959.70 in terms of beginning-of-the-year dollars.

If inflation is anticipated, the rate of inflation will be built into the interest rate so that creditors will be compensated for the loss of purchasing power of the interest and principal payments. But the greater the *unanticipated* inflation rate, the better off are the borrowers and the worse off are the creditors.

Since inflation and interest rates are tied together, purchasing power risk and interest rate risk are tied together. As expectations of inflation change, so do interest rates and, hence, the value of debt securities.

Marketability Risk

A security that can be readily sold at prevailing market prices is considered liquid or marketable. ***Marketability risk*** is the risk that investors will not be able to sell a security they hold for what it is worth: The greater is the marketability risk, the greater is the required return on the investment.

Small security issues and those with very "thin" markets—little trading—have greater marketability risk. A security having features that are unattractive to investors may be unmarketable.

DEBT RETIREMENT

With the rare exception of a perpetual debt, debt obligations have a fixed life, a maturity. But a borrower does not have to keep its debt outstanding for the debt's entire life. Debt can be retired prior to its maturity by

- Calling in callable debt.
- Issuing a sinking fund call.
- Forcing convertible bonds into stock.
- Purchasing the debt from the investor either through direct negotiation or by buying the debt in the open market.

There are a number of reasons to retire debt before its maturity.

First, the borrower may want to eliminate the fixed, legal obligations associated with debt. If the interest is too burdensome or the borrower does not have enough taxable income to use to offset the interest tax deduction, debt may be unattractive because it increases the firm's default risk.

Second, the borrower may find the indenture provisions too confining. Provisions such as a covenant that the firm maintain a specified ratio of current assets to current liabilities may restrict management decisions.

Third, the borrower may no longer need the funds represented in the debt. The borrower may be generating more cash from operations than needed for other purposes and, hence, may choose to use the excess to reduce debt.

And fourth, market interest rates may have fallen, making the interest rates on the outstanding debt too costly relative to current rates.

The first three reasons are part of what we refer to as the capital structure decision—a firm's mix of debt and equity to finance its operations. (We discuss capital structure decisions in a later chapter.)

But let's take a closer look at this last reason. Suppose we currently have $1 million of bonds outstanding with a 10 percent coupon rate. We issued these bonds five years ago, and they will mature in five years. Looking at current rates, we figure we can issue bonds today with a maturity of five years and a coupon rate of 6 percent. Should we buy back our outstanding 10 percent bonds and issue new 6 percent bonds in their place? This is called *re-funding.* Let's assume that it costs us $100,000 in underwriters' fees to refund these bonds. Does it pay to do this?

It all boils down to comparing the cost of the old bonds with the cost of the new ones. Suppose the current annualized yield to maturity is 6 percent (that is, 3 percent per six-month period). The value of the old bond is:

$$\text{Value of old bond} = \sum_{t=1}^{10} \frac{\$50}{(1 + 0.03)^t} + \frac{\$1,000}{(1 + 0.03)^{10}}$$

$$= \$426.51 + \$744.09$$

$$= \mathbf{\$1,170.60}$$

If the old bonds are not callable and we were to buy these bonds in the financial markets, we would have to pay $1,170.60 per bond, or $1,170,600 for the entire issue.

The premium on these bonds ($1,170.60 − $1,000.00 = $170.60 per bond, or $170,600 in total) and the flotation expenses—the $100,000 we pay the underwriters who help us sell the new bonds—are deductible for tax purposes. If we have a 40 percent tax rate, this means that the premium costs us only 60 percent of $170,600, or $102,360, and the flotation expenses cost only 60 percent of $100,000, or $60,000. The government pays for the difference by allowing us to lower our taxable income by $100,000 + $170,600 = $270,600:

Item	Cost	Firm's share	Government's share
Premium on old bonds	$ 170,600	$ 102,360	$ 68,240
Flotation costs on new bonds	100,000	60,000	40,000
Total	$270,600	$162,360	$108,240

Therefore, considering the flotation costs, we have to issue new 6 percent bonds with a face value of $1,170,600 − $68,240 + $60,000 = $1,162,360 to replace our 10 percent bonds. If we do this, we will have interest payments of 3 percent × $1,162,360 = $34,871 every six months instead of our 5 percent × $1,000,000 = $50,000 on the old bonds.

Are we better off with the new bonds? With the old bonds, we had an interest expense of $50,000 each period. But since interest is deductible for tax purposes, this really costs us only 60 percent of $50,000, or $30,000. For the new bonds, the after-tax cost is 60 percent of $34,871, or $20,922, every six months. We would save $9,078 every six months over the next five years by retiring the old bonds and issuing new bonds.

But that's not the whole story. The only way to figure out the answer is to look at the present value of the difference in cash flows between the old and the new debt. How do they differ? In two ways. First, every six months the new debt has a lower interest payment, which amounts to $9,078 after taxes. Second, the new debt requires us to pay a different maturity value in five years: $1,162,360 instead of $1,000,000.

$$\text{Present value of difference} = \underbrace{\sum_{t=1}^{10} \frac{\$9,078}{(1 + 0.03)^t}}_{\substack{\text{Present value} \\ \text{of difference in} \\ \text{after-tax interest} \\ \text{expense}}} - \underbrace{\frac{\$162,360}{(1 + 0.03)^{10}}}_{\substack{\text{Present value} \\ \text{of difference in} \\ \text{maturity values}}}$$

$$= \$77,437 - \$120,811$$

$$= -\$43,374$$

Therefore, we are worse off by $43,374 when we buy back the old 10 percent debt issue and issue the new 6 percent debt.

The refunding decision—the decision whether to retire old debt and issue new debt—requires us to look at whether the refunding increases the value of the firm by providing increased cash flows. The way we do this is to:

1. Determine the cash flows for the old and new debt, taking into account the difference in interest payments, any tax effects, and any flotation costs.
2. Calculate the difference in cash flows between the old and new debt.
3. Calculate the present value of the difference in cash flows.

If the present value of the difference is positive, the new issue provides a benefit; if negative, the new issue represents a cost.

LONG-TERM DEBT AS A SOURCE OF CAPITAL

Firms can raise new capital by issuing bonds, notes, preferred stock, or common stock. Why issue debt instead of equity? For these reasons:

- **Taxes.** The interest paid on debt is deductible for tax purposes; dividends paid on equity are not deductible.
- **Control.** By issuing debt, the firm does not dilute the voting rights or control of equity securities; creditors have a say in management only when the borrower is in default.
- **Cost of funds.** Due to the tax deductibility of interest expenses and the seniority of creditors' claims over shareholders' claims, debt is a cheaper source of capital than equity.

But we must look at the flip side: Why issue equity instead of debt?

- **Financial distress.** Debt obligations are legally binding contracts, and failure to pay these obligations as promised may force the firm into bankruptcy.
- **Debt capacity.** By financing more of its assets with equity, the firm preserves the ability to raise debt in future periods.

FIGURE 12-3

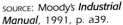

Debt, Preferred Stock, and Common Stock Issued by U.S. Corporations, 1950–1990

SOURCE: Moody's *Industrial Manual*, 1991, p. a39.

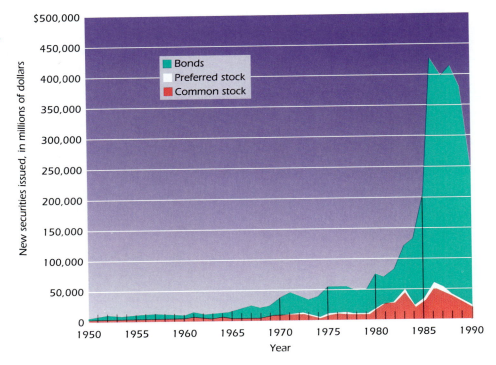

The decision regarding what type of capital to raise—the capital structure decision—involves a tradeoff between these debt and equity considerations.

U.S. corporations raise more funds with debt than with equity issues, as shown in Figure 12-3. Does that mean that corporations are increasing their debt relative to their equity? Not necessarily: Most debt has a fixed maturity; when it matures, the corporation usually replaces it with another issue. Most corporate debt securities have maturities of fifteen to thirty years. So if a firm wants to finance a portion of its assets with debt, it would have to issue new debt as its existing debt matures. Since some equity is raised internally (retained earnings) and since equity securities are perpetual securities (so replacement is not a consideration) firms do not issue equity securities very often.

SUMMARY

- Long-term debt securities—term loans, bonds, and notes—have characteristics that can be packaged in different ways.

- Debt securities may be denominated in any country's currency. They may have any maturity, though term loans tend to have shorter maturities than notes and bonds.

- Interest payments on debt securities may be variable or fixed, may start immediately or start some time in the future, and may allow debtholders to share in the good fortune of the firm.

- Debt securities may be backed by specific pledges of property or may be backed by the general credit of the firm. Some debt securities may have prior claims over other debt securities, though all debt securities have prior claim over owners.

- Many debt securities have optionlike features that give the issuer or the debt owner certain rights. Callability, conversion rights, putability, and warrant rights are valuable and affect the riskiness and attractiveness of the security they are attached to.

- The bond indenture is the contract between the borrower and the lenders and consists of provisions that protect the interests of the lenders, who are the bondholders. A trustee acts in their interest, monitoring the firm to ensure that the borrower is abiding by the contract provisions.

- The risk of debt securities includes the risk that the borrower will not abide by the debt agreement, referred to as default risk. Risks associated with market conditions and the structure of the debt payments include interest rate risk, reinvestment rate risk, purchasing power risk, and marketability risk.

- Debt is retired by issuers calling it in or buying it back in the marketplace and by investors converting it into other securities.

- The decision to refund debt—replace debt with a security that has a lower coupon—depends on the present value of the benefits of retirements, such as lower interest rates, compared to the present value of the costs of retirements, such as flotation costs.

- Long-term debt securities are the most often issued corporate security because they constantly need replenishment. As debt securities mature, firms issue more debt securities to replace the maturing issue.

QUESTIONS

12-1   What distinguishes a note from a bond? How are the terms "note" and "bond" commonly used?

12-2   What is the difference between a registered bond and a bearer bond?

12-3   At whose option is a callable bond exercised? At whose option is a convertible bond exercised?

12-4   What is the role of the trustee designated in a bond indenture?

12-5   If a corporation were to issue both a convertible and a nonconvertible bond—both identical except for the conversion feature—how would the prices of the two bonds compare? How would the yields on the two bonds compare?

12-6   Explain why a detachable warrant to buy the common stock of a corporation may have a value even though the exercise price of the warrant is above the current price of the common stock.

12-7   Why would a corporation attach warrants to a bond?

12-8   How does a put option affect the cost of debt for an issuer? Why would a put feature be attractive to the investor?

12-9   If the rate of inflation increases, which party (borrowers or creditors) loses? Which party wins? Why?

12-10 Why would a corporation decide to issue debt instead of stock?

12-11 Rank each of the following bonds on the basis of its interest rate risk:

- 5 percent coupon bond with a maturity of five years
- Zero-coupon bond with a maturity of five years
- 10 percent coupon bond with a maturity of five years

12-12 Rank each of the following bonds on the basis of its reinvestment rate risk:

- 5 percent coupon bond with a maturity of five years
- Zero-coupon bond with a maturity of five years
- 10 percent coupon bond with a maturity of five years

12-13 Rank each of the following securities on the basis of its default risk, assuming all of them are issued by the same company:

- Subordinated debenture
- Mortgage bond
- Debenture

12-14 If a corporation's bond issue is rated AAA by Standard & Poor's, does this mean the bond is risk free? Explain.

PROBLEMS

Interest

12-1 The Can Sell Company issued $1 million of 8 percent coupon bonds in 1990 at par value. These bonds mature in 1995 and pay interest semiannually. Calculate the amount of the interest to be paid each period on these bonds.

12-2 The Quarter Company has $2 million of 10 percent coupon bonds outstanding. These bonds have interest paid each quarter, that is, every three months. What is the dollar amount of interest Quarter Company pays each quarter?

12-3 The Drifter Corporation has $1 million in floating rate notes outstanding, with interest paid annually. The rate of interest is calculated as the sum of the ten-year U.S. Treasury bond rate plus 3 percent. Given the following forecasted Treasury bond rates, what are the expected annual interest payments on these notes for the years 2000 through 2005?

Year	Forecasted Treasury bond rate
2000	5.0%
2001	5.5
2002	6.0
2003	6.0
2004	6.3
2005	6.5

12-4 The Cipher Corporation issued a zero-coupon bond with a face value of $1,000 on January 1, 1992. The bond was issued at $400 and will mature on December 31, 2000.

    a. If you bought these bonds when they were issued and held them to maturity, what return would you earn?

    b. What is the amount of interest expense that Cipher deducts each year on the bond?

12-5 The Gator Corporation issued a zero-coupon bond with a face value of $1,000 on January 1, 1992. The bond was issued at $556.84 and will mature on December 31, 2003.

    a. If you bought these bonds when they were issued and held them to maturity, what return would you earn?

    b. What is the amount of interest expense on a bond that Gator deducts each year on the bond?

Optionlike features

12-6 The Basis Corporation issued $6 million of 5 percent coupon bonds, each with a warrant to buy a share of Basis Corporation common stock at $20 per share.

   a. If the price of a share of stock is $15, is the warrant worthless? Explain.

   b. If the price of a share of stock is $26, what is the minimum price you would be willing to pay for the warrant?

   c. If the price of a share of stock is $22, what is the minimum price you would be willing to pay for the warrant?

   d. If the warrant had an expiration date two years into the future, how would this warrant price compare with a similar, but perpetual, warrant?

12-7 Doppleganger Inc. notes have a face value of $1,000 each and are convertible into common shares at $50 per share.

   a. What is the conversion price of the shares?

   b. What is the conversion ratio for these notes?

   c. If the common stock is trading at $60 a share, what is the market conversion price of the notes?

   d. If the common stock is trading at $40 a share, what is the market conversion price of the notes?

   e. If the notes are trading at 110 or $1,100 per note, what is the effective conversion price?

12-8 Changeling Inc. bonds have a face value of $1,000 each and are convertible into common stock at $35 per share.

   a. What is the conversion price?

   b. What is the conversion ratio of these bonds?

   c. If the common stock is trading at $30 a share, what is the market conversion price of these bonds?

   d. If the common stock is trading at $40 a share, what is the market conversion price of these bonds?

   e. If the bond is trading at 90 or $900 per bond, what is the effective conversion price?

12-9 The Choice Corporation has $5 million of 6 percent coupon bonds outstanding, each with a face value of $1,000. The bonds are callable at 104 at any time, are putable at 105 in five years, are convertible into 20 shares of common stock, and have a warrant attached to each that gives the bondholder the right to buy a share of common stock at $50 per share.

   a. List all the options associated with these bonds, identifying the party that has the option.

   b. If each option is exercised, is there a cash inflow or outflow to Choice? What is the amount of the cash flow?

Risk and the value of debt

12-10 The Perry Corporation has $1 million of 5 percent coupon bonds outstanding, with interest paid semiannually, five years remaining to maturity, and a face value of $1,000 per bond.

   a. If these bonds are priced so that their annualized yield to maturity is 4 percent (that is, the six month yield is 2 percent), what is their value?

b. If the yield on these bonds changes from 4 percent to 6 percent, what is the change in the price of the bonds?

12-11 The Wakulla Corporation has $2 million of 8 percent coupon bonds outstanding with interest paid semiannually, ten years remaining to maturity, and a face value of $1,000 per bond.

a. If these bonds are priced so that their annualized yield to maturity is 8 percent (that is, their six-month yield is 4 percent), what is their value?
b. If the yield to maturity on these bonds changes from 8 percent to 6 percent, what is the percentage change in the bond's price?
c. If the yield to maturity on these bonds changes from 8 percent to 4 percent, what is the percentage change in the bond's price?

12-12 Consider two bonds, A and B, each with five years remaining to maturity, a face value of $1,000, and interest paid semiannually. Bond A has a 10 percent coupon, and Bond B has a 6 percent coupon.

a. If the annualized yield to maturity on these bonds changes from 4 percent to 6 percent, what is the percentage change in each bond's value?
b. If the annualized yield to maturity on these bonds changes from 6 percent to 8 percent, what is the percentage change in each bond's value?
c. If the annualized yield to maturity on these bonds changes from 4 percent to 8 percent, what is the percentage change in each bond's value?
d. Which bond's value is more sensitive to changes in interest rates?

12-13 Suppose you invest in a 6 percent coupon bond with interest paid semiannually and that has six years remaining to maturity.

a. If you can reinvest the coupons in an investment that has a six-month yield of 3 percent (therefore an annualized yield to maturity of 6 percent), what is your total return on this bond investment?
b. If you can reinvest the coupons in an investment that has a six-month yield of 2 percent, what is your total return on this bond investment?

12-14 Consider two bonds, C and D, each of which has annual coupons, a face value of $1,000, and three years remaining to maturity. Bond C has a 2 percent coupon, and Bond D has a 10 percent coupon.

a. If both bonds have a yield to maturity of 6 percent, what are their values?
b. If the yield to maturity on both bonds changes from 6 percent to 8 percent, what is the percentage change in each bond's value?
c. If the cash flows from each can be reinvested at 5 percent, what is the return on each bond if you hold them to maturity?
d. If the cash flows from each can be reinvested at 8 percent, what is the return on each bond if you hold them to maturity?
e. Which bond's return is more sensitive to changes in the reinvestment rate? Which bond's value is more sensitive to changes in interest rates?

Retiring debt

12-15 The Obligor Corporation currently has $5 million of 10 percent coupon bonds, with interest paid semiannually, a face value of $1,000 each, and ten years remaining to maturity. The bonds are callable at 105 and are trading to yield 6 percent (a 3 percent six-month yield). Obligor's marginal tax rate is 30 percent.

a. What is the total market value of the outstanding bonds?

b. Should Obligor Corporation buy the outstanding bonds in the open market or call in the bonds at this point in time? Why?

12-16 The Pact Company is evaluating its outstanding debt security in light of a recent drop in interest rates. Currently, it has $1 million of 8 percent coupon bonds (paid semiannually) outstanding that mature in five years and have a face value of $1,000 each. The bonds are callable at 106 at any time. Pact's outstanding bonds are priced to yield 6 percent (a six-month yield of 3 percent), and the company believes that if it could retire the existing bonds, it could issue new bonds at par with a 6 percent coupon rate. Pact Company's marginal tax rate is 40 percent.

    a. What is the total market value of the outstanding bonds?
    b. Should Pact Company buy the outstanding bonds in the open market or call in the bonds at this time? Why?
    c. If there are no flotation costs, what is the face value of new 6 percent bonds that must be issued to refund the existing bonds?
    d. Should Pact refund the 8 percent bonds?

Potpourri

12-17 **Research:** Select a U.S. corporation that has more than one debt issue outstanding and describe the debt obligations of the firm, noting for each security:

- The face value of the debt.
- The maturity date.
- The type of interest (fixed or variable).
- The seniority of the different debt obligations.
- Any security.

12-18 **Research:** Determine the current status of one of the debt issues described in this chapter, choosing among:

- USX's convertible zero-coupon bonds that mature in 2005.
- IBM's 9 percent notes that mature in May 1998.
- Disney's zero-coupon notes that mature in 2005.

If the debt has been retired, how and when was it retired? If the debt is currently outstanding, what is its price as of the end of the most recent calendar year?

FURTHER READINGS

The structure of many indenture agreements is similar. For a look at a model indenture agreement, see:
AMERICAN BAR FOUNDATION, *Mortgage Bond Indenture Form 1981*, Illinois: American Bar Foundation, Chicago, 1981.

There are a number of books that describe debt securities in detail. Two good references are:
RICHARD S. WILSON and FRANK J. FABOZZI, *The New Corporate Bond Market*, Probus, Chicago, 1990.
FRANK J. FABOZZI, *Bond Markets Analysis and Strategies*, 2d ed., Prentice-Hall, Englewood Cliffs, N.J., 1993.

CHAPTER 13

Capital Structure

INTRODUCTION 592

CAPITAL STRUCTURE AND FINANCIAL LEVERAGE 595

FINANCIAL LEVERAGE AND RISK 598

The Leverage Effect 598

Quantifying the Leverage Effect 599

CAPITAL STRUCTURE AND TAXES 600

What Modigliani and Miller Told Us 600

Interest Deductibility and Capital Structure 605

Personal Taxes and Capital Structure 609

Unused Tax Shields 610

CAPITAL STRUCTURE AND FINANCIAL DISTRESS 612

Costs of Financial Distress 612

The Role of Limited Liability 612

Bankruptcy and Bankruptcy Costs 615

Financial Distress and Capital Structure 616

PUTTING TOGETHER FINANCIAL LEVERAGE, TAXES, AND THE COSTS OF FINANCIAL DISTRESS 617

RECONCILING THEORY WITH PRACTICE 620

Capital Structures among Different Industries 620

Capital Structures within Industries 621

Trade-off Theories and Observed Capital Structures 622

ANOTHER POSSIBLE EXPLANATION 623

A CAPITAL STRUCTURE PRESCRIPTION 624

Factors Important in Selecting a Capital Structure 624

What's a Financial Manager to Do? 625

Summary 625

Airlines' Debt Ratings Take a Dive

The Airline Deregulation Act of 1978, which deregulated the airline industry, was expected to increase competition, increase air traffic to smaller cities in the United States, and reduce air fares. At the time the law was passed, there were twenty-one financially healthy airlines. Fifteen years later, there were twelve airlines, of which four were in bankruptcy and others were having financial difficulties (see Michael Oneal and Wendy Zellner, "Fly the Lucrative Skies of United American Delta," *Business Week,* Oct. 14, 1991, pp. 90–91).

In March 1993, Standard & Poor's Corporation (S&P) lowered its ratings of the debt of the three largest U.S. airlines to junk status. These three airlines, AMR Corporation, UAL Corporation, and Delta Air Lines, were responsible for approximately 75 percent of the airline industry's revenues and were the healthiest (financially speaking) in the industry.

Debt ratings reflect the ratings service's perception of the debtor's ability to meet the promised interest and principal repayments—the debtor's credit risk. Why did S&P lower these airlines' debt ratings? Let's take a brief look at their credit risk.

Operating earnings from 1982 through 1991 ranged from close to zero to almost 16 percent:

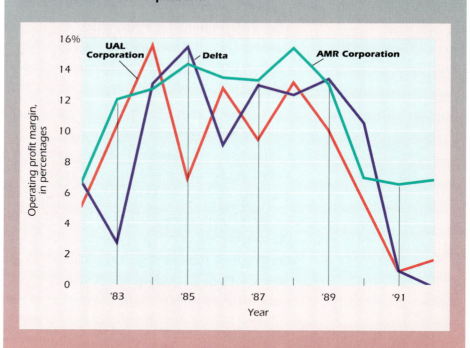

SOURCE: Standard & Poor's, *Compustat PC Plus* (CD-ROM); data are as of end of fiscal year.

But the recent trend is downward toward zero—and below! The airline industry is capital intensive, meaning that it is characterized by high fixed costs (relative to variable costs). As a result, airline operating earnings are very sensitive to changes in the number of passengers (referred to as the "load factor"). This sensitivity is evidenced by the volatile nature of operating earnings from 1982 through 1991. We refer to the sensitivity of operating earnings as business risk. And business risk increases a firm's credit risk.

And what about financial risk? The percentage of these three airlines' assets financed with long-term debt has varied widely, but the more recent trend appears to be a heavier reliance on debt financing:

SOURCE: Standard & Poor's, *Compustat PC Plus* (CD-ROM); data are as of end of fiscal year.

The three largest airlines have been taking on more debt in recent years, increasing their financial risk and, hence, their credit risk.

And adding to the woes of AMR, UAL, and Delta was the fact that some of their competitors were in bankruptcy. Continental Airlines and Trans World Airlines, both in bankruptcy, have been able to renegotiate labor contracts (cutting their operating costs) and their debt obligations (cutting their financing costs). Lower operating costs, combined with their "we have nothing to lose" status in bankruptcy, means that these bankrupt firms can conduct fare wars. So while the three largest airlines exercise considerable market power (having the lion's share of the air passenger traffic), they are at a competitive disadvantage with respect to some of the less financially healthy, smaller airlines.

These factors combine to paint a discouraging view of the future of AMR, Delta Air Lines, and UAL. The downgrade of their debt further exacerbates their situation, making it even more expensive for them to borrow money.

INTRODUCTION
A business invests in new plant and equipment to generate additional revenues and income—the basis of its growth. The funds raised from sources such as long-term debt and equity are referred to as *capital.*

One way to pay for investments is to generate capital from the firm's operations. Earnings belong to the owners and can either be paid to them—in the form of cash dividends—or plowed back into the firm. The owners' investment in the firm is referred to as *owners' equity* or, simply, *equity.* If management plows earnings back into the firm, the owners expect it to be invested in projects that will enhance the value of the firm and, hence, the value of their equity.

But earnings may not be sufficient to support *all* profitable investment opportunities. In that case the firm is faced with a decision: Forgo profitable investment opportunities or raise additional capital. A firm can raise new capital either by borrowing or by selling additional ownership interests or both.

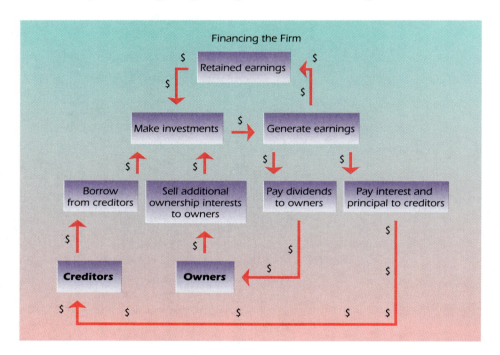

The combination of debt and equity used to finance a firm's projects is referred to as *capital structure.* The capital structure of a firm is some mix of debt, internally generated equity, and new equity. But what is the right mixture?

What capital structure is best depends on several factors. If a firm finances its activities with debt, the creditors expect the interest and principal—fixed, legal commitments—to be paid back as promised. Failure to pay may result in legal actions by the creditors.

Suppose you borrow $100 and promise to repay the $100 plus $5 in one year. Consider what may happen when you invest the $100:

- If you invest the $100 in a project that produces $120, you pay the lender the $105 you owe and keep the $15 profit.

- If your project produces $105, you pay the lender $105 and keep nothing.
- If your project produces $100, you pay the lender $105, with $5 coming out of your personal funds.

So if you reinvest the funds and get a return of more than the $5 (the cost of the funds) on the $100, you can keep all the profits. But if you get a return of $5 or less, the lender *still* gets her or his $5 back. This is the basic idea behind *financial leverage*—the use of financing that has fixed, but limited, payments.

If the firm has abundant earnings, the creditors are paid a fixed amount and the owners reap all that remains of the earnings after the creditors have been paid. If earnings are too low, the creditors *must* be paid what they are due, leaving the owners nothing out of earnings.

Failure to pay interest or principal as promised may result in financial distress. *Financial distress* is the condition under which a firm makes decisions under pressure to satisfy its legal obligations to its creditors. These decisions may not be in the best interests of the owners of the firm.

With equity financing there is no obligation. Though the firm may choose to distribute funds to the owners in the form of cash dividends there is no legal requirement to do so. Furthermore, interest paid on debt is deductible for tax purposes, whereas dividend payments are not tax deductible.

One measure of the extent to which debt is used to finance a firm is the *debt ratio,* the ratio of debt to equity:

$$\text{Debt ratio} = \frac{\text{debt}}{\text{equity}} \qquad [13\text{-}1]$$

The greater the debt ratio, the greater the use of debt for financing operations, relative to equity financing.

Another measure is the *debt-to-assets ratio,* which is the extent to which the assets of the firm are financed with debt:

$$\text{Debt-to-assets ratio} = \frac{\text{debt}}{\text{assets}} \qquad [13\text{-}2]$$

There is a tendency for firms in some industries to use more debt than others. We see this in the graph of the capital structure for different industries in Figure 13-1, in which the proportions of assets financed with debt and equity are shown graphically. We can make some generalizations about differences in capital structures across industries from this figure:

- Industries that are more reliant upon research and development for new products and technology—for example, chemical companies—tend to have lower debt-to-asset ratios than firms without such research and development needs—for example, grocery stores.
- Industries that require a relatively heavy investment in fixed assets, such as iron and steel foundries, tend to have lower debt-to-asset ratios.
- Industries with more volatile operating earnings, such as electronic computer firms, tend to finance assets more with equity than with debt.

FIGURE 13-1

Proportion of Capital from Debt and Equity, Selected Industries, 1991

SOURCE: Standard & Poor's, *Compustat PC Plus* (CD-ROM).

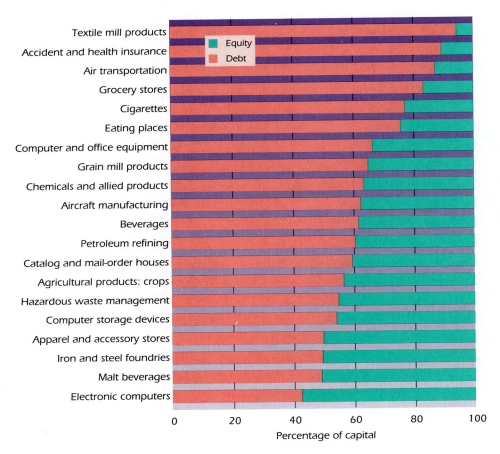

It is interesting to see how debt ratios compare among industries. For example, the aircraft manufacturing industry has a much higher use of debt than the malt beverage industry. Yet debt ratios vary among the firms within each industry. The percentage of each firm's assets that is financed with debt in 1991 for individual companies in the aircraft manufacturing industry and the malt beverage industries is graphed in Figures 13-2(*a*) and (*b*). For the aircraft manufacturing industry, Figure 13-2(*a*), debt finances 62 percent of assets, but varies from 49 to 99 percent for firms within the industry. In the malt beverage industry, Figure 13-2(*b*), the average proportion of debt is 49 percent and ranges from 33 to 83 percent.

Why do some industries tend to have firms with higher debt ratios than other industries? By examining the role of financial leveraging, financial distress, and taxes, we can explain some of the variation in debt ratios among industries. And by analyzing these factors we can explain how the firm's value may be affected by its capital structure.

FIGURE 13-2(a)

Proportion of Capital from Debt and Equity for Firms in the Aircraft Manufacturing Industry, 1991

SOURCE: Standard & Poor's, *Compustat PC Plus* (CD-ROM).

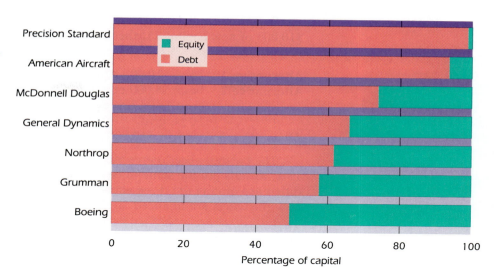

FIGURE 13-2(b)

Proportion of Capital from Debt and Equity for Firms in the Malt Beverage Industry, 1991

SOURCE: Standard & Poor's, *Compustat PC Plus* (CD-ROM).

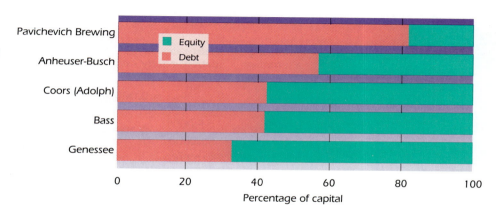

CAPITAL STRUCTURE AND FINANCIAL LEVERAGE

Debt and equity financing create different types of obligations for the firm. Debt financing obligates the firm to pay creditors interest and principal—usually a fixed amount—when promised. If the firm earns more than necessary to meet its debt payments, it can either distribute the surplus to the owners or reinvest.

Equity financing does *not* obligate the firm to distribute earnings. The firm may pay dividends or repurchase stock from the owners, but there is *no* obligation to do so.

The fixed and limited nature of the debt obligation affects the risk of the earnings to the owners. Consider Capital Corporation, which has $20,000 of assets, all financed with equity. There are 1,000 shares of Capital stock outstanding, valued at $20 per share. The firm's current balance sheet is simple:

Capital Corporation
Balance Sheet

| Assets | $20,000 | Liabilities | –0– |
| | | Equity (1,000 shares) | $20,000 |

Suppose Capital Corporation has investment opportunities requiring $10,000 of new capital. Further suppose Capital can raise the new capital in one of three ways:

Alternative 1   Issue $10,000 equity (500 shares of stock at $20 per share).
Alternative 2   Issue $5,000 of equity (250 shares of stock at $20 per share) and borrow $5,000 with an annual interest of 10 percent.
Alternative 3   Borrow $10,000 with an annual interest of 10 percent.[1]

The balance sheet representing each financing method is shown in Table 13-1. Results are the same in each case: assets increase to $30,000. The only difference among the three alternative means of financing is with respect to how the assets are financed:

Alternative 1   All equity.
Alternative 2   One-sixth debt, five-sixths equity.
Alternative 3   One-third debt, two-thirds equity.

Stated differently, the debt ratio and the debt-to-asset ratio of Capital under each alternative is:

Financing alternative	Debt ratio or debt-to-equity ratio	Debt-to-assets ratio
1	$\dfrac{\$0}{\$30,000} = $ **0.000** or **0%**	$\dfrac{\$0}{\$30,000} = $ **0.000** or **00.0%**
2	$\dfrac{\$5,000}{\$25,000} = $ **0.200** or **20%**	$\dfrac{\$5,000}{\$30,000} = $ **0.167** or **16.7%**
3	$\dfrac{\$10,000}{\$20,000} = $ **0.500** or **50%**	$\dfrac{\$10,000}{\$30,000} = $ **0.333** or **33.3%**

How do we interpret these ratios? Let's look at Alternative 2. The debt ratio of 20 percent tells us that the firm finances its assets using $1 of debt for every $5 of equity. The debt-to-assets ratio tells us that 16.7 percent of the assets are financed using debt or, putting it more clearly, almost 17 cents of every $1 of assets are financed with debt.

The return on assets is the ratio to assets of earnings before interest and taxes (EBIT), also referred to as operating earnings:

$$ROA = \frac{EBIT}{total\ assets}$$

[1] It may be unrealistic to assume that the interest rate on the debt in Alternative 3 will be the same as the interest rate for Alternative 2, since Alternative 3 involves more credit risk. For purposes of illustrating the point of leverage, however, let's keep the interest rate the same.

TABLE 13-1

Capital Corporation
Projected Balance Sheet for
Three Financing Alternatives

ALTERNATIVE 1: $10,000 EQUITY, $0 DEBT

| Assets | $30,000 | Liabilities | –0– |
| | | Equity (1,500 shares) | $30,000 |

ALTERNATIVE 2: $5,000 EQUITY, $5,000 DEBT

| Assets | $30,000 | Liabilities | $ 5,000 | *borrowing* |
| | | Equity (1,250 shares) | 25,000 | |

ALTERNATIVE 3: $0 EQUITY, $10,000 DEBT

| Assets | $30,000 | Liabilities | $10,000 |
| | | Equity (1,000 shares) | 20,000 |

Suppose Capital has $4,500 of operating earnings. This means it has a $4,500/$30,000 = 15 percent return on assets (ROA = 15 percent). And suppose there are no taxes. What are the earnings per share (EPS) under the different alternatives?

	Alternative 1: $10,000 equity	Alternative 2: $5,000 equity and $5,000 debt	Alternative 3: $10,000 debt
Operating earnings	$4,500.00	$4,500.00	$4,500.00
Less interest expense	0.00	500.00	1,000.00
Net income	$4,500.00	$4,000.00	$3,500.00
Divide by no. of shares	1,500	1,250	1,000
Earnings per share	$ 3.00	$ 3.20	$ 3.50

Suppose that the return on assets is 10 percent instead of 15 percent. Then:

	Alternative 1: $10,000 equity	Alternative 2: $5,000 equity and $5,000 debt	Alternative 3: $10,000 debt
Operating earnings	$3,000.00	$3,000.00	$3,000.00
Less interest expense	0.00	500.00	1,000.00
Net income	$3,000.00	$2,500.00	$2,000.00
Divide by no. of shares	1,500	1,250	1,000
Earnings per share	$ 2.00	$ 2.00	$ 2.00

If we are earning a return that is the same as the cost of debt, 10 percent, the earnings per share are not affected by the choice of financing.

Now suppose that the return on assets is 5 percent. The net income under each alternative is:

	Alternative 1: $10,000 equity	Alternative 2: $5,000 equity and $5,000 debt	Alternative 3: $10,000 debt
Operating earnings	$1,500.00	$1,500.00	$1,500.00
Less interest expense	0.00	500.00	1,000.00
Net income	$1,500.00	$1,000.00	$ 500.00
Divide by no. of shares	1,500	1,250	1,000
Earnings per share	$ 1.00	$ 0.80	$ 0.50

If the return on assets is 15 percent, Alternative 3 has the highest earnings per share, but if the return on assets is 5 percent, Alternative 3 has the lowest earnings per share.

We cannot say ahead of time what next period's earnings will be. So what can we do? Well, we can make projections of earnings under different economic climates and make judgments regarding the likelihood that these economic climates will occur.

Comparing the results of each of the alternative financing methods provides information on the effects of using debt financing. The greater is the amount of debt used in the capital structure, the greater will be the "swing" in the EPS.

Summarizing the EPS under each financing alternative and each economic climate:

	Earnings per share under different economic conditions		
Financing alternative	Slow (ROA = 5%)	Normal (ROA = 10%)	Boom (ROA = 15%)
1: $10,000 equity	$1.00	$2.00	$3.00
2: $5,000 equity, $5,000 debt	$0.80	$2.00	$3.20
3: $10,000 debt	$0.50	$2.00	$3.50

When debt financing is used instead of equity (Alternative 3), the owners don't share the earnings—all they must do is pay their creditors the interest on debt. But when equity financing is used instead of debt (Alternative 1), the owners must share the increased earnings with the additional owners, diluting the original owners' return on equity and earnings per share.

FINANCIAL LEVERAGE AND RISK

The Leverage Effect

Equity owners can reap most of the rewards through financial leverage when their firm does well. But there is a downside they may suffer when the firm does very poorly. What happens if earnings are down so low they are not high enough to pay interest? Interest must be paid no matter how low the earnings. How can money be obtained with which to pay interest when earnings are insufficient? It can be obtained:

- By reducing the assets in some way, such as by using working capital needed for operations or by selling buildings or equipment.
- By taking on more debt obligations.
- By issuing more shares of stock.

Whichever course the firm chooses, the burden ultimately falls upon the owners.

This leveraging effect is illustrated in Figure 13-3 for Capital Corporation where we have broadened the number of possible return-on-assets outcomes, extending them from 0 percent to 30 percent. Alternative 3 provides for the most upside potential for the equity holders; it also provides for the most downside potential. Hence, Alternative 1—all equity—offers the more conservative method of financing operations—the least to lose, yet the least to gain.

The three alternatives have identical earnings per share when there is a 10 percent return on assets. Capital Corporation's 10 percent return on assets is referred to as the ***EPS indifference point:*** the return at which the EPSs are the same under all the financing alternatives. Above a 10 percent return on assets (that is, above operating earnings of $3,000), Alternative 3 offers the most to owners. But Alternative 3 also has the most downside potential, producing the worst earnings to owners below this 10 percent return on assets.

Quantifying the Leverage Effect

We can see the effects of financial leverage by quantifying the uncertainty of the possible outcomes. Consider once again the three return-on-assets outcomes—5 percent, 10 percent, and 15 percent—but this time take a guess

FIGURE 13-3

Earnings per Share for Different Operating Earnings for the Three Financing Alternatives, Capital Corporation

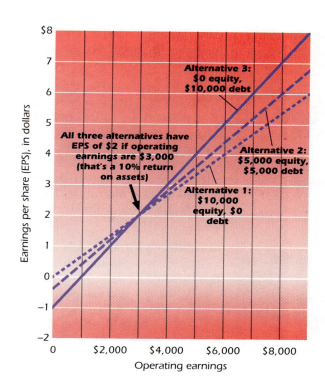

(somehow) at what the probability is that each of the outcomes will happen. Suppose that the probability associated with each outcome is as follows:

Economic climate	Return on assets	Probability
Slow	5%	20%
Normal	10	60
Boom	15	20

We can measure the risk associated with each alternative by calculating the standard deviation of the possible earnings per share. The larger is the standard deviation, the greater is the uncertainty associated with the alternative.

The calculation of the expected EPS, the standard deviation of EPS, and the coefficient of variation are shown in Table 13-2 for each of the three alternative financing arrangements. The expected values and corresponding standard deviations calculated in Table 13-2 are summarized as follows:

Financing alternative	Expected EPS	Standard deviation of EPS
1: $10,000 equity	$2.00	$0.6325
2: $5,000 equity, $5,000 debt	2.00	0.8944
3: $10,000 debt	2.00	0.9487

It happens that each alternative has the same expected EPS, but the standard deviations differ. All-debt financing (Alternative 3) results in the highest standard deviation of EPS. This result supports the notion that financial leverage increases the returns to owners but also increases the risk associated with the returns.

CAPITAL STRUCTURE AND TAXES

What Modigliani and Miller Told Us

The value of a firm—meaning the value of all its assets—is equal to the sum of its liabilities and its equity (the ownership interest). Does the way we finance the firm's assets affect the value of the firm and hence the value of its owners' equity? It depends.

The basic framework for the analysis of capital structure and how taxes affect it was developed by two Nobel Prize–winning economists, Franco Modigliani and Merton Miller.[2] Modigliani and Miller reasoned that if the following conditions hold, the value of the firm is not affected by its capital structure:

Condition 1 Individuals and corporations are able to borrow and lend at the same terms (referred to as "equal access").
Condition 2 There is no tax advantage associated with debt financing relative to equity financing.

Comparing Risk among Alternatives

In the Capital Corporation example, the expected values for alternatives are the same. However, if we are trying to compare risk among different probability distributions that have different expected values, we need to scale the standard deviation to make each comparable. To do this we divide the standard deviation by the expected value, which gives us a scaled down value of dispersion called the coefficient of variation, CV:

$$CV = \frac{\sigma(EPS)}{E(EPS)}$$

The larger is the coefficient of variation, the greater is the risk. See Appendix D for details on the calculation and interpretation of CV.

The work of Modigliani and Miller is cited so often that we frequently refer to them as M&M.

[2] "The Cost of Capital, Corporation Finance, and the Theory of Investment," *American Economic Review*, vol. 48, no. 3, June 1958, pp. 261–297.

The expected earnings per share for a given alternative are calculated by weighing the possible earnings per share (EPS) by the related probability:

$$E(\text{EPS}) = \sum_{i=1}^{N} p_i x_i$$

where $E(\text{EPS})$ = is the expected earnings per share
N = is the number of possible outcomes
x_i = is a possible earnings per share
p_i = is the probability associated with a possible earnings per share

The standard deviation, $\sigma(\text{EPS})$, is:

$$\sigma(\text{EPS}) = \sqrt{\sum_{i=1}^{N} p_i [x_i - E(\text{EPS})]^2}$$

The standard deviation is a measure of the dispersion of possible outcomes around the expected value: The larger is the standard deviation, the greater is the dispersion of possible values and, hence, the greater is the risk. For more discussion on the interpretation and calculation of the expected value and the standard deviation, see Appendix D.

Condition 3 Debt and equity trade in a market in which assets that are substitutes for one another trade at the same price. This is referred to as a ***perfect market.*** When assets are traded in a perfect market, the value of assets with the same risk and return characteristics trade for the same price.

Under the first condition, individuals can borrow and lend on the same terms as the business entities. Therefore, if individuals are seeking a given level of risk, they can either (1) borrow or lend on their own or (2) invest in a business that borrows or lends. In other words, if an individual wants to increase the risk of her investment, she could choose to invest in a company that uses debt to finance its assets. Alternatively, the individual could invest in a firm with no financial leverage and take out a personal loan—increasing her own financial leverage.

The second condition isolates the effect of financial leverage. If deducting interest from earnings is allowed in the analysis, it would be difficult to figure out what effect financial leverage itself has on the value of the firm.

The third condition ensures that assets are priced according to their risk and return characteristics.

Under these conditions, the value of Capital Corporation is the same, no matter which of the three financing alternatives it chooses. The *total* income

TABLE 13-2

Capital Corporation's Expected Earnings per Share and Standard Deviation of Possible Earnings per Share Associated with Three Financing Alternatives

ALTERNATIVE 1: $10,000 EQUITY, $0 DEBT

EPS	Probability	EPS × probability	Deviation from E(EPS)	Deviation squared	Squared deviation × probability
$1.00	20%	$0.20	−$1.00	1.0000	0.2000
2.00	60	1.20	0.00	0.0000	0.0000
3.00	20	0.60	1.00	1.0000	0.2000
		$E(\text{EPS}) = \$2.00$			$\sigma^2(\text{EPS}) = 0.4000$

$$\sigma(\text{EPS}) = \sqrt{0.4000} = \$0.6325$$

ALTERNATIVE 2: $5,000 EQUITY, $5,000 DEBT

EPS	Probability	EPS × probability	Deviation from E(EPS)	Deviation squared	Squared deviation × probability
$0.80	20%	$0.16	−$1.60	2.5600	0.5120
2.00	60	1.20	0.00	0.0000	0.0000
3.20	20	0.64	1.20	1.4400	0.2880
		$E(\text{EPS}) = \$2.00$			$\sigma^2(\text{EPS}) = 0.8000$

$$\sigma(\text{EPS}) = \sqrt{\$0.80} = \$0.8944$$

ALTERNATIVE 3: $0 EQUITY, $10,000 DEBT

EPS	Probability	EPS × probability	Deviation from E(EPS)	Deviation squared	Squared deviation × probability
$0.50	20%	$0.10	−$1.50	2.2500	0.4500
2.00	60	1.20	0.00	0.0000	0.0000
3.50	20	0.70	1.50	2.2500	0.4500
		$E(\text{EPS}) = \$2.00$			$\sigma^2(\text{EPS}) = 0.9000$

$$\sigma(\text{EPS}) = \sqrt{0.9000} = \$0.9487$$

NOTE: $E(\text{EPS})$ = expected earnings per share; $\sigma^2(\text{EPS})$ = variance of earnings per share; $\sigma(\text{EPS})$ = standard deviation of earnings per share.

to owners and creditors is the same. For example, if the return on assets is expected to be 15 percent, the *total* income to owners and creditors is $4,500 under each alternative:

Financing alternative	Income to owners	Income to creditors	Total income to owners and creditors
1: $10,000 equity	$4,500	$ 0	$4,500
2: $5,000 equity, $5,000 debt	4,000	500	4,500
3: $10,000 debt	3,500	1,000	4,500

This means Firm L, which has $10,000 of debt at an interest rate of 10 percent and a tax rate on income of 30 percent, has a $3,000 tax shield:

PVITS = 0.30($10,000) = **$3,000**

The fact that the Internal Revenue Code allows interest on debt to reduce taxable income *increases* the value of Firm L by $3,000.

Tax shields from interest deductibility are valuable: If a firm finances its assets with $50,000 of debt and has a tax rate of 30 percent, the tax shield from debt financing (and hence the increase in the value of the firm) is $15,000!

We can specify the value of the firm as:

$$\text{Value of the firm} = \frac{\text{value of the firm}}{\text{if all-equity financed}} + \frac{\text{present value}}{\text{of the interest tax shield}}$$

If the firm is expected to maintain the same amount of debt in its capital structure,

Value of the firm = value of the firm if all-equity financed + τD

Therefore, the value of the firm is supplemented by the tax subsidy resulting from the interest deducted from income.

Personal Taxes and Capital Structure

A firm's corporate taxes and debt affect its value: The more debt the firm uses, the more interest is deductible and the more income is shielded from taxes.

But personal taxes also enter into the picture. Who is going to buy this debt? Investors. But investors face personal taxes and have to make decisions about what investments they want to buy. And if their income from debt securities—their interest income—is taxed differently from their income on equity securities—their dividends and capital appreciation—this may affect how much they are willing to pay for the securities.[6] This affects the return the firm must offer investors on debt and equity to entice them to buy the securities.

We won't go through the mathematics of how personal taxes affect the interest rates a firm must offer. But we can look at the major conclusions regarding personal taxes and capital structure:

1. If debt income (interest) and equity income (dividends and capital appreciation) are taxed at the same rate, the interest tax shield is still τD and increasing leverage increases the value of the firm.
2. If debt income is taxed at higher rates than equity income, some of the tax advantage to debt is offset by a tax disadvantage to debt *income*. Whether the tax advantage from the deductibility of interest expenses is more than or less than the tax disadvantage of debt income depends on the firm's tax rate, the tax rate on debt income, and the tax rate on equity income. But since different investors are subject to different tax

---

[6] Equity income consists of dividends and capital appreciation. Under the present U.S. tax system capital appreciation is taxed more favorably (meaning at lower rates) than interest income, since (1) capital appreciation is not taxed until realized (for example, when shares of stock are sold) and (2) at times, a portion of the realized capital gain has been excluded from taxable income or taxed at lower rates.

rates (for example, pension funds are not taxed), determining whether there is a tax advantage or disadvantage is a problem.

3. If investors can use the tax laws effectively to reduce their tax on equity income to zero, firms will take on debt up to the point at which the tax advantage to debt is just offset by the tax disadvantage to debt income.[7]

The bottom line on incorporating personal taxes is that there is a benefit in using debt. It may not be as large as τD because of personal taxes, but it is generally viewed that personal taxes reduce some, but not all, of the benefit from the tax deductibility of debt.[8]

Unused Tax Shields

The value of an interest tax shield depends on whether or not the firm can use the interest expense deduction. In general, if a firm has deductions that *exceed* income, the result is a **net operating loss.** The firm need not pay taxes in the year of the loss and may "carry" this loss to another tax year.

This loss may be applied against previous years' taxable income (with some limits). The previous years' taxes are recalculated and a refund of taxes previously paid is requested. If there is insufficient previous years' taxable income to apply the loss against, any unused loss is carried over into future years (with some limits), reducing future years' taxable income.[9]

Therefore, when interest expense is larger than income before interest, the tax shield is realized immediately—*if* there is sufficient prior years' taxable income. If the prior years' taxable income is *insufficient* (that is, less than the operating loss created by the interest deduction), the tax shield is *less* valuable because the financial benefit is not received until some later tax year (if at all). In this case, we discount the tax shield to reflect both the uncertainty of benefiting from the shield and the time value of money.

To see how the value of an interest tax shield may become less valuable, let's suppose The Unfortunate Firm has the following financial results:

	THE UNFORTUNATE FIRM		
	Year 1	Year 2	Year 3
Taxable income before interest	$7,000	$ 8,000	$6,000
Interest expense	5,000	5,000	5,000
Taxable income	$2,000	$ 3,000	$1,000
Tax rate	0.40	0.40	0.40
Tax paid	$ 800	$1,200	$ 400

[7] This reasoning was developed by Merton Miller in "Debt and Taxes," *Journal of Finance*, vol. 34, no. 2, May 1977, pp. 261–276.

[8] Some argue that the benefit from $1 of debt is about 20 cents. See, for example, Ronald H. Masulis, "The Effect of Capital Structure Change on Security Prices: A Study of Exchange Offers," *Journal of Financial Economics*, vol. 8, no. 2, June 1980, pp. 139–177; and Ronald H. Masulis, "The Impact of Capital Structure Change on Firm Value," *Journal of Finance*, vol. 38, no. 1, March 1983, pp. 107–126.

[9] The tax code provisions, with respect to the number of years available for net operating loss carrybacks and carryovers has changed frequently. For example, under the Tax Reform Act of 1986, the Internal Revenue Code permits a carryback for three previous tax years and a carryforward for fifteen future tax years [IRC Sec. 172 (b), 1986 Code].

Suppose further that The Unfortunate Firm has the following result in Year 4:

THE UNFORTUNATE FIRM
Operating Results for Year 4

Taxable income before interest	$ 1,000
Less: Interest expense	8,000
Net operating loss	**−$7,000**

Suppose the tax code permits a carryback of three years and a carryover of fifteen years. The Unfortunate Firm can take the net operating loss of $7,000 and apply it against the taxable income of previous years, beginning with Year 1:

THE UNFORTUNATE FIRM

Calculation of tax refunds based on Year-4 net operating loss

	Year 1	Year 2	Year 3
Taxable income before interest	$7,000	$ 8,000	$6,000
Interest expense	5,000	5,000	5,000
Original taxable income	$2,000	$ 3,000	$1,000
Application of Year-4 loss	−2,000	−3,000	−1,000
Recalculated taxable income	$ 0	$ 0	$ 0
Recalculated tax due	$ 0	$ 0	$ 0
Refund of taxes paid	$ 800	$1,200	$ 400

By carrying back part of the loss, The Unfortunate Firm has applied $6,000 of its Year-4 loss against the previous years' taxable income: $2,000 (Year 1) + $3,000 (Year 2) + $1,000 (Year 3) and receives a tax refund of $2,400 (= $800 + $1,200 + $400). There remains an unused loss of $1,000 ($7,000 − $6,000). This loss can be applied toward future tax years' taxable income, reducing taxes in future years. But since we don't get the benefit from the $1,000 unused loss—the $1,000 reduction in taxes—until sometime in the future, the benefit is worth less than if we could use it today.

The Unfortunate Firm, with an interest deduction of $8,000, benefits from $7,000 of the deduction: $1,000 against current income and $6,000 against previous income. Therefore, the tax shield from the $8,000 is not $3,200 (40 percent of $8,000), but rather $2,800 (40 percent of $7,000) plus the present value of the taxes saved in future years. The present value of the taxes saved in future years depends on:

1. The uncertainty that The Unfortunate Firm will generate taxable income.
2. The time value of money.

The Unfortunate Firm's tax shield from the $8,000 interest expense is less than what it could have been because we couldn't use all of it now.

The bottom line of the analysis of unused tax shields is that the benefit from the interest deductibility of debt depends on whether or not the firm can use the interest deductions.

CAPITAL STRUCTURE AND FINAN- CIAL DISTRESS

A firm that has difficulty making payments to its creditors is in financial distress. Not all firms in financial distress ultimately enter into the legal status of bankruptcy. However, extreme financial distress may very well lead to bankruptcy.[10]

Costs of Financial Distress

The costs related to financial distress without legal bankruptcy can take different forms. For example, to meet creditors' demands, a firm may take on projects expected to provide a quick payback. In doing so, the financial manager may choose a project that decreases owners' wealth or may forgo a profitable project.

Another example of a cost of financial distress is the cost associated with lost sales. If a firm is having financial difficulties, potential customers may shy away from its products because they may perceive the firm as unable to provide maintenance, replacement parts, and warranties. If you are arranging your travel plans for your next vacation, do you want to buy a ticket to fly on an airline that is in financial difficulty and may not be around much longer? Lost sales due to customer concern represent a cost of financial distress—an opportunity cost, something of value (sales) that the firm would have had if it were not in financial difficulty.

Still another example of costs of financial distress are costs associated with suppliers. If there is concern over the ability of the firm to meet its obligations to creditors, many suppliers may be unwilling to extend trade credit or, if willing, may extend trade credit at less favorable terms. Also, suppliers may be unwilling to enter into long-term contracts to supply goods or materials. As a firm loses its long-term guarantees to certain goods or materials, the greater becomes the uncertainty that it will be able to obtain these items in the future and the higher will be the costs associated with renegotiating contracts.

> A profitable investment is one that provides a greater return than required by the suppliers of capital (that is, it has a positive net present value); an unprofitable investment is one that does not.

The Role of Limited Liability

Limited liability limits owners' liability for obligations to the amount of their original investment. Limited liability for owners of some forms of business creates a valuable right and an interesting incentive for owners. This valuable right is the right to default on obligations to creditors—that is, the right not to pay creditors. Since, with limited liability, the most owners can lose is their investment, there is an incentive for the firm to take on very risky projects. If the projects turn out well, the firm pays creditors only what is owed and keeps the rest, and if the projects turn out poorly, it pays creditors what is owed—*if* there is anything left.

We can see the benefit to owners from limited liability by comparing the Unlimited Company, whose owners have unlimited liability, and the Limited

---

[10] While bankruptcy is often a result of financial difficulties arising from problems in paying creditors, some bankruptcy filings are made prior to distress, when a large claim is made on assets (for example, a class-action liability suit).

The right to default is a call option: The owners have the option to buy back the entire firm by paying off the creditors at the face value of their debt. As with other types of options, the riskier are the cash flows, the more valuable is the option.

Company, whose owners have limited liability. Suppose that the two firms have the following identical capital structure in Year 1:

	Year 1	
	Unlimited Company	**Limited Company**
Debt	$ 1,000	$ 1,000
Equity	3,000	3,000
Total value of firm's assets	**$4,000**	**$4,000**

Owners' equity—their investment—is $3,000 in both cases.

If the value of the assets of both firms in Year 2 is increased to $5,000 (without increasing debt), the value of both debt and equity is the same for both firms:

	Year 2	
	Unlimited Company	**Limited Company**
Debt	$ 1,000	$ 1,000
Equity	4,000	4,000
Total value of firm's assets	**$5,000**	**$5,000**

Now suppose the total value of both firms' assets in Year 2 is instead $500. If there are insufficient assets to pay creditors the $1,000 owed them, the owners with unlimited liability must pay the difference (the $500). The owners with limited liability do not make up the difference, and the most the creditors can recover is the $500. The following table depicts the distribution of assets among creditors and owners:

	Year 2	
	Unlimited Company	**Limited Company**
Debt	$1,000	$ 500
Equity	−500	0
Total value of firm's assets	**$ 500**	**$500**

In this case, the Unlimited Company's owners must pay $500 to its creditors because the claim of the creditors is greater than the assets available to satisfy their claims. The Limited Company's creditors do not receive their full claim, and since the owners are shielded by limited liability, the creditors cannot approach the owners to pay the remaining $500 owed to them.

We can see the role of limited liability for a wider range of asset values by comparing the creditors' and owners' claims in Figures 13-6(*a*) for the Unlimited Company and Figure 13-6(*b*) for the Limited Company. In the case of

FIGURE 13-6(a)
Claims on Assets, Unlimited Company

If the firm's asset value is less than $1,000, creditors claim $1,000 and owners make up the difference out of their personal assets.

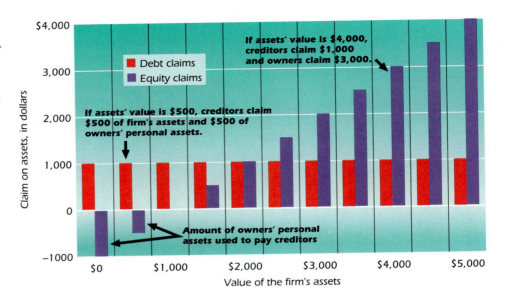

FIGURE 13-6(b)
Claims on Assets, Limited Company

If the firm's asset value is less than $1,000, the creditors can claim only the assets of the firm—they cannot claim the personal assets of the owners.

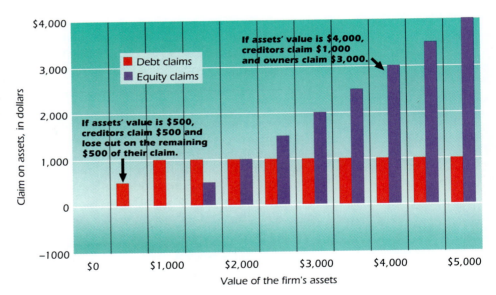

the Unlimited Company the creditors make their claims at the expense of the owners for asset values of less than $1,000. If the value of assets of the Unlimited Company is $500, the creditors recover the remaining $500 of their claim from the owners' personal assets (if there are any such assets). In the case of the Limited Company, however, if the assets' value is less than $1,000, the creditors cannot recover the full $1,000 owed them—they can't touch the personal assets of the owners![11]

---

[11] Lenders are aware of this dilemma and, for small businesses, often require managers (who are also shareholders) to be *personally* liable for the corporation's debts. This allows lenders to avoid the problem of limited owners' liability.

The fact that owners with limited liability can lose only their initial investment—the amount they pay for their shares—creates an incentive for owners to take on riskier projects than if they had unlimited liability: They have little to lose and much to gain. Owners of the Limited Company have an incentive to take on risky projects, since they can lose only their investment in the firm. But they can benefit substantially if the payoff on the investment is high.

For firms whose owners have limited liability, the more the assets are financed with debt, the greater the incentive to take on risky projects, leaving creditors "holding the bag" if the projects turn out to be unprofitable. This is a problem: There is a conflict of interest between owners' interests and creditors' interests. The investment decisions are made by managers (who represent the owners) and, because of limited liability, there is an incentive for managers to select risky projects that may harm creditors who have entrusted their funds (by lending them) to the firm.

> We refer to the relationship between creditors and owners as an *agency relationship:* the creditors are the *principals* and the owners (through the managers) are the *agents*.

However, creditors are aware of this and demand a higher return on debt (and hence a higher cost to the firm).[12] The result is that owners ultimately bear a higher cost of debt.

Bankruptcy and Bankruptcy Costs

When a firm is having difficulty paying its debts, there is a possibility that creditors will foreclose (that is, demand payment) on loans, causing the firm to sell assets which could impair the firm's operations or cause it to cease operations entirely. But if some creditors force payment, this may be disadvantageous to other creditors. As a result, what has developed is a process of dealing in an orderly way with a firm's payments to its creditors when the firm is having payment difficulties—the process is called *bankruptcy*.

Bankruptcy in the United States is governed by the Bankruptcy Code, created by the Bankruptcy Reform Act of 1978. A firm may be reorganized under Chapter 11 of this code, resulting in a restructuring of its claims, or liquidated under Chapter 7.[13]

Chapter 11 bankruptcy provides the troubled firm with protection from its creditors while it tries to overcome its financial difficulties.[14] A firm that files for bankruptcy under Chapter 11 continues as a going concern during the process of sorting out which of its creditors get paid and how much. On the other hand, a firm that files for bankruptcy under Chapter 7 is placed under the management of a trustee, who terminates the firm's operations, sells its assets, and distributes the proceeds to creditors and owners.

We can classify *bankruptcy costs* into direct and indirect costs. Direct costs include the legal, administrative, and accounting costs associated with the filing for bankruptcy and the administration of bankruptcy. These costs

---

[12] Michael Jensen and William H. Meckling analyze the agency problems associated with limited liability in "Theory of the Firm: Managerial Behavior, Agency Costs and Ownership Structure," *Journal of Financial Economics*, vol. 3, no. 4, 1976, pp. 305–360. They argue that creditors are aware of the firm's incentives to take on risky projects. Creditors will demand a higher return and may also require protective provisions in the loan contract.

[13] Bankruptcy Reform Act of 1978, P.L. 95-598.92 Stat. 2549.

[14] We should note that a firm filing for bankruptcy need not be technically insolvent. Some firms file for bankruptcy when faced with large expected liabilities (for example, A. H. Robbins), whereas others may file to avoid a potential insolvency (for example, Chicago Central Pacific Railroads).

are estimated to be 6.2 percent of the value of the firm prior to bankruptcy.[15] For example, the fees and expenses for attorneys representing shareholders and creditors' committees in the Zale Corporation's 1992 bankruptcy were approximately $1 million per week, which are quite large compared to Zale's assets of less than $2 billion.[16]

The indirect costs of bankruptcy are more difficult to evaluate. Operating a firm while in bankruptcy is difficult, since there are often delays in making decisions, creditors may not agree on the operations of the firm, and the objectives of creditors may be at variance with the objective of efficient operation of the firm, which is intended to maximize the wealth of the owners. One estimate of the indirect costs of bankruptcy, calculated by comparing actual and expected profits prior to bankruptcy, is 10.5 percent of the value of the firm prior to bankruptcy.[17]

Another indirect cost of bankruptcy is the loss in the value of certain assets. Since many intangible assets derive their value from the continuing operations of the firm, the disruption of operations in bankruptcy may change the value of the firm. The extent to which the value of a business enterprise depends on intangibles varies among industries and among firms; so the potential loss in value from financial distress varies as well. For example, a drug company may experience a greater disruption in its business activities, than say, a steel manufacturer, since much of the value of the drug company may be derived from research and development, leading to new products.

Financial Distress and Capital Structure

The relationship between financial distress and capital structure is simple: As more debt financing is used, fixed, legal obligations (interest and principal payments) increase, and the ability of the firm to satisfy these increasing, fixed payments decreases. Therefore, as more debt financing is used, the probability of financial distress and then bankruptcy increases.

For a given decrease in operating earnings, the greater the extent to which a firm uses debt in its capital structure (that is, the greater the firm's use of financial leverage), the greater is the firm's risk of not being able to satisfy its debt obligations and the greater the risk to owners' earnings.

Another factor to consider in assessing the probability of distress is the business risk of the firm. **Business risk** is the uncertainty associated with the earnings from operations. Business risk is uncertainty inherent in the type of business and can be thought of as comprising sales risk and operating risk.

Sales risk is the risk associated with sales as a result of economic and market forces that affect the volume and prices of goods or services sold.

Operating risk is the risk associated with the cost structure of the firm's assets. A cost structure is composed of both fixed and variable costs. The

We presented a more detailed discussion about business risk, sales risk, and operating risk in Chapter 7. In that chapter, we examined the sensitivity of a firm's earnings and cash flows to these sources of risk.

[15] The direct cost is taken from the report by Edward I. Altman, "A Further Empirical Investigation of the Bankruptcy Cost Question," *Journal of Finance*, vol. 39, no. 4, Sept. 1984, pp. 1067–1089, based on his study of industrial firms. An earlier study (Jerold B. Warner, "Bankruptcy Costs: Some Evidence," *Journal of Finance*, vol. 34, no. 2, May 1977, pp. 337–347) estimated the direct costs of bankruptcy to be approximately 5 percent of the prebankruptcy market value of the firm.

[16] *Business Week*, January 25, 1993, p. 37.

[17] The indirect cost estimate is taken from Altman, "A Further Empirical Investigation," p. 1077.

greater the use of fixed costs, relative to variable costs, the greater is the operating risk. If sales were to decline, the greater use of fixed costs in the operating cost structure would have an exaggerated effect on operating earnings. When an airline flies between any two cities, most of its costs are the same whether there is one passenger or one hundred passengers on board. Its costs are mostly fixed (fuel, pilot, gate fees, etc.), with very little in the way of variable costs (the cost of the meal and some fuel). Therefore, an airline's operating earnings are very sensitive to the number of tickets sold.

The effect of the mixture of fixed and variable costs on operating earnings is akin to the effect of debt financing (financial leverage) on earnings to owners. Here it is referred to as *operating leverage:* The greater are the fixed costs in the operating cost structure, the greater is the leveraging effect on operating earnings for a given change in sales. The greater is the business risk of the firm, the greater is the probability of financial distress.

Our concern in assessing the effect of distress on the value of the firm is the present value of the expected costs of distress. And the present value depends on the probability of financial distress: The greater is the probability of distress, the greater are the expected costs of distress.

The present value of the costs of financial distress increase with the increasing relative use of debt financing, since the probability of distress increases with increases in financial leverage. In other words, as the debt ratio increases, the present value of the costs of distress increases, lessening some of the value gained from the use of the tax deductibility feature of interest expense.

Summarizing the factors that influence the present value of the cost of financial distress:

1. The probability of financial distress increases with increases in business risk.
2. The probability of financial distress increases with increases in financial risk.
3. Limited liability increases the incentives for owners to take on greater business risk.
4. The costs of bankruptcy increase the more the value of the firm depends on intangible assets.

We do not know the precise manner in which the probability of distress increases as we increase the debt-to-equity ratio. Yet, it is reasonable to think that the probability of distress increases as a greater proportion of the firm's assets are financed with debt.

DOL and DFL

We saw in Chapter 7 how to calculate the degree of operating leverage (DOL), which is a measure of the sensitivity of operating earnings to a given change in units sold. The greater the DOL, the greater the firm's operating leverage and, hence, its operating risk.

We also saw how to calculate the degree of financial leverage (DFL), which is a measure of the sensitivity of owners' earnings to a given change in operating earnings. The greater is the DFL, the greater is the firm's financial leverage and, hence, its financial risk.

PUTTING TOGETHER FINANCIAL LEVERAGE, TAXES, AND THE COSTS OF FINANCIAL DISTRESS

As we increase the relative use of debt in the capital structure, we see that the value of the firm increases as a result of the tax shield of interest deductibility but that this benefit is eventually offset by the expected costs of financial distress. Weighing the value of the tax shield from interest against the costs of financial distress, we can see that there is some ratio of debt to equity that maximizes the value of the firm. Since we do not know the precise relationship between the tax shield and distress costs, we cannot specify, for a given firm, what the optimal debt-to-equity ratio should be. And although we have not yet considered other factors that may play a role in determining the value of the firm, we can say that:

- The benefit from the tax deductibility of interest increases as the debt-to-equity ratio increases.
- The present value of the cost of financial distress increases as the debt-to-equity ratio increases.

This trade-off between the tax deductibility of interest and the cost of distress can be summarized in terms of the value of the firm in the context of the Modigliani-Miller model:

$$\text{Value of the firm} = \text{value of the firm if all-equity financed} + \text{present value of the interest tax shield} - \text{present value of financial distress}$$

The value of the firm is affected by taxes and the costs of financial distress. As a firm becomes more leveraged financially (using more debt financing relative to equity financing), its value increases. And the costs associated with financial distress (both direct and indirect costs) reduce the value of the firm as financial leverage increases. Hence, the trade-off between the tax deductibility of interest and the costs of financial distress.

These considerations help to explain the choice between debt and equity in a firm's capital structure. As more debt is used in the capital structure, the benefit from taxes increases the firm's value, while the detriment from financial distress decreases its value. This trade-off is illustrated in the three graphs in Figures 13-7(*a*), 13-7(*b*), and 13-7(*c*), in which the value of the firm is plotted against the debt ratio:

Case 1   No interest tax deductibility and no costs of financial distress [Figure 13-7(*a*)].

Case 2   Tax deductibility of interest, but no costs of financial distress [Figure 13-7(*b*)].

Case 3   Tax deductibility of interest and costs of financial distress [Figure 13-7(*c*)].

Case 3 is the most comprehensive (and realistic) case. At moderate levels of financial leverage (low debt ratios), the value contributed by tax shields more than offsets the costs associated with financial distress. However, at some level of the debt ratio the detriment from financial distress may outweigh the benefit from corporate taxes, reducing the value of the firm as more debt is used. Hence, the value of the firm increases as more debt is taken on, up to some point, and then decreases.

At that point, the value of the firm begins to diminish as the probability of financial distress increases and the present value of the costs of distress outweighs the benefit from interest deductibility. The mix of debt and equity that maximizes the value of the firm is referred to as the ***optimal capital structure.*** This is the point at which the marginal benefit from taxes exactly offsets the marginal detriment from financial distress. The optimal capital structure is that mix of debt and equity that produces the highest value of the firm.

At first glance, the value enhancement from tax shields appears simple to calculate: Multiply the corporate tax rate times the face value of debt. How-

FIGURE 13-7(a)
Case 1

The value of the firm, assuming no interest deductibility and no costs of financial distress

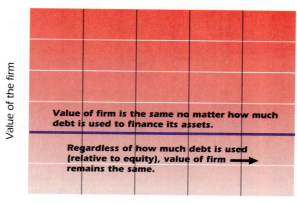

Value of firm is the same no matter how much debt is used to finance its assets.

Regardless of how much debt is used (relative to equity), value of firm → remains the same.

Value of the firm

Debt ratio

FIGURE 13-7(b)
Case 2

The value of the firm, assuming interest deductibility but no costs of financial distress

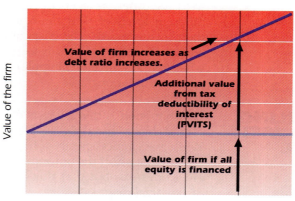

Value of firm increases as debt ratio increases.

Additional value from tax deductibility of interest (PVITS)

Value of firm if all equity is financed

Value of the firm

Debt ratio

FIGURE 13-7(c)
Case 3

The value of the firm, assuming interest deductibility and costs of financial distress

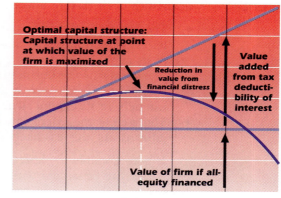

Optimal capital structure: Capital structure at point at which value of the firm is maximized

Reduction in value from financial distress

Value added from tax deductibility of interest

Value of firm if all-equity financed

Value of the firm

Debt ratio

ever, it is not that simple, for many reasons. The use of τD for valuation assumes that:

1. The marginal corporate tax rate remains constant.
2. Debt can be refinanced at current interest rates.
3. The firm will earn sufficient taxable income (before interest payments) to be able to use the interest deduction.

Marginal corporate tax rates change frequently, at the discretion of Congress. Interest rates change over time, and it is very unlikely that refinancing in, say, twenty years will be at current interest rates. Further, you cannot always predict that a company will generate future income that will be sufficient to cover interest expenses.

Furthermore, the expected costs of financial distress are difficult to calculate. You cannot simply look at a firm and figure out the probability of distress for different levels of financial leverage. The probability of distress at different levels of debt financing may differ among firms, depending upon their business risk. The costs of distress are also difficult to measure. These costs will differ from firm to firm, depending on the type of asset (that is, whether intangible or tangible) and the nature of the firm's suppliers and its customer relationships.

RECONCILING THEORY WITH PRACTICE

So what good is this analysis of the trade-off between the value of the interest tax shields and the costs of distress if we cannot apply it to a specific firm? While we cannot specify a firm's optimal capital structure, we *do* know the factors that affect the optimum. The analysis demonstrates that there is a benefit from taxes but that this benefit may eventually be reduced by the costs of financial distress.

Capital Structures among Different Industries

The analysis of the capital structure trade-off points up several financial characteristics of firms that affect the choice of capital structure:

*   The greater is the marginal tax rate, the greater is the benefit from interest deductibility and, hence, the more likely the firm is to use debt in its capital structure.
*   The greater is the business risk of a firm, the greater is the present value of financial distress and, therefore, the less likely the firm is to use debt in its capital structure.
*   The greater the extent to which the value of the firm depends on intangible assets, the less likely it is to use debt in its capital structure.

It is reasonable to expect these financial characteristics to differ among industries, but be similar within an industry. The marginal tax rate should be consistent within an industry, since:

*   The marginal tax rates are the same for all profitable firms;
*   The tax law provides specific tax deductions and credits (for example, depreciation allowances and research and development credits) that create some differences across industries, but generally apply to all firms within an industry since the asset structure and the nature of investment is consistent within an industry.

FASB Statement No. 94 and Capital Structure

FASB Statement No. 94 requires consolidation (combining together) of majority-owned subsidiaries in a firm's financial statements, even if their operations are quite different from the parent corporation's. It does not change a firm's capital structure, but it does alter a *source of information* we use for capital structure—the balance sheet. Using accounting rules, let's look at General Motors Corporation's 1991 liabilities, with and without consolidating its finance subsidiary, General Motors Acceptance Corporation:

	Without consolidation	With consolidation
Current liabilities	$30,221	$94,150
Long-term debt	19,057	40,683

If we are looking at General Motor's capital structure, do we use the debt figures with or without consolidation? If the parent corporation is ultimately liable for the debts of the subsidiary (such as through a guarantee), we should use the combined debt figure. If the parent corporation is not liable for the debts of the subsidiary, we should use the figures without consolidation.

SOURCE: Standard & Poor's *Compustat PC Plus* (CD-ROM).

- All the firms in an industry are subject to the same economic and market forces that may cause tax shields to be unusable. Therefore, it is reasonable to assume that the capital structures will be similar within industry groups.

Capital Structures within Industries

The capital structures differ among firms within industries for several possible reasons.

First, an industry may not be composed of a homogeneous group of firms. For example, Walt Disney Company, Caesars World, and Bowl America are all considered members of the amusement industry, but they have quite different types of business risk. The problem of industry groupings is exacerbated by the recent acquisitions boom—many industries now include firms with dissimilar product lines.

Adding to the difficulty in comparing firms is the recent Financial Standards Accounting Board (FASB) requirement that firms consolidate the accounting data of majority-owned subsidiaries.[18] The capital structure of the automobile manufacturers (for example, General Motors and Ford Motor Company) look quite different when the financing subsidiaries are included in the calculation of their debt ratios.

[18] Statement of Financial Accounting Standards No. 94, FASB, Stamford, Conn., 1987.

Book vs. Market Value of Equity

The **book value of equity,** also referred to as stockholders' equity, is the amount reported in the balance sheet. The book value of equity is the sum of the capital stock, paid-in capital, and retained earnings accounts, all of which reflect historical values, not current values.

The **market value of equity** is the value of owners' equity in the financial marketplace. We calculate it by multiplying the market price per share of stock times the number of shares outstanding.

Another reason an industry may appear to comprise firms with different capital structures is due to the way the debt ratio is calculated. We can see this in Table 13-3, in which the ratios of debt to the market value of equity are shown alongside the ratios for debt to the book value of equity for firms in the chemical industry.[19] Using book value of equity, the debt ratios range from 8.59 to 774.64 percent in the chemical industry; using the market value of equity, the debt ratios range from 9.62 to 104.56 percent.

Trade-off Theories and Observed Capital Structures

Trade-off theories can explain some of the capital structure variations that we observe. Firms whose value depends to a greater extent on intangibles than on tangibles, such as companies in the semiconductor and drug industries,

[19] The book value of debt is used in the calculation of both ratios in this table. This is necessitated by the lack of current market value data on long-term debt.

TABLE 13-3

Comparison of Debt-to-Equity Ratios, Book vs. Market Value of Equity, Corporations in the Chemical Industry, 1990

| | Ratio | | |
Corporation	Debt to book value of equity	Debt to market value of equity	Debt to total assets
Aceto	8.59%	9.62%	5.86%
Wisconsin Pharmaceuticals	9.19	4.52	6.03
Great Lakes Chemical	14.05	3.37	5.38
Chemdesign	15.26	11.80	10.87
Detrex	15.72	28.17	9.70
American Cyanamid	16.59	7.88	7.61
Imperial Chemical Industries	35.75	27.59	15.46
Akzo NV	36.62	51.50	12.43
Ferro	41.30	29.26	17.60
Monsanto	62.01	27.22	17.89
Olin	76.52	57.02	24.97
Dow Chemical	111.37	40.19	21.75
W. R. Grace	144.80	95.27	31.55
ICN Biomedical	279.82	49.66	22.91
FMC	774.64	104.56	39.15

SOURCE: Standard & Poor's, *Compustat PC Plus* (CD-ROM).

tend to have lower debt ratios. Firms in more volatile product markets, such as the electronics and telecommunications industries, tend to have lower debt ratios.

However, the trade-off theories cannot explain all observed capital structure behavior. We observe several profitable firms in the drug manufacturing industry that have no long-term debt (American Home products, Forest Laboratories, and Marion Laboratories). Though these firms do have a large investment in intangibles, they choose not to take on *any* debt at all. By taking on some debt, they could enhance the value of their firms. Yet they choose not to do so.

We also see firms that have high business risk and high debt ratios. Firms in the air transportation industry experience a volatile product market, with a high degree of operating leverage. Firms in this industry must invest heavily in jets, airport gates, and reservations systems, and have a history of difficulty with labor. However, these firms also have high debt ratios, averaging 86 percent of their assets financed with debt. One possible explanation for the large amount of financial leverage airlines take on in addition to their already high operating leverage is that their assets, such as jets and gates, can be sold quickly, offsetting the effects of the greater volatility in the companies' operating earnings. Whereas the high business risk increases the probability of financial distress, the liquidity of the assets reduces the probability of distress. But hindsight tells us more about the airline industry. The overcapacity of the industry just prior to the recession of 1989–1991 meant that there wasn't much of a market for used jets and planes. The airlines suffered during this economic recession: Of the fourteen firms in existence just prior to 1989, by 1993 four had entered bankruptcy (Continental, Pan Am, Midway, and America West), and two were liquidated (Eastern Airlines and Braniff).

ANOTHER POSSIBLE EXPLANATION

Looking at the financing behavior of firms in conjunction with their dividend and investment opportunities, we can make several observations:

- Firms prefer using internally generated capital (retained earnings) to externally raised funds (the proceeds of equity or debt issues).
- Firms try to avoid sudden changes in dividends.
- When internally generated funds are greater than needed for investment opportunities, firms pay off debt or invest in marketable securities.
- When internally generated funds are less than needed for investment opportunities, firms use existing cash balances or sell off marketable securities.
- If firms need to raise capital externally, they issue the safest security first, for example, debt is issued before preferred stock, which is issued before common stock.

The trade-off among taxes and the costs of financial distress leads to the belief that there is some optimal capital structure that maximizes the value of the firm. Yet, it is difficult to reconcile this with some observations of actual situations. Why?

One possible explanation is that the trade-off analysis is incomplete. We didn't consider the relative costs of raising funds from debt and equity. Since there are no out-of-pocket costs to raising internally generated funds (retained earnings), internal equity may be preferred to debt and to externally raised funds. Since the cost of issuing debt is less than the cost of raising a similar amount of external funds (issuing common stock), debt may be preferable to external funds.

Another explanation for the differences between what we observe and what we believe should exist is that firms may wish to build up ***financial slack,*** in the form of cash, marketable securities, or unused debt capacity, in order to avoid the high cost of issuing new equity.

Still another explanation is that financial managers may be concerned about the signal given to investors when equity is issued. It has been observed that the announcement of a new common stock issue is viewed as a negative signal, since the announcement is accompanied by a drop in the value of the equity of the firm. It has also been observed that the announcement of the issuance of debt does not affect the market value of equity. Therefore, the financial manager must consider the effect that the new security announcement may have on the value of equity, and hence, may shy away from issuing new equity.

The concern over the relative costs of debt and equity and over the interpretation by investors of the announcement of equity financing leads to a preferred ordering, or ***pecking order,*** of sources of capital: first internal equity, then debt, then preferred stock, then new common stock. It follows from this ordering that firms prefer to build up funds in the form of cash and marketable securities, so as not to be forced to issue equity at times when internal equity (retained earnings) is inadequate to meet new profitable investment opportunities.[20]

A CAPITAL STRUCTURE PRESCRIPTION

Factors Important in Selecting a Capital Structure

The analysis of the trade-off and pecking order explanations of capital structure suggests that there is no satisfactory explanation of capital structure. What is learned from an examination of these possible explanations is that there are several factors to consider in making the capital structure decision:

- *Taxes.* The tax deductibility of interest makes debt financing attractive. However, the benefit from debt financing is reduced if the firm cannot use the tax shields.
- *Risk.* Since financial distress is costly, even without legal bankruptcy, the likelihood of financial distress depends on the business risk of the firm, in addition to any risk from financial leverage.
- *Type of asset.* The cost of financial distress is likely to be higher for firms whose value depends on intangible assets and growth opportunities.
- *Financial slack.* The availability of funds to take advantage of profitable investment opportunities is advantageous. Therefore, having a store of cash, marketable securities, and unused debt capacity is advantageous.

---

[20] For a more complete discussion of the pecking order explanation, especially the role of asymmetric information, see Stewart C. Myers, "The Capital Structure Puzzle," *Journal of Finance,* vol. 39, no. 3, July 1984, pp. 575–592.

What's a Financial Manager to Do?

The financial manager's task is to assess the business risk of the firm, predicting the usability of future tax deductions, evaluating the likely effects of distress on asset values, and estimating the relative issuance costs of the alternative sources of capital. In the context of all these considerations, the financial manager can observe other firms in similar situations, using their decisions and consequences as a guide.

- Financial leverage is the use of fixed cost sources of funds. The effect of using financial leverage is to increase both the expected returns and the risk to owners.

- Taxes provide an incentive to take on debt, since interest paid on debt is a deductible expense for tax purposes, shielding income from taxation. But the possibility of incurring direct and indirect costs of financial distress discourages the taking on of high levels of debt.

- Taxes and financial distress costs result in a trade-off. For low debt ratios, the benefit of taxes more than overcomes the present value of costs of distress, resulting in increases in the value of the firm for increasing debt ratios. But beyond some debt ratio, the benefit of taxes is overcome by the costs of financial distress; the value of the firm decreases as debt is increased beyond this point.

- An explanation for the capital structures that we observe is that firms prefer to raise capital internally, but will raise capital externally according to a pecking order ranging from safe to riskier securities.

- We cannot figure out *the* best capital structure for a firm. We can, however, provide a checklist of factors to consider in the capital structure decision: taxes, business risk, asset type, issuance costs, and investor interpretations of security issuance announcements.

13-1 What is financial leverage and how does it affect the risk associated with future earnings to shareholders?

13-2 If the marginal tax rate on corporate income were to increase, what do you expect would be the effect of the increase on the tax shield from interest deductibility?

13-3 Consider three financing alternatives:

Alternative A Finance solely with equity
Alternative B Finance using half debt, half equity
Alternative C Finance solely with debt

a. Which of the three alternatives involves the greatest financial leverage?
b. Which of the three alternatives involves the least financial leverage?

13-4   List the potential costs associated with financial distress.

13-5   How does limited liability affect the incentives of shareholders to encourage investment in riskier projects?

13-6   List the potential direct and indirect costs associated with bankruptcy.

13-7   Shareholders may be viewed as having a call option on the firm. What is this call option? Identify the elements of an option in the context of the equity of a firm, specifically the:

    a. Exercise price
    b. Expiration date

13-8   Explain why firms in the electric utility industry tend to have higher debt ratios than firms in other industries.

13-9   Rank the following sources of capital in order of preference, according to the pecking order explanation of capital structure:

- Issue debt
- Sell shares of stock
- Use retained earnings

13-10   What is financial slack? Why do firms wish to have financial slack?

PROBLEMS

13-1   Consider the following information on the three firms A, B, and C:

Capital	Firm A	Firm B	Firm C
Debt	$1,000	$2,000	$3,000
Equity	3,000	2,000	1,000

    a. Calculate the debt ratio for each firm.
    b. Calculate the debt-to-assets ratio for each firm.

13-2   The Chew-Z Corporation is considering three possible financing arrangements to raise $10,000 of new capital. Currently, the capital structure of Chew-Z consists of no debt and $10,000 of equity. There are 500 shares of common stock currently outstanding, selling at $20 per share. In the next period, Chew-Z expects to generate $12,000 of earnings before interest and taxes. It is expected that the interest rate on any debt would be 10 percent. The three possible financing alternatives are:

    Alternative 1   Finance entirely with new equity
    Alternative 2   Finance using 50 percent debt and 50 percent new equity
    Alternative 3   Finance entirely with new debt

a. Calculate the following items for each alternative, assuming that there are no taxes on corporate income:

- Earnings to owners
- Earnings per share
- Distribution of income between creditors and shareholders

b. Calculate the following items for each alternative, assuming that the marginal rate of tax on corporate income is 40 percent:

- Earnings to owners
- Earnings per share
- Distribution of income among creditors, shareholders, and the government

13-3 The financial manager of the Variable Corporation has looked into the department's crystal ball and estimated the earnings per share for Variable under three possible outcomes. This crystal ball is a bit limited, for it can only make projections regarding earnings per share and the probability of their occurrence. Unfortunately, it cannot tell the financial manager which of the three possible outcomes will occur. The data provided by the crystal ball indicates:

Economic environment	Probability	Earnings per share
Good	50%	$10
OK	20	5
Bad	30	1

Help the financial manager assess these data by calculating expected earnings per share and its standard deviation.

13-4 Calculate the capitalization rate (discount rate) for equity for Firms D, E, and F:

Capital	Firm D	Firm E	Firm F
Debt	$1,500	$1,000	$2,000
Equity	1,500	2,000	1,000

Assume that there are no corporate income taxes and that the cost of equity for an unleveraged firm is 10 percent and the cost of risk-free debt is 6 percent.

13-5 The I. O. Corporation has $10,000 of debt in its capital structure. The interest rate on this debt is 10 percent. What is the present value of the tax shield from interest deductibility if the tax rate on corporate income is:

a. 0 percent?
b. 20 percent?
c. 40 percent?
d. 60 percent?
e. 80 percent?

13-6 The I. R. S. Corporation has $10,000 of debt in its capital structure. The interest rate on this debt is 10 percent. What is the present value of the tax shield from interest deductibility if the tax rate on corporate income is 45 percent?

13-7 The Lou Zer Corporation generated a net operating loss of $5,000 in 1995. Assume that the current tax law allows the loss to be carried back three years to reduce the previous years' taxes and that previous tax returns reveal the following information:

Tax year	Taxable income	Taxes paid
1994	$1,000	$ 400
1993	2,000	800
1992	3,000	1,200
1991	2,000	800

   a. What is the amount of tax refund that Lou Zer can apply for as a result of the 1995 loss?
   b. How would your answer differ if the tax law permitted the loss to be carried back only two years?

PC+ **13-8** **Research:** Select two industries and calculate the debt ratio and the debt-to-assets ratio for the three largest firms in the industry.
   a. Explain why the capital structure may differ between the two industries.
   b. Explain why the capital structure may differ among the firms in each industry.

   Recommended sources of information:

   - *Industrial Manual,* Moody's
   - *Compustat PC Plus* (CD-ROM), Standard & Poor's
   - *Value Line Investment Survey*

PC+ **13-9** **Research:** Select a corporation and describe its capital structure over the past five years, using the debt ratio and the debt-to-assets ratio.
   a. Has there been a change in capital structure over the years? If so, what has been this change?
   b. What is the corporation's marginal tax rate? What is the corporation's average tax rate?
   c. How does this corporation's capital structure differ from that of other firms in the same industry?
   d. What are the corporation's debt ratings? Is the corporation's debt investment grade?

   Recommended sources of information: See Problem 13-8.

PC+ **13-10** **Research:** Take a look at the airline industry and answer the following:
   a. How many firms are there in existence today?
   b. How many firms are currently in bankruptcy?
   c. How many firms currently have investment grade debt outstanding?

   Recommended sources of information: See Problem 13-8.

FURTHER READINGS

For an overview of the issues related to capital structure decision, see:
STEWART C. MYERS, "The Search for Optimal Capital Structure," *Midland Corporate Finance Journal*, vol.1, no.1, Spring 1983.

For a recent discussion and debate on the Modigliani and Miller propositions, see:
SUDIPTO BHATTACHARYA, "Corporate Finance and the Legacy of Miller and Modigliani," *Journal of Economic Perspectives*, vol. 2, no. 4, Fall 1988, pp. 135–148.
MERTON H. MILLER, "The Modigliani-Miller Propositions After Thirty Years," ibid., pp. 99–120.
FRANCO MODIGLIANI, "MM—Past, Present, and Future," ibid., pp. 149–158.
STEPHEN A. ROSS, "Comment on the Modigliani-Miller Propositions," ibid., vol. 2, no. 5, Fall 1988, pp. 127–134.
JOSEPH E. STIGLITZ, "Why Financial Structure Matters," ibid., vol. 2, no. 4, Fall 1988, pp. 121–126.

For an overview of the issues and evidence on capital structure, see:
RONALD W. MASULIS, *The Debt/Equity Choice*, The Institutional Investor Series in Finance, Cambridge, Massachusetts: Ballinger, 1988.
STEWART C. MYERS, "The Capital Structure Puzzle," *Journal of Finance*, vol. 39, no. 3, July 1984, pp. 575–592.

For an historical perspective on financing patterns, see:
ROBERT A. TAGGART, JR., "Corporate Financing: Too Much Debt?" *Financial Analysts Journal*, vol. 42, no. 3, May/June 1986, pp. 35–42.

For a discussion of the bankruptcy law and strategy, see:
MICHELLE J. WHITE, "The Corporate Bankruptcy Decision," *Journal of Economic Perspectives*, vol. 3, no. 2, Spring 1989, pp. 129–151.

CHAPTER 14

The Cost of Capital

INTRODUCTION 633

DETERMINING THE PROPORTION OF EACH CAPITAL COMPONENT 635

DETERMINING THE COST OF EACH CAPITAL COMPONENT 636

The Cost of Debt 636

The Cost of Preferred Stock 644

The Cost of Common Stock 646

    Cost of Common Stock Using the Dividend Valuation Model 647

    Cost of Common Stock Using the Capital Asset Pricing Model 650

PUTTING IT ALL TOGETHER: THE COST OF CAPITAL 653

The Marginal-Cost-of-Capital Schedule 653

The Marginal Cost of Capital and Shareholder Wealth Maximization 657

Practical Problems with the Marginal Cost of Capital 658

ESTIMATING THE COST OF CAPITAL FOR AN ACTUAL COMPANY 660

Step 1: Determine the Proportion of Each Capital Component 660

Step 2: Determine the Cost of Each Source of Capital 662

    The Cost of Debt 662

    The Cost of Preferred Stock 663

    The Cost of Common Stock 664

Step 3: Put It All Together 668

Caveats 669

Summary 670

Of Course, They Have a Lower Cost of Capital!

During the 1980s and early 1990s, U.S. competitiveness in the global market has been eroding and Japan's has increased. Some observers say this happened because the United States has a higher cost of capital than Japan. If this were true (that is, Japan had the lower cost of capital) it would mean that Japan would have more profitable (shareholder wealth-maximizing) investments.

Is the cost of capital in Japan really lower than in the United States? Evidence supporting this includes the following:

- Nominal yen interest rates are lower than nominal dollar interest rates.
- The savings rate in Japan is higher (increasing the supply of capital).

But there doesn't seem to be much difference between real interest rates (nominal rates adjusted for inflation) in the United States and Japan. And Japan's higher savings rate was accompanied by a higher demand for funds, which would be expected to offset the downward pressure on the opportunity cost of funds of Japanese investors.

There is another consideration, too. Firms in the United States, Japan, Europe, Africa, and elsewhere all compete for funds in the global marketplace. The world's financial markets are all interconnected. Because all firms compete in the global marketplace for the same capital, the cost of capital should reflect the firm's risk and the opportunity cost of the providers of capital. This means that U.S. firms are not necessarily disadvantaged relative to Japanese firms in the cost of capital.

But what about Japan, where the government provides cheaper capital? This assistance is usually provided with strings attached: a lower-cost capital is available *if* a firm invests in certain projects or in certain geographic areas. This is no different than the U.S. government's providing tax breaks for certain types of investment and providing the tax deductibility of interest!

And what about these lower-cost bank loans we observe for Japanese firms? Though the interest rates on these loans are typically lower than the rates U.S. firms experience, there are many implicit costs in the Japanese firm-bank relationship (such as high compensating balances) that end up increasing the effective cost of bank financing.

So why did the Japanese firms gain on U.S. firms in the past two decades? Probably not because of a cheaper cost of capital. Most likely because Japanese firms have different goals. U.S. firms consider the cost of capital in investment decisions and select projects whose returns exceed the returns required by the providers of capital. Japanese firms, on the other hand, most often are concerned with a different goal: maintaining or enhancing their position in the Japanese power system. It appears that Japanese firms are more concerned about the strategic goal of increasing the firm's market power, worrying about how to finance it (and the cost of this financing) once the investment decision is made.

The upshot of the difference in goals is that Japanese firms do not necessarily consider risk explicitly in their investment decision, leading them to take on riskier projects than might be acceptable to U.S. firms in similar situations. This is beneficial as long as optimistic conditions (such as a booming economy) exist. But this is detrimental if pessimistic conditions (such as a worldwide recession) exist.

NOTE: For a more detailed look at the differences in the costs of capital between the United States and Japan, see W. Carl Kester and Timothy A. Luehrman, "The Myth of Japan's Low-Cost Capital," *Harvard Business Review,* May/June 1992, pp. 130–138.

INTRODUCTION

You should already understand that to value an asset you need to know (1) the amount and timing of the future cash flows the asset is expected to produce and (2) the discount rate used to translate those future cash flows into a current value. This discount rate reflects how much an investor is willing to pay today for the right to receive a future cash flow. Or, saying that another way, the discount rate is the rate of return you require on your investment, given the price you are willing to pay for the expected future cash flow.

Suppose you are evaluating an investment that promises $10 every year forever. The value of this investment is the present value of the stream of $10s to be received each year to infinity, ∞, where each $10 is discounted at some rate r:

$$
\text{Present value of investment} = \frac{\$10}{(1+r)^1} + \frac{\$10}{(1+r)^2} + \frac{\$10}{(1+r)^3} + \cdots + \frac{\$10}{(1+r)^\infty}
$$

$$
= \sum_{t=1}^{\infty} \frac{\$10}{(1+r)^t}
$$

Because this is a perpetual stream:

$$
\text{Present value of investment} = \frac{\$10}{r}
$$

If the rate used to translate this future stream into a present value is 10 percent per year, the value of the investment is:

$$
\text{Present value of investment} = \frac{\$10}{0.10} = \$100
$$

Looking at this investment from another angle, if you consider the investment to be worth $100 today, you are valuing the future cash flows using a discount rate of 10 percent per year, which is also referred to as the ***capitalization rate.***

The discount rate for any perpetual stream of cash flow (CF) per period and present value (PV) is given by:

$$
PV = \frac{CV}{r} \qquad \text{or} \qquad r = \frac{CF}{PV}
$$

If you are willing to pay PV to receive a promised stream of CF per period *forever*, then you should require a return of r on your investment. In other words, r is the investor's ***required rate of return.*** From the perspective of the promisor of this stream, r is the ***cost of capital***—it's the borrower's cost to obtain the investor's funds.

The required rate of return on an investment and the value of the investment are intertwined. If you buy a bond, you expect to receive interest and the repayment of the principal in the future. The price you pay reflects your required rate of return. What determines your required rate? Your opportunity cost—the return you could have received on an investment with similar risk. Suppose that after you buy this bond, market interest rates increase. Your own required rate of return also rises. When your required rate of return increases, the value of your bond's future interest and principal fall, since the discount rate—the rate you would use to translate future cash flows into today's value—increases. The discount rate increases because it is a reflection of market interest rates.

The cost of capital and the required rate of return are *marginal* concepts. That is, the cost of capital is the cost associated with raising one more dollar of capital, and the required rate of return is the return expected on the investment of one more dollar.

Suppose you have already borrowed $10,000, promising to pay 5 percent interest per year. And suppose that if you need to borrow any more, you would have to pay 6 percent per year of the amount you borrow above $10,000. Then 6 percent is the *marginal* cost. The cost of what you have already borrowed is, in effect, history. How much you have already borrowed and what you are committed to pay will influence what you will have to pay to borrow further. That's because the more you are already paying for your borrowings, the greater the rate lenders will require of you to lend you more. That's why when we analyze the cost of a new investment, we need to think about the marginal costs of capital.

To make investment decisions of any kind, we need to know the cost of capital. In economics, you learned that a firm should produce goods to the point at which the firm's marginal benefit of producing them equals the marginal cost of their production. At that level of production, profit is maximized.

It's the same in investment and financing decisions: Invest in a project until the marginal cost of funds is equal to the marginal benefit the project provides. The benefit from an investment is its return, which we refer to as its **internal rate of return** (from the investor's perspective) or the **marginal efficiency of capital** (from the firm's perspective). This means that we keep on raising funds to invest in projects until the marginal cost of these funds is equal to the marginal benefit of the projects (which decreases as we take on more and more projects). Therefore, we need to know the marginal cost of funds before we can determine how much to invest in projects in our attempt to maximize shareholder wealth.

When we refer to the cost of capital for a firm, we are usually referring to the cost of financing its assets. In other words, it is the cost of capital for all the firm's projects taken together and, hence, is the cost of capital for the average-risk project of the firm.

When we refer to the cost of capital of a project, we are referring to the cost of capital that reflects the risk of that project. So why determine the cost of capital for the firm as a whole? For two reasons. First, the cost of capital for the firm is often used as a starting point (a benchmark) for determining the cost of capital for a specific project. The firm's cost of capital is adjusted upward or downward depending on whether the project's risk is more than or less than the firm's typical project.

Second, many of a firm's projects have risk similar to the risk of the firm as a whole. So the cost of the capital of the firm is a reasonable approximation for the cost of capital of any one of its possible projects that is under consideration for investment.

A firm's cost of capital is the cost of its long-term sources of funds: debt, preferred stock, and common stock. And the cost of each source reflects the risk of the assets the firm invests in. A firm that invests in assets having lit-

---

The terms "cost of capital" and "required rate of return" are often used as synonyms. Both terms reflect the same concept, but from a different perspective. As we shall see later in this chapter, the difference between the cost of capital and the required rate of return is due to taxes (in the case of debt) and the costs of issuing securities.

Marginal cost. Cost of producing the next unit of a good.
Marginal benefit. Benefit from selling the next unit of a good.

tle risk in producing income will be able to bear lower costs of capital than a firm that invests in assets having a higher risk of producing income. For example, a discount retail store has much less risk than an oil-drilling firm. Moreover, the cost of each source of funds reflects the hierarchy of the risk associated with its seniority over the other sources. For a given firm, the cost of funds raised through debt is less than the cost of funds from preferred stock, which, in turn, is less than the cost of funds from common stock. Why? Because creditors have seniority over preferred shareholders, who have seniority over common shareholders. If there are difficulties in meeting obligations, the creditors receive their promised interest and principal before the preferred shareholders, who, in turn, receive their promised dividends before the common shareholders. If the firm is liquidated, the funds from the sale of its assets are distributed first to debtholders, then to preferred shareholders, and then to common shareholders (*if* anything is left).

For a given firm, debt is less risky than preferred stock, which is less risky than common stock. Therefore, preferred shareholders require a greater return than the creditors, and common shareholders require a greater return than preferred shareholders.

Figuring out the cost of capital requires us to first determine the cost of each source of capital we expect the firm to use, along with the relative amounts of each source of capital we expect the firm to raise. Then we can determine the marginal cost of raising additional capital.

We can do this in three steps:

Step 1 Determine the proportions of each source to be raised as capital.
Step 2 Determine the marginal cost of each source.
Step 3 Calculate the weighted average cost of capital.

In this chapter, we look at each step. We first discuss how to determine the proportion of each source of capital to be used in our calculations. Next we calculate the cost of each source. The proportions of each source must be determined before calculating the cost of each source, since the proportions may affect the cost of the sources of capital.

Finally, we put together the cost and proportions of each source to calculate the firm's marginal cost of capital. We also demonstrate the calculation of the marginal cost of capital for an actual company, showing just how much judgment and how many assumptions go into calculating the cost of capital; that is, we show that it's an estimate.

DETERMINING THE PROPORTION OF EACH CAPITAL COMPONENT

The cost of capital for a firm is the cost of raising an additional dollar of capital. Suppose that a firm raises capital in the following proportions: debt 40 percent, preferred stock 10 percent, and common stock 50 percent. This means an additional dollar of capital will comprise 40 cents of debt, 10 cents of preferred stock, and 50 cents of common stock. We need to take into account the different costs of these different sources of capital.

Our goal as financial managers is to estimate the *optimum proportion* of each type of new capital for our firm to issue—not just in the next period, but well beyond.

If we assume that the firm maintains the same **capital structure**—the mix of debt, preferred stock, and common stock—throughout time, our task is simple. We just figure out the proportions of capital the firm has at present. If we look at the firm's balance sheet, we can calculate the book value of its debt, its preferred stock, and its common stock. With these three book values, we can calculate the proportion of debt, preferred stock, and common stock that the firm presently has. We could even look at these proportions over time to get a better idea of the typical mix of debt, preferred stock, and common stock.

But are book values going to tell us what we want to know? Probably not. What we are trying to determine is the mix of capital that the firm considers appropriate. It is reasonable to assume that the financial manager recognizes that the book values of capital are historical measures and looks instead at the market values of capital. Therefore, we must obtain the market value of debt, preferred stock, and common stock.

If the securities represented in a firm's capital are publicly traded—that is, listed on exchanges or traded in the over-the-counter market—we can obtain market values. If some capital is privately placed, such as an entire debt issue that was bought by an insurance company, or is not actively traded, our job is tougher but not impossible. For example, if we know the interest, maturity value, and maturity of a bond that is not traded and the yield on similar-risk bonds, we can get a rough estimate of the market value of that bond even though it is not traded.

Once we determine the market value of debt, preferred stock, and common stock, we calculate the sum of the market values of each and then figure out what proportion of this sum each source of capital represents.

But the mix of debt, preferred stock, and common stock that a firm has now may not be the mix it intends to use in the future. So while we may use the present capital structure as an approximation of the future, we really are interested in the firm's analysis and resulting decision regarding its *future* capital structure.

DETERMINING THE COST OF EACH CAPITAL COMPONENT

The Cost of Debt

The ***cost of debt*** is the cost associated with raising one more dollar by issuing debt. Suppose you borrow one dollar and promise to repay it in one year as well as an additional 10 cents to compensate the lender for the use of his money.

Since Congress allows you to deduct the interest you paid from your income, how much does this dollar of debt *really* cost you? It depends on your ***marginal tax rate***—the tax rate on your next dollar of taxable income. Why the marginal tax rate? Because we are interested in seeing how the interest deduction changes your tax bill. To see how, we will compare your tax expense with and without the interest deduction.

Suppose that before considering interest expense you have $2 of taxable income subject to a tax rate of 40 percent:

Taxable income	$2.00
Tax rate	×.40
Taxes	**$0.80**

Suppose your interest expense reduces your taxable income by 10 cents, reducing your taxes from 80 cents to 76 cents:

Taxable income	$1.90
Tax rate	×.40
Taxes	**$0.76**

By deducting the 10-cent interest expense, you have reduced your tax bill by 4 cents. You pay out the 10 cents and get a benefit of 4 cents. In effect, the cost of your debt is not 10 cents, but 6 cents—4 cents is the government's subsidy of your debt financing!

We can generalize this benefit of the tax deductibility of interest. Let r_d represent the cost of debt per year before considering the tax deductibility of interest; r_d^* represent the cost of debt after considering the tax deductibility of interest; and τ be the marginal tax rate. The effective cost of debt for a year is:

$$r_d^* = r_d(1 - \tau)$$

[14-1]

Using our example:

$$r_d = \frac{\$0.10}{\$1.00} = 10\% \quad \text{and} \quad \tau = \mathbf{40\%}$$

The effective cost of debt is:

$$r_d^* = 0.10(1 - 0.40) = \mathbf{0.06} \text{ or } \mathbf{6\%} \text{ per year}$$

Creditors *require* a return of 10 percent per year on the funds they lend. But it only *costs* you 6 percent per year.

In our example, the required rate of return is easy to figure out: You borrow $1 and repay $1.10; so your lender's required rate of return is 10 percent per year. But your cost of debt capital is 6 percent per year—less than the required rate of return—thanks to Congress. Most debt financing is not as straightforward, requiring us to figure out the yield on the debt—the lender's required rate of return—given information about interest payments and maturity value.

Let's look at an example of the firm's cost of a straight coupon bond. Suppose a firm issues new bonds that have a face value of $1,000, mature in twenty years, and pay interest at a rate of 10 percent semiannually. If these bonds are issued at face value, the required rate of return of this new debt capital, r_d, is the yield to maturity, YTM, of the bonds. The **yield to maturity** for these bonds is the discount rate that causes the present value of the future cash flows—the interest and maturity value—to equal today's price of the bonds:[1]

> We looked at yield to maturity in greater detail in Chapter 6.

$$\text{Present value of a coupon bond} = \text{present value of interest payments} + \text{present value of maturity value}$$

---

[1] Solving for the yield to maturity of a bond may be tedious without the use of a financial calculator. Solving for r_d without a financial calculator involves trial and error. Most financial calculators have special programming for solutions to bond problems.

The present value of the interest payments is the present value of an annuity. Let C indicate the interest payment, t the period, and T the number of periods left until maturity:

$$\text{Present value of interest payments} = \sum_{t=1}^{T} \frac{C}{(1 + r_{d,\text{six-months}})^t}$$

Since the maturity value, M, is a lump sum received at the end of the life of the bond:

$$\text{Present value of maturity value} = \frac{M}{(1 + r_{d,\text{six-months}})^T}$$

Putting together the present values of the interest payments and the maturity value:

$$\begin{array}{l}\text{Present value of}\\\text{a coupon bond}\end{array} = \sum_{t=1}^{T} \frac{C}{(1 + r_{d,\text{six-months}})^t} + \frac{M}{(1 + r_{d,\text{six-months}})^T} \qquad [14\text{-}2]$$

or, stated differently,

$$\begin{array}{l}\text{Present value of}\\\text{a coupon bond}\end{array} = C \underbrace{\sum_{t=1}^{T} \frac{1}{(1 + r_{d,\text{six-months}})^t}}_{\substack{\uparrow \\ \text{Present value} \\ \text{annuity factor}}} + M \underbrace{\frac{1}{(1 + r_{d,\text{six-months}})^T}}_{\substack{\uparrow \\ \text{Discount} \\ \text{factor}}}$$

We can solve for the yield to maturity in two ways:

1. Trial and error: Try different values for r_d until the right-hand side of the equation (the discounted value of interest and principal) is equal to the left-hand side (the value of the bond).
2. By using calculator or spreadsheet programs.

Investors are willing to pay a price today for the bond that reflects the present value of its future cash flows, so today's price is the bond's present value. Let's apply this valuation to the bond in our example, solving first for the six-month yield, $r_{d,\text{six-months}}$, and then translating this six-month yield into an effective annual yield to maturity, r_d:

Present value of bond = $1,000

$$\text{Interest, C} \qquad = \$1,000 \times \frac{10\%}{2} = \$50 \text{ every six months}$$

Number of periods, T = 20 × 2 = 40 six-month periods

Maturity value, M   = $1,000

We solve for $r_{d,\text{six-months}}$, the six-month yield:

$$\$1,000 \quad = \sum_{t=1}^{40} \frac{\$50}{(1 + r_{d,\text{six-months}})^t} + \frac{\$1,000}{(1 + r_{d,\text{six-months}})^{40}}$$

$r_{d,\text{six-months}} = 5\%$

This six-month yield is equivalent to an effective annual yield, r_d:

$r_d = (1 + 0.05)^2 - 1 = \mathbf{10.25\%}$ **per year**

Yielding on Yields

The annualized yield to maturity is calculated by multiplying the six-month yield by 2. If the six-month yield is 5 percent, then the annualized yield to maturity = $0.05 \times 2 = 10\%$ per year. This is the yield to maturity often quoted for debt instruments and is consistent with the practice of quoting coupon rates on an annualized basis. For example, a bond with a 10 percent coupon and with interest paid semiannually, pays 5 percent interest every six months.

However, the annualized yield to maturity is not the *effective* annual yield, since we know that interest is compounded; that is, investors receive the interest after the first six months and can reinvest the amount they receive during the second six months. Therefore, the *effective* annual yield, which takes compounding into consideration, is:

$$r_d = (1 + r_{d,\text{six-months}})^2 - 1 = (1 + 0.05)^2 - 1 = \mathbf{10.25\%} \text{ per year}$$

It is very important that all the costs of different sources of capital are stated on an effective annual basis. When we refer to the yield to maturity in our discussion of the cost of capital, we are referring to the effective annual rate, which we designate as r_d.

Suppose the firm is able to issue the 10 percent bonds at a price of $900 per bond and interest is not deductible from the firm's income.[2] The cost of debt would be greater than 10 percent because we are paying 10 percent based on the face value of $1,000, but we only get the use of $900. Using the equation for the present value of the bond, we first identify what we know:

Present value of bond = $900

Interest, C $\qquad = \$1,000 \times \dfrac{10\%}{2} = \$50$ every six months

Number of periods, T = $20 \times 2 = 40$ six-month periods

Maturity value, M $\quad = \$1,000$

Again, solve for $r_{d,\text{six-months}}$

$$\$900 \quad = \sum_{t=1}^{40} \frac{\$50}{(1 + r_{d,\text{six-months}})^t} + \frac{\$1,000}{(1 + r_{d,\text{six-months}})^{40}}$$

$r_{d,\text{six-months}} = \mathbf{5.6342\%}$ per period

which we convert into an effective annual yield:

$$r_d = (1 + 0.056342)^2 - 1 = \mathbf{11.59\%} \text{ per year}$$

---

[2] Realistically, firms do not typically issue bonds with such a large discount unless they issue a zero-coupon bond. However, since there is some lag between setting the coupon rate and the actual sale of the bonds to investors, many bonds sell for a slight premium or discount from face value because interest rates change quite often.

In this case, the return expected on the bond (the lender's required rate of return) and the cost of funds for the firm (the cost of debt) are 11.59 percent, since there is no other cost associated with raising funds from debt. Any costs associated with the issuance of debt—borrowing—are incorporated directly into the calculation of the cost of debt to the issuer, since the present value of the bond is the proceeds of the bond's issuer—the price of the bond less costs of issuance.

Now let's consider the costs of issuance, called the **flotation costs,** which are the payments to lawyers, accountants, and investment bankers who assist the firm in issuing debt securities (as well as preferred stock and common stock).[3] If these bonds are sold at $900 per bond, investors will require a rate of return of 11.59 percent, as we just determined.

But if the firm gets only $890 per bond (the flotation costs are $10 per bond), this means the cost to the firm is *more* than 11.59 percent per year:

$$\$890 = \sum_{t=1}^{40} \frac{\$50}{(1 + r_{d,\text{six-months}})^t} + \frac{\$1,000}{(1 + r_{d,\text{six-months}})^{40}}$$

$$r_{d,\text{six-months}} = \mathbf{5.7040\%} \text{ per period}$$

which we convert into an annual yield:

$$r_d = (1 + 0.057040)^2 - 1 = \mathbf{11.73\%} \text{ per year}$$

Flotation costs of $10 per bond increase the cost of the bond to the firm from 11.59 percent to 11.73 percent. But investors pay $900 a bond, which reflects their *required rate of return* of 11.59%.

Next we consider the tax deductibility of interest. If a dollar of interest is paid, is the interest cost to the firm one dollar? No, because interest on debt *is* deductible for tax purposes.[4] Since interest expense reduces income, a dollar of interest reduces taxable income by one dollar. If the firm issues the 10 percent bonds at par, with interest paid annually and no flotation costs, and has a 40 percent marginal tax rate, the after-tax cost of debt is 6 percent per year:

$$r_d^* = 0.10(1 - 0.40) = \mathbf{0.06} \text{ or } \mathbf{6\%} \text{ per year}$$

If the firm issues the 10 percent bonds at 90 (this is financial reporting shorthand, so to speak, meaning 90 percent of the bond's face value, or $900 per bond), with no flotation costs, the before-tax cost of debt is 11.59 percent and the after-tax cost is:

$$r_d^* = 0.1159(1 - 0.40) = \mathbf{0.0695} \text{ or } \mathbf{6.95\%} \text{ per year}$$

But to be complete we must include flotation costs. If the firm issues the 10 percent bonds at 90, receiving only $890 per bond after flotation costs (a before-tax cost of 11.73 percent), the after-tax cost of debt, r_d^*, is:

$$r_d^* = 0.1173(1 - 0.40) = \mathbf{0.0704} \text{ or } \mathbf{7.04\%} \text{ per year}$$

[3] The process of issuing securities and the costs of issuance are discussed in Appendix 14A.

[4] It is generally the case that interest on debt is deductible for tax purposes. However, the Tax Reform Act of 1986 reduced or eliminated the deductibility of interest paid on some forms of personal debt.

Therefore, the tax deductibility of interest reduces the cost of debt to the borrower.

The greater is the marginal tax rate, the greater is the benefit from deductibility and, hence, the lower is the cost of debt. For example, the cost of 10 percent coupon bonds for different marginal tax rates, with annual interest and no flotation costs, is:

Marginal tax rate	After-tax cost of debt (r_d^*)
20%	8%
40	6
60	4
80	2

Not all bonds are straight coupon bonds. Suppose we issue a zero-coupon bond. Though there is no interest paid in cash each year, there is *implicit* interest. We are allowed to deduct the implicit interest each period for tax purposes, even though we do not pay interest each period.[5]

Suppose we issue a zero-coupon bond at the beginning of 1996 that matures in five years and has a face value of $1,000. If this bond does not pay interest—not explicitly at least—no one will buy it at its face value. Instead, investors will pay some amount *less* than the face value, and the return they will require will be based on the difference between what they pay for the bond and (assuming they hold it to maturity) the face value. If the bonds are issued at 60, which means 60 percent of the $1,000 face value or $600, what is the yield to maturity? We compare today's value—the present value of the bond, which is $600—with the future value of the bond—the maturity value, which is $1,000. We can start with the basic valuation relation:

$$FV = PV (1 + r)^T$$

where FV = future value
     PV = present value
      r = interest per period
      T = number of periods

Modifying this to fit our needs:

Maturity value = present value $(1 + r_d)^T$

First, let's identify the known values:

Maturity value, M = $1,000
Present value, PV = $600
Number of periods, T = 5

---

[5] The flip side to this is that investors report interest income on their tax returns for the amount of the implicit income, even though they do not receive any cash.

We then insert these known values into the equation and solve for the one unknown, r_d:

$$\$1{,}000 = \$600\,(1 + r_d)^5$$

$$\frac{\$1{,}000}{\$600} = (1 + r_d)^5$$

$$1.6667 = (1 + r_d)^5$$

$$r_d = \sqrt[5]{1.6667} - 1 = \textbf{0.1076} \text{ or } \textbf{10.76\%} \text{ per year}$$

The implicit interest over the life of the bond is the difference between the face value and the issue price, $600. The implicit interest for a *given year* is the growth in the value of the bond during the year that is expected *at the time the bond is issued*.[6] For example, the implicit interest for the first year is the difference between the $600 issue price and the amount grown—accrued—in one year at 10.76% per year:

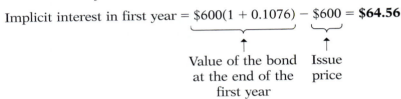

Implicit interest in first year = $600(1 + 0.1076) − $600 = **$64.56**

Value of the bond at the end of the first year   Issue price

We can see the growth in the implicit interest (due to compounding) for each year by comparing the end-of-period accrued value of the bond with the previous period's accrued value:

Year	End-of-period accrued value	Previous-period accrued value	Implicit interest
1996	$ 664.56	$600.00	$64.56
1997	736.07	664.56	71.51
1998	815.27	736.07	79.20
1999	902.99	815.27	87.72
2000	1,000.00	902.99	97.01

Each period, we deduct the implicit interest expense on our tax return to arrive at taxable income.

There is a tax benefit from interest deductibility, just as there was with a coupon bond. For example, in the year 2000, the accrued interest is $64.56, which is 10.76 percent of the beginning-of-the-year value of $600.00. The issuer deducts $64.56 interest from her income for tax purposes. If the marginal tax rate is 40 percent, the effective cost per bond is:

$$r_d^* = 0.1076(1 - 0.40) = \textbf{0.0646} \text{ or } \textbf{6.46\%} \text{ per year}$$

---

[6] The implicit interest does not depend on what happens to the actual price of the bond; rather, it depends only on the price of the bond at issuance and its time path, assuming the bond is held to maturity.

Riding the Yield Curve

Even for debt that has similar credit risk, the yields may be different among securities because these securities have different times remaining to maturity. The relation between the yield on securities and the time remaining to maturity is called the **term structure of interest rates.** This relationship is depicted using a graphical representation referred to as a **yield curve,** which is typically upward sloping, with longer term securities having higher yields than shorter term securities,

but at times has been downward sloping.

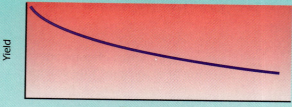

There are several explanations for the different yields for different maturities. The first explanation is the **expectations hypothesis,** which states that the relation depends on expectations about future inflation. An upward sloping term structure indicates that inflation is expected to increase in the future.

The second explanation is the **market segmentation hypothesis,** which states that the relation between yield and time to maturity is influenced by the supply and demand for securities of different maturities. An upward sloping curve would indicate a greater demand for shorter maturity securities relative to longer maturities.

The last explanation is the **liquidity preference theory,** which suggests that the curve should be upward sloping because investors prefer shorter term securities to longer term securities. Thus, a higher yield is necessary to entice investors to invest in longer term securities.

All three explanations have some validity. The relation between yield and maturity is most likely influenced by inflation expectations, supply and demand forces, and investors' preference for liquidity.

The term structure of interest rates affects a firm's cost of capital since the firm has different costs of capital depending on the maturity of the security.

As you can see from our calculations for a straight coupon bond and a zero-coupon bond, the starting point is the investor's required rate of return. Once we have that rate, we adjust it for flotation costs and the issuer's tax benefit from interest deductibility.

The Cost of Preferred Stock

The *cost of preferred stock* is the cost associated with raising one more dollar of capital by issuing shares of preferred stock. Preferred stock is a perpetual security—it never matures. Consider the typical preferred stock with a fixed dividend rate, where the dividend is expressed as a percentage of the par value of a share.[7]

The value of preferred stock is the present value of all future dividends to be received by the investor. If a share of preferred stock has a 5 percent dividend (based on a $100 par value) paid at the end of each year, the value of the stock today is the present value of the stream of $5s forever:

$$\text{Present value of preferred stock} = \frac{\$5}{(1+r)^1} + \frac{\$5}{(1+r)^2} + \cdots + \frac{\$5}{(1+r)^\infty}$$

$$= \sum_{t=1}^{\infty} \frac{\$5}{(1+r)^t}$$

> We looked at the valuation and returns on preferred stock in Chapter 6.

This series of constant amounts divided by a denominator that is growing at a constant rate collapses to:

$$\text{Present value of preferred stock} = \frac{\$5}{r}$$

If the discount rate is 10 percent per year:

$$\text{Present value of preferred stock} = \frac{\$5}{0.10} = \mathbf{\$50}$$

That is, investors are willing to pay $50 today for the promised stream of $5 per year because they consider 10 percent per year to be sufficient compensation for the time value of money and the risk associated with the perpetual stream of $5 annual dividends.

Let's rephrase this relationship letting P_p indicate today's price, which is the present value of the preferred stock; D_p indicate the perpetual dividend per share per period; and r_p indicate the discount rate, which is the cost of preferred stock capital. Then:

$$P_p = \frac{D_p}{r_p}$$

We can turn this equation around to solve for r_p, given P_p and D_p:

$$r_p = \frac{D_p}{P_p} \qquad [14\text{-}3]$$

[7] The determination of the cost of preferred equity becomes much more complex for dividend rates that are not fixed or nearly constant. If the dividend rate is adjusted frequently, the preferred shares will trade around their par value and the required rate of return (and hence the cost of capital) will fluctuate as market rates on preferred shares fluctuate.

Consider a share of preferred stock with a price of $100 and a dividend rate of 12 percent per year:

$D_p = \$100 \times 12\% = \$12$ per share
$P_p = \$100$

We want to solve for the discount rate that equates the discounted value of future dividends with today's price. This discount rate is the cost of preferred stock, r_p, which is also the required rate of return on preferred stock:

$$r_p = \frac{\$12}{\$100} = \textbf{0.12} \text{ or } \textbf{12\%}$$

But an issuer must pay flotation costs. In this case, the proceeds of the issue would not be $100 per share, but less. If the flotation costs are 2 percent of the price of the stock when it is issued (thus, $2 per share), the issuer's proceeds from the sale of a share of preferred stock would be $98 instead of $100. Therefore, the issuer's cost of preferred stock is *more* than 12 percent because of the flotation costs. We know:

$D_p = \$100 \times 12\% = \$12$ per share   and $P_p = \$98$

and wish to solve for the issuer's cost of preferred stock, r_p:

$$r_p = \frac{\$12}{\$98} = \textbf{0.1225} \text{ or } \textbf{12.25\%} \text{ per year}$$

But the investors' required rate of return on the preferred stock is 12 percent per year, since they are willing to pay $100 to get a future perpetual stream of $12 per year.

We can rewrite the equation for the cost of preferred stock to include flotation costs. Let f represent the percentage of the share's price that is paid in flotation costs. Then:

$$r_p = \frac{D_p}{P_p(1 - f)} \qquad\qquad\qquad [14\text{-}4]$$

Substituting the figures in our example:

$$r_p = \frac{\$12}{\$100(1 - 0.02)} = \frac{\$12}{\$98} = \textbf{0.1225} \text{ or } \textbf{12.25\%} \text{ per year}$$

Since dividends paid on preferred stock are not deductible as an expense for the issuer's tax purposes, the cost of preferred stock is not adjusted for taxes—dividends paid on this stock are paid out of *after-tax* dollars. Therefore, the difference between the investor's required rate of return and the issuer's cost of preferred stock is due only to flotation costs.

Up to now, we have simplified the yield on preferred stock by assuming that dividends are paid at the end of the year, so the r_p we calculate is the effective rate of return on preferred stock. But dividends on preferred stock are typically paid on a quarterly basis, so we need first to calculate the yield on a quarterly basis and then transform the result into an effective annual rate.

To see how to do this, suppose we have a preferred stock with a par value and a price of $100 that pays dividends of 12 percent per year, paid quarterly ($3 each quarter). The quarterly yield, $r_{p,quarterly}$, is:

$$r_{p,quarterly} = \frac{\$3}{\$100} = 3\%$$

and the effective annual yield on the preferred stock is:

$$r_p = (1 + 0.03)^4 - 1 = \mathbf{12.55\%} \text{ per year}$$

If it costs the firm $2 per share to issue this stock, then:

$$r_{p,quarterly} = \frac{\$3}{\$98} = 3.06\% \quad \text{and} \quad r_p = (1 + 0.0306)^4 - 1 = \mathbf{12.81\%}$$

You can see that taking into account the reinvestment of the quarterly dividends increases the required rate of return on preferred stock and the cost of preferred capital.

The Cost of Common Stock

The **cost of common stock** is the cost of raising one more dollar of common equity capital, either internally (from earnings retained in the firm) or externally (by issuing new shares of common stock). There are costs associated with both internally and externally generated capital.

"Equity" is the ownership interest of a firm. When referring to a corporation, we can use the terms "equity," "owners' equity," and "stock" interchangeably. When we want to be specific about the type of stock, preferred or common, we can use the terms "preferred equity" and "preferred stock" interchangeably and the terms "common equity" and "common stock" interchangeably.

How can internally generated capital—retained earnings—have a cost? As a firm generates internal funds, some portion is used to pay off creditors and preferred shareholders. The remainder are funds owned by the common shareholders. The firm may either retain these funds (investing in assets) or pay them out to the shareholders in the form of cash dividends.

Retained Earnings Is *Not* a Cash Account

The balance sheet account Retained Earnings is a record of the accumulation of earnings generated by the firm, less any dividends paid to owners. This accumulation starts when the firm first incorporates; so it is the sum of *all* past earnings less *all* past dividends.

Shareholders will require their firm to use retained earnings to generate a return that is at least as large as the return they could have generated for themselves if they had received as dividends the amount of funds represented in the retained earnings.

Retained funds are *not* a free source of capital. The cost of internal equity funds is the opportunity cost of funds of the firm's shareholders. This opportunity cost is what shareholders could earn on these funds at the same level of risk.

The only difference between the cost of internally and externally generated funds is the cost of issuing new common stock. The cost of internally generated funds is the opportunity cost of those funds—what shareholders could have earned on these funds. But the cost of externally generated funds (that is, funds obtained by selling new shares of stock) is the sum of the opportunity cost and the cost of issuing the new stock.

The cost of issuing common stock is difficult to estimate because of the nature of the cash flow streams to common shareholders. Common shareholders receive their return (on their investment in the stock) in the form of dividends and changes in the price of the shares they own. The dividend stream is not fixed, as in the case of preferred stock. How often and how much is paid as dividends is at the discretion of the board of directors. Therefore, this stream is unknown (and its value is therefore difficult to determine).

The change in the price of shares is also difficult to estimate; the price of the stock at any future point in time is influenced by investors' expectations of cash flows further into the future beyond that point.

Nevertheless, there are two methods commonly used to estimate the cost of common stock: the dividend valuation model and the capital asset pricing model. Each method relies on different assumptions regarding the cost of equity; each produces different estimates of the cost of common equity.

Cost of Common Stock Using the Dividend Valuation Model

The ***dividend valuation model*** (DVM) states that the price of a share of stock is the present value of all its future cash dividends, where the future dividends are discounted at the required rate of return on equity, r:[8]

$$\text{Price of common stock} = \frac{\text{dividends in first period}}{(1 + r)^1} + \frac{\text{dividends in second period}}{(1 + r)^2} + \cdots$$

If these dividends are constant forever (similar to the dividends of preferred stock, which we just covered), the cost of common stock is derived from the value of a perpetuity. Let D represent the constant dividend per share of common stock that is expected next period and each period after that forever; P_0, the current price of a share of stock; and r_e, the cost of common stock. The current price of a share of common stock is:

$$P_0 = \frac{D}{r_e}$$

[8] The DVM is attributed to Myron Gordon. A more formal presentation of this model can be found in his "Dividends, Earnings and Stock Prices," *Review of Economics and Statistics*, May 1959, pp. 99–105, and *The Investment Financing and Valuation of the Corporation*, Irwin, Homewood, Ill., 1962.

We can solve for r_e:

$$r_e = \frac{D}{P_0}$$

However, common stock dividends do not usually remain constant. It's typical for dividends to grow at a constant rate. Let D_0 indicate this period's dividend. If dividends grow at a constant rate, g, forever, the present value of the common stock is the present value of all *future* dividends:

$$P_0 = \frac{D_0(1 + g)^1}{(1 + r_e)^1} + \frac{D_0(1 + g)^2}{(1 + r_e)^2} + \cdots + \frac{D_0(1 + g)^\infty}{(1 + r_e)^\infty}$$

Pulling today's dividend, D_0, from each term,

$$P_0 = D_0\left[\frac{(1 + g)^1}{(1 + r_e)^1} + \frac{(1 + g)^2}{(1 + r_e)^2} + \cdots + \frac{(1 + g)^\infty}{(1 + r_e)^\infty}\right]$$

Expressing this in summation notation:

$$P_0 = D_0\sum_{t=1}^{\infty}\frac{(1 + g)^t}{(1 + r_e)^t}$$

The summation term is approximately equal to $(1 + g)/(r_e - g)$, so we can rewrite the price of the common stock as:

$$P_0 = D_0\frac{(1 + g)}{(r_e - g)}$$

If we refer to the next period's dividend, D_1, as this period's dividend, D_0, compounded one period at the rate g,

$$D_1 = D_0(1 + g)$$

then

$$P_0 = \frac{D_1}{(r_e - g)}$$

Rearranging this equation to solve for r_e:

$$r_e = \frac{D_1}{P_0} + g \qquad\qquad\qquad\qquad [14\text{-}5]$$

we see that the cost of common stock is the sum of next period's **dividend yield,** D_1/P_0, plus the growth rate of dividends:

Cost of common stock = dividend yield + growth rate of dividends

Consider a firm expected to pay a constant dividend of $2 per share per year forever. If the firm issues stock at $20 a share, the firm's cost of common stock is:

$$r_e = \frac{\$2}{\$20} = \mathbf{0.10}\text{ or }\mathbf{10\%}\text{ per year}$$

But if dividends are expected to be $2 in the next period and to grow at a rate of 3 percent per year, and the required rate of return is 10 percent per year, the expected price per share (with $D_1 = \$2$ and $g = 3$ percent) is:

$$P_0 = \frac{\$2}{0.10 - 0.03} = \mathbf{\$28.57}$$

which is more than $8 above the price if there is no expected growth in dividends.

As with preferred stock and bonds, we can be more precise in our estimate of the cost of common stock if we take into account the reinvestment of the dividends during the year, since common stock dividends are typically received quarterly. Let's take the example of the common stock whose dividend is $2 per year and whose price is $20 per share. If these dividends are paid quarterly ($0.50 per quarter), the cost of common stock is determined by first calculating the quarterly yield and then compounding that result for the entire year:

$$r_{e,\text{quarterly}} = \frac{\$0.50}{\$20} = 0.025$$

The effective annual cost of common equity is:

$$r_e = (1 + 0.025)^4 - 1 = \mathbf{10.38\%} \text{ per year}$$

While the compounding of the quarterly cost of common stock is palatable (in terms of accounting for the reinvestment of dividends), there is a problem with this approach: We observe that for many firms, it's the annual dividend that tends to grow at a constant rate, not the quarterly dividend. This means that using the dividend valuation model to determine the effective cost of common equity when dividends grow annually is a bit more complicated than what we've presented here. So what do we do? Typically, the annual approximation (ignoring the reinvestment of dividends during the year) is used, as shown in Equation 14-5, with D_1 being next year's total dividend. This results in a slight understatement of the cost of common equity. [9]

The DVM regarding the relation between the cost of equity and the dividend payments reflects two ideas that make some sense:

- The greater is the current dividend yield, the greater is the cost of equity.
- The greater is the growth in dividends, the greater is the cost of equity.

However, the DVM has some drawbacks:

- How do you deal with dividends that do not grow at a constant rate? This model does not accommodate nonconstant growth easily.

---

[9] A possible solution to this dilemma is presented by Charles M. Linke and J. Kenton Zumwalt, "Estimation Biases in Discounted Cash Flow Analyses of Equity Capital Cost in Rate Regulation," *Financial Management*, vol. 13, no. 3, Autumn 1984, pp. 15–21. This solution requires translating the annual growth rate into a quarterly growth rate, producing an approximation for the cost of common stock.

- What if the firm does not pay dividends now? In that case, D_1 would be zero and the expected price would be zero. But a zero price for stock does not make any sense! And if dividends are expected in the future, but there are no current dividends, what do you do?
- What if the growth rate of dividends is greater than the required rate of return? This implies a negative stock price, which isn't possible.
- What if the stock price is not readily available, say, in the case of a privately held firm? This would require an estimate of the share price.

Therefore, the DVM may be appropriate to use to determine the cost of equity for companies with stable dividend policies, but it may not be applicable to all firms.

Cost of Common Stock Using the Capital Asset Pricing Model

The investor's required rate of return is compensation for both the time value of money and risk. To figure out how much compensation there should be for risk, we first have to understand *what* risk we are talking about.

The *capital asset pricing model* (CAPM) assumes that an investor holds a *diversified portfolio*—a collection of investments whose returns are not in synch with one another. The returns on the assets in a diversified portfolio do not all move in the same direction nor at the same time nor by the same amount. The result is that the only risk left in the portfolio as a whole is the risk related to movements in the market as a whole—*market risk.*

If investors hold diversified portfolios, the only risk they have is market risk. Investors are *risk averse,* meaning they don't like risk. And if they are going to take on risk they want to be compensated for it. Investors who bear only market risk need be compensated only for market risk.

If we assume all shareholders hold diversified portfolios, the risk that is relevant in valuing a particular investment is the market risk of that investment. It is this market risk that determines the investment's value. The greater is the market risk, the greater is the compensation—meaning the higher the yield—for bearing this risk. And the greater is the yield, the lower is the present value of the asset because expected future cash flows are discounted at a higher rate that reflects the higher risk.

The cost of common stock is the sum of the investor's compensation for the time value of money and the investor's compensation for the market risk of the stock:

$$\text{Cost of common stock} = \frac{\text{compensation for the}}{\text{time value of money}} + \frac{\text{compensation}}{\text{for market risk}}$$

Let's represent the compensation for the time value of money as the expected risk-free rate of interest, r_f. If a particular common stock has market risk that is the *same* as the risk of the market as a whole, then the compensation for that stock's market risk is the *market risk premium.* The market's risk premium is the difference between the expected return on the market, r_m, and the expected risk-free rate, r_f:

$$\text{Market risk premium} = r_m - r_f$$

The *risk-free rate of interest* is the rate that is earned on an asset that has no risk.

Market Risk Is a Portfolio's Relevant Risk

A portfolio may have assets whose returns are not perfectly positively correlated; that is, the assets' prices do not all move in the same direction nor at exactly the same time nor by precisely the same amount.

We can eliminate some—but not all—of the risk in our portfolio by adding assets that are "out of step." There is some risk, such as the risk related to the economy in general, that affects the cash flows of all our assets and therefore cannot be eliminated by diversifying our portfolio.

We refer to the risk that can be diversified away as ***diversifiable risk*** and the risk that cannot be diversified away as ***nondiversifiable risk*** or *market risk*. For a more in-depth discussion of diversification and market risk, take a look back at the discussion of portfolios and the capital asset pricing model in Chapter 7.

If the expected risk-free rate is 3 percent and the expected return on the market is 11 percent, the market risk premium is 8 percent.

But if a particular common stock has market risk that is *different* from the risk of the market as a whole, we need to adjust that stock's market risk premium to reflect its different risk. Suppose the market risk premium is 8 percent. If a stock's market risk is twice the whole market's risk, the stock's premium for its market risk is 2×8 percent, or 16 percent. If a stock's market risk is half the risk of the market as a whole, the stock's premium for market risk is 0.5×8 percent, or 4 percent. What we are doing here is fine-tuning our estimate of the compensation investors will want before accepting that stock's market risk. We fine-tune by adjusting our benchmark, which is the risk of the market as a whole, to reflect the market's premium for the stock's relative market risk. The result is the stock's premium.

Let β represent the adjustment factor. Then the compensation for market risk is:

Compensation for market risk = $\beta(r_m - r_f)$

Since we know the compensation for the time value of money, r_f, and now we know the compensation for market risk, we see that the cost of common stock, r_e, is:

$$r_e = r_f + \beta(r_m - r_f) \qquad [14\text{-}6]$$

- The term $(r_m - r_f)$ represents the risk premium required by investors for bearing the risk of owning the market portfolio.
- The multiplier, β, fine-tunes this risk premium to compensate for the market risk associated with the individual firm. β, commonly referred to as ***beta,*** is a measure of the sensitivity of the returns on a particular security (or group of securities) to changes in the returns on the market—a measure of market risk.

And It Works for a Portfolio of Assets as Well

The analysis of the market risk of a stock can also be broadened to describe the risk associated with a *group* of assets, a **portfolio.**

Suppose we invest $10,000 in each of two assets, one with a beta of 2.0 and the other with a beta of 0.80. These two assets make up our portfolio. The portfolio's beta is the weighted average of the betas of the assets in our portfolio:

$$\text{Portfolio beta} = \left(\frac{\$10,000}{\$20,000}\right)2.0 + \left(\frac{\$10,000}{\$20,000}\right)0.80$$
$$= 1.0 + 0.40 = \mathbf{1.40}$$

Since the beta is greater than 1.0, it means that this portfolio's return is more sensitive to changes in the returns on the market than the average asset in the market.

A common stock having a β greater than 1.0 has more risk than the average security in the market. A common stock having a β of less than 1.0 has less risk than the average security in the market.

Suppose a firm's stock has a β of 2.0. This means its market risk is twice the risk of the average security in the market. If the expected risk-free rate of interest is 6 percent and the expected return on the market is 10 percent, the cost of common stock, r_e, is:[10]

$$r_e = 0.06 + 2.0(0.10 - 0.06)$$
$$= 0.06 + 2.0(0.04)$$
$$= 0.06 + 0.08$$
$$= \mathbf{0.14} \text{ or } \mathbf{14\%}$$

In this example, the market risk premium is (10 percent − 6 percent) = 4 percent. A market risk premium of 4 percent means that if you own a portfolio with the same risk as the market as a whole (that is, with a beta of 1.0), you would expect to receive a 10 percent return, of which 6 percent compensates you for the price of time and 4 percent compensates you for the price of market risk. If you invest in a security with a β of 2.0, you would expect a return of 14 percent: 6 percent to compensate you for the price of time and 2.0 times 4 percent = 8 percent to compensate you for the price of that security's particular risk.

The CAPM is based on two ideas that make sense: Investors are risk averse, and they hold diversified portfolios. But the CAPM is not without its drawbacks. First, the estimates rely heavily on historical values: returns on the

---

[10] You'll notice that in using the CAPM we did not need to transform the cost of equity into an effective annual cost. This is because we assume that r_m and r_f are already expected effective annual yields. If r_m, r_f, and β were, say, in terms of monthly data, we would have to translate the monthly r_e into an effective annual r_e: $r_e = (1 + r_{e,monthly})^{12} - 1$.

stock and returns on the market. These historical values may not be representative of the future, which is what we are trying to gauge. Also, the sensitivity of a firm's stock returns may change over time, for example, when the firm changes its capital structure. Second, if the firm's stock is not publicly traded, there is no data source even for historical values.

PUTTING IT ALL TOGETHER: THE COST OF CAPITAL

Average *and* Marginal?!

The weighted average cost of capital is a *weighted average* of the different costs of capital. But each of these costs is a *marginal* cost—the cost of raising additional capital using that source. So the WACC is a *marginal* cost—what it costs to raise additional capital—*averaged* across the different sources of capital.

The cost of capital is the average of the cost of each source, weighted by the proportion of total capital it represents. Hence, it is also referred to as the **weighted average cost of capital** (WACC) or the **weighted cost of capital** (WCC).

Let w_d, w_p, and w_e represent the proportion of debt, preferred stock, and common stock in the capital structure, respectively, and r_d^*, r_p, and r_e equal the after-tax cost of debt, the cost of preferred stock, and the cost of common stock, respectively. The weighted average cost of capital is:

$$WACC = w_d r_d^* + w_p r_p + w_e r_e \qquad [14\text{-}7]$$

Consider the following weights and marginal costs of the different sources of capital:

Source	Weight	Cost of capital
Debt	40%	$r_d^* = 6\%$
Preferred stock	10	$r_p = 12\%$
Common stock	50	$r_e = 14\%$

and

$$WACC = 0.40(0.06) + 0.10(0.12) + 0.50(0.14)$$
$$= 0.024 + 0.012 + 0.070$$
$$= \textbf{0.106} \text{ or } \textbf{10.6\%}$$

The Marginal-Cost-of-Capital Schedule

As you raise more and more money, the cost of each additional dollar of new capital may increase. This may be due to a couple of factors: the flotation costs and the demand for the security representing the capital to be raised.

For example, the cost of internal funds from retained earnings will differ from the cost of funds from issuing common stock due to flotation costs. If a firm expects to generate $1,000,000 entirely from what's available in internal funds—retained earnings—there are no flotation costs. But if the firm needs $1,000,001, that $1 above $1,000,000 will have to be raised *externally*, requiring flotation costs.

Let's consider a simple example using the dividend valuation method for the cost of common stock. Suppose a firm pays a dividend of $5 per share this year and dividends are expected to grow at a rate of 5 percent per year forever. The current price of the stock is $50. The cost of this internal source of funds is:

$$r_e = \frac{\$5(1 + 0.05)}{\$50} + 0.05$$
$$= 0.1050 + 0.05$$
$$= \textbf{0.1550} \text{ or } \textbf{15.5\%} \text{ per year}$$

If the firm is expected to generate $2 million in retained earnings in the next period, the cost to use this amount as capital will be 15.5 percent per year.

If the firm needs *more than* $2 million, each additional dollar of equity capital will cost more than 15.5 percent because it will be raised from a source that requires paying flotation costs.

Suppose in addition to the retained earnings, the firm expects to be able to issue new shares at $50 per share but receives only $48 per share—the investment bankers get the $2 difference. The cost of this external equity is:

$$r_e = \frac{\$5(1 + 0.05)}{\$48} + 0.05$$

$$= 0.1094 + 0.05$$

$$= \mathbf{0.1594} \text{ or } \mathbf{15.94\%} \text{ per year}$$

The first $2 million costs 15.5 percent per year, and anything over that costs 15.94 percent per year. Therefore, the marginal cost of raising any amount from $1 to $2 million from equity (common stock) is 15.5 percent per year and the marginal cost of raising each dollar above $2 million from equity is 15.94 percent per year.

Flotation Costs

How much do you have to pay underwriters to help you raise additional capital? It depends on how you do it. For example, you can raise additional equity capital by issuing stock to the public or through a rights offering (selling shares directly to your current shareholders). If you are selling shares of stock to the public for the first time (going public), it costs somewhat more. In 1991, the flotation costs for a public common stock issue were 3.88 percent of the total offering (the price of shares to investors) and the costs for an initial public offering were 6.28%.

SOURCE: George Anders, "Time Warner Holders Are Irked by Advisory Fees in Rights Deal," *The Wall Street Journal,* June 12, 1992, p. C1.

Flotation costs also play a role in creating layers of cost for debt. For example, a firm may expect to be able to privately place a debt issue of $1 million with an insurance company. If more than $1 million of new debt capital is needed, the firm would have to sell another debt issue publicly, incurring higher issuance costs. The first $1 million of debt capital would be at one cost, and any additional debt capital is at a higher cost.

Additional capital may be more costly, since the firm must offer higher yields to entice investors to purchase ever larger issues of securities.

Considering the effects of flotation costs and the additional yield necessary to entice investors, we most likely face a schedule of marginal costs of debt capital and a schedule of marginal costs of equity capital. Hence, we need to determine at what level of fund raising the marginal cost of capital for the firm changes.

Capital structure is the mix of long-term sources of funds.

Suppose a firm has a target capital structure of 40 percent debt and 60 percent common stock and will raise new funds in these proportions. In consultation with its investment bankers, the firm has determined the cost of raising new capital from debt and equity for different levels of financing:

Amount of new debt	Marginal cost of debt per year
$1 to $1,000,000	5%
$1,000,001 to $2,000,000	6
$2,000,001 to $3,000,000	7
$3,000,001 to $4,000,000	8
$4,000,001 to $5,000,000	9

Amount of new equity	Marginal cost of common stock per year
$1 to $1,000,000	9%
$1,000,001 to $3,000,000	10
$3,000,001 to $5,000,000	11
$5,000,001 to $8,000,000	12

For example, if the firm issues $1.5 million of new debt, the first $1 million will cost 5 percent per year and the next $0.5 million will cost 6 percent per year.

Suppose the firm raises capital in the proportions of 40 percent debt and 60 percent equity and raises $2 million of new capital of which $0.8 million is debt and $1.2 million is common stock. Looking at the schedules, we see that the cost of debt is 5 percent for the first $1 million of debt. However, the cost of equity changes once we have raised $1 million: The first $1 million of equity costs 9 percent and the additional $0.2 million costs 10 percent. Therefore:

$$\text{Cost of capital for first } \$2,000,000 = \underbrace{\frac{\$800,000}{\$2,000,000}\,0.05}_{\text{Debt}} + \underbrace{\frac{\$1,000,000}{\$2,000,000}\,0.09}_{\text{Equity at 9\%}} + \underbrace{\frac{\$200,000}{\$2,000,000}\,0.10}_{\text{Equity at 10\%}}$$

$$= 0.020 \quad + \quad 0.045 \quad + \quad 0.010$$

$$= \mathbf{0.075} \text{ or } \mathbf{7.5\%} \text{ per year}$$

The average cost of raising a dollar of capital for the first $2 million of capital is 7.5 percent. The marginal costs of capital are:

$$\text{Marginal cost of capital for first } \$1,800,000 = \frac{\$720,000}{\$1,800,000}\,0.05 + \frac{\$1,080,000}{\$1,800,000}\,0.09$$

$$= \mathbf{7.4\%} \text{ per year}$$

and

$$\text{Marginal cost of capital for next \$200,000} = \frac{\$80,000}{\$200,000}\,0.05 + \frac{\$120,000}{\$200,000}\,0.10$$

$$= \textbf{8\% per year}$$

If we raise one more dollar of capital beyond the $2 million, but not more than $1 million in total debt or more than $3 million in total equity, then it costs 5 percent for the additional debt and 10 percent for the additional equity:

$$\text{Weighted average cost of capital beyond \$2,000,000 but less than \$4,000,000} = 0.40(0.05) + 0.60(0.10)$$

$$= 0.02 + 0.06$$

$$= \textbf{0.08 or 8\%} \text{ per year}$$

The marginal cost of capital is 8 percent for $2,000,001 of new capital.

The marginal cost of capital for $4 million of capital ($1.6 million of debt and $2.4 million of equity) is 8.4 percent: The marginal cost of debt is 6 percent, the marginal cost of equity is 10 percent, and

$$\text{Weighted average cost of capital} = 0.40(0.06) + 0.60(0.10)$$

$$= 0.024 + 0.060$$

$$= \textbf{0.084 or 8.4\%} \text{ per year}$$

Each time the marginal cost of *either* the equity or the debt changes, the marginal cost of capital changes. These changes are referred to as ***breakpoints.*** We can see breakpoints for this example in Figure 14-1, which represents graphically the marginal cost of capital ratcheting upward as the total dollars raised increase and kinking at each breakpoint. The set of marginal costs of capital for different levels of capital raised makes up the ***marginal-cost-of-capital schedule.***

We can figure out where these breakpoints occur by looking at:

- The marginal-cost-of-debt schedule.
- The marginal-cost-of-stock schedule.
- The capital structure proportions.

Let's first look at the marginal-cost-of-debt schedule. The marginal cost of capital breaks when the marginal cost of debt changes from 5 percent to 6 percent, that is, once we have used up the first $1 million of debt capital. Since 40 percent of our total capital structure consists of debt:

$$0.40(\text{total capital raised}) = \$1,000,000$$

Using a bit of algebra:

$$\text{Total capital raised} = \frac{\$1,000,000}{0.40} = \textbf{\$2,500,000}$$

Once we have raised $2.5 million of capital, we have hit the $1 million break in the marginal-cost-of-debt schedule.

We can repeat this for each break in the marginal-cost-of-debt schedule and each break in the marginal-cost-of-equity-capital schedule. The results of

FIGURE 14-1

Marginal Cost of Capital for Different Levels of Capital

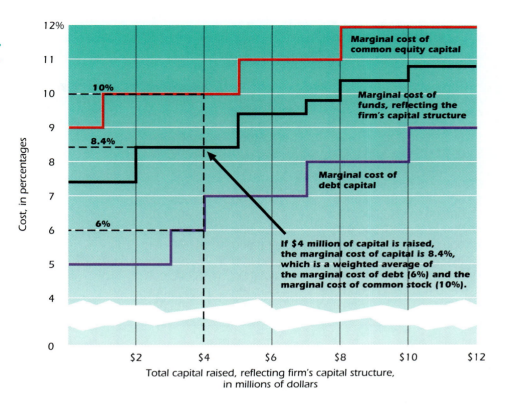

computing the breaks in the marginal-cost-of-capital schedule are shown in Table 14-1. By comparing the data in this table with the graph in Figure 14-1, you can see a correspondence between the breakpoints in the graph and the shifts in the marginal-cost-of-capital schedule in the table.

We can generalize the calculation of the breakpoint in the marginal-cost-of-capital schedule as follows:

$$\text{Breakpoint in marginal cost of capital} = \frac{\text{breakpoint in marginal cost of capital from source}}{\text{proportion of capital from source}} \qquad [14\text{-}8]$$

In general, as the marginal cost of any component of capital changes, so does the marginal cost of capital.

The Marginal Cost of Capital and Shareholder Wealth Maximization

Let's see what maximizing shareholder wealth means in terms of making investment and financing decisions.

To maximize shareholder wealth we must invest in a project until the marginal cost of capital is equal to its marginal benefit. What is the benefit from an investment? It is the internal rate of return, which is also known as the marginal efficiency of capital. If we begin by investing in the best projects (those with the highest returns), and then proceed by investing in the next-best projects, and so on, the marginal benefit from investing in more and more projects declines.

657

TABLE 14-1

Marginal-Cost-of-Capital Schedule

Amount of new capital raised	Amount of debt raised	Amount of common stock raised	Marginal cost of debt	Marginal cost of common stock	Marginal cost of capital
$1 to $1,000,000	$ 400,000	$ 600,000	5%	9%	7.4%
$1,000,001 to $2,000,000	800,000	1,200,000	5	10	8.0
$2,000,001 to $3,000,000	1,200,000	1,800,000	6	10	8.4
$3,000,001 to $4,000,000	1,600,000	2,400,000	6	10	8.4
$4,000,001 to $5,000,000	2,000,000	3,000,000	7	10	8.4
$5,000,001 to $6,000,000	2,400,000	3,600,000	7	11	9.4
$6,000,001 to $7,000,000	2,800,000	4,200,000	7	11	9.4
$7,000,001 to $8,000,000	3,200,000	4,800,000	8	11	9.8
$8,000,001 to $9,000,000	3,600,000	5,400,000	8	12	10.4
$9,000,001 to $10,000,000	4,000,000	6,000,000	8	12	10.4
$10,000,001 to $11,000,000	4,400,000	6,600,000	9	12	10.8
$11,000,001 to $12,000,000	4,800,000	7,200,000	9	12	10.8

Also, as we keep on raising funds and investing them, the marginal cost of funds increases. To maximize shareholders' wealth, we should invest in projects to the point at which the increasing marginal cost of funds is equal to the marginal benefit from our investment.

We can see this concept illustrated in Figure 14-2. Here we plot the marginal cost of capital and marginal efficiency of investment against the capital expenditure. The **optimal capital budget** is the capital expenditure at the point at which the marginal cost of capital intersects the marginal efficiency of capital. In this graph, the optimal capital budget is $2,750,000. This is the amount of capital investment at which the marginal cost = the marginal benefit = 8.85 percent. This means that the firm should take on an investment as long as its marginal return exceeds or is equal to the marginal cost of capital incurred in order to make the investment.

Practical Problems with the Marginal Cost of Capital

Determining the cost of capital appears straightforward: Find the cost of each source of capital and weight it by the proportion it will represent of the firm's new capital. But it is *not* so simple. There are many problems in determining the cost of capital for an individual firm. Consider the following, for example:

- How do you know what it will cost to raise an additional dollar of new debt? You may seek the advice of an investment banker. You may look at recent offerings of debt with risk similar to yours. But until you issue your debt, you will not know for sure.
- The cost of preferred stock looks easy. But how do you know, for a given dividend rate, what the price of the preferred stock will be? Again, you can seek advice or look at similar risk issues. But until you issue your preferred stock, you will not know for sure.

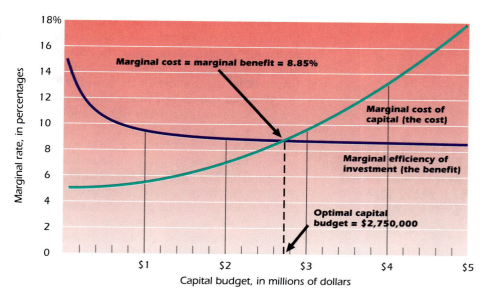

- The cost of common stock is more perplexing. There are problems associated with both the DVM and the CAPM.
- In the case of the DVM: What if dividends are not constant? What if there are no current dividends? And the expected growth rate of dividends is merely an estimate of the future.
- In the case of the CAPM: What is the expected risk-free rate of interest into the future? What is the expected return on the market into the future? What is the expected sensitivity of a particular asset's returns to that of the market's return? To answer many of these questions, we may derive estimates by looking at historical data. But this can be hazardous.

Estimating the cost of capital requires a good deal of judgment. It requires an understanding of the current risk and return associated with the firm and its securities as well as of the firm's and the securities' risk and return in the future.

If you are able to derive estimates of the costs of each of the sources of capital, you then need to determine the proportions in which the firm will raise capital. If your firm is content with its current capital structure and you expect to raise capital according to the proportions already in place, your job is simpler. In this case, the proportions can be determined by estimating the market value of existing capital and calculating the weights.

On the other hand, if your firm raises capital in proportions *other* than its current capital structure, there is a problem of estimating how this change in capital structure affects the costs of the components. Consider a firm that has a current capital structure, in market value terms, of 50% debt and 50% common stock. What happens to the market value of each component if the firm undergoes a large expansion and raises new funds solely from debt? This increase in debt may *increase* the cost of debt and the cost of common stock.

This will occur if this additional debt is viewed as significantly increasing the financial risk of the firm—the chance that the firm may encounter financial problems—thereby increasing the cost of capital. But this increase in the use of debt may also *decrease* the cost of capital. This could result because the firm will be using more of the lower-cost capital—debt.

Whether the cost of financial risk outweighs the benefit from the tax deductibility of interest is not clear—and cannot be reasonably forecast.

ESTIMATING THE COST OF CAPITAL FOR AN ACTUAL COMPANY

Although a precise determination of the cost of capital is not possible, we can develop estimates that may help in decision making. Let's estimate the cost of capital for E. I. du Pont Corporation, a large U.S. chemical company, whose products range from oil to pharmaceuticals. Though we do not have the benefit of talking to its investment bankers and can only look at published financial data, we can get an idea of how this firm estimates its cost of capital. Let's estimate Du Pont's cost of capital for 1992, using all published financial data through 1991.

Step 1: Determine the Proportion of Each Capital Component

If new capital is raised in the same proportions as existing capital, the weights applied to the costs of capital would be the market-value proportions of capital—the firm's use of each source of capital, based on its market value. For example, if the market value of debt is $100 and the market value of common stock is $400, the market-value proportion of debt is 20 percent and the market-value proportion of common stock is 80 percent.

Since many firms maintain a relatively stable capital structure, that makes it easier to determine the proportions of each capital component.

One practical problem is determining the market value of the components of capital. The market values of publicly traded common stock are readily available. But not all debt is publicly traded—some may be privately placed. If the firm has securities that are not publicly traded, their market values may not be available.

Du Pont has raised capital from three sources: long-term debt, preferred stock, and common stock. The debt and equity proportions, based on book values and market values, are shown in Table 14-2.

Calculating the Market Values

The calculation of the market value of debt is no easy task. At the end of 1991, Du Pont had eleven different debt issues that were publicly traded, with several other issues that were privately placed.

The market values of publicly traded issues were obtained from Moody's *Bond Record*, using January issues of *each subsequent year* to arrive at year-end prices of the debt of the previous year. The market value of privately placed debt was estimated from information on the coupon and maturity of the security obtained from Moody's *Industrial Manual*, assuming a yield similar to other Du Pont debt.

The market value of the preferred and common stock was calculated from information provided in Standard and Poor's *Daily Stock Price Record*.

TABLE 14-2

Capital Structure and Capital Proportions, E. I. du Pont Corporation, 1987–1991

Year	Book values, in millions				Market values, in millions			
	Book value of debt	Book value of preferred stock	Book value of common stock	Total book value	Market value of debt	Market value of preferred stock	Market value of common stock	Total market value
1987	$3,102	$237	$15,561	$18,900	$2,942	$120	$21,039	$24,102
1988	3,232	237	15,343	18,812	3,055	116	20,138	23,309
1989	4,149	237	15,561	19,947	4,067	128	28,771	32,966
1990	5,663	237	16,418	22,318	5,189	123	24,639	29,951
1991	6,725	237	16,715	23,677	6,433	140	31,550	38,123

Year	Weights using book values			Weights using market values		
	Proportion of debt	Proportion of preferred stock	Proportion of common stock	Proportion of debt	Proportion of preferred stock	Proportion of common stock
1987	16.41%	1.25%	82.33%	12.21%	0.50%	87.30%
1988	17.18	1.26	81.56	13.11	0.50	86.39
1989	20.80	1.19	78.01	12.34	0.39	87.27
1990	25.37	1.06	73.56	17.32	0.41	82.27
1991	28.40	1.00	70.60	16.87	0.37	82.76
Average	21.63	1.15	77.22	14.37	0.40	85.20

SOURCE: Moody's *Industrial Manual* and Standard & Poor's *Daily Stock Price Record.*

If we look at book values over the same period, we get a slightly different idea of the proportions: 21.63 percent debt, 1.15 percent preferred stock, 77.22 percent common stock. If we assume Du Pont will issue new securities in proportion to its capital structure based on recent years' market values, we would expect the firm to raise capital in the following proportions: 14.37 percent of debt, 0.40 percent preferred stock, and 85.20 percent common stock.

Comparing the book and market values, we see that the book value of common stock understates the stock's market value. For example, at the end of 1991 the book value of common stock was $16,715 million and the market value was $31,550 million. One reason for this discrepancy is that retained earnings (which typically represent a large portion of common stock) are the accumulation of earnings less any dividends paid since the beginning of the corporation's existence. These accumulated earnings are a sum of earnings for the *entire* corporate life of the firm, so in Du Pont's case, earnings in 1990 are added to earnings from 1950, say, which are added to earnings from 1935, and so on back to its beginnings as a public corporation in 1915.

Aside from this problem, the sum of earnings reinvested in the firm does not reflect what the firm does with them when they are reinvested, whereas the market value of equity reflects these earnings' growth potential.

The book value of debt overstates the true value of Du Pont debt by several hundred million dollars. Most of the Du Pont debt sells at a discount from face value, implying that the coupon rates of outstanding debt are below the market rates at the end of 1991. This is because interest rates at the end of 1991 were at higher rates than when the debt was issued.

The use of book values results in an understatement of the use of common stock—the highest cost source—and an overstatement of the use of debt—the lowest cost source. And since the firm's decision makers are most likely to look at market values in assessing the firm's current and future capital structure, it seems reasonable to focus more on the market-value proportions.

Step 2: Determine the Cost of Each Source of Capital

We must estimate the cost of each of Du Pont's sources of capital. To simplify our chore, let's ignore flotation costs.

The Cost of Debt

There are several ways by which we could estimate the cost of raising an additional dollar of new debt. We could look at:

1. Yields on recent debt offerings with similar risk.
2. Yields on recent debt offerings made by Du Pont.
3. Yields on outstanding debt of Du Pont.

Du Pont debt is rated Aa2 in Moody's system and AA in Standard & Poor's system. This means that the debt is considered to be of high quality in terms of default risk. That is, there is little risk Du Pont will be unable to pay the promised interest and principal on its current debt issues.

Using the three ways to estimate Du Pont's cost of new debt, we obtain the following results:

1. *Recent debt offerings with similar risk.* For firms with Aa-rated debt that was issued during the last two weeks of 1991, the yield was about 8.57 percent per year.[11]
2. *Recent Du Pont offerings.* Looking at Du Pont's Aa-rated debt issues, we see that the most recent was the 8.25 percent sinking fund debentures issued in September 1991. Since these debentures have sinking fund protection, investors demand a lower yield than if the debt did not have the sinking fund. These debentures had a yield to maturity of 7.59 percent at the end of 1991, according to Moody's *Bond Record*.
3. *Outstanding Du Pont debt.* Yields on Du Pont's current debt issues, according to Moody's *Bond Record*, ranged from 6.85 percent to 8.4 percent per year, and the yields on the sinking fund and shorter-maturity debt were in the lower part of this range.

---

[11] According to Moody's *Industrial Manual*, the average yield on Aa-rated debt in the last week of 1991 was 8.56 percent, and in the second-to-last week of 1991 the yield was 8.58 percent.

Compiling these estimates we can see that there is quite a discrepancy among the rates, with estimates between 6.85 and 8.57 percent per year:

Approach	Yield, in percentages
Yield on recently issued debt of similar risk	8.57
Yield on most recently issued debt	7.59
Yield on currently outstanding debt	6.85 to 8.40

Which do we use? Which one will be enough to get investors to put their money into new Du Pont debt? Most of Du Pont debt now consists of debentures without any sinking fund and with maturities of at least ten years. This persuades us to choose a cost at the upper end of the possible estimates. Since the debt yielding about 8.4 percent per year is more typical of the debt Du Pont issues, let's estimate the yield on new debt to be 8.4 percent.

Though the required rate of return on new Du Pont debt is estimated to be 8.4 percent, the *cost* of debt to Du Pont is less, since the interest on debt is tax deductible. Considering the tax rates on corporations for 1991, with a top marginal rate of 34%, the estimated cost of debt, r_d^*, is:

$$r_d^* = 0.084(1 - 0.34) = \mathbf{0.0554} \text{ or } \mathbf{5.54\%} \text{ per year}$$

The Cost of Preferred Stock

The cost of preferred stock can be estimated in a manner similar to that of debt. But since firms do not issue preferred stock with the same frequency as debt, it is likely that there is no recent preferred stock issue by the same company. We can, however, look at recent issues of preferred stock of similar risk and current yields on existing issues.

Looking at recent issues of preferred stock, we see that during the last two weeks of 1991 preferred stock of similar risk yielded approximately 7.625 percent per year.[12]

We can also look at the yield on Du Pont's currently outstanding preferred stock. At the end of 1991, Du Pont had two preferred stock issues outstanding, one with a $3.50 dividend and the other with a $4.50 dividend. We can calculate the yield on the preferred stock by using the current market value of the preferred stock and the amount of the dividend. In Standard & Poor's *Daily Stock Price Record*, we see that for the stock with the $3.50 dividend, the price at the end of 1991 was $49.25. Therefore, the required rate of return on this preferred stock, with $P_p = \$49.25$ and $D_p = \$3.50$, is:[13]

$$r_p = \frac{\$3.50}{\$49.25} = \mathbf{0.0711} \text{ or } \mathbf{7.11\%} \text{ per year}$$

[12] According to Moody's *Industrial Manual*, high-grade preferred stock issues yielded 7.59 percent in the last week of 1991 and 7.66 percent in the second-to-last week in 1991.

[13] We are ignoring any reinvestment of dividends during the year. We are comparing our calculated yield (based on the annual dividend and the current market price) with published yields, which are in terms of annualized yields (ignoring compounding). It is more convenient to compare yields stated on the same basis. Since we are seeking a ballpark estimate, adding precision to a ballpark estimate may be going a bit too far afield. We should understand, however, that these annualized yields understate the true cost slightly.

Looking at the same source, we see that the price of the stock that pays $4.50 per share is $63.00 at the end of 1991. Therefore the required rate of return on this preferred stock is:

$$r_p = \frac{\$4.50}{\$63.00} = \mathbf{0.0714} \text{ or } \mathbf{7.14\%} \text{ per year}$$

We arrive at three estimates of the cost of preferred stock:

Approach	Yield
Recent issues of preferred stock of similar risk	7.625%
Current yield on preferred stock with $3.50 dividend	7.11
Current yield on preferred stock with $4.50 dividend	7.14

Since the current yield on Du Pont's preferred stock is significantly lower than that of recent issues by other firms, we may wish to use a yield on preferred stock closer to the yields on Du Pont's own issues, since this lower yield is probably what investors will require on Du Pont's preferred stock. Let's use an estimate midway between the two current yields: 7.125% per year.

The Cost of Common Stock

We can estimate the cost of equity using either the DVM or the CAPM. We'll do both.

Using the Dividend Valuation Model

One of the key ingredients in the DVM is the growth rate of dividends. Ideally, we would like to have an estimate of the growth rate of future dividends in perpetuity. But this information is not available.

As an alternative, we look at the dividend history of Du Pont and see if the pattern of dividend payments indicates a trend. The yearly dividends per share paid over the period 1960–1991 are shown in Figure 14-3. They do not follow a constant pattern in the earlier years. But if we focus on the past five years, we get a pattern that resembles constant dividend growth.

Du Pont paid dividends on common stock over the past five years as follows:

Year	Dividends per share
1987	$1.10
1988	1.23
1989	1.45
1990	1.62
1991	1.68

We can calculate the growth rate of dividends by applying the basic valuation equation:

$$FV = PV(1 + r)^t$$

Let the present value be the dividends for 1987, $1.10, and the future value of dividends be the dividends four years later, $1.68. The growth rate, g, is the rate by which the dividends change each year, which is r in the basic valuation equation. Dividends have grown from $1.10 to $1.68 over four years. Therefore:

$$\$1.68 = \$1.10(1 + g)^4$$

and we solve this equation for the growth rate in dividends, g:

$$(1 + g)^4 = \frac{\$1.68}{\$1.10}$$

$$g = \sqrt[4]{\frac{\$1.68}{\$1.10}} - 1 = \mathbf{0.1117} \text{ or } \mathbf{11.17\%} \text{ per year}$$

Since the most recent dividend, D_0, is $1.68 per share, the estimate of next period's dividend, D_1, is:

$$D_1 = \$1.68(1 + 0.1117) = \mathbf{\$1.87}$$

The price of the stock at the end of 1991 is $46\frac{5}{8}$, or $46.625 per share. Substituting the known values of D_1 and P into the equation:

$$r_e = \frac{\$1.87}{\$46.625} + 0.1117$$

$$= 0.0401 + 0.1117$$

$$= \mathbf{0.1518} \text{ or } \mathbf{15.18\%} \text{ per year}$$

Using the Capital Asset Pricing Model

To estimate the cost of equity using the CAPM we first need to estimate:

- r_f, the expected risk free rate of interest
- r_m, the expected return on the market
- β, the sensitivity of the stock's return to changes in the market's return

FIGURE 14-3

Common Stock Dividends per Share, E. I. du Pont Corporation, 1976–1991

SOURCE: Standard & Poor's *Compustat PC Plus* (CD-ROM).

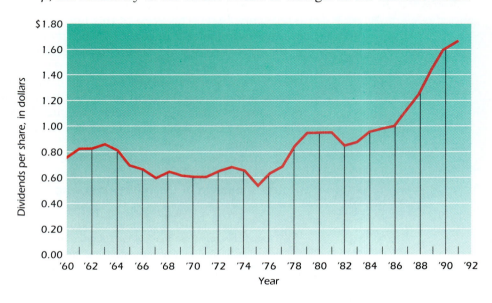

We first need an estimate of the risk-free rate that is expected in the long term. Though there are no risk-free perpetual securities, we can use the yield on a long-term government bond. Using the yield on 30-year U.S. Treasury bonds as of the end of 1991, we estimate the risk-free rate of interest to be 7.5 percent per year.[14]

We also need an estimate of the expected market return in the future. The best we can do is determine a typical recent return on the market. If we assume that the market is represented well by an index, say Standard & Poor's 500 Stock Index, we could look at the typical return on the index and use that as our best estimate of the future market return. We can estimate the return on the market by looking at the most recent year's return or at an average market return over a broader time period. The average annual return on the S&P 500 for the past ten years is 15.9 percent.

Since the sensitivity of returns on common stock to returns on the market is specific to the individual stock, we need information on the returns on Du Pont stock. We can see the relation between the returns on Du Pont's common stock and the returns on the market by looking at Figure 14-4. In this graph, each point represents a month's return on Du Pont common stock and a month's return on the S&P 500 Index, which we use to represent the entire market. For example, during the month of July 1989, the return on Du Pont common stock was 4.6 percent and the return on the S&P 500 was 8.84 percent.

We can describe the relation between the returns on the stock and returns of the market by looking at their relation over time. To do this we use regression analysis, which measures the sensitivity of one variable (in our example, the returns on Du Pont stock) to changes in another (the returns on the S&P 500).

The regression of the monthly returns on Du Pont common stock against the monthly returns on the market, represented by the S&P 500, for the sixty months from January 1987 through December 1991 produces a measure of the average relation between the returns on Du Pont's stock and the returns of the market. This average is represented graphically by the regression line (see Figure 14-4). The slope of this line —1.15—indicates the sensitivity—on average over the sixty months—of the returns on Du Pont stock to changes in the returns on the market and is our estimate of the market risk, beta (β).[15]

We could also obtain an estimate of β from financial services, such as the *Value Line Investment Survey*. Since there are many different ways to estimate β such as by using a different period of time or a different market index, there may be slight differences between estimates from different financial services. The β for Du Pont taken from *Value Line* is 1.15, which just happens to match our estimate.

Is an historical beta a good estimate of the future beta? For some stocks yes, for others no. It depends on whether the market risk of the firm is expected to change in the future. Perusing financial news on Du Pont during

Return on Standard & Poor's 500 Stock Index, 1982–1991

Year	Return per year
1982	−0.76%
1983	22.38
1984	6.10
1985	31.57
1986	18.55
1987	5.23
1988	17.07
1989	31.53
1990	−3.18
1991	30.51
Average	15.90% per year

SOURCE: *The Wall Street Journal*, various issues.

[14] We found this rate in Moody's *Bond Record*, Jan. 1992.

[15] The statistical technique of regression and the calculations necessary to estimate a regression line are provided in Appendix D.

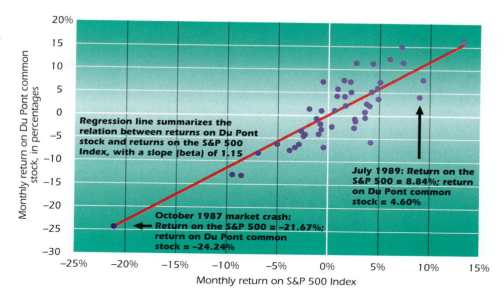

FIGURE 14-4

Relation between Returns on Du Pont Common Stock and Returns on the S&P 500 Stock Index, Monthly, 1987–1991

SOURCE: Standard & Poor's *Daily Stock Price Index.*

1991, we see that Du Pont is restructuring its operations in an effort to cut costs. This should improve the profitability of Du Pont in the long run and ensure its competitiveness in the marketplace. This move may reduce the operating risk of Du Pont somewhat and, hence, reduce the sensitivity of the return on its stock to changes in the market return. Therefore, we could use a β estimate slightly lower than our historical beta and Value Line's estimate.

We have gathered the following:

r_f = 7.5% per year, which is 0.6% per month
r_m = 15.9% per year, which is 1.24% per month
β = 1.15

Putting these pieces together, we find that the cost of common stock is:

r_e = 0.006 + 1.15(0.0124 − 0.006)
  = 0.006 + 1.15(0.0064)
  = 0.006 + 0.0074
  = **0.0134** per month

which, on an annual basis translates to:

r_e = (1 + 0.0134)^{12} − 1
  = **0.1726** or **17.26%** per year

What does this result mean? It means that we expect the market as a whole to generate a return of 15.9 percent per year in the future, which is above the expected risk-free rate. Our estimate suggests that investors require a return of 17.26 percent per year on Du Pont stock, since it is riskier than the market as a whole.

Reconciling the Two Estimates

The different models produced different estimates for the cost of common stock:

CAPM: $r_e = 17.26\%$ per year   DVM: $r_e = 15.18\%$ per year

This is to be expected, since we are approaching the estimate from different paths. The CAPM evaluates the cost on the assumption that investors hold diversified portfolios and are concerned only about market risk. The DVM evaluates the cost on the assumption that dividends will follow a particular pattern in the future. Moreover, the different approaches of these two models require us to make certain estimates along the way.

Then which approach is better? The one that provides the best estimate of the cost of common stock. Which does that? It's the model that fits our firm's situation better than the other. To determine the better fit in the case of Du Pont, we could ask ourselves:

- Do dividends grow at approximately a constant rate?
- Do changes in the market return tend to explain movements in the returns on the common stock?

Du Pont's dividends do not appear to grow at a constant rate, at least when we look at them over a broad period, as shown in Figure 14-3. But they do tend to be explained by movements in the market's return. We can see this in Figure 14-4, where the points that represent the return on Du Pont stock in relation to the market's return tend to be clustered around the regression line, telling us that the market return does explain some portion of the returns on Du Pont's stock.

The answers to these questions—the growth in dividends and the fit of the regression line—tell us to rely more heavily on the CAPM in estimating the cost of equity for Du Pont rather than on the DVM. Therefore, we will use the cost of equity obtained from our CAPM analysis to estimate our marginal cost of capital.

Step 3: Put It All Together

Using the market-value weights of capital, we estimate the marginal cost of capital for Du Pont as:

Source of capital	Weight	Marginal cost	Weight times cost
Debt	14.4%	5.54%	0.0080
Preferred stock	0.4	7.13	0.0003
Common stock	85.2	17.26	0.1471
Weighted average cost of capital			**0.1554** or **15.54%** per year

We estimate the cost of capital for Du Pont to be 15.80 percent per year. In other words, if Du Pont raises additional capital, we estimate that the cost of this additional capital will be 15.54 percent per year.

Caveats

The calculations we made to determine the cost of capital can mislead us into thinking that the result we obtain is precise. Rather, what we get is a ballpark estimate. Our estimate is accompanied by a number of caveats:

- *We get different estimates of the marginal cost of capital using different costs of components.* For example, we get a cost of capital of 13.76 percent instead of 15.54 percent if we use the DVM instead of the CAPM. Each model relies on different assumptions.
- *We get different estimates of the marginal cost of capital using different weights.* For example if we used book weights instead of market weights, the cost of capital would be 14.62 percent, instead of 15.80 percent.[16] Also, if we look at the change in the capital structure over time, we see that Du Pont is using more debt in recent years; so we may wish to use a greater proportion for debt.
- *Flotations costs must be considered.* We have ignored flotation costs, but these could be substantial, especially if we are raising a large proportion of common equity capital.
- *Changes in costs for different levels of capital need to be considered.* There may be quite a difference in the cost of capital if Du Pont raised, say, $2 billion rather than $20 billion in new capital.

The cost of capital of 15.54 percent is an estimate. Despite all the assumptions and judgments that go into this figure, we at least have a starting point—an estimate of the cost of capital. Knowing more about Du Pont's target capital structure, future dividend plans, and flotation costs would help us refine our estimate, providing a more useful figure for decision making.

---

[16] Using book value weights:

Source of capital	Weight	Marginal cost	Weight times cost
Debt	21.6%	5.54%	0.0120
Preferred stock	1.2	7.13	0.0009
Common stock	77.2	17.26	0.1333
Weighted average cost of capital			**0.1462**

SUMMARY

■   The cost of capital is the marginal cost of raising additional funds. This cost is important in our investment decision making because we ultimately want to compare the cost of funds with the benefits from investing these funds.

■   The cost of capital is determined in three steps: (1) Determine what proportions of each source of capital we intend to use; (2) calculate the cost of each source of capital; and (3) put the cost and the proportions together to determine the weighted average cost of capital.

■   The required rate of return on debt is the yield demanded by investors to compensate them for the time value of money and the risk they bear in lending their money. The cost of debt to the firm differs from this required rate of return because of (1) flotation costs and (2) the tax benefit from the deductibility of interest expense.

■   The required rate of return on preferred stock is the yield demanded by investors and differs from the firm's cost of preferred stock because of the costs of issuing additional shares (the flotation costs).

■   The required rate of return on common stock is more difficult to estimate than the cost of debt or preferred stock because of the nature of the return on stock: Dividends are not guaranteed or fixed in amount, and part of the return results from the changes in the value of the stock.

■   The dividend valuation model and the capital asset pricing model are two methods commonly used to estimate the required rate of return on common stock. The DVM deals with the expected dividend yield and is based on an assumption that dividends grow at some constant rate into the future. The CAPM assumes that investors hold diversified portfolios and therefore require compensation for the time value of money and the market risk they bear in owning the stock.

■   The proportion of each source of capital that we use in calculating the cost of capital is based on the mix of debt and equity in the new capital the firm seeks to raise. If the firm already has a capital structure—a mix of debt and equity—it feels appropriate, then that same proportion of each source of capital, in market-value terms, is a good estimate of the proportions of debt and equity in new capital.

■   The cost of capital is the cost of raising new capital. The weighted average cost of capital is the cost of all new capital for a given level of financing. The cost of capital is a *marginal* cost—the cost of an additional dollar of new capital at a given level of financing.

■   In determining the optimal amount to spend on investments, the relevant cost is the marginal cost, since we are interested in investing to the point at which the marginal cost of the funds is equal to the marginal benefit from our investment. The point at which marginal cost = marginal benefit results in the optimal capital budget.

■   The actual estimation of the cost of capital for a firm requires a bit of educated guesswork and lots of reasonable assumptions. Using readily available financial data, we can, however, arrive at a good enough estimate of the cost of capital.

QUESTIONS

14-1   Why does the cost of debt differ from the required rate of return on debt for the same firm?

14-2   How does a change in the corporate tax rate affect the cost of debt? In particular, how would an increase in the corporate tax rate affect the cost of debt?

14-3   What is the difference between the required rate of return on common stock and the cost of common stock?

14-4   Why is it that there is a cost to the firm for internally generated capital? Why does the cost of externally generated equity capital differ from the cost of internally generated equity capital?

14-5   Why is it that, for a given firm, the required rate of return on equity is greater than the required rate of return on debt?

14-6   Why are market-value proportions preferred to book value proportions in the calculation of the weighted average cost of capital?

14-7   List at least three problems that are encountered in calculating the cost of capital of an actual firm.

14-8   List at least two drawbacks associated with the dividend valuation model in the calculation of the cost of common stock. List at least two drawbacks associated with the capital asset pricing model in the calculation of the cost of common stock.

14-9   If both the dividend valuation model and the capital asset pricing model produce estimates of the cost of common stock, how is it possible to end up with two different numerical estimates?

14-10   What are flotation costs? Explain how flotation costs affect the cost of capital.

PROBLEMS

Cost of debt

14-1 The Athens Airline Company has consulted with its investment bankers and determined that it could issue new debt with a yield of 8 percent. If the company's marginal tax rate is 40 percent, what is the after-tax cost of debt to Athens?

14-2 The Oshkosh Travel Company is considering issuing additional debt. Oshkosh wishes to use the yield on its existing debt as a guide to the cost of new debt. Oshkosh currently has a 5 percent coupon bond that pays interest semiannually, matures in ten years, and has a current market price of 80, or $800 per $1,000 face value bond. If Oshkosh's marginal tax rate is 30 percent, what is the firm's expected cost of new debt?

14-3 The Richardson Oil Company is considering issuing additional debt. The firm wishes to use the yield on its existing debt as a guide to the cost of new debt. Richardson currently has a zero-coupon bond outstanding that has five years to maturity and a current market price of $74\frac{6}{8}$, or $747.50 per $1,000 par value.

   a. If Richardson's marginal tax rate is 20 percent, what is the cost of debt?
   b. If Richardson's marginal tax rate is 30 percent, what is the cost of debt?

Cost of preferred stock

14-4 The Oxford Company is evaluating its financing strategy. Oxford estimates that it can sell an issue of $50 par value preferred stock that has a dividend rate of 6 percent, with dividends to be paid at the end of each year.

   a. What is the cost of preferred stock if Oxford sells the issue at par value with no flotation costs?
   b. What is the cost of preferred stock if the firm sells the issue at par value with flotation costs of $3 per share?
   c. What is the cost of preferred stock if the firm sells the issue at par value with flotation costs of 1 percent of par value?
   d. What is the cost of preferred stock if the firm sells the issue at $52 per share and incurs no flotation costs?
   e. What is the cost of preferred stock if the firm sells the issue at $52 per share and incurs flotation costs of $1 per share?

14-5 The Bloomington Flower Corporation is evaluating its cost of preferred stock. Bloomington's management believes that it can issue new preferred stock at yields close to that of its outstanding preferred stock issues. There are three outstanding preferred stock issues, A, B, and C. The following information has been gathered on these issues:

Issue	Dividend per share	Current market price per share
A	$3.00	$35\frac{1}{4}$
B	$2.50	$29\frac{1}{2}$
C	$4.50	$52\frac{7}{8}$

Assume, for simplicity, that dividends are paid at the end of each year.

a. What is the current yield on each of these preferred stock issues?
b. What would you estimate to be the expected yield on preferred stock?

Cost of common stock

14-6   The Clemson Cat Supply Company is considering issuing new stock and has requested your assistance in evaluating the cost of common stock. The current dividend per share is $2, and the current price of the stock is $40 per share. The management of Clemson expects dividends to grow at a rate of 10 percent per year for the foreseeable future. Using the dividend valuation model, what is the cost of common stock to Clemson?

14-7   The Charlotte Honey Company is considering issuing new stock and is evaluating its cost of equity capital. Charlotte expects a risk-free rate of interest of 5 percent and a return on the market of 12 percent.

a. If Charlotte's common stock has a beta of 1.0, what is the expected cost of common stock using the capital asset pricing model?
b. If Charlotte's common stock has a beta of 2.0, what is the expected cost of common stock using the capital asset pricing model?
c. If Charlotte's common stock has a beta of 3.0, what is the expected cost of common stock using the capital asset pricing model?

Proportions of capital

14-8   The Gainesville Gas Company is evaluating its cost of capital. To calculate the weighted average cost of capital, Gainesville needs to figure out the best weights to use once the company has determined the cost of each source of capital. The following information is available:

Security	Book value	Market value
Mortgage bonds	$100,000,000	$110,000,000
Debentures	100,000,000	150,000,000
Subordinated debentures	200,000,000	230,000,000
Preferred stock	100,000,000	110,000,000
Common stock	300,000,000	600,000,000

a. What are the proportions of debt, preferred stock, and common stock if book value weights are used?
b. What are the proportions of debt, preferred stock, and common stock if market value weights are used?
c. Which do you recommend—book value or market value weights—in advising the Gainesville management?

Weighted average cost of capital

14-9   Yellowjacket Honey Inc. is evaluating its cost of capital under alternative financing arrangements. In consultation with investment bankers, Yellowjacket expects to be able to issue new debt at par with a coupon rate of 10 percent and to issue new preferred stock with a dividend of $4.00 per share at $25 per share. The common stock of Yellowjacket is currently selling for $20.00 per share. Yellowjacket expects to pay a dividend of $2.50 per common share next year. Market analysts foresee a growth in dividends in Yellowjacket stock at a rate of 5 percent per year. Yellowjacket does not expect its cost of debt, preferred stock, or common stock to be different under the two possible financing arrangements. Yellowjacket's marginal tax rate is 40 percent.

The two arrangements are:

	Percentage of new capital raised		
Financing arrangement	Debt	Preferred stock	Common stock
1	20%	30%	50%
2	50	30	20

What is the cost of capital to Yellowjacket Honey Inc. under each financing arrangement?

Marginal-cost-of-capital schedule

14-10 The Walla Walla Washing Company has a capital structure consisting of 40 percent debt and 60 percent equity. If the required rate of return on debt is 10 percent and the cost of common stock is 16 percent, what is the cost of capital to Walla Walla if there are no flotation costs and

a. The marginal tax rate on corporate income is 40 percent?
b. The marginal tax rate on corporate income is 60 percent?

14-11 As financial manager of True Devalue Company, you have been given the following information on investment opportunities and the cost of raising alternative levels of capital.

Capital raised	Marginal cost of capital
$1 to $2,000,000	10%
$2,000,001 to $4,000,000	12
$4,000,001 to $6,000,000	14
$6,000,001 to $8,000,000	16

Investment opportunity	Cost	Internal rate of return
A	$ 300,000	8%
B	500,000	12
C	1,500,000	16
D	1,200,000	14
E	600,000	10
F	800,000	18

a. What is the optimal capital budget?
b. Which projects should be chosen, given this information?

14-12 The Stillwater Corporation is evaluating its marginal-cost-of-capital schedule. The company does not presently use debt or preferred stock in its capi-

Trends in Investment Banking

As a response to some of the abusive banking practices that contributed to the 1929 stock market crash and the ensuing economic depression, the Glass-Steagall Act of 1933 separated the commercial banking and investment banking business. But over the years, the distinction between commercial banking and investment banking has become blurred, as commercial banks have formed nonbank affiliates and investment banks have formed nonbank banks.

This blurring, along with relaxing of restrictions on banking affiliates' activities by the Federal Reserve, may eventually lead to the undoing of the separation of commercial and investment banking.

SUMMARY

- Issuing new securities is selling a product. Just as Procter & Gamble sells toothpaste to consumers, a firm that wants to raise capital must sell its securities to investors. The difference between a security and a product like toothpaste is that a security does not represent something tangible. Rather, it represents a claim on the firm's future cash flows, which is an intangible asset. So selling a security is a bit more challenging than selling toothpaste because the investor is interested in the certainty of receiving those future cash flows. Securities laws, which require disclosures in registration statements and prospectuses, are designed to provide the investor with information necessary to adjudge the security's risk and expected return.

- Like consumer products, the firm can sell its securities either wholesale (through an underwriter) or retail (privately placed or through, say, a rights offering). The cost to the firm of selling these securities depends on whether they are sold at wholesale or at retail.

- The cost of issuing securities depends on the type of security and the size of the offering. Debt is less costly than equity, and larger issues are less costly than smaller ones.

FURTHER READINGS

The effects of the method of issuing securities on a firm's share price is examined in:

CLIFFORD W. SMITH, JR., "Raising Capital: Theory and Evidence," *Midland Corporate Finance Journal*, vol. 4, no. 1, Spring 1986, pp. 6–22.

CLIFFORD W. SMITH, JR., "Investment Banking and the Capital Acquisition Process," *Journal of Financial Economics*, vol. 15, no. 1, Jan.-Feb. 1986, pp. 3–29.

PART VI

Management of Working Capital

15 Management of Short-Term Assets 684

16 Management of Short-Term Financing 736

CHAPTER 15

Management of Short-Term Assets

INTRODUCTION 687

CASH MANAGEMENT 690
Reasons for Holding Cash Balances 690
Costs Associated with Cash 691
Determining the Investment in Cash 691
    The Baumol Model 691
    The Miller-Orr Model 696
    Other Considerations 699
Cash Management Techniques 699
    The Check-Clearing Process 699
    Lockbox Systems 702
    Controlled Disbursements 704
Monitoring Cash Needs 704
Marketable Securities 705
    Reasons for Holding Marketable Securities 705
    Types of Marketable Securities 706

RECEIVABLES MANAGEMENT 709
Reasons for Extending Credit 709
Costs Associated with Credit 709
    The Cost of Discounts 709
    Other Costs 711
    Credit and the Demand for a Firm's Goods and Services 712
Credit and Collection Policies 713
    Credit Policies 713
    Evaluation of Creditworthiness 714
    Collection Policies 714
Monitoring Accounts Receivable 715
Establishing and Changing Credit Policies 717
    Analyzing a Change in Credit and Collection Policies: An Example 717
    Caveats 719
Captive Finance Subsidiaries 720

INVENTORY MANAGEMENT 720
Reasons for Holding Inventory 720
Costs Associated with Inventory 721
Models of Inventory Management 722
    The Economic Order Quantity Model 722
    Just-in-Time Inventory 725
    Other Considerations 727
Monitoring Inventory Management 727

Summary 728

A Look at the Operating Cycle

The operating cycle is the time it takes a firm to turn its investment of cash in inventory and accounts receivable back into cash. Specifically, the operating cycle is the sum of the number of days of inventory (the time it takes to produce and sell inventory) and the number of days of credit (the time it takes customers to pay):

$$\text{Operating cycle} = \frac{\text{number of days}}{\text{of inventory}} + \frac{\text{number of}}{\text{days of credit}}$$

Looking at companies in 1991, we see vast differences among their operating cycles:

Company	Business	Number of days of inventory	Number of days of credit	Operating cycle, in days
McDonald's	Restaurants	4	14	18
Shoney's	Restaurants	15	7	22
Kroger	Grocery retailing	33	5	38
Winn-Dixie Stores	Grocery retailing	43	4	47
Boeing	Aircraft manufacturing	51	26	77
Wal-Mart Stores	Discount retailing	70	7	77
Inland Steel	Steel production	48	41	89
Apple Computer	Computer manufacturing	60	48	108
Procter & Gamble	Consumer products	72	40	112
Service Merchandise	Retailing	112	5	117
Child-World	Toy retailing	117	5	122
Union Carbide	Chemical production	61	132	193
Diebold	Teller machine manufacturing	116	81	197
Chrysler	Automobile manufacturing	50	226	276
Tiffany	Jewelry retailing	294	35	329

SOURCE: Standard & Poor's *Compustat PC Plus* (CD-ROM).

Some of these differences are due to the nature of the firm's business. For example, we would hope that McDonald's inventory would not be around too long. And we can see that Tiffany's jewelry, a luxury item, does not sell quickly.

Also, the process of producing inventory differs. It takes Diebold longer to make its automated teller machines than it takes

McDonald's to process and sell hamburgers. Therefore, Diebold is likely to have more inventory that is work-in-process than McDonald's.

Differences also arise from customary business practice. McDonald's does not extend credit to its customers, but Chrysler, through its financing subsidiary, does. Chrysler's major competitors, General Motors and Ford, offer credit to their customers, but McDonald's major competitors, Wendy's and Burger King, do not.

Some generalizations about operating cycles:

- Firms in the retail industry tend to have shorter operating cycles, with firms dealing in food products having the shortest operating cycles and firms dealing in luxury items having the longest.
- Firms involved in manufacturing tend to have longer operating cycles than retailers because of the amount of time necessary to produce goods for sale.
- Firms such as automobile manufacturers, which customarily extend credit to their customers, tend to have longer operating cycles, but the length of time it takes customers to pay varies among industries.

A firm's investment in working capital (its current assets) depends, in part, on the length of its operating cycle. The longer this cycle, the longer it takes to generate cash from the firm's investment in its goods and services. This longer cycle increases a firm's risk and cost associated with its working capital investment.

INTRODUCTION

The world sometimes turns upside down and only those with light, liquid assets float to the top again.

Anthony H. Allen, 1933

When we evaluate an investment in a long-lived project, we consider the future cash flows from that project, the uncertainty of those cash flows, and the opportunity cost of the funds invested in that project. Evaluating an investment in an asset that is not around very long—categorized under current assets—is done in exactly the same way, but over a much shorter time horizon.

The time value of money plays an important role in our valuation of long-term investments because these investments produce expected cash flows far into the future. But current assets (cash, marketable securities, accounts receivable, inventory) provide expected cash flows only in the near future. So the time value of money plays a lesser role in evaluating current assets.

When we decide to develop and market a new product, we are making a capital investment. Aside from the outlay for any equipment or other assets to produce the product, the investment may require:

- More cash (to handle the increased volume of transactions).
- More inventory (raw materials, work in process, finished goods).
- More accounts receivable (because selling more goods on credit means increasing the credit extended to our customers).

Investments in current assets support the day-to-day operations of the firm. Therefore, when we invest in a long-lived project we have to invest in current assets also in order to support the day-to-day activities that will be required by the long-lived project. Current assets are *working capital*—we put them to work to generate the benefits from our capital investment.

We can consider that we invest in current assets for the same reason we invest in long-term (capital) assets: to maximize owners' wealth. But because we evaluate current assets over a shorter time frame (less than a year) we focus more on their cash flows and less on the time value of money.

How much should a firm invest in current assets? That depends on several factors:

- The type of business and product.
- The length of the operating cycle.
- Customs, traditions, and industry practices.
- The degree of uncertainty of the business.

The type of business, whether extractive, retail, manufacturing, or service, affects the way a firm invests. In some industries, large investments in machinery and equipment are necessary. In other industries, such as retail firms, less is invested in plant and equipment and other long-term assets, and more is invested in current assets such as inventory.

The firm's operating cycle—the time it takes the firm to turn its investment in inventory into cash—affects how much the firm ties up in current assets. The operating cycle includes the time it takes to manufacture the goods, sell them, and collect on their sale. The longer the operating cycle, the larger the investment in current assets.

Capital Notions

A firm's capital consists of the firm's resources—its assets. We tend to distinguish between long-lived assets and short-lived assets, since different factors are important in making these investment decisions. Current assets are short-lived assets. Since they are used in the day-to-day operations of the firm, we usually refer to them as the firm's *working capital*. We refer to the long-lived assets as the firm's *capital assets.*

Working Capital, Also Known as:

- Current assets
- Current capital
- Circulating capital

Customs and traditions developed over time also affect how much a firm invests in current assets. Some industries, such as those selling raw materials, traditionally require cash on delivery. This tradition developed when there was such a small profit margin on these goods that the seller could not bear the cost of extending credit. What competitors are doing is also an influence. If competitors are extending credit to customers on generous terms, your firm may have to do the same.

The greater the uncertainty firms experience regarding the supply and cost of raw material, the larger is the investment they tend to make in current assets. If the price of raw materials (such as sugar, silver, or cocoa) fluctuates widely, a firm that needs these materials may have to keep either a large store of these goods on hand or a sufficient supply of cash (or cash equivalents) at the ready in order to be able to take advantage of price fluctuations. If it is likely that the supply of raw materials may be interrupted (say, by a labor strike), the firm may want to keep on hand a large quantity of raw materials whose prices are volatile. Furthermore, the greater the uncertainty firms face regarding the sale of their goods and services, the larger is the investment they tend to make in current assets to ensure that there will be enough in case demand increases.

Let's look at the investment in current assets of a few industries, as graphed in Figure 15-1. The percentage invested in current and noncurrent (long-term) assets varies among these industries. Firms that manufacture goods such as steel tend to have more invested in long-term assets than, say, retail record and tape stores. Of the manufacturing firms, those with greater raw material price uncertainty, such as sugar and confectionery processors and beverage producers, tend to have more invested in current assets.

The influence of the nature of the business can be seen in these differences. What is the inventory of a waste management business? Nuts and bolts to keep the trucks operating, which don't amount to too much. What is the inventory of a hospital? Medicine? Bed pans?

The differences in how these industries invest in current assets is illustrated in more detail in Figure 15-2. Here, current assets are broken down by type: cash, marketable securities, accounts receivable, inventory, and "other."[1] Inventory plays a small role in hospitals and waste management firms, but is significant in variety stores and retail record and tape stores. Accounts receivable, however, are not important to record and tape stores and variety stores, since they typically do not extend credit to customers, but are important to hospitals and waste management firms, which typically do.

Beverage producers tend to have more invested in cash than, say, paper mills. This may be due to the greater uncertainty regarding raw materials for beverages, requiring the producers to have more cash (or marketable securities) on hand in case of major fluctuations in the price of raw materials, such as sugar. Since many paper mills own timberland, their supply of raw materials is more certain than that of food processors. Hospitals have a large in-

---

[1] "Other" includes prepaid expenses (which is a short-term asset because these are expenses paid but not yet incurred) and income tax refunds (because they are refunds that are coming, but have not yet arrived). We do not discuss either in detail in this chapter.

FIGURE 15-1

Investment in Current and Noncurrent Assets, Selected Industries, 1991

SOURCE: Standard & Poor's *Compustat PC Plus* (CD-ROM).

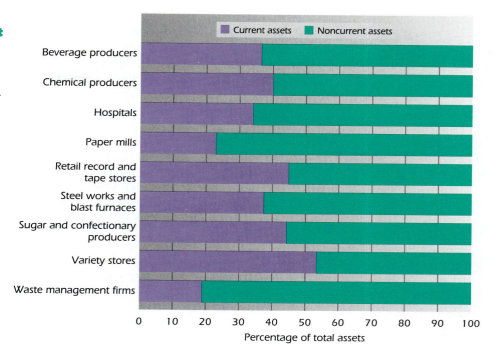

Percentage of total assets

FIGURE 15-2

Breakdown of Current Assets by Type, Selected Industries, 1991

SOURCE: Standard & Poor's *Compustat PC Plus* (CD-ROM).

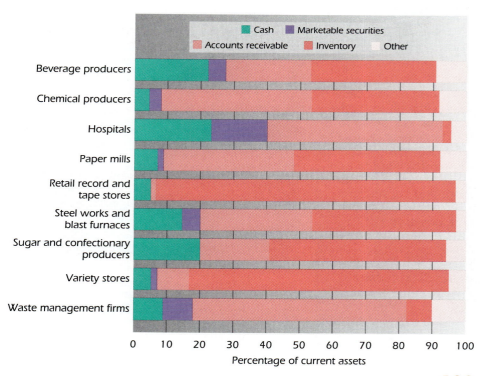

Percentage of current assets

vestment in cash, marketable securities, and accounts receivable, probably because they extend credit to patients who are subsequently unable to pay.

The working capital decision requires an evaluation of the benefits and costs associated with each component. In this chapter, we look at the management of cash and marketable securities, accounts receivable, and inventory, and see how we can evaluate the benefits and costs associated with the investment in working capital.

CASH MANAGEMENT

Cash flows *out of* the firm as we pay for the goods and services we purchase from others. Cash flows *into* the firm as our customers pay for the goods and services they purchase from us. When we refer to *cash*, we mean the amount of cash and cashlike assets: currency, coin, and bank balances. When we refer to *cash management*, we mean the management of the cash inflows and outflows as well as the stock of cash on hand.

Reasons for Holding Cash Balances

Firms hold some of their assets in the form of cash for several reasons. They need cash to meet the transactions of their day-to-day operations. Referred to as the ***transactions balance,*** the amount of cash needed for this purpose differs from firm to firm, depending on the particular flow of cash into and out of the firm. The amount depends on:

1. The size of the transactions made by the firm.
2. The firm's operating cycle—which determines its cash outflow and inflow, both depending on the firm's production process, purchasing policies, and collection policies.

Reasons for Holding Cash

- Transaction needs
- Precautionary needs
- Speculative needs
- Banking services

"Partly on reasonable and partly on instinctive grounds, our desire to hold money as a store of wealth is a barometer of the degree of our distrust of our own calculations and conventions concerning the future. The possession of money lulls our disquietude; the premium which we require to make us part with money is a measure of the degree of our disquietude" (John Maynard Keynes, 1930).

The Operating Cycle

Cash → Purchase raw material and produce goods (Generating cash) → Sell goods (Generating sales) → Extend credit (Creating accounts receivables) → Collect accounts receivables (Generating cash) → Cash

There is always *some* degree of uncertainty about future cash needs. Firms typically hold an additional balance, referred to as a ***precautionary balance,*** just in case transaction *needs* exceed the transactions *balance.* But how much to keep as a precaution depends on the degree of uncertainty of the transactions—how well we can predict our transaction needs.

In addition to the precautionary balances, firms may keep cash on hand for unexpected future opportunities. Referred to as a ***speculative balance,*** this is the amount of cash or securities that can be easily turned into cash, above what is needed for transactions and precaution, and it enables a firm to take advantage of investment opportunities on short notice and to meet extraordinary demands for cash. For example, an automobile manufacturer may need an additional cash cushion to pay its bills in case a wildcat strike closes down a plant.

In addition to the cash balances for transaction, precautionary, and speculative needs, a firm may keep cash in a bank account in the form of a ***compensating balance***—a cash balance required by banks in exchange for banking services. By keeping a balance in an account that is noninterest earning or low-interest earning, the firm is effectively compensating the bank for the loans and other services it provides. Some bank loans and bank services require that a specified amount or average balance be maintained in an account.

Costs Associated with Cash

There is a cost to holding assets in the form of cash. Since cash does not generate earnings, the cost of holding assets in the form of cash, referred to as the ***holding cost,*** is an opportunity cost: what the cash *could* have earned if invested in another asset.

If we need cash, we must either sell an asset or borrow cash. There are transaction costs associated with both. Transaction costs are the fees, commissions, or other costs associated with selling assets or borrowing to get cash; they are analogous to the ordering costs for inventory.

Determining the Investment in Cash

How much cash should a firm hold? For transaction purposes, enough to meet the demands of day-to-day operations. To determine how much is enough for transaction purposes, we compare the cost of having *too* much cash to the cost of getting cash—we compare the holding cost and the transaction cost.

As you hold more cash, its holding cost increases. With more cash on hand, the cost of making transactions to meet your cash needs for operations declines. That's because with larger cash balances, you need fewer transactions (selling marketable securities or borrowing from a bank) to meet your cash needs.

We want to have on hand the amount of cash that minimizes the sum of the cost of making transactions to get the cash (selling securities or borrowing) and the opportunity cost of holding more cash than we need.

We will look at the Baumol and the Miller-Orr models to help us decide what level of cash we need and when we need it.

The Baumol Model

The Baumol model is based on the ***economic order quantity*** (EOQ) model developed for inventory management.[2] Applied to the management of cash,

---

[2] William J. Baumol, "The Transactions Demand for Cash: An Inventory Theoretic Approach," *Quarterly Journal of Economics*, vol. 66, Nov. 1952, pp. 545–556.

the EOQ model determines the amount of cash that minimizes the sum of the holding cost and the transaction cost. The holding cost includes costs of administration (keeping track of the cash) and the opportunity cost of not investing the cash elsewhere. The *transaction cost* is the cost of getting more cash—either by selling marketable securities or by borrowing. The economic order quantity is the level of cash infusion (from selling marketable securities or borrowing) that minimizes the total cost associated with cash.

Suppose each time our cash balance is zero we generate $100,000 (by borrowing or selling securities). Further suppose that our opportunity cost for holding cash is 5 percent. We could have invested the cash in something that earns 5 percent instead of holding it. Our holding cost is the product of the average cash balance and the opportunity cost. If we start with $0 cash and end up with $100,000 after an infusion, our average cash balance is $100,000/2 = $50,000, so our holding cost is:

$$\text{Holding cost} = 0.05 \underbrace{}_{\substack{\uparrow \\ \text{Opportunity} \\ \text{cost}}} \underbrace{\left(\frac{\$100,000}{2} \right)}_{\substack{\uparrow \\ \text{Average} \\ \text{balance}}} = \mathbf{\$2,500}$$

If we did not hold $50,000 of cash on average, we could have earned $2,500 by investing it.

Now suppose we need $1 million in cash for transactions over the period. If we need $1 million in total and we get $100,000 in cash at a time, we need to make ten transactions during the period. If it costs us $200 every time we make a cash infusion our transaction cost is $2,000:

$$\text{Transaction cost} = \underbrace{\$200 \text{ per transaction}}_{\substack{\uparrow \\ \text{Cost per transaction}}} \underbrace{\left(\frac{\$1,000,000}{\$100,000 \text{ per transaction}} \right)}_{\substack{\uparrow \\ \text{Number of transactions}}}$$

$$= \$200(10)$$
$$= \mathbf{\$2,000}$$

The total cost associated with cash is the sum of the holding cost and the transaction cost:

Total cost = $2,500 + $2,000 = **$4,500**

Will cash infusions of $100,000 at a time produce the lowest cost of getting cash? We can't control the cash needed for transaction purposes or the cost per transaction. But we can control how many cash infusions we make. And how many we make affects both the holding cost and the transaction cost.

To minimize the costs of cash, we need to find the amount of cash infusion that minimizes these costs. The holding cost is a function of the amount of the cash infusion: With larger cash infusions, we hold more cash. The more cash we hold, the greater is our opportunity cost of holding it. The transaction cost is also a function of the amount of cash infusion: The larger is the

The Average Cash Balance

Suppose we have $300,000 in cash at the beginning of September. If we use cash *evenly throughout the month*— $10,000 per day—we have $0 at the end of the period. How much cash do we have on hand on *average* during September? $300,000/2 = $150,000.

The cash balance starts at $300,000, but is $0 by the end of the month. On average, we have $150,000 invested in cash during the month. If our opportunity cost of holding cash is 1 percent per month, our holding costs are 1 percent of $150,000 or $1,500.

cash infusion, the fewer are the transactions, and therefore the lower are our transaction costs.

Let's use these considerations and what we know about the economic order quantity to determine the minimum cost of cash.

If we get cash in the amount of Q at the beginning of a period and wait until the cash balance is zero before we get more cash, the average cash balance over the period is Q/2. The cost of holding cash during this period is determined by the average cash balance, Q/2, and the opportunity cost of holding the cash, k:

$$\text{Holding cost} = k\,\frac{Q}{2}$$

But each time we get cash, we have to make a transaction. If we demand a total of S dollars of cash each period, we end up making S/Q transactions per period. If it costs K to make a transaction, the transaction cost for the period is:

$$\text{Transaction cost} = K\,\frac{S}{Q}$$

Putting the holding cost and transaction cost together, we find that the total cost associated with the cash balance is:

$$\text{Total cost} = \text{holding cost} + \text{transaction cost}$$

$$= k\,\frac{Q}{2} \qquad + K\,\frac{S}{Q}$$

The total costs are minimized at some value of Q. From calculus, we find that the economic order quantity, designated as Q*, is:

$$Q^* = \sqrt{\frac{2(\text{cost per transaction})(\text{total demand for cash})}{\text{opportunity cost of holding cash}}}$$

or:

$$Q^* = \sqrt{\frac{2\,K\,S}{k}} \qquad\qquad\qquad [15\text{-}1]$$

What does this mean? If we look at the relations among Q* and K, S, and k in this equation, we see that:

- The larger is the cost per transaction, K, the greater is the optimal amount of cash, Q*, infused in a single transaction—the larger the transaction cost, the fewer transactions we make.
- The larger is the demand for cash, S, the larger is the optimal amount of cash, Q*, infused in a single transaction.
- The larger is the opportunity cost of holding cash, k, the smaller is the optimal amount of cash, Q*, infused in a single transaction.

In our example:

K = $200 per transaction
S = $1,000,000
k = 5%

The total cost associated with any given level of inventory ordering Q is:

$$\text{Total cost} = k\,\frac{Q}{2} + K\,\frac{S}{Q}$$

To calculate the minimum total cost with respect to the amount of inventory we get each time, we:

1. Calculate the first derivative of the total cost equation with respect to Q.
2. Set this first derivative equal to zero.
3. Solve for Q.

The first derivative of the total cost with respect to Q (where "d" indicates "change") is:

$$\frac{d(\text{total cost})}{d(Q)} = \frac{k}{2} - \frac{S}{Q^2}\,K$$

Setting the first derivative equal to zero:

$$0 = \frac{k}{2} - \frac{S}{Q^2}\,K$$

Solving for the level of Q that minimizes the total cost, Q*:

$$Q^* = \sqrt{\frac{2KS}{k}}$$

and

$$Q^* = \sqrt{\frac{2(\$200)(\$1{,}000{,}000)}{0.05}} = \mathbf{\$89{,}443}$$

If every time we need a cash infusion, we get \$89,443, the costs associated with cash will be minimized.

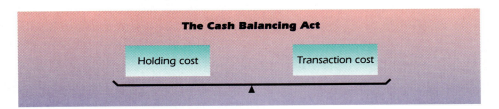

The Cash Balancing Act

Holding cost   Transaction cost

We can check our work by looking at the total cost of cash for levels of Q on either side of Q* = $89,443. If Q = $100,000,

Total cost = $2,500 + $2,000 = **$4,500**

as we saw before. If Q = $50,000:

$$\text{Total costs} = 0.05\left(\frac{\$50,000}{2}\right) + \$200\left(\frac{\$1,000,000}{\$50,000}\right)$$
$$= \$1,250 \qquad + \$4,000$$
$$= \mathbf{\$5,250}$$

If Q = $89,443:

$$\text{Total costs} = 0.05\left(\frac{\$89,443}{2}\right) + \$200\left(\frac{\$1,000,000}{\$89,443}\right)$$
$$= \$2,236 \qquad + \$2,236$$
$$= \mathbf{\$4,472}$$

We can see in Figure 15-3 that the minimum of the total cost curve is at a cash infusion level of $89,443, which corresponds to a total cost of $4,472. If the level of cash infusion is less than or more than $89,443, the cost of cash will be higher.

The EOQ and Time

The EOQ model can be applied to any time framework—whether the period is a year, a month, a week, or any other unit of time. It is only necessary to make sure that all the elements that depend on the chosen unit of time—the holding costs, k, and transactions demand, S—are for that same unit of time.

FIGURE 15-3

Cost of Cash for Different Levels of Cash Infusion

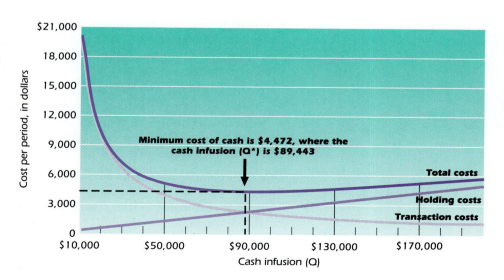

Minimum cost of cash is $4,472, where the cash infusion (Q*) is $89,443

The economic order quantity model can be modified to suit the circumstances of different cash situations. For example, the EOQ model for cash can be modified to include a **safety stock**—a cash balance for precautionary purposes. The safety stock is a level of cash balance that acts as a cushion in case a firm's needs are suddenly greater than expected.

The Miller-Orr Model

The Baumol model assumes that cash is used uniformly throughout the period. The Miller-Orr model recognizes that cash flows vary throughout the period in an unpredictable manner.[3]

To see how the Miller-Orr model takes account of changes in the need for cash, look at the following diagram:

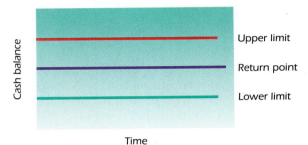

The lower limit is really a safety stock of cash—the cash on hand must never fall below this level. We need to apply experience and judgment in determining the lower level.

Based on (1) how much needs are expected to vary each day, (2) the cost of a transaction, and (3) the opportunity cost of cash expressed on a daily basis, this model tells us:

1. *The level of cash immediately after a new cash infusion.* This level is referred to as the **return point** (not to be confused with the level of safety stock). Levels of cash below the safety stock cannot be tolerated; levels below the return point are tolerated—until they hit the safety stock level, of course.
2. *The upper limit of cash.* If the cash balance exceeds this limit we invest in marketable securities, so that the amount of cash on hand after the investment is the return point balance.

The return point and the upper limit are determined by the model as the levels necessary to minimize costs of cash, considering (1) daily swings in cash needs, (2) the transaction cost, and (3) the opportunity cost of cash.

The Miller-Orr model provides us with a few decision rules:

- Our cash balance can be at any level between the upper and lower limit.
- There is a cash balance (the return point) that we aim for if our cash balance exceeds the upper limit or falls below the lower limit:

[3] Merton H. Miller and Daniel Orr, "A Model of the Demand for Money by Firms," *Quarterly Journal of Economics*, vol. 80, July 1966, pp. 413–435.

If our cash balance *exceeds the upper limit*, any cash in excess of the return point is invested in marketable securities.

If our cash balance is *below the lower limit*, any deficiency up to the return point is made up by selling marketable securities or borrowing.

The return point is a function of:

1. The lower limit.
2. The cost per transaction.
3. The opportunity cost of holding cash (per day).
4. The variability of daily cash flows, which we measure as the variance of daily cash flows.

and is determined mathematically as follows:

$$\text{Return point} = \text{lower limit} + \sqrt[3]{\frac{0.75\left(\begin{array}{c}\text{cost per}\\\text{transaction}\end{array}\right)\left(\begin{array}{c}\text{variance of}\\\text{daily cash flows}\end{array}\right)}{\text{opportunity cost per day}}} \qquad [15\text{-}2]$$

In this equation, we see that:

- The higher is the safety stock (the lower limit), the higher is the return point.
- The higher is the cost of making a transaction, the higher is the return point.
- The greater is the variability of cash flows, the higher is the return point.
- The greater is the holding cost of cash, the lower is the return point.

The upper limit is the sum of the lower limit and three times the return point:

$$\begin{array}{l}\text{Upper limit} =\\ \quad \text{lower limit} + 3\left[\sqrt[3]{0.75\left(\begin{array}{c}\text{cost per}\\\text{transaction}\end{array}\right)\left(\begin{array}{c}\text{variance of}\\\text{daily cash flows}\end{array}\right)}\right]\end{array} \qquad [15\text{-}3]$$

To see how this model works, suppose we solve it using the following data:

Opportunity cost per day   = 0.01%
Variance of daily cash flows = $20,000
Cost per transaction   = $200
Lower limit   = $10,000

Then:

Lower limit   = $10,000

$$\text{Return point} = \$10,000 + \sqrt[3]{\frac{0.75(\$200)(\$20,000)}{0.0001}}$$

$$= \$10,000 + \sqrt[3]{\frac{\$3,000,000}{.0001}}$$

$$= \mathbf{\$13,107}$$

Upper limit = $10,000 + 3($3,107)

$$= \mathbf{\$19,321}$$

What we have just determined using the Miller-Orr model is that the cash balance can be allowed to fluctuate between $10,000 and $19,321. If the cash balance exceeds $19,321, we invest the difference between the cash balance and the return point, restoring the cash balance to the return point. If the cash balance is below the lower limit, we sell marketable securities to bring the cash balance to the return point. Each time the cash balance is outside either the lower or the upper limit, we take action to bounce the cash balance back to the return point.

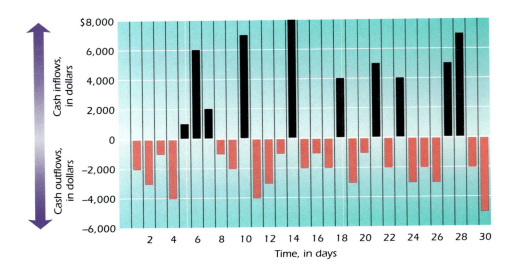

This "bouncing" is illustrated in Figures 15-4(*a*) and 15-4(*b*). In Figure 15-4(*a*), the cash flow per day is graphed against time and, as the figure shows, sometimes cash flows in, sometimes cash flows out. In Figure 15-4(*b*), the cash balance is plotted for each day using the Miller-Orr model. Each time the balance hits $10,000, it bounces back to $13,107 and each time the balance hits $19,321, it bounces back to $13,107.

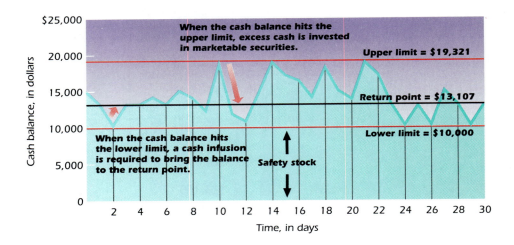

Other Considerations

The Baumol and Miller-Orr models both try to help us minimize the costs of cash.[4] The Baumol model assumes a predictable, steady use of cash. The Miller-Orr model incorporates an estimate of the variability of cash flows.

But there are other factors that affect cash management. One is the seasonality of our cash needs. If our sales and collections on sales are seasonal, we must factor the pattern of cash into our cash balance. However, the Baumol model does not consider changing cash needs.

Another factor is doing business in other countries. If we do business in a foreign country, we have added complications, including:

- The need to keep cash in different currencies.
- Restrictions on transferring currencies across borders.
- Laws in many countries that require holdings in that country's domestic currency.
- The risk that the value of the foreign currency may change relative to the firm's domestic currency.

We must look very closely at our cash flows and the factors that affect our cash needs. Once we understand our cash flow needs and the predictability of these needs, we can use either model as a basis to determine cash infusions and holdings to minimize costs.

Cash Management Techniques

Cash management has very simple goals:

- Have enough cash on hand to meet immediate needs, but not too much.
- Get cash from those who owe it to you as soon as possible and pay it out to those you owe as late as possible.

The Baumol and Miller-Orr models help us in managing our cash to satisfy the first goal. But the second requires methods that speed up incoming cash and slow down outgoing cash. To understand these methods, we need first to understand the check-clearing process.

The Check-Clearing Process

The process of receiving cash from customers involves several time-consuming steps:

- The customer sends the check.
- The check is processed within the firm, so that the customer can be credited with the payment.
- The check is sent to the firm's bank.
- The bank sends the check through the clearing system.
- The firm is credited with the amount of the check.

[4] Tests of these models indicate that while they may not accurately depict the cash flows of a firm, they perform fairly well in applications (with slight modifications) and are useful in reducing the time managers spend on managing cash (David Wiley Mullins, Jr., and Richard B. Homonoff, "Applications of Inventory Cash Management Models," *Modern Developments in Financial Management*, ed. Stewart C. Myers, Dryden Press, Hinsdale, Ill., 1976, pp. 494–527).

The Check-Clearing Process

Steps in the Process

Process Started
Customer mails the check to the firm.

Mail Float
The check is in the mail.
1–5 days

Firm Float
The check is processed by the
receiving firm and sent to the bank.
Up to 1 day

Clearing Float
The bank sends the check to the
Federal Reserve bank or the
Federal Reserve check-processing center.
Up to 2 days

Process Completed
The receiving firm is given credit for the deposit.

A Sample Time Line Representing the Check-Clearing Process

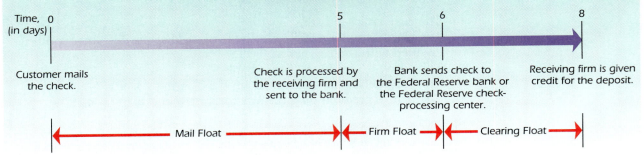

Time, 0   5   6   8
(in days)

Customer mails
the check.

Check is processed by
the receiving firm and
sent to the bank.

Bank sends check to
the Federal Reserve bank or
the Federal Reserve check-
processing center.

Receiving firm is given
credit for the deposit.

Mail Float   Firm Float   Clearing Float

700

Several days may elapse between the time when the firm receives the check and the time when the firm is credited with the amount of the check. During that time, the firm cannot use the funds. The amount of funds tied up in transit and in the banking system is referred to as the *float*. The float occurs because of the time the check is tied up in the mail, in check processing within the firm, and in check processing in the banking system.

The float can be costly to those who are on the receiving end. Suppose on average our customers make $1 million in payments each day. If our float is seven days, we therefore have 7 times $1,000,000 = $7,000,000 coming to us that we cannot use. If we can speed up our collections to five days, we can reduce our float to $5 million—using the $2 million freed up for other things.

But float can be beneficial to the payor. If a firm is credited with paying an account before it actually loses the use of the funds represented in that payment, that's a float from the perspective of the paying firm, and it increases the firm's available funds—but, only until the firm loses the use of the funds.

Suppose we make payments to our suppliers of $1 million per day, on average. And suppose it takes our suppliers five days after they receive our checks to complete the check-clearing process. We have $5 million in float per day. If we could slow down the check processing by one day, we could increase the float by $1 million to $6 million. That's $1 million more in cash available for us to use each day.

There are several ways we can speed up incoming cash:

- *Lockbox system.* Customers send their checks to post office boxes, and banks pick up and begin processing the checks immediately.
- *Selection of banks.* Choosing banks that are well connected in the banking system, such as clearinghouse banks or correspondent banks, can speed up the collection of checks.
- *Check processing within the firm.* Speed up processing of checks within the firm so that deposits are made quickly.
- *Electronic collection.* Avoid the use of paper checks, dealing only with electronic entries.
- *Concentration banking.* Select a bank or banks located near customers, reducing the mail float.

Clearinghouse and Correspondent Banks

A *clearinghouse* is a location where banks meet to exchange checks drawn on each other, and a *clearinghouse bank* is a participant in a clearinghouse. Clearinghouses may involve local banks or other banks. Check clearing through a clearinghouse can be half a day faster than through the Federal Reserve system.

A *correspondent bank* is a bank that has an agreement with a clearinghouse bank to exchange its checks in the clearinghouse. Banks can become correspondents to clearinghouses in other parts of the country, reducing their check-clearing time relative to the time needed for clearing checks through the Federal Reserve System.

In addition, there are several methods we can use to slow up our payments of cash:

- *Controlled disbursements.* Minimizing bank balances by depositing only what is needed to make immediate demands on the account.
- *Remote disbursement.* Paying what is owed with checks drawn on a bank that is not readily accessible to the payee, increasing the check-processing float.

We have to remember that whichever way we speed up the receipt of cash (reducing the float to us) or slow down the payment of cash (increasing the float to others), there is a cost. We have to weigh the benefits against the costs of altering the float.

We will look at one speedup device closely—the lockbox system—and one slowdown device—controlled disbursements—to see how the float can be altered.

Lockbox Systems

With a *lockbox system* a firm's customers send their payments directly to a post office box controlled by the firm's bank. Doing this skips the step in which the firm receives and handles the check and paperwork, removing that step from the process. The lockbox system can cut down on the time it takes to process checks in two ways. First, the firm can use post office boxes (and collecting banks) throughout the country, reducing the time a check spends in the mail—reducing the mail float. Second, because the bank processes the checks and paperwork, we avoid the time the checks spend at the receiving firm—eliminating the time it takes to process checks within the firm.

To see the savings realized by using a lockbox, suppose that it can reduce our total float from six to three days. If we collect $1.5 million per year through the lockbox system, three days' worth of collections frees up $12,329 for investment during the year ($1,500,000/365 × 3 days = $12,329). If we can earn 12 percent a year by investing in marketable securities, the three-day reduction amounts to an increase in earnings of $12,329 × 0.12 = $1,479. As long as the cost of the lockbox system is less than $1,479 per year, there is a benefit in using it.

We can state the increased earnings from the lockbox system as follows:

$$\text{Benefit from lockbox system} = \left(\begin{array}{c}\text{collections}\\\text{per day}\end{array}\right)\left(\begin{array}{c}\text{reduction of}\\\text{float in days}\end{array}\right)\left(\begin{array}{c}\text{opportunity cost}\\\text{of funds per year}\end{array}\right) \quad [15\text{-}4]$$

To decide whether or not to use such a system involves comparing the benefit obtained from the lockbox system with the lockbox fees charged by the bank.

There are a couple of drawbacks to a lockbox system. Because the bank receives the check and documents, it takes longer for the firm to record who has paid—the bank must forward the documents to the firm. Also, customers may become a bit confused over the addresses, since payments are sent to the lockbox address and all other correspondence is sent to the firm's business address.

The Lockbox Process

Steps in the Process

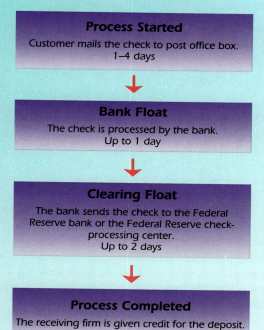

Process Started

Customer mails the check to post office box.
1–4 days

Bank Float

The check is processed by the bank.
Up to 1 day

Clearing Float

The bank sends the check to the Federal Reserve bank or the Federal Reserve check-processing center.
Up to 2 days

Process Completed

The receiving firm is given credit for the deposit.

An Example of the Time Line Corresponding to a Lockbox System

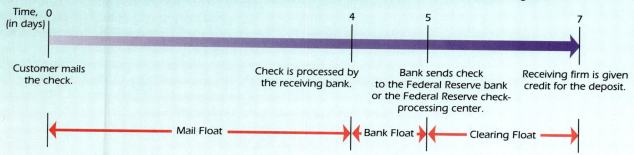

Time, 0 (in days)   4   5   7

Customer mails the check.

Check is processed by the receiving bank.

Bank sends check to the Federal Reserve bank or the Federal Reserve check-processing center.

Receiving firm is given credit for the deposit.

Mail Float — Bank Float — Clearing Float

The lockbox system may reduce the mail float (due to the placement of the lockboxes in locations near the customer) and changes what was the "firm float" to a "bank float," since the bank now processes the checks received from customers.

Setting up a lockbox system requires answers to several questions:

1. How many lockboxes?
2. Where to locate the lockboxes to cut down on mail time?
3. Where to direct which customers to send their payments?

Determining the optimal lockbox setup requires evaluating the cost of each lockbox and the opportunity cost of having checks in the mail.

Controlled Disbursements

If you want to have more cash available for your own use, slow down the payments you make, thus increasing the float to others. You could use *remote disbursements:* writing checks on banks that are relatively inaccessible to your payees. However, remote disbursements are discouraged by the Monetary Control Act of 1980. The Federal Reserve now charges banks for float at the federal funds rate, and banks pass along the charges to their customers in the form of fees.

An alternative to remote disbursements is controlled disbursements. *Controlled disbursements* is an arrangement with a bank to minimize the amount you hold in bank balances to pay what you owe. Under this system, you keep in your account only the funds you need for immediate disbursement. To succeed in this, you need to work closely with the bank: The bank notifies you of checks being cashed on your account and you immediately wire the necessary funds.

An extreme disbursement method is referred to as a *zero-balance account* (ZBA). In a ZBA arrangement, you keep no funds in the bank: You simply deposit funds as the checks you wrote out are presented for payment through the banking system. Since this account can save you two to three days of float and cost anywhere from $20 to $200 per month in bank fees, zero-balance accounts are attractive. Some banks also make ZBA arrangements attractive by offering to automatically invest funds in excess of the firm's payment needs in short-term securities, thus ensuring that there are no idle funds.

As you can imagine, a controlled disbursements system requires coordination between you and your bank. If you are off just a little bit, you can lose goodwill with your suppliers or other payees. Also, this system is not costless; the bank is performing a service and charges a fee.

Monitoring Cash Needs

We can monitor our cash needs through cash forecasting. *Cash forecasting* is analyzing how much and when cash is needed, and how much and when to generate it. Cash forecasting requires pulling together and consolidating the short-term projections that relate to cash inflows and outflows. These cash flows may be a part of your capital budget, production plans, sales forecasts, or collection on accounts.

To understand the cash needs and generation, you have to understand how long it takes to generate cash once an investment in inventory is made. We're referring to the operating cycle—the time it takes to make cash out of cash.

> Cash forecasting is discussed in Chapter 17.

Current Advances in Lockboxes

There are a number of recent advances in lockbox systems that need to be considered in selecting a lockbox system, including:

Lockbox networks. Collections of banks that link lockboxes from different parts of the country to speed up the bank float.

Image-based processing. Computer coding, such as bar coding of envelopes, that speeds up processing by the bank.

Mail interception. Banks pick up mail at the post office to reduce the mail float.

Nonbank lockbox systems. Lockbox systems established by firms other than banks.

In selecting a lockbox system, we need to evaluate the speed with which we have access to funds, the record-keeping of accounts paid, and the costs of the system.

If we consider cash disbursements, we get a better picture of the **net operating cycle**—the time it takes to make cash from cash plus the time we delay payment on our purchases:

Net operating cycle = operating cycle – number of days of purchases

Estimating our net operating cycle gives us information on how long it takes to generate cash from our current assets. The longer the net operating cycle, the more cash we need on hand.

To understand our cash flows, we also have to have a fairly good idea of the uncertainty of our cash needs and cash generation. Cash flows are uncertain because sales are uncertain, and so is the uncertainty regarding when we will collect payment on what we do sell, as well as uncertainty about production costs and capital outlays. Forecasting cash flows requires the coordination of marketing, purchasing, production, and financial management.

Marketable Securities

Reasons for Holding Marketable Securities

An integral part of cash management is storing excess cash in an asset that earns a return, such as marketable securities. Precautionary and speculative needs for cash can often be satisfied by funds stored in marketable securities, selling the securities as needs for cash arise. In our models of cash management, we assume that we stash cash we don't need right away into marketable securities and convert them to cash as needed. In this way, marketable securities are a substitute for cash.

If cash flows of a firm are uneven—perhaps seasonal—the firm can deal with the uneven demands for cash by either borrowing for the short term or selling marketable securities. If short-term borrowing is not possible or is costly, marketable securities can be used: Buy marketable securities when cash inflows exceed outflows; sell marketable securities when cash inflows are less than outflows. In this way, marketable securities are a temporary investment.

Aside from the uneven cash demands from operations, marketable securities may be a convenient way of storing funds for planned expenditures. If you generate cash from operations or from the sale of securities for an investment in the near future, the funds can be kept in marketable securities until needed.

Types of Marketable Securities

The primary role of marketable securities is to back up the cash balances—the securities are a place to store cash that isn't needed immediately, but may be needed soon. We should therefore consider only marketable securities that provide safety and liquidity. In evaluating safety and liquidity, we need to look at the risks we accept in investing in securities. The relevant risks to consider are:

Default risk	The risk that the issuer will not pay interest and/or principal as promised.
Purchasing power risk	The risk that inflation will erode the purchasing power of the money you receive in the form of interest and principal in the future.
Interest rate risk	The risk that interest rates will change, changing the value of your investment.
Reinvestment rate risk	The risk that interest rates will change, affecting the rate of return you can earn on reinvesting the interest and principal from your investment.
Liquidity risk	Also referred to as marketability risk, the risk that the security will not be marketable, at least at its true value, because of a lack of investor interest in the security.

The marketable securities that satisfy the criteria of safety and liquidity are most likely money market securities. Money market securities include:

Banker's acceptances	Debt issued by banks that originates most often from international trade transactions. Since this debt is backed by both the issuing bank and the purchaser of goods, the likelihood of default is very small.
Certificates of deposit	Debt issued by banks and sold in large denominations. This debt has maturities ranging generally up to one year. Since this debt is issued by banks, but exceeds the amount for deposit guaranteed by bank insurance, there is some default risk.

Commercial paper	Debt issued by large corporations that is sold in large denominations and generally matures in thirty days. While the debt is unsecured credit and is issued by corporations, there is some default risk, though this is minimized by the backup lines of credit at commercial banks.
Eurodollar deposits	Loans and certificates of deposit of non-U.S. banks that are denominated in the U.S. dollar. These debts are generally in large denominations and have maturities up to six months. As with loans and certificates of U.S. banks, there is some default risk.
Money market preferred	Preferred stock whose dividend rates are reset periodically (usually by a Dutch auction). Investors can decide whether to sell the stock back to the issuer or hold it at each Dutch auction (typically every seven weeks). Dividends received by corporations are, in large part, excluded from taxation.
Repurchase agreements	Short-term financing arrangements in which the seller of a security—say, a Treasury bill—agrees to buy back the security after a few days, but at a higher price. Since the security acts as collateral for this financing, there is little risk.
Treasury bills	Securities issued by the U.S. government that have maturities of 91, 192, or 365 days. These securities are considered default free and are readily marketable.

Some money market securities, such as government securities, have no default risk; the ones that do have default risk have very little. Because of the short maturity of money market securities and the fact that they are generally issued by large banks or corporations (who are not likely to get into deep financial trouble in a short time), their default risk is low. Even so, you can look at the credit ratings by financial services such as Moody's and Standard & Poor's for an evaluation of the default risk of any particular money market security.

Money market securities have relatively little purchasing power risk. The chance that inflation will change over the short term is slight, though a possibility. Money market securities also have relatively little interest rate risk. Since these securities are short term, their values are not as affected by changes in interest rates as, say, a thirty-year corporate bond.

The short maturities of money market securities, however, subject the investor to reinvestment rate risk. If rates fall and the security matures, the investor must roll over—or reinvest—the funds in another security with lower rates. But since this investment's purpose is short term, that is a risk we must bear.

Cash Investment Strategies from around the World

The management of a firm's investment of cash in marketable securities differs around the world. Let's look at four companies and their marketable securities investments:

Toyota Motor Corporation (Japan)

- Keeps cash in yen to avoid currency risk, though subsidiaries hold cash in the currency of nation in which they do business (for example, Toyota Motor Sales U.S.A. invests in securities denominated in the U.S. dollar).
- Invests in time deposits of Japanese city banks with maturities of three to six months, in commercial paper, and in short-term bonds issued by the Japanese government and large Japanese cities.
- Will not invest in stocks or corporate bonds.

AB Volvo (Sweden)

- Due to government restrictions, can invest only in Swedish kroner-denominated securities.
- By law, it must deposit 15 percent of any excess cash in a low-interest account in the Swedish central bank.
- Invests its cash in Swedish government securities, certificates of deposit, and commercial paper with maturities of less than one year.
- Also invests in government bonds and high-quality mortgage-backed bonds with maturities of up to five years.

Siemens (Germany)

- Most of the investments are denominated in deutschemarks, though some investments are denominated in U.S. dollars (such as U.S. Treasury and agency securities).
- Invests in time deposits (with maturities of less than six months), commercial paper, fixed rate bonds and notes with maturities of less than five years, and equity securities.

Chrysler Corporation (United States)

- Invests primarily in dollar-denominated securities, but does some hedging of foreign currency risk.
- Invests in loan participation (short-term loans arranged by banks and sold to third parties) and other short-term securities, but avoids investment in bonds.

SOURCE: These policies are covered in more detail in Claire Makin and Ida Picker, "A Portfolio of Cash Management Strategies," *Institutional Investor*, vol. 19, Feb. 1989, pp. 128–139.

RECEIVABLES MANAGEMENT

When we allow customers to pay for goods and services at some time after the purchase, we create **accounts receivable.** By allowing our customers to pay some time after they receive the goods or services, we are granting credit, which we refer to as **trade credit.** Trade credit, also referred to as **merchandise credit** or **dealer credit,** is an informal credit arrangement. Unlike other forms of credit, trade credit is not usually evidenced by notes, but rather is generated spontaneously: Trade credit is granted when a customer buys goods or services.

Reasons for Extending Credit

Firms extend credit to customers to help stimulate sales. Suppose you offer a product for sale at $20, demanding cash at the time of the sale. And suppose your competitor offers the same product for sale, but allows customers thirty days to pay. Who's going to sell the product? If the product and its price are the same, your competitor, of course. So the benefit of extending credit is the profit from the increased sales.

Extending credit is both a financial and a marketing decision. When a firm extends credit to its customers, it does so to encourage the sale of its goods and services. The most direct benefit is the profit on the increased sales. If the firm has a **variable cost margin** (that is, variable costs/sales) of 80 percent, then increasing sales by $100,000 increases the firm's profit before taxes by $20,000. Another way of stating this is that the **contribution margin** (funds available to cover fixed costs) is 20 percent: for every $1 of sales, 20 cents is available *after* variable costs.

The benefit from extending credit is:

$$\text{Benefit from extending credit} = (\text{contribution margin})(\text{change in sales}) \qquad [15\text{-}5]$$

If a firm liberalizes the credit terms it grants to customers, and thereby increases sales by $5 million and if its contribution margin is 25 percent, the benefit from liberalizing credit is 25 percent of $5 million, or $1.25 million.

Costs Associated with Credit

But like any credit, trade credit has a cost. The firm granting the credit is forgoing the use of the funds for a period, so there is an opportunity cost associated with giving credit. In addition, there are costs of administering the accounts receivable—keeping track of what is owed. And there is a chance that the customer may not pay what is due when it is due.

The Cost of Discounts

Do firms grant credit at no cost to the customer? No, because as we just explained, a firm has costs in granting credit. So firms generally give credit with an implicit or hidden cost:

- The customer that pays cash on delivery or within a specified time thereafter—called a discount period—gets a discount from the invoice price.
- The customer that pays after this discount period pays the *full* invoice price.

Paying after the discount period is really borrowing. The customer pays the difference between the discounted price and the full invoice price. How much has been borrowed? A customer paying in cash within the discount period pays the discounted price. So what is effectively borrowed is the cash price.

In analyses of credit terms, the dollar cost of granting a discount is:

Cost of discount = discount percentage × credit sales using discount   [15-6]

But wait. Is this the only effect of granting a discount? *Only* if you assume that when the firm establishes the discount it does not adjust the full invoice price of its goods. But is this reasonable? Probably not. If the firm decides to alter its credit policy to institute a discount, most likely it will increase the full invoice price sufficiently to be compensated for the time value of money and the risk borne when extending credit.

The difference between the cash price and the invoice price is a cost to the customer—and, effectively, a return to the firm for this trade credit. Consider a customer who purchases an item for $100, on terms of 2/10, net 30 days. This means that if she pays within ten days, she receives a 2 percent discount, paying only $98 (the cash price). If she pays on the eleventh day, she pays $100. Is the seller losing $2 if the customer pays on day 10? Yes and no. We have to assume that the seller would not establish a discount as a means of cutting prices. Rather, a firm establishes the full invoice price to reflect the profit from selling the item *and* a return from extending credit.[5]

Suppose Discount Warehouse revises its credit terms—payment in full in thirty days—and introduces a discount of 2 percent for accounts paid within ten days. And suppose Discount's contribution margin is 20 percent. To analyze the effect of these changes, we have to project the increase in Discount's future sales and estimate how soon Discount's customers will pay.

Let's first assume that Discount does not change its sales prices. And let's assume that Discount's sales will increase by $100,000 to $1.1 million, with 30 percent of its customers paying within ten days and the rest paying within thirty days. The benefit from this discount is the increased contribution toward before-tax profit of $100,000 × 20 percent = $20,000. The cost of the discount is the forgone profit of 2 percent on 30 percent of the $1.1 million sales, or $6,600.

Now let's assume that Discount changes its sales prices when it institutes the discount so that the profit margin (available to cover the firm's fixed costs) after the discount is still 20 percent:

Contribution margin$(1 - 0.02) = 20\%$

Contribution margin $= \dfrac{0.20}{(1 - 0.02)} = \mathbf{20.408\%}$

---

[5] If the customer pays within the discount period, there is a cost to the firm—the opportunity cost of not getting the cash at the exact date of the sale but, rather, at some later time. With the 2/10, net 30 terms, if the customer pays on the tenth day, the seller has just given a ten-day interest-free loan to the customer. That is part of the carrying cost of accounts receivable, which we discuss later in this chapter.

If sales increase to $1.1 million, the benefit of the difference is the profit:

Before the discount:	20% of $1,000,000	= **$200,000**
After the discount:	20.408% of $1,100,000	= **$224,490**

The incremental benefit is $24,490, and the cost, in terms of the discounts taken, is 2 percent of 30 percent of $1.1 million or $6,600.

While we haven't taken into consideration the other costs involved (such as the carrying cost of the accounts and bad debts), we see that we get a different picture of the benefits and costs of discounts depending on what the firm does to the price of its goods and services when the discount is instituted. So what appears to be the "cost" of the discounts taken doesn't give us the whole picture because the firm most likely changes its contribution margin at the same time to include compensation for granting credit and in that way increases the benefit from the change in the policy.

Other Costs

There are a number of costs of credit in addition to the cost of the discount. These costs include:

- The carrying cost of tying up funds in accounts receivable instead of investing them elsewhere.
- The cost of administering and collecting the accounts.
- The risk of bad debts.

The carrying cost is similar to the holding cost that we looked at in our discussion of cash balances: the product of the opportunity cost of investing in accounts receivable and the investment in the accounts. The opportunity cost is the return the firm could have earned on its next best opportunity. The investment is the amount the firm has invested to generate sales. Consider a product that is sold for $100. If its contribution margin is 25 percent, this means that the firm has invested $75 in the sold item (in raw materials, labor, and other variable costs).

Suppose a firm liberalizes its credit policy, resulting in an increase in accounts receivable of $1 million. And suppose the firm's contribution margin is 40 percent (which means its variable cost ratio is 60 percent). The firm's increased investment in accounts receivable is 60 percent of $1 million, or $600,000. If the firm's opportunity cost is 5 percent, the carrying cost of accounts receivable is:

Carrying cost of accounts receivable = 5% of $600,000 = **$30,000**

We can state the carrying cost more formally as:

$$\text{Carrying cost of accounts receivable} = \left(\begin{array}{c}\text{opportunity}\\\text{cost}\end{array}\right)\left(\begin{array}{c}\text{variable}\\\text{cost ratio}\end{array}\right)\left(\begin{array}{c}\text{change in}\\\text{accounts receivable}\end{array}\right) \quad [15\text{-}7]$$

In addition to the carrying cost, there are costs of administering and collecting accounts. Extending credit involves record-keeping, and there are also costs that are incurred just in personnel and paperwork keeping track of which customers owe what amount. In addition to simply recording these accounts,

The Implicit Cost of Trade Credit to the Customer

Trade credit is often stated in terms of a rate of discount, a discount period, and a net period when payment in full is due. The effective cost of trade credit to the customer can be calculated by first determining the effective interest cost for the credit period and then placing this effective cost on an annual basis so that we can compare it with the cost of other forms of credit.

If the credit terms are stated as "2/10, net 30," this means that the customer can take a 2 percent discount from the invoice price if payment is made within ten days; otherwise the full price is due within thirty days. If you purchased an item that costs $100, you would either pay $98 within the first ten days after purchase or the full price of $100 if you paid after ten days.

The effective cost of credit is the discount forgone. For a $100 purchase, this is $2. Putting this in percentage terms, you pay 2 percent of the invoice price to borrow 98 percent of the invoice price:

$$\text{Cost of credit} = r = \frac{0.02}{0.98} = \textbf{0.0204} \text{ or } \textbf{2.04\%} \text{ per credit period}$$

The effective *annual* cost is calculated by determining the compounded annual cost if this form of financing is done *throughout the year*. Assuming that payment is made on the net day (thirty days after the sale), the credit period (the difference between the net period and the discount period) is twenty days and there are $t = 365/20 = 18.25$ such credit periods in a year. Therefore:

$$\text{Effective annual cost} = (1 + r)^t - 1$$
$$= (1 + 0.0204)^{18.25} - 1 = \textbf{44.56\%} \text{ per year}$$

The flip side of this trade credit is that the firm granting credit has an effective return on credit of 44.56 percent per year.

there are expenses in collecting accounts that are past due. Whether the firm collects its own accounts or hires a collection agency to collect them, there are costs involved in making sure that customers pay.

Still another cost of trade credit is unpaid accounts—bad debts. If the firm demanded cash for each sale, there would be no unpaid accounts. By allowing customers to pay after the sale, the firm is taking on risk that the customer will not pay as promised. And by liberalizing its credit terms (for example, allowing a longer time to pay) or its criteria concerning to whom to extend credit, the firm may attract customers who are less able to pay their obligations when promised.

Credit and the Demand for a Firm's Goods and Services

When a firm that did not grant credit decides to do so, it has to consider the effect of this change on its pricing and sales. Let's return to the case in which your competitor offers credit terms of payment in thirty days and your firm does not. While on the surface it may seem that your competitor has an advantage, this may not be so. What if your competitor also has higher prices for its goods? Perhaps these prices are just high enough to compensate for the expected costs of bad debts and the time value of money. Does this mean that your firm will increase sales if it extends credit? Yes, if your firm does not change its prices; maybe, if your firm increases prices when it extends credit.

To analyze the effect of extending credit, you have to understand a number of factors:

- *The price elasticity of your goods and services.* How sensitive are your sales to the prices of your goods and services?
- *The probability of bad debts.* When you extend credit, how likely is it that some customers may pay late or never pay? How much compensation do you require to bear this risk?
- *When customers are most likely to pay.* If you offer discount terms, will all your customers pay at the end of the discount period? What proportion of your customers will pay within the discount period?

As you can see, there are many variables to consider, and they will differ from firm to firm and industry to industry. An understanding of the market for your goods and services as well as an understanding of your customers' needs are required in analyzing the effects of a change in your credit policy.

Credit and Collection Policies

A firm has a set of credit and collection policies dealing with the terms for extending credit, the guidelines prescribing who gets credit, and procedures for collecting delinquent accounts. In deciding what its credit and collection policies will be, a firm considers the trade-off between the costs of accounts receivable—the opportunity cost of investing in receivables, the cost of administering the receivables, and the cost of delinquent accounts—and the benefits of accounts receivable—the expected increase in profits and the return received from its trade credit.

Credit Policies

The **credit terms** consist of the maximum amount of credit, the length of period allowed for payment (that is, the net period), and the discount rate and

---

Tailoring Your Terms to Fit Your Customers

If your customers have seasonal cash flows (as a toy retailer would) you could have terms with **seasonal dating,** in which the discount period begins at the start of the customers' busy season. Seasonal dating is useful as a marketing tool, since it encourages customers to purchase goods from your firm early—without the obligation to pay until the time when they begin to receive cash from the sale of their goods.

discount period, if any. The purpose of discounts is to attract customers—thereby increasing sales, and to encourage the early payment of accounts, thereby reducing the amount tied up in accounts receivable.

Credit terms should somehow balance the marketing needs (increased sales) and the costs of these receivables (the cost of administration of receivables, the risk of bad debts, and the opportunity cost of funds). To design terms to meet our marketing needs, we must consider:

1. *Our customers' cash flow patterns.* Do our customers have seasonal cash flows? How long are our customers' operating cycles?
2. *The terms our competitors are offering.*
3. *The equitability of our credit terms among customers.* Firms must be careful not to discriminate among customers. While different terms can be applied to customers with different credit risks, there must be some basis for classifying the customers according to risk.

Evaluation of Creditworthiness

The *five Cs of credit* that must be considered in evaluating a customer's creditworthiness are:

Capacity	Ability of the customer to pay.
Capital	Financial condition.
Character	Willingness of the customer to pay debts.
Collateral	Ability of creditors to collect on bad debts if the customer liquidates its assets.
Conditions	Sensitivity of the customer's ability to pay to underlying economic and market factors.

Sources of information to assess the creditworthiness of customers in terms of these five factors include:

- Your firm's prior experience with the customer.
- Credit agency ratings and reports on the customer, such as those of Dun & Bradstreet and TRW.
- Contact with the customer's bank or other creditors.
- Analysis of the customer's financial condition.

We need to consider the cost of these sources, such as fees for credit reports, as well as the costs of staff personnel and other resources used in evaluating the information contained in the credit reports.

Often firms will extend a small amount of credit to new customers to get experience with them—to see whether they actually do pay on time.

Collection Policies

Collection policies specify the procedures for collecting delinquent accounts. Collection could start with polite reminders, continuing in progressive steps, and ending by placing the account in the hands of a collection agency, a firm that specializes in collecting accounts. For example,

1. When an account is a few days overdue, a letter is sent, reminding the customer of the amount due and the credit terms.

2. When an account is a month overdue, a telephone call is made, reminding the customer of the amount due, the credit terms, and efforts to collect the account by letter.
3. When an account is two months overdue, it is handed over to a collection agency.

In designing the collection procedures, we have to keep in mind that aggressive efforts to collect may result in lost future sales. We also have to consider the customers' circumstances. For example, if the customer is in the midst of a labor strike, you may wish to avoid collection tactics detrimental to your relationship with this particular customer.

The Bill Collectors

When firms do not or cannot collect payments on their customers' accounts, they sometimes let collection agencies do it. Collection agencies, which specialize in collecting on delinquent accounts, are limited as to what they can do. The Fair Debt Collection Practices Act protects the debtor from harassment, prohibiting collectors from calling at unusual times of the day, making misleading statements, or calling the debtor's place of work without permission. Despite these protections, there are a number of reports of abusive tactics by bill collectors (Lucinda Harper, "Debt Collectors' Aggressive Tactics Bring Mounting Protests from Irate Consumers," *The Wall Street Journal*, Dec. 3, 1991, p. B1).

Monitoring Accounts Receivable

We can monitor how well accounts receivable are managed by using financial ratios and aging schedules. Financial ratios can be used to get an overall picture of how fast we collect on accounts receivable, and aging schedules, which are breakdowns of the accounts receivable by the length of time they have been around, help us get a more detailed picture of our collection efforts.

We can get an idea of how quickly we collect our accounts receivable by calculating the **number of days of credit,** which is the ratio of the balance in accounts receivable at a point in time (say, at the end of a year) to the credit sales per day (on average, the dollar amount of credit sales during a single day):

$$\text{Number of days of credit} = \frac{\text{accounts receivable}}{\text{credit sales per day}} \qquad [15\text{-}8]$$

where credit sales per day is the ratio of credit sales over a period divided by the number of business days in that period. For example, averaging over a year:

$$\text{Credit sales per day} = \frac{\text{credit sales}}{365 \text{ days}} \qquad [15\text{-}9]$$

The number-of-days-of-credit ratio, also referred to as the **average collection period** or **days sales outstanding** (DSO), measures how long, on average, it takes us to collect on our accounts receivable.

If we have $1 million in credit sales per year and currently have a balance in accounts receivable of $80,000, then:

$$\text{Credit sales per day} = \frac{\$1,000,000}{365 \text{ days}} = \textbf{\$2,740 per day}$$

and

$$\text{Number of days of credit} = \frac{\$80,000}{\$2,740 \text{ per day}} = \textbf{29 days}$$

This means the firm has, on average, twenty-nine days worth of sales that have not been paid for as yet.

We can use this measure to evaluate the effectiveness of our collection policies, comparing the number of days of credit we determine with the net period allowed by credit terms. We can also use this information to help us in our cash forecasting, since it tells us the length of time, on average, before each credit sale turns into cash.

But we need to consider certain factors in applying this measure. For example, if our sales are seasonal, which accounts receivable balance do we use? Over what period are we measuring credit sales per day? We must be careful when we interpret this ratio, since both the numerator and denominator are influenced by our pattern of sales.

We can also monitor receivables by using an aging schedule. Preparing an aging schedule allows us to look at all our receivables and group them according to how long they were outstanding, such as 1 to 30 days, 31 to 40 days, and so on. For example:

Number of days outstanding	Number of accounts	Amount outstanding
1–30	120	$320,000
31–40	40	80,000
41–50	10	18,000
51–60	5	15,000
Over 60	3	3,000

This schedule can represent the receivables according to how *many* there are in each age group or according to the *total dollars* the receivables represent in each age group. The higher the number of accounts or the number of dollars in the shortest-term groups, the faster the collection.

Looking at a breakdown of accounts receivable in an aging schedule, we can:

1. Estimate the extent of our customers' compliance with our credit terms.
2. Estimate our cash inflows from collections in the near future.
3. Identify accounts that are the longest overdue.

We have to keep in mind that the age of our receivables may change from month to month if our credit sales change. For example, our 31-to-60-day–old accounts receivable may increase from June to July simply because credit

Low Tide

Firms tend to select the end of their accounting year to be the *low* point of their operating cycle. This is when business is slowest, which means that inventory and, possibly, receivables will be at their lowest levels. If we evaluate receivables at a firm's year end, we may not get the best measure of collections. It is preferable (though not always possible) to look at quarterly or monthly averages of receivables.

sales increased from May to June—not because collections of receivables became slower.

Establishing and Changing Credit Policies

Credit decisions involve trade-offs: the profit from the additional sales versus the costs of extending credit:

Benefits	Costs
• Increased profits from increased sales.	• The opportunity cost of funds. • Administration and collection costs. • Bad debts.

It is difficult to measure the benefit of extending credit or changing credit terms because there are many variables to consider: If the firm liberalizes its credit policy, extending credit to more customers, do the costs associated with this increased credit change? Most likely. Do they change in a predictable manner? Most likely not, because you won't know the costs associated with these additional sales until you change the credit policy.

Ideally, a firm wants to design its credit (and collection) policy so that the marginal benefits from extending credit equal its marginal cost of extending credit. At this point, the firm maximizes owners' wealth. But the benefits and costs are uncertain. The best the firm can do in forecasting the benefits and costs from its credit and collection policies is to learn from its own experience (make changes and see what happens) or from the experience of others (look at what happens when a competitor changes its policies).

Analyzing a Change in Credit and Collection Policies: An Example

Let's look at an example of a change in credit policy by a firm. Books-R-Us Company is a wholesale distributor of books, and all its sales are on credit. For every book it sells, its variable costs are 70 percent of the sales price; in other words, its variable cost ratio is 70 percent and its contribution margin is 30 percent. If Books-R-Us sells $100,000 worth of books, it has $30,000 left after deducting variable costs.

Books-R-Us is proposing a change in its credit policy:

From	To
• Payment due in 30 days • Moderate collection efforts, costing 1 cent per dollar of accounts receivable	• Payment due in 40 days • Intense collection efforts, costing 1 cent per dollar of accounts receivable for accounts paying within 40 days, 3 cents per dollar of accounts receivable for accounts paying beyond 40 days

Without the changes, Books-R-Us expects $3 million in sales and $1 million in accounts receivable; with the changes, Books-R-Us expects sales to be

$4 million and accounts receivable to be $1.5 million (an increase of $0.5 million). But where will these extra sales come from? We assume that the additional sales will come from slower-paying customers who like the new forty-day credit period.

To analyze the benefits and costs, we need to know Books-R-Us's opportunity cost of funds: what the firm could do with the funds if they weren't tied up in receivables. Let's assume that the firm's opportunity cost of funds (on a before-tax basis) is 20 percent.[6]

The Benefits

The benefits from the change in policies are the profits from the increased sales. For each dollar of increased sales, Books-R-Us makes 30 cents before taxes. So the added $1 million in sales increase translates into $300,000 in increased profits before taxes:

$$\text{Benefit from extending credit} = (\text{contribution margin})(\text{change in sales})$$
$$= 30\%(\$1,000,000)$$
$$= \mathbf{\$300,000}$$

The Costs

The opportunity cost of funds is the cost of what the firm has tied up in accounts receivable. How much more will the firm invest in these accounts? The full $0.5 million? Not really, because only a portion of that represents funds the firm has actually invested. Suppose a book sells for $10. What has that book cost Books-R-Us? As long as Books-R-Us is not operating at full capacity (so it doesn't have to increase its investment in its fixed assets, such as plant and equipment), the firm has invested $7 in that book. Therefore, although accounts receivable increase by $10 when the book is sold, Books-R-Us has invested only $7.

The cost of funds is therefore the variable cost portion of the increased accounts receivable:

$$\begin{array}{l}\text{Carrying cost of} \\ \text{accounts receivable}\end{array} = \begin{pmatrix}\text{opportunity} \\ \text{cost}\end{pmatrix}\begin{pmatrix}\text{variable} \\ \text{cost ratio}\end{pmatrix}\begin{pmatrix}\text{change in} \\ \text{accounts receivable}\end{pmatrix}$$
$$= 20\%(70\%)\$500,000$$
$$= \mathbf{\$70,000}$$

Another cost associated with the change in policy is the additional collection cost. Before the change, collection costs were 1 cent per dollar of accounts, or $10,000. After the change, collections costs are 1 cent per dollar for the accounts that tend to pay within forty days, but increase to 3 cents per dollar for the added $0.5 million of accounts, or $15,000. Therefore, the incremental collection costs are $15,000.

---

[6] You'll notice that our analysis is in terms of the before-tax costs. It is important that we be consistent in our analysis and deal exclusively either with before-tax benefits and costs or with after-tax benefits and costs. Since dealing with the before-tax benefits and costs saves us the adjustment for taxes, let's stick with these to make our analysis simpler.

Benefits	Costs
• Increased profits before taxes: $300,000	• Carrying cost of accounts receivable: $70,000 • Increased collection costs: $15,000

Comparing the benefits, $300,000, with the costs, $70,000 + $15,000 = $85,000, it appears that Books-R-Us would be better off with the change in its policies.

Caveats

We've simplified the Books-R-Us policy change, leaving out many factors that would likely change. Consider the following:

- When the credit period is liberalized, customers that used to pay within thirty days may now pay within forty days, increasing accounts receivable (and the cost of funds tied up in these accounts) but probably not increasing collection costs for these customers, since the cost of collecting should not increase as they stretch out their payments.
- When the credit period is liberalized, not only is the firm likely to increase its sales from customers that like the longer credit period, but may attract customers whose probability of bad debt is higher than that of its customers under the old policy. But it is unclear how much bad debts will increase because collection policies are being enhanced.

As you can see from the Books-R-Us example and the caveats, there are many factors to consider when a firm adjusts its credit or collection policies. As one element is changed, there may be a "domino" effect. A lengthening in the credit period may increase expected sales, which increases the expected profit from sales but may also increase the expected level of accounts receivable. In turn, these effects may increase (1) the expected opportunity cost of funds tied up in accounts receivable, (2) the expected costs of administering accounts receivable, and (3) the expected loss from the increase in bad debts.

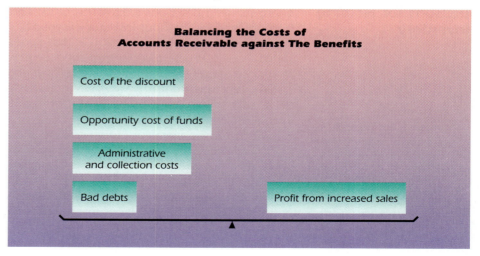

Balancing the Costs of Accounts Receivable against The Benefits

Cost of the discount

Opportunity cost of funds

Administrative and collection costs

Bad debts

Profit from increased sales

Captive Finance Subsidiaries

Some firms choose to form a wholly owned subsidiary—a corporation owned by the parent firm—to provide the credit-granting and collection functions of the parent firm. For example, if you buy a General Motors car, you can conveniently finance your purchase through General Motors Acceptance Corporation (GMAC), a lender that is a wholly owned subsidiary of General Motors.

These subsidiaries are referred to as *captive finance subsidiaries.* They are companies wholly owned by—or in a sense "captives of"—the parent corporation, and their sole purpose is to finance the customers' purchases of the parent firm's products. GMAC is the captive finance subsidiary of its parent, General Motors Corporation.

There are a number of motives behind the decision of firms to establish these subsidiaries. One is to stimulate sales. By providing easy access to loans, the parent firm can sell more of its product. For example, Hyundai Motors of America found that customers were having difficulty getting auto loans for their cars, since loan defaults were typically higher for loans on low-priced autos. So Hyundai established its own finance company, Hyundai Motor Finance Co. (HMFC), to finance customers' purchases of Hyundai cars and increase sales.

Another motive to establish a finance subsidiary is to separate the credit function from the rest of the firm's operations. By operating the credit-granting and collection functions as a separate subsidiary—and therefore as a separate profit center—it is easier to evaluate how well accounts receivable are managed.

INVENTORY MANAGEMENT

Inventory is the stock of physical goods held for eventual sale. Inventory consists of raw material, work in process, and finished goods available for sale. There are many factors involved in our decision on how much inventory to have on hand. There is a trade-off between the costs of investing in inventory and the costs of insufficient inventory. There's a cost in holding too much inventory and there's a cost in holding too little inventory.

Reasons for Holding Inventory

There are several reasons to have inventory. The most obvious is that you can't transact business without inventory if your business involves selling a physical good. Another obvious reason is that goods cannot be manufactured instantaneously. If you manufacture goods, you will likely have some inventory in various stages of production—work in process.

We also may want to have some inventory of finished goods in case sales are greater than expected. This is a cushion representing a precautionary balance in inventory.

Moreover, we may want to hold some inventory for speculative purposes in dealing with events such as a change in the product or a change in the cost of the raw materials. A good example of speculative inventory with respect to a change in product is Coca-Cola. When Coca-Cola introduced New Coke to replace the "old" Coke, many retailers hoarded supplies of the "old" Coke product—since renamed Classic Coke—in anticipation of continued customer demand for the original product.

Further, some firms may hold inventory to satisfy contractual agreements. For example, a retail outlet that is the sole distributor or representative of a

Reasons for Holding Inventory

- Transaction needs
- Work in process
- Precautionary needs
- Speculative needs
- Contractual requirements

Added Borrowing Power—A Dubious Motive

Another motive sometimes cited for establishing a finance subsidiary is to increase the firm's ability to borrow. The basis for this motive is as follows: Accounts receivable are liquid assets—they are collected within a short time and could be factored ("factored" means sold for cash to another party). Therefore, the finance subsidiary could not only borrow against its receivables (its only assets) but borrow more than if the parent held these assets, because 100 percent of the subsidiary's assets are more liquid than the parent's assets. The flaw in this reasoning is that even though management of the accounts receivable may be physically apart from the rest of the firm, there is still a legal link between the parent and the subsidiary. That is, the assets of the subsidiary are assets of the parent firm and the debts of the subsidiary are debts of the parent firm. Hence, lenders are not likely to lend more on these receivables to the subsidiary than they would to the parent.

But the jury is still out on whether ownership of a finance subsidiary does in fact increase the borrowing power of the parent firm. Some evidence suggests that firms forming a captive finance subsidiary tend to increase the amount of debt they take on, since they allow the subsidiary to finance more of its assets with debt than the parent. This may not be because lenders are more likely to lend to the subsidiary, but rather because the firm's management permits the subsidiary to take on relatively more debt.

NOTE: Shehzad L. Mian and Clifford W. Smith, Jr., looked at the reaction of share prices to the announcement of the formation of captive finance subsidiaries and found that (1) share price does not change when these subsidiaries are formed, (2) finance subsidiaries tend to take on relatively more debt than the parent corporation, and (3) the amount of lending to customers increases significantly following the formation of the captive finance subsidiary ("Accounts Receivable Management Policy: Theory and Evidence," *Journal of Finance*, vol. 47, no. 1, March 1992, pp. 169–200).

product in a region may be required to carry a specified inventory of goods for sale.

The decision to invest in inventory involves, ultimately, determining the level of inventory at which the marginal benefit of investing in inventory (such as providing for transactions and precautionary needs) equals the marginal cost of investing in inventory (such as carrying costs). The level of inventory at the point at which the marginal benefits equal the marginal cost is the owners' wealth-maximizing level.

Costs Associated with Inventory

There are two types of inventory cost—the cost of holding inventory and the cost of getting more inventory.

The holding cost for inventory, also referred to as the ***carrying cost,*** is the cost of keeping inventory—storage, depreciation, and obsolescence—and the opportunity cost of tying up funds in inventory. If we estimate holding costs on a per-unit basis, we have the following relationship:

Holding cost = (average quantity)(holding cost per unit)

Replenishing inventory is costly. We must place orders—by phone, fax, or computer—and pay shipping charges for each order. These costs make up the *ordering cost*. Given a cost per order, we calculate our ordering costs as:

Ordering cost = (fixed cost per order)(number of orders per period)

The total cost of inventory is the sum of the holding cost and ordering cost:

Total inventory cost = holding cost + ordering cost

Let c = holding or carrying cost, in dollars per unit
   Q = quantity ordered
   K = cost per transaction
   S = total number of units needed during the period

Then:

$$\text{Total inventory cost} = \underset{\substack{\uparrow \\ \text{Carrying} \\ \text{cost} \\ \text{per unit}}}{c} \; \underset{\substack{\uparrow \\ \text{Average} \\ \text{balance}}}{\frac{Q}{2}} + \underset{\substack{\uparrow \\ \text{Cost} \\ \text{per} \\ \text{order}}}{K} \; \underset{\substack{\uparrow \\ \text{Number} \\ \text{of} \\ \text{orders}}}{\frac{S}{Q}}$$

Suppose we have a total demand for 500,000 units during a month. If we order 50,000 units each time we put in an order during the month, that's ten orders. If it costs us $100 each time we place an order, the ordering costs are $10 \times \$100 = \$1,000$. If we order 50,000 units each time we run out, we have, on average, 25,000 units on hand. Suppose the carrying cost per unit is 20 cents. If we have 25,000 units on hand, on average, we have holding costs of $\$0.20 \times 25,000$, or $5,000. Hence:

$$
\begin{aligned}
\text{Total inventory cost} &= \$0.20\left(\frac{50,000}{2}\right) + \$100\left(\frac{500,000}{50,000}\right) \\
&= \$0.20(25,000) + \$100(10) \\
&= \$5,000 + \$1,000 \\
&= \mathbf{\$6,000}
\end{aligned}
$$

Models of Inventory Management

There are alternative models for inventory management, but the basic idea for all of them is the same: Minimize inventory costs. We will look at two—the economic order quantity model and the just-in-time inventory model—to see how they minimize costs.

The Economic Order Quantity Model

The economic order quantity (EOQ) model helps us determine what quantity of inventory to order at one time so that total inventory costs throughout the period will be minimized. The EOQ model assumes that:

- Inventory is received instantaneously.
- Inventory is used uniformly throughout the period.
- Inventory shortages are not desirable.

With these assumptions, we can minimize the costs of inventory—the sum of the carrying costs and the ordering costs—by ordering a specific amount of inventory, referred to as the ***economic order quantity,*** each time we run out of inventory.

The economic order quantity is the value of Q in:

$$\text{Total inventory cost} = c\frac{Q}{2} + K\frac{S}{Q}$$

that minimizes the total cost. Invoking a bit of calculus to minimize total costs with respect to Q, d(total cost)/d(Q), it turns out that the economic order quantity, Q*, is:

$$\text{Economic order quantity} = \sqrt{\frac{2(\text{cost per transaction})(\text{total demand})}{\text{carrying cost per unit}}}$$

Or:

$$Q^* = \sqrt{\frac{2KS}{c}} \qquad\qquad [15\text{-}10]$$

If c = $0.20 per unit
  K = $100 per transaction
  S = 500,000 units

then:

$$Q^* = \sqrt{\frac{2(\$100)(500,000)}{\$0.20}} = \textbf{22,361 units}$$

Then for this order quantity:

$$\text{Total inventory cost} = \text{holding cost} \quad + \text{ordering cost}$$

$$= \$0.20\left(\frac{22,361}{2}\right) + \$100\left(\frac{500,000}{22,361}\right)$$

$$= \$2,236 \qquad\quad + \$2,236$$

$$= \textbf{\$4,472}$$

Are costs minimized at this point? Let's check it out by looking at the costs of a couple of other order quantities. If the order quantity were 10,000 units, total costs would be:

$$\text{Total costs at Q of 20,000} = \$0.20\left(\frac{20,000}{2}\right) + \$100\left(\frac{500,000}{20,000}\right)$$

$$= \$2,000 + \$2,500$$

$$= \textbf{\$4,500}$$

If the order quantity were 30,000 units, total costs would be:

$$\text{Total costs at Q of 30,000} = \$0.20\left(\frac{30,000}{2}\right) + \$100\left(\frac{500,000}{30,000}\right)$$

$$= \$3,000 + \$1,667$$

$$= \textbf{\$4,667}$$

The costs are lowest at Q = 22,361 units.

FIGURE 15-5

Cost of Inventory and the Economic Order Quantity

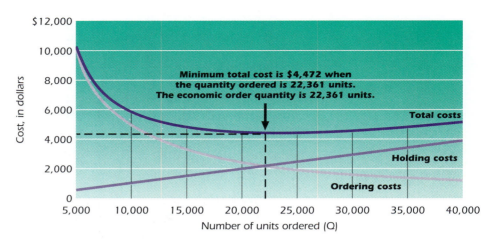

We can see how total costs are minimized at the EOQ in the graph shown in Figure 15-5. In this graph, carrying costs, ordering costs, and total costs are plotted for different order quantities. Total costs are minimized at an order quantity of 22,361 units.[7]

We can modify the EOQ model to include factors such as:

Safety stock	An additional level of inventory intended to enable the firm to continue to meet demand in case sales levels turn out to be higher than predicted and in case there are unexpected delays either in receiving raw materials or in producing goods. The level of safety stock depends on the degree of uncertainty in the firm's sales and production and the cost of lost sales (where the cost of lost sales comprises sales lost and the loss of customer goodwill).
Lead time	The time it takes between placing an order for more inventory and the time when it is received or produced. We can modify the EOQ model so that ordering takes place early enough to ensure that the new inventory will arrive just as the existing inventory runs out.

---

[7] Though inventory costs are lowest at 22,361 units ordered ($2,236.10 + $2,236.04 = $4,472.14, to be precise), there is a range of order quantities around that optimum that are still quite low. For example, if the order quantity is 22,300 units, the inventory costs are $2,230.00 + $2,242.15 = $4,472.15, a difference of 1 cent!

Allowance for stock-out   The tolerance for a shortage of goods for sale. We can modify the EOQ model to permit shortages—though we risk the loss of sales and customer goodwill.

The EOQ model for inventory management is difficult to apply when:

- Inventory is kept in several locations
- There are different types of inventory
- Sales are seasonal
- Quantity discounts are available

The EOQ model is useful in pointing out the trade-off between holding and ordering costs. But there are some problems in applying it to actual inventory management. One problem is that it does not consider the possibility that inventory may be held in several locations. For example, if a firm has many retail outlets and regional warehouses, the model has to be altered to consider order quantities for the firm as a whole, for each warehouse, and for each store. Another problem is that there may be different types of inventory—raw materials, work in process, and finished goods—and many different goods, requiring EOQ models for each one. Still another problem is that the EOQ is not useful if the demand for inventory is seasonal. Furthermore, the EOQ is not readily adapted to cases in which quantity discounts are available.

Just-in-Time Inventory

The goal of the ***just-in-time*** (JIT) inventory model is to cut down on the firm's need to keep inventory on hand by coordinating the supply of raw materials with the production and marketing of the goods. In JIT, the raw materials are acquired only *precisely* when they are needed—just in time. The idea of JIT is to have zero or as near zero inventory as possible without adversely affecting production or sales. The goal of this strategy is to cut down on inventory costs by:

1. Holding less inventory, so that there are lower storage costs, lower levels of spoilage, and less risk of obsolescence.
2. Coordinating with suppliers to minimize the cost of reordering inventory.

JIT requires coordination between a firm and its suppliers. To make JIT work, we must have timely, reliable delivery of goods and materials. Further, we must have a predictable production process, so that we can figure out our input needs in advance, which requires a high degree of production automation. In addition, demand must be predictable. If production is constantly modified to suit the demand for the product, JIT will not work well or may not work at all.

JIT, TQC, and EI

A revolution in management styles and techniques in U.S. business is under way. The keys to this revolution are in *just-in-time* (JIT) inventory management, *total quality control* (TQC), and *employee involvement* (EI). These principles—which work hand-in-hand—have been applied in Japan and are catching on in the United States.

JIT is a strategy of coordination between a firm's suppliers and its production and marketing operations. The purpose is to maintain the amount of inventory at the point at which it is always possible to supply exactly what consumers demand. Supplies and raw materials are delivered only when needed for production. The firm produces only those items that are needed for anticipated demand. This requires lots of coordination and falls apart if there is poor quality in any one part of the process—a defective bolt can gum up the works.

TQC is the principle that quality goods and services must be a goal of *all* efforts of the firm—production, accounting, marketing, etc. Part of TQC is recognizing that some personnel of the firm are customers of other personnel. For example, the financial manager serves the production managers by evaluating any proposed expansion of production facilities, and the accounting staff serves the financial manager, supplying financial data necessary for the financial manager's evaluation of the expansion.

EI is the philosophy that employees at all levels should be involved in the firm's decision making. By participating in decision making, employees will be able to understand and perform their tasks better. Also, employees will be able to make significant contributions to the decision-making process because of their unique perspective regarding the practical effects of the decision.

U.S. companies are adopting these principles to increase their competitiveness in the global market. Although there are legal, economic, and cultural differences between the United States and Japan that inhibit the direct application of Japanese management principles to U.S. firms, TQC, JIT, and EI are quickly becoming a part of the management style of U.S. firms.

JIT and ZBA

The management strategy of just-in-time inventory management is similar to the zero-balance account (ZBA) disbursement technique for cash management. Both are based on the idea that we can reduce costs if we carry a lower balance, and both require coordination and planning to make them work.

JIT is not just an inventory method, but rather a management strategy that blends well with the management strategies of total quality control and employee involvement.

JIT has been used extensively in Japan, but now many U.S. firms are adapting JIT principles to inventory management. For example, Ford Motor Company allows its suppliers to tap into its inventory management system computer, so that they can figure out what supplies are needed and when to deliver them to Ford's production plants. This helps Ford's suppliers in their own planning, which benefits Ford through more efficient delivery of the goods it needs.

Other Considerations

The goal of both EOQ and JIT is to minimize the costs of holding and ordering inventory. The EOQ model does this by determining the quantity of goods to order that will minimize costs. JIT inventory management does this somewhat differently, by focusing on the source of these costs and minimizing holding costs.

Which model is appropriate for our use? EOQ, JIT, or some variation of these models may be appropriate; the choice depends on our management structure, the predictability of our demand, and our ability to coordinate with our suppliers.

In addition to the holding and ordering costs, there are other considerations in determining the appropriate level of inventory. One consideration is taxes on inventory. For example, there may be a state tax based on the value of inventory held as of a specified date, say December 31. In that case we would hold the smallest amount of inventory on that date that would not cause a shortage of goods for our customers.

Another consideration is the possibility of expropriation. If we are doing business in another country, there may be a risk that the foreign government may expropriate—take over—our goods without compensating us. When doing business in other countries, we must assess the risk of expropriation and, if high, minimize our inventory holdings there.

Still another consideration is export-import quotas. For example, if we produce goods in the United States and sell them in Japan, there may be a limit on the amount Japan will import. Suppose the limit on imports into Japan is 50,000 units per month. If demand in Japan is seasonal—say, 20,000 per month every month except June, when the demand shoots up to 200,000 units—the importer in Japan will have to import more than needed for several months to build up inventory for June.

Monitoring Inventory Management

We can monitor inventory by looking at financial ratios in much the same way that we monitor receivables. The **number of days of inventory** is the ratio of the inventory at a point in time to the cost of goods sold per day:

$$\text{Number of days of inventory} = \frac{\text{inventory}}{\text{average day's cost of goods sold}} \qquad [15\text{-}11]$$

This ratio gives us an idea of the number of days' worth of sales we have on hand at a specific point in time. Combined with an estimate of the demand for our goods, this ratio helps us in planning our production and purchasing of goods.

Another way to monitor inventory is to use the inventory turnover ratio—the ratio of what we sell over a period (the cost of goods sold) to what we have on hand at the end of that period (inventory):

$$\text{Inventory turnover} = \frac{\text{cost of goods sold}}{\text{inventory}} \qquad [15\text{-}12]$$

The inventory turnover ratio tells us how many times, on average, inventory flows through the firm—from raw materials to goods sold—during the period.

We must be careful, however, in interpreting these ratios. Since the production and sale of those goods may be seasonal—and not always in synch—the values we put into our calculations may not be representative of what is actually going on.

Also, interpretation of an inventory turnover ratio is not straightforward. Is a higher turnover good or bad? It could be either. A high turnover may mean that the firm is using its investment in inventory efficiently. But it might mean that the firm is risking a shortage of inventory. Not keeping enough on hand (relative to what is sold) incurs a greater chance of lost sales and customer goodwill. Using inventory turnover ratios along with measures of profitability can give us a better idea of whether we are getting an adequate return on our investment in inventory.

SUMMARY

- The management of short-term assets involves decisions related to cash, marketable securities, accounts receivable, and inventory. Since short-term assets support the long-term investments of the firm, they are linked to the firm's capital budgeting decision.

- The objective of short-term investments is the same as for long-term investment decisions: Maximize owners' wealth. But since we are basing our decision on cash flows received over the short term, we focus less on the time value of money and more on identifying the costs and benefits associated with our decisions.

- The common purpose of our decisions related to cash, marketable securities, accounts receivable, and inventory is to minimize our investment in the short-term asset. But in all cases, we must have *some* investment in the asset because we will incur costs if we do not have enough of it. If we don't pay our bills, we may be unable to buy goods from our suppliers in the future. We may be unable to borrow in the future because we can't pay our debts on time. If we don't have enough inventory or we don't offer competitive credit terms we may lose sales to our competitors.

- We need to strike the right balance between the cost of having and not having the asset. The "right balance" is different for each firm. Each firm must assess its costs of having and not having the asset.

- Cash management involves a trade-off between the benefits of having enough cash to meet day-to-day operations and the costs of having cash (e.g., the opportunity cost of funds and the costs of getting and storing cash). The Baumol and Miller-Orr models can be used in the management of cash to determine the amount of funds to transfer in and out of cash.

- Marketable securities are a store of excess cash. A firm invests funds in marketable securities in order to have a readily available, or liquid, source of cash. Marketable securities include U.S. Treasury bills, commercial paper, and certificates of deposit.

- Receivables management involves a trade-off between the benefits of increased sales and the costs of credit (e.g., the opportunity cost of funds and defaults by credit customers). Credit and collection policies must be formulated to consider the benefits arising from sales and the costs associated with extending credit.

- Inventory management involves a trade-off between the benefits of having sufficient inventory to meet demand and the costs of inventory (e.g., the opportunity cost of funds, storage, and obsolescence). Models of inventory management, such as economic order quantity and just-in-time, can be used to analyze and minimize the costs of inventory.

QUESTIONS

15-1 Why do firms hold some of their assets in the form of cash?

15-2 What is the benefit of using a lockbox system?

15-3 Suppose the post office develops new technology that speeds up mail delivery. How would such a development affect a firm's cash management decision?

15-4 The Peach Company has determined that its cash EOQ is $100,000. What does this mean?

15-5 The Pear Company applies the Miller-Orr model to its cash management. Pear has determined that the return point is $12,000, the lower limit is $5,000, and the upper limit is $26,000. Explain what this information means for Pear's cash management.

15-6 What are the primary differences between the Baumol and Miller-Orr models of cash management?

15-7 Preferred stock is a long-term source of capital for a corporation. How can it serve as both a long-term source of capital *and* a short-term investment of funds?

15-8 Granting credit to customers means that the firm will not receive the cash from sales for some time after the sale. Why do firms extend credit to customers?

15-9 What do the credit terms "2/10, net 30" mean? If a firm changes its credit terms from "2/10, net 30" to "3/10, net 30," what do you expect would happen to its investment in accounts receivable?

15-10 List the five Cs of credit. Suppose you own a small landscaping business and are considering granting credit to your customers. How would you apply the five Cs to your landscape customers?

15-11 "Where inventory occupies a prominent position in business operations, it will usually play a key role in deciding the success of the venture." Comment.

15-12 Why do firms invest in inventory? What are the benefits of the investment in inventory? What are the costs of investing in inventory?

15-13 Compare and contrast the motives for holding cash and inventory. What are the similarities in these motives? What are the differences in these motives?

15-14 Distinguish between the economic order quantity and the just-in-time inventory models of inventory management.

15-15 If you are doing business in a foreign country, what factors must you consider in determining the level of your investment in inventory?

15-16 We observe that the amount firms invest in working capital varies from industry to industry and from firm to firm. We also observe that the amount invested in working capital varies according to the business cycle. Explain why a firm's working capital investment may vary according to the business cycle.

PROBLEMS

Cash management

15-1 Suppose you start each month with a cash balance of $100,000 and you use cash evenly throughout the month, ending each month with a zero cash balance.

    a. What is the average cash balance each month?
    b. If you could earn 1 percent per month by investing your cash, what is the opportunity cost per month associated with your cash balance?

15-2 The Bulldog Company has cash needs of $5 million per month. If Bulldog needs more cash, it can sell marketable securities, incurring a fee of $300 for each transaction. If Bulldog leaves its funds in marketable securities, it expects to earn approximately 0.50 percent per month on its investment.

    a. If Bulldog gets a cash infusion of $1 million each time it needs cash, what are the holding costs associated with its cash investment?
    b. If Bulldog gets a cash infusion of $1 million each time it needs cash, what are the transaction costs per month associated with its cash infusions?
    c. Using the EOQ model, what level of cash infusion minimizes Bulldog's costs associated with cash?

15-3 Buccaneer Inc. has determined that it needs $10 million in cash per week. If Buccaneer needs additional cash, it can sell marketable securities, incurring a fee of $100 for each transaction. If Buccaneer leaves funds in its marketable securities, it expects to earn approximately 0.2 percent per week on its investment. Using the economic order quantity model, determine how much cash Buccaneer should raise by selling securities each week to minimize its costs of cash.

15-4 The Seminole Company wishes to apply the Miller-Orr model to the management of its cash investment. Seminole's managers have collected the following estimates:

Cost per transaction = $200
Variance of daily cash flows = $10,000
Opportunity cost of cash, per day = 0.05%

Based on their experience in dealing with the cash flows of the company, Seminole's managers have figured out that there should be a cushion—a safety stock—of cash of $20,000. Calculate the following:

a. The lower limit
b. The return point
c. The upper limit

15-5 The financial managers of the Book Warehouse Company wish to apply the Miller-Orr model to the firm's cash investment. They have determined that the cost of either investing in or selling marketable securities is $100. By looking at Book Warehouse's past cash needs, they have determined that the variance of daily cash flows is $20,000. Book Warehouse's opportunity cost of cash per day is estimated to be 0.03 percent. Based on experience, the managers have determined that the cash balance should never fall below $10,000. Calculate the lower limit, the return point, and the upper limit, using the Miller-Orr model of cash management.

15-6 The Gator Corporation has determined that it can reduce its float by three days if it applies a number of different cash management techniques. If Gator typically receives $100,000 in payments from its customers per day and can earn 10 percent on its investments, what are the savings per year from the float reduction?

15-7 SNK Inc. is considering evaluating its collection and deposit procedures. SNK typically has sales of $5 million per day. SNK's opportunity cost of investing in cash is 10 percent. If SNK can reduce the time needed to clear its payments from customers from seven to six days, what is the benefit to SNK? How much should SNK be willing to pay in annual fees to accomplish this float reduction?

15-8 Consider the following five different lockbox arrangements:

Arrangement	Float reduction, in days	Opportunity cost per year	Annual collections	Bank fee for lockbox
A	3	10%	$1,000,000	$ 500
B	5	10	1,000,000	600
C	5	10	1,000,000	1,500
D	4	12	500,000	500
E	3	5	1,200,000	500

a. For each arrangement, calculate the benefits of using the lockbox system.
b. Considering the bank fee for each arrangement, which lockbox systems are attractive?

Receivables management

15-9 Calculate the cost of trade credit to your customers for each of the following credit terms, assuming they pay on the net day:

- **a.** 2/10, net 30
- **b.** 1/10, net 30
- **c.** 3/20, net 30
- **d.** 1/10, net 40
- **e.** 3/10, net 40

15-10 The AR Company had sales of $5 million in 1991. It is estimated that 80 percent of all sales are on credit.

- **a.** If the balance in accounts receivable at the end of 1991 was $0.5 million, how long did it take AR's customers to pay?
- **b.** If the balance in accounts receivable at the end of 1991 was $0.75 million, how long did it take AR's customers to pay?
- **c.** Suppose AR extends credit to customers on the basis of 2/10, net 30. How does the actual time it takes customers to pay compare with these credit terms if the accounts receivable balance is $0.5 million? If the accounts receivable balance is $0.75 million?
- **d.** Criticize the use of the number of days of credit to evaluate AR's collections.

15-11 The COMP Computer Company is reevaluating its credit terms. Presently it is granting credit terms to customers of 1/10, net 40. COMP's competitors give their customers terms of 2/5, net 40. If COMP's customers miss the discount period, they typically pay on the net day.

- **a.** Compare COMP's credit terms with those of its competitors. Which has a higher implicit cost to the customer?
- **b.** If COMP switched its terms to those of its competitors, what do you expect would happen to the amount of COMP's accounts receivable? Why?

15-12 The El Cheapo Company typically has $1 million in sales each year and a contribution margin of 20 percent. El Cheapo is considering offering its customers a 1 percent discount if they pay within five days of the sale; otherwise, full payment would be due within twenty days.

- **a.** What is the effective annual cost of credit to its customers if El Cheapo changes its policy and customers pay on the net day?
- **b.** If sales are expected to increase to $2 million per year when this discount is instituted and if 30 percent of El Cheapo's customers are predicted to take advantage of this discount, what is the cost of the discount to the firm?
- **c.** What contribution margin would El Cheapo need to insure a 20 percent profit margin on those accounts paid within five days (ignoring any costs of carrying accounts receivable)?

15-13 UO Inc. is evaluating its present credit policy and is concerned that it may not be offering terms that are competitive. Presently, UO offers terms of 1/10, net 30, with 50 percent of its customers paying within the discount period and the remainder paying within the net period. UO's credit department has projected that if the terms were changed to 2/10, net 30 without changing the 25 percent contribution margin, annual credit sales would increase from $20 million to $30 million, with 75 percent of the customers paying within ten days and the remainder paying within the net period.

This change will decrease UO's days of credit from twenty to fifteen days. UO's opportunity cost for its accounts receivable investment is 15 percent before taxes.

a. What would be the cost to UO of changing its discount?
b. What would be the change in UO's carrying cost of accounts receivable if UO changes its terms?
c. Should UO change its discount? Explain.

Inventory management

15-14 Hurricane Inc. is evaluating its management of inventory. Hurricane's management estimates that the firm needs 100,000 units per month. Each order it places to replenish inventory costs Hurricane $50, and the cost of carrying one unit is approximately 5 cents per month.

a. If Hurricane orders 20,000 units each time it places an order, what are its ordering costs per month?
b. If Hurricane orders 20,000 units each time it places an order, what are the holding costs of inventory per month?
c. What is the economic order quantity for Hurricane? How do the inventory costs change if Hurricane orders 1,000 units more than the EOQ each time? How do the inventory costs change if Hurricane orders 1,000 units less than the EOQ each time?

15-15 Consider the following information from 1991 financial statements, with dollar amounts in millions:

Corporation	Inventory	Cost of goods sold	Primary product
Abbott Laboratories	$ 815.385	$ 2,760.955	Drugs and health care
American Brands	2,141.000	3,975.400	Tobacco products
Amoco	1,147.000	17,932.000	Oil and gasoline
Campbell Soup	706.700	3,915.000	Food
Digital Equipment	1,595.150	6,506.066	Computers
General Mills	493.600	3,727.000	Food

SOURCE: Standard & Poor's *Compustat PC Plus* (CD-ROM).

a. Calculate the inventory turnover for each firm for 1991.
b. Calculate the number of days of inventory for each firm for 1991.
c. Why might the inventory turnovers and number of days of inventory differ among these firms?

Potpourri

15-16 Paul's Pawn Shop is reevaluating the credit terms for its customers in light of a new state law that limits interest rates on secured credit (which includes pawn shop credit) to an annual percentage rate of 45 percent (that is, rate × number of credit periods in a year = 45 percent). Paul's currently has terms that require repayment of the loan plus 25 percent interest paid after 45 days.

a. What is the effective annual rate for Paul's customers before the change if they pay on the net day?

b. If Paul's wants to keep terms requiring payment within forty-five days, what interest rate should it charge for this period to comply with the law? What is the effective annual rate on these new terms?

PC+ 15-17 **Research:** Select a corporation and find the amount invested in working capital over a ten-year period.

a. Calculate the ratio of working capital to total assets for each year. Plot this ratio over time.

b. How does the firm's investment in working capital relative to total assets change over the ten-year period?

c. Does the change in the firm's working capital investment relate in any way to the change in the economic environment?

d. Does the change in the firm's working capital investment relate to other factors, such as the demand for raw materials or technological obsolescence?

Recommended sources of information:

- Annual reports
- *Industrial Manual*, Moody's
- *Compustat PC Plus* (CD-ROM), Standard & Poor's

15-18 **Research:** What is the current annual return on the following short-term investments:

- 90-day Treasury bills
- Repurchase agreements
- Certificates of deposit
- Commercial paper

Recommended sources of information:

- *Federal Reserve Bulletin*
- *Industrial Manual*, Moody's

PC+ 15-19 **Research:** Select a corporation and calculate the inventory turnover and the number of days of inventory in each of the past five years.

a. What is the trend in turnover and number of days over this five-year period?

b. What factors, such as the line of business of the selected corporation, influence the turnover and number of days?

Recommended sources of information: See Problem 15-17.

PC+ 15-20 **Research:** Select a corporation and determine the proportion of current assets invested in cash, marketable securities, accounts receivable, and inventory for each of the past five years.

a. Have these proportions changed much over the five years? If so, what has been the change?

b. What firm- or industry-specific factors influence this distribution of current assets?

Recommended sources of information: See Problem 15-17.

FURTHER READINGS

A survey of cash and marketable securities management practices of U.S. firms is provided in:
Ravinda R. Kamath, et al., "Management of Excess Cash: Practices and Developments," *Financial Management*, vol. 14, no. 3, Autumn 1985, pp. 70–77.

A survey of trade credit policies of U.S. firms is provided in:
Scott Besley and Jerome S. Osteryoung, "Survey of Current Practices in Establishing Trade-Credit Limits," *Financial Review*, vol. 20, no. 1, Feb. 1985, pp. 70–82.
P. J. Davey, *Managing Trade Receivables*, The Conference Board, New York, 1972.
P. R. A. Kirkman, *Modern Credit Management: A Study of the Management of Trade Credit under Inflationary Conditions*, George Allen and Unwin, London, 1977.

The use of the EOQ model in minimizing inventory costs is demonstrated in:
Frank M. Tiernan and Dennis A. Tanner, "How Economic Order Quantity Controls Inventory Expense," *Financial Executive*, July 1983, pp. 46–47, 49–52.

CHAPTER

16

Management of Short-Term Financing

INTRODUCTION 739

COSTS OF SHORT-TERM FINANCING 740

Single-Payment Interest 742

Discount Interest 742

Compensating Balance 745

Other Costs 747

UNSECURED FINANCING 748

Trade Credit 749

    Cost of Trade Credit 749

    Accounts Payable Management 751

Bank Financing 753

    Single-Payment Loan 753

    Line of Credit 754

    Revolving Credit 755

    Letter of Credit 755

    Comparing Forms of Bank Financing 756

Money Market Securities 758

    Commercial Paper 758

    Bankers' Acceptances 761

SECURED FINANCING 764

Repurchase Agreements 764

Accounts Receivable 765

Inventory 768

ACTUAL COSTS OF SHORT-TERM FINANCING 771

Summary 773

The Reliance of Firms on Short-Term Financing

Large U.S. corporations use short-term indebtedness, such as trade credit, bank loans, and commercial paper, to satisfy their temporary financing needs. Looking at the firms that comprise the Standard & Poor's 500 Stock Index as representative of large U.S. firms, we find that, on average, trade credit finances 10 percent of a firm's assets, while other sources, including bank loans and commercial paper, combine to make up another 10 percent [calculated using data from Standard & Poor's *Compustat PC Plus* (CD-ROM)]. But the relative use of these sources varies among industries:

Industry	Percentage of 1991 assets financed with trade credit	Percentage of 1991 assets financed with other short-term indebtedness
Steel pipes and tubes	60%	3%
Meat-packing plants	42	2
Advertising	36	1
Paperboard mills	31	4
Printer circuit boards	19	1
Variety stores	18	1
Drug stores	16	1
Nonresidential building contractors	16	1
Farm machinery and equipment	14	14
Motor vehicles and car bodies	11	18
Computer storage devices	14	0
Jewelry stores	9	39
Plastic products	8	6
Ball and roller bearings	7	11
Concrete, gypsum, and plaster	7	29

SOURCE: Standard & Poor's *Compustat PC Plus* (CD-ROM).

Whether or not trade credit is extended depends on a number of factors, including the business customs of the industry. Trade credit typically is extended to customers that are retail firms, such as variety stores. Trade credit is also used in some manufacturing industries, but not others. For example, trade credit is used extensively by producers of steel pipes and tubes, but not much by bearings producers.

We can also see that the use of trade credit varies within an industry. For example, in the food-processing industry, we find that the largest firms, Kraft General Foods and Philip Morris Companies Inc., use trade credit less than the others:

Industry	Percentage of 1991 assets financed with trade credit	Percentage of 1991 assets financed with other short-term indebtedness	1991 sales, in billions
Philip Morris Companies	6%	1%	$48.1
Kraft General Foods	5	2	28.1
Pet	5	0	13.7
Borden	11	7	7.2
Campbell Soup Company	12	1	6.3
Quaker Oats Company	12	3	5.6
Universal Foods Corporation	19	1	0.8

SOURCE: Standard & Poor's *Compustat PC Plus* (CD-ROM).

Aside from the customs of the business, we observe that trade credit is used as a means of short-term financing more often by smaller firms, who may not be able to sell commercial paper or secure large bank loans.

Only 360 Days in a Year?

Before inexpensive calculators and computers came along, calculating interest required a great deal of effort. Now it's a simple computation. To simplify matters back then, calculations were performed using a 360-day year instead of the actual 365- or 366-day year. What started out as a convenience has developed into a convention for quoting rates.

Some rates are quoted on a 360-day year. While quibbling over five or six days makes little numerical difference for small loans, it can make quite a difference with larger ones.

We can easily convert a rate quoted on a 360-day basis into a quotation based on a 365-day basis. An APR of 12 percent on financing with daily compounding, using a 360-day year, means that the daily rate, r, is

$$r = \frac{0.12}{360} = \mathbf{0.00033}$$

The effective annual rate is higher than 12 percent

$$EAR = (1 + 0.00033)^{365} - 1 = \mathbf{0.1280} \text{ or } \mathbf{12.80\%} \text{ per year.}$$

We can also translate an APR on a 360-day basis into an APR on a 365-day basis. For example, a 12 percent APR on a 360-day basis with daily compounding has a rate per day of:

$$r \times 360 = 0.12 \qquad \text{or} \qquad r = \frac{0.12}{360} = \mathbf{0.00033}$$

Annualized on a 365-day basis:

$$r \times 365 = 0.00033 \times 365 = \mathbf{0.1205} \text{ or } \mathbf{12.05\%} \text{ per year}$$

Combining these two steps, we can convert an APR with a 360-day year (APR_{360}) into an APR with a 365-day year (APR_{365}) by multiplying by the ratio of 365 to 360:

$$APR_{360}\left(\frac{365}{360}\right) = APR_{365}$$

Given the daily rate, the effective rate for a 360-day year is:

$$EAR = (1 + 0.00033)^{360} - 1 = \mathbf{0.1261} \text{ or } \mathbf{12.61\%} \text{ per year}$$

and on a 365-day basis is:

$$EAR = (1 + 0.00033)^{365} - 1 = \mathbf{0.1280} \text{ or } \mathbf{12.80\%} \text{ per year}$$

Since we are interested in the effective rate of interest per year so that we can compare this rate with alternative financing, we should calculate the rate that takes into account compounding and is most accurate, namely, the EAR based on a 365-day year. For a $1 million loan, the difference between EARs calculated on a 360-day basis and a 365-day basis using the rates above is $1,900!

$10,000 difference is the interest on the loan—the discount interest. You effectively pay $10,000/$190,000 = 0.0526 or 5.26% for the use of the $190,000 for four months.

The effective annual rate of a discount loan is calculated in the same way as the EAR of a single-payment loan once you have figured out r, the effective cost for the period. In this example, r = 0.0526 and there are three four-month periods in a year. Therefore:

$$EAR = (1 + 0.0526)^3 - 1 = 1.1662 - 1 = \mathbf{0.1662} \text{ or } \mathbf{16.62\%} \text{ per year}$$

The only difference in our calculation between the single-payment and the discount loan cost is in how we determine r: For the single payment loan we determine r using the end-of-period interest, whereas for the discount loan we use the amount of the discount relative to the funds available for use.

Suppose we are given only the discount rate and the time to maturity for the loan. We can still determine the effective annual rate without knowing the amount of the loan. The rate per period is:

$$r = \frac{costs}{funds\ available}$$

If there is a 1 percent discount (the cost) we have use of 99 percent of the funds (funds available). If there is a 5 percent discount, we have use of 95 percent of the funds. And so on. If we let d represent the discount rate, the rate per period is:

$$r = \frac{d}{1 - d} \tag{16-3}$$

For example, if there is a 1 percent discount, the funds available are 99 percent of the face value of the loan and the rate per period is:

$$r = \frac{0.01}{0.99} = \mathbf{0.0101} \text{ or } \mathbf{1.01\%} \text{ per period}$$

FIGURE 16-2

Effective Cost per Period of a Discount Loan for Various Discount Percentages

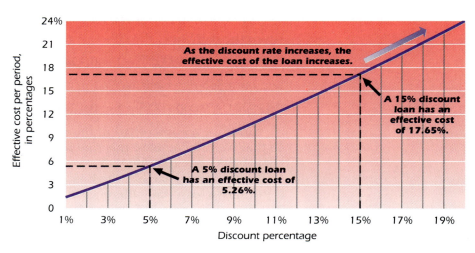

Adding On the Interest

Another way of stating interest is ***add-on interest,*** where the total interest is *added* to the principal amount of the loan and interest is paid on both the amount borrowed and the interest to be paid on the loan. Used primarily in consumer installment loans, add-on interest increases the cost of the loan.

Consider a loan of $1,000 for five years with 10 percent add-on interest; the loan is to be paid off in five year-end installments. The funds that are borrowed (available to the borrower) are $1,000, and the "interest" is $100 × 5 = $500. The installments are calculated on the basis of the loan principal amount of $1,000 + $500 = $1,500: $1,500/5 = $300 each.

How much is the borrower really paying to borrow $1,000? Let's restate this loan in more familiar terms:

Present value = $1,000
Number of payments = 5
Amount of each payment = $300

and

$1,000 = $300(present value of an annuity for T = 5 and r = ?)

The effective annual cost, r, of this loan is 15.24 percent, which is more than one and one-half times the stated rate of 10 percent!

If the discount rate is 5%:

$$r = \frac{0.05}{0.95} = \textbf{0.0526} \text{ or } \textbf{5.26\%} \text{ per period}$$

which is what we figured out earlier by using the comparison of the discount and the funds available.

The greater the discount rate, the higher the effective cost per period. We can see this in Figure 16-2, where the effective cost is plotted against the discount percentage. For larger discounts, the effective cost is larger than the discount percentage. As another example, a 15 percent discount results in an effective cost of r = 0.15/0.85 = 0.1765 or 17.65 percent per period.

Compensating Balance

Some financing arrangements require that a balance be maintained in a non-interest-bearing account with the lender. This balance is referred to as a ***compensating balance,*** since it compensates the lender for making the loan. As in the case of a discount loan, this arrangement may have the effect of raising your cost of borrowing, since you do not have the use of the funds you deposited in this account for the period of the loan.[1]

The amount of the compensating balance depends on the amount of the loan and typically ranges from 5 percent to 20 percent of the amount of the loan. Once required with nearly all bank loans, the use of compensating balances has declined in the United States over the years and has been replaced by service and other direct fees. However, more than two-thirds of U.S. banks still require compensating balances in their lending arrangements.[2]

Let's figure out the effective cost of a compensating balance loan. First, suppose you borrow $300,000 for one year from a bank with a single-payment loan that requires interest of 10 percent payable at the end of the year. The cost of this financing is $30,000 or 10 percent. We don't have to worry about compounding of interest here, since interest is paid at the end of the year.

Now suppose the bank will lend to you on these same terms, with an additional stipulation: You leave 5 percent of the loan amount (hence, it's a discount loan) in a non-interest-bearing account for the entire year. What is the cost of the loan now? The cost is more than the 10 percent, since we now are paying 10 percent of $300,000, but have the use of only 95 percent of the funds, or $285,000. The effective cost is:

$$\text{Effective cost} = \frac{\$30,000}{\$285,000} = \mathbf{0.1053} \text{ or } \mathbf{10.53\%} \text{ per year}$$

The compensating balance requirement increases the cost of the financing from 10 percent to 10.53 percent.

We can generalize the cost of financing with a compensating balance. Let r once again represent the effective cost per period, i represent the stated interest rate per compounding period on the face value of the loan, and b represent the compensating balance as a percentage of the loan face value. Then,

$$r = \frac{\text{costs}}{\text{funds available}} = \frac{i(\text{loan amount})}{(1 - b)(\text{loan amount})}$$

$$r = \frac{i}{1 - b} \qquad\qquad\qquad [16\text{-}4]$$

Suppose you borrow $500,000 from the bank for three months, at a nominal annual rate of 12 percent compounded every three months, and the bank requires you to maintain a compensating balance of 10 percent of the loan. Then, the stated quarterly rate is:

$$i = \frac{0.12}{4} = 0.03 \text{ or } 3\% \qquad \text{for a three-month period}$$

[1] If you would have left funds equal to the compensating balance on deposit with the bank whether or not you were borrowing, the compensating balance would not increase the cost of the loan. However, with all the available short-term investment opportunities, it is quite possible that a firm would not have had the funds on deposit without the compensating balance requirement.

[2] The survey by Thomas A. Ulrich and William E. Blouch, "Compensating Balance Practices by Southwestern Banks," *Southwest Journal of Business and Economics*, vol. 5, no. 4, Summer 1988, pp. 44–55, provides an overview of typical compensating balance arrangements.

and the compensating balance, b, is 10 percent. The *effective* cost for a three-month period is:

$$r = \frac{0.03}{1 - 0.10} = \textbf{0.0333} \text{ or } \textbf{3.33\%} \text{ per period}$$

Since there are four three-month periods in a year:

$$\text{EAR} = (1 + 0.0333)^4 - 1 = \textbf{0.1400} \text{ or } \textbf{14\%} \text{ per year}$$

If there were no compensating balance requirement:

$$\text{EAR} = (1 + 0.03)^4 - 1 = \textbf{0.1255} \text{ or } \textbf{12.55\%} \text{ per year}$$

The compensating balance requirement raises the effective annual cost from 12.55 percent to 14 percent. We can see the effect of the compensating balance requirement on the effective cost of a loan in Figure 16-3, where the cost of the 12 percent loan is plotted against the compensating balance as a percentage of the loan's face value. The higher the compensating balance percentage, the higher the effective cost of the loan.

Other Costs

Besides interest, discount interest, and compensating balances, there may be other costs associated with financing. The lender may charge a **loan origination fee,** which covers the lender's costs of credit checks and legal fees to make the loan available to you. A lender may also charge a **commitment fee,** which is compensation for the promise to make a loan, since the bank stands ready to lend the funds whether used or not. All these fees increase the cost of financing.

Suppose you arrange to borrow $50,000 from the bank for three months with a single-payment loan at a rate of 2.5 percent for three months. The effective annual cost of this credit is:

$$\text{EAR} = (1 + 0.025)^4 - 1 = \textbf{0.1038} \text{ or } \textbf{10.38\%} \text{ per year}$$

FIGURE 16-3

Effective Annual Cost of a Bank Loan with an APR of 12 Percent Compounded Quarterly for Various Compensating Balances

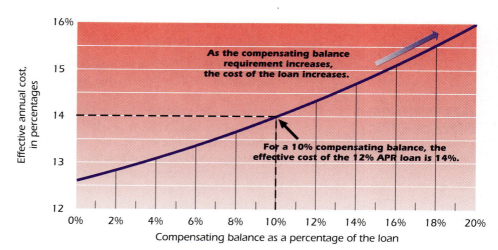

As the compensating balance requirement increases, the cost of the loan increases.

For a 10% compensating balance, the effective cost of the 12% APR loan is 14%.

Upfront Fees vs. End-of-Period Fees

It makes a difference whether the fees are paid at the beginning of the period or the end of the period. Consider a one-year loan of $10,000 with single-payment interest of 5 percent. If there were no fees, the effective cost of credit would be 5 percent per year.

Suppose there is a fee of $300 associated with this loan. If the fees are paid at the beginning, you are effectively borrowing $10,000 less the fee, or $9,700. The effective cost is:

$$r = \frac{\$500 + \$300}{\$9,700} = 0.0825 \text{ or } 8.25\%$$

Suppose instead that the $300 fee is paid at the end of the loan period. You then have $10,000 to use during the entire year; so the effective cost is:

$$r = \frac{\$500 + \$300}{\$10,000} = 0.0800 \text{ or } 8\%$$

Paying the fee up front effectively increases the cost of financing compared to paying the same fee at the end of the loan period.

If the bank charges a loan origination fee of $500, taken as a discount from the amount loaned, the effective cost for the three-month period is:

$$r = \frac{\text{costs}}{\text{funds available}} = \frac{0.025(\$50,000) + \$500}{\$50,000 - \$500}$$

$$= \frac{\$1,750}{\$49,500}$$

$$= 0.0354 \text{ or } 3.54\% \text{ per period}$$

Taking into consideration the origination fee as a discount from the face value of the loan, the effective annual cost is:

$$\text{EAR} = (1 + 0.0354)^4 - 1$$
$$= 1.1493 - 1$$
$$= 0.1493 \text{ or } 14.93\% \text{ per year}$$

The fee raises the effective annual cost from 10.38 percent to 14.93 percent. The higher are the fees, the higher is the effective cost of the loan.

UNSECURED FINANCING

In some types of financing, the creditor is counting on being paid the promised interest and principal, relying on the general creditworthiness of the borrower. But other creditors want more assurance of being paid back. This assurance is provided by requiring that specified property belonging to the borrower be transferred to the lender if the borrower fails to pay as promised. The lender can count on getting paid the interest and principal of the loan from the proceeds of the sale of the specified property.

A loan that is "backed" by specific property is a **secured loan.** A loan that is backed only by the general credit of the borrower is an **unsecured loan.** There are several different types of unsecured loans. We take a look at the more widely used types of unsecured credit: trade credit, bank loans, and money market securities.

Trade Credit

Trade credit is granted by a supplier to a customer purchasing goods or services. Trade credit arises spontaneously as the customer acquires goods or services and promises to pay some time in the future. From the seller's point of view, trade credit is a way of making more sales. By extending credit (their own credit), they hope to sell more goods and services. From the customer's point of view, trade credit is a very easy way to finance the purchase of goods. Once a satisfactory relationship is established between the seller and the customer, trade credit is granted automatically. For the seller, trade credit creates accounts receivable; for the customer, trade credit creates accounts payable.

Cost of Trade Credit

There is no explicitly stated interest rate for trade credit. But there is an *implicit* cost. Suppliers allow customers to pay at a later date but offer a discount if payment is made within a specified time period. The implicit cost is the difference between the cash price (the cost after the discount) and the full invoice price. Trade credit terms customarily state the discount terms: the discount percentage, the period within which the payment must be received to take advantage of the discount, and the final due date.

For example, the terms 1/15, net 30 mean that if payment is made during the first fifteen days, there is a 1 percent discount from the invoice amount; otherwise, full payment of the invoice amount must be made by day 30. Let's look at a time line that represents the amounts due on a $100 purchase:

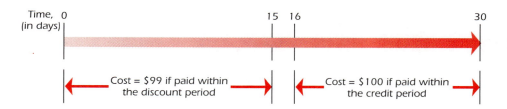

If you pay *on* or *before* the fifteenth day, your cost of the goods is $99. If you pay *after* the fifteenth day, your cost of the goods is $100. The credit period begins after day 15. You start incurring a higher cost on day 16, and the cost of the credit is $1 (the difference between $100 and $99). The credit period covers the number of days payment is delayed *beyond* the fifteenth day.

In turn, the effective cost of credit depends on the length of the credit period. Because terms of credit from different suppliers may not be all alike and because we may wish to compare the cost of alternative forms of credit, it is convenient to calculate the effective cost of trade credit for some common period, say a year.

What is the effective annual cost of using trade credit if terms are 1/15, net 30 and payment is made on the tenth day? Since the cash price is paid on day 10, there is no cost of credit: EAR = 0%.

What if payment is made on the twentieth day under these terms? The rate of interest is 1 percent of invoice price, but how much are you really borrowing? If you paid within fifteen days from the date of purchase, the cost was $99. If you paid *after* fifteen days, the cost was $100. Therefore, by paying on day 20, you have paid $1 to borrow $99 for five days:

$$r = \frac{\$1}{\$99} = \mathbf{0.0101} \text{ or } \mathbf{1.01\%} \text{ per period (5 days in this case)}$$

If you pay on day 20, you have effectively borrowed funds for five days (from day 16 through day 20). How many five-day periods (compounding periods) are there in a year?

$$t = \frac{365}{5} = 73$$

The effective annual cost of trade credit if you pay twenty days after your purchase is:

$$\text{EAR} = (1 + 0.0101)^{73} - 1$$
$$= \mathbf{1.0826} \text{ or } \mathbf{108.26\%} \text{ per year}$$

What this means is that you effectively borrowed $1 from the sixteenth day to the twentieth day and paid an annual rate of 108.26 percent for these five days.

What if you pay on the "net" day—thirty days after purchase? The interest rate for the credit period remains the same, since you are still paying 1 percent of the invoice price to borrow 99% of the invoice:

$$r = \frac{0.01}{0.99} = \mathbf{0.0101} \text{ or } \mathbf{1.01\%} \text{ per period (15 days in this case)}$$

But the credit period is now fifteen days, so there are fewer compounding periods in a year:

$$t = \frac{365}{15} = \mathbf{24.33}$$

The effective annual rate when you pay thirty days after the purchase is:

$$\text{EAR} = (1 + 0.0101)^{24.33} - 1$$
$$= \mathbf{0.2770} \text{ or } \mathbf{27.70\%} \text{ per year}$$

As the credit period is lengthened, the cost of trade credit declines. The cost of trade credit for alternative payment dates under the terms 1/15, net 30, illustrates the point:

THE COST OF TRADE CREDIT IF TERMS ARE 1/15, NET 30

Payment day	Length of credit period, in days	Number of credit periods, per year	Effective annual cost of credit
20	5	73.00	108.26%
25	10	36.50	44.31
30	15	24.33	27.70

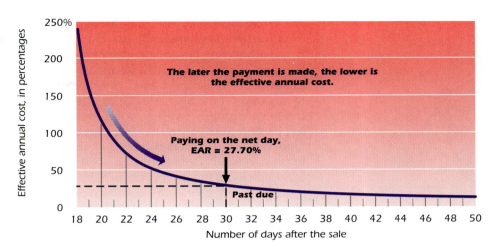

FIGURE 16-4

Effective Annual Cost of 1/15, net 30, Trade Credit Financing, with Payments Eighteen to Fifty Days after the Sale

The later the payment is made, the lower is the effective annual cost.

Paying on the net day, EAR = 27.70%

Past due

Effective annual cost, in percentages

Number of days after the sale

Why does the EAR decline as you stretch out payments? The later within the credit period that you pay your bill, the longer you have the creditor's $1 and the lower the effective annual cost. The cost of credit for the credit period remains the same once you pay after the fifteenth day and through the thirtieth day, 1.01 percent, but the credit period *lengthens*. You can see this in Figure 16-4, where the effective annual rate of trade credit under these terms is plotted against the number of days payment is made after the purchase date, starting with the eighteenth day.[3] You can see that the effective rate drops swiftly as we stretch out our payments beyond the discount period.

Accounts Payable Management

Managing accounts payable involves negotiating the terms of purchases as well as deciding when to pay amounts due. Remember that accounts payable are the "flip side" of accounts receivable—your accounts payable are someone else's accounts receivable. Your suppliers are trying to minimize their costs in terms of funds tied up in accounts receivable and bad debts. Yet, at the same time, they are extending credit to generate more sales.

Firms try to set their trade credit policies with an eye on the policies of their competitors, so we end up with terms of credit that are similar within industries. However, if your firm is an important customer of a particular supplier, you may be able to negotiate better terms of credit.

In calculating the cost of trade credit, we know that:

- If you pay within the discount period you are using free credit: You can delay payment by, say, ten days and the amount you pay will be the same as if you paid in cash on the date of purchase.
- If you pay beyond the discount period, the later you pay, the lower will be your cost of credit.

[3] You'll notice that we did not start graphing the effective cost in Figure 16-4 until three days into the credit period (eighteen days from the sale). This is because the effective interest cost is extraordinarily high for days 16 and 17 after the sale, rendering the graph difficult to read:

EAR, paying 16 days after the sale = $(1.0101)^{365} - 1 = $ **38.17** or **3,817%**

EAR, paying 17 days after the sale = $(1.0101)^{182.5} - 1 = $ **5.26** or **526%**

751

While paying beyond the due date does reduce the cost of trade credit even further, there are some issues that arise. First, there may be legal problems with paying beyond the due date. Paying taxes, insurance, or license fees late may cost you dearly in legal costs and sanctions. Second, there may be direct costs to late payments. Your creditors may impose penalties for payments beyond the due date. Third, there may be indirect costs to paying late. If you consistently pay late, you may damage your relationship with a creditor, perhaps a supplier, that you may need later. Also, paying beyond the due date may hurt your credit rating, making it more difficult or more expensive to borrow funds from banks or to purchase goods on credit in the future.

Aside from the legal costs and the indirect and direct costs of paying late, there is an important ethical issue: You agree to specific terms when you purchase the goods on credit. Intentionally (or even unintentionally) violating these terms is unethical business behavior.

It is important to monitor accounts payable to ensure that discounts are taken when possible and not to make payments beyond the specified period. We can get an idea of our accounts payable management by looking at the accounts payable turnover. The turnover is a measure of how many times within a period of time the accounts payable are created and paid:

$$\text{Accounts payable turnover} = \frac{\text{credit purchases}}{\text{accounts payable}} \qquad \text{[16-5]}$$

The numerator is the total amount of credit purchases made in the period. The denominator is a typical accounts payable balance over this period. The larger the turnover, the more quickly we are paying our accounts. For example, if we have $2 million in credit purchases in a year and our ending balance in accounts payable (using the ending balance as the typical accounts payable figure) is $200,000, the turnover is ten times:

$$\text{Accounts payable turnover} = \frac{\$2,000,000}{\$200,000} = \mathbf{10\ times}$$

A high turnover may be good news or bad news: good news, since we are probably establishing goodwill with our suppliers by paying quickly; bad news if we are not taking discounts but paying our bills before they are due.

A low turnover also may be good news or bad news: good news, since we are stretching our payments out, lowering the effective cost of trade credit; bad news if we are paying beyond the due date, which may harm our credit standing.

Deciding whether a specific accounts payable turnover ratio tells us good news or bad news requires somewhat more information.

We can learn more about our accounts payable management by calculating how long, on average, it takes us to pay. If we know the accounts payable amount we generate on a typical day and we know our typical balance of accounts payable, we can calculate the number of days' worth of payables we have in accounts payable:

$$\frac{\text{Number of days}}{\text{in accounts payable}} = \frac{\text{accounts payable}}{\text{average daily credit purchases}} \qquad \text{[16-6]}$$

If total credit purchases for the year are $2 million, our average daily credit sales are $2,000,000/365 = **$5,479.** This implies that the number of days in our accounts payable balance is $200,000/$5,479 per day = **36.5 days.** This tells us that it takes, on average, 36.5 days to pay our accounts. Is this good or bad? It depends on our credit terms. If our credit terms all have net days of 30, then having 36.5 days in our ending balance tells us that we are, on average, paying late.[4] If our credit terms all have net days of 60, then having 36.5 days in our ending balance tells us that we are, on average, paying too early.

If the credit terms you face are varied, it is difficult to evaluate the number of days in accounts payable. A more detailed breakdown of accounts payable is necessary. One way to break them down is to classify them into three groups:

- Payables that are still within the discount period.
- Payables that are beyond the discount period, yet are not overdue.
- Payables that are overdue.

Once you have this classification, you can focus on why each of the accounts payable is not paid when due and why discounts were not taken. This also allows you to plan for discounts that can be taken in the near future.

Another classification scheme is to "age" the accounts payable, that is, classify the accounts by the number of days since the purchase. This breakdown allows you to identify the older accounts payable as well as to plan ahead for the ones that must soon be paid.

Accounts payable management is a balancing act: The cost of trade credit must be balanced against the cost of alternative sources of financing. For example, if bank loans effectively cost 10 percent per year, should the firm borrow from the bank or use trade credit with terms of 1/15, net 30? Answer: Borrow from the bank, since it costs less (10 percent versus 27.70 percent). But many times, especially for small businesses, bank loans may not be available and trade credit is the only source for financing the purchases.

Bank Financing

Banks lend money to firms under different financing arrangements. The financing arrangement may be straightforward, such as a single-payment loan. Or a firm may obtain a promise from a bank to extend a loan, such as a line of credit or revolving credit.

Single-Payment Loan

A single-payment loan is the simplest short-term financing arrangement. In a single-payment loan, the borrower negotiates a loan of a specific sum from the lender, usually a bank, and agrees to repay the loaned amount at the end of a specified period.

Short-term bank loans are generally self-liquidating, that is, they are used to acquire assets, and the cash flows from these assets are sufficient to pay

---

[4] Of course, we are assuming that as soon as we purchase goods we record the obligation and as soon as we pay our accounts we record the payment, and so the accounts payable balance accurately reflects our obligations. If it takes time to record obligations or to record payments, the number of days in accounts payable may differ from the credit period and still be timely.

off the loan. Bank loans are represented in the form of a promissory note, which specifies the amount of the loan, the maturity date, and any interest.

The interest on a single-payment loan may be either discount interest or single-payment interest. With discount interest, the borrower receives less than the amount of the loan, paying back the full amount of the loan at maturity. The interest is the difference between the amount of the loan—the face value—and the funds actually available to the borrower. With single-payment interest, the borrower receives the amount of the loan, paying back the full amount of the loan plus interest at maturity.

The interest rate in a single-payment loan may be either fixed or variable; that is, the amount of interest may be fixed at the beginning of the loan period at a specified amount or may vary according to some specified formula.

Rates are often quoted relative to the ***prime rate,*** which is the rate banks charge their most creditworthy customers. A variable rate may change during the life of the loan, adjusting periodically as some other rate changes. For example, a variable interest rate may be specified as 50 basis points, or 0.5 percent, above the average yield on the six-month U.S. Treasury bill (T-bill) for the issue just prior to the maturity of the loan. Or, the rate may be 50 basis points above the T-bill rate, adjusted each week.

Line of Credit

A ***line of credit*** is an agreement that the bank will make available to a firm a loan of funds up to a specific limit—the line—if the firm requests these funds. The bank extends this line of credit for a specified period, typically one year.

Example: Mattel Inc. has seasonal sales, with its highest sales in the third quarter of the year and its lowest sales in the first quarter. Mattel negotiates lines of credit for both its domestic and foreign operations. Mattel's line of credit for 1991 with foreign banks (which it uses to meet seasonal working capital needs in its non-U.S. operations) was for $300 million.[5] This means that Mattel could borrow up to $300 million from these banks during 1991.

A line of credit is a flexible source of credit. The firm borrows funds only as needed, borrowing up to the line, if necessary, although usually the borrowing is uneven throughout the period. A line of credit is convenient if a firm's cash flow is uneven throughout the year, as happens with a seasonal business. When a firm borrows under a line of credit, it takes out notes payable to the bank, which range in maturity from one to ninety days. A bank may require that the borrower "clean up" the line—pay off the borrowings completely—for a specified period of time.

A line of credit may be uncommitted or committed. In an ***uncommitted line of credit,*** the bank makes a verbal agreement to lend funds up to the line within the specified period, but is not legally bound to do so. In a ***committed line of credit,*** the bank agrees in writing to lend funds and is legally bound to do so in accordance with the specific terms of the line-of-credit agreement.

The cost of the line of credit may comprise two costs. First, the borrower pays interest at a specified rate only on the funds borrowed and for the time borrowed. Second, if the agreement is a committed line of credit, the bor-

[5] Mattel Inc., *Annual Report, 1991,* p. 44.

rower pays either a commitment fee—from 0.25 to 0.5 of the unused portion of the line of credit—or must maintain a specified compensating balance for the period of the line of credit. Either way, the firm incurs some cost, though likely quite small, for the line of credit even if it does not borrow anything against the line.

McCredit

During 1990, McDonald's had a $1 billion line-of-credit agreement, with a commitment fee of 0.15 of 1 percent per year for any unused portion. The line of credit was not used during 1990; so McDonald's paid 0.15 of 1 percent of $1 billion = $1.5 million in commitment fees in 1990.

SOURCE: McDonald's, *Annual Report, 1990,* p. 38.

In addition to the fee or compensating balance, there may be some *covenants*—conditions that limit the actions of the borrower. Covenants may require that the borrower provide financial statements periodically or that certain financial ratios, such as a minimum interest coverage or current ratio, be satisfied. These covenants do not usually restrict the decision making of the borrower, but do serve to protect the lender in extreme cases.

Revolving Credit

A *revolving credit agreement* is similar to a line-of-credit agreement, but is usually for a longer period—two to three years. The borrower can borrow and repay the credit many times *within* this period in a series of short-term notes.

The cost of the revolving credit comprises two parts: (1) the commitment fee or compensating balance and (2) the interest on any borrowings under the agreement. Unlike the line of credit, revolving credit agreements usually specify a variable interest rate—an interest rate that varies according to some benchmark interest rate.

Typically, the borrower and lender renegotiate the revolving line of credit prior to maturity, ensuring a continuous source of funds for the borrower.

Letter of Credit

Suppose you just started an export-import business and you are importing calculators made in Taiwan. Your supplier in Taiwan may not want to grant you trade credit for your purchase of the calculators—it may be too expensive or time-consuming for the supplier to evaluate your creditworthiness. But since your business is just getting started and you have very little funds, you may not want to pay outright for the calculators. You can solve this dilemma by getting a letter of credit from your local bank.

A *letter of credit* is a written promise by a bank to make a loan if specific conditions are met; for example, if you are importing calculators from Taiwan, the condition may be that you receive the goods. The Taiwanese sup-

---

The Flowers of Revolving Credit

In 1991 and 1992, Flowers Industries, a food processor, entered into three-year revolving credit agreements with three different banks for $40 million each, or total possible borrowings of $120 million. Two of the three banks required a commitment fee of 0.125 percent of the unused portion of the line of credit. At the end of their 1992 fiscal year, Flowers had borrowed $30 million of the possible $120 million.

SOURCE: Flowers Industries Inc., *Annual Report, 1992,* p. 39

plier may be willing to ship the goods to you if you have the promise from your bank that payment will be made as soon as the goods are received. In effect, the letter of credit serves as a loan to you from the bank in the amount due the supplier, so that you can pay for the goods.

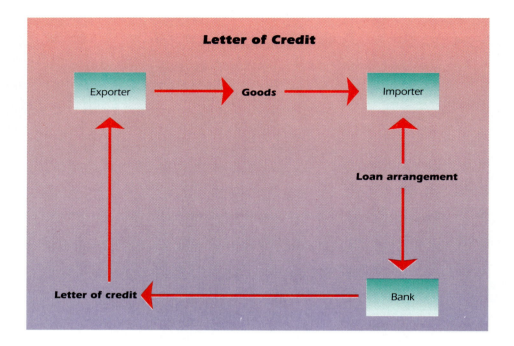

A letter of credit may be either revocable or irrevocable. If revocable, the bank can cancel the letter of credit; if irrevocable, the bank is committed to making the loan.

The cost of a letter of credit consists of a commitment fee for writing the letter of credit plus the interest on the loan once it is made. The loan typically has a fixed interest rate.

Comparing Forms of Bank Financing

Let's see what the alternative ways of stating the costs for bank credit do to the borrower's cash flows and the effective cost of financing. Suppose there are four alternative loan arrangements.

Alternative 1 A loan with a single interest payment of 10 percent.
Alternative 2 A loan with a 10 percent discount.
Alternative 3 A loan with a single interest payment of 10 percent and a 20 percent compensating balance.
Alternative 4 A $150,000 line of credit from which any borrowings incur a single interest payment of 10 percent; in addition, there is a 1 percent fee on any unused credit.

If you need to borrow $100,000 for one year, which of these alternatives has the lowest effective cost of financing? Let's look at each.

Alternative 1

Since there is only a single interest payment of 10 percent, the effective cost of credit is 10 percent. The cash flows to the borrower are:

Alternative 2

If $100,000 of funds are needed, we must first determine the principal amount of the loan:

Loan amount − 0.10(loan amount) = $100,000

$$\text{Loan amount} = \frac{\$100,000}{0.90} = \textbf{\$111,111}$$

The principal amount of the loan is $111,111 and the discount is 10 percent of $111,111, or $11,111. Therefore, the effective cost of the loan is:

$$r = \frac{\$11,111}{\$100,000} = \textbf{0.1111 or 11.11\%}$$

At the beginning of the year, you receive $100,000 and pay $111,111 at the end of the year:

Alternative 3

If you want to borrow $100,000 and there is a 20 percent compensating balance, you need to borrow more than $100,000:

Loan amount − 0.20(loan amount) = $100,000

$$\text{Loan amount} = \frac{\$100,000}{0.80} = \textbf{\$125,000}$$

You therefore need to borrow $125,000 in order to have $100,000 to use during the year, leaving $25,000 on deposit at the bank. At the end of the year you pay the interest of 10 percent on $125,000, or $12,500; so the effective cost of the loan is:

$$r = \frac{\$12,500}{\$100,000} = \textbf{0.1250 or 12.50\%}$$

At the end of the year, you repay the loan amount, $125,000, plus the $12,500 interest. And since you get back the use of the compensating balance, your payment to the bank (after taking into consideration the return to you of the compensating balance) is $125,000 + $12,500 − $25,000 = $112,500:

Alternative 4

If you borrow only $100,000 of the $150,000 line, your cost is composed of two parts: (1) the 10 percent interest on the $100,000 you borrowed, or $10,000, and (2) the 1 percent fee for the $50,000 unused line of credit, or $500. The effective cost of financing is:

$$r = \frac{\$10,000 + 500}{\$100,000} = \mathbf{0.1050} \text{ or } \mathbf{10.50\%}$$

At the end of the year, you repay the $100,000 borrowed and pay the $10,000 interest and $500 fee:

Comparing the Four Alternatives

The compensating balance, discount, and fees increase the effective cost of the loan above the 10 percent cost of a single-payment loan:

Alternative	Effective cost of financing
1: Single payment	10.00%
2: Discount loan	11.11
3: Compensating balance	12.50
4: Line of credit	10.50

Money Market Securities

In addition to trade credit and bank loans, there are loans that become marketable—loans that can be bought and sold on the open market. Two short-term financing arrangements that create a *money market security*— short-term securities that can be bought or sold in financial markets by investors—are commercial paper and bankers' acceptances.

Commercial Paper

Commercial paper is an unsecured promissory note with a fixed maturity issued by the borrower. Commercial paper originated during the nineteenth century as a substitute for bank loans and became popular in the United States during the 1920s because banks were restricted from operating across state lines. Most state laws prohibited banks from branching out across state lines, and some even prohibited branches within the same state. Bank borrowing became cumbersome because one bank could not service the banking needs of a firm that had operations across the country. Though restrictions on interstate and intrastate bank branching have eased, the commercial paper market is still a growing source of short-term financing.

Commercial paper notes have denominations (face values) starting at $25,000 each, although most have denominations of $100,000 or larger.

Commercial paper is unsecured, so the lender (the party buying the commercial paper) is counting on the borrower's being able to pay the face amount of the note at maturity. Nevertheless, almost all commercial paper is backed by a line of credit from a bank. If commercial paper is backed and the borrower is unable to pay the lender at maturity, the bank stands ready (for a fee) to lend the borrower funds to pay off the maturing paper.

Most commercial paper issued in the United States has maturities ranging from 3 to 270 days. Though these maturities are relatively short, some firms tend to use commercial paper for financing over longer periods of time. They do this by rolling over the paper: As the paper matures, they issue new commercial paper to pay off the maturing paper.

Both finance and nonfinance companies issue commercial paper. Finance companies, such as General Motors Acceptance Corporation (GMAC) and C.I.T. Financial Corporation, are in the business of lending funds to consumers, usually for the purchase of consumer durables, such as automobiles. Finance companies tend to continually roll over their commercial paper, since it is the major source of funds they use for their lending business. Nonfinancial companies, such as manufacturing firms and public utilities, tend to issue commercial paper to meet their seasonal financing needs.

A firm can issue commercial paper either directly—selling the paper to the investor itself—or indirectly through dealers. Finance companies issue commercial paper either directly or through a dealer; larger finance companies, such as GMAC, tend to issue their paper directly.

> Why does commercial paper have a maturity of less than 270 days? Because if a security has a maturity over 270 days, the issuer must register it with the Securities and Exchange Commission. Doing so would delay the issuance and increase the cost of issuing the paper.

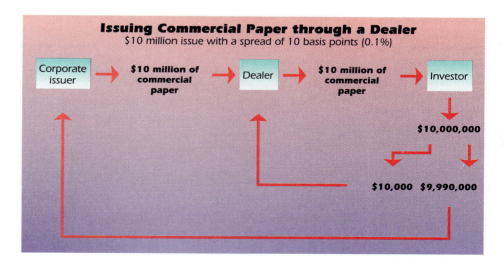

Issuing Commercial Paper through a Dealer
$10 million issue with a spread of 10 basis points (0.1%)

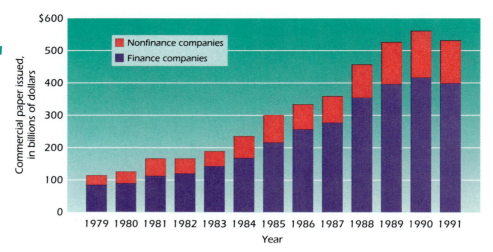

Large industrial companies, bank holding companies, and small finance companies tend to issue commercial paper through a dealer, who is compensated through the **spread**—the difference between what the dealer pays the issuer and what investors pay the dealer. The spread is usually around 5 to 15 basis points, or 0.05 to 0.15 percent of the amount of the issue.

We can see in Figure 16-5, which shows the growth in the commercial paper market for both finance and nonfinance companies, that the finance companies tend to dominate the market.

The interest on commercial paper is generally stated as discount interest, though in recent years some commercial paper with single-payment interest—interest bearing—has been issued. The interest is quoted on the basis of a 360-day year and is fixed for the maturity of the paper.

Investors can get an idea of the quality of the commercial paper by looking up the ratings by financial service companies such as Moody's, Standard & Poor's, Fitch Investors Services, and Duff & Phelps Credit Rating Company. The rating classes used by Moody's Investors' Service and Standard & Poor's are described in Table 16-1. The vast majority of commercial paper is of high quality, with ratings in the top one or two classes.

TABLE 16-1

Commercial Paper Ratings by Standard & Poor's and Moody's Investors' Service

Judgment	Standard & Poor's	Moody's
High degree of safety	A-1	Prime 1
Satisfactory ability to make timely payments	A-2	Prime 2
Adequate capacity to make timely payments, but vulnerable to adverse effects of changes in circumstances	A-3	Prime 3
Speculative	B	Not prime
Doubtful capacity to make timely payments	C	Not prime
In default	D	Not prime

SOURCE: Moody's *Bond Record* and Standard & Poor's *Bond Guide.*

Protecting Its Rating

General Motors (GM), is the largest U.S. automobile manufacturer. Long viewed as a "blue chip" investment, GM has been in jeopardy of losing its status as a high-quality investment. During the late 1980s and early 1990s, GM lost some of its market share to U.S. and non-U.S. rivals. Accompanying this loss, GM's earnings slid, resulting in a cash drain.

General Motors finances its business from many sources, including trade credit (informal credit by suppliers), commercial paper (short-term IOUs), and bank loans. Losing the top-tier rating of the commercial paper issued by its financing subsidiary, General Motors Acceptance Corporation (GMAC), would be a major blow to GM, since the Securities and Exchange Commission does not permit money market funds (by far the largest investor in commercial paper) to invest in any commercial paper not rated as top-tier by at least two rating services. Any downgrade in the ratings of its commercial paper or its debt would increase GM's cost of capital, sending it into that vicious circle of borrowing to cover increasing costs of financing.

In recent years, General Motors has taken many measures (including issuing preferred and common stock and selling its accounts receivable) to stop its cash drain and to prevent a possible downgrade of its commercial paper rating.

The most noteworthy defaults on commercial paper were those of Penn Central, in 1970, and the Manville Corporation, in 1982.

Some commercial paper, however, is "junk," listed as not-prime by the rating services or not rated at all. While investors generally do not have to worry about default risk—the risk that the amount due will not be paid at maturity—there have been a few defaults on commercial paper.

The cost of commercial paper varies along with other market interest rates, such as the rate on a 91-day Treasury bill. In addition to general market rates, the quality of the issuer of commercial paper affects the cost of this form of financing. Historically, there was little difference in yields among commercial paper with different ratings. The shakeup of the commercial paper market in 1990 that resulted from defaults by Integrated Resources and Drexel, Burnham & Lambert, among others, caused a greater difference in yields among commercial paper with different default risk.

The default risk of commercial paper is a function of both the creditworthiness of the issuer and the backup line of credit. With the recent defaults in commercial paper, this backup line of credit has become more important to investors.

Bankers' Acceptances

A *banker's acceptance* is a bank's commitment to honor someone else's promise to pay a specified amount at a specified date to a third party. With a banker's acceptance, the bank commits itself to make the specified payment at the maturity of the draft *if* the issuer of the draft does not pay. Bankers' acceptances are typically used in international trade, though they may be used domestically as well. They generally have maturities of less than 270 days; hence, they are time drafts.

Although there are a variety of ways to arrange a banker's acceptance, the basic idea behind all of them is that a letter of credit is transformed into a security that can be bought and sold in the open market.

Suppose a bank issues a letter of credit to assist an importer in the payment of goods. The exporter wants cash now, not the letter of credit. So the exporter takes the letter of credit to his bank and receives his funds now. But he receives *less* than the face value of the letter of credit. By cashing it in, rather than waiting for maturity, he receives less money. The exporter's bank may not want to hold onto the letter of credit until maturity; so the exporter's bank exchanges it for funds with the importer's bank. First the letter of credit is exchanged for a time draft—a promise of the importer's bank to pay. Then the draft is exchanged into funds with the importer's bank. The importer's bank is now holding a time draft that has not matured. The bank can either hold it as an investment or sell it to an investor. This process is diagrammed in Figure 16-6.

The cost of a banker's acceptance comprises a commitment fee, or commission for the commitment, and the interest rate on the loan if the bank

FIGURE 16-6

How Bankers' Acceptances Provide Financing for Export-Import Transactions

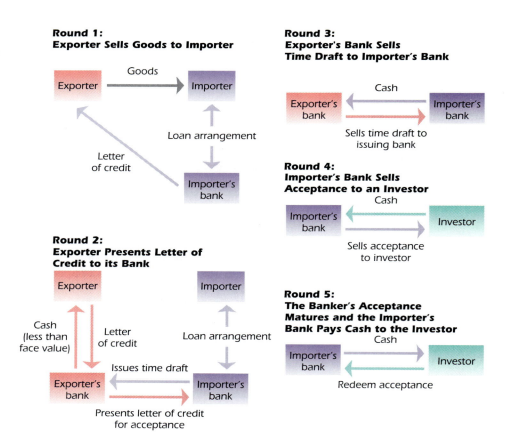

Round 1:
Exporter Sells Goods to Importer

Round 2:
Exporter Presents Letter of Credit to its Bank

Round 3:
Exporter's Bank Sells Time Draft to Importer's Bank

Round 4:
Importer's Bank Sells Acceptance to an Investor

Round 5:
The Banker's Acceptance Matures and the Importer's Bank Pays Cash to the Investor

makes the payment for the issuer. The interest is usually stated as discount interest—the difference between the price paid and the face value. The amount specified in the letter of credit is for the price of the goods plus interest; the face value of the acceptance is some amount larger than the price of the goods, with the difference being the interest on the loan. This is similar to trade credit: By cashing in the letter of credit, the exporter gets the cash price of the goods, but if he had waited, he would have received this cash price plus interest.

When the banker's acceptance is sold to investors, it is sold at a discount from the face value, so when the acceptance matures, the purchaser of the goods (the importer in our example) pays face value. If the purchaser cannot pay the face value, the bank will because it has accepted responsibility for the payment.

A banker's acceptance is similar to commercial paper. Both can be traded among investors, both have maturities of less than 270 days, and both generally have discount interest. But they differ in two ways:

1. In the way in which they are created.
2. In their risk. Commercial paper is backed by the issuer, which *may* have a backup line of credit; a banker's acceptance is backed by the issuer; yet the bank stands ready to pay the face value. The lower risk on bankers' acceptances results in slightly lower yields than those on commercial paper.

The use of bankers' acceptances for import and export transactions has been relatively constant in recent years, though their use for other purposes has varied, as shown in Figure 16-7.

FIGURE 16-7

Use of Bankers' Acceptances to Finance Exports and Imports, 1980–1991

SOURCE: *Federal Reserve Bulletin.*

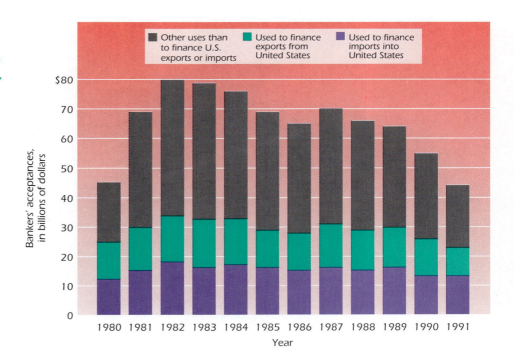

SECURED FINANCING

Secured financing is "backed" by some specific asset or assets of the borrower. Borrowers' assets used in this way are referred to as **collateral.** The collateral acts as a backup source of funds for the lender: If the borrower fails to abide by the terms of the loan, the lender can take possession of the collateral and dispose of it to recover the amount of the loan and interest, or at least some part of both.

In most secured credit arrangements, the collateral is a secondary source of repayment on a loan. The lender generally does not consider it likely that the need to take possession of the collateral will occur. But having collateral may have some psychological value, encouraging payment of the loan. The collateral for short-term financing arrangements is usually current assets, such as marketable securities, accounts receivable, or inventory.

Repurchase Agreements

A *repurchase agreement* (sometimes referred to as a "repo") has two parts: a sale of a marketable security and the subsequent repurchase of that same security from the purchaser. The agreement involves borrowing funds for a period shorter than the maturity of the marketable securities used in the agreement. Suppose you need funds for twenty days and you own U.S. Treasury bills that mature in forty days. You can sell your T-bills with a repurchase agreement, promising to buy them back within twenty days. This is a secured loan, since the T-bills are marketable securities; they are the collateral. If you fail to repurchase them, the buyer takes ownership of them. The value of the collateral exceeds the cash paid in the initial sale—that is, the loan is over-collateralized—and this difference is referred to as the "haircut."

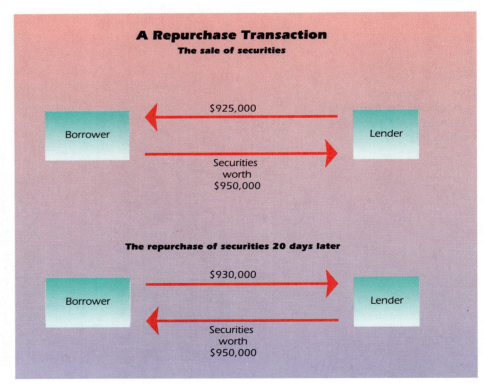

A Repurchase Transaction
The sale of securities

Borrower ← $925,000 Lender

Borrower → Securities worth $950,000 → Lender

The repurchase of securities 20 days later

Borrower → $930,000 → Lender

Borrower ← Securities worth $950,000 ← Lender

The cost of a repurchase agreement is the difference between what you sell the securities for and what you pay to buy them back. Suppose you make a repurchase agreement to sell Treasury bills that have a face value of $1 million and a current market value of $950,000. If you sell them for $925,000—a haircut of $25,000—and promise to buy them back for $930,000 twenty days later, you are effectively paying $5,000 for the use of $925,000 for twenty days. The effective cost, r, is:

$$r = \frac{\$5,000}{\$925,000}$$

$$= \mathbf{0.0054} \text{ or } \mathbf{0.54\%} \text{ per period} \qquad (20 \text{ days in this example})$$

The effective annual cost of this repurchase agreement—the EAR—with $365/20 = 18.25$ twenty-day periods in a year, is:

$$EAR = (1 + 0.0054)^{18.25} - 1$$

$$= \mathbf{0.1034} \text{ or } \mathbf{10.34\%} \text{ per year}$$

The buyer (and subsequently the seller) in this agreement has a very secure position. If you fail to repurchase the securities, the lender has given you $925,000 for securities that are worth $950,000. Since these are marketable securities—which, by definition, can be readily sold—there is little risk from the lender's point of view. If the borrower fails to pay the $930,000, the lender is left with $950,000 worth of securities that she can easily sell.

Accounts Receivable

Accounts receivable can be used as collateral for a secured loan. The simplest form of accounts receivable financing is the assignment of receivables. In an

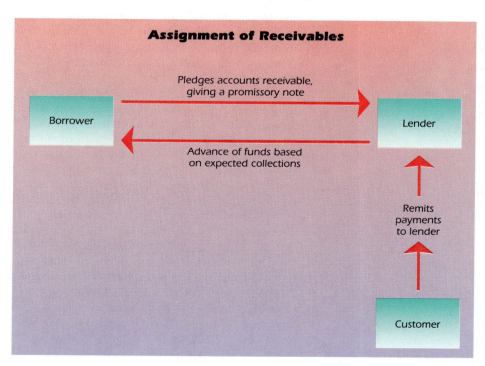

Assignment of Receivables

Pledges accounts receivable, giving a promissory note

Borrower

Lender

Advance of funds based on expected collections

Remits payments to lender

Customer

assignment of receivables, the lender makes a loan, accepting the borrower's accounts receivable as the collateral. The borrower receives immediate cash in exchange for a promissory note to the lender. The borrower's customers are generally instructed to send their payments to the lender, who uses these payments to reduce the amount of the loan. This type of financing is flexible, since the lender increases the loan as more receivables are generated (as acceptable collateral by the borrower) and reduces the loan as these receivables are paid off. Therefore, the loan fluctuates with the needs of the borrower.

If payments on the accounts receivable are sent directly to the lender, there are potential problems.

First, part of the motivation that customers have to repay their trade credit is to maintain the customer-supplier relationship. If payments are made to a party (the lender) *other* than the supplier, the customer may not be as highly motivated to pay.

Second, if there are disputes over goods or services, it is difficult to resolve them if payments are made to a third party. Suppose the customer refuses to pay because the goods were defective. The third party (the lender) is not in a position to resolve this dispute, and part of the loan collateral may not have value.

In general, lenders loan up to 70 to 85 percent of the value of the accounts receivable. Lenders do not accept accounts receivable that are grossly past due.

The cost of a loan that is secured with accounts receivable depends on a number of factors, including the amount of the loan, the turnover (the rate of collection), and the creditworthiness of the accounts receivable. The interest rates charged on loans backed by accounts receivable are usually variable, tied to the interest rate on some other security. For example, a loan backed by accounts receivable may be specified as 50 basis points (that's 0.5 percent) above the prime rate. If the lender performs any credit functions, such as approving credit or collecting accounts, service fees will increase the cost of the loan.

A borrower can go a step further in financing with its accounts receivable. Instead of simply using accounts receivable as collateral, the borrower can sell them outright to another party—called a *factor*—typically a bank or a commercial finance company. Selling the receivables—called *factoring*—may be done with or without recourse. In a factoring arrangement *without recourse*, the factor performs all the accounts receivable functions: evaluating customers' credit, approving credit, and collecting on accounts receivable. If any of the accounts turn out to be uncollectable, the factor bears the loss of the bad debt. If a borrower's arrangement with a factor is *with recourse* and the borrower grants credit without permission from the factor, the borrower assumes the responsibility for collection of the account.

There are basically two types of factoring, maturity factoring and conventional factoring. They differ with respect to when the seller receives cash for the receivables. In *maturity factoring,* the customer sends cash to the factor, who then sends the cash (less a commission) to the seller. In *conventional factoring,* the factor advances cash to the seller when the accounts are factored and then keeps the customers' payments as they come in.

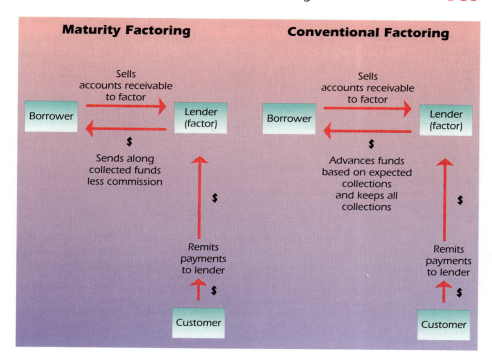

Factors charge a commission of 0.75 to 1.5 percent of the face value of the accounts receivable. In addition, if funds are advanced, as in the case of conventional factoring, the factor charges interest on those funds, usually at a rate of 2.5 to 3 percent above the prime rate. Since factoring replaces accounts receivable personnel, a firm's decision to use factoring requires comparing the cost of operating the receivables function with the factor's commission.

Suppose a firm borrows using conventional factoring for its $10 million in accounts receivable. And suppose the factor charges a fee of 1 percent of the face value of the receivables, payable up front, and interest at 3 percent over prime. If the prime rate is 12 percent APR, what does it effectively cost the firm to borrow under these terms for one month?

If the factor lends the firm $10 million but then charges a fee of 1 percent at the beginning of the loan, the firm has the use of only 99 percent of the $10 million, of $9.9 million. Interest is 3 percent over prime, or 15 percent a year. Since the prime rate is an annual percentage rate, the monthly rate is 15%/12 = 0.0125 or 1.25%. The interest is therefore 1.25 percent of $10 million, or $125,000. The effective cost for a month is:

$$r = \frac{\$125{,}000 + \$100{,}000}{\$9{,}900{,}000} = 0.0227 \text{ or } 2.27\%$$

and the effective annual rate is:

$$\text{EAR} = (1 + 0.0227)^{12} - 1 = 0.3091 \text{ or } 30.91\%$$

Receivables can also be used to generate immediate cash through securitization. **Securitization** of assets creates a security out of a collection of assets, such as accounts receivable. The return is dependent on the cash flow from the assets that constitute the security. Securitization is carried out in two steps:

Step 1 Accounts receivable are grouped together and sold to a trust. A trust is a legal arrangement in which assets are transferred to the trust and managed by an individual or a firm (the trustee) for a specific purpose.

Step 2 The trust sells securities, which represent interests in the trust, to investors.

Investors—those buying the securities from the trust—receive a return in the form of cash flows from the accounts receivable that constitute the created security.

Securitizing is only possible with accounts receivable that have good collection records. By selling the assets to the trust, the seller is transferring the risk of collecting on these accounts to the investors. But a problem with securitization is that the best assets are sold to the trust, leaving the firm with the accounts receivable that are more difficult to collect.

Inventory

Inventory can also be used as collateral for financing, since it is a fairly liquid asset. Not all inventory is of equal importance as security: The amount of funds loaned depends on how easy it is for the lender to turn the inventory into cash. In general:

- Standardized inventory is much better than specialized inventory.
- Nonperishable inventory is better than perishable inventory.
- Raw materials and finished goods are better than work in process.

There are several different types of loan arrangements that involve inventory as collateral. These arrangements differ in terms of the control the lender has over the location and disposition of the inventory.

A **floating lien** is the most flexible type of inventory loan. A floating lien gives the lender a lien on all inventory of the borrower—that is, all inventory is security for the loan. Therefore the security of the loan changes as the borrower buys and sells inventory.

A **chattel mortgage** is a loan secured by specified inventory. In other words, inventory items are uniquely identified, such as by serial number, as collateral for the loan. The borrower retains title in the inventory. And although the borrower still owns the inventory, she or he cannot sell it unless the lender gives permission. This type of loan is best suited for inventory that consists of large, slow-moving items.

In a **trust receipts loan,** the borrower holds the inventory in trust for the lender. As the inventory is sold, the borrower keeps the proceeds in trust for the lender. This type of arrangement is also referred to as **floor planning** and is often used with auto dealerships. First, the borrower arranges a loan with the finance company. The borrower then orders and receives the inventory,

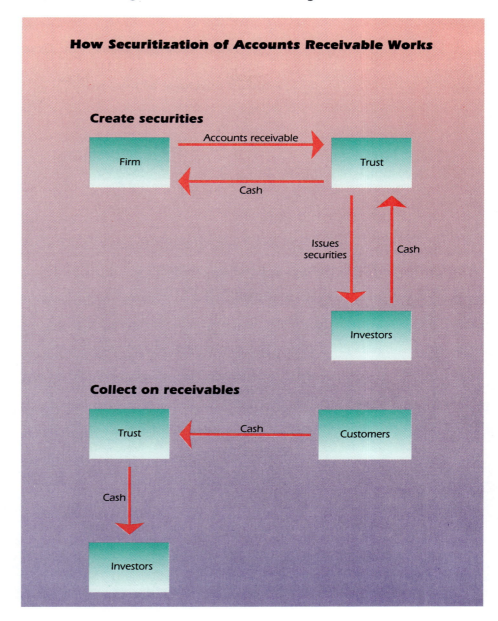

How Securitization of Accounts Receivable Works

Create securities

with the finance company paying the supplier. As the borrower sells the inventory items, the borrower remits the payments to the finance company, reducing the amount of the loan. Since the finance company is counting on the borrower to maintain the inventory (keep it in good condition) and to send the payments when sales are made, the lender must devise a way to monitor the borrower.

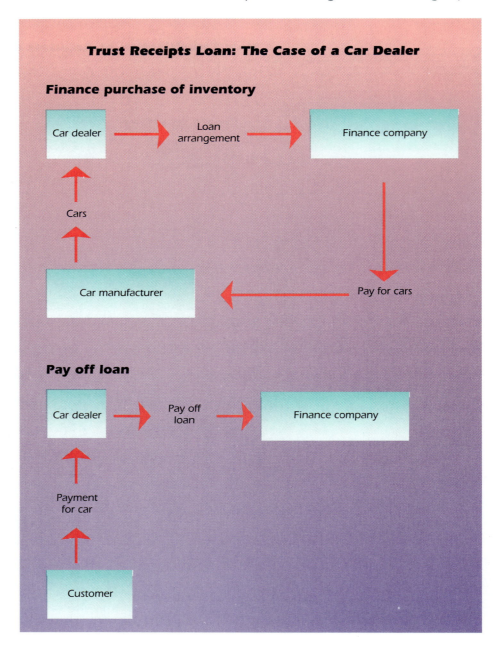

In a **field warehouse loan** the lender has tighter control over the inventory. The collateral (the inventory) is kept in a separate, secured area within the borrower's premises and is monitored by a field warehouse agent. This agent keeps control over the inventory in this area and issues receipts to the lender, indicating the existence of the inventory. As the lender receives these receipts, he makes a loan based on the collateral value of the inventory. This arrangement is more expensive than the floating lien, chattel mortgage, and trust receipts arrangements because a third party—the field warehouser—must be compensated for his services. This arrangement offers the lender more peace of mind over the inventory.

Suppose a firm borrows $1 million for one month under a field warehousing arrangement. And suppose the APR on the loan is 12 percent. The interest on the loan is therefore 1 percent of $1 million, or $10,000. If the field warehouse charges a $5,000 fee, payable at the end of the month, the cost of this financing is:

$$r = \frac{\$10,000 + \$5,000}{\$1,000,000} = 0.0150 \text{ or } 1.50\%$$

and:

$$EAR = (1 + 0.0150)^{12} - 1 = 0.1956 \text{ or } 19.56\%$$

If the field warehouse charges the $5,000 fee at the *beginning* of the month, the cost for the month is higher, since effectively the firm has borrowed only $995,000:

$$r = \frac{\$10,000 + \$5,000}{\$995,000} = 0.0151 \text{ or } 1.51\%$$

and:

$$EAR = (1 + 0.0151)^{12} - 1 = 0.1970 \text{ or } 19.70$$

Even tighter control over collateral inventory is maintained in a public warehouse loan arrangement. In a ***public warehouse loan,*** collateral inventory is kept in a secured area away from the borrower's premises, such as in a public warehouse, and is released to the borrower only if the lender gives permission. The warehouser issues receipts to the lender (similar to the field warehouse arrangement) which the lender acknowledges in the form of money loaned to the borrower. In this arrangement, the *lender* has title to the goods instead of the borrower.

ACTUAL COSTS OF SHORT-TERM FINANCING

The cost of short-term financing is a function of many factors, including:

- Prevailing interest rates
- Creditworthiness of borrower
- Length of maturity of borrowing
- Amount borrowed
- Security
- Backup line of credit

The cost of the different forms of financing varies because of these factors. We can see the difference in cost of several different forms of short-term financing in Figure 16-8, where the cost of several types of businesses' financing are shown along with the rate on the 90-day T-bill—the government's cost of short-term financing. We use the T-bill rate for comparison purposes, since this is the rate on a short-term security with no risk of default—the U.S. government can always print more money to cover its debts.

FIGURE 16-8
Annual Cost of Short-Term Financing Alternatives, 1970–1991

SOURCE: Moody's, "Selected Money Market Rates," *Bank and Finance Manual*, 1992, p. a12.

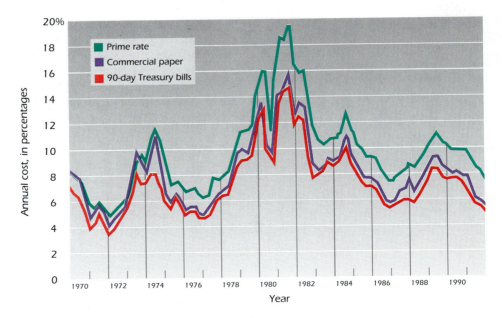

For a closer look at the difference in rates, we show the average rates on these securities at the end of 1990 and 1991:[6]

Security	End of 1990	End of 1991
90-day T-bill	7.02%	4.58%
Bankers' acceptances	7.76	4.83
Commercial paper	7.90	4.98
Prime rate	10.00	7.60

We see that bankers' acceptances rates are higher than the T-bill rates. This is because there is some default risk with acceptances. Commercial paper rates are slightly higher than those for acceptances, since they are also considered to have little default risk but may or may not be backed by a line of credit. The prime rate, which is what banks use as a base rate for their loans, is above the commercial paper rate, reflecting a generally greater risk associated with bank loans relative to commercial paper, which is issued by large, creditworthy corporations.

[6] Moody's, *Bank and Finance Manual*, 1992, p. a12.

SUMMARY

- Short-term financing is used to finance the seasonal needs of a business and includes trade credit, bank financing, money market securities, and secured financing.

- We need to calculate the effective cost of short-term financing arrangements in order to be able to compare them. Putting the cost of financing on an effective annual basis facilitates this comparison. In calculating an effective cost, we need to consider any discount interest, compensating balance requirements, and fees.

- Trade credit arises out of our ordinary business transactions whenever our suppliers permit us to pay at some time after the purchase of the goods or services. The cost of trade credit arises from any forgone discount.

- Accounts payable management requires us to compare the cost of trade credit with the cost of other forms of credit. We also must weigh the benefits of paying our accounts later with the cost of late payments in terms of their effects on our relationship with suppliers.

- Bank financing comes in many forms, including single-payment loans, which may arise from simple lending arrangements or from promises to lend in the form of lines of credit, revolving credit agreements, or letters of credit.

- Short-term financing can also be obtained by using loans that create marketable securities, such as commercial paper and bankers' acceptances. Since these securities have low risk owing to the creditworthiness of the parties that issue the security and the backup credit by banks, they are also low-cost ways of financing.

- There are a variety of secured financing arrangements involving marketable securities (repurchase agreements), accounts receivable (assignment and factoring), and inventory (floating liens, chattel mortgages, trust receipts, and warehousing).

- The costs of short-term financing depend on many features of the loan, including the creditworthiness of the borrower, the amount borrowed, any backup line of credit, and the maturity of the loan. Generally, commercial paper and bankers' acceptances have lower costs than bank loans and loans secured with accounts receivable or inventory.

QUESTIONS

16-1 Consider a single-payment loan with interest of 10 percent and a discount loan with a discount of 10 percent. If the loan amounts and the loan periods are the same for both loans, which loan has a higher effective cost of financing? Why?

16-2 If a bank states 5 percent interest on a 360-day basis, is this stated rate less than, equal to, or more than 5 percent interest on a 365-day basis? Why?

16-3 Consider two loans with equal maturity and identical face values: a discount loan that has a discount of 10 percent and a single-payment loan with a 10 percent compensating balance requirement. Which loan has the higher interest rate? Explain.

16-4 Consider two loans with equal maturity and identical loaned amounts: a discount loan that has a discount of 10 percent and a single-payment loan with no interest but an origination fee of 10 percent. Which loan has the higher interest rate? Explain.

16-5 Explain the advantages and disadvantages of stretching payments on trade credit.

16-6 In a repurchase agreement, which parties are borrowing and which parties are lending? What is the collateral in a repurchase agreement? What is a "haircut," and why do these types of agreements require a "haircut"?

16-7 A firm can use its inventory as collateral in financing arrangements in several different ways. How do these alternative arrangements differ?

16-8 At the end of its 1992 fiscal year, OEA Inc., a manufacturer of aerospace and automobile products, had a $2.5 million line of credit, with the interest rate equal to the lending institution's prime interest rate minus 0.5 percent. OEA is required to keep a compensating balance on deposit with the lending institution equal to 5 percent of the line of credit, and, in addition, pays 5 percent of any usage (OEA, *35th Annual Report*, 1992, p. 14).

    a. What do you need to consider in determining OEA's cost of the line of credit?

    b. How does the compensating balance affect OEA's cost of borrowing?

PROBLEMS

Cost of credit

16-1 Calculate the effective annual rate that corresponds to the annual percentage rates for each of the following financing alternatives:

Alternative	APR	Frequency of compounding
A	12%	Annually
B	12	Semiannually
C	18	Monthly
D	10	Weekly
E	5	Quarterly

16-2 In the following pairs of financing costs, which has the lower effective annual cost?

	Financing alternative A	Financing alternative B
Pair 1	12% APR—interest compounded monthly	11% APR—interest compounded quarterly
Pair 2	8% APR—interest compounded quarterly	7.2% APR—interest compounded monthly
Pair 3	6% APR—interest compounded semiannually	5.2% APR—interest compounded weekly

Cost of trade credit

16-3 Calculate the effective annual cost for each of the following trade credit terms and payment dates:
  a. 1/10, net 30, paying on day 20.
  b. 2/10, net 40, paying on day 30.
  c. 3/15, net 60, paying on day 60.
  d. 5/15, net 50, paying on day 50.

16-4 Calculate the effective annual cost of trade credit for terms of 1/10, net 40, if payment is made:
  a. 9 days after the sale.
  b. 11 days after the sale.
  c. 20 days after the sale.
  d. 30 days after the sale.
  e. 40 days after the sale.

Cost of bank loans

16-5   What is the effective annual cost of a single-payment loan that requires interest of 6 percent after three months?

16-6   What is the effective annual cost of a discount loan that has a discount of 5 percent and a loan period of four months?

16-7   Calculate the effective annual cost of a six-month loan of $100,000 that has a 7 percent interest rate and:
  a. No compensating balance or loan origination fee.
  b. A 20 percent compensating balance and no loan origination fee.
  c. A 20 percent compensating balance and a loan origination fee of $1,000 taken as a discount.

16-8   Calculate the effective annual cost of a three-month loan of $1 million that has a 16 percent APR and:
  a. No compensating balance or loan origination fee.
  b. A 10 percent compensating balance and no loan origination fee.
  c. A 10 percent compensating balance and a loan origination fee of $1,000, paid at the beginning of the loan.

Monitoring accounts payable

16-9   The Dieu Company had sales of $1 million in 1992, with 60 percent of its purchases made on credit. If the average accounts payable is $100,000, what is Dieu's accounts payable turnover?

16-10   At the end of 1992, General Motors Corporation had $10 billion in accounts payable. If this balance is representative of GM's payables, and if it takes GM thirty days to pay on its accounts, how much did GM have in credit purchases during 1992?

The cost of secured credit

16-11   REPO Corporation used a repurchase agreement, selling $2 billion in face amount of U.S. Treasury bills with a market value of $1.99 billion for $1.95 billion, and repurchasing them twenty-five days later for $1.975 billion.
  a. What is the amount of the haircut in REPO's transaction?
  b. What is REPO's cost of credit for the twenty-five days?
  c. What is REPO's effective annual cost of credit using repurchases?

16-12   Transmutant Company is in the process of negotiating a repurchase agreement. Transmutant has U.S. Treasury bills with a face value of $1 million and a current market value of $990,000 that it wants to sell and then repurchase twenty days later. If Transmutant sells these securities for $950,000 and if the lender wants an effective annual return of 15 percent, what price would Transmutant need to pay in order to repurchase these securities?

16-13   The Cash Poor Company is considering using its $1 million in accounts receivable to secure financing for the next month. Cash Poor has approached two financing firms, each offering different arrangements. Firm A is willing to lend Cash Poor 75 percent of the face value of the receivables at 60 basis points above the prime rate. Firm B is willing to factor Cash Poor's receivables, advancing 75 percent of the receivables, collecting a fee up front of

1 percent of all receivables, and charging interest at 30 basis points above the prime rate. In the case of Firm A's arrangement, Cash Poor continues with its evaluation and collection of credit, but in the case of Firm B's arrangement, Firm B performs all the credit functions, saving Cash Poor an estimated $10,000 over the next month. If the prime APR is 12 percent, which arrangement is less costly for Cash Poor?

16-14 A firm is considering using a field warehousing arrangement as part of its short-term financing. The field warehouse requires a once-a-year payment of $10,000, paid at the beginning of the year, no matter how much the firm borrows. Interest on the loan is a single payment of 10 percent per year, paid at the end of the year. What is the effective annual cost of borrowing using field warehousing if the amount borrowed is:

   a. $150,000
   b. $200,000
   c. $300,000
   d. $500,000

Potpourri

16-15 Evaluate the effective annual cost of each of the following credit terms:

   a. Trade credit, with terms of 2/10, net 30, paying on the net day.
   b. Bank loan with single-payment interest of 5 percent for six months.
   c. Bank loan with discount interest of 4 percent for six months.
   d. Bank loan with single-payment interest of 2 percent for three months, with a compensating balance of 10 percent.
   e. Bank loan with single-payment interest of 3 percent for three months, with a compensating balance of 5 percent.
   f. A one-year loan secured with accounts receivable, with a service fee of 5 percent (payable at the end of the loan) and a 5 percent rate of interest.

16-16 Which of the following financing arrangements provides the lowest effective annual cost to the borrower?

Arrangement 1	Repurchase agreement in which securities with a face value of $5 million and a market value of $4.5 million are sold for $4.3 million and repurchased thirty days later for $4.35 million.
Arrangement 2	Commercial paper with a maturity of 91 days, which is sold at a 4 percent discount from its face value.
Arrangement 3	A one-year bank loan with no compensating balance, but with discount interest of 14 percent.
Arrangement 4	A one-year bank loan with a 10 percent compensating balance and single-payment interest of 5 percent.

16-17 **Research:** Select a company and describe any lines of credit or revolving credit agreements it may have as of the most recent fiscal year end. This information is usually provided in a footnote to the annual report.

   a. What fees does the company pay for these agreements?
   b. Did the company use some or all of these credit agreements during the most recent fiscal year?

16-18 **Research:** What were the prevailing costs of bankers' acceptances and commercial paper as of the end of the last calendar year. How did these costs change during the past calendar year? Explain why these rates may have changed over the past year.

Recommended sources of information:

- *Bond Record*, Moody's
- *Bank and Finance Manual*, Moody's

FURTHER READINGS

A detailed description of the growing popularity of commercial paper as a source of short-term financing is provided in:

MITCHELL A. POST, MICHAEL A. SCHOENBECK, and JOYCE A. PAYNE, "The Evolution of the U.S. Commercial Paper Market Since 1980," *Federal Reserve Bulletin*, vol. 78, no. 12, Dec. 1992, pp. 879–891.

PART VII

Financial Management and Planning

17 Strategy and Financial Planning 780

Strategy and Financial Planning

INTRODUCTION 783

STRATEGY 784

Comparative and Competitive Advantage 784

Strategy and Owners' Wealth Maximization 785

FINANCIAL PLANNING AND BUDGETING 786

Sales Forecasting 788

    Forecasting with Regression 790

    Market Surveys 794

    Management Forecasts 794

Seasonal Considerations 795

Budgeting 796

    The Cash Budget 797

    Pro Forma Financial Statements 802

Long-Term Financial Planning 806

FINANCIAL MODELING 808

**BUDGETING AND FINANCIAL PLANNING
   PRACTICES 811**

Summary 812

Socks 'n Stocks

Sears, Roebuck & Co., one of the largest U.S. retailers, has fallen on hard times, closing its 97-year-old catalog operation and selling some of its businesses. How could such a large, established retailer fall on hard times? Part of the problem was the company's strategy of becoming a one-stop–shopping retailer, where customers could buy wrenches, clothing, stocks, and real estate in one store— hence, the strategy's nickname of Socks 'n Stocks.

In late 1981, to follow this strategy, Sears acquired Coldwell Banker & Co., a real estate sales company, and Dean Witter Reynolds, a securities brokerage firm. Along with Allstate Insurance, which had been a part of Sears for some time, these acquisitions were key to the Sears strategy of becoming a financial supermarket. In 1984, Sears entered into the Prodigy joint venture with IBM and CBS to provide an on-line computer shopping and information network. In 1985, Sears launched the Discover card.

What may have looked good on paper to Sears did not always work. Most of their difficulties in fitting together companies with diverse business lines and diverse corporate cultures began after all the pieces of the financial supermarket were in place, in 1986. We can see this in the revenues and net income for the different divisions following the acquisitions.

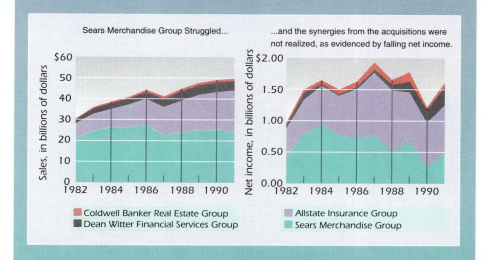

What was expected to create synergies (benefits from combining the firms) instead caused headaches. For example, in many states Sears was prevented from offering merchandise discounts to buyers of homes sold through its Coldwell Banker unit. And subscribers to the Prodigy system were able to purchase securities without a stock broker, thus undercutting Dean Witter Reynolds, the Sears brokerage division.

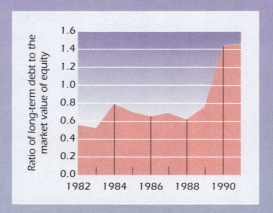

Sears began to rely more on debt financing as its troubles grew. Declining profits and increasing use of financial leverage resulted in the inevitable—the downgrading of the company's debt, beginning in 1989.

Among the actions the company took to stop its downward financial spiral and to raise cash:

- In 1988, Sears tried to sell its office tower in Chicago for $1 billion. After one year, Sears could not find a buyer and instead renegotiated its financing on the building.
- In 1989, Sears sold a portion of its ownership interest in Coldwell Banker.
- In 1990, the Sears merchandise group began layoffs and salary freezes.
- In late 1992, Sears began selling off its investments in Dean Witter Reynolds (packaged with the Discover card), the remainder of its Coldwell Banker interest, and a portion of its Allstate Insurance unit.
- In late 1992, the Sears merchandise group closed its catalog operation.
- In early 1993, the merchandise group embarked on a major store renovation plan.

In hindsight, we see that the Sears strategy of becoming a financial supermarket and the acquisitions it made to accomplish this strategy were not in its (and its shareholders) best interests. Why didn't the strategy work out as planned? Perhaps the firm's analysis of the purchase of these companies was too optimistic. Or maybe Sears did not follow through after these acquisitions to realize the synergies that were attainable. It's even possible that the Sears strategy was not a good one.

INTRODUCTION

A business that operates in such a way as to maximize its owners' wealth allocates its own resources more efficiently, resulting in a more efficient allocation of resources for society as a whole. Owners, employees, customers, and anyone else who has a stake in the business enterprise are all better off when its managers make decisions that maximize the value of the firm.

Just as there may be alternative routes to a destination, there may be alternative ways to maximize owners' wealth. A ***strategy*** is a sense of how to reach an objective, such as wealth maximization. And just as some routes may get you where you are going faster than others, so some strategies may be better than others.

Suppose a firm has decided it has an advantage over its competitors in marketing and distributing its products in the global market. The firm's strategy for maximizing that advantage may be to expand into the European market, followed by an expansion into the Asian market. Once the firm has its strategy, it needs a plan, in particular the ***strategic plan,*** which is the set of actions the firm intends to take to carry out its strategy.

The investment opportunities that enable the firm to carry out its strategy constitute the firm's ***investment strategy.*** The firm may pursue its strategy of expanding into the European and Asian markets either by establishing itself in those markets or by acquiring businesses already located there. This is where capital budgeting analysis comes in: We evaluate the possible investment opportunities to see which ones, if any, provide a return greater than necessary for the investment's risk. And let's not forget the investment in working capital, the resources the firm needs to support its day-to-day operations.

Suppose as a result of evaluating whether to establish or acquire businesses, our firm decides it is better—in terms of maximizing the value of the firm—to acquire selected European businesses. The firm's next step is to figure out how it is going to *pay* for these acquisitions. The financial managers must make sure that the firm has sufficient funds to meet its operating needs as well as its investment needs. This is where the firm's ***financing strategy*** enters the picture. Planning is needed: Where should the needed funds come from? What is the precise timing of the need for funds? To answer these questions, working capital management (in particular, with respect to short-term financing) and the capital structure decision (the chosen mix of long-term sources of financing) come into play.

When we look at our firm's investment decisions and at the same time consider how we are going to finance them, we are budgeting. ***Budgeting*** is mapping out the sources and uses of funds for future periods. In budgeting we use both economic analysis (including forecasting) and accounting. Economic analysis includes both marketing and production analysis to develop forecasts of future sales and costs. We use accounting techniques, adapted to our particular purpose, as a measurement device. But instead of using accounting to summarize what has happened (its common use), in budgeting we use accounting to represent what we expect to happen in the future.

Once these plans are put into effect, we must compare what happens with what was planned. This is ***postauditing,*** which we use to:

- Evaluate the performance of the management of the firm.
- Analyze any deviations of actual results from planned results.
- Evaluate the planning process to determine just how good it is.

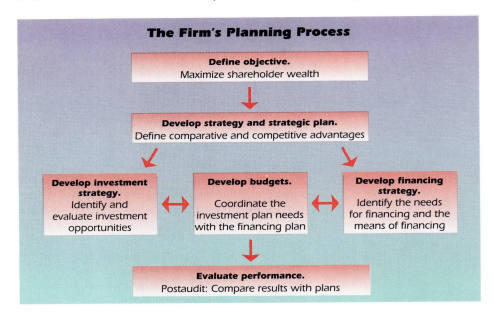

STRATEGY

Whilst every man is free to employ his capital where he pleases, he will natu-
rally seek for it that employment which is most advantageous; he will natu-
rally be dissatisfied with a profit of 10 per cent, if by removing his capital he
can obtain a profit of 15 per cent.

David Ricardo, *The Principles of Political Economy and Taxation*, London, 1817.

The way to create wealth from investments is to invest in projects that have positive net present values. But where do these positive net present values come from? From the firm's comparative or competitive advantage.

Comparative and Competitive Advantage

A **comparative advantage** is the edge one firm has over others in terms of the cost of producing or distributing goods or services. Wal-Mart Stores Inc. has developed a comparative advantage over its competitors (such as K Mart) through its vast network of warehouses and its distribution system. Wal-Mart invested in a system of regional warehouses and in its own trucking operation. By using the regional warehouse system instead of a national warehouse system or no warehouse system, Wal-Mart reduced its need for inventory. And by having its own truck fleet, Wal-Mart is able to replenish store inventories more frequently than its competitors. Combined with bulk purchasing and a unique customer approach (including its "greeters"), Wal-Mart's comparative advantages in its warehousing and distribution systems have helped it grow to be a major (and very profitable) retailer in a very short span of time.

A **competitive advantage** is the edge one firm has over others because of the structure of the input and output markets they all operate in. For example, one firm may have a competitive advantage because of barriers in the way of other firms that seek to enter the same market. This happens in the case of government regulations that limit the number of firms in a market, as with banks, or in the case of government-granted monopolies, as with lo-

NPV > 0

A positive net present value (NPV) project is a project whose expected return is greater than its cost of capital, where this cost of capital reflects the project's perceived risk. A positive NPV project is "profitable" in economic terms but not necessarily in accounting terms.

cal cable companies.[1] A firm may itself create barriers to entry (although with the help of the government) that include patents and trademarks.

How Sweet It Was

NutraSweet Company, a unit of the Monsanto Company, had the exclusive patent on the artificial sweetener aspartame, which it markets under the brand name NutraSweet. However, this patent expired December 14, 1992. The loss of the monopoly on the artificial sweetener was expected to reduce the price of aspartame from $45 per pound to $30 per pound, since other firms could produce and sell aspartame products starting December 15, 1992 (Lois Therrien, Patrick Oster, and Chuck Hawkins, "How Sweet It Isn't at NutraSweet," *Business Week*, Dec. 14, 1992, p. 42).

NutraSweet had a competitive advantage as long as it had the patent. But as soon as the patent expired, the competitive advantage was lost and competitors began to line up to enter the market.

Only by having some type of advantage can a firm invest in something and get more back in return. So first you have to figure out what your firm's comparative or competitive advantage is before you can determine your firm's strategy.

Strategy and Owners' Wealth Maximization

Often we think of strategy in terms of the consumers of the firm's goods and services. For example, we may have a strategy to become the world's leading producer of microcomputer chips. How do we do this? By developing a comparative or competitive advantage: producing the best-quality chip or producing chips at the lowest cost, thus developing a cost (and price) advantage over our competitors. So our focus is on product quality and cost. Is this strategy in conflict with the goal of maximizing owners' wealth? No.

To maximize owners' wealth, we focus on the returns and risks of future cash flows to the firm's owners. And we look at a project's net present value in deciding whether to invest in it.

Is a strategy of gaining a competitive or comparative advantage consistent with the goal of maximizing shareholder wealth? Yes. Because projects with positive net present value do not arise out of thin air—they arise because the firm has a competitive or comparative advantage over other firms.

Suppose a firm is evaluating a new piece of equipment and analysis reveals that the product has a positive net present value; that is, it is expected to generate a return greater than what is expected in terms of the project's risk (its cost of capital). But how can a firm create value simply by investing in a piece of equipment? If investing in this equipment can create value, wouldn't the firm's competitors also want this equipment? Of course. If they could use it to create value, they would surely be interested in it.

Strategy Isn't Mickey Mouse Stuff

"The Walt Disney Company has several strategic and financial objectives that guide management decision-making in creating value for its shareholders. Its overriding objective is to sustain Disney as the world's premier entertainment company from a creative, strategic and financial standpoint" (*The Walt Disney Company 1992 Annual Report*, p. 45).

---

[1] But monopolies are not given away. For example, cable companies typically pay a "franchise fee" of a percentage of their revenues (say, 5 percent) to the local government in exchange for the privilege of operating the local cable monopoly.

First, suppose the firm's competitors face no barriers in buying the equipment and exploiting its benefits. What would happen? The firm and its competitors would compete for the equipment, bidding up the price of the equipment. When does it all end? When the net present value of the equipment is zero.

Now suppose, instead, that the firm can keep its competitors from exploiting the equipment's benefits (say, the firm has a patent on the process). Then there would be no competition for the equipment and the firm would be able to exploit the equipment in order to increase the wealth of the firm's owners.

Strategy and Owners' Wealth

Consider a case in which trying to gain a comparative advantage went wrong. Schlitz Brewing Company attempted to reduce its costs to gain an advantage over its competitors: It reduced its labor costs and shortened the brewing cycle. Reducing costs allowed it to reduce its prices below its competitors' prices. But product quality suffered— so much so that Schlitz lost market share instead of gaining it.

Schlitz attempted to gain a comparative advantage, but was not true to a larger strategy of satisfying its customers, who apparently wanted quality beer more than they wanted cheap beer. And the loss of market share was reflected in Schlitz's declining stock price.

A firm has to keep an eye on its strategy. In the long run, the strategy of satisfying its customers and maximizing owners' wealth do converge.

SOURCE: The case of Schlitz Brewing is detailed in George S. Day and Liam Fahey, "Putting Strategy into Shareholder Value Analysis," *Harvard Business Review*, March–April 1990, pp. 156–162.

Value can be created only when the firm has a competitive or comparative advantage. If a firm analyzes a project and determines that the project has a positive net present value, the first question to answer should be: What is the source of that positive value?

FINANCIAL PLANNING AND BUDGETING

As certainly as financial planning centers about commitments and utilization of capital, the protective function of management is also germane to the process. This function comprehends the integrity of capital, the profitable survival of the business entity, and the safe-guarding of the rights of the capital contributors.

Paul M. Van Arsdell, *Corporation Finance*, Ronald Press, New York, 1968, p. 550.

A strategy is the direction a firm takes to meet its objective. A strategic plan describes how a firm intends to go in that direction. In financial management, a strategic investment plan includes policies to seek out possible investment opportunities: Do we spend more on research and development? Do we look globally? Do we attempt to increase market share?

A strategic plan also includes resource allocation. If a firm intends to expand, where does it get the capital to do so? If a firm requires more capital, the timing, amount, and type of capital (whether equity or debt) constitute elements of a firm's financial strategic plan. These elements must be planned as a part of the process of implementing the strategy.

Financial planning allocates a firm's resources to achieve its investment objectives. Financial planning is important for several reasons.

First, financial planning assists managers to assess the impact of a particular strategy on their firm's financial position, its cash flows, its reported earnings, and its need for external financing.

Second, by formulating financial plans, the firm's management is in a better position to react to any changes in market conditions, such as slower-than-expected sales, or unexpected problems, such as a reduction in the supply of raw materials. By constructing a financial plan, managers become more familiar with the sensitivity of the firm's cash flows and its financing needs to changes in sales or some other factor.

Third, creating a financial plan helps managers understand the trade-offs inherent in its investment and financing plans. For example, by developing a financial plan, the financial manager is better able to understand the trade-off that exists between having sufficient inventory to satisfy customer demands and the need to finance the investment in inventory.

Financial planning consists of the firm's investment and financing plans. Once we know the firm's investment plan, we need to figure out when funds are needed and where they will come from. We do this by developing a *budget*, which is basically the firm's investment and financing plans expressed in dollar terms. A budget can represent details, such as what to do with cash in excess of needs on a daily basis, or it can reflect broad statements of a firm's business strategy over the next decade.

Budgeting for the short term (less than a year) is usually referred to as *operational budgeting;* budgeting for the long term (typically three to five years ahead) is referred to as *long-run planning* or *long-term planning.* But since long-term planning depends on what is done in the short term, operational budgeting and long-term planning are closely related.

The budgeting process involves putting together the financing and investment strategies in terms that allow the financial manager to determine what investments can be made and how these investments should be financed. In other words, budgeting pulls together decisions regarding capital budgeting, capital structure, and working capital. And we do this by preparing financial statements that represent these decisions.

Consider Sears. Its store renovation plan is part of its overall strategy of regaining its share of the retail market by offering customers better quality and service. Fixing up its stores is seen as an investment strategy. Sears evaluates its renovation plan by using capital-budgeting techniques (e.g., net present value). But the renovation program requires financing, and this is where the capital structure decision comes in. If the program needs more funds, where should they come from? Debt? Equity? Both? And let's not forget the working capital decisions. If Sears renovates its stores, will this change its need for cash on hand? Will the renovation affect inventory needs? If Sears expects to increase sales through this program, how will any increase affect

The "Purse Strings"

The term "budget" originates from the French *bouge,* meaning a bag and its contents. We use the term budget to refer to the allocation of a firm's resources (in dollars) over future periods. The bag is therefore the firm; its contents are the firm's resources, its funds.

the company's investment in accounts receivable? And what about short-term financing? Will Sears need more or less short-term financing when it renovates?

Since Sears is undergoing a renovation program, it needs some idea of what funds it will have on hand and what it needs, in both the short run and the long run. This is where a cash budget and pro forma financial statements are useful. The starting point is generally long-term and short-term sales forecasts which are related closely to the purchasing, production, and other forecasts of the firm. The amount Sears expects to sell affects its purchases, sales personnel, and advertising forecasts. Clearly, putting together forecasts requires cooperation among the firm's marketing, purchasing, and financial management.

Once Sears has its sales and related forecasts, the next step is a cash budget, detailing the cash inflows and outflows each period. Once the cash budget is established, the pro forma balance sheet and income statements can be constructed. Following this, Sears must verify that what is budgeted is consistent with its objective and strategies.

Budgeting generally begins four to six months prior to the end of the current fiscal period. Most firms have a set of procedures that must be followed in compiling the budget. The budget process is usually managed by either a vice president of planning, the director of the budget, the vice president of finance, the chief financial officer, or the corporate controller. Each division or department provides its own budget, and the budgets are then merged into a company budget by the budget manager.

A budget looks forward and backward. It identifies resources the firm will generate or need in the near and long term, and it serves as a measure of the current and past performance of departments, divisions, and individual managers. But we have to be careful when we measure deviations between budgeted and actual results. We must distinguish between deviations that were controllable and deviations that were uncontrollable. For example, suppose we develop a budget based on the expectation that we will achieve $10 million in sales from a new product. If actual sales turn out to be $6 million, do we interpret this result as poor performance on the part of management? Maybe; maybe not. If the lower-than-expected sales are due to an unexpected downturn in the economy, probably not. But yes, if they are due to obviously poor management forecasts of consumer demand.

Sales Forecasting

Sales forecasts are an important part of financial planning. Inaccurate forecasts can result in shortages of inventory, inadequate short-term financing arrangements, and so on.

To predict cash flows we forecast sales, but our forecasts are uncertain because they are affected by future economic, industry, and market conditions. Nevertheless, we can usually assign meaningful degrees of uncertainty to our forecasts. We forecast sales using one or more of the following:

- Regression analysis
- Market surveys
- Management opinions

The Budgeting Process

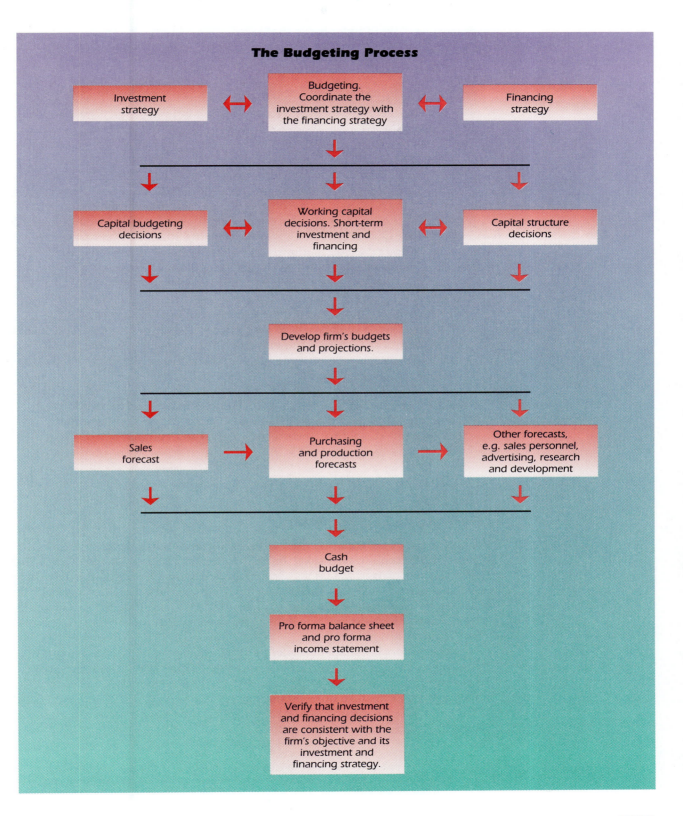

Too Much of a Good Thing

Coleco Industries Inc. introduced a toy product in 1983, its Cabbage Patch doll, which enjoyed runaway popularity. In fact, the doll was so popular that Coleco could not keep up with demand. The doll was in such demand and inventory was so depleted that fights broke out in toy stores; some parents bribed store personnel to get scarce dolls just before Christmas; and fake dolls were smuggled into the country.

Coleco missed its mark, significantly underestimating the demand for the dolls. While having a popular toy may seem like a dream for a toy manufacturer, the doll turned into a nightmare. With no Cabbage Patch dolls on the toy shelves, other toy manufacturers introduced dolls with similar (but not identical) features, capturing some of Coleco's market. Also, many consumers—the parents—became irate at Coleco for creating demand for the toy through advertising, but not having a sufficient number of dolls to satisfy the demand.

And the nightmare continued. Each Cabbage Patch doll sold was promised a birthday card on its first birthday. But since Coleco was caught off guard by the unexpected demand, it was not able to deliver these cards on time, causing further public relations damage.

Coleco Industries tried but failed to introduce other toys as successful as the Cabbage Patch doll. The company filed for bankruptcy in 1988, and most of its assets (including its Cabbage Patch doll line) were sold to Hasbro Inc., a rival toy company.

Forecasting with Regression

One way regression can be used is to simply extrapolate future sales on the basis of the trend in past sales. In Figure 17-1(a), let's look at the sales of International Business Machines over the period from 1976 through 1990. During this period, sales increased each year; hence, the sales trend is positive. If we were to connect each point representing sales and time the result would look almost like a straight line that slopes upward. But we can't do much with an "almost" straight line.

Regression is a statistical method that enables us to "fit" a straight line that on average represents the best possible graphical relationship between sales and time. This best "fit" is called the *regression line.* Let's simplify the regression against time by noting the years 1976, 1977, . . . , 1990 as 1, 2, . . . , 15. Regressing IBM's sales against time we estimate a regression line described as:[2]

---

[2] We have to be careful to keep track of how we measure time. In this case, we used 1, 2, 3, and so on. This means that if we forecast sales for 1991, we substitute "16" for "time," not "1991." While we could have estimated the regression using 1976, 1977, and so on to represent time, the calculations are somewhat easier to work with if we use 1, 2, and so on.

FIGURE 17-1(*a*)

Sales of International Business Machines, 1976–1990

SOURCE: *Value Line Investment Survey.*

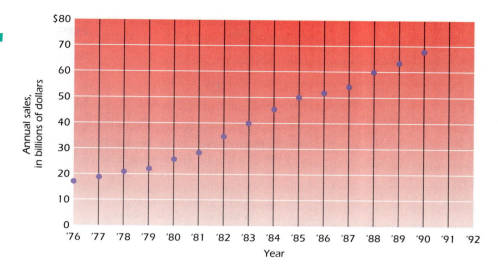

IBM annual sales, in billions = $9.11   + $3.87 × time

↑   ↑
Intercept   Slope of
of line with   the line, in
vertical axis,   billions of
in billions   dollars per year

Appendix D details the procedure for estimating a regression line.

While we won't concern ourselves here with the data that went into estimating this line, we can interpret what this line means. This line tells us that on average, from 1976 through 1990, IBM's sales increased by $3.87 billion each year. This regression line is plotted in Figure 17-1(*b*). You'll notice that the line intersects the vertical axis at $9.11 billion sales and has a slope (a rate of change in sales each year) of $3.87 billion.

FIGURE 17-1(*b*)

Sales of International Business Machines, 1976–1990, with Regression Line Summarizing Relation between Annual Sales and Time

SOURCE: *Value Line Investment Survey.*

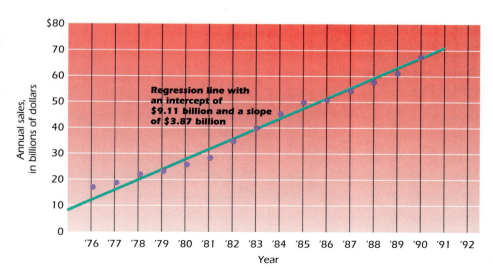

Regression line with an intercept of $9.11 billion and a slope of $3.87 billion

If we assume the current trend continues, we would predict sales to increase in 1991. Let 1991 be represented as time = 16; then:

IBM 1991 sales, in billions = $9.11 + $3.87(16) = $71.03

And for 1992 (time = 17):

IBM 1992 sales, in billions = $9.11 + $3.87(17) = $74.90

The difference between what was forecast and what actually occurred is the *forecast error*. Were actual 1991 and 1992 sales close to what we predicted? Not really: We have predicted higher sales than actually occurred.

	Actual sales, in billions	Sales predicted by regression line, in billions	Forecast error, in billions
1991	$64.89	$71.03	$6.14
1992	64.52	74.90	10.38

Predicted and actual 1991 and 1992 sales are shown in Figure 17-1(*c*). You'll notice that we overestimated sales. This illustrates a problem with regression analysis: Past trends do not always continue. Sales growth slowed in 1991 and 1992 as IBM lost more market share to its rivals.

Another way of using regression analysis is to look at the relation between two measures, say, sales and capital expenditures. If we look at the relation between sales and capital expenditures for the period from 1976 through 1990, as shown in Figure 17-2, we see that the greater the capital expenditures, the greater IBM's sales. The straight line shown in this figure is the regression line, which represents the best summary of the relation between IBM's sales and capital expenditures from 1976 through 1990. If we expect 1991 capital expenditures to be, say, $6.5 billion, we would expect (based on the average

FIGURE 17-1(c)

Sales of International Business Machines, 1976–1990, with Forecasts for 1991 and 1992

SOURCE: *Value Line Investment Survey.*

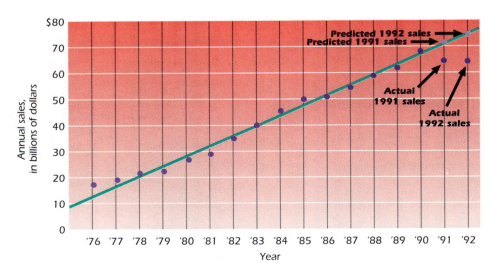

FIGURE 17-2

Sales and Capital Expenditures of International Business Machines, 1976–1990, with Forecasts for 1991 and 1992

SOURCE: *Value Line Investment Survey.*

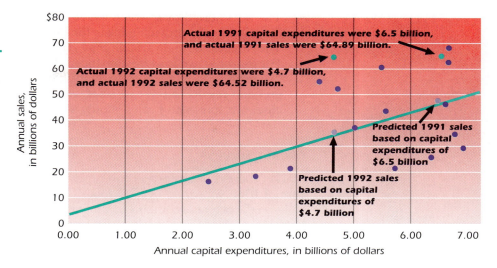

relation between sales and capital expenditures) sales to be $47 billion.[3] As it turns out, IBM spent $6.5 billion and had sales of $64.89 billion. We have *under*estimated IBM's sales in this case.

We could also look at the relation between IBM's sales and the combination of a number of factors, such as IBM's capital expenditures, a measure of economic activity such as gross domestic product (GDP), and the capital expenditures of IBM's competitors. By estimating the relation among these factors over a number of years and combining the results with forecasts of GDP and competitors' expenditures, we could predict IBM's sales for 1991. The more factors we include, the more accurate should be our predictions.

While regression analysis gives us what may seem to be a precise measure of the relationship among variables, we have to be careful in using it and interpreting what we get out of it. There are a number of warnings that the financial manager must heed in using regression analysis:

- Using historical data to predict the future assumes that past relationships will continue into the future, which is not always true.
- The period over which the regression is estimated may not be representative of the typical environment the firm will face next. For example, looking at data from a recessionary period of time may not tell us much about a future period that is predicted to be a time of economic boom.
- The reliability of the estimate is important: If there is a high degree of error in the estimate (that is, the observed data points—the actual past data—do not cluster tightly around the estimated regression line), the regression estimates may not be useful.

---

[3] A more precise estimate of sales for capital expenditures of $6.5 billion is $47.397 billion, based on the regression of sales on capital expenditures from 1976 through 1990.

- The time period over which the regression is estimated may not be long enough to provide a basis for projecting long-term trends;
- The forecast of one variable may require forecasts of other variables. For example, we may be convinced that sales are affected by GDP and use regression techniques to analyze this relationship. But to use regression results to forecast sales, we must first forecast GDP. In this case, our forecast of sales is only as good as our forecast of GDP.

Market Surveys

Market surveys of customers can provide estimates of future revenues. In the case of IBM, we would need to focus on the computer industry and, specifically, on the personal computer, minicomputer, and mainframe computer markets. For each of these markets, we would have to assess IBM's market share and expected sales in each market. We should expect to learn from these market surveys:

- Product development and introductions by IBM's competitors.
- The general economic climate of the computer market.
- Projected customer expenditures on computers.

A firm can use its own market survey department to survey its customers. Or it can employ outside market survey specialists.

Management Forecasts

Besides using market survey results, the firm's managers may themselves be able to develop forecasts of future sales. The experience of a firm's managers and their familiarity with the firm's products, customers, and competitors make them reliable forecasters of future sales.

The firm's own managers should have the expertise to predict the market for the company's goods and services and to evaluate the costs of producing and marketing them. But there are potential problems in using management forecasts. Consider the case of a manager who forecasts rosy outcomes for a new product. These forecasts may persuade the firm to allocate more resources, such as a larger capital budget and additional personnel, to that manager. If these forecasts come true, the firm will be glad these additional resources were allocated. But if these forecasts turn out to be too rosy, the firm has unnecessarily allocated these resources.

Forecasting is an important element in planning for both the short term and the long term. But we have to keep in mind that forecasts are made by people. Forecasters tend to be optimistic, which usually results in rosier than deserved forecasts of future sales. In addition, people tend to focus on what worked in the past, with past successes carrying more weight in developing forecasts than an analysis of the future.

One way to avoid this is to make managers responsible for their forecasts, rewarding accurate forecasts and penalizing the ones that are way off the mark.

Seasonal Considerations

The operating activities of a firm typically vary throughout the year, depending on seasonal demand and supply factors. Seasonality influences a firm's short-term investment and financing activities.

Let's look at the quarterly revenues of a few U.S. corporations to get an idea of different seasonal patterns of activity:

- Coca-Cola, a beverage producer
- Service Merchandise, a catalog–retail store chain
- Walt Disney, a film and amusement firm
- Warner-Lambert, a drug manufacturer
- Delta Airlines, a national airline

The quarterly revenues for each of these firms is plotted in Figure 17-3 from the first quarter 1989 through the fourth quarter 1992. The seasonal patterns are quite different:

- Coca-Cola tends to have increased sales in the summer months, driven, most likely, by their largest segment, soft drinks.
- Service Merchandise has the highest degree of seasonality, with sales dependent on the December holiday season and therefore highest in the fourth quarter.
- Walt Disney Company has sales that tend to increase in the fourth quarter of each year, influenced by the company's two major product lines, movie production and amusement parks.
- Warner-Lambert's revenues do not appear to have any seasonality. The demand for the drugs apparently is not influenced by the time of the year.
- Delta's sales increase somewhat during the summer months because of summer vacation travel, but this seasonality is not as pronounced as that of, say, Service Merchandise or Disney.

FIGURE 17-3

Sales of Selected U.S. Companies, Quarterly, 1989–1992

SOURCE: Standard & Poor's *Compustat PC Plus* (CD-ROM) and Moody's *Industrial Manual.*

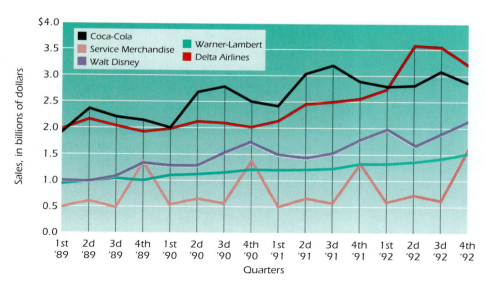

To understand our cash flows we must first understand the patterns associated with our operating activities.

Looking closer at what seasonality has to do with cash flows, let's focus on the likely cash flow pattern for Service Merchandise. Sales are greatest in the fourth quarter of the year because of holiday shopping. As a retail operation that does not extend credit, this company also experiences its highest cash inflows in the fourth quarter.

But what about cash *out*flows? To have the merchandise to sell in the fourth quarter, Service Merchandise must increase its inventory prior to or during the fourth quarter. Depending on its credit arrangements with its suppliers, cash will be flowing out of the firm prior to or during the fourth quarter. This means that for some period of time Service Merchandise will have more cash going out than coming in, and then more cash coming in than going out.

Budgeting

In budgeting, we bring together analyses of cash flows, projected income statements, and projected balance sheets. The cash flow analyses are most important, though we also need to generate the income statements and balance sheets.

Most firms extend or receive credit; so cash flows and net income do not coincide. Typically, we must determine cash flows from accounting information on revenues and expenses.

Projecting sales, either through regression or market analysis, provides information we can use in our planning. Combining sales projections with our estimates of collections of accounts receivable results in an estimate of cash receipts.

Suppose you have the following sales projections for the next six months:

Month	Sales
July	$300,000
August	600,000
September	900,000
October	600,000
November	300,000
December	300,000

How do we translate these sales estimates into cash receipts? First, we need an estimate of how long it takes to collect on our accounts. Where do our estimates of collections come from?

We could estimate the typical time it takes to collect on our accounts, using the financial ratio,

$$\text{Number of days of credit} = \frac{\text{accounts receivable}}{\text{credit sales per day}}$$

This tells us how long it takes, on average, to collect on accounts receivable. Suppose the number of days of credit is thirty. This means that a sale made in January is collected in February, a sale made in February is collected in

March, and so on. If we have sales of $300,000 in the previous June, our estimate of cash receipts for July through December is:

Month	Sales	Collections on receivables	
July	$300,000	$300,000	← From June sales
August	600,000	300,000	
September	900,000	600,000	
October	600,000	900,000	
November	300,000	600,000	
December	300,000	300,000	

An alternative, and more precise, method is to look at the aging of the receivables—how long each account has been outstanding—and use this information to better track collections. However, using aging for the analysis of cash receipts requires a detailed estimate of the age of all accounts and their typical collection period.

Whether we use an overall average or an aging approach, we need to consider several factors in our cash collections estimate:

- An estimate of bad debts—accounts that will not be collected at all.
- An analysis of the trend in the number of days it takes customers to pay on account.
- An estimate of the seasonal nature of collections of accounts since customers' ability to pay is often influenced by the operating cycle of their own firms.

As with revenues and cash receipts, there is a relation between expenses and cash disbursements. Firms typically do not pay cash for all the goods and services they acquire; purchases are generally bought on account (creating accounts payable) and wages and salaries are paid periodically (weekly, semimonthly, or monthly). Therefore, there's a lagged relationship between expenses and cash payments.

We can get an idea of the time it takes us to pay for our purchases on account by looking at the number of days of purchases:

$$\text{Number of days of purchases} = \frac{\text{accounts payable}}{\text{average day's purchases}}$$

And we can determine the time it takes to pay for wages and salaries by looking at the firm's personnel policies. Putting these two pieces together, we can estimate how long it takes to pay for the goods and services we acquire.

The Cash Budget

A *cash budget* is a detailed statement of the cash inflows and outflows expected in future periods. This budget helps us identify our financing and investment needs. We can also use a cash budget to compare our actual cash flows with planned cash flows so that we can evaluate both our performance and our forecasting ability.

Cash flows *into* the firm as a result of:

1. Operations such as sales (receipts) and collections on accounts receivable.
2. Financing decisions, such as borrowings, sales of shares of common stock, and sales of preferred stock.
3. Investment decisions, such as sales of assets and income from marketable securities.

Cash flows *out* of the firm as a result of:

1. Operations, such as payments on accounts payable, purchases of goods, and payment of taxes.
2. Financing obligations, such as the payment of dividends and interest and the repurchase of shares of stock or the redemption of bonds.
3. Investments, such as the purchase of plant and equipment.

As we noted before, the cash budget is driven by the sales forecast. Consider the following sales forecasts for the Imagined Company for January through June of 1999:

Month	Forecasted sales
January	$1,000
February	2,000
March	3,000
April	2,000
May	1,000
June	1,000

Using the forecasted sales, along with a host of assumptions about credit sales, collections on accounts receivable, payments for purchases, and financing, we can construct a cash budget, which tells us about the cash inflows and outflows.

Let's look at Imagined's cash budget for January 1999. Sales are expected to be $1,000. Now let's translate sales into cash flows, focusing first on the cash flows from operations.

Let's assume that an analysis of accounts receivable over the past year reveals that:

- 10 percent of a month's sales are paid in the month of the sale.
- 60 percent of a month's sales are paid in the month following the sale.
- 30 percent of a month's sales are paid in the second month following the sale.

This means that only 10 percent of the $1,000 in sales, or $100, is collected in January. But this also means that in January Imagined collects 60 percent of 1998's December sales and 30 percent of 1998's November sales. If December 1998 sales were $1,000 and November 1998 sales were $2,000, then in January 1999, total cash inflow from collections is $1,300, as follows:

Collections on January 1999 sales	$100	← 10% of $1,000
Collections on December 1998 sales	600	← 60% of $1,000
Collections on November 1998 sales	600	← 30% of $2,000
Total cash inflow from collections	**$1,300**	

Now let's look at the cash flows related to Imagined's payments for its goods. We first have to make an assumption about how much Imagined buys and when it pays for its goods and services. First, assume that Imagined has a cost of goods (other than labor) of 50 percent. This means that for every $1 it sells, it has a cost of 50 cents. Next, assume that Imagined purchases goods two months in advance of when the firm sells it. (This means the number of days of inventory is about 60.) Finally, let's assume that Imagined pays 20 percent of its accounts payable in the month it purchases the goods and 80 percent in the month after it purchases the goods.

Putting all this together, we forecast that in January, Imagined will purchase 50 percent of March's forecasted sales, or 50 percent of $3,000 = $1,500. Imagined will pay 20 percent of these purchases in January, or 20 percent of $1,500 = $300. In addition, Imagined will be paying 80 percent of the purchases made in December 1998. And December's purchases are 50 percent of *February's* projected sales. So in January, Imagined will pay 50 percent of 80 percent of $2,000, which is 50 percent of $1,600, or $800.

We assume that Imagined has additional cash outflows for wages (5 percent of current month's sales) and selling and administrative expenses (10 percent of current month's sales). Imagined's cash outflows related to operations in January consist of:

Payments for current month's purchases	$300	← 20% of $1,500
Payments for previous month's purchases	800	← 50% of $1,600
Wages	50	← 5% of $1,000
Selling and administrative expenses	100	← 10% of $1,000
Operating cash outflows	**$1,250**	

The cash budget for Imagined Company is shown in Table 17-1. The cash budget is presented in three parts: (1) cash flows from operations, (2) nonoperating cash flows, and (3) analysis of cash and marketable securities. In the first two parts, inflows are presented first, followed by outflows. The assumptions that we have to make to budget these cash flows are shown at the bottom of the table.

Looking at the cash flows from Imagined Company's operations in Table 17-1, we see that in January, there is a net cash *in*flow from operations of $50. Extending what we did for January's cash flows to the next five months as well, we get a projection of cash inflows and outflows from operations. As you can see, there are net outflows from operations in February and net inflows in other months.

But cash flows from operations do not tell us the complete picture. We also need to know about Imagined's nonoperating cash flows. Does it intend to buy or retire any plant and equipment? Does it intend to retire any debt?

TABLE 17-1

Imagined Company Monthly Cash Budget, January–June 1999

	January	February	March	April	May	June
OPERATING CASH FLOWS						
Cash inflows						
Collections on accounts receivable						
Collections on current month's sales	$ 100	$ 200	$ 300	$ 200	$ 100	$ 100
Collections from preceding month's sales	600	600	1,200	1,800	1,200	600
Collections from second preceding month's sales	600	300	300	600	900	600
Operating cash inflows	$1,300	$1,100	$1,800	$2,600	$2,200	$1,300
Cash outflows						
Payments of purchases on account						
Payments for current month's purchases	$ 300	$ 200	$ 100	$ 100	$ 100	$ 100
Payments for previous month's purchases	800	1,200	800	400	400	400
Wages	50	100	150	100	50	50
Selling and administrative expenses	100	200	300	200	100	100
Operating cash outflows	$1,250	$1,700	$1,350	$ 800	$ 650	$ 650
Operating net cash flow	$ 50	−$ 600	$ 450	$1,800	$1,550	$ 650
NONOPERATING CASH FLOWS						
Cash inflows						
Retirement of plant and equipment	–0–	–0–	–0–	$500	–0–	–0–
Issuance of long-term debt	–0–	$3,000	–0–	–0–	–0–	–0–
Issuance of common stock	–0–	–0–	–0–	–0–	–0–	–0–
Nonoperating cash inflows	–0–	$3,000	–0–	$500	–0–	–0–
Cash outflows						
Acquisition of plant and equipment	$1,000	$3,000	–0–	–0–	$3,500	–0–
Payment of cash dividends	–0–	–0–	$100	–0–	–0–	$ 100
Retirement of long-term debt	–0–	–0–	–0–	–0–	–0–	1,000
Retirement of common stock	–0–	–0–	–0–	–0–	–0–	–0–
Interest on long-term debt	10	10	10	10	10	10
Taxes	69	165	271	$168	53	53
Nonoperating cash outflows	$1,079	$3,175	$381	$178	$3,563	$1,163
Nonoperating cash flows	−$1,079	−$ 175	−$381	$322	−$3,563	−$1,163
ANALYSIS OF CASH AND MARKETABLE SECURITIES						
Balance, beginning of month	$1,500	$1,000	$1,000	$1,069	$2,000	$1,000
Net cash flows for the month	−1,029	−775	69	2,122	−2,013	−513
Balance without any change in bank loans	$ 471	$ 225	$1,069	$3,192	−$ 13	$ 487
Bank loans to maintain minimum balance	529	775	–0–	–0–	1,013	513
Cash available to pay off bank loans	–0–	–0–	–0–	1,192	–0–	–0–
Balance, end of month	$1,000	$1,000	$1,069	$2,000	$1,000	$1,000

ASSUMPTIONS: (1) Cash sales are 10 percent of current month's sales. (2) Collections on accounts receivable are 60 percent of preceding month's sales and 30 percent of the second preceding month's sales. (3) Purchases are 50 percent of sales two months ahead. (4) Payments on accounts are 20 percent of current month's purchases plus 80 percent of previous month's purchases. (5) Wages are 5 percent of current month's sales. (6) Selling and administrative expenses are 5 percent of current month's sales. (7) July and August sales are forecast to be $1,000 each month.

Does it need to pay interest on any debt? And so on. These projections are inserted in the lower portion of Table 17-1.

But there is one catch here: Cash inflows must equal cash outflows (unless Imagined has found a way to create cash!). So we have to decide where Imagined is going to get its cash if its *in*flows are less than its *out*flows. And we have to decide where it is going to invest its cash if its *out*flows are less than its *in*flows.

Let's assume that Imagined will borrow from the bank when it needs short-term financing and will pay off its bank loans or invest in marketable securities (if it has no outstanding bank loans) when it has more cash than needed. In our example, let's group cash and marketable securities into one item, referred to as "cash."

The bank loan–marketable securities decision is a residual decision: We decide when we pay our accounts, for example, and we use the bank loan or marketable securities investment as a "plug" figure to help balance our cash inflows and outflows. But this "plug" is very important: It tells us what financing arrangement we need to have in place (such as a line of credit) or what decisions we need to make regarding short-term investments, such as U.S. Treasury bills.

Comparing inflows with outflows from operations, we see that if Imagined requires a minimum cash balance of $1,000, it needs to use bank financing in January, February, May, and June. We also see that if Imagined does not need to maintain a cash balance higher than $2,000, it can pay off some of its bank loans in April.

We've forecasted cash inflows and outflows for several months into the future. But these are forecasts and since lots of things can happen between now and then, the actual cash flows can easily differ from the forecasted ones. Furthermore, we've made a host of assumptions and decisions along the way, some that we have control over, such as dividend payments, and some that we have no control over, such as how long customers take to pay. Economic conditions, market conditions, and other factors will affect actual cash flows.

Two methods to help us look at the uncertainty of cash flows are sensitivity analysis and simulation analysis. ***Sensitivity analysis*** involves changing one of the variables in our analysis, such as the number of units sold, and looking at its effect on the cash flows. This gives us an idea of what cash flows may be under certain circumstances. We can pose different scenarios: What if customers take sixty days to pay instead of thirty? What if sales are actually $1,000 in February instead of $2,000?

But sensitivity analysis can become unmanageable if we start changing two or more things at a time. A more manageable approach to doing this is with computer simulation. ***Simulation analysis*** allows us to develop a probability distribution of possible outcomes, given a probability distribution for each variable that may change.[4]

Suppose we can develop a probability distribution—that is, a list of possible outcomes and their related likelihood of occurring—for sales. And sup-

A ***probability distribution*** is the set of possible outcomes and their likelihood of occurrence.

---

[4] Simulation analysis and sensitivity analysis are discussed in detail in Chapter 10 in the context of the capital budgeting decision.

pose we can develop a probability distribution for the costs of the raw materials that are needed in producing the product. Using simulation, a probability distribution of cash flows can be produced, providing information on the degree of uncertainty of the firm's future cash flows.

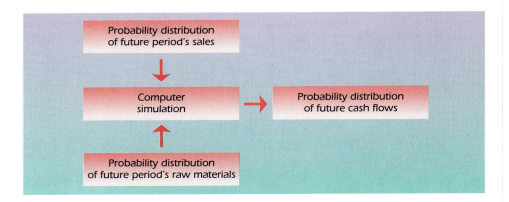

Once we produce the probability distribution of future cash flows, we have an idea of the possible cash flows and can plan accordingly. The cash budget produced using the possible cash flows is a *flexible budget.* With this information, we can then determine which are the most appropriate short-term financing and investments to consider.

Pro Forma Financial Statements

A *pro forma balance sheet* is a projected balance sheet for a future period—a month, a quarter, or a year—that summarizes assets, liabilities, and equity. A *pro forma income statement* is the projected income statement for a future period—a month, a quarter, or a year—that summarizes revenues and expenses. Taken together, the projections help us to identify our firm's investment and financing needs.

The analysis of accounts and the percent-of-sales methods are two ways of projecting financial statements.

Analysis-of-Accounts Method

The *analysis of accounts* starts with the cash budget. Before putting together the pro forma income statement and balance sheet, we need to see how the various asset, liability, and equity accounts change from month to month, based on the information provided in the cash budget. The analysis of accounts is shown in Table 17-2, in which each account is analyzed, starting with the beginning balance and making any necessary adjustments to arrive at the ending balance.

TABLE 17-2

Imagined Company Analysis of Monthly Changes in Accounts, January–June 1999

	January	February	March	April	May	June
Accounts receivable						
Month's beginning balance	$ 2,000	$ 1,700	$ 2,600	$ 3,800	$ 3,200	$ 2,000
Plus credit sales during the month	900	1,800	2,700	1,800	900	900
Less collections on accounts	1,200	900	1,500	2,400	2,100	1,200
Month's ending balance	$ 1,700	$ 2,600	$ 3,800	$ 3,200	$ 2,000	$ 1,700
Inventory						
Month's beginning balance	$ 2,500	$ 3,500	$ 3,500	$ 2,500	$ 2,000	$ 2,000
Plus purchases	1,500	1,000	500	500	500	500
Plus wages and other production expenses	50	100	150	100	50	50
Less goods sold	550	1,100	1,650	1,100	550	550
Month's ending balance	$ 3,500	$ 3,500	$ 2,500	$ 2,000	$ 2,000	$ 2,000
Accounts payable						
Month's beginning balance	$ 2,000	$ 2,400	$ 2,000	$ 1,600	$ 1,600	$ 1,600
Plus purchases on account	1,200	800	400	400	400	400
Less payments on account	800	1,200	800	400	400	400
Month's ending balance	$ 2,400	$ 2,000	$ 1,600	$ 1,600	$ 1,600	$ 1,600
Bank loans						
Month's beginning balance	$ 1,000	$ 1,529	$ 2,304	$ 2,304	$ 1,113	$ 2,125
Plus borrowings	529	775	–0–	–0–	1,013	513
Less repayment of loans	–0–	–0–	–0–	1,192	–0–	–0–
Month's ending balance	$ 1,529	$ 2,304	$ 2,304	$ 1,113	$ 2,125	$ 2,638
Plant and equipment						
Month's beginning balance	$10,000	$10,890	$13,751	$13,614	$12,982	$16,318
Plus acquisitions	1,000	3,000	–0–	–0–	3,500	–0–
Less retirements	–0–	–0–	–0–	500	–0–	–0–
Less depreciation (1% of gross plant and equipment)	110	139	138	131	165	163
Month's ending balance	$10,890	$13,751	$13,614	$12,982	$16,318	$16,154
Long-term debt						
Month's beginning balance	$ 5,000	$ 5,000	$ 8,000	$ 8,000	$ 8,000	$ 8,000
Plus issuances of long-term debt	–0–	3,000	–0–	–0–	–0–	–0–
Less retirements of long-term debt	–0–	–0–	–0–	–0–	–0–	1,000
Month's ending balance	$ 5,000	$ 8,000	$ 8,000	$ 8,000	$ 8,000	$ 7,000
Common equity						
Month's beginning balance	$ 8,000	$ 8,161	$ 8,547	$ 9,079	$ 9,470	$ 9,592
Plus earnings retained during the month	161	386	532	391	123	24
Plus issuances of common stock	–0–	–0–	–0–	–0–	–0–	–0–
Less retirements of common stock	–0–	–0–	–0–	–0–	–0–	–0–
Month's ending balance	$ 8,161	$ 8,547	$ 9,079	$ 9,470	$ 9,592	$ 9,616

We can see how the cash budget interacts with the pro forma income statement and balance sheet by looking at the change in accounts receivable. Consider what happens in January:

The analysis of accounts receivable . . .		. . . affects financial planning through the . . .
Balance at the beginning of the month	$2,000 →	pro forma balance sheet (accounts receivable)
Plus credit sales during January	+900 →	pro forma income statement (sales) and pro forma balance sheet (accounts receivable)
Less collections on accounts during January	−1,200 →	cash budget (cash flow from operations)
Balance at the end of the month	$1,700 →	pro forma balance sheet (accounts receivable)

As you can see, the balances in these accounts are all interrelated with the cash budget.

In doing our cash budget, we have begun our projections:

- Changes in the cash account are determined by the difference between our cash inflows and outflows.
- Changes in accounts receivable are determined by our sales and collections projections.
- Changes in inventory are determined by our purchase and sales projections.
- Changes in plant and equipment are determined by our capital budgeting.
- Changes in long-term debt are determined by our financing projections.
- Changes in common equity are determined by both the financing projections and the projected retained earnings.
- Changes in retained earnings are determined by the projected income.

If we put together all these pieces, we have a pro forma balance sheet for Imagined Company, as shown in Table 17-3. Looking at the cash budget in Table 17-1, the analysis of accounts in Table 17-2, and the balance sheet in Table 17-3, we can follow through to see the interactions among the various assets, liabilities, equity accounts, and cash flows, as we did for accounts receivable.

The pro forma income statement for Imagined Company is shown in the lower part of Table 17-3. Though our interest is ultimately in cash flows, the income statement provides useful summary information on the expected performance of the firm in months to come. As you can see in Table 17-3, net income tends to increase in March, accompanying the month's increased revenues.

We are interested in the pro forma balance sheet and income statement not just as a product of our cash flow analysis. Suppose our bank financing

TABLE 17-3

Imagined Company Pro Forma Balance Sheet and Income Statement, Monthly, January–June 1999

PRO FORMA BALANCE SHEET

	January	February	March	April	May	June
ASSETS						
Cash and marketable securities	$ 1,000	$ 1,000	$ 1,069	$ 2,000	$ 1,000	$ 1,000
Accounts receivable	1,700	2,600	3,800	3,200	2,000	1,700
Inventories	3,500	3,500	2,500	2,000	2,000	2,000
Plant and equipment	10,890	13,751	13,614	12,982	16,318	16,154
Total assets	$17,090	$20,851	$20,983	$20,182	$21,318	$20,854
LIABILITIES AND EQUITY						
Accounts payable	$ 2,400	$ 2,000	$ 1,600	$ 1,600	$ 1,600	$ 1,600
Bank loans	$ 1,529	$ 2,304	$ 2,304	$ 1,113	$ 2,125	$ 2,638
Long-term debt	5,000	8,000	8,000	8,000	8,000	7,000
Common equity	8,161	8,547	9,079	9,470	9,592	9,616
Total liabilities and equity	$17,090	$20,851	$20,983	$20,182	$21,318	$20,854

PRO FORMA INCOME STATEMENT

	January	February	March	April	May	June
Sales	$1,000	$2,000	$3,000	$2,000	$1,000	$1,000
Less cost of goods sold	550	1,100	1,650	1,100	550	550
Less depreciation	110	139	138	131	165	163
Gross profit	$ 340	$ 761	$1,212	$ 769	$ 285	$ 287
Less selling and administrative expenses	100	200	300	200	100	100
Earnings before interest and taxes	$ 240	$ 561	$ 912	$ 569	$ 185	$ 187
Less interest	10	10	10	10	10	10
Earnings before taxes	$ 230	$ 551	$ 902	$ 559	$ 175	$ 177
Less taxes	69	165	271	168	53	53
Net income	$ 161	$ 386	$ 632	$ 391	$ 123	$ 124
Less cash dividends	–0–	–0–	100	–0–	–0–	100
Retained earnings	$ 161	$ 386	$ 532	$ 391	$ 123	$ 24

is secured financing, limited to 80 percent of accounts receivable. If this is the case, we may be limited in how much we can borrow from the bank in any particular month. We are also interested in the balance sheet, since some of our short-term or long-term debt may have covenants that require the firm to maintain specific relations among its accounts, for example, a current ratio of 2:1. In addition, we may be concerned about the firm's perceived riskiness. If we must borrow heavily at certain times within a year, does this affect the riskiness of our debt securities, increasing the cost of financing?

These considerations point out the importance of reviewing the projected balance sheet. In fact, these considerations may point out the need for the financial manager to explicitly build constraints into the budget to ensure that, say, a current ratio of 2 is maintained each month. These constraints add complexity to an already complex system of relationships, the detail of which is beyond the scope of this text.

Percent-of-Sales Method

The **percent-of-sales method** uses historical relationships between sales and each of the other income statement accounts and between sales and each of the balance sheet accounts. There are two steps to this method.

First, the previous periods' income statement and balance sheet accounts are restated in terms of a percentage of sales for the year. Let's look at the items in the Imagined Corporation balance sheet and income statement for 1998, which are shown in the left-most column of Table 17-4. Since we are projecting monthly sales, each item in both statements is restated as a percentage of December 1998 sales, as shown in the second column of the table.

Second, based on the forecasted sales for the future years and the percentages each account represents, projections for January through June are calculated. For example, cost of goods sold is 55 percent of sales. Since January sales are predicted to be $1,000, cost of goods sold is predicted to be 55 percent of $1,000, or $550. And since sales for February are predicted to be $2,000, cost of goods sold for February is predicted to be $1,100. Likewise for balance sheet accounts. Cash and marketable securities are 75 percent of monthly sales, so we expect $750 in this account in January. As shown in Table 17-4, each item in the balance sheet and income statement accounts is forecast for January through June.

This method of creating pro forma statements is simple. But it may make inappropriate assumptions, such as that (1) all costs vary with sales, even though most firms have some fixed costs, or that (2) assets and liabilities change along with sales, even though firms tend to make capital investments that generate cash flows far into the future, not necessarily in the year they are put in place.

And there is another drawback: The percent-of-sales method focuses on accounts in the financial statements, not cash flows. As a result, it cannot help us figure out when a firm needs cash and when it has excess cash to invest.

Nevertheless, the percent-of-sales method is used frequently because of its simplicity. Furthermore, since we are dealing with forecasts, which are themselves estimates (and not actual fact), the simpler approach is sometimes attractive.

Long-Term Financial Planning

Long-term planning is similar to what we have just completed for the operational budget for January through June 1999, but is carried out for a longer span of time into the future and in less detail.

TABLE 17-4

Imagined Corporation Pro Forma Financial Statements Based on Percent-of-Sales Method, Monthly, January–June 1999

PRO FORMA BALANCE SHEET

	As of end of 1998	Percentage of December 1998 sales	Forecasted accounts for 1999					
			January	February	March	April	May	June
ASSETS								
Cash and marketable securities	$ 1,500	75%	$ 750	$ 1,500	$ 2,250	$ 1,500	$ 750	$ 750
Accounts receivable	2,000	100	1,000	2,000	3,000	2,000	1,000	1,000
Inventories	2,500	125	1,250	2,500	3,750	2,500	1,250	1,250
Plant and equipment	10,000	500	5,000	10,000	15,000	10,000	5,000	5,000
Total assets	$16,000	800%	$8,000	$16,000	$24,000	$16,000	$8,000	$8,000
LIABILITIES AND EQUITY								
Accounts payable	$ 2,000	100%	$1,000	$ 2,000	$ 3,000	$ 2,000	$1,000	$1,000
Bank loans	1,000	50	500	1,000	1,500	1,000	500	500
Long-term debt	5,000	250	2,500	5,000	7,500	5,000	2,500	2,500
Common stock and paid-in capital	2,000	100	1,000	2,000	3,000	2,000	1,000	1,000
Retained earnings	7,000	350	3,500	7,000	10,500	7,000	3,500	3,500
Total liabilities and equity	$16,000	800%	$8,000	$16,000	$24,000	$16,000	$8,000	$8,000

PRO FORMA INCOME STATEMENT

	As of end of 1998	Percentage of December 1998 sales	Forecasted accounts for 1999					
			January	February	March	April	May	June
Sales	$ 2,000	100.0%	$1,000	$2,000	$3,000	$2,000	$1,000	$1,000
Less cost of goods sold	1,100	55.0	550	1,100	1,650	1,100	550	550
Less depreciation	200	10.0	100	200	300	200	100	$ 100
Gross profit	$ 700	35.0%	$ 350	$ 700	$1,050	$ 700	$ 350	$ 350
Less selling and administrative expenses	10	0.5	5	10	15	10	5	5
Earnings before interest and taxes	$ 690	34.5%	$ 345	$ 690	$1,035	$ 690	$ 345	$ 345
Less interest	20	1.0	10	20	30	20	10	10
Earnings before taxes	$ 670	33.5%	$ 335	$ 670	$1,005	$ 670	$ 335	$ 335
Less taxes	12	0.5	6	12	18	12	6	6
Net income	$ 658	33.0%	$ 329	$ 658	$ 987	$ 658	$ 329	$ 329

Consider the sales forecasts for the next five years:

Year	Forecasted sales
1999	$20,000
2000	22,000
2001	25,000
2002	26,000
2003	27,000

Projections of the cash budget for 1999 through 2003 are shown in Table 17-5(a), and those for the pro forma financial statements are shown in Table 17-5(b). You'll notice that we are not as concerned about the details regarding, say, the source of cash flows from operations, but rather the bottom line. However, we must compile these statements as we did those for the operational budget: We integrate the investment decisions with the financing decisions on the basis of projections and assumptions that are built into our cash budget.

By looking at the long-term plan, we get an idea of how the firm intends to meet its objective of maximizing shareholder wealth. For example, in the operational budget we are concerned about meeting monthly cash demands and we assumed Imagined Company borrows from banks to meet any cash shortages. But with the long-term plan, we can address the issue of what capital structure (the mix of debt and equity) the firm wants in the long run. In the case of Imagined Company, we assume:

- Any bank loans are reduced to $1,000 at the end of each year;
- When long-term capital is needed, we raise half using debt and half by issuing new equity.
- When the firm is able to reduce its reliance on external funds, it will reduce its long-term debt.

Long-term plans should be evaluated periodically as are operational budgets. And since the two are closely tied (what we do in the short term influences what happens in the long term), it is convenient to update both types of budgets simultaneously.

FINANCIAL MODELING

A *financial model* is the set of relationships that are behind the calculations we perform in putting together the cash budget and the pro forma statements. In financial modeling, we generally focus on the essential features of the budget and statements and try not to get bogged down in the details. In our Imagined Company example, we looked at the relation between cash and marketable securities, but we avoided getting into the detail of where the cash is held or which securities we buy or sell.

In the case of Imagined Company, the following relations between cash inflows and sales are "modeled":

$$\text{Cash inflows} = 10\%\left(\begin{array}{c}\text{this}\\\text{month's sales}\end{array}\right) + 60\%\left(\begin{array}{c}\text{preceding}\\\text{month's sales}\end{array}\right) + 30\%\left(\begin{array}{c}\text{second}\\\text{preceding}\\\text{month's sales}\end{array}\right)$$

TABLE 17-5(a)

Imagined Company Long-Term Planning: Cash Budget 1999–2003

	1999	2000	2001	2002	2003
OPERATING CASH FLOWS					
Cash inflows					
Cash sales	$ 2,000	$ 2,200	$ 2,500	$ 2,600	$ 2,700
Collections on account	19,000	19,820	21,250	22,040	24,100
Operating cash inflows	$21,000	$22,020	$23,750	$24,640	$26,800
Cash outflows					
Payments of purchases on account	$10,067	$10,917	$12,375	$12,958	$13,458
Wages	1,000	1,100	1,250	1,300	1,350
Selling and administrative expenses	2,000	2,200	2,500	2,600	2,700
Operating cash outflows	$13,067	$14,217	$16,125	$16,858	$17,508
Operating net cash flows	$ 7,933	$ 7,803	$ 7,625	$ 7,782	$ 9,292
NONOPERATING CASH FLOWS					
Cash inflows					
Retirement of plant and equipment	$ 500	–0–	–0–	–0–	$1,000
Nonoperating cash inflows	$ 500	–0–	–0–	–0–	$1,000
Cash outflows					
Maturing long-term debt	$ 1,000	$ 1,000	$ 1,000	$1,000	$1,000
Acquisitions of plant and equipment	10,000	7,500	7,500	5,000	1,000
Payment of cash dividends	400	400	400	400	400
Interest on long-term debt	300	350	400	350	300
Taxes	1,308	1,317	1,454	1,520	1,773
Nonoperating cash outflows	$13,008	$10,567	$10,754	$8,270	$4,473
Nonoperating net cash flows	−$12,508	−$10,567	−$10,754	−$8,270	−$3,473
ANALYSIS OF CASH					
Cash balance beginning of year	$1,500	$1,500	$1,500	$1,500	$1,500
Net cash flows during year	−4,575	−2,764	−3,129	−488	5,819
Cash balance without any financing	−$3,075	−$1,264	−$1,629	$1,012	7,319
Long-term debt issuance	2,287	1,382	1,564	244	–0–
Common stock issuance	2,287	1,382	1,564	244	–0–
Available to pay off long-term debt	–0–	–0–	–0–	–0–	3,319
Cash balance, end of year	$1,500	$1,500	$1,500	$1,500	$4,000

TABLE 17-5(b)

Imagined Company Long-Term Planning: Pro Forma Financial Statements 1999–2003

PRO FORMA BALANCE SHEET

	1999	2000	2001	2002	2003
ASSETS					
Cash and marketable securities	$ 1,500	$ 1,500	$ 1,500	$ 1,500	$ 4,000
Accounts receivable	1,000	980	2,230	3,590	3,790
Inventories	2,500	2,500	2,500	2,500	2,500
Plant and equipment	17,160	21,701	25,697	27,013	23,772
Total assets	$22,160	$26,681	$31,927	$34,603	$34,062
LIABILITIES AND EQUITY					
Accounts payable	$ 1,933	$ 2,017	$ 2,142	$ 2,183	$ 2,225
Bank loans	1,000	1,000	1,000	1,000	1,000
Long-term debt	6,287	6,669	7,234	6,478	2,159
Stockholders' equity	12,939	16,995	21,551	24,942	28,678
Total liabilities and equity	$22,160	$26,681	$31,927	$34,603	$34,062

PRO FORMA INCOME STATEMENT

	1999	2000	2001	2002	2003
Sales	$20,000	$22,000	$25,000	$26,000	$27,000
Less cost of goods sold	11,000	12,100	13,750	14,300	14,850
Less depreciation	2,340	2,959	3,504	3,684	3,242
Gross profit	$ 6,660	$ 6,941	$ 7,746	$ 8,016	$ 8,908
Less selling and administrative expenses	2,000	2,200	2,500	2,600	2,700
Earnings before interest and taxes	$ 4,660	$ 4,741	$ 5,246	$ 5,416	$ 6,208
Less interest	300	350	400	350	300
Earnings before taxes	$ 4,360	$ 4,391	$ 4,846	$ 5,066	$ 5,908
Less taxes	1,308	1,317	1,454	1,520	1,773
Net income	$ 3,052	$ 3,074	$ 3,392	$ 3,546	$ 4,136
Less cash dividends	400	400	400	400	400
Retained earnings	$ 2,652	$ 2,674	$ 2,992	$ 3,146	$ 3,736

Cash outflows are similar, but instead of collecting on sales and receivables, we are meeting expenses and paying on our accounts payable:

$$\underset{\text{outflows}}{\text{Cash}} = \underbrace{20\%\left(\begin{array}{c}\text{this}\\\text{month's}\\\text{purchases}\end{array}\right) + 80\%\left(\begin{array}{c}\text{last}\\\text{month's}\\\text{purchases}\end{array}\right)}_{\substack{\uparrow\\\text{Payments on}\\\text{purchases}}} + \underbrace{5\%\left(\begin{array}{c}\text{this}\\\text{month's}\\\text{sales}\end{array}\right)}_{\substack{\uparrow\\\text{Wages}}} + \underbrace{10\%\left(\begin{array}{c}\text{this}\\\text{month's}\\\text{sales}\end{array}\right)}_{\substack{\uparrow\\\text{Other expenses}}}$$

Since purchases are determined by projected sales, we can rewrite this as:

$$\begin{array}{l}\text{Cash} \\ \text{outflows}\end{array} = 20\%\begin{pmatrix}\text{sales} \\ \text{forecasted} \\ \text{two months} \\ \text{out}\end{pmatrix} + 80\%\begin{pmatrix}\text{next} \\ \text{month's} \\ \text{sales}\end{pmatrix} + 15\%\begin{pmatrix}\text{this} \\ \text{month's} \\ \text{sales}\end{pmatrix}$$

The cash inflows and outflows from operations are therefore dependent on the forecast of sales in future periods. Changing forecasted sales changes the cash inflows and outflows as well.

We could continue modeling the relations expressed in the cash budget and pro forma financial statements until we have represented all the relationships. Once we have done this, we have our financial model. By playing "what if" with the model—changing one item and observing what happens to the rest—managers can see the consequences of their decisions.

Software and Modeling

The task of modeling financial relationships is made easier by computer programs. Many software packages are available, including:

Excel (Microsoft Corporation)
Lotus 1-2-3 (Lotus Development Corporation)
VisiCalc (Lotus Development Corporation)
Multiplan (Microsoft Corporation)

These programs reduce the modeling effort because they enable the user to program a financial model using understandable phrases instead of programming code.

Building the financial model forces the manager to think through the relationships and consequences of investment and financing decisions. Much of the computation in financial modeling can be accomplished using computers and spreadsheet programs.

BUDGETING AND FINANCIAL PLANNING PRACTICES

On the basis of numerous surveys of budgeting practices in U.S. companies, we can make some general statements regarding budgeting and financial planning practices:[5]

- Most firms start with sales forecasts.
- Most use historical data analysis to forecast sales and expenses, though some use opinions of management and economic models.
- Most firms have budget manuals, detailing budget procedures and forms to be completed.

[5] See Srinivasan Umapathy, *Current Budgeting Practices in U.S. Industry,* Quorum, New York, 1987, for a detailed survey of budgeting and planning practices.

The surveys indicate these recent changes in firms' financial planning:

- An increasing number of firms have established formal budget programs.
- The role of boards of directors in approving budgets is decreasing.
- Strategy is becoming more centralized within companies.
- There is more frequent updating of long-run plans.
- The use of flexible budgets that separate controllable and uncontrollable revenues and expenses is increasing.

Over time, the level of sophistication of capital budgeting in the United States has increased. This is due to two factors. First, there is an increased awareness of the need to plan a firm's finances to meet its objective of maximizing owners' wealth. Second, technological advances in computer software and hardware make financial planning less time consuming and less costly.

SUMMARY

- The goal of financial management is to maximize shareholder wealth. Like any goal, it requires a strategy.
- As part of its strategy, the firm needs to plan the sources and uses of funds. The investment strategy is the plan that identifies the investment opportunities needed to meet the firm's goals. The financing strategy is the plan that specifies the sources of the funds needed to make those investments.
- Financial planning brings together decisions, actions, and goals with forecasts about the firm's sales.
- In financial planning we need to forecast sales in order to determine what our cash flows will be. We can forecast sales by using regression analysis, market surveys, or management forecasts.
- The cash budget is used to coordinate the investment decisions—which often require cash outlays—with the financing decisions—which specify where the cash is coming from.
- Pro forma financial statements can be generated by using the percent-of-sales method or by analyzing accounts based on the cash budget. Whereas the percent-of-sales method is simpler, the analysis of accounts gives the financial manager a better idea of the cash flows of the firm and their relation to the financial statements.
- Long-term financial planning is less detailed than the operational budgets, but not less important. Long-term planning helps keep financial managers focused on the objective of the firm and the strategy to achieve it.
- Financial modeling is a useful tool in looking at the array of relationships that exist in financial planning. It enables managers to examine the consequences of their decisions.
- Budgeting practices of U.S. companies have become more sophisticated, with more formalized procedures and more attention to long-term financial planning.

QUESTIONS

17-1 Suppose the financial manager of the Sooner Company had projected sales in 1991 of $4 million and actual sales for that year were $3 million. What should you consider in evaluating this difference? Why?

17-2 How does the process of selecting projects on the basis of net present values, as is done in capital budgeting, relate to a firm's strategy? Explain.

17-3 How does a firm's capital structure decision relate to its strategy? Explain.

17-4 Consider a discount retail store chain. List the factors that influence future sales of the chain. Identify the factors over which the firm's management exercises some control.

17-5 What are the advantages and disadvantages of using the percent-of-sales method in constructing pro forma financial statements?

17-6 Describe the methods a financial manager could use to assess the uncertainty of a firm's future cash flows.

17-7 Explain how long-term financial planning is related to operational budgeting.

17-8 What is financial modeling and how does it assist the financial manager in planning?

PROBLEMS

Forecasting

17-1 The quarterly sales for Olin Corporation for the period from the first quarter of 1989 through the second quarter of 1992 are as follows:

Quarter	Sales, in millions	Quarter	Sales, in millions
1Q89	$671	4Q90	$640
2Q89	658	1Q91	561
3Q89	580	2Q91	568
4Q89	600	3Q91	551
1Q90	636	4Q91	595
2Q90	660	1Q92	614
3Q90	656	2Q92	633

SOURCE: *Value Line Investment Survey.*

Olin Corporation's products include chemicals, metal products, and ammunition.

a. Plot these sales over time.

b. Do you detect any seasonality in Olin's sales? What do you envision to be Olin's pattern of cash flows from operations?

c. Looking at your graph, what sales do you predict for Olin for the third quarter of 1992?

17-2 The quarterly sales of Chiquita Brands International Inc. from the first quarter of 1989 through the second quarter of 1992 are as follows:

Quarter	Sales, in millions	Quarter	Sales, in millions
1Q89	$ 895	4Q90	$1,050
2Q89	1,023	1Q91	1,179
3Q89	903	2Q91	1,256
4Q89	1,004	3Q91	1,036
1Q90	1,025	4Q91	1,156
2Q90	1,137	1Q92	1,158
3Q90	1,060	2Q92	1,230

SOURCE: *Value Line Investment Survey.*

Chiquita Brands products include bananas, other fruits, and packaged meats.

a. Plot these sales over time.

b. Do you detect any seasonality in Chiquita's sales? What do you envision to be the pattern of Chiquita's cash flows?

c. Looking at your graph, what sales do you predict for Chiquita Brands for the third quarter of 1992?

Budgets

17-3 Consider the financial statements for the Pretend Corporation for 1995:

BALANCE SHEET		INCOME STATEMENT	
Current assets	$ 1,000	Sales	$15,000
Plant and equipment	8,500	Cost of goods sold	10,000
Other assets	500	Gross profit	$ 5,000
Total assets	$10,000	Other operating expenses	500
		Operating profit	$ 4,500
Current liabilities	$ 500	Interest expense	200
Long-term liabilities	5,000	Taxes	1,720
Stockholders' equity	4,500		
Total liabilities and equity	$10,000	Net profit	$ 2,580
		Dividends	1,032
		Retained earnings	$ 1,548

Forecasted sales for the years 1996 through 1998 are as follows:

Year	Forecasted sales
1996	$17,000
1997	18,000
1998	19,000

  a. Using the percent-of-sales method, create a pro forma balance sheet for each year from 1996 through 1998 for the Pretend Corporation.
  b. Using the percent-of-sales method, create a pro forma income statement for each year from 1996 through 1998 for the Pretend Corporation.

17-4 Consider the financial statements for the Monsanto Corporation for 1990, stated in millions:

BALANCE SHEET		INCOME STATEMENT	
Current assets	$3,513	Sales	$8,995
Net plant, property, and equipment	3,492	Cost of goods sold	4,901
Other assets	2,231	Gross profit	$4,094
Total assets	$9,236	Selling, general, and administrative expenses	2,485
		Depreciation	700
Current liabilities	$2,190	Operating profit	$ 909
Long-term liabilities	2,957	Interest expense	208
Stockholders' equity	$4,089	Other nonoperating items	108
Total liabilities and equity	$9,236	Taxes	263
		Net profit	$ 546
		Dividends	245
		Retained earnings	$ 301

SOURCE: Standard & Poor's *Compustat PC Plus* (CD-ROM).

SOURCE: Standard & Poor's *Compustat PC Plus* (CD-ROM).

Forecasted sales for the years 1991 through 1993 are as follows:

Year	Forecasted sales, in millions
1991	$ 9,000
1992	9,500
1993	10,000

  a. Using the percent-of-sales method, create a pro forma balance sheet for each year from 1991 through 1993 for the Monsanto Corporation.
  b. Using the percent-of-sales method, create a pro forma income statement for each year from 1991 through 1993 for the Monsanto Corporation.

17-5 Forecasted sales for Outlook Inc. for the months of March through June are as follows:

Month	Forecasted sales
March	$100,000
April	250,000
May	125,000
June	150,000

Actual sales in February were $150,000. Outlook generally collects 20 percent of its sales in cash and 80 percent the following month. Outlook's purchases amount to 70 percent of the current month's sales. It pays 50 percent of its purchases during the current month and 50 percent during the following month. Determine the projected net cash flows from operations for each of the four months.

Potpourri

17-6   The financial manager of the AppleCart Company has prepared the following pro forma balance sheet for the next month:

ASSETS		**LIABILITIES AND EQUITY**	
Cash	$ 150	Accounts payable	$ 200
Accounts receivable	50	Long-term debt	200
Inventory	200	Common equity	600
Plant and equipment	600	Total liabilities and equity	$1,000
Total assets	$1,000		

a.   After preparing this budget, the financial manager learned that Apple-Cart needs to maintain a current ratio of 3 (current assets are three times the current liabilities) at all times. If the only way this can be accomplished is to reduce the amount of cash on hand, propose an alternative pro forma balance sheet that satisfies this constraint.

b.   How does the reduction in cash on hand alter AppleCart's risk?

c.   Propose two other approaches AppleCart could use to satisfy the current ratio constraint. What risks are involved in each?

PC+   **17-7**   **Research:** Evaluate Sears's change in strategy from seeking to become a financial supermarket to concentrating on its retail stores.

a.   How has Sears fared since 1992 in terms of revenues and profits?

b.   Calculate the return on Sears's common stock in each month since 1992. How has Sears fared since 1992 in terms of returns to shareholders? How do the returns to shareholders compare with the returns in the stock market as a whole?

Recommended sources of information:

- *Industrial Manual*, Moody's
- Sears, Roebuck annual reports
- *Compustat PC Plus* (CD-ROM), Standard & Poor's
- *Value Line Investment Survey*

PC+   **17-8**   **Research:** Select a corporation and find its financial statements for the past five fiscal years.

a.   Given the pattern of sales over the past five fiscal years, predict sales for the next fiscal year.

b.   Locate sales forecasts for the company in a published financial service, such as *Value Line Investment Survey*, or in articles in the financial press, such as *The Wall Street Journal*. How do these compare with your forecasts?

c.   Using the percent-of-sales method, create pro forma balance sheets and income statements for the next three years.

Recommended sources of information:

- Annual reports
- *Industrial Manual*, Moody's
- *Compustat PC Plus* (CD-ROM), Standard and Poor's
- *Value Line Investment Survey*

17-9 **Research:** Locate an article in the financial press that provides forecasts of a company's future prospects made by the company's own management.

17-10 **Research:** Locate a statement of corporate strategy in a firm's published annual reports or in articles published in the financial press (such as *The Wall Street Journal*).

FURTHER READINGS

The relation between strategy and the objective of maximizing owners' wealth is discussed in several articles:
PATRICK BARWISE, PAUL R. MARSH, and ROBIN WENSLEY, "Must Finance and Strategy Clash?" *Harvard Business Review*, Sept.–Oct. 1989, pp. 85–90.
GEORGE S. DAY and LIAM FAHEY, "Putting Strategy into Shareholder Value Analysis," *Harvard Business Review*, March-April 1990, pp. 156–162.
ALFRED RAPPAPORT, "CFOs and Strategists: Forging a Common Framework," *Harvard Business Review*, May–June 1992, pp. 84–91.

The relation between corporate strategy and comparative and competitive advantages, with many examples of actual cases, is discussed by:
GEORGE STALK, PHILIP EVANS, and LAWRENCE E. SHULMAN, "Competing on Capabilities: The New Rules of Corporate Strategy," *Harvard Business Review*, March–April 1992, pp. 57–69.

Financial modeling concepts and procedures are discussed in detail in:
JAMES R. MORRIS, *The Dow Jones–Irwin Guide to Financial Modeling*, Dow Jones–Irwin, Homewood, Ill., 1987.

The budgeting practices of U.S. corporations are examined and summarized in:
SRINIVASAN UMAPATHY, *Current Budgeting Practices in U.S. Industry*, Quorum, New York, 1987.

APPENDIX

A

Keeping Up with Security Prices

INTRODUCTION 819

HOW TO READ STOCK QUOTATIONS 819

HOW TO READ BOND QUOTATIONS 822

HOW TO READ OPTIONS QUOTATIONS 824

HOW TO READ FUTURES CONTRACT QUOTATIONS 827

INTRODUCTION

A security's current price, often referred to as the "price quotation" or, simply, "quotation" or "quote," can be found in many financial media. To illustrate how to read and understand securities quotes, we look at some examples from the "Money and Investing" section of *The Wall Street Journal*.[1] These quotes are reported in much the same way in any local newspaper.

What we read in today's newspaper is a report of what happened yesterday. It's the same for the prices and trading activity. They are reports of the *previous* day's trading. This means that on Tuesday you would find Monday's security trading information, and so on.

We will look at quotes for stocks, corporate bonds, options, and futures. Once we do, you will be able to determine the prices for any type of security.

HOW TO READ STOCK QUOTATIONS

Let's try to make sense out of a segment of the February 2, 1993, stock quotes for the New York Stock Exchange composite transactions shown in Table A-1. The title, "New York Stock Exchange Composite Transactions," tells us we are reading a summary of the trading activity of the securities listed on the New York Stock Exchange (NYSE) and traded on the NYSE and on any regional exchanges. Since one full day's trading activity cannot be reported until the following day, the stock quotes in the Tuesday, February 2, 1993, issue of *The Wall Street Journal* reflect trading on Monday, February 1, 1993. The column headings and notation used in *The Wall Street Journal* are described in Table A-1.

Stock prices are quoted in points; "one point" is just another way of saying $1.00. You will notice that most stock prices are quoted in increments of one-eighth of a point (or $0.125), though low-priced stocks may be quoted in units of one-sixteenth (or $0.0625) or one-thirty-second (or $0.03125).

The column for volume of shares traded ("Vol 100s") indicates how many hundreds of shares were traded that day. To find out total shares traded, simply multiply the reported figure by 100.

Let's interpret some stock quotes. Look at the stock report segment for Acme-Cleveland Corporation, abbreviated "AcmeCleve," on the fourth line. That line describes everything we need to know about the trading that took place in shares of Acme-Cleveland's common stock on February 1, 1993.

To identify each common stock, there is a unique label, called a ticker symbol, which contains up to five characters. Acme-Cleveland's ticker symbol is AMT. If no ticker symbol is provided in the quotation, the quotation is for some security of the company other than its common stock, such as a preferred stock or a warrant. If a "pf" follows the company-name abbreviation, this tells us it's a type of preferred stock. In the case of the Alabama Power (AlaPwr) quote in Table A-1, the letters "pfA" to the right of the company-name abbreviation indicate Class A preferred stock.

Focusing on the Acme-Cleveland common stock, we see that its shares traded in a price range between $8\frac{5}{8}$ and $8\frac{3}{4}$ on February 1, 1993, closing at $8\frac{5}{8}$. In other words, the highest price of the day was $8.75, the lowest price of the day was $8.625, and the closing price was $8.625. The change in price

---

[1] *The Wall Street Journal* is published each business day by Dow Jones & Company.

TABLE A-1
Dissecting Stock Quotations

NEW YORK STOCK EXCHANGE COMPOSITE TRANSACTIONS
Quotations for Monday, February 1, 1993

	52 Weeks Hi	52 Weeks Lo	Stock	Sym	Div	Yld %	PE	Vol 100s	Hi	Lo	Close	Net Chg
s	34	$26\frac{1}{8}$	AbbotLab	ABT	.60	12.2	19	11126	$27\frac{7}{8}$	$27\frac{1}{8}$	$27\frac{1}{2}$	$\cdots$
n	$9\frac{7}{8}$	$3\frac{3}{4}$	Abex	ABE	$\cdots$	$\cdots$	$\cdots$	573	$4\frac{1}{8}$	4	$4\frac{1}{8}$	$+\frac{1}{8}$
s	15	6	AcceptIns	AIF	$\cdots$	$\cdots$	dd	1098	$11\frac{1}{8}$	$10\frac{7}{8}$	$10\frac{7}{8}$	$+\frac{1}{4}$
s	$11\frac{3}{4}$	$4\frac{3}{4}$	<u>AcmeCleve</u>	AMT	.40	4.6	18	113	$8\frac{3}{4}$	$8\frac{5}{8}$	$8\frac{5}{8}$	$-\frac{1}{8}$
	$29\frac{3}{4}$	$12\frac{1}{2}$	AirbornFrght	ABF	.30	1.4	cc	1017	21	$20\frac{5}{8}$	21	$+\frac{1}{2}$
s	**23**	$11\frac{3}{8}$	**Airgas**	**ARG**	$\cdots$		**28**	**380**	**20**	$10\frac{1}{8}$	$19\frac{7}{8}$	**+1**
	$12\frac{3}{8}$	$9\frac{1}{8}$	Airlease	FLY	1.60	14.2	9	206	$11\frac{3}{8}$	$11\frac{1}{8}$	$11\frac{1}{8}$	$-\frac{1}{8}$
n	26	$23\frac{5}{8}$	AlaPwr pfA		1.90	7.3	$\cdots$	20	$25\frac{7}{8}$	$25\frac{5}{8}$	$25\frac{7}{8}$	$\cdots$

Explanation of column headings:

52 Weeks Hi The highest traded price during the last 52 weeks.
52 Weeks Lo The lowest traded price during the last 52 weeks.
Stock Abbreviated company name. If this security is other than common stock, or if there is more than one type of common stock for the company, an additional description is provided.
Sym Ticker symbol.
Div Cash dividend per share of stock. This dividend is the expected annual dividend per share. If this is blank, the company does not currently pay a dividend. Expected annual dividend is calculated based on last dividend payment.
Yld % Dividend yield, calculated by dividing the expected annual dividend (Div) by the closing stock price.
PE Price-to-earnings ratio. The ratio of the closing price per share to the expected annual earnings per share. If this is blank, the earnings per share are either zero or negative.
Vol 100s Volume of shares traded, in hundreds of shares.
Hi Highest price for the day.
Lo Lowest price for the day.
Close Closing price for the day.
Net Chg Change in price during the day from the day's opening price.

Explanation of notation:

cc Price-earnings ratio is 100 or more.
dd A loss in the last fiscal quarter.
n New stock, issued within the past 52 weeks.
s Recent stock split.
Boldface Indicates price changed by more than 5 percent.
Underline Indicates higher than normal volume of trading.

SOURCE: *The Wall Street Journal*, Tuesday, Feb. 2, 1993, p. C3.

from the trading day's opening price was minus one-eighth, or down 12.5 cents.

How many shares of Acme-Cleveland stock traded on February 1? The volume is shown as 113 hundreds, so 113×100, or 11,300 shares, were traded.

In addition to the day's high, low, and closing prices, the quote tells us the annual dividends per share (in dollars and cents), the dividend yield (the dollar amount of the dividends per share divided by the closing price per share), and the price-earnings ratio (PE), where PE = price per share/earnings per share. Given this information we can determine Acme-Cleveland's earnings per share as:

$$\text{Earnings per share} = \frac{\text{price per share}}{\text{PE}} = \frac{\$8.625}{18} = \mathbf{\$0.48}$$

Let's take a closer look at the line containing the Acme-Cleveland quotation:

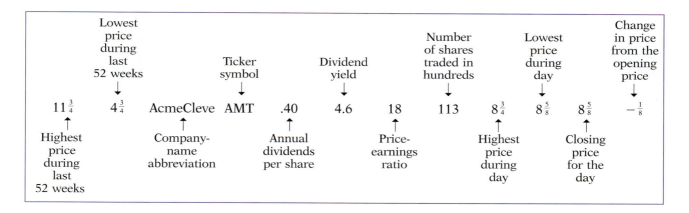

From this one line of information, we know that:

- Acme-Cleveland paid 40 cents in dividends over the past year.
- The dividend yield on Acme-Cleveland is 4.6 percent, which is the ratio of the dividends, 40 cents, to the closing price, $8.625.
- Annual earnings per share are 48 cents.

Let's look at Abbott Laboratories common stock, abbreviated as AbbotLab. On February 1, 1993, 1,112,600 shares of Abbott Laboratories stock changed hands. The price of Abbott stock ranged from $27.125 to $27.875, closing for the day at $27.50. There was no change from the trading day's opening price. Abbott Laboratories paid a dividend of 60 cents per share of common stock during the prior year. Given a PE of 19 and the closing price of $27.50, we also know that Abbott's previous year's earnings per share were $1.45.

In addition to the quotation information, stocks that had a price change of more than 5 percent in one day are indicated in boldface, as in the case of Airgas in Table A-1, and stocks with an unusually high trading volume are underlined, as in the case of Acceptance Insurance (AcceptIns). In addition, there are footnotes that tell us a bit more about the stock or its trading. Notations commonly found in quotation tables include the following:

cc   The price-earnings ratio is 100 or more.
dd   The company has incurred a loss in the last fiscal quarter.
n   This is a new stock, issued within the past fifty-two weeks.
pf   The quote is for a preferred stock, not a common stock.
rt   The quote is for rights, not common stock.
s   The stock has been split in the past fifty-two weeks.
vj   The company is in bankruptcy or receivership or is being reorganized under the Bankruptcy Act.
wt   The quote is for a warrant, not a common stock.
x   The stock is trading without the next dividend (ex-dividend).
z   Sales volume is reported as actual numbers of shares, not in hundreds.

If we know how to read it, a single line from the stock quote tables provides a great deal of information.

HOW TO READ BOND QUOTATIONS

Bond quotes are somewhat different from stock quotes because the characteristics of the underlying securities differ somewhat.[2] A segment of the bond quotes published in *The Wall Street Journal* for New York Exchange bonds is shown in Table A-2 along with an explanation of the column headings and footnotes. As in the stock quotation tables, the company name is abbreviated; it is followed immediately by a description of the bond, using its coupon rate and the year it matures.[3] However, there is no ticker symbol for bonds. For example, "AirbF $6\frac{3}{4}$01" indicates Airborne Freight's $6\frac{3}{4}$ percent coupon bonds that mature in 2001 and "AlldC zr96" indicates Allied Chemical's zero-coupon bonds ("zr") that mature in 1996.

A bond price is quoted as a percentage of its face value. For example, if a bond has a $1,000.00 face value and it closed at 98, its price at closing was 98 percent of $1,000.00 or $980.00. The net change in the price of a bond for a given day is a *percentage of its face value*. A change of, say, one-fourth tells us that the price of the bond changed by one-fourth of 1 percent of its face value. For a bond with a face value of $1,000.00, that means the price changed by $2.50:

$$\tfrac{1}{4} \text{ of } 1\% \text{ of } \$1,000.00 = \tfrac{1}{4}\% \text{ of } \$1,000.00 = 0.0025 \times \$1,000.00 = \textbf{\$2.50}$$

The volume of trading on the exchange is quoted differently for bonds. For stocks, the volume is reported in hundreds of shares. For bonds, the volume is reported in terms of the actual number of bonds traded.

---

[2] Though the financial section in the paper is entitled "Bonds," these quotes are for *both* bonds and notes. We will use the financial reporting convention here and simply refer to both notes and bonds as "bonds."

[3] Comparing Tables A-1 and A-2, you'll notice that the abbreviated name for Airborne Freight differs (AirbornFrght in Table A-1, AirbF in Table A-2). This is because the quotations are from different computerized sources, and they sometimes identify security issuers a bit differently. Note also that if the coupon rate is a whole number (say 8 percent), an "s" is inserted to separate the coupon rate from the year of maturity. So "8s06" tells us the bond has an 8 percent coupon rate and matures in the year 2006.

NEW YORK EXCHANGE BONDS
Quotations for Monday, February 1, 1993

Bonds	Cur Yld	Vol	Close	Net Chg
AirbF $6\frac{3}{4}$01	cv	70	$93\frac{1}{4}$	$+\frac{1}{4}$
AlaP $8\frac{1}{4}$03	7.9	10	104	...
AlskAr $6\frac{7}{8}$14	cv	30	77	-1
AlskAr zr06	...	12	$34\frac{1}{2}$	$+\frac{3}{4}$
AlldC zr96	...	20	$83\frac{7}{8}$	$-\frac{1}{8}$
AlldC zr2000	...	37	$58\frac{7}{8}$	$+2\frac{5}{8}$
AlldC zr99	...	30	$63\frac{1}{4}$	$+\frac{3}{8}$
AlldC zr05	...	5	$36\frac{1}{2}$	$-1\frac{1}{2}$
Allwst $7\frac{1}{4}$14	cv	40	97	...
AAirl $5\frac{1}{4}$98	5.8	2	90	...

Explanation of column headings:

Bonds — Abbreviated company name or organization that issued the bond, with brief description of the bond (coupon rate and maturity date). The maturity date is abbreviated using the last two digits of the year.

Cur Yld — Current yield, calculated as the ratio of the current annual interest to the closing price of the bond. If blank, the bond pays no interest. If cv, then the bond is convertible and the current yield is not necessarily a good indicator of the bond's return.

Vol — Thousands of dollars of bonds traded during the day.

Close — Closing price.

Net Chg — Change in price from the day's opening price, quoted in terms of a fraction of 1 percent of par value.

Explanation of notation:

cv — Convertible bond.

s — Placeholder to separate the coupon rate and the maturity date; used when the coupon rate has no fraction.

zr — Zero-coupon bond.

SOURCE: *The Wall Street Journal*, Tuesday, Feb. 2, 1993, p. C16.

Let's look at examples of bond quotes. Find the quote for the Alabama Power Corporation bonds that have a coupon rate of $8\frac{1}{4}$ percent and mature in 2003 (second line down). Ten of these bonds traded on February 1, 1993,

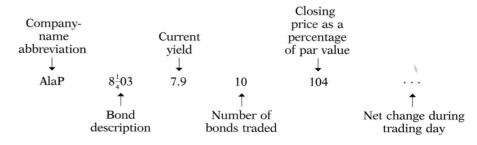

The reported current yield on these bonds is 7.9 percent. However, you can calculate the yield from information in the quote, remembering that the current yield is the ratio of the annual interest to the closing price:[4]

Closing price   = $1,040.00
Annual interest = $8\frac{1}{4}\%$ of $1,000, or $82.50

Since:

$$\text{Current yield} = \frac{\text{annual interest}}{\text{closing price}}$$

For the Alabama Power $8\frac{1}{4}\%$ bond:

$$\text{Current yield} = \frac{\$82.50}{\$1,040} = 0.079 \text{ or } \textbf{7.9\%}$$

Let's look at the quote for the Alaska Airlines convertible bonds, AlskAr $6\frac{7}{8}14$ (third line down). We know it's a convertible bond because of the "cv" listed in the current-yield column. There is no current yield reported for convertible bonds because they can be converted to common stock at the investor's discretion. The Alaska Airline convertible bonds have a coupon rate of $6\frac{7}{8}$ percent and closed at a price of $770 per bond. On the following line, for Alaska Airline zero-coupon bonds maturing in 2006, there is no current yield because, by definition, zero coupons have no coupon.

Like the stock quotations, the bond quotations include numerous footnotes that provide additional information about the bond, its trading, and the bond's issuer:

dc   The bond is sold at a deep discount from its face value.
ec   The bond is denominated in European currency units.
f   The bond is "dealt in flat," which means it is not currently paying its promised interest.
rp   The bond's principal has been reduced from its original face value.
t   The bond's interest rate is a floating rate.
vj   The issuer is in bankruptcy or receivership or being reorganized under the Bankruptcy Act.
x   The bond is trading without the right to the next interest payment.

As you can see, these footnotes provide valuable information to the investor, especially with respect to the security's risk.

HOW TO READ OPTIONS QUOTATIONS

An example of options quotes, taken from the February 2, 1993, issue of *The Wall Street Journal*, is shown in Table A-3. These quotes are reports of options contracts traded on February 1, 1993.

The key elements of an options contract are:

- *The strike price or exercise price.* The price at which the buyer of the options contract can buy (in the case of a call option) or sell (in the case of a put option) the common stock.

---

[4] The current yield is *not* the yield to maturity on the bond. It is simply a quick approximation of the yield and does not reflect the timing, the amount, and the risk of the future cash flows (interest and principal) of the bond.

Future value = FV = PV(compound factor) = $PV(1 + r)^t$ where FV = future value, t periods into the future
PV = present value
r = interest rate per period
t = number of periods

Interest rate per period, r

Number of periods, t	1%	2%	3%	4%	5%	6%	7%	8%	9%	10%	11%	12%
1	1.0100	1.0200	1.0300	1.0400	1.0500	1.0600	1.0700	1.0800	1.0900	1.1000	1.1100	1.1200
2	1.0201	1.0404	1.0609	1.0816	1.1025	1.1236	1.1449	1.1664	1.1881	1.2100	1.2321	1.2544
3	1.0303	1.0612	1.0927	1.1249	1.1576	1.1910	1.2250	1.2597	1.2950	1.3310	1.3676	1.4049
4	1.0406	1.0824	1.1255	1.1699	1.2155	1.2625	1.3108	1.3605	1.4116	1.4641	1.5181	1.5735
5	1.0510	1.1041	1.1593	1.2167	1.2763	1.3382	1.4026	1.4693	1.5386	1.6105	1.6851	1.7623
6	1.0615	1.1262	1.1941	1.2653	1.3401	1.4185	1.5007	1.5869	1.6771	1.7716	1.8704	1.9738
7	1.0721	1.1487	1.2299	1.3159	1.4071	1.5036	1.6058	1.7138	1.8280	1.9487	2.0762	2.2107
8	1.0829	1.1717	1.2668	1.3686	1.4775	1.5938	1.7182	1.8509	1.9926	2.1436	2.3045	2.4760
9	1.0937	1.1951	1.3048	1.4233	1.5513	1.6895	1.8385	1.9990	2.1719	2.3579	2.5580	2.7731
10	1.1046	1.2190	1.3439	1.4802	1.6289	1.7908	1.9672	2.1589	2.3674	2.5937	2.8394	3.1058
11	1.1157	1.2434	1.3842	1.5395	1.7103	1.8983	2.1049	2.3316	2.5804	2.8531	3.1518	3.4785
12	1.1268	1.2682	1.4258	1.6010	1.7959	2.0122	2.2522	2.5182	2.8127	3.1384	3.4985	3.8960
13	1.1381	1.2936	1.4685	1.6651	1.8856	2.1329	2.4098	2.7196	3.0658	3.4523	3.8833	4.3635
14	1.1495	1.3195	1.5126	1.7317	1.9799	2.2609	2.5785	2.9372	3.3417	3.7975	4.3104	4.8871
15	1.1610	1.3459	1.5580	1.8009	2.0789	2.3966	2.7590	3.1722	3.6425	4.1772	4.7846	5.4736
16	1.1726	1.3728	1.6047	1.8730	2.1829	2.5404	2.9522	3.4259	3.9703	4.5950	5.3109	6.1304
17	1.1843	1.4002	1.6528	1.9479	2.2920	2.6928	3.1588	3.7000	4.3276	5.0545	5.8951	6.8660
18	1.1961	1.4282	1.7024	2.0258	2.4066	2.8543	3.3799	3.9960	4.7171	5.5599	6.5436	7.6900
19	1.2081	1.4568	1.7535	2.1068	2.5270	3.0256	3.6165	4.3157	5.1417	6.1159	7.2633	8.6128
20	1.2202	1.4859	1.8061	2.1911	2.6533	3.2071	3.8697	4.6610	5.6044	6.7275	8.0623	9.6463
21	1.2324	1.5157	1.8603	2.2788	2.7860	3.3996	4.1406	5.0338	6.1088	7.4002	8.9492	10.8038
22	1.2447	1.5460	1.9161	2.3699	2.9253	3.6035	4.4304	5.4365	6.6586	8.1403	9.9336	12.1003
23	1.2572	1.5769	1.9736	2.4647	3.0715	3.8197	4.7405	5.8715	7.2579	8.9543	11.0263	13.5523
24	1.2697	1.6084	2.0328	2.5633	3.2251	4.0489	5.0724	6.3412	7.9111	9.8497	12.2392	15.1786
25	1.2824	1.6406	2.0938	2.6658	3.3864	4.2919	5.4274	6.8485	8.6231	10.8347	13.5855	17.0001
26	1.2953	1.6734	2.1566	2.7725	3.5557	4.5494	5.8074	7.3964	9.3992	11.9182	15.0799	19.0401
27	1.3082	1.7069	2.2213	2.8834	3.7335	4.8223	6.2139	7.9881	10.2451	13.1100	16.7386	21.3249
28	1.3213	1.7410	2.2879	2.9987	3.9201	5.1117	6.6488	8.6271	11.1671	14.4210	18.5799	23.8839
29	1.3345	1.7758	2.3566	3.1187	4.1161	5.4184	7.1143	9.3173	12.1722	15.8631	20.6237	26.7499
30	1.3478	1.8114	2.4273	3.2434	4.3219	5.7435	7.6123	10.0627	13.2677	17.4494	22.8923	29.9599
31	1.3613	1.8476	2.5001	3.3731	4.5380	6.0881	8.1451	10.8677	14.4618	19.1943	25.4104	33.5551
32	1.3749	1.8845	2.5751	3.5081	4.7649	6.4534	8.7153	11.7371	15.7633	21.1138	28.2056	37.5817
33	1.3887	1.9222	2.6523	3.6484	5.0032	6.8406	9.3253	12.6760	17.1820	23.3252	31.3082	42.0915
34	1.4026	1.9607	2.7319	3.7943	5.2533	7.2510	9.9781	13.6901	18.7284	25.5477	34.7521	47.1425
35	1.4166	1.9999	2.8139	3.9461	5.5160	7.6861	10.6766	14.7853	20.4140	28.1024	38.5749	52.7996
36	1.4308	2.0399	2.8983	4.1039	5.7918	8.1473	11.4239	15.9682	22.2512	30.9127	42.8181	59.1356
37	1.4451	2.0807	2.9852	4.2681	6.0814	8.6361	12.2236	17.2456	24.2538	34.0039	47.5281	66.2318
38	1.4595	2.1223	3.0748	4.4388	6.3855	9.1543	13.0793	18.6253	26.4367	37.4043	52.7562	74.1797
39	1.4741	2.1647	3.1670	4.6164	6.7048	9.7035	13.9948	20.1153	28.8160	41.1448	58.5593	83.0812
40	1.4889	2.2080	3.2620	4.8010	7.0400	10.2857	14.9745	21.7245	31.4094	45.2593	65.0009	93.0510

TABLE B-1 (CONT.)
Compound Factors

Future value = FV = PV(compound factor) = $PV(1 + r)^t$ where FV = future value, t periods into the future
PV = present value
r = interest rate per period
t = number of periods

Interest rate per period, r

Number of periods, t	13%	14%	15%	16%	20%	24%	28%	32%	36%	40%
1	1.1300	1.1400	1.1500	1.1600	1.2000	1.2400	1.2800	1.3200	1.3600	1.4000
2	1.2769	1.2996	1.3225	1.3456	1.4400	1.5376	1.6384	1.7424	1.8496	1.9600
3	1.4429	1.4815	1.5209	1.5609	1.7280	1.9066	2.0972	2.3000	2.5155	2.7440
4	1.6305	1.6890	1.7490	1.8106	2.0736	2.3642	2.6844	3.0360	3.4210	3.8416
5	1.8424	1.9254	2.0114	2.1003	2.4883	2.9316	3.4360	4.0075	4.6526	5.3782
6	2.0820	2.1950	2.3131	2.4364	2.9860	3.6352	4.3980	5.2899	6.3275	7.5295
7	2.3526	2.5023	2.6600	2.8262	3.5832	4.5077	5.6295	6.9826	8.6054	10.5414
8	2.6584	2.8526	3.0590	3.2784	4.2998	5.5895	7.2058	9.2170	11.7034	14.7579
9	3.0040	3.2519	3.5179	3.8030	5.1598	6.9310	9.2234	12.1665	15.9166	20.6610
10	3.3946	3.7072	4.0456	4.4114	6.1917	8.5944	11.8059	16.0598	21.6466	28.9255
11	3.8359	4.2262	4.6524	5.1173	7.4301	10.6571	15.1116	21.1989	29.4393	40.4957
12	4.3345	4.8179	5.3503	5.9360	8.9161	13.2148	19.3428	27.9825	40.0375	56.6939
13	4.8980	5.4924	6.1528	6.8858	10.6993	16.3863	24.7588	36.9370	54.4510	79.3715
14	5.5348	6.2613	7.0757	7.9875	12.8392	20.3191	31.6913	48.7568	74.0534	111.1201
15	6.2543	7.1379	8.1371	9.2655	15.4070	25.1956	40.5648	64.3590	100.7126	155.5681
16	7.0673	8.1372	9.3576	10.7480	18.4884	31.2426	51.9230	84.9538	136.9691	217.7953
17	7.9861	9.2765	10.7613	12.4677	22.1861	38.7408	66.4614	112.1390	186.2779	304.9135
18	9.0243	10.5752	12.3755	14.4625	26.6233	48.0386	85.0706	148.0235	253.3380	426.8789
19	10.1974	12.0557	14.2318	16.7765	31.9480	59.5679	108.8904	195.3911	344.5397	597.6304
20	11.5231	13.7435	16.3665	19.4608	38.3376	73.8641	139.3797	257.9162	468.5740	836.6826
21	13.0211	15.6676	18.8215	22.5745	46.0051	91.5915	178.4060	340.4494	637.2606	1171.3556
22	14.7138	17.8610	21.6447	26.1864	55.2061	113.5735	228.3596	449.3932	866.6744	1639.8978
23	16.6266	20.3616	24.8915	30.3762	66.2474	140.8312	292.3003	593.1990	1178.6772	2295.8569
24	18.7881	23.2122	28.6252	35.2364	79.4968	174.6306	374.1444	783.0227	1603.0010	3214.1997
25	21.2305	26.4619	32.9190	40.8742	95.3962	216.5420	478.9049	1033.5900	2180.0814	4499.8796
26	23.9905	30.1666	37.8568	47.4141	114.4755	268.5121	612.9982	1364.3387	2964.9107	6299.8314
27	27.1093	34.3899	43.5353	55.0004	137.3706	332.9550	784.6377	1800.9271	4032.2786	8819.7640
28	30.6335	39.2045	50.0656	63.8004	164.8447	412.8642	1004.3363	2377.2238	5483.8988	12347.6696
29	34.6158	44.6931	57.5755	74.0085	197.8136	511.9516	1285.5504	3137.9354	7458.1024	17286.7374
30	39.1159	50.9502	66.2118	85.8499	237.3763	634.8199	1645.5046	4142.0748	10143.0193	24201.4324
31	44.2010	58.0832	76.1435	99.5859	284.8516	787.1767	2106.2458	5467.5387	13794.5062	33882.0053
32	49.9471	66.2148	87.5651	115.5196	341.8219	976.0991	2695.9947	7217.1511	18760.5285	47434.8074
33	56.4402	75.4849	100.6998	134.0027	410.1863	1210.3629	3450.8732	9526.6395	25514.3187	66408.7304
34	63.7774	86.0528	115.8048	155.4432	492.2235	1500.8500	4417.1177	12575.1641	34699.4734	92972.2225
35	72.0685	98.1002	133.1755	180.3141	590.6682	1861.0540	5653.9106	16599.2166	47191.2839	130161.1116
36	81.4374	111.8342	153.1519	209.1643	708.8019	2307.7070	7237.0056	21910.9659	64180.1461	182225.5562
37	92.0243	127.4910	176.1246	242.6306	850.5622	2861.5567	9263.3671	28922.4750	87284.9987	255115.7786
38	103.9874	145.3397	202.5433	281.4515	1020.6747	3548.3303	11857.1099	38177.6670	118707.5982	357162.0901
39	117.5058	165.6873	232.9248	326.4838	1224.8096	4399.9295	15177.1007	50394.5205	161442.3336	500026.9261
40	132.7816	188.8835	267.8635	378.7212	1469.7716	5455.9126	19426.6889	66520.7670	219561.5736	700037.6966

TABLE B-2
Discount Factors

Present value $= PV = FV\left(\dfrac{\text{discount}}{\text{factor}}\right) = FV\left(\dfrac{1}{1+r}\right)^t = \dfrac{FV}{(1+r)^t}$

where FV = future value, t periods into the future
PV = present value
r = interest rate per period
t = number of periods

Interest rate per period, r

Number of periods, t	1%	2%	3%	4%	5%	6%	7%	8%	9%	10%	11%	12%
1	0.9901	0.9804	0.9709	0.9615	0.9524	0.9434	0.9346	0.9259	0.9174	0.9091	0.9009	0.8929
2	0.9803	0.9612	0.9426	0.9246	0.9070	0.8900	0.8734	0.8573	0.8417	0.8264	0.8116	0.7972
3	0.9706	0.9423	0.9151	0.8890	0.8638	0.8396	0.8163	0.7938	0.7722	0.7513	0.7312	0.7118
4	0.9610	0.9238	0.8885	0.8548	0.8227	0.7921	0.7629	0.7350	0.7084	0.6830	0.6587	0.6355
5	0.9515	0.9057	0.8626	0.8219	0.7835	0.7473	0.7130	0.6806	0.6499	0.6209	0.5935	0.5674
6	0.9420	0.8880	0.8375	0.7903	0.7462	0.7050	0.6663	0.6302	0.5963	0.5645	0.5346	0.5066
7	0.9327	0.8706	0.8131	0.7599	0.7107	0.6651	0.6227	0.5835	0.5470	0.5132	0.4817	0.4523
8	0.9235	0.8535	0.7894	0.7307	0.6768	0.6274	0.5820	0.5403	0.5019	0.4665	0.4339	0.4039
9	0.9143	0.8368	0.7664	0.7026	0.6446	0.5919	0.5439	0.5002	0.4604	0.4241	0.3909	0.3606
10	0.9053	0.8203	0.7441	0.6756	0.6139	0.5584	0.5083	0.4632	0.4224	0.3855	0.3522	0.3220
11	0.8963	0.8043	0.7224	0.6496	0.5847	0.5268	0.4751	0.4289	0.3875	0.3505	0.3173	0.2875
12	0.8874	0.7885	0.7014	0.6246	0.5568	0.4970	0.4440	0.3971	0.3555	0.3186	0.2858	0.2567
13	0.8787	0.7730	0.6810	0.6006	0.5303	0.4688	0.4150	0.3677	0.3262	0.2897	0.2575	0.2292
14	0.8700	0.7579	0.6611	0.5775	0.5051	0.4423	0.3878	0.3405	0.2992	0.2633	0.2320	0.2046
15	0.8613	0.7430	0.6419	0.5553	0.4810	0.4173	0.3624	0.3152	0.2745	0.2394	0.2090	0.1827
16	0.8528	0.7284	0.6232	0.5339	0.4581	0.3936	0.3387	0.2919	0.2519	0.2176	0.1883	0.1631
17	0.8444	0.7142	0.6050	0.5134	0.4363	0.3714	0.3166	0.2703	0.2311	0.1978	0.1696	0.1456
18	0.8360	0.7002	0.5874	0.4936	0.4155	0.3503	0.2959	0.2502	0.2120	0.1799	0.1528	0.1300
19	0.8277	0.6864	0.5703	0.4746	0.3957	0.3305	0.2765	0.2317	0.1945	0.1635	0.1377	0.1161
20	0.8195	0.6730	0.5537	0.4564	0.3769	0.3118	0.2584	0.2145	0.1784	0.1486	0.1240	0.1037
21	0.8114	0.6598	0.5375	0.4388	0.3589	0.2942	0.2415	0.1987	0.1637	0.1351	0.1117	0.0926
22	0.8034	0.6468	0.5219	0.4220	0.3418	0.2775	0.2257	0.1839	0.1502	0.1228	0.1007	0.0826
23	0.7954	0.6342	0.5067	0.4057	0.3256	0.2618	0.2109	0.1703	0.1378	0.1117	0.0907	0.0738
24	0.7876	0.6217	0.4919	0.3901	0.3101	0.2470	0.1971	0.1577	0.1264	0.1015	0.0817	0.0659
25	0.7798	0.6095	0.4776	0.3751	0.2953	0.2330	0.1842	0.1460	0.1160	0.0923	0.0736	0.0588
26	0.7720	0.5976	0.4637	0.3607	0.2812	0.2198	0.1722	0.1352	0.1064	0.0839	0.0663	0.0525
27	0.7644	0.5859	0.4502	0.3468	0.2678	0.2074	0.1609	0.1252	0.0976	0.0763	0.0597	0.0469
28	0.7568	0.5744	0.4371	0.3335	0.2551	0.1956	0.1504	0.1159	0.0895	0.0693	0.0538	0.0419
29	0.7493	0.5631	0.4243	0.3207	0.2429	0.1846	0.1406	0.1073	0.0822	0.0630	0.0485	0.0374
30	0.7419	0.5521	0.4120	0.3083	0.2314	0.1741	0.1314	0.0994	0.0754	0.0573	0.0437	0.0334
31	0.7346	0.5412	0.4000	0.2965	0.2204	0.1643	0.1228	0.0920	0.0691	0.0521	0.0394	0.0298
32	0.7273	0.5306	0.3883	0.2851	0.2099	0.1550	0.1147	0.0852	0.0634	0.0474	0.0355	0.0266
33	0.7201	0.5202	0.3770	0.2741	0.1999	0.1462	0.1072	0.0789	0.0582	0.0431	0.0319	0.0238
34	0.7130	0.5100	0.3660	0.2636	0.1904	0.1379	0.1002	0.0730	0.0534	0.0391	0.0288	0.0212
35	0.7059	0.5000	0.3554	0.2534	0.1813	0.1301	0.0937	0.0676	0.0490	0.0356	0.0259	0.0189
36	0.6989	0.4902	0.3450	0.2437	0.1727	0.1227	0.0875	0.0626	0.0449	0.0323	0.0234	0.0169
37	0.6920	0.4806	0.3350	0.2343	0.1644	0.1158	0.0818	0.0580	0.0412	0.0294	0.0210	0.0151
38	0.6852	0.4712	0.3252	0.2253	0.1566	0.1092	0.0765	0.0537	0.0378	0.0267	0.0190	0.0135
39	0.6784	0.4619	0.3158	0.2166	0.1491	0.1031	0.0715	0.0497	0.0347	0.0243	0.0171	0.0120
40	0.6717	0.4529	0.3066	0.2083	0.1420	0.0972	0.0668	0.0460	0.0318	0.0221	0.0154	0.0107

TABLE B-2 (CONT.)

Discount Factors

Present value $= PV = FV\left(\dfrac{\text{discount}}{\text{factor}}\right) = FV\left(\dfrac{1}{1+r}\right)^t = \dfrac{FV}{(1+r)^t}$

where FV = future value, t periods into the future
PV = present value
r = interest rate per period
t = number of periods

Interest rate per period, r

Number of periods, t	13%	14%	15%	16%	20%	24%	28%	32%	36%	40%
1	0.8850	0.8722	0.8696	0.8621	0.8333	0.806 45	0.781 250	0.757 576	0.735 294	0.714 286
2	0.7831	0.7695	0.7561	0.7432	0.6944	0.650 36	0.610 352	0.573 921	0.540 657	0.510 204
3	0.6931	0.6750	0.6575	0.6407	0.5787	0.524 49	0.476 837	0.434 789	0.397 542	0.364 431
4	0.6133	0.5921	0.5718	0.5523	0.4823	0.422 97	0.372 529	0.329 385	0.292 310	0.260 308
5	0.5428	0.5194	0.4972	0.4761	0.4019	0.341 11	0.291 038	0.249 534	0.214 934	0.185 934
6	0.4803	0.4556	0.4323	0.4104	0.3349	0.275 09	0.227 374	0.189 041	0.158 040	0.132 810
7	0.4251	0.3996	0.3759	0.3538	0.2791	0.221 84	0.177 636	0.143 213	0.116 206	0.094 865
8	0.3762	0.3506	0.3269	0.3050	0.2326	0.178 91	0.138 778	0.108 495	0.085 445	0.067 760
9	0.3329	0.3075	0.2843	0.2630	0.1938	0.144 28	0.108 420	0.082 193	0.062 828	0.048 400
10	0.2946	0.2697	0.2472	0.2267	0.1615	0.116 35	0.084 703	0.062 267	0.046 197	0.034 572
11	0.2607	0.2366	0.2149	0.1954	0.1346	0.093 83	0.066 174	0.047 172	0.033 968	0.024 694
12	0.2307	0.2076	0.1869	0.1685	0.1122	0.075 67	0.051 699	0.035 737	0.024 977	0.017 639
13	0.2042	0.1821	0.1625	0.1452	0.0935	0.061 03	0.040 390	0.027 073	0.018 365	0.012 599
14	0.1807	0.1597	0.1413	0.1252	0.0779	0.049 21	0.031 554	0.020 510	0.013 504	0.008 999
15	0.1599	0.1401	0.1229	0.1079	0.0649	0.039 69	0.024 652	0.015 538	0.009 929	0.006 428
16	0.1415	0.1229	0.1069	0.0930	0.0541	0.032 01	0.019 259	0.011 771	0.007 301	0.004 591
17	0.1252	0.1078	0.0929	0.0802	0.0451	0.025 81	0.015 046	0.008 918	0.005 368	0.003 280
18	0.1108	0.0946	0.0808	0.0691	0.0376	0.020 82	0.011 755	0.006 756	0.003 947	0.002 343
19	0.0981	0.0829	0.0703	0.0596	0.0313	0.016 79	0.009 184	0.005 118	0.002 902	0.001 673
20	0.0868	0.0728	0.0611	0.0514	0.0261	0.013 54	0.007 175	0.003 877	0.002 134	0.001 195
21	0.0768	0.0638	0.0531	0.0443	0.0217	0.010 92	0.005 605	0.002 937	0.001 569	0.000 854
22	0.0680	0.0560	0.0462	0.0382	0.0181	0.008 80	0.004 379	0.002 225	0.001 154	0.000 610
23	0.0601	0.0491	0.0402	0.0329	0.0151	0.007 10	0.003 421	0.001 686	0.000 848	0.000 436
24	0.0532	0.0431	0.0349	0.0284	0.0126	0.005 73	0.002 673	0.001 277	0.000 624	0.000 311
25	0.0471	0.0378	0.0304	0.0245	0.0105	0.004 62	0.002 088	0.000 968	0.000 459	0.000 222
26	0.0417	0.0331	0.0264	0.0211	0.0087	0.003 72	0.001 631	0.000 733	0.000 337	0.000 159
27	0.0369	0.0291	0.0230	0.0182	0.0073	0.003 00	0.001 274	0.000 555	0.000 248	0.000 113
28	0.0326	0.0255	0.0200	0.0157	0.0061	0.002 42	0.000 996	0.000 421	0.000 182	0.000 081
29	0.0289	0.0224	0.0174	0.0135	0.0051	0.001 95	0.000 778	0.000 319	0.000 134	0.000 058
30	0.0256	0.0196	0.0151	0.0116	0.0042	0.001 58	0.000 608	0.000 241	0.000 099	0.000 041
31	0.0226	0.0172	0.0131	0.0100	0.0035	0.001 27	0.000 475	0.000 183	0.000 072	0.000 030
32	0.0200	0.0151	0.0114	0.0087	0.0029	0.001 02	0.000 371	0.000 139	0.000 053	0.000 021
33	0.0177	0.0132	0.0099	0.0075	0.0024	0.000 83	0.000 290	0.000 105	0.000 039	0.000 015
34	0.0157	0.0116	0.0086	0.0064	0.0020	0.000 67	0.000 226	0.000 080	0.000 029	0.000 011
35	0.0139	0.0102	0.0075	0.0055	0.0017	0.000 54	0.000 177	0.000 060	0.000 021	0.000 008
36	0.0123	0.0089	0.0065	0.0048	0.0014	0.000 43	0.000 138	0.000 046	0.000 016	0.000 005
37	0.0109	0.0078	0.0057	0.0041	0.0012	0.000 35	0.000 108	0.000 035	0.000 011	0.000 004
38	0.0096	0.0069	0.0049	0.0036	0.0010	0.000 28	0.000 084	0.000 026	0.000 008	0.000 003
39	0.0085	0.0060	0.0043	0.0031	0.0008	0.000 23	0.000 066	0.000 020	0.000 006	0.000 002
40	0.0075	0.0053	0.0037	0.0026	0.0007	0.000 18	0.000 051	0.000 015	0.000 005	0.000 001

NOTE: A space has been provided between the third and fourth decimal places in columns 24%–40% to enhance readability.

TABLE B-3

Future Value Annuity Factors

Future value of a T-cash-flow ordinary annuity $= FV = CF\left(\dfrac{\text{future value}}{\text{annuity factor}}\right) = CF\left[\displaystyle\sum_{t=1}^{T}(1+r)^{T-t}\right] = CF\left[\dfrac{(1+r)^T - 1}{r}\right]$

where FV = future value of annuity
  CF = level cash flow each period
  r = interest rate per period
  T = number of cash flows

Interest rate per period, r

Number of cash flows, T	1%	2%	3%	4%	5%	6%	7%	8%	9%	10%	11%	12%
1	1.0000	1.0000	1.0000	1.0000	1.0000	1.0000	1.0000	1.0000	1.0000	1.0000	1.0000	1.0000
2	2.0100	2.0200	2.0300	2.0400	2.0500	2.0600	2.0700	2.0800	2.0900	2.1000	2.1100	2.1200
3	3.0301	3.0604	3.0909	3.1216	3.1525	3.1836	3.2149	3.2464	3.2781	3.3100	3.3421	3.3744
4	4.0604	4.1216	4.1836	4.2465	4.3101	4.3746	4.4399	4.5061	4.5731	4.6410	4.7097	4.7793
5	5.1010	5.2040	5.3091	5.4163	5.5256	5.6371	5.7507	5.8666	5.9847	6.1051	6.2278	6.3528
6	6.1520	6.3081	6.4684	6.6330	6.8019	6.9753	7.1533	7.3359	7.5233	7.7156	7.9129	8.1152
7	7.2135	7.4343	7.6625	7.8983	8.1420	8.3938	8.6540	8.9228	9.2004	9.4872	9.7833	10.0890
8	8.2857	8.5830	8.8923	9.2142	9.5491	9.8975	10.2598	10.6366	11.0285	11.4359	11.8594	12.2997
9	9.3685	9.7546	10.1591	10.5828	11.0266	11.4913	11.9780	12.4876	13.0210	13.5795	14.1640	14.7757
10	10.4622	10.9497	11.4639	12.0061	12.5779	13.1808	13.8164	14.4866	15.1929	15.9374	16.7220	17.5487
11	11.5668	12.1687	12.8078	13.4864	14.2068	14.9716	15.7836	16.6455	17.5603	18.5312	19.5614	20.6546
12	12.6825	13.4121	14.1920	15.0258	15.9171	16.8699	17.8885	18.9771	20.1407	21.3843	22.7132	24.1331
13	13.8093	14.6803	15.6178	16.6268	17.7130	18.8821	20.1406	21.4953	22.9534	24.5227	26.2116	28.0291
14	14.9474	15.9739	17.0863	18.2919	19.5986	21.0151	22.5505	24.2149	26.0192	27.9750	30.0949	32.3926
15	16.0969	17.2934	18.5989	20.0236	21.5786	23.2760	25.1290	27.1521	29.3609	31.7725	34.4054	37.2797
16	17.2579	18.6393	20.1569	21.8245	23.6575	25.6725	27.8881	30.3243	33.0034	35.9497	39.1899	42.7533
17	18.4304	20.0121	21.7616	23.6975	25.8404	28.2129	30.8402	33.7502	36.9737	40.5447	44.5008	48.8837
18	19.6147	21.4123	23.4144	25.6454	28.1324	30.9057	33.9990	37.4502	41.3013	45.5992	50.3959	55.7497
19	20.8109	22.8406	25.1169	27.6712	30.5390	33.7600	37.3790	41.4463	46.0185	51.1591	56.9395	63.4397
20	22.0190	24.2974	26.8704	29.7781	33.0660	36.7856	40.9955	45.7620	51.1601	57.2750	64.2028	72.0524
21	23.2392	25.7833	28.6765	31.9692	35.7193	39.9927	44.8652	50.4229	56.7645	64.0025	72.2651	81.6987
22	24.4716	27.2990	30.5368	34.2480	38.5052	43.3923	49.0057	55.4568	62.8733	71.4027	81.2143	92.5026
23	25.7163	28.8450	32.4529	36.6179	41.4305	46.9958	53.4361	60.8933	69.5319	79.5430	91.1479	104.6029
24	26.9735	30.4219	34.4265	39.0826	44.5020	50.8156	58.1767	66.7648	76.7898	88.4973	102.1742	118.1552
25	28.2432	32.0303	36.4593	41.6459	47.7271	54.8645	63.2490	73.1059	84.7009	98.3471	114.4133	133.3339
26	29.5256	33.6709	38.5530	44.3117	51.1135	59.1564	68.6765	79.9544	93.3240	109.1818	127.9988	150.3339
27	30.8209	35.3443	40.7096	47.0842	54.6691	63.7058	74.4838	87.3508	102.7231	121.0999	143.0786	169.3740
28	32.1291	37.0512	42.9309	49.9676	58.4026	68.5281	80.6977	95.3388	112.9682	134.2099	159.8173	190.6989
29	33.4504	38.7922	45.2189	52.9663	62.3227	73.6398	87.3465	103.9659	124.1354	148.6309	178.3972	214.5828
30	34.7849	40.5681	47.5754	56.0849	66.4388	79.0582	94.4608	113.2832	136.3075	164.4940	199.0209	241.3327
31	36.1327	42.3794	50.0027	59.3283	70.7608	84.8017	102.0730	123.3459	149.5752	181.9434	221.9132	271.2926
32	37.4941	44.2270	52.5028	62.7015	75.2988	90.8898	110.2182	134.2135	164.0370	201.1378	247.3236	304.8477
33	38.8690	46.1116	55.0778	66.2095	80.0638	97.3432	118.9334	145.9506	179.8003	222.2515	275.5292	342.4294
34	40.2577	48.0338	57.7302	69.8579	85.0670	104.1838	128.2588	158.6267	196.9823	245.4767	306.8374	384.5210
35	41.6603	49.9945	60.4621	73.6522	90.3203	111.4348	138.2369	172.3168	215.7108	271.0244	341.5896	431.6635
36	43.0769	51.9944	63.2759	77.5983	95.8363	119.1209	148.9135	187.1021	236.1247	299.1268	380.1644	484.4631
37	44.5076	54.0343	66.1742	81.7022	101.6281	127.2681	160.3374	203.0703	258.3759	330.0395	422.9825	543.5987
38	45.9527	56.1149	69.1594	85.9703	107.7095	135.9042	172.5610	220.3159	282.6298	364.0434	470.5106	609.8305
39	47.4123	58.2372	72.2342	90.4091	114.0950	145.0585	185.6403	238.9412	309.0665	401.4478	523.2667	684.0102
40	48.8864	60.4020	75.4013	95.0255	120.7998	154.7620	199.6351	259.0565	337.8824	442.5926	581.8261	767.0914

TABLE B-3 (CONT.)

Future Value Annuity Factors

Future value of a T-cash-flow ordinary annuity $= FV = CF\left(\dfrac{\text{future value}}{\text{annuity factor}}\right) = CF\left[\displaystyle\sum_{t=1}^{T}(1+r)^{T-t}\right] = CF\left[\dfrac{(1+r)^{T}-1}{r}\right]$

where FV = future value of annuity
CF = level cash flow each period
r = interest rate per period
T = number of cash flows

Interest rate per period, r

	13%	14%	15%	16%	20%	24%	28%	32%	36%	40%
1	1.0000	1.0000	1.0000	1.0000	1.0000	1.0000	1.0000	1.0000	1.0000	1.0000
2	2.1300	2.1400	2.1500	2.1600	2.2000	2.2400	2.2800	2.3200	2.3600	2.4000
3	3.4069	3.4396	3.4725	3.5056	3.6400	3.7776	3.9184	4.0624	4.2096	4.3600
4	4.8498	4.9211	4.9934	5.0665	5.3680	5.6842	6.0156	6.3624	6.7251	7.1040
5	6.4803	6.6101	6.7424	6.8771	7.4416	8.0484	8.6999	9.3983	10.1461	10.9456
6	8.3227	8.5355	8.7537	8.9775	9.9299	10.9801	12.1359	13.4058	14.7987	16.3238
7	10.4047	10.7305	11.0668	11.4139	12.9159	14.6153	16.5339	18.6956	21.1262	23.8534
8	12.7573	13.2328	13.7268	14.2401	16.4991	19.1229	22.1634	25.6782	29.7316	34.3947
9	15.4157	16.0853	16.7858	17.5185	20.7989	24.7125	29.3692	34.8953	41.4350	49.1526
10	18.4197	19.3373	20.3037	21.3215	25.9587	31.6434	38.5926	47.0618	57.3516	69.8137
11	21.8143	23.0445	24.3493	25.7329	32.1504	40.2379	50.3985	63.1215	78.9982	98.7391
12	25.6502	27.2707	29.0017	30.8502	39.5805	50.8950	65.5100	84.3204	108.4375	139.2348
13	29.9847	32.0887	34.3519	36.7862	48.4966	64.1097	84.8529	112.3030	148.4750	195.9287
14	34.8827	37.5811	40.5047	43.6720	59.1959	80.4961	109.6117	149.2399	202.9260	275.3002
15	40.4175	43.8424	47.5804	51.6595	72.0351	100.8151	141.3029	197.9967	276.9793	386.4202
16	46.6717	50.9804	55.7175	60.9250	87.4421	126.0108	181.8677	262.3557	377.6919	541.9883
17	53.7391	59.1176	65.0751	71.6730	105.9306	157.2534	233.7907	347.3095	514.6610	759.7837
18	61.7251	68.3941	75.8364	84.1407	128.1167	195.9942	300.2521	459.4485	700.9389	1064.6971
19	70.7494	78.9692	88.2118	98.6032	154.7400	244.0328	385.3227	607.4721	954.2769	1491.5760
20	80.9468	91.0249	102.4436	115.3797	186.6880	303.6006	494.2131	802.8631	1298.8166	2089.2064
21	92.4699	104.7684	118.8101	134.8405	225.0256	377.4648	633.5927	1060.0793	1767.3906	2925.8889
22	105.4910	120.4360	137.6316	157.4150	271.0307	469.0563	811.9987	1401.2287	2404.6512	4097.2445
23	120.2048	138.2970	159.2764	183.6014	326.2369	582.6298	1040.3583	1850.6219	3271.3256	5737.1423
24	136.8315	158.6586	184.1678	213.9776	392.4842	723.4610	1332.6586	2443.8209	4450.0029	8032.9993
25	155.6196	181.8708	212.7930	249.2140	471.9811	898.0916	1706.8031	3226.8436	6053.0039	11247.1990
26	176.8501	208.3327	245.7120	290.0883	567.3773	1114.6336	2185.7079	4260.4336	8233.0853	15747.0785
27	200.8406	238.4993	283.5688	337.5024	681.8528	1383.1457	2798.7061	5624.7723	11197.9960	22046.9099
28	227.9499	272.8892	327.1041	392.5028	819.2233	1716.1007	3583.3438	7425.6994	15230.2745	30866.6739
29	258.5834	312.0937	377.1697	456.3032	984.0680	2128.9648	4587.6801	9802.9233	20714.1734	43214.3435
30	293.1992	356.7868	434.7451	530.3117	1181.8816	2640.9164	5873.2306	12940.8587	28172.2758	60501.0809
31	332.3151	407.7370	500.9569	616.1616	1419.2579	3275.7363	7518.7351	17082.9335	38315.2951	84702.5132
32	376.5161	465.8202	577.1005	715.7475	1704.1095	4062.9130	9624.9810	22550.4722	52109.8013	118584.5185
33	426.4632	532.0350	664.6655	831.2671	2045.9314	5039.0122	12320.9756	29767.6233	70870.3298	166019.3260
34	482.9034	607.5199	765.3654	965.2698	2456.1176	6249.3751	15771.8488	39294.2628	96384.6485	232428.0563
35	546.6808	693.5727	881.1702	1120.7130	2948.3411	7750.2251	20188.9665	51869.4269	131084.1219	325400.2789
36	618.7493	791.6729	1014.3457	1301.0270	3539.0094	9611.2791	25842.8771	68468.6435	178275.4058	455561.3904
37	700.1867	903.5071	1167.4975	1510.1914	4247.8112	11918.9861	33079.8826	90379.6094	242455.5519	637786.9466
38	792.2110	1030.9981	1343.6222	1752.8220	5098.3735	14780.5428	42343.2498	119302.0844	329740.5506	892902.7252
39	896.1984	1176.3378	1546.1655	2034.2735	6119.0482	18328.8731	54200.3597	157479.7515	448448.1488	1250064.8153
40	1013.7042	1342.0251	1779.0903	2360.7572	7343.8578	22728.8026	69377.4604	207874.2719	609890.4824	1750091.7415

Number of cash flows, T

TABLE B-4
Present Value Annuity Factors

Present value of a T-cash-flow ordinary annuity $= PV = CF\left(\dfrac{\text{present value}}{\text{annuity factor}}\right) = CF\left[\sum_{t=1}^{T}\left(\dfrac{1}{1+r}\right)^{t}\right] = CF\left[\dfrac{1 - \dfrac{1}{(1+r)^{T}}}{r}\right]$

where PV = present value of annuity
CF = level cash flow each period
r = interest rate per period
T = number of cash flows

Interest rate per period, r

Number of cash flows, T	1%	2%	3%	4%	5%	6%	7%	8%	9%	10%	11%	12%
1	0.9901	0.9804	0.9709	0.9615	0.9524	0.9434	0.9346	0.9259	0.9174	0.9091	0.9009	0.8929
2	1.9704	1.9416	1.9135	1.8861	1.8594	1.8334	1.8080	1.7833	1.7591	1.7355	1.7125	1.6901
3	2.9410	2.8839	2.8286	2.7751	2.7232	2.6730	2.6243	2.5771	2.5313	2.4869	2.4437	2.4018
4	3.9020	3.8077	3.7171	3.6299	3.5460	3.4651	3.3872	3.3121	3.2397	3.1699	3.1024	3.0373
5	4.8534	4.7135	4.5797	4.4518	4.3295	4.2124	4.1002	3.9927	3.8897	3.7908	3.6959	3.6048
6	5.7955	5.6014	5.4172	5.2421	5.0757	4.9173	4.7665	4.6229	4.4859	4.3553	4.2305	4.1114
7	6.7282	6.4720	6.2303	6.0021	5.7864	5.5824	5.3893	5.2064	5.0330	4.8684	4.7122	4.5638
8	7.6517	7.3255	7.0197	6.7327	6.4632	6.2098	5.9713	5.7466	5.5348	5.3349	5.1461	4.9676
9	8.5660	8.1622	7.7861	7.4353	7.1078	6.8017	6.5152	6.2469	5.9952	5.7590	5.5370	5.3282
10	9.4713	8.9826	8.5302	8.1109	7.7217	7.3601	7.0236	6.7101	6.4177	6.1446	5.8892	5.6502
11	10.3676	9.7868	9.2526	8.7605	8.3064	7.8869	7.4987	7.1390	6.8052	6.4951	6.2065	5.9377
12	11.2551	10.5753	9.9540	9.3851	8.8633	8.3838	7.9427	7.5361	7.1607	6.8137	6.4924	6.1944
13	12.1337	11.3484	10.6350	9.9856	9.3936	8.8527	8.3577	7.9038	7.4869	7.1034	6.7499	6.4235
14	13.0037	12.1062	11.2961	10.5631	9.8986	9.2950	8.7455	8.2442	7.7862	7.3667	6.9819	6.6282
15	13.8651	12.8493	11.9379	11.1184	10.3797	9.7122	9.1079	8.5595	8.0607	7.6061	7.1909	6.8109
16	14.7179	13.5777	12.5611	11.6523	10.8378	10.1059	9.4466	8.8514	8.3126	7.8237	7.3792	6.9740
17	15.5623	14.2919	13.1661	12.1657	11.2741	10.4773	9.7632	9.1216	8.5436	8.0216	7.5488	7.1196
18	16.3983	14.9920	13.7535	12.6593	11.6896	10.8276	10.0591	9.3719	8.7556	8.2014	7.7016	7.2497
19	17.2260	15.6785	14.3238	13.1339	12.0853	11.1581	10.3356	9.6036	8.9501	8.3649	7.8393	7.3658
20	18.0456	16.3514	14.8775	13.5903	12.4622	11.4699	10.5940	9.8181	9.1285	8.5136	7.9633	7.4694
21	18.8570	17.0112	15.4150	14.0292	12.8212	11.7641	10.8355	10.0168	9.2922	8.6487	8.0751	7.5620
22	19.6604	17.6580	15.9369	14.4511	13.1630	12.0416	11.0612	10.2007	9.4424	8.7715	8.1757	7.6446
23	20.4558	18.2922	16.4436	14.8568	13.4886	12.3034	11.2722	10.3711	9.5802	8.8832	8.2664	7.7184
24	21.2434	18.9139	16.9355	15.2470	13.7986	12.5504	11.4693	10.5288	9.7066	8.9847	8.3481	7.7843
25	22.0232	19.5235	17.4131	15.6221	14.0939	12.7834	11.6536	10.6748	9.8226	9.0770	8.4217	7.8431
26	22.7952	20.1210	17.8768	15.9828	14.3752	13.0032	11.8258	10.8100	9.9290	9.1609	8.4881	7.8957
27	23.5596	20.7069	18.3270	16.3296	14.6430	13.2105	11.9867	10.9352	10.0266	9.2372	8.5478	7.9426
28	24.3164	21.2813	18.7641	16.6631	14.8981	13.4062	12.1371	11.0511	10.1161	9.3066	8.6016	7.9844
29	25.0658	21.8444	19.1885	16.9837	15.1411	13.5907	12.2777	11.1584	10.1983	9.3696	8.6501	8.0218
30	25.8077	22.3965	19.6004	17.2920	15.3725	13.7648	12.4090	11.2578	10.2737	9.4269	8.6938	8.0552
31	26.5423	22.9377	20.0004	17.5885	15.5928	13.9291	12.5318	11.3498	10.3428	9.4790	8.7331	8.0850
32	27.2696	23.4683	20.3888	17.8736	15.8027	14.0840	12.6466	11.4350	10.4062	9.5264	8.7686	8.1116
33	27.9897	23.9886	20.7658	18.1476	16.0025	14.2302	12.7538	11.5139	10.4644	9.5694	8.8005	8.1354
34	28.7027	24.4986	21.1318	18.4112	16.1929	14.3681	12.8540	11.5869	10.5178	9.6086	8.8293	8.1566
35	29.4086	24.9986	21.4872	18.6646	16.3742	14.4982	12.9477	11.6546	10.5668	9.6442	8.8552	8.1755
36	30.1075	25.4888	21.8323	18.9083	16.5469	14.6210	13.0352	11.7172	10.6118	9.6765	8.8786	8.1924
37	30.7995	25.9695	22.1672	19.1426	16.7113	14.7368	13.1170	11.7752	10.6530	9.7059	8.8996	8.2075
38	31.4847	26.4406	22.4925	19.3679	16.8679	14.8460	13.1935	11.8289	10.6908	9.7327	8.9186	8.2210
39	32.1630	26.9026	22.8082	19.5845	17.0170	14.9491	13.2649	11.8786	10.7255	9.7570	8.9357	8.2330
40	32.8347	27.3555	23.1148	19.7928	17.1591	15.0463	13.3317	11.9246	10.7574	9.7791	8.9511	8.2438

TABLE B-4 (CONT.)
Present Value of Annuity Factors

Present value of a T-cash-flow ordinary annuity $= PV = CF\left(\dfrac{\text{present value}}{\text{annuity factor}}\right) = CF\left[\displaystyle\sum_{t=1}^{T}\left(\dfrac{1}{1+r}\right)^{t}\right] = CF\left[\dfrac{1 - \dfrac{1}{(1+r)^{T}}}{r}\right]$

where PV = present value of annuity
CF = level cash flow each period
r = interest rate per period
T = number of cash flows

Interest rate per period, r

Number of cash flows, T	13%	14%	15%	16%	20%	24%	28%	32%	36%	40%
1	0.8850	0.8772	0.8696	0.8621	0.8333	0.8065	0.7813	0.7576	0.7353	0.7143
2	1.6681	1.6467	1.6257	1.6052	1.5278	1.4568	1.3916	1.3315	1.2760	1.2245
3	2.3612	2.3216	2.2832	2.2459	2.1065	1.9813	1.8684	1.7663	1.6735	1.5889
4	2.9745	2.9137	2.8550	2.7982	2.5887	2.4043	2.2410	2.0957	1.9658	1.8492
5	3.5172	3.4331	3.3522	3.2743	2.9906	2.7454	2.5320	2.3452	2.1807	2.0352
6	3.9975	3.8887	3.7845	3.6847	3.3255	3.0205	2.7594	2.5342	2.3388	2.1680
7	4.4226	4.2883	4.1604	4.0386	3.6046	3.2423	2.9370	2.6775	2.4550	2.2628
8	4.7988	4.6389	4.4873	4.3436	3.8372	3.4212	3.0758	2.7860	2.5404	2.3306
9	5.1317	4.9464	4.7716	4.6065	4.0310	3.5655	3.1842	2.8681	2.6033	2.3790
10	5.4262	5.2161	5.0188	4.8332	4.1925	3.6819	3.2689	2.9304	2.6495	2.4136
11	5.6869	5.4527	5.2337	5.0286	4.3271	3.7757	3.3351	2.9776	2.6834	2.4383
12	5.9176	5.6603	5.4206	5.1971	4.4392	3.8514	3.3868	3.0133	2.7084	2.4559
13	6.1218	5.8424	5.5831	5.3423	4.5327	3.9124	3.4272	3.0404	2.7268	2.4685
14	6.3025	6.0021	5.7245	5.4675	4.6106	3.9616	3.4587	3.0609	2.7403	2.4775
15	6.4624	6.1422	5.8474	5.5755	4.6755	4.0013	3.4834	3.0764	2.7502	2.4839
16	6.6039	6.2651	5.9542	5.6685	4.7296	4.0333	3.5026	3.0882	2.7575	2.4885
17	6.7291	6.3729	6.0472	5.7487	4.7746	4.0591	3.5177	3.0971	2.7629	2.4918
18	6.8399	6.4674	6.1280	5.8178	4.8122	4.0799	3.5294	3.1039	2.7668	2.4941
19	6.9380	6.5504	6.1982	5.8775	4.8435	4.0967	3.5386	3.1090	2.7697	2.4958
20	7.0248	6.6231	6.2593	5.9288	4.8696	4.1103	3.5458	3.1129	2.7718	2.4970
21	7.1016	6.6870	6.3125	5.9731	4.8913	4.1212	3.5514	3.1158	2.7734	2.4979
22	7.1695	6.7429	6.3587	6.0113	4.9094	4.1300	3.5558	3.1180	2.7746	2.4985
23	7.2297	6.7921	6.3988	6.0442	4.9245	4.1371	3.5592	3.1197	2.7754	2.4989
24	7.2829	6.8351	6.4338	6.0726	4.9371	4.1428	3.5619	3.1210	2.7760	2.4992
25	7.3300	6.8729	6.4641	6.0971	4.9476	4.1474	3.5640	3.1220	2.7765	2.4994
26	7.3717	6.9061	6.4906	6.1182	4.9563	4.1511	3.5656	3.1227	2.7768	2.4996
27	7.4086	6.9352	6.5135	6.1364	4.9636	4.1542	3.5669	3.1233	2.7771	2.4997
28	7.4412	6.9607	6.5335	6.1520	4.9697	4.1566	3.5679	3.1237	2.7773	2.4998
29	7.4701	6.9830	6.5509	6.1656	4.9747	4.1585	3.5687	3.1240	2.7774	2.4999
30	7.4957	7.0027	6.5660	6.1772	4.9789	4.1601	3.5693	3.1242	2.7775	2.4999
31	7.5183	7.0199	6.5791	6.1872	4.9824	4.1614	3.5697	3.1244	2.7776	2.4999
32	7.5383	7.0350	6.5905	6.1959	4.9854	4.1624	3.5701	3.1246	2.7776	2.4999
33	7.5560	7.0482	6.6005	6.2034	4.9878	4.1632	3.5704	3.1247	2.7777	2.5000
34	7.5717	7.0599	6.6091	6.2098	4.9898	4.1639	3.5706	3.1248	2.7777	2.5000
35	7.5856	7.0700	6.6166	6.2153	4.9915	4.1644	3.5708	3.1248	2.7777	2.5000
36	7.5979	7.0790	6.6231	6.2201	4.9929	4.1649	3.5709	3.1249	2.7777	2.5000
37	7.6087	7.0868	6.6288	6.2242	4.9941	4.1652	3.5710	3.1249	2.7777	2.5000
38	7.6183	7.0937	6.6338	6.2278	4.9951	4.1655	3.5711	3.1249	2.7778	2.5000
39	7.6268	7.0997	6.6380	6.2309	4.9959	4.1657	3.5712	3.1249	2.7778	2.5000
40	7.6344	7.1050	6.6418	6.2335	4.9966	4.1659	3.5712	3.1250	2.7778	2.5000

APPENDIX

Financial Math with Calculators

INTRODUCTION 840

GETTING TO KNOW YOUR CALCULATOR 840

HELPFUL HINTS AND WARNINGS 848

Helpful Hints 848

    Check Your Work 848

    The Number of Digits to Display 848

    Shortcuts 848

Warnings 848

    Getting Your Calculator Ready to Use 848

    Clearing the Calculator's Registers 849

    Checking the Timing of the Cash Flows 849

    Checking the Frequency of Payments 850

INTRODUCTION

Financial calculators can reduce the burden of financial mathematics, but only if you understand the financial mathematics you expect them to perform. To see what this means, let's look at the basic valuation equation:

$$FV = PV(1 + r)^t$$

where FV is the future value, PV is the present value, r is the interest rate per period, and t is the number of periods. All financial math usually involves an equation like this, consisting of several values, one of which is unknown. Though we can usually solve these kinds of equations for an unknown value using algebra, we can do so in less time with calculators programmed to do financial math.

The more complex calculations, such as those involving uneven cash flows, can be performed only on some advanced financial calculators. But you must be careful to input the cash flows in the correct order so that the calculator program applies the correct time value of money in its calculations.

The applications in this appendix use six different financial calculators:

- Hewlett Packard Model 10B (HP10B)
- Hewlett Packard Model 12C (HP12C)
- Hewlett Packard Model 19B (HP19B)
- Sharp EL-733 (SHARP)
- Texas Instruments Business Analyst II (TIBAII)
- Texas Instruments BAII Plus (TIBAII+)

Even if your calculator brand or model is not among these six, this appendix may still be useful to you, since many of the basic functions and procedures we discuss are similar among all financial calculators.

GETTING TO KNOW YOUR CALCULATOR

To keep hand-held calculators small but useful for many different types of calculations, most models have been designed so that many keys serve double duty: Each key is capable of doing two or more things. For example, in the HP10B calculator, the key labeled:

is used for both multiplication ($\times$) and for raising a value to a power ("y^x"). How do we raise some value to a power? We first strike the solid-colored key, ■, and then ▦. Striking the ■ tells the computer to use the second function of the ▦ key.

To multiply one value by another (for example, 3×4):

$$\boxed{3} \; \boxed{x} \; \boxed{4} \; \boxed{=}$$

with an answer of 12.

To raise a value to a power (for example, 3^4):

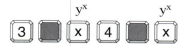

with an answer of 81. You'll notice that we had to strike the ■ and ⌧ keys twice in this calculation, but we did not have to use the ⌸ key. Some models have triple-level as well as double-level keys.

Access to the double- or triple-level functions differs among calculators. For the HP10B, the alternative function of a key is accessed by using the solid-colored key ■. In other models the alternative function may be accessed through, for example, a ⌷ key or a ⌷ key. You need to refer to the manual that came with your financial calculator to see how to access these second- or third-level functions.

In addition to access to different levels through a single key, some calculators, such as the HP19B, have a set of unidentified keys (just below the display) that will perform a function assigned to them based on the "screen" shown in the display. For example, if you select the time-value-of-money screen (by striking the ■ below FIN and then the ■ below TVM), these keys are assigned to represent PV, N, FV, and so on.

In the instructions that follow, we will describe what key to hit by showing the sequence of keystrokes; for example, to calculate 3^4 on the HP10B, the sequence is:

putting the key's label *in* the box representing the key to indicate which key to hit. In the case of keys identified by a display screen, such as on the HP19B, we indicate the keystroke by placing the identity of the key *above* the box (e.g. ▦).

The basic math calculations (such as addition, subtraction, multiplication, and division) are similar among the different brands and models. With the exception of the HP12C, the math is performed much as you would if you were doing it without the calculator.

Consider again the problem of multiplying 3 by 4:

All models except HP12C | 3 | | x | | 4 | | = | Display: 12

HP12C | 3 | | ENTER | | 4 | | x | Display: 12

Division, addition, and subtraction are performed in a like manner.

To understand how to use your calculator to perform financial mathematics, it is important that you first understand how to do the math *without* the calculator.

Financial mathematics calculations using each of the six calculators listed earlier are illustrated in Figures C-1 through C-5. To see how to use these calculators, let's look closely at the example shown in Figure C-1, using the HP10B calculator to solve a future value problem: If an investor deposits $1,000 today in an account that pays 5 percent interest each year, how much will be in the account at the end of ten years?

We are given:

PV = $1,000
r = 5% per year
t = 10 years

and we want to solve for FV.

The first thing we need to do is tell the computer the present value. However, in the HP10B (like most financial calculators), we have to change the sign on the present value in order for the calculator's program to work. This is because the calculator's program uses the basic valuation equation,

$$FV = PV(1 + r)^t$$

and rearranges it to put all values on one side:

$$0 = FV - PV(1 + r)^t$$

So we need to enter the value of −PV, not PV. We input $1,000 as the present value and change its sign,

We then need to tell the computer the interest rate, in whole numbers (that is, 5 percent is "5"):

The number of compounding periods is next:

And we solve for the future value by striking the FV key:

The future value, $1,628.90, will then be displayed.[1] These steps are summarized for the HP10B in the top left panel of Figure C-1.

To try out the examples in the figures, first see whether your calculator is among the six shown. If not, determine which model's keys and functions are closest to those of your calculator. Then strike the keys as instructed in the appropriate part of each figure, keeping an eye on your calculator's display to make sure you are keying in the correct information.

---

[1] If we had forgotten to change the sign on the present value, the displayed future value would have been −1,628.90. If we had been solving for the number of periods or the interest rate (that is, given FV, PV, and r, solve for t or given FV, PV, and t, solve for r) and had forgotten to change the sign on the present value, we would have gotten an error message in the display instead of a solution.

FIGURE C-1

Translating a Present Value into a Future Value

Suppose an investor places $1,000 in a bank account that promises to pay 5 percent interest each year, payable at the end of each year. If the investment is held for ten years, how much will the investment be worth at the end of the ten years?

The three known values are:

- The present value, PV = $1,000.
- The interest rate, r = 5 percent per year.
- The number of compounding periods, t = 10 years.

The unknown value is the future value, FV. Using the basic valuation equation and inserting the known values:

$$FV = \$1,000.00(1 + 0.05)^{10} + \$1,000.00(1.6289) = \mathbf{\$1,628.90}$$

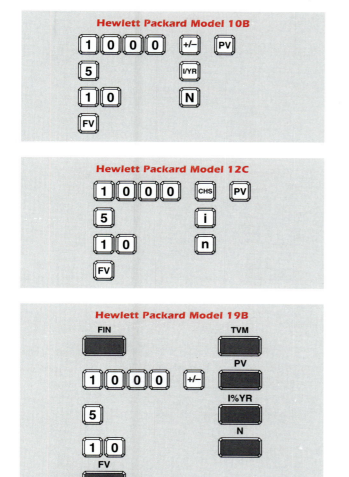

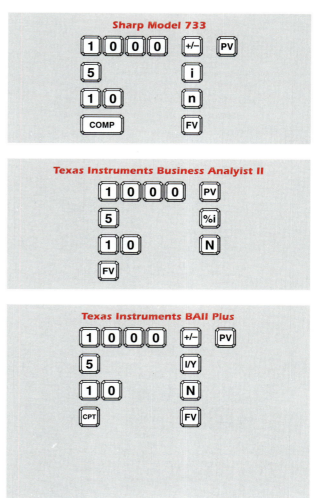

FIGURE C-2
Present Value of a Series of Uneven Cash Flows

Suppose you are promised the following set of cash flows:

End of period	Cash flow
0	$1,000
1	2,000
2	3,000

Using a discount rate of 5 percent per year, the present value of this series at time period 0 is:

$$PV = \frac{\$1,000.00}{(1 + 0.05)^0} + \frac{\$2,000.00}{(1 + 0.05)^1} + \frac{\$3,000.00}{(1 + 0.05)^2}$$

$$= \$1,000.00 + \$1,904.76 + \$2,721.09$$

$$= \mathbf{\$5,625.85}$$

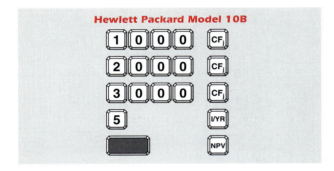

Hewlett Packard Model 10B

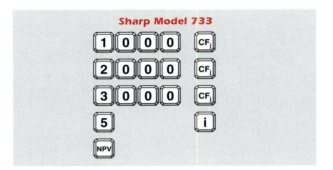

Sharp Model 733

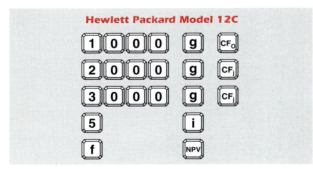

Hewlett Packard Model 12C

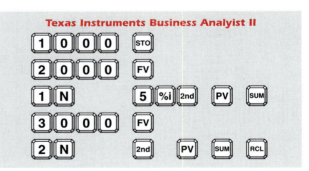

Texas Instruments Business Analyist II

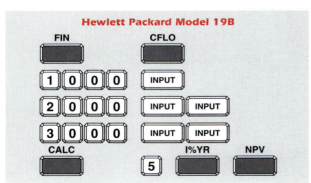

Hewlett Packard Model 19B

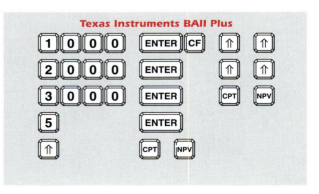

Texas Instruments BAII Plus

FIGURE C-3

Present Value of an Annuity

Consider an annuity consisting of five annual cash flows of $3,000 each, with the first cash flow one year from today. If these cash flows were deposited in a savings account that earns 4 percent interest compounded annually, what would be the value today of receiving these five future cash flows?

$$PV = \frac{\$3,000.00}{(1 + 0.04)^1} + \frac{\$3,000.00}{(1 + 0.04)^2} + \frac{\$3,000.00}{(1 + 0.04)^3} + \frac{\$3,000.00}{(1 + 0.04)^4} + \frac{\$3,000.00}{(1 + 0.04)^5}$$

$$= \$2,884.62 + \$2,773.67 + \$2,666.99 + \$2,564.41 + \$2,465.78$$

$$= \mathbf{\$13,355.47}$$

Hewlett Packard Model 10B

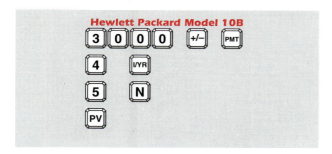

Sharp Model 733

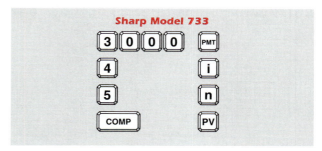

Hewlett Packard Model 12C

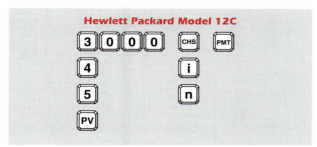

Texas Instruments Business Analyist II

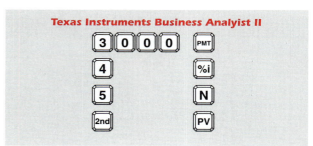

Hewlett Packard Model 19B

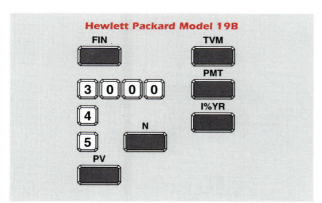

Texas Instruments BAII Plus

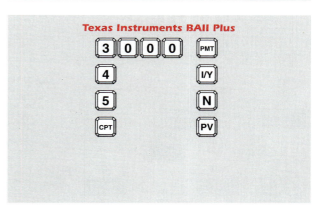

FIGURE C-4
Annualized Yield to Maturity of a Bond

Suppose you wish to calculate the yield to maturity on a $1,000-face-value bond that has a current market price of $900, an 8 percent coupon rate with interest paid semiannually, and five years remaining to maturity. What is the annualized yield to maturity (YTM) on this bond?

We first solve for the six-month yield (internal rate of return) and then annualize this rate to arrive at the YTM:

$$\$900 = \sum_{t=1}^{10} \frac{\$40}{(1 + r)^t} + \frac{\$1,000}{(1 + r)^{10}}$$

Through trial and error, we find that the six-month yield is between 5 and 6 percent. Therefore, the yield to maturity is between 10 percent and 12 percent and is closer to 10 percent. Precise answer: six-month yield, 5.3149 percent; annualized yield to maturity, 10.6299 percent.

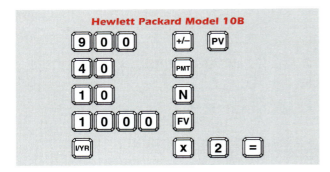

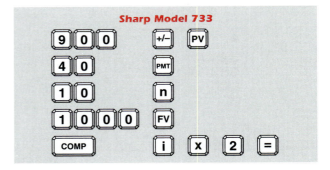

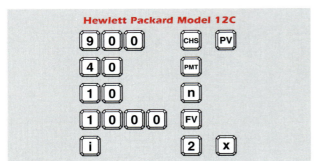

Texas Instruments Business Analyist II

The yield to maturity cannot be calculated directly using this calculator

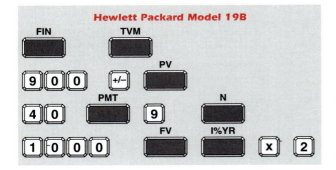

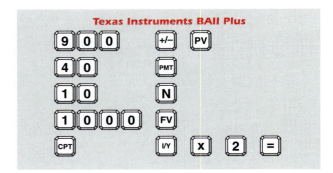

846

FIGURE C-5

Continuous Compounding of an Account

Suppose you want to calculate the future value of $100 deposited in an account that has a stated rate of 12 percent and on which interest is compounded continuously. The continuous compounded future value after one year is:

$$FV = \$100(e^{0.12}) = \mathbf{\$112.75}$$

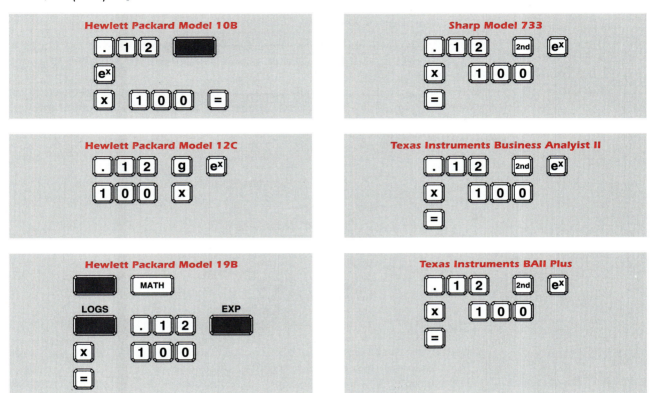

HELPFUL HINTS AND WARNINGS

Helpful Hints

Check Your Work

Always check for the reasonableness of your calculations; it's very easy to hit the wrong key—especially when taking tests. Learn to do your problem with your calculator, and then learn how to quickly evaluate your work and your answers using another method, such as with algebra or tables of factors (see Appendix B).

The Number of Digits to Display

Use at least four places to the right of the decimal place for all calculations. When working with interest rates, it is very important to use more than two decimal places.

You can set your calculator's display program to show a specified number of decimal places. To change the setting to display four decimal places:

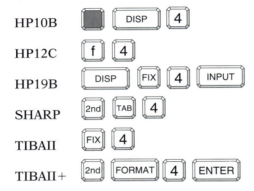

Shortcuts

Use shortcuts for entries that are repeated. Many calculators allow you to key in a value and then key in the number of times that value is to be repeated. For example, if you have to input six consecutive cash flows of $1 each in your HP12C:

where the sequence ⑥ Ⓖ Ⓝⱼ tells the calculator's program that the $1 cash flow is repeated six times.

Warnings

Getting Your Calculator Ready to Use

Your calculator may come from the factory with certain display and calculation settings. For example, the HP10B comes ready to perform calculations using two decimal places (a display setting) and twelve payments per year (a calculation setting). If you need more precision, you need to adjust the display. Also, if you require one payment per period, as in most of our calculations, you need to adjust the payments-per-year setting.

Clearing the Calculator's Registers

The information you input and the results of the calculations you perform are stored in the computer's registers (its memory for the bits and pieces of information). Clear your registers before starting a new calculation. If you fail to clear the registers in your calculator, you will find that the next problem you do will use data left over from the *last* problem—even if you had turned off your calculator since you did the last problem. To clear your calculator:

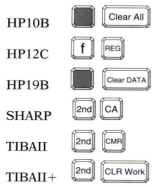

HP10B	▪	Clear All
HP12C	f	REG
HP19B	▪	Clear DATA
SHARP	2nd	CA
TIBAII	2nd	CMR
TIBAII+	2nd	CLR Work

Checking the Timing of the Cash Flows

Check to see whether your calculator is programmed to assume cash flows at the end of the period or at the beginning.

Many calculator brands allow you to specify when cash flows occur (beginning or end of the period), which is useful for annuity due calculations. However, like most registers in the calculator, the calculator remembers the last way you specified the cash flows; so you must change this register if you, say, switch from an annuity due to an ordinary annuity calculation.

For example, to change the setting from end of period to beginning of period:

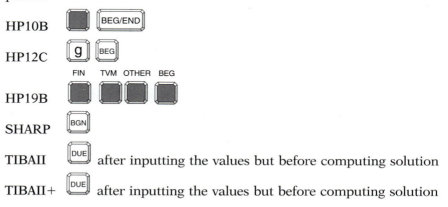

HP10B	▪	BEG/END		
HP12C	g	BEG		
	FIN	TVM OTHER	BEG	
HP19B	▪	▪ ▪	▪	
SHARP	BGN			
TIBAII	DUE	after inputting the values but before computing solution		
TIBAII+	DUE	after inputting the values but before computing solution		

Let's look at a simple example, using the HP10B. Suppose we have a three-cash flow annuity where each cash flow is $1,000 and the discount rate is 6 percent. If we want to calculate the present value of these cash flows on the assumption that they occur at the *end* of each period (that is, this is an ordinary annuity), we first look at the display. If the display consists simply of zeroes (but not the word "BEGIN") we can proceed:

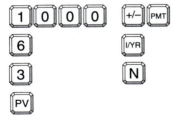

and the answer displayed is 2,673.0119, or $2,673.01. If "BEGIN" appears in the initial display, we must first strike ■ and BEG/END and then proceed as above.

   If we want to calculate the present value of these cash flows on the assumption that they occur at the *beginning* of each period (that is, this is an annuity due) and "BEGIN" is *not* displayed:

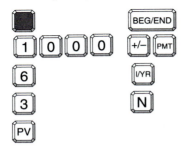

and the answer displayed is 2,833.3927 or $2,833.39.

Checking the Frequency of Payments

Most calculations require one interest compounding per period. Since this is the case, we need to make sure that the calculator program we are using considers only one compounding per period.

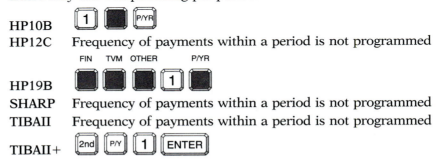

HP10B

HP12C   Frequency of payments within a period is not programmed

HP19B

SHARP   Frequency of payments within a period is not programmed

TIBAII   Frequency of payments within a period is not programmed

TIBAII+

FURTHER READINGS

Additional calculator instruction can be found in:

MARK A. WHITE, "Financial Problem-Solving with an Electronic Calculator," *Financial Practice and Education*, vol. 1, no. 2, Fall/Winter 1991, pp. 73–88.

APPENDIX D

Statistics Primer

INTRODUCTION 853

UNCERTAINTY STATISTICS 853

Probability Distributions 853

Summary Measures 854

Measures of Dispersion 855

    The Range 855

    The Standard Deviation of the Probability Distribution 856

    The Coefficient of Variation 859

    Portfolio Statistics 860

SAMPLE STATISTICS 865

Sample Statistics: One Sample 865

    Summary Measures 865

    Measures of Dispersion 866

    Tests of Hypotheses 869

Regression and Correlation Statistics 869

    Regression 869

    Correlation 879

Caveats 880

INTRODUCTION

Investment and financing decisions depend on the return and risk associated with them. Measuring return and risk requires the use of statistics. This appendix introduces the statistics frequently used in financial management and analysis.

UNCERTAINTY STATISTICS

Most decisions by financial managers are made in the context of uncertainty. Through research and experience, managers can get some measures of the possible outcomes and the likelihood that each will occur. These can be translated into the expected return and risk we need in our decision making.

Probability Distributions

Suppose you believe it to be equally likely that sales next year will be either $0.5 million or $1 million—a 50 percent probability of $0.5 million and a 50 percent probability of $1 million. The figure of 50 percent is the probability that the particular outcome will occur.

The collection of possible outcomes and their probabilities is referred to as a ***probability distribution.*** So the probability distribution of next year's sales is:

Possible outcome	Probability
$ 500,000	50%
1,000,000	50

Suppose we have the probability distribution of next year's sales for the Zoroastrian Company. There are thirteen possible outcomes:

Possible sales	Probability	Possible sales	Probability
$400,000	00.02%	$ 750,000	19.34
450,000	00.29	800,000	12.08
500,000	01.61	850,000	05.38
550,000	05.38	900,000	01.61
600,000	12.08	950,000	00.29
650,000	19.34	1,000,000	00.02
700,000	22.56		

We can represent a probability distribution graphically by plotting the possible outcomes (the sales in our example) on the horizontal axis and the probabilities on the vertical axis. Each vertical bar represents a possible outcome: The taller is the bar, the greater is the outcome's probability. The probability distribution shown in Figure D-1 is referred to as a ***discrete distribution,*** since there are a finite, or discrete, number of possible outcomes.

For convenience, we sometimes approximate a discrete distribution by using a ***continuous distribution,*** which represents an infinite number of possible outcomes. While a continuous distribution may not fit the distribution of our data precisely, we can use it to provide general statements regarding the probability distribution.

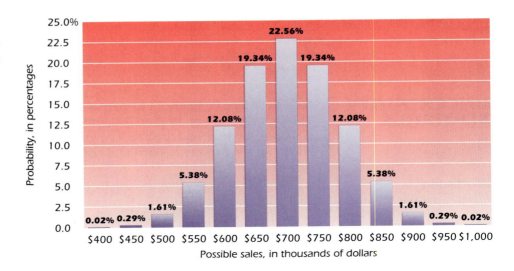

Possible sales, in thousands of dollars

Summary Measures

The probability distribution provides useful information on what may happen and on the likelihood that it will happen. But this may not be precise enough for making decisions. Consider the following probability distribution for the future price of a pound of filet mignon:

Possible outcome	Probability of outcome
$ 5.00	20%
10.00	50
15.00	30

There are two measures that are typically used to "summarize" a probability distribution like this. One is the ***most likely outcome***—the specific outcome with the highest probability (in this example, $10.00).

The other is the ***expected value***—the weighted average of all the possible outcomes, using the probabilities of occurrence as the weights:

$$\text{Expected value} = \begin{pmatrix}\text{probability}\\\text{of first}\\\text{outcome}\end{pmatrix}\begin{pmatrix}\text{first}\\\text{possible}\\\text{outcome}\end{pmatrix} + \begin{pmatrix}\text{probability}\\\text{of second}\\\text{outcome}\end{pmatrix}\begin{pmatrix}\text{second}\\\text{possible}\\\text{outcome}\end{pmatrix}$$

$$+ \cdots + \begin{pmatrix}\text{probability}\\\text{of last}\\\text{outcome}\end{pmatrix}\begin{pmatrix}\text{last}\\\text{possible}\\\text{outcome}\end{pmatrix}$$

In notation form this equation becomes:

$$E(x) = p_1x_1 + p_2x_2 + p_3x_3 + \cdots + p_Nx_N$$

where $E(x)$ = expected value
  N = number of possible outcomes
  i = individual outcome
  x_i = ith possible outcome
  p_i = probability of ith possible outcome

or, using a summation notation:

$$E(x) = \sum_{i=1}^{N} p_i x_i \qquad\qquad [D\text{-}1]$$

The expected price per pound for filet mignon is:

$$E(x) = (0.20 \times \$5.00) + (0.50 \times \$10.00) + (0.30 \times \$15.00)$$
$$= \$1.00 + \$5.00 + \$4.50$$
$$= \mathbf{\$10.50}$$

The *most likely price* is \$10.00, but the *expected price* (considering all possible outcomes and their probabilities) is \$10.50.

In Zoroastrian's sales probability distribution (Figure D-1), we see that the most likely outcome is \$700,000. The expected outcome is calculated in Table D-1. Alas, the expected outcome is equal to the most likely outcome. Why? Because in this example, the probability distribution is *symmetric* about the expected value; that is, the probabilities on either side of the expected value are equal.

Measures of Dispersion

We are often concerned not with a single future outcome but with all possible future outcomes and how each outcome differs from the others.

The degree to which future outcomes differ from one another is referred to as their **dispersion;** it is measured in terms of the range, standard deviation, and coefficient of variation of the probability distribution of the outcomes.

The Range

The **range** is a statistical measure that describes how far apart the two extreme outcomes are. It is the difference between the highest and lowest values of the possible outcomes:

TABLE D-1

Calculation of the Expected Value of the Probability Distribution of Zoroastrian's Next Year's Sales

Probability, p_i	Possible sales, x_i	$p_i x_i$
00.02%	\$ 400,000	\$ 80
00.29	450,000	1,305
01.61	500,000	8,050
05.38	550,000	29,590
12.08	600,000	72,480
19.34	650,000	125,710
22.56	700,000	157,920
19.34	750,000	145,050
12.08	800,000	96,640
05.38	850,000	45,730
01.61	900,000	14,490
00.29	950,000	2,755
00.02	1,000,000	200
		$E(x) = \mathbf{\$700,000}$

Range = highest value − lowest value

The wider the range, the further apart are the two extreme possible outcomes. In the filet mignon example, the range is $15.00 − $5.00 = $10.00. For Zoroastrian's sales, the range is $1,000,000 − $400,000 = $600,000.

The Standard Deviation of the Probability Distribution

Range tells us nothing about the likelihood of the possible outcomes at or between the extremes. However, we are usually interested in *all* possible outcomes.

One way to measure the dispersion of the possible outcomes is to look at how each outcome differs from each of the others. This would require looking at the differences between all possible outcomes and summarizing these differences in a measure we could use. Another is to look at how each possible future outcome differs from the expected outcome.

The **standard deviation** is a measure of how all the possible outcomes deviate, or differ, from the expected value. The standard deviation provides information on each outcome, its distance from the expected value, and its likelihood of occurrence.

The standard deviation is calculated in five steps:

Step 1   Calculate the deviation of each possible outcome from the expected value (that is, the difference between the possible outcome and the expected outcome).

Step 2   Square each individual outcome's deviation from the expected value.

Step 3   Weight each of the squared individual deviations by multiplying the probability of the outcome by the squared deviations.

Step 4   Sum these weighted squared deviations. This is referred to as the **variance** of the probability distribution, denoted $\sigma^2(x)$.

Step 5   Calculate the square root of the variance. This is the standard deviation, $\sigma(x)$. (Note that if the possible outcomes are in dollars, the variance is in terms of squared dollars, which is not very meaningful or easy to interpret, and the standard deviation is in terms of dollars.)

To demonstrate, we calculate the standard deviation for the filet mignon example, where the expected price is $10.50:

Possible outcome	Probability of outcome	Step 1: Deviation from expected value	Step 2: Squared deviation	Step 3: Weighted squared deviation
$ 5.00	20%	−$5.50	30.25	6.050
10.00	50	−0.50	0.25	0.125
15.00	30	+4.50	20.25	6.075
		Step 4	Variance =	**12.25**

Step 5   Standard deviation = $\sqrt{12.25}$ = **$3.50**

We can represent the standard deviation mathematically:

$$\sigma(x) = \sqrt{\sum_{i=1}^{N} p_i[x_i - E(x)]^2} \qquad \text{[D-2]}$$

This measure of a probability distribution tells us:

- *A standard deviation of zero means there is no risk.* If the standard deviation is zero, all possible outcomes *equal* the expected value.
- *The greater the standard deviation, the more the possible outcomes differ from the expected value and therefore the greater is the risk.* The standard deviation is calculated using deviations of outcomes from the expected value; so the greater are these differences, the more dispersed are the possible outcomes and hence the greater is the risk.
- *The standard deviation is in the same unit of measurement as the expected value.* The variance of a distribution is in squared units, but the standard deviation is in the same unit of measure as the expected value.

If a probability distribution is a **normal distribution,** that is, a continuous distribution that is bell-shaped and has certain other characteristics, we can make the following statements about its possible outcomes:

- The expected value is also the most likely value.
- The probability distribution is symmetric about the expected value; that is, there is an equal probability of the actual values falling above or below the expected value.
- The probability distribution can be described completely using only the expected value and the standard deviation.

If we know that the future outcomes are normally distributed and we also know the expected value and the standard deviation, we know that:

- There is a 68.3 percent probability that the outcome will be in the range within minus and plus one standard deviation from the expected value.

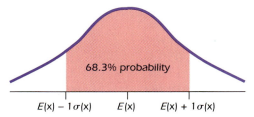

- There is a 95.4 percent probability that the outcome will be in the range within minus and plus two times the standard deviation from the expected value.

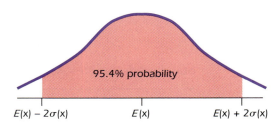

- There is a 99.7 percent probability that the outcome will be in the range within minus and plus three times the standard deviation from the expected value.

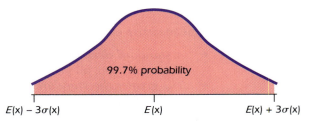

	99.7% probability	
$E(x) - 3\sigma(x)$	$E(x)$	$E(x) + 3\sigma(x)$

The probability distribution in the Zoroastrian example is approximately normally distributed around the expected value, $700,000. Using the standard deviation, calculated in Table D-2, we get a rough idea of how the possible outcomes differ from the expected value:

- There is a 68.3 percent probability that sales will be between ($700,000 − $86,548) = $613,452 and ($700,000 + $86,548) = $786,548.
- There is a 95.4 percent probability that sales will be between [$700,000 − (2 × $86,548)] = $526,904 and [$700,000 + (2 × $86,548)] = $873,096.
- There is a 99.7 percent probability that sales will be between [$700,000 − (3 × $86,548)] = $440,356 and [$700,000 + (3 × $86,548)] = $959,644.

TABLE D-2

Calculation of the Standard Deviation of Zoroastrian's Next Year's Sales

$E(x) = \$700,000.$

Probability, p_i	Possible sales, x_i	$x_i - E(x)$	$[(x_i - E(x)]^2$	$p_i[x_i - E(x)]^2$
00.02%	$ 400,000	−$300,000	90,000,000,000	18,000,000
00.29	450,000	−250,000	62,500,000,000	181,250,000
01.61	500,000	−200,000	40,000,000,000	644,000,000
05.38	550,000	−150,000	22,500,000,000	1,210,500,000
12.08	600,000	−100,000	10,000,000,000	1,208,000,000
19.34	650,000	−50,000	2,500,000,000	483,500,000
22.56	700,000	0	0	0
19.34	750,000	50,000	2,500,000,000	483,500,000
12.08	800,000	100,000	10,000,000,000	1,208,000,000
05.38	850,000	150,000	22,500,000,000	1,210,500,000
01.61	900,000	200,000	40,000,000,000	644,000,000
00.29	950,000	250,000	62,500,000,000	181,250,000
00.02	1,000,000	300,000	90,000,000,000	18,000,000

Variance = **7,490,500,000**

Standard deviation = $\sqrt{7,490,500,000}$ = **$86,548**

Looking at Figure D-1 and comparing the probabilities lying between values if the distribution were normally distributed with the probabilities lying between values as displayed in Figure D-1, we find that if the distribution were normal, the probabilities are somewhat different:[1]

Interval	Expected probability	Actual probability
One standard deviation from the expected value	68.3%	61.24%
Two standard deviations from the expected value	95.4	96.16
Three standard deviations from the expected value	99.7	99.96

The Coefficient of Variation

Often we are not looking at only one probability distribution. For example, when comparing the expected return and risk of two projects, we cannot merely compare the standard deviation of each project in order to decide which has more risk. Remember: The standard deviation gives us a measure of dispersion *about the expected value*. If the expected values of the projects are different, their standard deviations will not be comparable. But generally, that's just what we need to do: Compare projects that have different expected values.

The way we can do this is to divide each project's standard deviation by its expected value. This produces a measure of dispersion, called the ***coefficient of variation,*** which we can use to draw conclusions about which probability distribution has more dispersion. Because the coefficient of variation gives us a measure of the standard deviation per unit of expected value, and because the standard deviation is a measure of risk, the coefficient of variation tells us how much risk there is per unit of expected value.

$$\text{Coefficient of variation} = \frac{\text{standard deviation}}{\text{expected value}} = \frac{\sigma}{E(x)} \qquad [D\text{-}3]$$

Let's look at two probability distributions, each pertaining to possible returns for a product:

PRODUCT 1			**PRODUCT 2**		
Market scenario	Probability	Possible return	Market scenario	Probability	Possible return
Good	20%	30%	Good	20%	20%
Normal	50	20	Normal	50	0
Bad	30	−20	Bad	30	−10

The calculation of the expected return and standard deviation of the possible returns is shown in Table D-3 for both products. Which product has

[1] The probability of Zoroastrian's sales in the range from $613,452 to $786,548 is 19.34 percent + 22.56 percent + 19.34 percent = 61.24 percent.

TABLE D-3

Calculation of the Expected Return and Standard Deviation of the Returns for Products 1 and 2

Probability, p_i	Possible return on assets, x_i	$p_i x_i$	$x_i - E(x)$	$[x_i - E(x)]^2$	$p_i[x_i - E(x)]^2$
		PRODUCT 1			
20%	30%	0.06	0.20	0.0400	0.00800
50	20	0.10	0.10	0.0100	0.00500
30	−20	−0.06	−0.30	0.0900	0.02700
		$E(x) = \mathbf{0.10}$			$\sigma^2(x) = \mathbf{0.04000}$

$\sigma(x) = \sqrt{0.04000} = \mathbf{0.2000}$ or **20.00%**

		PRODUCT 2			
20%	20%	0.04	0.19	0.0361	0.00722
50	0	0.00	−0.01	0.0001	0.00005
30	−10	−0.03	−0.11	0.0121	0.00363
		$E(x) = \mathbf{0.01}$			$\sigma^2(x) = \mathbf{0.01090}$

$\sigma(x) = \sqrt{0.01090} = \mathbf{0.1044}$ or **10.44%**

more risk? Product 1 has a higher standard deviation, but it also has a higher expected return. And because the standard deviation is a measure of deviations from the expected value, we can't just compare standard deviations to see which is riskier. But we can calculate the coefficient of variation for each product.

$$\text{Coefficient of variation, Product 1} = \frac{20\%}{10\%} = \mathbf{2} \qquad \text{Coefficient of variation, Product 2} = \frac{10.44\%}{1\%} = \mathbf{10.44}$$

Product 1 has a smaller coefficient of variation, which means that it has less risk per unit of expected return.

Portfolio Statistics

Suppose a firm is considering investing in *both* Product 1 and Product 2. This means we are interested in determining the risk and expected return of a collection of investments—a portfolio. Determining the expected return and risk associated with a portfolio composed of Products 1 and 2 requires knowing how much the firm invests in each. Suppose the firm invests $40 million in Product 1 and $60 million in Product 2. The portfolio, therefore, is 40 percent invested in Product 1 and 60 percent in Product 2.

Portfolio Expected Return

The return on a portfolio is the weighted average of the returns on the assets in that portfolio, where the weights are the proportions of the portfolio invested in each asset. If the "Good" scenario takes place, we would expect a

860

return of 24 percent on the portfolio of which 40 percent is the return on Product 1 and 60 percent is the return on Product 2:

Portfolio return, good scenario $= (40\% \times 30\%) + (60\% \times 20\%)$
$$= 0.12 \qquad + 0.12$$
$$= \mathbf{0.24} \text{ or } \mathbf{24\%}$$

We can calculate the portfolio return for the other two possible scenarios in the same way:

Portfolio return, normal scenario $= (40\% \times 20\%) + (60\% \times 0\%) = \mathbf{8\%}$

Portfolio return, bad scenario $= [40\% \times (-20\%)] + [60\% \times (-10\%)] = \mathbf{-14\%}$

The calculation of the expected return on the portfolio composed of Products 1 and 2 is shown in Table D-4(a).

Portfolio Risk

The portfolio's risk can be measured using the standard deviation of the possible outcomes just as for a single probability distribution. For the portfolio of Products 1 and 2, there are three different outcomes: 24 percent, 8 percent, and -14 percent. The portfolio standard deviation, as calculated in Table D-4(a), is 13.60 percent, which is less than that of Product 1 alone, but more than that of Product 2 alone.

TABLE D-4

Statistics for the Portfolio Composed of Products 1 and 2

(a) Calculation of return on assets.

Probability, p_i	Possible return on assets, x_i	$p_i x_i$	$x_i - E(x)$	$[x_i - E(x)]^2$	$p_i[x_i - E(x)]^2$
20%	24%	0.048	0.1940	0.03764	0.00753
50	8	0.040	0.0340	0.00116	0.00058
30	-14	-0.042	-0.1860	0.03460	0.01038
		$E(x) = \mathbf{0.046}$			$\sigma^2(x) = \mathbf{0.01849}$

$\sigma(x) = \sqrt{0.01849} = \mathbf{0.1360}$ or $\mathbf{13.60\%}$

(b) Calculation of the covariance between the possible returns for Products 1 and 2.

Probability, p_i	Deviation of Product 1's return from its expected return	Deviation of Product 2's return from its expected return	Multiply deviations	Weight by probability
20%	0.20	0.19	0.038	0.0076
50	0.10	-0.01	-0.001	-0.0005
30	-0.30	-0.11	0.033	0.0099
			Covariance $= \mathbf{0.0170}$	

There is a direct relation between the portfolio's standard deviation (and its variance) and the standard deviation of each of the assets in the portfolio. The link between the individual assets' standard deviations and the portfolio's risk is the covariance. The ***covariance*** is a measure of how the assets' returns are related: Do they tend to go up at the same time? Do they tend to go down at the same time? Do they tend to move in opposite directions?

The statistical measure of covariance is:

$$\text{Covariance of returns for assets designated as 1 and 2} = \sum_{i=1}^{N} p_i \, [x_{1i} - E(x_{1i})][x_{2i} - E(x_{2i})] \qquad [\text{D-4}]$$

where x_{1i} and x_{2i} are the ith possible returns for asset 1 and asset 2, respectively. You can see in Equation D-4 that a positive covariance will result if the first asset's returns are above their expected values when the second asset's returns are above their expected values and if the first asset's returns are below their expected values when the second asset's returns are below their expected values. If, however, the first asset's returns tend to be above their expected values when the second asset's returns tend to be below their expected values (and vice versa), a negative covariance will result.

The covariance between Products 1 and 2 is 0.0170, as shown in Table D-4(*b*). Since the covariance is in squared units of measure (in our example, returns of Product 1 multiplied by returns of Product 2), it is not easily interpreted. So we convert the covariance to make interpretation easier. If we divide the covariance by the product of the standard deviations of the two assets, we arrive at a statistic called the ***correlation:***

$$\text{Correlation of returns for assets 1 and 2} = \frac{\text{covariance of returns on assets 1 and 2}}{\left(\begin{array}{c}\text{standard deviation} \\ \text{of returns} \\ \text{on asset 1}\end{array}\right)\left(\begin{array}{c}\text{standard deviation} \\ \text{of returns} \\ \text{on asset 2}\end{array}\right)} \qquad [\text{D-5}]$$

Like the covariance, the correlation is a measure of the association between the returns on the two assets, that is, a measure of how their future returns are expected to move together. The correlation, by construction, is bounded by $+1$ and -1.

- If the assets' returns move together in tandem, the correlation between them is $+1$ and we say they are ***perfectly positively correlated.***
- If the assets' returns tend to move together, but not perfectly, the correlation between them is between zero and $+1$ and we say they are ***positively correlated.***
- If the assets' returns do not move together in any way, the correlation between them is zero and we say they are ***uncorrelated.***
- If the assets' returns move in opposite directions, but not always to the same degree, the correlation between them is between zero and -1 and we say they are ***negatively correlated.***
- If the assets' returns move in opposite directions to one another and in the same degree, the correlation between them is -1 and we say they are ***perfectly negatively correlated.***

The correlation between the returns on Products 1 and 2 is:

$$\text{Correlation of returns for Products 1 and 2} = \frac{0.0170}{(0.2000)(0.1044)} = \mathbf{0.8142}$$

This means that the returns on Products 1 and 2 are *positively correlated*: Their returns tend to move together in the same direction but not precisely by the same degree, that is, the correlation is not *perfect*.

There is a direct relation between the portfolio standard deviation (and its variance) and the covariance of the two products' returns on assets. The portfolio standard deviation is affected by:

1. The proportion invested in each asset.
2. The variance of each asset's possible returns.
3. The covariance between the assets' returns.

Let w_1 and w_2 represent the proportion of the portfolio invested in assets 1 and 2, respectively; let σ_1^2 and σ_2^2 represent the variance of assets 1 and 2, respectively; and let $\text{cov}_{1,2}$ represent the covariance between the returns on the two assets. Then:

$$\text{Portfolio variance} = w_1^2\sigma_1^2 + w_2^2\sigma_2^2 + 2\,\text{cov}_{1,2}w_1w_2$$

and:

$$\text{Portfolio standard deviation} = \sqrt{w_1^2\sigma_1^2 + w_2^2\sigma_2^2 + 2\,\text{cov}_{1,2}w_1w_2} \qquad \text{[D-6]}$$

To calculate the portfolio variance and standard deviation for the portfolio consisting of Products 1 and 2:

where
$$w_1 = 0.40 \qquad w_2 = 0.60$$
$$\sigma_1^2 = 0.04000 \qquad \sigma_2^2 = 0.01090$$
$$\text{cov}_{1,2} = 0.0170$$

$$\begin{aligned}
\text{Portfolio variance} &= (0.16 \times 0.04000) + (0.36 \times 0.01090) + (2 \times 0.0170 \times 0.40 \times 0.60) \\
&= 0.00640 + 0.00392 + 0.00816 \\
&= \mathbf{0.01848}
\end{aligned}$$

and the standard deviation is the square root of the variance:

$$\text{Portfolio standard deviation} = \sqrt{0.01848} = \mathbf{0.1360} \text{ or } \mathbf{13.60\%}$$

which is the same standard deviation we calculated in Table D-4(*a*).

Taking a closer look at the relation between the covariance, correlation, and portfolio risk, we can make some generalizations.

Generalization 1   *If the correlation is perfect and positive, the portfolio standard deviation is the weighted average of the individual assets' standard deviations.* If the correlation is perfect (correlation = +1), this means that the covariance is $\sigma_1\sigma_2$. Substituting $\sigma_1\sigma_2$ for $\text{cov}_{1,2}$ in the equation for the portfolio standard deviation:

$$\begin{aligned}
\text{Portfolio standard deviation} &= \sqrt{w_1^2\sigma_1^2 + w_2^2\sigma_2^2 + 2\sigma_1\sigma_2w_1w_2} \\
&= w_1\sigma_1 + w_2\sigma_2
\end{aligned}$$

which is the same as saying the portfolio standard deviation is the weighted average of the individual assets' standard deviations. In the case of Products 1 and 2, if their returns were *not* correlated, the portfolio standard deviation would be: $(0.40 \times 0.2000) + (0.60 \times 0.1044) = 0.1426$ or 14.26 percent.

Generalization 2   *If there is less than perfect positive correlation among the assets' returns, the portfolio standard deviation is less than the weighted average of the individual assets' standard deviations.* If the correlation is less than $+1$, the portfolio standard deviation is less than the weighted average of the individual assets' standard deviations. In the case of Products 1 and 2, we see that since they are positively, but not perfectly, correlated, the portfolio standard deviation is 13.60 percent which is less than 14.26 percent. This is the idea behind **diversification:** adding assets to a portfolio whose returns are not perfectly positively correlated will result in a reduction of portfolio risk, to a point.

Generalization 3   *If there is no correlation among the assets' returns, the portfolio variance is the weighted average of the individual assets' variances.* If the correlation is zero (and, therefore, $\text{cov}_{1,2} = 0$):

Portfolio variance $= w_1^2\sigma_1^2 + w_2^2\sigma_2^2$

and

Portfolio standard deviation $= \sqrt{w_1^2\sigma_1^2 + w_2^2\sigma_2^2}$

which is the same as saying the portfolio variance is the weighted average of the individual securities' variances. If the returns on Product 1 and Product 2 were not correlated, the portfolio variance would be 0.01032 and the standard deviation would be 0.1016, or 10.16 percent. But since the returns on these two products *are* correlated, the portfolio standard deviation is above 10.16 percent.

Generalization 4   *If the assets' returns are perfectly negatively correlated, the portfolio standard deviation is reduced.* If the assets' returns are perfectly negatively correlated (correlation $= -1$), the covariance is equal to $-\sigma_1\sigma_2$, and

$$\text{Portfolio standard deviation} = \sqrt{w_1^2\sigma_1^2 + w_2^2\sigma_2^2 - 2\sigma_1\sigma_2 w_1 w_2}$$

which means that risk is *reduced substantially* by combining the two assets. If the assets were combined to form a portfolio such that $w_1\sigma_1 = w_2\sigma_2$, the portfolio would have no risk: When one asset's returns were up, the other assets' returns would be down by a like amount, and there would be no portfolio risk. This is diversification taken to the extreme.

SAMPLE STATISTICS

Financial managers look at past information to gauge performance over a previous period and to predict the future. When we look at the past, we are generally looking at representative values from a sample of observations. And we look at the dispersion of sample values to see how widely they differ as well as to help us judge the reliability of how representative they are.

Sample Statistics: One Sample

Summary Measures

Often, we want to get a single, representative measure from the sample. The two most common measures to describe a sample are the **mean,** also referred to as the **average,** and the **median,** the middle value. Together, they are referred to as **measures of central tendency.**

Let's look at a sample of different firms' sales for the past year.

Firm	Sales
A	$100
B	200
C	300
D	200
E	100

The mean sales value is the sum of the individual sales figures divided by the sum of the number of firms:

$$\text{Mean sales} = \frac{\$900}{5 \text{ firms}} = \mathbf{\$180} \text{ per firm}$$

To determine median sales, first rank the sales in numerical order (from lowest to highest dollar amount) and then find the middle value:

Firm	Sales
A	$100
E	100
B	200
D	200
C	300

The median sales value is $200.

Let's look at another example, a sample of current ratios for 1991 for firms in the retail department store industry, shown in Table D-5.

Current Ratios of Department Store Retailers, 1991

Corporation	Current ratio, 1991	Corporation	Current ratio, 1991
Alexander's	1.761	Neiman-Marcus Group	1.970
Bon-Ton Stores	2.872	Peebles	2.371
Carter Hawley Hale Stores	2.465	Penney (J. C.)	2.779
Crowley Milner	1.752	Proffitts	4.686
Dillard Department Stores	2.833	Pubco	1.828
Federated Department Stores	2.003	Schottenstein Stores	2.277
Gottschalks	2.092	Sears, Roebuck	1.576
Jacobson Stores	2.962	Strawbridge & Clothier	2.424
Macy (R. H.)	1.280	Valley Fair	4.385
May Department Stores	3.005	Younkers	2.288
Mercantile Stores	6.438	Zions	2.696
Meyer (Fred)	1.557		

SOURCE: Standard & Poor's *Compustat PC Plus* (CD-ROM).

The sample mean, $\overline{X}$, is calculated by summing all the sample values and dividing by the number of values, where X_i designates each value and n is the total number of values:

$$\overline{X} = \frac{\text{sum of all sample values}}{\text{number of observations in the sample}} = \frac{\sum_{i=1}^{n} X_i}{n} \qquad [D\text{-}7]$$

The sum of all the current ratios is 60.3. Dividing this sum by the number of ratios, twenty-three, we get a mean current ratio of 2.622.

To determine the median of the sample of current ratios, we first rank the sample firms by their current ratio. Since the sample has twenty-three firms, the median is the current ratio for the twelfth firm when they are ranked. As shown in Table D-6, Peebles has the median current ratio, 2.371. There are eleven firms with current ratios above and eleven firms with current ratios below this value.

Ala Mode

In addition to the mean and the median, another measure of central tendency is the **mode,** or **modal value:** the most frequently observed value in the sample. In our current-ratio example, as in many cases using financial data, there is no mode.

Measures of Dispersion

There are several measures of dispersion we can use to tell us how widely the sample observations differ from one another.

- *Range.* The difference between the highest and lowest values.
- *Variance.* The average of the squared deviations from the mean.

TABLE D-6

Calculation of Department Store Retailers, Median Current Ratio, 1991

Rank[a]	Corporation	Current ratio, 1991
1	Macy (R. H.)	1.280
2	Sears, Roebuck	1.576
3	Crowley Milner	1.752
4	Alexander's	1.761
5	Meyer (Fred)	1.557
6	Neiman-Marcus Group	1.970
7	Pubco	1.828
8	Federated Department Stores	2.003
9	Gottschalks	2.092
10	Schottenstein Stores	2.277
11	Younkers	2.288
12	Peebles	2.371 ← Sample median
13	Strawbridge & Clothier	2.424
14	Carter Hawley Hale Stores	2.465
15	Zions	2.696
16	Penney (J. C.)	2.779
17	Bon-Ton Stores	2.872
18	Dillard Department Stores	2.833
19	Jacobson Stores	2.962
20	May Department Stores	3.005
21	Valley Fair	4.385
22	Proffitts	4.686
23	Mercantile Stores	6.438

[a]1 = lowest, 23 = highest rank.

- *Standard deviation.* The square root of the variance.
- *Coefficient of variation.* The ratio of the standard deviation to the mean.

The standard deviation of a sample is calculated using five steps that are similar, but not identical, to the steps we used to calculate the standard deviation of a probability distribution:

Step 1 Calculate the deviation of each sample observation from the sample mean.

Step 2 Calculate the squared deviation of each sample observation from the sample mean.

Step 3 Sum the squared deviations. This is called the **variation.**

Step 4 Divide the variation by the number of sample observations minus one. This is the **sample variance.**

Step 5 Take the square root of the variance. This is the **sample standard deviation.**

The standard deviation for the sample of sales for the five firms is calculated by first summing the squared deviations from the mean of $180:

Firm	Sales	Step 1: Deviation from sample mean	Step 2: Squared deviation
A	$100	−$ 80	6,400
B	200	20	400
C	300	120	14,400
D	200	20	400
E	100	−80	6,400

Step 3   Variation = **28,000**

Step 4   Sample variance = $\dfrac{28,000}{4}$ = **7,000**

Step 5   Sample standard deviation = $\sqrt{7,000}$ = **$83.67**

In mathematical notation the variation is given as:

$$\text{Variation} = \sum_{i=1}^{n} (X_i - \overline{X})^2$$

and the sample variance by:

$$\text{Sample variance} = \frac{\sum_{i=1}^{n}(X_i - \overline{X})^2}{n - 1}$$

Using notation, the sample standard deviation, s, is:

$$s = \sqrt{\frac{\sum_{i=1}^{n}(X_i - \overline{X})^2}{n - 1}} \qquad\qquad [D\text{-}8]$$

The larger is s, the more dispersed (spread out) are the sample values.
    If we want to compare dispersion between *samples*, we need to adjust the standard deviation by the sample mean, which gives us the coefficient of variation:

$$\text{Coefficient of variation} = \frac{s}{\overline{X}} \qquad\qquad [D\text{-}9]$$

The coefficient of variation for the sample of five firms' sales is:

$$\text{Coefficient of variation} = \frac{\$83.67}{\$180.00} = \mathbf{0.465}$$

This means that the standard deviation is almost half the mean.

Tests of Hypotheses

The mean and sample standard deviation are descriptive statistics—they describe the sample. But we may also want to test specific hypotheses using the sample information. Consider our example of sales of five stores. Mean sales are $180. Is that significantly different from, say, $200? We looked at only five firms, and the sales of these firms ranged from $100 to $300. Considering that we are looking at a sample of just five firms with differing sales, we can't answer the question using only the sample mean.

To test a hypothesis, we need to calculate a test statistic. While the testing of hypotheses is beyond the scope of this text, to perform a test of a hypothesis we would need the sample mean, the sample standard deviation, and the sample size. Given this information, along with some judgment about how confident we want to be regarding our test, we could test a particular hypothesis.

Regression and Correlation Statistics

By looking at the trend in a firm's sales over time, can we predict what the firm's sales might be in the future? Looking at the firm's capital expenditures and its market share can we tell if spending more on capital projects results in an increase in market share? What about the relation between a firm's sales and the economy? Does the firm do well when the economy is doing well? Does the firm do well when the economy is doing badly?

Regression and correlation statistics, which are based on historical data, help us represent relations among variables. By looking at historical relations among variables, we can formulate expectations about their *future* relationships.

Regression

One way of looking at relationships among variables is to determine how one variable may explain another. For example, it seems reasonable to assume that car sales may be explained by how well the economy is doing. Using gross domestic product (GDP) to measure the performance of the economy, we could apply regression analysis to see whether GDP explains car sales.

The variable we want to explain, say, car sales, is referred to as the ***dependent variable,*** since we are looking at how it *depends* on the GDP. GDP in our example is referred to as the ***independent variable*** or the ***explanatory variable,*** since we are using it to *explain* car sales. If we are using only one independent variable, the regression is referred to as a ***simple regression.*** If we are using more than one variable to explain the dependent variable (say, GDP and interest rates to explain car sales), the regression is referred to as a ***multiple regression.***

Before looking at formulas and crunching numbers, let's look at what regression can do for us. The objective of regression is to explain why a variable varies. In Figure D-2, look at the variation in monthly returns for McDonald's Corporation common stock for 1985. The mean return over the period is 4.06 percent, the low is −3.69 percent, and the high is 11.99 percent.

**Returns on the Mc-
Donald's Corporation
Common Stock,
Monthly, 1985**

SOURCE: Standard & Poor's *Daily
Stock Price Record.*

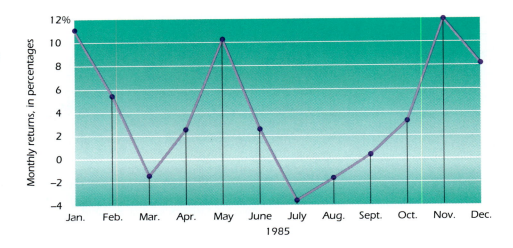

Why this variation? In statistical terms, we are asking; Why do the Mc-Donald's returns differ from month to month? Or, why do the McDonald's monthly returns differ from their average return?

Perhaps the returns on a particular stock change because returns in the market in general change. Over this same period, the mean monthly return on the Standard & Poor's 500 Stock Index (S&P 500) is 2.02 percent, and ranges from -3.47 percent to 7.41 percent. If we look at the McDonald's returns and the returns on the S&P 500 in Figure D-3, we see that the returns on the McDonald's common stock do tend to move along with those of the S&P 500: When the McDonald's returns are up, the returns on the S&P 500 Index are up, and vice versa. But this is not a perfect relation.

Let's represent the monthly returns for McDonald's stock as $Y_1, Y_2, \ldots, Y_{12}$, where Y_1 represents the return for January 1985, Y_2 the return for February 1985, and so on; and let's represent the market's returns (the returns on the S&P 500) as $X_1, X_2, \ldots, X_{12}$. The plot of the Y_i's and X_i's, with the Y_i's on the vertical axis and the X_i's on the horizontal axis, is shown in Figure D-4. We can see that there is, basically, a positive relation between these vari-

FIGURE D-3

**Returns on the Mc-
Donald's Corporation
Common Stock and
on S&P 500 Stock In-
dex, Monthly, 1985**

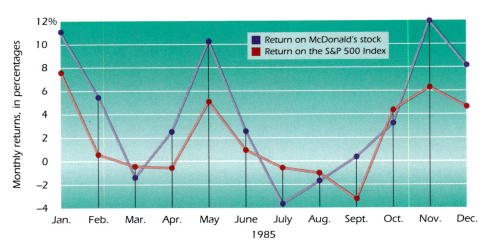

FIGURE D-4

Returns on McDonald's Common Stock vs. Returns on S&P 500 Stock Index, Monthly, 1985

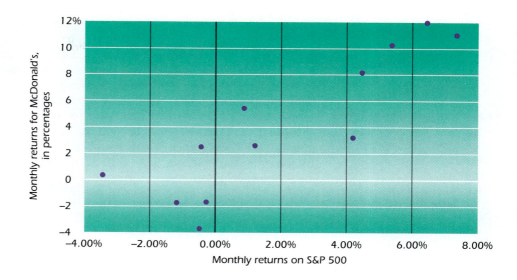

ables: when the McDonald's returns are up, so are those of the market; when the McDonald's returns are down, so are the market's.

We can specify the relation between McDonald's (the Y_i's) and the market (the X_i's) using a ***regression equation:***

$$Y_i = \alpha + \beta X_i \qquad\qquad [D\text{-}10]$$

Equation D-10 states that there is a linear (straight-line) relationship between the common stock returns of McDonald's and the returns on the market. The slope of the line is β, and the intercept on the Y axis is α. We represent this equation graphically with the ***regression line.***

Another way of representing this relation is with a ***regression model:***

$$Y_i = \alpha + \beta X_i + \epsilon_i \qquad\qquad [D\text{-}11]$$

The relation between the X's and Y's may not be a perfect straight line—some of the Y and X combinations may be off the line. That's where ϵ_i comes in: ϵ_i is the error term, which represents how much of the McDonald's return is *not* explained (predicted) by this straight-line equation.

Estimation

To determine the slope and intercept that best fit the relation between the McDonald's returns and the returns on the S&P 500 we use the ***ordinary least squares*** (OLS) method. We realize that there will be some difference, or error, between any line we try to fit to the observed data and the actual values, and the idea of OLS is to minimize that difference by minimizing the square of the "errors" in order to obtain the line that best fits the data.

Using OLS, the slope is estimated as the ratio of the covariance between the independent and dependent variables to the variance of the independent variable:

$$\beta = \frac{\text{covariance between independent and dependent variables}}{\text{variance of independent variable}}$$

> ϵ_i has many names, including the ***residual term,*** the ***disturbance term,*** and the ***error term.***

871

The slope is the measure of how much, on average, the dependent variable changes in response to a change in the independent variable. For example, if the slope is 3, then a one-unit (dollars, percent, whatever the measure) change in the independent variable will cause the dependent variable to change by three units. The slope is therefore a measure of the sensitivity of the dependent variable to changes in the independent variable.

To solve for β we must first solve for the covariance of the independent (X) and dependent (Y) variables and for the variance of the independent variable (X). The covariance is a measure of how much one variable differs from its mean as the *other* variable differs from *its* mean (that is, how two variables "co-vary"):

$$\text{Covariance of X and Y} = \frac{\sum_{i=1}^{n}(X_i - \overline{X})(Y_i - \overline{Y})}{n - 1} \qquad \text{[D-12]}$$

where $\overline{X}$ is the mean of the X_i's, $\overline{Y}$ is the mean of the Y_i's, and n is the number of observations.

In our McDonald's example:

$\overline{X} = 2.02\%$
$\overline{Y} = 4.06\%$
$n = 12$

The calculation of $\sum_{i=1}^{n}(X_i - \overline{X})(Y_i - \overline{Y})$ is shown in Table D-7. Using these data,

$$\text{Covariance of X and Y} = \frac{0.0177}{11} = \textbf{0.00161}$$

The equation used to solve for the variance of the independent variable, X, is:

$$\text{Variance of X} = \frac{\sum_{i=1}^{n}(X_i - \overline{X})^2}{n - 1}$$

The calculation of $\sum_{i=1}^{n}(X_i - \overline{X})^2$ is given in Table D-7:

$$\text{Variance of X} = \frac{0.0132}{11} = \textbf{0.0012}$$

The slope of the line is the ratio of the covariance of the two variables to the variance of the independent variable:

$$\hat{\beta} = \frac{\dfrac{\sum_{i=1}^{n}(X_i - \overline{X})(Y_i - \overline{Y})}{n - 1}}{\dfrac{\sum_{i=1}^{n}(X_i - \overline{X})^2}{n - 1}} \qquad \text{[D-13]}$$

Earlier in the appendix, we calculated the co-variance between the returns for two different probability distributions. The sample covariance calculated here is similar: The difference between an observation on a variable and its mean is multiplied by the difference between an observation on the other variable and its mean.

TABLE D-7

Calculation of Regression Line for McDonald's Corporation Common Stock Returns vs. Returns on Standard & Poor's 500 Stock Index, Monthly, 1985

Month in 1985	Returns on McDonald's stock, Y_i	Returns on S&P 500 Stock Index, X_i	$Y_i - \overline{Y}$	$(Y_i - \overline{Y})^2$	$X_i - \overline{X}$	$(X_i - \overline{X})^2$	$(Y_i - \overline{Y})(X_i - \overline{X})$
January	0.1105	0.0741	0.0699	0.0049	0.0539	0.0029	0.0038
February	0.0547	0.0087	0.0141	0.0002	−0.0115	0.0001	−0.0002
March	−0.0166	−0.0029	−0.0572	0.0033	−0.0231	0.0005	0.0013
April	0.0253	−0.0046	−0.0153	0.0002	−0.0248	0.0006	0.0004
May	0.1025	0.0541	0.0619	0.0038	0.0339	0.0011	0.0021
June	0.0262	0.0121	−0.0144	0.0002	−0.0081	0.0001	0.0001
July	−0.0369	−0.0049	−0.0775	0.0060	−0.0251	0.0006	0.0019
August	−0.0171	−0.0120	−0.0577	0.0033	−0.0322	0.0010	0.0019
September	0.0039	−0.0347	−0.0367	0.0013	−0.0549	0.0030	0.0020
October	0.0324	0.0425	−0.0082	0.0001	0.0223	0.0005	−0.0002
November	0.1199	0.0651	0.0793	0.0063	0.0449	0.0020	0.0036
December	0.0819	0.0451	0.0413	0.0017	0.0249	0.0006	0.0010
Total	**0.4872**	**0.2424**	**0.0000**	**0.0314**	**0.0000**	**0.0132**	**0.0177**

$$\overline{Y} = \frac{0.4872}{12} = \textbf{0.0406 or 4.06\%.}$$

$$\overline{X} = \frac{0.2424}{12} = \textbf{0.0202 or 2.02\%.}$$

$$\text{Standard deviation of Y} = \sqrt{\frac{0.0314}{11}} = \textbf{0.0534}$$

$$\text{Standard deviation of X} = \sqrt{\frac{0.0132}{11}} = \textbf{0.0346}$$

$\hat{\beta}$ is the estimated slope. Because we are working with a sample of values, the best we can do is calculate an estimate of the true slope, β. For the McDonald's regression line:

$$\hat{\beta} = \frac{0.00161}{0.0012} = \textbf{1.3417}$$

The *intercept*, α, is the value of the point at which the regression line intersects the dependent-variable axis. It is the value of the dependent variable if the independent variable is zero. In a simple regression, we calculate the intercept as:

$$\hat{\alpha} = \overline{Y} - \hat{\beta}\overline{X} \tag{D-14}$$

In the McDonald's example, the intercept is:

$$\hat{\alpha} = \overline{Y} - \hat{\beta}\overline{X}$$
$$= 0.0406 - (1.3417 \times 0.0202)$$
$$= \textbf{0.0135}$$

Since most calculators and spreadsheet software have regression programs, let's focus on the interpretation of the estimates. Using Equation D-10:

$$\text{Monthly return on McDonald's stock} = 0.0135 + 1.3417 \left(\text{monthly return on S\&P 500 Index} \right)$$

This means that:

- If the monthly return on the S&P 500 is 0 percent, we expect a return of 1.35 percent on McDonald's stock.
- If the S&P 500 Index has a return of 2 percent, we predict the return on McDonald's stock will be $0.0135 + (1.3417 \times 2$ percent$) = 4.03$ percent.
- If the monthly return on the S&P 500 goes *up* 1 percent, we expect the monthly return on the McDonald's stock to go up by 1.3417×1 percent, or 1.3417 percent.
- If the monthly return on the S&P 500 goes down 1 percent, we expect the monthly return on the McDonald's stock to go down by 1.3417×1 percent, or 1.3417 percent.

For each value of the independent variable we observe, we can predict a value of the dependent value according to the regression line, $\hat{Y}_i$. For exam-

---

TABLE D-8

Actual Returns on McDonald's Common Stock vs. Returns Predicted Using Regression Line Estimated for 1985

Month in 1985	Actual return on McDonald's stock, Y_i	Predicted return on McDonald's stock, $\hat{Y}_i$	Residual, $\epsilon_i = Y_i - \hat{Y}_i$
January	0.1105	0.1129	−0.0024
February	0.0547	0.0252	0.0295
March	−0.0166	0.0096	−0.0262
April	0.0253	0.0073	0.0180
May	0.1025	0.0861	0.0164
June	0.0262	0.0297	−0.0035
July	−0.0369	0.0069	−0.0438
August	−0.0171	−0.0026	−0.0145
September	0.0039	−0.0331	0.0370
October	0.0324	0.0705	−0.0381
November	0.1199	0.1008	0.0191
December	0.0819	0.0740	0.0079

EXAMPLES:

$\hat{Y}_{Feb} = 0.0135 + (1.3417 \times 0.0087) = 2.52\%$

$\hat{Y}_{Oct} = 0.0135 + (1.3417 \times 0.0425) = 7.05\%$

For each value of the independent variable we observe, we can predict a value of the dependent value according to the regression line, $\hat{Y}_i$. For example, the return on the S&P 500 in February 1985 was 0.87 percent. If the regression line were a perfect fit, the McDonald's return would be:

$$\hat{Y}_{Feb} = 0.0135 + (1.3417 \times 0.0087) = 2.52\%$$

But the actual return on the McDonald's common stock in February was 5.47 percent. So the line is not a perfect fit: The difference between the actual return, Y_{Feb}, and the predicted return, $\hat{Y}_{Feb}$, is the error of 5.47 percent $- 2.52$ percent $= 2.95$ percent. The error ("residual") for each observation is calculated and shown in Table D-8. The regression line is plotted in Figure D-5. The vertical distance between the actual return on the McDonald's stock and the return predicted from the regression line is the error.

The regression line we just estimated used only twelve observations. If we expand the number of observations to, say, sixty months, we get a more reliable estimate of the relation between McDonald's stock returns and the returns on the market. The regression line estimate based on monthly observations from 1985 through 1989 (sixty months) is:

$$\text{Monthly return on McDonald's stock} = 0.007 + 1.02 \left(\text{monthly return on S\&P 500 Index} \right)$$

Over the longer period, we estimate a lower slope coefficient (1.02 versus 1.34) and a lower intercept (0.007 versus 0.0135). But the interpretation is similar: For a 1 percent change in the market return we expect a 1.02 percent change in McDonald's return. The observations and the estimated regression line for this sixty-month period are shown in Figure D-6.

If we have a multiple regression (that is, more than one independent variable), the regression model is expanded. For example, if there are j independent variables:

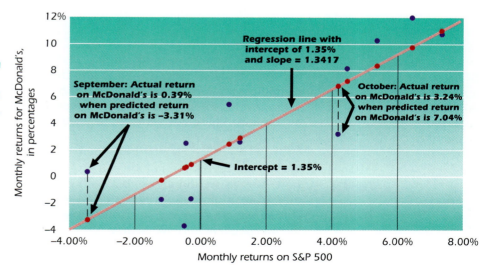

FIGURE D-5

Regression Line Summarizing Relation between the Returns on McDonald's Common Stock and Returns on S&P 500 Stock Index, Monthly, 1985

FIGURE D-6

Estimated Regression Line Summarizing Relation between McDonald's Corporation Common Stock Returns and Returns on S&P 500 Stock Index, Monthly, 1985–1989

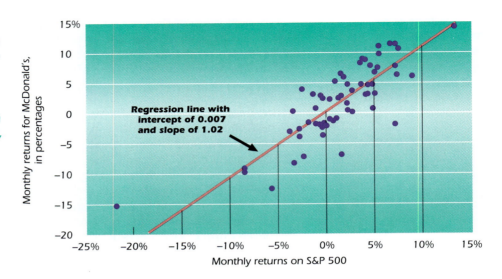

$$Y_i = \alpha + \beta_1 X_{1i} + \beta_2 X_{2i} + \cdots + \beta_j X_{ji} + \epsilon_i \qquad \text{[D-15]}$$

where β_j is the slope coefficient on the jth independent variable; and X_{ji} is the ith observation on the jth variable. The calculations of the slopes and intercept become more complicated when there is more than one explanatory variable, but it can be done easily enough using computer statistical programs.

Regression statistics can be used to test whether the relation among variables is a strong one and to test specific hypotheses. Using the estimated regression line and related statistics, we can:

- Describe what proportion of the variation in the dependent variable we were able to explain by introducing the independent variables.
- Test whether the independent variables explain a significant portion of the dependent variable's variation.
- Test whether a slope or the intercept is equal to a specific value (say, zero).

Testing hypotheses and judging whether the regression line is a good fit use the estimated regression line and the estimation errors. Most statistical computer programs (such as SAS, SPSS, and Minitab) will generate the statistics needed to evaluate the fit of the regression and to perform any tests of hypotheses. These test statistics are beyond the scope of this text.

Time Series and Forecasting

We can use regression to look at a single series of data over time in much the same way as we did above, but with one twist: The independent variable is time instead of market returns or GDP or interest rates or some other variable. If we are studying sales over time, the dependent variable is sales and the independent variable is time. We can represent time several ways, for example, by actual years (1981, 1982, and so on) or by counters (1, 2, and so on) denoting succession of years.

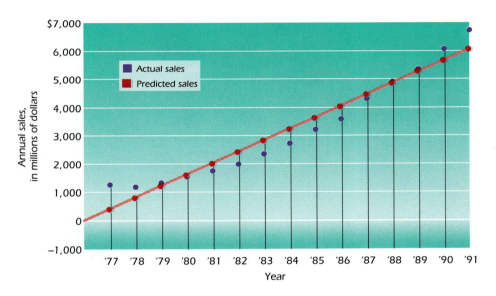

Let's look at annual sales for the Walgreen Company, a retail drug chain, from 1977 through 1991 (fifteen annual observations), plotted in Figure D-7(a). The regression line is estimated over the time series of sales in Figure D-7(b). The line is:[2]

[2] If we were to represent time in terms of years, 1977, 1978, and so on, the estimated regression for Walgreens would differ only in the intercept:

$$\text{Walgreen's annual sales, in millions} = -\$797{,}091 \text{ million} + (\$403.38 \times \text{time})$$

But the meaning is the same: predicted 1991 sales are:

$$\hat{Y}_{1991} = -\$797{,}091 \text{ million} + (\$403.38 \times 1991) = \$6{,}046 \text{ million}$$

Since it is simpler to work in the time units of 1, 2, et cetera, we tend to use this representation of time to make the interpretation and calculations a bit easier.

Walgreen's annual sales, in millions $= -\$5.043$ million $+ (\$403.38$ million $\times$ time$)$

We see that there is a positive slope, which means that sales are increasing through time, by an average of $403.38 million per year—a positive trend. If Walgreen's sales were to fit along the regression line, the predicted sales for 1991, $\hat{Y}_{15}$ would be:

Walgreen's annual sales, in millions $= -\$5.043$ million $+ (\$403.38$ million $\times$ 15$)$
$= \$6,046$ million

Actual 1991 sales were $6,733 million, a difference (an error) of $687 million.

Using this regression line to predict Walgreen's sales in 1992 (the sixteenth year, which is just outside of our sample data), where $\hat{Y}_{16}$ represents predicted 1992 sales:

$\hat{Y}_{16} = -\$5.043 + (\$403.38$ million $\times$ 16$)$
$= \$6,449$ million

Comparing this forecast with the actual 1992 sales of $7,475 million, we see that the forecast is off by over $1 billion. (See also Figure D-8.)

Keep in mind that we have less and less confidence about predictions the further we go in the future. For example, the data suggest we can be fairly confident (based on the trend we observed for 1977 through 1991) that Walgreen's sales will increase in 1992. But what about 1993? 1994?

With time-series regression we need to heed several caveats:

FIGURE D-8

Walgreen Company Actual Sales, Annually, 1977–1991, Estimated Regression Line, and Predicted Sales for 1992

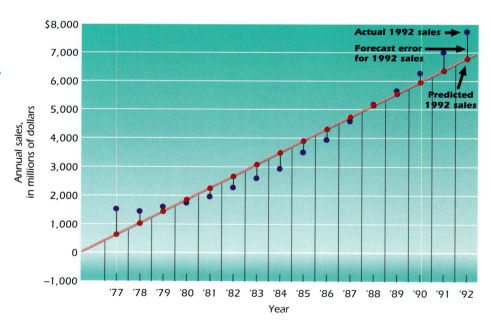

present in the data, one way to remove it is to transform the nominal data into real data.

- If a variable grows at a constant rate, the relation between that variable and time is not linear, but rather *curvi*linear. Hence, the relation is graphically represented as a curve, not a straight line. Techniques are available to estimate this nonlinear relation (which are beyond the scope of this text).
- Seasonality affects the fit of a straight line, especially with quarterly data. Techniques are available to adjust for seasonality of data in estimating a regression line (also beyond the scope of this text).

Correlation

Two variables are **correlated** if they tend to vary together. **Correlation** is a measure of the strength of the relationship between (or among) variables. A statistical measure of how variables vary with each other is referred to as the **correlation coefficient.** If we are talking about only two variables and how they are related to each other, we refer to this measure as the **simple correlation coefficient.**

We determine this coefficient by comparing the variables' covariance (a measure of how they covary), relative to how they tend to vary from their own means (the standard deviations). Let's label two variables X and Y and consider their correlation coefficient.

$$\text{Correlation coefficient} = \frac{\text{covariance of X and Y}}{(\text{standard deviation of X})(\text{standard deviation of Y})}$$

$$\text{Correlation coefficient} = \frac{\dfrac{\sum\limits_{i=1}^{n}(X_i - \overline{X})(Y_i - \overline{Y})}{n-1}}{\sqrt{\dfrac{\sum\limits_{i=1}^{n}(X_i - \overline{X})^2}{n-1}}\sqrt{\dfrac{\sum\limits_{i=1}^{n}(Y_i - \overline{Y})^2}{n-1}}} \qquad [\text{D-16}]$$

The correlation coefficient is similar to the concept of correlation we used with respect to uncertainty statistics. In the case of uncertainty statistics, we look at how the returns of two assets are correlated under different possible scenarios *in the future*. In the case of sample statistics, we want to see whether two variables have moved together *in the past*.

By dividing the covariance of X and Y by the product of their standard deviations, the correlation coefficient is placed within the range from -1 to $+1$. If this coefficient is negative, this means that when the X's are above their mean, the Y's tend to be below their mean. If this coefficient is positive, this means that when the X's are above their mean, the Y's tend to be above their mean. If the correlation coefficient is zero, this means that there is no co-movement between the two series.

The correlation between McDonald's monthly returns and the market's returns during 1985 is:

$$\text{Correlation coefficient} = \frac{0.00161}{0.0346 \times 0.0534} = \mathbf{0.8714}$$

McDonald's monthly returns are positively correlated with those of the market.[3]

Caveats

In using statistical analysis, the financial manager and analyst must be wary: Is the sample representative? Is the sample size sufficiently large to get a good idea of what they are trying to measure? Is the statistic meaningful? Is what happened in the past indicative of the future?

[3] Aside from just estimating the correlation coefficient, we can assess the strength of the correlation. We can perform a test to see whether the correlation is different from zero, that is, whether the correlation is statistically significant.

Glossary

A

Abnormal profit The difference between the actual return on an asset and the expected return, taking into account the time value of money and the compensation for the asset's market risk.

Accelerated depreciation A system of reducing income by an amount representing the loss in its value, where the reduction is greater in the earlier years of the asset's life.

Accounting profit The difference between revenues and expenses, determined according to accounting principles.

Accounts payable The amount that is owed to trade creditors (suppliers) for purchases made on credit.

Accounts receivable The amount due from customers who have purchased goods and services and have not yet paid for them.

Accounts receivable turnover The number of times during a period that a firm converts its credit sales into cash; the ratio of credit sales to accounts receivable.

Accumulated depreciation The total amount of depreciation attributed to an asset since its acquisition. The account referred to as Accumulated Depreciation in financial statements is the sum of accumulated depreciation for all depreciable assets.

Acid-test ratio See *quick ratio*.

Activity ratio A ratio that measures how effectively a firm manages its assets.

Additional paid-in capital The amount paid by shareholders for newly issued stock in excess of its par or stated value.

Add-on interest A method of computing a loan repayment: The interest to be paid over the life of the loan is added to the principal, thus increasing the effective interest paid above the stated interest rate.

Adjustable rate preferred stock (ARPS) Preferred stock whose dividend rate changes according to a prescribed formula when some other specified rate changes.

Adjusted gross income (AGI) Applicable to individual income taxes, it is the gross income less certain deductions, such as for an IRA contribution. An income figure used as a base for many individual income tax calculations.

Agency cost The implicit or explicit cost that arises when the interests of the principal and agent conflict.

Agency relationship Relationship between agent and principal, in which the agent represents, and acts on behalf of, the principal.

Agent A person or persons acting on behalf of another person, or an organization.

Allocative efficiency The allocation of resources to the production of goods and services demanded by consumers, where the allocation is such that any other allocation would benefit someone to the detriment of someone else.

American Depository Receipt (ADR) A certificate indicating a unit of ownership in the securities held by a trust.

American Stock Exchange (AMEX) A national securities exchange located in New York City, it is the second largest stock exchange in the United States.

Amortization The systematic allocation of an intangible's cost over the time the asset contributes value to the firm.

Analysis of accounts A technique for creating pro forma balance sheets and income statements, beginning with the cash budget and then determining the changes in the financial statements that result from the cash budget.

Annualized rate A representation of an interest rate on an annual basis, in which the interest rate per period is multiplied by the number of compounding periods in a year.

Annualized yield to maturity The annual return on an investment, assuming it is held to maturity, represented as the product of the yield per compounding period and the number of compounding periods in a year.

Annual percentage rate (APR) A representation of the annual interest rate, in which interest per compounding period is multiplied by the number of compounding periods in a year; the annual cost of financing, ignoring the effects of compound interest.

Annuity A series of level cash flows that occur (paid or received) at even intervals of time.

Annuity due A series of level cash flows that occur at even intervals of time, with the first cash flow occurring at the beginning of the first period.

Arbitrage The process of buying and selling identical assets in different markets at different prices until the assets have the same price everywhere.

Arbitrage pricing model A theory of asset pricing that describes asset prices as determined by several economic factors.

Arithmetic average return The return calculated by summing a set of returns and dividing the sum by the number of returns in the set.

Arrearage The accumulation of unpaid dividends on cumulative preferred stock.

Arrears A corporation's status when dividends on cumulative preferred stock have not been paid; the corporation is then said to be in *arrears*.

Articles of incorporation Descriptive statement of the business that constitutes the contract between the corporation and its shareholders; also referred to as the *certificate of incorporation*.

Ask price The price at which an asset is offered for sale.

Asset Tangible or intangible property expected to generate future cash flows.

Asset-backed security (ABS) A security that represents an interest in the future cash flows of an asset or group of assets, such as mortgages.

Asset beta A measure of the market risk of an asset; a measure of the sensitivity of an asset's returns to changes in the returns on all assets in the market.

Assignment of receivables Short-term borrowing secured (backed) by accounts receivable.

At the money In options, the situation in which the exercise price is the same as the price of the underlying asset.

Authorized shares The shares that a corporation is permitted to issue, as stated in the corporation's articles of incorporation.

Average The sum of a set of values divided by the number of values in the set; also referred to as the *mean*.

Average collection period The average time it takes to collect amounts due from customers; also referred to as the *number of days of credit*; the ratio of accounts receivable to average credit sales per day.

Average day's cost of goods sold The average day's purchases made in a day; cost of goods sold divided by the number of days in a year. Also referred to as the *average day's purchases*.

Average day's purchases See *average day's cost of goods sold*.

Average tax rate The rate of tax paid per dollar of taxable income; calculated by dividing the amount of taxes by taxable income.

B

Baby bond A bond with a face value (maturity value) of less than $1,000.

Balance sheet A financial statement that summarizes the assets, liabilities, and equity of a firm at a point in time.

Bankers' acceptances Debt issued by banks, and backed by both the issuing bank and the purchaser of goods; a form of short-term borrowing used extensively in international trade.

Bankruptcy A legal status, provided under Chapter 11 of the Bankruptcy Act of 1978, that allows an individual or business to continue operations in order to be able to satisfy its creditors.

Bankruptcy costs Expenses associated with bankruptcy, including direct costs (e.g., fees for lawyers and accountants) and indirect costs (e.g., lost sales).

Basic earning power ratio A measure of a firm's return on operations; the ratio of operating earnings to total assets.

Basic valuation equation $FV = PV (1 + r)^t$, where the future value, FV, is stated as a function of the present value, PV, the interest rate per compounding period, r, and the number of compounding periods, t.

Basis point One one-hundredth of 1 percent (0.01 percent); a convention for quoting interest rates on debt; if a bond's yield changes from 10.37 percent to 10.40 percent, we say that the yield has gone up 3 *basis points*; from 10.5 percent to 10.6 percent, it's up 10 *basis points*.

Bearer debt A debt obligation whose owner is not registered or recorded; the owner is whoever physically possesses the debt certificate.

Benefit-cost ratio See *profitability index*.

Beta The sensitivity of an asset's returns to changes in the returns on the market.

Bid price The price an investor is willing to pay for an asset.

Blanket indenture An indenture agreement that covers more than one bond issue.

Board of directors A group of persons elected by the shareholders and charged with the fiduciary duty to these shareholders, of monitoring the activities of the corporation and making decisions that are in the best interest of shareholders.

Bond An agreement between a lender (the issuer) and a borrower (the investor).

Bondholder An owner of (investor in) a bond.

Bond indenture A contract specifying the responsibilities of the bond's trustee and the issuer (the borrower).

Bonding costs A type of agency cost incurred by the agent to ensure that he or she will act in the interests of the principal.

Bonus Cash compensation based on some measure of performance, such as earnings per share.

Book value of equity The value of the ownership interest in the firm as determined by the accounting principles that summarize a firm's activities; the difference between the book value of total assets and the book value of liabilities.

Book value (of equity) per share The value of the ownership interest per share of stock, as reported in the firm's financial statements.

Break point A level of new capital at which the cost of capital is expected to change.

Budget A plan of the expected future cash flows of a firm, enabling its managers to identify short-term and long-term financing and investment needs.

Budgeting Planning the sources and uses of funds for future periods.

Business risk The degree of uncertainty associated with the economy, the market for a firm's product, the market for the inputs to the firm's product, and the operation of the firm; the degree of uncertainty pertaining to a firm's cash flows from operations.

Bylaws The rules of governance of an organization; for a corporation, the bylaws (along with the articles of incorporation) become a part of its corporate charter.

C

Callable preferred stock Preferred shares that can be bought back by the issuer at a specified price.

Call feature A provision of a security (often preferred stock or bonds) that allows the security's issuer to buy it back at a specified price (the call price).

Call option The right to buy a specified asset at a specified price within a specified period.

Call premium The difference between the price the issuer must pay when calling a security (the call price) and the security's face value.

Call price The price that must be paid by the issuer of a security to buy it back from the investor.

Call risk The uncertainty that a callable security will be bought back by the issuer prior to the security's maturity.

Capital A firm's resources; funds raised from long-term sources, such as bonds and stock.

Capital appreciation See *capital gain*.

Capital asset A tangible or intangible asset expected to provide future cash flows.

Capital asset pricing model (CAPM) A theory that explains asset pricing in terms of a return composed of the risk-free rate of interest and a risk premium for bearing market, or nondiversifiable, risk.

Capital budgeting Screening, evaluation, and selection of alternative investment opportunities whose benefits extend into the future.

Capital expenditure An outlay of cash for an investment whose benefits are realized over future periods.

Capital gain The increase or appreciation in the value of an asset; in taxation, the amount by which the sales price of a capital asset exceeds its original cost.

Capital investment See *capital expenditure*.

Capitalization rate The discount rate used to translate a series of future cash flows into a present value.

Capital lease A long-term rental agreement that essentially transfers the benefits and risks of property ownership to the lessee (the party using the asset); also referred to as a *financial lease*; a lease that satisfies the requirements contained in Statement of Financial Accounting Standards no. 13.

Capital loss The decrease in the value of an asset; in taxation, the amount by which the selling price of an asset is below its book value for tax purposes.

Capital market Market in which long-term securities, such as bonds and stocks, are traded.

Capital market line (CML). The possible portfolios that can be formed by combining the risk-free asset and the market portfolio in different proportions.

Capital market security A long-term security issued by a corporation, the U.S. government, or a state or local government.

Capital project An investment whose benefits are expected to be realized in future years; it may consist of several related assets.

Capital rationing Limit on the amount of spending on long-term investment projects.

Capital recovery period See *payback period*.

Capital structure The mixture of debt, preferred equity, and common equity used to finance the operations and investments of the business.

Capital yield The return arising from the change in the asset's value from one point in time to another.

Captive finance subsidiary A subsidiary formed to extend credit to the parent company's customers.

Carrying cost See *holding cost*.

Cash Coin and currency; sometimes used to describe coins, currency, and cashlike deposits that can be readily transformed into cash.

Cash budget Planning the sources and uses of cash for future periods.

Cash flow from financing activities Cash that flows into or out of the firm from the issuance, repurchase, and maturation of its securities.

Cash flow from investing activities Cash that flows into or out of the firm from the purchase or retirement of long-lived assets.

Cash flow interest coverage ratio Measure of a firm's ability to satisfy its interest obligations using the cash flow it generates during the period.

Cash flow risk The degree of uncertainty concerning the expected future cash flows from an investment.

Cash forecasting Predicting future cash inflows and outflows.

Cashless stock option An employee stock option accompanied by a loan for the amount of the exercise price of the option, requiring no cash outlay by the employee to exercise the option.

Certainty equivalent The certain cash flow that is considered to have the same value as a particular uncertain cash flow.

Certificate of deposit (CD) A receipt that is issued by a financial institution and that represents deposits held for the depositor. The financial institution pays interest on these deposits; maturity is typically less than one year.

Certificate of incorporation See *articles of incorporation*.

Chattel mortgage A loan secured by specific inventory (uniquely identified), in which the borrower retains title to the inventory and the lender must give the borrower permission to sell such inventory.

Chicago Board Options Exchange (CBOE) The first organized exchange for the trading of standardized options contracts, established in 1973.

Classified board of directors A board of directors whose members' terms of office are grouped into more than one class: Each class is elected in a different year so that the terms of the entire membership do not expire in the same year; also referred to as a *staggered board of directors*.

Close corporation or **closely held corporation** A corporation having few owners who exercise complete control over its decisions.

Coefficient of variation A statistical measure of the dispersion of outcomes in a sample; it is the ratio of the standard deviation to the mean, or expected, value.

Collar The minimum and maximum interest rate or dividend rate specified on a security whose rate may change (because it is a floating rate or because the rate is reset by periodic auction).

Collateral Property security for a debt obligation; in a case of default, the proceeds from the sale of the property can be used to pay the amount due the investor (the bond or note owner).

Collateralized mortgage obligation (CMO) Securities that represent the rights to payment on a group of home mortgages.

Collateral trust debt Indebtedness secured (backed) with equipment.

Collection policies Guidelines and procedures for collecting what is due.

Commercial banker A financial institution that accepts deposits from and lends funds to businesses and individuals.

Commercial paper An unsecured promissory note issued by a large corporation (typically a finance company); generally has a maturity of less than or equal to 270 days.

Commitment fee Fee paid to a financial institution in exchange for its promise to lend funds up to a specified amount within a specified period.

Committed line of credit Legally binding promise by a financial institution to lend up to a specified amount of funds within a specified period of time.

Commodity Futures Trading Commission (CFTC) Federal agency that regulates commodity futures and options.

Common size analysis Analysis of the proportion of each item comprising a financial statement.

Common size balance sheet A balance sheet in which each item is represented as a proportion of total assets.

Common size income statement An income statement in which each item is reported as a proportion of sales.

Common stock The ownership interest in a corporation; units of ownership are represented by shares.

Company-specific risk See *unsystematic risk*.

Comparative advantage The edge one firm has over another in terms of the cost of producing or distributing goods and services.

Compensating balance Deposit balance maintained at a financial institution during the period of a loan or a line of credit; usually expressed as a percentage of the loaned funds or line of credit.

Competitive advantage The edge one firm has over another in terms of the structure of the market for its inputs or outputs.

Complementary projects Investments that enhance the cash flows of each other.

Component percentage Financial data for an item (such as inventory) expressed as a percentage of the financial data of another item (such as total assets).

Compound factor $(1 + r)^t$, where r is the rate of interest per compounding period and t is the number of compounding periods; it is the rate of translation of values into the future.

Compounding Translating values from one period into a future period, taking into account that interest is paid on both the principal investment and any interest earned to date.

Compounding period A unit of time such that interest is paid or earned only at the end of the period.

Compound interest The payment of interest based on both the principal amount and accumulated interest.

Consumer Price Index (CPI) An index of the rate of inflation in prices of consumer goods and services.

Contingent projects Investments whose profitability depends on the outcome of another investment.

Contingent voting rights Rights to vote for representation on the board of directors of a corporation; these rights are valid only under specific conditions, such as if there are arrearages on cumulative preferred dividends.

Continuous compounding Interest paid on interest where the compounding period is the smallest unit of time possible; compounding where there are an infinite number of compounding periods.

Continuous distribution Probability distribution with an infinite number of possible outcomes.

Contribution margin The difference between the sales price of an item and its variable cost; the operating profit available to cover fixed operating costs.

Controlled disbursements An arrangement that minimizes the balances left on deposit with a bank; the objective is to maintain deposits at a level just sufficient to meet withdrawals by checks drawn on the account.

Conventional factoring An arrangement in which someone purchases accounts receivable, paying cash, and then collects on the accounts.

Conversion feature A provision of a security that permits its owner to exchange it for another specified security.

Conversion premium The difference between the market value of a convertible security and the market value of the securities into which it can be exchanged.

Conversion price The price paid for shares of stock when a debt obligation is exchanged for shares, assuming the investment in the debt is equal to its face value; also, the face value of the debt divided by the conversion ratio.

Conversion ratio The number of shares for which a convertible security may be exchanged.

Conversion value See *market conversion price*.

Convertible debt or **convertible bond** A debt obligation that may be exchanged for another security, such as common stock, at the discretion of the debt's owner.

Convertible feature An attribute of a security that gives its owner the right to exchange it for another security at a specified exchange rate.

Convertible preferred stock Preferred shares that may be converted into another security (usually common stock) at the option of the investor.

Corporate charter The contract between the state and the corporation, between the shareholders and the corporation, and between the shareholders and the state; contains the articles of incorporation, the corporate by-laws, and the state corporate laws.

Corporate democracy The system whereby the owners of a corporation have a say in the management of its business.

Corporate strategy The broad goals for the future of the firm.

Corporation A form of business that comes into being when the state grants a charter to the enterprise, enabling it to conduct business, incur liabilities, and enter into contracts.

Correlation The comovement between the values of two or more variables.

Correlation coefficient A statistical measure of the degree of comovement between two variables; the measure is bounded by -1 and $+1$.

Cost of capital The marginal cost of funds; the cost of using one more dollar of funds from additional long-term sources.

Cost of common stock Cost of using one more dollar of equity either internally (to add to retained earnings) or externally (to issue new shares).

Cost of debt The *marginal cost* of borrowed funds.

Cost of goods sold The cost of the goods and services produced during a period.

Cost of preferred stock The *marginal cost* of funds from preferred equity sources.

Cost of sales See *cost of goods sold*.

Coupon The interest on debt.

Coupon bond A bond that has a specified fixed rate of interest; also referred to as a *straight-coupon bond*.

Coupon-equivalent yield The return on a coupon-bearing security; it is a compounded annual return and its calculation takes account of the reinvestment of cash flows during the period.

Coupon rate The annual interest on an interest-bearing debt obligation, expressed as a percentage of the security's face value.

Coupon yield The return on a debt security during the period.

Covariance A statistical measure of the extent to which changes in two variables move together at the same time.

Covenant A provision in a bond indenture, stipulating a limit or restriction on the issuer to ensure that the promised interest payments and principal repayment are made when due.

Coverage ratio The relation between the funds available to satisfy an obligation and the amount of the obligation.

Creditor The lender; the party that lends money, expecting repayment at a future time.

Credit risk See *default risk*.

Credit terms The policy regarding the amount of credit, the length of the period for payments, and the amount of any discount and the discount period.

Crossover discount rate The discount rate at which the net present values of two projects are equal; the internal rate of return of the differences in the cash flows of two projects.

Cumulative feature Characteristic of a dividend-paying security requiring that any dividends not paid in one period be accumulated and payable in the subsequent period or periods.

Cumulative preferred stock Preferred shares on which dividends not paid in one period must accumulate until paid.

Cumulative voting A system that allows voters to stack up their votes, applying them to one or more positions on the board of directors, thus facilitating minority representation on the board; for example, if there are three director positions up for vote and you own 100 shares of stock, you get 300 votes to cast toward one, two, or three of the positions.

Currency risk Uncertainty associated with the change in the relative value of two or more nations' currencies.

Current assets Assets that can be transformed into cash within one operating cycle or one year, whichever is longer; generally includes cash, accounts receivable, inventories, and marketable securities.

Current liabilities Obligations due within one year or one operating cycle, whichever is longer.

Current ratio The ratio of current assets to current liabilities; a measure of a firm's liquidity.

D

Days' sales outstanding (DSO) See *number of days of credit*.

Debenture A debt obligation not secured by specific property, but backed solely by the general credit of the issuer.

Debt An obligation to repay borrowed funds; also referred to as *indebtedness* or a *liability*.

Debtholder The lender of funds; the owner of a debt security.

Debtor The party who borrows funds and must repay them.

Debt ratio The ratio of debt to equity, which is one measure of the use of debt to finance operations of the firm; a measure of financial leverage.

Debt-to-assets ratio The ratio of debt to total assets; a measure of financial leverage.

Decision criteria Rules guiding the decision whether to invest in a project.

Declaration date The date on which the board of directors declares a dividend.

Declining balance method of depreciation A system of allocating the cost of an asset over time at a fixed percentage of its declining undepreciated cost.

Default risk The degree of uncertainty regarding whether the borrower can pay what has been promised (e.g., interest and the repayment of principal).

Defease Effectively to retire debt by placing it in trust and using the trust proceeds to pay the interest and principal obligations of the debt.

Deferred annuity A series of level cash flows that occur at regular intervals, although the first cash flow occurs after the end of the first interval.

Deferred call A call provision that prohibits the issuer from calling (buying back) the security for a specified period of time after it is issued.

Deferred interest Interest not due for some period after the debt security was issued.

Deferred taxes A liability for taxes to be paid in future years, but for which no immediate payment is due.

Degree of financial leverage (DFL) The sensitivity of cash flows to owners to changes in operating cash flows.

Degree of operating leverage (DOL) The sensitivity of operating cash flows to changes in the number of units produced and sold.

Degree of total leverage (DTL) The sensitivity of the cash flow to owners to changes in the number of units produced and sold.

Dependent variable In regression analysis, the variable whose variation is determined, or "explained," by the other ("independent") variables.

Depositary preferred shares Units of ownership created when preferred shares are held in trust and shares of the trust are sold as securities.

Depreciable cost or **depreciable basis** The amount of an asset's cost that is depreciated for tax purposes.

Depreciation The systematic allocation of an asset's cost over its useful life.

Depreciation tax shield The reduction in taxes arising from the deduction for depreciation for tax purposes; the product of the marginal tax rate and the depreciation expense.

Derivative security A security whose value is dependent on the value of another asset.

Detachable warrant A warrant that may be sold apart from the security with which it was originally issued and traded as a separate security.

Direct lease A rental arrangement in which the lessee rents an asset not previously owned by the lessee.

Discount The amount by which the price of a security is below its face, or par, value.

Discount basis or **discounted basis** The method of reporting the interest on a loan or security as a percentage of the sum of the principal and all interest; the result is an understatement of the effective interest.

Discounted payback period The time it takes for the initial investment to be paid back in terms of discounted future cash flows.

Discount factor $1/(1 + r)^t$, where r is the interest rate per period, and t is the number of periods; it is the rate that translates values in one period into values that pertain to previous time periods.

Discounting Translating values at some future point of time into values at some earlier point in time, recognizing that interest is paid on both the principal and any interest earned between both points in time.

Discount interest Interest paid at the beginning of the loan directly from the loan proceeds.

Discount loan A loan whose interest is paid at the beginning of the loan period.

Discrete distribution A probability distribution with a finite number of possible outcomes.

Dispersion The differences among possible outcomes or sample items.

Disturbance term In regression analysis, the difference between the actual values of the dependent variable and the values predicted by the regression line; also referred to as the *error term* or the *residual term*.

Diversifiable risk Risk that can be eliminated by investing in assets whose expected returns are less than perfectly positively correlated.

Diversification Reducing risk by investing in assets whose expected returns are less than perfectly positively correlated.

Diversified portfolio A collection of assets that have no diversifiable risk.

Dividend A payment, in the form of cash, property, or stock, to the owners of the firm; the timing and amount of this payment are determined by the firm's board of directors.

Dividend payout (DPO) The percentage of earnings available to owners and paid out to them in the form of cash dividends; also referred to as the *dividend payout ratio*.

Dividend policy The policy regarding the payment of dividends to the firm's owners.

Dividend reinvestment plan (DRP) A program allowing shareholders to reinvest their cash dividends directly into shares of stock of the corporation paying the dividends.

Dividends per share (DPS) The dollar amount of cash paid during a period for each share of stock; it is the total amount paid in dividends divided by the number of shares of stock outstanding.

Dividends-received deduction The tax deduction for dividends received by one corporation from another corporation; the reduction in dividend income (generally stated as a percentage of the dividend income) that lessens the effects of multiple layers of taxation of income arising from dividend payments among corporations.

Dividend valuation model (DVM) A model that specifies that the current price of a share of stock is the present value of all future dividends to be paid from that stock.

Dividend yield The return expressed as a percentage and calculated by dividing the cash dividend per share by the price per share of stock.

Dow Jones Industrial Average (DJIA) The average price of the group of thirty large U.S. industrial corporations selected by Dow Jones as representative of all U.S. industrial corporations.

Draft A document that requires one party to pay funds to another party, such as a check that requires a financial institution to pay someone the amount of the funds stated on the check upon its presentation to the institution.

Du Pont system A system of breaking down return ratios into their profit margin and asset turnover components.

Dutch auction A type of auction in which a security's price or rate is determined by bidding and results in the lowest rate or highest price necessary to sell the security.

E

Earnings available to common shareholders Net income after payment of interest to creditors and dividends to preferred shareholders.

Earnings before interest and taxes (EBIT) Profits that result from operations; also referred to as *operating income, operating profit, operating earnings*.

Earnings per share (EPS) Net income available to shareholders divided by the number of shares of stock outstanding.

Earnings-per-share indifference point Identical earnings per share that could be obtained from alternative financing plans being considered.

Economic life The expected length of time an asset is expected to provide benefits to the user; also referred to as the asset's *useful life*.

Economic order quantity (EOQ) For inventory, the amount of goods that must be ordered to minimize total inventory costs; for cash, the size of the cash infusion necessary to minimize the costs of cash.

Economic profit The difference between revenues and the costs comprising expenditures, opportunity cost of funds, and normal profits.

Effective annual rate or **effective annual return (EAR)** The rate of interest for an annual period that takes into consideration any compounding within the year; the true, or economic, rate of return for an annual period.

Effective conversion price In an exchange of one security for another, the effective price paid after taking into account the value of the security given up in the exchange.

Effective rate of interest The interest rate that takes into consideration any compounding within the period; also referred to as the *effective annual rate* or the *effective annual return*.

Effective yield to maturity The annual return on a security bought and held to maturity after taking into account the reinvestment of any of its periodic cash flows, e.g., interest.

Efficient frontier The set of portfolios that have the least risk for a given expected return or the greatest expected return for a given level of risk.

Efficient market A market in which information is rapidly reflected in asset prices; a market may be described as being weak, semistrong-form efficient, or strong-form efficient, depending on the information reflected in asset prices.

8-K statement Filed with the SEC to inform it of any material events, such as a merger, that may affect a firm's financial condition.

Employee involvement (EI) A management philosophy that encourages employees' participation in the firm's decision making.

Employment tax A tax based on the salary and wages paid to employees.

Equipment obligation or **equipment trust certificates** or **equipment trust debt** Indebtedness secured (backed) by equipment.

Equity The ownership interest in a business enterprise.

Equity multiplier 1/[1-(total debt/total assets)]; the inverse of one minus the debt-to-total-asset ratio; the factor that adjusts the return on assets to produce a return on equity.

Equivalent annual annuity approach Method of selecting among mutually exclusive projects that have different useful lives; the procedure translates each project's future cash flows into an annual annuity with an identical present value.

Error term See *disturbance term*.

Eurobond or **Euronote** Debt issued in a country other than the country in whose currency the debt is denominated.

Eurodollar certificates of deposit Certificates of deposit of non-U.S. banks that are denominated in U.S. dollars.

Eurodollar deposits Loans of non-U.S. banks that are denominated in U.S. dollars.

Exchange A formal market that has a physical trading floor, such as the New York Stock Exchange.

Excise tax A tax levied against certain commodities.

Ex-dividend date The date when a buyer of shares of stock is no longer entitled to receive the forthcoming dividend.

Executive stock option A right given to a manager of a corporation that enables him or her to buy shares of stock in the corporation at a specified price within a specified period of time.

Exercise price The price at which an option to buy or sell can be exercised; also referred to as the *strike price*.

Expansion project An investment that broadens a firm's existing product line or broadens the firm's distribution within existing markets.

Expected return A statistical measure of return in the future, considering all possible returns and their likelihoods.

Expected value A measure of central tendency of a probability distribution; calculated as the weighted average of the possible outcomes, where the weights are the probabilities that the outcomes will occur.

Expiration date The date on which the right to exercise an option ends; maturity date of an option.

Explanatory variable See *independent variable*.

Export tax A tax or tariff levied on exported goods.

Externalities The side effects of actions, such as the loss of sales of one product of a firm resulting from the introduction of another product by the same firm.

Extraordinary items Nonrecurring profits or losses of a business during an accounting period.

F

Face value The principal amount of a security; the amount a security owner receives at the security's maturity; see also *principal*, *maturity value*, or *par value*.

Factor Purchaser of a firm's accounts receivable.

Factoring Selling accounts receivable to another party, where the factor (the purchaser) grants the credit assumed in the purchase and collects the receivables.

Fiduciary duty The responsibility of one party to act in the best interests of another party; for example, the members of the board of directors of a corporation have an obligation to make decisions in the best interests of the shareholders they represent.

Field warehouse loan A lending arrangement in which inventory is used as collateral and is kept in a warehouse area monitored by an agent.

Final prospectus A document that describes a security and its issuer and is released to the public following the Securities and Exchange Commission's decision that the security's registration statement has satisfied disclosure requirements.

Finance The study of the management of the acquisition and allocation of funds for profit.

Financial Accounting Standards Board (FASB) The organization that determines the standards to be used in financial accounting and financial reporting.

Financial analysis The evaluation of financial statement data, economic and market information, and forecasts to produce an assessment of a firm's past or projected operating performance and financial condition.

Financial distress A condition in which the firm is under pressure to pay its creditors.

Financial engineering Innovative design of financial securities.

Financial future An agreement obligating the buyer to buy and the seller to sell a specified amount of a financial instrument or security, such as Treasury bills, Treasury bonds, or commercial paper.

Financial institutions Banks, savings and loans, insurance companies, and other firms whose primary business is to act as a financial intermediary, taking in deposits and loaning funds; as one of the three broad categories of finance, deals with banks and other firms that specialize in bringing suppliers of funds together with the users of funds.

Financial lease See *capital lease*.

Financial leverage The extent to which a firm uses sources of capital that have fixed, limited payouts (for example, bonds).

Financial leverage ratios Ratios that measure the extent to which a firm finances its operations with debt.

Financial management The investment and financing decision-making process of a business enterprise.

Financial model A set of relationships among elements, reflecting the investment and financing decisions of a firm.

Financial planning The process of determining the sources of funds to meet investment objectives.

Financial risk The degree of uncertainty regarding a firm's cash flows arising from its fixed financing obligations, such as interest.

Financial slack The sum of cash, marketable securities, and unused debt capacity, which provides a cushion enabling a firm to avoid issuing additional securities.

Financing strategy The financing that the firm intends to use to achieve its objective of maximizing owners' wealth.

Fisher effect The relationship between the nominal return, expected inflation, and the real return.

Five Cs of credit Capacity, capital, character, collateral, and conditions; the factors to consider in determining whether to extend credit to a customer.

Fixed asset turnover The dollar amount of sales generated per dollar invested in total assets; the ratio of sales to fixed assets.

Fixed charge coverage ratio The earnings available to satisfy fixed financing obligations as a ratio to the fixed financial obligations (such as interest and lease payments).

Flexible budget A budget produced considering the probability distributions of possible future outcomes.

Float The amount of funds tied up in transit and in the banking system, representing payments made, but not yet credited to or available for use by, the payee.

Floating lien A flexible type of financing that uses inventory as collateral for a loan.

Floating rate The rate on a debt security that periodically changes according to changes in the rate of some other security.

Floor planning See *trust receipts loan*.

Flotation costs Expenses associated with the issuance of a security.

Footnotes In financial statements, additional disclosures regarding accounting policies and the details of specific financial statement items.

Forecast error The difference between an actual value and the forecasted value.

Foreign currency future A contract that obligates the buyer to buy or seller to sell a specified amount of foreign currency at a specified future time.

Forward stock split See *stock split*.

Free cash flow The cash flow generated in excess of what is needed to maintain existing production capabilities.

Fully diluted earnings per share The profits earned for each share of stock, considering the outstanding shares as well as the potential shares if all convertible securities and other dilutive securities were converted into shares.

Fully underwritten A security issue purchased in its entirety from the issuer for resale to the public.

Futures contract An agreement committing the investor (the buyer) to purchase a specified commodity at some specified future time at a specified price.

Future value (FV) The value, as of some future time, of a current value or a series of cash flows.

Future value annuity factor The factor that translates a series of even cash flows into a future value; the sum of compound factors.

G

Generally accepted accounting principles (GAAP) Principles and rules applied by accountants to report financial data that summarize the results of a firm's operations over a period of time and its financial condition at a point of time.

General obligation bond A municipality's debt obligation whose promised interest and principal payments are guaranteed by the municipality's tax resources.

General partner A partner who participates fully in the management of the business and shares in its profits or losses and is liable for its debts.

General partnership A business enterprise in which each owner is liable for the obligations of the business.

Geometric average return An average annual return that reflects the compounding in the growth of values from one period to another.

Golden parachute A lucrative compensation agreement for the manager of a firm; it goes into effect if the manager is dismissed because of a change in the control of the business, such as a merger.

Greenmail The threat of a takeover created by purchasing shares of stock in a corporation, where the threat is eliminated when the corporation purchases these same shares (generally at a higher price); also referred to as a *targeted block repurchase*.

Gross domestic product (GDP) The sum of all the goods and services produced within the borders of a nation during a particular period of time.

Gross plant and equipment or **gross plant assets** The sum of the costs of all long-lived, physical assets of a firm.

Gross profit The difference between sales revenues and the costs to produce the sold goods and services.

Gross profit margin The earnings left after deducting the cost of goods sold from sales revenues; sometimes expressed as a percentage of sales.

Growth rate The rate of change in a value over a specified period of time.

H

Half-year convention The method of depreciation in which the asset is assumed to be owned for one-half year during its first year no matter when it was acquired in that year.

Hedger A person who executes transactions to reduce risk on a particular asset investment.

High-grade bond or **high-grade debt, high-grade note, high-quality debt** Indebtedness ranked in the top two rating classes (Aaa and Aa for Moody's, AAA and AA for Standard & Poor's).

Holding costs The cost of carrying an asset; for inventory, it's the cost of storage and obsolescence, plus the opportunity cost of the funds tied up in the investment; for cash, it's the opportunity cost of funds.

Homemade leverage An individual's financing of his or her investments with debt which, in the Modigliani and Miller capital structure theory, is a substitute for the firm's debt.

Hostile takeover The takeover of one firm by another, where the management of the target firm objects to the takeover.

Human capital A person's value, which consists of her or his investment in education, training, and experience.

Hurdle rate The cost of capital, reflecting a project's risk.

I

Illegal insider trading Buying or selling securities on the basis of material, nonpublic information.

Import tax A tax or tariff levied on imported goods.

Income bond A bond whose interest is paid only when the firm has earnings sufficient to pay it.

Income statement Summary of the financial results of operations during a period of time.

Income tax A tax that is based on income.

Incorporation Creation of a corporate entity under state law.

Incremental cash flow The amount a firm's cash flow changes when a new investment is taken on.

Indebtedness See *loan*.

Indenture agreement An agreement specifying the trustee, the responsibilities of the trustee, the schedule of payments for interest and repayment of principal, and any restrictions (covenants) on the issuer.

Independent projects Investments whose cash flows are unaffected by one another.

Independent variable In regression analysis, a variable that determines, or "explains," the variation in another ("dependent") variable; also referred to as the *explanatory variable*.

Inflation premium The additional return necessary to compensate an investor for expected inflation.

Inside director A member of the board of directors who is also an employee of the corporation.

Institutional investor An investor that is an entity, such as a pension fund, that invests funds for another person or group of persons.

Intangible asset Asset having no physical attributes but which provides cash flows, for example, a patent.

Intercept In regression analysis, the value of the dependent variable when the independent variables take on a value of zero; the point of intersection of the regression line with the vertical (dependent variable) axis.

Interest A periodic cash payment to lenders of funds to compensate them for the time value of money and the uncertainty associated with the repayment of the amount loaned.

Interest coverage ratio A measure of a firm's ability to satisfy interest payment obligations; the ratio of earnings available to pay interest (earnings before interest and taxes) to interest.

Interest rate Interest specified as a percentage of some value, such as the face value of the security.

Interest rate future Contract on future delivery of interest-bearing securities, such as Treasury bills and bonds.

Interest rate risk Degree of uncertainty regarding future interest rates and its effect on the current value of an asset.

Interest tax shield The amount of tax avoided due to the tax deductibility of interest.

Intermarket Trading System (ITS) A system of interconnections among security markets, enabling brokers and dealers to trade securities in markets other than their own.

Intermediary The party who acts between the buyer and seller to facilitate the trade of the asset; in the case of financial assets, intermediaries include banks and investment bankers.

Internal rate of return (IRR) The discount rate that, when applied to an investment's incremental cash flows, results in a net present value of zero; the discount rate that equates the present value of the future cash inflows with the present value of future cash outflows; yield on an investment.

Internal Revenue Code (IRC) Tax provisions written by Congress that, in combination with court cases, make up the tax law of the United States.

In the money Either a call option's exercise price that is less than the value of the underlying asset or a put option's exercise price that is greater than the value of the underlying asset.

Inventory Goods held for sale; may include raw materials, work in process, and finished goods.

Inventory turnover ratio Number of times inventory flows into the firm (in the form of raw materials) and out of the firm (in the form of sold goods) during a period of time.

Investment Property that is expected to produce future cash flows; in the context of financial statements, the account that records long-term holdings of securities.

Investment banker An intermediary that assists firms and government bodies to obtain funds through the sale of securities.

Investment cash flows Cash flows associated with the purchase or sale of the assets related to an investment project.

Investment-grade debt Indebtedness in the top four rating classes (Aaa through Baa for Moody's, AAA through BBB for Standard & Poor's).

Investment profile Graphical representation of the net present value of a project for different discount rates.

Investments The area of finance that deals primarily with financial markets and the securities that trade in those markets.

Investment strategy Investment opportunities the firm intends to use to achieve its objective of maximizing owners' wealth.

Investment tax credit (ITC) A direct reduction of taxes based on a specified percentage of an asset's cost.

Issued shares Shares of stock sold to investors.

J

Joint venture A partnership or corporation formed to conduct a specific business transaction.

Junior The status of having a lower claim than another claimant on the income or assets of a firm.

Junk bond See *speculative debt*.

Just-in-time (JIT) inventory system An inventory management system that minimizes ordering and holding costs by streamlining the ordering system; success depends on cooperation of suppliers.

L

Lead time The time it takes to replenish inventory.

Lease A contract specifying that the owner of an asset (the lessor) gives the right to use it to another party (the lessee) for a period in exchange for a payment.

Lessee The party to a lease who pays rent to the owner (lessor) of an asset for its use.

Lessor The party to a lease who owns the asset leased to another party, the lessee.

Letter of credit Written promise by a bank to make a loan if specific conditions (such as the importing of goods) are met.

Leveraged lease A lease (rental agreement) by which the lessor borrows a substantial portion of the funds needed to finance the purchase of the leased asset.

Liability An obligation to pay at some time in the future.

Limited liability Liability limited to the amount of the investment, such as is the case of shareholders of a corporation.

Limited partner A partner who does not participate in the management of the partnership business and is not liable for its debts.

Limited partnership A partnership composed of at least one general partner and one limited partner.

Line of credit A promise by a financial institution to lend up to a specific amount of funds over a specified period; the financial institution is compensated either by a fee payment or by the potential borrower's maintaining a specified compensating balance with the institution.

Liquid asset Property that can be readily transformed into cash.

Liquidation value Value of a security in the event the firm ceases business, sells its assets, and distributes the proceeds to claimants.

Liquidity The ability of a firm to meet its short-term obligations using assets that can be readily transformed into cash.

Liquidity risk Degree of uncertainty regarding whether an asset can be sold for an amount equal to its value.

Listed Status of a corporation's stock that has become eligible to trade on a particular market.

Loan An obligation to repay borrowed funds; also referred to as *indebtedness*.

Loan amortization Schedule of periodic payments on indebtedness, specifying interest and principal components.

Loan origination fee The fee paid to the lender at the beginning of the loan period.

Lockbox system A process in which payments received from customers are handled directly by the bank in which the payments are deposited.

Long-run planning or **long-term planning** Planning the sources and uses of funds over a long time horizon, such as five years into the future.

Long-term debt-to-assets ratio A measure of the financial risk of a firm; the ratio of long-term debt obligations to total assets; the extent to which assets are financed by long-term debt obligations.

Long-term debt-to-equity ratio A measure of the financial risk of a firm; the ratio of long-term debt obligations to shareholders' equity; the amount of debt financing used relative to equity financing.

Long-term investment The acquisition of assets whose benefits, in the form of changes in the firm's cash flows, are expected to be realized in future years.

Long-term liability An obligation to render a payment at some time beyond one year.

M

Managerial finance The area of finance that deals with investment and financing decision making of a business enterprise.

Managing underwriter The investment banker (underwriter) that manages the issuance of a security, coordinating sales efforts among all the underwriters in an underwriting syndicate.

Mandated project Investment required to satisfy some law or regulation.

Mandatory convertible preferred stock Preferred shares that must be exchanged by the investor into shares of common stock within a specified period.

Marginal cost The cost associated with producing one more unit of a good or service.

Marginal cost of capital The cost associated with raising one more dollar of capital.

Marginal-cost-of-capital schedule The tabular representation of the marginal cost of capital for different levels of capital.

Marginal efficiency of capital The additional (marginal) return from investing an additional dollar on capital investments.

Marginal revenue Benefit received from the sale of one more unit of a good or service.

Marginal tax rate Tax rate on the next dollar of taxable income.

Marketability risk The uncertainty associated with the salability of a security at its current value.

Marketable securities Investments in securities (notes, bonds, and stocks) that can be readily sold.

Market conversion price Market value obtained by converting convertible securities. See also *conversion value*.

Market equilibrium Prices reflecting the valuation of the marginal investor.

Market portfolio Comprises all assets, including the risk-free asset, resulting in a portfolio that has the best combination of risk and expected return.

Market risk The component of an asset's risk that cannot be diversified away.

Market risk premium Compensation for bearing the same amount of nondiversifiable risk as the market portfolio; the premium or additional return demanded for bearing market risk.

Market solution The result obtained when buyers and sellers trade an asset; the determination of an asset's value through trading among market participants.

Market value The worth of an asset, as determined by buyers' and sellers' trading.

Market value of equity The value of the ownership interest; for a corporation, the product of the price per share of stock and the number of shares outstanding.

Market value of shareholders' equity The total worth of the ownership interest in a corporation, including the market value of both common and preferred equity.

Master limited partnership A limited partnership whose shares of ownership are traded in security markets.

Maturity The length of the period between the time when a debt is incurred and the time when it must be repaid.

Maturity date The date on which the amount borrowed must be repaid.

Maturity factoring An arrangement whereby the buyer of accounts receivable (the factor) collects on them and remits the payments (less a commission) to the firm from which it bought the accounts receivable.

Maturity value The amount of the indebtedness repaid at the end of the period of the loan, at maturity; see also *par value* and *face value*.

Mean See *average*.

Median The middle value when all observations are ranked in numerical order.

Modal value or **mode** The most frequently observed value in a sample.

Modern portfolio theory (MPT) The theory that examines the role of diversification in a portfolio's risk.

Modified internal rate of return (MIRR) The yield that takes account of intermediate cash flows reinvested at a rate other than the internal rate of return.

Money market The market for trading short-term securities.

Money market preferred stock Preferred stock whose dividend is reset periodically by Dutch auction.

Money market security Short-term security, e.g., T-bill, negotiable certificate of deposit, or commercial paper; low-risk security having an original maturity of less than one year.

Monitoring cost Costs incurred by a principal to make sure that the agent acts in the best interests of the principal.

Mortgage A debt obligation secured (backed) by real property, such as land or buildings.

Mortgagee The creditor or lender of funds representing debt secured by real property.

Mortgagor The borrower of funds, where the resulting debt is secured by real property.

Most likely outcome The future outcome having the highest probability of occurrence among all possible outcomes.

Multiple regression Regression analysis with more than one independent variable.

Municipal bond Debt obligation issued by a local government body, such as a city or a county.

Mutually exclusive projects Investments whose acceptance precludes the acceptance of the other project(s).

N

National Association of Securities Dealers (NASD) An association of brokers and dealers who trade securities over the counter.

National Association of Securities Dealers Automated Quotation (NASDAQ) system A computerized market through which brokers and dealers of over-the-counter securities trade.

National Market System (NMS) A subset of NASDAQ securities for which more trading information (such as high, low, and last price quotations) is made available to NASDAQ.

Negative correlation The situation in which one variable tends to be above its mean or expected value while a related variable tends to be below its mean or expected value.

Negotiable certificate of deposit A large-denomination short-term promissory note traded in the secondary market.

Net cash flow (NCF) A period's cash flow, including the cash flows from operations as well as from acquiring and disposing of assets.

Net income Earnings or profits of an enterprise; income after interest and taxes are deducted from operating earnings.

Net operating cycle The length of the period between the time when cash is invested in a project and the time when that project is considered transformed back into cash; takes into account the length of time required to transform the investment in inventory back into cash through the collections on accounts receivable and the length of time the firm takes to pay its accounts payable.

Net operating loss (NOL) A negative taxable income that can be carried to and applied against taxable income in other years in order to obtain either a refund of prior taxes paid or a reduction in future taxes.

Net plant and equipment or **net plant assets** Gross plant assets less accumulated depreciation.

Net present value (NPV) The difference between the present value of the future cash inflows of a project and the present value of its future cash outflows, where all flows are discounted at the project's cost of capital.

Net present value profile See *investment profile*.

Net profit margin Net income divided by sales.

Net working capital The difference between current assets and current liabilities.

Net working capital-to-sales ratio The ratio of net working capital to sales; a measure of a firm's liquidity.

New York Stock Exchange (NYSE) The largest U.S. exchange in terms of the market value of securities traded; located in New York City.

Nominal interest rate or **nominal rate** For a specified period, the rate of interest that does not take into account the effects of compounding; also referred to as the *stated interest rate* or *annual percentage rate*.

Nominal return Stated return that includes both the real return and a premium for expected inflation.

Noncumulative preferred stock Preferred shares that do not require that passed over dividends (dividends not paid) be paid in the future.

Nondiversifiable risk The degree of uncertainty of an asset's cash flows that cannot be reduced by combining it in a portfolio with assets whose cash flows are not perfectly positively correlated with its cash flows; also referred to as *market risk*.

No-par stock Shares of stock that does not have a par, or stated, value.

Normal distribution A continuous probability distribution that is symmetric and bell-shaped and can be fully described by its expected value and standard deviation.

Normal profit The minimum return necessary for a firm to continue operating.

Note A debt obligation that does not have an indenture agreement; generally considered to be debt that has a short maturity.

Noteholder The owner of (investor in) a note.

Number of days of credit The average number of days needed to collect on accounts receivable.

Number of days of inventory The average time inventory takes to go from raw materials to sold finished goods.

Number of days of purchases The average number of days a firm takes to pay on its accounts payable.

O

Operating cash flow (OCF) Cash flow from operations.

Operating cycle The time required for an investment of cash in the production of goods and services to produce cash from the sale of the goods and services that result from that investment.

Operating earnings See *earnings before interest and taxes*.

Operating income See *earnings before interest and taxes*.

Operating lease A rental arrangement whose term is less than the leased asset's economic life and is typically cancelable.

Operating leverage The mixture of fixed costs and variable costs in a firm's operating cost structure; the greater are the fixed costs (relative to variable costs), the greater is the potential risk associated with operating earnings.

Operating profit See *earnings before interest and taxes*.

Operating profit margin Earnings generated from operations, sometimes expressed in terms of per dollar of revenue.

Operating risk Uncertainty attributed to the firm's mix of fixed and variable operating costs.

Operational budgeting The process of planning the sources and uses of funds over a short time horizon, such as one year.

Opportunity cost The return on the next best available investment opportunity.

Optimal capital budget The amount of spending on capital projects that maximizes the value of the firm; spending on capital projects up to the point at which the marginal efficiency of capital equals its marginal cost.

Optimal capital structure The mixture of debt and equity that maximizes the value of the firm; in the trade-off theory of capital structure, it is the mixture of debt and equity at which the marginal benefit from the tax deductibility of interest equals the marginal cost associated with financial distress.

Option A contract that gives the buyer the right to buy (a call) or the seller the right to sell (a put) a particular asset at a specified price within a specified period.

Ordering cost Expenses incurred to place an order.

Ordinary annuity A series of level cash flows occurring at regular intervals, although the first cash flow occurs at the end of the first period.

Ordinary least squares (OLS) A statistical technique for estimating a regression line; it requires finding the line that minimizes the sum of the square of each difference between the actual sample (observed) value of the dependent variable and the value predicted by the regression line.

Original maturity The maturity of a debt security at the time it is issued.

Out of the money For a call option, the situation in which the exercise price of an option is greater than the value of the underlying asset; for a put option, the situation in which the exercise price of an option is less than the value of the underlying asset.

Outside director A member of the board of directors who is not an employee of the corporation.

Outstanding shares Shares of stock that have been issued and not subsequently bought back by the issuer.

Over-the-counter (OTC) market The market for securities traded over some medium, such as a computer or a phone line, in contrast to an exchange market, which is organized and is at a physical location.

Owners' equity See *equity*.

P

Participating debt A debt obligation whose interest is determined, in part or in whole, as a percentage of the debtor's (issuer's) earnings.

Participating security A type of security whose income (interest or dividend) is determined, in part or in whole, by the firm's earnings.

Partnership A contractual agreement between two or more persons to operate a business.

Par value The stated value of a security; it is printed on the security's certificate; see also *face value*, or *maturity value*.

Payback period The time it takes for the initial investment to be recovered in terms of future cash inflows; also referred to as the *payoff period*.

Payment date The date on which a dividend or interest on a security is paid.

Payoff period See *payback period*.

Pecking order A preferred ordering; in capital structure theory, an explanation of a firm's preference for internal rather than external capital.

Penny stock Low-priced stock, usually under $1 per share.

Percent-of-sales method A technique used to construct pro forma financial statements; relates each item in a financial statement to sales.

Perfectly negatively correlated A situation in which two variables move in exactly opposite directions to precisely the same degree.

Perfectly positively correlated A situation in which two variables move in exactly the same direction and by precisely the same degree.

Perfect market A market in which there are no taxes, no transaction costs, no costs in issuing securities, and no costs associated with the receiving or sending of information.

Performance shares Shares of stock given to employees on the basis of some measure of operating performance, such as earnings per share.

Permanent working capital The minimum amount of current assets needed for the operation of the business, aside from its seasonal needs.

Perpetual debt Indebtedness that never matures.

Perpetual warrant A warrant (an option to buy shares of stock at a specified price) that does not expire.

Perpetuity A series consisting of identical cash flows that occur at regular intervals forever.

Perquisites (perks) Fringe benefits enjoyed by employees.

Plant assets Physical property expected to produce cash flows in the future.

Poison pill A provision, usually specified in terms of rights given to existing shareholders, that makes a firm unattractive in the event of a hostile takeover; for example, a *shareholder rights plan* gives shareholders the right to buy shares of the firm at a substantial discount from market value.

Poison put Put feature of a security designed to discourage a takeover of the issuer by another firm.

Portfolio A collection of assets.

Positively correlated A situation in which two variables tend to move in the same direction at the same time.

Postauditing Comparing actual results with what was budgeted; can be used to evaluate performance and budgeting techniques.

Postcompletion audit Review of the realized and projected cash flows from an investment.

Postpayback duration Time beyond an investment's payback period during which the investment continues to generate cash inflows.

Potentially dilutive securities Securities that can be transformed (either through exercise or exchange) into common stock.

Precautionary balance The amount of an asset that is held in case of extraordinary demand for it.

Preemptive right A privilege granted by a corporate charter to current shareholders giving them the opportunity to purchase shares of any new stock issue, thus enabling them to preserve their proportionate share of ownership in the corporation.

Preferred stock Ownership interest in a corporation; has priority over common stock with regard to the receipt of dividends and, in the event of a liquidation, the claim on assets.

Preliminary prospectus Document provided to the Securities and Exchange Commission, describing a security issue and its issuer; since a disclaimer is made in red ink on the front page, specifying that the preliminary prospectus is not an offer of the security for sale, this document has become known as the *red herring*.

Premium The amount by which the value of a debt exceeds its face value.

Premium-priced option A stock option whose exercise price is above the current market price of a share of stock; often granted to employees of a corporation.

Prepayment risk The risk that the issuer will prepay (pay prior to maturity) a portion or all of an investment's principal.

Present value (PV) The current value of a cash flow or series of future cash flows.

Present value annuity factor The rate that translates a series of future level cash flows into a single current equivalent value.

Present value of the interest tax shield (PVITS) The value today of expected tax reductions resulting from future deductions of interest payments from taxable income.

Price-earnings (P/E) ratio The ratio of the current market price of a share of common stock to the earnings available for common stock.

Primary dealer A securities dealer who purchases securities directly from the U.S. government for resale to investors.

Primary earnings per share Earnings per share of common stock outstanding, without considering the potentially dilutive effects of other securities (e.g., convertible securities).

Primary market The market in which an asset is originally sold; for securities, it is the market in which the security issuer receives funds from investors.

Prime rate The interest rate a financial institution charges its most creditworthy customers on indebtedness.

Principal For a loan, it's the amount borrowed; in the context of a security, it's the face amount of the security; when talking about agency relations, it's the party represented by another party (the agent).

Private corporation See *privately held corporation*.

Privately held corporation A corporation whose securities are not traded in the public markets; also referred to as a *private corporation*.

Private placement Sale of a security by the issuer directly to investors.

Probability The likelihood that an uncertain outcome will occur.

Probability distribution A measure representing the likelihood that each possible future outcome will occur.

Production efficiency The allocation of resources to producers who produce goods and services at the level at which average total cost is minimized.

Professional corporation A form of business enterprise with all the characteristics of a corporation except limited liability.

Profitability index (PI) The ratio of the present value of future cash inflows to the present value of future cash outflows.

Profit margin ratio The ratio that represents the earnings generated for each dollar of revenues.

Profit-sharing Basing a debt security's interest income, in part, on the income of the firm issuing the debt.

Pro forma balance sheet The projected balance sheet for one or more periods into the future.

Pro forma income statement The projected income statement for one or more periods into the future.

Progressive taxation A tax rate system in which greater increments of income are taxed at increasing rates.

Project tracking A system of periodically keeping track of realized cash inflows and outflows in order to help detect unanticipated events, such as cost overruns.

Proprietor The sole owner of a business.

Prospectus The document that describes a security issue and its issuer.

Proxy A written authorization giving one person the right to act for another.

Proxy card A document that gives one party the right to act on behalf of another.

Proxy statement A document that describes the matters to be voted on by shareholders, the compensation of officers and directors, and the candidates for the board of directors.

Public corporation or **publicly held corporation** A corporation whose securities are traded in the securities markets.

Public warehouse loan A loan that uses inventory as collateral, whereby the lender takes title to the inventory and must give permission to the borrower before any item may be sold.

Purchasing power risk The uncertainty associated with changes in the purchasing power of a currency (i.e., changes resulting from inflation or deflation).

Pureplay A firm in a single line of business.

Putable bond or **putable debt** Indebtedness that gives the investor the right to sell a security to its issuer at a specified price, usually under specified conditions.

Put feature A characteristic of a security that gives its owner (the investor) the right to sell it back to its issuer at a specified price.

Put option A contract that gives its buyer the right to sell the specified asset at a specified price and within a specified period.

Q

Quick ratio The ratio of the most liquid current assets (usually cash, marketable securities, and accounts receivable) to current liabilities; also referred to as the *acid-test ratio*.

R

Range A statistical measure of dispersion; for a probability distribution, it's the difference between the highest and lowest possible outcomes; for a sample, it's the difference between the highest and lowest sample observations.

Ratio A mathematical relation between one quantity and another.

Real return Return on an asset after taking into account the loss in its value due to inflation.

Recapture of depreciation The amount by which an asset's selling price (or original cost if sold for more than original cost) exceeds its book value, representing the amount it has been overdepreciated during its life, which is taxed as ordinary income.

Red herring See *preliminary prospectus*.

Refunding Retiring existing debt while simultaneously issuing new debt, usually to replace debt with a lower coupon security.

Registered debt A note or bond whose ownership is known to the issuer and for which payments of interest and principal are made by the firm according to these records of ownership.

Registration statement Document filed with the Securities and Exchange Commission, describing a firm and the security it plans to issue to the investing public.

Regression A statistical technique for describing the relationship between one variable (the dependent variable) and one or more other variables (the independent or explanatory variables).

Regression equation Symbolic representation of the relation between one variable and two or more other variables.

Regression line Graphical representation of the relationship between one variable (the dependent variable) and one or more other variables (the independent or explanatory variables); represented symbolically as the *regression equation*.

Regression model The specific mathematical relationship between two variables.

Reinvestment rate (RR) The rate of return earned on the reinvestment of an asset's cash flows.

Reinvestment rate risk The degree of uncertainty regarding the return available on the reinvestment of cash flows from an investment.

Relevant risk The risk of an asset for which investors demand compensation for bearing; in the capital asset pricing model, this is referred to as the *market risk*.

Remote disbursements Payment by checks drawn on distant banks and intended to slow check processing, hence increasing the float.

Replacement chain method Method of selecting among mutually exclusive projects that have different useful lives; the procedure restates each project's net present value considering a finite number of replacements of the project so that all projects (considering replacement) have a common life.

Replacement project An investment that involves replacing an existing asset with another asset that performs essentially the same function.

Repurchase agreement Financing in which an investor sells a security (generally low-risk, short-term money market securities such as U.S. Treasury bills) and agrees to buy them back within a short time.

Required rate of return (RRR) Minimum rate of return needed to undertake an investment, taking into account the time value of money and the uncertainty of the investment's future cash flows.

Residual loss In an agency relationship, the difference between the value of a firm with and without monitoring and bonding efforts to ensure that agents act in the best interests of the principals.

Residual term See *disturbance term*.

Residual value See *salvage value*.

Restricted stock grant A grant of shares of stock that prohibits the recipient from selling them prior to a specified time.

Retained earnings The firm's earnings that are not paid out as dividends to owners, but which instead are reinvested in the firm's assets.

Return Profit or loss over time, generally expressed annually and as a percentage of some other value; also referred to as *yield*.

Return on assets The profit earned for each dollar invested in assets.

Return on common equity The profit earned for each dollar of common shareholders' equity.

Return on equity The profit earned for each dollar of shareholders' equity.

Return-on-investment ratio A measure of the profit generated per dollar invested in assets.

Return point In the Miller-Orr cash management model, the amount of cash the firm aims toward each time the level of cash hits either an upper limit (requiring an investment in marketable securities) or a lower limit (requiring a cash infusion).

Return ratio A ratio measuring the profit generated per dollar invested.

Revenue See *sales*.

Revenue bond A debt obligation that is issued by a municipality and whose promised interest and principal are paid from the revenues of a particular asset.

Reverse stock split Fewer shares given in exchange for existing shares.

Revolving credit agreement A line of credit given by a lending institution; allows the borrower to borrow up to a specified amount, usually within two or three years.

Right The grant of an option to buy a specified number of shares of common stock of the grantor at a specified price within a specified period.

Rights offering Shares of stock offered for sale to current shareholders.

Risk The degree of uncertainty of future outcomes.

Risk-adjusted discount rate The discount rate that reflects the time value of money and compensation for bearing risk.

Risk averse The trait of dislike of risk.

Risk aversion The dislike of risk.

Risk neutral The trait of indifference toward risk.

Risk preference The trait of liking risk.

Risk premium Compensation for bearing risk; the difference between the discount rate applied to a risky cash flow stream and the discount rate applied to a risk-free cash flow stream.

S

Safety stock The amount of an asset kept to meet extraordinary demands for it.

Salary Cash compensation for employment.

Sale-leaseback arrangement An agreement whereby the owner of an asset sells it to another party and then leases it from its new owner.

Sales Receipts from the sale of goods and services; also referred to as *revenue*.

Sales risk The degree of uncertainty (as a result of economic and market forces) associated with the number of units of goods and services expected to be sold and the price of those goods and services.

Salvage value The expected value of an asset at the end of its useful life; also referred to as the asset's *residual value*.

Sample A collection of observations.

Sample mean Average of sample observations; the sum of the sample observations, divided by the number of observations.

Sample standard deviation Standard deviation of sample observations; the square root of the sample variance.

Sample variance A measure of dispersion of values in a sample; the sum of the squared deviations of sample values from the sample mean, divided by the number of observations in the sample less one.

Seasonal dating Credit terms tailored to accommodate customers' seasonal business.

Secondary market Market in which assets are traded among investors.

Secured bond or **secured debt** or **secured note** Debt that is backed by specified property; if the debt issuer fails to make interest or principal payments when due, the creditor can recover what is due from the proceeds of the sale of the property.

Secured loan A loan that is backed by specific property (referred to as the loan's security); if the borrower is unable to pay its obligations, the lender may receive the interest and repayment of the loan from the proceeds of the sale of the property.

Securities and Exchange Commission (SEC) The federal agency that administers the securities laws of the United States; created by the Securities Exchange Act of 1934.

Securities market A market in which securities are bought and sold; it can have either a physical location (an exchange) or can be without a physical location (over the counter).

Securitization Creating a security by grouping together assets and selling the rights to the cash flows from the group.

Security Ownership in future cash flows of an asset; specific property that is collateral for the secured debt.

Security market line (SML) The relation between the expected return on an asset and the asset's beta.

Semistrong form of market efficiency A degree of market efficiency whereby asset prices reflect all publicly available information.

Senior debt Indebtedness whose owners have a prior claim over the owners of other indebtedness of the same firm.

Seniority The status of a security that has a prior claim on income or assets over another security of the same firm.

Sensitivity analysis Analysis of alternative scenarios that could affect future outcomes.

Serial debt Indebtedness issued at the same time but that matures at different times in the future.

Share A unit of ownership of the stock of a corporation.

Shareholder The owner of shares of stock of a corporation; also referred to as a *stockholder*.

Shareholder democracy The system of corporate governance that provides for the election of directors by the shareholders and voting by shareholders on major decisions of the corporation.

Shareholder ratios Financial ratios that restate financial data in terms of one share of stock.

Shareholder rights plan See *poison pill*.

Shareholders Owners of a corporation.

Shareholders' equity Ownership interest in a corporation; composed of preferred stock, common stock, paid-in capital in excess of par, and retained earnings.

Shark repellants Tactics (such as golden parachutes and poison pills) that discourage unwanted takeover attempts.

Shelf registration Registration of securities under SEC Rule 415: A master statement is filed with the SEC, and securities can be issued under that statement any time within two years of the filing.

Shirking Not expending one's best efforts; in an agency relationship, the problem of a manager (the agent) not expending his or her best efforts in the interests of the owners (the principal).

Short-term investment An investment whose benefits are generally realized within one year.

Sight draft A document that requires payment upon presentation.

Simple correlation coefficient A statistical measure of association between two variables.

Simple interest Payment of interest at the end of the loan period, where interest is paid on only the principal (not paid on accumulated interest).

Simple regression Regression analysis with one independent variable.

Simulation analysis Examination of possible outcomes, taking into account the probability distributions of uncertain elements.

Single-payment interest Interest paid at the end of the loan's term.

Single-payment loan A loan requiring interest to be paid only at the end of the loan's term.

Sinking fund A trust fund created by the security issuer to pay obligations on the security: the security issuer deposits funds in the trust, which are used either to pay interest and principal or to repurchase the security through a call or by open market purchases.

Sinking fund call price The price at which the security can be bought back by the issuer in the case in which the security is retired in whole or in part by a sinking fund.

Soft put The feature of a security that allows the investor to exchange it with its issuer, although the choice of what is given in exchange is determined by the security's issuer.

Sole proprietorship A business enterprise owned by one person; see *proprietor*.

Speculative balance The amount of an asset kept to be prepared for future investment opportunities.

Speculative debt or **speculative bond** Indebtedness for which there is significant risk of default; noninvestment-grade debt obligations; also referred to as *junk bond*.

Speculator A person who buys an asset, assuming the risks of unfavorable asset price movements.

Spread In underwriting, the difference between the price an investor pays for a security and the proceeds the issuer receives, which is paid to the party (the underwriter) that facilitates the security's sale; in a market, the difference between what a seller is willing to sell an asset for (the ask price) and what the buyer is willing to pay for it (the bid price).

Staggered board of directors See *classified board of directors*.

Stakeholders The parties who are affected by the actions of some other party; a corporation's stakeholders include its shareholders and employees and the members of the communities in which it operates.

Stand-alone risk The total risk of a project.

Standard & Poor's 500 Stock Index (S&P 500) An index composed of security prices of a selected group of five hundred U.S. corporations; serves as a barometer of general market movements.

Standard deviation With respect to a probability distribution, it's a measure of the differences between the possible outcomes and the expected value; in the context of a sample of observations, it's the measure of the difference between the sample observations and the sample mean.

Standby underwriting An agreement between a security issuer and the underwriter(s) who will purchase any shares of stock unsold following a rights offering.

Stated rate See *annual percentage rate*.

Stated value The nominal value assigned by a firm's management to an accounting item for financial statement purposes.

Statement of cash flows The financial statement that identifies the cash flows from operations, from financing activities, and investment activities; a financial statement required by Statement of Financial Accounting Standards no. 95.

Stock The ownership interest in a corporation.

Stock appreciation rights Privilege enabling the recipient to receive in cash the amount by which a specified number of shares of stock increase in value over a specified period of time.

Stockbroker An individual who buys and sells securities for her or his clients.

Stock dividend A distribution in the form of additional shares of stock to shareholders.

Stockholder See *shareholder*.

Stockholders' equity See *shareholders' equity*.

Stock option A contract that gives the owner the right to buy shares of stock at a specified price within a specified period.

Stock purchase program An arrangement under which a corporation sells its shares of stock directly to investors.

Stock split An exchange of shareholders' current shares for an increased number of shares; also referred to as a *forward stock split*.

Straight coupon Interest specified as a fixed percentage of the security's face value.

Straight-line depreciation An even allocation of the cost of an asset over its economic life.

Strategic plan A set of actions used to carry out a strategy, comprising financing and investment activities.

Strategy A sense of how to reach objectives.

Strike price See *exercise price*.

Strong form of market efficiency A degree of market efficiency whereby all information (both public and private) is reflected in asset prices.

Subchapter S corporation or **Sub S corporation** A corporation electing a special tax status that allows income to be taxed only once, at the individual shareholder level; generally a small business owned by a small number of shareholders.

Subordinated debt Indebtedness in which the priority of claims to income or assets is less than the priority of other securities.

Sum-of-the-years' digits method of depreciation Allocating the cost of an asset over its economic life so that the rate of depreciation is the ratio of the remaining years of its life to the sum of the digits of all the years that make up its life.

Sunk cost Past expenditure having no bearing on the attractiveness of current and future investments.

Syndicate A group of investment bankers who underwrite the issuance of a security.

Systematic risk The degree of uncertainty of an asset's returns that cannot be eliminated through diversification.

T

Targeted block repurchase See *greenmail*.

Tax A required payment to the government that has the effect of redistributing income from the private sector to the government sector.

Tax clientele The clustering of ownership of shares of stock according to the dividends paid by the corporations and the investors' tax situation.

Tax shield The reduction in taxes payable that results from a deduction from taxable income.

Temporary working capital Current assets above what is minimally required for the operation of the business; generally due to seasonal variations in the firm's operations or sales.

Tender offer An offer made directly to owners to purchase their shares of the security.

10-K statement Filed annually with the SEC; includes the annual report to shareholders and detailed information on the firm's operations and financing.

10-Q statement Filed quarterly with the SEC; provides information on the firm's operating and financial activities.

Terminal value The future value of an investment's cash flows, assuming a return on reinvested cash flows at some reinvestment rate.

Term loan A loan with a specified maturity date.

Time draft A draft payable only after a specific period.

Time line A graphical depiction of cash flows at different points in time.

Time path The values a debt has throughout its life, assuming a constant yield to maturity, with its value eventually converging upon its maturity value at maturity.

Times interest coverage ratio See *interest coverage ratio*.

Time value of money The idea that a dollar at one time is not worth the same as a dollar at another point in time.

Tombstone ad An advertisement in the financial press.

Total asset turnover A measure of a firm's ability to put its assets to use in generating sales; ratio of dollar sales to the amount invested in assets.

Total debt-to-assets ratio A measure of a firm's use of debt to finance its assets; the ratio of total debt to the amount invested in assets.

Total quality control (TQC) A management philosophy requiring that all aspects of the firm be involved in ensuring the quality of the goods and services it produces.

Trade credit Spontaneous, informal credit granted to customers specifically for the purchase of the firm's goods and services.

Transaction costs The costs of buying or selling a security, paid to an intermediary, such as a broker.

Transactions balance Amount of an asset on hand to meet the day-to-day operations of a business.

Treasury bill or **T-bill** A short-term debt obligation of the U.S. government that pays no interest but, instead, is sold at a discount from its face value.

Treasury stock The value of stock purchased by the issuing firm and not retired.

Triple-witching day A trading day on which stock index futures contracts, index options, and individual stock options all expire.

Trustee The party that represents the interests of the bondholders.

Trust receipts loan A lending arrangement in which the borrower holds the inventory in trust for the lender and remits proceeds from the sale of the inventory to the lender. The holding of the inventory is referred to as *floor planning*.

Turnover ratio A measure of the number of times an investment in an asset has generated sales equal to its value during a period of time.

U

Uncertainty The situation in which future outcomes are not known.

Uncommitted line of credit A nonlegally binding promise to lend up to a specified amount of funds within a specified period of time.

Underwriter An investment banker that buys a security issue from the issuer and resells it to investors.

Underwriting Buying securities from the issuer and reselling them to investors.

Unit The combination of two or more securities, such as a bond and a warrant, that can trade as one security.

Unit trust A trust in which securities are deposited and units of ownership in the trust are sold to investors.

Unsecured debt Indebtedness not backed by specific property but by the general credit of the debtor (that is, the debtor's ability to generate funds to pay the debt obligations).

Unsecured loan A loan that is not backed by any specific asset but by the general credit of the firm.

Unsystematic risk The degree of uncertainty of an asset's returns that can be eliminated through diversification; also referred to as *company-specific risk*.

Useful life See *economic life*.

W

Wages and salaries payable Short-term liability representing the amount due to employees.

Warrant A security that gives its owner the right to buy a specified number of shares of stock at a specified price within a specified period.

Weak form of market efficiency A degree of market efficiency whereby all past prices of an asset are reflected in its current price.

Weighted average cost of capital (WACC) or **weighted cost of capital** The marginal cost of raising additional capital; the marginal cost of each source of capital is weighted by its proportion in the capital structure.

Working capital Assets used in the day-to-day operations of the firm; see also *current assets*.

Y

Yankee certificate of deposit Certificates of deposit issued by foreign banks located in the United States.

Yield See *return*.

Yield to call The effective annual return earned by a security if it is bought and held until it is called (bought back) by the issuer.

Yield to maturity The annual return earned by a security if it is bought and held until it matures; as commonly used, yield to maturity is an annualized rate.

Z

Zero-balance account (ZBA) A form of controlled disbursements: only amounts necessary to meet checks presented are deposited in the bank account.

Zero-coupon debt Indebtedness on which no explicit interest is paid; a bond or note whose only cash flow to the investor is its face value at maturity.

Brief Solutions to End-of-Chapter Problems

END-OF-CHAPTER SOLUTION HINTS

Chapter 1 Hints

1-1   **a.**   Mary: $6,000

1-2   **a.**   Ivan: $25,000

1-3   Shareholders receive $0.42 of every dollar of Flow Through's income

1-4   Shareholders receive $0.21 of every dollar of Halfling's income

1-5   Corning: $7,298 billion

Chapter 2 Hints

2-1   Rank 2: Commercial paper

Chapter 3 Hints

3-1   **d.**   Tax = $340,000; marginal tax rate = 34%; average tax rate = 34%

3-2   **c.** $88,875.50; 31%; 29.6%

3-3   Depreciable cost = $800,000

3-4   Declining balance rate = 36.9% per year

3-5   **a.**   Dividends received deduction = $2.1 million

3-6   **b.**   Dividend income included in taxable income = $2 million

3-7   Apply to 1992, then 1993, then 1994 income

3-8   Carry back loss to 1991

3-9   **a.**   Year 1: $20,000
       b.   Year 1: $20,000 $\times$ 34% = $6,800

3-10   **a.**   Year 2: $1,000,000 $\times$ 24.49% = $244,900
       b.   Year 2: $244,900 $\times$ 34% = $83,266

3-11   **a.**   Taxable income = $102,000

3-12   **a.**   Taxable income = $490,000

Chapter 4 Hints

4-1   **j.** $1,050 $\div$ $6,000 = 17.5%

4-2   **a.**   Average day's cost of goods sold = $29,589 million
       b.   Credit sales per day = $32.877 million
       c.   Average day's purchases = $27.398 million

4-3   Firm X's debt-to-assets = 33.33%

4-4   Dividend payout $= \dfrac{\$2.50}{\$4.00}$

4-5   **b.**   Return on assets = 2% net profit margin $\times$ 12 total asset turnover

4-6   **c.**   Break return on assets down into net profit margin and total asset turnover
       d.   Break return on equity down into return on assets and equity multiplier

4-7   **a.**   Current ratio, Jan. '92: $\dfrac{\$1,926.85}{\$1,594.28}$

4-8   **a.**   Average growth rate of sales is 21.6% over the nine years

Chapter 5 Hints

5-1   PV = $100 and r = 8%

5-2   PV = $1,000 and r = 4%

5-3   **c.**   Compare balance with compound interest to balance with simple interest

5-4   **a.** $t = 2$

5-5   FV = $100 and r = 8%

5-6   **a.** $r = 5\%$ and $t = 2$

5-7 $t = 16$ and $r = 0.5\%$

5-8   **c.** $t = 20$ and $r = 3\%$

5-9   FV of Period 0 cash flow = $121

5-10   FV of Year 1999 cash flow = $5,000

5-11   PV of Period 1 cash flow = $189

5-12   **a.**   PV of 2003 cash flow = $-$863.84
　　　　b.   PV of 2003 cash flow = $-$822.70

5-13   Factor = 3.1525

5-14   Factor = 2.7232

5-15   **a.**   Factor = 3.4651

5-16   CF = $10; r = 6%; and T = infinity

5-17 $r = 1.88\%$

5-18   PV = $40 and CF = $2

5-19   Factor = $1 + 0.9434 + 0.8900 = 2.8334$

5-20   Factor = $3.1936 \times 1.06 = 3.3746$

5-21   Annuity due

5-22   10 payment ordinary annuity, discounted 4 periods

5-23   39 deposits, 20 withdrawals

5-24   10 payment ordinary annuity, deferred 2 years

5-25   PV = $2,000; FV = $4,000; and t = 6

5-26   PV $-$ $20,000; CF = $5,276; and T = 5

5-27   PV = 15; FV = 28; and t = 11

5-28   **a.**   PV = $10,000; r = 5%; and FV = $15,000

5-29   **a.**   PV = $1; FV = $2; and r = 5%

5-30   FV = $5,000; PV = $2,500; and r = 4%

5-31   **a.** $r = 5\%$ and $t = 4$

5-32   **d.** $r - 50\%$ and $t = 2$

5-33   3.78% per quarter

5-34 $r = 1\%$

5-35   Pawnshop r = 25% and t = 7.3

5-36   **a.**   Solve for PV of an amount　　　　**c.**   Solve for FV of an ordinary annuity

　　　　b.   Solve for PV of an ordinary annuity　　　　**d.**   Solve for FV of an amount

5-37   FV = $7,321.14

5-38   Compare balance using compounded interest with balance using simple interest

5-39 $r = 12\%$; $T = 10$; and $CF = \$1,000$

5-40 $r = 3\%$ and $T = 12$

5-41   **Plan 1:** 41 deposits, 30 withdrawals
            Plan 2: 40 deposits; 30 withdrawals
            Plan 3: 39 deposits; 30 withdrawals

5-42 $T = 16$ and $CF = \$240,245$

5-43 $t = 21$; $PV = \$0.28$; and $FV = \$1.35$

Chapter 6 Hints

6-1   PV of $\$1,200 = \$1,090.91$

6-2 $PV = \$50,000$

6-3 $D_1 = \$2.63$

6-4 $g = 8.01\%$

6-5 $D_1 = \$6.24$

6-6   **a.** $D_1 = \$2.10$ **b.** $D_1 = \$2.04$ **c.** $P_5 = \$32.55$

6-7   **a.** $D_1 = \$3.06$ **b.** $D_1 = \$3.12$ **c.** $P_4 = \$119.33$

6-8 $r_p = 10\%$; $D = \$5$

6-9   **b.**   PV of dividends + PV of call price

6-10 $D = \$9$; $P_p = \$90$

6-11 P_p (if $r_p = 8\%$) $= \$62.50$

6-12 $D = \$5$; $P_p = \$80$

6-13 $M = \$1,000$; $C = \$80$; $r_d = 6\%$; and $T = 3$

6-14 $M = \$1,000$; $C = \$50$; $r_d = 4\%$; and $T = 5$

6-15 $M = \$1,000$; $C = \$30$; $r_d = 4\%$; and $T = 10$

6-16 $M = \$1,000$; $C = \$50$; $r_d = 4\%$; and $T = 20$

6-17 $M = \$1,000$; $C = \$30$; and $T = 6$

6-18 $M = \$1,000$; $C = \$40$; $r_d = 3\%$; and $T = 10$

6-19 $M = \$1,000$; $C = \$80$; $r_d = 6\%$; and $T = 10$

6-20 $PV = \$3,000$; $FV = \$3,200$; and $t = 3$

6-21   **a.** $PV = \$3,000$; $FV = \$2,500$; and $t = 6$
         b. $PV = \$3,030$; $FV = \$2,475$; and $t = 6$

6-22   **a.** $PV = \$500$; $FV = \$750$; and $t = 12$
         b. $PV = \$510$; $FV = \$735$; and $t = 12$

6-23   **a.** $C = \$30$; $PV = \$800$; $M = \$900$; and $T = 2$
         b. $C = \$30$; $PV = \$800$; $M = \$1,000$; and $T = 4$
         c. $C = \$30$; $PV = \$800$; $M = \$1,000$; and $T = 8$

6-24 $M = \$1,000$; $C = \$30$; and $r_d = 5\%$ for six months

6-25 $M = \$1,000$; $C = \$60$; and $T = 6$

6-26   **a.** $r = 3$ and $t = 2$

6-27 $PV = \$1,081.11$; $M = \$1000$; $C = \$50$; and $T = 10$

6-28   M = \$1,000; and t = 5

6-29   M = \$1,000; T = 10; PV = \$900; and r_d = 5% per six months

6-30   Cash flows: $-$ \$1,000,000; $+$\$800,000; $+$\$400,000; $+$\$600,000

6-31   **a.** P_0 of common = \$23.75
          b. P_0 of common = \$27.94

Chapter 7 Hints

7-1   EBIT = \$100,000

7-2   Hi-Gear EBIT = \$200,000 and Lo-Gear EBIT = \$200,000

7-3   If r = 6%, Bond MM value = \$1,000 and Bond NN value = \$829.40

7-4   If r = 5%, Bond OO value = \$613.91 and Bond PP value = \$1,389.73

7-5   real return $\times$ inflation rate = 0.32%

7-6   nominal = 4% + real rate + (real rate $\times$ 4%)

7-7   **b.**   Variance = 12,960,000,000,000

7-8   **b.**   Investment 1 variance = 77,500; Investment 2 variance = 150,727

7-9   **b.**   Investment A variance = 14,185,000; Investment B variance = 24,090,000

7-10   Return if yield is 15%: HI bond: $-$16.8%; LI Bond: $-$17.9%

7-11   If correlation = 0, portfolio variance = $(0.25 \times 0.0016) + (0.25 \times 0.0036) = 0.0013$

7-12   If correlation = 0, portfolio variance = $(0.25 \times 0.0016) + (0.25 \times 0.0001) = 0.000425$

7-13   If invest equally, portfolio variance = 0.003700

7-14   If invest equally, portfolio variance = 0.000625

7-15 r_f = 5% and $r_m - r_f$ = 4%

7-16 r_f = 5% and r_m = 8%; $r_m - r_f$ = 3%

7-17 r_f = 5% and $r_m - r_f$ = 7%

7-18 r_f = 4% and $r_m - r_f$ = 8%

Chapter 8 Hints

8-1   Shipping and installation are part of investment outlay

8-2   Book value after five years = \$75,000

8-3   **a.**   Include cost of set-up in investment outlay
          b.   Both machines are fully depreciated at the end of ten years (book value = \$0)

8-4   **b.**   Tax on sale = \$4,000   **c.**   Tax on sale = \$26,544

8-5   **b.**   Tax on sale = \$2,518

8-6   **a.**   Change in taxes = \$16,000   **c.**   Change in taxes = \$32,000
          b.   Change in taxes = \$24,000   **d.**   Change in taxes = \$40,000

8-7   Year 4: Difference in depreciation = \$11,520 $-$ 20,000 = $-$\$8,480

8-8   Tax-shield from selling machine at a loss is \$23,040

8-9   Tax-shield from loss on sale is \$3,456

8-10   Disposition cash flow in third year = $+$\$243,345

8-11   Disposition cash flow in Year 7 = $+$\$240,000

8-12   Tax-shield from sale of old machine = $45,000

8-13   Tax on sale of new machine in Year 5 = $115,808

8-14   Cash flow from disposition of new equipment in Year 5 = +$140,000

Chapter 9 Hints

9-1   **d.**   Present value of cash inflows = $111,031
      i.   Terminal value of cash inflows = $140,108

9-2   **d.**   Present value of cash inflows = $108,919.14
      i.   Terminal value of cash inflows = $144,971.38

9-3   **d.**   Present value of cash inflows = $246,401.14
      i.   Terminal value of cash inflows = $396,831.50

9-4   **d.**   Present value of cash inflows = $119,459.74
      i.   Terminal value of cash inflows = $174,901

9-5   **d.**   Present value of cash inflows = $107,159.06
      h.   Net present value if discount rate is 8% = $100,442.01

9-6   **a.**   NPV of Thing 1 = $1,676.82; NPV of Thing 2 = $2,045.19

9-7   **a.**   NPV of Thing 3 = $2,421.47; NPV of Thing 4 = $5,950.56

9-8   **a.**   NPV of Thing 5 = $3,000.00; NPV of Thing 6 = $3,500.00

9-9   Eliminate EE from consideration

9-10 **a.**   Use PI, NPV, or IRR

9-11 **a.**   NPV of capital budget with KK, JJ, and LL is $210,000

9-12 **a.**   Acquisition cash flow, Year 0 = −$500,000; Disposition cash flow, Year 5 = +$78,640
      b.   Present value of cash inflows = $557,959.89
      h.   Terminal value of cash inflows = $818,600.80

9-13 **a.**   Net cash flow, Year 3 = $320,000
      h.   Terminal value of cash inflows = $750,500

9-14 Present value of Year 2005's cash flow = $298,630

9-15 Present value of fifth year's cash flow = $61,250

Appendix 9A Hints

9A-1 NPV of Felix, one replacement = $1,770.98; NPV of Oscar, two replacements = $385.62

9A-2 NPV of UX, using the equivalent annual annuity approach = $34,762.49

9A-3 NPV of Project 1 using the equivalent annual annuity approach = $17,884.52

Appendix 9B Hints

9B-1 Factor = 3.5770

9B-2 Interest in first year = $73,142

9B-3 **a.**   Factor = 4.1698   **c.**   Net cash flow from lease, Year 1 = −$167,873

9B-4 **a.**   Factor = 2.7355   **c.**   Net cash flow from lease, Year 1 = −$21,934

9B-5 Present value of future benefits = $568,618

Chapter 10 Hints

10-1 **c.**   Variance = 400,000

10-2 **c.**   Variance = 360,000

10-3 **c.** GHI variance = 25,410,000; JKL variance = 6,360,000

10-4 **c.** MNO variance = 96,000,000; PQR variance = 550,000,000

10-5 **a.** Cash flow, 2001: $17,500 + 25,000 = $42,500

10-6 **a.** Cash flow from disposition = +$120,000
b. Cash flow from disposition = +$60,000
c. Cash flow from disposition = +$180,000

10-7 Assign roll of die to outcomes: 1 for $2,000; 2,3,4,5 for $4,000; 6 for $6,000

10-8 **a.** 2% + 5% = 7%

10-9 **a.** 3% + (1.0 × 4%) = 7%

10-10 Airborne beta = 1.6 × 0.6858 = 1.0973

Chapter 11 Hints

11-1 **a.** 1981: DPS = $\dfrac{\$3,000}{1,000}$ = $3.00   **b.** 1981: DPO = $\dfrac{\$3,000}{\$5,000}$ = 60%

11-2 **a.** Fall to one-half pre-split price
b. Fall to one-half pre-dividend price
c. Fall to one-fourth pre-split price
d. Fall to two-thirds pre-dividend price

11-3 Expect price to be four times the pre-split price

11-4 **b.** 900,000 shares outstanding after repurchase

11-5 Need to double shares outstanding

11-6 Reduce shares to at least one-fourth of pre-split shares

11-7 **a.** Before 100 shares; After 150 shares

11-8 Dividends in one year = $9 million

11-9 **a.** Conversion value = 1,000 × 40 × $20

11-10 **a.** Dividend = 1 million shares × $100 par × 5%

Chapter 12 Hints

12-1 4% of $1 million

12-2 2.5% of $2 million

12-3 2001: 8.5% of $1 million = $85,000

12-4 **a.** FV = $1,000; PV = $400; and t = 9
b. End of 1992 value = $400 + 42.87 = $442.87

12-5 **a.** FV = $1,000; PV = $556.84; and t = 12
b. End of 1992 value = $556.84 + 27.84 = $584.68

12-6 Consider the likelihood of the price rising

12-7 **e.** Effective conversion price = $\dfrac{\$1,100}{20}$

12-8 **e.** Effective conversion price = $\dfrac{\$900}{28.57}$

12-9 **b.** Warrant: 5,000 bonds at $50 per share

12-10 M = $1,000, C = $25, and T = 10

12-11 M = $1,000, C = $40, and T = 20

12-12 **Bond A:** M = $1,000, C = $50, and T = 10
Bond B: M = $1,000, C = $30, and T = 10

12-13 **a.** Future value of investment = $1,425.76
b. Future value of investment = $1,402.36

12-14 **Bond C:** M = $1,000; C = $20; and T = 3
Bond D: M = $1,000; C = $100; and T = 3

12-15 **a.** M = $1,000, C = $50, T = 20, and r = 3%

12-16 **a.** M = $1,000, C = $40, T = 10, and r = 3%

Chapter 13 Hints

13-1 **a.** Firm A: $\dfrac{\$1,000}{\$3,000}$ **b.** Firm A: $\dfrac{\$1,000}{\$4,000}$

13-2 **a.** Earnings to owners: Alt. 1 = $12,000; Alt. 2 = $11,500; Alt. 3: $11,000
b. Earnings to owners: Alt. 1 = $7,200; Alt. 2 = $6,900; Alt. 3: $6,600

13-3 Variance = 15.610

13-4 Firm D: 10% + 4%

13-5 **b.** 20% of $10,000

13-6 45% of $10,000

13-7 **a.** Apply entire $5,000 to prior years' taxes
b. Apply only $3,000 to prior years' taxes

Chapter 14 Hints

14-1 60% of 8%

14-2 M = $1,000, C = $25, T = 20, PV = $800, and six-month yield = 3.9674%

14-3 **a.** 80% of 5.99% **b.** 70% of 5.99%

14-4 **c.** $\dfrac{\$3}{\$49.50}$

14-5 **a.** A: $\dfrac{\$3}{\$35.35}$

14-6 D_1 = $2.20

14-7 **b.** r_e = 5% + (2 × 7%)

14-8 **a.** Mortgage bonds = 12.5% **b.** Mortgage bonds = 9.17%

14-9 After-tax cost of debt = 6%; Cost of preferred = 16%; Cost of common = 17.5%

14-10 **a.** After tax cost of debt = 6%; Cost of equity = 16%

14-11 Marginal benefit from both E and A is less than marginal cost

14-12 **a.** D_1 = $3.15

14-13 **a.** $400,000 debt at 5%; $600,000 equity at 10%

Chapter 15 Hints

15-1 **b.** 1% of $50,000

15-2 k = 0.5%; K = $300; and S = $5 million

15-3 k = 0.2%; K = $100; and S = $10 million

15-4 Return point = $20,000 + 1,442

15-5 Cost per transaction = $100; Variance = $20,000; and Opportunity cost = 0.03%

15-6   3 days $\times$ \$100,000 $\times$ 10%

15-7   1 day $\times$ \$5 million $\times$ 10%

15-8   A: \$2,740 $\times$ 3 $\times$ 10%

15-9   **a.**   r = \$2.04% and t = 18.25

15-10   Credit sales per year = \$4 million; Credit sales per day = \$10,959

15-11   **a.**   COMP's EAR = 13.01%

15-12   **a.**   r = 1.01% and t = 24.333

15-13   Cost of discount = 2% $\times$ 75% $\times$ \$30 million

15-14   c = 5%, S = 20,000, and K = \$50

15-15   Abbott Lab: $\dfrac{\$2,760.955}{\$815.385}$

15-16   **b.**   r = 25% and t = 8.1111

Chapter 16 Hints

16-1   D: r = 0.19% and t = 52

16-2   Pair #1: Financing #A: 12.68% and Financing #B: 11.46%

16-3   **a.**   r = 1.01% and t = 36.5

16-4   **c:**   r = 1.01% and t = 36.5

16-5   r = 6% and t = 4

16-6   r = 5.26% and t = 4

16-7   **b.**   r = 4.375% and t = 2

16-8   **b.**   r = 4.44% and t = 4

16-9   Credit sales = \$600,000

16-10   Use "number of days in accounts payable" and solve for average daily credit purchases

16-11   **b.**   r = 1.28%

16-12   r = 0.77%

16-13   Firm A's proposal EAR = 13.35%; Firm B's proposal EAR = 13.21%

16-14   Add fee to numerator and denominator for interest rate

16-15   **a.**   r = 2.04% and t = 18.25

16-16   Arrangement #1: r = 1.16% and t = 12.1667

Chapter 17 Hints

17-1   Plot sales on vertical axis, time on horizontal axis

17-2   Plot sales on vertical axis, time on horizontal axis

17-3   Percentage of 1995 sales: Current assets = 6.67%; Plant and equipment = 56.67%; Long-term liabilities = 33.33%

17-4   Percentage of 1990 sales: Current assets = 39.06%; Current liabilities = 24.35%; Stockholders' equity = 45.46%

17-5   Collections on current month's sales: \$20,000; \$50,000; \$25,000; \$30,000

17-6   Current ratio = (\$400 $-$ X)/(\$200 $-$ X) = 3.0

END-OF-CHAPTER SOLUTIONS

More detailed solutions to each problem can be found in the *Solutions Manual to accompany Financial Management and Analysis*

Chapter 1

1-1 **a.** Mary: $6,000
Martin: $9,000
Michael: $15,000

1-2 **a.** Ivan: Owes $25,000
Dennis: Owes $75,000

1-3 58%

1-4 44%

1-5 Corning: $7,298 million   Monsanto: $7,020 million
Fisher Price: $785 million   Wal-Mart: $73,538 million
Lockheed: $3,448 million   Walt Disney: $22,541 million
Mattel: $2,485 million

Chapter 2

2-1 **1** 3.15%: U.S. T-bills
2 3.39%: Commercial paper
3 6.95%: High-quality long-term corporate bond
4 12.18%: Low-quality long-term corporate bond

Chapter 3

3-1 **a.** $5,250; 15%; 15%   **d.** $340,000; 34%; 34%
b. $30,050; 39%; 25%   **e.** $680,000; 34%; 34%
c. $100,250; 39%; 33.4%

3-2 **a.** $7,155; 28%; 20.4%   **d.** $305,876; 31%; 30.6%
b. $33,076; 31%; 27.6%   **e.** $615,876; 31%; 30.8%
c. $88,875.50; 31%; 29.6%

3-3 $160,000 per year

3-4 **a.** Straight-line: $360,000 per year
Declining balance: $738,000; $465,678; $293,843; $185,415; $116,997
b. Straight-line: $640,000 per year
Declining balance: $262,000; $534,322; $706,157; $814,585; $883,003

3-5 **a.** $360,000   **b.** $360,000   **c.** $0

3-6 **a.** $4,500,000   **b.** $3,600,000   **c.** $3,450,000

3-7 **a.** $270,000   **b.** $100,000

3-8 **a.** $80,000   **b.** $0

3-9 **a.** $20,000; $32,000; $19,200; $11,520; $11,520; $5,760
b. $6,800; $10,880; $6,528; $3,917; $3,917; $1,958

3-10 **a.** $142,900; $244,900; $174,900; $124,900; $89,300; $89,200; $89,300; $44,600
b. $48,586; $83,266; $59,466; $42,466; $30,362; $30,328; $30,362; $15,164

3-11 **a.** $398,000   **b.** $498,000   **c.** −$100,000   **d.** −$300,000

3-12 **a.** $553,000   **b.** $1,053,000   **c.** −$150,000   **d.** −$300,000

Chapter 4

4-1 **a.** 4 times   **b.** 2 times   **c.** 10.8 times   **d.** 2 times   **e.** 10%
f. 8.75%   **g.** 5%   **h.** 16.67%   **i.** 8.33%   **j.** 17.5%
k. 12%

4-2   **a.**   33.796 days   **b.**   18.25 days   **c.**   10.95 days   **d.**   52.046 days
     e.   41.096 days

4-3   Firm Y

4-4   **a.**   62.5%   **b.**   10 times

4-5   **a.** $12 million   **b.**   24%   **c.**   40%

4-6   **a.**   14%; 14.4%; 15.6%; 17.7%; 17.4%   **b.**   30.4%; 30.2%; 30.5%; 31.5%; 34.1%
     c.   Increased, attributed to both increased profit margin and asset turnover
     d.   Increased, attributed to increased return on assets

4-7   **a.**   Current ratio (Jan. '92) = 1.21; Quick ratio (Jan. '92) = 0.32
         Inventory turnover (Jan. '92) = 3.08; Total asset turnover (Jan. '92) = 1.35
         Operating profit margin (Jan. '92) = 9.52%; Net profit margin (Jan. '92) = 5.54%
         Interest coverage (Jan. '92) = 8.69; Total debt-to-assets (Jan. '92) = 46.66%

4-8   **a.**   Predict sales over $7 billion

Chapter 5

5-1   **a.** $108   **b.** $116.64   **c.** $125.97   **d.** $136.08   **e.** $146.93
     f. $2,172.45

5-2   **a.** $1,081.60   **b.** $1,169.86   **c.** $1,265.32   **d.** $2,191.12

5-3   **a.** $11,236   **b.** $1,200   **c.** $36

5-4   **a.** $1,440   **b.** $2,488.30   **c.** $15,407

5-5   **a.** $92.59   **b.** $85.73   **c.** $79.38   **d.** $73.50   **e.** $68.06
     f. $4.60

5-6   **a.** $907.03   **b.** $826.45   **c.** $756.14

5-7 $1,846.60

5-8   **a.** $2,837.13   **b.** $2,791.97   **c.** $2,768.38   **d.** $2,752.25

5-9 $741

5-10 $15,692

5-11 $645

5-12   **a.** $88.54   **b.** $84.33

5-13 $6,305

5-14 $2,723.20

5-15   **a.** $2,885.91   **b.**   Year 2: interest = $462.85; principal reduction = $2,423.06

5-16 $166.67

5-17 $2,659.57

5-18   5%

5-19 $2,833.40

5-20 $3,374.60

5-21 $8,428,428

5-22 $6,352.64

5-23 $1,092.26

5-24 $26,201.96

5-25　12.25%

5-26　10%

5-27　5.8384%

5-28　**a.**　9 years　　**b.**　15 years　　**c.**　23 years

5-29　**a.**　15 years　　**b.**　23 years

5-30　18 quarters

5-31　**a.**　20%　　**b.**　21.55%

5-32　**a.**　6 months　　**b.**　50%　　**c.**　100%　　**d.**　125%

5-33　15.12%

5-34　$1,172.60

5-35　14% bank loan

5-36　**a.**　$1,246.33　　**b.**　$25,122.20　　**c.**　$40,313.76　　**d.**　$3,209.41

5-37　$1,321.14

5-38　$221.02

5-39　$5,650.22

5-40　$354.80

5-41　**Plan 1:** $6,928.83　　**Plan 2:** $7,278.85　　**Plan 3:** $7,650.57

5-42　**a.**　$2,799,405.76　　**b.**　$2,427,890.81　　**c.**　8.9761%

5-43　7.78%

Chapter 6

6-1　Yes

6-2　$50,000

6-3　$87.50

6-4　$136.68

6-5　$208.00

6-6　**a.**　$42.00　　**b.**　$25.50　　**c.**　$28.93

6-7　**a.**　$102.00　　**b.**　$312.00　　**c.**　$109.89

6-8　10%

6-9　**a.**　$60　　**b.**　$60.00

6-10　10%

6-11　Increase

6-12　6.25%

6-13　$1,053.46

6-14　$1,044.52

6-15　$918.89

6-16　$1,135.90

6-17　**a.**　Loss of $52.43　　**b.**　Gain of $56.01　　**c.**　Loss of $101.51

6-18 $972.14

6-19 $895.38

6-20 **a.** 2.17%   **b.** 1.5%

6-21 **a.** −2.99%   **b.** −3.32%

6-22 **a.** 3.44%   **b.** 3.09%

6-23 **a.** 20.36%   **b.** 19.25%   **c.** 12.90%

6-24 **a.** $870.74   **b.** $898.49   **c.** $929.08

6-25 **a.** $1,104.84   **b.** $1,050.76   **c.** $1,000.00   **d.** $952.33
e. $907.54

6-26 **a.** 6.09%   **b.** 8.16%   **c.** 10.25%   **d.** 12.36%   **e.** 14.49%

6-27 **a.** 8.16%   **b.** $1,067.33   **c.** $1,052.42

6-28 **a.** $783.53   **b.** $680.58   **c.** 620.92   **d.** 567.43   **e.** 519.37

6-29 7.41%

6-30 39.5%

6-31 **a.** Buy preferred   **b.** Buy common

Chapter 7

7-1 **a.** 2.0   **b.** 2.0   **c.** 4.0   **d.** 2% increase   **e.** 12% decrease

7-2 **a.** Hi-Gear: 3.0; Lo-Gear: 2.5   **b.** Hi-Gear: 2.0; Lo-Gear: 1.33
c. Hi-Gear: 6.0; Lo-Gear: 3.325   **d.** Hi-Gear's

7-3 **a.** Bond NN   **b.** Bond NN   **c.** Bond MM

7-4 **a.** Bond OO   **b.** Bond OO   **c.** Bond PP

7-5 12.32%

7-6 5.77%

7-7 **a.** $2,800,000   **b.** $3,600,000

7-8 **a.** Investment 1: $650   Investment 2: $650
b. Investment 1: $278   Investment 2: $388
c. Investment 2

7-9 **a.** Investment A: $2,700   Investment B: $1,100
b. Investment A: $4,100   Investment B: $4,908
c. Investment B

7-10 **a.** HI bond: −4.56%; LI bond: −4.81%
b. HI bond: 11.75%; LI bond: 12.67%
c. LI bond

7-11

4%	0.0024	0.0025	5.00%
4	0.0012	0.0019	4.36
4	0.0000	0.0013	3.61
4	−0.0012	0.0007	2.65
4	−0.0024	0.0001	1.00

7-12

3.5%	0.0004	0.000625	2.50%
3.5	0.0002	0.000525	2.29
3.5	0.0000	0.000425	2.06
3.5	−0.0002	0.000325	1.80
3.5	−0.0004	0.000225	1.50

7-13	10.0%	0.0024	0.003600	6.00%
	12.0	0.0024	0.006400	8.00
	11.0	0.0024	0.003700	6.08
	11.5	0.0024	0.004725	6.87
	10.5	0.0024	0.003325	5.77

7-14	10.0%	0.0000	0.002500	5.00%
	6.0	0.0000	0.000000	0.00
	8.0	0.0000	0.000625	2.50
	7.0	0.0000	0.000156	1.25
	9.0	0.0000	0.001406	3.75

7-15 **a.** 5% **b.** 7% **c.** 9% **d.** 10% **e.** 13%

7-16 **a.** 8% **b.** 8.75% **c.** 9.5% **d.** 10.25% **e.** 11%

7-17 **a.** AA: 12%; BB: 13.75%; CC: 15.5%; DD: 12%
b. 1.1875 **c.** 13.31%

7-18 **a.** EE: 8%; FF: 10%; GG: 12%; HH: 14%
b. 0.875 **c.** 11%

Chapter 8

8-1 $1,100,000

8-2 **a.** Capital gain = $25,000; Recapture = $25,000
b. Capital gain = $0; Recapture = $25,000
c. Capital gain = $0; Recapture = $0
d. Capital loss = $25,000

8-3 **a.** Machine 1: $120,000; Machine 2: $110,000
b. Machine 1: $13,000; Machine 2: $6,500

8-4 **a.** $150,000 **b.** $56,000 **c.** $48,456

8-5 **a.** $50,000 **b.** $7,428

8-6 **a.** $84,000 **b.** $76,000 **c.** $68,000 **d.** $60,000

8-7 $0; +$4,800; −$320; −$3,392; −$3,392; +$2,304

8-8 −$1,010,000; +$170,000; +$170,000; +$170,000; +$170,000; +$203,040

8-9 −$1,010,000; +$85,500; +$126,300; +$82,520; $56,668; +$71,276

8-10 −$990,000; +$215,985; +$266,025; +$375,990

8-11 **a.** −$1,500,000 **b.** + $240,000 **c.** +$240,000; +$312,000; +$235,200; +$189,120; +$189,120; +$154,560; +$120,000 **d.** −$1,500,000; +$240,000; +$312,000; +$235,200; +$189,120; +$189,120; +$154,560; +$360,000

8-12 **a.** −$600,000 **b.** +$145,000 **c.** $0 **d.** +$120,000 each year
e. Year 0: −$455,000; Years 1–5: +$120,000

8-13 **a.** −$1,200,000 **b.** + $150,160 **c.** +$284,192
d. +$193,840; +$264,250; +$210,640; +$178,384; +$178,384
e. −$1,049,800; +$193,840; +$264,250; +$210,640; +$178,384; +$462,576

8-14 **a.** −$120,000 **b.** +$7,000 **c.** +$140,000
d. +$25,999; +$30,002; +$19,332; +$16,668; +$14,000
e. −$113,000; +$25,999; +$30,002; +$19,332; +$16,668; +$154,000

Chapter 9

9-1 **a.** 3 periods **b.** 4 periods **c.** Undefined **d.** $11,031
e. −$1,988 **f.** 1.1103 **g.** 0.9801 **h.** 15% **i.** 8.8%
j. 12.92%

9-2   **a.** 3 periods   **b.** 3 periods   **c.** 3 periods   **d.** $8,919.14
  e. $1,692.84   **f.** 1.098   **g.** 1.017   **h.** 15%   **i.** 13.178%
  j. 14.64%

9-3   **a.** 4 periods   **b.** 4 periods   **c.** 5 periods   **d.** $46,401.14
  e. $17,890.09   **f.** 1.232   **g.** 1.0895   **h.** 18.72%   **i.** 14.69%
  j. 16.99%

9-4   **a.** 4 periods   **b.** 4 periods   **c.** 4 periods   **d.** $19,459.74
  e. $11,152.75   **f.** 1.1946   **g.** 1.1115   **h.** 15%   **i.** 15%

9-5   **a.** 3 periods   **b.** 3 periods   **c.** Undefined   **d.** $7,159.06
  e. −$3,681.44   **f.** 1.0716   **g.** 0.9632   **h.** 8.2%

9-6   **a.** Thing 2   **b.** Thing 1   **c.** Thing 1   **d.** Neither   **e.** 7.09%

9-7   **a.** Thing 4   **b.** Thing 4   **c.** Thing 4   **d.** Neither   **e.** 22.13%

9-8   **a.** Thing 6   **b.** Thing 5   **c.** Neither   **d.** Neither   **e.** 5.49%

9-9   DD and BB

9-10   **a.** FF and GG   **b.** FF and GG

9-11   KK, JJ, and LL

9-12   **a.** −$500,000; +$135,000; +$153,000; +$133,800; +$122,280; +$200,920
  b. $57,959.89   **c.** $140,942.02   **d.** 1.28   **e.** 4 years
  f. 5 years   **g.** 14.26%   **h.** 10.36%   **i.** Yes

9-13   **a.** −$600,000; +200,000; +$200,000; +$320,000   **b.** −$12,471.82
  c. $48,310.12   **d.** 1.0805   **e.** 3 years   **f.** 3 years
  g. 8.9%   **h.** 7.75%   **i.** No

9-14   +$112,383

9-15   +$55,871

Appendix 9A

9A-1   Choose Felix

9A-2   Choose UX

9A-3   Choose Project 2

Appendix 9B

9B-1   Rent = $55,912

9B-2   Loan payment = $537,167

9B-3   **a.** Rent = $239,819   **b.** Loan payment = $239,819
  c. Borrow to buy

9B-4   **a.** Rent = $36,556   **b.** Loan payment = $37,173
  c. Buy the asset instead of lease

9B-5   Open the store

Chapter 10

10-1   **a.** $2,000   **b.** $2,000   **c.** 632.46   **d.** 0.3162

10-2   **a.** $2,000   **b.** $2,200   **c.** $600   **d.** 0.2727

10-3   **a.** GHI: $12,000; JKL: $6,000   **b.** GHI: $1,300; JKL: $1,800
  c. GHI: $5,040.83; JKL: $2,521.90   **d.** GHI: 3.8776; JKL: 1.4011
  e. GHI is riskier

10-4
a. MNO: $30,000; PQR: $60,000
b. MNO: $2,000; PQR: $20,000
c. MNO: $9,797.96; PQR: $23,452.08
d. MNO: 4.8990; PQR: 1.1726
e. PQR is riskier

10-5
a. $42,500; $60,000; $42,500; $25,000
b. $40,000; $55,000; $40,000; $25,000
c. $37,500; $50,000; $37,500; $25,000
d. Year 2001: $38,750; $1,677.05

10-6
a. 9%　b. 5%　c. 13%　d. 8.81%; 2.84%

10-7 Approximately: $\frac{1}{6}$ 1's; $\frac{2}{3}$ 2's, 3's, 4's, and 5's; $\frac{1}{6}$ 6's

10-8
a. 7%　b. 10%　c. 10%　d. 10%

10-9
a. 7%　b. 6.5%　c. 14%　d. 8%　e. 10%

10-10
Airborne:	1.0973
Albertson's:	0.7645
Arco Chemical:	1.0395
Arkla:	0.3403
Arrow Electronics:	0.6463

Chapter 11

11-1
a. $3.00; $3.10; $3.20; $3.30; $3.50; $3.725; $3.975; $4.20; $4.50
b. 60%; 60.78%; 71.11%; 61.11%; 63.64%; 70.28%; 76.44%; 75.00%; 77.59%
c. GHI's dividends per share have been increasing at an increasing rate

11-2
a. Approximately $50 per share
b. Approximately $50 per share
c. Approximately $25 per share
d. Approximately $67 per share

11-3 Approximately $8 per share

11-4
a. $900,000
b. $1.11 per share

11-5
a. 100% stock dividend
b. 2:1 stock split

11-6 At least 1:4

11-7
a. 50%　b. 100%　c. 200%　d. 40%

11-8 $18 million

11-9
a. $800,000
b. $1,200,000
c. $1,600,000

11-10
a. $1.25 million
b. Do nothing; Buy shares; Call stock
c. No

Chapter 12

12-1 $40,000 every six months

12-2 $50,000 every three months

12-3 $80,000; $85,000; $90,000; $90,000; $93,000; $95,000

12-4
a. 10.7173%
b. Implied interest: $42.87; $47.46; $52.55; $58.18; $64.42; $71.32; $78.97; $87.43; $96.80

12-5
a. 5%
b. Implied interest: $27.84; $29.23; $30.70; $32.23; $33.84; $35.53; $37.31; $39.18; $41.14; $43.19; $45.35; $47.62

12-6
a. No　b. Minimum $6　c. Minimum $2
d. Warrant with 2 years to expiration is worth less than warrant with no expiration

12-7
a. $50 per share
b. 20 shares
c. $1,200
d. $800
e. $55 per share

12-8
a. $35 per share
b. 28.57 shares
c. $857
d. $1,143
e. $31.50 per share

12-9 **a.** Choice (call option); Investor (Put option); Investor (Conversion: call option); Investor (Warrant: call option)

      b. Call option = $5.2 million outflow; Put option = $5.25 million outflow; Conversion: no outflow or inflow; Warrant: $0.25 million inflow

12-10 **a.** $1,044,910   **b.** $957,350; −9.15%

12-11 **a.** $1,000   **b.** 14.88%   **c.** 32.70%

12-12 **a.** Bond A: −7.79%; Bond B: −8.24%   **b.** Bond A: −7.64%; Bond B: −8.11%

      c. Bond A: −14.84%; Bond B: −15.69%

      d. Bond B's value is more sensitive

12-13 **a.** 6% annualized   **b.** 5.716% annualized

12-14 **a.** Bond C: $893.08; Bond D: $1,106.82   **b.** Bond C: −5.34%; Bond D: −5%

      c. Bond C: 2.059%; Bond D: 9.564%   **d.** Bond C: 2.119%; Bond D: 9.825%

      e. Bond C: more sensitive to interest rate changes; Bond D: more sensitive to reinvestment rate changes

12-15 **a.** $6,487,750   **b.** Calling in bonds would cost less

12-16 **a.** $1,085,300   **b.** Call   **c.** $1,036,000   **d.** $18,866.27; Yes

Chapter 13

13-1 **a.** Firm A: 0.33; Firm B: 1.00; Firm C: 3.00

      b. Firm B: 0.25; Firm B: 0.50; Firm C: 0.75

13-2

Tax rate = 0%	Alternative 1	Alternative 2	Alternative 3
Earnings	$12,000	$11,500	$11,000
Earnings per share	$ 24.00	$ 15.33	$ 11.00
Earnings to shareholders	$12,000	$11,500	$11,000
Earnings to bondholders	$ 0	$ 500	$ 1,000

13-3 Expected EPS = $6.30; Standard deviation = $3.95

13-4 Firm D: 14%; Firm E: 12%; Firm F: 18%

13-5 **a.** $0   **b.** $2,000   **c.** $4,000   **d.** $6,000   **e.** $8,000

13-6 $4,500

13-7 **a.** $2,000 refund   **b.** $1,200 refund and $2,000 loss carried forward

Chapter 14

14-1 4.8%

14-2 5.66%

14-3 **a.** 4.79%

      b. 4.19%

14-4 **a.** 6%   **b.** 6.38%   **c.** 6.06%   **d.** 5.77%   **e.** 5.88%

14-5 **a.** A: 8.51%; B: 8.47%; C: 8.51%   **b.** 8.5%

14-6 15.5%

14-7 **a.** 12%   **b.** 19%   **c.** 26%

14-8 **a.** 12.5%; 12.5%; 25%; 12.5%; 37.5%   **b.** 9.17%; 12.5%; 19.17%; 9.16%; 50%

      c. Market value

14-9 Arrangement #1: 14.75%; Arrangement #2: 11.30%

14-10 **a.** 12%   **b.** 11.2%

14-11 **a.** $4 million **b.** F, C, D & B

14-12 **a.** 15.5% **b.** 15.86% **c.** $1 million

14-13 **a.** 8% **b.** 8%; 8.8%; 10.8%; 12%

Chapter 15

15-1 **a.** $50,000 **b.** $500

15-2 **a.** $2,500 **b.** $1,500 **c.** $774,597

15-3 $1 million

15-4 **a.** $20,000 **b.** $21,442 **c.** $24,326

15-5 Lower limit = $10,000; Return point = $11,710; Upper limit = $15,130

15-6 $30,000 savings per year

15-7 $500,000; < $500,000

15-8 **a.** A: $822; B: $1,370; C: $1,370; D: $658; E: $493 **b.** Attractive: A, B, D

15-9 **a.** 44.56% **b.** 20.13% **c.** 203.67% **d.** 13.01% **e.** 44.83%

15-10 **a.** 45.62 days **b.** 68.44 days
  c. Customers are taking longer to pay than specified in credit terms
  d. (1) Representativeness of receivable balance; (2) Influence of particular accounts on average

15-11 **a.** Competitors have higher cost of credit
  b. Likely to reduce accounts receivable

15-12 **a.** 27.703% **b.** $6,000 **c.** 20.202%

15-13 **a.** $350,000 **b.** $136,987 **c.** Yes

15-14 **a.** $250 **b.** $500 **c.** 14,142 units

15-15 **a.** 3.387; 1.857; 15.634; 5.540; 4.079; 7.551
  b. 107.794; 196.575; 23.347; 65.885; 89.490; 48.339

15-16 **a.** 202.78% **b.** 511.01% **c.** APR = 45%; EAR = 54.98%

Chapter 16

16-1 A: 12%; B: 12.36%; C: 19.56%; D: 10.51%; E: 5.09%

16-2 B; B; B

16-3 **a.** 44.32% **b.** 44.56% **c.** 28.00% **d.** 70.73%

16-4 **a.** 0% **b.** 3,818.81% **c.** 44.32% **d.** 20.13% **e.** 13.01%

16-5 26.25%

16-6 16.64%

16-7 **a.** 7.12% **b.** 8.94% **c.** 11.73%

16-8 **a.** 16.99% **b.** 19.00% **c.** 19.53%

16-9 6 times

16-10 $122 billion

16-11 **a.** $40 million **b.** 1.28% **c.** 20.41%

16-12 $957,304

16-13 Firm B's is less costly than Firm A's

16-14 **a.** 17.86% **b.** 15.79% **c.** 13.79% **d.** 12.24%

16-15 **a.** 44.56%   **b.** 10.25%   **c.** 8.51%
d. 9.18%   **e.** 13.25%   **f.** 10%

16-16 #1: 15.06%; #2: 17.75%; #3: 16.28%; #4: 5.56%

Chapter 17

17-1 **c.** Approximately $650 million

17-2 **c.** Approximately $1.2 million

17-3 **a.** Pro forma Balance Sheet, 1996–1998

	1996	1997	1998
Current assets	$ 1,133	$ 1,200	$ 1,267
Plant and equipment	9,633	10,200	10,767
Other assets	567	600	633
Total assets	$11,333	$12,000	$12,667
Current liabilities	$ 567	$ 600	$ 633
Long-term liabilities	5,667	6,000	6,333
Stockholders' equity	5,100	5,400	5,700
Total liabilities and equity	$11,333	$12,000	$12,667

b. Pro forma Income Statement, 1996–1998

	1996	1997	1998
Sales	$17,000	$18,000	$19,000
Cost of goods sold	11,333	12,000	12,667
Gross profit	5,667	6,000	6,333
Other operating expenses	567	600	633
Operating profit	$ 5,100	$ 5,400	$ 5,700
Interest expense	227	240	253
Taxes	1,949	2,064	2,179
Net profit	$ 2,924	$ 3,096	$ 3,268
Dividends	1,170	1,238	2,307
Retained Earnings	$ 1,754	$ 1,858	$ 1,961

17-4 **a.** Pro forma Balance Sheet, 1991–1993

	1991	1992	1993
Current assets	$3,515	$3,710	$ 3,906
Net plant, property and equipment	3,494	3,688	3,882
Other assets	2,232	2,356	2,480
Total assets	$9,241	$9,755	$10,268
Current liabilities	$2,191	$2,313	$ 2,435
Long-term liabilities	2,959	3,123	3,287
Stockholders' equity	4,091	4,319	4,546
Total liabilities and equity	$9,241	$9,755	$10,268

b. Pro forma Income Statements, 1991–1993

	1991	1992	1993
Sales	$9,000	$9,500	$10,000
Cost of goods sold	4,904	5,176	5,449
Gross profit	$4,096	$4,324	$ 4,551
Selling, general, admin. exp.	2,486	2,625	2,763
Depreciation	700	739	778
Operating profit	$ 910	$ 960	$ 1,011
Interest expense	208	202	231
Other non-operating items	108	114	120
Taxes	263	278	292
Net profit	$ 546	$ 577	$ 607
Dividends	245	259	273
Retained earnings	$ 301	$ 318	$ 334

17-5 Net cash flows: +$52,500; +$7,500; +$93,750; +$33,750

17-6 **a.** Pay off $100 of accounts payable with $100 cash, reducing the current ratio to 3

b. Increases risk of not having sufficient cash to meet transactions needs

c. Reduce other working capital accounts to generate cash to pay off accounts payable or borrow using long-term debt

Index

Note: *Italicized* page numbers indicate material in tables, figures, and boxes.

A

AB Volvo, 13, *708*
Abnormal profit, 51
Accelerated depreciation, 69, 70–72
  comparison of straight-line depreciation with, 71–72
  declining balance method, 70, 71–72
  sum-of-the-years' digits method, 71–72
  for tax purposes, 77–79, 82–83, 89–90
Accounting data:
  problems of using, 143–145
  sources, 163
Accounting profit:
  defined, 19
  economic profit versus, *18*
Accounts payable:
  defined, 63
  management of, 751–753
Accounts payable turnover, 752
Accounts receivable:
  as collateral for loan, 765–768
  defined, 63
  factoring, 765–768
  (*See also* Receivables management)
Accounts receivable turnover ratio, 111–112, *158, 161*
Accumulated depreciation, 63
Acid-test ratio, 107
Acme-Cleveland, 819–822
Acquisitions (*see* Mergers and acquisitions)
Activity ratios, 111–113, *158*
  accounts receivable turnover ratio, 111–112, *158, 161*
  fixed asset turnover, 112, *158, 161*
  inventory turnover ratio, 111, *158, 161,* 727–728
  purpose of, 111
  total asset turnover, 112, *158, 161*
  Wal-Mart Stores Inc., 135–136
Add-on interest, *745*
Additional paid-in capital, 64–65
Adjustable rate preferred stock (ARPS), 535
Adjusted gross income (AGI), 84
Agency costs, 21–22
Agency relationship:
  costs, 21–22
  defined, 20
  and dividend decision, 525, 527–528
  and insider information, 52
  problems, 20
  social responsibility in, 22–23
Agent, 20, 527
Aging schedule:
  for accounts payable, 753
  for receivables, 716–717
Aharony, Joseph, 523n
Airline Deregulation Act of 1978, *590–591*
Allen, Anthony H., 687
Allowance for stock-out, 725
Altman, Edward I., 142, 142n, 616n
American Depository Receipts (ADRs), 50
American Stock Exchange (AMEX), 44, *45,* 46, *49,* 512
Amortization, 196
  defined, 63

Amortization (*Cont.*):
  (*See also* Discounting cash flows, series of payments)
AMR Corporation, *590–591*
Analysis-of-accounts method, 802–806
Ang, James, 527n, 561n
Annual percentage rate (APR), 213–214
  calculation of, 741–742, *743*
Annual report, 98
Annualized yield to maturity, *574*
Annuities:
  deferred, 204–207
  future value of, 189–191, 192–194, 196–198
  present value of, 191–192, 194–198, 638–640, *845*
Annuity due, valuation of, 199–203
Apple Computer Inc., *225*
Arbitrage pricing model, 332–333
Arithmetic average return, *257*
Arrearage, preferred stock, 535–536
Arrears, preferred stock, 535–536
Articles of incorporation, 9–10, 503
Asset-backed securities (ABS), 39
Asset beta, 481–483
Asset valuation, 230–255
  common stock, 234–235, 236–243
  long-term debt securities, 235, 245–251, *475*
  marketplace, role of, 233–234
  methods, 230–233
  options, 251–255
  perpetuity, 198–199, *231, 538*
  preferred stock, 235, 243–245
  risk in, 233–234
Assets:
  categories of, 61–63
  defined, 61
  intangible, 63
  return on, 119, 121–122, *124, 159, 162,* 596
  securitization of, 38, 768, *769*
Assignment of receivables, 766
At the money, 252
AT&T, 518
Authorized shares, 503
Average, 865, 866
Average annual return, *174,* 256
  geometric versus arithmetic, *257*
Average cash balance, *692*
Average cost of capital, 486
Average day's cost of goods sold, 104, *157, 160*
Average day's purchases, 105–106, *157, 160*
Average tax rate, 76–77
  marginal tax rate versus, *608*

B

Baby bonds, 555
Bad debts, 712
Balance sheet, 61–65
  assets, 61–63
  common-size, 128, *129, 139*
  equity, 61, 64–65
  example, *62*
  liabilities, 61, 63–64
  postretirement obligations, *59*
  pro forma, 802, *805, 807, 810*
Bank financing, 753–758
  comparing forms of, 756–758

Bank financing (*Cont.*):
  compensating balances, 691, 745–747, 757–758
  letter of credit, 755–756
  line of credit, 754–755
  revolving credit, 755
  single-payment loans, 742, 753–754, 757
Bankers' acceptances, 35, *36*
  default risk, 772
  investing in, 706
  issuing, 761–763
  rates, 772
Banking Act of 1933 (Glass-Steagall Act), *41, 681*
Bankruptcy:
  airline industry, *590–591*
  Chapter 7, 615
  Chapter 11, 615
  costs of, 457–458, 615–616
  defined, 615
  predicting, 142
Bankruptcy Reform Act of 1978, 615
Basic valuation equation, 172
Basis points, *754*
Baumol, William J., 691n
Baumol model, 691–696, 699
Bearer bonds, 554
Best-efforts offerings, 680
Beta:
  asset, 481–483
  estimation of, 329, 871–873
  portfolio, 330–331, *652*
  security, 328–331, 481–483, *484,* 651
Black, Fischer, 528n
Blanket indenture, 569
Blouch, William E., 746n
Board of directors, 10
  classified (staggered), 514, *515*
  and corporate democracy, 517–519
  and executive compensation plans, 22
  and voting rights of shareholders, 512–513
Bondholders, 37, 553
Bonding costs, of agency relationship, 21
Bonds, 37, 37n
  call feature, 276–277, *551,* 562, 563
  characteristics:
    denomination, 555
    interest, 556–560
    maturity, 556
    optionlike features, 562–567
    packaging, 567–568
    security, 560–562
    seniority, 562
  conversion feature, 254, *551,* 562, 563–565, *568*
  determining cost of, 636–644, 662–663
  government, 37–38
  income, 559–560
  indentures, 37n, 554, 569
  junk, 140, 570, *572*
  markets, 46
  putable, 254, *551,* 562, 565
  quotations, 822–824
  retirement of, 579–581

Bonds (*Cont.*):
  return on investment, 265–277
    effective annual return, 266–268
    yield to maturity, 268–276
  revenue, 37
  and risk, 570–579
  risk and return, *288–289*
  secured, 37
  as source of capital, 581–582, 583
  speculative, 140
  straight-coupon
    determining cost of, 637–640, 662–663
    interest on, 556–557
    valuation of, 245–249, *250*
    yield to maturity, 269–271, *846*
  transaction costs, 278
  valuation of, 235, 245–251, *475*
  yield to call, 276–277
  zero-coupon, *551*
    determining cost of, 641–644
    interest on, 557–558
    valuation of, 245, 250–251
    yield to maturity, 268–269
  (*See also* Debt securities)
Bonds payable, 64
Bonus, 21, 22
Book value of equity, 64, *622*
Book value of equity per share, *159*, *162*
Book value per share, 125
Boston Stock Exchange, 44
Boulding, Kenneth, *412*
Bower, Richard S., *453n*
Braude, Jacob M., 553
Break-even analysis, payback period as, 392
Breakpoints, 656–657
Brickley, James A., *515*
Budgeting, 783, 787–788, *789*, 796–806
  capital (*see* Capital budgeting)
  cash budget, 797–802
  operational, 787
  practical applications, 811–812
  pro forma financial statements in, 802–806
Business organization, forms of, 8–15
  corporations, 9–12, 13, *14*, *15*
  distribution of, in U.S., *14*
  joint ventures, 13
  master limited partnerships, 13
  partnerships, 8–9, 13, *14*, *15*, *19*
  professional corporations, 13
  sole proprietorships, 8, *14*, *15*
  virtual enterprises, *13*
Business risk, 291–294
  and capital structure, 616, 625
  in investment decisions, 347–348
Bylaws, 10

C

Calculators, financial, 840–850
Call feature, 38, 244–245, 254
  long-term debt, 276–277, *551*, 562, 563
  preferred stock, 38, 537–538, 539, 540
  yield to call, 276–277
Call options, 38
  defined, *825*
  in investment decisions, 255
  put options compared to, *253*, 254
  right to default as, *613*
  valuation of, 251–252
Call premium, 563
Call price, 244–245, 537–538, 563
Call risk, 300–301
Callable preferred stock, 38, 537–538, 539, 540
Canada, 50
  securities markets, 48, *49*
  taxation in, 86, *87*

Canadian Pacific Limited, 556
Capital:
  defined, 346, 592
  sources of
    common stock, 541–542, *582*, 677–681
    long-term debt, 553, 581–582
    preferred stock, 541–542, *582*
    primary markets, *40*, 40–41, 541–542
    private placements, 40, 677
    public offerings, 677–681
    retained earnings, 541
    for sole proprietorship, 8
Capital asset pricing model (CAPM), 326–331
  in determining cost of capital, 650–653,
    665–667, 668, 669
Capital assets, 80*n*, 687
Capital budgeting:
  capital investments in, 346–347
  cash flow estimation
    checklist, *369*
    examples, 368–378, *379*
    investment cash flows in, 354–359, *369*
    net cash flows in, 367–368
    operating cash flows in, 354, 359–367, *369*,
      800, *809*
    practical applications, 378–380
    simplifications in, 368
  classifying investment projects
    according to dependence on other projects,
      352–353, *353*
    according to economic life, 350–351, *353*,
      444–448
    according to risk, 351–352, *353*, 368–378
  corporate strategy in, 349
  defined, 348–349
  evaluation techniques, 389–434
    and capital rationing, 410, 416–417, *430*
    comparison of, 428–432
    discounted payback period, 394–399, *429*,
      431
    for independent projects, 410, 416–417
    internal rate of return (IRR) (*see* Internal
      rate of return)
    for investments with unequal lives, 444–448
    for leasing decision, 451–458
    modified internal rate of return (MIRR),
      260, *300*, 420–428, *429*, *432*, *578*
    for mutually exclusive projects, 402,
      414–416, *430*
    net present value (*see* Net present value)
    payback period, 391–394, *429*, *431*, 433–434
    practical applications, 432–434
    profitability index, 406–410, *429*, *431*
    scale differences, *409*, 409–410, *430*
  and maximization of owners' wealth, 347–349,
    394, 399, 408–410, 418, 428
  optimal capital budget in, 658
  project risk in, 463–484
    certainty equivalents, 486–487
    market, 465–466, 481–483, *484*, 485
    measurement of, 466–484
    practical applications, 487–488
    relevant cash flow, 464–465
    risk-adjusted rates, 484–486
    sources of, 464
    stand-alone, 465–466, 467–481, 485
  stages of, 349–350
Capital expenditure, 351
Capital gains, in evaluating asset cash flows, 356
Capital gains tax, 80–82
  cap, 80–81
  exclusion, 81–82
  on stock repurchases, 529–533
  tax on cash dividends versus, 526–527

Capital investments, 346–347
  (*See also* Capital budgeting)
Capital leases, 64, *64*, *64n*, 451–458
Capital loss, *82*
  in evaluating asset cash flows, 356–357
Capital market line (CML), 327
Capital market securities, 35–38
  defined, 35
  equity, 36
  indebtedness, 37–38
Capital projects, 347
  (*See also* Capital budgeting)
Capital rationing, 410, 416–417, *430*
Capital recovery period (*see* Payback period)
Capital structure, 590–625
  airline industry, *590–591*
  and business risk, 616, 625
  debt ratios in, 593, 594, *595*, 596
  defined, 592, *655*
  in determining cost of capital, 635–636,
    655–656, 660–662
  factors in selecting, 624
  and financial distress, *590–591*, 593, 616–617
  and financial leverage, 593, 595–600, 616,
    617–620
  industry differences, 593–594, 620–623
  Modigliani-Miller model of, 600–612, 617–620
  optimal, 618–620, 623–625
  and pecking order, 624
  and trade-off theories, 622–624
Capital yield:
  bond, 268
  common stock, 242, 261
  in dividend policy, 525–526
Capitalization rate, 232, 603, 633
Captive finance subsidiaries, 720, *721*
Carrying cost:
  of accounts receivable, 711, 718
  of inventory, 721
Cash:
  decisions concerning, 5
  defined, 62
Cash budget, 797–802
Cash dividends, 505
  (*See also* Dividends)
Cash flow interest coverage ratio, 117–118, *159*,
  161
Cash flow risk, 291–298
  business, 291–294, 347–348, 616, 625
  default, 297–298, 570–572, 612–615, 706, 707,
    761, 772
  financial, 113, 294–297
  operating and financial, combined, 296–297
Cash flows, 88–90
  in capital budgeting decisions (*see* Capital
    budgeting)
  compounding (*see* Compounding cash flows)
  depreciation tax shields in, 89–90
  discounting (*see* Discounting cash flows)
  operating (*see* Operating cash flows)
  outflows and inflows, 88
  predicting, 88–90
  risk and (*see* Cash flow risk)
  (*See also* Statement of cash flows)
Cash forecasting, 704–705
Cash management, 690–708
  costs associated with, 691
  determining investment in cash, 691–699
    Baumol model, 691–696, 699
    international considerations, 699, *708*
    Miller-Orr model, 696–698, 699
    seasonality in, 699, 796
  marketable securities in, 62–63, 705–708
  reasons for holding cash, 690–691

Cash management (*Cont.*):
  techniques, 699–705
    cash forecasting, 704–705
    to slow up payments of cash, 702, 704
    to speed up incoming cash, 699–701,
      702–704
CBS Inc., Prodigy system joint venture, 13
Central tendency, measures of, 865–866
Certainty equivalents, 486–487
Certificates of deposit (CDs), 35, *36*
  investing in, 706
Certificates of indebtedness, 554
    (*See also* Bonds; Notes)
Champion International Corporation, 563
Charitable organizations, owners of, 7
Chatfield, Robert E., 542*n*
Chattel mortgages, 768
Check-clearing process, 699–705
  controlled disbursements, 702, 704
  float in, 701, *702*
  lockbox systems in, 701, 702–704, *705*
Chicago Board of Trade (CBOT), 46
Chicago Board Options Exchange (CBOE), 46
Chicago Mercantile Exchange, 46
Chrysler Corporation, *708*
Cincinnati Stock Exchange, 44
Circulating capital (*see* Working capital)
C.I.T. Financial Corporation, 759
Classified board of directors, 514, *515*
Classified stock, 510–511
  in mergers and acquisitions, 510–511
  voting rights, 511–512
Clearinghouse bank, *701*
Closely held corporations, 11, *504*
Code of Hammurabi, *171*
Coefficient of variation, 473–474, *600*, 859–860,
  867, 868
Coleco Industries Inc., *790*
Collar, 535
Collateral, 35, 37, 560, 764, 765–768
Collateral trust debt, 561
Collateralized mortgage obligations (CMOs), 768
Collection agencies, *715*
Collection policies, 714–715, 717–719
Commercial bankers:
  defined, *41*
  investment bankers versus, *41*, 681
Commercial paper, 35, *36*
  as investment, 707
  issuing, 758–761
  rates, 772
Commitment fee, 747
Committed line of credit, 754
Commodity Futures Trading Commission
    (CFTC), 48*n*
Common life, 445
Common-size analysis, 128, *129, 130*
  Wal-Mart Stores Inc., 138, *139*
Common stock, 36, 510–533
  characteristics of, 234–235, *235*, 502–510
  classified, 510–512
  corporate democracy, 517–519
  cost of issuing, 527, *527*
  determining cost of, 646–653
    with capital asset pricing model (CAPM),
      650–653, 665–667, 668, 669
    with dividend valuation model (DVM),
      647–650, 653–654, 664–665, 668, 669
  dividends, 36, 234–235, 505–510, 520–533
  in executive compensation plans, 21–22
  market share of shareholders' equity, 16–17
  market value, 16–17
  quotations, 819–822
  as residual ownership, 502

Common stock (*Cont.*):
  return on investment, 260–265, 288–289
    with dividends at end of period, 260–265
    with no dividends, 260
  rights of shareholders
    other rights, 517
    preemptive right, 514–516
    voting rights, 511–514
  risk, *288–289*
  as source of capital, 541–542, 582, 677–681
  transaction costs, 278
  valuation of, 234–235
    dividend valuation model, 236–243
Company-specific risk, 328
Comparative advantage, 784
Compensating balances, 691, 745–747, 757–758
Competitive advantage, 784–785
Complementary projects, 353
Component percentage, 102
Compound factor, 172
Compound interest, 170, 740
Compounding cash flows:
  average annual return, *174*, 256, *257*
  basic equation for future value, 172
  compounding periods
    continuous, *216, 847*
    number of, 210–213
  defined, 168
  interest rate determination, 207–210
  series of payments, 181–188
    annuities, 189–191, 192–194, 196–198
    annuity due, 200–201
    deferred annuity, 204–207
    tables, *835–836*
  shortcuts
    annuities, 189–191, 192–194, 196–198
    compound value tables, 178–181, 196–198,
      835–836
    future value annuity factor, 192–194,
      835–836
    logarithms, *212*
    summation notation, 187–188
  single payment, 168–174, *843*
    tables, *178–181, 831–832*
  time lines in, 184, *185, 186, 193, 201, 203,* 378
  time periods in, *182*
ConAgra Inc., 503
Concentration banking, 701
Consolidated financial statements, *621,* 621
Consumer Price Index (CPI), 132–133
Contingent projects, 353
Contingent voting rights, 539
Continuous compounding, *216, 847*
Continuous distributions, 853, *854*
Contribution margin, 292, 709
Controlled disbursements, 702, 704
Conventional factoring, 766, *767*
Conversion feature, 38, 254
  long-term debt, 254, *551,* 562, 563–565, *568*
  preferred stock, 38, 536–537, *538,* 540
Conversion premium, *536*
Conversion price, 563–564
Conversion ratio, *536,* 563–564
Corporate charter, 10, 503
Corporate democracy, 517–519
  proxy fights in, 518–519
  shareholder proposals in, 517–518
  shareholders' rights movement in, 519
Corporate finance (*see* Financial management;
    Financial planning)
Corporations, 9–12
  and agency relationship, 20–23, 52, 525,
    527–528
  articles of incorporation, 9–10, 503

Corporations (*Cont.*):
  bonds (*see* Bonds)
  characteristics of, *15,* 502–503
  closely held, 11, *504*
  common stock (*see* Common stock)
  defined, 9
  distribution of, in U.S., *14*
  foreign investors in, 50
  incorporation process, 9, *503*
  and limited liability, 502, 612–615
  number of shares, 503–504
  ownership of (*see* Ownership interest)
  preferred stock (*see* Preferred stock)
  professional, 13
  relationships within, *10*
  Subchapter S, 85–86
  taxation (*see* Tax, corporate)
Correlation, 862–865, 879–880
  defined, 321
  and portfolio risk, *323*
Correlation coefficient, 321–322, 879
  covariance and, *322*
Correspondent bank, *701*
Cost of capital, 348, 464, *465,* 484–486, 631–669,
    633–634
  capital structure in, 635–636, 655–656,
    660–662
  common stock, 646–653, 664–668
    capital asset pricing model, 650–653,
      665–667, 668, 669
    dividend valuation model, 647–650,
      653–654, 664–665, 668, 669
  debt, 636–644, 662–663
    deductibility of interest, 640–641
    flotation costs, 640
    implicit interest, 642
    yield to maturity, 637–639
  defined, 389
  in discounted payback period, 394–399, *429,*
    431
  and internal rate of return, 417
  in Japan, *487,* 631–632
  marginal:
    marginal-cost-of-capital schedule, 653–657
    problems with, 658–660
    and shareholder wealth maximization,
      657–658
  as opportunity cost, *395*
  practical application of, 660–669
  preferred stock, 644–646, 663–664
  weighted average, 488, 653
    (*See also* Required rate of return)
Cost of goods sold (cost of sales), 65, 104, *157,*
    160
Coupon bond, 299
Coupon equivalent yield, 275
Coupon rate, 245, *574*
Coupon yield, 268
Coupons, 245, 556
Covariance, 862
  calculation of, 318–320
  and correlation coefficient, *322*
  negative, 320
Covenants, 569, 755
Coverage ratio, 101
Crabbe, Leland, 565*n*
Credit, tax, 79–80, 80*n,* 81
  in evaluating asset cash flows, 354, 354*n*
Credit cards, interest rate on, *217*
Credit risk (*see* Default risk)
Credit sales per day, 104, *157, 160*
Credit terms:
  establishing, 713–714, 717–719
  honoring, 751–753

Creditor, 553
Creditworthiness, 714
Crossover discount rate, 405, *406*
Cumulative preferred stock, 235, 535–536, 539
Cumulative voting, 513–514
Currency risk, 307
  and Principal Exchange-Rate Linked
    Securities (PERLs), *308*
Current assets, 61–63, 67, *67*
  (*See also* Working capital)
Current capital (*see* Working capital)
Current liabilities, 63, 67, *67*
Current ratio, 106–107, *157, 160*

D
Dambolena, Ismael G., 142*n*
Dann, Larry, 533*n*
Day, George, *786n*
Dealer credit (*see* Trade credit)
Debentures, 37, 560
Debt (indebtedness), 37–38, 553
Debt ratio:
  in capital structure, 593, 594, *595*, 596
  variations in calculation, 622, *622*
Debt securities:
  call feature, 38, 254, 276–277, *551*, 562, 563
  characteristics of, 235, *235*
  convertible feature, 38, 254, *551*, 563–565, *568*
  determining cost of, 636–644, 662–663
  evaluating quality of, 140–142
  face value, 235, 555
  marginal tax rate, 636–637
  maturity value, 34, 235, 555
  put feature, 38, 254, 551, 562, 565
  straight-coupon, 245–249, *250*
  zero-coupon, 245, 250–251
  (*See also* Bonds; Notes)
Debt-to-assets ratio, 593, 596
Debtholder, 37
Debtor, 553
Declaration date, dividend, 508, *509*
Declining balance method of depreciation, 70,
  71–72
Deductions, tax, 81, 83–84
  interest, 605–609, 640–641
Default risk, 297–298, 570–572
  bankers' acceptance, 772
  commercial paper, 761
  and limited liability, 612–615
  and marketable securities, 706, 707
Defeasance, 561–562
Deferred annuity, 204–207
Deferred call, 563
Deferred interest, on long-term debt, 558–559
Deferred taxes, 64, 64*n*, 144–145
Degree of financial leverage (DFL), 294–295,
  296–297, *617*
Degree of operating leverage (DOL), 291–293,
  296–297, *617*
Degree of total leverage (DTL), 297
Delta Air Lines, *590–591*
Denomination, of long-term debt, 555
Dependent variable, in regression, 869
Depositary preferred shares, *534*
Depreciation, 69–72
  accumulated, 63
  in capital budgeting analysis, 360–363
  comparison of methods, 71–72, 362–363
  declining balance method, 70, 71–72
  defined, 63
  purpose of, 69
  recapture of, for tax purposes, 82–83, 356
  salvage value in, 69, 77, 361
  straight-line, 69, 70, 71–72, 77–79, 82–83
  sum-of-the-years' digits method, 71–72

Depreciation (*Cont.*):
  for tax purposes, 77–79, 82–83, 89–90,
    360–363
  tax shields, 89–90, 362–363
Derivative securities, 38–39
  asset-backed, 39
  defined, 38
  futures, 39, 46–48, 827–829
  options, 21–22, 38–39, 251–255, 824–827
Detachable warrants, 254, 566
Dewing, Arthur Stone, *688*
Dilution, *126–127*
Direct lease, 451
Discount, bond, 247–248, 276
Discount factor, 176
Discount interest, 742–745, 760
Discount loans, 742–745
Discount rate, 395, *574*
  crossover, 405, *406*
Discounted basis, and Treasury bills, 34–35
Discounted payback period, 394–399, *429, 431*
  decision rule, 395–396
  defined, 394
  as evaluation technique, 396–399
Discounting cash flows:
  in asset valuation
    common stock, 236–243
    debt securities, 245–251
    options, 251–255
    preferred stock, 243–245
  basic equation for present value, 178
  compounding periods, number of, 210–213
  defined, 168
  interest rate determination, 207–210
  series of payments, 188–189, *844*
    annuities, 191–192, 194–198, 638–640, *845*
    annuity due, 199–200, 201–203
    in capital budgeting decisions, 394–399,
      429, 431
    deferred annuity, 204–207
    perpetuity, 198–199
    tables, *837–838*
  shortcuts, *177*
    annuities, 191–192, 194–198
    discount factor tables, 178–181, 196–198,
      833–834, 837–838
    logarithms, *212*
    present value annuity factor, 194–196
    summation notation, 187–188
  single payment, 174–178
    tables, *178–181, 833–834*
  time lines in, 184, *186, 189, 194, 203*
  time periods in, *182*
  with zero interest rate, *178*
Discounts, cost of, 709–711
Discover credit card, *217*
Discrete distributions, 853, *854*
Dispersion, 468
  measures of, 855–865, 866–868
Diversifiable (unsystematic) risk, 324, 328, *466*,
  651
Diversification:
  correlation as measure of, 321–322
  defined, 321
  and portfolio risk, 317–323
  and size of portfolio, 324
Dividend payout (DPO) ratio, 126, *159, 162*,
  520–522, *522, 524*
Dividend per share (DPS), 125, *159, 162*,
  520–521, *521, 523*
Dividend policy, 520–528
Dividend-received deduction, 540
Dividend reinvestment plans (DRPs), 528–529,
  679

Dividend valuation model (DVM), 236–243
  basic equation, 237
  in determining cost of capital, 647–650,
    653–654, 664–665, 668, 669
  growth rate of future dividends, 242–243
  and P/E ratio, *241*
  required rate of return, 236, 241–242
Dividend yield, 242, 261, 265, 525–526, 648
Dividends, 505–510
  on common stock, 36, 234–235, 505–510,
    520–533
    agency explanation, 525, 527–528
    bird-in-hard explanation, 525–526
    dividend irrelevance explanation, 524, 525
    dividend policy, 520–524
    dividend reinvestment plans, 528–529, *679*
    signaling explanation, 525, 527
    stock repurchases as, 529–533
    tax-preference explanation, 525, 526–527
  defined, 10, 505
  in determination of market value, 16
  and double taxation, 10–11, 83–84, 85–86, 526
  mechanics of paying, 508–510
  on preferred stock, 36, 235, 505–510, 534–536
    versus common stock, 501–502
    cumulative versus noncumulative, 235,
      535–536, 539
    and depositary preferred shares, *534*
    fixed versus variable rate, 535
    participating versus nonparticipating, 536
  property, 506
  stock, 506–507
  stock repurchases versus, 529, 531
Dividends-received deduction, 83–84, 526
Double taxation, 10–11, 83–84, 85–86, 526
Dow Jones Industrial Average (DJIA), 51
Drafts, *762*
Dravid, Ajay, 508*n*
Du Pont System, 121–123, *124*
Duff & Phelps Credit Rating Company, 570–572,
  760
Dun & Bradstreet, credit ratings, 140
Dutch auction, 529, *530*, 558
  for preferred stock dividend determination,
    535, 548–549

E
E. I. du Pont Corporation:
  cost of capital of, 660–669
  Du Pont System, 121–123, *124*
Earnings available to common shareholders, 66
Earnings before interest and taxes (EBIT), 65,
  596
Earnings per share (EPS), 19, 124, *126–127*,
  159, 162
  dilution, *126–127*
  expected, *601, 602*
  indifference point, 599
  standard deviation, *601, 602*
  and stock repurchase, 531
East India Company, *501*
Economic conditions, 464
Economic data, 98, *100, 132–133, 163*
Economic life (useful life), 69, 350–351, *353*
  in capital budgeting decisions, 444–448
Economic order quantity (EOQ):
  in Baumol model of cash management,
    691–696, 699
  determining, *694*
  for inventory management, 722–725, 727
  and time, *695*
Economic profit:
  accounting profit versus, *18*
  defined, 18
Effective annual rate (EAR), 214–218

Effective annual rate (EAR) (*Cont.*):
    calculation of, 741, *743*
    continuous compounding, *216*
    on credit cards, *217*
Effective annual return, 259, *639*
    bond, 266–268
    common stock, *264*
    from quarterly returns, *264*
Effective conversion price, 564
Effective cost of borrowing, 740
Effective yield to maturity, 248–249
Efficient frontier, 325, 326
Efficient markets:
    characteristics of, 51–52
    defined, 19
    and market value, 19
8-K statement, 99
Employee involvement (EI), *726*
Employment taxes, 73
    (*See also* Tax)
EPS indifference point, 599
Equipment obligation debt, 561
Equipment trust certificates, 561
Equipment trust debt, 561
Equity, 36, 592, *646*
    defined, 61, 64–65
    market value of, 16–17
    (*See also* Common stock; Ownership interest;
        Preferred stock)
Equity markets:
    international, 48–50
    United States, 44–46
Equity multiplier, 123
Equivalent annual annuity approach, 446–448,
    448
Eurobonds and Euronotes, *555*
Eurodollar deposits, 35, *707*
Ex-dividend date, *509*, 509–510
Exchanges, 43, 44–50
Excise taxes, 73, *73*
    (*See also* Tax)
Executive compensation:
    components of, 21–22, 38
    disclosure requirements, 22, *512*, 513
    golden parachutes, 20, *512*
Executive stock options, 21, 22, 38
Exercise price:
    option, 21–22, 38, 251, 824
    warrant, 566
Expansion projects, 351, 352, 368–374
Expectations hypothesis, *643*
Expected return:
    asset, 307–309, 328
    portfolio, 315–316, 860–861
Expected value, 469, 854–855
    calculation of, *314*, *319*
Expiration date, option, 251, 825
Export-import quotas, 727
Expropriation risk, 727
Externalities, 23
Extraordinary items, in ratio analysis, 144
F
Face value, 34, 235, 555
Factoring, *721*, 766–767
Fahey, Liam, *786n*
Fair Debt Collection Practices Act, *715*
Fama, Eugene F., *51n*
Federal Securities Act of 1964, *42*
Fiduciary duty, 21
Field warehouse loan, 770–771
Final prospectus, 677
Finance, as term, 4
Financial Accounting Standards Board (FASB),
    60

Financial Accounting Standards Board (FASB)
    (*Cont.*):
    Statement No. 94, *621*, 621
    Statement of Financial Accounting Concepts
        No. 1, *60n*
    Statement of Financial Accounting Standards
        No. 106, *59*
Financial analysis:
    accounting data in, 143–145, 163
    and additional disclosures, *99*
    applications of, 7
    for bankruptcy prediction, 142
    common-size analysis, 128, *129*, *130*, 138, *139*
    defined, 7, 98
    economic data in, 98, *100*, 132–133, 163
    to evaluate creditworthiness, 140–142
    to evaluate debt quality, 140–142
    industry data in, 98, *100*, 131–132, 163
    information sources for, 98, *100*, 131–133, 163
    problems and dilemmas, 143–146
    of Wal-Mart Stores Inc., 130–139, 146–147
    (*See also* Financial ratios)
Financial distress:
    airline industry, *590–591*, 623
    bankruptcy, 142, 457–458, *590–591*, 615–616
    and capital structure, *590–591*, 593, 616–617
    costs of, 612
    and limited liability, 612–615
Financial engineering, 554
Financial institutions, *4*, 40
Financial intermediaries, *41*, *681*
Financial leases (*see* Operating leases)
Financial leverage, 481–483
    capital structure, 593, 595–600, 616, 617–620
    degree of, 294–295, 296–297, *617*
    and risk, 598–600
Financial leverage ratios, *158–159*
    cash flow interest coverage ratio, 117–118,
        159, *161*
    fixed charge coverage ratio, 116–117, *158–159*,
        161
    interest coverage ratio (times interest earned),
        115–116, *158*, *161*
    long-term debt-to-assets ratio, 113, *158*, *161*
    long-term debt-to-equity ratio, 114–115, *158*,
        161
    purpose, 113
    total debt-to-assets ratio, 113, *158*, *161*
    Wal-Mart Stores Inc., 136
Financial management, *4*
    agency relationship in, 20–23
    applications of, 6–7
    decision-making in, 4–6, 16–19
    international (*see* International finance)
    objective of, 15–19
Financial modeling, 808–811
Financial planning, 787
    budgeting in, 783, 796–806, 811–812
    long-term, 806–808
    practical applications, 811–812
    sales forecasting in, 788–794
    seasonality in, 699, 739, 795–796
Financial ratios:
    and accounting data problems, 143–145
    and accounting methods, 144
    activity, 111–113
    benchmarks in, 130, 145
    classification of, 100–102
    defined, 100–101
    extraordinary items in, 144
    financial leverage, 113–119
    forecasting with, 142, 146–147
    and "fuzzy" items, 144–145
    historical costs and inflation in, 143–144

Financial ratios (*Cont.*):
    liquidity, 102–108
    profitability, 109–110
    return-on-investment, 119–123
    selecting and interpreting, 145–146
    shareholder, 123–128
    of Wal-Mart Stores Inc., 130–139
Financial risk, 113, 294–297
Financial slack, 624
Financial statements, 60–72
    balance sheet, *59*, 61–65, 128, *129*, *139*, 802,
        805, *807*, *810*
    common-size analysis, 128, *129*, *130*
    consolidated, *621*, 621
    depreciation in (*see* Depreciation)
    income statement, 65–66, 128, *130*, 802, *805*,
        807, *810*
    pro forma, 802–806, *807*, *810*
    standards, *59*, 60
    statement of cash flows, 67–69, 88
Financing decisions, 5–6
Financing strategy, 783
First Boston Corporation, 44, 46
First-in first-out inventory method (FIFO), *144*
Fisher, Irving, *306n*
Fisher effect, 306
Fitch Investors Services, credit ratings, 570–572,
    760
Fitzpatrick, Paul J., *142n*
Five-day settlement plan, 509
Fixed asset turnover ratio, 112, *158*, *161*
Fixed charge coverage ratio, 116–117, *158–159*,
    161
Fixed costs, and operating risk, 291–294,
    296–297
Flexible budget, 802
Float, in cash management, 701, *702*
Floating liens, 768
Floating rate, 558
Floor planning, 768–769
Flotation costs, 527, *527*, *654*, 669
    debt, 580, 640
    of issuing securities, 680
    preferred stock, 645
Flowers Industries, *755*
Footnotes, to financial statements, 69
Ford Motor Company, 510, 537, 726
Forecast error, 792
Forecasting:
    analysts' forecasts, 147
    cash, 704–705
    management, 794
    methods of, 146–147
    sales, 788–794
    time series in, 876–879
France:
    securities markets, 48, *49*
    taxation in, *87*
Frankfurt Stock Exchange, 48, *49*
Free cash flow, 527–528
Frequency distribution, 479
Fuller, Beverly R., *680n*
Fully diluted earnings per share, *127*
Fully-underwritten offerings, 680
Future value:
    calculation of, 169–174
    defined, 169
    (*See also* Compounding cash flows)
Future value annuity factors, 192–194, *835–
    836*
Futures contracts, 39
    index, *47*
    markets, 46–48
    quotations, 827–829

G

General Electric, 521–522, *523, 524*
General Motors (GM), 13, 510–511, *761*
General Motors Acceptance Corporation
  (GMAC), *621,* 720, 759, *761*
General obligation bonds, 37
General partners, 8
General partnerships, 8
Generally accepted accounting principles
  (GAAP), 60
Geometric average return, *257*
Germany, 48, *49*
  taxation in, *87*
Gilbert, John and Lewis, 519
Glass-Steagall Act of 1933, *41,* 681
Golden parachutes, 20, *512*
Gordon, Myron, 237*n,* 647*n*
Gosh, Chinmoy, *523n*
Government regulation, 23
Government-sponsored enterprises, 37*n*
Greenmail, 519, 530
Griffiths, Susan H., *746*
Grinblatt, Mark, 508*n*
Gross domestic product (GDP), 132
Gross plant and equipment (gross plant assets),
  63
Gross profit, 65
Gross profit margin, 109, *157, 160*
Growth rate, 172
Gulf States Utilities, 535–536

H

Half-year convention, 77, 79
Hamada, Robert S., 482*n*
Hansen, Robert S., 680*n*
Hara, Lloyd F., *702*
Harsco Corporation, *352*
Hasbro Inc., *790*
Hedgers, 39
Helms, Roy J., Jr., 487*n*
Hershey Foods, 350
Hertz, David B., 463
High-grade debt, 140, 570
Historical costs, and accounting information,
  143–144
Holding cost:
  cash, 691, 692, 693
  inventory, 721
Homonoff, Richard B., 699*n*
Hostile takeovers, 20
Hughes Aircraft Co., 510–511
Human capital, 5
Hurdle rate, 414
Hypothesis testing, 869
Hyundai Motor Finance Co. (HMFC), 720

I

Illegal insider trading, 52
Import and export taxes, 73
  (*See also* Tax)
In the money, 252
Income bonds, 559–560
Income statement, 65–66
  common-size, 128, *130*
  example, *66*
  pro forma, 802, *805, 807, 810*
  retained earnings, *66*
Income taxes, 73–86
  (*See also* Tax)
Incorporation, 9, *503*
  (*See also* Corporations)
Incremental cash flows, 353
  from investment, 353, 354–359
  from operations, 353, 359–367
Indenture agreement, 37*n,* 554, 569
Independent projects, 353

Independent variable, in regression, 869
Industry data, 98, *100,* 131–132, 163
  and capital structure, 593–594, 620–623
  in financial analysis, 98, *100,* 131–132, 163
  on working capital management, 688–690
Inflation:
  and accounting information, 143–144
  as component of yield, 37
  1941–1990, *306*
  and purchasing power risk, 304–307, 579, 706,
    707
Inflation premium, 306
Initial public offering, 680
Inside directors, 10
Insider information, 52
Insider trading, *42*
Insider Trading and Securities Fraud
  Enforcement Act of 1988, *42*
Insider Trading Sanctions Act of 1984, *42*
Institutional Brokers Estimate System (I/B/E/S),
  147
Institutional investors, *518*
Intangible assets, 63
Interest, 553
  add-on, *745*
  and Code of Hammurabi, *171*
  compound, 170, 740
  deductibility of
    and capital structure, 605–609
    and cost of capital, 636–637
  defined, 169
  discount, 742–745, 760
  on long-term debt, 556–560
    deferred interest, 558–559
    fixed rate, 556–557
    floating rate, 558
    income bonds, 559–560
    participating debt, 560
    zero-coupon, 557–558
  price of risk in, 169
  price of time in, 169
  simple, 170, 740
  single-payment, 742, 753–754, 757
Interest coverage ratio (times interest earned),
  115–116, *158, 161*
Interest rate:
  annual percentage rate (APR), 213–214,
    741–742, *743*
  on credit cards, *217*
  determination of, 207–210, 741–742, *743*
  effective annual rate (EAR), 214–218, *741,* 743
  as growth rate, 172
  on long-term debt, 556
  prime, 754
  as return, 173–174
  risk-adjusted, 484–486
  risk-free, 650
  as source of uncertainty, 464
  and usury, *169*
Interest rate of return (*see* Internal rate of
  return)
Interest rate risk, 301–304, 573–576, 706
Intermark, Inc., 536
Intermarket Trading System (ITS), 50
Intermountain Stock Exchange, 44
Internal rate of return (IRR), 256–260, 411–420,
  429, 432, 634
  decision rule, 414–417
  defined, 411–412
  as evaluation technique, 417–420
  modified, 260, *300,* 420–428, *429, 432,* 578
  multiple rates, 418–420
  net present value versus, 414–417
  origins of concept, *412*

Internal rate of return (IRR) (*Cont.*):
  practical application of, 433–434, 476–477
  in sensitivity analysis, 476–477, 801
  and yield, 414
Internal Revenue Code (IRC), 73–74
  (*See also* Tax)
Internal Revenue Service (IRS), 73–74
  (*See also* Tax)
International Business Machines Corporation
  (IBM), 557, 791–793
  dividends per share, *3, 19*
  earnings per share, *3, 19*
  market value, *3, 19*
  number of shares, 10
  Prodigy system joint venture, 13
International finance:
  cash management in, 699, *708*
  and currency risk, 307
  Japanese cost of capital, 487, 631–632
  markets and securities:
    bankers' acceptances in, *763*
    certificates of deposit, 35
    Eurobonds and Euronotes in, *555*
    exchanges, 48–49, *49*
  as source of uncertainty, 464
  taxation in, 86–88
International Paper Company, *509*
Inventory:
  as collateral for loan, 768–771
  defined, 63
  first-in first-out versus last-in first-out, *144*
Inventory management, 720–728
  costs associated with inventory, 721–722
  models, 722–727
    economic order quantity (EOQ), 722–725,
      727
    just-in-time (JIT) inventory, 725–726, 727
    other considerations, 727
  monitoring, 727–728
  reasons for holding inventory, 720–721
Inventory turnover ratio, 111, *158, 161,* 727–728
Investment Advisers Act of 1940, *42*
Investment bankers:
  commercial bankers versus, *41,* 681
  defined, *41*
Investment cash flows, 354–359, *369*
  in asset acquisition, 354–355
  in asset disposition, 355–359
  defined, 354
Investment Company Act of 1940, *42*
Investment decisions, 4–5, 6, 254–255
Investment-grade debt, 140, 570
Investment profile, 404–405
Investment strategy, 783
Investment tax credit (ITC), 79–80, 80*n*
Investments, *4*
  long-term, 351
Irrelevance, dividend, 524, 525
Issued shares, 503
Issuer, 553

J

J. C. Penney Company, *557*
J. M. Smucker Co., 483–484
Janjigian, Vahan, 680*n*
Japan:
  cash management in, *708*
  compensating balances in, *746*
  cost of capital in, 487, 631–632
  just-in-time (JIT) inventory in, 726
  securities markets, 49, *49*
  taxation in, 86–88
Jarrell, Gregg A., *515*
Jensen, Michael, 615*n*
"Joint and several" liability, 8, *9*

Joint venture, 13
Junk bonds, 140, 570, *572*
Just-in-time (JIT) inventory, 725–726, 727

K

K Mart Corporation, *33*, 41
Kester, W. Carl, 632*n*
Keynes, John Maynard, *690*

L

Larami Corporation, *462*
Last-in first-out inventory method (LIFO), *144*
Lead time, 724
Lease, Ronald C., 453*n*
Leases:
    capital, 64, *64*, 64*n*, *451*, 451–458
        alternative forms, 451
        and lease vs. buy decision, 452–457
        and perfect markets, 457–458
    defined, 451
    operating, 64*n*, *451*
    as ordinary annuities, 192
Lender, 553
Lessee, 451
Lessor, 451
Letter of credit, 755–756
Leverage:
    degree of financial, 294–295, 296–297, *617*
    degree of operating, 291–293, 296–297, *617*
    degree of total, 297
    financial, 481–483
Leverage effect, 598–600
Leveraged lease, 451
Liabilities:
    categories of, 63–64
    defined, 61, 63
Limited liability, 502, 612–615
Limited partners, 9
Limited partnerships, 9
Line of credit agreements, 754–755
Linke, Charles M., 649*n*
Liquid assets, 102
Liquidation value, preferred stock, 534
Liquidity preference theory, *643*
Liquidity ratios, 102–108
    average day's cost of goods sold, 104, *157*, *160*
    average day's purchases, 105–106, *157*, *160*
    credit sales per day, 104, *157*, *160*
    current ratio, 106–107, *157*, *160*
    liquidity, defined, 102
    net operating cycle, 106, *157*, *160*, 705
    net working capital-to-sales ratio, 107–108, *157*, *160*
    number of days of credit, 105, *157*, *160*, 715–717
    number of days of inventory, 104, *157*, *160*, 727–728
    number of days of purchases, 106, *157*, *160*, 797
    purpose of, 102–103
    quick ratio, 107, *157*, *160*
    Wal-Mart Stores Inc., 133–134
Listed securities, 43
Loan, 553
Loan amortization, 196
Loan origination fee, 747
Lockbox systems, 701, 702–704, *705*
Logarithms, *212*
Logue, Dennis E., 515*n*
London Interbank Offered Rate (LIBOR), 535, 558
London Stock Exchange, 48, *49*
Long-term debt:
    bonds (*see* Bonds)
    notes (*see* Notes)
    term loans, 553–554

Long-term debt-to-assets ratio, 113, *158*, *161*
Long-term debt-to-equity ratio, 114–115, *158*, *161*
Long-term financial planning, 806–808
Long-term investment, 351
Long-term liabilities, 64
Long-term planning, 787
Lotteries, *315*
Lough, William H., *518*
Luehman, Timothy A., 632*n*

M

McConnell, John J., 453*n*
McDonald's Corporation, *755*, 870–876
McGraw-Hill Inc., 520–521, *521*, *522*
McNichols, Maureen, 508*n*
Malatesta, Paul H., 519*n*
Malkiel, Burton G., 290
Management forecasts, 794
Managers:
    and agency relationship, 20–23
    and executive compensation, 20, 21–22, 38, *512*, 513
Managing underwriters, 679
Mandated projects, 351, 352
Mandatory convertible preferred stock, 537
Manufacturers Hanover Corporation, 558
Marginal benefit, defined, *634*
Marginal cost, defined, *634*
Marginal cost of capital:
    problems with, 658–660
    schedule, 653–657
    and shareholder wealth maximization, 657–658
Marginal efficiency of capital (*see* Internal rate of return)
Marginal tax rate, 76–77, 607, 620, 636–637
    average tax rate versus, *608*
Markel, F. Lynn, 378*n*
Market conditions, 464
Market conversion price, *536*, *564*
Market equilibrium, 234
Market makers, 46
Market portfolio, 326–327
Market risk, 324, 328, *466*
    in capital budgeting decisions, 465–466
        financial leverage, 481–483
        pureplay, 483–484
    in determining cost of capital, 650, *651*
    required return for, 485
Market risk premium, 328, 485, 650
Market segmentation hypothesis, *643*
Market solution, 23
Market surveys, 794
Market value:
    defined, 16
    and efficient markets, 19
Market value of shareholders' equity, *622*
    defined, 16
    and stock splits, *17*
Marketability risk, 46, 579
Marketable securities, 705–708
    defined, 62–63
    reasons for holding, 705–706
    risks of, 706, 707
    types of, 706–707
    (*See also specific types of securities*)
Markowitz, Harry, 325
Marr, M. Wayne, 542*n*
Master limited partnership, 13
Master's of Business Administration (MBA), as investment decision, *345*
Masulis, Ronald H., 508*n*, 610*n*
Mattel Inc., 349, 739, 754
Maturity date, 34, 556

Maturity factoring, 766, *767*
Maturity value, 34, 235, 555
Mean, 865, 866
Measures of central tendency, 865–866
Measures of dispersion, 855–865, 866–868
Meckling, William H., 615*n*
Median, 865, 866
Medicare, 59
Merchandise credit (*see* Trade credit)
Mergers and acquisitions:
    and classified board of directors, 514, *515*
    classified stock, 510–511
    conflicts of interest in, 20, *515*
    greenmail, 519, 530
    hostile takeovers, 20
    impact on stock price, *499–500*
    poison pills, *519*, 519
    poison puts, 565
Merrill Lynch & Co., 44
Mian, Shehzad L., *721n*
Mid-America Commodity Exchange, 46
Midwest Stock Exchange, 44, *49*
Miller, Merton H., 525, 527*n*, 600–605, 610*n*, 696–698
Miller-Orr model, 696–698, 699
Mode, *866*
Model Business Corporation Act, 10*n*
Modeling, 808–811
Modern portfolio theory (MPT), 324–325
    arbitrage pricing model, 332–333
    capital asset pricing model (CAPM), 326–331, 650–653, 665–667, 668, 669
Modified accelerated cost recovery system (MACRS), 77–79, *361*, *363*
Modified internal rate of return (MIRR), 260, *300*, 420–428, *429*, *432*, *578*
    decision rule, 425–426
    defined, 421–422
    as evaluation technique, 426–428
Modigliani, Franco, 525, 600–605
Modigliani-Miller model of capital structure, 600–612, 617–620
Monetary Control Act of 1980, 704
Money market securities, 34–35
    defined, 34
    investing in, 706–707
    issuing, 758–763
    markets for, 44
    types of, 34–35, *36*, 706–707
Monitoring costs, 21, 527
Monsanto Company, *785*
Moody's:
    Bond Record, *660*, 662
    credit ratings, 140, *141*, 570–572, 760
    Industrial Manual, *660*, 662*n*, 663*n*
Mortgagee, *560*
Mortgages, 560
Mortgagor, *560*
Most likely outcome, 854
Moyer, R. Charles, 542*n*
Mukherjee, Tarun K., 433*n*
Mullins, David Wiley, Jr., 699*n*
Multiple regression, 869
Municipal bonds, 37
Mutually exclusive projects, 353, 402, 414–416, *430*
Myers, Stewart C., 624*n*

N

National Association of Securities Dealers Automated Quotation System (NASDAQ), 44–45, *45*, 46, *49*, 512
National Market System (NMS), 45
NCR, 518
Negative covariance, 320

Negotiable certificates of deposit, 35, *36*
Net cash flows (NCF), 367–368
Net income, 66
Net operating cycle, 106, *157, 160*, 705
Net operating loss, 84–85, 610
Net plant and equipment (net plant assets), 63
Net present value (NPV), 399–406, *429, 431*
  additional considerations, 405–406
  and crossover discount rate, 405, *406*
  decision rule, 401–402
  defined, 400
  as evaluation technique, 402–404
  internal rate of return versus, 414–417
  and investment profile, 404–405
  for investments with unequal lives, 444–448
  practical application of, 432–434
  and profitability index, 408–410
  and project risk, 464
Net present value profile, 404–405
Net profit margin, 110, *157, 160*
Net working capital, 103
  in capital budgeting analysis, 363–365
  defined, 363
Net working capital-to-sales ratio, 107–108, *157, 160*
Netter, Jeffrey M., *515*
New York Futures Exchange, 46
New York Stock Exchange (NYSE), 44, *45*, 46, *49*
  classified stock regulations, 512
  Designated Order System, *47*
  voting rights regulation, 539
No-par stock, 502
Nominal rate (*see* Annual percentage rate)
Nominal return, 306
Noncumulative preferred stock, 535–536
Nondiversifiable (systematic) risk (*see* Market risk)
Normal profit, 18
Noteholders, 37, 553
Notes:
  characteristics, 554–567
    denomination, 555
    indentures, lack of, 34*n*, 554, 569
    interest, 556–560
    maturity, 556
    optionlike features, 562–567
    packaging, 567–568
    security, 560–562
    seniority, 562
  defined, 37, 37*n*
  determining cost of, 636–644, 662–663
  government, 37–38
  retirement of, 579–581
  and risk, 570–579
  secured, 37
  as source of capital, 581–582
  straight-coupon, 245–249, *250*
  zero-coupon, 245, 250–251
  (*See also* Debt securities)
Notes payable, 64
Number of days in accounts payable, 752–753
Number of days of credit, 105, *157, 160*, 715–717
Number of days of inventory, 104, *157, 160*, 727–728
Number of days of purchases, 106, *157, 160*, 797
NutraSweet Company, *785*

O

Oblak, David J., 487*n*
Operating cash flows, 354, 359–367, *800, 809*
  analysis of, application, 365–367
  defined, 354

Operating cycle, 61–63, 103–106, *157, 160*
  and cash management, *690*
  net, 106, *157, 160*, 705
  in working capital management, 685–686, 687
Operating earnings/income (*see* Earnings before interest and taxes)
Operating leases, *64*, 451
Operating leverage:
  and capital structure, 617
  degree of, 294–295, 296–297, *617*
Operating profit (*see* Earnings before interest and taxes)
Operating profit margin, 109–110, *157, 160*
Operating risk, 291–294, 296–297, 347
  and capital structure, 616–617
Operational budgeting, 787
Opportunity cost, 18
  as component of yield, 37
  and replacement projects, 352
  required rate of return as, 236, 241–242
Optimal capital budget, 658
Optimal capital structure, 618–620, 623–625
Options, 38–39, 251–255
  index, *47*
  markets, 46
  quotations, 824–827
  stock, 21–22, 38, 251–254
  types of, 254
  valuation of, 251–255
Ordering cost, inventory, 722
Ordinary annuity, 192
Ordinary least squares (OLS), 871–872
Original maturity, 34
Orr, Daniel, 696–698
Out of the money, 251–252
Outside directors, 10, 517
Outstanding shares, 503–504
Over-the-counter (OTC) markets, 43, 44–46
Overstreet, Robert, 255*n*
Owners' equity, 592, *646*
  (*See also* Common stock; Ownership interest; Preferred stock)
Ownership interest, 11–12
  maximization of:
    in capital budgeting decisions, 347–349, 394, 399, 408–410, 418, 428
    and cost of capital, 657–658
    as objective of financial management, 16–19
    and social responsibility, 22–23
    and stock repurchase plans, *532*
    strategy in, 785–786
  (*See also* Common stock; Equity; Preferred stock)

P

Pacific Stock Exchange, 44, 46
Par value, 34, *64*, 502
  long-term debt, 555
  preferred stock, 533
Paris Stock Exchange, 48, *49*
Participating bonds or notes, 560
Participating preferred stock, 536
Partnership agreement, 9
Partnerships:
  characteristics of, *15*
  defined, 8
  distribution of, in U.S., *14*
  general, 8
  liability in, 8, *9*
  limited, 9, 13
  master limited, 13
  termination of, 9
Patton, George S., 466
Payback period, 391–394, *429, 431*
  decision rule, 392–393

Payback period (*Cont.*):
  defined, 391
  as evaluation technique, 393–394
  and fractional payback, *392*
  practical application of, 433–434
Payment date, dividend, 508, *509*
Payoff period (*see* Payback period)
Pecking order, 624
Penny stocks, 507, 507*n*
Percent-of-sales method, 806
Perfect markets, 601
  and dividend irrelevance, 525
  and leasing, 457–458
Performance shares, 21, 22
Permanent working capital, 739
Perpetual debt, 556
Perpetual warrants, 566
Perpetuity:
  common stock and preferred stock as, 36, 234–235
  valuation of, 198–199, *231, 538*
Perquisites (perks), 20, 21–22, 38
Peterson, David, 508*n*, 527*n*, 561*n*
Peterson, Pamela, 508*n*, 527*n*, 561*n*
Pettit, Richardson, 523*n*
Petty, J. William II, 433*n*, 487*n*
Philadelphia Stock Exchange, 44, 46
Pike, Richard H., 433*n*
Plant assets, defined, 63
Plautus, 391
Pohlman, Randolph A., 378*n*
Poison pill, *519*, 519
Poison puts, 565
Pollution control, 23
Portfolio, defined, 315
Portfolio return, and diversification, 317–323
Portfolio risk:
  and capital asset pricing model (CAPM), 326–331
  in capital budgeting decisions, 465
  and correlation, *323*
  diversifiable (unsystematic), 317–323, 324, 328
  nondiversifiable (systematic), 324, 328, *466*
  as relevant risk to investors, 326
  and size of portfolio, 323–325
  stand-alone:
    sensitivity analysis, 475–477, 801
    simulation analysis, 477–481, 801
    statistical measures, 467–474
Portfolio statistics, 860–865
  expected return, 860–861
  risk, 861–865
  (*See also* Portfolio risk)
Positive net present value (NPV), *784*
Postauditing, 783
Postcompletion audit, 350
Postpayback duration, 392
Postretirement benefits, accounting for, *59*
Potentially dilutive securities, *126–127*
Pound, John, 513*n*
Precautionary balance, cash, 690
Preemptive rights, 514–516
Preferred stock, 36, 533–542
  adjustable rate, 535
  call feature, 38, 537–538, 539, 540
  characteristics of, 235, *235*, 502–510
  classified, 510–512
  conversion feature, 38, 536–537, *538*, 540
  cumulative feature, 235, 535–536, 539
  depositary preferred shares, *534*
  determining cost of, 644–646, 663–664
  dividends, 36, 235, 505–510, 534–536, 539, 540
  liquidation value, 534

Preferred stock (*Cont.*):
  money market, 707
  packaging features, 539–540
  par value, 533
  preference over common stock, 501–502, 533
  sinking funds, 539
  as source of capital, 541–542, *582*
  valuation of, 235, 243–245
  voting rights, 539
Preliminary prospectus, 677
Premium, bond, 246–247
Prepayment risk, 300
Present value, 16
Present value annuity factors, 194–196, *837–838*
Present value of cash flows:
  defined, 169
  (*See also* Discounting cash flows)
Present value of interest tax shield, 608–609
Price-earnings (P/E) ratio, *159, 162, 241*
Primary dealers, 44
Primary earnings per share, *127*
Primary market, *40,* 40–41, 541–542
Prime rate, 754
Principal:
  in agency relationship, 20, 527
  of security, 34, 169, 553
Principal Exchange-Rate Linked Securities
    (PERLS), *308*
Private (privately held) corporation, 504–505
Private placement, 40, 677
Pro forma financial statements, 802–806, *807,
    810*
  analysis-of-accounts method, 802–806
  percent-of-sales method, 806
Probability, *467*
Probability distributions, 310, *311, 467, 471,
    473, 801, 853, 854, 856–859*
Professional corporation, 13
Profit:
  abnormal, 51
  economic vs. accounting, 17–19
  normal, 18
Profit-sharing bonds or notes, 560
Profitability index (PI), 406–410, *429, 431*
  decision rule, 407
  defined, 406
  as evaluation technique, 407–410
  and net present value (NPV), 408–410
  and scale differences, *409,* 409–410, *430*
Profitability ratios, 109–110
  gross profit margin, 109, *157, 160*
  net profit margin, 110, *157, 160*
  operating profit margin, 109–110, *157, 160*
  purpose of, 109
  Wal-Mart Stores Inc., 134–135
Progressive taxation, 76, 84*n*
Project risk, in capital budgeting decisions:
  certainty equivalents, 486–487
  market, 465–466, 481–483, *484,* 485
  measurement, 466–484
  practical applications, 487–488
  relevant cash flow risk in, 464–465
  risk-adjusted rates, 484–486
  sources of, 464
  stand-alone, 465–466, 467–481, 485
Project tracking, 350
Property dividends, 506
Prospectus, 677
Proxy, 22, 512–513
Proxy card, 513
Proxy fights, 518–519
Proxy statements, 22, *512,* 513
Prudential Insurance Company, *388*
Public (publicly held) corporation, 11, 504–505

Public offerings, 677–681
  flotation costs, 680
  methods of issuing securities, 678–680
  registration procedures, 677–678
Public warehouse loan, 771
Purchasing power risk, 304–307, 579, 706, 707
Pureplay, 483–484
Put options, 38
  call options compared to, *253,* 254
  defined, 565, *825*
  in investment decisions, 255
  valuation of, 253–254
Putable bonds, 254, *551, 562,* 565

Q
Quick ratio, 107, *157, 160*
Quotas, export-import, 727

R
Random numbers, generation of, 479
Range, 310, 468–469, *855–856, 866*
Rating services, debt, 570–572, *590–591*
Ratio, defined, 100–101
Real return, 306
Receivables management, 709–720
  captive finance subsidiaries in, 720, *721*
  collection policies, 714–715, 717–719
  costs associated with credit, 709–713
  credit policies, 713–714, 717–719
  monitoring accounts receivable, 715–717
  reasons for extending credit, 709
Record date, dividend, 508, *509*
Red herring, 677
Refunding, debt, 580–581
Regional exchanges, 44, *45*
Registered bonds, 554
Registration statement, 12, *99,* 677
Regression, 869–879
  defined, 790
  estimation of intercept in, 873–876
  estimation of slope in, 871–873
  sales forecasting with, 790–794
Regression equation, 871
Regression line, 790, 871
Regression model, 871
Reinvestment assumption:
  and internal rate of return, 415
  and modified internal rate of return, 421–425
Reinvestment rate risk, 298–301, 576–579, 706
Reliance Financial Services, *531*
Remote disbursement, 702, 704
Replacement chain method, 445–446, *448*
Replacement projects, 351–352, 374–378, *379*
Repurchase agreements:
  investing in, 707
  as secured loans, 764–765
Required rate of return (RRR), 348, *395,* 464,
    465, 633–634
  in common stock valuation, 236, 241–242
  (*See also* Cost of capital)
Residual loss, 21
Restricted stock grant, 22
Retained earnings, 65, *66, 646*
  as source of funds, 541
Retirement of debt, 579–581
Return:
  average annual, *174,* 256, *257*
  defined, 173, 255
  portfolio, calculation of, 316
  and risk-tolerance, 315
  (*See also* Yield)
Return on assets (basic earning power ratio),
    119, 121–122, *124, 159, 162, 596*
Return on common equity, 120, 122–123, *124,
    159, 162, 596*
Return on equity, 120, 122–123, *124, 159, 162*

Return on investment, 255–278
  bonds, 265–277
  with even cash flows, 256–258
  with no intermediate cash flows, 255–256
  and reinvestment assumption, 258–260
  stocks, 260–265, 288–289
  of tax refund, *167*
  transaction costs in, 278
  with uneven cash flows, 258
Return-on-investment ratios, 119–123
  Du Pont System, 121–123, *124*
  purpose, 119
  return on assets (basic earning power ratio),
    119, 121–122, *124, 159, 162, 596*
  return on common equity, 120, 122–123, *124,
    159, 162*
  return on equity, 120, 122–123, *124, 159, 162*
Return ratios, 101
  Wal-Mart Stores Inc., 137
Revenue bonds, 37
Revenues (sales), 65
  in capital budgeting analysis, 359–360
  cash flows from change in, 359–360
Reverse stock splits, 507–508
Revolving credit agreements, 755
Ricardo, David, 784
Rights, 38, 254
Rights offerings, 514–516, *679*
@Risk (software), 479
Risk:
  in asset valuation, 233–234
  as component of yield, 37
  defined, 290, 463
  diversifiable (unsystematic), 324, 328, *466,
    651*
  and expected return, 307–309
  financial, 113, 294–297
  market (*see* Market risk)
  operating, 291–294, 296–297, 347, 616–617
  portfolio (*see* Portfolio risk)
  project (*see* Project risk, in capital budgeting
    decision)
  sales, 291, 294, 347, 616
  and standard deviation, 309–314
  types of, 290–307
    cash flow, 291–298, 329, 347–348, 464–466,
        570–572
    currency, 307, *308*
    interest rate, 301–304, 573–576, 706
    marketability, 46, 579
    purchasing power, 304–307, 579, 706, 707
    reinvestment rate, 298–301, 576–579, 706
  uncertainty versus, 290, 290*n*
Risk-adjusted rate, 484–486
Risk-averse investors, 233–234, 315, 650
Risk-free asset, defined, 326
Risk-free rate of interest, defined, *650*
Risk-neutral investors, 315
Risk preference, 315
Risk premium, 327, 603
  market, 328, 485, 650
Risk-tolerance, 315
RJR Nabisco, *499–500,* 565
Robertson, Nigel J., *746*
Rogers, Will, 43
Ross, Stephen, 332–333
Runyon, L. R., 487*n*
Ryngaert, Michael, *519n*

S
Safety stock, 696, 724
Salary, 21, 22
Sale-leaseback arrangement, 451
Sales (*see* Revenues)
Sales forecasting, 788–794

Sales forecasting (*Cont.*):
  management forecasts, 794
  market surveys, 794
  with regression, 790–794
Sales risk, 291, 294, 347, 616
Salomon Brothers, Inc., 44*n*
Salvage value (residual value), 69, 77, 361
Sample statistics, 865–880
  correlation, 879–880
  measures of dispersion, 866–868
  regression, 869–879
  summary measures, 865–866
  tests of hyptheses, 869
Santiago, Emmanuel S., 378*n*
Scale differences, *409*, 409–410, *430*
Scenario analysis, 475–477
Schallheim, James S., 453*n*
Schlitz Brewing Company, *786*
Scholes, Myron, 527*n*
Scott, David F., Jr., 433*n*, 487*n*
Sears, Roebuck & Co., 13, *781–782*, 787–788
Seasonal dating, *713*
Seasonality:
  in cash management, 699, 796
  and short-term sources of capital, 739
Secondary market, 41–43
Secured debt, 553
Secured loans, 748, 764–771
  accounts receivable as collateral for, 765–768
  inventory as collateral for, 768–771
  repurchase agreements, 764–765
Securities, 34–39
  capital market, 35–38
  defined, 34
  derivative, 38–39
  money market, 34–35
  (*See also specific types of securities*)
Securities Act of 1933, *42*, 677
Securities and Exchange Commission (SEC), *12*, 12, 43, 677
  and disclosure of executive compensation, 22, *512*, 513
  regulation of Eurobonds and Euronotes, *555*
Securities Exchange Act of 1934, 11–12, *42*, 504, 505, 513
Securities exchanges:
  international, 48–49
  United States, 44, 46–48
Securities Investor Protection Act of 1970, *42*
Securities markets, 11, 39–52
  classification of, 40–43
  defined, 34
  efficient, 19, 51–52
  exchanges, 43, 44–49
  international, 48–50
  market indicators, 50–52
  over-the-counter, 43, 44–46, 46
  purpose of, 39–40
  United States, *42*, 43–48
    bond, 46
    crash of 1987, *47*
    equity markets, 44–46, *47*, *49*
    futures, 46–48
    money markets, 44
    options, 46
    regulation, 23, *42*, 43
Securitization of assets, 39, 768, *769*
Security, 553
Security market line (SML), 328–331
Semistrong form of market efficiency, 51–52
Seniority, of long-term debt, 562
Sensitivity analysis, 475–477, 801
Serial debt, 556
Seward, James K., 515*n*

Shakespeare, William, 317
Shareholder ratios, 123–128
  book value per share, 125
  dividend payout ratio, 126, *159*, *162*, 520–522, *522*, *524*
  dividends per share (DPS), 125, 520–521, *521*, *523*
  earnings per share (EPS), 124, *126–127*, *601*, *602*
  purpose, 123
  Wal-Mart Stores Inc., 137–138
Shareholder rights plans (poison pills), *519*, 519
Shareholders, 10, 501
Shareholders' equity (*see* Equity; Ownership interest)
Shareholders' rights movement, 519
Shares, 10
  defined, 501
Sharpe, William, 325–326
Shelf registration, 678
Shirking, 20
Short-term financing:
  costs of, 740–748, 771–772
  permanent working capital, 739
  reliance on, 737–738
  secured, 748, 764–771
  temporary working capital, 739
  unsecured, 748–763
Short-term investment, 351
Shulman, Joel M., 142*n*
Siemens, *708*
Sight drafts, *762*
Signaling, 525, 527, 529, 532–533
Simple correlation coefficient, 879
Simple interest, 170, 740
Simple regression, 869
Simulation analysis, 477–481, 801
Single-payment loans, 742, 753–754, 757
Sinking fund call price, 539
Sinking funds:
  long-term debt, 561
  preferred stock, 539
Smith, Clifford W., Jr., 721*n*
Smith, Raymond F., 142*n*
Smucker (J. M.) Co., 483–484
Social responsibility, 22–23
Soft put, 565
Sole proprietorships:
  characteristics of, 8, *15*
  defined, 8
  distribution of, in U.S., *14*
Speculative balance, cash, 691
Speculative bonds, 140
Speculators, 39
Spokane Stock Exchange, 44
Spread, underwriter, 678–680, 760
Stakeholders, 23
Stand-alone risk, 465–466
  measuring, 467–481
Standard & Poor's:
  credit ratings, 140, *141*, 570–572, 760
  Daily Stock Price Record, 663–664
  debt ratings, *590–591*
  Earnings Forecaster, 147
  500 Stock Index (S&P 500), 51, 666, 737–738
Standard deviation, 469–473, 867
  calculation of, 312–314, *314*, *319*, *470*, *472*, 856–859
  and coefficient of variation, 473–474
  defined, 469, 856
  earnings per share, *601*
  of frequency distribution, 479*n*
  as measure of risk, 309–312
  portfolio, 318, 320–321, 863–865

Standard deviation (*Cont.*):
  of probability distribution, 856–859
  properties of, *470*
  sample, 867–869
  and size of portfolio, 324
  and variance, *313*
Standby underwriting, 679
Stated rate (*see* Annual percentage rate)
Stated value, 64, 502
  preferred stock, 533
Statement of cash flows, 67–69, 88
  cash flows from financing activities, 68–69
  cash flows from investing, 67–68
  cash flows from operating activities, 67, *67*
  example, *68*
Stock, *646*
  defined, 501
Stock (*see* Ownership interest)
Stock appreciation right, 21, 22
Stock brokers, 41
Stock dividends:
  defined, 506
  reasons for, 506–507
  stock splits, *117*, 507–508
Stock market:
  crash of 1987, *47*
  exchanges, 44, *45*, 46, 48–49, *49*
  indicators, 50–52
  international, 48–49
  over-the-counter, 44–46
  United States, 44–46
Stock options, 21–22, 38
  valuation of, 251–254
Stock purchase programs, *679*
Stock repurchases, 529–533
  open market purchases, 529
  reasons for, 530–533
  targeted block repurchase, 530
  tender offers, 529
Stock splits, 507–508
  and market value of shareholders' equity, *17*
  reverse, 507–508
Stockholders, 501
Stockholders' equity (*see* Equity; Ownership interest)
Straight-line depreciation, 69, 70
  comparison of accelerated methods with, 71–72
  for tax purposes, 77–79, 82–83
Strategic plan, 783
Strategy, 349, 784–786
  comparative advantage in, 784
  competitive advantage in, 784–785
  defined, 783
  and maximization of owners' wealth, 785–786
Strike price, option, 38, 251, 824
Strong form of market efficiency, 52
Stuart-James Co., 507*n*
Student Loan Marketing Association (Sallie Mae), *308*
Subchapter S corporations, 85–86
Subordinated debt, 562
Sum-of-the-years' digits method of depreciation, 71–72
Summary measures, 854–855, 865–866
Summation notation, 187–188
Sunk costs, 355
Swary, Itzhak, 523*n*
Sweden, taxation in, *87*
Syndicate, underwriting, 679, 680
Synergy, *781*

T
Targeted block repurchase, 530
Tax, 72–88

Tax (*Cont.*):
  capital gains, 80–82, 526–527, 529–533
  corporate, 10–11
    before- versus after-tax dollars, *117*
    in capital budgeting analysis, 360–363
    capital gains tax, 80–82
    and capital structure, 600–612, 617–620
    cash flows from change in, 360–363
    deferred taxes on balance sheet, 64, 64*n*,
      144–145
    and demand for leasing, 457–458
    depreciation for tax purposes, 77–79, 82–83,
      89–90
    and dividend policy, 525, 526–527
    double, 10–11, 83–84, 85–86, 526
    and inventory management, 727
    investment tax credit (ITC), 79–80, 80*n*
    net operating loss carrybacks and
      carryovers, 84–85, 610
    Subchapter S, 85–86
    tax rates, 74–77
    taxable income, 83–84
  government securities, 37
  individual
    capital gains tax, 80–82, 526
    and capital structure, 609–610
    net operating loss carrybacks and
      carryovers, 84–85
    refunds, economics of speeding up, *167*
    tax rates, 74–77
    taxable income, 84
  marginal rate, 76–77, 607, 608, 620, 636–637
  in other countries, 86–88
  partnership, 9
  progressive, 76, 84*n*
  sole proprietorship, 8
  as source of uncertainty, 464
  state and local, 86
  of stock repurchases, 529
  tax, defined, 73
  types of taxes, 73
  in the United States, 73–86
Tax clientele, 526
Tax shield:
  capital loss, 356–357
  defined, *607*
  depreciation, 89–90, 362–363
  interest, 607–609, 608–609
  unused, 610–612
Temporary working capital, 739
10-K statement, *99*
10-Q statement, *99*
Tender offers, 529
  Dutch auction, 529, *530*
Term loans, 553–554
Term structure of interest rates, *643*
Terminal value, 421, *578*
Time drafts, *762*
Time lines:
  for compounding cash flows, 184, *185*, *186*,
    193, *201*, *203*, 378
  defined, 184
  for discounting cash flows, *186*, *189*, *194*,
    203
Time series analysis, 876–879
Time value of money, 168 (*See also*
  Compounding cash flows; Discounting
  cash flows)
Time Warner, 515–516
Times interest covered ratio, 115–116
Titman, Sheridan, 508*n*
Tokyo Stock Exchange, 49, *49*
Tombstone advertisement, 677
Toronto Stock Exchange, 48, *49*

Total asset turnover ratio, 112, *158*, *161*
Total debt-to-assets ratio, 113, *158*, *161*
Total quality control (TQC), *726*
Toyota Motor Corporation, *708*
Trade credit:
  cost of, 749–751
  defined, 709, 749
  extension of:
    costs associated with, 709–713
    implicit cost to the customer, *712*
    reasons for, 709
  using, 749–751
  (*See also* Accounts payable; Accounts
    receivable; Receivables management)
Transaction costs, 278, 529, 691, 692, 693
Transactions balance, 690
Treasury bills (T-bills), 34–35, *36*
  investing in, 707
  rates, 772
  transaction costs, 278
Treasury bonds, 37–38, 278, 535
Treasury notes, 278
Treasury stock, 65
Triple-witching day, *47*
True yield (*see* Internal rate of return)
Trust Indenture Act of 1939 (TIA), 569
Trust receipts loans, 768–769
Trustees, 569
Turner Broadcasting, *511*
Turnover ratio, 101–102
UAL Corporation, *590–591*
Ulrich, Thomas A., 746*n*
Uncertainty:
  risk versus, 290, 290*n*
  sources of, 464
Uncertainty statistics:
  measures of dispersion, 855–865
  probability distributions, 853, *854*
  summary measures, 854–855
Uncommitted line of credit, 754
Underwriters, 678–680
Underwriting, 41
Unit trusts, 50
United Kingdom, 50
  securities markets, 48, *49*
  taxation in, 86, *87*
Unsecured debt, 553
Unsecured loans, 748–763
  accounts payable management, 751–753
  bank financing, 753–758
  money market securities, 758–763
  trade credit, 749–751
Unsystematic risk, 328
Useful (economic) life, 350–351, *353*
Useful life (economic life):
  in capital budgeting decisions, 444–448
USX Corporation, 518
  bonds, features of, *551–552*, *564*
Valuation (*see* Asset valuation)
Value Line Investment Survey, 147, 666
Van Arsdell, Paul M., *786*
Variable cost margin, 709
Variable costs, and operating risk, 291–294,
  296–297
Variance, *313*, 866
  portfolio, 320
View-Master Ideal Group, *568*
Virtual enterprise, 13
Volvo of Sweden, 13, *780*
Voting rights:
  common stock, 511–514
  preferred stock, 539

W

Wages and salaries payable, defined, 63
Wal-Mart Stores Inc.:
  business analysis, 130–131
  common-size analysis, 138, *139*
  economic analysis, 132–133
  financial analysis of, 130–139
  and forecasting, 146–147
  industry analysis, 131–132
  ratio analysis, 133–138
Walgreen Company, 877–879
Walkling, Ralph A., 519*n*
Walt Disney Company, 86, 145, *531*, 557, 562,
  567, *785*
Wang Laboratories, 97
Warner, Jerold B., 616*n*
Warrants, 38, 254
  defined, 566
  detachable, 254, 566
  with long-term debt securities, 566–567
  in rights offerings, 514
Weak form of market efficiency, 51
Weighted average cost of capital (WACC), 488, 653
Westinghouse Electric, *532*
Williams, John Burr, 233, 234, 236, 237*n*
Winakor, Arthur, 142*n*
Woolridge, J. Randall, 523*n*
Working capital, 103
  in capital budgeting analysis, 347, 363–365
  cash flows from change in, 363–365
  defined, 687
  net, 103, 107–108, *157*, *160*, 363–365
  permanent, 739
  temporary, 739
Working capital management:
  cash management in, 690–708
  industry data on, 688–690
  inventory management in, 720–728
  operating cycle in, *685–686*, 687
  receivables management in, 709–720
  short-term financing in (*see* Short-term
    financing)
  size of working capital, 688–690

Y

Yankee certificates of deposit, 35
Yield, 245, 255
  capital, 242, 261, 268, 525–526
  components of, *37*
  coupon, 268
  defined, 37
  dividend, 242, 261, 265, 525–526, 648
  (*See also* Return)
Yield curve, *643*
Yield to call, 276–277
Yield to maturity, 248–249, 574
  annualized versus effective, *639*, *846*
  bond, 268–276
    as maturity approaches, 271–273
    straight-coupon, 269–271
    as yields change, 273–276
    zero-coupon, 268–269
  in determining cost of debt, 637–639
  (*See also* Internal rate of return)

Z

Zacks Investment Research Inc., 147
Zale Corporation, 616
Zero-balance account (ZBA), 704, *726*
Zero-coupon bonds, *551*
  determining cost of, 641–644
  Disney, 567–568
  interest on, 557–558
  valuation of, 245, 250–251
  yield to maturity, 268–269
Zumwalt, J. Kenton, 649*n*